THE PAPERS OF
THOMAS JEFFERSON

BARBARA B. OBERG
GENERAL EDITOR

THE PAPERS OF
Thomas Jefferson

Volume 30
1 January 1798 to 31 January 1799

BARBARA B. OBERG, EDITOR

JAMES P. McCLURE AND ELAINE WEBER PASCU,
ASSOCIATE EDITORS

SHANE BLACKMAN AND F. ANDREW McMICHAEL,
ASSISTANT EDITORS

LINDA MONACO, EDITORIAL ASSISTANT

JOHN E. LITTLE, RESEARCH ASSOCIATE

PRINCETON AND OXFORD

PRINCETON UNIVERSITY PRESS

2003

As INDICATED in the first volume, this edition was made possible by a grant of $200,000 from The New York Times Company to Princeton University. Since this initial subvention, its continuance has been assured by additional contributions from The New York Times Company and The New York Times Company Foundation; by grants of the Ford Foundation, the National Historical Publications and Records Commission, and the National Endowment for the Humanities; by grants of the Andrew W. Mellon Foundation, the Packard Humanities Institute, the Pew Charitable Trusts, the John Ben Snow Memorial Trust, and the L. J. Skaggs and Mary C. Skaggs Foundation to Founding Fathers Papers, Inc.; by benefactions from the Barkley Fund and the Lyn and Norman Lear Foundation through the National Trust for the Humanities, the Florence Gould Foundation, the Charlotte Palmer Phillips Foundation, Time Inc., the Dyson Foundation, and the Lucius N. Littauer Foundation; and by gifts from Robert C. Baron, James Russell Wiggins, David K. E. Bruce, and B. Batmanghelidj. In common with other editions of historical documents, THE PAPERS OF THOMAS JEFFERSON is a beneficiary of the good offices of the National Historical Publications and Records Commission, tendered in many useful forms through its officers and dedicated staff. For these and other indispensable aids generously given by librarians, archivists, scholars, and collectors of manuscripts, the Editors record their sincere gratitude.

FOREWORD

DURING the thirteen months covered by this volume, Vice President Thomas Jefferson spent more than half of his time in Philadelphia, serving as president of a Senate that was dominated by Federalists and from which he expected little good. At the same time, he counseled his fellow Republicans on what he took to be the ill-advised policies of the Adams Administration. In this critical year, approaching the midpoint of his vice-presidency, Jefferson was plunged into a difficult period of his political life. He participated in the life of the Senate, presiding as it considered the House's impeachment of William Blount. The vice president made notes on the framing of oaths for impeachments and went back to his English law books to study the role of juries in impeachment trials. But in the main he expressed frustration at how little real business there was to transact in the first months of the second session of the Fifth Congress. They had merely postponed the Stamp Act until July, decided not to consider the land tax, and were waiting, in a "state of extraordinary suspense," for dispatches from Elbridge Gerry, Charles C. Pinckney, and John Marshall, the American envoys to France. When dispatches arrived in March and their contents were partially revealed, Republicans suspected the administration of controlling the release of information to further a goal of provoking war with France. Jefferson proclaimed that when the reports were fully known, the Directory's peaceful intentions would be clear and Republican beliefs triumphant. When the full truth of the XYZ affair became public, however, to many Americans Adams seemed vindicated and Jefferson too optimistic.

Following Adams's revelation of the XYZ dispatches, the nation debated the possibility of war and made preparations for it. The augmentation of the army and creation of a navy, the arming of merchant vessels, the appointment of George Washington as commander of the new provisional army, and the raising of taxes to sustain these measures engaged the attention of Congress. Patriotic addresses poured in on the president. If the Republicans could only beat back offensive measures during that session, Jefferson hoped, members of Congress could go home to their constituents and the real public sentiment would make itself felt. In the meantime, he bid farewell to acquaintances departing for Europe: Tadeusz Kosciuszko, slipping away in secret as "Thomas Kanberg"; George Logan, whose journey to France provoked accusations of unauthorized meddling in diplomacy; and the Comte de Volney and others pushed along by pending anti-French legislation. In June, two days after the Alien Friends Act was signed into law and almost three weeks before the session ended, Jefferson, having criticized Republican legislators for deserting their posts, left for Monticello. He stayed long enough in Philadelphia to see John Marshall return a hero from the mission to France and then stopped at Montpelier to convey all the latest news to James Madison

Debates in Congress took place against a backdrop of bitter partisan rivalry, characterized most famously by the near-brawl on the floor of the House between Matthew Lyon and Roger Griswold. There existed, Jefferson wrote to his old friend, Angelica Church, Alexander Hamilton's sister-in-law, a "wall of separation between those who differ in political sentiments." Jefferson himself referred to Adams's 19 Mch. message to Congress as "almost insane," and Madison called the president's politics "heretical." Jefferson was quite prepared, in a matter-of-fact way, to equate the terms Federalist, aristocrat, monocrat, and Tory. The partisan press, on both sides, was equally vivid in its language.

Following his inquisitive mind and as a relief from politics, Jefferson continued to engage in scientific pursuits and fulfill his role as a promoter of American science and learning. He was reelected in 1798 and 1799 to the presidency of the American Philosophical Society, to which he presented his paper on the moldboard plow. In Philadelphia he recorded winter temperature readings, worried about their accuracy, and decided to rely on David Rittenhouse's after all. He corresponded with William Linn on Indian languages and with Bishop James Madison on astronomy, prepared an ambitious course of reading for William Munford, a student at the College of William and Mary, and wrote on the Anglo-Saxon language.

Jefferson longed for Monticello and his family, contrasting the distasteful bickering of Philadelphia with the sanctuary of his mountaintop. Letters from his daughters were, he said, "gleams of light," and he lamented to his new son-in-law, John Wayles Eppes, "I never was more home-sick, or heart-sick." As Jefferson had learned before, his property suffered from his "long abandonment" of it while away on public business. Renovations to the house slowed, supplies for the nailery were disrupted, and he had to arrange for the sale of his crops through intermediaries. With the prices of wheat low and tobacco high, he was drawn back into dependence on the very crop he had hoped to abandon.

Jefferson's correspondence reveals glimpses of his life as absentee plantation owner and slaveholder. Thomas Mann Randolph and Jefferson's daughter, Martha, reported breaches of trust, idleness, and other lapses by slaves and tradesmen. Jefferson's room was broken into, but the culprit was caught and the stolen items recovered. Isaac was deemed "dissatisfied and rebellious." Randolph, with his father-in-law's blessing, halted the beginnings of individual cultivation of tobacco by Jefferson's slaves. In contrast, necessity required giving responsibility to a few slaves, including George, foreman at Monticello, and Jupiter, who was entrusted to take the horses to Fredericksburg to meet the master when he returned from Philadelphia and to deliver important letters and wait for replies. And although he gave no sign of changing his views, Jefferson saw two striking alternative models to slavery and slave labor in 1798. With Jefferson's aid Kosciuszko prepared a will authorizing his American friend to employ his estate to purchase, free, and educate black slaves, and Jefferson's protégé, William Short, eloquently and insistently refused to base his farming on slave labor.

Provoked by the Alien and Sedition Acts and by "the passions & the power of a majority in Congress," Jefferson penned the famous resolutions adopted in November 1798 by the Kentucky legislature. He kept his authorship a secret, however, seeking to avoid any appearance of "rashness" by Republicans. And, as if settling in for the indefinite continuation of the political conflict he found so distasteful, in late 1798 and early 1799 he strove to recall to the nation's citizens the true principles of their government. He urged Madison to publish his debates from the Constitutional Convention, which would "bring about a revulsion of public sentiment" against the administration's current anti-Republican measures, and he pleaded with Edmund Pendleton, "like the patriarch of old," to rally the people to the truth. He also sought to build a consensus among individuals, reaching out to those like Gerry, who he thought was really much closer in spirit to Republicanism than to Federalism. In a long and impassioned epistle to Gerry, Jefferson offered a "profession of my political faith." This letter and the Kentucky Resolutions reflect Jefferson's struggle to understand and define the political direction of the nation in times that he could neither comprehend nor accept.

Readers who have followed this edition since its inception or even simply in its most recent volumes will notice some changes in our treatment of the texts. We call your attention to the revised statement of editorial method in the Editorial Method and Apparatus.

ACKNOWLEDGMENTS

MANY individuals have given the Editors the benefit of their aid in the preparation of this volume, and to them we offer our gratitude. Those who helped us use manuscript collections or answered research queries are Robert Darnton, Charles C. Gillispie, William C. Jordan, and Georgia Nugent, Princeton University; in the libraries at Princeton, Karin A. Trainer, University Librarian, and William Blair, Mary George, Sooni K. Johnson, Susanne McNatt, Lara Moore, and Rosemary A. Little, whose many years of extraordinary help to us will be greatly missed; Timothy Connelly, Dane Hartgrove, and Michael Meier of the National Historical Publications and Records Commission; James H. Hutson and his staff at the Manuscript Division of the Library of Congress, especially Fred Bauman, Jeffrey Flannery, Gerard W. Gawalt, and Mary Wolfskill; Oona E. Beauchard, Peter Drummey, Nicholas Graham, Brenda M. Lawson, and Virginia H. Smith at the Massachusetts Historical Society; Robert C. Ritchie, John Rhodehamel, and others at the Huntington Library; James Horn and Lucia C. Stanton of the Thomas Jefferson Foundation at Monticello; Michael Plunkett and the staff of the Special Collections Department, the University of Virginia Library; Kristina Gray-Perez and Dennis Northcott, Missouri Historical Society; at the Library of Virginia, Brent Tarter and Minor T. Weisiger; Whitfield J. Bell, Jr., Robert Cox, Scott DeHaven, and Roy Goodman at the American Philosophical Society; Curtis Wilson, St. John's College (retired); Victor Bers, Yale University; at the North Carolina Division of Archives and History, Robert J. Cain and Donna Kelly; Paul Romaine of the Gilder Lehrman Collection and Leslie Fields at the Morgan Library; Cynthia Miller, University of Pittsburgh Press, and Anne Rawlinson; at the Maine Historical Society, Stephanie Philbrick; the staff of the New York Public Library; and our fellow editors at the Adams Papers at the Massachusetts Historical Society, the Papers of George Washington and the Papers of James Madison at the University of Virginia, the Thomas Jefferson Retirement Series at Monticello, the Papers of Benjamin Franklin at Yale University, and the Papers of Nathanael Greene at the Rhode Island Historical Society. William Howard Adams, Yvonne Brooks, Jacklyn Burns, Alfred L. Bush, Erin Chase, Tino Gipponi, Christin Giviskos, Ewa Gorniak, Leslie Graham, Robert Morgan, Jacqueline O'Regan, and Nicole Wells assisted in the search for illustrations. And we give special thanks to Walter Lippincott, director of Princeton University Press, and those at the Press who have given their

ACKNOWLEDGMENTS

meticulous attention to this and recent volumes: Alice Calaprice, Chuck Creesy, Dimitri Karetnikov, Thomas LeBien, Jan Lilly, Neil Litt, Elizabeth Litz, Gretchen Oberfranc, Maura Roessner, and Linny Schenck.

EDITORIAL METHOD AND
APPARATUS

1. RENDERING THE TEXT

Julian P. Boyd eloquently set forth a comprehensive editorial policy in Volume 1 of *The Papers of Thomas Jefferson*. Adopting what he described as a "middle course" for rendering eighteenth-century handwritten materials into print, Boyd set the standards for modern historical editing. His successors, Charles T. Cullen and John Catanzariti, reaffirmed Boyd's high standards. At the same time, they made changes in textual policy and editorial apparatus as they deemed appropriate. For discussions of these modifications, readers are encouraged to consult Vol. 1:xxix-xxiv; Vol. 22:vii-xi; and Vol. 24:vii-viii.

The revised, more literal textual method, which appears for the first time in Volume 30, will adhere to the following guidelines: Abbreviations will be retained as written. Where the meaning is sufficiently unclear to require editorial intervention, the expansion will be given in the explanatory annotation. Capitalization will follow the usage of the writer. Most dramatically, perhaps, readers will notice that Jefferson rarely begins his sentences with an uppercase letter, and we now conform to his usage. Because the line between uppercase and lowercase can be a very fine and fluctuating one, when it is impossible to make an absolute determination of the author's intention, we adopt modern usage. Punctuation will be retained as written and double marks of punctuation, such as a period followed by a dash, will be allowed to stand. Misspellings or so-called slips of the pen will not be silently corrected but will be allowed to stand or recorded in a subjoined textual note.

English translations or translation summaries will be supplied for foreign-language documents, which in Jefferson's papers are primarily French or Spanish. As in the past, in some instances, when documents are lengthy and not especially pertinent to Jefferson's concerns or if our edition's typography cannot adequately represent the script of a language, we will provide only a summary in English. In most cases, however, we shall print in full the text in its original language and also provide a full English translation. If a contemporary translation that Jefferson made or would have used is extant, we will likely choose to print it along with the most authoritative text in the original language. Otherwise, the Editors will supplement the text with a modern translation designed to provide a basic readable English text for the modern user rather than preserving all aspects of the original diction and language.

2. TEXTUAL DEVICES

The following devices are employed throughout the work to clarify the presentation of the text.

[. . .]	Text missing and not conjecturable.
[ ]	Number or part of a number missing or illegible.
[roman]	Conjectural reading for missing or illegible matter. A question mark follows when the reading is doubtful.
[*italic*]	Editorial comment inserted in the text.
⟨*italic*⟩	Matter deleted in the MS but restored in our text.

3. DESCRIPTIVE SYMBOLS

The following symbols are employed throughout the work to describe the various kinds of manuscript originals. When a series of versions is recorded, *the first to be recorded is the version used for the printed text.*

Dft	draft (usually a composition or rough draft; later drafts, when identifiable as such, are designated "2d Dft," &c.)
Dupl	duplicate
MS	manuscript (arbitrarily applied to most documents other than letters)
N	note, notes (memoranda, fragments, &c.)
PoC	polygraph copy
PrC	press copy
RC	recipient's copy
SC	stylograph copy
Tripl	triplicate

All manuscripts of the above types are assumed to be in the hand of the author of the document to which the descriptive symbol pertains. If not, that fact is stated. On the other hand, the following types of manuscripts are assumed *not* to be in the hand of the author, and exceptions will be noted:

FC	file copy (applied to all contemporary copies retained by the author or his agents)
Lb	letterbook (ordinarily used with FC and Tr to denote texts copied into bound volumes)

Tr   transcript (applied to all contemporary and later copies ex-
          cept file copies; period of transcription, unless clear by
          implication, will be given when known)

4. LOCATION SYMBOLS

The locations of documents printed in this edition from originals in
private hands and from printed sources are recorded in self-explanatory
form in the descriptive note following each document. The locations of
documents printed from originals held by public and private institutions in the United States are recorded by means of the symbols used in
the National Union Catalog in the Library of Congress; an explanation
of how these symbols are formed is given in Vol. 1: xl. The symbols
DLC and MHi by themselves stand for the collections of Jefferson Papers proper in these repositories; when texts are drawn from other collections held by these two institutions, the names of those collections
will be added. Location symbols for documents held by institutions outside the United States are given in a subjoined list. The lists of symbols
are limited to the institutions represented by documents printed or referred to in this volume.

CLU-C	University of California, Los Angeles, William An-drews Clark Memorial Library
CSmH	The Huntington Library, San Marino, California
CtHi	Connecticut Historical Society, Hartford
DLC	Library of Congress
DNA	The National Archives, with identifications of series (preceded by record group number) as follows:
	DL Domestic Letters
	PCC Papers of the Continental Congress
DSI	Smithsonian Institution
MHi	Massachusetts Historical Society, Boston
MWA	American Antiquarian Society, Worcester
MdAN	United States Naval Academy Library, Annapolis, Maryland
MeHi	Maine Historical Society, Portland
MoSHi	Missouri Historical Society, St. Louis
MoSW	Washington University Library, St. Louis
NHi	New-York Historical Society, New York City
NN	New York Public Library
NNPM	Pierpont Morgan Library, New York City
NRom	Jervis Library, Rome, New York
NjMoHP	Morristown National Historical Park, New Jersey

PHC	Haverford College Library, Pennsylvania
PHi	Historical Society of Pennsylvania, Philadelphia
PP	Free Library of Philadelphia
PPAmP	American Philosophical Society, Philadelphia
PPRF	Rosenbach Foundation, Philadelphia
PWacD	David Library of the American Revolution, Washington Crossing, Pennsylvania
Vi	Library of Virginia, Richmond
ViHi	Virginia Historical Society, Richmond
ViU	University of Virginia Library, Charlottesville
ViW	College of William and Mary Library, Williamsburg, Virginia
ViWC	Colonial Williamsburg, Inc., Williamsburg
WHi	State Historical Society of Wisconsin, Madison

The following symbol represents a repository located outside of the United States:

BPUG	Bibliothèque Publique et Universitaire de Genève, Switzerland
PRO	Public Record Office, London, with identification of series as follows:
	T Treasury

5. OTHER SYMBOLS AND ABBREVIATIONS

The following symbols and abbreviations are commonly employed in the annotation throughout the work.

Second Series   The topical series to be published as part of this edition, comprising those materials which are best suited to a topical rather than a chronological arrangement (see Vol. 1: xv-xvi)

TJ   Thomas Jefferson

TJ Editorial Files   Photoduplicates and other editorial materials in the office of *The Papers of Thomas Jefferson*, Princeton University Library

TJ Papers   Jefferson Papers (applied to a collection of manuscripts when the precise location of an undated, misdated, or otherwise problematic document must be furnished, and always preceded by the symbol for the institutional repository; thus "DLC: TJ Papers, 4: 628-9" represents a document in the Library of Congress, Jefferson Papers, volume 4, pages 628 and 629. Citations to volumes and folio numbers of the Jefferson Papers at the Library of Congress refer to the collection as it was arranged at the time the first microfilm edition was made in 1944-45. Access to the microfilm edition of the collection as it was rearranged under the Library's Presidential Papers Program is provided by the *Index to the Thomas Jefferson Papers* [Washington, D.C., 1976])

RG   Record Group (used in designating the location of documents in the National Archives)

SJL   Jefferson's "Summary Journal of Letters" written and received for the period 11 Nov. 1783 to 25 June 1826 (in DLC: TJ Papers). This register, kept in Jefferson's hand, has been checked against the TJ Editorial Files. It is to be assumed that all outgoing letters are recorded in SJL unless there is a note to the contrary. When the date of receipt of an incoming letter is recorded in SJL, it is incorporated in the notes. Information and discrepancies revealed in SJL but not found in the letter itself are also noted. Missing letters recorded in SJL are, where possible, accounted for in the notes to documents mentioning them or in related documents. A more detailed discussion of this register and its use in this edition appears in Vol. 6: vii-x

SJPL   "Summary Journal of Public Letters," an incomplete list of letters and documents written by TJ from 16 Apr. 1784 to 31 Dec. 1793, with brief summaries, in an amanuensis's hand. This is supplemented by six pages in TJ's hand, compiled at a later date, listing private and confidential memorandums and notes as well as official reports and communications by and to him as Secretary of State, 11 Oct. 1789 to 31 Dec. 1793 (in DLC: TJ Papers, Epistolary Record, 514-59 and 209-11, respectively; see Vol. 22: ix-x). Since nearly all documents in the amanuensis's list are registered in SJL, while few in TJ's list are so recorded, it is to be assumed that all references to SJPL are to the list in TJ's hand unless there is a statement to the contrary

V   Ecu

ƒ   Florin

£   Pound sterling or livre, depending upon context (in doubtful cases, a clarifying note will be given)

s   Shilling or sou (also expressed as /)

d   Penny or denier

₶   Livre Tournois

℔   Per (occasionally used for pro, pre)

6. SHORT TITLES

The following list includes short titles of works cited frequently in this edition. Since it is impossible to anticipate all the works to be cited in abbreviated form, the list is revised from volume to volume.

Abernethy, *Western Lands*   Thomas Perkins Abernethy, *Western Lands and the American Revolution*, New York, 1937

Adams, *Diary*   L. H. Butterfield and others, eds., *Diary and Autobiography of John Adams*, Cambridge, Mass., 1961, 4 vols.

Adams, *Works*   Charles Francis Adams, ed., *The Works of John Adams*, Boston, 1850-56, 10 vols.

AHR   *American Historical Review*, 1895-

Ammon, *Monroe*   Harry Ammon, *James Monroe: The Quest for National Identity*, New York, 1971

ANB   John A. Garraty and Mark C. Carnes, eds., *American National Biography*, New York and Oxford, 1999, 24 vols.

Annals   *Annals of the Congress of the United States: The Debates and Proceedings in the Congress of the United States ... Compiled from Authentic Materials*, Washington, D.C., Gales & Seaton, 1834-56, 42 vols. All editions are undependable and pagination varies from one printing to another. The first two volumes of the set cited here have "Compiled ... by Joseph Gales, Senior" on the title page and bear the caption "Gales & Seatons History" on verso and "of Debates in Congress" on recto pages. The remaining volumes bear the caption "History of Congress" on both recto and verso pages. Those using the first two volumes with the latter caption will need to employ the date of the debate or the indexes of debates and speakers.

APS   American Philosophical Society

ASP   *American State Papers: Documents, Legislative and Executive, of the Congress of the United States*, Washington, D.C., 1832-61, 38 vols.

Bear, *Family Letters*   Edwin M. Betts and James A. Bear, Jr., eds., *Family Letters of Thomas Jefferson*, Columbia, Mo., 1966

Bemis, *Pinckney's Treaty*   Samuel Flagg Bemis, *Pinckney's Treaty: America's Advantage from Europe's Distress, 1783-1800*, rev. ed., New Haven, 1960

Berkeley, *Beckley*   Edmund Berkeley and Dorothy Smith Berkeley, *John Beckley: Zealous Partisan in a Nation Divided*, Philadelphia, 1973

Betts, *Farm Book*   Edwin M. Betts, ed., *Thomas Jefferson's Farm Book*, Princeton, 1953

Betts, *Garden Book*   Edwin M. Betts, ed., *Thomas Jefferson's Garden Book, 1766-1824*, Philadelphia, 1944

Biog. Dir. Cong.   *Biographical Directory of the United States Congress, 1774-1989*, Washington, D.C., 1989

Biographie universelle   *Biographie universelle, ancienne et moderne*, new ed., Paris, 1843-65, 45 vols.

Bowman, *Neutrality*   Albert H. Bowman, *The Struggle for Neutrality: Franco-American Diplomacy during the Federalist Era*, Knoxville, 1974

Brant, *Madison*   Irving Brant, *James Madison*, Indianapolis, 1941-61, 6 vols.

Brigham, *American Newspapers*   Clarence S. Brigham, *History and Bibliography of American Newspapers, 1690-1820*, Worcester, Mass., 1947, 2 vols.

Bush, *Life Portraits*   Alfred L. Bush, *The Life Portraits of Thomas Jefferson*, rev. ed., Charlottesville, 1987

Callender, *Sedgwick & Co.*   James Thomson Callender, *Sedgwick & Co. or A Key to the Six Per Cent Cabinet*, Philadelphia, 1798

Cooke, *Coxe*   Jacob E. Cooke, *Tench Coxe and the Early Republic*, Chapel Hill, 1978

CVSP   William P. Palmer and others, eds., *Calendar of Virginia State Papers . . . Preserved in the Capitol at Richmond*, Richmond, 1875-93, 11 vols.

DAB   Allen Johnson and Dumas Malone, eds., *Dictionary of American Biography*, New York, 1928-36, 20 vols.

Dauer, *Adams Federalists*   Manning J. Dauer, *The Adams Federalists*, Baltimore, 1953

DeConde, *Quasi-War*   Alexander DeConde, *The Quasi-War: The Politics and Diplomacy of the Undeclared War with France, 1797-1801*, New York, 1966

DHSC   Maeva Marcus and others, eds., *The Documentary History of the Supreme Court of the United States, 1789-1800*, New York, 1985- , 6 vols.

Dictionnaire   *Dictionnaire de biographie française*, Paris, 1933- , 18 vols.

DNB   Leslie Stephen and Sidney Lee, eds., *Dictionary of National Biography*, 2d ed., New York, 1908-09, 22 vols.

DSB   Charles C. Gillispie, ed., *Dictionary of Scientific Biography*, New York, 1970-80, 16 vols.

Durey, *Callender*   Michael Durey, *"With the Hammer of Truth": James Thomson Callender and America's Early National Heroes*, Charlottesville, 1990

Duvergier, *Lois*   Jean B. Duvergier and others, eds., *Collection Complète des Lois, Décrets, Ordonnances, Réglemens, avis du Conseil-d'État*, Paris, 1834-1908, 108 vols.

EG   Dickinson W. Adams and Ruth W. Lester, eds., *Jefferson's Extracts from the Gospels*, Princeton, 1983, *The Papers of Thomas Jefferson*, Second Series

Ehrman, *Pitt*   John Ehrman, *The Younger Pitt: The Consuming Struggle*, London, 1996

Elkins and McKitrick, *Age of Federalism*   Stanley Elkins and Eric McKitrick, *The Age of Federalism*, New York, 1993

Evans   Charles Evans, Clifford K. Shipton, and Roger P. Bristol, comps., *American Bibliography: A Chronological Dictionary of all Books, Pamphlets and Periodical Publications Printed in the United States of America from . . . 1639 . . . to . . . 1820*, Chicago and Worcester, Mass., 1903-59, 14 vols.

Fitzpatrick, *Writings*   John C. Fitzpatrick, ed., *The Writings of George Washington*, Washington, D.C., 1931-44, 39 vols.

Ford   Paul Leicester Ford, ed., *The Writings of Thomas Jefferson*, Letterpress Edition, New York, 1892-99, 10 vols.

Freeman, *Washington*   Douglas Southall Freeman, *George Washington*, New York, 1948-57, 7 vols.; 7th volume by J. A. Carroll and M. W. Ashworth

Gaines, *Randolph*   William H. Gaines, Jr., *Thomas Mann Randolph: Jefferson's Son-in-Law*, Baton Rouge, 1966

Gibbs, *Memoirs*   George Gibbs, ed., *Memoirs of the Administration of Washington and John Adams, edited from the Papers of Oliver Wolcott, Secretary of the Treasury*, New York, 1846, 2 vols.

Greene, *American Science*   John C. Greene, *American Science in the Age of Jefferson*, Ames, Iowa, 1984

Haiman, *Kosciuszko*   Miecislaus Haiman, *Kosciuszko: Leader and Exile*, New York, 1977

HAW   Henry A. Washington, ed., *The Writings of Thomas Jefferson*, New York, 1853-54, 9 vols.

Heitman, *Dictionary*   Francis B. Heitman, comp., *Historical Register and Dictionary of the United States Army . . .* , Washington, D.C., 1903, 2 vols.

Heitman, *Register*   Francis B. Heitman, *Historical Register of Officers of the Continental Army during the War of the Revolution, April, 1775, to December, 1793*, new ed., Washington, D.C., 1914

Hening   William Waller Hening, ed., *The Statutes at Large; Being a Collection of All the Laws of Virginia*, Richmond, 1809-23, 13 vols.

Hoefer, *Nouv. biog. générale*   J. C. F. Hoefer, *Nouvelle biographie générale depuis les temps les plus reculés jusqu'a nos jours*, Paris, 1855-66, 46 vols.

JAH   *Journal of American History*, 1964-

JCC   Worthington C. Ford and others, eds., *Journals of the Continental Congress, 1774-1789*, Washington, D.C., 1904-37, 34 vols.

Jefferson Correspondence, Bixby   Worthington C. Ford, ed., *Thomas Jefferson Correspondence Printed from the Originals in the Collections of William K. Bixby*, Boston, 1916

JEP   *Journal of the Executive Proceedings of the Senate of the United States . . . to the Termination of the Nineteenth Congress*, Washington, D.C., 1828

JHD   *Journal of the House of Delegates of the Commonwealth of Virginia* (cited by session and date of publication)

JHR   *Journal of the House of Representatives of the United States*, Washington, D.C., 1826, 9 vols.

JS   *Journal of the Senate of the United States*, Washington, D.C., 1820-21, 5 vols.

Kimball, *Jefferson, Architect*   Fiske Kimball, *Thomas Jefferson, Architect*, Boston, 1916

King, *Life*   Charles R. King, ed. *The Life and Correspondence of Rufus King: Comprising His Letters, Private and Official, His Public Documents and His Speeches*, New York, 1894-1900, 6 vols.

Kline, *Burr*   Mary-Jo Kline, ed., *Political Correspondence and Public Papers of Aaron Burr*, Princeton, 1983, 2 vols.

Kohn, *Eagle and Sword*   Richard H. Kohn, *Eagle and Sword: The Federalists and the Creation of the Military Establishment in America 1783-1802*, New York, 1975

Kurtz, *Presidency of John Adams*   Stephen G. Kurtz, *The Presidency of John Adams: The Collapse of Federalism, 1795-1800*, Philadelphia, 1957

L & B   Andrew A. Lipscomb and Albert E. Bergh, eds., *The Writings of Thomas Jefferson*, Washington, D.C., 1903-04, 20 vols.

Latrobe, *Virginia Journals*   Edward C. Carter II and others, eds., *The Virginia Journals of Benjamin Henry Latrobe, 1795-1798*, New Haven, 1977, 2 vols.

LCB   Douglas L. Wilson, ed., *Jefferson's Literary Commonplace Book*, Princeton, 1989, *The Papers of Thomas Jefferson*, Second Series

Leonard, *General Assembly*   Cynthia Miller Leonard, comp., *The General Assembly of Virginia, July 30, 1619-January 11, 1978: A Bicentennial Register of Members*, Richmond, 1978

List of Patents   *A List of Patents granted by the United States from April 10, 1792, to December 31, 1836*, Washington, D.C., 1872

Logan, *Memoir*   Francis A. Logan, ed., *Memoir of Dr. George Logan of Stenton, by his widow Deborah Norris Logan*, Philadelphia, 1899

Lyons, *France Under the Directory*   Martyn Lyons, *France Under the Directory*, Cambridge, 1975

McColley, *Slavery*   Robert McColley, *Slavery and Jeffersonian Virginia*, Urbana, Ill., 1964

Madison, *Letters*   William C. Rives and Philip R. Fendall, eds., *Letters and Other Writings of James Madison . . . Published by Order of Congress*, Philadelphia, 1865, 4 vols.

Madison, *Papers*   William T. Hutchinson, Robert A. Rutland, J. C. A. Stagg, and others, eds., *The Papers of James Madison*, Chicago and Charlottesville, 1962- , 27 vols.

    Sec. of State Ser., 5 vols.

Malone, *Jefferson*   Dumas Malone, *Jefferson and his Time*, Boston, 1948-81, 6 vols.

Marshall, *Papers*   Herbert A. Johnson, Charles T. Cullen, Charles F. Hobson, and others, eds., *The Papers of John Marshall*, Chapel Hill, 1974- , 8 vols.

Mason, *Papers*   Robert A. Rutland, ed., *The Papers of George Mason 1725-1792*, Chapel Hill, 1970, 3 vols.

MB   James A. Bear, Jr., and Lucia C. Stanton, eds., *Jefferson's Memorandum Books: Accounts, with Legal Records and Miscellany, 1767-1826*, Princeton, 1997, *The Papers of Thomas Jefferson*, Second Series

Melton, *First Impeachment*   Buckner F. Melton, Jr., *The First Impeachment: The Constitution's Framers and the Case of Senator William Blount*, Macon, Ga., 1998

Merrill, *Jefferson's Nephews*   Boynton Merrill, Jr., *Jefferson's Nephews: A Frontier Tragedy*, Princeton, 1976

Miller, *Treaties*   Hunter Miller, ed., *Treaties and other International Acts of the United States of America*, Washington, D.C., 1931-48, 8 vols.

Monroe, *Writings*   Stanislas Murray Hamilton, ed., *The Writings of James Monroe*, New York, 1898-1903, 7 vols.

MVHR   *Mississippi Valley Historical Review*, 1914-64

National State Papers: Adams   Martin P. Claussen, ed., *National State Papers of the United States, 1789-1817. Part II: Texts of Documents. Administration of John Adams, 1797-1801*, Wilmington, 1980, 24 vols.

NDQW   Dudley W. Knox, ed., *Naval Documents Related to the Quasi-War between the United States and France*, Washington, 1935-38, 7 vols.

    Naval Operations from February 1797 to October 1798
    Naval Operations from November 1798 to March 1799

Nichols, *Architectural Drawings*   Frederick Doveton Nichols, *Thomas Jefferson's Architectural Drawings, Compiled and with Commentary and a Check List*, Charlottesville, 1978

Niemcewicz, *Under their Vine*   Julian Ursin Niemcewicz, *Under their Vine and Fig Tree: Travels through America in 1797-1799, 1805, with some Further Account of Life in New Jersey*, Elizabeth, N.J., 1965

Notes, ed. Peden   Thomas Jefferson, *Notes on the State of Virginia*, ed. William Peden, Chapel Hill, 1955

OED   Sir James Murray and others, eds., *A New English Dictionary on Historical Principles*, Oxford, 1888-1933

Palmer, *Democratic Revolution*   R. R. Palmer, *The Age of the Democratic Revolution: A Political History of Europe and America, 1760-1800*, Princeton, 1959-64, 2 vols.

Peale, *Papers*   Lillian B. Miller and others, eds., *The Selected Papers of Charles Willson Peale and His Family*, New Haven, 1983-2000, 5 vols. in 6

Perkins, *First Rapprochement*   Bradford Perkins, *The First Rapprochement: England and the United States, 1795-1805*, Philadelphia, 1955; Berkeley, 1967

Peterson, *Jefferson*   Merrill D. Peterson, *Thomas Jefferson and the New Nation*, New York, 1970

PMHB   *Pennsylvania Magazine of History and Biography*, 1877-

Prince, *Federalists*   Carl E. Prince, *The Federalists and the Origins of the U.S. Civil Service*, New York, 1977

PW   Wilbur S. Howell, ed., *Jefferson's Parliamentary Writings*, Princeton, 1988, *The Papers of Thomas Jefferson*, Second Series

Randall, *Life*   Henry S. Randall, *The Life of Thomas Jefferson*, New York, 1858, 3 vols.

Randolph, *Domestic Life*   Sarah N. Randolph, *The Domestic Life of Thomas Jefferson, Compiled from Family Letters and Reminiscences by His Great-Granddaughter*, 3d ed., Cambridge, Mass., 1939

Rose, *Prologue to Democracy*   Lisle A. Rose, *Prologue to Democracy: The Federalists in the South, 1789-1800*, Lexington, Ky., 1968

Scott and Rothaus, *Historical Dictionary*   Samuel F. Scott and Barry Rothaus, eds., *Historical Dictionary of the French Revolution, 1789-1799*, Westport, Conn., 1985, 2 vols.

Shackelford, *Jefferson's Adoptive Son*   George Green Shackelford, *Jefferson's Adoptive Son: The Life of William Short, 1759-1848*, Lexington, Ky., 1993

Shepherd, *Statutes*   Samuel Shepherd, ed., *The Statutes at Large of Virginia, from October Session 1792, to December Session 1806 . . .*, Richmond, 1835-36, 3 vols.

Smelser, *Navy*   Marshall Smelser, *The Congress Founds the Navy, 1787-1798*, South Bend, Ind., 1959

Smith, *Freedom's Fetters*   James Morton Smith, *Freedom's Fetters: The Alien and Sedition Laws and American Civil Liberties*, Ithaca, N.Y., 1956

Sowerby   E. Millicent Sowerby, comp., *Catalogue of the Library of Thomas Jefferson*, Washington, D.C., 1952-59, 5 vols.

Stewart, *French Revolution*   John H. Stewart, *A Documentary Survey of the French Revolution*, New York, 1951

Stewart, *Opposition Press*   Donald H. Stewart, *The Opposition Press of the Federalist Period*, Albany, 1969

Stinchcombe, *XYZ Affair*   William Stinchcombe, *The XYZ Affair*, Westport, Conn., 1980

Syrett, *Hamilton*   Harold C. Syrett and others, eds., *The Papers of Alexander Hamilton*, New York, 1961-87, 27 vols.

Tagg, *Bache*   James Tagg, *Benjamin Franklin Bache and the Philadelphia Aurora*, Philadelphia, 1991

Terr. Papers   Clarence E. Carter and John Porter Bloom, eds., *The Territorial Papers of the United States*, Washington, D.C., 1934-75, 28 vols.

TJR   Thomas Jefferson Randolph, ed., *Memoir, Correspondence, and Miscellanies, from the Papers of Thomas Jefferson*, Charlottesville, 1829, 4 vols.

Tolles, *Logan*   Frederick B. Tolles, *George Logan of Philadelphia*, New York, 1953

TQHGM   L. G. Tyler, ed., *Tyler's Quarterly Historical and Genealogical Magazine*, Richmond, 1919-52, 34 vols. in 33

Tucker, *Life*   George Tucker, *The Life of Thomas Jefferson*, Philadelphia, 1837, 2 vols.

U.S. Statutes at Large   Richard Peters, ed., *The Public Statutes at Large of the United States . . . 1789 to March 3, 1845*, Boston, 1855-56, 8 vols.

Van Horne, *Latrobe*   John C. Van Horne, ed., *The Correspondence and Miscellaneous Papers of Benjamin Henry Latrobe*, New Haven, 1984-88, 3 vols.

VMHB   *Virginia Magazine of History and Biography*, 1893-

Washington, *Diaries*   Donald Jackson and Dorothy Twohig, eds., *The Diaries of George Washington*, Charlottesville, 1976-79, 6 vols.

Washington, *Papers*   W. W. Abbot, Dorothy Twohig, Philander D. Chase, and others, eds., *The Papers of George Washington*, Charlottesville, 1983- , 43 vols.
   Pres. Ser., 1987- , 11 vols.
   Ret. Ser., 1998-99, 4 vols.

White, *Federalists*   Leonard White, *The Federalists: A Study in Administrative History*, New York, 1948

White, *Middle Ground*   Richard White, *The Middle Ground: Indians, Empires, and Republics in the Great Lakes Region, 1650-1815*, Cambridge, 1991

WMQ   *William and Mary Quarterly*, 1892-

Woods, *Albemarle*   Edgar Woods, *Albemarle County in Virginia*, Charlottesville, 1901

CONTENTS

CONTENTS

CONTENTS

CONTENTS

CONTENTS

CONTENTS

CONTENTS

CONTENTS

CONTENTS

CONTENTS

CONTENTS

1799

CONTENTS

ILLUSTRATIONS

Following page 364

THOMAS JEFFERSON BY ROBERT FIELD

This unfinished and now faded watercolor portrait on cardboard, $9\frac{1}{2}$ by $13\frac{1}{2}$ inches in size, is inscribed, apparently by the artist, "Painted by R. Field." Information about Field, who was evidently born in England, is fragmentary, but he was in Philadelphia by the mid-1790s, moved to Washington after it became the capital, and relocated to Boston in 1805. He left the United States three years later. This portrait was at one time thought to date from Jefferson's presidency, and a signature by him as president, clipped from a franked envelope, has been affixed to the lower left corner. But Jefferson's countenance in the picture, Field's known activity as a portraitist in Philadelphia in the later 1790s, and a chain of provenance that leads back to Charles Chauncy of Philadelphia all suggest that the painting dates from Jefferson's vice presidency. It does not resemble any other known portrait of him, and although it is thought to have been made from life, there is no record of his sitting for it (Bush, *Life Portraits*, 31-3; Harry Piers, *Robert Field: Portrait Painter in Oils, Miniature and Water-Colours and Engraver* [New York, 1927], 8-12, 19, 23-4, 186-7; DAB, 6:370-1).

Courtesy of the New-York Historical Society.

LUTHER MARTIN

Robert Field also painted this miniature on ivory of Luther Martin, the attorney general of Maryland whom an embittered Jefferson once described as a "federal bull-dog." This volume opens with one of the series of condemnatory letters that Martin addressed to Jefferson and published in Federalist newspapers. Martin excoriated Jefferson for his treatment in the *Notes on the State of Virginia* of the 1774 statement by the Mingo Indian Logan, who blamed Michael Cresap, Martin's deceased father-in-law, for the murder of members of his family. Martin's accusations prompted Jefferson to seek out additional information on the incident (Vol. 29:409-10n, 454-5n).

Field's miniature portraits, as distinguished from his watercolors, were painted on ivory, almost all of them ovals about $2\frac{1}{2}$ to $3\frac{1}{2}$ inches high mounted in a gold case or locket. In the late 1790s and early years of the nineteenth century Field painted miniatures of several prominent Americans, including two of Martha Washington and, in addition to Martin, members of influential Maryland families. Field charged $50 to execute one of these keepsake portraits on ivory (Piers, *Field*, 103, 109, 145-6, 168-74).

Courtesy of The Evergreen House Foundation, The Johns Hopkins University, Baltimore, Maryland.

"CINQUE-TETES, OR THE PARIS MONSTER"

Jefferson called the XYZ affair a "dish cooked up by Marshall." It was "the X.Y.Z. delusion," "the X.Y.Z. fever," "the XYZ. inflammation" (to Stevens Thomson Mason, 11 Oct. 1798; John Taylor, 26 Nov.; Monroe, 23 Jan. 1799;

Gerry, 26 Jan.; Edmund Pendleton, 29 Jan.; Nicholas Lewis and Madison, both 30 Jan.). But although Jefferson, insisting that the French government was not behind the solicitation of payments from the American envoys, rued the uses to which his political opponents put the diplomatic crisis, the sordid affair nonetheless provided convenient material for anyone seeking to influence American opinion against the French. In this well-known cartoon, the Directory, the five-member executive council of France, takes the form of a person with five viciously coarse heads ("cinque têtes") who snarls, " 'Il faut de l'argent, il faut beaucoup d'argent.'—Money, Money, Money!!" The uncowed envoys respond with a version of their famous retort: "Cease bawling, Monster! We will not give you six pence." To the side, the guillotine and a frightful woman, holding the French flag and liberty cap, represent the Terror, while a group including a well-dressed black from Saint-Domingue sit down to a plate of live frogs at a "Civic Feast." The verses below the image refer to American spoliation claims against France. The poem concludes, "Americans never From freedom will sever, Nor ADAMS, the voice of their mind; The Monster may roar, And make his throat sore, Till th' Devil & death stop his wind."

The vivid caricature has no date, and its artist is unknown. The envoys' account of their meeting of 27 Oct. 1797—at which Jean Conrad Hottinguer ("X") pressed them, "gentlemen, you do not speak to the point; it is money: it is expected that you will offer money," and the Americans rebuffed him with "no; no; not a sixpence"—was among dispatches that the Adams Administration sent to Congress on 3 Apr. 1798. The famous rejoinder was uttered by Charles Cotesworth Pinckney, as John Marshall recorded in his journal (ASP, *Foreign Relations*, 2:161; Marshall, *Papers*, 3:171).

Courtesy of the Huntington Library, San Marino, California.

TADEUSZ KOSCIUSZKO BY BENJAMIN WEST

In June 1797 American-born painter Benjamin West, then president of the Royal Academy, called on Tadeusz Kosciuszko at a hotel on Leicester Square in London, accompanied by Edward Bancroft and John Trumbull. Although the Polish exile's mobility was limited by slowly healing back and leg wounds and he spent much of his time sitting or reclining, Kosciuszko generally refused requests to pose for portraitists, and West began this picture from memory on the same day as his visit. Other artists who also managed to capture Kosciuszko's likeness included Richard Cosway, whose drawing of Kosciuszko is owned by the Fondazione Cosway in Lodi, Italy; Catherine Andras, who made portrait sculptures in wax; and an artist in Sweden. Their images of the much-feted Pole were reproduced as prints. Those portraits depicted Kosciuszko as West did, propped on a couch in a military-looking coat and boots, a bandage or scarf of silk, often narrow and black, around his head. Cosway, like West, placed a writing table with pen and inkwell close to the subject's hand, books and papers at his feet, a distinctive soft, high hat on a low table or footstool, and a sword visible but not dominating the picture. Cosway made the sword a saber, and the engravings of his work label it as the one bestowed on the general by the Whig Club, although that ceremonial gift was actually not ready until after its recipient had left England (see Julian Ursin Niemcewicz to TJ, 9 June 1798, and TJ to Kosciuszko, 18 June). Cosway may have made his drawing of Kosciuszko in preparation for a painting commissioned by the club. According to

ILLUSTRATIONS

legend Cosway peeked through a keyhole to draw the portrait-shy general or used his wife, Maria Cosway, to distract Kosciuszko as he sketched, although the details of any meeting between Cosway and Kosciuszko during the latter's two-week stay in London are not known (Chloe Hamilton, "A Portrait of General Kosciusko by Benjamin West," *Allen Memorial Art Museum Bulletin*, 9 [1952], 81-91; [Fondazione Cosway], *Maria e Richard Cosway*, Tino Gipponi, curator [Torino, 1998], 15; Niemcewicz, *Under their Vine*, fig. 7; Feliks Koneczny, *Tadeusz Kosciuszko: Na Setna Rocznice Zgonu Naczelnika; Zycie, Czyny, Duch* [Poznan, Poland, 1917], 347).

Apart from the particulars of the London setting, with St. Paul's visible through the window, West's picture shows Kosciuszko much as a caller would have seen him in the United States between August 1797 and May 1798. He continued to wear the kerchief to cover a scar on his forehead. The Irish radical Archibald Hamilton Rowan, who visited Kosciuszko in Philadelphia, left this description: "He sits in an arm chair, his head bound up with a broad black ribbon, dark curling hair, sparkling eye, *nez retrousé*"—that is, an upturned or snub nose—"his coat what we call Hussar, his legs bandaged, and the left one on a stool; he cannot walk, but thinks he is acquiring strength." Benjamin Rush observed that Kosciuszko's wounded leg and hip were mending, if slowly, and by the time he left the U.S. he was able to travel without the servant upon whom he had relied for assistance (William H. Drummond, ed., *The Autobiography of Archibald Hamilton Rowan* [Shannon, Ireland, 1972], 320; Julian Allen, *Autocrasy in Poland and Russia; or, A Description of Russian Misrule in Poland, and an Account of the Surveillance of Russian Spies at Home and Abroad* [New York, 1854], 127; Haiman, *Kosciuszko*, 50; Niemcewicz, *Under their Vine*, 65-6).

At a little over 12 by 17 inches, this oil painting by West is tiny compared to the huge historical works for which the artist is best known. It was displayed at the Royal Academy in 1798. An engraving of Kosciuszko hung at Monticello, although it has been suggested that that work was a head-and-shoulders portrait by Christian Josi after Joseph Grassi (Hamilton, "Portrait," 81n, 88; Susan R. Stein, *The Worlds of Thomas Jefferson at Monticello* [New York, 1993], 170-1).

Courtesy of Allen Memorial Art Museum, Oberlin College.

WEST'S "THE FRIGHT OF ASTYANAX"

During West's acquaintance with Kosciuszko in England the artist presented the Polish hero with this drawing, which is in ink with brown wash and blue and white coloring on brown paper, $12\frac{1}{2}$ by $18\frac{1}{8}$ inches in size. The scene is from book 6 of the *Iliad*, where Hector and his wife Andromache say goodbye. Their young son Astyanax, frightened by his father's flashing armor and crested helmet, cowers in the arms of a servant. Jefferson noted that West made the picture "for his own purposes," and the artist completed two paintings of the subject, neither of which has survived. In the panel on the left in the picture West inscribed: "From Benjn. West, Esq. to Genl. Kosciusko London June 10th. 1797." Kosciuszko in turn, on leaving the United States in the spring of 1798, gave the drawing to Jefferson, who considered it a watercolor painting. "Hector & Andromache," as Jefferson called it, hung at Monticello for many years. After his death, when other art from his estate was sold in 1833, the West drawing was one of a handful of works his granddaughter, Ellen Randolph Coolidge, held back from the sale. "I thought it a pity," she explained, "to

[xli]

sacrifice them as the others were sacrificed" (Stein, *Worlds*, 150, 447n; William Thornton to TJ, 11 Dec., TJ to Thornton, 24 Dec. 1814).
Courtesy of the J. Paul Getty Museum, Los Angeles.

JEFFERSON BY TADEUSZ KOSCIUSZKO

The convalescent Kosciuszko may have disliked having his own picture drawn but, forced to sit for extended periods, passed the time by making sketches of acquaintances and callers. The former military engineer also liked to draw landscapes. He carelessly discarded most of the portraits he made, but among those preserved are pictures of the master and the cabin boy of the ship *Adriana*, on which Kosciuszko traveled to America in 1797, and a young woman who was among the general's callers in Philadelphia. Like Kosciuszko's likeness of Jefferson, those examples are all profiles, and the portrait of Captain Lee of the *Adriana* also has the same upturned chin seen here (Haiman, *Kosciuszko*, 37, 52, 62, 65, 81, 168; Hamilton, "Portrait," 85).

Kosciuszko's original rendering of Jefferson, which he must have drawn during his residence in the United States during 1797-98, is known through examples of this colored aquatint engraving made by another Pole, Michel Sokolnicki, in Europe before the end of 1799. A copy was displayed at Monticello, and while Thomas Jefferson Randolph thought it a good likeness, his mother, Jefferson's daughter Martha, did not. Writing critically of another portrait, William Thornton wrote Jefferson: "Never was such injustice done to you, except by Sign Painters, and Genl. Kosciusko; than which *last* nothing can be so bad." Thornton said of Kosciuszko's portrait of Jefferson, "when I saw it, I did not wonder that he lost Poland—not that it is necessary a Genl. should be a Painter, but he should be a man of such Sense as to discover that he is not a Painter." But Jefferson, who ignored Thornton's scornful comment, kept a copy of this engraving in his quarters in the President's House in Washington in addition to the one hanging at Monticello. During Franklin Delano Roosevelt's administration, some of his admirers thought that Kosciuszko's likeness of Jefferson presaged the tilt of the later president's famous profile (Bush, *Life Portraits*, 28-30; Stein, *Worlds*, 170-1, 448n; Merrill D. Peterson, *The Jefferson Image in the American Mind* [New York, 1960], 360, 508; TJ to Isaac Coles, 29 Nov., Coles to TJ, 29 Dec. 1809; Thornton to TJ, 20 July, TJ to Thornton, 27 July 1816).
Courtesy of Yale University Art Gallery, Mabel Brady Garvan Collection.

JEFFERSON'S DOCKETING OF SENATE BILL CONCERNING ALIENS

As Jefferson presided over the Senate during the second session of the Fifth Congress, he recorded the progress of many bills through endorsements on the docketing panels, which identified the documents when filed. No record for a bill is fuller than that which he kept for the bill respecting aliens, which became known as the Alien Friends Act to distinguish it from the Alien Enemies Act, which would only come into effect during times of war (see TJ to Madison, 3 May 1798). While a Senate clerk wrote the bill's title on the panel, the chronological entries are all in Jefferson's hand and provide a complete legislative history of the bill from 4 May 1798, when it was brought in by Samuel Livermore, until it was passed by the Senate and sent to the House on 8 June. Jefferson continued to record on this handwritten copy of the bill even after the Senate began using a printed version that included many emendations in the vice president's hand. His endorsements also appear on its precursor, the 25 Apr. motion by James Hillhouse to bring in a bill for the removal of aliens dangerous to the "peace and safety" of the United States. Notations and emendations by the vice president appear on other extant documents in the Senate records relating to the alien friends legislation, including three amendments considered before the bill was recommitted on 1 June and the amendments sent by the House on 21 June (see Appendix). Although Jefferson paid close attention to actions taken, his markings are clerical in nature. It is in his correspondence that he expressed his concerns about the alien bill. On 26 Apr. he reported to Madison that Hillhouse had introduced a motion "for giving power to send away suspected aliens. this is understood to be meant for Volney & Collot." In writing to Thomas Mann Randolph on 9 May, he characterized the Senate bill as "worthy of the 8th. or 9th. century."

Courtesy of the National Archives.

"THE TIMES; A POLITICAL PORTRAIT"

Like the "Cinque-Tetes," this partisan cartoon, with its unflattering portrayal of Jefferson, has also been widely reproduced from a single rare example. Although the artist is unknown, this picture shows the influence of William Cobbett, at least as a source of references recognizable to many Americans at the time. Dressed in uniform and driving a version of a chariot, George Washington leads a disciplined volunteer army to meet the French, who in the left of the picture, identified by their liberty-cap insignia on poles, are capturing and killing unarmed Americans. A caption below the marauders proclaims, "The Cannibals are landing," an allusion to Cobbett's 1798 propaganda pamphlet, *Cannibals' Progress*, which accused the French military of terrible deeds against German civilians (see Benjamin H. Latrobe to TJ, 22 Sep. 1798). The trio of malcontents trying to impede Washington's progress are usually identified as Jefferson on the right, Albert Gallatin tugging at the wheel of the vehicle, and James Madison. Here again Cobbett's influence is evident, for the caption near Gallatin says "Stop de wheels of de gouvernement," words that Cobbett had earlier put into the immigrant Gallatin's mouth and that had been used in another mocking cartoon with a similar profile of Gallatin. The hapless figure on the ground, trampled by Washington's unswerving escort, is generally thought to be Benjamin Franklin Bache, Cobbett's great rival and the editor of the *Aurora*, a copy of which lies on the ground before him. Bache died of yellow fever in mid-September 1798. This undated broadsheet cartoon, therefore, was probably made sometime after Washington's appointment early in July as lieutenant general and commander in chief of the army and before Bache's death (William Cobbett, *Peter Porcupine in America: Pamphlets on Republicanism and Revolution*, ed. David A. Wilson [Ithaca, 1994], 141, 237; William Murrell, *A History of American Graphic Humor*, 2 vols. [New York, 1933-38], 1:35, 38, 48-9; Jeffrey A. Smith, *Franklin and Bache: Envisioning the Enlightened Republic* [New York, 1990], frontispiece; Bernard Fay, *The Two Franklins: Fathers of American Democracy* [Boston, 1933], xvi; Thomas C. Blaisdell, Jr., Peter Selz, and others, *The American Presidency in Political Cartoons: 1776-1976*, rev. ed. [Salt Lake City, 1976], 40-1; Henry Tazewell to TJ, 5 July 1798; James Thomson Callender to TJ, 26 Oct. 1798).

Courtesy of the New-York Historical Society.

Volume 30

1 January 1798 to 31 January 1799

JEFFERSON CHRONOLOGY

1743 · 1826

1743	Born at Shadwell, 13 Apr. (New Style).
1760	Entered the College of William and Mary.
1762	"quitted college."
1762-1767	Self-education and preparation for law.
1769-1774	Albemarle delegate to House of Burgesses.
1772	Married Martha Wayles Skelton, 1 Jan.
1775-1776	In Continental Congress.
1776	Drafted Declaration of Independence.
1776-1779	In Virginia House of Delegates.
1779	Submitted Bill for Establishing Religious Freedom.
1779-1781	Governor of Virginia.
1782	His wife died, 6 Sep.
1783-1784	In Continental Congress.
1784-1789	In France as Minister Plenipotentiary to negotiate commercial treaties and as Minister Plenipotentiary resident at Versailles.
1790-1793	Secretary of State of the United States.
1797-1801	Vice President of the United States.
1801-1809	President of the United States.
1814-1826	Established the University of Virginia.
1826	Died at Monticello, 4 July.

VOLUME 30

1 January 1798 to 31 January 1799

2 Jan. 1798	Writes Mann Page that "Congress have done nothing interesting."
27 Jan.	Provides Tazewell with notes on jury trials and impeachments.
23 Mch.	Writes description of moldboard plow for Sir John Sinclair.
3 Apr.	Adams sends XYZ dispatches to Congress.
5 May	Aids Tadeusz Kosciuszko in his secret departure from Philadelphia.
28 May	Adams signs act authorizing provisional army.
4 June	Writes attestation for George Logan, who soon embarks for Europe.
7 June	Volney, Victor Marie du Pont, and others leave for France.
25 June	Alien Friends Act signed by Adams.
27 June	Departs Philadelphia, arriving at Montpelier 2 July and at Monticello the next day.
6 July	Alien Enemies Act signed by Adams.
14 July	Sedition Act and act for laying direct tax signed by Adams.
July	Concern for daughter Mary's health.
by 4 Oct.	Writes resolutions against Alien and Sedition Acts (adopted by Kentucky legislature in November).
5-9 Oct.	Matthew Lyon is the first to be prosecuted under the Sedition Act.
ca. 15 Oct.	Madison visits Monticello.
ca. 9 Nov.	Logan returns from Europe.
23 Nov.	Will delay trip to Philadelphia to oversee work at Monticello.
26 Nov.	Writes John Taylor he is resuming emphasis on tobacco as a crop.
3 Dec.	Third session of Fifth Congress opens.
18 Dec.	Leaves Monticello, spending first night at Montpelier and arriving in Philadelphia on Christmas.
24 Dec.	Petition for election of grand jurors presented to the Virginia House of Delegates.
11 Jan. 1799	Senate votes to dismiss impeachment charges against William Blount.
26 Jan.	Articulates political principles in letter to Elbridge Gerry.
30 Jan.	Logan Act becomes law.

THE PAPERS OF
THOMAS JEFFERSON

·《════════》·

From Luther Martin

Sir,   Baltimore, January 1st, 1798.

It has been repeatedly suggested to me by my friends, that I am under no obligation to pursue any further the subject of discussion between us.—That having already publicly denied the charges made by you against Col. Cresap, and demanded from you the authority upon which you published them, your *silence* ought to convince the world those charges are *false*.—And I have been advised by them to leave it in this situation.

With these friends most certainly I should perfectly concur in sentiment, were all mankind in forming their judgments, uniformly influenced solely by unbiassed and impartial reason; and, were there not among your friends and adherents, persons of sense and merit, it is most probable I should have followed their advice; for why should I be very solicitous what those of a *different character* might think of myself or my connexions? But, sir, I am disposed to do you justice;—I will acknowledge that in the number of those devoted to you, there are persons of real worth, warmly attached to the Constitution of the United States, zealous supporters of our Government, and of the just, wise and enlightened system of politics it hath pursued.

These persons *do*, and *will*, make for that your silence a variety of excuses, however weak they may be, rather than to admit from it the conclusion, which impartial reason would necessarily infer.

Yes, sir, there are persons, and those too not deficient in understanding, who will not allow that your silence respecting the letter to Mazzei, is sufficient to induce a belief of your being its author, or of your approving the sentiments expressed therein!!!

A knowledge of this forbids me to leave any undertaking incomplete, and impels me to proceed until I enforce conviction on minds, over the most prejudiced and most partial.

Here let me observe, should the *Speech* of Logan be genuine, which however I controvert, I am willing to admit him, if you please, to be

[3]

answerable for the facts contained therein; but even this cannot *lessen your responsibility* for the *facts* contained in his *Story*.

Logan it is true, if that speech be genuine, declared that "Col. Cresap, in cold blood, and unprovoked, murdered all his relations, not sparing his women, and children;" an assertion, which from a savage would have had very little weight, except among certain philosophers, either in Europe or America. But it is *you*, sir, who in the *Story* pledge your character, as a man and historian, for the *Truth* of this savage's assertion.—It is *you*, who *minutely detail* the circumstances, which *you* aver attended this murder. And it is *you*, sir, who declared Col. Cresap to have been infamous for the many murders committed by him upon the much injured Indians!!

Be so good, Sir, as to to keep this in your mind; it may serve you as a *preparative* for certain remarks, which, in the sequel of these letters, I probably shall make, and which, however correct they may be, I am inclined to think will not perfectly harmonize with your feelings.

Had you, when you thought proper to introduce the name of Col. Cresap, confined yourself simply to what was connected with Logan and his family, my task would have been as easy as short; but as you have also declared him to *have been infamous* for his many murders of the Indians, I am under the necessity of investigating the lives of the only two of the name of Cresap, to either of whom, as I have in a former letter observed, the *calumny* could have been meant to be applied.

Having thus made these cursory observations, I shall now proceed to shew the *falshood* of those allegations, which you as a *gentleman* and *man of honor* ought either to have *authenticated* or *retracted*, and for that purpose, taking upon myself to establish *the negative* to the satisfaction of the most prejudiced among your friends, I mean to prove

1st. That Colonel Thomas Cresap, or Mr. Michael Cresap, his son, were not reputed infamous for murders committed upon the Indians; and that neither of them deserved to have been so reputed.

2d. That Colonel Cresap, Mr. Michael Cresap, or any other of the name of Cresap had not any share in the death of Logan's family.

3d. That the speech of Logan is fictitious.

And 4th, which to be sure is of very little consequence, that if Logan was a chief of the Mingoes, he owed his promotion not to his nation, but to the author of the Notes of Virginia.

In the prosecution of what I have now undertaken I shall first introduce to you, and give you a

Short sketch of the history of Colonel Thomas Cresap.

This gentleman was born in England, in the county of Yorkshire. He came in the early part of his life, but not before his arrival at manhood, to America. He married Hannah, one of the daughters of Mr. Daniel Johnson, who lived in New Jersey.

If I am not much mistaken, my relation Colonel Ephraim Martin, who commanded a regiment at the battle of Long Island, in which he was severely wounded, and who was afterwards one of the council in my native state, that of New Jersey, was the son of another of the daughters.

Before the year 1732, Mr. Cresap had established himself in Baltimore county, on the northern frontier of Maryland, on the river Susquehanna. Among other lands which he there held, is that beautiful and valuable tract at Wright's ferry on the west side of that river, including the spot where the buildings are erected, and where the ferry is kept. This tract was granted to him by a particular order, given by the then Lord Baltimore.

About the latter part of the year 1732, very serious disputes arose between the proprietors of Maryland and Pennsylvania, and between the settlers under those proprietors, concerning their respective rights to the lands on that part of the Susquehanna. These disputes continued several years. A number of inhabitants were induced to settle there, by virtue of a proclamation issued by Lord Baltimore, on the 2d day of March 1732, inviting and encouraging persons to seat themselves in that part of his province, and promising them protection. Mr. Cresap, who was ever on the frontier, was seated there for some time before.

On the part of the Pennsylvanians various efforts were made to detach those settlers from the jurisdiction of Maryland, and to dispossess by force those whom they could not influence by persuasion.

A petty war raged there for some years. A considerable number were wounded. Some lives were lost. Mr. Cresap's zeal for the interest of the proprietor of Maryland, and his intrepidity and address in repelling their attacks rendered him, as might naturally be expected, peculiarly obnoxious to the Pennsylvanian settlers.

About the first of Feb. in the year 1733, —— and —— with a number of armed men broke into his house, but were repulsed by him and his family; and one of the assailants being wounded by a bullet discharged from his rifle, they sought their safety in flight. After this time various attempts were made to waylay and carry him off. At length rewards were offered to those who would apprehend him dead or alive.

He, however, triumphed over all these efforts, until sometime in the month of November, in the year 1736, when a great number of persons armed with guns and other weapons, headed by —— and —— of Lancaster county, laid siege to his house, and after a most obstinate resistance, they at length "set it on fire, when himself, his wife, his children, and six others were in it, and burned the same to the ground, and while

[5]

those persons endeavoured *to escape the flames* several *guns were fired at them*, whereby one was killed, and others wounded, and several taken prisoners, and carried to the jails in Pennsylvania."

Here, sir, is an instance of cruelty, which might excite the indignation of any person, except a philosopher, almost as much as the destruction of Logan's family.

The foregoing statement of facts I have copied with fidelity from a proclamation issued by his Britannic Majesty, in council, dated at his court at Kensington, on the 25th day of May 1738.*

You will observe in this narrative of the injuries inflicted on Mr. Cresap, I have not introduced any names, not even their initials. I wish not to wound the feelings of any individual, but of *yourself*. Nor should I be solicitous, were it in my power, to transmit any person, an account of his conduct towards myself or any connexions, to posterity as deserving of *infamy*; I shall, however, take some pains to transmit *you*, sir, to the *latest posterity* as deserving *severe censure*.

But to return to my subject;—Mr. Cresap, at the time captain Cresap, was one of those, who were wounded and made prisoners. He was carried in *irons*, and I could name, sir, the man by whom they were made, to the jail of Philadelphia, and threatened to be brought to trial for his life. I possess the original plea to the jurisdiction of the courts of Pennsylvania, prepared by the then attorney general of Maryland, and sent to Mr. Cresap by governor Ogle, to be used, had an attempt been made to carry the threat into execution.

He remained imprisoned until on or about the 29th day of August 1738, when governor Thomas discharged him and several of his fellow sufferers from their confinement by virtue of an order of his Majesty [in] council, of the same date with the beforementioned proclamation.

But I fear, lest I may fatigue you, therefore here close this letter, And am, with all *due* respect,

Your obedient servant,   LUTHER MARTIN

---

* *Extract of a Proclamation, issued by* Governor Ogle *in council, dated at the city of Annapolis, March 29th*, 1737.

"Whereas it appears to this board, by *the testimony* of several *witnesses*, that ———— of Lancaster county, and ———— of the same county, with a *great number*† of other persons, armed with guns and other weapons, assembled themselves together in a riotous and unlawful manner, at the late dwelling house of Captain Thomas Cresap, in Baltimore county sometime in November last, and being there assembled killed and *murdered* one Michael Malone, and *burned the dwelling house* of the said Cresap, with *all his goods and chattels* being *in* and *about the said dwelling house*; the attorney general is hereby ordered to prosecute all the aforesaid offenders, for the said crimes, according to the utmost rigour of the law, &c." I have rather better authority for the facts I state, than can, I suspect, be produced in support of the speech and story of Logan.

† All these against Col. Cresap his *wife* some young *children*, and six other men!

Printed in *Porcupine's Gazette*, 4 Jan. 1798; at head of text: "No. 3." and "To the Honourable Thomas Jefferson, Esqr. Vice-President of the United States."

THE CHARGES MADE BY YOU AGAINST COL. CRESAP: see TJ to John Gibson, 31 May 1797. LETTER TO MAZZEI: see Jefferson's Letter to Philip Mazzei, 24 Apr. 1796.

To John Page

MY DEAR PAGE   Philadelphia [1] Jan. 1798.

You have probably seen or heard of some very abusive letters addressed to me in the publick papers by a mr Martin of Baltimore, on the subject of Logan's speech, cited in the Notes on Virginia. I do not mean to notice mr Martin, or go into the newspapers on the subject. but I am still anxious to enquire into the foundation of that story, & if I find any thing wrong in it it shall be corrected, & what is right supported either in some new edition of that work or in an Appendix to it. you and I were so much together about the year 1774. that I take for granted that whatsoever I heard, you heard also, and therefore that your memory can assist mine in recollecting the substance of the story, how it came to us, and who could now be applied to to give information relative to it. you were more in Ld. Dunmore's & Foy's company than I was, & probably heard more of it from that family than I did. I must pray you to rub up your recollection & communicate to me as fully as you can what you can recall to your mind relative to it. and if you can procure me the evidence, or the recollections of any other person on it it will much oblige me.

We have now been met 7. weeks and have done nothing except put off the stamp act to July next. nor does it seem as if there would be any thing to do. we are waiting for news from France. a letter from Taleyrand (French minister of foreign affairs) to mr Le Tombe Consul here, dated the day after the arrival of our ministers at Paris, says they will be well received, and that every disposition exists on the side of France to accomodate their differences with us. I imagine you will have seen Monroe's work, as many copies were sent to Richmond by Bache. we hourly expect Fauchet's pamphlet from the same press. I will send you a copy. present me respectfully to mrs Page and accept assurances of the constant friendship of my dear Sir

Your's affectionately   TH: JEFFERSON

RC (NHi); day of month in dateline supplied from PrC; addressed: "John Page of the General assembly of Virginia now at Richmond"; last three words of address struck through, "York" interlined, and the notation "forwd" made in an unknown hand; franked and postmarked. PrC (DLC); TJ inserted "1." in ink in dateline. Not recorded in SJL.

For the STAMP ACT that was originally supposed to go into effect on New Year's

Day, see TJ to Madison, 29 June 1797, and TJ to Thomas Mann Randolph, 14 Dec. 1797. A letter of 29 Sep. 1797 from Charles Maurice de Talleyrand-Périgord, the FRENCH MINISTER OF FOREIGN AFFAIRS, to Philippe de Létombe, his government's CONSUL in the United States, had noted the arrival of Charles Cotesworth Pinckney, Elbridge Gerry, and John Marshall in Paris (TJ to John Taylor, 23 Dec. 1797). MONROE'S WORK, *A View of the Conduct of the Executive*, had been published in December (see note to Monroe to TJ, [22] Oct. 1797). For Joseph FAUCHET'S PAMPHLET, *Coup d'oeil sur l'état actuel des nos rapports politiques avec les États-Unis*, see TJ's 23 Dec. letter to Taylor.

To Mann Page

DEAR SIR   Philadelphia Jan. 2. 1798.

I do not know whether you have seen some very furious abuse of me in the Baltimore papers by a mr Luther Martin, on account of Logan's speech published in the Notes on Virginia. he supposes both the speech & story made by me to support an argument against Buffon. I mean not to enter into a newspaper contest with mr Martin. but I wish to collect, as well as the lapse of time will permit the evidence on which we received that story. it was brought to us I remember by Ld. Dunmore & his officers on their return from the expedition of 1774. I am sure it was from them I got it. as you were very much in the same circle of society in Wms.burg with myself, I am in hopes your memory will be able to help out mine, and recall some facts which have escaped me. I ask it as a great favor of you to endeavor to recollect & to communicate to me all the circumstances you possibly can relative to this matter, particularly the authority on which we recieved it & the names of any persons who you think can give me information. I mean to fix the fact with all possible care & truth, and either to establish or correct the former statement in an Appendix to the Notes on Virginia, or in the first republication of the work.

Congress have done nothing interesting except postponing the Stamp act. an act continuing the currency of the foreign coins 3. years longer has past the Representatives, but hangs in the Senate. we have hopes that our envoys will be received decently at Paris and some compromise agreed on. there seems to be little appearance of peace in Europe. those among us who were so timid when they apprehended war with England, are now bold in propositions to arm. I do not think however that the Representatives will change the policy pursued by them at their summer session. the land tax will not be brought forward this year. Congress of course have no real business to be employed on. we may expect in a month or six weeks to hear so far from our commissioners at Paris as to judge what will be the aspect of our situation with France. if

peaceable, as we hope, I know of nothing which should keep us together.—in my late journey to this place I came through Culpeper, &
Prince William to Georgetown. when I return, it will be through the
Eastern shore (a country I have never seen) by Norfolk & Petersburg.
so that I shall fail then also of the pleasure of seeing you. present my
respectful compliments to mrs Page, and accept assurances of the sincere esteem of Dr. Sir

Your friend & servt.   TH: JEFFERSON

PrC (DLC); at foot of first page: "Mann
Page esquire."

For the history of the ACT CONTINUING
THE CURRENCY OF THE FOREIGN COINS, see
TJ to Thomas Mann Randolph, 14 Dec.
1797. The issue of a direct or LAND TAX
arose at the beginning of 1797 but did not
then come to a vote. In spite of TJ's prediction of continued inaction during 1798,
however, the measure was BROUGHT FOR-
WARD during the spring and became law
in July (Madison to TJ, 15 Jan. 1797; TJ
to Madison, 17 May 1798).

To James Madison

DEAR SIR   Jany 3. 1798.

Your's of Dec. 25. came to hand yesterday. I shall observe your directions with respect to the post day. I have spoken with the Depy. Post.
M. Genl. on the subject of our Fredericksburg post. he never knew
before that the Fredsbg printer had taken the contract of the rider. he
will be glad if either in your neighborhood or ours some good person
will undertake to ride from April next. the price given this year is 330.
D. & it will go to the lowest bidder who can be depended on. I understand (tho not from him) that Wyatt will be changed; and in general
they determine that printers shall not be postmasters or riders.—before
the receipt of your letter, I had informed Colo. Monroe of the paper you
had put into my hands for him. the draught was accepted & paiment
will be made at the proper term. Genl Van Cortlandt lodging in the
same house with me, I had shewn him Bailey's note, & he said he would
let him know that I was the holder of it.—all the nails you desire can be
furnished from Monticello. I will give directions accordingly by my
letter of this day. but as we can furnish the whole demand at any time in
3. weeks, and I presume you will not want them till your walls are done,
I shall only direct that they go about them whenever they receive notice
from you that you will soon want them. if you can give the second notification one month before your actual want, they will be in readiness.—
our weather here has been as with you, cold & dry. the thermometer[1]
has been at 8°. the river closed here the first week of December, which
has caught a vast number of vessels destined for departure. it deadens

also the demand for wheat. the price at New York is 1.75 & of flour 8.50 to 9. tobacco 11. to 12 D. there need be no doubt of greater prices. the bankruptcies here continue; the prison is full of the most reputable merchants, & it is understood that the scene is not yet got to it's height. prices have fallen greatly. the market is cheaper than it has been for 4. years. labour & house rent much reduced. dry goods somewhat. it is expected that they will fall till they get nearly to old prices. money scarce beyond all example.

The Representatives have rejected the President's proposition for enabling him to prorogue them. a law is past putting off the Stamp act till July next. the land tax will not be brought on. the Secretary of the Treasury says he has money enough. no doubt these two measures may be taken up more boldly at the next session when most of the elections will be over. it is imagined the Stamp act will be extended or attempted on every possible object. a bill has past the Repr. to suspend for 3. years the law arresting the currency of foreign coins. the Senate propose an amendment continuing[2] the currency of the foreign gold only. very possibly the bill may be lost. the object of opposing the bill is to make the French crowns a subject of speculation (for it seems they fell on the President's proclamation to a Dollar in most of the states) and to force bank paper (for want of other medium), through all the states generally.   Tenche Coxe is displaced, & no reason even spoken of. it is therefore understood to be for his activity[3] during the late election. it is said that the people from hence quite to the Eastern extremity are beginning to be sensible that their government has been playing a foul game. in Vermont Chipman was elected Senator by a majority of one against the republican candidate. in Maryland Loyd by a majority of one against Winder the republican candidate. Tichenor chosen Governor of Vermont by a very small majority. the house of Representatives of this state is become republican by a firm majority of 6. two counties it is said have come over generally to the republican side. it is thought the republicans have also a majority in the N. York H. of representatives. hard elections are expected there between Jay & Livingston, & here between Ross & McKean. in the H. of Representatives of Congress the Republican interest has at present on strong questions a majority of about half a dozen as is conjectured & there are as many of their firmest men absent; not one of the Antirepublicans is from his post. the bill for permitting private vessels to arm, was put off to the 1st. Monday in February by a sudden vote & a majority of 5. it was considered as an index of their dispositions on that subject, tho' some voted both ways on other ground. it is most evident that the Antireps wish to get rid off Blount's impeachment. many metaphysical niceties are handing about in conversation to shew that it cannot be sustained. to shew the contrary it is evident must be the task of the Republicans, or of no body. Monroe's book is considered as masterly by all those who are not opposed in principle, and it is deemed unanswerable. an answer however is commenced in Fenno's paper of yesterday under the signature of Scipio. the real author not yet conjectured. as I take these papers merely to preserve them, I will forward them to you, as you can easily return them to me on my arrival at home; for I shall not[4] see you on my way, as I mean to go by the Eastern shore & Petersburg. perhaps the paragraphs in some of these abominable papers may draw from you now & then a squib. a pamphlet of Fauchet's appeared yesterday. I send you a copy under another cover.—a handbill is just arrived here from N.Y. where they learn from a vessel which left Havre about the 9th. of Nov. that the emperor had signed the definitive articles, given up Mantua, evacuated Mentz, agreed to give passage to the French troops into Hanover, and that the Portuguese Ambassador had been ordered to quit Paris on account of the seisure of fort St. Julian's by the English, supposed with the connivance of Portugal.[5] tho' this is ordinary mercantile news, it looks like truth. the latest official intelligence from Paris is from Taleyrand Perigord to the French Consul here (Letombe) dated Sep. 28. saying that our envoys were arrived & would find every disposition on the part of his government to accomodate with us. my affectionate respects to mrs Madison; to yourself health & friendship. Adieu.

RC (DLC: Madison Papers); at foot of first page: "Mr. Madison." PrC (DLC). Listed in SJL as "1 Jan." but written between entries for 2 and 3 Jan. 1798.

FREDSBG PRINTER: Timothy Green of the *Virginia Herald* (Prince, *The Federalists*, 209, 223). For the benefits enjoyed by PRINTERS serving as POSTMASTERS, see same, 208-12. By 1800 Green had succeeded William Wiatt as postmaster at Fredericksburg (Madison, *Papers*, 17:67; ASP, *Miscellaneous*, 1:292). For the PRESIDENT'S PROPOSITION to postpone the meeting of Congress under certain circumstances such as yellow fever epidemics, see Madison to TJ, 25 Dec. 1797. The House defeated the measure on 18 Dec. by a 58 to 32 vote (JHR, 3:106; *Annals*, 7:739).

BILL FOR PERMITTING PRIVATE VESSELS TO ARM: see TJ to Francis Walker, 21 Dec. 1797. On 26 Dec. the first vote on the postponement of the bill carried 40 to 37. Another vote the same day to reconsider the postponement was defeated 44 to 38 (JHR, 3:115; *Annals*, 7:764-74).

The response to MONROE'S BOOK, which appeared as fifteen essays in John FENNO'S PAPER, the *Gazette of the United States*, between 2 and 27 Jan. 1798 UNDER THE SIGNATURE OF SCIPIO, was written by Connecticut Federalist Senator Uriah Tracy (DAB; Oliver Wolcott, Jr., to George Washington, 30 Jan. 1798, in Washington, *Papers, Ret. Ser.*, 2:61-2). Shortly after the last installment appeared, the essays were published in Philadelphia as a pamphlet entitled *Reflections on Monroe's View, of the Conduct of the Executive, as Published in the Gazette of the United States, under the Signature of Scipio. In which the Commercial Warfare of France is Traced to the French Faction in this Country, as Its Source, and the Motives of Opposition, &c.* Monroe's letter to George Logan, 24 June 1795, and an extract of TJ's letter to Philip Mazzei, 24 Apr. 1796, were appended to the last essay. Criticizing Monroe for discussing "confidential" State

Department communications, Tracy identified and charged Monroe with "acts of misconduct" and concluded that the "general tenor" of his actions throughout the mission was servile to France and "disrespectful, if not disobedient, to the Executive of the United States." "Scipio" argued that Monroe's misdeeds were "sufficient cause for his recall" (same, 5, 7, 9-74).

The same news that TJ reported from the HANDBILL appeared in the *Philadelphia Gazette*, 3 Jan. 1798, as "Important Intelligence" from the brig *Rosetta* which had arrived from HAVRE with information on the Treaty of Campoformio signed by Austria and France on 17 Oct. 1797. Austria surrendered its claims to the Low Countries, the left bank of the Rhine, and Milan, and recognized the Cisalpine Republic, receiving in

exchange territorial concessions in Venice, Salzburg, and elsewhere (Alexandre Jehan Henry de Clercq, ed., *Recueil des traités de la France*, 23 vols. in 24 [Paris, 1864-1917], 1:335-44). On 26 Oct. 1797 the French Directory ordered the PORTUGUESE AMBASSADOR António de Araújo Azevedo TO QUIT PARIS, charging that PORTUGAL had violated its recent treaty with France by allowing the British army to take over its military posts and forts (same, 344-5).

[1] TJ here canceled "here." PrC lacks emendation.
[2] Word interlined in place of "restraining."
[3] TJ here canceled "against."
[4] Word interlined.
[5] Word interlined in place of "England."

From George Jefferson

DEAR SIR,   Richmond Janr. 4th. 1798.

Mr. Boyce somewhat contrary to my expectation this day took up Mr. Barnes's draft—I have paid Mr. Walker $103.92. & to an order of Mr. Millers, a part of the sum which you direct to be paid him.

I am Very respectfully Dear Sir Your Mt. Obt. servt.

GEO. JEFFERSON

RC (MHi); at foot of text: "Thomas Jefferson esqr. Philada."; endorsed by TJ as received 11 Jan. 1798 and so recorded in SJL.

On 21 Dec. 1797 TJ sent Isaac Miller AN ORDER on George Jefferson for $73.62 (MB, 2:976). Letters from TJ to Miller of 3 Feb. 1794, 10 Sep. 1796, and 21 Dec. 1797, recorded in SJL, have not been found.

From Stevens Thomson Mason

DEAR SIR   Phila Jany 4th 1798

I subjoin an extract of a letter which I informed you I had received from Colo Normand Bruce of Frederick County Maryland and am

With great regard Your Obt Sert   STES. THON. MASON

"I am just informed that Mr Jefferson has requested Capt Perry Fitzhugh to procure information of Michael Cresap's conduct relating to the murder of the Indians in spring 1774. I have no doubt but that Capt Fitzhugh (who is a most friendly man) will exert himself to serve

[12]

Mr Jefferson. but the great distance he lives from where the affair happened, as well as his want of sight, must render this very inconvenient to him. it may be doubtful whether he may be able to obtain a satisfactory statement of facts, to procure which, it would seem, that Mr Jefferson ought to apply to some intelligent person near the neighbourhood where the transactions happened, which was, about cross creek in Ohio County; where no doubt many persons are yet to be found who were in that part of the Country at the time. Being a stranger to Mr. Jefferson you will excuse my intimating this to you. I know little of Cresap and nothing of the transactions but from hearsay. but he [. . .] censured at the time."

RC (DLC); bottom edge mutilated; endorsed by TJ as received 4 Jan. 1798 and so recorded in SJL.

Scion of an influential Stafford County family, Stevens Thomson Mason (1760-1803), a son of Thomson Mason and a nephew of George Mason, studied at the College of William and Mary and read law, subsequently establishing himself at his family's Raspberry Plain plantation in Loudoun County. He began his political career with election to the Virginia House of Delegates in 1783, later serving in the state senate and as a delegate to the ratifying convention, where he opposed the adoption of the federal Constitution. Elected to the United States Senate in 1794 and serving there for the remainder of his life, he gained notoriety for releasing the text of the Jay Treaty in 1795 and assisted Matthew Lyon and James T. Callender when they were prosecuted under the Sedition Act (DAB).

Notes on the Formation of the Federal Government

1798. Jan. 5. I recieve a very remarkeable fact indeed in our history from Baldwin & Skinner. before the establishment of our present government a very extensive combination had taken place in N. York & the Eastern states among that description of people who were partly monarchical in principle or frightened with Shays's rebellion & the impotence of the old Congress. delegates in different places[1] had actually had consultations on the subject of seizing on the powers of a government & establishing them by force, had corresponded with one another, and had sent a deputy to Genl. Washington to sollicit his co-operation. he calculated too well to join them. the new Convention was in the mean time proposed by Virginia & appointed. these people believed it impossible the states should ever agree on a government, as this must include the impost and all the other powers which the states had a thousand times refused to the general authority. they therefore let the proposed convention go on, not doubting it's failure, & confiding that on it's failure would be a still more favorable moment for their enterprize. they therefore wished it to fail, & especially when Hamilton their leader brought forward his plan of govmt, failed entirely in carrying it & retired in disgust from the Convention. his associates then took every method to prevent any form of govmt being agreed to. but the well intentioned never ceased trying first one thing then another till they could get something agreed to. the final passage & adoption of the constitution compleatly defeated the views of the combination, & saved us from an attempt to establish a govmt over us by force. this fact throws a blaze of light on the conduct of several members from N.Y. & the Eastern states in the Convention of Annapolis & the Grand convention. at that of Annapolis several Eastern members most vehemently opposed Madison's proposition for a more General Convention with more general powers. they wished things to get more & more into confusion to justify the violent measure they proposed. the idea of establishing a govmt by reasoning & agreemt they publicly ridiculed as an [. . .]

MS (DLC: TJ Papers, 102:17524); entirely in TJ's hand; incomplete, with remainder of sheet torn away; written on verso of sheet with Notes on Comments by John Adams and Robert Goodloe Harper, 26 Dec. 1797, and Notes on a Conversation with Tench Coxe, [27 Dec. 1797].

Congressmen Abraham BALDWIN of Georgia and Thomson J. SKINNER of Massachusetts resided with TJ at Francis's hotel. Baldwin had served as a delegate to the Constitutional Convention of 1787 and often made reference to its deliberations in his speeches (DAB; A List of the Names, and Places of Residence, of the Members of the Senate and House of Representatives of the United States [Philadelphia, 1797]). On 13 Jan. the PLAN OF GOVMT, which Alexander Hamilton included in his speech before the Constitutional Convention on 18 June

1787, appeared in the Philadelphia *Aurora* with the caption "Proposition *Of Colonel Hamilton of New-York, in the Convention for establishing a Constitution of Government for the United States*" and a note that the document was obtained "thro' a *certain* tho' indirect channel, from a member of the *Grand Convention.*" Of the four men known to have taken notes on Hamilton's speech during the secret deliberations—James Madison, Rufus King, delegate from Massachusetts, and New Yorkers John Lansing, Jr., and Robert Yates—the account in the *Aurora* most closely followed that of Madison. Hamilton left the CONVENTION on 29 June 1787 but returned to Philadelphia about five weeks later and by the middle of August was again taking part in the debates (Syrett, *Hamilton*, 4:178, 207-11, 223).

[1] Preceding three words interlined.

To Mary Jefferson Eppes

Philadelphia Jan. 7. 98.

I acknowleged, my dear Maria, the reciept of yours in a letter I wrote to mr Eppes. it gave me the welcome news that your sprain was well. but you are not to suppose it entirely so. the joint will remain weak for a considerable time, & give you occasional pains much longer.   the state of things at Chesnut grove is truly distressing. mr B.'s habitual intoxication will destroy himself, his fortune & family. of all calamities this is the greatest. I wish my sister could bear his misconduct with more patience. it might lessen his attachment to the bottle, & at any rate would make her own time more tolerable. when we see ourselves in a situation which must be endured & gone through, it is best to make up our minds to it, meet it with firmness, & accomodate every thing to it in the best way practicable. this lessens the evil. while fretting & fuming only serves to increase our own torment. the errors and misfortunes of others should be a school for our own instruction. harmony in the marriage state is the very[1] first object to be aimed at. nothing can preserve affections uninterrupted but a firm resolution never to differ in will, and a determination in each to consider the love of the other as of more value than any object whatever on which a wish has been fixed. how light in fact is the sacrifice of any other wish, when weighed against the affections of one with whom we are to pass our whole life. and though opposition in a single instance will hardly of itself produce alienation; yet every one has their pouch into which all these little oppositions are put: while that is filling, the alienation is insensibly going on, & when filled, it is complete. it would puzzle either to say why; because no one difference of opinion has been marked enough to produce a serious effect by itself. but he finds his affections wearied out by a constant stream of little checks & obstacles. other sources of discontent, very common indeed, are the little cross purposes of husband & wife in common conversation, a disposition in either to criticise & question whatever the other says, a desire always to demonstrate & make him feel himself in the wrong, & especially in company. nothing is so goading. much better therefore, if our companion views a thing in a light different from what we do, to leave him in quiet possession of his view. what is the use of rectifying him if the thing be unimportant; & if important let it pass for the present, & wait a softer moment, and more conciliatory occasion of revising the subject together. it is wonderful how many persons are rendered unhappy by inattention to these little rules of prudence.   I have been insensibly led, by the particular case you mention, to sermonize to you on the subject generally. however if it be the means of saving you from a single heart-ache, it will have contributed a great deal to my happiness. but before I finish the sermon, I must add a word on economy. the unprofitable condition of Virginia estates in general, leaves it now next to impossible for the holder of one to avoid ruin. and this condition will continue until some change takes place in the mode of working them. in the mean time nothing can save us & our children from beggary but a determination to get a year before hand, & restrain ourselves rigorously this year to the clear profits of the last. if a debt is once contracted by a farmer, it is never paid but by a sale. the article of dress is perhaps that in which economy is the least to be recommended. it is so important to each to continue to please the other, that the happiness of both requires the most pointed attention to whatever may contribute to it. and the more as time makes greater inroads on our person. yet generally we become slovenly in proportion as personal decay requires the contrary. I have great comfort in believing that your understanding & dispositions will engage your attention to these considerations: and that you are connected with a person & family who, of all within the circle of my acquaintance, are most in the dispositions which will make you happy. cultivate their affections my dear, with assiduity. think every sacrifice a gain which shall tend to attach them to you. my only object in life is to see yourself & your sister, & those deservedly dear to you, not only happy, but in no danger of becoming unhappy.

I have lately recieved a letter from your friend Kitty Church. I inclose it to you, & think the affectionate expressions relative to yourself, & the advance she has made, will require a letter from you to her.   it will be impossible to get a chrystal here to fit your watch without the watch itself. if you should know of any one coming to Philadelphia, send it to me, & I will get you a stock of chrystals.   the river being frozen up, I shall not be able to send your things till it opens, which will probably be some time in February.—I inclose to mr Eppes some pamphlets. present me affectionately to all the family, & be assured of my tenderest love to yourself. Adieu   TH: JEFFERSON

PrC (MHi). Tr (M. Howard Bradley, Decatur, Ga., 1955); 19th-century copy, with a TJ signature apparently clipped from another document and attached here; addressed: "Mrs. John W. Eppes. Eppington [in] Chesterfield Virginia." Enclosures not found, but see note below.

LETTER I WROTE: TJ to John Wayles Eppes, 21 Dec. 1797.

MR B'S HABITUAL INTOXICATION: John Bolling was married to TJ's sister Mary (note to TJ to John Page, 25 Dec. 1762). LETTER FROM YOUR FRIEND KITTY CHURCH: see TJ to Catherine Church, 11 Jan. 1798.

[1] Word interlined.

From Luther Martin

SIR,   Baltimore, January 8th, 1798.

Having in my last seen my much respected old friend Col. Cresap freed from his irons and discharged from an imprisonment of twenty months duration, which to give it its softest epithet was *most unmerited*, I will now accompany him to Maryland, and restore him to an affectionate wife and beloved children, who most providentially had escaped the relentless flames which had consumed his property, and the more relentless weapons of those by whom those flames had been enkindled; and who, during his confinement, had depended for the supplies of the necessary wants of nature, on the affection of relatives or the bounty of friends.

Returned again to his family to whose happiness he was devoted,— and to his adopted province for the interest of which he had suffered, he again betook himself to its frontier.

He established himself almost immediately in Prince George's County, which at that time extended to the western boundary of the Province, (as did Baltimore to its northern boundary) and included the whole, or nearly the whole that is now comprized in Prince George's, Montgomery, Frederick, Washington and Allegheny counties.

The precise time when he first became an inhabitant of that county is not within my researches, but I find that on the 15th day of June, in the year 1739, he was appointed one of the Justice's of Prince George's county court, and that he was regularly continued in the commission until the twenty first day of November, in the year 1748; when Frederick county was laid off out of Prince George's, including all the western part of the Province.—On the seventeenth day of November, in the year 1749, he was appointed second in the commission of the peace for that county, and remained in that office until the twenty sixth day of May, in the year 1756, when he was appointed Chief Justice of Frederick county court, which appointment he held until the sixth day of November, 1758.—On the fifteenth day of August, in the year 1774, he was again appointed Chief Justice of that county, and continued in that appointment until the revolution took place.

In a short time after his thus settling in Prince George's, he was also appointed by the Governor and council of Maryland county lieutenant of that county. I do not recollect the time, and though I have the commission among my papers, I have not leisure to look for it, but I think it was about the year 1740. He was also many years one of the members of the lower House of Assembly of the Province of Maryland; and for several years surveyor of Prince George's county.

From the land records of this state, it appears that before the year 1743, Col. Cresap had obtained patents for land, situate on the north branch of the Potowmac, about one hundred and seventy miles from the city of Annapolis, and but fifteen miles this side of where Fort Cumberland was afterwards erected. And I find that at an Indian treaty held at Lancaster, on the twenty ninth day of June, in the year 1744, at which commissioners from Virginia and Maryland, attended, the great object of which was the settlement of disputes concerning territory which subsisted between those provinces and the Six Nations, Connasatego one of their chiefs, declares they are ready to settle the bounds of the lands to which they admitted the province of Maryland, entitled, "by renouncing all right to Lord Baltimore, of all lands lying 2 miles above the uppermost fork of Potowmack, or Cohongarnton river, near where Thomas Cresap hath a hunting or trading cabin, by a north line to the bounds of Pennsylvania."

By which it appears Col. Cresap, at that time, had established himself even at the *remotest* western part of the province, to which the Indians admitted Lord Baltimore to be entitled, under any cession which they had at that time made.

Very early after the peace of Aix la Chapelle, the policy of the French government was particularly attended to by Colonel Cresap. Possessed of the country on the Mississippi, and also of the colonies on the St. Lawrence, France had formed the design of establishing a chain of posts on our frontiers from the one river to the other, and thereby to confine us in territory to our Atlantic settlements, and monopolize to itself the trade of the Indians, and secure their interest. To prevent this and to obtain for the British nation the advantages of which the French wished to deprive it, he was extremely anxious for the British government to authorize settlements to be made to the westward of the Alleghany mountains on the waters of the Ohio, and to encourage and support a commercial intercourse with the Indians, thereby to detach them from the French and to secure their interest and friendship to the British. This being an object of too much magnitude for an individual of but small property and moderate influence to undertake, he communicated his idea to a number of very respectable and influential characters in Virginia and Maryland, and proposed that they should obtain a grant of lands on the waters of the Ohio, and form themselves into a company for the purpose of seating the said lands and prosecuting an extensive Indian trade among their different nations.

For the obtention of a grant of lands his Britannic majesty was to be petitioned, and Mr. Hanbury a most respectable British merchant, was appointed their agent to advocate the measure and solicit the grant.

I have now in my possession the original rough draught of the petition in col. Cresap's hand writing, at the conclusion of which he adds with all that honest frankness and bluntness, which was ever a striking trait in his character "I should be heartily glad that your majesty had as good a personal knowledge of the situation of the country and of the trade which might be carried on to the advantage of your majesty, and many of your subjects who would be concerned therein, as I have."

In consequence of the means thus used by col. Cresap, and those associated with him, on the sixteenth of March 1748-9, instructions were made out by his Britannic majesty, at his court at St. James, and transmitted to sir William Gooch the then lieutenant governor of Virginia, whereby he was directed to grant unto John Hanbury, merchant of London, Thomas Lee, Esq. a member of the council, and one of the judges of the supreme court of judicature in the colony of Virginia, Thomas Nelson, Esq. also a member of the same council, col. Cresap, col. William Thornton, William Nimmo, Daniel Cresap, John Carlisle, Lawrence Washington, Augustine Washington, George Fairfax, Jacob Giles, Nathaniel Chapman and James Wardrope and others their associates two hundred thousand acres of land on the western waters, subject to certain conditions in the said instructions specified; and on those conditions being complied with, to grant to them the additional quantity of five hundred thousand acres.

Among those interested, whose names are not abovementioned, were I believe, Presley Thornton, Francis Thornton, Richard Lee, George Mason, John Taylor and James Scott of Virginia and James Baxter and Hugh Parker merchants of Maryland.

These gentlemen or the most of them formed themselves into a company called the Ohio company, and were extensively engaged in carrying on a trade with the Indians, and also in locating and endeavouring to secure lands on the waters of the Ohio, until hostilities commenced between France and Great Britain and between their colonies, about the year 1753 or 1754.

Among these gentlemen no person, I believe, embarked a greater proportion of his fortune or devoted more of his time and attention to those objects than colonel Cresap.

That col. Cresap possessed the good opinion and confidence of the government of Maryland is sufficiently evinced by the appointments bestowed upon him; and that he was respected and confided in by governor Dinwiddie of Virginia, appears from several letters, written by him to col. Cresap, in the year 1752, which I have before me. In these letters the governor solicits from him "an account of the several nations of Indians, their names, their numbers of each separate, viz, their fighting men, their women and children; and his advice how to engage them to the British interest,"—he also assures him of his "good opinion of his understanding and integrity;" that "the matters contained in his letters were of great consequence to his majesty's service, and the interest of the colony of Virginia;" that he is "sensible from his letters he is well acquainted with Indian affairs, and that he is obliged to him for the information received from him." He declares to him further, that "he has the success of the Ohio company much at heart, and that he thinks his (col. Cresap's) good offices will be very necessary, and will be acknowledged by the company."

In the year one thousand seven hundred and forty-two a treaty being proposed to be held with the Indians of the six nations, the governor and council of Maryland appointed commissioners to attend on the part of that province one of whom was the honorable col. Levin Gale, Esq. of Somerset county, on that occasion Conrod Wieser, who long acted as an interpreter at the Indian treaties, being informed a wish was entertained that col. Cresap should attend with the Maryland commissioners, and for some reason being desirous to prevent his attendance, wrote to col. Gale, expressing his sentiments that it would not be advantageous for col. Cresap to come to the treaty with the Maryland commissioners as he believed the Indians of the Six Nations did not think well of him on account of his having endeavored to purchase some lands from their warriors.

In the year 1751 a dispute having taken place between col. Cresap and a party of Indians of the Six Nations, who passing through that part of the country, had as was their usual custom, encamped at his plantation, some of the young men of whom, not satisfied with the provisions he gave them, killed several of his cattle and hogs, the principal warriors of the party finding that he was much irritated at their conduct sent a message to the governor of Maryland, informing him that their brother Cresap appeared angry with them, and was not disposed to give them victuals enough, that they had thought their brother, the governor, always paid him for the victuals he gave them, but understanding that was not the case, they hoped hereafter their brother the governor would make proper provision that they should be supplied when passing through that part of the province.

That from the commencement of hostilities on the frontiers until peace took place in the year one thousand seven hundred and sixty three, col. Cresap and all of his family who were able to bear arms took a most active and decided part is a fact of public notoriety. They were ever on the posts of danger, and ever among the foremost in exposing themselves to danger. His oldest son Thomas Cresap, a most amiable and respectable character fell during that war, bravely combating the savage foe.

In the year 1769 or 1770, Colonel Cresap went to Great Britain, he returned about the beginning of the year 1771: in the summer of 1772 or 1773, I first became acquainted with him. *I aver* that from that time he never was on the western side of the Alleghany mountains.—And Logan's family were not killed even as you state, and as I know the fact is, until in the spring of 1774.

In the spring of 1783, Colonel Cresap having made a conditional purchase from Capt. F——, of Deer island, situate in Passamaquoddy bay near the mouth of the river Saint Croix, just within the eastern limits of the United States, he went there to take possession of his purchase, but disliking his bargain, he left that place and arrived at Baltimore some time in the month of December the same year. On the Christmas following I married his grand daughter, and returning from Old Town with Mrs. M. to Baltimore early in January, from that time Colonel Cresap resided in my family until the May following, and though he was to a very great degree blind and deaf, and about one hundred years old, I found him a most entertaining and agreeable companion, still possessing a strong and vigorous mind, and as free from the fretfulness and peevishness of old age, as I ever knew a man of twenty-five.

In the month of May, 1783, he returned to Old Town, where, or in its vicinity, he remained until his death, which happened about thirty five minutes after one o'clock in the morning of Wednesday the thirty first day of January, in the year one thousand seven hundred and eighty seven.

I shall here, Sir, give you a short respite, And remain with *due* respect,

Your very obedient servant,   LUTHER MARTIN

Printed in *Porcupine's Gazette*, 13 Jan. 1798; at head of text: "No. 4." and "To the Honourable Thomas Jefferson, Esqr. Vice-President of the United States."

From James Monroe

DEAR SIR   Alb: Jany. 8. 1798.

I have yours of the 27. Decr., for which I thank you. I have made some comments on one item in it to a person who will probably see you.

I rejoice that the land tax is postponed, & hope when revived it will be under the auspices of those who have imposed on the publick the necessity of such an increase of their burden. It wod. be entertaining to see the friends of an accumulation of [the] debt, in principle, who have benefitted by it also in practice, standing aloof or modestly opposing such a tax, whilst the œconomic part of the legislature who had opposed the accumulation of the debt, took the lead in providing the tax, and with it the odium attending the provision. This is not the natural course of things, nor wod. the effect be salutary. Direct taxes must be laid but let them proceed from the quarter whence all mischief has proceeded.

The contest between a bare majority in the reps. against the Senate & President, exhibits an interesting spectacle. The details you have been so kind as note give cause to hope the result will be on the right side. But still we have been going wrong so long, under circumstances too more favorable than the present, that we ought not to be too sanguine. I heartily wish the Session was closed, for I expect no good from it. Indeed the only hope is to prevent harm.

You will have seen the resolutions of our assembly upon the petition from our district. I thi[nk] the resolutions sound and well drawn. I hope [the] measure of the district and assembly, will produce a good effect, generally.

I write you only to acknowledge the receit of yours: to tell you we are well—still on the no. side of the mountain and likely to [be] so on yr. return & to assure you that I am sir

yr. friend & servant   JAS. MONROE

I have requested Mr. D. to confer with you whether my coming up will be useful in any view in respect to publick or private concerns.

You have seen the discovery of a plot I had laid for blowing up the admn., by correcting the misrepresentation of the English prints, in handing to my countrymen occasionally a sketch of [. . .] of the French revolution to be printed in Bach[e's pa]per. I really suspect the project alarmed them, [for they] have wished to monopolize the publick mind to themselves, wh. they cod. not do, but by keeping the people ignorant of their affairs. Yet the chief of the admn. [deems] it harmless to trample on the constitution, by [rejecting?] its channel of a publick minister, & carry on an intrigue with the British govt.

RC (DLC); edges torn; endorsed by TJ as received 22 Jan. 1798 and so recorded in SJL.

MR. D.: John Dawson, one of the intermediaries in Monroe's dispute with Alexander Hamilton (see Monroe to TJ, 2 Dec., and TJ to Monroe, 27 Dec. 1797).

HANDING TO MY COUNTRYMEN OCCASIONALLY A SKETCH: on this day Monroe also wrote to John Taylor about letters he had written while minister to France for publication in American newspapers, especially the enclosure to his letter to TJ of 27 June 1795 (Massachusetts Historical Society, Proceedings, 42 [1909], 323-4).

To Angelica Church

Dear Madam   Philadelphia Jan. 11. 1798.

Your favor of July 6. was to have found me here: but I had departed before it reached this. it followed me home, & of necessity the enquiries after our friend Madame de Corny were obliged to await mrs Monroe's arrival at her own house. this was delayed longer than was expected; so that by the time I could make the enquiries, I was looking again to my return to Philadelphia. this must apologize for the delay which has taken place.   Mrs. Monroe tells me that Made. de Corny was at one time in extreme distress, her revenue being in rents, & these paid in assignats worth nothing. since their abolition however she recieves her rents in cash, & is now entirely at her ease. she lives in hired lodgings, furnished by herself, & every thing about her as nice as you know she always had. she visited mrs Monroe familiarly and freely in a family way, but would never dine when she had company, nor remain if company came. she speaks seriously sometimes of a purpose to come to America; but she surely mistakes a wish for a purpose. you & I know her constitution too well, her horror of the sea, to believe she could pass or attempt the Atlantic. Mrs. Monroe could not give me her address, so as to enable me to write to her.[1] in all events it is a great consolation that her situation is easy.

We have here a Mr. Niemcewitz, a Polish gentleman, who was with us at Paris while Mrs. Cosway was there, & who was of her society in London the last summer. he mentions the loss of her daughter, the gloom into which that & other circumstances have thrown her, that it has taken the hue of religion, that she is solely devoted to religious exercises, & the superintendance of a school she has instituted for Catholic children. but that she still speaks of her friends here with tenderness & desire. our letters have been rare. but they have let me see that her gaiety was gone, & her mind entirely placed on a world to come.[2]

I have recieved from my young friend Catharine a letter which gratifies me much, as it proves that our friendly impressions have not grown out of her memory. I am indebted to her too, for an acquaintance with your son, whose connections suffice to raise the strongest prepossessions in his favor. be so good as to present my respects to mr Church.[3] I hope he will find the state of society different in New York from what it is in this place. party animosities here[4] have raised a wall of separation between those who differ in political sentiments.[5] they must love misery indeed, who would,[6] at the sight of an honest man, feel the torment of hatred & aversion rather than the[7] benign spasms of benevolence and esteem. accept assurances of the unalterable attachment of, my dear Madam, your sincere and affectionate friend & servant

TH: JEFFERSON

RC (ViU); addressed: "Mrs. Church New York"; with addition in unknown hand: "Lalor, 88 Chatham Street." PrC (DLC). Dft (MHi); undated; heavily emended.

Church's FAVOR OF 6 July 1797, recorded in SJL as received eight days later, has not been found. Another letter from Church to TJ of 30 May 1797, which according to SJL was received from New York on 2 June 1797, is also missing.

For the LETTER from Catherine Church, see the following document and note.

[1] In Dft TJ here canceled "but I have an acquce. however in Paris who I am sure will find her out."

[2] Preceding paragraph written in left-hand margin of Dft.

[3] Following three sentences written on verso of Dft, where TJ first wrote "I am in hopes he will find the state of society better in N.Y. than it is here" before altering the sentence to read as above.

[4] Preceding two words interlined in Dft in place of "spirit."

[5] At this point in Dft TJ canceled "⟨the oldest friends will cross the street to avoid meeting each other. people must have a wonderful propensity to self torment who can prefer to the harsher feelings of the mind who would rather that⟩ the temperament of that mind must be lamentably" and then continued as above.

[6] TJ here canceled "rather." Emendation not in PrC. In Dft sentence interlined to this point including "would rather ⟨. . .⟩ at."

[7] In Dft TJ first wrote "heavenly feelings of benevolence and friendly society" before altering the remainder of the sentence to read as above.

To Catherine Church

Philadelphia Jan. 11. 98.

I recieved, my dear Catharine, from the hands of your brother, the letter you have done me the favor to write me. I see in that the excellent dispositions which I knew in you in an[1] earlier period of life. these have led you to mistake, to your own prejudice,[2] the character of our attentions to you. they were not favors, but gratifications of our own affections to an object which had every quality which might endear her to us. be assured we have all continued to love you as if still of our fireside,[3] & to make you the very frequent theme of our family conversations. your friend Maria has, as you supposed, changed her condition. she is now mrs Eppes. she & her sister, mrs Randolph retain all their affections for you, & never fail in their friendly enquiries after you when an opportunity offers. during my winter's absence, Maria is with the family with which she is become allied: but on my return, they will also return to reside with me. my daughter Randolph has hitherto done the same; but lately has removed with mr Randolph to live & build on a farm of their own adjoining me. but I still count on their passing the greater part of

[24]

their time at Monticello. why should we forbid ourselves to believe that, some day or other, some circumstance may gather you also to our little society, & renew the recollections of former scenes very dear to our memory. hope is so much more chearing than fears and[4] forebodings that we will not set it down among impossible things. we will calculate on the circumstance that you have already passed the wide ocean which laid between us, & that, in comparison with that, the space which remains[5] is little. who knows but you may travel to see our springs & our curiosities; not, I hope, for your health, but to vary your summer scenes, & enlarge your knolege of your own country. for all the good are fellow-citizens of the same country. in that case, we are on your road, & will endeavor to relieve the fatigues of it by all the offices of friendship and hospitality. I thank you for making me acquainted with your brother. the relations he bears to the best of people are a sufficient voucher to me of his worth. he must be of your party when you come to Monticello. Adieu, my dear Catharine. I consign in a separate letter my respects to your good mother. I have here therefore only to claim your acceptance of the sincere attachment of

Your's affectionately   TH: JEFFERSON

RC (ViU). PrC (DLC). Dft (MHi); un-dated; heavily emended; at foot of first page: "miss Catherine Church."

Church's LETTER to TJ of 17 Dec. 1797, recorded in SJL as received from New York two weeks later, has not been found.

[1] In Dft TJ first wrote "a much" before altering it to read as above.

[2] Preceding four words interlined in Dft.

[3] Word interlined in place of "family" in Dft.

[4] Preceding two words interlined in Dft.

[5] Preceding three words interlined in Dft in place of "land between us."

To Thomas Mann Randolph

TH:J. TO TMR.   Philadelphia Jan. 11. 98.

I am in hopes you are by this time in the regular reciept of Bache's papers; and in a few days you may expect the Chronicle from Boston. both are to begin Jan. 1. so that your year may end always at a marked period. tho we hear nothing official from our envoys at Paris, yet the rumors are very unfavorable. I begin to fear, not war from them, but that they will refuse to have any settlement with us, only perhaps confining their depredations to provision vessels going to their enemies, & to enemy's goods in our ships, according to the English example: and that this may excite a war cry with us. the best anchor of our hope is an invasion of England. if they republicanize that country, all will be safe with us, whatever mortifying things we may suffer in the mean time.

Congress has done nothing & has nothing to do. I hardly see how it will be possible to protract our session beyond February. mr Trist sets out in a day or two for Albemarle, but will be 10. days or a fortnight on the road. I shall take the liberty of giving him a letter to you, & as he is a stranger to the state of things with us, & inexperienced, I will request you to keep an eye on his negociations, and to give him friendly hints, even without his asking them. he is a very good young man, & will take it kindly of you. he will of course make Charlottesville his head quarters while in the neighborhood. I had a letter to-day from mr Eppes informing me that they were well. I hope I have some letters on the road from Patsy or yourself, not having as yet heard from you since I left home. my tender love to Patsy & the children, and affectionate esteem to you. Adieu.

RC (DLC); endorsed by Randolph as received 3 Feb. 1798. PrC (CSmH).

YOU MAY EXPECT THE CHRONICLE: Thomas Adams's and Isaac Larkin's semi-weekly *Independent Chronicle* was the leading Jeffersonian-Republican newspaper in New England (MB, 2:964). See Sowerby, No. 589.

The LETTER from John Wayles EPPES to TJ of 28 Dec. 1797, recorded in SJL as received from Bermuda Hundred 11 Jan. 1798, has not been found. A letter from Eppes to TJ of 5 Jan. 1798, which according to SJL was received from Eppington on 17 Jan. 1798, is also missing.

From John Gibson

DEAR SIR, Pittsburg Jany. 12th 1798.

I this moment have Been honoured with yours of the 31st. Ulto. But having just returned from the Country and the post Being to set out in a few minutes, I am prevented from giving you the Information you require, you may rest Assured of my making Every Inquiry of other persons, and giving you a full detail of the whole transaction by the next post.

In the Mean time, permit me to Assure you that, I am Dear Sir, with sincere Respect your most Obedient humble Servt. JNO. GIBSON

RC (DLC); at foot of text: "The Honble. T. Jefferson Esqr."; endorsed by TJ as received 21 Jan. 1798 and so recorded in SJL.

From Thomas Mann Randolph

TH: M. RANDOLPH TO TH: JEFFERSON, Belmont Jan. 13. :98

your letter of the 14th. Dec. did not arrive at Belmont till the 1st. inst: it did not lie in Charlottesville as we send thither regularly every week: I cannot explain its delay there was no failure that I have heard of in the

Fredericksburg as happened in the Richmond Mail about that time. Martha undertook to write the post after; that is last Monday, and being out myself I lost the opportunity of supplying her omission. The inhabitants of Milton and we of the vicinage are subjected to a serious trouble of sending to Charl'lle. every week for letters and papers, which we might be saved by a regulation for opening the Mails from Fredericksburg and Richmond there; both of them pass thro' the place going & returning and any Merchant in it will undertake to open & shut them without reward for the benefit of geting his own letters and papers so easily and timely. I suppose such a regulation can be made only in Philad'a. at the head of the P. Office: if it is so we ask of you the favor to procure it for us. The Factor of Ro: Rives & Co. David Higinbotham, desires me to say that he will undertake the opening and shuting the mail, free. I cannot answer for the Carrier, it is probable they will demand something for stoping alltho' they constantly do stop at present: Milton you know is on the high road from Fredericksburg (we may say); and the Richmond mail departs from and returns to Milton regularly, the Undertaker being one of the Inspectors of Tobacco there.

we have had the most variable weather I ever witnessed—there have been one or two falls of the Therm: of 2°. an hour for 15 hours and one of $2\frac{1}{2}$ for the same time: I copy my Diary for Dec: that you may have an opportunity of comparing the two climates as to positive cold and changeableness.

5.	11. 31.	17.	30. 40	29.	14. 40
6.	15. 37.	18.	36. 43	30.	15. 45
7.	20. 41.	19.	13. 33	31.	20. 50.
8.	31. 46. Misty rain	20.	30. 43		
9.	31. 36. very light snow	21.	$4\frac{1}{2}$. 19		
10.	21. 26.	22.	17. 28		
11.	22. 42.	23.	6. 26		
12.	35. 51. Smoky	24.	1. 31		
13.	45. 63.	25.	30. 55.		
14.	45. 66.	26.	34. 53. Rain—light snow & hail		
15.	54. 56. Rain	27.	19. 30		
16.	39. 47.	28.	14. 35		

The Earth has never been more than sprinkled with snow: it has been the severest winter for Wheat &c I ever knew—where it was not very thick sown there cannot be a tolerable crop so much is killed.

Fearing the effects of great failures in Philad'a. and supposing 8/6 w'd. be about the height of the Market this year from your letter I have sold my Varina crop for 8/. the Red & 8/6 the White pay'le. in 90 days—we were so unlucky as to have it all (1491 bushels) caught in the river by the Ice but the breaking up has done us no harm. B. Clarke has delivered our Bedford Wheat & is to get for it 1$. certain or whatever you receive in Albemarle.

I have a letter from Mr. Eppes of the 30th. ult—they were both perfectly well then—he despaired of settling Pantops this year every person in his neighbourhood who had negroes to hire refusing to let them come up to Albemarle: upon this he has hired his Blacksmith to me: I had been disappointed in every other attempt to get one and was about to write to Bauer to prevail upon one from Philad'a. to come on any terms. The negroe men belonging to the Woods hired at 22 £. round, $\frac{1}{3}$ Cash. I have been disappointed every where from the same cause with Mr. Eppes, tho I had empowered several persons in different parts to hire for me—I have no hope of geting farther than one flank of my house next summer—*that* I must make a sacrifice in my crop to obtain and will, for one flank with a temporary roof must be our habitation next winter as we cannot remain here.

There have been some severe illnesses among the *old* Negroes at Mont'o. but no death has happened except that of Sallies child. Affairs are not seriously backward either at Mont'o. or Shadwell tho' insubordination at the one and discontent at the other have greatly cloged their operations. I have been frequently called on and have not hezitated to interfere tho' without authority I have made known to all I had none that my interference if not productive of wholesome effects might be rejected.   Martha is in the finest health she ever enjoyed—the children quite well except Ellen who has 3 jaw teeth now coming thro' & yet is scarcely sick.

 with the most sincere affection y'r.   TH: M. RANDOLPH

RC (MHi); endorsed by TJ as received 23 Jan. 1798 and so recorded in SJL.

To James Brown

DEAR SIR   Philadelphia Jan. 14. 1798.

Having to remit to mr Higginbottom on account of Rives & co. at Milton 217.64 D I have his advice that I cannot do it more properly (as paiment is to be made in Richmond) than by placing it in your hands. I therefore take the liberty of inclosing you an order on George Jefferson & co. of Richmond for 217.64 D as abovementioned, which be pleased to recieve on account of the concern of Rives & co. at Milton.

We have nothing new here to communicate to you, except the state of extraordinary suspense in which we are till we hear from our envoys at Paris. how their mission will terminate is as yet difficult to conjecture. I am with great esteem Dear Sir

Your friend & servt.   TH: JEFFERSON

RC (WHi); addressed: "Mr. James Brown mercht Richmond," TJ having originally addressed it as a letter to John Forbes "near Goochland court house"; franked; endorsed by Brown.

In his financial memoranda TJ noted that £16.10 of this PAIMENT was to be credited to Lucy Wood for the hire of a slave in 1797, £18.15.10 was to the credit of Richard Richardson, and the remaining £30 was for TJ's own account with Rives & Co., being "about the balance I owe to that store" (MB, 2:977).

David Higginbotham was the factor of Rives & Co. at Milton (MB, 2:988). Six let-

ters from TJ to him written between 14 Nov. 1797 and 23 Jan. 1801, as well as four from Higginbotham to TJ dated 22 Dec. 1798, 29 Mch., 15 Nov. 1800, and 17 Jan. 1801, received on 1 Jan. 1799, 5 Apr., 15 Nov. 1800, and 22 Jan. 1801 respectively, are recorded in SJL but have not been found. Also recorded in SJL but missing are letters from TJ to John Forbes of 30 Oct. 1797, 14 Jan., and 7 Mch. 1798, and two from Forbes to TJ of 28 Sep. 1797 and 4 Feb. 1798 received on 7 Oct. 1797 and 6 Mch. 1798 respectively.

A letter that Brown wrote to TJ on 25 July 1797, recorded in SJL as received on 29 July, has not been found.

To George Jefferson

DEAR SIR   Philadelphia Jan. 14. 1798.

I enclose you mr Barnes's note for 500. Dollars to mr Hopkins to be taken up at ten days sight, as also letters of advice to mr Hopkin's & mr Boyce both of whom will attend to the note. as I have some paiments to make in Richmond which are already some days in arrear, I can only admit the interval of one post before I must send on draughts on you, as follows.

	D	
Colo. John Harvie	49.28	⎫
John Forbes of Goochland	23.	⎬ at ten days sight
Peter Derieux of Goochland	50.	⎪
James Brown	217.64	⎭
Colo. Thos. Bell	165.	

This will be at 3. days' sight: but the draught will have to go to Charlottesville and cannot be presented to you till the 3d. of February. the 1st. & 4th. draught will be presented probably in [. . .] days after you get this. The 3d. in a few days the 2d. not so soon. I am in hopes the punctuality of mr Barnes's correspondent will save you from any difficulty.

Your favors of Dec. 30. & Jan. 4. came to hand in due time. I am Dear Sir

Your affectionate friend & servt.   TH: JEFFERSON

PrC (MHi); faint; at foot of text: "Mr. George Jefferson"; endorsed by TJ in ink on verso. Enclosures not found.

For BARNES'S NOTE to John HOPKINS for $500, see MB, 2:977.

The remittance to JOHN HARVIE included TJ's payment of almost £15 to John Rogers for beef (MB, 2:974, 977). Letters from TJ to Rogers of 14 Jan. 1798 and 7 Jan. 1801, both recorded in SJL, have not been found.

TJ noted that his draft to PETER DERIEUX was "in charity" (MB, 2:977). A letter from

TJ to Derieux of 14 Jan. 1798, recorded in SJL, has not been found.

TJ directed Thomas BELL, with part of his draft, to pay notes due 1 Jan. 1798 totaling £49.10 to the Wood family for the hire of three slaves (MB, 2:952, 977). Letters from TJ to Bell of 11, 14 Jan., 15 Feb. 1798, 22 Jan., 11 July 1799, and 4 Apr. 1800, recorded in SJL, have not been found. Letters from Bell to TJ of 28 Jan., 11, 25 Feb., and 21 Apr. 1798, recorded in SJL as received 9, 22 Feb., 6 Mch., and 1 May, respectively, are also missing.

From Luther Martin

SIR,   Baltimore, 14th January, 1798.

I have in my last indisputably proved that Col. Cresap was not concerned in the death of Logan's family, since it is admitted that they were killed on some part of the waters of the Ohio, on the west side of the Alleghany Mountains, and not until the spring of the year 1774: whereas Colonel Cresap never was on the western side of those mountains after the summer of 1773.

I now proceed to prove from the different facts I have stated in the sketch of his life, that Col. Cresap was not considered infamous for his murders of the inoffensive Indians; and that he ought not to have been so reputed.

In my letter to Mr. Fennell, I have said "he was a man of most undaunted bravery;" were these letters designed to circulate no farther than Col. Cresap was, or than I am personally known, I would not here introduce the testimony of two of his most respectable cotemporaries, in support of this my assertion.—I have before me a certificate dated the 31st of August, in the year 1747, in the hand writing of the Honorable Daniel Dulany, Esqr. signed by him, and the Hon. Benjamin Tasker, Esqr. both of the Province of Maryland, wherein they certify, "that they had been many years acquainted with Col. Thomas Cresap, that he Mr. Dulany had dealt considerably with him, and found him to be an honest and fair man:" They add, "which is his general character, except among some *few* Pennsylvanians, who have treated him with great cruelty, and in view of causing him to be disliked by others, have aspersed him; and that he is a man of *unquestionable resolution*, will not, we believe, be denied by his *worst enemies*, as the proofs he has given of it are too *notorious to be contradicted*."

That a man *truly brave* will not be guilty of perfidious, treacherous murder, though generally true, I will admit is not absolutely conclusive; but I assert even *that* general presumption ought to be admitted sufficient evidence to [repel] a charge of infamy on account of murder, which charge is totally unsupported by testimony; and the author of which, when called on for proof, *shrinks* from the undertaking.

But I rest not here; I have shewn that, before the year 1732, Col. Cresap was settled on the northern frontiers of Maryland, in the immediate vicinity of the Indians; every motive of personal safety and personal interest must have most forcibly influenced him to keep fair with them, and to conciliate and preserve their affection; and as, while there, he for several years had a cruel enemy in the Pennsylvania settlers, it furnished an additional motive for his avoiding every thing which might excite the resentment of the Indians. Can then even *prejudice* itself believe that on the contrary he was during that time perfidiously and wantonly murdering those Indians?

Again, I have shewn that in the year 1742, the executive of Maryland had in contemplation to send Col. Cresap with their commissioners to a treaty to be held with the Six Nations, and their dependencies: would that executive have even thought of promoting the interest of that province by sending to the treaty a man stained with the blood of the individuals of some of those nations, and infamous for the many murders he had committed upon them?

Conrod Wieser was anxious to prevent Colonel Cresap's attendance. No man was better acquainted with the affairs of the Six Nations and their dependencies than Conrod Wieser. He was for a great length of time their interpreter, and possessed their confidence.

He was also in the confidence and interest of the government of Pennsylvania. Colonel Cresap was known to be warmly devoted to the government of Maryland, and was irritated against, and extremely obnoxious to that of Pennsylvania.

To this we may naturally attribute Conrod's solicitude to prevent Colonel Cresap's attendance at the treaty, or any other event which might be likely to give him consequence with the Six Nations.

But his objection to him did not arise from his having been guilty of murdering the Indians, or his being disapproved for any acts of violence inflicted upon them;—No, he trumps up as an excuse for his objection, that they were displeased with him for wanting to buy lands from their warriors—and that this was a mere pretext fabricated for the purpose I am well satisfied.

We have already seen that Colonel Cresap even before the year 1743, had obtained grants from the province of Maryland on the north branch of Potowmack, at Old Town. At the time when he first had in view the securing those lands, they were occupied by the Indians: Before he applied to the government of Maryland for a grant, he thought it prudent first to procure the approbation of the Indians in that neighborhood, and for that purpose contracted with certain of their warriors; this he did to avoid giving them offence, as at that time the line of cession between them and the province of Maryland was in dispute. And I have shewn that more that two years after, when at the treaty held at Lancaster in the year 1744-5, they ascertained that line; they so fixed it as only just to include that very settlement of their brother Cresap, which he had so purchased from their warriors. This, I believe, was the purchase to which Conrad Wieser alluded; it is, I believe, the only one he had made or attempted before that time to have made from them, but which I am satisfied was not offensive to the Six Nations or any of them, or complained of by them, as I can find no trace of such complaint.

Had Colonel Cresap before that period, been guilty of murders committed upon the Indians; had he been reputed infamous for these murders, no man would have been more likely to have known that fact than Conrod Wieser; nor can it be doubted he would have assigned *that*, which would have been so much better a cause why Colonel Cresap was an improper person to accompany the Maryland commissioners to the treaty.

I therefore infer, that at the period of 1742, Colonel Cresap was not reputed infamous for the many murders committed upon the inoffensive Indians; and that he did not *then* merit to be so reputed.

Again, in the year 1751 a party of indians belonging to the six nations complained to the governor of Maryland that their brother Cresap, seemed angry with them, and was not disposed to give them victuals enough; but I have examined the archives of Maryland, and can find no complaint or insinuation made by the indians of his having committed any acts of violence whatever against them or any of them.

Is it to be presumed that the governor of Virginia should have shewn that respect for and confidence in, or that the government of Maryland should have bestowed, from the year 1739 to the year 1775, so many respectable appointments upon—a man who was infamous for the many murders he had committed, if they had known that fact; Were they not as likely to have knowledge of that fact as you were? If they were ignorant, how came you by your information?

I have not heard that you *ever* pretended a belief in *inspiration*; you will not, I presume, insinuate you received it from *that* source; of those murders you could not know from your own personal knowledge: If then you derive your information from any other evidence, while *I aver* its *falsity* I *again call* on *you* to produce it.

But I proceed; between the beginning of the year 1748 and end of the year 1749, a considerable number of the most respectable gentlemen in Virginia and Maryland formed a connexion with col. Cresap to embark in important engagements for acquiring western lands, then occupied by the indians, and for carrying on an extensive trade with the indian nations: to effect either of which objects, their good will and friendship were essentially necessary. If these gentlemen had had an idea that col. Cresap had been concerned in cruel murders committed on the indians; if these gentlemen had known that he was reputed infamous on account of such murders, would not he have been the last man with whom they would have thought of entering into such a connexion?

In fine, from the earliest period of col. Cresap's life, after he first settled in Maryland, 'till he ceased being *actively* engaged in business, all his pursuits, as far as they related to his private emolument and the interest of his family, were of that nature as in a peculiar manner to require that he should be on good terms with the indians, and to excite his solicitude for their friendship.

A further argument to prove the falsity of your charge may be drawn from *that character* which you, sir, have given of the indians. You say that either education or nature "has made the *point of honor* with the indians consist in the destruction of an enemy by stratagem, and in the preservation of his own person freed from injury;" you also say "they are as bitter and determined in their resentments, as they are sincere in their friendships, and often pursue their enemies *several hundred miles* through the woods, *surmounting every difficulty* to be *revenged*."

If then col. Cresap had been guilty of so many murders, how came it, that there were no indians inspired with a spirit of resentment on the occasion? How came it, that all the friends and relations of these thus murdered were so entirely lost to that their "point of honor" when so few stratagems would have been requisite, and the preservation of their persons so probable? How came it, that when for so long a life he was living in their vicinity, where to have wreaked their vengeance upon him, they would have had so small a distance to go, and so few difficulties to surmount, he lived safe from that spirit of revenge; and after so very protracted an old age died in his bed?

How, I ask, shall all these things be accounted for, since even we, who are *yet weak* enough to believe in a *Providence*, have never supposed the *infamous murderer* to be the object of *its* particular favour and protection!

One observation more I shall make to shew the falsity of the charge, and shall for that purpose here introduce a name, which by you, sir, and many of your warmest friends, I am inclined to think, *will*, and I am sure, *ought* to be received with respect, that of the deceased col. George Mason.

In a letter written by him to Col. Cresap, dated the 12th of March 1783, after he had been acquainted with him near forty years, he concludes with this paragraph "Capt. B. tells me you have some thoughts of paying me a visit next summer, which gave me *great pleasure*, as I can with *great sincerity* assure you there are *few men in the world*, whom I should rejoice *more to see* than Col. Cresap."

Those, sir, who knew the late Col. George Mason, will not easily believe he would have so written to a man, who he supposed to be *infamous* for murder,—or *infamous* for any other cause.

I here rest the defence of Col. Thomas Cresap.

In my next I shall proceed to examine the charges, as they relate to his youngest son, the late Michael Cresap, Esq. who, if any of the name of Cresap, were *really meant* to be implicated in the charge of killing Logan's family, was the person so meant. This I infer from my knowledge that he alone of that name was on the western side of the Alleghany mountains at the time of that event.

I have said, "if any of that name were *really meant* to be implicated," because I have no reason to believe, that either of the name was ever thought to be concerned in the death of any individual of Logan's family, before you wrote your notes upon Virginia.

My own ideas are these;—that in your controversy with the celebrated Buffon, being anxious to support the reputation of your American savage, and having some where picked up the *fictitious* speech of Logan, you thought it might be made useful;—that to increase its celebrity, *you introduced into it* the name of Col. Cresap, a name well known in America, and partially in Europe;—and particularly known, as connected with the wars, which had taken place between the colonists and the indians;—and as to the *story*;—that you exercised that ingenuity, which I know you to possess, to *form one* that might *suit* the *speech*.

For the entertaining and avowal of these ideas, I shall hold myself perfectly free from censure, until you shall think proper to shew them incorrect.

I must now, sir, attend to *other* duties and remain, as heretofore, with *due* respect.

Your very obedient servant.   LUTHER MARTIN

Printed in *Porcupine's Gazette*, 20 Jan. 1798; at head of text: "No. V." and "To the Honourable Thomas Jefferson, Esqr. Vice-President of the United States."

MY LETTER TO MR. FENNELL: see note to

TJ to John Gibson, 31 May 1797. TJ conveyed his opinions of the CHARACTER . . . OF THE INDIANS in Query VI of the *Notes on Virginia*, which included Logan's declamation (*Notes*, ed. Peden, 58-63).

To Edmund Pendleton

DEAR SIR   Philadelphia Jan. 14. 1798.

I recieved some time ago from mr Edmund Randolph a note signed by mr Lyons & yourself undertaking to pay the amount of a decree of Royle's admrs v. yourselves as admrs of Robinson, to mr Short or myself as his attorney. this undertaking is perfectly satisfactory, and I only wait your pleasure to be signified as to the time when, and place where it may suit you to make the paiment. as it was to depend on the sale of stock, I should suppose this the best market. but of this you will judge.

We receive this day through the public papers news by the way of Norfolk of some stern interrogatories put to our envoys by the French directory. they look so like truth that they cannot fail to make an impression. we are willing to hope that France will not push her resentments to a declaration of war. but we have not entire confidence in the moderation of certain people among ourselves. on the whole our situation is truly perilous. Congress is at present lying on it's oars. there is nothing of the least importance to be taken up. they will begin tomorrow to talk about Blount and mr Liston. this may fill up some hours, as well as lounging, and furnish something for the blank pages of their journals. but unless our envoys furnish us something to do, I do not see how we can contrive even the semblance of business through February.   I avail myself with great pleasure of this opportunity of recalling our antient recollections: and it has been with very great satisfaction that I have heard from time to time of the great portion of health you have enjoyed & still enjoy. that it may continue thro all the years you wish is the prayer of my Dear Sir

Your affectionate friend & servt.   TH: JEFFERSON

RC (MHi: Washburn Collection); at foot of text: "Honble Edmund Pendleton"; endorsed. PrC (DLC: Short Papers); endorsed by TJ in ink on verso.

For the NOTE SIGNED BY MR LYONS & YOURSELF, see Edmund Randolph to TJ, 21 Nov. 1797.

According to a report that came to Philadelphia by way of London, Glasgow, and NORFOLK of STERN INTERROGATORIES PUT TO OUR ENVOYS, the Directory demanded to know if the American representatives had the power "to give satisfaction for the outrage offered to the French government, in the speech the President made on the 16th of May last," and "Whether they are authorised to re-establish the respective position in which the States stood in 1778, and to annul in the posterior treaties all the causes injurious to the interests of the French Republic" (*Philadelphia Gazette*, 15 Jan. 1798).

A letter from Pendleton to TJ, written 15 May 1797 and received on 29 May of that year, is recorded in SJL but has not been found.

To Edmund Randolph

DEAR SIR   Philadelphia Jan. 14. 1798

Your favor of the 7th. inst. came to hand yesterday. those of Nov. 15. 21. & 28. had been recieved in due time. that of the 21st. covered the assumpsit of Messrs. Pendleton and Lyons to pay the amount of the decree of Royle's admrs v. Robinson's admrs, to the use of mr Short. I should sooner have acknoleged these but that in that of the 21st. you mentioned that you had arranged the balance also equally well for mr Short and that I *should hear from you* the beginning of the ensuing year. the last phrase occasioned my delaying post after post to send you an acknolegement expecting to make one answer for the whole. I now write to mr Pendleton to recieve his pleasure as to the time & manner of making his remittance, which I shall immediately invest according to mr Short's directions.

We have today very sinister news by the way of Norfolk through the publick papers, as to the reception of our envoys to Paris. it looks so like truth that it cannot fail to make impression. Congress are waiting in anxiety for information of what may be expected from that quarter. we[1] have really nothing to do, and unless our envoys cut out something for us, I see nothing which can keep us here through February. be so good as to present my respects to mrs Randolph, & to yourself health & happiness. Adieu affectionately,   TH: JEFFERSON

PrC (DLC: Short Papers); at foot of text: "E. Randolph"; endorsed by TJ in ink on verso.

Randolph's FAVOR OF THE 7TH. INST., recorded in SJL as received 13 Jan. 1798, has not been found. Randolph's letter to TJ of 28 NOV., which according to SJL was received 13 Dec. 1797, is also missing.

[1] Preceding word interlined in place of "they."

From Samuel Magaw

SIR,   Philadelphia, Janry. 19. 1798

A stated meeting of the American Philosophical Society, is to be held, this evening, at the usual hour—six o'clock—in their hall; where Your presence is respectfully requested. It is matter of sincerest pleasure to every Well-wisher of Science, that One deep in its researches, & distinguished for its diffusion, is to honour its Chair again in this City; invited thereto by an unanimous suffrage.—The Secretaries ought to have announced to the President, his reelection, at an earlier time: But, for want of due arrangement among themselves, an omission has taken place; which, while needing an Apology,—they nevertheless, hope for

an excuse, in Your Kindness & Generosity.   In sentiments & Assurances of high Consideration,
   I am Your Obedient Servant,

SAM. MAGAW
Sec'ry.

RC (MHi); addressed: "The Hon. Thomas Jefferson"; endorsed by TJ as received 19 Jan. 1798 and so recorded in SJL.

Since his arrival in Philadelphia for the session of Congress TJ had not attended meetings of the society on 15 Dec. 1797 or 5 Jan. 1798, at the latter of which he had been reelected the group's PRESIDENT. He did attend on 19 Jan. 1798, at which time he gave the society a mammoth bone from Virginia. He also presented a Swedish coin, the gift of Tadeusz Kosciuszko. The membership tendered TJ "acknowledgement of the constant sense they entertain of his valuable Communications & Offices of Friendship" (APS, *Proceedings*, 22, pt. 3 [1884], 264-7; Philip Turpin to TJ, 18 July 1796; TJ to Thomas Mann Randolph, 7 May 1797; and TJ to John Barnes, [18] July 1797).

Two communications, nominally addressed to TJ as president of the society but almost certainly had not been dealt with by him individually, had been received by the society during his absence from Philadelphia. A long missive written by Dr. Benjamin Shultz in Philadelphia on 7 Nov. 1797 described a method for examining certain structures of plants "to distinguish between such plants as are esculent and such as are noxious to animals" (RC in PPAmP: Manuscript Communications, Natural History; at foot of text: "To Thomas Jefferson Esqr. President of the American Philosophical Society, & the present vice President of the United States of America, as well as to the

Members of the just-named respectable Society"; with author's footnotes; endorsed by an officer of the society). Thomas Coulter of Bedford County, Pennsylvania, wrote on 4 Dec. 1797 to identify himself as the author of an essay submitted in a society-sponsored competition seeking solutions to the problem of "Premature death in Peach trees," and to indicate that "The Author has Som reason to believe that Mr. George Elder, which he Got to Transscribe his Peace, has, Sent a Coppy to the Socity for him Self—If So, it, will appear (as I Suppose) in the Same hand writing as Mine does" (RC in same; addressed: "To the American Philosophical Society. In Phia. Or, the President (or) Vice President thereof"; endorsed by an officer of the society). Neither letter bears any endorsement by TJ or is recorded in SJL. Shultz's communication was read at a meeting on 1 Dec. 1797 and referred to a committee, which did not report until 7 Dec. 1798. At that time a vote by the members sustained the committee's "objections to publishing" the paper, the particular reasons for the rejection not being recorded in the minutes. The society received Coulter's essay on peach trees at the meeting of 19 Jan. 1798, then in October 1800 determined that no submission in that competition deserved the full prize. The society split the premium between Coulter and another entrant, and published both of the brief essays (APS, *Proceedings*, 22, pt. 3 [1884], 264, 266, 275, 303; APS, *Transactions*, 5 [1802], 325-8).

From Mann Page

DEAR SIR   Mann'sfield Jany. 19th. 1798

   Since the Rect. of your Letter, which was long in coming to hand, I have seen two most abusive Attacks upon you by Luther Martin. What he seems so positively to deny, viz. the Authenticity of Logan's Speech & Story I have no doubt may upon proper Enquiry be verified. I have endeavoured, but in vain, to recollect the Source from whence we derived the Information, but I well remember that it came from such Authority that at that Time no Body doubted the Authenticity of the Facts. Perhaps my Brother, who in such Matters is pretty accurate, may be able to give you some Information. Probably Govr. Wood or some of the old upland Officers may be able to ascertain the Fact at least, nor may it be a fruitless Search to examine the Journals of the Assembly about that Time, for frequently Communications upon Indian Affairs were made by the Executive to the Legislature, & Reports made by Indian Comrs. If any thing farther on this Subject should occur to me I will inform you.

I am much concerned to find that I am again to be disappointed in having the Pleasure of your Company. Farewell! my dear sir,

Your sincere Friend   MANN PAGE

RC (DLC); endorsed by TJ as received   LETTER: TJ to Page, 2 Jan. 1798.
29 Jan. 1798 and so recorded in SJL.

Stevens Thomson Mason's Copy of Logan's Speech

Logan's Speech deliver'd at the Treaty after the Battle in which Colo. Lewis was killed in 1774

I appeal to any white Man to say that he ever entered Logan's Cabin but I gave him meat; that he ever came naked but I clothed him. In the Course of the last War Logan remained in his Cabin an Advocate for Peace. I had such an affection for the white People that I was pointed at by my own Nation: I should have ever lived with them, had it not been for Colo Cressop who last Year cut off in cold Blood all the Relations of Logan, not sparing Women and Children, there runs not a drop of my Blood in the Veins of any human Creature. This called upon me for Revenge. I have sought it, I have killed many, and fully glutted my Revenge; I'm glad there is a Prospect of Peace on Account of the Nation; but I beg you will not entertain a thought that any thing I have said proceeds from fear. Logan disdains the Thought, He will not turn on his Heel to safe his Life, who is there to mourn for Logan—No one.

The foregoing is a copy taken by me when a boy at school in the year 1775 or at farthest in 1776 and lately found in an old pocket book, containing papers and manuscripts of that period.

STES. THON. MASON
Jany 20th. 1798

MS (DLC: TJ Papers, 1:32); entirely in Mason's hand and endorsed by him: "Logan's Speech," consisting of Logan's declamation as Mason first copied it, ca. 1775, Mason adding his memorandum, signature, and dateline to the paper on 20 Jan. 1798. In 1800 TJ printed the memorandum in his *Appendix to the Notes on Virginia* but omitted Mason's text of Logan's speech as "agreeing verbatim with that printed in Dixon and Hunter's Virginia Gazette of February 4, 1775, under the Williamsburg head" (*Notes*, ed. Peden, 245).

Notes on a Conversation with Uriah Springer

Jan. 20. 1798. Cap Uriah Springer of Fayette county Pensva calls on me (with Judge Turner) and informs me he was on the Monongehela in 1774. he lived there. that Logan's family was killed by one Greathouse & others. that they had been over yellow[1] creek a water of the Ohio 60. miles below Pittsbg & 130. above Kanhaway to the Shawanee encampment in a friendly way. that the Indians came over in a canoe after the whites & on their coming to the shore were shot by Greathouse's party.[2] Greathouse himself shot a woman who was ashore on the land, deliberately, after promising her not. that either a little before or after this, Michael Cressop (who was improving land on the Ohio) with others attacked a party of Shawanese & killed three. this brought on Dunmore's war. Judge Turner says Govr. Howard informed him he saw Cresap at Baltimore soon after with the scalps.

MS (DLC); entirely in TJ's hand.

Uriah Springer (ca. 1755-1826), a native of New Jersey who migrated to the transAppalachian frontier at a young age, began his military career as an ensign of Virginia militia under Lord Dunmore in 1774, served as an officer in Virginia regiments of the Continental Line during the Revolutionary War, was a captain of United States infantry from 1792 to 1796, and was commissioned a brigade inspector during the War of 1812 (Louise Phelps Kellogg, ed., *Frontier Retreat on the Upper Ohio 1779-1781*, Collections 24, Draper Series 5, of *Publications of the State Historical Society of Wisconsin* [Madison, 1917], 278n; Heitman, *Continental Army*, 512).

From Philadelphia on 11 June 1798 George TURNER, who had been a judge of the Northwest Territory, addressed a letter to TJ as the president of the American Philosophical Society. The letter, which TJ did not endorse or record in SJL, consisted of a description of an animal that Turner had observed at Vincennes in 1794 and called the prairie squirrel. Endorsed by an officer of the society as received on 16 June, Turner's letter was actually presented at a meeting held the day before. It was referred to Benjamin Smith Barton for consideration, but the society considered it too preliminary an observation to merit publication (RC in PPAmP: Manuscript Communications, Natural History; APS, *Proceedings*, 22, pt. 3 [1884], 272-3). Another letter from Turner to TJ, dated 2 Mch. 1794 and recorded in SJL as received from Cincinnati on 21 May of that year, has not been found. Elected to the APS in 1790, Turner was an active member, had chaired some meetings in the president's absence, and in January

1800 was elected one of three curators. The following month, however, the society learned that he had diverted most of a $500 gift. Turner resigned under threat of expulsion and had to give the APS a bond and a mortgage on land in Virginia to assure repayment of the missing funds (APS, *Proceedings*, 22, pt. 3 [1884], 179, 214, 221, 237, 251-2, 269-70, 286, 288, 290, 295-7, 312, 313; APS, *Transactions*, 4:334-5, 510-18; Vol. 24:604n).

[1] TJ interlined the text from this word through "Kanhaway" in place of "the river."

[2] Word interlined in place of "family."

From James Madison

DEAR SIR   Orange Jany. 21. 1798

When your favor of the 3d. instant arrived I was on a journey to the neighbourhood of Richmond, from which I did not return till the 18th. The mail on the day following brought me the packet of newspapers under your cover. Col. Bell has written me, that the nails ordered as stated in my last to you, are all ready for me. I had not requested them to be prepared in parcells as I shall use them, because I want some for out-houses immediately, and I wished to avoid the necessity of more than one trip. The attack on Monroe's publication evidently issues from or is aided by[1] an official source, and is a proof that the bitten bites. I have not yet seen a copy of it, and was astonished to learn in Richmond, where I passed a day, that a single copy only had reached that place, which from the length of it, not more than 2 or 3 persons had read. By them it was said that if this did not open the eyes of the people, their blindness must be incurable. If a sufficient number of copies do not arrive there before the adjournment of the Assembly, the only opportunity of circulating the information in this State, will be lost for a year, that is till the subject has lost its flavor. The enormous price also was complained of as a probable obstacle to an extensive circulation. You will have seen in the Newspapers, the proceedings on the Amherst Memorial, on the Glebes & Churches, and on the proposition for revising the Constitution. The first was the only test of party strength, and so far deceptive as it confounds scrupulous Republicans with their adversaries, in the vote agst. a legislative censure on the Grand jury. I did not understand the presentment was vindicated positively by a single member in the debate. The unfavorable accts. as to our three Plenipos. got to Richmond while I was there by the way of Norfolk. It seemed to give extreme uneasiness to the warm & well informed[2] friends of Republicanism, who saw in a war on the side of England, the most formidable means put into the hands of her partizans, for warping the public mind towards Monarchy. This consideration certainly merits the strictest regard as an argument for peace, as long as we have a fair choice on the question. The public will have a right to expect also from our Ex. & the Negociators, the fullest communication of every circumstance that may attend the experiment if it should miscarry. The British Treaty has placed such difficulties in the way of an adjustment, that nothing but the most cordial dispositions on both sides can overcome them; and such have been the indications on the side of our Executive, even during the negociation, that it will not be easily believed, in case of a rupture, that it was not promoted, if not caused, by our own Counsels.

We have had a fine spell of open weather with plentiful rains at proper intervals. This has been favorable to our winter operations, but otherwise to some of those of Nature, particularly in our Wheat fields which continue to present the most unpromising aspect. Accept the most affectionate farewel

RC (DLC: Madison Papers); torn by seal at closing; addressed: "The Vice President of the United States Philadelphia"; franked; endorsed by TJ as received 30 Jan. 1798 and so recorded in SJL.

AMHERST MEMORIAL: see Editorial Note and group of documents on petition to Virginia House of Delegates, printed at 3 Aug. 1797.

In January 1798 the Virginia House of Delegates debated a bill to revoke Virginia laws that promoted the "reestablishment of a National Church" and interfered with the state's statute on protection of religious freedom. The section of the bill which called for the sale of Episcopalian GLEBES AND CHURCHES as parishes became vacant (with the proceeds going for the education of poor children) was deleted during the House debate. The entire bill was defeated when the House would not agree to Senate amendments that further diluted it (JHD, Dec. 1797-Jan. 1798, p. 73, 78, 80-1, 85, 94, 96, 105-6; Philadelphia *Aurora*, 18, 24 Jan. 1798; Thomas E. Buckley, "Evangelicals Triumphant: The Baptists' Assault on the

Virginia Glebes, 1786-1801," WMQ, 3d ser., 45 [1988], 49-54).

On 8 Jan. 1798 a PROPOSITION FOR REVISING the Federal CONSTITUTION was introduced in the Virginia House of Delegates instructing Virginia congressmen to "use all constitutional exertions" to obtain amendments that would cut the term of United States senators in half, limit the president to two consecutive terms followed by a four-year interval before seeking a third term, and require that treaties needing appropriations would be considered "obligatory" only with the consent of the House of Representatives. Consideration of this three-part resolution was continuously postponed and did not come to a vote during the session (JHD, Dec. 1797-Jan. 1798, p. 85-6, 114). On 9 Jan. 1798 the House of Delegates defeated a motion to call a convention to revise the Virginia state constitution (same, 87; Philadelphia *Aurora*, 24 Jan. 1798).

[1] Preceding four words interlined.
[2] Preceding two words and ampersand interlined.

To Peter Legaux

SIR   Jan. 22. 1798.

I have to acknolege the favor of your's of the 8th. inst. I took the first occasion in my power of calling at No. 71. Chesnut street in hopes of finding you there & discussing more fully than can be done by letter, the subject of yours to me, and the way in which I might be useful. not finding you there, I still deferred answering in hopes of meeting you at the Philosophical society on Friday last but failed in that also. the difficulty which your proposition presents arises from this, that there has never, that I know of, been an application to Congress to take on itself the introduction of any new branch of agriculture or of any new art. whether they have such a power given them by the constitution, is therefore a question on which they have never decided, and it is the opinion, of some at least, that they have no such power. should you however chuse to propose to them the taking your enterprize under their patronage, it would be better that it should be done by petition to the House of representatives. in this case the representatives of this state, wherein the work is going on, would of course be the most able to represent it's situation & prospects, and previously to counsel you whether it would be proper or not to make the proposition. I sincerely regret the crisis in which this enterprize is placed, as I should consider the culture of the vine as an useful introduction to a certain degree. with every wish that you may still be enabled to prosecute it to a final establishment, I am with great esteem Sir

Your most obedt. & most humble servt   TH: JEFFERSON

RC (Charles Tome, Wilmington, Delaware, 1944); at foot of text: "M. Legaux."

Peter (Pierre) Legaux (1748-1827), born and educated in Lorraine, France, came from a prominent family, practiced law, and held government positions in the French West Indies before emigrating to Pennsylvania in 1785. At "Mt. Joy," his estate at Spring Mill on the Schuylkill River thirteen miles from Philadelphia, he operated a ferry, produced lime and glass, had a joinery, raised bees and livestock, and planted vineyards in which he cultivated European and American varieties of grapes. In 1793 the Pennsylvania General Assembly authorized the incorporation of a company to promote Legaux's vineyard by subscription, but most of the vines did not thrive. In 1806 the General Assembly tried unsuccessfully to implement a lottery to help the Vine Company recover its debts, and the vineyard project became defunct by 1812. Legaux made an important contribution to American horticulture by spreading the cultivation of a few hardy varieties of grapes, which although he did not call them such have been identified as strains native to America, and some of which he sent to TJ for planting at Monticello. In 1787 Legaux, who for a number of years made regular meteorological observations at Spring Mill, was elected to membership in the American Philosophical Society (S. Gordon Smyth, "Peter Legaux, A Noted Frenchman who Settled at Spring Mill in 1786," *Historical Sketches: A Collection of Papers Prepared for the Historical Society of Montgomery County, Pennsylvania*, 2 [1900], 92-125; Stevenson Whitcomb Fletcher, *Pennsylvania Agriculture and Country Life 1640-1840* [Harrisburg, 1950], 223-5; APS, *Proceedings*, 22, pt. 3 [1884], 162, 172, 371; MB, 2:1072).

Legaux's letter OF THE 8TH. INST. is recorded in SJL as received on 15 Jan. 1798 but has not been found. Also recorded in SJL but missing are letters from Legaux to TJ of 4 May 1798 and 26 and 29 Mch. 1800, received respectively on 4 May 1798 and 27 and 30 Mch. 1800, and one from TJ to Legaux of 8 May 1798.

From John Page

MY DEAR JEFFERSON   Richmond Jany. 22d. 1798

My long Absence from hence, occasioned by Sickness which prevented my return, & the Post-master's officious good intentioned Effort to convey your letters to me at Rosewell, where he supposed I should remain during the present Session of Assembly, put it out of my Power to acknowledge the Receipt of them 'till now. I thank you for your Letter, & for Fauchet's Pamphlet.

At present I can not recollect any Circumstance respecting Logan's Speech: & I do not remember that I ever heard it in Lord Dunmore's or Foy's Company; or, indeed where, or when I first heard it—I will however enquire how the Story came to us, & who you may apply to for Information respecting it—We are hurrying on to finish our Session in three days more—I am in a Tavern crouded—when in my bed-room I have no Retirement that can be relied on for a Moment, as I have but a Moiety of the Room & *the Table* in it. Accept therefore of this from your Friend—   JOHN PAGE

RC (DLC); endorsed by TJ as received 30 Jan. 1798 and so recorded in SJL.

YOUR LETTER: TJ to Page, [1] Jan. 1798.

From Martha Jefferson Randolph

Bellmont Jan. 22, 1798

Jupiter had given us so terrible an account of your sufferings from the ice on the patowmac that we began to be seriously alarmed about you, before the arrival of your letters, which came both to gether; it was with infinite pleasure than that we learned you had got the better of your cold and were at least *comfortably* if not agreably fixed for the winter. it is much more than we can boast of, for the extreme dampness of the situation and an absolute want of offices of every kind to shelter the servants whilst in the performance of their duties, have occasioned more sickness than I ever saw in a family in my life. pleurisie, rhumatism, and every disorder proceeding from cold have been so frequent that we have scarcely had at any one time *well* enough to tend the sick—our intercourse with Monticello has been allmost *daily* they have been generally well there except Tom and Goliah who are both *about* again and poor little Harriot who died a few days after you left us. I shall joyfully accept of the offer you make of executing my comissions in Philadelphia. Mr Randolph has some money remaining in Barnes's hands which I should

[43]

be extremely obliged to you to lay out in plate, table spoons tea spoons &c as far as it will go. I imagine there is enough of it for that purpose and as much (considering the many other urgent calls for money building will occasion) as will be convenient to bestow upon that article. and if such a thing is to be had *a game of the goose* it was a promise made to the children which Richmond does not furnish the means of paying. I look forward with great impatience to March I am afraid to flatter my self with the prospect of seeing you sooner and I feel every day more strongly the impossibility of becoming habituated to your absence— sepparated in my infancy from every other friend, and accustomed to look up to you alone, every sentiment of tenderness my nature was susceptible of was for many years centered in you, and no connexion formed since that could weaken a sentiment interwoven with my very existence. I have heard from Maria thru Mr Eppes she deals much in promises but very little in deeds that are to be performed with a pen she was in as good health and better spirits than usual adieu my dearest Father the children unanimously join in love to you and believe me with every sentiment of tenderness gratitude and respect your affectionate child—   M. RANDOLPH

RC (MHi); conjoined to RC of Thomas Mann Randolph to TJ, 28 Jan. 1798; addressed: "Thomas Jefferson Vice President Philadelphia"; endorsed by TJ as received 6 Feb. 1798 and so recorded in SJL.

ARRIVAL OF YOUR LETTERS: TJ to Thomas Mann Randolph, 14 Dec. 1797, and TJ to Martha Jefferson Randolph, 27 Dec. 1797.

Jefferson, the *Aurora*, and Delamotte's Letter from France

I. DELAMOTTE TO JEFFERSON,
23 JANUARY 1798

II. LETTER FROM A WELL INFORMED MERCHANT IN FRANCE,
1 FEBRUARY 1798

EDITORIAL NOTE

When the Philadelphia *Aurora* of 3 Apr. 1798 printed a translation of "a letter from a well informed merchant in France to his friend in this city," the newspaper gave no hint that the "friend" was Jefferson, or that the "merchant" was the U. S. vice-consul at Le Havre, F. C. A. Delamotte. The date of the letter had also been altered, from 23 Jan. to 1 Feb. 1798. Jefferson himself did not advertise his role in making the letter available for publication. To Madison on 5 Apr. he called attention to a letter that he had furnished for Bache's newspaper, mistakenly referring to its publication "yesterday." However, to Edmund Pendleton on 2 Apr. and to Monroe on 5 Apr. he made only vague reference to "letters from France," pointing neither to his role as recipient nor to the publication of the letter from Delamotte. In using the plural form, "letters," he may have meant correspondence addressed to others as well as to himself: the letters that Jefferson received from France on 30 Mch. 1798 in addition to Delamotte's were those written by Charles Louis Clérisseau on 23 May and William Short on 27 Dec. 1797, and neither of those seems to have introduced anything fresh on the subject of relations between the United States and France. They and Delamotte's of 23 Jan. were the only letters that Jefferson received from France during late March and early April 1798.

In both its timing and its content, Delamotte's communication must have seemed propitious for Jefferson and his political allies. Early in the document Delamotte unequivocally announced that the United States was mistaken ("vous vous trompés") to think that France was about to declare war. That was not to say, however, that careful attention was not required to repair the effects of American "disdain" toward a nation that seemed to be on the verge of global dominance. Perhaps no message could be better suited, at the moment of its arrival, to cool war fever and stimulate thought about relations with France. Any felicitous effect the letter might have had, however, evaporated within days of its publication as details of the U.S. envoys' dispatches on the XYZ affair became public.

There is no evidence that Jefferson made the translation that appeared in the *Aurora*. Bache was certainly fluent in French, although it is unclear when he resumed active direction of the newspaper from James Callender, who edited it during Bache's absence in March (Durey, *Callender*, 106-7). The published translation omitted the opening and closing paragraphs of the original letter and other passages identified in notes to Document I. Delamotte evidently enclosed a newspaper, which has not been found but may have been one of the "Latest Paris Papers" from which the editors of the *Aurora* translated items for inclusion in their columns during the first days of April. Despite Delamotte's comment that Jefferson should be apprised of the situation in France "le plus fréquemment possible," SJL records no further correspondence between them until 1800.

I. Delamotte to Jefferson

MONSIEUR   havre 23. Janvier [l'an] [. . .]

Je n'ai point eû l'honneur de vous ecrire depuis votre promotion á la presidence du Senat; Je vous prie pourtant de Croire que j'y ai pris tout l'Interet que j'y devois prendre & que je prendrai toujours á tout ce qui vous Arrivera d'important.[1]

La Situation Actuelle des Affaires d'Europe m'engage á vous adresser la presente, pour vous mettre, Autant qu'il dépend de moi, au Cours de nos Affaires politiques, qui deviennent celles de toute l'Europe

& même du Nouveau Monde & qui ont une Marche Si rapide, qu'il devient interessant pour vous, Soit pour votre gouvernemt.,[2] d'en etre informé le plus fréquemment possible, n'importe par quelle main, pourvû que vous puissiés Compter Sur la véracité et les bonnes intention de votre Correspondant.

les Commissaires d'Amerique bien Convaincûs qu'ils n'avanceront á rien dans leur Mission, parlent, me dit Mr. Mountflorence,[3] de quitter ce pays-ci. Je voudrois qu'ils fussent dejá chez vous, pour vous donner une juste idée des choses, Car Il me semble par le discours du President á la Session derniere, ou Actuelle, du Corps législatif, que vous Craignés une rupture ouverte, une déclaration de guerre de la part de la france & je suis d'opinion que vous vous trompés.

Je crois que le traité de 1794. Avec l'Angleterre est le moindre grief de la france Contre l'Amerique, du moins est-il Certain que ce traité, nuisible ou non á la france, est pour elle d'un bien petit interet; á Côté des vuës vastes que notre gouvernement a formées Contre l'Angleterre, contre Son immense Marine & Contre le Commerce qu'elle a envahi Sur tout le globe; vuës que notre gouvernement poursuit avec Activité & qu'il réalisera: n'en doutés pas. le veritable grief (j'ignore [S'il] est fondé ou Non Sur des faits) C'est le dedain Avec lequel on reproche á l'Amerique d'Avoir regardé la france, lorsque tous Ses ennemis Coalisés Sembloient devoir la détruire. toute nation est chatouilleuse Sur ce point, Surtout lorsqu'au lieu d'etre Abaissée par Ses ennemis, elle les a tous Surmontés.

pour Montrer á l'Amerique le ressentiment de ce dédain, on a d'Abord rompû les Communications politiqu[es;] ensuite on vous a cherché Une Mauvaise querelle Sur les rôles d'Equipage, au moyen de laquelle on vous a pris de riches Cargaisons, dont, Selon Moi, vous ne recouvrerés jamais un Sol. les Americains qui Sont en france ont ensuitte Craint qu'on ne Saisit leurs proprietés. on ne l'a pas fait & on ne le fera pas. le ressentiment n'ira, je Crois, pas plus loin & les choses resteront dans l'état oú elles sont, jusqu'apres qu'on aura reussi ou échoué dans les projets contre l'Angleterre. Si la paix avec l'Angleterre Avoit [eu] lieu dans l'une ou l'autre des tentatives du Lord Malmesbury, Je crois bien que la querelle de l'Amerique Auroit été bientot reglée,[4] mais quand vous verrés par le papier que je vous joins ici, ce qu'on veut faire de l'Electorât d'Hanovre, vous jugerés facilement qui vouloit la paix, qui ne la vouloit point. Au reste, à quoi bon la france vous feroit elle la guerre, avec quoi vous la feroit-elle? J'espere au contraire vous voir par la Suite Aussi bons alliés de la france que jamais, parceque je Crois que C'est l'interet de tous deux, mais je voudrois voir dés ce moment le gouvernemt Americain ouvrir la Voye á ce racco-

modement & cheminer doucement á coté du pot de fer. quand ce racco-
modement Aura lieu, il faut vous attendre âu Sacrifice d'une partie de
vos Connections Avec l'Angleter[re] & que nous voudrons vous fournir
Au moins Une partie des objets Manufacturés que vous ne tirés que
d'elle. [5] plût á Dieu, Monsieur, que vous fussiés venû en france;
vous ne le pouviés gueres, mais je ne fais Aucun doute que vous Auriés
été écouté & il eut peut etre été d'un grand Avantage pour votre pays,
que vous, qui Connoissiés la france d'autrefois, vous Connoissiés la
france d'Aujourd'huy.

Maintenant que vous Connoissés nos Succés en Italie, notre traité de
paix de Campo-formio Avec l'Empereur, l'Etablissement de la republique Cisalpine, le sort des gouvernements de Venise et de Gênes &a.
voyés dans le papier inclus le remuë-menage que nous faisons en Al-
lemagne pour nous donner la rive gauche du Rhin & vous dirés Sure-
ment que notre gouvernement n'a pas moins d'energie par Sa politique
que par Ses Armes. Il ne vous échappera pas que toutes les puissances,
grandes ou petites, auxquelles on donne des Compensations, gagnent á
l'échange et en deviennent plus Amies de la france; que les villes
Anséatiques tombant entre les Mains de grandes puissances, ces puissances Seront invitées á en fermer les ports Aux Anglois, Comme les
puissances, ci devant nos ennemies, maintenant nos alliées, leur ferment
les leurs. C'est le Sistême décidé du Directoire, de Couper les vivres [6]
aux Anglois, en empêchant l'écoulement de leurs Marchandises fabri-
quées. Voici depuis peû de jours un nouveau décret qui Statuë que la
qualité de Neutre ou d'"ennemi" d'un Navire ne Sera plus Constatée
que par l'Espece de Cargaison qu'il aura á bord & qu'un Navire quel-
conque, qui Sera chargé *en tout, ou en partie*, de Marchandises An-
gloises, ou *provenantes du Commerce* de l'Angleterre, Sera réputé ennemi & condamné de bonne prise, *à qui que ce soit* qu'appartienne la
Marchandise. vous voyés qu'on ne Ménage pas plus en Celá les Suedois
et Danois que les Americains & tel est Aujourd'huy l'ascendance de la
france, qu'elle peut Se permettre impunément ces choses Contraires á
l'ordre ordinaire—& que Si le Dannemarck & la Suede venoient Se
plaindre, on leur diroit "Nous travaillons en celá pour vous, dans
l'Avenir, autant que pour nous Même; Ce n'est plus pour Amener une
paix plus ou Moins Avantageuse, que nous guerroyons l'Angleterre,
C'est pour qu'elle rende á chacun Sa part de l'empire des Mers, Sa part
du Commerce qu'elle a envahi.   Nous préparons une flotte de
descente; les troupes Se rassemblent Sur les Cotes de la manche; les
Armements, les Constructions, tout nous dit que la tentative Sera ef-
fectuée cet été. les préparatifs qui Se font ne permettent pas de Croire
qu'ils Se réduiront á un Simulacre. nous n'avons point de marine, dira-

t'on? nous invoquerons le Calme qui rend á peû prés inutile celle de l'ennemi. les vaisseaux, que nous Avons retirés de l'Arsenal de Venise, qui Sont á Toulon, les notres, pour peû qu'il en reste, Ceux de l'espagne, de la hollande, Une Armée de Canonieres Armées de chacune trois Canons de 24. & de 36. une Armée de terre qui ne Connoit plus les dangers, n'en voilâ t'il pas assés pour porter en Angleterre une force redoutable Sur des bateux á rames? qui Sçait encore Si les Danois & les Suedois ne Céderont point á la prépondérance de la france et ne Se trouveront point obligés de Concourir á cette expédition & d'y Amener leurs vaisseaux?

Veuillés, Monsieur, ne point me taxer de legereté Sur ce que j'ai l'honneur de vous ecrire. J'Avoüe que vous pourrés bien en etre tenté. que Cette descente projettée Ait lieu, ou non, je n'en mettrai mon doigt au feu, mais vous pouvés Solidement Compter Sur Ceci; que le gouvernement françois ne Conteste plus Avec l'Angleterre Seulement pour faire un traité plus honorable, mais bien Certainemt, pour abattre Sa puissance; que C'est un point qui devient Necessaire á notre existence future, depuis que nous devenons de Si grands proprietaires terriens, & qu'il n'y a plus chés nous d'etat pour les particuliers que le Commerce & ce qui y a rapport; Enfin, que l'occasion est belle & qu'elle ne Se retrouveroit pas en plusieurs Siécles peut etre.

Je Conclus de tout celá que le gouvernement Americain ne doit point craindre la guerre de notre part, mais qu'il doit ménager beaucoup la france, même la Caresser Comme la puissance qui dictera Aux autres pendant un Siécle, par la Seule impulsion que lui a donné sa révolution & beaucoup plus longtems Si elle est gouvernée Avec des principes d'équité & de moderation envers les autres. [7]

Cutting, qui a voulu rester á Paris jusqu'a present peut etre dans la vuë de Se faire une fortune (tous nos chers Americains Veulent une fortune &c tout de Suite) me mande qu'au lieu de prosperer, Ses affaires ne Sont pas plus Avancées. Je le presse de venir prendre Son Consulat & je crois qu'il le fera, parce que je lui Ai en Même tems fait Savoir qu'un Mr. James Prince, Capitaine de Navire, de Boston, qui est resté ici depuis deux Ans & qui voudroi[t] bien que le Consulat l'aidât á Accaparer les affaires d'Amerique, veut obtenir cette Commission [ici] du fait que Cutting reste á Paris & qu'il n'y a point de Consul au Havre. M. Prince part en effet pour l'Amerique & se vante dejá de Ses esperances. Il n'est point douteux, Monsieur, que vous pouvés etre favorable á Cutting, & Si ma priere peut quelque chose Auprés de vous, je vous la fais de grand Cœur.

J'ai l'honneur d'etre avec respect & affection Sincere Monsieur Votre trés humble Servit.   DELAMOTTE

RC (DLC: TJ Papers, 53:9073-4); torn; with one word translated interlinearly, possibly by TJ (see note 6 below); endorsed by TJ as received 30 Mch. 1798 and so recorded in SJL. Editors' translations of passages omitted from English version in Philadelphia *Aurora* (see next document) are provided in notes below. Enclosure not found.

LE DISCOURS DU PRESIDENT À LA SESSION . . . DU CORPS LÉGISLATIF: John Adams's address to Congress of 23 Nov. 1797. For the French *arreté* that required American ships to have crew rosters, LES RÔLES D'EQUI-PAGE, of specified form to avoid capture, see Delamotte's letter to TJ of 31 July 1797. ET CHEMINER DOUCEMENT À COTÉ DU POT DE FER: in La Fontaine's version of a fable by Aesop, the clay pot, reluctant to leave the safety of home, is convinced by the iron pot that they should take a trip together, the iron pot to protect its more fragile companion; as they proceed down the road, however, they bump against one another and the clay pot is soon broken to pieces (Jean de La Fontaine, *Fables: Psyché-Œuvres Diverses*, ed. Roger Delbiausse [Paris, 1947], 85-6).

In addition to declaring that a ship with any cargo of British origin was a valid prize, the DÉCRET passed by the Directory on 18 Jan. 1798 closed French ports to vessels that had stopped in English ports (Duvergier, *Lois*, 10:182-3).

[1] Paragraph lacking in *Aurora*. Editors' translation: "I have not had the honor of writing to you since your promotion to the presidency of the Senate; nevertheless I beg you to believe that I paid it all the interest I should have taken and that I shall always take in everything important that happens to you."

[2] Phrase lacking in *Aurora* ("your government").

[3] Phrase lacking in *Aurora* ("Mr. Mountflorence tells me").

[4] Remainder of sentence lacking in *Aurora*. Translation: "but when you read the document I attach here, about what is to be done with the electorate of Hanover, you will easily judge who wanted peace, and who did not."

[5] Remainder of paragraph lacking in *Aurora*. Translation: "would to Heaven, sir, that you had come to France; you could scarcely do so, but I do not have the slightest doubt that you would have been listened to and that it would perhaps have been a great advantage for your country and for yourself, you who knew the former France, for you to know today's France."

[6] The word "aliment" appears in pencil above the preceding two words, possibly by TJ.

[7] *Aurora* omits final paragraph and closing. Translation: "Cutting, who desired to remain in Paris up until now, perhaps with a view to making a fortune (all our dear Americans want a fortune, and right away) writes that, instead of prospering, his affairs are no further advanced. I am urging him to take on his consulate, and I think he will do so, because at the same time I advised him that a Mr. James Prince, a ship captain from Boston, who has been staying here for two years, and who would like the consulship to help him take over the American business, has wanted to obtain that commission here ever since Cutting has been staying in Paris and there is no consul in Le Havre. In fact Mr. Prince is leaving for America, and is already boasting of his expectations. There is no doubt, sir, that you may be favorable to Cutting, and if my request may have any influence over you, I make it with all my heart.

"I have the honor to be with respect and sincere affection sir your very humble servant."

II. Letter from a
Well Informed Merchant in France

Translation of a letter from a well informed merchant in France to his friend in this city, dated Feb. 1st. '98.

The present situation of Europe induces me to address you, in order to inform you, as much as I can, of our political affairs which become those of all Europe and even of the New-World; and which are so quick in their progress, that it becomes interesting for you to be informed as to them as frequently as possible, no matter by what hand, provided you may depend upon the veracity and good intentions of your correspondent.

The American commissioners, well convinced that they will make no progress in their mission, speak of leaving this country. I wish they were already at home that they may give you a just idea of things; for it appears to me by the speech of the president at the last session, or the present one of the legislature, that you fear an open rupture, a declaration of war from France, & I am of opinion you are mistaken.

I believe, that the treaty of 1794 with England is one of the least grievances of which France complains against America; at least, it is certain that this treaty, however injurious it may be to France, is for her of very little interest compared to the vast views that our government has against England, against her immense navy, and against the commerce she has usurped in every quarter of the globe; views which our government pursues with activity, and which they will realise be assured. The principal grievance (I do not know whether it is or is not founded in fact) is the disdain with which America is reproached with having looked upon France, when all her enemies coalised seemed ready to destroy her. Every nation is ticklish upon this point; especially when instead of being depressed by its enemies, it has triumphed over all of them.

To shew America our resentment at this disdain, our political correspondence has first been cut short; then ill founded exceptions have been taken on the score of the *Role d'Equipage*; by means of which you have lost rich cargoes, for which, in my opinion, you will never receive a penny of compensation. Then the Americans in France feared, that their property would be seized; this has not and will not be done. Resentment will not carry us further, I believe; and things will remain in the state in which they are, until we have succeeded or miscarried in the expedition against England. If peace with England had been the issue of either of Lord Malmesbury's attempts, I believe the differences with America would soon have been arranged. But what should France make war upon you for; and how could they? I hope, on the contrary to see you shortly as good allies of France, as ever; because I believe it is the interest of both nations: but I should like now to see the American government opening the way to a reconciliation, and moving gently along side of the iron pot. When that reconciliation takes place, you must expect to sacrifice a portion of your commerce with England, and that we shall wish to supply you at least with a portion of the manufactured articles which at present you draw thence exclusively.

Now that you are acquainted with our successes in Italy, our treaty of Campo Formio with the Emperor, the establishment of the Cisalpine Republic; the fate of the governments of Venice and of Genoa, &c. see in the inclosed paper the movements which we make in Germany, in order to get possession of the left bank of the Rhine, and you will surely agree, that our government has not less energy in negociation than in the field.

It will not escape your attention, that all the powers little or big, to whom compensations are given, gain in the exchange, and become thereby more friendly to France; that the Hanse-towns falling into the hands of great powers, those powers will be invited to shut up their ports to the English, as has been done by the powers formerly our enemies, now our allies, who shut theirs. It is the determined system of the Directory, to cut off supplies from the English, by preventing the spreading of their manufactured goods. A few days since a new decree has passed, which declares, that the nature of the cargo shall in future make the vessel neutral or enemy; and that every vessel whatever, which shall be laden *in whole, or in part*, with English merchandise, or *arising from the commerce* of England, shall be considered as enemy and condemned as good prize, to *whomsoever* the merchandize may belong. You see, that in this, the Swedes and Danes are not more tenderly treated than the Americans, and such is at this time the asendancy of France, that she can with impunity do these things, contrary to the ordinary course of things: and that if Denmark or Sweden should complain, they would be told: "We labour, in this in your favor, as to the future, as well as for ourselves. It is no longer to secure a peace more or less advantageous, that we combat England; it is to make her give up to each his portion of the empire of the sea, his portion of the commerce, she has usurped." We are preparing a fleet for landing in England; the troops are mustering upon the coasts of the channel; the armaments and equipments, every thing tells us, that the attempt will be made this summer. The preparations which are making, do not permit a belief, that they are making only to excite uneasiness in England. It will be said we have no navy. We shall make choice of a calm, which renders that of the enemy useless. The vessels we got at Venice, which are at Toulon; our own, be those that remain ever so few, those of Spain and Holland; a number of gun-boats, each mounting three guns, 24 and 36 pounders; a land army, which knows no danger—are not those sufficient to carry to England a formidable force upon row boats? Who knows, also, whether the Danes and Swedes will not be inclined by the preponderancy of France, and find it in their interest to assist in this expedition with their fleets?

Do not I pray you, accuse me of levity on the score of what I write. I own you may be tempted to do it. But whether this landing takes place or not, you may fully depend on this: that the French government no longer can treat with England only for a treaty more or less honorable; but to destroy her power; that this is a point which becomes necessary to our future welfare, since we become such immense landed proprietors, and that there is no longer among us any avocation for individuals besides commerce, and what relates to commerce. Finally that the occasion is a good one, and that it might not occur again for many centuries.

I conclude, from all this, that the American government ought not to fear war from us; but that they ought to treat France with caution, and even seek her friendship, as a power, whose influence will preponderate for a century to come, by the impulse given it by its revolution, and much longer, if it is governed by principles of equity & moderation towards other nations.

Printed in Philadelphia *Aurora*, 3 Apr. 1798. For translation of passages omitted by *Aurora*, see textual notes to Document I.

From William Short

Jefferson. Jan. 23.—an abridgt. of that of Dec. 27. (see above)—except such parts are marked thus ( ).—The present sent by dup.—contains one for my brother—shall continue writing from time to time— (send on the 1st.—the letter of Mr. P[. . .] &)—

FC (DLC: Short Papers); entirely in Short's hand; part of an epistolary record of his letters to TJ and others from 26 Dec. 1797 to 9 Oct. 1798; endorsed by Short in margin at head of text: "(ans)." Enclosure: William Short to Peyton Short, 24 Jan. 1798, an abridgment of his letter of 26 Dec. 1797, noting in addition Henry Skipwith's failure to provide any account of his oversight of William Short's financial affairs (MS in same; consisting of a memorandum in the same epistolary record). Recorded in SJL as received from La Roche-Guyon on 25 Apr. 1798.

To James Madison

Philadelphia Jan. 24.[1] 98.

I wrote you last on the 2d. inst. on which day I recieved yours of Dec. 25. I have not resumed my pen because there has really been nothing worth writing about but what you would see in the newspapers. there is as yet no certainty what will be the aspect of our affairs with France. either the Envoys have not written to the government, or their communications are hushed up. this last is suspected because so many arrivals have happened from Bordeaux & Havre. the letters from American correspondents in France have been always to Boston: & the experience we had last summer of their adroitness in counterfeiting this kind of intelligence, inspires doubts as to their late paragraphs. a letter is certainly recieved here by an individual from Taleyrand, which says our envoys have been heard, that their pretensions are high, that possibly no arrangement may take place, but that there will be no declaration of war by France. it is said that Bournonville has written that he has hopes of an accomodation (3. audiences having then, Nov. 3. been had) and to be himself a member of a new diplomatic mission to this country. on the whole I am entirely suspended as to what is to be expected.—the Representatives have been several days in debate on the bill for foreign intercourse. a motion has been made to reduce it to what it was before the extension of 1796. the debate will probably have good effects in several ways on the public mind, but the advocates for the reformation expect to lose the question. they find themselves decieved in the expectation entertained in the beginning of the session, that they had a majority. they now think the majority is on the other side by 2. or 3. and there are moreover 2. or 3 of them absent.—Blount's affair is to come on next. in the mean time the Senate have before them a bill for regulating proceedings in impeachment. this will be made the occasion of offering a clause for the introduction of juries into these trials. (compare the paragraph in the constitution which says that the trial of all crimes, *except in cases of impeachment*, shall be by jury, with the VIIIth. amendment which says that in *all* criminal prosecutions, the trial shall be by jury.) there is no expectation of carrying this; because the division in the Senate is of 2. to 1. but it will draw forth the principles of the parties, and concur in accumulating proofs on which side all the sound principles are to be found.—very acrimonious altercations are going on between the Spanish minister & Executive, and at the Natchez something worse than mere altercation. if hostilities have not begun there, it has not been for want of endeavors to bring them on by our agents.—Marshall of Kentuckey, this day proposed in Senate some amendments to the constitu-

[53]

tion. they were barely read just as we were adjourning, & not a word of explanation given. as far as I caught them in my ear, they went only to modifications of the elections of President & V. President, by authorising voters to add the office for which they name each, &[2] giving to the Senate the decision of a disputed election of President & to the Representatives that of Vice-President. but I am apprehensive I caught the thing imperfectly, & probably incorrectly.[3] perhaps this occasion may be taken of proposing again the Virginia amendments, as also to condemn elections by the legislatures themselves, to transfer the power of trying impeachments from the Senate to some better constituted court &c. &c.

Good tobo. here is 13. Doll. flour 8.50 Wheat 1.50 but dull, because only the millers buy. the river however is nearly open & the merchants will now come to market & give a spur to the price. but their competition will not be what it has been. bankruptcies thicken, & the height of them is by no means yet come on. it is thought this winter will be very trying. friendly salutations to mrs Madison. Adieu affectionately.

Jan. 25.[4] I inclose Marshall's propositions. they have been this day postponed to the 1st. of June, chiefly by the vote of the Antirepublicans under the acknoleged fear that other amendments would be also proposed, and that this is not the time for agitating the public mind.

RC (DLC: Madison Papers); with change in dateline by TJ (see note 1 below); at foot of first page: "Mr. Madison"; listed in SJL at 25 Jan. 1798. PrC (DLC); lacks change in dateline and date in postscript (see note 4 below). Enclosure: see note below.

TJ's LAST letter to Madison was actually dated 3 Jan. 1798. The news that Charles François BOURNONVILLE, former secretary of the French legation in Philadelphia, would return to the United States as a MEMBER OF A NEW DIPLOMATIC MISSION was reported in the *Philadelphia Gazette*, 23 Jan. 1798.

On 18 Jan. the House of Representatives began DEBATE ON THE BILL FOR FOREIGN INTERCOURSE. Introduced by Robert Goodloe Harper, it would provide appropriations for the diplomatic corps. On the same day Virginia congressman John Nicholas moved to REDUCE significantly the size of the diplomatic establishment TO WHAT IT WAS BEFORE THE EXTENSION of 1796. He argued that the executive branch was using patronage appointments to increase its power over the legislative branch and that congressmen, eager for an appointment, were "willing to sacrifice all independent political opinions and bend at the shrine of Executive wisdom." The House debated Nicholas's amendment for about a week, and a month later again took up the measure. On 5 Mch. the amendment was defeated by a 52 to 48 vote. The next day the House passed the bill with the appropriations sought by Harper (*Annals*, 7:847-945, 1083-1215; 8:1217-34).

BILL FOR REGULATING PROCEEDINGS IN IMPEACHMENT: see TJ to Henry Tazewell, 27 Jan. 1798, for a discussion of this bill and for TJ's contribution to the argument in support of the INTRODUCTION OF JURIES at impeachment TRIALS.

VIIITH AMENDMENT: the Sixth Amendment as ratified.

The ACRIMONIOUS ALTERCATIONS between the SPANISH MINISTER Carlos Fernando Martinez de Irujo and Timothy Pickering were brought before Congress in a report by the secretary of state submitted on 23 Jan. 1798, in which he characterized Spain's refusal to carry out the provisions of

Pinckney's Treaty of 1795, especially de-lays in the joint survey to run the boundary line between the United States and Louisi-ana and Spain's retention of certain military posts such as the one at NATCHEZ, from whence the survey was to begin and where United States troops were congregating to aid in the project. Spain used the Blount af-fair to further support her delays (ASP, *For-eign Relations*, 2:78-103; Bemis, *Pinckney's Treaty*, 294-311).

In the four AMENDMENTS TO THE CON-STITUTION introduced by Humphrey Mar-shall on 24 Jan., the electors not the VOTERS were to distinguish between their choice for president and that for vice president; the Senate would settle disputes over electoral votes for president and the House those for the vice president. The final amendment gave the Senate the power to elect the vice president, from among those who had re-ceived votes, if no person had received a majority (JS, 2:430). Marshall's PROPOSI-TIONS immediately appeared as a broad-side printed by John Fenno (Evans, No. 48657). On 25 Jan., by a 15 to 13 vote, the Senate POSTPONED TO THE 1ST OF JUNE consideration of the amendments (JS, 2:430).

[1] TJ first wrote "5" and later altered it to read as above. Change lacking in PrC.

[2] TJ first wrote "transferring to the Sen-ate the right now held by the Representa-tives of chusing a President in the case of indecision" before altering the remainder of the sentence to read as above.

[3] Sentence interlined.

[4] Preceding two digits lacking in PrC.

From George Jefferson & Company

DEAR SIR,   Richmond Janr. 25th. 1798.

Your favor of the 14th. instant enclosing a note of Mr. Barnes's for $500. to be taken up by Mr. Hopkins, came to hand by last post. Mr. H. is out of Town, and the note is therefore not accepted; but that will make no difference, as it will be paid in the same manner as if it had. The draught you mention shall be duly attended to.

We have heard nothing yet of the Anvil Vice & beak Iron, shipped by Mr. Barnes on board the Schooner John Brown; at which we are sur-prised, as we suppose the Ice has been gone long enough for them to have arrived.

We are Very respectfully Your Mt. Obt. servts.

GEO. JEFFERSON & CO.

RC (MHi); at foot of text: "Thomas Jefferson esqr."; endorsed by TJ as received 1 Feb. 1798 and so recorded in SJL.

To Thomas Mann Randolph

TH:J. TO TMR.   Philadelphia Jan. 25. 98.

Yours of the 13th. came to hand yesterday, and relieves my anxiety as to the health of the family. I thank you for your interference at Monti-cello & Shadwell. I had directed the managers at both to apply to you for your counsel when at a loss, and have only been prevented by the state of your health from asking a more onerous attention. George needs to be supported & Page to be moderated. Davy and John also to be questioned as to their progress in the execution of my written instructions.[1] Richardson (whom I expect here daily) wrote me word he had hired 3. hands for me, & expected to get some more. they are to work with John. you will of course take Isaac when you please. I expect some new tools I have sent on for George will be in Richmond by the time you get this. as soon as smith George recieves them, Isaac is to have his anvil, vice and beak iron, as also the large new bellows nearly finished when I left home.   I must get you to write a line to Bates, & send Jupiter with it to bring me a certain answer from him whether I am to depend on him for my flooring plank. you will be so good as to send on the answer by post. I am uneasy about it, as I have never heard from him in answer to my letter, inclosing him the bill of the plank. George should be hurried to get his tobacco down. I have never learned whether he & Page have delivered all their wheat & how much. good tobo. sells here at 13. D. flour $8\frac{1}{2}$. wheat $1\frac{1}{2}$. but as yet only the millers have bought. the river is now opening & the merchants will be coming to market. however their distresses will repress their purchases. the winter has been very dry here. I find my position in the center of the town makes my thermometrical observations so fallacious, that I have ceased to take them. but I shall be able to get proper ones from mrs Rittenhouse. I shall therefore be glad of the continuance of yours. a post-office will be established at Milton in April, and mr Watson will be the postmaster. he spoke to me first. it would be established there now, but that the rider asked an unconscionable allowance for stopping.[2] if a good person in our neighborhood could be got to undertake the Fredericksburg post, the postmaster would be glad of it. 330. D. are given for the present year. the newspapers will keep you informed of the occupations of Congress. there are some interesting debates going on on the subject of foreign intercourse. we shall lose the question however, as they have a small majority. Blount's affair will come on next. we are entirely uninformed *officially* of the state of our negociation at Paris. we suspect the paragraphs from Boston to be in a considerable degree fabricated. there are some private letters here from Paris as late as Nov. 3. from these we might conjecture that tho' France will not arrange with us on the principles of our government, that still they will leave it to us to declare war. but all this is so uncertain that I keep my own opinion unformed. perhaps something will depend on the question whether peace will be made this winter between England & France. if it is not, I do not think they will declare war against us. if peace take place between them, perhaps they may be willing we should feel that we are not entirely out of their reach. my warmest love to my dear Martha. remind the children of me. Adieu affectionately.

RC (DLC); endorsed by Randolph as received 3 Feb. 1798. PrC (MHi); endorsed by TJ in ink on verso.

A letter from Richard RICHARDSON to TJ of 6 Jan. 1798, recorded in SJL as received from Richmond a week later, has not been found.

ANSWER TO MY LETTER: TJ recorded letters to "Bates" (presumably William) in SJL on 17 Nov. and 2 Dec. 1797, which are now missing, as is a letter from William Bates to TJ of 20 Jan. 1797, recorded in SJL as received on the same day.

[1] Preceding seven words interlined.
[2] Preceding two words interlined.

From James Monroe

DEAR SIR   Richmond Jany 27. 1798.

I came here abt. 6. days past to use my endeavors to raise money to pay the expences upon importation of my furniture. I have drawn on Mr. Barnes for 250. dolrs. wh. I hope he will pay. I think the time is expired when you intimated the sum plac'd in his hands wod. become due. I hope to get thro this heavy business without any very serious loss.   Our assembly adjourned two days since. Of a political nature, the resolutions on the amherst &ca, petition is the most important measure. These are sound & good. The next in pt. of importance is the passage of a law wh. subjects the Printer of the State to an annual election for his office. This will probably change the tone of that paper.

It is surprising that only one copy of my book has yet reached this place. It wod. have been well to have had the quota intended for this place during the session. I hope Mr. Bache will still send them on, as there still remains sufficient curiosity to enduce people to read them. I hear there is an attack made on it under the signature of Scipio supposed to be Chs. Lee. I hope some one will refute him in the gazette, as it may otherwise produce an ill effect. Is he supposed to be the author with you

The publick in this quarter are very anxious to hear the result of our mission to France. Shortly it must be known, unless purposely kept back by the admn.—

I have thoughts of coming to this place to resume the practice of the law. what think you of it? sincerely I am yr. friend & servant

JAS. MONROE

I observe Mr. Scipio takes the ground of attack on me by way of rescuing the admn. from that of defence. I commit this to Mr. Giles who will supply my omissions.

RC (DLC); endorsed by TJ as received 7 Feb. 1798 and so recorded in SJL.

The LAW concerning the public PRINTER OF THE STATE, "An Act directing the Mode of appointing the Public Printer, prescribing his Duties, and for other Purposes therein mentioned," passed on 22 Jan. It provided for the selection of a printer annually by a vote of both houses of the General Assembly and allowed the current printer, Augustine Davis, to continue in the position until the first election of a printer could be held at the next session of the legislature (*Acts Passed at a General Assembly of the Commonwealth of Virginia: Begun and Held at the Capitol, in the City of Richmond, on Monday, the Fourth Day of December, One Thousand Seven Hundred and Ninety-Seven* [Richmond, 1798], 32).

To Henry Tazewell

TH:J. TO MR TAZEWELL.   Jan. 27. 98.

As you mentioned that some of your commee admitted that the introduction of juries into trials by impeachment under the VIIIth. amendment depended on the question Whether an impeachment for a misdemeanor be a criminal prosecution? I devoted yesterday evening to the extracting passages from Law authors shewing that in Law-language the term crimes is in common use applied to *misdemeanors*, and that *impeachments*, even when for *misdemeanors* only are *criminal prosecutions*. these proofs were so numerous that my patience would go no further than two authors, Blackstone & Wooddeson. they shew that you may meet that question without the danger of being contradicted. the constitution closes the proofs by explaining it's own meaning when speaking of *impeachments, crimes, misdemeanors*.

the object in supporting this engraftment into impeachments is to lessen the dangers of the court of impeachment under it's present form, and to induce dispositions in all parties in favor of a better constituted court of impeachment,[1] which I own I consider as an useful thing, if so composed as to be clear of the spirit of faction.

Do not let the inclosed paper be seen in my hand writing.

PrC (DLC). Not recorded in SJL.

YOUR COMMITTEE: on 23 Jan. 1798 Tazewell was appointed to consider a bill on impeachment procedures that had been introduced by Humphrey Marshall of Kentucky the preceding day. Federalists Samuel Livermore, James Ross, and Uriah Tracy joined Marshall and Tazewell on this committee, one of several established in the next few weeks to consider rules and forms for impeachment trials. It was the only one to which a Republican was appointed. When the Senate considered the committee's report on 14 Feb., Tazewell called for the INTRODUCTION OF JURIES into the trials. The full debate began two days later, when, according to a report in the Philadelphia *Aurora*, the vice president read the section of the impeachment bill under consideration. Tazewell moved the following amendment: "And a Jury shall be summoned for the trial thereof in the manner, and under the directions herein after prescribed." He argued that while the Constitution guaranteed that all persons accused of crimes were to be tried before a jury except in cases of impeachment, the Bill of Rights had extended the protection to impeachment trials as well and that in Great Britain impeachment had "uniformly" been considered a CRIMINAL PROSECUTION. According to the newspaper account, Tazewell supported his case with passages from William BLACKSTONE and Richard WOODDESON. A long debate on 16 Feb. 1798 was concluded three days later when the amendment was defeated 26 to 3, with only Stevens Thomson Mason and Andrew Jackson joining Tazewell in support of the proposition (JS, 2:428, 440-2; Philadelphia *Aurora*, 16, 20, 28 Feb. and 1, 3 Mch. 1798). For an analysis of the debate and vote, see Melton, *First Impeachment*, 170-81.

[1] Word interlined in place of "appeals."

Notes on
Criminal Prosecutions and Impeachment

[26 Jan. 1798]

4. Blackstone.

5. 'a crime or misdemeanor is an act &c
'crimes & misdemeanors, *properly* speaking, are mere synonimous terms: tho' in *common* usage 'crimes' denote offences of a deeper & more atrocious dye, while smaller faults are comprised under the gentler name of 'misdemeanors' only.
'the distinction of *crimes & misdemeanors* from *civil injuries* &c.

battery[1]
[nuisance]

6. 'there are *crimes* of an inferior nature, for instance *battery*. the aggressor may be punished *criminally* by fine & imprisonment. so a *nuisance* &c

16. 'to steal a pig or a fowl was a *capital misdemeanor*'

[heresy][2]

49. *heresy* called a *crime* even now; when only cognisable spiritually & by censure.

reviling }
nonconformity }

50. '*reviling* the ordinances of the church is a *crime* of grosser nature than *non conformity*.'

[witch]craft.

60. 'witchcraft a *crime* punishable by imprisonment & pillory.'

[adultery].

65. 'the *crime* of *adultery*.'

[embezzling]

122 '*embezzling* the public money is not a *capital crime*.'

[oppression] }
[impeachment] }

140. 'oppression of judges is a *crime* of deep malignity & when prosecuted by *impeachment* [&c]

[libel] [. . .]

150. 'in a *civil action* [a libel must] appear false, but *in a criminal prosecution* &c

205. 'of these *crimes*, some are felonious & capital, others are simple *misdemeanors*'

imprisonment

218. 'the two remaining *crimes*, to wit, *false imprisonment* & *kidnapping* &c

[kid]napping.

219. '*kidnapping* is a very heinous crime, punishable with fine, imprisonment & pillory'

256. 'a commoner can be *impeached* only for a *misdemeanor*, a peer for *any crime*.'

275. 'if the offense be inter minora crimina or a
    misdemeanor only &c

[qu]i tam   303. '*informations* on penal statutes are a sort of *qui tam*
                     actions, carried on by a *criminal* instead of a *civil*
                     [*process*]

informations.   305. '*information*. when a grand jury informs on oath that
                     there is ground for a *criminal* suit.'
                     'these *informations* [are confined] to *misdemeanors*, &
                     go not to capital offences.'

[appeals]   308. 'an *appeal* when spoken of as a *criminal prosecution* &c.
                368. 'the next stage of *criminal prosecution* in such crimes &
                     misdemeanors as are too high or *too low* for benefit
                     of clergy, is judgment.'
                369. 'the court must pronounce the judgment annexed to
                     the *crime*. of these some are capital, some are pun-
                     ished *by exile, imprisonment, confiscation, fine* &c

[fines]   [372.] 'the reasonableness of *fines* in *criminal cases* has been
                     regulated by magna charta.'

[2.]³ Wooddeson. 501. '1. treasons. 2. felonies capital. 3. felonies not capital.
[misdemeanors]   4. *inferior misdemeanors*. between these several kinds
                     of *crimes* there are the strongest lines of legal
                     distinction.'

perjury   513. '*perjury* is a *crime* against public justice.' 'these *misde-
                     meanors* however are &c

atheism.   515. 'the *crime* of *atheistical tenets*' 'reformation of the
                     criminal.'

blasphemy.   517. '*blasphemous words* a *crime* against the laws &c.

nonconformity. 524. '*nonconformity* or dissent from the established
                     worship a civil *crime*.'

information   551.⁴ '*crimes* are brought to trial by indictment or
                     information.'

criminal   561. 'this mode of *criminal allegation* (information) cannot
  prosecuti[ons]   be brought in capital cases, nor misprision of
                     treason.'
                563. 'proceeding on a penal statute is a *criminal
                     prosecution*.
                569. 'such are the ordinary modes of commencing *criminal
                     prosecutions*.' viz. ba[. . .], appeal, indictmt,
                     information.

appeals.   575. '*appeals* in parliament a *criminal prosecution*.'
                578. '*appeals* in parl. were not only of treason & felony, but
                     of *misdemeanors* also.'

impeachments   580. 'the other occasions of exercising *criminal judicature*
                     by the lords, are the trials of indicted peers, the pro-
                     ceedings on *impeachments* &c.
                596. 'two distinct modes of *criminal prosecution*, namely
                     impeachments and penal acts.'
                601. 'a peer may be accused before his peers of *any crime*, a
                     commoner of misdemeanors only.'

[writing] & speaking	605.	*'impeachments* for *high crimes & misdemeanors* by *writing or speaking.'*
misdemeanors.	606.	'this was allowed in *misdemeanors,* & for *higher crimes* also'
impeachment.	619.	'the nature of the *crimes* adducible to justice by *impeachment.'*
	621.	'all the modes of *criminal prosecutions* whether by *impeachment* or otherwise'⁵

Constitution. Art. 2.§.4.		'the President &c. shall be removed from office on *impeachment* for & conviction of treason, *bribery,* or *other high crimes & misdemeanors.'*
Art. 3.§.2.		'the trial of all *crimes,* except in cases of *impeachment,* shall be by jury'⁶ and by Art. 1.§.3. 'the judgment in impeachments no further than removal from office & disqualificat[ion.]
VIIIth. Amendment.		'In all *criminal prosecutions* the accused shall enjoy the right to trial by an impartial jury [&c]⁷

Note. In the preceeding quotations the emphatic words are strictly copied. the others [are] sometimes brought together from some distance,⁸ omitting intervening words of the context not affecting the [sense, to?] abridge the trouble of writing. the words here expressed however are always the very words of the author.

PrC (DLC: TJ Papers, 102:7565-6); entirely in TJ's hand; undated, with date being determined by letter above; faint and left margin clipped. Dft (same, 102:17563); undated; includes variations in arrangement of text, with citations from Woodeson appearing before those from Blackstone and key words appearing to the right of citations; endorsed by TJ: "Impeachment." PrC of Dft (same, 102:17564); with two pages pressed on single sheet.

¹ Here in Dft TJ wrote and enclosed in brackets "battery & nuisance, *crimes.*"
² This word and the remaining key words for the Blackstone citations are missing in Dft.

³ In Dft this citation appears at head of first page with a canceled passage appearing above it which reads "high crimes & misdemeanors by writing or speaking. 2. Woodd. 605."
⁴ Above this citation in Dft TJ wrote and canceled "550. 'criminal prosecutions' 'criminal appeals.' " He left the key word "appeals" to the right uncanceled.
⁵ In Dft TJ wrote the following paragraph on the "Constitution" in a different ink and in a smaller hand at a later sitting. PrC of Dft ends at this point.
⁶ TJ inserted the remainder of this sentence in Dft.
⁷ Dft ends at this point.
⁸ Preceding three words interlined.

To Samuel Livermore

DEAR SIR   Jan. 28. 98

Having found it necessary, for my own government, to [consult?] the writers on Parliamentary law, a Summary of their proceeding in [. . .] I have thought it might not be unuseful to put it into the hands of one of the Committee to which the bill on impeachment is referred. I take [the] liberty therefore of inclosing it to you. it may serve to refresh your me[mory] on a subject in which you probably have not your books with you to [. . .] and to enable you to judge on what points [. . .] stands, and to keep up analogies where changes are necessary. [within a?] paragraph of a new law, we should ask ourselves these questions. How [reads the?] law now? is a change necessary? what changes would be best? [if?] it is to be our guide in the impeachment now [. . .] and be upon us before the bill can be passed which [warrants? so]ber side[ration.] that bill will probably undergo far [more study? than others do. considering] this, [it] would be adviseable to [take up the bill?] [. . .] [. . .]tially [. . .] these [situa]tions. [. . .] my [provision?] being *order* [. . .] should be accomplished [. . .] that subject. accept assurances of [. . .] Dear Sir

    Your most obedt. hum[ble servt.]   TH: JEFFERSON

PrC (DLC); faint, with several illegible phrases of three or more words; at foot of text: "Judge Livermore." Enclosure not found but see note below.

WRITERS ON PARLIAMENTARY LAW, A SUMMARY OF THEIR PROCEEDING: TJ probably enclosed paragraphs from his "Parliamentary Pocket-Book" which described the impeachment process in the British Parliament (PW, 12-13, 153-7). For other members of this COMMITTEE appointed on 23 Jan. to consider a BILL ON IMPEACHMENT procedures, see TJ to Henry Tazewell, 27 Jan. 1798.

From Thomas Mann Randolph

TH:M.R. TO TH: JEFFERSON,   Belmont Jan. 28. 98

    We had no mail last week from Richmond or Fredericksburg which lost us our weekly joy of reading your letter or knowing you are well. I rec'd. your present of Fauchet's pamphlet which I read eagerly myself and communicated to our friends: I have not yet learnt the character it bears: I believe it myself to be just in all its statements & views, and I admire greatly the moderation with which it is written when I consider the mortifications the Author underwent while in the situation which gave him the information he shews.

    The Gazette allso containing the proclamation of the Directory of determined hostility to England came at the same time. It was highly pleasant to me for if there is a matter which concerns me in the affairs of nations it is the humiliation of England. I feel yet the rapines and indignities of '82: I have seen the haughty air and base spirit of the government & have witnessed with contempt the groveling unmanly character it strives to inspire into the nation, and to diffuse abroad. All favors of this kind will be most gratefully rec'd. when you have not leisure to write.

Martha and the children are as well today as they were on the 22d. Jefferson has had no shoes and no cold as yet—P. Carrs adopted son has been a fortnight with us and tho' well complains daily that the water gets thro' his shoes and flannel socks. We wished much for a spot of White soil to build on when we were chusing our situation: we did not know then the disadvantage of that kind in this neighbourhood: tis so retentive of moisture that our yard is mud to the ancles long after the red land has dried perfectly. There is another much more serious disadvantage in our situation here—the cellar after every rain is full of water—we have been obliged to dig a well in the middle of it and now draw off the water as it collects in that: I have great apprehension for the health of my family on this account: My own has suddenly begun to decline when I considered it as absolutely confirmed and had assumed all the habits of full vigor which indeed I felt.

Yours most affectionately   Tʜ: M. Rᴀɴᴅᴏʟᴘʜ

RC (MHi); on same sheet as Martha Jefferson Randolph to TJ, 22 Jan. 1798; addressed in Martha Jefferson Randolph's hand: "Thomas Jefferson Vice President Philadelphia"; endorsed by TJ as received 6 Feb. 1798 and so recorded in SJL.

The 4 Jan. 1798 issue of the *Philadelphia Gazette* included a ᴘʀᴏᴄʟᴀᴍᴀᴛɪᴏɴ ᴏꜰ ᴛʜᴇ ᴅɪʀᴇᴄᴛᴏʀʏ calling for the assemblage of troops along the coast of France under Napoleon Bonaparte's command to be known as the "army of England." In the same issue a "Gentleman in Havre" declared in a letter dated 6 Nov. 1797 that there was "now a project of an absolute Descent on England!" Another witness arriving from France reported "that the most active preparations were making to invade England, and that 150,000 men were to be employed in this undertaking."

From John Wise

Sɪʀ,   Richmond Jany. 28th. 1798

It having been communicated to me by a friend, that he had understood you had, some short time since, in a public company, at Francis's Hotel, in the city of Philadelphia, used expressions to my injury and discredit, I have thought proper to address you, with intent as well to ascertain the truth of the report, as to be informed, if it be true what motive induced the observation and what Idea was intended to be conveyed by it.—The expressions reported to have been used by you were to this effect, if not precisely in these words, "That altho' the Virginian Assembly was as Republican as any in the union, yet they had elected a Tory Governor, a Tory Speaker, a Tory clerk and a Tory Printer."—

I was not a little surprised, Sir, nor was I less mortified, to understand that you, for whose character I profess to have, hitherto, entertained the highest Respect, should, unprovokedly and without sufficient knowledge or information of my Character to warrant it, bestow upon me Epithets, in their general acceptation,[1] disrespectfull and opprobrious.—Indeed I candidly confess, so little was a thing of this kind to be expected by me from you, that I have been led to doubt the accuracy of the report, and to suppose Your observation must have been misunderstood by the gentleman from whom my information is derived, and who is said to have been present when it was made.—I have, However, thought it proper to make this enquiry of you, and must, therefore, request you to give me an answer, As soon as convenient, to be directed to me in Accomack County, for which place I shall set out tomorrow.—

With due consideration I am, sir, Your obt. Sert.   JNO. WISE

RC (CSmH); endorsed by TJ as received 3 Feb. 1798 and so recorded in SJL.

John Wise (d. 1812) of Accomac County, an attorney and planter, sat in the Virginia House of Delegates from 1791 to January 1801 and was speaker from 1794 to 1799 (Barton H. Wise, *The Life of Henry A. Wise*

of Virginia, 1806-1876 [New York, 1899], 5-6, 9; Leonard, *General Assembly*, 183, 187, 191, 195, 199, 203, 207, 211, 215, 219).

[1] Preceding five words written over an erased and illegible passage.

From Edmund Pendleton

DEAR SIR   Virga. Jany. 29th. 1798.

As soon as I shall have communed with Mr. Lyons on the propriety of selling our stock, you shall be informed when payment shall be made of Royal's decree vs. Robinson's Admors; the place I suppose will be Richmond. The rise or fall of that market price, probably depends on events rather likely to produce the latter, & may dictate a present sale, but the scarcity of Cash, it is said, will render a sale difficult, however justice to the Creditor will prevent our being over over scrupulous on the Occasion.

The receipt of your Favr. did indeed awaken pleasing recollections of past transactions in which we were connected; not unmix'd however wth. a sad lamentation that the Revolutionary Spirit of *Union* & *Patriotism*, which conducted America to an happy issue of that great contest, had not continued to direct our National Counsels since, which I am perswaded would have preserved Us From the perilous state in which we are now placed.

I hope the Norfolk intelligence is a Fabrication, as it is said here to be, however I expect an high tone From the Directory to our Envoys, whatever may be the result, I flatter my self they will not proceed to a Declaration of War, since I do not discover a possible motive For it, but resentment to our Executive, a passion which I should think them too wise to gratify: On the same ground I trust our Government will be too prudent to declare or provoke a War, From which every evil, & no possible good can be expected. May Heaven direct our Counsels, & all those with which we are connected to Peace and a *free* Commerce, that great blessing to Mankind, but preserve us From all attempts to Force a trade by a Ruinous Navy, which may indeed increase the *Power* of the *Executive*, and the *proffit* of the *Merchant*, but Oppression & final ruin to the bulk of the Society: an Effect which serious contemplation will discover From the boasted of British Navy; a Gulph in which has been swallowed All the Fruits of the most persevering labour & industry ever manifested by a people!!

Your concern For, & congrations on my state of health, (wch. is indeed better than For the ten preceeding years) demand my Warmest acknowledgements, wch. you will please to accept, with my reciprocal cordial wishes that you may enjoy every Felicity. I am

My Dear Sir, Yr. very Affecte. Friend & Servt.

EDMD PENDLETON

My Complts. to Messrs. Tazwell & Mason.

RC (DLC); endorsed by TJ as received 3 Feb. 1798 and so recorded in SJL. RECEIPT OF YOUR FAVR: TJ to Pendleton, 14 Jan. 1798.

From La Rochefoucauld-Liancourt

Hambourg Le 30 Jer 1798.

chés Mr Matthiessen Selem & Co

Je n'ai pas oublié Monsieur, l'engagement que j'ay Contracté de vous ecrire d'europe mais j'aurois mieux aimé datter ma lettre de france, et je n'y suis pas encor. Vous aprendrés par les papiers publics que buonaparte est a paris, et que la Sagesse de Sa Conduite est egale au brillant de ses exploits & a la grandeur de Ses talents. on avoit annoncé son arrivée Comme l'epoque d'une Nouvelle Comotion, il Semble que cette funeste prediction est evanouie, et que la france en est quitte au moins pour quelque tems. Mais le dix huit fructidor jette une grande allarme parmi les bons Citoyens. quoiqu'il soit très vray qu'il y ait eu alors une Conspiration reelle Contre le Sisteme républicain, et que les Sots, qui Comme tous les mauvais partisans de l'angleterre, fussent extremement repandus, il n'est pas moins vray qu'il y a eu des Victimes innocentes frappées et des Victimes vraiment amies de la libertée, qui auraient ete frappées encor Si l'autre parti eut reussi. il n'est pas moins vray qui toutes les formes Constitutionnelles & juridiques ont ete violées, et C'est le plus grand mal de tous, quoique le Malheur d'individus innocens en soit par luy meme un bien grand aussy. il est a desirer qu'une loy Sanctionnée par le peuple prévienne le retour d'un tel evenement qui mettroit en danger la liberté publique. d'ailleurs par tous Mes raports avec la france j'aprends que le Sisteme republicain y est aimé, que Sa Conservation en est generalement desirée. J'espere donc que nous Sortirons encor heureusement de ces Malheurs, et que lor de l angleterre perdra Successivement de Son influence. il doit aussy devenir un peu rare. dailleurs on n'est occupé en france que de la descente en angleterre, et je n'ay aucun doute quelle n'ait lieu Si la paix ne Se fait pas d'icy la; Ce qui toutefois pourroit bien etre. C'est autour de la republique que doivent aujourdhuy Se reunir tous les francois qui aiment la liberté, qui aiment leur patrie, et encor Ceux qui aiment leurs interets & qui Savent bien les Connoitre. Il est a craindre que vos envoyés qui ne sont pas encor reçus le soient jamais. j'en Suis Sincerement afligé parce que Ce Sera un grand Malheur pour les deux pays. et que quoique Ce Mal ait ete prévu et provoqué par Votre Coté de la Mer, il ne peut pas moins avoir des Suites facheuses pour nos deux patries, et pour l'independance de la votre, le premier de tous les biens pour un Etat. On craint fortement en angleterre le projet de descente, et Sil Se tente, il S'effectuera et vous y verrés l'employ de moyens jusqu'icy inimaginés. Le batiment qui vous porte cette Lettre vous portera aussi la nouvelle du dr evenement d'hollande, il est pareil au 18 fructidor de france. on nous dit icy qu'il fera aller les affaires plus vite, et que tous les obstacles a l'achevement de la Constitution Sont levés. On Saccorde aussy a dire qu'un plus grand nombre de victimes meritait de l'etre Mais quune douzaine d'honnetes & purs Republicains ont ete enveloppes dans le Coup. il y a, a mon avis, peu de bonnes choses faites Sans fumée. Voila Rome ou au moins Son Sacerdoce Couronné, a la fin de Sa Carriere politique. Voila la suisse en revolution. L'angleterre ne l'echappera pas, et toute l'europe s'en suivra.

Nous irons encor vous faire une visite en amerique. quant a moy c'est mon project arreté, Si d'icy a six mois les portes de france ne me sont pas rouvertes. on me flatte a chaque Courrier, que les Circonstances Seules retardent Ce Moment tant desiré. C'est mon plus cher desir. mais Si je Suis destiné au Malheur de le voir Sans Succès, Je vais finir en Amerique Ma Carriere. et j'y Conteray au nombre de mes plus grandes douceurs Celle de Me retrouver avec Vous—J'aprends que

Miss Polly est mariée, recevés-en Mon Compliment, puisse-t-elle etre aussy heureuse que belle.

Voudriés vous bien Monsieur me rappeller au souvenir de tous vos amis et demeurer Convaincu des Sentimens d'estime & d'attachement dont je fais profession pour vous   LIANCOURT

E D I T O R S'   T R A N S L A T I O N

Hamburg 30 Jan. 1798
c/o Mr. Matthiessen Selem & Co.

I have not forgotten, Sir, the promise I made you to write to you from Europe but I should have preferred to date my letter from France, and I am not yet there. You will learn from the newspapers that Bonaparte is in Paris and that the discretion of his conduct is equal to the brilliance of his exploits and the greatness of his talents. His arrival had been foretold as the time for a new turbulence, it seems that that fatal prediction has faded away, and that France is free of it at least for some time. But the eighteenth of Fructidor has greatly alarmed many good Citizens. Although it is perfectly true that there was at the time a real Plot against the Republican system, and that the Fools, who, like all the bad partisans of England, were very much mixed up in it, it is nonetheless true that innocent victims were stricken, victims truly friends of Freedom, who would still have been stricken if the other party had succeeded. It is nonetheless true that all Constitutional and juridical forms were violated, and that is the greatest evil of all, although the misfortune of innocent individuals is in itself a very great one also. It is to be desired that a law sanctioned by the people would forestall the repetition of such an event that would put the public liberty in danger. Moreover through all my relations with France I learn that the republican system is beloved there, that its preservation is generally desired. So I hope that we shall still emerge successfully from these misfortunes and that the gold of England will gradually lose its influence. It must also be becoming a trifle rare. Besides, in France the only preoccupation is the invasion of England, and I have no doubt that it will take place if peace does not occur before then; which all the same might happen. Around the Republic all Frenchmen who love liberty, who love their fatherland, and even those who love their own interests and who know how to recognize them must unite today. It is to be feared that your envoys who have not yet been received may never be. I am sincerely sorrowful about that because it will be a great misfortune for both our countries. And although this mischief has been anticipated and provoked by your side of the ocean, it has no less unfortunate results for our two homelands, and for the independence of yours, the greatest of all good things for a country. In England, the invasion plan is greatly feared, and if it is attempted it will succeed, and you will see in it the use of means hitherto unimagined. The ship that bears you this letter will also bear you the news of the latest happening in Holland, it equals the eighteenth of Fructidor in France. Here we are told that it will speed up events and that all the obstacles to the completion of the Constitution have been removed. People are also in agreement in saying that a greater number of victims deserved to be, but that a dozen honest and pure Republicans were swept up in the coup. In my opinion, very few good things are accomplished without casualties. Now you have Rome, or at least its priesthood, crowned, at the end of his political career. Now you have Switzerland in revolution. England will not escape it, and all Europe will follow.

We shall yet visit you in America. As for myself the decision is made if within six months the gates of France have not yet been reopened. With each mail I am encouraged, that only circumstances are delaying this much hoped-for moment. It is my dearest desire. But if I am destined to the misfortune of never seeing it succeed, I am going to America to finish my career. and I shall count among the sweetest events meeting with you again—I have learned that Miss Polly is married, please accept my compliments on it, may she be as happy as she is beautiful.

Kindly remember me, Sir, to all your friends and remain convinced of the feelings of esteem and affection that I entertain for you.   LIANCOURT

RC (MoSHi: Jefferson Papers); endorsed by TJ, the date of receipt being torn away but recorded in SJL as 4 May 1798.

EVENEMENT D'HOLLANDE: ending a deadlock in which no one commanded a majority in a constitutional convention for the Batavian Republic, on 22 Jan. 1798 the democrats, with French complicity, staged a coup by expelling the more moderate delegates and clearing the way for a democratic constitution that was subsequently ratified. Political turmoil in ROME late in 1797 prompted intervention by French troops, the eviction of the Pope to Siena, and, in February 1798, the establishment of a closely supervised Roman Republic (Palmer, *Democratic Revolution*, 2:199-202, 368-9; Georges Lefebvre, *The French Revolution*, trans. Elizabeth M. Evanson and others, 2 vols. [New York, 1962-64], 2:224).

From Thomas Mann Randolph

T. M. RANDOLPH TO TH: JEFFERSON,   Belmont Jan. 30. :98

You will be alarmed at a report Richardson will make of an occurrence at Monticello which I have had notice of only since my indisposition & have not been able to go over & learn the truth of the matter & the magnitude of the Mischief, if any has been done. Jupiter came over to me yesterday evening—he says there has never been the smallest mark about the Door or lock, of the room having been entered by anyone. I think it possible the villain may have contrived to get loose that part of the lock into which the bolt of it enters & have replaced it carefully so as to give it exactly the same appearance: I am confident however but little mischief can have been done, for if any thing curious or valuable had been taken it must have been seen about the person as those things were which gave rise to the suspicion: his stupidity w'd. have prevented his concealing it I am certain. Three or 4 days before I heard of this affair, I observed a Negroe with a gun skulking about my yard just at the close of day I went out immediately and seized him it proved to be *York* who had been some time here for a wound he got in his arm from a knife in an affray at Mont'o.; which I had cured & had returned him to George some time. The gun exciting suspicion I had him searched; one pair &

an odd stocking marked T.I. were upon him a copy of Brackens Farri-
ery & a pen-knife: which might all have been obtained elsewhere than
in your room for my people remembered some of your stocki[ngs
ha]ving been stolen from the wash house and the bo[ok was] not one,
I thought, of your library. The gun I suspect to be yours but cannot
positively decide being familiar only with the Pistoias. I find myself
mending fast and hope tomorrow to ride to Mont'o. to have the door
properly secured. By next post I shall be able to inform you fully on this
affair.

Will you do me the favor to get 6 panes of Glass $16\frac{3}{8}$ by $14\frac{1}{4}$ for Martha's bookcase? If the last edition of Linnaeuses genera plantarum can
be had in Philad'a. I will thank you to procure it for me and a small ivory
Mem'd. book for the pocket.

Yours most affectionately   Th: M. Randolph

RC (ViU: Edgehill-RAndolph Papers);
torn; addressed: "Thomas Jefferson Vice-
President U.S. Philad'a."; endorsed by TJ
as received 9 Feb. 1798 and so recorded in
SJL.

BRACKENS: probably Henry Bracken,
The Traveller's Pocket Farrier (London,
1744). See Sowerby, No. 943.

From Mary Jefferson Eppes

Eppington February 1st 1798

May I thank you my Dear Papa for your last letter, The advice with
which it is fill'd, I feel the importance of, & the solicitude it expresses for
my happiness makes me sensible[1] how gratefully I will endeavour to
follow it. I hope I shall never do otherwise for I feel more & more every
day how much the, happiness of my life depends[2] on deserving your
approbation. you will have heard I suppose before you recieve this of my
aunt Skipwiths death an event which was render'd by her situation *before it*, a relief to her friends, who began to apprehend a long life of
insanity. she had been for two months before she died, tho quite well
otherwise so perfectly out of her senses that she knew no one about her,
& expir'd in that situation. the family here will go in a week to her
funeral we shall stay some time[3] there to comfort the poor children &
most of all poor Betsy whose sufferings for her mothers situation have
but too much allready affected her health. we left Richmond a
few days ago & I should have written to you there, but I had not time.
we saw Mr W. Hylton there, who inform'd us that his son, with Mr
Lawrence, had rented Richneck of him for 1000 pounds a year, in consequence of which he goes to live in Berkely where he has bought land
of a gentleman who is engaged to Mrs Campbell his daughter, & will be

married to her this spring, this piece of news I thought would not be disagreable to you as he has given over all thoughts of settling in our neighbourhood. I will write to Kitty Church soon & enclose my letter in one to you. Adieu dear Papa. I am your affectionate daughter

ME

RC (MHi); endorsed by TJ as received 15 Feb. 1798 and so recorded in SJL.

YOUR LAST LETTER: TJ to Mary Jefferson Eppes, 7 Jan. 1798. ADVICE WITH WHICH IT IS FILL'D: included in TJ's papers are two pages of undated notes in Mary Jefferson Eppes's hand on the duties of a wife that she probably copied from a published work. The notes begin: "Sweetness of temper, affection to a husband & attention to his inter-

ests, constitute the duties of wife & form the basis of matrimonial felicity" (MS in DLC: TJ Papers, 234:41985).

[1] Word interlined in place of "assure you," which was interlined in place of an illegibly canceled word.
[2] Word interlined.
[3] Eppes first wrote "I shall stay [gladly as long?]" before altering the passage to read as above.

From Peter Charles Varlé

Susquehanna Canal, 1 Feb. 1798. Having observed the ravages of yellow fever in Philadelphia in 1793 he developed a plan for countering the disease, which was favorably received by the people to whom he communicated it. Their attention to the subject lessened with the decline of the epidemic, but the return of the fever last year shows that the malady has not been eradicated. As this is a subject in which everyone concerned with the good of humanity will have an interest, he feels that he could do no better than to address himself to TJ as president of the American Philosophical Society. He is sending the explanation and plans of his idea, since the society makes itself acquainted with new inventions and will be able to appreciate the usefulness of his idea as well as correct any defects in it.

RC (PPAmP: Manuscript Communications, Medicine); 3 p.; in French; endorsed by the society as read on 20 Apr. 1798 and "Accompanying a project to prevent the Yellow fever from Visiting Philadelphia." Enclosure not found, but see below.

Peter Charles Varlé learned civil engineering in his native France, worked under the supervision of the chief engineer of the island of Saint-Domingue from about the beginning of the French Revolution until 1793, then moved to the United States where he was employed on various canal projects. By 1798 he was superintendent of the Susquehanna Canal Company in Maryland. Beginning in the mid-1790s he published several maps, including one in 1808 of Frederick and Washington counties in

Maryland that was the first county map in the United States to show land ownership as well as such features as roads, mills, taverns, and political boundaries. Varlé, who also submitted papers to the American Philosophical Society on other occasions, was active into the 1830s (Richard W. Stephenson, "Charles Varlé: Nineteenth Century Cartographer," *Proceedings of the American Congress on Surveying and Mapping: 32nd Annual Meeting* [Washington, D.C., 1972], 189-98).

TJ probably did not deal personally with the contents of this letter, which he did not endorse or record in SJL. He attended a meeting of the society on 20 Apr. 1798 that authorized payment of two dollars in postage for Varlé's communication, but the further disposition of the engineer's proposal is unknown. A four-page undated paper by Varlé now in the society's archives, "Reflexions Sur les Causes de la Fievre Jaune de Philadelphie, et Sur les Moyens d'en Preserver les habitants," attributed yellow fever in Philadelphia to impure atmosphere resulting from industrial and commercial activities and a concentration of population, and suggested devices and measures for purifying the city's air and water. Varlé also submitted a paper on yellow fever to the society in 1814, and it is uncertain whether the "Reflexions" formed part of his earlier or his later submission on that topic (MS in PPAmP: Manuscript Communications, written in French in Varlé's hand, undated, with an endorsement, "Plan of a Lock C. Navigation 1796," which evidently refers to a paper on locks for inland navigation that Varlé submitted to the society in 1807; APS, *Proceedings*, 22, pt. 3 [1884], 270, 393-5, 443-4).

From Arthur Campbell

SIR   Montgomery County Feb. 2d. 98

Your very friendly letter of September last aroused my watchfulness, and induced a recurrence to first principles and first practices I have now *more* than a suspicion that a Counter revolution is aimed at.—A judicious person lately said "that a certain Foreign Minister had a more regular intelligence by means of the post-offices than the President or Vice-President of the United States."—I have lately observed an extreme eagerness for certain Foreigners to be appointed Contractors,—postmasters, and even post-Riders, and I have been told of extreme curiosity on the arrival of a Mail at certain offices, to look at, handle and even open letters. This may be part of a *plan* by means of Merchants, Traders, & Consuls to forward intelligence to philadelphia. It may only be a Shred of a plan already detected, of course impotent. Legislative provisions may be necessary to counteract such evil designs.—Or in time of peace the head of the Department can silently remedy the imperfection by removing all foreigners, that have emigrated from the British dominions since the peace, and to avoid appointing any such in future.—Let them first prove their civism, by marrying an American Woman, or by some other satisfactory evidence.—

I believe our Country, is near an important crisis, to a Brother Whig my solicitude or even jealousy—will not be unacceptable.

I am Sir, with highest Esteem, Your obedient servant

ARTHUR CAMPBELL

N.B. No answer is expected, by the post your hand write, or name on the outside, would prevent it being received.

RC (DLC); with *"private"* written to the left of signature; endorsed by TJ as received 22 Feb. 1798 and so recorded in SJL.

LETTER OF SEPTEMBER LAST: TJ to Campbell, 1 Sep. 1797.

From John Gibson

DEAR SIR   Pittsburg Feby. 2d 1798.

I shoud have wrote you sooner, but have Been waiting to Obtain some Information from Colo. Zanes of Ohio County, respecting the Transaction of Cresap and Party in the Spring of 1774, as soon as I Obtain it shall transmit to you or Bring it Myself as I Entend Being in Philada. next Month and unless you wish to have it sooner, shall have then the Oppurtunity of Communicating what further I know on the Subject, in person.

Our Mutual friend Genl. Irwin has informed me that there is a prospect of an Appointment taken Place in the Indian Department in this Quarter, as a large Appropiation has been made, shoud that take Place, permit me to Sollicit your Interest and that of your friends.

I am, Dear Sir, very respectfully your most Obdt. very humble Servt

JNO. GIBSON

RC (DLC); endorsed by TJ as received 10 Feb. 1798 and so recorded in SJL.

From Hugh Williamson

DEAR SIR   Hartford 2nd Feby 1798.

At Boston, from which I am now returning on my way to New York, a gentleman of much Information expressed a wish to me that some of the southern Members would, before the arming bill passes or without Delay, introduce a Bill for a Law in perfect conformity to the British Navigation Act. Such a Bill if opposed by the Eastern Brito-Americans would as he conceives effectually turn New England Politicks the other side up. And if not opposed by them it would effectually serve the Interest of our Country. Therefore the Bill whether it passes or not must render effectual service to the U:S:

I don't know which of my acquaintance in the House of Reps:, not affected by the Anglomania, is best acquainted with the Spirit of the British Navigation Act and accustomed to drawing Bills so that he could draw a Navigation Act correctly with proper Technical Terms, that it may whether it passes or not be fully understood and make a respectable appearance when it shall be published & read; for it will be read & meditated upon in every mercantile Town in the Union. If you think as I do on this subject you will suggest the Idea to some Gentleman who can & will immediately prepare & bring in a Bill for an American Navigation Act. The Representatives from N Carolina are not any of them Lawyers.

I am with the utmost Respect Dr sir Your most obedient and very hble Servant   Hu Williamson

RC (CSmH); endorsed by TJ as received 7 Feb. 1798 and so recorded in SJL.

E N C L O S U R E

Memorandum on Exports of North Carolina

Some Accot of the Exports of No: Carolina.

Tar Pitch Turpentine annually @   120,000 Brls.
   Tobacco   10,000 Hhds
 ⎧ Indian Corn   20 @   50,000 [Brls?]
 ⎨ Peas   5,000 Bushels
 ⎩ Herring   3 &   4,000 Brls
     These 3 last articles are chiefly for the west India market.
     Pipe & Hhd Staves in great plenty and of the best kind that are produced in America
     Boards & lumber of all sorts; fit for the West India market; for building Ware Houses &c to any Amot: that can be in demand also
     Shingles—Cypress & Juniper 18 Inches @ 3 feet.
     Indigo & Rice—from Wilmington.
     Wheat—a considerable Quantity is annually exported—also Bees Wax
     Pork—a great Quantity—the cheapest in America—

MS (CSmH); entirely in Williamson's hand.

From Luther Martin

Baltimore, Feb. 3, 1798.

Unaccustomed, Sir, to ask favors even from my friends, yet I feel myself under the necessity of soliciting *your* forgiveness for my *apparent* neglect, in suffering such a length of time to elapse since I last addressed myself to you; be assured, Sir, it is to be attributed to the pressure of my official and professional engagements, together with certain intervening duties, which I have been bound to pay to outraged society, and not to any intentional deficiency in those attentions which from me you so distinguishedly merit.

I now will proceed to the vindication of *my father-in-law*, the late capt. *Michael Cresap.*—His life, unfortunately for his country—unfortunately for his family, was too short for much difficulty in tracing its great outlines; and the whole of it has passed within so recent a period, that no part of it can be shrouded in the shade of obscurity: in truth, there are now *many* persons *living* who can bear testimony to, and where neces-

[73]

sary, explain, almost every important incident of that life from his cradle to his grave.

Born at Old Town in the year 1747, a time when the Indians were frequent in that neighborhood, his eyes were familiarized, to their sight almost from the time they were opened; and by his parents and brothers accustomed to see them treated with kindness and humanity, the infant ideas of one of the most benevolent and generous of minds were not likely to be tinged with cruelty or inhumanity towards that unhappy race.

When hostilities commenced between the British and French colonies he was about seven years of age.—When peace took place he was about sixteen. Much of the intervening time was spent in his education; but on several occasions, though in years and in stature a child, and of strength scarcely able to bear the weight of his rifle, he has joined his father and his brothers in their military excursions, when in pursuit of a savage foe, and shared with them their fatigues and their dangers with all the firmness and fortitude of the man, and the hero. Was this the *dawn* to a *day* of *infamy*!!

During the principal parts of the years 1755, 1756 and I believe part of 1757, he was under the care and tuition of the rev. Mr. Craddock, who at that time kept an academy in this county about twelve miles from this city. In the year 1776, I believe, and when not more than twenty years of age, he married Miss Whitehead whose father was a native of the Jerseys; with her he returned to Old Town, which was the place of his residence until death—He there possessed a very handsome landed estate, situate partly in Maryland and partly in Virginia, the north branch of Potowmack running through his possessions. In the year 1770 on the second day of April he was appointed by the government of Maryland one of the magistrates of the county in which he lived, and continued in the commission of the peace for that county to the time of the late revolution.

He early in life engaged in commerce, and having established stores at Old Town and at Ford Redstone, carried on an extensive trade with the western inhabitants of Maryland and with the inhabitants on the west side of the Allegany mountains; and on the breaking out of Indian hostilities in 1774, between six and ten thousand pounds were owing to him; a great part of which was due from those who lived on the western waters. Besides which he had expended large sums of money in the purchases of most valuable lands at Fort Redstone and in its vicinity, as also in the forming various settlements on the Ohio, quite down to the Great Shanhawa, in effecting which last he had at times even been in hazard of his life, for inheriting all that bravery and all that enterprising disposition which had ever characterised his father, he too had formed all his plans, and devoted his cares and attentions to the settlement, cultivation, and improvement of the western wilderness.

In prosecution of these views, very early in the year 1774, he had determined on an expedition for exploring the Tenessee and the country adjacent, and had made all the necessary preparations for that purpose. In the spring of that year he sent forward a party to one of his settlements on the Ohio, there to remain until he himself with the remainder of his party should join them.—They met at the appointed place, but before they proceeded on their intended journey, a number of canoes filled with the scattered inhabitants below, came pushing up the river, with their families and effects, in the deepest consternation from the apprehensions of an immediate Indian invasion.

These apprehensions arose from the insolent behaviour of the Indians themselves, and from a message they had received from their Commandant at Pittsburg, requiring them to be on their guard, as he had received certain information that some of the Indian tribes, I believe the Shawanese and Mingoes were about to take up the hatchet, and to commit immediate hostilities;—Mr. Cresap and his party immediately decamped, and with them also passed up the river to the mouth of Wheelan. Every thing he there heard, confirmed the impressions he had already received: he was informed several murders had already been committed, and that a number of Indians were at that time collected at the mouth of Yellow Creek, conducting themselves towards the Whites with the utmost insolence, and threatening them with violence; and such was in reality the fact.

Well acquainted with the nature of the Indians and of their warfare, and well knowing that in general the first notification of war they gave was with the tomahawk and scalping knife, Mr. Cresap placed himself at the head of a small party, consisting principally of his own men, and left Wheelan with the design to proceed to the mouth of Yellow Creek, and disperse the Indians so collected at that place. In the *mean time* Logan's family were killed, and the Indians left Yellow Creek; of which Mr. Cresap being informed while on his way, he and his party immediately returned to the mouth of Wheelan. But before their return a canoe, in which it was supposed there were hostile Indians, being discovered standing down the river, Mr. Cresap, and a few of his men, passed over to the northwest side thereof, the better to reconnoitre their movements, when the canoe proceeding for the opposite shore was fired upon by the party remaining there, and two Indians were killed.

Soon after his return to the mouth of Wheelan, being informed a considerable party of Indians had passed down the river, Mr. Cresap with his party went in pursuit of them; they fell in with each other on the Ohio, near the Round Bottom, a skirmish ensued, one Indian was killed, and one whiteman was wounded. Mr. Cresap then again returned to the mouth of Wheelan, and seeing it utterly impossible to pursue his expedition to the Tenessee until the Indians should be reduced to reason, with a view of assisting in the attainment of that object, he returned to Old Town, where he instantly raised a company principally at his own expence, and marched them over the mountains, for the assistance and protection of the western inhabitants; and had he on that occasion been suffered to pursue the dictates of his own judgment, I doubt not the savages would have been speedily humbled, the lives of many innocent men, women and children preserved, and the state of Virginia saved from a heavy debt incurred in the two expeditions of the year 1774, the first under Major M'Donald, the other under Lord Dunmore. But no sooner was his arrival announced, than superior authority, instead of thankfully accepting his services, sent him a positive command to disband his company, and to return home. He foresaw what would be to the western inhabitants the *baleful consequences* of obedience to the mandate, but he did obey it; and with a heart suffering the most bitter chagrin, he returned to his home.

What *those consequences* were, may be collected from the following letter written to him by Mr. Caldwell, "Buffaloe Creek Settlement, 31st May, 1774, Dear Sir, I would acquaint you with the deplorable state of our country *since your departure* from us, we are credibly informed that some parties of Indians are actually set out from their towns in order to annoy the inhabitants. Adam Roe, an inhabitant of Fish creek, offers to be on oath, that he saw a party of five Indians, carry off Joseph Proctor over the Ohio, at the mouth of Grave creek. The said Roe's family, and one Harris, being on the river at the same time, are not to be found since, and it is believed they are totally destroyed. The whole country is chiefly in confusion, and taken up in making places of defence; so that it is much talked of; yet no scouts are gone out; and I am apprehensive that instead of turning out spiritedly to prevent the enemy from coming in among us *according to the late commendable motion you was pleased to make in our favour,* that they will be *suffered* to make a breach *on us without any let* or *hindrance.* I hope, dear Sir, that the *necessity* of the *poor and helpless country* will *balance* the *affront,* which —— did you, and that *you will return to our relief* with all convenient speed; for the *desire* of our young men in general is to be led out *by you* against the Indians. And a scout from Fort Pitt some time ago, on their return home, told me at my own house, that if Mr. Cresap had called at Fort Pitt, a *number* of men *would have followed you,* excuse Sir, my freedom, I am Sir, your most obedient &c.   *WILLIAM CALDWELL.*

To Michael Cresap, esq."

And also from the following letter, written by Thomas Brown, now deceased, the late proprietor of Bromsville on the Monongahala,

"*To Michael Cresap, esq.*   "*June* 8, 1794.

"DEAR SIR

"As the present juncture is very difficult and dangerous, I take this opportunity to acquaint you of a barbarous massacre by a party of Indians on the bodies of Henry Spicer, his wife and five children on the waters of Whitely creek, which happened on Saturday evening last; and on Monday last, a man was killed and scalped near the same place. It is commonly reported that the whole Six Nations are taking up arms against us, and as the chiefest inhabitants have crossed the mountain, it is generally supposed that the remnant must feel the ravages of a heavy war, unless some assistance can be given us from below.—Mr. —— has sent expresses all over the inhabitants, only here, directing them how to proceed; and a few neighbours of us. as we thought it proper to make some defence against the enemy, we have erected four block houses, and shall stockade them, if time will permit, as we have become the frontiers.—There is scarcely a family but what is forted, I am, Sir, with respect, your humble servant and well wisher,

"*THOMAS BROWN.*"

"P.S. The *whole inhabitants* are *wishing for your coming out.*"

The aforegoing letters not only shew the situation in which the inhabitants were reduced, but also their confidence in Mr. Cresap, and their solicitude for his services. As a further proof of the last, I shall give you a petition addressed and sent to him, signed by *two hundred and ten* of the most respectable inhabitants at Redstone and its vicinity; I shall give it to you precisely as I find it; the language it is true is a little inaccurate, but I pray you do not view it with too fastidious an eye.— That they were not well calculated to write *notes upon Virginia*, I will readily admit, but they were honest and useful citizens; I wish the same could with justice be said of many of the philosophers of the present day, and at least knew how to express their feelings in such a manner as to make themselves understood.

"*To the Honourable Captain Michael Cresap, Esq.*

"The humble petition of Red Stone settlement and the ajacent inhabitants humbly sheweth, that your honour's Petitioners expects daily to be attacked by the savage enemy; and as your petitioners is fully convinced and satisfied, that you are a gentleman of courage and conduct, there is nothing that would *revive their spirits* at this critical juncture as much as *your appearance*; as they should look upon *you* the *preserver* of their *lives* and *estates*, under the Providence of God—and the people in general in this quarter, have *unanimously agreed* to assist *you* with their *lives* and *fortunes* in any thing, which *you* think will be requisite and necessary towards the suppression of the enemy.—Now as your Honour was *always a lover of your country*, your petitioners begs your *aid* and *assistance*, and your *appearance* as soon as possible; and yur petitioners as in duty bound, will ever pray."—I have now before me several other petitions of a similar purport, from different settlements, but I will not surfeit you with them.—At the same time, letters were also addressed to his Father, with a view through his means, the more effectually to influence the Son; I will *only trouble you* with an extract from *one* of them, written by a Mr. Hardin, and dated the 13th of June, in the year 1774. It is as follows: "I am sorry to hear Mr. Michael Cresap met with so *cold a reception*, when he was among us," (alluding to the peremptory command then given to him, to disband his company, and to return home): "had he continued, he surely must have been a great support to our frontiers. Nevertheless I hope his *interest* in the *country*, and his *love* for his *fellow creatures*, will cause him to *stifle* his resentment, and *once more* march with such active men as he can collect; which must of consequence *closely attach him to the breasts* of every *thinking* man, who *wishes* the *welfare* of *his country*."

But, I must here for the present, break off, as I do not think you or I have so much merit with Mr. Cobbett, as to entitle us to claim a whole news-paper to ourselves.

I *continue* to be, with *due* respect, your very humble servant,

LUTHER MARTIN

Printed in *Porcupine's Gazette*, 8 Feb. 1798; at head of text: "No. VI." and "To the Honourable Thomas Jefferson, Esquire, Vice President of the United States."

GREAT SHANHAWA: that is, the Kanawha River. MESSAGE THEY HAD RECEIVED FROM THEIR COMMANDANT AT PITTSBURG: Michael Cresap contended that in the spring of 1774 he acted in response to a circular letter from John Connolly, who under Lord Dunmore's authority commanded Virginia militia around Pittsburgh (Reuben Gold Thwaites and Louise Phelps Kellogg, eds., *Documentary History of Dunmore's War,* 1774 [Madison, Wis., 1905], 12n; above in this series, 1:235n). Thomas Brown's letter would have been dated 1774, not 1794.

From Thomas Mann Randolph

T.M.R. TO TH: JEFFERSON, Belmont Feb. 3. 98.

I visited Monticello yesterday and entered your room with great anxiety but was soon much comforted by finding little change in the position of the different things which are exposed to the eye: I had got the general order of the room very much in my mind from the many visits I had paid and am satisfied from its being so little broken that no great mischief has been done. Indeed the villain (he is allmost an Idiot it appears to me) has confessed many & I believe every thing he stole: a waistcoat or two & some breeches of Nankin, thread, tape, some impressions in lead & tin of Dies of the Medals & Coins & the gun, &c. which *I* recovered, I am satisfied make the whole, of all these he tells himself and his simplicity is such I think he conceals nothing: all these things were seen in his possession by the Negroes soon after your departure and nothing more can be traced. I have some hope of recovering the proofs of Medals (tis from the description I conclude they are out) I have traced one to a Negroe of the neighbourhood who b't. it of York but he says he has lost it. I found the door locked yesterday as I left it, exactly, but upon examining soon discovered that the skrews of the lock had all been taken out for they were not close skrewed, the lock being quite loose. York says he was twice in the room, once before Jupiters return from Georgetown which was before I went over & again when it was discovered. I have taken effectual measures to secure it against all future attempts even the most violent. Agricultural affairs proceed both at Mont'o. and Shadwell: George is steady & industrious—Page I think is as anxious about his duties as any Overseer I ever knew. The thorough confidence you place in the companies of tradesmen is less abused than I expected but I am still convinced that being under no command whatever they will become idle and dissipated tho' I am clear that it confirms them in honesty.

Martha and the children are in fine health: I am tolerably well recovered from my fit of languor tho' not in such health as before; the proximate cause of this attack was a weting I got; the remote, (which I cannot help inquiring after allways) perhaps the use of Coffee, for it is so pleasant a Stimulus to the Stomach I cannot refrain from it when I am tolerably well and yet tis probable it disposes that organ to receive impressions which w'd. fall elsewhere. In these cases without cough or change in my pulse or inclination for food I become weak, flatulent, heavy, melancholic, I lose flesh, sleep profoundly; am afflicted with Rheumatic pains upon the least exposure to fresh or damp air: these symptoms continue sometimes several weeks with Atrophy and not infrequently go off with one smart attack in the bowels and an obstinate constipation after, during which I lose the flatulency, acquire a great appetite which increases even as far as the 4th. or 5th. day, and get as light & heartsome as ever.

We have not heard from you since your letter to Martha of Dec. 27th.

Peter Carr has been ill in Char'lle. 10 or 12 days, with a pain in the side & bad cough: his friends were much alarmed at first but he is now out of danger: Mrs Carr is with him at Joüts: they move to Carrsbrook (the low grounds) in the first spring weather.

I send my Diary for January

	Thermom at Sunrise	Thermom at 3 o clock	
1.	40.	55	
2.	32.	50	
3.	28.	43	
4.	31.	36	
5.	33.	46	
6.	32.	54	
7.	25.	47	
8.	29.	39	
9.	35.	37	
10.	24.	35	
11.	23.	42.	
12.	20.	45.	
13.	35.	58.	
14.	43.	58	
15.	54.	60	only 14 fair days in the month
16.	44.	54	
17.	34.	54	
18.	40.	44	
19.	30.	37	
20.	32.	50	
21.	40.	54	
22.	40.	47	
23.	34.	30	
24.	16.	32	
25.	23.	43	
26.	36.	49	
27.	35.	32	
28.	23.	43	
29.	28.	43	
30.	26.	56	
31.	31.	46	

yours most affectionately   TH: M. RANDOLPH

RC (MHi); addressed: "Thomas Jefferson Vice-President U. S. Philada:"; franked; endorsed by TJ as received 13 Feb. 1798 and so recorded in SJL.

To William Linn

SIR   Philadelphia Feb. 5. 179[8]

I had the honor before of acknoleging the receipt of [your] favor of [May] [. . .] and of stating that on my return home I would see whether [the papers?] [. . .] there would [enable] me to contribute any thing to the general subj[ect of the in]quiry contained in the printed paper you enclosed [me. on examination] of my papers I found that I could not with certainty establish from [them] any thing more th[an] had been published in the Notes on Virginia. [in] fact my [absence] from the US. on other employments [. . .] [the] [. . .] the time of that publication had not left it in my power [. . .] addition [. . .] former stock of information. [I sh]all add [however] [. . .] [reason?] which may remove a doubt or two [on certain Indian names?]. it says "there are [besides] [. . .] [them], such as [. . .] are the same called on my list [Ouiàtonons (according to the French] orthography) or Wiatonons of the English, [. . .] called Wawia[tons] [. . .] and shortly Weeaws. the [. . .] I [. . .] are those called Mache[cous] in my list, according to the orthography of the [Fre]nch travellers. the Hurons are the Wyan[dots] & the [. . .] of Chippewas.   I have long wished to make as extensive a collection of vocabul[aries] of Indian languages as possible and after form[ing] a vocabulary of the names of natural objects chiefly, I had a [. . .] and sent out some of [them]. my success however has not yet been [consi?]derable. should the enterp[rise] [. . .] which is the subject of your letter I should be very glad to be [permitted to communicate] one of my [plans?] which [. . .] [consist of] [. . .] for the use of [your missionaries]. [uni]formity in the vocabularies is essential to the [object of] [. . .] the history of the Indians by the a[ffinities?] of their languages.

I have the honor to be with great respect & esteem Your most obedt humble se[rvt]   TH: JEFFERSON

PrC (DLC: TJ Papers, 99:17031); faint, with several illegible phrases of three or more words; at foot of text: "Revd. Wm. Linn"; endorsed by TJ in ink on verso as a letter of 5 Feb. 1796, but recorded in SJL under 5 Feb. 1798.

TJ probably acknowledged Linn's FAVOR of 25 May 1797 in a letter of 3 June 1797, which is recorded in SJL but has not been found.

COLLECTION OF VOCABULARIES: some years earlier, in an effort to research the origins of Native American tribes through a comparative study of languages, TJ had created a printed form, titled "Vocabulary," that listed 282 English words and infinitives in four columns, beginning with "fire," "water," and "earth," and ending with "to break," "to bend," "yes," and "no." The form left space in each column for providing the equivalent terms from another language; a surviving example is the one returned by William Vans Murray with his letter to TJ of 18 Sep. 1792, filled in with words of the Nanticoke language. Writing on 2 Apr. 1798 to Linn, one of the directors of the New York Missionary Society, TJ made his blank form available to the fledgling organization, which began its evangelical work with one minister sent to the Chickasaws in 1799. The directors' instructions to missionaries that year referred obliquely to TJ's word list, acknowledging as well his reason for recording vocabularies: "Every thing which relates to the Indians, is an object not only of curiosity, but of real utility. By their language and customs we are most likely to arrive at their origin. A vocabulary of English words, prepared and already sent out by a Gentleman engaged in inquiries of this kind, will be put into your hands, and you are desired to mark the Indian names for these things, that so the number of languages and the different dialects may be ascertained." Unfortunately most of the information that TJ gathered about American Indian languages was lost in 1809 (*The New-York Missionary Magazine, and Repository of Religious Intelligence*, 1 [1800], 10-11, 15, 23; Vol. 20:450-2).

During his sojourn in the United States, C. F. C. Volney used one of TJ's printed forms to record words from the Miami language, returning the list to TJ in March 1798. Volney collected the data in Philadelphia during January and February of that year by interviewing William Wells, who had worked as an interpreter during Anthony Wayne's négotiations with the western tribes, and Wells's father-in-law, the Miami leader Michikinikwa (Little Turtle). Volney included his Miami word list, in a different arrangement and with additional information drawn from the studies of Benjamin Smith Barton, in his book about America (MS in PPAmP, with Miami words inserted by Volney, who also wrote a note in English at the head of the text concerning pronunciation and another in French at the foot of the document to explain the circumstances of his gathering the information, concluding: "Copie offerte a mr jefferson en mars 1798, par son Serviteur et ami C: Volney," endorsed by TJ, who also wrote and handprinted at head of text: "A Vocabulary of the Miami language, by Volney"; C. F. C. Volney, *A View of the Soil and Climate of the United States of America*, trans. Charles Brockden Brown [Philadelphia, 1804; repr. 1968], 356-8, 429-39; DAB, 11:300).

To David Longworth

Sir   Philadelphia Feb. 5. 98.

I received while in Virginia your obliging letter with the 1st number of your new edition of Telemachus, and deferred answering it till I should come to this place. I came here later than should have been and have been prevented by other business from acknowleging your letter till now. I shall be glad to become a subscriber for a couple of copies, to be delivered bound when the whole work is finished. it is really a fine specimen of the typographical art, and would do honor to the presses of Europe where it has been so much longer exercised. the price shall be paid either here or in New York as you shall be pleased to direct. I am Sir

Your very humble servt   Th: Jefferson

RC (George W. Grill, Chicago, 1950); addressed: "Mr. David Longworth No. 66. Nassau street New York"; franked and postmarked.

In 1796 David Longworth (ca. 1765-1821) published the first number of *Longworth's American Almanack*, a New York City directory that appeared annually thereafter and became the staple of his business, which also included the sale of books and prints at an establishment he came to denote the Shakespeare Gallery. Initially using T. and J. Swords as printers, by 1800 he acquired his own press. He published and perhaps contributed to *Salmagundi*, an enormously popular collection of social satire written pseudonymously by Washington Irving, William Irving, and James Kirke Paulding, which first appeared as a periodical during 1807-8. The work's authors and publisher later had a falling out over distribution of the proceeds, Longworth having taken out a copyright on the work after Irving and the others rejected his suggestion that they do so. Beginning in 1802 Longworth played a significant role in the publication and sale of theatrical works, including those of American playwrights (Jacob Blanck, "*Salmagundi* and Its Publisher," *Papers of the Bibliographical Society of America*, 41 [1947], 1-12; Roger E. Stoddard, "A Catalogue of the Dramatic Imprints of David and Thomas Longworth, 1802-1821," *Proceedings of the American Antiquarian Society*, 84 [1974], 317-18; Stoddard, "Notes on American Play Publishing, 1765-1865," same, 81 [1971], 173-7).

Longworth's OBLIGING LETTER of 21 Aug. 1797, which according to SJL TJ received from 66 Nassau St. in New York on 1 Sep. 1797, has not been found. YOUR NEW EDITION OF TELEMACHUS: Longworth published a two-volume edition of *The Adventures of Telemachus Son of Ulysses* (New York, 1796-97), an English translation of a work by François de Salignac de La Mothe-Fénelon, first published in 1700, which presented a classical tale in the context of a political novel. TJ, who acquired at least three other versions of the story, did not record the Longworth edition in his library catalogues (Evans, Nos. 30414, 32126; Sowerby, Nos. 4305-7).

Notes on Anti-French Sentiment in the Washington Administration

[before 6 Feb. 1798]

[. . .][1] one of the Secretaries that a resolution was formed to give no office to any person who did not approve of the proceedings of the Executive, and that it was determined to recall Monroe whose conduct was not consonant with the views of the Executive. Davy said they expressed very hostile dispositions towards France, and he wished Logan to apprise Adet of it, who he observed was a good kind of man, ought to know it, & to put his government on their guard.

MS (DLC: TJ Papers, 102:17525); entirely in TJ's hand; incomplete, with beginning of text on previous sheet torn away (see Notes on the Formation of the Federal Government, 5 Jan. 1798); written on same sheet as document below.

George LOGAN entertained French diplomats, including Pierre Auguste ADET, at Stenton, his home near Philadelphia (Tolles, *Logan*, 148).

[1] Beginning of text torn away.

Notes on a Conversation with Abraham Baldwin

Feb. 6. mr Baldwin tells me that in a conversn yesterday with Goodhue, on the state of our affairs, Goodhue said 'I'll tell you what, I have made up my mind on this subject; I would rather the old ship should go down than not.' (meaning the union of the states.) mr Hillhouse coming up, 'well says mr Baldwin I'll tell my old friend Hillhouse what you say,' & he told him 'well says Goodhue I repeat that I would rather the old ship should go down, if we are to be always kept pumping so.' 'mr Hillhouse, says Baldwin, you remember when we were learning logic together at school, there was the case *categorical* & the case *hypothetical*. mr Goodhue stated it to me first as the case categorical.' I am glad to see that he now changes it to the case hypothetical, by adding 'if we are always to be kept pumping so.' Baldwin went on then to remind Goodhue what an advocate he had been for our tonnage duty wanting to make it 1 Doll. instead of 50. cents, and[1] how impatiently he bore the delays of Congress in proceeding to retaliate on Gr. Br. before mr Madison's proposns came on; Goodhue acknoleged that his opinions had changed since that.

MS (DLC: TJ Papers, 102:17525); entirely in TJ's hand; on same sheet as preceding document; with opening quotation mark to "well says mr Baldwin" and closing quotation mark following "as the case categorical" supplied by Editors.

LEARNING LOGIC TOGETHER: Baldwin and James Hillhouse graduated from Yale in 1772 and 1773, respectively (Franklin Bowditch Dexter, *Biographical Sketches of the Graduates of Yale College with Annals of the College History*, 6 vols. [New York, 1883-1912], 3:432-4, 486-90).

[1] Preceding passage beginning with "wanting" interlined by TJ.

From Samuel Sitgreaves

SIR,   Tuesday 6. Feb. 1798

I have the Honor to inform you that, if it shall be convenient and agreeable to the Senate, the Managers for the House of Representatives will, tomorrow at 12 o'Clock, exhibit Articles in Maintenance of their Impeachment against William Blount for High Crimes and Misdemeanors—

As the Managers are desirous to conform to any Ceremonial which the Senate may deem it proper to prescribe in this Case, I request you will take the Trouble to cause me to be informed of any such, which it shall be necessary for us to attend to—

I have the Honor to be, with just Consideration, Sir, Your most obed Serv.   S SITGREAVES

RC (DNA: RG 46, Senate Records, 5th Cong., 2d sess.); in a clerk's hand, with part of complimentary close and signature by Sitgreaves; at foot of text: "The Vice President of the United States"; endorsed in clerk's hand: "Legis: 2d. Sess: 5th. Cong: Letter to Vice President from Mr. Sitgreaves relative to exhibiting Articles of Impeachment against William Blount. February 6th. 1798."

Samuel Sitgreaves (1764-1827) received a classical education and was admitted to the bar in Philadelphia in 1783. Three years later he moved to Easton, Northampton County, Pennsylvania where he practiced law and was elected as a delegate to the state constitutional convention of 1790. As a Federalist congressman in 1795 he led the House investigation into the activities of William Blount. Appointed to the five-man commission established under the 6th Article of the Jay Treaty to settle British claims, he resigned from Congress in August 1798. When the commission came to a close in July 1799, Sitgreaves returned to Easton, resumed the practice of law, took an active role in local politics and in promoting internal improvements and economic development (*Biog. Dir. Cong.*; JEP, 1:296-7; PMHB, 13 [1889], 128, 254-5; 22 [1898], 364; 34 [1910], 239-40).

There is no indication that this letter was officially presented to the Senate or that the Senate considered receiving the MANAGERS FOR THE HOUSE OF REPRESENTATIVES to exhibit the ARTICLES of IMPEACHMENT on this date (JS, 2:434-5). As the first item of business the next day, however, Jonathan W. Condy, clerk of the House of Representatives, addressed TJ and the Senate as follows: "*Mr. President*: The House of Representatives have resolved that articles agreed by the House to be exhibited in the name of themselves and of all the people of the United States against William Blount, in maintenance of their impeachment against him for high crimes and misdemeanors, be carried to the Senate by the managers, Messrs. Sitgreaves, Bayard, Harper, Gordon, Pinckney, Dana, Sewall, Hosmer, Dennis, Evans, and Imlay, appointed to conduct the said impeachment" (JS, 2:435). For the election of the impeachment managers, see note to Senate Resolution on William Blount, [4 July 1797]. After hearing this message, the Senate resolved to receive the congressmen at noon (JS, 2:435).

Address from Samuel Sitgreaves
to the Senate

MR. VICE PRESIDENT,   [7 Feb 1798]

The House of Representatives having agreed upon Articles in Maintenance of their Impeachment against William Blount for High Crimes & Misdemeanors, and having appointed on their Part Managers of the said Impeachment, the Managers have now the Honor to attend the Senate for the Purpose of exhibiting the said Articles

MS (DNA: RG 46, Senate Records, 5th Cong., 2d sess.); in an unknown hand; endorsed in clerk's hand: "Legis: 2d: Sess: 5th. Cong: Address of the Chairman of the Managers appointed to conduct the Impeachment against William Blount. February 7th. 1798."

Upon receiving the managers from the House of Representatives FOR THE PURPOSE OF EXHIBITING the impeachment ARTICLES, the Senate followed procedures that they had adopted on 5 Feb. including designating James Mathers, doorkeeper of the Senate, to serve as sergeant-at-arms. Upon TJ's order, Mathers issued a proclamation for silence in the Senate as Sitgreaves read the document. TJ reportedly responded as directed in the procedures: "Gentlemen, managers on the part of the House of Representatives: The Senate will take such order on the articles of impeachment which you have exhibited before them as shall seem to them proper; of which due notice will be given to the House of Representatives" (JS, 2:433-5; *Annals*, 7:970). The House members then left the Senate chamber and Samuel A. Otis entered the articles in the Senate journal (JS, 2:435-7).

From William Linn

Sir,   New-York, Feb. 8th. 1798.

I feel honored & obliged by your communication of the 5th instant. I have lately formed a table of the Indians within the territory of the United States, in which I have followed yours as to the arrangement, spelling, & lists of the numbers of the warriors. I have added an anonymous list published 1797, & a column marking their languages. I have inserted the Weeas & Eelriver, finding them mentioned in one of the treaties, but shall attend to the remarks made in your letter. In determining the places of residence, I have consulted Dr Morse's Gazetteer, a late work, & compared it with your table. The Mohiecons, spelled in the History of the Mission of the United Brethren Mahikans & Mahikanders I have supposed to be the same who are called Mohegans, & in their own language Muhhekanneew. Part of these now reside at New Stockbridge & are called Stockbridge Indians; part at Brothertown in the Oneida reservation; & part, if I am not mistaken in all this, removed with the Missionaries first to Bethlehem, & after various emigrations & afflictions, are settled near Sandosky. It is extremely difficult to arrive at accuracy in this business. My table is only in manuscript & still incorrect.

I find that your opinion as to the languages of the Indians differs from what is asserted in the "History of the Mission of the United Brethren" compiled by George Henry Loskiel & translated by La Trobe; & by Dr Edwards in his "Observations on the Muhhekaneew language" The history extends from 1735 till the middle of 1787. Some of the Missionaries have learned the Delaware language, & have had intercourse with many tribes, & yet they say that there are only two languages radically different; the Delaware & the language of the six nations. The words in the history are; "Our Missionaries at least, who were particularly attentive to this subject, have never met with any which had not some similitude with either one or the other: But the Delaware language bears no resemblance to the Iroquois." This too is the opinion of Dr Edwards who early learned the Mohegan language, (a dialect of the Delaware,) & still retains a knowledge of it. In his observations, he shows its affinity to the Shawenese & Chippewa, &, in some respects to the Hebrew. I know not whether you have seen either of these publications. The first is a large Octavo volume, the last a small pamphlet which I could easily inclose to you. I would also send the first, with cheerfulness, if I knew of a conveyance, & take my chance for a copy here. Besides the history of the Mission, it contains a history of the Delawares & Iroquois, their customs &c.

It is certain that there is a great variety of dialects—that information comes chiefly from illiterate captives, traders & interpreters—& that petty tribes are known to affect to be a distinct nation & to have a distinct language. This is a subject of useful inquiry, & would be a certain indication of the part of the world from which the Indians have emigrated. Bishop Ettwein of Bethlehem, in a letter to me, says that "Mr. John Heckewelder, a Missionary has found that a Tartar nation about Mount Caucasus, agrees so much with the Delawares, that he thinks he could as well converse with said Tartars, as he can with the Delawares, whose language he can speak."

I request you to favor me with one of your Blanks, which I shall present to the Directors of the Society, to whom it will be very acceptable.

I have the honor to be—with great respect & esteem, Sir, Your most Obedient humble servt   WM LINN

RC (DLC); addressed: "The Honorable Thomas Jefferson Vice President of the United States Philadelphia"; endorsed by TJ as received 10 Feb. 1798 and so recorded in SJL.

DR. MORSE'S GAZETTEER: Jedidiah Morse, *The American Gazetteer* (Boston, 1797). The work by Moravian bishop GEORGE HENRY LOSKIEL that Christian Ig-natius LA TROBE translated from German was *History of the Mission of the United Brethren among the Indians in North America* (London, 1794). The Connecticut Society of Arts and Sciences had published the paper of Jonathan EDWARDS the younger reporting his *Observations on the Language of the Muhhekaneew Indians* (New Haven, Conn., 1788). See Sowerby, Nos. 3964, 4011, 4050.

To James Madison

Philadelphia Feb. 8. 98.

I wrote you last on the 25th. Ult. since which yours of the 21st. has been recieved. Bache had put 500. copies of Monroe's book on board a vessel, which was stopped by the early & unexpected freezing of the river. he then tried in vain to get them sent on by fifties at a time by the stage. the river is now open here, the vessels have fallen down and if they can get through the ice below, the one with Bache's packet will soon be at Richmond. it is surmised here that Scipio is written by C. Lee. Articles of impeachment were yesterday given in against Blount; but many knotty preliminary questions will arise. must not a *formal law* settle the oath of the Senators, forms of pleadings, process against person & goods &c. may he not appear by attorney? must he not be tried by jury? is a Senator impeachable? is an ex-Senator impeachable? you will readily concieve that these questions to be settled by 29. lawyers are not likely to come to speedy issue.—a very disagreeable question of privilege has suspended all other proceedings for several days. you will see this in the newspapers.—the question of arming was to have come on on Monday last. that morning the President sent in an inflammatory message about a vessel taken & burnt by a French privateer near Charleston. of this he had been possessed some time, and it had run through all the newspapers. it seemed to come in very apropos for spurring on the disposition to arm. however the question is not come on. in the mean time the general spirit, even of the merchants, is becoming adverse to it. New hampshire &, Rhodeisland, are unanimously against arming. so is Baltimore. this place becoming more so. Boston divided & desponding. I know nothing of New York. but I think there is no danger of the question being carried, unless something favorable to it is recieved from our envoys. from them we hear nothing. yet it seems reasonably believed that the Executive has heard, & that it is something which would not promote their views of arming. for every action of theirs shew they are panting to come to blows.—Walker's bill will be applied to answer a draught of Colo. Monroe's on Barnes. I have not heard yet from Bailey. I wrote to you about procuring a rider for the Fredsbg post. the propositions should be here by the 14th. inst. but I can get it kept open a little longer. there is no bidder yet but Green the printer. £100. Virga will be given.—Giles is arrived. my friendly salutations to mrs Madison Adieu affectionately.

RC (DLC: Madison Papers).

See TJ to Madison, 24 Jan. 1798, for the letter which TJ completed on the 25TH. ULT.

DISAGREEABLE QUESTION OF PRIVILEGE: on 30 Jan. 1798 Republican Matthew Lyon, Irish-born representative from Vermont, spit in the face of Roger Griswold after the Federalist congressman repeated charges that Lyon was punished for cowardly behavior during the Revolutionary War. Shortly thereafter Massachusetts Federalist Samuel Sewall introduced a resolution seeking Lyon's expulsion for the "violent attack and gross indecency" committed against Griswold. The resolution was immediately referred to a committee of privileges, which three days later reported that Lyon was guilty of conduct "unworthy of a member of this House" and should be expelled. In the midst of the debate Robert Goodloe Harper added the charge that during his defense on 8 Feb., Lyon had used "an expression so outrageous, so gross, and indecent, that no gentleman yet had been able

to repeat it." On 12 Feb. an amendment to reprimand rather than expel Lyon was defeated by a 44 to 52 vote. The House then voted by the same margin to expel Lyon, but lacking the two-thirds vote required for expulsion, the resolution did not carry. Three days later, Griswold sought retribution by attacking Lyon with a walking stick as he sat in his seat in the House. Lyon defended himself with tongs from the fireplace. The next day Thomas T. Davis of Kentucky called for the expulsion of both Griswold and Lyon for "violent and disorderly behaviour committed in the House." On 20 Feb. the committee of privileges presented a report against expulsion. Three days later the House, by a 73 to 21 vote, agreed with the committee's recommendation. A resolution to reprimand the two congressmen also failed (*Annals*, 7:955-1029, 1034-43, 1047-58, 1063-7).

On 5 Feb. 1798 President Adams sent a MESSAGE to Congress describing the actions of a FRENCH PRIVATEER NEAR CHARLESTON. Adams had received the information in a letter from South Carolina Governor Charles

Pinckney of 22 Oct. 1797. Adams noted that he was transmitting the letter and enclosed depositions to encourage the passage of legislation that would allow the executive to take proper defensive measures to protect United States citizens and those of friendly foreign nations (JS, 2:434; JHR, 3:161).

To James Monroe

TH:J. TO COLO. MONROE [8 Feb. 1798]

I recieved yesterday by mr Giles yours of Jan. 27. and am well pleased with the indications of republicanism in our assembly. their law respecting the printer is a good one. I only wish they would give the printing of the laws to one & journals to another. this would secure two, as each portion of the business would be object enough to a printer, and two places in their gift would keep within bounds the other printers also who would be in expectancy of catching something in case of either vacancy.—Bache was prevented sending 500 copies of your book to Richmond by the freezing of this river after they were aboard the vessel. he tried in vain to get boxes of fifties carried on by the stages. however, the river is now open here, the vessels have fallen down and if they find it open below, that with Bache's packets will soon be in Richmond. it has been said here that C. Lee was the author of Scipio, but I know of no authority for it. I had expected Hamilton would have taken the field, and that in that case you might have come forward yourself very shortly merely to strengthen and present in a compact view those points which you expected yourself they would lay hold of; particularly the disposition expressed to acquiesce under their spoliatory decree. Scipio's attack is so weak as to make no impression. I understand that the opposite party admit there is nothing in your conduct which can be blamed, except the divulging secrets: & this I think might be answered by a few sentences, discussing the question Whether an Ambassador is the representative of his country or of the President. Barnes has accepted your bill. as to the question of your practising the law in Richmond, I have been too long out of the way in Virginia, to give an opinion on it worth attention. I have understood the business is very profitable, much more so than in my time: and an opening of great importance must be made by the retirement of Marshall & Washington, which will be filled by somebody. I do expect that your farm will not sufficiently employ your time to shield you from ennui. your mind is active, & would suffer if unemployed. perhaps it's energies could not be more justifiably employed than for your own comfort. I should doubt very much however whether you should combine with this the idea of living in Richmond,

[89]

at least till you see farther before you. I have always seen that tho' a residence at the seat of government gave some advantages yet it increased expences also so seriously as to overbalance the advantages. I have always seen too that a good stand in the country intercepted more business than was shared by the residents of the city. yours is a good stand. you need only visit Staunton &c sometimes to put yourself in the way of seeing clients.—The articles of impeachment against Blount were yesterday recieved by the Senate. some great questions will immediately arise. 1. Can they prescribe their own oath, the forms of pleadings, issue process against person or goods by their own orders, without the formality of a law authorising it? has not the 8th. amendment of the constitution rendered trial by jury necessary? is a Senator impeachable? these and other questions promise no very short issue. the Representatives have a dirty business now before them on a question of privilege. this you will see in the public papers.—the question of arming our vessels was to have come on on Monday last. accordingly the President that morning sent in an inflammatory message about a vessel taken near Charleston & burnt by a French privateer, of which fact he had been sometime possessed, & it had been in all the newspapers. it seemed thrown in on that day precisely to give a spur to the question. however it did not come on. in the mean time the spirit of the merchants is going fast over to the safe side of the question. in New hampshire and Rhode island they are unanimous; in Baltimore also. in this place becoming more so. in Boston divided & desponding. of New York I have no information. but I think the proposition will not be carried, unless something befriending it should come from our envoys. nothing transpires yet of their mission. yet it cannot be well doubted but that the Executive must have recieved information. perhaps it is of a nature to damp the spirit for arming.—pray tell Colo. Bell (to whom I wrote about getting a rider for the Fredsbg post) that the 14th. inst. is the day by which the proposition should come in. I can get it kept open a little longer. £100. our money will be given. my friendly salutations to mrs Monroe. Adieu affectionately.

RC (DLC: Monroe Papers); undated, but supplied from PrC; addressed: "James Monroe near Charlottesville"; franked and postmarked; endorsed by Monroe. PrC (DLC); consists of first page only; dated by TJ in ink: "Feb. 8. 98." PrC (MHi); consists of second page only.

Notes on the Framing of Oaths

[ca. 8-9 Feb. 1798]

In an oath are to be distinguished 1. the formal or ceremonial parts & 2. the substance.

the 1st. dependg. on the religious opns of the party, & is to be accomodated thereto[1] by the discretion of the judge.

2. the substance must have been prescribed either by the Common law, or a legislative act. a principle

the substance of the oath now under considn has not been prescribed by the Constitution

a resoln of the Senate is not a legislative act

peculiarly indelicate for the Senate to prescribe contents of their own oath.

     unsafe to the citizen. if Senate may frame the oath on their honour

      they might as well be trusted to try on honour

MS (DLC: TJ Papers, 6:1039); entirely in TJ's hand; undated, but see below for date supplied.

On 8 Feb. 1798 the Senate began to consider the SUBSTANCE OF THE OATH to be administered to senators when sitting for an impeachment trial. The subject was introduced three days earlier in one of the reports on impeachment procedures. Debate centered on whether a RESOLUTION could prescribe an oath or whether a LEGISLATIVE ACT was required, in which case the concurrence of the House of Representatives would be necessary. Some senators believed that this would be a check by the House on the Senate's impeachment power. For a summary of the debate, see Melton, *First Impeachment*, 164-9. On 9 Feb. the Senate passed a resolution prescribing the oath, in which they would swear to "do impartial justice, according to law" (JS, 2:437-9).

[1] Preceding two words interlined in place of "indulged."

To Martha Jefferson Randolph

Philadelphia Feb. 8. 98.

I ought oftener, my dear Martha, to recieve your letters, for the very great pleasure they give me, & especially when they express your affections for me. for though I cannot doubt them, yet they are among those truths which tho' not doubted we love to hear repeated. here too they serve like gleams of light, to chear a dreary scene, where envy, hatred, malice, revenge, & all the worst passions of men are marshalled to make one another as miserable as possible. I turn from this with pleasure to contrast it with your fire side, where the single evening I passed at it was worth more than ages here. indeed I feel myself detaching very fast, perhaps too fast, from every thing but yourself, your sister, & those who are identified with you. these form the last hold the world will have on me, the cords which will be cut only when I am loosened from this state of being.   I am looking forward to the spring with all the fondness of desire to meet you all once more, and with the change of season, to enjoy also a change of scene & of society. yet the time of our leaving this is not yet talked of.   I am much concerned to hear the state of health of mr Randolph & the family, mentioned in your letters of Jan. 22. & 28. surely, my dear, it would be better for you to remove to Monticello. the south pavillion,[1] the Parlour & Study, will accomodate your family; & I should think mr Randolph would find less inconvenience in the riding it would occasion him than in the loss of his own & his family's health. let me beseech you then to go there, and to use every thing & every body as if I were there. if mr Randolph will take on himself to command the usual functions of the servants, carts, waggon, and other resources of the place, you may make yourselves comfortable there. I shall anxiously hope to hear that you adopt this plan.   I wrote to mr Randolph on the subject of a rider for our Fredericksburg post who may be relied on. the proposition should be here, if any one will undertake it, by the 14th. inst. but the postmaster has promised to keep it open a little longer. £100. Virginia money will be given, if the person be approvedly trustworthy.—all your commissions shall be executed, not forgetting the game of the goose, if we can find out what it is; for there is some difficulty in that. kiss all the little ones for me: present me affectionately to mr Randolph, & my warmest love to yourself. Adieu.

RC (NNPM); at foot of text: "Mrs. Randolph." PrC (MHi); endorsed by TJ in ink on verso.

[1] Preceding word written over "chamber," erased. Change lacking in PrC.

Notes for a Letter to Hugh Williamson

TH: JEFFERSON TO DOCTR. WILLIAMSON   Phila [11 Feb. 1798]

'Have they not Moses & the prophets? verily verily I say unto thee that if they will not hear them, neither will they be persuaded though one should rise from the dead.' this was the answer of a Southern member to whom I shewed your lre of the 2d Inst. and who had formerly been in favor of Madisons proposns which he quoted to me as going[1] precisely to the object of the Brit. navign act as proposed in your lre, he observed that they were supported by the Southern & rejected by the Northern delegations, that it was a liberal offer of sacrifice of the interests of the former to the latter, that in the last vote on the subject the 3. states of Mass. R.I. & Conn. gave 20. votes agt. & 2. for them, while the 3. states of Virga., Kent. & N.C. wherein not a single topmast vessel is probably owned by a native[2] gave 25. for & 4. against them. if this record, said he, will not evince the Northern & Southern politics in Congress, neither would the same proposition were it now raised from the dead.

Dft (DLC: TJ Papers, 103:17912); entirely in TJ's hand, heavily revised; undated, but supplied from the document that follows.

Perpendicularly on the same sheet TJ made two heavily emended lists of votes of 98 members of the House of Representatives on 5 Feb. 1794 on a motion to postpone consideration of Madison's resolutions to implement the legislative recommendations in the Report on Commerce (Vol. 27: 535; *Annals*, 4:431-2). TJ arranged the members' names by state and in columns of yeas and nays. On the later of the two lists he tallied votes from certain states and calculated totals of 2 yea and 20 nay votes from Massachusetts, Connecticut, and Rhode Island and 25 yeas to 4 nays from Virginia, Kentucky, and North Carolina. He used a similar method to count the votes from New York, New Jersey, Pennsylvania, and Delaware, but without computing the totals for that group of states, which were 13 yea and 15 nay. Alongside the full lists TJ wrote and canceled two shorter lists of names of members of the House.

[1] Preceding fifteen words interlined in place of "proceeded to quote the inclosed experiment of Madison's propositions, [a transaction] which went."

[2] Preceding twelve words interlined.

To Hugh Williamson

DEAR SIR   Philadelphia Feb. 11. 98.

I have to acknolege the reciept of your favor of the 2d. inst. I [will] with great pleasure sound opinions on the subject you mention, & [see] whether [it] can be brought forward with any degree of strength. I doubt it however, & for [this] reason. you may recollect that a report which I gave in to Congress in [. . .] [93. and] mr Madison's propositions of Jan. 94 went directly to establish a Navigation act on the British principle. on the last vote given on this (which was in Feb. 94.) from the three states of Massachusets, Connecticut & Rhode island there were 2. votes for it and 20. against it; and from the 3. states of Virginia, Kentuckey & N. Carolina wherein not a single topmast vessel is, I believe, owned by a native citizen, there were 25. votes for & 4. against the measure. I very much suspect that were the same proposition now brought forward, the Northern vote would be [nearly the] same, while the Southern one, I am afraid, would be [. . .]ally varied. [. . .] [. . .]jections of their disinterested endeavors for placing our navigation on an independent footing & forcing on them the British treaty have not had a tendency to [. . .] new offers of sacrifice, and especially under the prospect of a new rejection. you observe that the rejection 'would change the politics of New England.' but it would [afford] no evidence which they have not already in the records of Jan. & Feb. 94. however as I before mentioned, I will with pleasure sound the dispositions [on that] subject. if [the proposition] should be likely to obtain a reputable vote, [it may] do good. as to myself I sincerely wish that the whole Union may accomodate their interests to each other, & play into their hands mutually as members of the same family, that the wealth & strength of any one part should be viewed as the wealth & strength of the whole. the Countervailing act of G. [Britain] lately laid before us by the President, offers a just occasion of looking [to our] navigation: for the merchants here say that the effect of it will be that they themselves shall never think of employing an American vessel to carry [provision] to Gr. Britain after a peace. not having [. . .] any conversation on this subject, [I cannot] say whether it has excited sensibility either in the North or South. it shall be tried however. accept assurances of the sincere esteem of Dear Sir Your friend & servt.   TH: JEFFERSON

PrC (DLC); faint; at foot of text: "Dr. Hugh Williamson."

THE COUNTERVAILING ACT: with a message of 2 Feb. 1798 the president gave Congress copies of two acts of Parliament, one of which, approved on 4 July 1797, implemented articles of the Jay Treaty. In order "to countervail the Difference of Duty" that favored imports brought to the United States by American vessels over those carried in foreign ships, the act imposed additional duties on American goods brought to Britain in American ships beginning 5 Jan. 1798. Rufus King had protested in vain to the British government that the additional duties went beyond merely putting American and British shipping on an equal footing. The other act of Parliament that Adams sent to Congress, also passed in July 1797, permitted countries friendly to Great Britain to trade with British possessions in India and confirmed the role of the East India Company in regulating that trade (Sir Thomas Edlyne Tomlins and John Raithby, eds., *The Statutes at Large, of England and Great Britain*, 20 vols. [London, 1811], 19:382-3, 419-20; Perkins, *First Rapprochement*, 76-7; JS, 2:433).

From James Madison

DEAR SIR   Orange Feby. 12. 1798

The last mail brought neither letters nor papers from Philada. By the preceding one I recd your favor of Jany. 24. and a bundle of the Gazettes down to the 25th. inclusive, with an omission only of that of the 23d. which it may be proper for you to supply in order to keep your Sett entire. Your account of the probable fortune of the negociation at Paris, is less decisively unfavorable than the reports prevailing here. It will be happy if a good issue should result from the crisis: But I have great apprehensions from two sources; 1. the spirit in which the negociation will be conducted on the side of our Executive, if not on the other side also; 2. the real difficulties, which the British Treaty has thrown in the way. It is pretty clear that France will not acquiesce under the advantage which that insidious instrument gives to her enemy, and the House of Representatives at the last Session admitted that the condition of the two nations ought to be equalized. How can this now be done? in one of two ways only; either by dissolving the British Treaty, or by stipulating with France that she may plunder us as we have stipulated that Britain may plunder us. To the first mode the objections on the American side are obvious. To the second, will not France refuse so far to sanction the principle that free ships do *not* make goods free, as to enter into a positive stipulation to that effect, chusing rather to equalize her own situation on the principle of retaliation which indirectly supports instead of surrendering her favorite object. Should this be her course, the U. States will have no option but to go directly to war in defence of the British Treaty which was adopted as a defence against war, and in defence of the principle that free ships do *not* make free goods,[1] in opposition both to their own principles & their essential interests,—or to go indirectly to war, by using the frigates as convoys and arming private vessels of which the owners & mariners will often be British subjects under American colours—or to try some defensive regulation of a commercial nature. The first will not be done, because the people are not yet confided in to tolerate it. The last will not be done because it will be difficult to frame such a regulation as will not injure Britain as well as ourselves more than France. The second expedient I conclude therefore will be persisted in; and as there is likely to be a majority ready to back the hostility of the Executive; the best that can be done by the Republicans, will be to leave the responsibility on the real authors of whatever evils may ensue. I am not surprised at the extremity to which the dispute at the Natchez is pushed. I never had a doubt that in proportion as war with France is contemplated, a war with Spain will be provoked by the present administration. The former would not be relished even by the New England privaters, without the prospect of plunder presented by the latter, A war with Spain would also be a most convenient grave for the misdemeanours of Liston and his partizans.

I returned from Albemarle on Monday last, where I consulted with your Nailor on the subject of the Sprigs & lathing nails not included in the parcels prepared for me. I found that the cutting machine has never been reestablished, & I did not request that this slight kind of nails should be made in the common way. If you mean however that the machine shall be set up again, or it be a part of your plan to make such nails in the common way, there will be time eno' for either before I shall want them. I was at Mr. Randolphs & found all well there, as you will doubtless learn to be the case from himself. I was astonished to find that even Monroe himself had not yet seen a printed copy of his publication. In the mean time Scipio's mad representations & sophistries are filling the public mind with all the poison which P.s malice can distil into it. Where the book is not seen first, & an antidote does not quickly follow from the same center which gives circulation to the poison, innocence & truth can not have fair play. Present my friendly respects to Mr Giles who I hear has gone on to Phia. also to Mr Tazewell & Mr. Dawson. I have been sorry to hear of the ill health of the former. As I perceive by the votes in the Senate that he has resumed his seat, I hope he is well again.

Yrs. always & affecy.

RC (DLC: Madison Papers); addressed: "Thomas Jefferson Philadelphia," with "*private*" appearing above address; endorsed by TJ as received 20 Feb. 1798 and so recorded in SJL.

P.S MALICE: Madison believed Timothy Pickering was Scipio. In fact it was Uriah Tracy; see note to TJ to Madison, 3 Jan. 1798.

[1] MS: "good."

From James Monroe

DEAR SIR   Albemarle Feby 12. 1798.

Mr. Fauchetts pamphlet was the last communication from you. Mine by Mr. Giles you doubtless have before this. We are here so barren of incident that we have nothing worthy yr. notice. We look to the admn. for the coloring we are to have of European or rather our affrs. with France, and we know enough of the admn. to know that it will be black or white according to circumstances. If for example the admn. thinks things ready for an immediate expln., a ground work for it will be laid before Congress. And if it thinks it better to practise upon the two countries, by keeping our agents in Paris another year, it will do so. In short I think it will take precisely that course wh. will be best calculated to promote a rupture with France & overthrow our own govt.—I have serious doubts whether it were not better the admn. shod. carry the question of arming &ca. whether it were not better it shod. carry all its measures & completely open its views to the publick—I mean the measures it avows. Till they are all carried, the trouble & losses of the publick are ascribed to those who defeat them, & perhaps eventually half the blame be laid to this account. But if the admn. carried its measures this wod. not be the case. One effect which permission to arm wod. produce—I think wod. be this, the mass of *real* American merchants wod. conclude war was declared, & retire their ships. The British merchants (called american) & some bold adventurers of our own, hoping to profit by plunder especially of the Spaniards, wod. fit out large vessels, called merchant vessels, but wh. wod. in truth be privateers. Thus we shod. be at work at once, with both France & Spn., & the crisis be completely brot. on, whose object on one side wod. be, to connect us with Engld., assimilate our govt. to hers, & seperate the western country from the Union, objects which that side has long pursued with great system. I only state the idea of the admn. carrying its measures, being the best way to complete its over throw & save us from infinite trouble, as an hypothesis, in favor of which my opinion is not made up. Admitting however it wod. promote the cause of republican govt., yet the majority ought to be very small, & the consequences of the measures fully and ably anticipated in debate by the minority. If it is deemed best to put off the crisis by negotiating another campaign, I conclude the question abt. arming will be put off till the next session, & Congress adjourn.

Nothing or very little is done to yr. house since you left it—& I suppose will not till you return. My cabbins are yet to be seen only on paper. & in the history of the neighbourhood nothing new has occurred. I am making a great effort for tobo., having already cleared ground enough to make 20.000. at least.

As yet not more than 3. copies of my book have reached Virga. that I know of. One at Richmond only when I was there. In consequence whereof it is industriously circulated that the work is suppressed, with a train of inferences to wh. that idea leads. It was unfortunate Mr. B. did not send a few trunks full to Richmond while the assembly was sitting. I stipulated with him that he shod. send it all over the continent as soon as published—and sell it cheap—I made no other stipulation—of the price I say nothing for I wished him if possible, without injury to the circulation, to make something by it. But greatly has he erred in not pushing the circulation. I earnestly hope he will do it now without delay. He ought to send 6. or 800. into this State at least.

I requested yr. opinion upon a private subject in my letter by Mr. Giles wh. I hope will not escape you.

RC (DLC); endorsed by TJ as received 22 Feb. 1798 and so recorded in SJL.

TJ's LAST COMMUNICATION with Monroe by letter was dated 27 Dec. 1797. William Branch GILES carried Monroe's letter of 27 Jan. 1798 to TJ.

To John Wise

SIR,   [Phila]delphia Feby 12th. 1798

I have duly recieved yours of the 28 Ult. mentioning that it had been communicated to you that in a Conversation in Francis's hotel (where I lodge) I had Spoken of you as of tory politics: & you make enquiry as to the fact, & the Idea intended to be Conveyed:[1] I Shall answer you with frankness. It is now well understood that two political sects have arisen within the US. the one believeing that the Executive is the branch of our Government which the most needs support: the other that, like the analogous branch in the English government, it is already too strong for the republican parts of the Constitution, and therefore, in equivocal cases, they incline to the Legislative powers. the former of these are called Federalists, sometimes Aristocrats or monocrats and Sometimes tories, after the corresponding sect in the English government, of exactly the same definition: the latter are Stiled Republicans, Whigs, Jacobins, Anarchists, Disorganisers &c. these terms are in familiar use with most persons and which of those of the first Class I used on the occation alluded to I do not particularly remember. they are all well understood to designate persons who are for Strengthening the Executive rather than the Legislative branches of the government. but probably I used the last of those terms, & for these reasons, both parties claim to be Federalists and Republicans, & I believe with truth, as to the great Mass of them: these appellations therefore designate neither exclusively: and all the others are Slanders, except those of Whig & tory, which alone charactarise the Distinguishing principles of the two sects as I have before explained them, as they have been known and named in England for more than a Century, and as they are growing into daily use here with those whose respect for the right of private Judgment in others, as well as themselves does not permit them to use the other terms which either imply against themselves, or Charge others, Injuriously.

I remark with real Sensibility the Sentiments of esteem you are pleased to express for my Character, and do not Suffer myself to believe they will be lessened by any Difference which may happen to exist in our political opinions, if any there be. the most upright and conscientious Characters are on both Sides of the question; & as to myself, I Can say with truth that political tenets have never taken away my esteem for a moral and good man. on this head I have never uttered a word, nor entertained a thought to your prejudice: & even as to politics, I Could say nothing of my own Knowledge,[2] as you must be sensible, but only from the information of Others, having understood on Different Occasions, that on public questions you have generally Concurred with those

[98]

who were on the side of Executive powers. if in this I have been misinformed I shall with pleasure correct the error: if otherwise, your Conviction of the solidity of your opinions will render it Satisfactory to you that they have not been mistaken. this is the Sentiment which each side entertains of it's own opinions, and neither thinks them the Subject of imputation.

I am really Sorry that any one should have found gratification in paining you or myself by such Communication, the Circumstance took place in a familiar conversation with gentlemen who, with myself mess together every day at our lodgings, and was therefore the less guarded. & I do not recollect that there was a person present but of our ordinary Society. the occasion too was as clear of exception being used in proof how little of party Spirit there is in Virginia, & how little it influences public proceedings there: & so transient withal, that I dare say it has not been since thought of nor repeated but to[3] yourself: with what view is not for me to Consider.

I have thought I owed to your private and public character this Candid declaration and[4] I have no fear you will mistake the Motives which lead to it.

I have the honour to be with great respect Sir Your most Obt. Servt.

THO. JEFFERSON

Tr (MHi: Timothy Pickering Papers); in an unidentified hand; torn at top of sheet; at foot of text: "The Honble. John Wise"; endorsed by Pickering: "T. Jefferson's letter to Mr. Wise   Tory" and "Jefferson to Wise." Tr (MWA); entirely in Dwight Foster's hand; at head of text: "Copy of a Letter from *Thomas Jefferson* to the Honble. Mr. Wise—Speaker of the House of Delegates in Virginia"; at foot of text: "NB. The above is confidentially communicated & not to be printed—D.F. See Bache's Paper March 21. 1798 Letter Feb. 15. 1798. Also — — April 25. 1798 another —." Tr (photostat in DLC: James McHenry Papers); in an unidentified hand; at foot of text: "Vide Bache's paper of March 21: & April 25. 1798. two letters purporting to be written from a Citizen of Pennsylvania, the one bearing date Feby. 15, being 3 days after the present letter, & the other April 10: 1798.—Whether they proceeded from the same hand with the present, or whether at least they must not have been written in concert with the author of the present, let candour decide—And if either should be the case, what are we to think of the views of a man, standing in his honorable & influential station, in the present state of our affairs?— 'You ought to know that the diplomatic skill of France & the means she possesses in your Country, are sufficient to enable her, *with the French Party in America*, to throw &c. And you may assure yourselves *this will be done*.'—What further proof is necessary?," the embedded quotation being extracted from comments of Pierre Bellamy ("Y") to the American envoys as recorded in John Marshall's journal and contained in a dispatch from Charles Cotesworth Pinckney, Marshall, and Elbridge Gerry to Pickering on 8 Nov. 1797, which Pickering transmitted to Congress on 3 Apr. 1798 (Marshall, *Papers*, 3:180, 276, 285; ASP, *Foreign Relations*, 2:157, 164); endorsed: "Copy of a Letter to J. Wise Esquire"; also endorsed, possibly by McHenry: "*Copy of Mr. Jefferson's letter* to Mr J Wise—explanatory of the use he made of the epethet tory to Mr Wise recd. from. Mr Evans," possibly referring to Federalist Congressman Thomas Evans of Accomac County, Virginia. Tr (PHi: Fisher Family Papers); in an unidentified hand; endorsed in part: "Curiosity, political." Tr (PHi: Spackman Papers); probably a 19th-century copy; with same distinctive variation as Tr in PHi: Fisher Family Papers. Printed in AHR, 3 (1897-98), 488-9 (from Tr in PHi: Spackman Papers); in VMHB, 12 (1905), 257-9 (from McHenry Tr); and in University of Virginia, *Alumni Bulletin*, 3d ser., 12 (1919), 195-7 (also from McHenry Tr). Although no version of this letter in TJ's hand has been located, TJ did record a missive to Wise under this date in SJL.

In the application of the label TORY from English usage to the Federalists, the frank acknowledgment that TWO POLITICAL SECTS HAVE ARISEN WITHIN THE US, and the presumed identification of each party with a different BRANCH OF OUR GOVERNMENT, the letter printed above shares certain characteristics with the two communications in Benjamin Franklin Bache's *Aurora* that Federalists—to judge from the notations on Foster's and McHenry's copies of this letter—thought came from TJ's pen or were written with his collusion. However, the length and style of the letters in the *Aurora*, their confrontational tone, and their appearance at a time when, in the aftermath of the

publication of his controversial letter of 24 Apr. 1796 to Philip Mazzei, TJ was particularly averse to the publication of his opinions, would all seem to contradict the idea that he wrote the two *Aurora* letters. Moreover, one of the letters refers to $202.50 received for 81 subscriptions to the *Aurora*, a transaction that does not appear to have been associated with TJ. Both letters were unsigned but attributed to "a citizen of Pennsylvania." The first, to the writer's "friend in Baltimore," was dated 15 Feb. 1798 and appeared in the *Aurora* on 21 Mch. 1798, when James Thomson Callender acted as editor in Bache's absence (Durey, *Callender*, 106-7). The second, addressed on 10 Apr. 1798 to a "Friend in *Delaware*," appeared on 25 Apr. 1798.

[1] In McHenry Tr and Trs in MWA and PHi: Spackman Papers the preceding five words are enclosed in quotation marks.
[2] Preceding four words lacking in McHenry Tr.
[3] Tr in PHi: Fisher Family Papers and Tr in PHi: Spackman Papers: "repeated to any other person than."
[4] In Tr in MWA Foster interlined "2" and "1" above "declaration" and "and," respectively.

To John Gibson

DEAR GENERAL   Philadelphia Feb. 13. 98.

Your favor of the 2d. inst. is recieved. should our session be continued to a greater length than I expect, it would be a circumstance of great pleasure to me to see you here. but I do not think we can continue here much longer than the present month as there is really nothing to do but to recieve information from our envoys at Paris. if that bear a peaceable aspect, as I hope it will we ought not to remain here a week longer for any thing we have to do. I must therefore trouble you to give me by way of letter the information respecting Cresap & his party and the murder of Logan's family. it seems Logan has mistaken the title of Cresap if not the person. I wish to get a minute history of the whole transaction in order to correct or confirm that which has been before given.—we are very anxious here to get some information from our envoys in order to know on what ground we are to stand with our former allies. they appear to have established peace with all their continental neighbors, and to be collecting all their energies to invade England. their objects seem to be to republicanize her government, and to bring her power on the ocean within more reasonable and safe limits.—I shall with great pleasure make myself useful to you here, should any thing turn up in which I can be so. I shall thereby be discharging a duty of conscience & at the same time of friendship. I am with sentiments of great esteem Dear General

Your most obedt. servt   TH: JEFFERSON

PrC (DLC); at foot of text: "Gen[l.] Gibson"; mistakenly recorded in SJL as a letter to George Gibson.

From Mann Page

DEAR SIR   Mann'sfield Feby. 13th. 1798

Since I wrote to you I have been so fortunate as to obtain such Proofs of the general Authenticity of your Publication in the Notes on Virginia, as will fully justify what you have said respecting Cresop's Murder, & Logan's Speech, & must entirely confute Mr. Martins impudent unfounded Assertions. I enclose them for your Satisfaction. You will no doubt wish to know who this Mr. Anderson is, whose Narrative I have taken from his own Lips, which I read to him, & which he affirmed to be substantially true.

He has for *several*[1] Years past been settled in Fredsburg in the Mercantile Line. I have known him in prosperous & adverse Situations. He has always shewn the greatest Degree of Equanimity. His Honesty & Veracity are unimpeachable. These things can be attested by all the respectable Part of the Town & Neighbourhood.

If what I now send you should not be satisfactory, return Anderson's Narrative. He will certify it, & I will obtain an ample Certificate of his Character.

Colo. Lewis Willis has favoured me with the enclosed Copy of Logan's Speech for your Use. He says it was given to him by the late Genl. Mercer twenty odd Years ago.

Should I be able to obtain any farther Information on the Subject I will communicate it to you. Accept the best Respects of all at Mann'sfield, & the sincerest Assurances of Regard from

Yr. Friend &c   MANN PAGE

RC (DLC); endorsed by TJ as received on 20 Feb. 1798 and so recorded in SJL.

[1] Above this word Page interlined "*many*" without canceling either word.

I
Statement of John Anderson

Mr. John Anderson a merchant in Fredsburg says that in the Year 1774, being a Trader in the Indian Country, he was at Pittsburg, to which place he had a Cargo brought up the River in a Boat navigated by a Delaware & Shawnese [1] Indian & a white Man. That on their Return down the River with a Cargo belonging to Messrs Butler [2] *Colo. [3] Michael Cresop with a Party fired on the Boat & killed the two Indians. [4] After which two Men of the Name of Gatewood & others of the Name of Tumblestone, who lived on the opposite Side of the River from the Indians, with whom they were on the most friendly Terms, invited a Party of them to come over & drink with them, & that when the Indians were drunk they murdered them to the Number of six, among whom was Logan's mother.√ That five other [5] Indians uneasy at the Absence of their Friends, came over the River to enquire after them, when they were fired upon, & two were killed & the others wounded. This was the Origin of the War.

As to Logan's Speech, he says, that Colo. John Gibson, (who he believes is now living at Pittsburg,) who was at that Time Interpreter to the Indians, informed him that he delivered the Speech to Lord Dunmore. He farther says, that when Gibson shewed him Anderson the Speech he observed that he suspected that he had made it for Logan, but he assured him that he had not, & that tho' he had translated it literally, he could by no Means come up to the Force of Expression in the Original.

---

* Logan in the Original of his Speech does not give Cresop the Title of Colo.

√ There was another Indian Squaw killed, perhaps some Relation of Logan; for farther particulars apply to Colo. John Gibson.

MS (DLC: TJ Papers, 106:18201); undated; entirely in Mann Page's hand. Tr (same, 106:18199); entirely in TJ's hand; with variations, not recorded, in punctuation, capitalization, abbreviations, and symbol used to key author's second footnote; endorsed by TJ: "Logan's speech Anderson John." Printed in *An Appendix to the Notes on Virginia Relative to the Murder of Logan's Family* (Philadelphia, 1800; see Sowerby, No. 3225); consists of first paragraph only; lacks author's footnotes; with minor variations of punctuation and capitalization not recorded, and significant variations recorded in notes below; with three numbers inserted in text in brackets, this being TJ's system for keying, in the *Appendix*, specific instances of violence in 1774; identified at head of text as Anderson's "Certificate," quoting Page's comments about Anderson from the letter of 13 Feb. 1798 above; adds at foot of text: "I certify the above to be true to the best of my recollection. JOHN ANDERSON," with attestation by David Blair dated 30 June 1798 (*Notes*, ed. Peden, 231, 237-8; see TJ to Page, 6 Mch. 1798).

It is likely that the name Anderson recalled as GATEWOOD was actually Greathouse. A note that TJ keyed to the name TUMBLESTONE in the *Appendix to the Notes on Virginia* calls it "the proper pronunciation of Tomlinson, which was the real name" (*Notes*, ed. Peden, 238, 301n).

[1] Preceding word and ampersand omitted in *Appendix*.

[2] Preceding seven words interlined.

[3] Abbreviation lacking in *Appendix*.

[4] *Appendix*: "Michael Cresap fired on the boat, and killed the Indian."

[5] Preceding two words interlined in place of "the."

II
Hugh Mercer's Copy of Logan's Speech

The Speech of Logan a Shawanees Cheif to Ld. Dunmore

I appeal to any white man to say if ever he[1] enter.d Logans Cabin hungrey and I gave him not Meat if ever he came Cold, or naked and I gave him not cloths, during the course of the last long & bloody War, Logan remained Idle in his Tent[2] an advocate for peace nay such was my love for the Whites that those of my own Country pointed at me as they passed by & said Logan is the friend of white Men, I had even thoughts of living with You but for the Injustice of one Man, Colo. Cressap, the last spring in cold blood & unprovock.d cut of all the relations of Logan not sparing even my Women & Children. There runs not a drop of the[3] blood of Logan in the Veins of any human creature, This call.d on me for revenge, I have saught it, I have kill.d many. I have fully gluted my Vengeance for my Country, I rejoice at the beams of peace. but do not harbour a thought that mine is the Joy of fear. Logan never felt fear he will not turn his heel[4] to save his life. who is there left to mourn for Logan. not one

MS (DLC: TJ Papers, 1:131); undated; in an unidentified hand; endorsed in same hand: "Logans Spe[ech]"; endorsed by TJ: "copy of Logan's speech given by the late Genl. Mercer upwards of 20. years ago (from the date of Feb. 98) to Lewis Willis, who delivered it to Mann Page to be forwarded to Th:J. See M. Page's letter Feb. 13. 98."

TJ gave this version of Logan's lamentation a place in the *Appendix to the Notes on Virginia*, but only by way of a heading that traced the document's provenance, TJ omitting the text of the address as "agreeing verbatim with that in the Notes on Virginia." There are a few variations in wording between the speech in TJ's *Notes* and the document above (*Notes*, ed. Peden, 63, 245).

LOGAN A SHAWANEES CHEIF: although the Shawnees were prominent in Dunmore's War, Logan was a Mingo; see note to TJ to John Gibson, 31 May 1797.

[1] The word "came" is canceled here.
[2] Word interlined in place of "Cabbin."
[3] Word interlined in place of an illegible cancellation.
[4] Word interlined in place of "head."

To George Jefferson

DEAR SIR   Philadelphia Feb. 14. 98.

Yours of Jan. 28th. is duly recieved. in mine of Jan. 14. I mentioned that Colo. Thos. Bell would be authorized to draw on you for 165.D. this was intended to answer two notes I had given Feb. 12. 1797. the one to Lucy Wood senr. for £33. the other to Lucy Wood junr. for £16.10 for the hire of negroes. I did not know into what hands these notes had got and desired Colo. Bell to seek them out & pay them. the last post brings me a letter from mr. Jourdan Harris informing me he has one of them, but does not say which. be so good therefore as to pay it on his presenting it legally assigned, and to take it in. this will lessen so much Colo. Bell's draught on you if he should find out the other. so long ago as Nov. 18. Joseph Roberts shipped from hence for me 2. open stoves & [. . .] 7. bundles of hoop iron. they were probably addressed to mr Johnston: but I have never heard whether they were recieved & have been forwarded. will you be so good as to enquire? the schooner John Brown took from hence the package described in the within receipt of Saml. De[sear] for Capt Stratton. I believe she had also on board an anvil, vice, & beak iron formerly mentioned. I think she was one of the vessels which got out at a short opening of the river which took place a fortnight ago. I hope she is arrived safe. all these articles are to be forwarded by the Milton boats. I must also get the favor of you to get mr Hay to bottle two casks (of 30 galls each) of his best beer for me, to have it packed in crates or barrels, & to pay him for it and forward them to Milton to the care of Fleming & Mc.lenahan. another office I have to impose on you which will be troublesome. Sr. John Sinclair President of the Board of agriculture in London, has desired me to send them some of our May wheat. I must get the favour of you to seek out some which is genuine & fine; as much as will fill two light flour barrels will suffice. the difficulty is to prevent it's heating, a small degree of which you know destroys it's vegetating power. let the cooper therefore make so many heads or round [boards] for the casks that after putting in a layer of wheat of 3. inches thick a head may be dropped in loose, then another layer of 3. Inches & another head, & so on till it be full. the layers will thus be so thin as not to contract much heat and what they do contract will not be communicated through the board. if to this could be added through the favor of the captain's to take the [casks?] into the cabbin, it would be [secure?]. the [casks] must be addressed to Sr. John Sinclair, President of the board of Agriculture, Whitehall, London, and be sent by two different vessels bound to London. I have sold my [flour] this year at a price which is to be fixed by the highest price which shall be given at Richmond or Manchester from Nov. 1[0] (the date of the sale) to the last of March I believe, for I [cite] by memory, and am not entirely certain but it [run] to the last of April. I will ask the favor of you to keep an eye on the sales at those places, and to preserve for me proofs of the highest.—one other little commission for you & I am done. I own a lot of land in Richmond on the river, not far from Mayo's bridge. mr Buchanan knows it, and was so kind as to undertake to pay whatever taxes were due on it, which were trifling if any. will you be so good as to enquire of him what he paid, to reimburse him, and hereafter to take it under your charge. you can also suggest to me whether it could without expence be put under some kind of occupation, to preserve the bounds and titles. I am with great esteem Dear Sir

Your friend & servt   TH: JEFFERSON

PrC (MHi); badly blurred; endorsed in ink by TJ.

Letters from TJ to LUCY WOOD SENR. of 17 Dec. 1796 and 21 July 1797, recorded in SJL, have not been found. Also missing is a letter from her to TJ of 11 Dec., recorded in SJL as received 12 Dec. 1796. A letter from TJ to LUCY WOOD JUNR. of 18 Nov. 1797 and her response of 20 Nov., recorded in SJL as received 26 Nov. 1797, have not been found.

SJL records a LETTER FROM Jordan HARRIS of 5 Feb. 1798, received by TJ eight days later, which has not been found. A letter recorded in SJL from TJ to Harris of 14 Feb. 1798 is also missing.

On 19 Jan. 1798 TJ ordered John Barnes to pay JOSEPH ROBERTS $128.85, the balance of payment for three tons of iron rod shipped from Philadelphia on 18 Oct. 1797 and received at Monticello early in December, and on 19 Feb. 1798 TJ wrote another draft on Barnes to pay Roberts $73.40, $36 of which was for two stoves that TJ had ordered on Reuben Lindsay's behalf (MB, 2:968, 978, 979). TJ also wrote a draft on 23 Jan. 1798 ordering Barnes to pay $100 to Robert Aitken, recorded in MB as a payment on account for the MILTON firm of FLEMING & McClenahan (drafts all in MHi, written and signed by TJ, endorsed by Barnes).

DATE OF THE SALE: TJ sold his crop of wheat to Fleming & McClenahan on 10 Nov. 1797 (MB, 2:973).

From Luther Martin

Baltimore, Feb. 14*th*, 1798.

In the conclusion of my last letter you have seen the anxiety which the western inhabitants expressed for the aid of Mr. Cresap, and their hopes that he would not yield to his resentment so far as to deny them that aid.

Though no man, perhaps, felt more sensibly than Mr. Cresap an indignity offered to him, yet was he not of a disposition to sacrifice the innocent for the guilty, or the happiness of that infant country to his injured feelings; the dying groans of its butchered inhabitants; the flames ascending from their dwellings through the dark horrors of the night could not afford music to his ears, or pleasure to his eyes; on the contrary they added the most poignant anguish to a heart already oppressed with chagrin.

But to what purpose should he again have embodied a company, and again have crossed the mountains, when he could only count upon useless expence to himself, fatigue and loss of time to his soldiers; a fresh insult, and no benefit to his country?

Fortunately however, for those western settlements, the earl of Dunmore better appreciated his merits; and notwithstanding Mr. Cresap was a citizen of Maryland, on the tenth day of June in the year 1774, a commission was made out for him at Williamsburgh, and sent him as speedily as the distance would permit; by which he was appointed a captain in the service of the colony of Virginia; authorized to raise a company to act against the Indians, and for that purpose to join major August M'Donald, to whom was given the command of the expedition.

By this conduct of lord Dunmore, who soon after made him a friendly visit, his wounded feelings were not only soothed, but he found himself invested with an authority, that could no longer be questioned. He immediately repaired to the defence of those settlements, and at the appearance of their favorite hero, joy beamed on every countenance, while confidence animated with every heart; the inhabitants hailed him as their expected deliverer, and thronged in such number to his standard, that although several captains, previously appointed, had already raised their companies among them, he scarcely had arrived at Redstone when not only his own, but the companies of his nephew Michael Cresap and captain H. L. who were with him, were compleated; and so far were these people from being persons of no consequence or the refuge of society, that on the contrary the *privates* of his company were in general among the worthiest citizens of his own neighbourhood; of the mountains, and of the settlements on the other side of these mountains, many of whom have since filled respectable appointments in the civil and military departments of our governments and discharged the duties of those appointments with honor and fidelity.

Mr. Cresap served that summer and the succeeding autum in the two expeditions which took place, the first under major M'Donald against the Muskingum, the other under lord Dunmore to the great Kanhawa; and to his exertions and the confidence the inhabitants reposed in him was in a great degree owing to the facility with which the army was furnished with provisions and other necessaries during those expeditions; the last of which ended on the 26th day of November in the aforegoing year; a treaty having in the intermediate time been held at Chiliothi, on the Scioto, which terminated in a peace with the Indian nations.

Upon that event taking place Mr. Cresap returned to his family, and during the succeeding winter he devoted himself to every necessary preparation for resuming his favorite undertaking, with which the Indian hostilities of the preceding year had so totally interfered.

George Rogers Clarke, the present general Clarke of Kentucky, who during the American revolution, so nobly distinguished himself to the westward, was at that time a young man of a bold and enterprizing disposition, but destitute of fortune, and almost as destitute of friends. Mr. Cresap had served with him under lord Dunmore; an Intimacy and attachment had taken place between them. Him Mr. Cresap associated with himself in his expedition to the Tenesee, and as early as possible, in the spring of 1775, they proceeded together to that place, accompanied by a number of men engaged by Mr. Cresap for that purpose, and furnished with every necessary for exploring, and making settlements in the wilderness.

After their arrival, Mr. Cresap continued with them until he had sufficiently examined the country, and fixed on the part which he thought the most eligible for the intended settlements; when finding his constitution much shattered, and his health greatly impaired, by the hardships and fatigues to which he had been exposed during the *antecedent* year, and his *then* expedition, he left the improvements to be made,—the persons employed thereon, and the necessaries provided for that purpose, under the care and superintendance of his friend Clarke, and returned with the intention, for a time, of enjoying repose and seeking for health in the bosom of his family.

During his absence, the disputes which were before subsisting between Great Britain and her colonies had assumed a new aspect;—an appeal had been made to arms;—the battle of Lexington had been fought; and the siege of Boston had been commenced. The Congress of 1775 on the 14th day of June, seven days before you first took your seat in it, had voted six rifle companies, two of them from Maryland, to be raised to march and join the American army at Boston. And during his absence, to that department authorised to appoint officers for the Maryland companies, Col. Cresap had pledged himself that his son should accept the command of one of those companies.

When Mr. Cresap returned and was informed of these events, a respect for his father's engagement and a love for his country superseded every other consideration—not withstanding his ill state of health he hesitated not a moment;—he tore himself from the tender embraces of a beloved wife, and the endearing caresses of four lovely children, the oldest of whom, the late Mrs. M. was then but eight years of age. It was their last adieu! Their longing eyes were no more to be blest with the sight of an affectionate husband, a tender and indulgent father! He marched with his company to the siege of Boston;—he lived not to return.

To the pious care of the generous citizens of New-York was entrusted his body, all of him that was mortal.—His generous spirit, that portion of ethereal flame which during their union warmed and animated it here, ascended to the bosom of its Creator, where the shafts of malevolence cannot assail it; nor the envenomed calumnies of philosophers disturb its repose.

The following is an account of his death, taken from a New-York paper, published in October 1775:—"Yesterday died at at his lodgings in this city, Michael Cresap, Esq. of the colony of Virginia†, *first captain* in the corps of riflemen, a gentleman of great reputation as a soldier, and

† † This was a mistake, both Col. Cresap and his son lived on the Maryland side of the North branch of the Potomack, although both lived within a few hundred yards of Virginia.

highly esteemed as a citizen. His remains will be interred to-morrow evening with the honours of war, attended by all the military of this city."

And in a subsequent paper, his funeral was thus announced, "On the 12th instant arrived here on his return from the Provincial camp at Cambridge, and on the 18th instant departed this life of a fever, in the twenty-eighth year of his age, Michael Cresap, Esq. youngest son of Col. Thomas Cresap, of Potowmack in Virginia†; he was captain of a rifle company now in the continental army before Boston.—He served as a captain under the command of Lord Dunmore, in the late expedition against the Indians; in which he eminently distinguished himself by his prudence, firmness and intrepidity as a brave officer. And in the present contest between the parent state and the colonies, gave proofs of his attachment to the rights and liberties of his country. He has left a widow and four children to deplore the loss of a husband and a father; and by his death, his country is deprived of a worthy and esteemed citizen. His remains were interred the day following in Trinity Church Yard with military honours, attended by a vast concourse of people!"

How sincerely he was esteemed, and how dearly he was beloved, while living, by the inhabitants of the western parts of Maryland, and of the western side of the Alleghany mountains, and how bitterly they lamented his death, thousands yet living can testify.

As to the inhabitants of the western side of those mountains, it may with truth be said he was *more* than beloved and esteemed; he was by many of them even idolized;—he was considered almost as their tutelar deity:—as the being to whom next to their God they looked up in the hour of danger and distress for relief and protection.

And is *this* the man to whom you alluded in your notes upon Virginia?—Is *this* the man, whom of all others you selected to declare him an infamous murderer! The wanton, the cruel, the cowardly assassin of every individual in whose vein the blood of Logan flowed, not even excepting his women and children!

What would my noble minded, generous spirited father-in-law have felt, when just closing this sublunary scene, could he have supposed it possible that one of his compatriots distinguishedly enagaged in the cabinet in the same cause, in which he had been employed in the field, would almost before his ashes were cold have attempted to eternize his memory *only* by devoting it to infamy!—That in order to raise a monument to some worthless insignificant savage, you should unite the powers of your eloquence with the charms of your diction to blast a name, the doing justice to which might have given you fame as an historian! That *you* should have exerted all those talents you possess for the purpose of transmitting him to every part of the globe where civilization and science might shed their enlightening beams, and to remotest ages, as the proper object of their horror and execration!

Would to heaven he had lived—but unless his life would have prevented the execrable page I retract the wish.

I am not ashamed to avow, on the contrary I make it my boast, as a proof of my understanding‡, that I believe in a religion the pure precepts of which, in spite of the artful casuistry of false honour, or the powerful pleadings of the passions, prohibit every attempt, in whatever manner may be made on the life of a fellow creature, for reparation satisfaction of injuries committed:—I rejoice that he did not essay the trial, nor incur the guilt.

Yet shall not the injury you have done to his memory pass unavenged.—For offences such as your's there is a punishment the inflicting of which, reason, religion, and the good order of society, equally not only permit but applaud;—that punishment I am inflicting, and will continue to inflict, until its measure be full.

And now, Sir, on what transaction in the short life of Mr. Cresap will you fix to establish his infamy?—Like his father, from the time he entered upon life, he was actively and extensively engaged in pursuits, the success of which depended upon a good understanding and friendly intercourse with the Indians:—He had embarked in those pursuits a large portion of his fortune.—No *one* individual I believe had a greater stake than himself on the western side of the Alleghany mountains, or was more interested in the welfare and prosperity of those settlements, was he then likely to do any act which might expose them to the ravages of a relentless foe? At the moment the Indian hostilities commenced, he was on a journey to extend his researches into the wilderness, and to make new settlements therein, for which purpose he had incurred a heavy expence, all which was lost to him by reason of those hostilities.

The inhabitants of that country, who best knew him, and were most intimately acquainted with all his conduct, never charged him with a single act, the tendency of which was to excite the Indians to make war upon them; and when in their danger they so fervently sought his assistance and protection, they never insinuated that he had been in any degree the cause of their being threatened with those calamities which they so greatly apprehended; on the contrary they expressed the deepest regret

‡ Many persons I am well satisfied, have possessed a disbelief of revalation from motives of vanity, having thereby to pass for men of soperior genius and abilities to the common class of mankind,—I differ from them so widely, that I always consider this *want* of *belief* one of the strongest proofs of the *want* of *information* or the *want* of *understanding*. For these sentiments the philosophers of the present age, have my free permission to bestow upon me as much of their pity or contempt as they please.

that those measures had not been adopted, which he had recommended. I must now for a short time dismiss you, and am as before, With *due* respect,

your very humble servant. LUTHER MARTIN

Printed in *Porcupine's Gazette*, 20 Feb. 1798; at head of text: "Mr. Martin's 7th Letter to the Philosopher Jefferson" and "To the Honorable Thomas Jefferson, Esquire, Vice President of the United States."

From Horatio Gates

DEAR SIR   New York 15th. Febry: 1798.

I take the Liberty to Inclose you a Letter For my Highly esteemed Friend General Kuscuiusko, perhaps you may like to call upon him with it; Men, who so Sincerely seek the Happyness of Man, must be Intimate with each Other. I like, (so far as it respects Us;) what we hear, Via Norfolk from Europe. After what we have been *Guilty* of, we cannot expect, immediately, any thing better than to be amused by the Government of France—a change of Men, & a change of Measures, may work better things for Us—War, of all Evils, is the worst that could befall Us: & to cut the Throats of our Friends, for the Amusement of our Enemies, is certainly the most Diabolical of all War. In regard to Commerce, we are certainly Milking the Cow; and if some Spoon fulls falls out of the Pail, we must charge it to Profit, & Loss; I am rejoiced my Friend Monroe has been so Generously Distinguish'd by his Countrymen at Richmond. The Hour will come, when his book will be Noticed as an Excelling Patern of Diplomatic Integrity, & Abillity;—nay, for Once—, Our Republic be Gratefull, to a good, and Faithfull, Servant. You see I write to you, as a Confidential good Friend; & not as V.P. of The US! I hope to see you at Rose Hill, before you return to Virginia as I wish to Introduce you to my Cousin Mr: John Garnet, a Man of much Science who is come to riside in America; he has brought his Family, and a handsome Independence with Him; but what may in Future prove much better to This Country he has brought his Talents with Him. I wrote you a Letter of Introduction, when he went in November to Philadelphia; but he brought it back, as you was not [then?] come to Congress. Mrs: Gates Joins me in respectfull Compliments, & our Sincere invitation to Rose Hill—with the Truest Attachment I am Your Faithfull and Obedient Servant   HORATIO GATES

RC (DLC); word obscured by tape; endorsed by TJ as received 16 Feb. 1798 and so recorded in SJL. Enclosure not found.

On 26 Jan. 1798, the day following the adjournment of the Virginia legislature, MONROE WAS DISTINGUISHED BY HIS COUN-

TRYMEN at a gathering at Eagle Tavern in RICHMOND, where he was toasted as "our late minister to France—May America honor him as the true friend of Liberty, which he has never failed to support" (Philadelphia *Aurora*, 8 Feb. 1798).

To James Madison

Philadelphia Feb. 15. 98.

I wrote you last on the 8th. we have still not a word from our envoys. this long silence (if they have been silent) proves things are not going on very roughly. if they have not been silent, it proves their information if made public would check the disposition to arm. I had flattered myself, from the progress of the public sentiment against arming, that the same progress had taken place in the legislature. but I am assured, by those who have better opportunities of forming a good judgment, that if the question against arming is carried at all, it will not be by more than a majority of two: & particularly that there will not be more than 4. votes against it from the 5. eastern states, or 5. votes at the utmost. you will have percieved that Dayton is gone over compleatly. he expects to be appointed Secretary of war in the room of Mc.Henry who it is said will retire. he has been told, as report goes, that they would not have confidence enough in him to appoint him. the desire of inspiring them with more seems the only way to account for the eclat which he chuses to give to his conversion. you will have seen the disgusting proceedings in the case of Lyon. if they would have accepted even of a commitment to the Serjeant it might have been had. but to get rid of his vote was the most material object. these proceedings must degrade the General government, and lead the people to lean more on their state governments, which have been sunk under the early popularity of the former. this day the question of the jury in cases of impeachment comes on. there is no doubt how it will go. the general division in the Senate is 22. and 10. and under the probable prospect of what they will for ever be, I see nothing in the mode of proceeding by impeachment, but the most formidable weapon for the purposes of a dominant faction that ever was contrived. it would be the most effectual one for getting rid of any man whom they consider as dangerous to their views, and I do not know that we could count on one third on an emergency. it depends then on the H. of Representatives, who are the impeachers: & there the majorities are of 1. 2. or 3 only & these sometimes one way & sometimes another: in a question of pure party they have the majority, & we do not know what circumstances may turn up to increase that majority temporarily if not permanently. I know of no solid purpose of punishment which the courts of law are not equal to, and history shews that in England, Impeachment has been an engine more of passion than justice.   a great ball is to be given here on the 22d. and in other great towns of the Union. this is at least very indelicate, & probably excites uneasy sensations in some. I see in it however this useful deduction, that the birthdays which have been kept have been, not those of the President, but of the General.—I inclose with the newspapers the two acts of parliament passed on the subject of our commerce which are interesting. the merchants here say that the effect of the countervailing tonnage on American vessels, will throw them completely out of employ as soon as there is peace. The Eastern members say nothing but among themselves. but it is said that it is working like gravel in their stomachs. our only comfort is that they have brought it on themselves. my respectful salutations to mrs Madison & to yourself friendship & Adieu.

RC (DLC: Madison Papers); addressed: "James Madison junr. near Orange Courthouse"; stamped, franked, and postmarked. PrC (DLC).

During the second session of the Fifth Congress, Jonathan DAYTON, Speaker of the House of Representatives, began to side with the high Federalists. On 5 Mch. 1798 the *Aurora* published a piece which insinuated that Dayton's political change was due to the fact that he expected to lose his seat in Congress and thus desired to please President Adams to increase his chances of being APPOINTED SECRETARY OF WAR (Richard A. Harrison, *Princetonians, 1776-1783: A Biographical Dictionary* [Princeton, 1981], 37).

Although the GREAT BALL in celebration of Washington's birthday had become an annual event, Adams had previously expressed dissatisfaction with festivities that he interpreted as promoting the veneration of a military hero, a practice that he associated with the downfall of the Roman republic. He declined the invitation to the 1798 event, calling it an insult to the office of the presidency. A number of Federalists fol-

lowed the president's lead, thereby bringing to public notice a fissure within the Federalist party. Scheduled to take place ON THE 22D, the ball, less than a week before the event, was postponed a day because it conflicted with the special election held in Philadelphia. TJ, as he customarily did, declined to attend the ball but on 2 Feb. paid five dollars for a subscription to the affair (TJ to Thomas Willing, 23 Feb. 1798; Page Smith, *John Adams*, 2 vols. [New York, 1962], 2:950-1; MB, 2:978; *Claypoole's American Daily Advertiser*, 12, 17 Feb. 1798; Philadelphia *Aurora*, 17 Feb. 1798).

I INCLOSE. . .TWO ACTS OF PARLIAMENT: *Message from the President of the United States, Accompanying Copies of Two Acts of the Parliament of Great-Britain, Passed on the 4th and 19th of July 1797, Relative to the Carrying into Execution the Treaty of Amity, Commerce and Navigation, Concluded between His Majesty and the United States of America; And regulating the Trade to be carried on with the British possessions in India, by the ships of Nations in amity with his Majesty* [Philadelphia, 1798]. See Evans, No. 34802. For a discussion of these acts, see TJ to Hugh Williamson, 11 Feb. 1798.

Notes on a Conversation with John Adams

Feb. 15. 98. I dined this day with mr Adams (the Presidt.) the company was large. after dinner I was sitting next to him, & our conversn was first on the enormous price of *labour,[1] house rent, & other things. we both concurred in ascribing it chiefly to the floods of bank paper now afloat, and in condemning those institns. we then got on the constitn & in the course of our conversn he said, that no republic could ever last which had not a Senate & a Senate deeply & strongly rooted, strong enough to bear up against all popular[2] storms & passions.[3] that he thought our Senate as well constituted as it could have been, being chosen by the legislatures, for if these could not support them he did not know what could do it. that perhaps it might have been as well for them to be chosen by the state at large, as that would ensure a choice of distinguished men, since none but such could be known to a whole people; that the only fault in our Senate was that it was not durable enough. that hitherto it had behaved very well, however he was afraid they would give way in the end. that as to trusting to a popular assembly for the preservn of our liberties it was the merest chimaera imaginable. they never had any rule of decision but their own will, that he would as lieve be again in the hands of our old committees of safety who made the law & executed it at the same time. that it had been observed by some writer (I forget whom he named) that anarchy did more mischief in one night than tyranny in an age, and that in Modern times we might say with truth that in France anarchy had done more harm in one night than all the despotism of their kings had ever done in 20. or 30. years.' the point in which he views our Senate, as the Colossus of the[4] constitn. serves as a key to the politics of the Senate, who are two thirds of them in his sentiments, and accounts for the bold line of conduct they pursue.

* he observed that 8. or 10. years ago he gave only 50. D. to a common labourer for his farm, finding him food & lodging. now he gives 150. D. and even 200. D. to one.

MS (DLC: TJ Papers, 102:17525); entirely in TJ's hand; on same sheet as Notes on a Conversation with Abraham Baldwin, 6 Feb. 1798.

[1] TJ here canceled "& goods."
[2] MS: "popuplar."
[3] Word interlined in place of "tempests."
[4] TJ here canceled "govt."

To Thomas Mann Randolph

I have to acknolege the receipt of yours of Jan. 28. & 30. & Feb. 3. that
of the 30th. came by Richardson. mine to you have been of Jan. 11. &
25. & to Martha Feb. 8. I imagine yours of Feb. 3. was sent when you
sent to Charlottesville for your letters and that you received by the return of your messenger mine of Jan. 25. and I hope too that of Jan. 11.
tho' it was then a fortnight in arrear. it was chiefly to recommend mr
Trist to your friendly counsel in his purchases &c. he set out about a
week ago, & I imagine will arrive at Charlottesville about 10. days
hence. the contents of my lre of Jan. 25. were important. therefore I
hope you got that, it imposed on you a commission about Bates; for I
begin to feel with great anxiety my houseless situation. I write to Davenport by this post to inform me what he has done & is doing. I expect
that according to promise he has kept a strong force sawing sheeting
plank, & getting & preparing shingles, & that with the first open
weather of the spring he would begin to cover the house, so that I may
find that compleat on my return, and begin immediately to floor. as he
was to get the sheeting & shingles at Pouncey's, if you can spare mr
Duke a day he might go and see what is done. I am not quite certain
however whether Davenport did not propose to get the shingles at some
other place. is Arnold come to Monticello, & at work? how does Watson
answer your purpose? if you could sometimes take the trouble to make
John & Davy come to you & bring their written instructions, & question them as to their progress, it would probably keep them to their
metal. it will immediately be time for John to be doing something in the
garden. on this head Martha can question him from my little Calendar
of which she has a copy. great George should be spurred in his attention
to the employment of the waggon & carts. he must look out for some
plough horses, as I know he will want some. I will get the favor of you
to consult with him and judge what his want will be in that line &
inform me of it. I had hoped to have got mules in Connecticut but find
it too difficult. what is the price of corn? is it to be had conveniently &
in plenty? I directed Page to provide what I owe you whenever wanting
but if he cannot get it more convenient, I desired him to furnish it out of
his own stock, which we can replace by purchase.—I have occasion here
for 2. copies of my blank vocabularies, which are each of them a single
sheet of paper. there are 2. or 3. quires either in a box on the floor of my
study on the right hand as you enter, or in the Walnut presses standing
on the top of the desk. I must ask the favor of you to inclose me a couple.
I am drawing largely you see on your time.

Not a word yet from our Envoys. the length of their silence is certainly a favorable symptom. Congress are still without any thing to do, till they hear from them. and if what they hear shall be peaceable they may separate at a week or fortnight's notice. I send you by post another volume of Callendar's. do you get Bache's and Adams's papers regularly? I inclose a letter for mr Duke, covering an order for money. my tender love to my dear Martha & the children, and affectionate salutations to yourself. Adieu.

RC (DLC); endorsed by Randolph. PrC (MHi); endorsed by TJ in ink on verso. Enclosure: see note below.

The letter from TJ to William DAVENPORT, which according to SJL was written on 14 Feb. 1798, has not been found. COPIES OF MY BLANK VOCABULARIES: see TJ to William Linn, 5 Feb. 1798. I SEND YOU BY POST: on 9 Feb. TJ purchased five copies of James T. Callender's *Sketches of the History of America*, which was shortly to be published by the Philadelphia firm of Snowden & McCorkle (MB, 2:979). See Sowerby, No. 3516.

The letter enclosed by TJ to Henry DUKE of 15 Feb. 1798, recorded in SJL, has not been found. The ORDER FOR MONEY was probably one of this date drawn on Thomas Bell for $100 in partial payment of what TJ owed Duke for bricklaying during 1797. TJ funded that order by one drawn on John Barnes, also on 15 Feb., to pay $100 to Samuel Harrison Smith, who was to credit the amount to Alexander Garrett of Charlottesville, who would in turn make it available to Bell (MS in ViU: Edgehill-Randolph Papers, written and signed by TJ, endorsed by Barnes, receipt by Smith on same sheet). See also MB, 2:958, 974, 979.

To John Wayles Eppes

TH.J. to J. W. EPPES   Philadelphia Feb. 18. 9[8]

I wrote you last on the 1st. inst. and three days ago recieved Maria's of the same date. we have intelligence which seems to be authentic that the Spaniards have delivered up the posts on the Missisipi. this is the more welcome, as the commencement of war in that quarter seemed more imminent than it is with France. we are certainly more indebted for avoiding it to the good sense & moderation of the Spanish government than to the conduct of our agents. that was such as to have excited a suspicion that was the [object?] desired. it might be thought that if war should take place with France, we might, by forcing Spain into it, [. . .] subject that our hostilities might reach. we have no news yet from our Parisian envoys; but this is one of those cases when no news is good news. certainly if any thing very threatening existed, our envoys would have found an opportunity to put us on our guard. you will have seen that Congress has been occupied with a very dirty & degrading business. a resolution for expelling both members was referred to the Committee of privileges. they have agreed to report against the resolution.

how it will be finally decided we know not. the testimony bears hard on the Speaker. the surrender of the posts by Spain will give us something to do, as a temporary government must be established there. but this will be [a] short business, and little else appears to be done. still they do not begin to talk of the time of adjournment. I hope however it will be in the [first?] of next month. the price of wheat here is 1.50 D flour 8.50 tobacco (old) [11.6]. they will all rise somewhat. this river being closed again, no exportation takes place yet, & keeps the market dull.—I am happy to have it in my power to make you & Maria a present of my chariot, which is in possession of Quarrier at Richmond. it has no harness. I believe it is the best piece of work that ever crossed the ocean. I find I shall have no occasion for such a thing here, and it may be useful to you & Maria. it will require some caution to get it clear of a considerable expence of storage. Quarrier was to have a certain percent on it if sold, in lieu of storage. you must therefore tell him you have given me 400. dollars for it and that he is to draw on me for the per cent agreed on. I forget what it was. I inclose you a letter to him which makes the storage a matter of account merely between him & me. the wheels of the carriage were originally heavy & bad. I am in hopes they will hold out to carry you to Monticello, where I will have a set of good ones made for you.—I send by post a new volume of Callendar's for mr Eppes.—present me affectionately to mr & mrs Eppes & the family: and my most tender love to Maria. cordial salutations to yourself & Adieu.

PrC (CSmH); faint. Enclosure: TJ to Alexander Quarrier, 18 Feb. 1798 (recorded in SJL, but not found).

I WROTE YOU LAST: TJ's letter to Eppes of 1 Feb. 1798, recorded in SJL, has not been found. A letter from Eppes to TJ of 8 Feb. 1798, which according to SJL was received from Petersburg on 27 Feb. 1798, is also missing.
TESTIMONY BEARS HARD ON THE SPEAKER: during the debate on Lyon's ex-pulsion, Dayton was appalled when an attempt was made to alter the punishment to a reprimand and reportedly declared: "*If I could speak with a voice of Thunder that would blast him, I would do it!!*" Although Dayton expressed shock at Lyon's behavior, several congressmen testified that the speaker of the House took no action to stop the confrontation and restore order when Roger Griswold was the aggressor (Philadelphia *Aurora*, 15-17 Feb., 8 Mch. 1798; *Annals*, 7:1003-4, 1051-8).

From James Madison

DEAR SIR   [18 or 19 Feb. 1798]

Since my last I have recd. yours of Feby. 8. with a continuation of the Gazettes down to that date, with the exception only mentioned already, of the gazette of Jany. 23. I am glad to find the public opinion to be taking the turn you describe on the subject of arming. For the public opinion alone can now save us from the rash measures of our hot-heated

Executive; it being evident from some late votes of the House of Reps. particularly in the choice of Managers for the Impeachment, that a majority there as well as in the Senate are ready to go as far as the controul of their Constituents will permit. There never was perhaps a greater contrast between two characters, than between those of the present President & of his predecessor, altho' it is the boast & prop of the latter, that he treads in the steps of the former. The one cold considerate & cautious, the other headlong & kindled into flame by every spark that lights on his passions: the one ever scrutinizing into the public opinion, and ready to follow where he could not lead it: the other insulting it by the most adverse sentiments & pursuits: W. a hero in the field, yet overweighing every danger in the Cabinet—A. without a single pretension to the character of Soldier, a perfect Quixotte as a Statesman: the former chief Magistrate pursuing peace every where with sincerity, tho' mistaking the means: the latter taking as much pains to get into war, as the former took to keep out of it. The contrast might be pursued into a variety of other particulars—the policy of the one in shunning connections with the arrangements of Europe, of the other in holding out the U.S. as a makeweight in its Balances of power: the avowed exultation of W. in the progress of liberty every where, & his eulogy on the Revolution & people of France posterior even to the bloody reign & fate of Robespierre—the open denunciations by Adams of the smallest disturbance of the antient discipline order & tranquility of Despotism. &c &c &c The affair of Lyon & Griswold is bad eno' every way; but worst of all in becoming a topic of tedious & disgraceful debates in Congress. There certainly could be no necessity for removing it from the decision of the parties themselves before that tribunal,[1] & its removal was evidently a sacrifice of the dignity of the latter, to the party-manœuvres of ruining a man whose popularity & activity were feared. If the state of the House suspended its rules in general, it was under no obligation to see any irregularity which did not force itself into public notice—and if Griswold be a man of the sword, he shd not have permitted the step to be taken; if not, he does not deserve to be avenged by the House. No man ought to reproach another with cowardice, who is not ready to give proof of his own courage. I have taken some pains but in vain to find out a person who will engage to carry the Mail from Fredg to Charlottesville. When I was in the neighbourhood of the latter I suggested the propriety of an effort there for that purpose, but do not know that it will be more successful. Our Winter has continued without snow & rather dry. and our Wheat-fields wear the most discouraging aspect. Adieu

RC (DLC: Madison Papers); undated, with date assigned from internal evidence and later correspondence (see TJ to Madison, 2 Mch. 1798); addressed: "Thomas Jefferson. Vice President of the United States Philadelphia"; endorsed by TJ as re-

ceived 27 Feb. and recorded in SJL under
that date in 1798; later endorsement by TJ:
"probably 98 Feby." For later emendations
to this letter, see Madison, *Papers*, 17:82-3.

[1] Remainder of text is written length-
wise in left margin, continuing at right angles to the first part of the letter.

From Nathaniel Cutting

Paris, 19 Feb. 1798. Although it has been several years since he has written,
he wishes to retain a place in TJ's memory. He congratulates the country on
TJ's acceptance of the vice presidency, but cannot commend the United States
on its foreign policy or "refrain from hazzarding an opinion" based on his observations. More than a year ago he foresaw that the French government's intentions to prevent the entry of English manufactures into the markets of Europe
would lead to measures against neutral vessels bearing British goods. This policy was made manifest by the recent decree of the Directory. France has solemnly pledged war to the death against Great Britain, and French people of all
political persuasions unite in "most formidable preparations for the actual Invasion of that insolent Dominatrice of the Seas." While he will not attempt to
characterize the entire political situation in Europe, he will communicate his
own fears and hopes concerning the United States. First among his fears is that
the British government has so influenced the United States as to put the peace
and perhaps even the independence of America at risk. A lack of "early and
accurate" information from Europe causes many in the United States to be
misled. Regrettably the American government squandered an opportunity to
become the guiding "Preceptor" of France and for the two republics to share a
bond of "reciprocal interest and mutual benefit." Once jealousy begins to dis-
lodge calm reflection and amity in human relations, if not resisted it can lead to
"the deadly blasts of Rancor." He has no intimacy with any member of the
French government but believes that he can characterize the attitude of the
Directory: that France regrets that those who govern the United States and
control its policy are under the sway of the Court of St. James; that the United
States cannot have forgotten the French expenditures of blood and treasure
during the American Revolution in defense of "sublime principles"; that France
might have expected American assistance in preserving the gains of the French
Revolution, and certainly would not have thought that the United States would
throw its influence in favor of France's greatest enemy, as seems now to have
occurred; that the British monarchy and the French republic "cannot long exist
together" and the destiny of all republics likely depends on the outcome; that
this great struggle may oblige France temporarily "to infringe the regulations
and injure the interests" that have heretofore governed relations of amity with
other nations; that the French will work to ameliorate such infringements by
"rational accommodation" with sympathetic nations, but not with any government that even covertly supports Britain, no matter how much affection the
French may feel for the people represented by the offending government; and
that France earnestly implores the American people not to subvert their republican virtue by heeding "vile Intriguers from proud Albion's shore." The Directory commands "such immense means" that clearly the United States "have
much to lose and nothing to gain by taking up the Cudgels against the gigantic
Republic of France!" He fears that the French government interprets the recall

and subsequent treatment of Monroe, whose conduct as minister merits esteem, to mean that Monroe's sentiments are not those of the United States. Hearing the government of his country censured, Cutting feels compelled to write this to TJ out of duty and not from any "party-spirit." Much of the harm to the reputation of the United States arose from the recall of Monroe, who had gone far to counter the deep feelings of "duplicity" felt by the French when they learned of Jay's Treaty. General Pinckney's "ill-timed importance" and "minute adhereance to unessential etiquette" on replacing Monroe were injurious to the interests of the United States. No well-informed American in Paris was surprised by the Directory's rebuff of Pinckney, although many were astonished that the American government immediately sent him back to France in a new capacity, which demonstrated either "an ignorance of human nature" or a deliberate intention to force a rupture with France. It is most unfortunate, given the currently sensitive state of the French government, that some expressions in the president's address to Congress in November could be construed here as disrespectful toward the French nation. "Many very enlightened men in the United States seem to be totally ignorant of the weight and influence that a few words or sentiments emaning from Public Characters acquire by traversing the Atlantic in a Newspaper," but "fugitive expressions, born of Indiscretion and ushered into the World by inadvertence," might make the difference between peace and war. Although some Americans might be inclined to defy France for reasons of national pride, war by the United States against "this Omnipotent Republic" would come at a frightful cost. He estimates that a war could cost the United States one hundred million dollars. Twenty million dollars of American property has been seized so far by the French, and similar losses after the onset of war would amount to even more than that total. Cutting suggests as an alternative that the United States offer France a loan of thirty million dollars, twenty million of it in the form of the property already seized by France, the whole without interest during the term of the present war and then to be repaid over ten years after the establishment of peace. "A suspicion is entertained by several Gentlemen of my acquaintance that whenever the Directory of France think proper to commence negociation with our Commissioners, *It* will peremptorily make certain demands which will be tantamount to a Loan; but probably the pecuniary aid they may *require*, will never be placed on so favorable a footing for America as that which I have indicated above." Expression of these sentiments might bring down on Cutting "the Epithet of *Jacobin*," but to see good relations between France and the United States is "the most ardent wish of my heart." He regrets that since his return from Algiers the state of commerce has made it inconvenient for him to resume his residence at Havre de Grace. Delamotte as vice consul has "faithfully discharged" the duties of the office, and Cutting considers himself to be, at Paris, within the district of his consular office even though the presence of the consul general has made it unnecessary for him to render any official duty. He now contemplates removing to Havre and in the event of a general peace will fix himself there permanently.

RC (DLC); 16 p.; at foot of recto of each sheet: "Mr. Jefferson"; endorsed by TJ as received 4 Sep. 1798 and so recorded in SJL. Dupl (CtHi: Oliver Wolcott Papers); at head of text: "Duplicate." FC (Lb in MHi: Cutting Letterbook); memorandum by Cutting at foot of text indicates that the RC was sent "₱ M. Grubb" via Havre and the Dupl "₱ M. Lee" via Bordeaux.

From James Monroe

Your favor in answer to mine by Mr. Giles gives me much comfort. I had almost concluded that the admn. wod. carry the project for arming our merchant vessels & thus involve us in war with France & Spain. That view of our affrs. was a disquieting one, but yet I was satisfied, as the war, in its consequences, wod. rouse the publick attention, that the result wod. be favorable to republican govt. & disgraceful to the admn. I was satisfied the people wod. shrink from it as from a pestilence, whereby the admn. wod. soon stand alone & become an object of publick scorn. But if we can get right without the aid of such a scourge happy indeed will it be for us. And nothing is wanting to get us right but a knowledge of our affrs. among the people wh. nothing will so essentially contribute to [dif]fuse as able, free, & comprehensive discussion on [the] part of the friends of republican govt. in the H. [of] R. I believe no admn. was ever before in such a d[ilem]ma, for if it carries its measures it must be d[isgraced] & if it does not carry them it must be so likewise. Mr. A. may thank himself for this. You did every thing [in] yr. power to unite the people[1] under his admn., & to give him in negotiation the aid of the republican character & interest to support the pretentions of our country & not without hazard to yrself.[2] But this he spurned with a degree of wantonness of wh. there is no example. He wod. have none in his ranks but tried men, whose political creed corresponded with his own. My opinion is if the measure is carried we have war, & if rejected the tone of the French govt. will change, since the regard they bear for America especially when thus pronounc'd thro' a constitutional organ agnst war will immediately operate. The H. of R. may therefore prevent war if it carries its measures & stands firm. But what is then the situation of the country? An unhappy one it is true, but still better than in war. Its unhappiness however proceeds from the past misconduct of the admn., wh. seeking war and favoring the cause of the kings agnst France, has so compromitted itself that it cannot become an useful organ of the publick sentiment, to extricate us from the dilemma into which it has brought us.

I think I shall enter into the practice of the law immediately & in that case move to Richmond. The organization of the courts is such that it is impossible for me to practice in the Supr cts & reside in the country. The expence of attendance at Richmond, wod. more than make up for the difference between that of living there & here, to [say] nothing of the objection to leaving my family for six months in the year.   I think with you that Scipio's performance is not a thing for a library—& therefore I think it must have been drawn by T.P. or C.L. It is quite in the admn. stile, much low spleen & malice, & otherwise without force. If any thing is to be said Mr. D. or some one of my friends on the ground had better do it, as they better know what is requisite & will suit. Giles, Nicholas, Brent & many others hold good pens, from whom it wod. come better than from me.

RC (DLC); torn, text in brackets supplied by conjecture; endorsed by TJ as received 27 Feb. 1798 and so recorded in SJL.

YOUR FAVOR: TJ to Monroe, 8 Feb. 1798.

T.P.: Timothy Pickering. C.L.: Charles Lee. MR. D.: John Dawson.

[1] Word interlined in place of "country."
[2] Preceding five words and ampersand interlined.

Emendations to the Senate Journal

[20 Feb. 1798]

The house having agreed to so much of the amendment reported by[1] the commee as proposed to strike out the 4th. section of the bill and proceeding to the question for inserting agreeably to the residue of the said amendment the following words to wit[2]

MS (DNA: RG 46, Senate Records, 5th Cong. 2d sess.); in TJ's hand except for one emendation (see note 1 below); with date supplied from endorsement; endorsed in Samuel A. Otis's hand: "Vice President amends the Journal of Feb 20th 1798 L. 5th Cons 2d Sess." Rough Journal (same); with text above appearing as emendation in Otis's hand (see note 2 below).

TJ drafted this introduction to a proposed amendment to the 4TH. SECTION OF THE BILL "regulating certain proceedings in cases of impeachment," originally presented by Humphrey Marshall, to amend an incomplete entry in the Rough Journal of the Senate. This part of the bill included procedures for summoning the impeached party to appear before the Senate. The amendment added language on the execution of the subpoena and provided that

"should the party fail to appear, the Senate may notwithstanding proceed to trial and judgment." It was defeated by a 6 to 18 vote, with Joseph Anderson requesting a record of the vote (JS, 2:443; [Humphrey Marshall], *A Bill Regulating Certain Procedures in Cases of Impeachment* [Philadelphia, 1798], 2). TJ's emendation appears again in the Rough Journal to introduce an amendment to the sixth section of the bill which dealt with the oath to be administered to the senators. This amendment was also defeated and the bill failed to receive a third reading (JS, 2:443).

[1] Preceding two words interlined in Otis's hand in place of "of."
[2] This entire passage is inserted in the Rough Journal in place of "On motion by Mr. Anderson to adopt this report & to amend the bill as follows."

To Jean Armand Tronchin

DEAR SIR   Philadelphia Feb. 20. 98.

You will have been justly surprised that your letter to me, dated so long ago as Nov. 17. 1796. should not yet have been answered. I know not through what channel it came, but it never got to my hands till Dec. 27. 1797. at that time I found it on my arrival at this place. our rivers being then and still frozen up, no vessels are sailing for Europe, and it will probably lie still some time before this answer can be put on it's way.

The information to your friend that a debt contracted in another country cannot be recovered in the courts of the United states, is entirely erroneous. such a debt is as recoverable here, as if it had been contracted here. the difficulty in the case of a foreign debt, is to produce due proof of it. if the debt be founded on a bill of exchange, bond, promisory note or other written title, the original must be produced, if it be in existence: but if it has been destroyed or lost by any accident, an authenticated copy may be used. when the original is sent here, the holder should in prudence have one or more copies of it taken authentically, that if the original miscarries, he may afterwards have copies to send on & supply it's place; and he should take notice by what ship or other channel the original is sent, that if the ship be lost or other accident happen to the paper, it's loss may be traced & proved. if the debt has already been sued for in Europe, and a judgment pronounced for it by any court there, then a copy of the proceedings and judgment of that court will be a sufficient foundation whereon to bring a suit here. these proceedings should be certified under the seal of the court. copies of bills of exchange, bonds & other written titles of a private nature should be authenticated under the seal of the Mayor & corporation of the town where the writing is produced; and this kind of seal is so much respected as evidence in our courts, that even if the proceedings of a court be sent under the seal of the court, it would not be amiss to have that seal authenticated by the seal of the Mayor & corporation. a copy of a bill under the hand & seal of a Notary, should be still authenticated by the seal of the Mayor, certifying that the Notary is really such. you ask in what manner your friend should constitute an attorney to prosecute his suit. a letter of procuration, drawn in the forms usual in Europe, and legalised under the seal of the Mayor & corporation of his town, will be good here. I am not able to answer the question whether an attorney would prosecute for a certain proportion of the sum to be recovered. this is probably sometimes done, but it is not reputable. but an attorney will prosecute the suit, and pay the expences out of the money recovered, so as to call for little or no money to be advanced by the client, and when he has recovered, he deducts expences, charges a fixed commission on the money when recovered & collected, & remits the nett balance. the expences of the law here are very moderate.

I shall be much gratified if this information is in time to be useful to your friend. it's delay I fear will have excited suspicions in your mind that I had become forgetful of the rights of acquaintance & friendship, which I hope will be effaced when you are informed of the delay of your letter. our distance & the state of things in Europe do not permit me to make any enquiries as to yourself of a political nature. I hope however you have not suffered by the events which have taken place in that part of the globe, and that you will accept assurances of the sincere esteem & respect with which I have the honour to be Dear Sir

Your most obedient & most humble servt.   TH: JEFFERSON

RC (BPUG); at foot of first page: "Monsr. Tronchin."

To Horatio Gates

DEAR GENERAL   Philadelphia Feb. 21. 98.

I recieved duly your welcome favor of the 15th. and had an opportunity of immediately delivering the one it inclosed to General Kosciusko. I see him often, and with great pleasure mixed with commiseration. he is as pure a son of liberty, as I have ever known, and of that liberty which is to go to all, and not to the few or the rich alone.   we are here under great anxiety to hear from our envoys. but I think this is one of the cases where no news is good news. if the dispositions at Paris threatened war, it is impossible that our envoys should not find some means of putting us on our guard, of warning us to begin our preparations: especially too when so many vessels have come from ports of France, and if writing were dangerous (which cannot be) there are so many of our countrymen at Paris who would bring us their vivâ voce communications. peace then must be probable. I agree with you that some of our merchants have been milking the cow: yet the great mass of them have become deranged, they are daily falling down by bankruptcies, and on the whole the condition of our commerce far less firm & really prosperous than it would have been by the regular operations and steady advances which a state of peace would have occasioned. were a war to take place and throw our agriculture into equal convulsions with our commerce our business would be done at both ends. but this I hope will not be. the good news from the Natchez has cut off the fear of a breach in that quarter, where a crisis was brought on which has astonished every one. how this mighty duel is to end between Gr. Britain and France is a momentous question. the sea which divides them makes it a game of chance; but it is narrow, and all the chances are not on one side. should they make peace, still our fate is problematical. the countervailing acts of Gr. Brit. now laid before Congress, threaten, in the opinion of merchants, the entire loss of our navigation to England. it makes a difference, from the present state of things, of 500. Guineas on a vessel of 350. tons. if, as the newspapers have told us, France has renewed her arret of 1789. laying a duty of 7. livres a hundred on all tobo. brought in foreign bottoms (even our own) and should extend it to rice & other commodities, we are done as navigators to that country also. in fact I apprehend that those two great nations will think it their interest not to permit us to be navigators. France had thought otherwise, and had then an equal desire to encourage our navigation as her own, while she hoped it's weight would at least not be thrown into the scale of her enemies. she sees now that that is not to be relied on, and will probably use her own means, and those of the nations under her influence to exclude us from the ocean. how far it may lessen our happiness to be rendered merely agricultural, how far that state is more[1] friendly to principles of virtue & liberty are questions yet to be solved.   Kosciusko has been disappointed by the sudden peace between France & Austria. a ray of hope[2] seemed to gleam on his mind for a moment that the extension of the revolutionising spirit through Italy and Germany might so have occupied the remnants of monarchy there as that his country might have risen again. I sincerely rejoice to find that you preserve your health so well. that you may so go on to the end of the chapter, & that it may be a long one, I sincerely pray. make my friendly salutations acceptable to mrs Gates, & accept yourself assurances of the great & constant esteem & respect of Dear Sir

Your friend & servt   TH: JEFFERSON

RC (ViU); addressed: "Majr. Genl. Gates New York"; stamped, franked, and postmarked; endorsed by Gates. PrC (DLC).

[1] Word interlined.
[2] Word interlined in place of "light."

Notes on Newspaper Articles

1797.

Nov. 30. good cautions to prevent fire. Adams & Larkin's paper of this date.

Dec. 1. Pleasant's paper. an excellent piece on the bank of the US.

shewing they draw 960,000 D. profits on 2. millions actual cash which is 48. per cent.

Bache's. Mc.kain's charge on the subject of libels.[1]

1798.

Feb. 3. & 5 16.[2] Brown's paper, 3[3] excellent pieces (by Tenche Coxe) the 1st. fixg. the dates of the commencemt of British & French spolians

Feb. 5. Greenleaf's paper. a piece signed Ecclesiasticus, shewing that the 1st. day of the week is not authorized as Sabbath by the example or precepts of our Saviour, or his apostles, or the primitive fathers. that they kept no Sabbath. that it was first ordained in the 4th. century by Constantine, & then only for the cities, leaving the country to pursue it's agriculture

21. do. answer by Sabbaticus.

MS (DLC: TJ Papers, 103:17593); written entirely in TJ's hand on a scrap of paper probably at two or more sittings; with notation by TJ on verso: "Newspapers, tracts & references."

The list of CAUTIONS TO PREVENT FIRE was printed in the Boston *Independent Chronicle* at the request of the Massachusetts Charitable Fire Society.

PLEASANT'S PAPER: Richmond *Virginia Argus*.

Thomas McKean, chief justice of the Pennsylvania supreme court, presented his CHARGE ON THE SUBJECT OF LIBELS to the grand jury on 27 Nov. 1797 (Philadelphia *Aurora*, 1 Dec. 1797). Tench COXE used the pseudonym "An American Merchant" for his articles on "Neutral Spoliations," which appeared in the *Philadelphia Gazette* on the dates listed by TJ. In his discussion of steps

taken by Great Britain and France against neutral shipping in 1792-93, Coxe blamed the British for initiating the interdiction of shipments of foodstuffs. At some unknown time TJ, perhaps prompted by Coxe's articles and perhaps after consulting some of the same sources of information, drew up a chronology of the same sequence of events (see Notes on Infractions of Neutral Rights by France and Great Britain, [after 21 July 1795], printed in Vol. 28: 411-12).

The article SIGNED ECCLESIASTICUS appeared in *Greenleaf's New York Journal* on 3 Feb. 1798.

[1] Preceding eight words inserted in different ink.

[2] Preceding date interlined by TJ.

[3] TJ first wrote "2" and then altered the digit to read as above.

To James Madison

Philadelphia Feb. 22. [1798]

Yours of the 12th. is recieved. I wrote you last on the 15th. but the letter getting misplaced, will only go by this post. we still hear nothing from our Envoys. whether the Executive hear we know not. but if war were to be apprehended, it is impossible our envoys should not find means of putting us on our guard, or that the Executive should hold back their information. no news therefore is good news. the countervailing act, which I sent you by the last post, will confessedly put American bottoms out of employ in our trade with Gr. Britain. so say well informed merchants. indeed it seems probable, when we consider that hitherto, with the advantage of our foreign tonnage, our vessels could only share with the British, and the countervailing duties will, it is said, make a difference of 500 guineas to our prejudice on a ship of 350. tons. still the Eastern men say nothing. every appearance & consideration render it probable that on the restoration of peace, both France & Britain will consider it their interest to exclude us from the ocean by such peaceable means as are in their power. should this take place, perhaps it may be thought just & politic to give to our *native* capitalists the monopoly of our internal commerce. this may at once relieve us from the danger of wars abroad and British thraldom at home.—the news from the Natchez of the delivery of the posts, which you will see in the papers, is to be relied on. we have escaped a dangerous crisis there.—the great contest between Israel & Morgan, of which you will see the papers full, is to be decided this day. it is snowing fast at this time, and the most sloppy walking I ever saw. this will be to the disadvantage of the party which has the most invalids. whether the event will be known this evening I am uncertain. I rather presume not, & therefore that you will not learn it till next post. you will see in the papers the ground on which the introduction of the jury into the trial by impeachment was advocated by mr Tazewell, & the fate of the question. Reade's motion, which I inclosed you, will probably be amended & established so as to declare a Senator unimpeachable, absolutely, and yesterday an opinion was declared that not only officers of the state governments but every private citizen of the US. is impeachable. whether they will think this the time to make the declaration I know not, but if they bring it on I think there will be not more than two votes North of Patowmac against the universality of the impeaching power. the system of the Senate may be inferred from their transactions heretofore, and from the following declaration made to me personally by their oracle.[1] 'no republic can ever be of any duration, without a Senate, & a Senate deeply & strongly rooted, strong enough to bear up against all popular storms & passions. the only fault in the constitution of our Senate is that their term of office is not durable enough. hitherto they have done well, but probably they will be forced to give way in time.' I suppose their having done well hitherto alluded to the stand they made on the British treaty. this declaration may be considered as their text; that they consider themselves as the bulwarks of the government, and will be rendering that the more secure, in proportion as they can assume greater powers. the foreign intercourse bill is set for to-day: but the parties are so equal on that in the Repr. that they seem mutually to fear the encounter.

Tho' it is my intention, & the orders I left were, that the cutting machine should be repaired, yet I think it would not be adviseable for you to depend on it, as to your sprigs & lathing nails if you want them before my return: as at my present distance, I could not rely sufficiently on the execution of my orders. immediately on my return my own wants will oblige me to recommence cutting. I imagine that by this time a large cargo of Monroe's book has arrived at Richmond, as the vessel which had them on board got out during the short interval the river was open. my friendly salutations to mrs Madison & the family. to yourself friendly adieux.

RC (DLC: Madison Papers); partially dated, with year added at later date in an unknown hand; addressed: "James Madison junr. near Orange court house"; stamped, franked, and postmarked. PrC (DLC); partially dated.

On 16 Feb. 1798, the Philadelphia newspapers carried information from New Orleans on the Spanish DELIVERY OF THE POSTS at Walnut Hills and Natchez (Philadelphia *Aurora* and *Philadelphia Gazette*, 16 Feb. 1798).

The GREAT CONTEST BETWEEN Republican Israel ISRAEL and Federalist Benjamin R. MORGAN took place in the special election of this date to fill the Pennsylvania state senate seat that was vacated on 7 Feb. when a special committee declared invalid Israel's 1797 election by only 38 votes because the eligibility of some voters was questionable. In the rematch the Federalist candidate won by 357 votes out of a total of 8,723 cast (*Philadelphia Gazette*, 7, 15, 24 Feb. 1798; Harry M. Tinkcom, *The Republicans and Federalists in Pennsylvania, 1790-1801: A Study in National Stimulus and Local Response* [Harrisburg, 1950], 176-9).

The introduction and emendations to a resolution brought in by Massachusetts Senator Theodore Sedgwick on 21 Feb., which referred Jacob Read's MOTION that senators are not impeachable to a committee appointed the previous day to respond to the articles of impeachment presented by the House of Representatives against Blount, are in TJ's hand and similar to Emendations to the Senate Journal, printed above at 20 Feb. 1798 (MS in DNA: RG 46, Senate Records, 5th Cong., 2d sess.; endorsed in clerk's hand, in part: "Mr. Sedgwicks motion on Mr. Reads motion of 14th Feby. respecting the impeachment of a Senator U.S. 21 Feb 1798"). For Sedgwick's resolution, see JS, 2:444. Records of the debate on Read's resolution have not been found.

THEIR ORACLE: John Adams (see Notes on a Conversation with John Adams, 15 Feb. 1798).

[1] "Mr. Adams" is written in right margin of PrC in pencil, probably in TJ's hand, to identify "their oracle."

To Thomas Mann Randolph

TH.J. TO TMR.   Philadelphia Feb. 22. 98.

I wrote you last on the 15th. since that we are quieted by an entire confidence in the account from the Natchez that the Spaniards will immediately deliver up the posts. the conduct of our agents there was so waspish as to have induced a suspicion that, if war was to take place against France, we meant to drive Spain into it also, that our Southern states might have something to conquer and amuse themselves by land,

& the Eastern states by water for their privateers. these golden views are disappointed by the moderation of Spain. we have still no information from our envoys. their silence is sufficient evidence that there is no danger of war. if there were it is inconcievable that they should not find means (and they cannot be difficult) to put us on our guard, and warn us to begin preparations. the English countervailing acts are now before Congress. the Eastern men, on whom they chiefly fall, are silent. it is affirmed by judicious merchants here, that they will completely exclude American bottoms from our intercourse with Gr. Britain. we could only share with them before, with all the benefit of our foreign tonnage. the countervails make a difference of 500. guineas on a vessel of 350. tons.—the river here, after having opened for a short time, closed up again and still continues shut. the prices of wheat, flour, & tobo. therefore continue stationary.—there is no talk as yet of fixing a day for our adjournment. some hold up an idea of a very distant one, tho' acknoleging there is not even the shadow of business to do, if matters with France appear peaceable. I therefore confide that as soon as the spring opens, the farmers & lawyers will not be restrained by those who had rather be here than at home. my tender love to my dear Martha & the children. to yourself affectionately Adieu.

RC (DLC); endorsed by Randolph as received 3 Mch. 1798. PrC (CSmH).

To Thomas Mann Randolph

Th:J. to TMR.   Philadelphia Feb. 22. 98.

Since writing my letter of this morning yours of the 12th. inst. is come to hand. I very much doubt Bates's not having recieved my bill. however it happens luckily that I have a copy of it with me, & therefore write him the inclosed letter subjoining the bill. he has still time to get it before the rise of the sap, & I will pray you to send Jupiter off immediately with the letter with orders not to return without finding him & bringing an answer. I had written to Davenport last week; but will write again now in consequence of what you mention.—my letter by last post desired that George should look out for horses for his ploughs. I must pray you to authorize the purchase of any you may deem necessary & at proper prices, without waiting further to consult me, as it will be fatal to have the ploughs stopped. he should obtain a credit till July 1st. that I may be sure of being in place to answer it. if you should at any time see Davenport I pray you to push him with my work. Adieu affectionately.

RC (DLC); endorsed by Randolph as received 3 Mch. 1798. Enclosure: TJ to William Bates, 22 Feb. 1798 (recorded in SJL, but not found).

Randolph's letter of the 12TH. INST., which according to SJL was received 22 Feb. 1798, has not been found. SJL records a letter from TJ to William DAVENPORT of 22 Feb. 1798, which is also missing. MY LETTER BY LAST POST: TJ to Randolph, 15 Feb.

Certificate for George Taylor, Jr.

Philadelphia.

I hereby certify that mr George Taylor acted as translating clerk for the French language to the Secretary of state's office, during the latter part of the time that I was in that department: that his translations were faithful and well done, and bespoke a full degree of knowlege of that language: and that he was very diligent and assiduous in this as in all his other duties. Given under my hand this 22d. day of February 1798

TH: JEFFERSON

MS (B. Altman & Company, New York, 1959); entirely in TJ's hand.

Given TJ's practices, an SJL entry of a letter to Taylor of 22 Feb. 1798 probably refers not to this document but to a now-missing cover letter in which it was enclosed. A letter from Taylor to TJ, written and received on 20 Feb. 1798, is also recorded in SJL but has not been found.

To Peregrine Fitzhugh

DEAR SIR   Philadelphia Feb. 23. 1798.

I have yet to acknolege your last favor which I recieved at Monticello, and therefore cannot now recur to the date. the perversion of the expressions of a former letter to you, which you mention to have been made in the newspapers, I had not till then heard of. yet the spirit of it was not new. I have been for some time used as the property of the newspapers, a fair mark for every man's dirt. some too have indulged themselves in this exercise who would not have done it, had they known me otherwise than thro' these impure and injurious channels. it is hard treatment, and for a singular kind of offence, that of having obtained by the labours of a life the indulgent opinions of a part of one's fellow citizens. however these moral evils must be submitted to, like the physical scourges of tempest, fire &c.—we are waiting with great anxiety to hear from our envoys at Paris. but the very circumstance of silence speaks I think plain enough. if there were danger of war we should certainly hear from them. it is impossible, if that were the aspect of their negociations, that they should not find or make occasion of putting us on our guard, & of warning us to prepare. I consider therefore their silence as a proof of peace. indeed I had before imagined that when France had thrown down the gauntlet to England, and was pointing all her energies to that object, her regard for the subsistence of her islands would keep her from cutting off our resources from them. I hope therefore we shall rub through the war, without engaging in it ourselves, and that when in a state of peace our legislature & executive will endeavor to provide peaceable means of obliging foreign nations to be just to us, and of making their injustice recoil on themselves. the advantages of our commerce to them may be made the engine for this purpose, provided we shall be willing to submit to occasional sacrifices, which will be nothing in comparison with the calamities of war. Congress has nothing of any importance before them, except the bill on foreign intercourse, & the proposition to arm our merchant vessels. these will be soon decided, and if we then get peaceable news from our envoys, I know of nothing which ought to prevent our immediate separation. it had been expected that we must have laid a land tax this session. however it is thought we can get along another year without it. some very disagreeable differences have taken place in Congress. they cannot fail to lessen the respect of the public for the general government, and to replace their state governments in a greater degree of comparative respectability. I do not think it for the interest of the general government itself, & still less of the Union at large, that the state governments should be so little respected as they have been. however I dare say that in time all these as well as their central government, like the planets revolving round their common Sun, acting & acted upon according to their respective weights & distances, will produce that beautiful equilibrium on which our constitution is founded, and which I believe it will exhibit to the world in a degree of perfection unexampled but in the planetary system itself. the enlightened statesman therefore will endeavor to preserve the weight & influence of every part, as too much given to any member of it would destroy the general equilibrium.   the ensuing month will probably be the most eventful ever yet seen in Modern Europe. it may probably be the season preferred for the projected invasion of England. it is indeed a game of chances. the sea which divides the combatants gives to fortune as well as to valour it's share of influence on the enterprize. but all the chances are not on one side. the subjugation of England would indeed be a general calamity: but, happily it is impossible. should it end in her being only republicanised, I know not on what principle a true republican of our country could lament it, whether he considers it as extending the blessings of a purer government to other portions of mankind, or strengthening the cause of liberty in our own country by the influence of that example. I do not indeed wish to see any nation have a form of government forced on them: but if it is to be done, I should rejoice at it's being a freer one.—permit me to place here the tribute of my regrets for the affecting loss lately sustained within your walls, and to add that of the esteem & respect with which I am Dear Sir

Your friend & servt.   TH: JEFFERSON

PrC (DLC); faint and partially overwritten by TJ in ink; at foot of first page: "Peregrine Fitzhugh esq."

Fitzhugh's LAST FAVOR was of 15 Oct. 1797. TRIBUTE OF MY REGRETS: Fitzhugh's

father, Col. William Fitzhugh, died 11 Feb. 1798 (VMHB, 8 [1900-1], 91-2).

A letter from Fitzhugh to TJ of 28 Mch., recorded in SJL as received 12 Apr. 1798, has not been found.

To James Martin

SIR   Philadelphia. Feb. 23. 1798.

I recieved after my return home in July last your obliging letter inclosing an oration pronounced at Jamaica in Long island on the 4th. of July 1796. a singular concurrence of name with one or two other circumstances occasioned me to ascribe it to another gentleman from whom I had parted a few days before only; and to write to him a letter of acknolegement. it was not till I had the pleasure of seeing Colo. Burr here lately that the error was discovered. permit me now to correct it, and to return my thanks for the piece inclosed to me. it contained sentiments of policy precious to my heart, and which have been the pursuit of my life, and expressed in language equal to the subject and occasion. it is a pity that such a pen should not be more employed. the times call for it: the cause is worthy of it; and if heaven is prospering the bloody energies of liberty on the other side the water, it could not be indifferent to the milder efforts of persuasion here. pardon this liberty; accept a repetition of my acknolegements and assurances of the esteem & respect with which I am Sir

Your most obedt. & most humble servt   TH: JEFFERSON

PrC (DLC); at foot of text: "Mr. James Martin."

YOUR OBLIGING LETTER: Martin to TJ, 20 July 1796. For the SINGULAR CONCUR-

RENCE OF NAME that caused TJ to send a LETTER OF ACKNOLEGEMENT to the wrong person, see TJ to Benjamin Vaughan, 31 Aug. 1797.

To Thomas Willing

Feb. 23. 98.

Th: Jefferson presents his respects to mr Willing, and other gentlemen managers of the ball of this evening. he hopes his non-attendance will not be misconstrued. he has not been at a ball these twenty years, nor for a long time permitted himself to go to any entertainments of the evening, from motives of attention to health. on these grounds he excused to Genl. Washington when living in the city his not going to his birthnights, to mrs Washington not attending her evenings, to mrs Adams the same, and to all his friends who have been so good as to invite him to tea- & card parties, the declining to go to[1] them. it is an indulgence which his age and habits will he hopes obtain and continue to him. he has always testified his homage to the occasion by his subscription to it.

RC (PPAmP: Francis Lewis Randolph Collection); addressed: "Mr. Willing one of the managers of the ball at Mr. Oellers'." PrC (DLC).

[1] Torn. Word supplied from PrC.

From George Jefferson

DEAR SIR,   Richmond February 24th. 1798.

I have received your favor of the 14th.—Your instructions respecting the wheat for the agricultural society, shall be strictly attended to.

I have been looking out for such as you describe, but have not yet been able to meet with any; though hope soon to procure some which is genuine.

Mr. Buchanan has shewn me your lot of ground. a Mr. Gaddy has enclosed a small part of it, on which he has built a stable. I called to speak to him upon the subject, but found he was out of Town, and probably will be for some time. The lot is much injured by having been used as a road—it is further injured by the washing of the river, which at a small expence I think might be remedied. Should Gaddy raise no difficulty I believe I will enclose it, and sow it in clover for my Horse, & perhaps put a stable on it.

Your stoves & hoop iron have been forwarded to Milton by Johnston. The Schooner John Brown has not yet arrived.

I am Dear Sir Very sincerely Yours   GEO. JEFFERSON

RC (MHi); at foot of text: "Thomas Jefferson esqr."; endorsed by TJ as received 5 Mch. 1798 and so recorded in SJL.

From James Monroe

DEAR SIR   Feby 25. 1798. Albemarle.

The trial of Mr. Lyon has taken much time & produc'd much irritation. I fear the division wh. took place there will be carried to other objects. It seems to be as if the antagonist of Lyon was the aggressor & that it wod. have been equally politic and just for some cool person to have brot. forward a resolution censuring both. But really we have been so long on the defensive, that we find it difficult to change the mode of warfare, even where a suitable occasion occurs. Certain it is the H. of Reps. as a body, have lost much ground in the squabble, and if our recovery to old principles &ca, is to be brot. abt., by *its* decline in the publick opinion, we are in the high road to a happy change.

I have great doubts as to my removal to Richmd., or in other words resuming the practice of the law, for upon the former depends the latter measure. In these courts I shod. make nothing at all—and at Richmd. I incur a heavy expence. And such is the present organizn. of the courts there, that I cannot follow them up, without residing there. Mr. D. will consult you upon all cases in wh. I am interested; and unfortunately it happens that I have some yet depending.

I think the discussion on the foreign intercourse bill will produce a good effect. The principle taken by the republicans is sound. If we had had no minister abroad thro' this war, I am sure we shod. have had no dispute with France. And Mr. Adams's appointment of his son to the moon, was a most reprehensible act. If you had appointed (being in his place) a remote relation to such an office, the noise wh. the royalists wod. have made, wod. never have ceased. The inattention wh. the enemies of such a mission; enemies from principle too, have previously shewn to the measure is a proof of their extreme supineness, in cases where they ought to be active, & might be active with effect.

I inclose you a letter for Martin wh. be so good as forward. Sincerely I am yr. friend & servt.

RC (DLC); endorsed by TJ as received 6   MR. D: John Dawson.
Mch. 1798 and so recorded in SJL. Enclosure not found.

From Luther Martin

Baltimore, February 26th, 1798.

If you have found me tedious, Sir, by reason of the number or length of my letters to you, be so good as to recollect you have no person to blame for it but yourself.—I called on you to inform me to whom of the Cresap's you alluded in your Notes upon Virginia.—You did not deign to give me an answer.—This obliged me to undertake the vindication of *two* of that name.

I also called upon you for the circumstances of time, place and persons, on which you founded your charge, that one of that family was infamous for the many murders he had committed on the unoffending Indians.—You refused me this information. A charge so general as you had made could only be refuted by an appeal to the general history of their lives.

However, I am *now* about to do, what alone would have been necessary for me to have done, had you confined yourself in your publication to the speech of Logan, and the death of his family; to lay before you that testimony which I possess to prove by whom they were killed; that none of the name of Cresap was concerned therein; that Logan was not a chief of the Mingoes; and that the speech is spurious.

And here let me observe, that you may the better understand the vouchers I shall produce, early last spring, wishing to obtain correct information, I sent to a friend near Fort Cumberland a series of questions, that he might procure me answers to each of them from gentlemen, whom he might find acquainted with the transactions to which those questions referred. To detail to you these interrogatories would be a needless waste of paper, they will be sufficiently understood by the answers which I shall give you.

Here again you will permit me further to observe, that the sole object I have in view being to vindicate my connexions against your malignant accusations, when I introduce the names of those by whom Logan's family were killed, it ought not to be supposed that I mean to charge them with having killed his family in the wanton, cruel, and cowardly manner you have represented. I do not hold myself bound to vindicate their conduct; still less do I feel myself bound to brand them with infamy, on account of that transaction. Perhaps neither you, nor myself, can at this time obtain so perfect a knowledge of every circumstance attending it, as we ought to possess before we should pass a sentence of acquittal or condemnation. However, it is but justice to those, whose names I am obliged to disclose to the public, to declare, that as you have shewn so total an ignorance of the place where, and the persons by whom, Logan's family were killed, so it is very probable that you are equally ignorant as to the circumstances attending their death, and the cause of that event. From the best information I have been able to obtain, and I have sought for information, which I believe you never did before you wrote your Notes upon Virginia, there were a number of

Indians collected at the mouth of Yellow Creek, conducting themselves with great insolence, insomuch that Mr. Baker, who lived there, thought it prudent to send from thence the women and children of his family, and the white men who remained, found it necessary to be armed: That Logan's younger brother, his mother and sister, were *of that party*; these three, and no others of his family were killed; that previous to their death, and but two or three days before, two white men had been murdered, and another wounded by the Indians, in that neighbourhood, near the mouth of little Beaver Creek; and that the attack upon the Indians, which proved fatal to Logan's family, arose not *solely* from a principle of retaliation, but was *more immediately occasioned* by the insolence of Logan's brother, who was about to carry off the coat of one of the Inhabitants. And that the circumstances you have so minutely detailed, of a party of the whites proceeding down the river in quest of vengeance; a canoe of unsuspecting women and children being discovered by them, their concealing themselves on the bank of the river; their singling out their objects as the canoe reached the shore, and killing every person in it, are as little to be depended on as that Mr. Cresap commanded the party, or that the transaction happened on the Kanhawa; in fine, that those circumstances have no other foundation but the fanciful reveries of a philosophical imagination. And as *no children were killed*, I presume *they* were introduced by you to render the story more pathetic.

Having made these observations, I shall now, furnish you in the first place, with the information I have received from Benjamin Tomlinson, Esq. a respectable inhabitant of Alleghany county, and at this time a member of the House of Delegates of this State; a gentleman with whom I have never conversed on this or any other subject, and whom I do not recollect ever to have seen; it is dated at Cumberland, April the 17th, 1797, and, as far as relates to the subject in discussion, is as follows:

"To your first questions—I answer, Logan's mother, younger brother,[1] and sister, who was Gibson's Squaw, were killed; this woman had a child half white, *which was not killed.*

To the second question—They were killed the third or fourth day of May, 1774, at the mouth of Yellow Creek: The circumstances attending this affair were, that two or three days before the Indians were killed at Yellow Creek by the whites, two men were killed, and one wounded, by the Indians, in a canoe belonging to a Mr. Butler, of Pittsburgh, as they were going down the river Ohio, near the mouth of little Beaver Creek; and this canoe was plundered of all the property; moreover the Indians were at this time threatening the inhabitants on the river Ohio.

I was also informed they committed some robbery on the property of Michael Cresap. The fact of the white men being killed, *I well know*, because I assisted at their burial.

To your third question—I state that the party (by whom Logan's family was killed) had no commander, I believe Logan's brother was killed by a man of the name of Sappington; I came to the spot just after they were shot, and *before they were dead*, yet I do not know *who in particular* killed the others; but *this I well know*, that captain *Michael Cresap*, or *any other of the name of Cresap were not there*, nor do I believe were *within many miles* of the place.

To the 4th question. I believe Logan's residence was on the Muskingum; his character was no ways particular, he was only a common man among the Indians; no *chief* nor *captain*.

To the 5th question. I do not know when he died (Logan) died, but was informed by Hugh Barclay, esq. of Bedford, that he became very vile, killed his own wife, and was himself killed by his wife's brother, but where or when I know not, but am certain it was after the treaty.

To the 6th question. I may first observe that I am certain Logan was not at the treaty. Perhaps Cornstalk, chief of the Shawanese nation, mentioned in the speech at the treaty, among other grievances, the Indians that were killed at Yellow creek; but, I believe, neither Cresap nor any other person, were charged as the perpetrators.

But this I perfectly recollect, that I was *that day*, to wit, the day of the treaty, officer of the guard, and stood *near* Dunmore's person, and consequently *saw* and *heard* what passed; as also that two or three days before, as I was on an out guard, Simon Girty passing by, stopped some time, sat down and conversed with me: He said he was going after Logan to bring him to the treaty, but that he did not like the business, for he (Logan) was a surly fellow. Girty however proceeded on his journey, and I saw him return on the day of the treaty, and Logan was not with him, at this time a circle was formed and the treaty was begun; I saw John Gibson on Girty's arrival get up, go out of the circle, and talk with Girty, upon which he, Gibson, went into a tent, I think colonel Stephens and after a short space he returned into the circle, drew out of his pocket a piece of *clean newspaper*, on which was written in *his own hand writing*, a speech for and in the name of Logan: this speech I *heard read three* times, *once* by *Gibson*, and *twice* by *Dunmore*, and the purport of that speech was, "that he (Logan) was the white man's friend; that on a journey to Pittsburgh to brighten this friendship, or on his return from thence, all his friends were killed at Yellow creek; that now when he died who should bury him, for the blood of Logan was now running in no living creatures veins, &c." but neither was *the name of Cresap*, or *any other person* particularized in this speech given in for Logan: nay, I believe no names were at all mentioned; but I recollect to see Dunmore put this speech among the treaty papers.

To the 7th question. In addition to what is stated above, I have *no doubt upon my mind but this Speech originated in, and was composed by John Gibson.*

To the 9th question. The Indian reason for Dunmore's war was, the killing the Indians at Yellow creek, Whetstone Point and Beach Bottom, but the Indians were the first aggressors, and committed the first hostilities.

To your 10th question. I assert that John Martin* and two of his men were killed on Hockhockan, and his canoe plundered of two hundred pounds worth of goods, about one year before this expedition, and consequently as above stated, the Indians were the first aggressors.

I lived on the river Ohio, and near the mouth of Yellow creek, from the year 1770, till the Indians were killed at that place, and *several years afterwards*: I was there *when the Indians were killed*, and present at the treaty in September or October, 1774, near Chilicothi on the Scioto, and certify that the foregoing statement of facts are true to the very best of my knowledge."

(Signed) BENJAMIN TOMLINSON.

I shall next, Sir, subjoin a certificate I received some time past from Joseph Cresap, esq. of Alleghany county, who was lately also one of the delegates in the legislature of this state, who was an officer under lord Dunmore, and present at the treaty; he also served in one of the rifle companies at the siege of Boston.

"In the Indian war of 1774, I was lieutenant in the company commanded by my uncle, captain Michael Cresap, I was on the expedition against Wappatomachee under major M'Donald, and also the expedition under the earl of Dunmore in person; I can therefore answer some of your questions from information, and others from personal knowledge; these I shall distinguish.

To your first question. As the Indians were killed at Yellow creek before I crossed the mountains, all I know is from information, but believe some of Logan's relations were killed at that place.

To your 2d. From the best of my recollection, these Indians were killed in April or May, in the year 1774; the place was the mouth of Yellow creek on the east side of the Ohio river; the circumstances attending the transaction were, that the Indians had a little before killed two men in a canoe in the river Ohio, not many miles from Yellow

* John Martin married the sister of Mr. Tomlinson.

creek; they were also very turbulent and saucy, and threatening to fall on the inhabitants about the river. The Indians in particular at Yellow creek were so uncommonly impudent, that the family which lived at the place to wit, Joshua Bakers, had removed away for fear, that is, all the women and children; and the people who killed those Indians were the *neighbouring men* who gathered on the occasion. Of this I am certain from the *best information*, that my uncle, captain *Michael Cresap, was not at Yellow creek*, nor *within fifty miles* of the place. This I am well assured is a fact, because *every person who was present say he was not there*, nor did I ever hear *any person* say that *he was there*.

To the 3d. As I was not present, it cannot be expected that I should know the particulars, but I believe no person commanded the party. There were present at the time and of the party, Nathaniel Tomlinson, Daniel Greathouse, Joshua Baker and John Sappington, the other names I know not. I have been informed Sappington killed Logan's brother, being provoked so to do by his putting on Nat. Tomlinson's coat.

To the 4th. I believe Logan's residence was the Wappatomachee, an Indian town on the river Muskingum. His character from the Indians themselves was that of a skulk; his prowess consisted in killing women and children, and he was called by the Indians an old woman; he was of no estimation as a *chief* or *warrior*, being *only a common man*.

To your 6th—Being present at the treaty held by lord Dunmore, near Scioto, in October 1774, I had an opportunity of seeing and knowing what passed. I know Logan was not present; nor did *I hear* of any speech made for, or in his name, or on his behalf, but recollect to have heard Cornstalk, the Chief of the Shawanese, in his speech mention Yellow creek, and some words in English, or *names* of *places* that I understood, but I believe he mentioned no *names* of *persons*, or charged any *individuals* with this or any other thing.

To your 9th—I will observe, that I believe the circumstances mentioned in my answer to your second question are some of those, which gave rise to the Indian war of 1774; to these may be added that the Indians had killed three men on Hockhockin, to wit, John Martin, an Indian trader; and two of his men near a year before, for this the white people had retaliated, and some were killed on both sides.

One thing is however certain, that the people west of the Alleghany (mountains) were so exasperated against the Indians, and so anxious and desirous to chastise them, that Dunmore's *whole expedition* was completed and finished without *one farthing of money* being *advanced* by government until the campaign was completely finished: neither was there an army ever more expeditiously raised, or rapidly marched, than this of Dunmore's notwithstanding *no pay* nor *absolute certainty of pay*.

I certify the fact before and above stated so far as they are within my own knowledge are true; and so far as I have learned them from information I verily believe them to be true."

(Signed) JOSEPH CRESAP.

I now, Sir, shall add an extract from a deposition, sent to me, and sworn to by a Mr. Thomas Chenoweth, who though a native of this county, many years past removed to the westward, and was with Mr. Cresap in the spring of 1774, at *the very time* when Logan's family were killed in manner as before stated.

"The said Thomas Chenoweth being sworn on the holy Evangels of Almighty God, deposeth and saith that early in the spring of the year 1774, he this deponent and his brother John Chenoweth set off in order to join some hands that capt. Michael Cresap had at work on the river Ohio, and to remain with the said hands until Mr. Cresap was ready to start on an adventure for exploring the Tenessee river. That he this deponent and his aforesaid brother did go to the Ohio, and at the place called the Round Bottom they met with *eleven* canoes with white inhabitants of the river below, passing up, and, as they said, flying from the Indians; and that they then returned with the said canoes and people to the mouth of Wheelen creek. That after they arrived at Wheelen the general conversation and expectation was an immediate Indian war; more especially that there were some Indians assembled at Yellow creek, who manifested an intention of hostility; upon which captain Cresap with a small party of men, this deponent being one of the number, set off from Wheelen in order to go up to Yellow creek, and chastise the insolence of those Indians; that on their way up they saw a canoe standing down the river, in which they suspected were hostile Indians, upon sight of which capt. Cresap with a few men crossed the river, to the Indian side, and the Indian canoe, as it proved to be, having discovered them crossing, stood in for the Virginia side, on which John, the brother of this deponent, and some others ran up the bank, fired upon and killed the two Indians, who were in the canoe. That about this time or sometime after, this deponent doth not precisely recollect, *they*, Mr. Cresap's party, *were informed* that a certain Daniel Greathouse and others had killed some, and dispersed others, of the party of Indians at Yellow creek. That the *party with capt. Cresap did not go to Yellow creek, but returned to the mouth of the Wheelen again.*"

This deposition was sworn to before, and is certified by, Gabriel Jacob, Esq. of Alleghany county.

In further support of the facts I have stated, I shall not hesitate to introduce the name of general Morgan, a representative in congress from your state, a gentleman whom I have not had the pleasure of seeing since he served in Virginia, in the summer of the year 1781, who a few weeks after Logan's family were killed, marched with his company to the place where that transaction happened; and also of captain Springer, who was lately in Philadelphia, whom I have never seen, but who was at that time also well acquainted in that part of the country, both of whom, I am *well informed*, have done myself and my connexions the justice to declare, that immediately after the death of Logan's family, it was a matter of notoriety that they were killed at the mouth of the Yellow creek by Daniel Greathouse and some other persons of that neighbourhood and that captain Michael Cresap was not at the time nearer to that place than fifty miles, or thereabouts; at the same time that I refer you to these gentlemen, I request them to accept my thanks, on behalf of myself and those connexions, for the justice which they have thus unsolicitedly done to us.

The *most zealous* of your friends cannot certainly *require farther testimony* to satisfy them of the injury which you have done to the ancestor of my children; but was it necessary, beside the names I have already introduced, and beside a variety of different characters, I am possessed of the names of thirteen *other officers*, who served under lord Dunmore, and were present at the treaty, who are now living all or the most of whom hold respectable, and some of them high appointments, who are I believe both able and ready to add the weight of their evidence in support of the cause I am now advocating.

And now, Sir, having among other subjects, endeavoured to investigate the true cause of the Indian war of 1774, with a view of freeing my countrymen of the westward from the stigma, which you have endeavoured to fix also upon them, in order to support the repution of *your* savages, and to shew that they were not the agressors, an act of justice to which I acknowledge them entitled, if for no other reason, for the affection they entertained for my father-in-law, I cannot avoid, notwithstanding the enormous length to which I foresee it will protract this letter, here to insert a sensible and judicious publication, which was printed in the newspapers of 1774, it is the "extract of a letter from Redstone;" take it as follows "It will not here be improper to investigate the cause of the Indian war, which broke out this spring, before I give you a sketch of the history of the expedition, which his Excellency Lord Dunmore has carried on successfully against the Shawanese, one of the richest, prowdest, and bravest of the Indian Nations.

In order to do this, it is necessary to look back as far as the year 1764, when Col. Bouquet made peace with that nation.

The Shawanese *never complied* with the terms of that treaty. They did not deliver up the white prisoners. There was no *lasting impression* made upon them by a stroke from the troops employed against them that campaign, and they *barely acquiesced* in *some articles* of the treaty by the *command* of the Six Nations. The Redhawk a Shawanese chief, insulted Col. Bouquet with impunity, and an indian killed the colonel's footman the *day after the peace was made*; this murder not being taken notice of, gave rise to several daring outrages committed immediately after. In the year following several murders were committed by the Indians on the New river, and soon after several men employed in the service of Wharton and company were killed on their passage to the Illinois and the goods belonging to the company carried off. Sometime after this outrage, a number of men employed to kill meat for the garrison at Fort Chartres, were killed, and their rifles, blankets, &c. carried to the Indian towns.

These *repeated* hostilities and outrages being committed *with impunity* made the Indians bold and daring. Although it was not the Shawanese alone that committed all those hostilities, yet letting *one nation* pass with impunity when mischief is done, inspires the *rest of the tribes* with courage, so that the officers commanding his majesty's troops on the[2] Ohio, at that time, not having *power* or *spirit* to *punish* the Indians, or *address* to *reclaim* them, mischief became *familiar* to them; they were *sure to kill and plunder* whenever it was in their power; and indeed they *panted* for an opportunity.

It is probable you will see Lord Dunmore's speech to some chiefs of the Six Nations, who waited on his Lordship to plead in favour of the Shawanese: in this speech his Lordship mentions the particular murders and outrages committed by them every year successively, since they pretended to make peace with Col. Bouquet.

The most recent murders committed by the Indians before the white people began to retaliate, was that of Capt. Russel's son, three more white, and two of his negroes, on the 15th day of October 1773. That of a Dutch family on the Kanhawa in the June of the same year, and of one Richard's in the July following; and that of Mr. Hogg and three white men on the great Kanhawa, early in April 1774. Things being in this situation, a message was sent to the Shawanese inviting them to bury the tomahawk, and brighten the chain of friendship. They *fired on the messengers*, and it was with difficulty they escaped with their lives. Immediately on their return, letters were wrote by some gentlemen at

Fort Pitt and dispersed among the inhabitants on the Ohio, assuring them that a war with the Shawanese was unavoidable, and desiring them to be on their guard, as it was uncertain where they would strike first. In the mean time two men of the names of Greathouse and Baker, sold some rum near the mouth of Yellow creek, and with them some Indians got drunk, and were killed. Lord Dunmore has ordered that the manner of their being killed be enquired into. Many officers, and other adventurers who were down the Ohio, in order to explore the country, and have lands surveyed, upon receiving the above intelligence, and seeing the letters from the gentlemen at Fort Pitt, thought proper to return; Capt. Michael Cresap was one of those gentleman. On their return up the river, they fell in with a party of Indians and being apprehensive that the Indians were now preparing to attack them, as appeared from their manœuvres, the white people, being the smallest number, thought it adviseable to have the first fire, whereupon they engaged, and after exchanging a few shot, killed two or three Indians and dispersed the rest; hostilities being thus commenced on both sides the matter became serious."

You will observe that Mr. Tomlinson, speaking from the best of his recollection, and having heard the original of what passes for Logan's speech, read three times declared that the *name of Cresap was not mentioned therein*; I cannot doubt but that his memory is correct, for which I will assign several reasons. Mr. Tomlinson had long been well acquainted with Mr. Cresap, they had served together that campaign, his name being familiar to him was not likely to pass unnoticed, and as he *perfectly knew* Mr. Cresap had no part in the death of Logan's family, any attempt to implicate him in the guilt of that transaction, could not but most powerfully have affected his mind, and in all probability would have made too deep an impression to be forgotten. Again, as it is absolutely certain Mr. Cresap was not concerned in the death of Logan's family, and it must be supposed that Logan himself was not unapprized of the circumstances attending their death, and of the persons by whom they were killed, there is no reason to suppose, even had the speech been genuine, that *he* would have introduced the name of a man who was perfectly innocent, and who had done him no injury; *much less* can it be supposed that Col. Gibson, who undoubtedly was the author of that speech, who well knew Logan's family, who lived in that part of the country, who it cannot be doubted, also well knew by whom Logan's family was killed, would *wantonly*, and contrary to the *well known fact*, have made such a charge against a man with whom he was so intimately acquainted, one who was so beloved by the inhabitants, and who was a brother officer, at that moment serving with him. To these let me add, that Captain Michael Cresap, his nephew, Michael Cresap, and Joseph Cresap, were then serving under Lord Dunmore, and present at the treaty, yet have I evidence the *most convincing to my mind*, that not one of the name had ever heard, or suspected, that a Cresap was charged with being concerned in the death of Logan's family, until within about three or four years past; nor do I believe there was a man in Lord Dunmore's army, who would have produced such a speech with Mr. Cresap's name inserted therein, unless he was weary of his life, or courted danger in preference to every other object. Believing therefore, upon such powerful evidence, that the *name of Cresap* was not *originally* in the pretended speech of Logan, I at least shall expect that you will account by whom, and how, that name was introduced therein, or that you submit to the justice of the sentiments I have already expressed on that subject.

Thus, Sir, I have effected the *great objects* I had in view. I have proved that neither Col. Cresap, nor his son Michael Cresap were infamous for the many murders committed on the unoffending Indians; that neither of them, nor any other of the name were concerned in the death of Logan's family; that your elegant specimen of Indian eloquence, to illustrate which you introduced your unfounded *story*, is entirely fictitious; and that your celebrated Mingo chief was an ignorant, insignificant, worthless savage, without merit and without consequence.

Thus having done, I now call on you, *Thomas Jefferson, Esquire, Vice-President of the United States;*

You have been *solemnly arraigned* at the *bar* of that *august* tribunal, *the public*, on a charge of *foul calumny.*—You have *refused* to plead, and have *stood mute*; of this no *advantage* has been taken; you have been *put upon a fair* a *candid* and an *impartial trial*; the *evidence has been heard*; you *stand convicted.*

And now, Sir, if *you have aught to say* in extenuation of your offence, or to shew why *sentence* should not be passed upon you, come forward, and you shall *yet be heard!*

Here for the present I *pause*. The *future* must determine whether any degree of respect whatever, shall be entertained for you, by

Your very humble servant,   LUTHER MARTIN.

Printed in *Porcupine's Gazette*, 3 Mch. 1798; at head of text: "Mr. Martin's VIIIth Letter to the Philosopher Jefferson" and "To the Honourable Thomas Jefferson, Esq. Vice-President of the United States."

[1] *Porcupine's Gazette*: "mother."
[2] *Porcupine's Gazette*: "he."

From Martha Jefferson Randolph

Bellmont February 26th[1] 1798

You tell me My dear Father that I ought to write oftener and enforce your request with an argument that has allways been irresistable with me "the pleasure it gives you" but the expression of a tenderness like mine is not easily rendered even by those endowed with the happy faculty of expressing their feelings. that fortunate gift however was never mine or else subjects for a letter could never fail while the heart that dictates them continued to beat, but there is so little consonance between the cold & inadequate language of a pen totally unversed in the art of describing them, and the glowing affections of a heart fraught with every tender sentiment the human mind is susceptible of, that I never can bear the weak and imperfect picture of my feelings which a letter presents. the solitude in which we live affords little else[2] to comunicate but the sensations and reflections of its inhabitants. our dwelling begins to be infinitely more comfortable by the addition and repairs of some offices and the arrival of our furniture from Varina perhaps allso having acquired a seasoning to the place, added to this Mr Randolph has taken all his workmen, wheel rights carpenters smiths &c under his own command which renders his presence indispensibly necessary here, and of course the acceptance of your attentive and affectionate offer impracticable. Isaac has given him a great deal of trouble allways dissatisfied and rebellious he at last eloped with an intention of going to Eppington but being twice taken by the patrol and escaping both times he returned home much humbled and apparently better disposed to work. my communications with John have been regular from the first of January according to the little callender you left me. your smoke house was under mined and[3] seventeen pieces of meat taken out the same accident happened at Dunlora about the same time and by the same means tho the loss they sustained was less rather than yours you have hardly I imagine been informed of poor Aunt Skipwith's death she had been perfectly insane for two months before it, tho well otherwise. she expired in a fit with out ever having had an interval of reason or knowing any one about her. we have Mr & Mrs P. Carr & their family with us at present consisting of his Sister & 2 children; of Browse we have not heard a word but by your letters. Mr Randolphs accompts as Executor guardian &c have prevented his writing to you this post but the next he will certainly do it and give you the information you demand respecting your affairs, Davenport's particularly who I fear has done little or nothing this winter this however is rather conjecture than any certain knowledge. we are all in perfect health but Ellen who looks wretchedly but I hope it is the effect of teething only adieu my Dear Papa I am afraid you will scarcely be able to decypher this scrawl, written within the noise and confusion of the children and chat of the Ladies believe me with unchangeable and truly ardent affection yours

M RANDOLPH

RC (ViU: Coolidge Deposit); endorsed by TJ as received 8 Mch. 1798 and so recorded in SJL.

[1] Randolph first wrote "18th" before altering date to read as above.
[2] Randolph here canceled "for a" and interlined the following two words.
[3] Randolph here canceled "robbed of."

From Thomas Mann Randolph

T.M.R: TO TH: JEFFERSON,   Belmont Feb. 26. 98

I did not expect to have written by this post as I was much engaged in preparing some papers & in the business of the farm my Overseer being abroad on some affairs of his own, and Martha had written fully this morning. I recollect however now (7 oclock in the Evening) that tis necessary to inform you the Nailery will soon be out of iron if it does not receive a supply from you. George came over some few days since to ask my advice: he told me he was then nearly upon working the half crews—I recommended sending the Waggon for a parcel which was lying in Columbia—it was done but not by 3 days so soon as I wished which reduced George truly to the half crews: he has been working it only a day or two however and today James has arrived with 36 bunches, most of it unluckily of the large kind. I shall write this moment to George Jefferson to ask if there is any in Richmond and to hurry it up if there is—I hope there has been time since the Delaware opened. George tells me the demand for nails is very brisk.

Will it be possible to prevail on a good journey man Blacksmith to come round from Philad'a. & work on a farm here? I w'd. give any wages within tolerable bounds. Nothing of Arnold yet. Page & George progress—the former anxious but peevish & too ready to strike—the latter absolutely wasting with care—Tobacco is his favorite crop he has 30.000 ready in the pack.

Yours most affectionately   TH: M. RANDOLPH

RC (ViU: Edgehill-Randolph Papers); addressed: "Thomas Jefferson Vice-president U.S. Philad'a."; franked and postmarked; endorsed by TJ as received 8 Mch. 1798 and so recorded in SJL.

From Horatio Gates

DEAR SIR   27th: Febry. 1798.

The post which arrived within an Hour from Boston, brings an account, that a Vessel had just put into Salem, from Bourdeaux in France, after a passage of Forty Days, with Intelligence; that every Vessel in The Ports of That Republic, from Forty Tons, & upwards, was put in Requisition. (The one arrived at Salem, Sliped Her Cable and got to Sea at Night;) I conclude the like has taken place in England, or somewhat Similar; which Accounts for Our not hearing also from thence. The Captain of the Vessel at Salem Says, Our Commissioners are Treated politely at paris, but not any Answer would be given to them, until The Directory heard from The US.—I had the pleasure to receive yours, with Kuscuiusko's inclosed—If the French are Determined upon The Invasion, as, from the Intelligence I conclude they are, The Contest will be as Important as that of Anthony & Cæsar, The Empire of the World—

with Sentiments of Esteem, & Regard I am Your Obedient Servant

HORATIO GATES

RC (DLC); endorsed by TJ as received 1 Mch. 1798 and so recorded in SJL.

The Boston *Independent Chronicle* of 26 Feb. included news from SALEM where Captain Townsend had just arrived after being detained by an embargo at Bordeaux from 18 Dec. 1797 to 10 Jan. 1798. He reported that every vessel of more than 15 tons was PUT IN a state of REQUISITION as France prepared for a three-pronged invasion of England.

From William Short

DEAR SIR   Paris Feb. 27. 1798

I had the pleasure of writing to you on the 27th. of Dec. & 23. ulto. the first was of very great length I do not recollect whether it was sent by duplicate, as was the last.—It was sent to M. de la Motte at Havre, to whom I addressed also the first copy of that of the 23d. ulto.—He has just informed me that having recd. it whilst the vessel on wch. he had put that of Dec. was in the road waiting for a wind, he had sent it also on board of the same, addressing it as he had done the other under the cover of the Sec. of State—this he informs me is his usage as to all letters destined for America having found it the only sure means to prevent the Captain's throwing them overboard or losing them.—(On reading over again M. de la Motte's letter I see it may be construed so as to leave some doubt whether he put mine under the cover of the S. of S. or gave them to the Capt.—but I suppose the former)—The vessel however by which they went was the James of New-York. Capt. Thos. Fitch, bound to New-York & sailed the 10th. of Febry. or thereabouts.—Mr. Fenwick writes me from Bordeaux that the one wch. I sent him (the 2d. of that of Jan. 23.) will go by the ship Pomona Capt. Waters bound for Baltimore—the present will be sent to Havre, in the hope of its being in time for an American gentleman who I learn is about sailing in a Danish vessel for Norfolk—If I had known of this vessel in time I should probably have made use of the opportunity notwithstanding the season is not of my choice, & notwithstanding I should prefer landing further north, being desirous to visit such parts of the U.S. as I am not acquainted with—Still I should have made use of this vessel from the uncertain prospect of finding another opportunity—& the prospect of being obliged to go via England, which augments the journey, the sea—& the risk of being stopped—On the whole the prospect of finding a favorable passage has probably been at no time so unpromising since my being in Europe—yet I am resolved to undertake it in the spring or the early summer—& I count with great impatience on the pleasure of seeing you, my friends & my country.—

Having made a divorce with politics as I have already mentioned I have only to trouble you on my personal affairs, for which I am really almost ashamed, seeing that your time must be at present fully employed between your own & those of a public nature—I count however for my excuse on your good will & friendship.—The principal & most pressing is that of the 9. m. dollars—If I were sure of my late letters getting safe across the sea I shd. have nothing to add—it is by way of greater caution that I repeat here my request to recover the sum, out of wch. I have been held, perhaps somewhat by my own negligence, beyond all kind of reason—the only possible difficulty that can be evoked & wch. the Sec. of State's letter of July 17th. 96. states, is in the case of Mr Randolph's acting as my private agent—to this I have only to add & I trust nothing else need be added, Mr Randolph was never my private agent in any instance before or after, & in this instance, every thing that passed was in our official despatches respectively—I beg them to be recurred to, as they will be found in the archives of the dept. of State— There can be certainly no right or reason in keeping me at present out of a sum to which I was entitled in the year 94.—& wch. I was prevented from recieving then by an arrangement in wch. I was not consulted, made by the then Sec. of State as appears by one of his subsequent letters without any regard to me, & solely for the purpose of accomodating one of the other foreign ministers (Col. Humphreys)—It may be necessary to observe here that I drew on the bankers of the U.S.

last spring at the moment that I was about to set out for America—but this has nothing to do with the 9. m. dollars—& was on acct. of the $\frac{1}{4}$ salary allowed for return—It enters of course into the final settlement of my acct. with the U.S.

I should wish if it were possible that Indian Camp should be tenanted out—I fear however it will be difficult to find tenants, where lands are so cheap & where there are slaves—Otherwise I should be glad to have the greater part if not the whole of my fortune vested in that way—the nearer your residence the better I should like it—if it were possible to have lands producing on the purchase money a clear & regular rent of 5. p.ct. I shd. prefer it to an interest of 6. p.ct. on the purchase money in the funds—& I understand that the 6. pct. funds yield on any sum that shd. be vested there at present, between 7 & 8. pct.—on account of their being below par.—If I could have purchased the whole of the Blenheim tract—or that part on the southern side of the mountains, & placed good tenants thereon producing a regular & suitable rent on the purchase money I should have liked it—but as I have said, I fear tenants cannot be counted on in that quarter, if in any quarter of Virginia—for it is in direct opposition to theory, as it presents itself to me, that free people at their ease can be found to cultivate the lands of others, where they are able to purchase lands of their own & where they are accustomed to see only slaves, working such lands—but I have learned so much to distrust theory in every respect that I do not lay this down as infallible & shall be happy to find it contradicted by fact—My first pursuit will be on arriving in America, to endeavour to realize what I have disponible, in this way—I see nothing secure in the world at present except real estate in our country—the clouds that have been so long hanging over property—the thunder that has from time to time been bursting—the hurricanes that have been raging—are if I do not mistake not an end—but will spread still further—No country wch. has not already been attained seems more exposed than England—It is true their affairs have so often given the lye to calculation in the course of this century that it would be rash to calculate the moment—but any person whose property is now in that country & who should think it safe there would seem to me to have a most robust faith. I should imagine that many prudent people there would be transferring something at least to the U.S.—this perhaps may raise our funds; & as it is probable many of the class of farmers may emigrate there, this may in time facilitate the letting out lands at rent—but it would not be prudent to count absolutely on this contingency until it should take place—

As to the canal shares of Richmond I do not know what is the rate of interest they produce or are likely to produce—I have seen Marshall but once since my arrival here & had not an opportunity of conversing with him much on the subject—I learned however from him that the canal is not to unite with the landing below Richmond, but to end in a bason on the hill—This must necessarily diminish exceedingly the value of that work, & must certainly render the city unwholesome—less so perhaps than the canals at Batavia but still in a great degree—This it may be said is nothing to the holders of shares provided they do not live in that place, & provided a good interest regularly accrues on their money.

You mentioned that certain sums that you shd. be re-imbursed on my acct. you shd. be at a loss how to dispose of, & that others were left in Philadelphia subject to my call on my arrival—As I shall have cash with me for my immediate expences I beg the favor of you to have whatever may be on hand immediately revested, & in future, as it may accrue, in some fund bearing interest—& in this class I consider, the deferred—it is that perhaps to wch. I shd. give the preference for present purchases although the interest does not begin before some years—

It is probable you will have followed in your mind the progress of the Philanthropic establishment at Sierra Leona—If you have not read, I recommend to you a work published two or three years ago in London by a Swede of the name of Wadstrom entitled an Essay on Colonization &c. & on Sierra Leona & Bulama[1]—It gives very encouraging hopes with respect to the perfectibility of the black race—It is more than probable that the establishment at S.L. will degenerate from its first principles & become in time an establishment merely commercial, shackled by the mother country & by the succeeding proprietors in England, with exclusions monopolies &c. &c.—but in the mean time it has done & will have done infinite good, by turning the researches of Philanthropes & of Philosophers, towards the black inhabitants of Africa—Several travellers have lately explored their country beyond what has been hitherto done—& it is even affirmed that one of them has discovered a city larger than London—we are expecting the publication of his work with impatience—Abating a great deal for exageration, still it leaves enough to suppose a state of civilization far advanced—What has been already seen & authentically established by late travellers leaves no doubt of their susceptibility of all the arts of civilization & gives sanguine hopes that our posterity at least will see improved, populous & extensive nations of the black color, formed into powerful societies who will par in every respect with whites under the same circumstances—

This will insure the restoration of the rights of citizenship of those blacks who inhabit the U.S. if it be not sooner done, as it may be expected, by the gradual & beneficial operation of our own laws—& will tend to remove the aversion (wch. it is so natural shd. exist, even among the least subjected to prejudice, with those who have been [bore & bred] among blacks all of them in the state of degradation inseparable from the most mitigated degree of slavery) to the mixture of the two colors—If this be an evil, is it not the least that can take place under present circumstances? It is certainly less than keeping 700,000 people & their descendants in perpetual slavery even if it were possible—Is it not less also than having that number of free people living in the same country & separated from the rest of the community by a marked & impassable line?—Is it not less even than the expopulation of the U.S. of so great a number of their inhabitants by any possible means? The revocation of the edict of Nantes, or what may perhaps be considered as still more in point, the expulsion of the Moors from Spain during the last century, shews us how deep such wounds go & how difficult, if not impossible, to cicatrize them. It will be said that the expulsed in these cases were the most industrious artisans & manufacturers of the country—many of them undoubtedly were—but the blacks with us are the tillers of the land & I can never believe that for any people (unquestionably for us it cannot be) the loss of their manufacturers is a greater evil than that of their agriculturers—

As to the evils to be apprehended from the mixture of the two colors (& I know that the most enlightened & virtuous minds do apprehend such) the subject is certainly worthy of serious attention—Facts are certainly wanting to guide us—It is impossible yet to know, notwithstanding the long systems drawn from short experiments, what influence the climate alone will produce on the black color—If I do not mistake the blacks in our country several generations removed from their imported ancestors are sensibly less dark than the Africans themselves—some part of this may be imputed perhaps to a mixture of the whites in their production, but a part also to the climate—Suppose a black family transplanted to Sweden, may we not presume, for as yet there is no possibility of the fact, that in a sufficient number of succeeding generations, the color would disappear from the meer effect of the climate—If the climate has this tendency by however gradual degrees, we may well suppose that in time the color of our inhabitants will revert to its present state, even if the blacks should be incorporated, as we may be assured that this incorporation will take place by slow & very slow degrees, owing to the real preference that the whites will give to their own color & the deep rooted prejudices against the other—But even admitting that this mixture should change our hue & that all of our Southern inhabitants should advance to the middle ground between their present color & the black (& this is granting more than can be asked as there are every where more whites than blacks[2]) still they would not be of a

[150]

darker color than the inhabitants of some of the provinces of Spain—& I do not see that these provinces labour under any inconvenience greater than the rest of the Spaniards or that the Spaniards in general labour under any inconvenience with respect to the rest of Europe, merely on account of their color—Even in our own country there are some people darker, than the gradual mixture of the blacks can ever make us, & yet I do not know[3] that they suffer from thence—I don't know if you ever saw, a Mrs. Randolph afterwards Mrs. Tucker,—There is no country that might not be content to have its women like her—There is no sentiment arising from the contemplation of beauty that they would not be capable of inspiring equally with those who can boast the perfect mixture of the rose & the lilly.

The next thing to be considered is, how is to be effected this great & momentous object, the transformation of 700,000 slaves into free citizens—& here I own a great many difficulties present themselves even to my contemplation & at this distance—how many more will be seen by a penetrating genius capable of diving into the bosom of futurity, & who examines the subject on the spot—The first desideratum is that such geniuses should turn their attention towards the examination of this subject, & certainly none can be more worthy to exercise the talents of the statesman, the philosopher, the philanthrope, in short all who have any regard to the interests of their country or the rights of humanity— but let them have always before their eyes this golden rule "ne soyez pas jaloux du tems"[4]—the longer I live in the world the more I see the danger of ever losing sight of this polar star of every political mariner— the best measures on earth may become the most disastrous by this means—Let Hispaniola & what has taken place there within these last seven years be adverted to—I hope it will operate on our citizens, as well those who have the misfortune to have slaves as those who having not, might from an impatient indignation, be disposed to break at once their irons & turn them loose, without preparation for that state, on the society—they cannot fail to become beasts of prey if their numbers surpass at once the means of subsistence—To avoid all such risks (& there must come many instances in time where there will be such risks either from external or internal enemies) let the owners of slaves begin to prepare them as well as themselves for the gradual transmutation—let the legislatures of the different states adopt also some gentle operation (this I fear is more to be wished than expected from some of them)—let the enlightened & virtuous citizens, who toil for public instruction, turn the public mind towards this subject, & endeavour to demonstrate that the owners of slaves would gain in point of interest, by the change—for it is perhaps a melancholy consideration but it is not the less true, that the only way to bring men in general to desire an event is to shew that they have an interest in it—if they see their interest on one side & humanity on the other, never count on the majority for the last—see how ingenious they are to satisfy their own conscience & then to prove to others that their interest is not opposed to the general good—how many good Christians are there, who consider themselves the beloved of Christ & the invariable followers of his gospel, who with all his precepts in their mind go to Africa, wrest the mother from the infant—the husband from the wife—chain them to the whip & lash, they & their posterity for ever, nay hold this scourge in their own hand & inflict it with all the *gout* of their abominable appetites, & who do not doubt that they are violating the whole doctrine of the author of their religion—To what absurdities may not the human mind bring itself when this can be thought by them less offensive to God, than eating meat on a friday?—

I wish the slave holders to be attacked by proofs that their interest would not suffer, because I think it the most certain way of converting them, & because I believe firmly that observation, & still more, experience, will shew this to be the case—As example will of course have more weight than precept, suppose some person of fortune & well known should attempt a plan somewhat like this—Let him ascertain what his slaves bring him of neat revenue, deduction made of taxes paid on them, food clothing &c. &c.—Let him if it be possible find a sufficient number of tenants (better if free blacks as being more convincing) & lease out a like quantity of land to them, & compare the neat rent wch. he may recieve—Or let him separate from among his slaves such as are most to be relied on for care & industry, & let him give them a certain portion of land on rent, & let him compare the neat revenue, produced by a like number of slaves—Let all the minute calculations of detail be entered into & published in the gazettes—Whatever may be the result of the first essays, time & repetition will I think infallibly shew the advantage of free, above forced, labor.

I have thought sometimes that one step wch. might be obtained towards an amelioration of the condition of our slaves, would be to assimilate them to the serfs of Europe, by attaching them to the glebe—the owners perhaps wd. not be averse to this, or at least many of them, & the slaves would thus gain an exemption from the cruel separations of father, mother, husband, wife, so often seen—& I believe also that this security of a permanent residence, would settle their minds towards improving any little lot of ground that might be given them to work for their own account, during the time allowed them—If the legislature should consider this change in the tenure of slaves as an attack on what is called property, let them, instead of a general law obliging this change, make one that shall authorize the holders of slaves to make this change & attach their own slaves to the glebe, so as to be binding on their heirs—Let them follow also the example of Spain & having each slave valued, oblige the owner to recieve that value, whenever the slave shall offer it—& further oblige them to yield to the slaves one day in the week more, or any other portion of their time, that the slaves shall have been able to purchase—It is easy to see that only the most industrious & most ripe for liberty will be emancipated in this way—Let humane societies be formed for the gradual emancipation & instruction of the blacks—let them recieve subscriptions & purchase such as appear most worthy, preferring always the females, because each individual thus manumitted stops one continual source of slavery—thus the purchasing all the female slaves at once, wch. would cost less than the same number of males, is purchasing in fact all future generations instead of one only—if any female purchased be unable to provide for her children, let them be provided for like other poor children—they can never be a charge[5] to a young country like ours—they may be bound for a time sufficient to pay for the food of their infancy.—

Notwithstanding the immense length of this letter I should have a great deal more to say to you if I were not afraid of wearing out your patience—I therefore put to a stop to this subject for the present, & will detain you no longer than to inclose you an acct. of a new typographical invention here—I have heard a great many disputes on the subject—a thousand plausible reasons, that I cannot answer are adduced by many argumenters to prove, that the invention cannot succeed—I must refer you to experience, the only sure guide—the only argument I make use of in favor of the invention is this—the type & impression (of wch a prospectus is already published) is beautiful—the authors say they will give a volume in 18.° for 15. sols—now gentlemen as I rely only on *resultats*, if as I dont doubt they will do this I shall certainly purchase their editions, notwithstanding all the reasonings however specious or unanswerable that you give me—& as I suppose every body else will prefer an equally good impression at a third or a fourth of the price, I shd. imagine that these printers will sell more than any others who sell dearer—The reply wch. I recieve is "C'est egal Monsieur—Je vous repond que cela ne reussira pas—c'est impossible—c'est moi qui vous le dis—& je vous le prouverai quand vous le voudrez."[6]—

Adieu; my dear Sir, & believe me sincerely & invariably your friend & servant   W: SHORT

RC (DLC); at foot of first page: "Thos. Jefferson, V.P. of the U.S."; endorsed by TJ as received 22 June 1798 and so recorded in SJL. FC (DLC: Short Papers);

consisting of an abbreviated summary entirely in Short's hand, part of the same epistolary record in which he summarized his letter to TJ of 23 Jan. 1798; at foot of text: "sent to Higginson [. . .], sailed in May." Enclosure: Clipping from a newspaper identified by Short in FC as the *Journal de Paris*, in French, containing news items as late as 13 Feb. 1798 as well as a notice, headed "Mélanges. Typographie," of a new printing method patented by Pierre Didot, Firmin Didot, and Louis Etienne Herhan, to commence with an edition of Virgil, the products of the new process being called "stéréotypes," the patentees' method allowing them to correct errors at low cost and create perfect editions at about half the price of books printed by traditional methods that are usually filled with errors (DLC: TJ Papers, 236:42346; incomplete; with a pointing hand drawn in ink next to the title of the notice).

Short's explanation of the 9. M. DOLLARS owed him for salary and expenses appears in his letter to TJ of 2 Sep. 1795; see also Timothy Pickering to TJ, 25 Apr. 1798.

An act of Parliament in 1791 incorporated the joint-stock Sierra Leone Company to facilitate the PHILANTHROPIC ESTABLISHMENT on the west coast of Africa, where settlement of British and American people of African descent had begun four years earlier (Ellen Gibson Wilson, *John Clarkson and the African Adventure* [London, 1980], 53-5). The reputed CITY LARGER THAN LONDON was likely Housa (Hausa), which according to an account published in the early 1790s had a population "equalled only . . . by that of London and Cairo" and was the seat of an empire. Its location was thought to be in the

watershed of the Niger River, in the same part of West Africa as the legendary trading center Tombouctou (Timbuktu), long an object of European curiosity. The region, seemingly impenetrable by Europeans, was a focus of attention of the Association for Promoting the Discovery of the Interior Parts of Africa, founded in London in 1788 by Sir Joseph Banks and others. Short may have been EXPECTING THE PUBLICATION of the account of Scottish physician Mungo Park, who had made an arduous journey under the association's auspices without locating either city and published his *Travels in the Interior Districts of Africa* in 1799, or Short may not have learned yet of the death of another explorer sponsored by the association, Daniel Houghton, who had set out for Tombouctou but died of dysentery short of his goal (Robin Hallett, ed., *Records of the African Association, 1788-1831* [London, 1964], 13, 27-9, 39, 103, 110-26, 130-9, 300-3).

Short later sent TJ a volume of Virgil produced by the NEW TYPOGRAPHICAL INVENTION of stereotype printing (TJ to Short, 13 Apr. 1800).

[1] Preceding clause interlined.
[2] Short interlined the preceding three words in place of "blacks than whites."
[3] Word interlined in place of "remember."
[4] Translation: "make haste slowly" (literally, "do not be jealous of time").
[5] Word interlined in place of "loss."
[6] Translation: "Never mind, Sir—I reply that it will not succeed—it is impossible—I am telling you—and I will prove it to you whenever you wish."

From George Jefferson

DEAR SIR   Richmond March 1st. 1798.

I received by yesterdays post a letter from Mr. Randolph in which he enquires of me whether you have any nail rod here? and desires if you have, that I will send it up immediately, as the naillery is almost at a stand for want of it.

I am induced to give you this information least Mr. R. should con-

clude I have some in my possession, and for that reason delay acquaint-
ing you with the want of it.

I am Mt. sincerely Dear Sir Your Very Obt. servt.

GEO. JEFFERSON

RC (MHi); at foot of text: "Thomas Jefferson esqr."; endorsed by TJ as received 8 Mch. 1798 and so recorded in SJL.

Notes on a Conversation with Henry Tazewell

Mar. 1. mr Tazewell tells me that when the appropriations for the British treaty were on the carpet and very uncertain, in the lower house, there being at that time a number of bills in the hands of Commees of the Senate, none reported, & the Senate idle for want of them, he, in his place, called on the commees to report, and particularly on mr King, who was of most of them. King said that it was true the Commees kept back their reports waiting the event of the question about appropria-tion: that if that was not carried, they considered legislation as at an end, that they might as well break up & consider the union as dissolved. Tazewell expressed his astonmt at these ideas & called on King to know if he had misapprehended him. King rose again & repeated the same words. the next day Cabot took an occasion in debate, & so awkward a one as to shew it was a thing agreed to be done, to repeat the same sentiments in stronger terms, and carried further by declaring a deter-mination on their side to break up and dissolve the govmt.[1]

MS (DLC: TJ Papers, 102:17525); en-tirely in TJ's hand; on same sheet as Notes on a Conversaton with John Adams, 15 Feb. 1798; with a long, partially illegible cancellation at the end of the entry.

For tactics used in the Federalist cam-paign to win APPROPRIATIONS FOR THE BRITISH TREATY, see Madison to TJ, 18 Apr. 1796.

[1] TJ here canceled more than five lines, part of the first being illegible, with the re-mainder as follows: "[as] one of those who [went to?] Annapolis ([at] the convention there) by an affectation of a too high-flying spirit of independance, endeavoured th[en] to prevent the calling a grand convention, who failing in that & coming to the grand convention did every thing in his power to prevent their agreeing in any thing, and was one of those who had been previously in the combination to seize the powers of govmt and erect one in a form of their own chusing: as told me by Baldwin ante Jan. 5. 98."

To James Madison

I wrote you last on the 22d. since which I have received yours without date, but probably of about the 18th. or 19th. an arrival to the Eastward brings us some news which you will see detailed in the papers. the new partition of Europe is sketched, but how far authentic we know not. it has some probability in it's form. the French appear busy in their preparations for the invasion of England: nor is there any appearance of movements on the part of Russia & Prussia which might divert them from it.

The late birthnight has certainly sown tares among the exclusive federals. it has winnowed the grain from the chaff. the sincerely Adamites did not go. the Washingtonians went religiously, & took the secession of the others in high dudgeon. the one sex threaten to desert the levees, the other the evening parties. the whigs went in number, to encourage the idea that the birthnights hitherto kept had been for the General & not the President, and of course that time would bring an end to them. Goodhue, Tracy, Sedgwick &c did not attend: but the three Secretaries & Attorney General did. we were surprised at the close of the last week with a symptom of a disposition to repeal the stamp act. petitions for that purpose had come from Rhode island & Virginia, & had been committed to rest with the Ways & Means. mr Harper, their chairman, in order to enter on the law for amending it,[1] observed it would be necessary first to put the petitions for repeal out of the way, and moved an immediate decision on them. the Rhode islanders begged & prayed for a postponement, that not expecting that question to be called up they were not at all prepared. but Harper would shew no mercy. not a moment's delay should be allowed. it was taken up, and on a question without debate determined in favor of the petitions by a majority of 10. astonished & confounded, when an order to bring in a bill for repeal was moved, they began in turn to beg for time 3 weeks, one week, 3 days, 1 day. not a moment would be yeilded. they made three attempts for adjournment. but the majorities appeared to grow. it was decided by a majority of 16. that the bill should be brought in. it was brought in the next day, & on the day after passed, sent up to the Senate, who instantly sent it back rejected by a silent vote of 15. to 12. R. I. & N. Hampshire voted for the repeal in Senate.[2] the act will therefore go into operation July 1. but probably without amendments. however I am persuaded it will be shortlived. it has already excited great commotion in Vermont, and grumblings in Connecticut. but they are so priest-ridden that nothing is to be expected from them but the most bigotted[3] passive obedience. no news yet from our commissioners. but their silence is admitted to augur peace. there is no talk yet of the time of adjourning, tho' admitted we have nothing to do, but what could be done in a fortnight or three weeks. when the spring opens and we hear from our commissioners, we shall probably draw pretty rapidly to conclusion.—a friend of mine here wishes to get a copy of Mazzei's Recherches historiques et politiques. where are they?　　　salutations & Adieu.

wheat 1.50. flour 8.50. tobo. 13.50

RC (DLC: Madison Papers); addressed: "James Madison junr. near Orange Court house," written over partially erased "Mr. Alexander F[. . .]"; franked. PrC (DLC); at foot of first page in ink: "Mr. Madison."

On 2 Mch. the *Philadelphia Gazette* carried the articles of peace to be ratified at the conference at Rastadt, which detailed the NEW PARTITION OF EUROPE.

On 11 Jan. Thomas Tillinghast presented a resolution from the Rhode Island legislature urging repeal of the Stamp Act. The next day Virginia congressman Carter B. Harrison presented a petition from three Virginia counties with the same request. The Virginia petition was referred to the ways and means committee, which reported a few days later that repeal would be inexpedient. In the committee of the whole house on 26 Feb., Robert G. HARPER noted that the secretary of the treasury was preparing to implement the tax and needed any amendments to it immediately. Despite the report of the ways and means committee, the House voted 47 to 37 IN FAVOR OF THE PETITIONS. Tillinghast then moved for a vote on his resolution in favor of repeal, which passed 49 to 36. Seeing that he was in the minority, Harper encouraged the House to delay action until more information was available from the Treasury Department. Motions for postponement and ADJOURNMENT were defeated, and a resolution to bring in a BILL to repeal the stamp tax was passed 52 to 36. The legislation was BROUGHT IN THE NEXT DAY and on 28 Feb. it passed by a 51 to 42 vote. Before adjourn-

ment that same day, the House received word that the Senate had REJECTED it (*Annals*, 7:820, 828, 830-1, 847, 1069-83, 1097-8; JHR, 3:203-9). COMMOTION IN VERMONT, AND GRUMBLINGS IN CONNECTICUT: on 31 Jan., *The Bee*, the Republican newspaper in New London, Connecticut, printed an essay entitled "Loyalty," which asserted that an "unqualified attachment to government" is "one of the most pernicious doctrines that can be admitted into a republic." It shackled Americans with "poll-taxes, excise laws, British treaties, and stamp duties." The same issue reported that protests against the "dreaded *Stamp Act*" erupted in parts of Vermont, Massachusetts, and New York state when it became known that the act was expected to go into effect on 1 Jan. Although some protesters were quieted by the news that the tax would fall primarily on seaports, the reporter remarked: "What kind of a law is that, the only argument in favour of which is, that the burden of it will be borne by a small part only of the community? *Grumblers call it unequal and unjust*."

In 1788 Madison received 164 copies of Philip MAZZEI's *Recherches historiques et politiques sur les États-Unis d'Amérique*, a work of four volumes that had been published in Paris. For the distribution of this publication, see Madison, *Papers*, 17:88n.

[1] Preceding five words interlined in place of "something else."

[2] Preceding two words interlined.

[3] Preceding word interlined in place of "abject."

To Thomas Mann Randolph

TH:J. TO TMR.   Philadelphia Mar. 2. 98.

All well. no news from our commissioners at Paris. no talk yet of the time of adjournment, though probably it will be very soon after we hear from Paris. I wrote you 2. letters on the 22d. of Feb. no change in the price of wheat or flour. old tobacco at 13.50. I write in the moment of the departure of the post so can only add kisses to my dear Martha & the little ones and an affectionate Adieu to yourselves.

P.S. if any mules can be got in the neighborhood for 100. Dollars of the breed of mrs Barclay's Jack, I had rather buy them than horses taking the credit before mentioned.

RC (DLC); addressed: "Thomas M. Randolph at Belmont near Charlottesville"; franked and postmarked at Baltimore, 4 Mch.; endorsed by Randolph as received 1[0] Mch. 1798. Not recorded in SJL.

From Hugh Williamson

DEAR SIR   New York 3rd March 1798

The Letter you did me the favour to write on the 11th: ult: had been left at my lodging by the Penny Post and was handed me on my return to this City. The Report of the Committee I have returned to be forwarded to whom it concerns in the State of Tennessee on Cumberland River.

Congress as I observe or rather the House of Reps. have given leave to bring in a Bill to repeal the Stamp Act, not as I presume because money is not wanted, but some People object, by antient Prejudice to the Word, *Stamp Act.* Is it probable that a Tax less oppressive or more tolerable in its Operation will be substituted to the Stamp Tax. I think recourse will be had to a Tax infinitely more severe in its operation, a land Tax. And that Tax will be adopted meerly to save the trouble of devising a more complex System, or to save trouble in legislating.

I took it into my head last spring before the stamp Act was brought forward to attempt a Scheme for raising 2 or 3 million of Dollars ℗ Annum by a Tax not oppressive to [the] poor in any possible Case and a Measure, the object of my constant wishes, that would lessen our Dependence upon England and assist in stopping that destructive Drain of our vital Strength the universal Use of English Manufactures. The shirt that Dejanira gave Hercules did not poison him more effectually than English Cloaths do the Americans in all their political morals. My plan

[158]

was an Excise on foreign Cloaths. It was published in Careys News Paper last Summer, perhaps on the second or third week of the Extra session of Congress. I am Dr sir

With great Esteem Your friend & servt   Hu WILLIAMSON

RC (CSmH); at foot of text: "Honble Thos Jefferson"; word torn away supplied in brackets; endorsed by TJ and recorded in SJL as received on 5 Mch. 1798.

REPORT OF THE COMMITTEE: the previous spring John Caffery, who discovered mammoth bones near the CUMBERLAND RIVER, had contacted the American Philosophical Society through Williamson. In a letter of 28 Feb. 1798 that is recorded in SJL but has not been found, TJ had evidently sent Williamson information concerning the society's appointment of a committee on 16 Feb. to determine the best means of preserving the fossils (APS, *Proceedings*, 22, pt. 3 [1884], 267-8; Williamson to TJ, 24, 28 May 1797). To address such issues on a larger scale, in 1797 the society had begun to develop a "Plan for collecting information respecting the remains of ancient natural and artificial productions" in North America. On 6 Apr. 1798 a standing committee was appointed, to consist of TJ, Caspar Wistar, Adam Seybert, Jonathan Williams, Charles Willson Peale, General James Wilkinson of the U.S. Army, who had recently been elected to membership in the society, and George Turner, who had already collected numerous fossils, artifacts, and natural specimens from the Ohio River frontier. The committee issued a circular letter soliciting information on topics relating to America, expecting to address the call "to such persons as were likely, in their opinion, to advance the object of the Society." In particular the circular requested: recovery of complete skeletons of mammoths and other poorly understood animals; detailed information about prehistoric earthworks and mounds; study of changes in the land's surface features; and research on the culture and languages of American Indians (APS, *Proceedings*, 22, pt. 3 [1884], 251-2, 253, 258, 260, 261, 266, 269-70; APS, *Transactions*, 5 [1802], ix-xi; printed circular in DLC: Thornton Papers, signed and dated 7 May 1798 by Williams).

Williamson's SCHEME for an EXCISE on imported clothing appeared in five "Letters to a Member of Congress, on the Subject of an Additional Revenue," signed "A Planter," that appeared in the Philadelphia *Daily Advertiser*, 15-19 May 1797. The letters, arguing the unlikelihood of raising additional funds from existing taxes, lamented a slavish devotion to European fashion and also touted the suggested excise for the salutary effects it might have on the balance of trade and on domestic manufacturing.

To Bishop James Madison

DEAR SIR   Philadelphia Mar. 4. 98

A person here imagines he has discovered a new property [. . .] [magne]tic needle, which however, for want of a well-made dipping needle, he can[. . .] at least to my satisfaction. there is no such instrument at this plac[e. I] think I recollect to have [seen a] very fine one at your college. I must the[refore] take the liberty of solliciting you to make an experiment for us, which [. . .] the less unwillingness as it is only an experiment of a single instant. [. . .] the meridian of the needle, so that the North end shall be to the South, [. . .] South end to the North, & mark it's dip with accuracy while in that posit[ion.] [. . .] not

certain that I recollect exactly the construction of the instrument, but
[. . .] it hung on a cross-axis, & had a brass meridian in the plain of the
needle, [. . .] was graduated on the inner edge so as to indicate the dip
of the needle or [decli]nation from the horizontal level. however whatever be it's construction [. . .] have no difficulty in managing it according to it's construction so as to [. . .] declination of the needle below the
horizontal level when it's ends are in [. . .] of the plain [but] [. . .]. repeat the experiment if you please several [. . .] we may be [satisfied]
whether the result be uniform & what it is. the [. . .] is poor, & expects
to make some thing by his discovery, if it be real. I am [. . .] not at
liberty [to say to] you what it is; but on the contrary have to [. . .] [may]
[. . .] about it till you hear further from me, which [. . .] experiments
result.

[. . .] a Professor Zach, Director of the Observatory [. . .] [Patterson]
of the Philosophical society, giving us some ob[. . .] [. . .] that Mr.
Schroter, astronomer at Lilienthal near [. . .] Hanover, with a [. . .]
[feet] refrac[tor], has [disc]overed a spot in two of Jupit[er's moons?]
by which [he has been able to] observe the ro[tation] of these satellites
on their ax[es.] that each [revolves] on it's axis exactly within the same
time as round it's pla[net] [. . .] [planetary rotation] [. . .], of which before we had no knowlege. [. . .] of our [. . .] be general to [. . .] second-
aries.[1]—de Zach has noted an error in mr Ellicot's observation of the
Polar star. he states it's true position as follows.

	Æ. media Polaris.	Var. ann.	Declin. media	Var. ann.
	° ′ ″	′ ″	° ′ ″	″
1796.	12–[52–58.90]	3– 10.45	88–13– 5.73	19.[516]
1797.	12– 56– 8.35	3– 11.46	88–13–[25.25]	19.[512]
1798.	12– 59–18.80	3– 12.51	88–13– 44.77	19.[508]
1799.	13– 2–30.26	3–[13.57]	88–14– 4.28	19.[504]
1800.	13– 5–42.77		88–14– 23.79	

he observes that three observations in 1795 at Blenheim, London &
Palermo made it's expolarity to be

$$1 - 47 - 13.\ 770$$
$$[1-]47-13.[688]$$
$$1 - 47-13.[790]$$

so that there is now not the single second's incertitude about it.—he has
calculated the longitude of Philadelphia from mr Rittenhouse's observation of the annual eclipse of the sun Apr. 3. 91. and makes it 5^H–10′–3″.
Euler by observation of the transit of ♀ had made it 5^H–10′–6″. he concludes therefore that Dr. Ewen[2] had made it too small by the eclipses of
Jupiter's satellites.

We had before had all our chemistry to learn over again, and also our calendaring time revolutionized. we have now to learn a new system of geography, if the partition of Europe in the papers of the day be authentic. [. . .] ourselves had set the example of reformation in the principles of politics: so that all our old books are becoming like old almanacs, and science itself like the shifting phantasms of the magic lanthern. we have nothing yet from our envoys at Paris. their silence however most certainly is an evidence of peace. I hope we shall be able to rub through the present war, without entering into it: and that during the next interval of peace our rulers will have the [. . .], & our people the self-denial, to establish such a system of commercial regulation as shall [. . .] any injustice of any nation towards our commerce or navigation react on itself as regularly as effect [follows] cause &[3] [. . .] and [. . .] entirely peaceable. the peculiar character of our commerce [. . .] them in our power as to this, and tho it would bring on our farmers temp[orary] [. . .], these [would] be nothing in comparison with the evils of war.   Congress [. . .] [any] thing to do. the moment we hear from our envoys, if the [. . .] we may all go home. an awful crisis [seems] impending over Great Britain. it is indeed a conflict of chances, but all the chances are not [on one side]: the issue therefore is in dubio. accept my salutations & assurances of friendly esteem & respect.

TH: JEFFERSON

PrC (DLC); at foot of first page: "Bishop Madison"; faint, torn along margin of first page, several phrases illegible; figures in brackets supplied from TJ's notes on Zach's letter (see below).

PERSON HERE: see TJ to Andrew Gwin, 24 Mch. 1798.

Franz Xavier von ZACH, an astronomer whose OBSERVATORY near Gotha was under the patronage of the Duke of Saxe-Coburg, had sent some of his published works to the American Philosophical Society, which acknowledged receipt of the books at a meeting of 17 Nov. 1797. TJ did not attend that meeting but presided over another on 19 Jan. 1798 at which Zach, an active disseminator of astronomical data who regularly exchanged information with American scientists, was elected to membership (DSB, 14:583; APS, Proceedings, 22, pt. 3 [1884], 262, 266; Greene, American Science, 135, 142, 154-5). Robert PATTERSON, who in 1797-1798 was a curator of the society and had recently served as one of its secretaries, was the recipient of a letter from Zach that

has not been found but evidently accompanied the books sent by the German astronomer (APS, Proceedings, 22, pt. 3 [1884], 235, 246, 266). TJ made notes on "de Zach's lre to mr Patterson" but did not record its date. The notes include the table of the right ascension and declination of Polaris and the other data from Zach that TJ reported to Bishop Madison in the letter above. TJ identified Zach as "Director of the Observatory at Seebourg in Saxony" (MS in DLC: TJ Papers, 232:41533; entirely in TJ's hand; undated; endorsed: "Astronomy"; see notes 1-2 below).

The observatory at LILIENTHAL, overseen by Johann Hieronymus Schröter, held some of the finest equipment in Europe and was a center for astronomical research (DSB, 12:226). Zach publicized Schröter's recent discovery in Allgemeine Geographische Ephemeriden, Verfasst von einer Gesellschaft Gelehrten und herausgegeben von F. Von Zach, H.S.G. Obristwachtmeister und Direktor der herzoglichen Sternewarte Seeberg bey Gotha, 1 [1798], 131-3, XVI-XVII.

OBSERVATION OF THE POLAR STAR: Andrew Ellicott had published tables and other data on the position of Polaris in APS, *Transactions*, 3 [1793], 116-18, and as a pamphlet, *Several Methods by Which Meridional Lines May be Found with Ease and Accuracy: Recommended to the Attention of the Surveyors in the United States* (Philadelphia, 1796). See Evans, No. 30385. By declaring that the table in the above letter represented the TRUE POSITION of the pole star, TJ probably meant that Zach's figures were more accurate than earlier data, not that the table took into account all variables affecting the star's apparent location in the sky, such as aberration and nutation. Zach's great compendium of star tables, the *Tabulae Speciales Aberrationis et Nutationis*, was not formally published until 1806, but portions were printed earlier. Apparently one of those incomplete versions was the work that the American Philosophical Society received from Zach in November 1797. Zach continually refined his data, and the figures for the pole star in the 1806 edition do not precisely match those in the letter above (Zach, *Tabulae Speciales Aberrationis et Nutationis in Ascensionem Rectam et in Declinationem* . . . , 2 vols. [Gotha, 1806], 1:76; *Connaissance des Tems*, Year 8 [1799-1800], 400; Year 10 [1801-1802], 326).

For his 1770 calculation of the LONGITUDE OF PHILADELPHIA, expressed in the letter above as hours, minutes, and seconds west of the meridian of the Paris Observatory, the renowned European mathematician and scientist Leonhard EULER drew on data from the TRANSIT of Venus between the earth and the sun in June 1769. Euler collected other calculations of the city's longitude as well, including one of 5 hours, 9 minutes, and 55 seconds west of Paris that had been derived using observations of the movements of JUPITER'S SATELLITES and was reported to the APS in 1769 by Presby-

terian minister and avid astronomer John Ewing, who long served as provost of the University of Pennsylvania. Bishop Madison and Ewing had been contentious rivals in 1784, when they represented Virginia and Pennsylvania respectively on a commission fixing the boundary between the two states (*Leonhardi Euleri Opera Omnia* [Leipzig and Berlin, 1911-], ser. 2, vol. 30:153, 225-6; APS, *Transactions*, 1 [1771], 55-9, 88; 6 [1809], 359; Royal Society of London, *Philosophical Transactions*, 59 [1769], 170-93, 228-40, 273-80, 327-58, 374-8, 407-31; Francisco de [i.e., Franz Xavier von] Zach, *Tabulae Motuum Solis Novae et Correctae ex Theoria Gravitatis et Observationibis Racentissimis Erutae* . . . [Gotha, 1792], 29; Brooke Hindle, *David Rittenhouse* [Princeton, 1964], 253-4; DAB, 6:236-7).

At a meeting presided over by TJ on 2 Mch. 1798 the Philosophical Society agreed to pay Samuel Lewis's bill of $5.24 for his work filling the diplomas of 31 new members over the previous eight months (bill in PPAmP, in Lewis's hand, with Samuel H. Smith's endorsement of the society's action, TJ's signature, and Lewis's receipt of payment on 6 Mch. 1798; APS, *Proceedings*, 22, pt. 3 [1884], 268).

¹ In his notes on Zach's letter to Patterson, TJ wrote: "Mr. Schröter astronomer at Lilienthal near Bremen in Hanover has discovered with his 27 feet refractor a spot in 2 of Jupiter's satellites, by which he observed the rotation of the satellite on it's axis to be in the same time as his revolution round his planet. this law of motion then may be supposed by analogy general to the secondary planets."

² TJ's notes on Zach's letter: "Ewing."

³ Preceding six words and ampersand interlined.

From James Madison

DEAR SIR   March 4. 1798

Your two favors of the 15 & 22 Ult: came to hand by friday's mail. I can wait without inconvenience for the Sprigs &c. till you return & reestablish your Cutting machine. Mr. Tazewell's Speech is really an able one in defence of his proposition to associate juries with the Senate in cases of impeachment. His views of the subject are so new to me, that I ought not to decide on them without more examination than I have had time for. My impression has always been that impeachments were somewhat sui generis, and excluded the use of Juries. The terms of the amendment to the Constitution are indeed strong, and Mr. T. has given them, as the French say, all their lustre. But it is at least questionable whether an application of that amendment to the case of impeachments would not push his doctrine farther than he himself would be disposed to follow it. It would seem also that the reservation of an ordinary trial by a jury must strongly imply that an impeachment was not to be a trial by jury. As removal & disqualification, the punishments within the impeaching jurisdiction, were *chiefly* intended for offences in the Executive line would it not also[1] be difficult to exclude Executive influence from the choice of juries; or would juries armed with the impeaching power, and under the influence of an unimpeachable Tribunal, be less formidable than the power as hitherto understood to be modified. The universality of this power is the most extravagant novelty that has been yet broached, especially coming from a quarter that denies the impeachability of a Senator. Hardy as these Innovators are, I can not believe they will venture yet to hold this inconsistent & insulting language to the public. If the conduct & sentiments of the Senate on some occasions were to be regarded as the natural & permanent fruit of the institution, they ought to produce not only disgust but despair in all who are really attached to free Government. But I can not help ascribing some part of the evil to personal characters, and a great deal of it to the present spirit of the Constituents of the Senate. Whenever the State Legislatures resume the tone natural to them, it will probably be seen, that the tone of their Representatives will vary also. If it should not, the inference will then be unavoidable that the present constitution of the Senate is at war with the public liberty. If the countervailing act does not open the mouths & eyes both, of the Eastern Carriers, it will be a political phenomenon without example. In the year 1789, G.B. had about 230 & America 43 thousand of the tonnage in the mutual trade. The encouragements given by Congress, & which G.B. did not dare to countervail till Jay tied our hands from continuing the advantage on the side of America, have brought up the American share to about one half. The bounties now secured to the British Tonnage will pretty certainly reduce our proportion below its original scantiness.[2] And if the French as may be expected, should suffer their disgust at the British Treaty to dictate their navigation policy towards us, Jay will have accomplished more than perhaps was ever done by the same personal talents; he will have annihilated the marine of a maritime Country by a single stroke of his pen; and what is still more extraordinary recd. the plaudits of the victims,[3] whom he has sacrificed. I am curious to see how the zealots for expelling Lyon will treat the deliberate riot of Griswold. The whole affair has been extremely disgraceful, but the dignity of the Body will be wounded, not by the misconduct of individual members which no public body ought to be answerable for, but by the misconduct of itself, that is of a majority, and it is to be feared that the majority in this case are ready for every sacrifice to the spirit of party which infatuates them. The greatest sinners among them are Sewal & Harper who forced the offensive business on the House. We have had lately about $4\frac{1}{2}$ inches of snow. On the 22d however, the day on which it was snowing as you observe in your letter, it was throughout fair here. On the 21st. day & night together there fell $\frac{5}{8}$ of an inch; & on the night of the 23 $\frac{1}{8}$ of an inch of rain.

Yrs always & Affecy.

RC (DLC: Madison Papers); addressed: "Thomas Jefferson Vice President of the United States" with "*private*" at head; endorsed by TJ as received 13 Mch. 1798 and so recorded in SJL. For later emendations, see note 2 below and Madison, *Papers*, 17:88-90.

[1] Preceding nine words interlined by Madison in place of "*Executive* offences may it not."

[2] At a later date a mark was placed above this word, which was keyed to the following note located below the close of the letter, probably in Madison's hand: "this prevented by the war in Europe & the neutrality of the U. States."

[3] Preceding word reworked from "[nation?] ⟨*for sacrificing*⟩."

From Edmund Pendleton

DEAR SIR   Caroline Virga. Mar. 5th. 1798.

Since my last Mr. Lyons hath held a Council with those learned in the Science, who are of Opinion that the present time is very unfavorable for the Sale of our Stock; what is called the market price being very low, & None or very few Purchasers at that; it is supposed that during the Month of April, it will be known whether a rise happens or is in near prospect, & our conclusion is to wait til then, wch. I hope will not be inconvenient to Mr. Short, & you'l please to appoint some person in Richmond to recieve the money, in case you should not return by the time, & let me know who it is, for we have fix'd an Agent there to Watch Occurrences, & strike at an Opportunity of a prudent Sale, should one offer.

perhaps it may be agreable to Mr. Short or to you to fund the money; if so, it may save trouble, & perhaps delay, to have the Stock transfer'd at the Current market price on a certain day, say April 25th., unless our Agent shall have disposed of it, before we recieve your letter acceding to such transfer.

It seems Congress, by the distribution of Saliva & sticks, have found other amusement than debate, to pass away time 'til they hear from Our Envoys at Paris. Is it not strange that no Account is recieved from them? I am always

Dr. Sir, Yr. Affe. & mo. Obt. Servt.   EDMD PENDLETON

RC (DLC: William Short Papers); endorsed by TJ as received 13 Mch. 1798 and so recorded in SJL.

To Mann Page

DEAR SIR   Philadelphia Mar. 6. 98.

I have to acknolege the receipt of your f[avor] of [Feb.] 13. and [. . .] thank you for the papers it contain[ed.] that of mr Anderson [is so much] [. . .] that I take the liberty of reques[ting you] [. . .] his signature, for which purpose I now inclose it to you. [it is possible] that whenever I shall have collected full evidence on the subject, I [shall] [. . .] from the whole [. . .] statement of the transaction [and publish it] in some way. [for?] this [reason] [I wish] to have in my possession auth[entic statements] to support [every] p[. . .] which may be questioned.

We have at length recieved despatches from our envoys. [such] of them as [were] in readiness were yester-day laid before [. . .]. I inclose you a copy. [you] will see by them that they do not expect to obtain the objects of their mission. what these were have not yet been explained to us however it does not seem [as] if open war would be de[clar]ed against us. the law indeed which the Directory proposes [wi]ll have many effects; but whether these [will fall hard]est on [us or] the English, will be better decided by merchants acquai[nted] with all th[eir business.] I apprehend that our navigation would [. . .] it to [continue]. [. . .] probably it's continuance will not be long. [that the?] conflict [for] which the two great combatants are preparing must soon [. . .] of [. . .] of [. . .] [war] between the [. . .] wisdom [. . .] to us, & [. . .] Mr. Nicholas's [amendment?] [. . .]ded[1] in the negative [. . .][2] not what will be [. . .], but it is evident we have [not] [. . .]. [be pleased] to present my [. . .][3]   TH: JEFFERSON

PrC (DLC); faint and torn, with multiple illegible passages, the longest of which are identified in notes below; at foot of text: "Mann Page Esq." Enclosures: (1) Enclosure No. 1 printed at Page to TJ, 13 Feb. 1798. (2) *The Message of the president of the*

United States, of 5th March, 1798; with a Letter from our Envoys Extraordinary at Paris, with Other Documents (Philadelphia, 1798); see Evans, No. 34809.

Five DESPATCHES from the American ENVOYS in Paris finally arrived at the Department of State late on 4 Mch. 1798. The next day the president sent Congress one of the communications, No. 5, dated 8 Jan. 1798. That dispatch enclosed a message from the Executive Directory of France to the Council of Five Hundred, 4 Jan. 1798, and a copy of the pending French LAW, which was subsequently approved, whereby the presence of British goods in a cargo would condemn a vessel and neutral ships would be refused admittance to French ports if they had stopped at British ports en route (see Jefferson, the *Aurora*, and Delamotte's Letter from France, at 23 Jan. 1798). "We can only repeat that there exists no hope of our being officially received by this Government," the three diplomats stated in dispatch No. 5, "or that the objects of our mission will be in any

way accomplished." That comment would be fully understood only in the context of the other four dispatches, written between 22 Oct. and 24 Dec. 1797, which revealed what became known as the XYZ affair. Explaining that those lengthy communications required "some days" for decipherment, Adams did not convey them to Congress on 5 Mch. 1798. In a bleak message to Congress on 19 Mch. he announced the failure of the mission to France but gave no details. On 3 Apr. 1798, in response to a resolution of the House of Representatives on the preceding day, he sent Congress the four dispatches, along with the instructions under which the envoys had gone to France (ASP, *Foreign Relations*, 2:150-68).

[1] Approximately one line of original text illegible.
[2] Approximately one line of original text illegible.
[3] Approximately one and a half lines of original text and complimentary closing illegible.

To Mary Jefferson Eppes

Philadelphia Mar. 7. 98.

I have recieved yours, my dear Maria, of Feb. 1. and with that extreme gratification with which I recieve all the marks of your affection. my impatience to get from hence is urged by the double motives of escaping from irksome scenes here, and meeting yourself and others dear to us both. no time is yet spoken of for our adjournment; yet as there is likely to arise nothing which might keep congress together, I cannot but hope we shall separate early in the next month. I still count on joining you at Eppington on my return. I recieve from home very discouraging accounts of Davenport's doing nothing towards covering the house. I have written to him strongly on the subject, expressing my expectations to find the roof finished at my return. but I fear it will not produce the effect desired. we are sure however of the Outchamber for you, and the Study for myself, and will not be long in getting a cover over some room for your sister. my last letter from Belmont was of Feb. 12. when they were all well. they have found the house there unhealthy, and their situation in general not pleasant. I pressed them to go to Monticello where they would be relieved from the inconvenience [to health?] of a cellar-full of water under them. I have not heard from them since. mr Trist is gone on to purchase mr Lewis's place. they will not remove there till the fall. he is to be married to a Miss Brown of this place, an amiable girl, and who I hope will be of value to you as a neighbor. having no news for mr Eppes but what he will find in a paper inclosed herewith, I do not write to him. my salutations to him, mr & mrs Eppes & the family at Eppington. to yourself my tenderest love.

TH: JEFFERSON

PrC (MHi); faint; at foot of text in ink: "Eppes Maria"; endorsed by TJ in ink on verso. Enclosure not found.

I HAVE WRITTEN TO HIM STRONGLY: for TJ's correspondence with William Davenport, see TJ to Thomas Mann Randolph,

15 and 22 Feb. (second letter) 1798. A letter from Davenport to TJ of 5 Mch. 1798, recorded in SJL as received eight days later, has not been found. LAST LETTER FROM BELMONT: see TJ to Thomas Mann Randolph, 22 Feb. 1798 (second letter).

To George Jefferson

DEAR SIR   Philadelphia Mar. 8. 98.

I this moment recieve your favor of the 1st. inst. & am alarmed at the account of my nailery being out of nailrod. I left them with a provision to last till late in April, but whether it had all got home, or was still at Richmond my memory does not tell me. a person happening to be with me when I opened your letter who tells me he was in mr Johnston's warehouse the 1st. of Feb. & saw a quantity of nailrod which the young man told him was mine. if this be so, it explains their running out at home. I will get the favor of you to enquire into it and have it forwarded by the boats without delay, if it were there & be not gone. to guard against the danger of mistake however in the person who gives me the information, I will tomorrow order three tons by the first vessel. I inclose you a bill of lading for a hogshead of molasses, a barrel of clover seed, & small box laden to your address on board the schooner Dove, Potter. I will endeavor to get the nail rod on board the same vessel if she is not gone. be so good as to forward the clover seed & the small box T.I. about a foot square by the first safe waggon to Charlottesville to Colo. Bell, who will pay the waggoner. this is important because I shall lose the season of [. . .] if it does not go on without delay. it ought to be [seeded the first] week in April. the Molasses & nail rods should [. . .] first boats to Milton to either messrs. Fleming [& Mc.lenahan?] or mr Watson.—there went some time ago by a [. . .] what one) some smith's tools, & a large very heavy box [. . .] chimney piece. I hope this will get to your hand in [time to][. . .] chimney [piece?] from being sent up from Richmond, [. . .] [relative to] it, which may perhaps render it

[. . .] [to order?] [. . .], and it's going on to Monticello [. . .] situation. be so good as to retain it [. . .]. I am Dear Sir with great esteem
Your friend & servt.   TH: JEFFERSON

PrC (MHi); faint, several phrases illegi-   A PERSON: Richard Richardson (see TJ to
ble; at foot of text: "[. . .]ge Jefferson." En-   Thomas Mann Randolph, 15 Mch. 1798).
closure not found.

To James Monroe

DEAR SIR   Philadelphia Mar. 8. 98.
    I have to acknolege the receipt of yours of Feb. 12. 19. & 25. at length the charm is broke, and letters have been recieved from our envoys at Paris. one only of them has been communicated, of which I inclose you a copy with the documents accompanying it. the decree therein proposed to be passed has struck the greatest alarm through the merchants I have ever yet witnessed. as it has not been known more than two or three days, it's particular operations are not yet developed. it will probably drive our vessels out of the British trade, because as they will not have the benefit of convoy they cannot bring a return cargo from Great Britain but on much higher insurance than the British vessels who will have convoy. nor can they carry out produce but on much higher freight because they will be to return empty, in which case the British will underwork them. it seems then as if one effect would be to increase the British navigation. unless indeed our vessels instead of laying themselves up in port, should go to other markets with their produce & for return cargoes. however it is not probable this state of things will last long enough to have any great effect. the month of April I think will see the experiment of the invasion, and that will be a short one. you will see in Bache's paper of this morning the 5th. number of some pieces written by T. Coxe, in which this proposed decree is well viewed. how it will operate on our question about arming, we do not yet know. some talk of letters of marque & reprisal, yet on the whole I rather believe it will not add to the number of voters for arming. this measure with the decrees of the British courts that British subjects adopted here since the peace and carrying on commerce from hence, are still British subjects, & their cargoes British property, has shaken these quasi-citizens in their condition. the French adopt the same principle as to their cargoes when captured. a privateer lately took near our coast an E. Indiaman worth 250,000 D. belonging to one of these lately emigrated houses. is it worth our while to go to war to support the contrary doctrine? the British principle is clearly against the law of nations. but which way our

interest lies is also worthy consideration. the influence of this description of merchants on our government & on the public opinion is not
merely innocent. it's absence would not weaken our union.—the issue
of the question on foreign intercourse has enabled us to count the
strength of the two parties in the H. of representatives. it is 51. & 55 if
all the members were present, the whigs being a minority of 4. but in
this computation all wavering characters are given to the other side.
Jersey has laid itself off into districts, which instead of an uniform delegation, will give one chequered as the state is. they will at their next
election send whigs from two districts. Pennsylvanvia, at her next election (in October) will add two more to the whig list. let us hope that
Morgan & Machir will give place to whig successors. I do not know
that this can be hoped for from our Eastern shore. this much I think
tolerably certain, besides the natural progress of public sentiment in
other quarters, & the effect of the events of the time. we do not think
then that the partizans of Republican government should despair.—
they do not yet talk of the time of adjournment though confessedly they
have nothing to do. yet I trust it will be early in the ensuing month.—
how far it may be eligible for you to engage in the practice of the law I
know not. on the question of your removal to Richmond, I may doubtless be under bias, when I suppose it's expediency questionable. the
expence to be incurred in the first moments will certainly be great.
could it be only deferred for a while it would enable you to judge
whether the prospect opened will be worth that dislocation of your affairs, whether some other career may not open on you. of these things no
body but yourself can judge. it is a question too for yourself whether a
seat among the judges of the state would be an object for you. on all
these points your friends can only offer motives for consideration: on
which none but yourself can decide avec connoissance de cause.[1] I really
believe that some employment, more than your farms will furnish, will
be necessary to your happiness. you are young, your mind active, &
your health vigorous. the languor of ennui would, in such a condition of
things, be intolerable. make my most respectful salutations to mrs Monroe, & accept friendly Adieux to yourself.

RC (DLC: Monroe Papers); addressed: "James Monroe near Charlottesville"; franked and postmarked; endorsed by Monroe. PrC (DLC); at foot of first page in ink: "Monroe James." Enclosure: Enclosure No. 2 listed at TJ to Mann Page, 6 Mch. 1798.

5TH. NUMBER OF SOME PIECES WRITTEN BY T. COXE: "No. V. Cursory reflections upon the Message of *the French Directory* of the 4th January 1798, concerning the seizure of *British* produce and manufactures," signed "An American Merchant." The *Aurora* of this day also carried news that a British admiralty court in the Bahamas had condemned a cargo intended for New Orleans by partners who were originally British subjects but resided in the United States, one for sixteen years and the other for seven.

Similarly, a French PRIVATEER had on 12 Feb. captured the *New Jersey*, homeward bound from Canton. The ship and cargo, together reputedly insured for a quarter of a million dollars, were owned by the firm of English-born Philadelphia merchant Philip Nicklin (PMHB, 49 [1925], 190-1).

[1] That is, "knowingly."

To Thomas Mann Randolph

TH:J. TO TMR.   Philadelphia Mar. 8. 98.

I wrote you last on the 22d. of Feb. and then acknoleged the receipt of yours of the 12th. Feb. which is the last come to hand. I am now sending off a hogshead of molasses and 4. bushels of clover seed. I write to mr Jefferson to forward the latter immediately by some waggon, as the season for sowing it will be far advanced. mr Page & George have written directions where to sow it; to wit the former in the strong patches in the East field, Mountain field & Triangle, & the latter in patches of the River field & Antient field, & the whole of the High field. I wish them to keep a look out for the arrival of the seed at Milton or Charlottesville that no time may be lost for sowing it. there goes with these things a box just recieved from mr Strickland, containing a bag of *true* Winter vetch & some hop-trefoil. the vetch is not to be sowed till autumn. the hop-trefoil immediately. John may chuse a patch somewhere within his enclosure, as the object would be only to gather seed from it, if found worth attention. the molasses will go up the river and should be carried home immediately on it's arrival at Milton, before the heats set in.—at length letters are come from our envoys. I send you a copy of the only one communicated. the decree proposed by the Directory has petrified the English merchants here, and the more as late decisions of the English courts, still consider them as English subjects, and their cargoes bound to or from enemy ports liable to condemnation. the French view them in the same light. this applies to all who have been citizenized since the peace. I do not know that our interests, well weighed, require us to be over tenacious of the contrary opinion, tho' unquestionably the sound one. the operation of this decree is not yet developed. but probably it will either occasion our ships to be laid up in port, or to seek other markets for our produce & for return cargoes. in the former case it will increase the British shipping as they will have the benefit of convoy. some here talk of embargo, & some of letters of marque & reprisal. probably neither will take place, nor is the information likely to increase the vote for[1] arming. it does not appear that the French will proceed to a declaration of war against us. the price of wheat & flour remains as it was. had I either I believe I should be for selling, because the present prices are good, and the prospect involved in impenetrable uncertainty. tobacco has started from half a dollar to a dollar. it is impossible that article should fall. the autumn price is well worth waiting for. no time for adjournment is yet spoken of. but it is evident enough we shall have nothing to do, unless another battle or two can be produced to give the appearance of employment. my warmest love to Martha and the little ones: affectionate Adieux to yourself.

RC (DLC); endorsed by Randolph as received 17 Mch. 1798. PrC (ViU: Edgehill-Randolph Papers); lacks second page.

TJ's LAST to Randolph was actually 2 Mch. 1798.

I SEND YOU A COPY: see Enclosure No. 2 listed at TJ to Mann Page, 6 Mch. 1798.

[1] PrC ends at this point.

From James Currie

SIR   Richmond March—11th. 1798
I take the liberty of writing you at this time solliciting once more your friendly agency, in a matter of debt between Mr R Morris, & me. our friend Mr L Burwell who you have seen, & is now in Philadelphia (unless he has just left it) & from the probability of which I have taken the Liberty—to inclose my Letter to him for your perusal: that you may be enabled *to afford* him your assistance & advice. in case he is *not gone*, you may if you please after perusing it, seal & send it to him. If he has left Philadelphia you'll be good enough to retain it,—as his last letter told me he should leave my Notes of RM & N. with you, for your agency thereon—Youll see in my Letter to LB. my Ideas & wishes in regard to the Notes & what ought to be done with them—& a PS of what came to my knowledge just as I was finishing my Letter. & if it is material can be ascertaind., undoubtedly. of this youll make what use you think proper, if—as I have told B—if any thing new has occurd, or if he is possesd of any information, which may lead him to delay Suits & try to Negotiate further. very well if not—the sooner the Suits are commencd—the better—to this matter if he is gone (& at all events (my good Sir) I must sollicit Your attention to & agency upon & to have done whatever you think most proper not only with those Notes—but with the residue of J T Griffins debt, left in the agency of Mr Ingersol, & who sometime ago, Obtaind—a judgem. for a part of it but which has not yet been productive & he seems to have had hardly any hope Of the remaining part of it ever being paid—however of all this I wish to be availd of your information after you have had an Oppty of informing yourself as to every thing concerning it—I still flatter myself if you will

do me the favor to Undertake the negotiation (if any negotiation is not too late to Ultimately secure me both debts) that you most probably can & will effect it—& if that could be done on a sure footing I would grant indulgence & receive it by Any Installments you might think proper to Stipulate—for me—at all Events—I commit it to your care to Negotiate or Sue for as you may Judge right—as my real friend—I must now apologize to you for thus having recourse to you on So many Urgent Occasions—having experiencd Your friendly aid before—causes the present application & enables me still to hope in your—assistance. & to give me full confidence it will not be in Vain—if any thing is possible to be done—I am at present Confind, & in very bad health indeed—my Strength greatly impaird by disorder & confinement.—Shall hope to have the honor of a letter from you after receipt & perusal of this & the inclosd—to be disposd of as above directed—at your discretion if LB. is gone & Still to act upon it whether he is gone or not—feeling weake & fainty I have Only to add, that I feel a lively gratitude to you for all your friendly offices, hitherto exercisd—towards me & that I always Am Dr Sir with the most Respectfull Regard Your, Most Obdt. hble Servt.

JAMES CURRIE

RC (CtHi: Aaron Burr Papers); addressed: "The honble. Thomas Jefferson Esqre. Vice President of the United States. Philadelphia"; franked and postmarked; endorsed by TJ as received 17 Mch. 1798 and so recorded in SJL.

RM & N.: the bankrupt Robert Morris, who had gone into debtor's prison the previous month, and John Nicholson, his associate in land speculation. Morris had purchased at least one tract in Goochland County from John Tayloe Griffin, and for several years Currie looked to TJ for assistance in collecting GRIFFINS DEBT to him.

TJ had arranged for Jared Ingersoll to represent Currie (Memorandum to Thomas Mann Randolph, [ca. 16-24 Jan. 1794]; Barbara Ann Chernow, *Robert Morris: Land Speculator, 1790-1801* [New York, 1978], 200, 216).

Letters from Currie to TJ of 30 May and 4 Nov. 1797, received respectively on 13 June and 8 Nov. 1797, and one that TJ wrote to Currie on 21 June 1797 are recorded in SJL but have not been found. According to SJL they exchanged an additional 24 letters between 11 Apr. 1798 and 18 Dec. 1799 that are also missing.

Notes on Conversations with Abraham Baldwin, John Brown, and John Hunter

Mar. 11. in conversn with Baldwin & Brown of Kentucky, Brown says that in a private company once consisting of Hamilton, King, Madison, himself & some one else making a fifth, speaking of the '*federal government*' 'Oh,' says Hamilton 'say the *federal monarchy* let us call things by their right names, for a monarchy it is'

Baldwin mentions at table the following fact. when the bank bill was under discussion in the H. of R. judge Wilson came in, & was standing by Baldwin. Baldwin reminded him of the following fact which passed in the grand convention. among the enumerated powers given to Congress was one to erect corporns. it was on debate struck out. several particular powers were then proposed. among others Rob. Morris proposed to give Congress a power to establish a National bank. Gouvernr. Morris opposed it, observing that it was extremely doubtful whether the constn they were framing could ever be passed at all by the people of America, that to give it it's best chance however, they should make it as palateable as possible, & put nothing into it not very essential which might raise up enemies. that his collegue (Rob. Morris) well knew that 'a bank' was in their state (Pensva) the very watchword of party. that *a bank* had been the great bone of contention, between the two parties of the state from the establmt of their constn, having been erected, put down & erected again as either party preponderated; that therefore to insert this power, would instantly enlist against the whole instrument the whole of the anti-bank party in Pensva, whereupon it was rejected, as was every other special power except that of giving copy-rights to authors & patents to inventors. the general power of incorporating being whittled down to this shred. Wilson agreed the fact.

Mr. Hunter of S. Carola who lodges with Rutledge[1] tells me that Rutledge was explaining to him the plan they proposed to pursue as to war measures when Otis came in. Rutledge addressed Otis. now Sir says he you must come forward with something liberal for the Southern states, fortify their harbours, & build gallies, in order to obtain their concurrence. Otis said we insist on Convoys for our European trade, & Guarde costas, on which condn alone we will give them gallies & fortificns. Rutledge observed that in the event of war Mc.Henry & Pickering must go out, Wolcot he thought might remain, but the others were incapable of conducting a war. Otis said the Eastern people would never abandon Pickering, he must be retained, Mc.Henry might go. they considered together whether Genl. Pinckney wd accept the office of Secy. at war. they apprehended he would not. it was agreed in this conversn that Sewall had more the ear of the President than any other person.

MS (DLC: TJ Papers, 102:17525); entirely in TJ's hand; on same sheet as Notes on a Conversation with Henry Tazewell, 1 Mch. 1798.

[1] At a later sitting TJ wrote in margin "J. Rutledge junr."

From Joel Barlow

DEAR SIR,   Paris 12 March 1798—

The extreme mortification with which I view the progress of a misintelligence between two nations that ought to cherish each other with peculiar symaphy has induced me to address to my Brother in law Mr. Baldwin my sentiments on that subject. But I am apprehensive that before my letter can arrive Congress will adjourn, & Baldwin be gone to Georgia. In that case the chance of its doing any good will be lost, as the present crisis of our affairs cannot continue long.

For this reason I enclose a copy of it to you, trusting in your prudence to make such use of it only as may do the most good to the cause of truth, & the least mischief to me. The bluntness & severity with which I have delivered some of my sentiments, you will see, are not calculated for your eye, but for those of a more intimate friend.

Permit me to thank you, as I sincerely do, for accepting the place of vice president. I know it must have been a sacrifice of feeling and of every personal consideration to the hope of rendering public service, at a time when I was afraid you had become quite discouraged.

I am with great attachment & respect Dear Sir Your obet. Sert.—

JOEL BARLOW

RC (DLC); at foot of first page: "Mr. Jefferson"; endorsed by TJ as received 26 July 1798 and so recorded in SJL. Enclosure: Barlow to Abraham Baldwin, Paris, 4 Mch. 1798, a treatise on worsening relations between the United States and France, attributing the deterioration to American measures that included the appointment of Gouverneur Morris as minister to France, the Jay Treaty, the recall of James Monroe, and the sending to France of Pinckney (whose return there after the French government's refusal to recognize him "was undoubtedly intended as an insult"), Marshall ("whose effigy had been burnt in Virginia for his violent defense of the English treaty"), and Gerry ("a little make-weight man, appointed with the intention that he should have no influence"); Barlow also rues Adams's failure to change the direction of policy and his "borrowing the cant of Edmond Burke" in his message of 23 Nov. 1797, to which Congress should have replied with "an order to send him to the madhouse"; he laments anti-French statements in Congress and the "dirty calumny against the French" in American newspapers; he fears that the envoys in Paris might call for strong measures and push Adams into "another desperate leap in to the region of madness" in his policy toward France; and he concludes: "When, in God's name are we to expect from America any just ideas relative to France? Look to England for a republic; but do not look to France for a monarchy" (Dupl in DLC; opening pages in a clerk's hand, remainder in Barlow's hand; at head of text: "Copy"). Enclosed in John Brown to TJ, 29 June 1798.

Matthew Lyon obtained, not from TJ, a copy of Barlow's letter to BALDWIN. Lyon had it published and also read portions to assemblies in Vermont. That dissemination of the letter became the basis of two counts of the indictment of Lyon later in 1798 under the Sedition Act. Federalist newspapers condemned Barlow's letter to Baldwin and reprinted it to demonstrate the character of opposition to the government (Smith, *Free-*

dom's Fetters, 226-33; James Woodress, *A Yankee's Odyssey: The Life of Joel Barlow* [Philadelphia, 1958], 193-8).

See the note to Fulwar Skipwith to TJ,

17 Mch. 1798, concerning William Lee's role as courier of this and the following document.

From Joel Barlow

Sir,   Paris 12 March 1798—

Mr. Wm. Lee of Boston has done me the favor to charge himself with a packet for you this day. He is a man of an excellent character & good connections in commerce. He wishes to obtain the consulate of Bordeaux or Paris, if vacant. Could you yield him assistance in this or any other object you would very much oblige your obet. Servt.

Joel Barlow

RC (DLC); at foot of text: "Thos. Jefferson vice President of the United States"; endorsed by TJ as received 26 July 1798 and recorded in SJL as received on that day "by mr Lee." Enclosed in John Brown to TJ, 29 June 1798.

From James Madison

Dear Sir   Mar. 12. 98

I have recd. your favor of Mar: 2. with a continuation of the Gazettes, with an omission however of Feby. 23. I apprized you before of a like omission of Jany. 23. I think the Whigs acted very properly in attending the Birthnight on the principle of appropriating it to the person and not to the office of the late President. It is a pity that the non-attendance of the adamites is not presented to the public in such a manner with their names, as to satisfy the real friends of Washington, as well as the people generally, of the true principles & views of those who have been loudest in their hypocritical professions of attachment to him. The proceedings relative to the stamp act mark strongly two things, one that the public feeling is not as is pretended in unison with all the measures of the Government, the other that it will whenever it shews itself, direct immediately the course of the H. of R. and no doubt finally the Senate also. The Eastern votes for the repeal are a demonstration of both these truths. The inclosed paper contains all the information I possess on the subject of Mazzei's Cargo of books. Notwithstanding the lapse of time I have never had a single return of sales. Whilst Congress sat in N.Y. I repeatedly enquired of Rivington without learning that any had taken place. [1] I beg you to preserve & return the paper. We have had warm & dry weather for 10 days till yesterday which gave us a fine rain. The Wheat fields in general retain their sickly countenance. In many places it is thought impossible to replace the seed, and it seems certain that the ensuing crop will be very short, whatever change for the better may happen in the residue of the season. Great efforts are generally on foot for crops of Tobo.—

RC (DLC: Madison Papers); endorsed by TJ as received 20 Mch. 1798 and so recorded in SJL. Enclosure not found.

[1] Preceding six words interlined in place of "hearing a word on the subject."

Notes on Senators' Comments about House Impeachment Committee

Mar. 12. when the bill for appropriations was before the Senate, Anderson moved to strike out a clause recognising (by way of appropriation) the appmt of a commee by the H. of R. to sit during their recess to collect evidence on Blount's case, denying they had power, but by a law, to authorize a commee to sit during recess. Tracy advocated the motion & said 'we may as well speak out. the commee was appd by the H. of R. to take care of the Brit. minister, to take care of the Span. min. to take care of the Sec. of state, in short to take care of the Pres. of the US. they were afraid the Pres. & Secy. of state wd not perform the office of collecting evidence faithfully, that there would be collusion &c therefore the House appointed a commee of their own. we shall have them next sending a commee to Europe to make a treaty &c suppose that the H. of R. should resolve that after the adjmt of Congress they should continue to sit as a commee of the whole house during the whole recess.' this shews how the appointment of that commee has been viewed by the President's friends.

MS (DLC: TJ Papers, 102:17525); entirely in TJ's hand; on same sheet as Notes on Conversations with Abraham Baldwin, John Brown, and John Hunter, 11 Mch. 1798.

In the SENATE on this day the bill to appropriate funds for the support of the government during 1798 received a third reading. Joseph ANDERSON MOVED TO STRIKE OUT A CLAUSE allocating $2,626 for salaries and expenses incurred by the committee of the House of Representatives that had investigated William BLOUNT'S CASE. Anderson's motion failed, 18 nays to 7 yeas (JS, 2:453-4).

From Thomas Mann Randolph

TH: M. RANDOLPH TO TH: JEFFERSON   Belmont March 12. 98

We rec'd. your two letters of the 22d. Feb. on the 3 inst. and that of the 2d. on the 10th. I have not been able to procure horses for George and Page yet tho' I have taken very considerable pains myself and they as far as the hurry of the season would permit them have been looking about. There are none worth having in the neighbourhood but many pass along the road from Kentucki, for sale, and may be bought for Cash on very moderate terms. This I am convinced is the only way in which you can get properly supplied. No person who owns a Mule of the Don Carlos breed but prizes him as high as we do—I have been trying all the Winter to get some & cannot tho' I w'd. willingly give 40£ a piece.

Mr. Trist arrived here on Saturday Morning & remained with us till today—I have little hope of his settling here, he passed thro' Frederic & Berkeley on his way from Philad'a. and was charmed with the appearance of that Country—ours is too unlike to please him. Indeed I perceived today as I accompanied him great part of the way to Charl'lle. that the face of the country which you know is gloomy enough in its present state made a strong impression on him. I join him tomorrow to shew him Lewises farm which he will I think soon turn from. We are all well & impatient for your return.

    yours most affectionately   TH: M. RANDOLPH

RC (ViU: Robert H. Kean deposit); endorsed by TJ as received 22 Mch. 1798 and so recorded in SJL.

From Bishop James Madison

DEAR SIR   Williamsburg, March 13th. 1798—

I take great Pleasure in transmitting the Result of the Experiment, which you wished to have made.

The Instrument is delicate, & appears well formed. The Needle, which is 9 Inches in Length, is supported as usual, by a transverse Axis; but each Extremity of the Axis rests upon three small Friction Wheels, whilst the Parts of the Axis which touch them are highly polished, & of Steel. The Circle, within which the Needle revolves, is very carefully divided into Degrees & $\frac{1}{2}$ Degrees. I had every Part of the Instrument examined, & touched the Needle with a Magnet of considerable power.

The Instrument was suspended in the Magnetic Meridian; every Thing which could affect the Needle removed, & the Dip noted, first, with the Needle in it's proper Position; or, with the North End directed to the North. A Variety of Trials shewed the Dip here to be 66°s. or perhaps more accurately, 66°15′.—I then reversed the Ends, the North End pointing to the South, & kept the Needle in a Line parallel with the Horizon; up on removing the Support, the North End, after vibrating, as usual, settled in its former Position, pointing out the same Declination below the horizontal Level, and, on the same Side, as before. The Expt. has been repeated, perhaps 50 Times, & always with the same uniform Result. This will be the Case, untill the N. End is raised nearly to the Line of Inclination, which the Needle in dipping takes. In that Position, it will remain stationary. A Few Degrees on either Side of that Line, will cause the Needle to come round, in one Case, by the North, in the other, by the South; settling however, in both Cases, in the same Point in which it would have settled, had the Needle been placed in the Magnetic Meridian with its North End direct to the North, and then left freely to indicate it's Dip.

I do not know how these Results may coincide with the Wishes of the Person who thinks he has made some Discovery in Magnetism; but, of their Accuracy there can be no Doubt.

I have a short Essay upon magnetic Attraction which I shall endeavour to forward to you, before you leave Philadelphia.

The Discovery relative to Jupiters Satellites is highly interesting to Astronomy. It is an additional Proof of the Purpose for which they are destined, & evinces a surprizing Uniformity in lunar Motions.—I wonder how the Discovery escaped Herschel; tho I never doubted of the superior Clearness of View which the Refractor had over the Reflector—

I thank you also for your other Communications, which are very valuable, particularly those respecting the Polar Star.

If you have published a Dissertation upon the Bones of the Mahmouth, as I have sometimes heard, I beg to have a Perusal of it.—I brought with me from Botetourt Cy, last Fall, a Part of one of those Bones, dug up, 25 Feet below the Surface, about 3 or 4 Miles from the Big-Lick in that County. It is the Extremity of the Thigh Bone; by completing the Circle, of which the Bone is a Part, it originally measured 15 Inches in Circumference.

With very sincere Respect & Esteem I am Dr Sir, Yr Friend & Sert

J MADISON

RC (DLC); endorsed by TJ as received 22 Mch. 1798 and so recorded in SJL.

THE EXPERIMENT, WHICH YOU WISHED TO HAVE MADE: see TJ to Bishop Madison, 4 Mch. 1798.

To George Jefferson

DEAR SIR   Philadelphia Mar. 14. 98.

I yesterday recieved a letter from mr Jordan Harris informing me that an irregularity in the assignment of Lucy Wood's bond to him occasions a demurrer to it's payment under the caution expressed in my letter to you that it should be *legally* assigned. the caution was a reasonable one, as we should naturally expect an assignee to take care that his title be *legal*. however not wishing to be scrupulous, and observing by his statement that the only irregularity is in the assignment's being made by Stephen Southall on behalf of Lucy Wood (tho' not under her signature) knowing that he has done business for mrs Wood his mother in law, I would wish you to pay it, taking in the bond. this will secure me against any action on it at Common law, and Chancery would not molest an obligor in such a case. I am still uninformed by mr Harris what is the amount of the bond, and there were two given to the same person on the same day, the one for £33. the other for £16–10. but this need not delay the payment. I shall hear of the other one, as Colo. Bell is enquiring after it & will draw on you for it if he finds it. there is a mr Charles L. Lewis here, son of the gentleman of the same name at Buckisland in Albemarle, and my nephew. he came to seek business in some counting house or office. there is very little prospect of getting a place for him, in which case he will come to Richmond on the same errand. he appears to be a prudent, good & regular young man, entirely docile, has worked a year or two in a country store, and is I believe equal to common business. my acquaintance in Richmond is so small that I cannot be of [assistance?] to him there. if he should come, I will take the liberty of ad[dressing] him to [you?], and in the mean time will ask the favor of you [. . .] know of any vacancy for him, to endeavor to keep it open [. . .] dropping me a line, he will go off immediately to Richmond. he [will] be easy in his terms, on being boarded. I am with great esteem Dear Sir

Your friend & servt   TH: JEFFERSON

PrC (MHi); faint; at foot of text: "Mr. George Jefferson"; endorsed in ink by TJ on verso.

The LETTER FROM MR. JORDAN HARRIS of 5 Mch. 1798, recorded in SJL as received eight days later, has not been found. TJ's response of 14 Mch. 1798 is also missing.

On 6 Mch. 1798 TJ had written a draft on John Barnes for $30 to CHARLES L. LEWIS, the payment "to be charged to Richd. Richardson" (MS in MHi, written and signed by TJ, endorsed by Barnes and canceled). See also MB, 2:980.

From John Beckley

Thursday evening
15th: March 1798

J: Beckley, returns enclosed Mr: Jefferson's parliamentary Notes.—
On the first part he has pencilled a few remarks.—On the Second part
'respecting priviledged questions' want of time now to consider it, induces a wish, that at the close of the Session Mr: Jefferson would permit
him to take a Copy of these, and any other Notes which Mr: J— may
add on the law of parliament generally, when an attentive revisal of the
whole subject will be endeavored to be made by JB— before the succeeding Session. A Copy of the notes on Conferences will be handed to
Mr: Jefferson tomorrow.

RC (DLC); endorsed by TJ. Not recorded in SJL. For enclosure, see note
below.

The PARLIAMENTARY NOTES returned by
Beckley were probably from TJ's "Parliamentary Pocket-Book," which included
paragraphs on PRIVILEDGED QUESTIONS
and CONFERENCES (see PW, 15-16). For a

description of the one-page document entitled "Extracts from Book of Minutes on
parliamentary proceeding," which Beckley
sent to TJ, perhaps at this time, see same.
The extracts are printed as an enclosure to
the letter above in Gerard W. Gawalt, ed.,
*Justifying Jefferson: The Political Writings
of John James Beckley* (Washington, D.C.,
1995), 141-2.

From George Jefferson

DEAR SIR,   Richmond March 15th. 1798

This post has brought me yours of the 8th. Johnston has no nail rod
of yours—the last he received for you he forwarded in November last. I
had made this enquiry previously to my last, but omitted to inform you
of it. That which was seen in his lumberhouse the first of February I
expect belonged to a person of his name in this place, which he informs
me was sent to him about that time by mistake.

The smiths tools & chimney-piece I have received, and have forwarded them about a week since to Milton. I hope you will not have to
return the latter.

I am sorry to inform you that I have not yet procured the May wheat
which you directed me to get for the agricultural society. I find much
greater difficulty in doing it than I immagined there would be; having
taken great pains to get some which is genuine, but hitherto without
effect.

I find that most of the persons in the neighbourhood on whom I could
rely have ground up their wheat; & from what I can learn it would be

improper to trust to others—as I understand that much, which passes for our May wheat, is mixed with our common white wheat. I am told further that if this wheat has been in bulk it will have got heated and will not come up, as it is particularly delicate. this makes it necessary that I should get it from some one in whom I have confidence. there is none though I believe at this season of the year as good as it is earlier. I hope soon to have it in my power to give you more pleasing intelligence upon this subject—& am most truly

Dear Sir Your Very Obt. servt.   GEO. JEFFERSON

RC (MHi); at foot of text: "Thomas Jefferson esquire"; with TJ's notation at foot of text: "8. hhds of tobo. recd."; endorsed by TJ and recorded in SJL under 22 Mch. 1798.

MY LAST: George Jefferson to TJ, 1 Mch. 1798.

To James Madison

Philadelphia Mar. 15. 98

I wrote you last on the 2d. inst. your's of the 4th. is now at hand. the public papers will give you the news of Europe. the French decree making the vessel friendly or enemy according to the hands by which the cargo was manufactured has produced a great sensation among the merchants here. it's operation is not yet perhaps well understood; but probably it will put our shipping out of competition because British bottoms which can come under convoy will alone be trusted with return cargoes. our's losing this benefit would need a higher freight out, in which therefore they will be underbid by the British. they must then retire from the competition. some no doubt will try other channels of commerce and return cargoes from other countries. this effect would be salutary. a very well informed merchant too (a Scotsman entirely in the English trade) told me he thought it would have another good effect, by checking & withdrawing our over-extensive commerce & navign (the fruit of our neutral position) within those bounds to which peace must necessarily bring them. that this being done by degrees will probably prevent those numerous failures produced generally by a peace coming on suddenly. notwithstanding this decree the sentiments of the merchants become more & more cooled & settled down against arming. yet it is believed the Representatives do not cool: and tho' we think the question against arming will be carried, yet probably by a majority of only 4. or 5. their plan is to have convoys furnished for our vessels' going to Europe, & smaller vessels for the coasting defence. on this condition they will agree to fortify Southern harbours & build some gallies. it has been concluded among them, that if war takes place, Woolcot is to be retained in office, that the P. must give up Mc.Henry; & as to Pickering they are divided, the Eastern men being determined to retain him, their middle & Southern brethren wishing to get rid of him. they have talked of Genl. Pinckney as successor to Mc.Henry. this information is certain. however I hope that we shall avoid war & save them the trouble of a change of ministry. the P. has nominated J. Q. Adams Commissioner Plenipoty. to renew the treaty with Sweden. Tazewell made a great stand against it on the general ground that we should let our treaties drop, & remain without any. he could only get 8. votes against 20. a trial will be made to day in another form which he thinks will give 10. or 11. against 16. or 17. declaring the renewal inexpedient. in this case, notwithstanding the nomination has been confirmed, it is supposed the P. would perhaps not act under it, on the probability that more than a third would be against the ratification. I believe however that he would act, & that a third could not be got to oppose the ratification. it is ackknoleged we have nothing to do but to decide the question about arming. yet not a word is said about adjourning, and some even talk of continuing the session permanently; others talk of July & August. an effort however will soon be made for an early adjournment. my friendly salutations to mrs Madison, to yourself affectionate Adieux.

RC (DLC: Madison Papers); addressed: "James Madison junr. near Orange Courthouse"; franked. PrC (DLC).

THEIR PLAN: see Notes on Conversations with Abraham Baldwin, John Brown, and John Hunter, 11 Mch. 1798.

During two days of closed executive proceedings following President Adams's 12 Mch. naming of his son, John Quincy Adams, as commissioner, Henry TAZEWELL MADE A GREAT STAND AGAINST the nomination and moved that the Senate "not advise and consent to the appointment of *a* commissioner." A question of order being raised, TJ argued "that on a message of appointment from the President, the Senate can answer only yea or nay, viz. that they do, or do not approve the appointment of J. Q. Adams. They cannot amend or modify, as by saying they do not approve the appointment of *a* commissioner &c." The Senate CONFIRMED the appointment on 14 Mch. (PW, 13-15; JEP, 1:265-6). For the decision to postpone Tazewell's effort to declare the RENEWAL of the treaty INEXPEDIENT, see TJ to Madison, 21 Mch. Tazewell gave an account of his opposition to John Q. Adams's appointment in a letter to Madison of 18 Mch. 1798 (see Madison, *Papers*, 17:94-5).

To Thomas Mann Randolph

TH:J. TO TMR.   Philadelphia Mar. 15. 98.

Your's of Feb. 26. came to hand on the 8th. inst. but after mine to you of that date was sealed. I at the same time recieved one from G. Jefferson informing me I had no nail rod in his possession. Richardson however, who happened to be present told me that on the 1st. of Feb. he saw in mr Johnston's warehouse a considerable parcel of nail rod which they told him was mine. I therefore wrote back instantly to G. Jefferson to enquire into that & forward it without delay, & the next morning (the 9th.) the vessel with my molasses, cloverseed &c being just about sailing, I got 3. tons of rod put on board her. so that perhaps by this time it may be at Richmond & will be forwaded by G. Jefferson by the Milton boats. I hope therefore there will be no great interval of want of this article. I will look out for a blacksmith for you, but observe at the same time that this is not a place for country work. I doubt whether there is a ploughshare made in the whole city. but I will not fail to make due enquiry.—I am in hopes you get Bache's & Adams's papers regularly so that from them you will have the European news. the new decree of the French does not seem to have increased the inclination of the merchants to arm. on the contrary they seem to become daily more & more sensible of the ruinous tendency of that measure. not so the H. of Representatives. they appear more kindled: so that tho' we believe there is a majority against arming, yet probably it will not be of more than 4. or 5. those for arming carry their views to measures which would bankrupt us in one year. for it is known from trial that we cannot borrow a dollar either in Europe or America. no day of adjournment is yet talked of. my kindest love to my dear Martha, kisses to the little ones & affectionate Adieux to yourself.

RC (DLC); endorsed by Randolph as received 24 Mch. 1798. PrC (CSmH); endorsed by TJ in ink on verso.

For the letter from George JEFFERSON, see 1 Mch. 1798.

From Fulwar Skipwith

MY DEAR SIR   Paris 17 March 1798

I leave to Mr. Barlow, who writes to you by Mr. Lee the confidential bearer of his and this letter, to trace the rise and progress of the present alarming indisposition of this Government towards ours; but being more frightened than perhaps my friend Mr. Barlow is at the dangers which threaten the peace and safety of my Country, I am irrisistably led to express my fears to the man of my Government, who I deem the best capacitated to appreciate their value, being well persuaded that he will not suspect the purity of the motive which induce me to hazard them.

Untill the issue of the late election of President of the United States was known to the Government here, its doubts, jealousies, and prejudices had been levelled against Individuals of our Administration only, and not against the Government or the Nation at large;—And surely had there then been a desire in our Cabinet to stand well with France revolutionized, or had pride and ignorance given place to the light of reason and of impartial information, a becoming and an *acceptable* atonement would have been devised and offered to the french Nation for the infatuated prostitution, which a misguided President and an intriguing Junto had made at the foot of the British throne, of what we sacredly owed to humanity, to character, to liberty and to France. But to return to the important event of the last election which gave a new President to the U. States—The moment the man was anounced to this Government, they thought they read in his character that of his Nation; or in other words they saw in the enemy of their Revolution and in the stiff necked bigot of aristocracy, the perverse blindness of the American Nation;—And from that instant their deportment and conduct towards us assumed and continues more and more to evidence marks of an inimical, if not an inveterate and extensive plan of hostilities against our Country, and which may e'er long threaten all that can be dear to her as a Nation—Yes, Sir, the moment is come that I see the fortunes nay Independence of my Country, at hazard, and in the hands of the most gigantic Nation on earth;—my solicitude therefore, while yet I think myself a free American, waves discretion and must speak.

France with almost the whole of the Continent of Europe at her feet, will soon reduce to the same humble posture the Power who alone supports life in her enemies in America; and as I cannot attribute to her so great a portion of magnimity as to suppose that, when she shall consummate the act, she will forego the occasion of satisfying her vengeance, and especially as she may gratify herself with the prospect of doing it with great commercial advantages, and aggrandizement, or even that she may league with the very Power that now caresses us; so do I every day see the cloud of calamity approaching nearer the peaceful shores of our common Country.—Already the language of planting new Colonies upon the borders of the Missipi is the language of frenchmen here, and if I had not been apprised of the fact, I should without any claim to foresight know, that Spain is disposed to cede her possessions upon that river whenever the Directory shall require it.—It may be also important for the American Cabinet to recollect, what possibly they may have forgotton, that the country over whom they preside the constituted guardians, has its weak parts—Their Western people, the Savages upon their frontiers, and the Slaves that swarm within their bosom are subjects whose situations do not, and whose uses would not escape the observation of this Government in case of War—But War may be prevented and our Country saved, if we can come forward and discharge the debt which our blunders have brought upon us, and which the strength and fortunes of France now lay claim to;—T"is to confess some of our errors, to lay their sins heavily upon the shoulders of a few persons who have perpetrated them, to modify or break the English treaty with Jay, and to lend France as much money, should she ask it, as she lent us in the hour of distress. I am aware that the pride of some, the knavery of many, and the ignorance of others would pretend to execrate the act; but imperious necessity commands, and the genius of Republican liberty would sanction it.

The blunders of our present as well as our late Administration must by this time appear in *large* characters from one end of our Continent to the other—in Europe they are read almost without eye sight; if therefore I touch upon one of them, t'is because it forms in this theatre the actual scene of their political-dramatical action.   When the news came that Genl. Pinckney was ordered to retake his post at Paris, and that Genl. Marshall, one of the declaiming Apostles of Jays treaty, was to support him, this Government I believe suspected that their mission was virtually destined for the Court of Louis the 18th. and not for the french Republic; for Mr. Adams when he composed it, did not dream of the event of the 18th fructidor, but in the language of the Gazette which I fancy publishes his official acts, he must have thought *the revolutionary and piratical* banditti of France near its dissolution. Be this as it may, no body expected from the nomination of those two persons that concord with the *French Republic* was their object, and their deportment since their arrival added to the Presidents ill judged and ill timed speech at the opening of your present session of Congress, have served powerfully to confirm that impression.—Every body here remarks, what those two Gentlemen do not attempt to conceal, that their doors are open only to the intriguants against and enemies of the present Government, and that they are among the first persons to hear and buz about the tales of new Coalitions and counter revolutions; the name of a true supporter of the french revolution is as grating to their ears as his sight is disgusting to their eyes.—from their arrival, their attentions and caresses have been confined to the families of the proscribed and of the transported, and their closet Counsellor seems to be Beaumarchais, of whose character you I know want no information.

When we heard that Mr. Gerry was nominated to the Mission the Directory were pleased, and the patriots in Paris of both Countries were delighted in the idea of seeing here one of the tryed patriots of 75 and one of the remaining republican chiefs of the American States; but painful is it to me to add that we behold him moving here but as the shadow of what we presumed he was, and we much fear that the longer he stays, the more apt will public opinion be to suscribe the neutrality of his character to the feebleness of his diplomatic talents. We learn in secret whispers from this good old Gentleman, (for I venerate the chastity of his moral character while I regret that he has not the courage to shape a political course congenial to the crisis here) that he has a hard and cruel task to think and act with his two associates, and that were he alone he would be able to stop the frightful breach between the two Countries—But I am apprehensive that his paralytic mind would prove too weak to invent, and his arm to feeble to apply the remedy which the disease demands.—In fact no one but a pronounced Republican and friend of the french revolution, and a man unfettered by the forms and school readings of Mr. Adams and Pickering, can stand a chance to heal the wounds which are now bleeding

In regard to both the internal and external situation of this Republic, let not our Governors any longer entertain the delusive hope of a decline in its power or its destinies—The late conquest of a part of Switzerland leaves to France the only inlet into her country, which remained open to a foreign foe, and I suspect at last teaches neighbo'ring despots that they are yet to die under the increasing rays of representative Government. The interior of the Republic exhibits perfect peace and plenty, and I believe contains no element that can shake its Government; on the contrary, all that can be wanted to increase its strength. Those innumerable insects which so many ages of monarch-craft and priest-craft had engendered and left upon the soil, are either returned to the muck of their first state of non existence, or are working thro' the digestive passages of its bowels in order that they may regenerate among the fair growth of its creation. Or to speak without a figure, the disaffected french men themselves are growing proud of the unexampled achievements and grandeur of their Country, and are daily becoming reconciled to its change of Government.

The certainty of this conveyance has induced me to discharge my mind of what I thought I owed to my Country—that you will treat both myself and what I have thrown upon paper with indulgence I have no doubt.   F.S.

RC (CtHi: Wolcott Papers); addressed: "Mr. Jefferson"; at head of text in Oliver Wolcott's hand: "(These Letters exhibit the secret Intriggues of France at this period). OW."

Although TJ received the two letters of 12 Mch. 1798 that Joel BARLOW entrusted to William LEE as a CONFIDENTIAL BEARER, this missive from Skipwith—which is not recorded in SJL, bears no endorsement in TJ's hand, and is located in Wolcott's papers rather than TJ's—was obviously meant to travel by the same means but never reached its intended destination. Under the circumstances, TJ's receipt of the communications from Barlow may be more surprising than the fact that Skipwith's letter ended up in Wolcott's possession. Lee, who arrived in the United States early in June, carried letters from France addressed to a variety of recipients. The secretary of the treasury, learning that some of the packets had originated in offices of the French government, traveled to New York to see Lee. Inquiring particularly if anything was addressed to TJ, Wolcott on 20 June received a negative answer, which perhaps referred only to letters with the seal of the French office of foreign affairs. He nonetheless took possession from Lee of an unknown quantity of letters. It seems likely that this one from Skipwith to TJ was either among them or was given to Wolcott by John Kidder, who traveled with Lee and for a time had some of the packets. As for Barlow's letters, Lee presumably concealed their existence from the inquisitive Wolcott on 20 June. Both were probably enclosed in John Brown's letter to TJ of 29 June and, after cautious conveyance through Thomas Bell, reached TJ at Monticello on 26 July. The affair of the sequestered correspondence was no secret: to allay suspicions that he was Talleyrand's hireling, Lee issued a public statement after his surrender of the documents to Wolcott, and one of the waylaid dispatches was the subject of a bitter newspaper battle between Benjamin Franklin Bache and his political opponents. Bache's published comments during the controversy led the government to charge him with seditious libel under common law prior to the passage of the Sedition Act (Smith, *Freedom's Fetters*, 194-200; Gibbs, *Memoirs*, 2:68, 70, 72, 158-61; Tagg, *Bache*, 378-88; Malone, *Jefferson*, 3:378-9; *Diary of William Dunlap (1766-1839)* . . . *Volume 1*, vol. 62 of *Collections of the New-York Historical Society* [New York, 1930], 294; MB, 2:986).

PRESIDENTS ILL JUDGED AND ILL TIMED SPEECH: Adams's address of 23 Nov. 1797. Early in 1798 military intervention by France joined with domestic revolutionary insurgence to give France control over several cantons of SWITZERLAND. A French-allied Helvetic Republic originated on 22 Mch. 1798 (Palmer, *Democratic Revolution*, 2:408-12).

Two letters from Skipwith to TJ, dated at Paris on 9 June and 6 Aug. 1798 and received on 27 Sep. and 25 Dec., respectively, are recorded in SJL but have not been found.

From Mary Jefferson Eppes

DEAR PAPA   Eppington March 20th 1798

We have been to Cumberland since I wrote to you last & saw while there the last melancholy rites paid to my Aunt Skipwith; I was never more affected, & never so sensible of the cruelty of requiring the presence of those who are most deeply afflicted at the ceremony. we came down immediately after it & brought poor Betsy[1] for who'm the scene had been too much with us, as her father fear'd her relapsing in to her former state of melancholy if left alone so soon after it. we had a dreadful journey down & thought ourselves fortunate in escaping with one over-setting only, in which except the fright, none of us suffer'd, for the roads were as bad as they could possibly be. I am sorry to hear that my sisters situation at Belmont is not as agreeable as she expected, tho I shall rejoice if it occasions her return to Monticello. how much do I wish for that day which will reunite us all after so long an absence! but I am afraid it will be some time yet before it arrives. the family here would all be allmost as much dissapointed as myself, were you not to return by this place, particularly my father, who can think he says of nothing but the improvements he saw at Monticello, & intends to get you to plan when you come, a cover'd way from the Maidens hall, to the house, with an alcove in it, & an octogon to the other wing. Aunt Carr is return'd from Celies in good health & is at present with Aunt Bolling, who is in tolerable health, the former will be here soon, where she will stay I expect & go up with us, Adieu Dear Papa that I may see you soon again & in good health is the earnest prayer of your affectionate daughter

ME

RC (MHi); endorsed by TJ as received   [1] Eppes here canceled "Skipwith."
31 Mch. 1798 and so recorded in SJL.

MY FATHER: her father-in-law, Francis
Eppes.

From James Thomson Callender

SIR   Philadelphia March 21st. 1798

Your interference with respect to my getting payment in a certain quarter has not had even the smallest effect. Before, or at the time of going there, I had a claim on a Gentleman for 34 dolls. and $\frac{1}{2}$. I have got, at length 19.—dols.—So want 15 & $\frac{5}{8}$. besides my gratuitous attendance now in the 4th, &, as I believe, in the last week. For I will, if I Can only get the balance *due*, to answer some Cogent demands, (I am asking no advances, nor pecuniary favours, but my own) proceed immediately to print my proposals for the next Volume; and the money I should raise by that wd serve to protract the burden of existence for a few months longer.

My Sale has been rapid beyond all hope. In less than 5 weeks, 700 have gone off, and Some commissions and Subscribers are yet unanswered. A gentleman came lately si[xty?] miles to Albany to buy a copy, and told our correspondent that in his country neighbourhood, he believed that he could sell 500.

The next is to be a book of only $\frac{1}{2}$ a dollar, good paper and print, and will I fancy sell fully faster than the other, as being of a more *come at able* Size & price—the type close, to Contain much matter.—The Six per Cents, in *quite a new light*—the Indian wars—the power of making treaties—A Review of Fenno's Gazette—are among the Chief Articles. I could have sold this week, for the Country, 150 of 1796 but they are all, or as good as all, gone.

If your good offices could get the bals due, I think I shall not run Scores with the Society again.—With a little help, and Mr. Bache's and other Correspondence I Could soon come to dispose of an edition of 2000. I will bring you a sample Sheet of the print, paper and i[. . .] agreeable, next week, one Gentleman has promised to pay down at least 30 dollars for the new Volume, as soon as printed. If I Could afford to lye out of my money, like other people, I Could Sell many more, but this I cannot do, which increases the wonder at my Sale of 700, of which only 190 are on Credit,—But after all I am in danger of Sticking for want of that help necessary to set up the Smallest huckster's store—If I Could find any 4th person to do what Mr. D—s, or $\frac{1}{2}$ of what L— or Mr. Jefferson have already done, I would make myself heard very distinctly, for a considerable distance.

I hope I need not add, that I have not mentd one word of the Society to any human being but you. If they would only keep their agreement for 3 months, till I get this piece out, I would do.

I am Sir with the greatest respect Your obedt Sert

J. T. CALLENDER

RC (DLC); torn; portions of words in right margin obscured by tape; addressed: "Mr. Jefferson"; endorsed by TJ as received 22 Mch. 1798 and so recorded in SJL.

IF I CAN ONLY GET THE BALANCE DUE: on 23 Mch. 1798 TJ had Thomas Leiper transmit $16 to Callender (MB, 2:980). MY SALE HAS BEEN RAPID: Callender's *Sketches*

of the History of America was published in Philadelphia in February 1798. His NEXT work, printed by the Philadelphia *Aurora* in May, entitled *Sedgwick & Co. or a Key to the Six Per Cent Cabinet*, was only 88 pages long; the *Sketches* ran to more than 260 pages (see Evans, Nos. 33484, 33485).

MR. D—S: Alexander J. Dallas. L—: Thomas Leiper.

To James Madison

Philadelphia. Mar. 21. 98.

I wrote you last on the 15th. since that yours of the 12th. is recieved. since that too a great change has taken place in the appearance of our political atmosphere. the merchants, as before, continue, a respectable part of them, to wish to avoid arming. the French decree operated on them as a sedative, producing more alarm than resentment. on the Representatives differently. it excited indignation highly in the war-party, tho' I do not know that it had added any new friends to that side of the question. we still hoped a majority of about 4. but the insane message which you will see in the public papers has had great effect. exultation on the one side & a certainty of victory; while the other is petrified with astonishment. our Evans, tho' his soul is wrapt[1] up in the sentiments of this message, yet afraid to give a vote openly for it, is going off tomor-

[189]

row as is said. those who count say there are still 2. members of the other side who will come over to that of peace. if so the numbers will be for war measures 52. against them 53. if all are present except Evans.— the question is What is to be attempted, supposing we have a majority. I suggest two things. 1. as the President declares he has withdrawn the Executive prohibition to arm, the Congress should pass a Legislative one. if that should fail in the Senate, it would heap coals of fire on their head. 2. as to do nothing, & to gain time, is every thing with us, I propose that they shall come to a resolution of adjournment 'in order to go home & consult their constituents on the great crisis of American affairs now existing.' besides gaining time enough by this to allow the descent on England to have it's effect here as well as there, it will be a means of exciting the whole body of the people from the state of inattention in which they are, it will require every member to call for the sense of his district by petition or instruction, it will shew the people with which side of the house their safety as well as their rights rest, by shewing them which is for war & which for peace, & their Representatives will return here invigorated by the avowed support of the American people. I do not know however whether this will be approved, as there has been little consultation on the subject. we see a new instance of the inefficacy of Constitutional guards. we had relied with great security on that provision which requires two thirds of the Legislature to declare war. but this is completely eluded by a majority's taking such measures as will be sure to produce war.—I wrote you in my last that an attempt was to be made on that day in Senate to declare an inexpediency to renew our treaties. but the measure is put off under a hope of it's being attempted under better auspices.—to return to the subject of war, it is quite impossible, when we consider all it's existing circumstances, to find any reason in it's favor, resulting from views either of interest or honour, & plausible enough to impose even on the weakest mind; and especially when it would be undertaken by a majority of one or two only. whatever then be our stock of charity or liberality we must resort to other views. and those so well known to have been entertained at Annapolis & afterwards at the grand convention by a particular set of men, present themselves as those alone which can account for so extraordinary a degree of impetuosity. perhaps instead of what was then in contemplation a separation of the union, which has been so much the topic to the Eastward of late, may be the thing aimed at.—I have written so far two days before the departure of our post. should any thing more occur to-day or tomorrow, it shall be added.

22d. at night. nothing more

RC (DLC: Madison Papers); addressed: "James Madison junr. Near Orange court house"; franked. PrC (DLC); lacks postscript.

INSANE MESSAGE: for John Adams's message to Congress of 19 Mch., which was printed in the Philadelphia *Aurora* the next day, see note to TJ to Mann Page, 6 Mch. 1798. Thomas EVANS received a leave of ab-

sence from the House of Representatives on 21 Mch. and was back in the House by 11 Apr. (JHR, 3:231, 257; *Annals*, 8:1402). For the views ENTERTAINED AT ANNAPOLIS and at the Constitutional CONVENTION, see Notes on the Formation of the Federal Government, 5 Jan. 1798.

[1] Word reworked from "[bent? on]."

To James Monroe

Philadelphia Mar. 21. 98.

The public papers will present to you the almost insane message sent to both houses of Congress 2. or 3. days ago. this has added to the alarm of the sounder and most respectable part of our merchants, I mean those who are natives & are solid in their circumstances & do not need the lottery of war to get themselves to rights. the effect of the French decree on the representatives had been to render the war party inveterate & more firm in their purpose without adding to their numbers. in that state of things we had hoped to avert war-measures by a majority of 4. at this time, those who count talk of it's being reduced to a majority of 1. or 2. if a majority be with us at all. this is produced by the weight of the Executive opinion. the first thing proposed by the whigs will be a call for papers. for if Congress are to act on the question of war, they have a right to information. the 2d. to pass a Legislative prohibition to arm vessels instead of the Executive one which the President informs them he has withdrawn. these questions will try the whig strength, on the ground of war. the 3d. to adjourn to consult our constituents on the great crisis of American affairs now existing. this measure appears to me under a very favorable aspect. it gives time for the French operations on England to have their effect here as well as there. it awakens the people from the slumber over public proceedings in which they are involved. it obliges every member to consult his district on the simple question of war or peace: it shews the people on which side of the house are the friends of their peace as well as their rights, & brings back those friends to the next session supported by the whole American people. I do not know however whether this last measure will be proposed. the late maneuvres have added another proof to the inefficacy of Constitutional barriers. we had reposed great confidence in that provision of the constitution which requires $\frac{2}{3}$ of the Legislature to declare war. yet it can be entirely eluded by a majority's taking such measures as will bring on war.—my last to you was of the 8th. inst. the last recd from you was of Feb. 25.

RC (DLC: Monroe Papers); addressed: "Colo. James Monroe near Charlottesville"; franked and postmarked; endorsed by Monroe. PrC (DLC).

To George Jefferson

DEAR SIR   Philadelphia. Mar. 22. 98.
I inclose you a bill of lading for a box containing a harpsichord, and another containing plants, sent by the Sloop Sally capt. Potter, who sails with a Northwester which will probably place him at our capes speedily. both packages should be sent up *by water*, and as the plants will fail unless they have a speedy passage I must pray your immediate attention to them, that they may go by the first boats to Milton.—be so good as to bear in mind what I lately wrote you that the box containing the chimney piece (formerly sent) is to wait at Richmond for further orders. I shall be glad to hear of the arrival of the John Brown & the Dove: as also to be apprised when & by what vessels you forward the two casks of wheat to Sr. John Sinclair, that I may write to him. I am Dear Sir
Your affectionate friend & servt   TH: JEFFERSON

PrC (MHi); at foot of text: "Mr. George Jefferson"; endorsed by TJ in ink on verso. Enclosure not found.   I LATELY WROTE YOU: TJ to George Jefferson, 8 Mch. 1798.

To Thomas Mann Randolph

TH:J. TO TMR.   Philadelphia Mar. 22. 98.
Your's of Mar. 5. was recieved after mine of the 15th. was sealed. I have observed for some time past that your letters come 2. days later than mr Madison's. I suspect therefore that your's come by the way of Richmond.
I think, considering the poor appearance of the wheat crop, & high price of tobacco, it will be best for Page & George to push at as much of the latter as they can. I should be glad to know how much tobo. George made the last year, & whether it is gone to Richmd. I pray you to direct Page to get your corn in time before you will want it. I have just had put on board the sloop Sally, capt Potter for Richmond, a harpsichord for Maria, and a box of plants, which I shall desire mr Jefferson

to forward up the river without delay. the plants are distinguished by numbers as follow.

No. 1. Rhododendron maximum 3. plants. to be planted in the Nursery.

2. Scotch pines.	3. plants	to be planted among the Kentuckey Coffee trees in
3. Norway firs.	2. do.	an open space between the Pride of China trees &
4. Balm of Gilead.	2. do.	the Grove, about S.W. & by W. from the house.
6. Dwarf Ewe	3. do.	they may be planted within 20. feet of one an-

other, therefore I suppose there will be space enough in the place I describe to receive them all, without disturbing the Coffee trees.

5. Juniper.　　　　3. plants.　　to be planted on the upper Roundabout between or in continuation of the Arbor vitaes & Cedars.

7. Aesculus Virginica. yellow Horse chesnut	1. plant.	on the Slope leading from
8.	hybrida	variegated	1. do.	the Pride of China trees
9.	Pavia.	Scarlet	1. do.	down to the shops, a-
10.	Alba	white	1. do	mong the Catalpas, Crab-
11. Sugar maple.		2. plants		apple trees &c wherever
12. Balsam poplars.		3. do.		there are vacant spaces.

13. Viburnum opulifolium. bush cranberry. 3. plants. in the curran or gooseberry squares

14. Alpine strawberries ⎫ in new & separate beds in the garden. both of these
15. Chili strawberries ⎭ kinds are immensely valuable.

16. Antwerp raspberry. twenty odd plants I expect. in some new row by themselves. it has the reputation of being among the finest fruits in the world.[1]

Peruvian winter grass. many roots of this are packed in among the plants. it is a most valuable grass for winter grazing. John had better take some favorable place under trees to set it out. the cherry trees in the garden would be good places, if there is not danger of too much trampling.

Many nuts of the yellow & scarlet Horse chesnut are stuck in among the moss. John must set them out in the nursery instantly, & before they dry.

I must ask the favor of you, the moment these things arrive at Milton, to send to James to go for them with his waggon, & to take a ride to Monticello, as soon as they get there, & direct John where to plant them. he would do well perhaps to dig his holes before hand, to mellow the earth. all the trees to be well staked, & the numbers preserved.

You will see in the public papers a message from the President declaring that he sees nothing further to be expected from negociation, and recommending measures for protecting our commerce by force. this has thrown an inexpressible gloom over the advocates for peace, while those for war are in the highest exultation. we had expected that war measures might have been rejected by a majority of about 4. but such is the weight of the executive opinion, & such the advantage that the warparty has by it's alliance with the Executive, that the issue is now become very doubtful. our Evans, who, from the exposed situation of his constituents,[2] was afraid to vote for war, and yet whose party attachment forbid his voting against it, went off yesterday home. another (a quaker) whose religious principles forbade the indulgence of his British attachments, is gone off. those who are most sanguine count now on no more than an equal division 52. and 52. our three members are exactly those who have carried every vote against us, and who make the scale of war-advocates preponderate. the steady, sure merchants, trading on real capital are in dismay. the tottering, and those foreigners whose attachment to their native[3] country is greater than to this, are well pleased. they will avail themselves of the President's having withdrawn his prohibition to arm. it is not yet certain what measures will be proposed by the whigs. but a proposition is spoken of to adjourn in order to consult their constituents on the great crisis in their affairs now existing. my warm affections to my dear Martha, & kisses to the little ones. Adieu affectionately.

RC (DLC); endorsed by Randolph as received 1 Apr. 1798.

A letter from Randolph to TJ OF MAR. 5, 1798, recorded in SJL as received ten days later, has not been found.

OUR THREE MEMBERS: Thomas Evans, James Machir, and Daniel Morgan, three

Virginia congressmen who voted with the Federalists (see TJ to James Madison, 18 May 1797).

[1] Sentence interlined.
[2] Word written over a partially erased and illegible word.
[3] Word interlined.

To Carlos Martínez de Irujo

Mar. 23d. 1798.

Th: Jefferson presents his compliments to the Chevalier d'Yrujo, and asks the favor of a passport for Thomas Kanberg, a friend of his who is going to Europe on private business. he is a native of the North of Europe (perhaps of Germany) has been known to Th:J. these twenty years, is a most excellent character, and entirely out of the political line. whether he will take his passage from Baltimore or Philadelphia, depends on the fact from which place he can get the best convenience for going to some port in France.

PrC (DLC); endorsed in ink on verso by TJ, who also wrote in ink at foot of text: "for Kosciuzko."

In 1795 the Spanish government named diplomat Carlos Fernando Martínez de Irujo (1763-1824) minister to the United States. He officially assumed the post the following year. Allied with Thomas McKean in an acrimonious political dispute

against publicist William Cobbett, Irujo married McKean's daughter Sarah (Sally) in 1798. Named Marquis of Casa-Irujo in 1802, beginning in 1808 he represented Spain in Brazil, Paris, and London, and held high government positions at home. He also translated into Spanish Condorcet's compendium of Adam Smith's *Wealth of Nations* (Germán Bleiberg, *Diccionario de Historia de España*, 2d ed., 3 vols. [Madrid,

1968-69], 1:753-4; G. S. Rowe, *Thomas McKean: The Shaping of an American Republicanism* [Boulder, Colo., 1978], 295-303; Fitzpatrick, *Writings*, 35:117).

For TJ's efforts to obtain travel papers for Tadeusz Kosciuszko as THOMAS KANBERG, see the next document and TJ's letters to Philippe de Létombe and Robert Liston of 23 and 27 Mch. Irujo replied to TJ on this day with a brief note written at High Street in Philadelphia that covered the requested passport and indicated that "The name of the port in Europe is left blank and may be filled up by Mr. Kanberg" (RC in MoSHi: Jefferson Papers; unsigned; endorsed by TJ; enclosure not found). On 26 Apr. the Portuguese minister to the United States, Cipriano Ribeiro Freire, sent TJ a brief letter enclosing a passport for "Mr. Thomas Kanburg" as TJ had requested earlier that day in a note that has not been found and was not recorded in SJL (RC in DLC; endorsed by TJ as received 26 Apr. 1798; enclosure not found).

From Tadeusz Kosciuszko

SIR   [on or before 23 Mch. 1798]

You had the goodness to take me under your care and protection. I beseech to continue to the end—

I send inclosed a Varrant for the letters of Exchange. I live to your jugement in what maner to be done that i may receive without trouble or loss of time. Six hundred eighty four out of the whole money will serve to pay my passage the rest out of this i would wish to have by me in hard Cash. I must know six or ten days before i go to prepare the things and in the maner that nobody should know it—it is requisit that I should have passports on the name of Mr *Kann*[1] from Ministers Engl[ish?] Portugal. Span. French. be so good to send a Pro curation for you to act in my absence not only wyth the money lay'd upon the Banck of Pensylwania but also wyth this that may Come to the Treasurer, for which i send you a letter inclosed. recomend me i beg you to your friend at Lisbon to help me in every thing—and as i am a stranger and will stay few days i would wish if posible that he should take me to his house upon any Condition—not forget to recomend me to the care of the Capitain in whose Ship i will go. in any thing you choose to be informed i beg you write me if you have not time to come to see me i will born all thos letters immidiatly. I take the Liberty to send you a Bear skin as a Token of my veneration, respect and Esteem for you for ever

  Humble Servant—   T KOSCIUSZKO

Soon i will got all my Shares upon the Banck of Pensylwania i will have have the honour to send imidiatly—

RC (MeHi: Fogg Collection); undated, but conjectured on the basis of TJ's correspondence of 23 Mch. 1798 (see below). Enclosure not found.

The youngest son of a family of the Polish gentry, Tadeusz (Thaddeus) Andrzej Bonawentura Kosciuszko (1746-1817) pursued a military career and studied engineering, artillery, and drafting at royal academies in Warsaw and France before going to the United States in 1776. During the Revolutionary War he supervised the construction of major fortifications and served under Horatio Gates and Nathanael Greene, achieving the brevet rank of brigadier general at the close of the war. He returned to Poland, and as lieutenant general led that nation's army in its war with Russia beginning in 1792. Defeated and wounded in October 1794, he spent two years as a Russian prisoner but was freed by Emperor Paul I upon swearing an oath of allegiance in order to effect the release of other Polish captives. Still ailing from his wounds, he was greeted by enthusiastic crowds in England in the spring of 1797 and when he arrived in the United States in August of that year. Almost immediately, however, using John Dawson as an intermediary Kosciuszko made contact with Philippe de Létombe, the French minister in Philadelphia, and expressed a desire to go to France, which in 1792 had accorded him honorary citizenship along with Washington, Paine, Joseph Priestley, and others. He also met often with TJ, whom he had previously known only slightly. Years later Kosciuszko attributed to TJ a hope that the Polish hero might help repair ties between France and the United States. Kosciuszko also thought that the French might be sympathetic to a restoration of Polish independence. Fawned over by many Americans, he nevertheless met a chilly reception from the most ardent Federalist newspapers, and he harbored suspicions that his movements were under surveillance. It was generally believed that he would settle on a country estate in America, but TJ clandestinely organized his departure, making arrangements so secret that even Julian Niemcewicz, who had accompanied the general to America, knew nothing of the plan until the last moment and even then had to remain behind. Under the guise of traveling to Virginia for his health, a ruse that was not entirely shattered for some months, Kosciuszko left Philadelphia in the predawn hours of 5 May 1798. TJ accompanied him part way to New Castle, Delaware, where the Pole boarded a ship for Europe. In Paris he met with members of the Directory and lobbied, as did George Logan and Volney, for improved relations with the United States. He remained an exile from his partitioned homeland, residing in France until 1801 and in Switzerland from that year onward. He maintained a warm correspondence with TJ until his death (ANB; Haiman, *Kosciuszko*, 31-6, 42-6, 62-4, 73-5, 79-80, 83-7; MB, 2:981-2; Stewart, *French Revolution*, 317-18).

In January 1798 Dawson had been instrumental in the passage of an act of Congress that authorized payment to Kosciuszko of six percent interest for the period 1793-97 on $12,280.54 owed him for his service to the United States during the Revolution (Haiman, *Kosciuszko*, 70-2; *Acts Passed at the Second Session of the Fifth Congress of the United States of America* [Philadelphia, 1798], 61; ASP, *Claims*, 207-8). TJ did not actually receive Kosciuszko's Treasury warrant, which he used to purchase bills of EXCHANGE for the general, until 12 Apr.; see Memorandum to Tadeusz Kosciuszko, [25 Apr. 1798].

Kosciuszko's request here for PASSPORTS under an assumed name, in conjunction with TJ's letters of 23 Mch. 1798 to Carlos Martínez de Irujo and to Létombe, implies that Kosciuszko wrote this letter no later than that day.

On TJ's advice Kosciuszko entrusted the management of his American finances to John Barnes, who initially invested the funds in 30 shares of the Bank of Pennsylvania (Haiman, *Kosciuszko*, 75, 119). THAT MAY COME TO THE TREASURER: on 13 Mch. 1798 Secretary of the Treasury Oliver Wolcott wrote to the Dutch banking firm of Willink, Van Staphorst & Hubbard to supersede an earlier arrangement whereby Kosciuszko was to receive payment in Europe of part of his claim. Wolcott asked the firm to credit the funds to the United States so that he could pay Kosciuszko in America (Tripl in MHi).

¹ Altered by TJ to read "Thomas Kannberg."

To Philippe de Létombe

Philadelphia Mar. 23d 98.

Th: Jefferson presents his compliments to M. Letombe Consul of France, and asks the favor of a passport for Thomas Kanberg, a friend of his who is going to Europe on private business. he is a native of the North of Europe (perhaps Germany) has been known to Th:J. these twenty years, is a most excellent character, and no ways connected with the politics of our country or of that to which he is going. it is uncertain whether he will take his passage from Baltimore or this place; it will depend on the fact at which place he can get the best convenience for going to some port in France.

PrC (DLC); endorsed in ink on verso by TJ, who also wrote in ink at foot of text: "this was for Kosciuzko."

Létombe replied to this letter on 24 Mch. with a brief note in French that covered the requested passport and offered to send another in a different form if that would be more suitable "à Monsieur Kanberg" (RC in MoSHi: Jefferson Papers; unsigned; dated "Ce Samedi"; endorsed by TJ as written and received on 24 Mch. 1798; enclosure not found).

In May 1797 Létombe, already in the United States as consul general of France, received the powers of minister plenipotentiary (Abraham P. Nasatir and Gary Elwyn Monell, *French Consuls in the United States: A Calendar of their Correspondence in the Archives Nationales* [Washington, 1967], 563). A letter from Létombe to TJ, written and received on 18 May 1797, and two from TJ to Létombe written on 2 and 29 June 1797 are recorded in SJL but have not been found.

To Sir John Sinclair

DEAR SIR   Philadelphia March 23. 1798.

I have to acknolege the receipt of your two favors of June 21. & July 15. & of several [separate] parcels of[1] the Agricultural reports. these now form a great mass of information on a s[ubject] of all in the world the most interesting to man; for none but the husbandman makes any thing [for him] to eat, & he who can double his food, as your exertions bid fair to do, deserves to rank, [among his] benefactors, next after his creator. among so many reports of transcendent merit, [one is un]willing to distinguish particulars: yet the application of the new chemistry to the subject of manur[es,[2] the] discussion of the question on the [size] of farms, the [treatise on the potatoe, from] their universality, have an advantage in other countries [over] those [which are topographical.] the work which shall be formed as the result of the whole [we shall ex]pect with impatience. Permit me, through you, to make here my acknowlegements to the board of Agriculture for the honor they have been pleased to confer on me, by [associating me to their institution. in] love for the art which gives bread to man, & virtue [to him] who makes it,[3] I am truly their [associate;] but even[ts have co]ntrouled my [predilection for[4] it's practice,] and denied to me that [uninterr]upted attention which alone can enable [us to advance in it with a sure step. perhaps] I may find opportunities of being useful to you as a centinel [at an outpost], by conveying intelligence of whatever may [occur] here [new & interesting to agriculture. this duty I] shall perform with[5] pleasure; as well in [respectful] return for the notice of the board, [as from] a zeal for improving the condition of human life by an interchange of it's comforts & of the information[6] which may [increase them].

Observing from your letter of July 15. that a sample of the Virginia May wheat would be acceptable, I have given orders at Richmond to have some of the most genuine procured, & to be so packed in a [barrel in layers with boards between each, as may pre]vent it's heating. for a very small [degree of heat destroys] it's [vegeta]ting power, and as the present unbridled state of things on the ocean, renders every thing committed to it precarious, I have directed a second parcel to be sent by a second vessel so as to double the chance of your getting it. it will be addressed to yourself by my correspondent there. this wheat has it's disadvantages; but it has also some properties[7] singularly advantageous under certain circumstances; and as under every accident of [season, soil or climate it is] desireable that the farmer should find something which may suit [his situation, this] newly discovered variety of wheat will often fill a plot which otherwise would be without resource. it may be sowed in Virginia 3. or 4 weeks later than the common wheat, & comes 3. or 4. weeks sooner, to wit, the last week in May. it thus lengthens the seed time, lengthens the harvest, & shortens the distresses arising from a preceding short crop. the grain to be sown must be carefully kept from heat. many crops were lost, before it's peculiar tenderness in that respect was known. it is more liable to sprout as it grows in the field in wet seasons, and yields less straw than the common. it is on the other hand a heavier grain, & makes the whitest & lightest bread we have ever seen; insomuch as to command a shilling more for the bushel. but it must be ground early in the season. it loses of it's colour if it lies unground till the spring. it does not answer equally[8] well in every part of our state. in the lower country it is invaluable: but in the temperate climate of the middle parts, where I live, it fails too frequently to be relied on. whether this proceeds from the mildness of our summer, or greater degree of winter, we have not yet had experience enough of this grain to decide.

I promised in a former letter to send you a drill invented by a mr Martin of Virginia, which I consider as perfect for sowing a single row.[9]

it will I hope, so far, supply this great desideratum which has so long existed, and still exists as mr Young informs us even for the farmer of England. you will find that the drill of mr Martin fulfills the requisites so properly exacted by mr Young, of simplicity & cheapness of construction, ease of repair, & the perfect performance of it's offices. it is made with us for 9. dollars or 40/6 your money. it opens it's furrow, sows the seed, & covers it, & that by a draught not too great for a man. I have myself drawn it through a row of several hundred paces without fatigue. the weakest & cheapest draught animal therefore [10] is equal to it. I expect one daily, which is on it's way here, from the inventor, made on his most approved construction; which shall be immediately forwarded to your address: [11] and I can recommend it with confidence, from my own experience, as well as from that of better judges. I have for some time contemplated the extending it to the sowing 3. or 4. rows at a time; in which way the sowing wheat in equidistant rows might be rendered as easy as it is advantageous.

We have a very simple contrivance for economising clover seed; which, considering the expence of that article, and the rapid extension of the clover husbandry, as well as the superior regularity with which it sheds it's seed, is of real value. it is a box of thin deal, or other light wood, 7. feet long, 6. Inches wide & 3. Inches deep, divided by thin partitions into 7. equal cells, in the bottom of each of which are holes of the size of the largest knitting needle, for knitting the coarsest woollen hose. a hole of $\frac{1}{4}$ of an inch should be first made through the wooden bottom, & that covered by a piece of tin an inch square, with such a hole through it's center, as is before described. two straps round the box about 18. I. or 2. feet from the center each way, serve as handles for the seedsman to hold by, & he walks on, sifting the seed over a band of about 9. feet breadth, and will sow about 8. or 10. acres a day. winds do not impede the operation; their effect being uniform on the falling of the seed. this circumstance I have found important, because the latter end of March, when I have usually sown, is for the most part very windy. those who sow by hand are in the habit with us of sowing about a gallon of seed to the acre. I can affirm after my own experience of several hundred acres sown in my farms within the last 4. or 5. years, that 3. pints sowed by this box are equal to a gallon by hand; & that for equality of distribution, no human hand can be compared with it. two such holes as I have mentioned in each cell will shed 3. pints to the acre. I know you are in the practice in England of sowing much more than a gallon of clover seed to the acre. [12] but whatever be the quantity which any farmer sows by hand, he will have the same effect from this box with three eighths of the seed. if he now sows two gallons by hand, let him have 4.

holes in each cell of the box; it will then shed 3. quarts, and the ground be as effectively covered with seed, & afterwards with plants. I believe the use of this seed-box to have originated here, & suggest it on that supposition, as the economy it presents is worthy the farmer's attention.

Another small practice, which I believe also to have originated here, [13] & now approved by an extensive [14] experience of several years, is the method of laying down & ploughing in buckwheat or other plants intended to be turned in as a green dressing. this has been practised in other countries by rakes or rollers preceding the plough. the imperfections & inconveniences of both these methods are known to every farmer. our method is to fix horizontally in the fore-end of the plough-beam, and at right angles to it, an iron or wooden pin [2.] feet long, on the side on which the mould board lies. to the end of this pin hang a heavy ox-chain, & fasten the other end of the chain round the beam, 2. or 3. feet from it's end, letting the chain swag to the ground. a little experience will teach the precise part of the beam where the hinder end of the chain should be fixed, & what sweep to give it. the ploughman then proceeding, the chain draws down the plants, & while the heads are held d[own by it, the] share cuts under the root, the whole plant is turned over, & immediately covered with earth by the mouldboard.

I observe you have considered the rafter-level as worthy notice in some of the Reports for the convenience with which, by it's aid, we trace the level for the rills of water in irrigation. as it seems that this use of it, so familiar with us, was new with you, perhaps another may be equally so, to which it is applied with peculiar advantage. I suppose this the more possible, as I do not know that it is used even here for this purpose but in my own neighborhood. [15] I mean the tracing on the side of a hill the line of regular ascent for a road. I live in a very hilly country. in my farms particularly I have found it necessary to pay great attention to the making roads of such easy & regular ascent as may in some degree lessen this natural disadvantage. I find that a rise of 1. foot in 10. being an angle of about 5°-45′ is a very practicable & convenient degree of ascent. to prepare the instrument for this, set it on a level floor, & then raising one of the feet one tenth of it's span, mark the cross bar where the plumbline intersects it. do the same with the other foot, & the instrument is ready for working with either foot foremost. place one foot at the foot of the hill, & raise the other up the face of it, till the plumb line crosses the bar at the corresponding mark. stick a pin in the ground at the forefoot; then advance setting the lower foot by that pin, & again moving the upper one till the line again covers the same mark, which gives you a point for a second pin; and so on to the height you mean to attain. if you wish to go round a hill at any particular height, on a dead level, you move the forefoot till the plumbline falls on the central mark which denotes the true level, & setting there a pin, you proceed step by step as before. these pins trace the line for the center of the road. dig half the breadth you propose for it into the hill, & draw the earth out to form the other half of the breadth, as in making a terras. [16] this process enables you to make the road with the least digging & other labor possible. having made many miles of such road, about 10. feet wide, I am enabled to say from my own experience that a mile requires from 25. to 100. days work, according as the hill is more or less steep or stony, & as it is open or covered with trees, which require to be taken up by the roots.

These details I know are small, & not important; & by those to whom they are familiar, will be thought too obvious for mention. I thought so of the use of the rafter level till I saw that it had not occurred with you. perhaps this may be the case with some other of these small details; & in that case the benefit cannot be less than the trouble of mentioning them. [17]

In a former letter to you I mentioned the construction of the mould board of a plough, which had occurred to me, as advantageous in it's form, as certain & invariable in the method of obtaining it with precision. I remember that mr Strickland of York, a member of your board, was so well satisfied with the principles on which it was formed that he took some drawings of it; and many others have considered it with the same approbation. an experience of 5. years has enabled me to say it answers in practice to what it promises in theory. [18] the mould board should be a continuation of the wing of the ploughshare, beginning at it's hinder edge and in the same plane. it's first office is to recieve the sod horizontally from the wing, to raise it to a proper height for being turned over, & to make in it's progress [19] the least resistance possible, & consequently to require a minimum in the moving power. [20] were this it's only office, the [21] wedge would offer itself as the most *eligible form in practice. but the sod is to be turned over also. to do this, the one edge of it is not to be raised at all: for to raise this would be a waste of labor. [22] the other edge is to be raised till it passes the perpendicular, that it may fall over with it's own weight. and that this may be done, so as to give also the least resistance, it must be made to rise gradually from the mo-

*I am aware that, were the turf only *to be raised* to a given height in a given length of mouldboard, & not to be turned over, the form of least resistance would not be rigorously a wedge with both faces strait, but with the upper one curved according to the laws of the solid of least resistance described by the mathematicians. but the difference between the effect of the curved & of the plain wedge, in the case of a mouldboard, is so minute, & the difficulty in the execution which the former would superinduce on common workmen is so great, that the plain wedge is the most eligible to be assumed in practice for the first basis of our construction.

ment the sod is recieved. the mould board then, in this second office, operates as a transverse or rising wedge, the point of which sliding back horizontally on the ground, the other end continues[23] rising till it passes the perpendicular. or, to vary the point of view, place on the ground a wedge of the breadth of the ploughshare, of it's length from the wing backwards, & as high at the heel as it is wide.[24] draw a diagonal on it's upper face from the left angle at the point to the right upper angle of the heel. bevil the [face] from the diagonal to the right bottom edge which lies on the ground. that half is then evidently in the best form for performing the two offices of raising & turning the sod gradually, & with the least effort: & if you will suppose the same bevil continues on[25] the left side of the diagonal, that is, if you will suppose a strait line, whose length is at least equal to[26] the breadth of the wedge,[27] applied on the face of the first bevil, and moved backwards on it, parallel with itself & with the ends of the wedge, the lower end of the line moving[28] along the right bottom edge, a curved plane will be generated whose characteristic will be a combination of the principle of the wedge in cross directions, & will give what we seek, *the mould-board of least resistance.* it offers too this great advantage that it may be made by the coarsest workman, by a process so exact, that it's form shall never be varied a single hair's breadth.[29] one fault of all other mouldboards is that, being copied by the eye, no two will be alike. in truth it is easier to form the mouldboard I speak of with precision, when the method has been once seen, than to describe that method either by words or figures. I will attempt however to describe it. whatever may not be intelligible from the description may be supplied from the model I send you.[30]

Let the breadth & depth of the furrow the farmer usually opens, as also the length of his plough-bar, from where it joins the wing to the hinder end, be given; as these fix the dimensions of the block of which the mould-board is to be made. suppose the furrow [9]. Inches wide, 6. Inches deep, & the plough bar 2. feet long. the block Fig. 1. must be 9. I. wide at bottom, (b.c.) $13\frac{1}{2}$ I. wide at top (a.d.) because if it were merely of the same width with the bottom (as a.e.) the sod, only raised to the perpendicular, would fall back into the furrow by it's own elasticity. I find from experience that[31] the top of the mould-board should over-jet[32] the perpendicular $4\frac{1}{2}$ I.[33] to ensure that the weight of the sod shall preponderate over it's elasticity.[34] the block must be 12. I. high, because, unless the mouldboard be in height double the depth of the furrow, in ploughing friable earth, it will be thrown in waves over the mouldboard. and it must be 3. feet long, one foot of which is added to form a tailpiece, by which it may be made fast to the plough handle. the first operation is to give the first form to this tailpiece, by sawing the block (Fig. 2.) across from a. to b. on it's left side, which is 12. Inches from it's hinder end, along the line b.c. to c.[35] within $1\frac{1}{2}$ Inch of the right side; & to the corresponding point in the bottom, $1\frac{1}{2}$ Inch also from the side. then saw in again at the hinder end from d.e. ($1\frac{1}{2}$ I. from the right side) along the line d.c. the block a.b.c.d.e.f.g. drops out, & leaves the tail-piece c.d.e.h.i.k. $1\frac{1}{2}$ I. thick. the fore part of the block a.b.c.k. l.m.n.[36] is what is to form the real mould-board. with a carpenter's square, make a scribe all round the block at every inch. there will of course be 23. of them. then from the point k. Fig. 2. & 3. draw the diagonals k.m. on the top, & k.o. Fig. 3. on the right side. enter a saw at the point m. being the left-fore-upper corner, & saw in, guiding the hinder part of the saw along the diagonal m.k. (Fig. 2.3.) & the fore part down the left edge of the block at the fore-end m.l. (Fig. 2) till it reaches k. & l. in a strait line. it will then have reached the true central diagonal of the block.[37] then [enter the saw at the point o.]

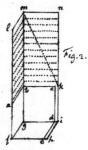

Fig. 2.

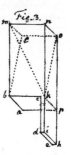

Fig. 3.

being the right fore-bottom corner, & saw in, guiding the hinder part of the saw along the diagonal o.k. Fig. 3. & the fore part along the bottom edge of the fore-end o.l. till it again reaches k.l.[38] the same central diagonal to which you had cut in the other direction. consequently the pyramid k.m.n.o.l. Fig. 4. drops out & leaves the block in the form Fig. 5. you will now observe that if, in the last operation, instead of stopping the saw at the central diagonal k.l. we had cut through the block in the same plane, we should have taken off a wedge l.m.n.o.k.b. Fig. 3. & left the block in the form of a wedge also l.o.k.b.a.p.k. which, when speaking of the principle of the mould board, I observed would be the most perfect form, if it had only to raise the sod. but as it is to be turned over also, the left half of the upper wedge is left on,[39] to furnish on the left side[40] the continuation of the bevil which was proposed to be made on the right half of the bottom edge.[41] we are now to proceed to this bevil; for which purpose the scribes round the block were formed, before the pyramidal piece was taken out; & attention must be used not to mismatch or mistake them now that they are disjoined by the withdrawing of that piece. enter the saw on the two points of the 1st. scribe, where it has been disjoined, which is exactly where it intersected the two superficial diagonals, & saw across the hollow of the block, guiding the saw both

Fig. 4.

Fig. 5.

before & behind along the same scribe, till the fore-part of the saw reaches the bottom edge of the right side & the middle of the saw reaches the central diagonal; the hinder part will of course continue the same strait line, which will issue somewhere on the top of the block. then enter the saw in like manner on the two projecting points of the 2d. scribe, & saw in, along the scribe before [&] behind, till it reaches the same bottom edge of the right side, & the central diagonal. then the 3d. 4th. 5th. &c. scribes successively. after cutting in several of the earlier scribes, the hinder part of the saw will issue at the left side of the block, & all the scribes being cut, the saw will have left strait lines from the bottom edge of the right side of the block across the central diagonal. with an adze dub off all the sawed parts to the bottoms of the saw marks, just leaving the traces visible, and the face of the mouldboard is finished. These traces will shew how the cross wedge rises gradually on the face of the direct wedge, which is preserved in the[42] central diago-nal.   a person may represent to himself sensibly and easily the manner in which the sod is raised on this mouldboard, by describing on

 the ground a parallelogram 2. feet long and 9 inches broad, as a.b.c.d.[43] then rest one end of a stick $27\frac{1}{2}$ I. long on the ground at b. & raise the other 12 I. high at e. which is $4\frac{1}{2}$ I. from d. & represents the overhanging of that side of the mouldboard. then present[44] another stick 12 I. long from a. to b. and move it backwards parallel with itself from a.b. to d.c. keeping one end of it always on the line a.d. and letting the other rise, as it recedes, along the diagonal stick b.e. which repre-sents our central diagonal. the motion of the cross stick will be that of our rising wedge, & will shew how every transverse line of the sod is conducted from it's first horizontal position, till it is raised so far beyond the perpendicular as to fall reversed by it's own weight. But, to return to our work. we have still to form the underside of the mouldboard. turn the block bottom up. enter the saw on the 1st. scribe, at what was the bottom edge of the left side, & cut in, guiding the instrument at both ends by the scribe, till it has approached within an inch, or any other distance according to the thickness[45] you chuse, of the face. then cut in like manner all the other scribes, &, with the adze dub out the sawed parts, & the mouldboard is done.   It is to be made fast to the plough by resting the toe in the hinder edge of the wing, which must be made double, like a comb case, to recieve & protect the fore-end of the mouldboard. then pass a screw through the mouldboard & helve of the plough-share where they touch each other, and two others through the tailpiece of the mouldboard, and right handle of the plough, & cut

off so much of the tailpiece as projects behind the handle, diagonally, & the whole is done.

I have described this operation in it's simplest mode that it might be the more easily understood. but, in practice, I have found some other modifications of it advantageous. thus instead of first forming my block as a.b.c.d. Fig. 7.[46] where ab. is 12. I. & the angle at b. a right one, I cut a wedge like piece b.c.e. off of the bottom through the whole length of the block, b.e. being equal to the thickness of the bar of the share (suppose $1\frac{1}{2}$ I.) be-cause,[47] the face of the wing declining from the top of the bar to the ground, were the block laid on the share, without an equivalent bevil at it's bottom, the side a.b. would decline from the perpendicular, and a.d. from it's horizontal position. again, instead of leaving the top of the block [$13\frac{1}{2}$] I. wide from m. to n. Fig. 8.[48] I cut a wedge from the right side n.k.i.c.p.n. $1\frac{1}{2}$ I. thick at top and taper-ing to nothing at bottom; because I find that the tail-piece,

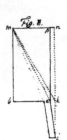

being by this means made oblique, as c.i. instead of k.i. is brought more advantageously to the side of the handle. the first superficial diagonal is consequently brought from m. to c. & not from m. to k. as in the first directions. these variations[49] will be seen in the models accompanying this, & will be easy to any one after understanding the general principle. the models represent the block in the different stages of the operation, & the mould-board as ultimately formed.[50]   While these mould-boards have been under trial, & essays have been making of greater or less projections for the upper right edge of the block, & of different heights in proportion to the depth of the furrow, I have continued to make them of wood. but now satisfied by a sufficient experience that, for a furrow of 9. I. by 6. I. the dimensions I have stated are the best, I propose to have the mould-board made of cast iron.

I am sensible that this description may be thought too lengthy & elaborate for a subject which has rarely[51] been deemed worthy the appli-cation of science. but if the plough be in truth the most useful of the instruments known to man, it's perfection cannot be an idle speculation. and in any case whatever, the combination of a *theory* which may satisfy the learned, with a *practice* intelligible to the most unlettered laborer, will be acceptable to the two most useful classes of society.[52]   Be this as it may, from the widow her mite only was expected. I have con-tributed according to my poverty: others will from their abundance. none so much as yourself who have been the animating principle of the institution from it's first germ. when I contemplate the extensive good which the proceedings under your direction are calculated to produce, I cannot but deplore every possibility of their interruption. I am fixed in awe at the mighty conflict to which two great nations are advancing, and recoil with horror at the ferociousness of man. will nations never devise a more rational umpire of differences than force? are there no means of coercing injustice more gratifying to our nature than a waste of the blood of thousands, & of the labor of millions of our fellow-creatures?[53] we see numerous societies of men (the aboriginals of this country) living together without the acknolegement of either laws or magistracy. yet they live in peace among themselves, & acts of violence & injury are as rare in their societies as in nations which keep the sword of the law in perpetual activity. public reproach, a refusal of common offices, interdiction of the commerce & comforts of society are found as effectual as the coarser instruments of force. nations, like these individuals, stand towards each other only in [the] relations of natural right. might they not, like them, be peaceably punished for violence & wrong? wonderful has been the progress of human improvement in other lines. let us hope then that that law of nature which makes a virtuous conduct produce benefit, & vice loss to the agent, in the long run, which has dictated[54] the common principle that honesty is the best policy, will in time influence the proceedings of nations as well as of individuals: & that we shall at length be sensible that war is an instrument entirely inefficient towards redressing wrong; that it multiplies, instead of indemnifying, losses. had the money which has been spent in the present war been employed in making roads, & conducting canals of navigation & irrigation through the country, not a hovel in the remotest corner of the highlands of Scotland, or mountains of Auvergne, would have been without a boat at it's door, a rill of water in every field, and a road to it's market town. had the money we have lost by the lawless depredations of all the belligerent powers been employed in the same way, what communications would have been opened of roads & waters! yet were we to go to war for redress, instead of redress, we should plunge deeper into loss, & disable ourselves for half a century more from attaining the same end. a war would cost us more than would cut through the isthmus of Darien; and that of Suez might have been opened by what a single year has seen thrown away on the rock of Gibraltar. these truths are palpable, & must in the progress of time have their influence on the minds & conduct of nations. an evidence that we are advancing towards a better state of things may be gathered from the public patronage of your labors, which tend eminently to ameliorate the condition of man. that they may meet the success they merit I sincerely pray; & that yourself may recieve the patriot's best reward, the applauding voice of present &

future times. accept, I beseech you, mine, with assurances of the sentiments [of] great & sincere respect & esteem with which I have the
honor to be Dear Sir

Your most obedient & most humble servt.[55]   TH: JEFFERSON

PrC (DLC); faint and torn, with text in brackets supplied from Dft and diagrams from MS at DLC; several words added in ink probably at the same time the author's note was appended (see notes 21-2, 26, 28-9), for other emendations see notes 19, 20, and 46; with author's note in margin probably added in response to Robert Patterson to TJ, 29 Mch. 1798 (see TJ to Patterson, 31 Mch. 1798); at foot of first page: "Sr John Sinclair." Dft (DLC); heavily emended; with several variations from PrC (see notes 1, 21, 41, 43, and 54); variations in capitalization, punctuation, and abbreviations not recorded; lacks author's note. MS (DLC: TJ Papers, 234:41813-4); entirely in TJ's hand and signed by him; undated; consists only of those paragraphs describing the moldboard plow, with author's note at foot of first page and diagrams in margin; at head of text: "Description of a Mouldboard of the least resistance, & of the easiest & most certain construction." MS (MHi); entirely in TJ's hand and signed by him; undated; consists of the same text as MS in DLC, similarly arranged, with identical title at head. Printed as "No. XXXVIII. The description of a Mould-board of the least resistence, and of the easiest and most certain construction, taken from a letter to Sir John Sinclair, President of the board of agriculture at London" in APS, *Transactions*, 4 [1799], 313-22; lacks second through seventh paragraphs; with diagrams at end of volume.

With this letter TJ fulfilled his promise to provide a description of his improved method for the construction of a moldboard plow of least resistance. His interest in this plow can be traced to his travels from Strasbourg to Meaux in April 1788, during which he noted that the "awkward figure of their mold board leads one to consider what should be it's form." Shortly thereafter TJ wrote a brief description with two diagrams for the construction of a moldboard. Upon his return to Monticello in 1790 he constructed a block demonstrating his method and built a model. When he retired there in

1794, he began using the moldboard plow on his farms. William Strickland was favorably impressed with a demonstration of it during his visit with TJ in 1795 and, upon his return to London, recommended it to the Board of Agriculture. During his years in Philadelphia as secretary of state TJ also worked on a detailed written description for the construction of the implement and evidently obtained David Rittenhouse's endorsement of it. Repeated encouragement by Sinclair to send "Some important Communication" to the British Board of Agriculture provided the final impetus for TJ to bring his paper before the public. Before he sent the letter to Sinclair TJ extracted the paragraphs on the moldboard and on 27 Mch. sent them to Robert Patterson, professor of mathematics at the University of Pennsylvania and his associate at the American Philosophical Society, for suggestions or corrections. Patterson's response on 29 Mch. led TJ to add an author's note and make other changes as indicated by several of the alterations in ink on the press copy. On 4 May TJ's description of the moldboard plow was read at the meeting of the APS and referred to Patterson, who recommended its publication in the society's *Transactions*. This publication of a lengthy extract of the letter provided wide publicity for his plow and made it unnecessary for TJ to send his description to state agricultural societies. Instead the agricultural societies reprinted the letter as found in the *Transactions*. On 4 June TJ sent John Taylor a press copy of one of the extracts, thereby fulfilling a promise he had made to him. TJ received more recognition for the moldboard when James Mease included the paragraphs on it from the *Transactions* in the American edition of A. F. M. Willich's five volume *The Domestic Encyclopædia; or, A Dictionary of Facts, and Useful Knowledge*, printed in Philadelphia in 1803 (4:288-92). In London, Sinclair, although no longer president of the organization, laid TJ's letter before the Board of Agriculture where it was read at the May 1798 meeting. The entire letter was reportedly published in an Edinburgh encyclopedia (ANB, s.v. "Patterson, Robert"; APS, *Proceedings*, 22, pt. 3 [1884]: 270-1; Henry S. Randall, "President Jefferson's Plow," in *Transactions of the New York State Agricultural Society*, 22 (1862), 66-73; Notes of a Tour through Holland and the Rhine Valley, printed in Vol. 13:xxv-xxvi, 27, 33-4n; Thomas Mann Randolph, Jr., to TJ, 23 Apr. 1790; TJ to Thomas Mann Randolph, Jr., 9, 31 May 1790; Sinclair to TJ, 28 May and 10 Sep. 1796, 21 June 1797, 4 June 1798; Lord Somerville to TJ, 28 May 1798; TJ to William Hendrick, 27 July 1806). TJ's interest in improving his moldboard continued into his presidency and in 1805 he circulated a supplementary note to the description he here sends to Sinclair ("A Supplementary note on the Mould board described in a letter to Sr. John Sinclair of Mar. 23. 1798. inserted in the American Philosophical transactions Vol. 4. and in Maese's Domestic Encyclopædia voce Plough," in DLC: TJ Papers, 147:25678; TJ to Mease, 11 Mch. 1805).

For the AGRICULTURAL REPORTS or surveys produced by the British Board, see Strickland to TJ, 20 May 1796, and Sinclair to TJ, 15 July 1797. I HAVE GIVEN ORDERS AT RICHMOND: see TJ to George Jefferson, 14 Feb. 1798. For TJ's promise to send a DRILL to the British Board of Agriculture, see TJ to Sinclair, 12 Mch. 1797. TJ earlier described the seed box, a CONTRIVANCE FOR ECONOMISING CLOVER SEED, in a letter to John Taylor dated 13 Apr. 1795. Not until 1814 did TJ HAVE THE MOULDBOARD MADE OF CAST IRON for use at Monticello (TJ to John Staples, 4 May 1814). On 21 Mch. 1815 TJ wrote Charles Willson Peale that he was using the iron moldboard and observed that it was so light it could be drawn by only two small horses or mules. He concluded: "it does beautiful work and is approved by every one."

¹ Dft and APS, *Transactions*: "containing."
² In Dft TJ here canceled "and the universality of ⟨that⟩ it's use, give it an advantage over those which are topographical."
³ Preceding eleven words and ampersand lacking in APS, *Transactions*.
⁴ Preceding two words interlined in Dft in place of "attachment to."
⁵ TJ here canceled "great" in Dft.

⁶ Preceding word interlined in Dft in place of "knolege."
⁷ Preceding word interlined in Dft in place of "qualities."
⁸ In Dft TJ wrote the remainder of the paragraph in the left margin.
⁹ In Dft TJ first wrote "it is on the principle of the chain pump, and for simplicity cheapness, and the perfect performance of it's offices leaves nothing ⟨more?⟩ to be desired on that head" before altering and expanding the passage into the next two sentences.
¹⁰ In Dft TJ began this sentence "an ass or any other [. . .] most trifling animal of the smallest value as" before altering it to read as above.
¹¹ Remainder of sentence interlined in Dft.
¹² In Dft TJ here canceled "to produce an equivalent effect with the box, must be increased in number, but still the same saving may be made of 5. parts out of 8."
¹³ In Dft TJ first wrote "which I [know?] to have ⟨been invented⟩ first practised [around] here" before altering the passage to read as above.
¹⁴ Preceding two words interlined in Dft in place of "a common."
¹⁵ Preceding four words interlined in Dft in place of "by myself."
¹⁶ Preceding five words interlined in Dft.
¹⁷ Preceding six paragraphs omitted from APS, *Transactions*.
¹⁸ MSS at DLC and MHi begin at this point.
¹⁹ Preceding two words interlined in place of "doing this." In Dft preceding four words interlined in place of "[. . .] on doing this."
²⁰ TJ first wrote "the minimum of force in the moving power" before altering the passage to read as above. In Dft TJ first wrote "least resistance possible to the progress of the draught cattle" before altering the passage to read as in altered PrC.
²¹ Remainder of sentence interlined in ink on PrC in place of "form of least resistance would evidently be a wedge," which is the phrasing TJ used in Dft. Author's note lacking in Dft.
²² TJ first wrote "be labor lost" before altering the phrase in ink on PrC. Dft similarly altered.
²³ Preceding two words interlined in Dft in place of "hinder edge should continue."

²⁴ In Dft TJ first wrote "⟨*let a strait line whose length*⟩ suppose a wedge of the breadth & length of the ploughshare from the wing backwards [. . .] & it's hinder end as high as it is wide" before altering the passage to read as above.

²⁵ MS at DLC, MS at MHi, and APS, *Transactions*: "continued across."

²⁶ TJ first wrote "is equal to or more than" before interlining "at least" in ink and altering the passage to read as above; Dft similarly altered.

²⁷ In Dft TJ first wrote "to be moved parallel with itself on the first bevil face of the first bevil" before altering and expanding the passage through "right bottom edge."

²⁸ Preceding word interlined in ink in place of "being guided"; Dft similarly altered.

²⁹ Preceding six words written in ink at bottom of page by TJ, probably to record words cut off when the press copy was made.

³⁰ Sentence lacking in MSS at DLC and MHi.

³¹ In MS at DLC, MS at MHi, and APS, *Transactions*, TJ here added "in my soil."

³² Altered in Dft from "over hang."

³³ In MSS at DLC and MHi TJ here added "in a height of 12. I." APS, *Transactions*, expanded "I" to "inches."

³⁴ In MS at DLC, MS at MHi, and APS, *Transactions*, TJ here added: "this is an angle of nearly 22°."

³⁵ In Dft TJ first wrote "the block across from a.b. which is 12 I. from the hinder end to c." before expanding the passage to read as above.

³⁶ In Dft TJ first wrote "block from a.b.c.k." before altering it to read as above.

³⁷ In MS at DLC, MS at MHi, and APS, *Transactions*, TJ here added "k.l. Fig.5."

³⁸ In MS at DLC, MS at MHi, and APS, *Transactions*, TJ here added "Fig.5."

³⁹ In MSS at DLC and MHi TJ interlined "preserved" in place of the preceding two words. APS, *Transactions*: "preserved."

⁴⁰ Preceding six words interlined in Dft in place of "that on it may."

⁴¹ Dft, MS at DLC, MS at MHi, and APS, *Transactions*: "wedge."

⁴² In MS at DLC, MS at MHi, and in APS, *Transactions*, TJ here added "trace of the."

⁴³ In Dft, in MS at DLC, MS at MHi, and APS, *Transactions*, TJ here added "Fig. 6."

⁴⁴ Word interlined in Dft in place of "hold one end of."

⁴⁵ Preceding four words interlined in Dft.

⁴⁶ TJ interlined the "Fig. 7." here and in Dft.

⁴⁷ In Dft TJ originally wrote the remainder of this sentence as: "as may be seen by laying the block on the share, and would tilt over, and the side a.b. would be no longer perpendicular nor a.d. horizontal."

⁴⁸ In Dft TJ interlined the "Fig. 8."

⁴⁹ Text from this point through ampersand lacking in MS at DLC, MS at MHi, and APS, *Transactions*.

⁵⁰ Preceding sentence lacking in MS at DLC, MS at MHi, and in APS, *Transactions*.

⁵¹ MS at DLC, MS at MHi, and APS, *Transactions*: "hardly."

⁵² MSS at DLC and MHi end here. In Dft TJ wrote the paragraph to this point in margin in place of "I am sensible that this lengthy and intricate description is more than the thing is worth. but."

⁵³ In Dft TJ here canceled "I am persuaded such means exist."

⁵⁴ "Sanctioned" interlined in Dft in place of preceding word; APS, *Transactions* follows Dft.

⁵⁵ APS, *Transactions*: "Your affectionate friend, and humble servant."

To William Strickland

DEAR SIR   Philadelphia March 23. 1798.

I have to acknoledge the reciept of your favors of Aug. 16. & 18. together with the box of seeds accompanying the former which has just come to hand.¹ the letter of the 4th. of June which you mention to have committed to mr King, has never been recieved. it has most likely been intercepted on the sea, now become a field of lawless & indiscriminate rapine & violence. the first box which came through mr Donald arrived safely the last year, but being a little too late for that season, it's contents have been divided between mr Randolph & myself, & will be committed to the earth now immediately. the peas & the vetch are most acceptable indeed. since you were here I have tried that species of your field pea which is cultivated in New York & begin to fear that that plant will scarcely bear our sun & soil. a late acquisition too of a species of our country pea, called the cow-pea, has pretty well supplied the place in my husbandry which I had destined for the European field pea. it is very productive, excellent food for man & beast, awaits without loss our leisure for gathering, & shades the ground[2] through the hotter months of the year. this with the loosening of the soil, I take to be the chief means by which the pea improves the soil. we know that the sun, in our cloudless climate, is the [most powerful] destroyer of fertility in naked grounds; & therefore that the [perpetual] fallows will not do here, which are so beneficial in a cloudy dripping [climate. still I] shall[3] with care try all the several kinds of pea you have been [so good as to sen]d me, & having tried all, hold fast that which is good. mr Ran[dolph is peculiarly] happy in having the barlies committed to him, as he had [been desirous of go]ing considerably into that culture. I was able, at the same [time to put into his] hands some Siberian barley sent me from France. I look forward with considerable anxiety to the success of the winter vetch. for if it [gives us a good winter] crop, & helps the succeeding summer one, it is something [like doubling the produce] of the field. I know it does well in Italy, & therefore [have the more hope here].

[My] experience leaves me no fear as to the success of clover. I have never [seen finer] than in some of my fields which have never been manured. my rotation is [triennial], to wit one year of wheat & two of clover in the stronger fields, or two of peas in the weaker, with a crop of Indian corn & potatoes between every other rotation, that is to say [once in seven] years. under this easy course of culture, aided with some manure, I hope my fields will recover their pristine fertility, which had, in some of them, been completely exhausted by perpetual crops of Indian corn & wheat alternately. the atmosphere is certainly the great[4] workshop of nature for elaborating the fertilizing principles, & insinuating them into the soil. it has been relied on as the sole means of regenerating our soil by most of the landholders in the canton I inhabit, and where rest has been re[sorted to] before a total exhaustion, the soil has never failed to recover. if indeed it [be so run down] as to be incapable of throwing up weeds or herbage of any kind to [shade the] soil from the sun, it either goes off in gullies & is entirely lost, or remains exhausted till a growth springs up of such trees as will rise in the poorest soils.

under the shade of these & the cover soon formed of their deciduous leaves and a commencing herbage, such fields sometimes recover in a long course of years. but this is too long to be taken into a course of husbandry. not so however is the term within which the atmosphere alone will reintegrate a soil rested in due season. a year of wheat will be balanced by one, two, or three years of rest & atmospheric influence,[5] according to the quality of the soil.   it has been said that no rotation of crops will keep the earth in the same degree of fertility without the aid of manure. but it is well known here that a space of rest greater or less in spontaneous herbage [will restore the] exhaustion of a single crop. this then is a rotation. and as it is not to be believed that spontaneous herbage is the only or best covering during rest, so may we expect that a substitute for it may be found which will yield profitable crops. such perhaps are clover, peas, vetches &c. a rotation then may be found which by giving time for the slow influence of the atmosphere, will keep the soil in a constant and equal state of fertility. but the advantage of manure is that it will do in one year what the atmosphere would require several years to do; & consequently enables you[6] so much the oftener to take exhausting crops from the soil;[7] a circumstance of importance [where] there is more labor than land.

I am much indebted to you for mr Kirwan's charming treatise on manures. science never appears so beautiful as when applied to the uses of human life, nor any use of it so engaging as agriculture & domestic economy. Doctr. Home had formerly applied the doctrines of chemistry to the analysis of soils & manures, but the revolution in that science had required the work to be done over again, & gives to mr Kirwan's the entire merit of a new work.   I thank you very much for the cones of the Larch. it was precisely the tree I wished to propagate; & if the loss of one season has not destroyed their vegetative power, I shall from these cones have a well stored nursery of them. the one you saw at Monticello continues to thrive very kindly; but it will be years yet before it will bear seed.

I again send you some seeds of what I before forwarded under the name of the Varina vetch. mr Randolph since that has had opportunities of seeing the plant at different periods of it's growth, and he finds it to be an Ononis, not a Vetch. the *stamina omnia connexa* is the distinctive line between them. it is non-descript. he has therefore furnished me with the following botanical description of it for you. Ononis, Calyx periantherum, quinque-partitum, longitudine fere carinae, laciniis linearibus acuminatis: Corolla papilionacea, vexillum cordatum striatum: [Stamina] filamenta X in cylindrum integrum connata: Antherae simplices: Pistillum germen oblongum subvillosum: Stigma bifidum barbatum: Pericarpium legumen rhombiforme glabrum, uniloculare, bivalve: Semina multa, X aut XII.   It grows about two feet high[;] best in meadow land; well in orchards, but not well in clay or sand, or even in loam if dry & hilly. it is an annual plant, should be sowed in September, [gives good] winter & spring grazing, & then a good crop of hay or seed, which ripens in the beginning of June, the season of our barley harvest. when once it possesses a field it is difficult to eradicate. if followed by wheat, this should be sown in drills to give opportunity for cleansing. it is known with us only at Varina, where, as far as we know, it is indigenous, and is there the richest winter herbage known. we are persuaded it will, in it's proper place, make a valuable addition [to the] subjects of farming. I have put a paper of the seed, under your address, into a box containing a model of my mould board, & sent to Sr. John Sinclair, for the board of agriculture.   I am much obliged for your information respecting my map of S. America in Faden's possession. I do not wish to withdraw it from him as long as it can [be useful towards rendering] that more perfect which he is about to give to the world.

[Stealing from occupation,] not a little irksome to me, and beguiled by the subject & the [garrulity natural to a farmer;] I have been insensibly led to obtrude on you a long letter. [My last revulsion] from retirement has overshadowed me with despair when I contemplate the [necessity of reformation in] my farms. that work finds obstacles enough in the ignorance & unwillingness of the instruments employed, even in the presence of the master. but when he is obliged [to be absent] the half of every year no hope remains of that steady perseverance in a fixed plan [which alone] can ensure it's success. three journeys to Philadelphia in the course of the last year [breaking] so often the thread of regular operations have lost much of the ground I had got [over[8] in the establish]ment of system in my farms, & the employments of this place do not make amends in point of happiness. time & experience have long since cured me of ambition. not [that I am] indifferent to the approbation of my fellow citizens. I feel that with a warmth, the want of which would be evidence that I did not deserve it.[9] but I am sensible too of it's di[vided] state: the natural result of the rise of party among us. we are now as regularly divided into whig & tory as you ever were in any period of your history. a part wish to in[crease] the powers of the Executive, some from apprehensions of it's weakness, others perhaps [from] the hope of it's favors. another part, believing it already too strong for the legislature, give their support to that as the republican branch of the constitution. these divisions were to be expected from the nature of man when free to think as he pleases, & speak as he thinks. perhaps too they are necessary for the preservation of the constitution in all it's parts. they appear threatening indeed at times in the angry declamations of passionate individuals. but these portend nothing [serious.] our citizens are intelligent, firm in the principles of their constitution, & too intent on their [private pur]suits to partake [10] much of party passion. their sparse situation too secures their minds, as [it does] their houses from the sudden flames which catch from person to person & [house to house] in the crowded population of large cities. while this state of things continues, they will remain cool & self-possessed; [11] they will support the rulers of their choice so long as these observe the limits of their constitution; and the known attachment of [our constituents] to this will long shield us from any open attempts to change it substantially. I have therefore the firmest confi[dence in the] stability of our government.

[Affairs on your] side the water [present at] this moment an awful aspect. I sincerely wish the conflict between your nation & it's [neighbor may end in leaving] to both the government they [chuse, and to all others] safety in the possess[ion of] their rights, & tranquility in the pursuit of their lawful [vocations. I feel the more] anxiety on acco[unt of some] excellent friends residing in both countries about [whose fortunes] I cannot be indifferent. I hope however that resources will still be found in the wisdom [12] [of both parties for preventing the extremities of the last] trial of force.   for your fortunes I feel the sin[cerest concern. the short time I had the happiness to] possess you at Monticello served to unfold your right [to my best esteem. and has been followed] by those [regrets] naturally excited by wishes which can never be realized. [13] [the gratification] next to [this will be in] the exercise of your permission sometimes to write to you, & in the expression [of those senti]ments of great & sincere esteem & attachment with which I am Dr Sir your friend & servt.   TH: JEFFERSON

P.S. I have put into the same paper a few seeds of the Wabash melon. it is a new member of the family of Cucurbita standing between the pumpkin & squash. it is eaten in the same way. it's most remarkeable characteristic is the extraordinary size of the fruit, which weighs sometimes [100?] ℔. it requires rich ground & a great space to run in. I think it will do in your climate as it's native region is the country of the Miamis at the head of the Wabash & thence to Lake Erie.

PrC (DLC); faint, with missing words supplied in brackets from Dft; day of month in dateline inserted in ink by TJ; postscript written in right margin, being completely illegible and supplied entirely from the Dft; at foot of first page: "William Strickland esq." Dft (DLC); evidently begun before the arrival of Strickland's letter and box of 16 Aug. 1797 (see note 1); variations from PrC consisting primarily of abbreviations and changes in punctuation, with one exception (see note 2).

For previous reference to Strickland's LETTER OF THE 4TH. OF JUNE 1797, which TJ never received, see Strickland to TJ, 18 Aug. 1797.

Randolph's BOTANICAL DESCRIPTION of what TJ called the Varina vetch is found in TJ's papers (MS in DLC: TJ Papers, 232:41555; undated; in Randolph's hand, with several words transcribed by TJ, including at foot of text: "Ononis. Calyx. 5-partitum"; endorsed by TJ: "Botany Ono-nis"). IT GROWS ABOUT TWO FEET HIGH: notes on the cultivation of "The Varina Vetch a species of Ononis," which TJ incorporated in his observations to Strickland, are also extant (same, 232:41554; undated; entirely in TJ's hand; with emendations).

¹ In Dft TJ first wrote "favors of May 20. 96. and Aug. 18. 97. the former did not come to hand Aug. 18. 97. but without the box of seeds which it announced as accompanying it. ⟨probably I shall still⟩ this however I shall probably hear of hereafter" before altering the sentence to read as above.

² In Dft TJ here included "very closely."

³ In Dft TJ first began the sentence "We shall however" before altering it to read as above.

⁴ In Dft TJ first wrote the remainder of the sentence as "⟨reservoir⟩ laboratory of nature for fabricating & communicating principles of fertility to the soil" before altering it.

⁵ In Dft TJ first wrote "by two, three or four years of rest" before altering the passage to read as above.

⁶ Word interlined in Dft in place of "us."

⁷ Remainder of sentence interlined in Dft.

⁸ In Dft TJ wrote preceding two words over an illegible word or words and interlined the remainder of the sentence.

⁹ Preceding sentence interlined in Dft in place of "for of that I have all the sensibility it is calculated to inspire."

¹⁰ In Dft TJ interlined preceding word in place of "feel."

¹¹ Sentence to this point and preceding sentence interlined in Dft, extending into the right margin.

¹² Word interlined in Dft in place of "moderation".

¹³ In Dft TJ here canceled "I ⟨cheerfully⟩ willingly therefore accept the proposn to exchange by way of letter those ⟨tokens⟩ sentiments of esteem to which no other means of communication are left."

To Elizabeth Wayles Eppes

DEAR MADAM   Philadelphia Mar. 24. 98.

I have to acknoledge the reciept of your friendly letter of the 5th instant. I had before heard of the melancholy situation of mrs Skipwith and, whatever reason might suggest as less painful than that was to herself and her friends, yet affection could not learn the event without a shock, and a tender recollection of former scenes on which the curtain is now forever drawn. but we shall join her again, and time and the tedium of life are preparing for us more of comfort than pain in that thought. I know nothing so dreary in prospect as old age surviving it's old friends and burthening it's young ones. it is a great comfort that I have still some of my antient affections left in whom my heart is wrapt up: and no where do I feel this truth so much as at Eppington. I have passed with you, my dear friend, & with mr Eppes, through so many scenes of animated happiness, that their recollection will be for ever dear to me. I have been flattering myself that I might have an opportunity of seeing you as I return to Virginia; & so I shall, if Congress does not protract it's session so as to render the 10. days or a fortnight, which it would lengthen my journey, too distressing. the situation of my house, entirely open & uncovered except two rooms, leaving me not only without a shelter for my friends, but almost for my family & myself, is very urging on my mind. I hope as soon as we get a cover there for you, we shall see yourself, mr Eppes & family there. I shall strive hard to hasten it. will you be so good as to tell Maria that I have sacrificed my own judgment to her wishes & bought her a harpsichord, which is gone off & will be on it's way up the river by the time you recieve this? it is one of Kirckman's highest priced, and of a fine silver tone: double-keyed, but not with as many pedals as her sister's. present my love to her, to mr Eppes father and son and all the young ones my friendly attachments, and accept yourself the sincere and affectionate esteem of a constant friend & servt   TH: JEFFERSON

PrC (MHi); at foot of text: "Mrs. Eppes."   EPPES'S LETTER OF THE 5TH INSTANT, re-corded in SJL as received 13 Mch. 1798, has not been found.

To Andrew Gwin

SIR   Philadelphia Mar. 24. 98.

I wrote to mr Madison, President of the college of Williamsburg, describing to him the experiment I wished him to try with the dipping needle of that college. I did not give him the least hint of the object, but only desired him to hold the meridian of the instrument in the meridian of the place, but with the North end pointing South, and to mark the dip. I inclose you his answer, by which you will percieve that it was not the latitude of the place, which is about $37° \frac{1}{2}$ but $66° \frac{1}{4}$ being exactly it's dip when held in the true position of the needle. when you shall have satisfied yourself with the contents of the letter, I will thank you to return it.

I am Sir Your most obedt. servt.   TH: JEFFERSON

PrC (DLC); at foot of text: "Capt. Gwinn No. 9. Penn street"; endorsed by TJ in ink on verso. Enclosure: Bishop James Madison to TJ, 13 Mch. 1798.

WROTE TO MR. MADISON: TJ to Bishop James Madison, 4 Mch. 1798.

To Samuel Brown

Dear Sir   Philadelphia Mar. 25. 98

You were a witness, before you left our side of the continent, to the endeavors of the tory party among us, to write me down as far as they could find or make materials. 'Oh! that mine enemy would write a book!' has been a well known prayer against an enemy. I had written a book, and it has furnished matter of abuse for want of something better. mr Martin's polite attack on the subject of Cresap & Logan, as stated in the Notes on Virginia, had begun before you left us. it has continued & still continues; tho' after the perusal of the first letter had shewn me what was to be the style of those subsequent, I have avoided reading a single one. a friend of mine having wished for a general explanation of the foundation of the case of Logan, I wrote him a letter of which I had a few copies printed, to give to particular friends for their satisfaction, & on whom I could rely against the danger of it's being published. I inclose you a copy as well for these purposes, as that I think it may be in your power to obtain some information for me. indeed I suppose it probable that General Clarke may know something of the facts relative to Logan or Cresap. I shall be much obliged to you for any information you can procure on the subject. you will see by the inclosed in what way I mean to make use of it. I am told you are preparing to give us an account of the General, which for it's matter I know, & for it's manner I doubt not, will be highly interesting. I am in hopes, in connecting with it some account of Kentucky, that your information & his together will be able to correct and supply what I had collected relative to it in a very early day. indeed it was to Genl. Clarke I was indebted for what degree of accuracy there was in most of my statements. I wish you to attend particularly to the overflowage of the Missisipi, in which I have been accused of error. present me affectionately to the General, & assure him of my constant remembrance & esteem: and accept yourself salutations & sentiments of sincere attachment from Dear Sir

Your friend & servt   TH: JEFFERSON

PrC (DLC); at foot of text: "Doctr. Samuel Brown." Enclosure: TJ to John Henry, 31 Dec. 1797 (printed copy).

OVERFLOWAGE OF THE MISSISIPI: see Volney to TJ, 24 Aug. 1796.

To Henry Remsen

DEAR SIR   Philadelphia Mar. 25. 98.

As I have probably not long to stay here, I must sollicit your information of the state of my accounts for Greenleaf's and Oram's papers, that I may remit to you before my departure, not only any arrears, but also for the current year which I should wish always to pay in advance. We are here in great fear of a war being brought on from France. a little more of that patience of which we have shewn so much would let us see the issue now making up between France & England, & which, whatever the event be, must bring on a peace. for us to enter into the war just as it is closing with all the rest of the world, would only be to sacrifice what still remains of our navigation, besides the contracting endless debt, and endangering our internal harmony. the H. of Representatives will take up the subject tomorrow, and will probably furnish interesting debates. still it will not be in their power alone to prevent the effect of taking off the prohibition to arm our merchant ships, announced by the President. we consider ourselves as standing on the brink of a precipice the depth of which no man sees. with every wish for your health & happiness I am Dear Sir

Your friend & servt   TH: JEFFERSON

RC (NjMoHP: Lloyd W. Smith Collection); addressed: "Mr. Henry Remsen New York"; franked and postmarked; endorsed by Remsen.

GREENLEAF'S AND ORAM'S PAPERS: on 15 May TJ asked John Barnes to pay Remsen $3.00 for a subscription from Thomas

Greenleaf to 1 July 1798, probably for the semi-weekly *Greenleaf's New York Journal* although Greenleaf also published the *Argus*, a daily. At the same time TJ ordered payment through Remsen of $3.75 for James Oram's *New York Price-Current* to 13 Aug. 1798 (Brigham, *American Newspapers*, 1:610, 646, 680; MB, 2:983).

From John Taylor

J. TAYLOR TO MR: JEFFERSON   Virga. Caroline March 25. 1798

Mr: Martin, for whom I solicited you to obtain a patent for a thrashing machine, has made several important improvements upon the model forwarded to you, and therefore wishes the taking out of a patent may be postponed, until his application can be so amended, as that it may include these improvements. For this End I will very shortly take the liberty of inclosing you the proper papers, together with drawings of the machine, relying upon you to finish a business, which you have been so good as to commence.

These improvements have roused the attention of a great part of our country. They bestow upon a machine to be turned by one man, a degree of velocity surpassing that of the machine originally constructed to go by water, and an equal degree of execution is looked for. Yet the machine is considerably simplified. Indeed it is hoped that the invention is now very little short of perfection. Farewell.

RC (DLC); endorsed by TJ as received 3 Apr. 1798 and so recorded in SJL.

To John Wickham

Dear Sir   Philadelphia Mar. 25. 98.

In fixing with you on the epoch of July 1. for the annual paiment of my instalments to the representatives of Cary & co. I had a view to my tobacco which I have heretofore sold in April or May, payable July 1. for some time past however, and especially by my sales of the last year, it has appeared, that the most advantageous time is not till September, and especially when sold at this place where it is not considered as old tobacco till frost, and it then commands from one to two dollars more in the hundred than in April. I lost the last year a dollar a hundred by selling in June. this sacrifice you will be sensible is a serious one: & as the case with Cary's representatives is not like that of a merchant in an active course of business who must recieve his paiments to a day in order to be enabled to fulfill his own engagements, I shall hope that preserving sacredly for the instalments the funds destined to pay them, you would think it not an unreasonable indulgence to suffer them to take the benefit of the highest market, which is not till the autumn. I wish therefore in future to defer the sales of my tobacco till the fall payable as usual at 60. or 90. days, which I know will make a difference of 15. per cent in the price. you shall immediately on the sale be authorised to recieve the amount of the instalment out of the money. as this sacrifice in price is out of all proportion to the time I shall hope your consent to it, recieving of course interest for the delay. I have thought that this early consultation with you on the subject might prevent any inconvenience to your principal which might otherwise have occurred, and shall be happy to have an answer from you as soon as convenient. I am with esteem Dear Sir

Your most obedt. servt   Th: Jefferson

RC (PHC); addressed: "Mr. Wickam Atty at law Richmond"; franked and postmarked. PrC (MHi); endorsed by TJ in ink on verso.

From Joel Barlow

DEAR SIR,   Paris 26 March 1798—

Notwithstanding I wrote you a few days ago by Mr. Lee I cannot omit this occasion to inform you that two of your commissioners, Pinckney & Marshall, are in all probability to leave this country in a few days, in consequence of an intimation from this Government. The message from the Minister Talleyrand was nearly in the following words: "If the American Government wishes to negotiate, it is inconcievable that among its three commissioners two should be men remarkable for nothing but their enemity to the existance of the French republic, & to the principles of liberty. I am charged at the same time to inform you that the presence of Mr. Gerry, in the absence of the other two, would be agreeable to the Directoire."

I am told it is Gerry's intention to stay when the others are gone. Should this be the case, & Mr. Adams should wish to terminate his dispute here by negotiation, it is presumable that he will consent to send a person or persons to join Gerry who are known to be agreeable to the French, & that they will have sufficient powers to act.—

respectfully yours   JOEL BARLOW

RC (DLC); endorsed by TJ as received 31 July 1798, changed by him to 1 Aug. 1798 but recorded in SJL as received 31 July.

WROTE YOU A FEW DAYS AGO: Barlow to TJ, 12 Mch. 1798.

From Andrew Gwin

Philadelphia March the 26th. 1798

The great attention your Excellancy has paid to My Universal quadrant and the trouble you have taken in writing to Virginia does Me honour beyond Expression and fully Convinces me of the great desire you have to encourage aney Usefull discoveries. Mr. Maddisons letter I have carefully examined but I find you did not give him aney directions Respecting the elevation of the Needle but I wish him to make a second trial With his diping needle and to be governed by the directions—first—let the horizontal Motion be confined: so that the instrument May be placed either: North-or-south—East-or-West then let the Needle be placed East and West and brought to nearly a true balance the North end rather the heaviest then turn the South end of the needle to the true North point let attention be paid to the: Degree of elivation on the arch where the Needle is checked by the polar

[219]

attraction—the South Virtue of the Magnet being much inferior in Strength to that of the North that its power except when verry highly touched is not Equal to hold the Needle Stationary for More then 30″ Seconds of time but the Magnetic Check is Easily percived if his needle does not hing two heavy on its axes he will find it to agree with the Latitude of the place of exhibition—Note—the instrument Must be kept in motion: and he will find the polar Check at the true Mile of Latitude—

My instrument is not yet Compleated but I have got the arch Devided to Degrees & half Degrees and to a Certanty the Needle cuts to a Mile the Lattitude of this City. My needle I have brought to Such perfection as to remain statioanary to the true polar attraction. I only now wait ain opertunity to give it a fair tryel at Sea—The inclosed is a Certificate of a discovery which I Made January last and concive it will be of the gratest utility to Navigation—the principles of which I wish to Communicate to you if agreeable—I also inclose Mr. Maddisons: letter. be pleased to return the Certificate.

I am respectfully Your Excellencys Most Obt. Servt.

ANDREW GWIN

RC (DLC); endorsed by TJ as received 27 Mch. 1798 and so recorded in SJL. Enclosure: Bishop James Madison to TJ, 13 Mch. 1798. Other enclosure not found.

From George Jefferson

DEAR SIR,   Richmond March 26th. 1798.

Capt. Potter with the nail rods Molasses and seeds did not arrive here until the day before yesterday.   I have this day sent up the seeds by a Waggon, & two Tons of the nail rod by a boat; the balance, and the Molasses, I expect to send tomorrow.

I have been endeavouring agreeably to your request to procure business for Mr. Lewis—but have not yet heard of any place; if I should, I will give you the earliest information of it. I fear though that I shall find it difficult, as there are generally many more applicants for places, than there are places to be filled. my fear however of being unsuccessful, shall not cause me to relax in my endeavours to oblige one, the serving of whom will ever be one of the most agreeable employments of

His Mt. grateful & Very Obt. servt.   GEO. JEFFERSON

We have paid J. Harris for your note to Mrs. Wood £33—

RC (MHi); at foot of text: "Thos. Jefferson esqr."; endorsed by TJ as received 31 Mch. 1798 and so recorded in SJL.

From James Monroe

Dear Sir   Albemarle March 26. 1798.

Yours of the 8. was the last with which I was favd. from you. The resolution of the French govt. to seize British manufactures is a severe stroke on the dry-goods traders, and all connected with them wh. comprehends the great mass of our people. On my part I wish they were permanently prohibited by law since I am satisfied the effect wod. be salutary to the general interests of America. But this is not the general opinion, and in consequence the measure will be considered as a new grievance, by those who suffer for the time in the current price of their produce. Still I think all these things must ultimately open the eyes of the people, if they are not the most stupid, and likewise the most worthless of all people ever collected in the form of a nation. And this I think is not the case: for I consider thier adherence to the measures wh. pass, as a proof of their virtue. The want of light is the great evil wh. overwhelms us, & this will not be remedied till more pens are put to work.

It has occurred to me it wod. be proper for my narrative to be inserted in the gazettes. I shod. suppose Bache wod. not object to it since it wod. most probably promote his interest by promoting the sale of the book. He has to apprehend it will be written down by the host of Scribblers who attack it, & thus the sale prevented. If he does not accede to this I shall be much surprised indeed.

I have repeatedly thought I wod. answer the flimsy scurrilous papers of Scipio, but whenever I took up the subject it really laid me up with the head ache. I cod. not answer them with my name & I shod. be known as well if I did not sign as if I did, from the precise tone of sentiment & stile wh. wod. be seen. And to defend my own book,[1] might rather weaken than support it. It seems to me that the line of propriety on my part is to rest quiet, & let calumny have its course. The book will remain & will be read in the course of 50. years if not sooner, and I think the facts it contains, will settle or contribute to settle, the opinion of posterity in the character of the admn., however indifferent to it the present race may be. And it will be some consolation to me to hope on reasonable ground, that I shall contribute to do justice to them with posterity, since a gang of greater scoundrels never lived. We are to dance on their birth night, forsooth, and say they are great & good men, when we know they are little people. I think the spirit of that idle propensity is dying away & that the good sense of the people is breaking thro the prejudice wh. has long chained them down.

Mr. Walcott sent me a bill (in Paris) for 120.000. dolrs. on a house there, to be remitted when the amt. was recd. to Holland. The trust was laborious & difficult beyond measure, in the execution. Mr. Skipwith took charge of it when recd, put it in boxes &ca to be forwarded when the order of the govt. was obtaind wh. however was at first refused, & acted without compensation. His house was robbed, and abt £1000 taken from it. He replac'd the sum at my request in expectation of being reimbursed on his draft on the secry. of the Treasury. The money was at length forwarded, & arrived safe in Holland. Mr. Skipwith was possessd of it (as above stated) 7. weeks. His bill on the secretary was protested & I was calumniated as having kept the money back unnecessarily to speculate with. I possess a copy of my correspondence with the French govt., bankers in Holland &ca, exhibiting in the clearest and most satisfactory manner that I did all in my power, was laborious, attentive &ca and of course was injured in any[2] imputation to the contrary—and essentially so in the protest of the bill. The truth is the whole transaction was managed by Jacob Van Staphorst one of our bankers, & I have his declaration to that effect with a history of the whole transaction. I see no ground in the documents more than in truth whereon the fairness and integrity of the transaction can be questioned, or how the Secry. can escape odium for his conduct. He says he protested the bill because Swan the drawer was to bear the expence & risk of transportation; Altho I had nothing to do with Mr. Swan and acted as a publick officer at the request of the Secry. He sent me at the same time an alternate set of bills on Hamburg to be resorted to in case those on Paris were not paid. We adhered to the latter under all the difficulties, because the secry. in his letter told us, it was the preferable exchge & because Mr. Van Staphorst was told by Dallarde, Swans partner, the money was not provided there for the payment of them. This was considered as a proof I kept the money back to speculate. Mr. Skipwith has sent me a power to act for him, tho' I doubt whether I ought not to consider the case as mine & present a petition to the congress for reimbursement, opening in the petition the whole affr. & printing all the documents wh. are lengthy. It merits consideration what mode is to be taken whether that course is the preferable one, and in whose name. Or whether a suit shod. be brot. agnst Walcott. I prefer the former & in my own name, if it is not presumeable that the spirit of party might oppose & defeat it agnst the favor of the most positive demonstration that can be conceived. If they will not vote that it is dark when it is light the law wod. pass. It is to be observed that all the injury is done that can be by underhanded slanders, and thence decided whether opening the affr. on them in that publick manner by surprise wod. not be of some use. I have mentioned this also to Mr. Dawson, as likewise another irritating incident in wh. yr. council may be useful. If a petition is proper, I ought to know it as soon as possible, & it shod. be hinted to whom I might write a letter to request to present it. If of our own state it is a thing of course, but perhaps a member from another might be preferred.

I see a piece in Davis's paper signed Thrasibulus in wh. there are some just views of the subject—perhaps some of these might be published to advantage.

RC (DLC); endorsed by TJ as received 3 Apr. 1798 and so recorded in SJL.

MY NARRATIVE: Monroe's *A View of the Conduct of the Executive*. For the accusations against Monroe and Fulwar SKIPWITH concerning their handling of a remittance to Amsterdam, see Monroe's letter to TJ of 30 July 1796.

A PIECE . . . SIGNED THRASIBULUS: as Augustine Davis's *Virginia Gazette* reprinted from the *Gazette of the United States* the criticisms by "Scipio" of Monroe's book, "Thrasybulus" offered detailed rebuttals (*Virginia Gazette and General Advertiser*, 28 Mch. 1798).

[1] Here Monroe canceled "myself."
[2] Word interlined in place of "every."

To Robert Liston

Mar. 27. 98.

Th: Jefferson presents his respects to mr Liston & asks the favor of the passport for his friend Thomas Kanberg of whom he spoke to him yesterday. he is a native of the North of Europe, (perhaps of Germany) has been known to Th:J. these twenty years in America, is of a most excellent character stands in no relation whatever to any of the belligerent powers, as to whom Th:J. is not afraid to be responsible for his political innocence, as he goes merely for his private affairs. he will sail from Baltimore if he finds there a good opportunity for France; & if not, he will come on here.

PrC (DLC); at foot of text by TJ in ink: "for Kosciuzko."

Career diplomat Robert Liston (1742-1836) was Great Britain's ambassador to the Ottoman Empire when, in February 1796, his government appointed him ambassador extraordinary and minister plenipotentiary to the United States. He held that post until 1802, when he became the British envoy to the Batavian Republic (DNB).

On 28 Mch. 1798 Liston replied with a brief note that enclosed the requested passport and acknowledged that he "shall be happy at all times to render every service in my power to any person in whom you are pleased to take an interest" (RC in MoSHi: Jefferson Papers; endorsed by TJ as received on the same day; enclosure not found).

To Robert Patterson

DEAR SIR   Philadelphia Mar. 27. 9[8]

In the lifetime of mr Rittenhouse I communicated to him the description of the mouldboard of a plough which I had constructed, and supposed to be what we might term *the mould-board of least resistance.* I asked not only his opinion but that he would submit it to you also. after he had considered it, he gave me his own opinion that it was demonstrably what I had supposed, and I think he said he had communicated it to you. of this however I am not sure, and therefore now take the liberty of sending you a description of it and a model, which I have prepared for the board of agriculture of England at their request. mr Strickland one of their members had seen the model, and also the thing itself in use in my farms, and thinking favorably of it, had mentioned it to them. my purpose in troubling you with it is to ask the favor of you to examine the description rigorously & suggest to me any corrections or alterations which you may think necessary, as I would wish to have the ideas go as correct as possible out of my hands. I had sometimes thought of giving it in to the Philosophical society; but I doubted whether it was worth their notice, and supposed it not exactly in the line of their ordinary publications: I had therefore contemplated the sending it to some of our agricultural societies, in whose way it was more particularly, when I recieved the request of the English board. the papers I inclose you are the latter part of a letter to Sr. John Sinclair their president. it is to go off by the packet, wherefore I will ask the favor of you to return them with the models in the course of the present week with any observations you will be so good as to favor me with. I am with great esteem Dear Sir

Your most obedt servt   TH: JEFFERSON

PrC (DLC); slightly torn; at foot of text: "Mr. Patterson." Enclosure: see note to TJ to Sir John Sinclair, 23 Mch. 1798.

From Benjamin H. Latrobe

SIR,   Francis's Hotel March 28th. 1798.

I should have taken the liberty to deliver to you the enclosed letter from Mr. Randolph immediately on my arrival two days ago, had he not told me, that he has therein done me the favor to recommend me to you, with a view to interest your kind offices for me in an application I had intended to make to the Executive of the United States, during my stay at Philadelphia.—I had understood that it was the intention of the Government to erect an Arsenal and a Manufactory of arms at Harpers ferry, and as I am now engaged in Virginia, in the Penitentiary house, and am consulted by several of the Canal companies,—to have designed & directed a Work of such magnitude as, I suppose, this Arsenal will be, would have at once decided me to sell my Pensylvanien property & consider myself as a Virginian for the rest of my life.—But upon some previous enquiry, I am told, that although I have very strong recommendations to several Gentlemen highly in the confidence of the President, I am not likely to succeed, should I apply; and that it will not avail me to have had an education entirely directed to the object of becoming useful as an Engineer & Architect, & to have given proofs of some degree of skill,—for I am [1] guilty of the crime of enjoying the friendship of many of the most independent & virtuous men in Virginia, & even was seen at the dinner given to Mr Monroe.—I have therefore resolved not to run the risk of a refusal, and should esteem it a mark of favor in you to permit the enclosed letter to pass for a *general* recommendation. Since my arrival in America, it is been my very anxious wish to become known to you, & to improve an old acquaintance with, and admiration of your works, into a personal Knowledge of you.

If you will permit me, I will do myself the honor to wait upon you, at your apartment tomorrow morning, being engaged for this evening to meet Mr Caleb Lownes.—

I am, with the sincerest respect Yours   B. HENRY LATROBE

RC (DLC); endorsed by TJ as received 28 Mch. 1798 and so recorded in SJL; second page bears faint image of text in TJ's hand, probably the result of coming into contact with PrC of TJ to Latrobe, 18 Oct. 1798, before the PrC had dried. Enclosure: Edmund Randolph to TJ, 11 Mch. 1798, which is recorded in SJL as received 28 Mch. 1798 but has not been found.

Born into a Moravian family in Yorkshire, his mother a native of Pennsylvania, Benjamin Henry Latrobe (1764-1820) was educated in German Moravian schools and then worked for prominent civil engineering and architectural practices in England before emigrating to Virginia in the spring of 1796. He immediately undertook architectural commissions, and in 1797 it was his design for a new Virginia PENITENTIARY that won out over several other plans, including one by TJ (see James Wood to TJ, 3 Mch., TJ to Wood, 31 Mch. 1797). In 1798 he relocated to Philadelphia, where he

received commissions for the Bank of Pennsylvania and the city's waterworks. He continued to work both as an architect and as an engineer, and in 1803 TJ appointed him surveyor of public buildings. The two collaborated as Latrobe redesigned significant portions of the U.S. Capitol. He also worked on the White House, designed government buildings in Washington and elsewhere, and completed a wide variety of private architectural commissions and engineering projects. He was elected to membership in the American Philosophical Society in July 1799 (ANB; APS, *Proceedings*, 22, pt. 3 [1884]: 283).

In March 1798 Latrobe could well consider himself NOT LIKELY TO SUCCEED in obtaining a commission from the U.S. government. In January he had written a play, *The Apology*, for a benefit performance by a Richmond theatrical company. The comedy, which from a variety of circumstances received only a single, poorly executed performance in Richmond, transparently spoofed Alexander Hamilton, William Cobbett (as "Skunk, a newspaper editor"), and other Federalists. Appearing only months after the revelation of Hamilton's affair with Maria Reynolds, the play also featured adultery in its plot. Soon after Latrobe wrote the above letter Cobbett's *Porcupine's Gazette* took acidic notice of *The Apology* and its author (Talbot Hamlin, *Benjamin Henry Latrobe* [New York, 1955], 86-9, 129-30). For the DINNER GIVEN TO MR MONROE,

which Latrobe attended, see Horatio Gates to TJ, 15 Feb. 1798. ADMIRATION OF YOUR WORKS: during his residence in Virginia Latrobe had consulted the *Notes on the State of Virginia* on a variety of topics (Latrobe, *Virginia Journals*, 1:112-13, 151; 2:336, 393-4).

[1] Word interlined in place of "have been."

From Isaac Ledyard

SIR   NYork 29th. Apl. [i.e., Mch.] 1798

After waiting a long time for further materials, the Travels of my kinsman are now prepared for the Press. The honor which you did me to hand me his Letters to you for publication, & the great respect with which he speaks of you in other Letters of this Compilation, make all the direct authority I have to transmit herewith several Subscription Proposals with the hope that it may be convenient to you to direct some of them to proper persons in the Southern States

Altho: this publication has been loudly called for from almost every part of the Union, yet as (from the infant state of the taste &[1] literature in America) no worthy Edition has yet paid the Author or Compiler, I am obliged to take security in a Subscription against too inconvenient a loss

You see Sir I take the liberty to address you as a philosopher & literary man, not as Vice President of the United States, fully persuaded that were you in the highest Trust which those States can give, & which has been the ardent wish of the virtuous & undeluded, these qualities would still maintain thier undiminished estimation in your mind, On them I rely for pardon for this confident intrusion and beg leave further to subscribe it with the utmost Respect & Esteem

Sir Your Obedt. & very humble Servt.   ISAAC LEDYARD

RC (CSmH); at foot of text: "Thos. Jefferson Esqr."; endorsed by TJ as received 4 Apr. 1798, where he noted also that the date of the letter "should be Mar. 29," recording it similarly in SJL.

Isaac Ledyard (1754-1803), a doctor, sought to gather papers documenting the adventurous global TRAVELS of his cousin, John Ledyard, who had died in Cairo in 1789. Philip Freneau expected to publish

the work, issuing anticipatory notices in September 1797 and August 1798, but Ledyard, concluding that he had assembled too thin a record of his cousin's life, abandoned the effort. Later Jared Sparks drew on the materials to produce a biography of John Ledyard (Stephen D. Watrous, ed., *John Ledyard's Journey Through Russia and Siberia, 1787-1788: The Journal and Selected Letters* [Madison, 1966], 4, 30, 82-4; Jared Sparks, *The Life of John Ledyard, the*

American Traveller; Comprising Selections from his Journals and Correspondence [Cambridge, Mass., 1828], v).

[1] Ledyard here canceled "science."

To James Madison

Philadelphia Mar. 29. 98.

I wrote you last on the 21st. your's of the 12th. therein acknoleged is the last recd. the measure I suggested in mine of adjourning for consultation with their constituents was not brought forward; but on Tuesday 3. resolutions were moved which you will see in the public papers. they were offered in committee to prevent their being suppressed by the previous question, & in the commee on the state of the Union to put it out of their power, by the rising of the commee & not sitting again, to get rid of them. they were taken by surprise, not expecting to be called to vote on such a proposition as 'that it is inexpedient to resort to war against the French republic.' after spending the first day in seeking[1] on every side some hole to get out at, like an animal first put into a cage, they gave up that resource. yesterday they came forward boldly, and openly combated the proposition. Mr. Harper & mr Pinckney pronounced bitter Philippics against France, selecting such circumstances & aggravations as to give the worst picture they could present. the latter on this, as in the affair of Lyon & Griswold, went far beyond that moderation he has on other occasions recommended. we know not how it will go. some think the resolution will be lost, some that it will be carried, but neither way by a majority of more than 1. or 2. the decision of the Executive, of two thirds of the Senate & half the house of representatives is too much for the other half of that house. we therefore fear it will be borne down, and are under the most gloomy apprehensions. in fact the question of war & peace depends now on a toss of cross & pile. if we could but gain this season, we should be saved. the affairs of Europe would of themselves relieve us. besides this there can be no doubt that a revolution of opinion in Massachusetts & Connecticut is working. two whig presses have been set up in each of those states.—there has been for some days a rumor that a treaty of alliance offensive & defensive with Gr. Britain is arrived. some circumstances have occasioned it to be listened to; to wit the arrival of mr King's Secretary, which is affirmed, the departure of mr Liston's secretary which I know is to take place on Wednesday next, the high tone of the executive measures at the last & present session, calculated to raise things to the unison of such a compact, and supported so desperately in both houses in opposition to the pacific wishes of the people & at the risque of their approbation at the ensuing election. Langdon yesterday in debate mentioned this current report. Tracy in reply declared he knew of no such thing, did not believe it, nor would be it's advocate. the Senate are proceeding on the plan communicated in mine of Mar. 15. they are now passing a bill to purchase 12. vessels of from 14. to 22. guns, which with our frigates are to be employed as convoys & guarda costas. they are estimated, when manned & fitted for sea, at 2. millions. they have past a bill for buying one or more founderies. they are about bringing in a bill for regulating private arming, and the defensive works in our harbors have been proceeded on some time since. an attempt has been made to get the Quakers to come forward with a petition to aid with the weight of their body the feeble band of peace. they have with some effort got a petition signed by a few of their society. the main body of their society refuse it, Mc.lay's peace motion in the assembly of Pensylvania was rejected with an unanimity of the Quaker vote, and it seems to be well understood that their attachment to England is stronger than to their principles or their country. the revolution war was a first proof of this. mr White from the federal city is here, solliciting money for the buildings at Washington. a bill for 200,000. D. has passed the H.R. & is before the Senate, where it's fate is entirely uncertain. he is become perfectly satisfied that mr A. is radically against the government's being there. Goodhue (his oracle) openly said in commee in presence of White, that he knew the government was obliged to go there, but they would not be obliged to stay there. mr A. said to White that it would be better that the President should rent a common house there, to live in; that no President would live in the one now building. this harmonises with Goodhue's idea of a short residence. I write this in the morning, but need not part with it till night. if any thing occurs in the day it shall be added.

P.M. Nothing material has occurred. Adieu.

RC (DLC: Madison Papers); addressed: "James Madison junr. near Orange courthouse." PrC (DLC).

On TUESDAY, 27 Mch. Maryland congressman Richard Sprigg, Jr., introduced three RESOLUTIONS in the committee of the whole concerning President Adams's address of 19 Mch., which were carried in the local PAPERS the next day. The first resolution declared that "under existing circumstances" it was "not expedient" to RESORT TO WAR AGAINST THE FRENCH REPUBLIC. The second advocated continuing restrictions against the arming of merchant vessels and the third called for measures for coastal protection and the internal defense of the country (*Annals*, 8:1319-20). For the response the next day by Robert Goodloe HARPER and Thomas PINCKNEY, see same, 1334-45.

REVOLUTION OF OPINION IN MASSACHUSETTS: TJ highly recommended the Boston *Independent Chronicle* published by Thomas Adams, but it was not a new publication and the reference to the second whig press in the state is not clear. In CONNECTICUT TJ supported *The Bee*, which Charles Holt began publishing in New London in June 1797, and the Philadelphia *Aurora* published articles from the Middletown *Middlesex Gazette*, which had been taken over by Tertius Dunning in October 1797 (TJ to Thomas Mann Randolph, 11 Jan. 1798; Brigham, *American Newspapers*, 1:35, 52, 307; Philadelphia *Aurora*, 25 Mch., 2 Apr. 1798). See also Sowerby, Nos. 589, 602. On 30 Mch. and 2 Apr. 1798 the Philadelphia *Aurora* carried rumors of a TREATY OF ALLIANCE OFFENSIVE AND DEFENSIVE with Britain.

On 23 Mch. the Senate began considering a bill that would authorize the executive to PURCHASE 12 VESSELS to be used as CONVOYS ("A Bill to provide an additional Armament for the further protection of the trade of the United States; and for other purposes," in DNA: RG 46, Senate Records, 5th Cong., 2d sess., in Samuel A. Otis's hand, with emendations and docketing on 23, 28, 29, 30 Mch. and 3, 9 Apr. in TJ's hand). The legislation passed by the Senate on 9 Apr. increased the number to up to 16 vessels (see also TJ to Thomas Mann Randolph, 19 Apr. 1798). When the House returned the bill to the Senate, the number of vessels had been reduced to 12 and all sections restricting the use eliminated. Republican Henry Tazewell's motion to postpone consideration of the changes until the next session was decisively defeated. When a tie vote resulted on consideration of the House amendment to strike out the fifth section of the bill, which restricted the use of convoys, TJ voted against the change. The Senate reversed his decision the next day and went on to accept all of the House amendments. On 27 Apr. the president signed the legislation that authorized the expenditure of $950,000 for the purchase and manning of up to 12 vessels (JS, 2:464, 469, 476-8; *Annals*, 8:1384; U.S. Statutes at Large, 1:552; Smelser, *Navy*, 141-7). On 22 Mch. the Senate passed and sent to the House a bill for the purchase or lease of ONE OR MORE FOUNDERIES. The House included an appropriation of $100,000 for the lease and establishment of foundries as part of a larger bill that also allowed the president to expend up to $800,000 to procure cannon, arms, and ammunition. The president signed the legislation on 4 May (JS, 2:460; JHR, 3:237, 287, 361; U.S. Statutes at Large, 1:555-6; Smelser, *Navy*, 140-1).

QUAKERS TO COME FORWARD WITH A PE-

TITION: on 23 Mch. Samuel Wetherill sent a petition to Congress noting that peace was essential to promote the happiness of the country. Three days later in *Porcupine's Gazette* William Cobbett warned members of the Society of Friends not to sign the document, claiming that it was the work not of Wetherill but of an "infamous society who were tools of France." Several Quakers withdrew their names from the petition (Richard G. Miller, *Philadelphia—The Federalist City: A Study of Urban Politics, 1789-1801* [Port Washington, New York, 1976], 104; Elaine Forman Crane, ed., *The Diary of Elizabeth Drinker*, 3 vols. [Boston, 1991], 2:1016). On 20 Mch. William Maclay introduced a PEACE MOTION in the Pennsylvania House of Representatives "against war in any shape, or with any nation, unless the territories of the United States should be invaded." It was defeated by a 33 to 37 vote, with Quakers Cadwalader Evans and Robert Waln arguing against it and noting that state legislators ought not to instruct Congress. According to the *Aurora*, "the Quietists and Quakers, whose doctrines disavow all resistance, voted, to a man, against the resolution." Forty members of the Pennsylvania General Assembly finally signed a modified, unofficial memorial by Maclay, which argued that the arming of merchant vessels would be a threat to the "neutrality and peace of the nation." Albert Gallatin laid it before the House of Representatives on 3 Apr. (JHR, 3:251; *Annals*, 8:1373-4; Philadelphia *Aurora*, 21, 23 Mch. 1798; *Journal of the First Session of the Eighth House of Representatives of the Commonwealth of Pennsylvania. . .* [Dec. 1797-Apr. 1798], [Philadelphia, 1797?], 305-7; Crane, *Drinker Diary*, 3:2145, 2225).

On 12 Apr. the Senate, by a 17 to 6 vote, passed an amended bill, which the House agreed to the next day, authorizing a $100,000 loan over two years for the BUILDINGS AT WASHINGTON. Benjamin GOODHUE voted against the measure (JS, 2:471; JHR, 3:260-1; U.S. Statutes at Large, 1:551). See also TJ to Madison, 5 Apr. 1798.

[1] Preceding word interlined in place of "trying."

From Robert Patterson

DR. SIR   March 29th. 1798—

The drawings, model, and description of your *mold-board of least resistance*, which you have been pleased to submit to my inspection, and which I had not seen before, I have now examined with much attention and pleasure; and do not hesitate in giving it my approbation, if that can be thought of any consequence after the one it has already received from Mr. Rittenhouse.

The doctrine of resistance is, indeed, still but little understood; no theory having yet been established on this subject, which will perfectly agree with practice—Induction, from well conducted experiments, will in this, as in most other cases of practical *science*, be our surest guide.

I should suppose that a good proof of a mold-board being of the best form, would be its *wearing evenly* in all its parts—And I think I have frequently observed that the mold-board of a plough, however formed by the carpenter, would in time, by the wearing or friction of the sod, acquire a figure exactly resembling that of your model—

Whether a *plane* sided wedge (as you have taken for granted) be a solid of the best form for removing an obstacle to one side, or simply in one direction, may perhaps be doubted—Emerson, in his doctrine of fluxions, makes it a solid of a *curvilineal* surface—Experiment however must determine this matter.

The sod, formed by all the ploughs which I have seen is a rectangular parallelopiped; and therefore if set on edge, perpendicularly to the horizon would have no tendency to turn over, but would stand in that position —nay if its dimensions be 6 I. by 9 it must be made to decline from the perpr. upwards of 40 degrees before it will fall over.

Quere, then, whether there might not be some advantage in having the sod cut with oblique angles, the coulter, for this purpose, inclining a little towards the left hand? The transverse section of the sod would then be a rhumboid, and could not stand perpendicularly but must fall over from the plough. Indeed it would have this tendency even before it arrived at a vertical position, viz. as soon as the center of gravity came to the right hand of the left-under-acute-angle of the sod. I conceive also that the surface of the plowed land would be less uneven or corrugated when plowed in this way, as the obtuse angles of the sods would be all turned upwards—

Quere 2d. As the figure of your mold-board is exactly that which a plane board would acquire by being *twisted*—whether, when made of wood, which, with the generality of farmers, would most frequently be

[230]

the case, mold-boards might not more easily be formed in this way, previously heating the board, either with steam or fire, as ship-builders do their planks? The friction also would be less on boards made by twisting than on those formed by the saw and adze, as it would be parallel to, and not accross the grain of the wood. Such mold-boards would moreover be much less liable to break.

Quere 3d Whether three or four *rollers*, with their surfaces projecting a little beyond the surface of the mold-board, might not be applied with advantage in lessening the friction from the sod?—

These crude remarks are however submitted with great diffidence, to one who is infinitely better acquainted with the subject, both in theory and practice, than I can pretend to be.

From Dr. Sir, with very great regard & esteem—Your Most obedt Servt   R. PATTERSON

RC (MHi); at foot of text: "*Mr. Jefferson*"; endorsed by TJ as received [29] Mch. 1798 and so recorded in SJL.

DOCTRINE OF FLUXIONS: William Emerson, *The Doctrine of Fluxions: not only* explaining the Elements thereof, but also its Application and use in the several parts of Mathematics and Natural Philosophy, 2d. ed. (London, 1757). See Sowerby, No. 3678.

To Thomas Mann Randolph

TH:J. TO TMR.   Philadelphia Mar. 29. 98.

My last to you was of the 22d. inst. & on the same day I recieved yours of the 12th. I have in mr Lott's hands something short of 200. Doll. should either the objects of horses or corn require this, be so good as to call on mr Lott for it, who will not need from you a formal order signed by me. he may be also informed that the order of Mar. 13. for 93.33 D given Richardson & notified to mr Lott in my letter of the 14th. will not be presented at all, as Richardson has answered his purpose in another way. I should suppose also that mr Clarke of Staunton may[1] have lodged money for me with Colo. Bell; if he has, make use of that also for the same purposes if necessary.—mr Trist is arrived here. he determines to remove to Charlottesville, and to confirm his purchase of mr Lewis. he is now seeking a vessel to send off furniture. you will see in the newspapers the resolutions brought forward by the peace party in answer to the President's late message. the first of them, 'that it is not expedient to resort to war against the republic of France' was yesterday openly and elaborately opposed by mr Pinckney & mr Harper. the debates will be interesting and long, and the issue extremely doubtful. the decisive cast of the Executive, two thirds of the Senate, & half the H. of

R. is too much to be withstood by the other half. we fear therefore they will be borne down. if one or two votes only can be withdrawn from them by either hopes or fears, we are gone. I now consider war as on a cross & pile chance. the present state of astonishment leaves it uncertain what & when prices will take a turn. the Senate are proceeding with a firm vote in war measures. it is yet to be seen which of them may pass the other house. we cannot yet fix on a day of adjournment. I hope Davenport is going on powerfully. my tender love to my dear Martha, & kisses to the little ones. affectionate salutations to yourself.

RC (DLC); endorsed by Randolph. PrC (MHi).

TJ's letter to Peter LOTT of 14 Mch. 1798, recorded in SJL, has not been found.

[1] Word interlined in place of "must."

From Louis of Parma

SIR   Aranjuez the 30. March. 1798.

I received about two months ago yours dated the 23d. of May 1797. I pray you to be well persuaded of my greatefull acknowledgement, and for the many other motives I am so much indebted to you for. In the first place, for the complaisance and great pains you were pleased to take to procure means of gratifying my desire, afterwards for the just picture you make of the state of things and persons, and for the good advices and councils which you give me on the subject with the same interest as if it had personally regarded you. In short, for the huge tusk of the mammoth which I received and a very estimable piece for its rarity; it is still more so for me; being a remembrance of your politeness, and complaisance; the sight of that enormous tusk augmented my desire of reading the account of that animal which make an article worthy of being inserted in a volume of your philosophical transactions which you promise me that did not yet come to hand, but I expect it with impatience.

I see what you say concerning Mr. Peale, and that his situation must certainly produce the effect of which you have informed me, and would distress me much on considering the great distance there is between us, and especially having no constant of fixed intercourse between the two countries.

It would be necessary that my correspondent ran with the expences of hunting, preparation, shipping of what he would send me here, and that of my side I should correspond with all his demands, provided that neither accompts nor money should from one another &c. which would be very incomodious. It appears to me to be very difficult, or almost impossible that a person in Mr. Peales's situation would aggree to such proposals without funds. Further, if his commerce be supported by other schemes, exclusive of his foundness for natural history, that is to say when interest interfares without which it is impossible he can subsist, as the expences cannot absolutely be balanced or equalled but by mutual returns which would give room to lawsuits and finish a commercial correspondence in a rupture. I doubt that Mr. Peale would be content with that, if however he did accept the commission, I send you a list of some articles of the animal kingdom, which I wished for, to give them to Mr. Peale, or to the person that would take upon him the obligation with the above mentioned conditions.

As to the mineral kingdom I will remit another list in case the negociation can be established. As to the vegetable kingdom, though I think that Mr. Bartram could be very useful, I cannot enter upon that negociation not having as yet formed a real botanic garden.

I must also prevent you, that if by chance the correspondence be established, any thing Mr. Peale, or any other should send me; 1st. I desire it to be well packed up: 2d. that it is to be shipped on board a vessel bound directly to some port of Spain: 3d. that the bale or case be addressed to me with the following directions.

A. S. A. S.
El Señor Infanta Principe de Parma
Madrid.

with a letter for me to the same address: 4th. that the master of the vessel instantly gives part to the director of the Exchequer in the same port, and he remits the box, and letter to me at Madrid. I pray also you to tell my correspondent (if he be there) to send with the list of what he intends, his address.

I am at this moment ashamed of having so much encroached upon your civility, I beg then of you to pardon me, and to be perfectly assured that I wish for every occasion of being useful to you in any thing, and to give, you a proof of the acknowledgement, and perfect esteem with which I am

Sir Your most affec,te. humble Servt.   LOUIS PRINCE OF PARMA

P.S. The adjoined list is a little too, but this is in order not to repeat it offen, and for the greater facility, and commodiousness of my correspondent, if it should be established.

RC (DLC); endorsed by TJ as received 18 Aug. 1798 and so recorded in SJL. Enclosure: List of fishes, reptiles, and birds, giving Linnaean names, and in some cases common names in French or English (MS in DSI; undated; in hand of Louis of Parma;

with note by Charles Willson Peale on a separate slip: "Subjects of Natural History wanted in exchange for those of Europe— for the Museum of the prince of Palma"). For TJ's transmittal of the list to Peale, see Peale, *Papers*, v. 2, pt. 1:237, 238n.

To Robert Patterson

DEAR SIR   Philadelphia Mar. 30. 98.

I am much obliged by your letter of yesterday. tho' I possess Emerson's fluxions at home, & it was the book I used at College, yet it had escaped me that he had treated the question of the best form of a body for removing an obstacle in a single direction. that of the wedge offered itself so readily as the best, that I did not think of questioning it. nor does it now occur to me on what principle it can be questioned. if you have Emerson and will be so good as to lend him to me a day or two, I will be obliged to you—I am with great esteem Dear Sir

Your friend & servt   TH: JEFFERSON

PrC (DLC); at foot of text: "Mr. Robert Patterson."

To Robert Patterson

DEAR SIR   Philadelphia Mar. 31. 98.

I return you Emerson with thanks. it has suggested a qualification of the expression in my letter, which had supposed the [wedge] the form offering least resistance to the rising sod.—I did at f[irst], as you do now, consider this mould board as a twisted plane. but a little reflection convinced me, as it will you, that it is not, and that it would be impossible to twist a board into that form. a second view of the mould board would shew you that the breadth of it's face varies much, and that parallel lines drawn on it horizontally would not be strait ones. I have sometimes thought however of making a mouldboard on that principle: that is to say take a block formed into a wedge 2. f. long, 12. I. high (the breadth of the wedge) & $13\frac{1}{2}$ I. wide at the thick end, as in the margin. Fig. 1. saw in, at a.b.c.d.e.f.g Fig. 2 in lines parallel to the ground, and at increasing depths from top to bottom, so that the saw shall enter $4\frac{1}{2}$ I in the bottom line at the but end of the wedge, & not at all at the point. then [dish] out the sawed stuff, and a face would be presented offering strait lines both longitudinally & transversely. such

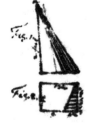

a surface would be generated by laying a stick h. k. (Fig. 3.) on the floor,[1] & another h.i. 12. I. above it parallel with the plane of the floor, the point h. of each[2] perpendicularly over or under the other & the end i. of the upper one[3] $4\frac{1}{2}$ I. to the right of the end k. of the under one. then move a strait line back from h. parallel with itself, keeping the lower end on h.k. & the upper on h.i. & the surface would be formed. this would be perfect for turning over the sod, but not at all for raising it. I am with great esteem Dear Sir Your friend & servt   TH: JEFFERSON

PrC (DLC); faint; at foot of text: "Mr. Patterson."

EXPRESSION IN MY LETTER: TJ to Sir John Sinclair, 23 Mch. 1798.

[1] Word interlined in place of "ground."
[2] TJ here canceled "[parallel?]."
[3] Preceding four words interlined by TJ.

To Mary Jefferson Eppes

MY DEAR MARIA   Philadelphia Apr. 1. 98.

Yours of Mar. 20. came to hand yesterday. you are not aware of the consequences of writing me a letter in so fair a hand, and one so easily read. it puts you in great danger of the office of private secretary at Monticello, which would sometimes be a laborious one. your letter was 11. days coming here, and mr Eppes's of Feb. 8. was 19. days on it's way. this shews that there is something wrong in the time they take to get into the mail; for from Richmond here is but about 5. or 6. days. I have feared some of my letters may have miscarried. I hope mr Eppes recieved that of Feb. 18. covering an order to Quarrier to deliver my chariot to him, and asking his & your acceptance of it. should that have miscarried, this serves to make the same tender. I have still hopes of being able to come by Eppington: but these become less firm in proportion as Congress lengthen their session; for that route would add a fortnight to the length of my journey. if I do not get home within a certain time, I shall not finish the hull of the house this year, & if I do not finish that this year, then I cannot build my mill the next. but whatever rout I am obliged to adopt, I will give you timely notice. they talk of not rising here till the last of this month. should I not be able to come by the way of Eppington, still, tell mr Eppes, I will make a visit from Monticello, rather than lose the colonnade & octagon. so he will not get off from his purposes by that excuse. my last letter from Belmont[1] was of the 19th. but mr Trist came from there since and reports that all were well. he is about sending off his furniture. he has taken the house in Charlottesville that was George Nicholas's, and will be living there before midsummer. my affectionate salutations to mrs Eppes, the gentlemen, & young ones, & kisses and everlasting love to yourself. Adieu.

Mar. 16. the 1st shad here.
28. the weeping willow begins to shew green leaves.

RC (Mrs. Harold W. Wilson, Miami, Florida, 1963). PrC (CSmH); endorsed by TJ in ink on verso.

[1] Interlined in place of "Monticello."

To Bishop James Madison

DEAR SIR   Philadelphia Apr. 1. 98.

I am to acknolege the reciept of your favor of Mar. 13. & to thank you for the trouble you have taken. the result of your observations [impress] me strongly with the belief that the person on whose account I [wrote] to you will be disappointed in his supposed discovery. however he has still hopes, and wishes me to ask you to take the trouble of trying again under certain precautions, which, as I do not understand them well, I will quote in the very words of his letter. 'I find you did not give Bishop Madison any directions respecting the elevation of the needle, but I wish him to make a second trial with his dipping needle, & to be governed by the directions; first, let the horizontal motion be confined, so that the instrument may be placed either North or South, East or West then let the needle be placed East & West and brought to nearly a true balance, the North end rather the heaviest. then turn the South end of the needle to the true North point. let attention be paid to the degree of elevation on the arch where the needle is checked by the polar attraction. the South virtue of the magnet being much inferior in strength to that of the North that it's power except when very highly touched is not equal to hold the needle stationary for more than 30. seconds of time but the magnetic check is easily perceived.'

I expect to remain here 3. or 4. weeks still, within which time shall be happy to recieve the result of the trials above proposed, as also your own essay on magnetic attraction if ready. I have never published any thing relative to the Mammoth except what is in the Notes of Virginia. I have given the Philosophical society a paper on the subject of the bones of another enormous animal of perhaps the Lion kind, whom I have called the Megalonyx. these bones were sent to me from Greenbriar, and deposited with the society, in whose volume now in press the account will appear. I have so nearly overrun the moment of the post that I must here end with my friendly salutations.

TH: JEFFERSON

PrC (DLC); faint; at foot of text: "Bishop Madison."

PERSON ON WHOSE ACCOUNT I WROTE TO YOU: Andrew Gwin. I HAVE GIVEN THE PHILOSOPHICAL SOCIETY A PAPER: Memoir on the Megalonyx, [10 Feb. 1797].

To Mathew Carey

Apr. 2. 98.

Th: Jefferson presents his compliments to mr Matthew Cary, & will be obliged to him if he can inform him how to address a letter to his brother John Carey in London, as he does not know the street, number &c where he would be found.

RC (NN); addressed: "Mr. Matthew Carey 118. Market street." Not recorded in SJL.

According to SJL on 2 Apr. 1798 TJ wrote a letter to JOHN CAREY "at mr. Hamilton's Falcon court Fleet street," which has not been found. John Carey wrote letters to TJ on 6 and 10 June 1797, which according to SJL were received from London on 8 Sep., with duplicates or a second set received on 13 Dec. 1797, none of which has been found. Letters from Carey to TJ of 21 May and 11 and 25 June 1798, the first being recorded in SJL as received 4 Sep. and the June letters on 25 Oct. 1798, are also missing.

On 21 May 1798 John Carey also wrote Philadelphia bookseller Henry Rice, who had charge of the sale of *The System of Short-Hand Practised by Mr. Thomas Lloyd, in Taking Down the Debates of Congress; and Now (with his permission) Published for General Use by J.C.*, printed in Philadelphia for Carey in 1793, the year he left for London (see Sowerby, No. 1133). He wished Rice to settle his accounts from the sale of that publication as well as for his edition of Washington's *Official Letters to the Honorable American Congress* and other books

Carey had left with him. Carey also requested that Rice send the income from the sale of personal items he had left in Philadelphia, including pistols and a "copying-press." Noting that perhaps Rice had not sent a remittance earlier because of the danger of interception at sea, he informed him that he was contacting TJ who, Carey was confident, would receive the monies from Rice and find a safe conveyance for the transfer of the funds. Carey mentioned that he was "in extreme need of money" and wanted the remittance sent as quickly as possible. He also noted that "Mr. Jefferson, in his zeal to promote the cause of literature, may perhaps think of some person who can assist in disposing of any copies" that remained unsold, in which case Rice was to turn the volumes over to that party (RC in DLC; addressed: "Mr. Rice, Bookseller, Philadelphia"; below the address in TJ's hand: "50. Market" and "16. S. 2 d."). To aid Rice in closing the accounts, Carey enclosed letters to "T. Grammer, Esqr. Petersburg, Virginia" and "Mr. Young, Bookseller, Charleston, S.C.," dated 21 May 1798, requesting them to remit payments to Rice for 20 and 25 copies of *Short-Hand*, respectively, that they had received in 1793 (same).

To William Linn

DEAR SIR   Philadelphia April 2. 98

I could not sooner acknolege the reciept of your favor of Feb. [8]th. because I had to write to Virginia for one of my blank vocabularies, and to await it's reciept. I now avail myself of your permission to inclose you one. the chief object is that as far as your society may attempt to collect vocabularies of the Indian languages, there may be as much uniformity as they can approach with what has been done before. I have several vocabularies in this form and have many out in the hands of my friends who are in situations to fill them up with the languages of different tribes. the opinion I hazarded on the multiplicity of Indian languages radically different, was not on such foundations as to give me entire reliance on it. much has been collected since that time by myself & some others, and I hope with the aid of your society we are still in time to save most of the native languages, and by them to obtain a clue to their origin. my object being the true fact, I do not permit myself to form as yet a decisive opinion, and therefore leave the slight one I had hazarded to the result of fuller enquiry. but neither does the enquiry, so far as we have yet made progress in it, render it very safe to say those radical languages are very few. I have obtained here a copy of Loskiel's book. Edwards's pamphlet on the Mohiccon language I cannot find. if therefore you have a spare copy, it will be thankfully recieved. when we shall have got in all our vocabularies, we shall be enabled to compare them with the Asiatic languages, by the help of the great collection of them published by the Empress of Russia, a copy of which was sent to Dr. Priestly & by him given to Dr. Barton. I am with great respect Dr. Sir

Your most obedt. servt.   TH: JEFFERSON

PrC (DLC); at foot of text: "Revd William Linn. New York." Enclosure not found, but see note to TJ to Linn, 5 Feb. 1798.

WRITE TO VIRGINIA: see TJ to Thomas Mann Randolph, 15 Feb. 1798.

For the GREAT COLLECTION of comparative vocabulary lists prepared under the sponsorship of Catherine II, the EMPRESS OF RUSSIA, see Benjamin Smith Barton to TJ, 25 Oct. 1796.

From James Madison

DEAR SIR   April 2d. 1797 [i.e. 1798]

Since my last I am in debt for your two favors of the 15th. & 22, the Gazettes of the 3. 6 7 & 8 Ulto, with a regular continuation to the 22d— two statements from the Treasury Department, and Payne's letter to the French people & armies.—The President's message is only a further developement to the public, of the violent passions, & heretical politics, which have been long privately known to govern him. It is to be hoped however that the H. of Reps. will not hastily eccho them. At least it may be expected that before war measures are instituted, they will recollect the principle asserted by 62 vs. 37. in the case of the Treaty, and insist on a full communication of the intelligence on which such measures are recommended. The present is a plainer, if it be not a stronger case, and if there has been sufficient defection to destroy the majority which was then so great & so decided, it is the worst symptom that has yet appeared in our Councils. The constitution supposes, what the History of all Govts. demonstrates, that the Ex. is the branch of power most interested in war, & most prone to it. It has accordingly with studied care, vested the question of war in the Legisl: But the Doctrines lately advanced strike at the root of all these provisions, and will deposit the peace of the Country in that Department which the Constitution distrusts as most ready without cause to renounce it. For if the opinion of the P. not the facts & proofs themselves are to sway the judgment of Congress in declaring war, and if[1] the President in the recess of Congress create a foreign mission, appt. the minister, & negociate a War Treaty, without the possibility of a check even from the Senate, untill the measures present alternatives overruling the freedom of its judgment; if again a Treaty when made obliges the Legis: to declare war contrary to its judgment, and in pursuance of the same doctrine, a law declaring war, imposes a like moral obligation, to grant the requisite supplies, until it be formally repealed with the consent of the P. & Senate, it is evident that the people are cheated out of the best ingredients in their Govt. the safeguards of peace which is the greatest of their blessings.—I like both your suggestions in the present crisis. Congress ought clearly to prohibit arming, & the P. ought to be brought to declare on what ground he undertook to grant an indirect licence to arm. The first instructions were no otherwise legal than as they were in pursuance of the law of Nations, & consequently in execution of the law of the land. The revocation of the instructions is a virtual change of the law, & consequently a Usurpation by the Ex. of a legislative power. It will not avail to say that the law of Nations leaves this point undecided, & that every nation is free to decide it for itself. If this be the case, the regulation being a Legislative not an Executive one, belongs to the former, not the latter Authority; and comes expressly within the power to "define the law of Nations" given to Congress by the Constitution. I do not expect however that the Constitutional party in the H. of R. is strong eno' [to][2] do what ought to be done in the present instance. Your

2d idea that an adjournment for the purpose of consulting the Constituents on the subject of war, is more practicable because it can be affected by that branch alone if it pleases, & because an opposition to such a measure, will be more striking to the public eye. The expedient is the more desirable as it will be utterly impossible to call forth the sense of the people generally before the season will be over, especially as the Towns &c. where there can be most despatch in such an operation are on the wrong side; and it is to be feared that a partial expression of the public voice, may be misconstrued or miscalled, an evidence in favor of the war party. On what do you ground the idea that a decl'n of war requires $\frac{2}{3}$ of the Legislature? The force of your remark however is not diminished by this mistake, for it remains true, that measures are taking or may be taken by the Ex. that will end in war, contrary to the wish of the Body which alone can declare it.

RC (DLC: Madison Papers); with last digit of year changed from "7" to "8," perhaps by TJ; addressed: "Thomas Jefferson Philada." with "private" at head; endorsed by TJ: "Madison James. Apr. 2. 97. for 98 recd. Apr. 10" and recorded in SJL under that date.

The second of TJ's TWO FAVORS is found under 21 Mch., the day he began the letter. TJ concluded the missive with a postscript on 22 Mch. TWO STATEMENTS FROM THE TREASURY DEPARTMENT: on 5 Mch. TJ presented to the Senate a letter he had received from Oliver Wolcott, Jr., dated the same day, transmitting the "Statement of goods, wares, and merchandize exported from the United States during one year prior to the 1st. of October 1797" as directed by a Senate resolution. Wolcott noted that the exports were estimated at about $27 million (RC in DNA: RG 46, Senate Records, 5th Cong., 2d sess.; in clerk's hand, signed by Wolcott; misdated 5

Feb. 1798; at foot of text: "The Honble The President of the Senate of the United States"). On the same day the Senate ordered that the letter and statement be printed for their use (JS, 2:449). For the report as printed for the House of Representatives, see Evans, No. 34859. The second statement has not been identified.

PAYNE'S LETTER: Thomas Paine, *Letter to the People of France, and the French Armies, on the Event of the 18th Fructidor—Sep. 4— and its Consequences* (New York, 1798). See Evans, No. 34292.

PRINCIPLE ASSERTED BY 62 VS. 37: the vote by which the House of Representatives requested President Washington to send them the papers relating to the Jay Treaty negotiations (see Madison to TJ, 6 Mch. 1796).

[1] Madison here canceled several illegible words.
[2] Word supplied.

To Edmund Pendleton

DEAR SIR   Philadelphia Apr. 2. 98.

I have to acknolege the reciept of your favor of Jan. 29. and as the rising of Congress seems now to be contemplated for about the last of this month, and it is necessary that I settle mr Short's matter with the treasury before my departure, I take the liberty of saying a word on that subject. the sum you are to pay is to go to the credit of a demand which mr Short has on the treasury of the US. and for which they consider mr Randolph as liable to them: so that the sum he pays to Short directly lessens so much the balance to be otherwise settled. mr Short, by a letter recieved a few days ago, has directed an immediate employment of the whole sum in a particular way. I wish your sum settled therefore that I may call on the treasury for the exact balance. I should have thought your best market for stock would have been here, and I am convinced the quicker sold, the better, as should the war measures recommended by the executive, & taken up by the legislature, be carried through, the fall of stock will be very sudden, war being then more than probable. mr Short holds some stock here, and should the first of mr Sprigg's resolutions, now under debate in the lower house, be rejected, I shall within 24. hours from the rejection sell out the whole of mr Short's stock. how that resolution will be disposed of (to wit, that against the expediency of war with the French republic) is very doubtful. those who count votes vary the issue from a majority of 4. against the resolution to 2 or 3. majority in it's favor. so that the scales of peace & war are very nearly in equilibrio. should the debate hold many days, we shall derive aid from the delay. letters recieved from France by a vessel just arrived, concur in assuring us that as all the French measures bear equally on the Swedes & Danes as on us, so they have no more purpose of declaring war against us than against them. besides this a wonderful stir is commencing in the Eastern states. the dirty business of Lyon & Griswold was of a nature to fly through the newspapers both whig & tory, & to excite the attention of all classes. it of course carried to their attention at the same time the debates out of which that affair sprung. the subject of these debates was whether the representatives of the people were to have no check on the expenditure of the public money, & the Executive to squander it at their will, leaving to the Legislature only the drudgery of furnishing the money. they begin to open their eyes on this to the Eastward & to suspect they have been hoodwinked. two or three whig presses have set up in Massachusets & as many more in Connecticut. the late war-message of the president has added new alarm. town meetings have begun in Massachusets and are sending in their petitions & remonstrances by great majorities against war-measures, and these meetings are likely to spread. the present debate as it gets abroad, will further shew them that it is their members who are for war measures. it happens fortunately that these gentlemen are obliged to bring themselves forward exactly in time for the Eastern elections to Congress which come on in the course of the ensuing summer. we have therefore great reason to expect some favorable changes in the representation from that quarter. the same is counted on with confidence from Jersey, Pensylvania & Maryland; perhaps one or two also in Virginia; so that after the next election the whigs think themselves certain of a very strong majority in the H. of R. and tho' against the other branches they can do nothing, good, yet they can hinder them from doing ill. the only source of anxiety therefore is to avoid war for the present moment. if we can defeat the measures leading to that during this session, so as to gain this summer, time will be given as well for the tide of the public mind to make itself felt, as for the operations of France to have their effect in England as well as here. if on the contrary war is forced on, the tory interest continues dominant, and to them alone must be left, as they alone desire to ride on the whirlwind & direct the storm. the present period therefore of two or three weeks is the most eventful ever known since that of 1775. and will decide whether the principles established by that contest are to prevail or give way to those they subverted. accept the friendly salutations & prayers for your health & happiness of Dear Sir

Your sincere & affectionate friend   TH: JEFFERSON

P.S. compliments to mr Taylor. I shall write to him in a few days.

RC (MHi: Washburn Collection); addressed: "The honble Edmund Pendleton near the Bowling-green"; franked and postmarked; endorsed by Pendleton. PrC (DLC).

The recently received letter from William SHORT that was dated 27 Dec. 1797, which TJ received on 30 Mch. 1798. LETTERS RECIEVED FROM FRANCE: see Editorial Note and group of documents on Jefferson, the *Aurora*, and Delamotte's letter from France, at 23 Jan. 1798. Recent TOWN MEETINGS in Roxbury and Milton, Massachusetts, had voiced opposition to the arming of merchant vessels. Both towns prepared PETITIONS, received by the House of Representatives on 30 Mch. and 2 Apr. 1798, addressing that issue and appealing for a peaceful resolution of the strained relations between the United States and France. In the weeks that followed, other towns in Massachusetts and elsewhere sent similar memorials to Congress, and by the end of April a countering movement of petitions from locales in support of the administration's measures had begun (Philadelphia *Aurora*, 30, 31 Mch., 2 Apr. 1798; JHR, 3:247, 248-9, 260, 262, 266, 269, 270, 277).

From John Wickham

DEAR SIR,   Richmond 2d. April 1798.

In reply to your Letter of the 25th. Ulto. I have to inform You that, though generally retained as Counsel for Mr. Welch, I am not his Attorney in Fact, Mr. Benjamin Waller of Wms.Burg acting in that Character, it was solely with a View to serve him that I undertook in his Stead to make the Adjustment which took place between us.—   I have inclosed your Letter to Mr. Waller, & doubt not he will be disposed to consult your Convenience with respect to the Times of payment as far as his Duty to his principal will admit.

I am very respectfully Dear Sir, Your obedt. Servt.

JNO: WICKHAM

RC (MHi); at foot of text: "The Hon. Thos. Jefferson"; endorsed by TJ as received 10 Apr. 1798 and so recorded in SJL.

From William Linn

DEAR SIR,   New York, April 4th. 1798.

I received this day your favor of the 2d instant inclosing one of your vocabularies. The Society here intend to establish a Mission, probably, among either the Western or Southern Indians, as soon as ever they can obtain proper persons. Some have already offered, but we are not yet ready for the execution of our purpose. Your vocabulary will be put into the hands of the Missionaries with directions to fill it up. When these vocabularies are filled by different hands, attention must be paid, I presume, to the spelling, for where the pronunciation may be nearly the same, the spelling may be extremely various. Hardly two writers spell the same Indian names & words exactly alike.

I have inclosed you Dr. Edward's pamphlet which may be of some use to you in your investigation. As far as he goes, he is more to be depended on than hundreds of those who have no knowledge of the structure of languages. I am with great respect, Dear Sir,

Your friend and humble servt.   WM LINN

RC (DLC); endorsed by TJ as received 6 Apr. 1798 and so recorded in SJL. Enclosure: see note to Linn to TJ, 8 Feb. 1798.

From John Taylor

J. TAYLOR TO THE VICE PRESIDENT.   April 4. 1798.

I now take the liberty of inclosing you the papers accompanied with a drawing to obtain Mr: Martin's patent, having by a reference to the law, discovered the error in having before omited this drawing.

Mr: Martin wishes the former papers to be withdrawn or to remain unnoticed, not only on account of this error, but also because several essential improvements have been added by him, since the model sent was made. But if there should be any difficulty in effecting this, he is willing to take the patent upon the old papers, not only because it is probable his right to these improvements will never be contested, but because if they should be, he is able to adduce ample testimony of his having invented them. If the papers are withdrawn, he wishes them to be forwarded to me, together with the patent, by Colo. Anthony New, the representative in Congress for this district. Among the inclosures, I have placed an order to the Secretary of state to deliver the patent to you, as the law seems to require it.

I hope I have not presumed farther than you are willing I should, in continuing to trouble you with this business. It is in truth one of prodigious expectation with us—several hundred machines have been applied for, and many are now in forwardness—therefore models are unnecessary, as they will immediately on the issuing of the patent, be scattered over a large space of country. But should a model be required, I hope the patent will not therefore be delayed, because it is a matter of discretion, and because I will undertake to forward one, if it is required, to the office of state, after the patent has issued.

God preserve you!

Should a patent be taken out upon the old papers, it is the wish of Mr: Martin, that these may be returned with it. If any farther expence is necessary, I will, on the first notice reimburse it—

RC (DLC); with date appearing above postscript; endorsed by TJ as received 12 Apr. but recorded in SJL at 11 Apr. 1798. Enclosures not found.

TJ filed the documents relating to Thomas C. MARTIN'S PATENT for a threshing machine with the State Department on 18 Apr. 1798. The following day Jacob Wagner, chief clerk, wrote TJ noting that he had found the former patent issued to Martin and therefore it was necessary "that it should be cancelled and a new one issued." Observing that the "original specification" was missing from Martin's papers, he inquired whether it had been mistakenly returned with the other papers WITHDRAWN by TJ (RC in MoSHi: Jefferson Papers).

To James Madison

Philadelphia Apr. 5. 98.

I wrote you last on the 29th. ult. since which I have no letter from you. these acknolegements regularly made and attended to will shew whether any of my letters are intercepted, and the impression of my seal on wax (which shall be constant hereafter) will discover whether they are opened by the way. the nature of some of my communications furnishes ground of inquietude for their safe conveyance. the bill for the federal buildings labors hard in Senate, tho' to lessen opposition the Maryland Senator himself proposed to reduce the 200,000 D. to one third of that sum. Sedgwick & Hillhouse violently opposed it. I conjecture that the votes will be either 13 for & 15 against it, or 14 & 14. every member declares he means to go there, but tho' charged with an intention to come away again not one of them disavowed it. this will engender incurable distrust.—the debate on mr Sprigg's resolutions has been interrupted by a motion to call for papers. this was carried by a great majority. in this case, there appeared a separate squad, to wit the Pinckney interest, which is a distinct thing, and will be seen sometimes to lurch the President. it is in truth the Hamilton party, whereof P. is only made the stalking horse. the papers have been sent in & read, & it is now under debate in both houses whether they shall be published. I write in the morning, & if determined in the course of the day in favor of publication, I will add in the evening a general idea of their character. private letters from France by a late vessel which sailed from Havre Feb. 5. assure us that France classing us in her measures with the Swedes & Danes, has no more notion of declaring war against us than them. you will see a letter in Bache's paper of yesterday which came addressed to me. still the fate of Sprigg's resolutions seems in perfect equilibrio.— you will see in Fenno two numbers of a paper signed Marcellus. they promise much mischief, and are ascribed, without any difference of opinion, to Hamilton. you must, my dear Sir, take up your pen against this champion. you know the ingenuity of his talents, & there is not a person but yourself who can foil him. for heaven's sake then, take up your pen, and do not desert the public cause altogether.

Thursday evening. The Senate have to-day voted the publication of the communications from our envoys. the House of Repr. decided against the publication by a majority of 75. to 24. the Senate adjourned over tomorrow (good Friday) to Saturday morning: but as the papers cannot be printed within that time, perhaps the vote of the H. of R. may induce the Senate to reconsider theirs. for this reason I think it my duty to be silent on them. Adieu.

RC (DLC: Madison Papers); addressed: "James Madison junr. near Orange court house"; franked. PrC (DLC).

The committee in charge of the BILL FOR THE FEDERAL BUILDINGS was chaired by MARYLAND SENATOR James Lloyd (JS, 2:459). A printed copy of the bill passed by the House on 20 Mch. 1798 can be found in the Senate records. On it the "two hundred thousand" is canceled with "66,666" interlined above it, perhaps in TJ's hand. The final clauses, which appropriated the $200,000 over three years from 1798 to 1800 at $66,667 per annum, are also deleted (DNA: RG 46, Senate Records, 5th Cong., 2d sess.; on verso in clerk's hand: "An act making appropriations for completing. . ." and "Messrs. Lloyd & others 5 Cong: 2 Sess:"; with the following appearing in TJ's hand: "buildings Washington. Mar. 20th. Read 1st. passed to 2d. 21st. read 2d. and refd. to Comme 28. reported. lie on table Apr. 2. made order of day for Wedn. 4th. Apr. 4. taken up. postponed 5. taken up. & postponed. 9. amended &

passed to 3d. reading 10. read 3d. & recommitted"). For the passage of the bill see note to TJ to Madison, 29 Mch. 1798.

For an analysis of the joint Federalist and Republican CALL FOR PAPERS, see Dauer, *Adams Federalists*, 141-2. For the PUBLICATION of the letters from the envoys to France, see TJ to John Wayles Eppes, 11 Apr. 1798. LATE VESSEL: the brig *James* from Le Havre arrived in New York on 28 Mch. (*Philadelphia Gazette*, 30 Mch. 1798). For the LETTER IN BACHE'S PAPER, see Editorial Note and group of documents

on Jefferson, the *Aurora*, and Delamotte's letter from France, at 23 Jan. 1798. No evidence has been found to prove that Hamilton wrote the TWO NUMBERS by MARCELLUS that appeared in John Fenno's *Gazette of the United States* on 31 Mch. Five days later, however, the same newspaper began publishing articles entitled "The Stand" under the signature "Titus Manlius," which Hamilton was submitting to the New York *Commercial Advertiser* (Syrett, *Hamilton*, 21:381-7).

To James Monroe

Philadelphia Apr. 5. 98.

I wrote you last on the 21st. of Mar. since which yours of the 26th. of March is recieved. Yesterday I had a consultation with mr Dawson on the matter respecting Skipwith. we have neither of us the least hesitation, on a view of the ground, to pronounce against your coming forward in it at all. your name would be the watchword of party at this moment, and the question[1] would give opportunities of slander, personal hatred, and injustice, the effect of which on the justice of the case cannot be calculated. let it therefore come forward in Skipwith's name, without your appearing even to know of it. but is it not a case which the Auditor can decide? if it is, that tribunal must be first resorted to.—I do not think Scipio worth your notice. he has not been noticed here but by those who were already determined. your narrative and letters wherever they are read produce irresistable conviction, and cannot be attacked but by a contradiction of facts, on which they do not venture. finding you unassailable in that quarter, I have reason to believe they are preparing a batch of small stuff, such as refusing to drink Genl. Washington's health, speaking ill of him & the government, withdrawing civilities from those attached to him, countenancing Paine to which they add connivance at the equipment of privateers by Americans. I am told some sort of an attack is preparing, founded on the depositions of 2. or 3. Americans. we are therefore of opinion here that Dr. Edwards's certificate (which he will give very fully) should not be published, but reserved to repel these slanders, adding to it such others as the nature of them may call for. mr Dawson thinks he can easily settle the disagreeable business with M. the difficulty & delicacy will be with G. he is to open the matter to them to day and will write to you this evening. it is really a most afflicting consideration that it is impossible for a man to act in any office for the public without encountering a persecution which even his retirement will not withdraw him from. at this moment my name is running through all the city as detected in a criminal correspondence with the French directory, & fixed upon me by the documents from our envoys now before the two houses. the detection of this by the publication of the papers, should they be published, will not relieve all the effects of the lie, and should they not be published, they may keep it up as long and as successfully as they did and do that of my being involved in Blount's conspiracy. the question for the publication of the communications from our envoys is now under consideration in both houses. but if published, you cannot get them till another post. the event of mr Sprigg's resolutions is extremely doubtful. the first one now under consideration (to wit that it is not expedient to resort to war) will perhaps be carried or rejected by a majority of 1. or 2. only. consequently it is impossible previously to say how it will be. all war-measures, dehors of our country will follow the fortune of that resolution. measures for internal defence will be agreed to. letters from France by a vessel which left Havre Feb. 5. express the greatest certainty that the French government, classing us in all her measures with Denmark & Sweden, has no more idea of declaring war against us than against them. consequently it rests with ourselves. present my best respects to mrs Monroe & accept yourself friendly salutations & Adieux.

P.S. I will hereafter seal my letters with wax, & the same seal. pay attention if you please to the state of the impression.

RC (DLC: Monroe Papers); addressed: "James Monroe near Charlottesville"; franked and postmarked; endorsed by Monroe. PrC (DLC).

MATTER RESPECTING SKIPWITH: Monroe had indicated to John Dawson that he might join Fulwar Skipwith, who sought reimbursement for advances he had made from his personal funds, in a petition to Congress. Dawson, like TJ, cautioned Monroe that associating himself with Skipwith's claims could unleash a barrage of Federalist attacks that would be difficult to counter (Henry Bartholomew Cox, *The Parisian American: Fulwar Skipwith of Virginia* [Washington, D.C., 1964], 53-4, 57-8; Ammon, *Monroe*, 165; Dawson to Monroe, 5 Apr. 1798, in DLC: Monroe Papers).

Monroe's NARRATIVE was the *View of* the *Conduct of the Executive* he published after his return from France. To refute partisan criticism of his conduct in Paris, especially false allegations that he had snubbed a toast to WASHINGTON'S HEALTH at a dinner in Paris on 4 July 1796 and encouraged Thomas PAINE to compose the inflammatory *Letter to George Washington*, Monroe on 12 Feb. 1798 had asked for Enoch EDWARDS's recollection of events, which Edwards provided later in April. M., Robert Morris's son William White Morris, furnished a statement about conflicting accounts of the July 1796 dinner, which he had attended and which had been the subject also of communication between William Branch Giles—G. in the above letter—and James Marshall, John Marshall's brother and Robert Morris's son-in-law (Monroe, *Writings*, 3:98-100; Ellis Paxson

Oberholtzer, *Robert Morris: Patriot and Financier* [New York, 1903], 266-9; Morris to Monroe, [before 14 Apr. 1798], Edwards to Dawson, 21 Apr. 1798, in DLC: Monroe Papers; Madison to TJ, 10 Jan. 1796).

LETTERS FROM FRANCE: see the preceding document and Editorial Note and group of documents on Jefferson, the *Aurora*, and Delamotte's letter from France, at 23 Jan. 1798.

[1] Word interlined in place of "vote."

Notes on a Conversation with Benjamin Rush

Apr. 5. Dr. Rush tells me he had it from mrs Adams that not a scrip of a pen has passed between the late & present Presidt. since he came into office.

MS (DLC: TJ Papers, 102:17525); entirely in TJ's hand; on same sheet as Notes on Senators' Comments about House Impeachment Committee, 12 Mch. 1798.

To Martha Jefferson Randolph

Philadelphia. Apr. 5. 98.

Mr. Randolph's letter of Mar. 26. informs me you are all well at Belmont. my last news from Eppington was of Mar. 20. when all were well there. I have myself had remarkeably good health through the winter, since the cold which I took on my way here. the advance of the season makes me long to get home. the first shad we had here was Mar. 16. and Mar. 28. was the first day we could observe a greenish hue on the weeping willow from it's young leaves. not the smallest symptom of blossoming yet on any species of fruit tree. all this proves that we have near two months in the year of vegetable life, and of animal happiness so far as they are connected, more in our canton than here. the issue of a debate now before the H. of Representatives will enable us to judge of the time of adjournment. but it will be some days before the issue is known. in the mean time they talk of the last of this month. letters by a late arrival from France give reason to believe they do not mean to declare war against us; but that they mean to destroy British commerce with all nations, neutral as well as belligerent. to this the Swedes & Danes submit, and so must we unless we prefer war. a letter from mr Short informs me of the death of the old Dutchess Danville. he talks of coming in this spring or summer. I have purchased an excellent harpsichord for Maria, which I hope is by this time arrived at Monticello, with a box of trees to which I asked mr Randolph's attention by the last post.

[248]

among these were cranberries, raspberries & strawberries of great value. I am afflicted with the difficulty of procuring horses for the farm, or rather for the waggon in place of the mules to be turned over to the farm, which is a good idea. I am afflicted too with the fear that the roof of the house is not going on as my necessities require. I have engaged a fine housejoiner here to go on with me. my most friendly salutations to mr Randolph & tenderest love to yourself and the little ones. Adieu affectionately.

RC (NNPM); at foot of text: "Mrs. Randolph." PrC (CSmH); endorsed by TJ in ink on verso.

Thomas Mann RANDOLPH'S LETTER of 26 Mch., recorded in SJL as received 3 Apr., has not been found. NEWS FROM EPPINGTON: Mary Jefferson Eppes to TJ, 20 Mch.

1798. For the letter from William SHORT to TJ, see 27 Dec. 1797. For the letter by the LAST POST, see TJ to Thomas Mann Randolph, 29 Mch. TJ engaged the services of the FINE HOUSEJOINER James Dinsmore, who arrived at Monticello in Oct. 1798 and served as the principal joiner in the renovation of Monticello until 1809 (MB, 2:985).

From Aaron Burr

DEAR SIR,   Albany 6 Apl. 1798

This will be presented to you by Captain Aupaumut Chief of the Moheakuns,—a Man of perfectly decent Manners and deportment and Who has been Useful to the U.S. in War and in Nigociation. He is solicitous to be made known to you, and I have thought that you would consider an estimable and intelligent Man of his Nation as a desireable acquaintance.

I am with very great Respect Your assured & Obt H st

AARON BURR

RC (DLC); at foot of text: "The Hon. Th. Jefferson"; endorsed by TJ as received 20 Apr. 1798 and recorded in SJL as received on that day "by Capt Aupaumut. Hendruc."

Hendrick AUPAUMUT was chief sachem of the Stockbridge branch of the Mahican (Mohican) Indians, who had lived in New York State since the mid-1780s. Aupaumut, who had continued on to Philadelphia after failing to win the New York legislature's approval of a claim from the tribe, had

been USEFUL TO THE U.S. as a soldier during the American Revolution and as an envoy to tribes in the Great Lakes region (Kline, Burr, 1:341-2; William C. Sturtevant, gen. ed., Handbook of North American Indians, 11 vols. to date [Washington, 1978-   ], 15:209; B. H. Coates, ed., "A Narrative of an Embassy to the Western Indians, from the Original Manuscript of Hendrick Aupaumut," Memoirs of the Historical Society of Pennsylvania, 2 [1827], 68-70).

To James Madison

So much of the communications from our envoys has got abroad, & so partially that there can now be no ground for reconsideration with the Senate. I may therefore consistently with duty do what every member of the body is doing. still I would rather you would use the communication with reserve till you see the whole papers. the first impressions from them are very disagreeable & confused. reflection however & analysis resolves them into this. mr A's speech to Congress in May is deemed such a national affront, that no explanation on other topics can be entered on till that, as a preliminary is wiped away, by humiliating disavowals or acknolegements. this working hard with our envoys, & indeed seeming impracticable for want of that sort of authority, submission to a heavy amercement (upwards of a million sterl.) was, at an after meeting suggested as an alternative which might be admitted if proposed by us. these overtures had been through informal agents; and both the alternatives bringing the envoys to their ne plus, they resolve to have no more communication through inofficial characters, but to address a letter directly to the government, to bring forward their pretensions. this letter had not yet however been prepared. there were interwoven with these overtures some base propositions on the part of Taleyrand through one of his agents, to sell his interest & influence with the Directory towards smoothing difficulties with them in consideration of a large sum (50,000 £) sterl.) and the arguments to which his agent resorted to induce compliance with this demand were very unworthy of a great nation (could they be imputed to them) and calculated to excite disgust & indignation in Americans generally, and alienation in the republicans particularly; whom they so far mistake as to presume an attachment to France, and hatred to the Federal party, & not the love of their country, to be their first passion. no difficulty was expressed towards an adjustment of all differences & misunderstandings or even ultimately a paiment for spoliations, if the insult from our Executive should be first wiped away. observe that I state all this from only a single hearing of the papers, & therefore it may not be rigorously correct. the little slanderous imputation before mentioned has been the bait which hurried the opposite party into this publication. the first impressions with the people will be disagreeable, but the last & permanent one will be that the speech in May is now the only obstacle to accomodation, and the real cause of war, if war takes place. and how much will be added to this by the speech of November is yet to be learnt. it is evident however on reflection, that these papers do not offer one motive the more for our

going to war. yet such is their effect on the minds of wavering characters, that I fear that to wipe off the imputation of being French partisans,
they will go over to the war-measures so furiously pushed by the other
party. it seems indeed as if they were afraid they should not be able to
get into war till Great-Britain will be blown up, and the prudence of our
countrymen from that circumstance have influence enough to prevent
it. the most artful mis-representations[1] of the contents of these papers
were published yesterday, & produced such a shock on the republican
mind as has never been seen since our independance. we are to dread the
effects of this dismay till their fuller information. Adieu.

P.M. the evening papers have come out since writing the above. I
therefore inclose them. be so good as to return Brown's by post, as I
keep his set here. the representations are still unfaithful.

RC (DLC: Madison Papers); addressed:
"James Madison junr. near Orange courthouse"; franked. PrC (DLC). Enclosures
not found, but see note below.

USE THE COMMUNICATION WITH RE-
SERVE: TJ probably enclosed an account
(now missing) of the dispatches that he had
made from memory after hearing them read
and debated in the Senate (TJ to Madison,
12 Apr.). The INFORMAL AGENTS indenti-
fied in the published correspondence only as
W, X, Y, and Z were Nicholas Hubbard,
Jean Conrad Hottinguer, Pierre Bellamy,
and Lucien Hauteval, respectively. For
information on Talleyrand, the French
agents, and their dealings with the American envoys, see Stinchcombe, *XYZ Affair*,
32-6, 40-4, 55-69. SLANDEROUS IMPUTA-
TION: the envoys reported that on 30 Oct.
1797, Bellamy warned them that they were
mistaken if they thought they could convince their "countrymen" that negotiations
failed because of the "unreasonableness" of
the French government. He continued:
"you ought to know that the diplomatic skill
of France, and the means she possesses in
your country, are sufficient to enable her,
with the French party in America, to throw
the blame which will attend the rupture of
the negotiations on the federalists, as you
term yourselves, but on the British party, as
France terms you; and you may assure yourselves this will be done." On 3 Nov. Bellamy
noted that if Burr and Madison had been

sent as envoys a settlement already would
have been arranged (ASP, *Foreign Relations*,
2:164-5). Versions of the former conversation appeared in Philadelphia newspapers
in the following days. On 6 Apr. the *Philadelphia Gazette* reported that the envoys
were advised "that the French had a strong
party in America, warmly attached to their
cause. That it would be impossible for the
United States, to carry on a war, because the
people were divided, and were unwilling to
fight the French." For Adams's speech of 23
NOVEMBER, see TJ to Francis Walker, 21
Dec. 1797.

One of the MOST ARTFUL MIS-REPRESEN-
TATIONS that PRODUCED SUCH A SHOCK ON
THE REPUBLICAN MIND was William Cobbett's piece in *Porcupine's Gazette* of 5 Apr.
He wrote that the envoy's communications
surpassed all that he had said "respecting
the malignity, the atrocity, and the insolence of the French." He continued: the
French have "*Spies* in every nook and corner" and "know their strength here, much
better than we do." They are "linked together by the indissoluble bond of Jacobin-
ism."

EVENING PAPERS: newspapers published
to appear in the evening included the *Gazette of the United States*, *Porcupine's Gazette*, *Carey's United States Recorder*, and
Andrew Brown's *Philadelphia Gazette*.

[1] TJ first wrote "representations" before
altering it to read as above.

[251]

To John Taylor

TH: JEFFERSON TO JOHN TAYLOR.   Philadelphia Apr. 6. 98.

I had just recieved from New York the box containing mr Martin's model of the hand-threshing machine, & the drill, when your favor of Mar. 25. came to hand, and I had nearly compleated a drawing to be filed in the Secretary of state's office. I suspend further proceeding till I hear from you. in the mean time mr Bingham had communicated to me a model which he had recieved from England. I think this so admirably simple that I made a drawing of it, and now inclose it for mr Martin's consideration. by making the axis of the great spur wheel serve as one of the feeding cylinders, you save the endless screw & 4. crown & spur wheels employed by mr Martin to communicate motion from the great spur to the feeding cylinders. this saves a great deal of work & friction. I know from experience that the drum wheel ought to turn ten times for once of the cylinders, which is the motion given here. the inclined plane is also better for feeding than the cloth & rollers used by mr Martin. these have long given way in Great Britain to the inclined plane.

Mr. Martin's improvement in the cups of his drill is a beautiful one, and it is now the most compleat machine in the world for sowing a single row. I have sent it to the board of agriculture in London, and informed them whose invention it is. I wish he could be induced to try to make me one which would sow 4. rows at a time 12. I. apart from row to row. this would add greatly to it's value, & is the only point in which Cook's famous drill plough has the advantage of it. in every thing else mr Martin's is preferable to Cook's. but it is most desirable to be able to sow in equidistant rows. perhaps by making an iron axis with a circle of cups at every 3. I. & a spout under each circle, it might be made to sow at any distance (of which 3. I. should be an aliquot part) by stopping intermediate spouts according to our purpose. but he will probably think of something better.

a great shock is communicated by the documents from our envoys. we are not yet at liberty to divulge them. but do not be alarmed. the last and permanent impression will be the reverse of the first. the votes for & against publication have been not at all party votes, but a perfect jumble. all see something they like & something they do not like. the only thing to be feared is that the first impressions will produce measures, which reflection & an analysis of the whole transactions will be too late to remedy. certainly no man can on reflection find one motive the more, in these papers for going to war. accept my affectionate salutations & Adieu.

RC (MHi: Washburn Collection); addressed: "John Taylor Caroline near the Bowling green"; franked and postmarked; endorsed by Taylor. PrC (DLC).

BOX CONTAINING MR MARTIN'S MODEL: see Taylor to TJ, 19 Nov. 1797. For the shipment of Thomas C. Martin's grain drill to the BOARD OF AGRICULTURE IN LONDON, see TJ to Sir John Sinclair, 23 Mch.

ENCLOSURE

Drawing of a Threshing Machine

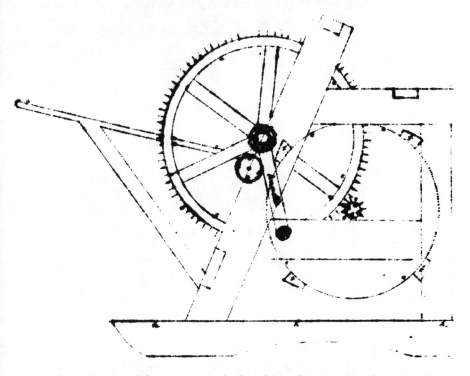

a.a.a.a. is the axis of the great spur wheel, and is at the same time the upper of the two cylinders for drawing in the grain. these cylinders are fluted

b.b.b.b. is the under cylinder. they are fluted, and the under one has a small cast iron wheel toothed on the edge (like those in a wheat fan) having a broken joint in it's axis (like those in Martin's drills) which permits the under cylinder to approach or recede from the upper one, without displacing the toothed wheel, which is moved by it's taking in a similar toothed wheel on the upper cylinder or axis.

c.c.c.c. is the great spur wheel.

d.d.d.d. is an iron toothed or pinion wheel, the number of whose teeth is one tenth of those of the great spur wheel. it is fixed on the axis of the drum wheel which is

e.e.e.e. of such a radius as with it's beater f. to pass the cylinders nearly by brushing them.

f.f.f.f. are 4. beaters mortised on the arms of the Drum wheel.

g.g. is an inclined plane for spreading the sheaf on and sliding it in between the cylinders.

h.h.h. are two sills made in the form of those of a sleigh for drawing the machine. they serve at the same time as sills for the frame which will be readily understood by the above drawing without particular explanation.

this drawing is strictly in the proportions of the model from which it is taken.

PrC (DLC).

From James Monroe

DEAR SIR   Albemarle April 8. 1798.

Yrs. of the 21. ulto. was the last recd. Mr. A: will never surprise me by any act of the wild & extravagant kind. If he was in a sober and discreet manner to repair the breach between this country & France, & heal the wounds wh. his predecessor has given to the reputation & interest of his country, I shod. be surprised. His passion is to out-do his predecessor, & thus I expect to find no difference, between the knight of the present day and the former one, than what the superior violence of his passion may lead to. I still think it of little importance, how great soever the errors be into wh. they run. A question for war with France, or for measures leading to war, carried by a feeble majority agnst the interest of the continent, & the judgmt. of the mercantile class of the community, & the wish & opinion of every other class, can have no other issue than of disgracing its authors. The further they plunge the sooner will the people recover the use of their intellects. Nor do I fear disunion, or any thing of the kind, because the eastern people are as averse to it as we. It becomes our members to be calm & collected at this crisis; firm yet to say nothing wh. may hereafter in retrospect dishonor them, their state, or cause. If they act thus they will soon be lookd up to by the eastern people, who will abandon their own representatives. Let the issue be what it may, I mean as to the passage or rejection of Mr. A:'s propositions, I date from the present epoch, the decline & perhaps the ruin of the party.

I have just return'd from Staunton, having attended the district court & resum'd my practice there. I shall do the same here & at Fredbg.— I take a house in Richmd. whither I repair from Fredbg. to attend the chy &ca. *Here* my domicil will be—my time will be divided between the places as professional duties require, since here I shall prefer to be.

Being without a horse Mr. Randolph was so kind as lend me yours to ride to Staunton. He is restored in excellent order. we are well & desire to be affecy. remembered. yr. friend & servt   JAS. MONROE

RC (DLC); endorsed by TJ as received 24 Apr. 1798 and so recorded in SJL.   MR. A: John Adams. CHY: chancery.

To Thomas Carstairs

SIR   Apr. 9. 98.

The bearer hereof, Richard Richardson, is a bricklayer who has worked a great deal for me in Virginia. being industrious & desirous of improving in his art, he is come here by my advice to learn what is to be learnt here. he wishes now to work a while with a plaisterer, and understands that a mr Johnston of your acquaintance is engaged in that line of business: I take the liberty therefore of asking your interest with mr Johnston to recieve him, and so employ him as that he may gain insight into the plaistering business, which will oblige Sir

Your most obedt. servt   TH: JEFFERSON

RC (PWacD: Feinstone Collection, on deposit PPAmP); recipient not identified by TJ, but this and other correspondence between TJ and Carstairs were previously in the possession of Mrs. L. Carstairs Pierce, Wayne, Pennsylvania (see also note below). Not recorded in SJL.

In 1793 TJ had called upon Carstairs, a carpenter and architect, to develop estimates for the construction of the United States Capitol (TJ to Carstairs, 14 July 1793). John JOHNSTON, stucco plasterer, was located at 39 Filbert Street (Cornelius William Stafford, *The Philadelphia Directory for 1798* [Philadelphia, 1798], 79).

From "Americanus"

SIR,   Virginia, April 10, 1793. [i.e. 1798]

About the time, or soon after you left home for Congress last, a paper called "the petition of the subscribers, inhabitants of Amherst, Albemarle, Fluvanna and Goochland," on the subject of a presentment of a grand jury in one of our Federal circuit courts, was presented to the Legislature of Virginia; which, from several circumstances attending it, was supposed to come from your pen. On hearing this opinion, which I thought an injurious, and I hoped an unfounded one respecting you,

I had determined to write you a private letter, merely to inform you of its existence, that you might have it in your power to contradict it. But scarcely had I formed this determination before I was convinced, by almost positive proof, that the opinion was too well founded. I then resolved to point out in the most striking and public manner I could, the extreme impropriety of your having engaged in such a business while Vice-President of America, not only as the time it employed was supposed to affect your attendance on Congress at the commencement of its present session, but on the principles laid down in the petition itself.

Having often heard you declare that you never had, nor never would write any thing for public view which did not either bear your name or which you would not readily and openly avow, I cannot help reminding you of that declaration, as a source from whence I derive considerable hope, that the people at least of the district immediately concerned, who are not all possessed of the same testimony of the fact with myself, will be informed, whether or not you were the author of that petition: For although I candidly own, that your silence on the subject of the letter to *Mazzei*, was no actual deviation from that declaration, since it is not very difficult to conceive that *that* letter was not one of the things *intended by you* for *public view*, yet, you must admit, on the other hand, that a petition intended for the approbation or disapprobation of a whole district, and afterwards for the public consideration and discussion of the General Legislature of a whole state, falls directly and strictly within the right we have to expect a compliance with the conditions of the declaration above alledged.

Whatever may be your reasons for not rendering an answer to the enquiries of an individual citizen on the subject of your conduct, which no one would be more sorry than myself you were obliged to do, yet, you will not deny, I am sure, that the "*sovereign people*" at large, who have the appointing you, and to whose scrutiny your conduct is subject before the repetition of your election, have a right to know whenever you deviate from those principles on which they have heretofore appointed you. That the majority who elected you, was formed on the belief, that you would give to the government, that republican tone, so far as the exercise of your office could affect it, which it was intended to have, I suppose will not be contested. The American government, if it has a feature likely to become stronger, by its operation, than its republican one, that feature is to be found in the means placed, by the constitution, in the hands of that branch over which you preside. Consequently, much depends upon the conduct of the members of that body.

By the constitution of the United States, the representative part of our government is divided into three distinct parts: the immediate rep-

resentatives of the people, who are invested solely with legislative powers; the Senate, who are a *remove further* from the *people*, and have a
mixture of legislative, executive, and in some instances, judiciary authorities; and the President, or executive, in whose hand, among other
things, is the nomination of all ministerial officers, a qualified negative
over the acts of the other two grand departments of state. The Senate is
the body who appoint those ministerial offices, or reject them under the
nomination of the President. The senate have the sole power of trying
all impeachments; and with the Chief Justice at their head, who they
appoint and are the judges of the conduct of in turn, have the trying of
the President himself, in case of impeachment. And *two thirds* of the
Senate, in concurrence with *two thirds* of the House of Representatives,
qualify the negative of the President, and render ineffectual, his voice, in
the general legislature of the whole.

It is easy to be perceived then, how these different and complicated
powers of that body, by a *pretended* attachment to the principles of republicanism, and a superior degree of attatchment to the rights and
interests of the people, may be made to draw into its own vortex, swal-
low up, and destroy entirely all the powers and independence of all the
other departments of government; and thereby produce in reality the
reverse of such principles as is *pretended*. By holding over the head of
the President the terror of rejecting his nominations, and thereby fixing
on him the character of an enemy to *their pretended* principles; by shaping their decisions in matters of impeachment by the same *pretended*
rule of patriotism and republicanism; and finally, by intriguing with the
immediate representatives of the people; they may, not only destroy all
the good which was intended by the President's nomination of officers;
render, the offices thus generated in party spirit and subject to their
dismissal, the immediate tools of their projects, and destroy entirely the
intended check of the negative of the President; but draw immediately
under their feet, all the other departments, and thereby produce all
those evil consequences complained of in the petition itself, which has
caused this enquiry.

The Senate, sir, not being the immediate representatives of the people, but a refined body; removed from them by the appointment of their
representatives in the State Legislatures; but few in number; and chosen for long periods; is to be considered, if there is an aristocratic feature
in the formation of our government, of that description. And the influence of that thin and incomplete branch of representation over all the
rest, produced by joining with one, and overawing others with the exercise of those various and complicated powers in the way already described, is the only mean by which the effects of aristocracy or an undue

executive influence as it is called, is to be felt by the operation of our government in the way complained of.

The Federal Judges, it is to be remembered, owe their appointments immediately to the Senate; and, in case of impeachment are subject entirely to their decisions. If therefore, there be any real reason for apprehending danger from the interference of the executive over other departments, thro' the medium of its influence over the judiciary, is there not reason for apprehending some danger from the interference and influence of the Senate in the same way? From the abundance of means, certainly in their hands, that body, I think, may be considered the strong and leading part of the government of the United States; and therefore are we led, when we hear so much of the existence of an aristocracy and aristocrats, the undue influence of the executive, &c. particularly from that body itself to turn our eyes *there*, as the only place where those things, in reality, can possibly exist. And although no such improper, such *pretended patriotic* attempts have yet been made, at least by *two thirds* of that body, to tyrannize over the President and the different ministerial branches of government, thereby to absorb the whole of their powers, control the representatives, and erect themselves into an oligarchic assembly; yet it naturally occurs to us, to enquire, from what we have already seen of the dispositions of the minority, what we are likely to be the consequences of the additional weight of an influential *head* thrown into the scale of their popular pretensions, by way of interference[1] among the other departments of government,[2] *or the people*, under the pretence of *superior*[3] *patriotism*, a great love for *liberty* and the *privileges* of the *representatives*?

The President of the Senate, although he is not appointed directly in the same way with the other members of that body, is appointed in a way, which places him at the same distance, precisely, from the people, appointed immediately with the President, by the same electors being eventually subject to fill his place, and holding the same permanent situation, nearly, in the government with the Senators themselves; his interference in the other branches of government may be considered as falling under either head, of an executive or senatorial usurpation of power, or incroachment on their rights; and it matters not whether that interference be with the open and avowed intention of increasing those executive or senatorial powers, or cloathed in the more artful appearance of increasing the influence of a more popular branch; the effects, when we consider the unnatural course of power operating to the diminution of itself, in favour of a *rival* authority, it must be expected, will be the same.

And if sir, from the organization of the Senate and the unnatural expectation that men in power and long habituated to power, would enter into a voluntary diminution of that power to encrease the power of others, the reverse is most natural to be expected, does it not result, as naturally, that some danger is to be apprehended, when we behold the head of that body descending from his exalted station, to become the petition drawer, even of the people, to increase the privileges of *another branch* of government? It is principles, and not professions or men we have to look to for security, as the best of us are liable to deceive ourselves, and the worst are certain to endeavour to deceive others. If therefore, upon principle, it is wrong for the executive, through its influence over the judiciary, to intrude its controul over the representative privileges of the people, is it not, at least suspicious, for one, subject himself to constitute that executive, to intrude his interference, in the management of those popular privileges, in circumscription of those *executive wrongs?*

Even admitting the professions of such an one to be sincere, in contradiction to the natural propensities of all human nature, it is, in my humble conception, as improper for the representative branch to interfere in the affairs of the executive and judiciary, as it is for the executive and judiciary to interfere in the affairs of the representatives; and considerably more alarming for the head of that body, which holds such strong influences over both the executive and judiciary, to be found intriguing with that representative branch to overawe[4] and control those other two. I have already observed, that it has been long easy to be perceived, from the formation of the government, how a Senate *pretending* an attachment to the principles of republicanism, and an increase of the right of the people, to the lessening of their own, by joining with the immediate representatives of the people, might work the whole of the powers of the government into their own hands, and thereby convert it into an aristocratic republic; but after the alarm of an *aristocracy* and *aristocrats* had been so loudly rung, it was hardly to have been expected, that, even amidst that frightful peal, we should have beheld an influential and important character of the only department where those things can ever possibly, in reality, exist, not only engaging with the representatives of the government to which he immediately belongs, but with the people at large, and the *state legislatures*, who elect the senators *over whom he presides*, to overawe all the other departments of government. Such an interference stops not at the erection of an aristocracy; it seems to be aiming at nothing less than the absolute grasp of of dictatorial authority itself!

Under this impression, and believing, as many others as well as myself do, that you were the author of the petition alluded to, I cannot do otherwise in justice to myself, and in candor to you, than lay before you those impressions; hoping thereby, if my ideas have been in any way unfounded, as candidly to be set right.

[259]

If it shall be asked, why I have thus *particularly* busied myself in a matter which so *generally* concerns all America?—I reply—that I am a member of that *particular* district, which, besides the *general* interest it has in all our public concerns, is, in my opinion, particularly disgraced in the composition of the petition itself. It is built, sir, I am sorry to say, upon a shameful, erroneous, and uncandid statement of facts; and what is worse, insults us by boldly presenting the falshood to view, as if we dare not, or cannot detect the fraud. The petition is founded on the idea of the Jury's having presented *all correspondence* between the representative and constituent; and not only tending to render odious the act itself of such correspondence, but absolutely asserts, it has a tendency to interrupt all *private intercourse* even "between citizen and citizen."—Whereas the presentment itself, which is placed in the very middle of those assertions, says, "the circular letters of *several* members of the late congress, and *particularly* letters with the signature of *Samuel I. Cabell*, endeavouring at a time of real public danger to *disseminate unfounded calumnies* against the happy government of the United States, and thereby to separate the people therefrom, & to increase or produce a foreign influence ruinous to the peace, happiness and independence of the United States."

Whether these letters were of that description or not, or whether the jury had a right to judge of what description they were, I will confess, depends upon opinion; but whether the jury presented the act itself of letter-writing, between the representative and constituent, and even "between citizen and citizen," is a matter of fact too plainly contradicted by the presentment itself, to insult the commonest understanding with an observation on. One remark, however, on the subject of the interference of the different branches of government with each other, here presents itself to view.

The petition states, that to put the representative in jeopardy of criminal prosecution, of vexation, expense, and punishment, before the judiciary, if his communications, private or public, do not exactly square with their ideas of right and fact, or with their designs of wrong, is to put the legislative department under the feet of the judiciary, &c."—and again, "is to do away the influence of the people over the proceedings of their representatives, by excluding from their knowledge by the terror of punishment, all but such information, or misinformation, as may suit their views;"—and yet, the petition admits, that the judiciary are the proper judges of all the infractions of the laws; and certainly very properly too: The representatives being the passers of the laws, it certainly would be improper for them to undertake to judge of the infraction of those laws, or engage in the execution of them.

To determine whether a thing be an actual infraction of the laws, or a matter of opinion, is certainly *itself* a judicial, and not a legislative right; and to punish that act, if it be adjudged the former, is properly an executive, and not a representative function. The legislature having no power to judge or punish acts, except those relating immediately to the rights of their own body, and not those but in actual session, how is the simple fact to be decided, whether a communication from a representative to his constituent, or even to an enemy, which shall have come to light after his term of service has expired, is one of those communications, proper to be made, as containing only mere matters of opinion, or an actual infraction of the laws intended to produce treason and sedition? Will any one say that, because such communication flowed from the hand of a representative, it ought not to be judged of, and punished, if found improper? Suppose, for instance, a disappointed minority should set to work, to stir up the people to oppose the proceedings of the majority, or join the *enemy* (which seems to have been the opinion of the jury, in the case of the letters presented), and that endeavour should only have come to light after the term for which that minority were appointed had expired, is there no tribunal competent to decide, no authority left to punish such an outrage? And yet, if the courts and juries have no right to judge, and the executive to act upon their decisions, it is not very difficult to discern, that there are no authorities left to examine into and punish the most abominable attempts that may be made to destroy the peace, the safety and happiness of the country, provided those attempts come from those most capable of executing them,—the *popular* representatives of the people!

These, Sir, are not the mere *air balloon* speculations of a *whimsical philosophy*, the suggestions of malice, the workings of *aristocracy*, or the mere chimeras of a distempered imagination; but, the solid and substantial conclusions, resulting from the attempts already made in the senate, by those who are known to agree with you in every instance of your *late* political persuasions.

In the memorable case of your *celebrated* electioneering *friend*, William Blount, it will never be forgotten, that your political friend and adherent, Senator Tazewell, *first* objected to the expulsion of that *worthy* brother senator, because he could not be tried *again* upon an impeachment for the *same offence*; *then*, that he could not be tried on the impeachment; but by the introduction of a *Jury* into the Senate; which farcical doctrine, could it have found *patriotic* and *republican* advocates enough to have sustained it, would have been next met by your Virginia *election*[5] *doctrine*, of the Jury's having no right to interfere with the *letters* of our *representatives*; and consequently, that Mr. Blount's offence, which was nothing more than just the writing of a *little private letter* to one of his *constituents* and friends was not to be punished. I will not suppose Sir, that these different *patriotic* doctrines have been started in different places and by different influential characters, for the valuable purpose of clearing that *honourable* and *inestimable* senator; but must leave it to those who have brought them forward to explain their strong appearances.

At any rate, whatever may have been the motives, the impropriety of the Vice President's *secretly* imploying the people to attack the government he is *sworn* to support; or, what is worse, his *secretly* engaging with them, in petitioning the legislatures who appoint the senators over whom he presides, to interfere and aid him in abridging the powers of the other branches of the government in which he acts; and the proofs to establish the fact, are too strong, to admit of a justification for your remaining silent in the case.

On my own part, however severe may be the charge, and however unnecessary it may be to subscribe a name which could add no weight to the observations here submitted to the public, I now engage, when you shall have fulfilled your promise of never writing any thing for "public view that shall not be freely and openly avowed," to render to you *that name*, as freely, as I shall now give you a fictitious one; Nay, more. Having never uttered a sentiment of any one in my life, which I would not be willing, and even chose to have communicated to them, under my real name if required, in the same way it was meant to be applied in any other, I now inform you, that my true name is with the editor of this paper for your *private* satisfaction, whilst I subscribe myself for public view (with all that *difference* and *respect* to which your *real merits* intitle you).

Your *sincere friend* and *devoted partizan*.   AMERICANUS.

Printed in *Porcupine's Gazette*, 28 Apr. 1798; at head of text: "To the Honourable Thomas Jefferson, Esq. Vice-President of America."

"Americanus" had criticized TJ in a series of articles in the *Virginia Gazette and General Advertiser* in 1797. George Washington, in an 8 Mch. 1798 letter to Bushrod Washington, identified the "reputed author" of the pieces as "Mr Nicholas," clerk of Albemarle County and "a respectable man; well disposed to the Government." He was

John Nicholas, Jr. (see Editorial Note to Jefferson's Letter to Philip Mazzei, Vol. 29:76, 78; Washington, *Papers, Ret. Ser.,* 2:129-30).

PETITION: Petition to Virginia House of Delegates, printed under 3 August 1797 (Vol. 29:491-504)."

¹ MS: "inteference."
² MS: "governmen."
³ MS: "suporior."
⁴ MS: "ouerawe."
⁵ MS: "electition."

To John Wayles Eppes

DEAR SIR   Philadelphia Apr. 11. 98.

My last letter from Maria was of Mar. 20. & from yourself of Feb. 8. the dates of my latest to Maria were of Apr. 1. Mar. 7. and to yourself of Feb. 18. you have seen in the papers the resolutions proposed by mr Sprigg, the first of which was that under existing circumstances it is not expedient to resort to war with France. it is very uncertain how this would have been decided. but the communication of the papers from our envoys by the President, of which I inclose you a copy, has altered the aspect of that resolution. you will see that in these communications some demands have been made of a large sum of money from us as a amulet, or satisfaction for the President's speech in May last. it was thought that were we now to resolve it is not expedient to resort to war, it might imply an acquiescence under their demand to purchase a peace. therefore the resolution has been postponed. still however the communications do not offer a single motive the more for going to war. there are as you will see some swindling propositions for a sum of £50,000 from certain inofficial characters, which probably were meant for themselves alone, or for themselves & Taleyrand (whose character we have always known to be very corrupt) but there is not the smallest ground to believe the Directory knew any thing of them. in the case of the Portuguese minister, where similar propositions were made & acceded to by him, he was imprisoned by the Directory, as soon as they knew it, as having attempted corruption. it is evident on the whole that the President's speech is the only obstacle to an amicable negociation, that satisfaction being given them for this by disavowals, acknolegements or money, they are willing to proceed to arrangements of our other differences & even to settle & acknolege themselves debtors for spoliations. the members of Congress had very generally fixed their minds on the last of this month for adjournment. these papers however seem to unfix their ideas in some degree. the peace party are of opinion they should agree to all reasonable measures of internal defence, but to nothing external. but I fear they are not strong enough to hold that ground. it is the opinion of many that we must absolutely resort to a land tax, to meet the expences of the war measures which the war-party are endeavoring[1] to force on us. should this take place, we shall be greatly delayed here. we have a report from Boston yesterday that the frigate built there was sunk in the storm of the 3d instant, her portholes having been left open. but it is not yet entirely credited. I am anxious to hear that Maria's harpsichord has arrived safe. it went from here about the 22d or 23d. of

March, and should by the 3d. of April have been in James river, where the storm would not endanger it. my friendly salutations to mr & mrs Eppes & family, & tenderest love to Maria. Adieu affectionately.

RC (ViU); at foot of first page: "J. W. Eppes." Enclosure: see note below.

For the letter from Eppes to TJ of feb. 8, see note to TJ to Eppes, 18 Feb.

The papers from our envoys were published in *Message of the President of the United States to both Houses of Congress. April 3d, 1798* (Philadelphia, 1798). For the printing by John Fenno, see Evans, No. 34812. For the copy in TJ's library printed by Thomas Dobson and John Ormrod, see Sowerby, No. 3210, and Evans, No. 34814. The publication included Secretary of State Pickering's instructions to the envoys and five letters sent from Paris by the negotiators to Pickering, dating from 22 Oct. 1797 to 8 Jan. 1798. The last letter, with its enclosure, was previously published with

Adams's message to Congress of 5 Mch. (see enclosure No. 2 listed at TJ to Mann Page, 6 Mch.).

In a letter to Rufus King dated 12 Apr., William Hindman reported that Republican members of the House in caucus agreed to strong measures of internal defence but, he asserted, "when We get upon Vessels of War for the protection of our Commerce I fear They will give Way" (King, *Life*, 2:313-14). For the land tax, see enclosure to TJ to Madison, 17 May 1798. The false report from boston on the sinking of the frigate *Constitution* is cited in Smelser, *Navy*, 144.

[1] TJ first wrote "will endeavor" and altered it to read as above.

To John Heckewelder

SIR   Philadelphia. Apr. 11. 98.

About the year 1787. I published a book entitled 'Notes on Virginia' in which was an account of the murder of the family of Logan an Indian chief in the year 1774. by some whites, at the head of whom was said to be one of the Cressaps. this was the general report & belief of that day. lately a mr Martin of Maryland, who married a Cressap, has undertaken to contradict the fact, to deny that either of the Cresaps was concerned in the murder, to deny the genuineness of the speech sent by Logan to Ld Dunmore & to represent Logan as a worthless, drunken, & unprincipled Indian, of no account in his tribe & of no abilities. I am told that your situation about that time was such as to enable you to give some information as to these facts, either from your own knowlege, or what you may have heard from others. my object is to learn the truth, and when I shall have got at an exact knolege of the transaction, to publish a correct statement of it, doing justice to Cressap if he has been injured or to Logan if mr Martin's imputations on him be found to be mere calumnies. I have no attachment which would induce me to conceal or discolour the truth. your character in the world gives me confidence that if you can contribute any thing towards fixing this transaction on it's true bottom, you will have no hesitation to bear testimony to the truth. may I take the liberty of asking you to give me any information you can on this subject, which if addressed to me in a letter to this place will readily find me. your compliance with this request will much oblige Sir

your most obedt. humble servt TH: JEFFERSON

PrC (DLC); at foot of text: "The revd. John Heckewelder." RC (Thomas A. Lingenfelter, Doylestown, Pennsylvania, 1994); consists of address cover only, addressed in TJ's hand to Heckewelder at Bethlehem, Pennsylvania; franked and with postmark of 12 Apr.

Born in England to parents from Moravia, John Gottlieb Ernestus Heckewelder (1743-1823) immigrated to America with his family when he was eleven. A member of the Moravian community at Bethlehem, Pennsylvania, he was an occasional courier to Indian towns, then became a missionary in 1771. Until 1786 he worked among settlements of Native American converts in Pennsylvania and what is now Ohio, subse-

quently assisting government commissions sent to negotiate with western tribes. From 1801 to 1810 he administered lands on the Muskingum River that were held in trust for christianized Indians. Encouraged by Caspar Wistar, to whom TJ had expressed a concern that Heckewelder's accumulated knowledge of indigenous peoples might be lost, Heckewelder wrote accounts of Indian customs and languages and a history of the Moravian missions. He also made observations in natural history and became a member of the American Philosophical Society in April 1797 (DAB; APS, *Proceedings*, 22, pt. 3 [1884], 238, 256, 365, 473; Heckewelder to Peter S. Du Ponceau, 21 Mch. 1819, in PPAmP).

From George Jefferson

DEAR SIR, Richmond April 11th. 1798.

The sloop Sally Capt. Potter did not arrive until yesterday—which was occasioned chiefly by a considerable fresh in the river which met him at Osburnes, where he was detained in consequence of it about a week. he called though I understand at Norfolk. The harpsichord & box of plants are forwarded to Milton by a boat as you directed.

I have at length sent the two barrels of wheat for Sir John Sinclair to Messrs. Gilliat & Taylor, our Correspondents in Norfolk, with a request that they will forward it by the very first two Vessels sailing for London. I did not forget to desire them to prevail on the Captains to take it in their Cabins—and to inform them of the reason. I will forward you bills of lading immediately on receiving them, and which I desired G & T. to send me as soon as possible—enclosing copies under blank covers to Sir J.S.

I have so long delayed executing this business for you, that I think it necessary to inform you of the reasons. I have been endeavouring all in my power ever since you first wrote to me upon the subject to get wheat of *the very first* quality; having spoken to all the millers in Town, and written to several in the Country, to procure me some—all of whom promised to do so. I have waited thus long in expectation of getting some in this way—but finding myself disappointed, & learning from many that the very best is not to be had at this season of the year, as those who cultivate it, generally send it to market early, knowing it is more liable to sustain injury by keeping than the common wheat—I concluded to send some which I got soon after the receipt of your first letter respecting it; and which I reserved least I should not be able to procure better. The only objection to it is, that the grain is rather small. I cleaned it very well though, having run it through a fan several times, by which as many of the small grains were got out as possible. it is a clear flinty grain, & weighed 64 ld. 14 ozs. which is within two ounces of being as heavy as any, of which I have heard. it has the further advantage of having been tried—as I planted 43 grains of it, 42 of which came up.

I am now sorry that I delayed sending it so long—as I fear it may not keep so well now that the warm weather is approaching—and likewise that it may have given you some uneasiness.

I certainly would not have put it off until this, had I foreseen how long it would have been. but I calculated confidently, from time to time upon getting some which was better. several persons at the distance of 20 or 30 miles having informed me that their neighbours had some which was *fine*, and promised to get them to send it—but as often disappointed me.

I am very respectfully, & most sincerely, Dear Sir Your friend & servt.   GEO. JEFFERSON

We have received two more Hhds: of your Tobacco—the ten weigh 16447 ld.

RC (MHi); addressed: "Thomas Jefferson esquire Philadelphia"; franked and postmarked; endorsed by TJ as received 17 Apr. 1798 and so recorded in SJL.

YOU FIRST WROTE TO ME ON THE SUBJECT: TJ to George Jefferson, 14 Feb.

To Peter Carr

TH:J. TO P. CARR.   Philadelphia Apr. 12. 98.

As the instructions to our envoys & their communications have excited a great deal of curiosity, I inclose you a copy. you will percieve that they have been assailed by swindlers whether with or without the participation of Taleyrand is not very apparent. the known corruption of his character renders it very possible he may have intended to share largely in the 50,000 £. demanded. but that the Directory knew any thing of it is neither proved nor probable. on the contrary, when the Portuguese ambassador yeilded to like attempts of swindlers, the conduct of the Directory in imprisoning him for an attempt at corruption, as well as their general conduct really magnanimous places them above suspicion. it is pretty evident that mr A's speech is in truth the only obstacle to negociation. that humiliating disavowals of that are demanded as a preliminary, or as a commutation for that a heavy sum of money, about a million sterling. this obstacle removed, they seem not to object to an arrangement of all differences and even to settle & acknolege themselves debtors for spoliations. nor does it seem that negociation is at an end, as the P's message says, but that it is in it's commencement only. the instructions comply with the wishes expressed in debate in the May session to place France on as good a footing as England, & not to make a sine qua non of the indemnification for spoliations. but they declare the war in which France is engaged is not a defensive one, they reject the[1] naturalization of French ships, that is to say the exchange of naturalization which France had formerly proposed to us, & which would lay open to us the unrestrained trade of her West Indies & all her other possessions, they declare the 10th. article of the British treaty, against sequestering debts, money in the funds bank stock &c to be founded in morality & therefore of perpetual obligation, & some other heterodoxies.

You will have seen in the newspapers some resolutions proposed by mr Sprigg, the first of which was that it is inexpedient under existing circumstances to resort to war with France. whether this could have been carried before is doubtful. but since it is known that a sum of money has been demanded, it is thought that this resolution, were it now to be passed, would imply a willingness to avoid war even by purchasing peace. it is therefore postponed. the peace party will agree to all reasonable measures of internal defence, but oppose all external preparations. tho' it is evident that these communications do not present one motive the more for going to war, yet it may be doubted whether we are now strong enough to keep within the defensive line. it is thought the expences contemplated will render a land tax necessary before we separate. if so, it will lengthen the session. the first impressions from these communications are disagreeable; but their ultimate effect on the public mind will not be favorable to the war party. they may have some effect in the first moment in stopping the movement in the Eastern states, which were on the creen, & were running into town meetings, yet it is believed this will be momentary only, and will be over before their elections. considerable expectations were formed of changes in the Eastern delegations favorable to the Whig interest. present my best respects to mrs Carr, & accept yourself assurances of affectionate esteem.

RC (MdAN); PrC (DLC). Enclosure: *Message of the President . . . April 3d, 1798* (see TJ to John Wayles Eppes, 11 Apr.)

For the DEBATE in the House of Representatives TO PLACE FRANCE ON AS GOOD A

FOOTING AS ENGLAND, see note to TJ to Madison, 18 May 1797.

SJL records a letter from TJ to Carr of 6 Nov. 1797 which has not been found.

[1] TJ here canceled "idea."

To James Madison

Philadelphia Apr. 12. 98.

I wrote you two letters on the 5th.[1] inst. since which I have recd yours of the 2d. I send you, in a separate package, the instructions to our envoys & their communications. you will find that my representation of their contents, from memory, was substantially just. the public mind appears still in a state of astonishment. there never was a moment in which the aid of an able pen was so important to place things in their just attitude. on this depends the inchoate movement in the Eastern mind, and the fate of the elections in that quarter, now beginning & to continue through the summer. I would not propose to you such a task on any ordinary occasion. but be assured that a well digested analysis of these papers would now decide the future turn of things which are at this moment on the creen. the merchants here are meeting under the auspices of Fitzsimmons to address the President & approve his operations. nothing will be spared on that side.—Sprigg's first resolution against the expediency of war, proper at the time it was moved, is now postponed, as improper, because to declare that, after we have understood it has been proposed to us to buy a peace, would imply an acquiescence under that proposition. all therefore which the advocates of peace can now attempt is to prevent war-measures *externally*, consenting to every rational measure of *internal* defence & preparation. great expences will be incurred; & it will be left to those whose measures render them necessary to provide to meet them. they already talk of stopping all paiments of interest, & of a land tax. these will probably not be opposed. the only question will be how to modify the land-tax. on this there may be great diversity of sentiment. one party will want to make it a new source of patronage & expence. if this business is taken up it will lengthen our session. we had pretty generally, till now, fixed on the beginning of May for adjournment. I shall return by my usual route, &

not by the Eastern shore, on account of the advance of the season. friendly salutations to mrs Madison & yourself. Adieu.

RC (DLC: Madison Papers); at foot of text: "Mr. Madison." PrC (DLC).

¹ In PrC TJ here interlined in ink at a later date "& 6th."

TJ wrote Madison TWO LETTERS, one on 5 Apr. and the other on 6 Apr.

To Thomas Mann Randolph

TH:J. TO TMR.   Philadelphia Apr. 12. 98.
I have still to acknolege your favors of Mar. 19. & 26. my last to you was of Mar. 29. I have recieved a letter from Arnold dated Apr. 1. in which he promises to set out for Monticello immediately after Easter: I suppose therefore about the 9th. and that he will be there before you recieve this. I inclose a memorandum for him, and propose that John Hemings shall work with him for the present. I would wish you to consider, on a view of Davy & Abram's employment, whether it would be better to continue Lewis with them, or place him also with Arnold. there is one article I must trouble you with. to wit, to endeavor to get Davenport to engage some sawyers express and to provide flooring plank for me according to the bill I now inclose. this is very essential to me. you will judge whether Bates or any other person might be engaged of preference to do this. much depends on their opportunity of getting good pine. I am in hopes Davenport is going on steadily, and that I shall find myself under cover on my arrival at home. I have a very fine housejoiner engaged here (@ 40. £ Virga. money) to go on with me to live. there will long be work enough for him & Arnold both.

I inclose you the instructions to our envoys & their communications. the tory party here were so much enchanted with a little scrap of slander against the whigs which was insinuated arguendo by the swindlers into whose hands our envoys appear to have fallen, that they published the whole pieces; not considering that while the first impressions of disgust at the corruption which probably attaches to Taleyrand (of most noted ill-fame) but not at all to the Directory, are momentary, the last & lasting impression will be that mr Adams's speech in May is the only obstacle to a friendly arrangement with France, and that if our pride revolts at¹ a disavowal of that, a heavy sum, as a commutation (a million sterling) is demanded: still also it is certain that these communications do not offer one motive the more for our going to war. they seem however to render mr Sprigg's 1st. resolution improper. because however wise it was to express an opinion against the inexpediency of war before, were it to be done after insinuations that we are expected to buy a peace, a resolution against war might now imply an acquiescence in that insinuation. the resolution therefore is postponed. the whig-party are willing to indulge the war-gentry with every reasonable measure of internal defence & preparation, but will oppose every thing external. but I fear they are not strong enough to hold this line. if other expences are incurred, it is admitted a land-tax must be laid. should this be done it will lengthen the session. if we could but pass over this session without thrusting ourselves into the war, it will be over before another. this is foreseen by some, and is the reason of their driving headlong into it now. they consider it as the only means of allying us with Gr. Britain & separating us from France. if we could stop where we are, we are on the most desireable ground, that of a separation (in politics) from every nation.

I wrote to Martha the last week. my tender love to her & the children & affectionate salutations to yourself.

---

300. square feet of flooring plank in cuts 31.f. long.

475. do.	do.	28.f.
1500. do.	do.	24.f.
1900. do.	do.	16.f.
450. do.	do.	14.f.
1300. do.	do.	12.f.
300. do.	do.	10.f.

to be got in flitches between the heart & sap, clear of both & of knots, and to be kiln-dried.

RC (DLC); addressed: "Thomas M. Randolph near Milton"; franked. PrC (MHi); endorsed by TJ in ink on verso. Enclosure: *Message of the President . . . April 3d, 1798* (see TJ to John Wayles Eppes, 11 Apr.). Second enclosure printed below.

Randolph's letter OF MAR. 19, recorded in SJL as received 31 Mch., has not been found. For his missive of 26 Mch., see TJ to Martha Jefferson Randolph, 5 Apr. The 1 Apr. LETTER FROM Samuel ARNOLD, which according to SJL was received by TJ on 10 Apr., has not been found. SJL records 11 other letters exchanged by TJ and Arnold, the first from Arnold to TJ on 24 Mch. 1797 from "N. Kent C.H." and the last from TJ to him, 9 July 1798, all of which are missing. No evidence of Arnold's employment at Monticello has been found.

TJ WROTE TO MARTHA on 5 Apr. 1798.

[1] Preceding two words interlined in place of "refuses."

Memorandum for Samuel Arnold

Memorandum for mr Arnold.

I left with old George written directions about the accomodation of mr Arnold. I also pointed out to him the place where I left written directions for his employment. I think it was on the top of the glass clock-case in the parlour.

I would have mr Arnold first prepare the architraves mentioned in those instructions, for the Alcoves & doors of all the rooms; because that will enable us to close them & make them inhabitable. then he may go on with the other work in the order mentioned in that paper, except the doors which are to be the last thing done.

John Hemings may work with him till I come home; and I think had better be employed in dressing the flooring plank got from Calvert and such other of the plank as will do tolerably for flooring. particularly some short plank sawed by Haden's people, which will do well to floor the alcoves, as they must be first floored.

No work is to be put up till I come home.   TH: JEFFERSON
                                                         Apr. 12. 98.

RC (DLC); endorsed by Randolph.

CALVERT: probably Benjamin Colvard,

Jr., who had worked at Monticello as an apprentice carpenter twenty years earlier (MB, 1:447).

Notes on British Instructions and on Clement Humphreys

Apr. 13. new instructions of the British govmt to their armed ships now appear which clearly infringe their treaty with us, by authorising them to take our vessels carrying produce of the French colonies from those colonies to Europe, & to *take* vessels bound to a blockaded port.[1] see them in Brown's paper of Apr. 18. in due form.

The Presidt. has sent a govmt brig to France, probably to carry dispatches. he has chosen as the bearer of these one Humphreys, the son of a ship carpenter, ignorant[2] under age, not speaking a word of French, most abusive of that nation[3] whose only merit is the having mobbed & beaten Bache on board the frigate built here, for which he was indicted & punished by fine.

MS (DLC: TJ Papers, 102:17525); entirely in TJ's hand; on same sheet as Notes on Senators' Comments about House Impeachment Committee, 12 Mch. 1798; with an addition by TJ at a later sitting.

The Duke of Portland signed the IN-

STRUCTIONS of 25 Jan. 1798 to the commanders of British SHIPS of war and privateers (*Philadelphia Gazette*, 18 Apr. 1798). Clement HUMPHREYS was selected to carry a letter to the envoys at Paris aboard the U.S. brig *Sophia* (Instructions from Timothy Pickering to Humphreys, 29 Mch. 1798, in

MHi: Pickering Papers; Pickering to Hamilton, 25 Mch. 1798, in Syrett, *Hamilton*, 21:378-9). For information on Humphreys's attack on BACHE ON BOARD THE FRIGATE *United States*, for which he received a $50 FINE, see Tagg, *Bache*, 328.

[1] Following sentence probably added by TJ at a later sitting.
[2] Word interlined.
[3] Preceding eleven words interlined.

From Tadeusz Kosciuszko

DEAR SIR   [14 Apr. 1798]

I lost the passage to Lisbon and I afraid of this to Bordeau. and when you will go to Virginia my hopes are at an end. it may perhaps be found one going to Lisbon. do not forget that i am under your protection. and you only my resource in this Country. your Humble and Obedient Servant.   T: KOSCIUSZKO

RC (NNPM); undated; endorsed by TJ as received 14 Apr. 1798 and so recorded in SJL.

From James Monroe

DEAR SIR   Alb: 14. April 1798.

I have yours of the 5 inst. The seal had no mark of violence on it. I shall attend to it for the future having no confidence in the admn., in any respect. The royalists are at a point wh. perplexes them & of course they will play a desperate game. Yet I hope the people will take alarm at their projects & forsake them, in wh. case their fall is inevitable, but this requires temper as well as firmness in the republicans to turn the crisis to good acct. in favor of republican govt. These virtues I think will be displayed by the members of that party. Their attacks on you will not injure you. They impose the necessity of great caution agst casualties & false friends, but this you will have.

The affr. with M. I hope is settled as it shod. be. It is indeed afflicting to be troubled with such an incident—but it only remains to settle it in the best possible manner & there let it rest. I commit whatever appertains to me to yourself & one or two others, to act on the spot as may be deemed eligible, & will by advice here take [an]y step on my own part that you think prop[er. The] affr. of Skipwith will of course rest for a year if necessary, and when brot. forward it will be as you propose.

With respect to our countrymen's privateering in France, I wish to know how I wd. prevent it had I known it. It will not I presume be intimated that I was a party. The truth is I discountinanc'd it all in my power, having objected to have Mr. Vans of Massachusetts recognized as Consul upon an intimation that he was engaged in that business, as he will depose. But he is in France. I know not upon what ground they will calumniate me till I see it. I despise them & their calumnies more than I can express, & hope that justice will sooner or later overtake them. Yr. friend.

RC (DLC); mutilated; endorsed by TJ as received 24 Apr. 1798 and so recorded in SJL.

m.: William White Morris.

From Bishop James Madison

DEAR SIR   Apl. 15th. 1798 Wmsburg

I have endeavoured to understand the Directions of the Gentleman, & would have been happy to have made such Experiments as he wished; but, before this can be done, he must express himself more clearly. At present, I am entirely at a Loss for his Meaning. Indeed, from some Expressions, I suspect he confounds the Compass with the Dipping Needle. Has he a clear Idea of the latter Instrument?—I can only add, that he may be assured, in every well constructed Dipping Needle, the Inclination, that is the Angle which the North End makes with the Horizon, will be the same, in all Cases, provided the Plane of the Instrument be in the Magnetic Meridian, except when the North End is turned South, & elevated nearly or exactly to the Magnetic *Line*.

I have inclosed a few Experiments in a particular Phœnomenon in Magnetism. I beg you to exercise the most rigorous Judgment upon them, & to throw them aside, should you think them unworthy of Notice,—

I am Dr Sir, very respectfully & sincerely—Yr Friend & Sert

J MADISON

RC (DLC); endorsed by TJ as received 24 Apr. 1798 and so recorded in SJL. Enclosure: MS, not found, of "Experiments upon Magnetism," a report taking the form of a letter from Bishop Madison to TJ, dated April 1798, describing three experiments in which Madison covered magnets with water and observed the movements of iron filings on the water's surface in an effort to understand better the means by which magnets exert their force; presented to the American Philosophical Society at a meeting of 4 May and referred to Thomas C. James, one of the society's secretaries; reported worthy of publication on 1 June and printed the following year (APS, *Transactions*, 4 [1799], 323-8; APS, *Proceedings*, 22, pt. 3 [1884], 270, 272).

DIRECTIONS OF THE GENTLEMAN: see TJ to Bishop Madison, 1 Apr. 1798.

From James Madison

My last answered yours of the 21. since which I recd. on friday last your three favors of the 29 Ult. of Apl. 5 & 6. I have no reason to suspect that any of your letters have miscarried, or been opened by the way. I am less able to say whether mine have all reached you, as I have generally written them in haste, & neglected to keep a note of their dates. I will thank you to mention in your acknowledgment of this, whether you recd. one from me inclosing a letter to F. A. Muhlenburg, & whether he certainly recd. it. It related to a case of humanity & required an answer which has never come to hand.

The effect of the P.s speech in F. is less to be wondered at, than the speech itself with other follies of a like tendency is to be deplored. Still the mode & degree of re[si]sting them is rather meeting folly with folly, than consulting the true dignity & interest which ought to prescribe[1] in such cases. The conduct of Taleyrand is so extraordinary as to be scarcely credible. I do not allude to its depravity, which however heinous, is not without examples. Its unparallelled stupidity is what fills one with astonishment. Is it possible that a man of sagacity as he is admitted to be, who has lived long eno' in this Country to understand the nature of our Govt. who could not be unaware of the impossibility of secresy & the improbability of success in pursuing his propositions thro' the necessary forms, who must have suspected the Ex. rather of a wish to seize pretexts for widening the breach between the two Republics, than to make use of any means however objectionable to reconcile their differences; who must have been equally suspicious of the probable inclination of some one or other of the Envoys—is it possible, that such a man under such circumstances, could have committed both his character & safety, by such a proposition? If the evidence be not perfectly conclusive, of which I cannot judge, the decision ought to be agst. the evidence, rather than on the side of the infatuation. It is easy to foresee however the zeal & plausibility with which this part of the despatches will be inculcated, not only for the general purpose of enforcing the war measures of the Ex. but for the particular purpose of diverting the public attention from the other more important part, which shews the speech & conduct of the P. to be now the great obstacle to accomodation. This interesting fact must nevertheless, finally take possession of thinking minds; and strengthen the suspicion, that whilst the Ex. were pursuing ostensible plans of reconciliation, and giving instructions which might wear that tendency, the success of them was indirectly counterworked by every irritation & disgust for which opportunities could be found in official speeches & messages, answers to private addresses harangues in Congress[2] and the vilest insults & calumnies of Newspapers under the patronage of the Government. The readyness with which the papers were communicated, & the quarter proposing the call for them, would be entitled to praise, if a mass of other circumstances did not force a belief that the view in both, was more to inflame than to inform the public mind. It is not improbable that the influence of the first impressions in checking the rising spirit in N. England, and bearing up the party of Jay in N.Y. whose re-election is brought into danger by the pestilent consequences experienced from his Treaty, had considerable share in the motive. The negative declaration proposed by Mr. S. is liable to so many specious objections that I shall be surprized if a willing majority does not take advantage of them. In ordinary cases, the mode of proceeding is certainly ineligible. But it seems equally obvious that cases may arise, for which that is the proper one: Three of these occur, where there does not appear any room to doubt on the subject. 1. where nothing less than a declaration of pacific intentions from the department entrusted with the power of war, will quiet the apprehensions of the constituent body, or remove an uncertainty which subjects one part of them, to the speculating arts of another. 2. where it may be a necessary antidote to the hostile measures or language of the Ex Departmt. If war Sentiments be delivered in a speech to Congress which admits of a direct answer, & the sentiments of Congress be against war, it is not doubted that the counter sentiments might & ought to be expressed in the answer. Where an extra message delivers like sentiments, and custom does not permit a like explanation of the sentiments of the Legislative,[3] there does not appear any equivalent mode of making it, except that of an abstract vote. 3. Where public measures or appearances, may mislead another nation into distrust of the real object of them, the error ought to be corrected; and in our Govt. where the question of war or peace lies with Congress, a satisfactory explanation cannot issue from any other Department. In Govts. where the power of deciding on war is an Ex. prerogative it is not unusual for Explanations of this kind to be given either on the demands of foreign Nations, or in order to prevent their improper suspicions. Should a demand of this sort be at any time made on our Govt. the answer must proceed[4] from the War prerogative, that is from Congs—and if an answer could be given, on demand, a declaration without a demand, may certainly be made with equal propriety, if there be equal occasion for it.—The discovery of Mr. A's dislike to the City of Washington will cause strong emotions. What sort of conscience is that which feels an obligation on the Govt. to remove thither, and a liberty to quit it the next day? The objection to the magnificence of the President's House belongs to a man of very different principles from those of Mr. A. The increase of expence therefore without a probable increase of Salary in proportion, must be the real ground of objection.—I have looked over the two papers which you consider as so threatening in their tendency. They do not, I own, appear to me exactly in the same light; nor am I by any means satisfied that they are from the pen you ascribe them to. If they are, there has certainly been a disguise aimed at in many features of the stile. I differ still more from you as to the source from which an antidote, if necessary, ought to come. But waving every thing of that sort, there is really a crowd & weight of *indispensable* occupations, on my time, which it would be very tedious to explain, but wch. I pledge myself, will justify me in leaving such tasks to others, not only commanding more time for them, but in every respect more favorably situated for executing them with advantage & effect. And it is with no small pleasure I observe that some pens are employed which promise the public all the lights with respect to their affairs, which can be conveyed to them thro' the channels of the press.

It is now become certain that not half crops of wheat can be made. Many will not get back more than their seed, & some not even that. We have lately had a severe spell of N.E. rain, which in this neighbourhood swept off at least 15 PrCt. of the Catch; and from accts. in different directions it appears to have been equally fatal. We are at present in the midst of a cold N.W. spell, which menaces the fruit. The tops of the Blue Mountains are tinged with snow, & the Thermr. this morning was at 31°. It does not appear however that the mischief is yet done. The coming night, if no sudden change takes place, must I think be fatal.

If Mr. Bailey has not yet taken up his note, Be so good as to have the inclosed forwarded to him.

RC (DLC: Madison Papers); endorsed by TJ as received from Orange 24 Apr. 1798 and so recorded in SJL. For later emendations, see note 4 below and Madison, *Papers*, 17:112-15. Enclosure not found.

It is not clear when Madison sent TJ the enclosure to Frederick MUHLENBURG.

MR. S.: Richard Sprigg, Jr. For the TWO PAPERS by "Marcellus" that TJ believed were written by Hamilton, see TJ to Madison, 5 Apr. 1798.

On 24 June 1798 TJ noted in his financial records that he had assigned Madison's

order on Theodorus BAILEY for $250 to John Barnes. The money was "to be applied to the credit of James Monroe in part of the quarter's interest he recd. on loan" from William Short. The money was to be charged to TJ's account with Short (MB, 2:986).

[1] Madison here canceled "the conduct of [ministers?]."

[2] Preceding three words interlined.

[3] Preceding seven words interlined in place of "answer."

[4] At a later date Madison here interlined "if thro' an Executive function."

From William Short

Jefferson. April. 15—by Ml.—my letter concise—have little time,—the bearer goes to morrow—had thoughts for some time to go with him on acct. of his safe conduct—my health—wish it to be better established for so long a voyage—press the 9. M. dollars—to employ my disponible cash in a productive fund—Indian camp to be tenanted out if practicable—send him the prospectus of the stereotype—

FC (DLC: Short Papers); entirely in Short's hand; part of an epistolary record of his letters to TJ and others from 26 Dec. 1797 to 9 Oct. 1798; recorded in SJL as received from Paris 22 June 1798. Enclosure: "Prospectus" of the Didots and Herhan (see Short to TJ, 27 Feb. 1798), announcing that they have joined together to produce editions under a new patent for the stereotype process that allows them to offer, in addition to printed books, sets of plates ready for printing, each set capable of producing at least 150,000 copies with replacement plates of individual pages available on demand, the partners expecting to produce about 100 volumes a year beginning with Virgil (DLC: TJ Papers, 236:42347-8; in French, undated, consisting of four printed pages; at head of text: "Éditions Stéréotypes"; bearing stamp of the French Republic; endorsed by TJ: "Printing").

ML.: John Marshall; see Short to TJ, 6 Aug. 1798.

On 3 Apr. TJ sent an order to the comptroller of the U.S. authorizing John Barnes to collect all dividends payable 1 Apr. on Short's U.S. bonds (RC in MoSW; at foot of text: "John Steele esq. comptroller of the US."; endorsed by Steele).

To John Beckley

DEAR SIR   April 16. 98.

It is with sincere concern that I learn your situation and find myself so unable to relieve it. I have not at this moment more than 50. dollars in the world at my command, and these are my only resource for a considerable time to come. I have been in the habit of keeping myself in a situation just to meet ordinary occurrences, & have been thrown behind by the necessities of two persons whom I could not avoid helping. having had very little to do with banks, I do not know whether my name would be taken at any of them for any thing. but if it would, and you can make it answer your purpose, I will endorse any paper which may enable you to relieve yourself. I am deeply afflicted at having nothing better to offer being sincerely Dear Sir

Your friend & servt   TH: JEFFERSON

PrC (MHi); at foot of text: "Mr. Beckley."

For Beckley's financial SITUATION at this time, see Berkeley, Beckley, 173-7. NECESSITIES OF TWO PERSONS: TJ may be referring to his aid to James T. Callender and to his nephew Charles L. Lewis, who was in

Philadelphia seeking employment (TJ to George Jefferson, 14 Mch.; Callender to TJ, 21 Mch.; MB, 2:980, 981).

A letter from Beckley to TJ of 16 Apr., which according to SJL TJ received the same day, has not been found.

To John Beckley

DEAR SIR   Philadelphia April 17th. 1798.

You mention that Colo. John Trigg will accomodate you with the sum of three hundred & forty dollars or part of it on an assurance that it shall be replaced to him in Richmond or Lynchburg within two or three months from this time. I will undertake to have it replaced to him the first week in July in Richmond, if that will suit him, for which this letter shall be my obligation. I sincerely wish that this may answer both his & your accomodation, being with esteem Dear Sir

Your friend & servt   TH: JEFFERSON

PrC (MHi); at foot of text: "Mr. Beckley."

YOU MENTION: SJL records a letter from Beckley to TJ of 17 Apr. 1798, that TJ received the same day, which has not been found. Serving as a security for Beckley, TJ gave JOHN TRIGG, congressman from Bedford County, Virginia, a note for $240 on 17 May, payable at Lynchburg on 7 July (MB, 2:983, 986, 988).

To John Beckley

DEAR SIR   Philadelphia Apr. 17. 1798.

If Colo. Trigg will be so good as to furnish you the two hundred & forty dollars, I will undertake that it shall be repaid to him at Lynchburg the first week of July in such way as shall be satisfactory to him; on which subject I will confer with him for explanation, and conform myself to his wish. I will call on him the first moment in my power, or be glad to see him at my lodgings if he should have a moment to spare before I have. I am with esteem Dear Sir

Your friend & servt   TH: JEFFERSON

PrC (MHi); at foot of text: "Mr. Beckley"; endorsed in ink by TJ on verso.

To James Madison

I wrote you last on the 12th. & then acknoleged your last at hand of the 2d inst. the sensations first occasioned by the late publications have been kept up and increased at this place. a petition[1] from the merchants & traders & others was so industriously pushed as to have obtained a very extensive signature. the same measure is pursuing in New York. as the election of their governor comes on next Tuesday, these impressions will just be in time to affect that. we have no information yet of their effect to the Eastward. in the mean time petitions to Congress against arming from the towns of Massachusetts were multiplying. they will no doubt have been immediately checked. the P's answer to the address of the merchants here you will see in Fenno of yesterday. it is a pretty strong declaration that a neutral & pacific conduct on our part is no longer the existing state of things. the vibraters in the H. of R. have chiefly gone over to the war party. still if our members were all here, it is believed the naval-bill would be thrown out. Giles, Clopton & Cabell are gone. the debate commenced yesterday, & tho' the question will be lost, the effect on the public mind will be victory. for certainly there is nothing new which may render war more palatable to the people. on the contrary the war-members themselves are becoming alarmed at the expences, & whittling down the estimates to the lowest sums. you will see by a report of the Secretary at war which I inclose you that he estimates the expences of preparation at seven[2] millions of Dollars; which it is proposed to lower to about 3. millions. if it can be reduced to this, a stoppage of public interest will suffice & is the project of some. this idea has already knocked down the public paper, which can no longer be sold at all. if the expences should exceed 3. M. they will undertake a land tax. indeed a land tax is the decided resource of many, perhaps of a majority. there is an idea of some of the Connecticut members to raise the whole money wanted by a tax on salt; so much do they dread a land tax. the middle or last of May is still counted on for adjournment.

Colo. Innes is just arrived here, heavily laden with gout & dropsy. it is scarcely thought he can ever get home again. the principles likely to be adopted by that board have thrown the administration into deep alarm. it is admitted they will be worse than the English, French & Algerine depredations added together. it is even suggested that, if persevered in, their proceedings will be stopped. these things are not public.—your letter, by occasioning my recurrence to the constitution, has corrected an error under which a former one of mine had been written. I had erroneously concieved that the declaration of war was among the things confided by the constitution to *two thirds* of the legislature. we are told here that you are probably elected to the state legislature. it has given great joy, as we know your presence will be felt any where, and the times do not admit of the inactivity of such talents as yours. I hope therefore it is true, as much good may be done by a proper direction of the local force. present my friendly salutations to mrs Madison & to yourself affectionately Adieu.

RC (DLC: Madison Papers); addressed: "James Madison junr. near Orange courthouse"; franked. PrC (DLC). Enclosure: *Letter from the Secretary at War, to the Chairman of the Committee, on so much of the President's Speech as Relates to the Protection of Commerce, and the Defence of the Country . . . 11th April, 1798, Committed to the Committee of the whole House, on the State of the Union* [Philadelphia, 1798], consisting of a letter from James McHenry to Samuel Sewall, 9 Apr. 1798, with an enclosure describing and estimating the cost of specific measures necessary for the protection of American trade and territory, including 20 vessels (2 of 22 guns, 8 of 20 guns, and 10 of 16 guns), 6 galleys, and an addition to the military establishment of one regiment each of infantry, artillery, and cavalry, with emergency powers given to the president to raise a provisional army of 20,000 men, if necessary, plus monies for additional fortifications for ports and a supply of cannons and other military stores (see Evans, No. 34888). Enclosed in following document.

At noon on 17 Apr. Philadelphia MER-CHANTS, underwriters, and TRADERS presented an address to President Adams,

signed by about 500, pledging firm support for measures that would protect "our rights as an independent people" in the crisis with France. Adams's ANSWER declared that no enemy of the United States had the power to injure the country's commerce "if protected by its own efforts, with such aids as are in the power of the government to afford." He indicated that if France had been willing to negotiate, the United States would have continued to pursue a "neutral, impartial, and pacific course," but citing that country's "spirit of hostility" Adams asserted that there were seasons when "tranquility may be fatal" (*Gazette of the United States,* 18 Apr. 1798).

For the death in August of James INNES, a member of the commission established under the Jay Treaty to settle prewar claims of British merchants, see TJ to Madison, 16 Jan. 1799. Madison was not ELECTED TO THE STATE LEGISLATURE until 1799 (Leonard, *General Assembly,* 213, 217).

[1] Preceding two words interlined in place of "an address."
[2] TJ wrote the preceding word over a partially erased, illegible word and canceled "or eight."

To James Madison

P.M.   [19 April 1798]
the inclosed was sealed before I recollected that I have mentioned a *petition* instead of *an address* to the President, which is to be corrected. a nomination of Govr. Secretary & three judges to the Missisipi territory is sent in to the Senate, four of whom are agents, or interested in the land speculations of that country, two of them bankrupt speculators, & the 5th. unknown. the Senate demur, and are going into an enquiry. the

nomination is George Matthews governor, Millar of Connecticut Secretary, Wetmore of Mass. Clarke of the Missis district (a merchant who
married a daur of Adam Hoops) and Tilton of New Hampshire judges.

RC (DLC: Madison Papers, Rives Collection); undated; addressed: "James Madison junr. near Orange court house";
franked. PrC (DLC). Enclosure: see preceding document.

President Adams sent his nominations
for officers of the Mississippi Territory TO
THE SENATE on 18 Apr. and the following
day they were referred to a committee for
consideration. On 2 May Adams withdrew
them and submitted a new slate with only

Daniel TILTON appearing on both lists. On 7
May, after several days of debate, Winthrop
Sargent was confirmed as governor by an 11
to 10 vote. The appointments of John Steele
as secretary, and Peter Bryan Bruin and Tilton as judges, were also approved that day.
On 26 June Adams completed the appointments by nominating William McGuire of
Virginia to serve as chief justice of the territory. The Senate approved the appointment
two days later (JEP, 1:269-74, 282).

To James Monroe

April 19. 98.

I wrote you on the 5th. inst. and on the 12th. I inclosed you a copy of
the instructions & communications from our envoys. in that of the 5th.
I acknoleged the receipt of your last at hand of Mar. 26. the impressions
first made by those communications continue strong & prejudicial here.
they have enabled the merchants to get a war-petition very extensively
signed. they have also carried over to the war-party most of the waverers
in the H. of R. this circumstance with the departure of 4. Southern
members, & others going, have given a strong majority to the other
party. the expences will probably bring them up: but in the mean time
great & dangerous follies will have been committed. a salt-tax, land tax,
& stoppage of interest on the public debt are the resources spoken of for
procuring from 3. to 7. millions of Dollars of preparatory expence. I
think it probable that France, instead of declaring war, will worry us
with decrees. a new one is proposed making neutral *armed* ships good
prize. such measures, and the bottom of our purse which we shall get to
even by the expences of preparation, may still prevent serious war.
bankruptcy is a terrible foundation to begin a war on, against the con-
querors of the universe. a governor, secretary & 3. judges are named for
the Missisipi territory. of these, two are agents for the land companies,
2 are bankrupt speculators, & the other unknown.—Your matter with
Morris is well settled. with respect to your accounts mr Dawson will
inclose you the difficulties objected by the Department of state. considering how much better items of an account can be explained vivâ voce,
how much more impressive personal remonstrance is than written, we

have imagined you will think it adviseable to come on yourself, and have these matters settled, or at least to narrow them down to a few articles as to which you may take measures from hence to procure vouchers from Europe if necessary. but of this you alone are the competent judge. present my affectionate salutations to mrs Monroe. friendly Adieux to yourself.

P.S. wheat & flour not saleable at this moment. tobacco (old) 13.50 D & likely to rise.

RC (DLC: Monroe Papers); addressed: "James Monroe near Charlottesville"; franked and postmarked; endorsed by Monroe. PrC (DLC).

No letter written by TJ to Monroe ON THE 12TH. has been found or is recorded in SJL. For the INSTRUCTIONS & COMMUNICATIONS TJ sent on that day, see his letter to John Wayles Eppes of 11 Apr.

MAKING NEUTRAL ARMED SHIPS GOOD PRIZE: American newspapers carried an un-substantiated report of a motion in the Council of Five Hundred of France "for the condemnation of all neutral vessels found with arms on board" (Philadelphia *Aurora*, 17 Apr. 1798). John DAWSON had been in communication with Timothy Pickering to identify those portions of Monroe's accounts with the DEPARTMENT OF STATE still in need of resolution (Pickering to Dawson, 13 Apr. 1798, in DLC: Monroe Papers; Ammon, *Monroe*, 162).

To Thomas Mann Randolph

TH:J. TO TMR.   Philadelphia Apr. 19. 98.

I wrote you last on the 12th. inst. two days after which I recieved yours of the 2d. from it's frequently happening that instead of arriving on Tuesday (as all letters do by the Fredericksburg post) your's arrive on Saturday, the day the Richmond letters come here, I presume they come by the way of Richmond. if they arrived on Tuesday, they would be acknoleged in my letters of Thursday, which is the day for writing hence to our neighborhood. I am in hopes the establishment of a post office at Milton will enable you to put your letters in in time for the Fredericsburg post, & gain a week in the date of the answer. a letter from George Jefferson of the 11th. informs me he had that day forwarded the harpsichord & box of plants by the Milton boats. I am in hopes therefore they are by this time planted at Monticello. since that I have forwarded by another opportunity (under the superintendance of C. L. Lewis who went passenger to Richmond in the same vessel) a Windsor sopha with a mattras, which I hope will get up safe. Clarke writes me he had forwarded my bacon &c to Columbia & written to you on the subject. his tobo. is all at Richmond where I hope George's will soon join it. I entirely approve your measure of breaking up Phill's cart & putting his mules to the plough. perhaps this may give me time to buy mules either at Georgetown or Richmond, which would be far preferable to horses at any price, but especially at such prices as they seem to have risen to. on the subject of Darlington, I have always ascribed his dullness, stumbling & weakness to sickness, and been confident that if his health becomes firm he will be highly valuable to me. and I trust that the long rest he has had will give him time to recover. though continuing mine he might still serve you the half of the year that I am from home: for I would rather you should keep & use him for your own riding in the neighborhood than leave him at Monticello. he must now be as well as rest can make him. I wish you therefore to take him till wanting for my journey.   I have got for you Bell's abridgment, the Edinburgh Dispensatory and the Ivory book: but there is no chance of getting the Genera of Linnaeus. I hope mr Davenport is going on with spirit. Richardson is here under inoculation: he is now in the fever, and so far doing well. his anxiety to learn the art of plaistering induces him to wish to pass as much of the summer here as possible. he was employed in cutting stone till lately, & will return here in the winter to perfect himself in that business. he wishes to send mr Duke a brick from this place as a model, & proof how much too careless our workmen are in making theirs.

I inclosed you the last week the instructions & communications of our ministers. their effect on the popular mind is artificaly increased & kept up here by the merchants & satellites of the administration. probably the same may be done in other large mercantile towns. but in the country we learn that it has no effect towards rendering war more palateable to the farmer. it will probably lessen the respect which many had entertained for the French government, who will not analyse and see that the government is really not implicated in the corrupt part of the business. we do expect also they will check the career of the Eastern sentiment which was rapidly getting into a direction very different from what it has been. however that will get to rights unless the Executive should be able to plunge us into war irrecoverably during the momentary operation & first impressions from these papers. a circumstance which will shorten the duration of their effect on the people is the entire stagnation of the sale of wheat & flour. they are still quoted indeed the former at 1.20 the latter 7. to 7.50 but they cannot be sold at any price. Baltimore & N. York have both suspended their shipments to the W. Indies. this place was shipping a little, in armed vessels, but probably the expectation of a decree of France making armed neutral vessels lawful prize will damp this kind of enteprize. the worst effect of these papers has been in the H. of Repr. they have carried over all the waverers to the other side. we now expect to lose every question which shall be proposed. they begin to talk of ways & means. the sum to be raised by new taxes is differently estimated from 3. to 7. millions of Dollars. if the former only, they can get it by stopping the interest of the public debt, which is the plan of some. if a larger sum, they will venture on a land tax. in every case it is believed we shall get away by the middle of May. the whigs in the H. of Repr. will oppose the bill for building &c 16. armed vessels, passed by the Senate, and endeavor to restrain private arming. they will fail in the questions, but the discussion will inform the public mind, from which source alone our safety & peace can be hoped. affections to my dear Martha, & kisses to the little ones. cordial salutations to yourself. Adieu.

P.S. since writing the above, the Secretary of state has applied to me for the loan of Escarbot's and Champlain's travels in N. America. Escarbot I know I have, & I believe Champlain also, but of this last I am not certain. will you be so good as to search for & forward one or both from my library? you will see by the Catalogue whether I have Champlain or not. I have an idea it is a 4to. volume. the government want them for the settlement of their dispute with England as to the St. Croix river. let them be very well wrapped up, first in paper, then coarse linen, and directed 'on public service' to myself, or *in my absence* to the Secretary of state, and sent by the Fredericksburg post under a particular charge to take care of them. from Fredericksburg they will come in the stage & safe. if they come by the first return of post they will find me here. they are rendered the more precious because the government has endeavored to have them procured in Europe & are assured on trial that they are not to be had.

RC (DLC); endorsed by Randolph as received 28 Apr. 1798. PrC (MHi); endorsed by TJ in ink on verso.

Randolph's letter OF THE 2D., recorded in SJL as received 14 Apr. 1798, has not been found. CLARKE WRITES ME: the letter from Bowling Clark to TJ of 25 Mch. 1798, recorded in SJL as received 10 Apr., has not been found.

ST. CROIX: Article 5 of the Jay Treaty authorized a bilateral commission to fix the boundary between Maine and the British possessions to the east as called for by the 1783 Treaty of Peace. At issue was the identification of the river called the St. Croix in the 1783 treaty, and Timothy Pickering not only borrowed Samuel de Champlain's *Voyages de la Nouvelle France* (Paris, 1632) and Marc Lescarbot's *Histoire de la Nouvelle-France* (Paris, 1618) from TJ but also did other research in Philadelphia. To simplify matters the two nations in March 1798 agreed to an explanatory article to the Jay Treaty that allowed the commissioners to describe the river they determined upon without a precise specification of the latitude and longitude of its source. Before the end of the year the commission reached a compromise that settled this portion of the U.S.-British boundary (ASP, *Foreign Relations*, 1:48; 2:183-5; Perkins, *First Rapprochement*, 48-53).

From David Redick

SIR,   Washington April 19th 1798
The evening before I left Philadelphia Messrs. Baird and Isreal waited
on me in my bedchamber, after I had got to bed, and Mentioned to me
your desire of Seeing me on the Subject of Mr Luther Martins attack I
Should with pleasure have done myself the honour but that the Stage in
which myself and Son had taken Seats for Lancaster Set out at 6
OClock the next morning—I haveing observed a letter in Porcupines
Gazette addressed to Mr Martin by a Mr Corbin, of whom I have Some
acquaintance, expressing his, and the publics Satisfaction, with respect
to Cresops inocence in the Murder of Logans friends and finding in
Several Circles a disposition to give Currency to[1] falshood, in this respect, I wrote a little heasty paper Stateing that I knew the universal
belief of Cresop having killed the Indians Alluded to, to have prevailed
in the Western Country, that the Indian tribes Charged him with it, that
Cresop and Greathouse were the Subjects of their Constant Execrations
and appealed to Mr Heckewelder one of the Moravian Missionaries for
the last flact—I sent the paper to Mr Feno, for publication in hopes it
might in Some degree check the Currant of untruth, but I find Mr
Fenno has Not published it. The only appology I can make for him, as
he told the boy who dilivered it, that it Should have a place, is, that he
being a printer of Correct taste, and the paper being heastily drawn up
without revision; he might have thought it undeserving a place—be this
as it may, I have been at Some pains to procure the Most Authentic
documents that this late day admits of, to establish the facts; and I believe I have not failed altogather. I enclose you a Certificate of William
Huston a man of Established reputation in point of Integrity I have been
in the Country to day makeing enqurey at a Mr Chambers who is intimate with Secrets on the Subject of killing the Indians at Bakers bottom, a few days after, Cresops, Skirmish he Also is in possession of the
real history of Cresops attack on Logan's family; he had it from a Mr
Smith one of Cresops party—his relation of the Case to me goes fully to
Justify the opinion of Mr Huston—Mr Chambers has promised to wait
on me Shortly and make an Affidavit of the Whole; which I hope to be
able to Send you ere long—I think, to take up the affair of killing the
Indians at Bakers bottom of Some importance, tho not appearently connected with the Subject principly in view at present: but as it will go far
in developeing Several important facts which has never been yet divulged, So far as I know, it will furnish Criticle documents for the Philosophical historian of Virginia, it will go compleatly to the depravity of

[285]

Mind which reigns in a frontier Country—Compariscon will be the better made between the Natives, intrely Savage, and the first adventurers[2] who claim Some Small Share of Civilization.—Mr Chambers will prove that Cresops party, particulary Mr Smith of Virginia whom he Mentions as having but one Arm Acknowledged that the Indians passed the encampment of Cresop in their Canoa without any apparent animosity and peaceably encamped at Some Small distance below them on the bank of the River that they went Silently down and fired on them, that the Indians took Arms and wounded one of Cresops Men Chambers will also prove that he was Solicited to be of a party to kill the Indians at Bakers bottom Several days before it hapned, that his intimate Companion, Edwd. King, was of the party. that Baker had been engaged by Greathouse to invite the Indians over and Make them drunk that they might become an easy prey—when the particulars are properly detailed it will make a horrid picture. these facts have Never been made known. even the greater part of Greathouses party were Ignorant of the true State of Things. Chambers refused being of the party least he Should become a Murderer of the inocent. I am Sir with Sentiments of very great Esteem

yours Sincerely

DAVID REDICK

RC (DLC); at foot of text: "Hon. Thomas Jefferson Esqr." Recorded in SJL as received 26 Apr. 1798. Enclosure: Certificate of William Huston of Washington County, Pennsylvania, 18 Apr. 1798, attesting to what he learned in 1774, from "a party of Armed men" led by Michael Cresap, about two instances in which they had killed Indians (MS in DLC; in Redick's hand, signed by Huston; printed in the *Appendix to the Notes on Virginia Relative to the Murder of Logan's Family*, with variations in spelling, punctuation, and capitalization, and the omission of the word "wouded"— i.e., "wounded"—from the clause "they had with them one man on a litter who was wouded in the skirmish"; see *Notes*, ed. Peden, 236-7). Other enclosure printed below.

MESSRS. BAIRD AND ISREAL seem likely to have been Thomas Baird, a Pittsburgh merchant who was part of an increasingly influential group of Republicans in western Pennsylvania, and either Israel Israel or John Israel, who during 1798 moved from Philadelphia to Washington, Pennsylvania,

to begin publication of the *Herald of Liberty* and involve himself energetically in Republican politics, founding the *Tree of Liberty* in Pittsburgh two years later (Russell J. Ferguson, *Early Western Pennsylvania Politics* [Pittsburgh, 1938], 164-5, 167; Carl E. Prince, "John Israel: Printer and Politician on the Pennsylvania Frontier, 1798-1805," PMHB, 91 [1967], 46-55).

In a letter of 10 Mch. 1798 addressed to Luther Martin and published in PORCU-PINES GAZETTE on the 28th of that month, Francis CORBIN declared that Martin had so "abundantly vindicated" the reputation of the Cresap family that TJ must certainly acknowledge the error of his assertions about the Logan affair: "Candid and a lover of truth, polite and a gentleman as he is, nothing can restrain him from this but pride or personal contempt. The avowed tenets of his political creed, if he be not inwardly an infidel, forbid us to suspect him of the former, and your respectability for talents and learning must, doubtless, protect you from the latter.—It follows then that being a republican and a philosopher (I use this last word as a literal compound of its derivatives) it is impossible for him to refuse you that satisfaction.—Having full credit in my estimation for the double character he sustains, I shall be extremely sorry indeed, if by his silence, he should forfeit his title to both or either." Corbin, of "The Reeds" in Caroline County and previously of Middlesex County, had been born in Virginia in 1759 but received his education at Cambridge University. During the Revolution he remained in England, where he was admitted to the Inner Temple. Serving in the Virginia House of Delegates from 1784 to 1794, in 1785 he strongly opposed TJ's bill for religious freedom. An active proponent of ratification of the U.S. Constitution, in 1788 he gained notoriety by mocking Patrick Henry in the General Assembly, only to be bettered by Henry's withering reply. Corbin aspired unsuccessfully to a seat in either the U.S. House of Representatives or the Senate (VMHB, 30 [1922], 315-17; Madison to TJ, 22 Apr. 1788, 23 Oct. 1792; Monroe to TJ, 12 July 1788, 16 Oct. 1792, 27 Mch. 1793; TJ to Short, 6 Apr. 1790; Vol. 2:548-9).

Corbin and TJ were in communication during the period in which Corbin's letter to Martin appeared in *Porcupine's Gazette*, but the subject of their correspondence is not known. According to SJL, they exchanged five letters between 11 Sep. 1797 and 8 Apr. 1798 and another nine between 5 Dec. 1798 and 20 Oct. 1800, none of which has been found. They do not appear to have communicated again until 1814, when they traded letters on the disposition of the estate of Lucy Ludwell Paradise (Corbin to TJ, 30 Apr., TJ to Corbin, 20 May 1814).

On 20 Apr. 1798 James CHAMBERS gave a deposition concerning what he knew of attacks led by Daniel Greathouse and Michael Cresap against Indians along the Ohio river in the spring of 1774. Redick sent the deposition to TJ, who included it in his *Appendix* in 1800 (MS in DLC; in Redick's hand, signed by Samuel Shannon, justice of the peace of Washington County, Pennsylvania, and by Chambers; with attestation by Redick, 26 Apr. 1798, as prothonotary of the court of common pleas for the county; endorsed by TJ; printed in the *Appendix* with minor variations in spelling, punctuation, and capitalization; see *Notes*, ed. Peden, 238-41).

[1] Redick here canceled "what I was fully persuaded."
[2] Word interlined in place of "Settlers."

ENCLOSURE

David Redick to John Fenno

Mr Fenno   Philadelphia 29th March 1798.
In Porcupines Gazatte of yesterday a letter Addressed to Mr Luther Martin by Frances Corbin, declares that on the Subject of Mr Martins charge against Mr Jefferson, he and the public are Satisfied; and that Mr Jefferson will be bound to render Satisfaction &c. I am of opinion that Mr Corbin has too hastily found himself Satisfied. I am a resident of the Ohio Country and have been Conversant in its affairs for more than 25 years, I was well Acquainted with "Logan" the Indian Chief whose family Mr Cresop was charged with Murdering I know that at the time of the horrid Act No one in that Country ever called in question, to my knowledge, Mr Cresops haveing been the perpetrater. I have heard him boasted of as the brave Warrior who in his Countrys cause had killed these Indians, by the ignorant and Savage part of our early frontier inhabitants— The Indian tribes in that Neighbourhood uniformly & universally charged him and Greathouse with it †Clesop & Gleathouse was Continually on their lips as the

† the Indians reject the R. Substituting the L.

Subjects of their executions. of this fact any one may be Certified by appealing to the Moravian Missionaries who at the time resided in the Indian Towns on the Moskindum of whom the Reverend Mr Hekewelder is Still liveing, and residing at Bethlehem in Pennsylvania, Genl Gibson of Pittsburgh, Colo. John Campbel at the Rapids of Ohio and divers others all must know that Cresop was believed to be the[1] person who killed Logans family—Logan was a man of probity[2] Men of probity are to be found amongst the Indians. he would not take up sole reports on Slight Grounds in my opinion—I am unknown to Mr Jefferson except perhaps by name only. I am unconnected in all respects with him but as a Citizen of America. As a lover of truth and honest fame, alone have I written this paper. I enclose my name that if it Should prove Necessary you may use it—

MS (DLC); in Redick's hand; torn; author's note written in margin; in TJ's hand at foot of text: "David Riddick Prothonotary of Washington county Pensylva"; endorsed by TJ.

MOSKINDUM: the Muskingum River. At some point TJ received the following statement by Thomas Meriwether, dated Richmond, 4 Apr. 1798, concerning John GIBSON: "Colo. John Gibson who commanded the 6th. Virginia Regimt. in the late revolutionary war, was for several years previous to that war a trader in the Delawar-nation; He has informed the writer hereof in the course of their acquaintance that he had had a wife of that nation, who with a child, were both kill'd by the White people about the mouth of Wheeling—the Writer thinks he mentioned the white people as being under the influence of the late Colo. Cresap— The Writer thinks Colo. Gibson understood the Indian language (perhaps the Delawarre) well, as he has heard him sing it and speak it fluently— Colo. Gibson was living a few months past, and resided at or near Pittsburg—" (MS in DLC; in Meriwether's hand, signed by initials; signed note added by Thomas Lomax: "This was written by Colo. Thos. Merriwether at the request of Thos. Lomax, who was in conversation with him in Richmd. on Luther Martin's attack up on Mr. Jefferson. given under my Hand this 6th. of Apl. 1798"; at foot of text in Mann Page's hand: "Test. Mann Page jr."). During the American Revolution Meriwether had served as an officer of the First State Regiment under Colonel George Gibson, the brother of John Gibson. He entered military service from Caroline County, of which Lomax was a prominent resident. For several years after the war Meriwether was clerk to the Council of Virginia (VMHB, 21 [1913], 339; CVSP, 4:282-3; 5:647; Thomas Elliott Campbell, *Colonial Caroline: A History of Caroline County, Virginia* [Richmond, 1954], 343, 344-5, 348; DAB, 7:252-3; Vol. 4:539).

[1] Redick here canceled "Murderer" and "killer."
[2] Redick first wrote, "man of as much probity and honour in my opinion as any one who has [. . .]," before altering the passage to read as above.

From Tadeusz Kosciuszko

[21 Apr. 1798]

I afraid to hurt your feelings by my reiterated impartunities, but I am so enxious of going away. that not one moment in a day I have a rest, if this occasion fall of going to Bourdeau. I should prefer to Lisbon to avoided of bieng taking by the Englishs. the Season far advenced. and rumour of this Country is very desigreable to a feeling heart. as we cannot talk fully upon this Subject. I beg you was kind to put me a paper like this for information how and when i expect to go—

RC (MHi); endorsed by TJ as received 21 Apr. 1798.

From James Madison

Dear Sir   Apl. 22 1798

My last was on the 15th. and acknowledged your preceding letters. I have since recd. that of the 12. under the same cover with the Gazettes; and, the instructions & despatches, under a separate cover. The interruptions of company added to the calls of business have not left me time as yet to read over the whole of those papers. A glance at them, with the abstracts given of their contents, fully account for the state of astonishment produced in the public mind. And yet the circumstance that ought to astonish most perhaps, is the publication of them by the Ex. & Senate. Whatever probability there may be of individual corruption within the pale of the French Govt. the evidence is certainly very insufficient to support such an attack on its reputation in the face of the world, even if we could separate the measure from its inevitable effect in blasting every chance of accomodation, if it should reach France before terms shall be finally settled. After this stroke in the politics of those two Branches of our Govt. no one who has not surrendered his reason, can believe them sincere in wishing to avoid extremities with the French Republic; to say nothing of the internal views to which they mean also to turn this extraordinary manœuvre. There has not been time for any impressions on the public sentiment in this quarter, which the Despatches are calculated to make. The first will no doubt pretty much correspond with those made elsewhere: But the final impressions will depend on the further & more authentic developments which can not be far behind, & wch. may by this time be arrived where you are. I find that in several places the people have turned out with their protests agst. the war measures urged by the Ex: Whether the proceeding will be general is what I can not pretend to decide. In this County a Petition is to be handed about, which will I presume be pretty fully signed, if sufficiently circulated; unless the disaffected few among us, should be embolded by the present crisis to circulate along with it, the impressions emanating from the Despatches wch. may stop the hands of wavering or cautious people.—Altho' the thermoter on the mornings of the 15 & 16 inst: was at 31 & 32°. the fruit was not materially injured except in low situations; but having sunk during the night following to 24°. vegitation of every kind seemed to feel the blow. The Peaches & Cherries appear to [be][1] totally destroyed, and most of the Apples. Even the young Hickory leaves are in considerable proportion compleatly killed. The weather has since been more natural to the season.

RC (DLC: Madison Papers, Rives Collection); addressed: "Thomas Jefferson Philadelphia" with *Private* at head; endorsed by TJ as received 1 May 1798 and so recorded in SJL.

PETITION IS TO BE HANDED ABOUT: on 22 May the House of Representatives acknowledged receipt of a petition from Orange County, Virginia, opposing the use of public authority to arm merchant vessels and encouraging the adoption of measures to prevent a war with France (JHR, 3:306).

[1] Word supplied.

From Thomas Mann Randolph

[22 Apr. 1798]

I am confident I could have served you considerably but I thought it better to trust to the motives upon which you depended than risk the consequences of a sudden relaxation of[1] strict command. I scarcely look to the Nailery at all—George I am sure could not stoop to my authority & I hope and believe he pushes your interests as well as I could.

The papers with the dispatches from our envoys have reached us and create very considerable emotion. The idea that our Commissioners have been attempted by a company of sharpers unconnected unauthorized by the French government and having no view but to swindle & then abscond prevails more generally than my fears of the Anglican faction w'd. let me hope at first. Tis the just view [of the?] affair I am certain: I cannot however help feeling some little suspicion of Talleyrands honesty. Is it not probable that the resentment the divulgation of these dispatches will produce in Paris may occasion hostilities immediately. A War with France as producing an intimate union with the English Monarchy destroys in my breast all interest in the United States. I think only of my Tobacco & beg your advice whether to take the present price which w'd. enable me to shift thro' the year tolerably or wait for the chance of one which might make me quite easy. W. Nicolas & F. Walker are our delegates.

We are all well & quite *impatient* for your return now—Summer & Monticello, Monticello and you are linked together in the fancy, which heightens the warmest feelings of the heart.

your's most affectionately   TH: M. RANDOLPH

RC (ViU: Edgehill-Randolph Papers); incomplete, consisting of last page only; torn; addressed: "Thomas Jefferson Vice-president of the U. States Philad'a."; en-dorsed by TJ as a letter of 22 Apr. received 1 May 1798 and so recorded in SJL.

¹ Randolph here canceled "pretty."

From John Heckewelder

SIR   Bethlehem Apr. 23d. 1798.

By this Mail I will just acknowledge the reciept of Your Letter—& inform You that I am preparing some account of the Murder of Logans family &c. & which will serve to show: that what You published in or about the Year 1787 of this transaction was precisely the report & belief of that day; nay more, from the time of that horrid Massacree untill the publication of Mr. Martins Letters, wherein he undertakes to contradict the fact, I never once heard that a doubt was entertained as to authentic-ity, altho I had so often been present when this transaction had been the subject of conversation, & even near the spot where it had happened. With respect to Logans Speech to Lord Dunmore I observe, that at that time I had gone on a Journey, & did not return untill Peace was con-cluded; but from similar Expressions of his, which were related to me afterwards by Indians, I find no reason to doubt this, moreover, being accustomed to hear Indians express themselves in this Style on various occasions, I gave credit to it. As for Logan himself I knew better from report than from personal acquaintance—yet I had seen him & con-versed with him. In my next I shall give some account of him. Was my time at present not so short & precious, (being about to set off for De-troit the last Day of this Month) I could on many occasions (respecting the above) be more particular, however truth may be supported by few Words.

I have the honour to be Sir Your most obedt. humble servt.

JOHN HECKEWELDER

RC (DLC); at foot of text: "The Honble. Thomas Jefferson Esqr."; endorsed by TJ as received 24 Apr. 1798 and so recorded in SJL.

YOUR LETTER: TJ to Heckewelder, 11 Apr. 1798.

To Tadeusz Kosciuszko

TH:J. TO GENL. KOSCIUSKO   Apr. 23. 98.

I had wished, my dear General, to have awaited the departure of the Benjamin Franklin, which I think still will not be delayed more than 3.

or 4. weeks. she is so fine a vessel & has so good a captain. but on reading your note, I yesterday set mr Barnes (my confidential agent here) to looking out for a vessel bound to any port of Europe from Nantes Southwardly. he sent me in the evening the inclosed note. for many reasons however the vessel therein mentioned will not do. he will be able in the course of a few days to give me an account of every vessel bound from this port to those before described. I communicate to him no more of my object than is necessary. you shall know as soon as we get any thing worth communicating to you; and be assured no pains shall be spared to fulfill your wishes. health, happiness & Adieu.

PrC (MHi); endorsed by TJ in ink on verso. Enclosure not found.

YOUR NOTE: Kosciusko to TJ, [21 Apr. 1798].

Memorandum to Tadeusz Kosciuszko

[25 Apr. 1798]

Memorandum.

The triplicate of both bills of exchange & the copy of the letters of advice enclosed to Messrs. Nicholas & Jacob Van Staphorst & Hubbard bankers of Amsterdam. therefore the [. . .] of the bills & letters must [. . . .]. they are [. . .] informed that the half yearly dividends [. . .] [return?] [. . .] to them. therefore they [. . .] with you [. . .] recieve [. . .] the conveni[. . .] [. . .] [much con]nected with [. . .] [counted] [. . .] Th: J. for which reasons he [. . .] resides at Paris, is an [. . .] [acquain]ted with, and [. . .] [applied to if the bills be not disposed?] of before you [. . .] particular position is not known to Th:J. letters for you will be addressed to them. they should consequently be kept always informed where you are. the person who acts for me at Philadelphia is mr John Barnes, merchant, South 3d. street Philadelphia. he will be particularly empowered to receive the halfyearly dividends & to remit them to Messrs. Nicholas & Jacob Van Staphorst & Hubbard at Amsterdam.

TH: JEFFERSON

PrC (MHi); faint, with numerous phrases of three or more words illegible; undated, assigned on basis of reference to bills of exchange (see below); endorsed by TJ in ink on verso: "Kosciusko."

BILLS OF EXCHANGE: on 12 Apr. Kosciuszko gave TJ a U.S. Treasury warrant for $3,684.54 with a request "to have bills of exchange bought for him." Barnes con-

verted $3,600 of the sum into two bills of exchange (see TJ to Van Staphorst & Hubbard, 1 May 1798). TJ delivered the bills to Kosciuszko on 25 Apr. along with $66 drawn in the form of a check by Barnes on the Bank of Pennsylvania, which was the remainder of Kosciuszko's warrant less the bills of exchange and Barnes's commission of one half of one percent (MB, 2:981, 982).

Notes on Conversation with Tench Coxe

Apr. 25. at a dinner given by the bar to the Federal judges, Chase & Peters, present about 24. lawyers and Wm. Tilghman in the chair, this toast was given 'Our *King* in old England.' observe the double entendre on the word King. DePonceau who was one of the bar present, told this to Tenche Coxe who told me in presence of H. Tazewell. Dallis was at the dinner; so was Colo. Charles Sims of Alexandria, who is here on a law suit v. Genl. Irving.

MS (DLC: TJ Papers, 102:17525); entirely in TJ's hand; on same sheet as Notes on British Instructions and on Clement Humphreys, 13 Apr. 1798, with two lines of canceled text separating them.

From Palisot de Beauvois

MONSIEUR,   Richmond 25 avril 1798.

persuadé que vous apprendrés avec plaisir de nouveaux details sur différens objets naturels et principalement sur l'animal curieux dont vous avéz donné des ossemens a la société philosophique, je m'empresse de vous en faire part par écrit, dans L'incertitude ou je suis de vous rencontrer encore a philadelphie lorsque je m'y rendrai pour y prendre mon passage pour france.

Dans une derniere tournée que je viens de faire, et dans laquelle j'ai été bien dedommagé des peines et des contrariétés que j'ai eprouvées, par le spectacle, pour moi ravissant, des beautés en tous genres que la Nature offrait a chaque instant a mes yeux avides de les contempler, je me suis arretté quelque tems a Green Briar. Le Col. Stuárd, notre digne collegue, s'est preté avec toute la complaisance et L'honneteté imaginables a m'accompagner partout où il a cru que mon gout pouvait trouver a se satisfaire. je ne vous detaillerai pas toutes les choses curieuses qui ont fixé mes regards et que j'ai ramassé, mais vous ne serés sans doute pas faché d'apprendre que ce comté est Extremement riche en plants, et en productions naturelles de tout genre. entre autres L'espece de Marbre bleu ou pierre a chaux qui y abonde est couverte de differentes productions Marines. j'y ai distinctement reconnu de Vers de Mer, des Lithophites, des Madrepores &c. le petrosilex que l'on rencontre aussi souvent disséminé sur la surface de la terre y est agatisé: il forme quelques fois des geodes zonées et couvertes au centre de petits cristaux.—Dans une caverne située a 4 miles du Col. Brown et dont

L'entrée est de 50 a 60 pieds perpendiculaires a été trouvé le squelette presqu'entier d'un Elk (*cervus elephas Canadensis? Lin. genes.*) notés que depuis environ une 30e. d'années on ne voit plus de ces animaux dans le quartier. les cornes ou bois fixés a L'un des cotés de cette caverne etaient couverts de stalactites; les os du crâne etaient decomposés et presque reduits a L'etat de chaux. toutes les circonstances indiquent que L'animal, tombé sans doute par accident, y etait depuis longtems; cependant un des os de la cuisse que quelqu'un trouva par hazard se trouva rempli de moëlle. elle etait blanchatre comme du suif dont elle conservait L'odeur. je ne ferai aucune reflexion sur ce fait a la connaissance des habitans de Lewisburg et des environs. mais il me parait interessant a remarquer.

je Viens Maintenant a L'objet principal de Ma Lettre. je me suis transporté dans la caverne ou ont été trouvés les ossemens de cet Animal curieux que vous me Montrates a Monticello en 1796, lorsque j'eus L'honneur de vous y aller rendre Mes devoirs, et que depuis Votre Amour pour les sciences vous a determiné a présenter a la société, avec un Memoire dont elle s'est empressé d'ordonner L'impression. un des ouvriers pour le Salpêtre que L'on retîre abondamment de ce souterrain me Montra et me donna une dent qu'il avait trouvé peu de jours Auparavant *dans la même place*. j'y fis fouiller dans L'esperance d'y trouver les Machoires qui probablement m'auraient Mis a Même de determiner a quelle famille appartient cet Animal. mais je n'y trouvai qu'un petît os brisé et peu interressant (j'ai appris qu'un M. Alexandre Courré qui demeure a 8 ou 10 miles de Stanton a plusieurs debris de ce Même Animal).

comme il y a quelques probabilités de croire que la dent que l'on m'a montrée a appartenu au Même Animal, je vous en Envoy une Esquisse de sa grandeur Naturelle. d'après la forme des griffes ou ongles vous avez pensé avec raison que cet Animal appartient a la famille des animaux carnassiers, a ongles retractiles et par consequent au Genre des *felis. Lin*. Mais combien ne serés-vous pas surpris a L'inspection de cette dent qui parait etre celle d'un animal de la famille des ruminans (pecores Lin) et par consequent dont les pieds sont a sabots ou ungulés.

ce fait bien singulier presente Naturellement plusieurs questions.
1o. cette dent peut-elle appartenir a un animal du genre des *felis*?
2o. est-elle dent incisive ou dent Molaire.
3o. enfin ne designerait-elle pas que L'animal est du genre des *bradypus. Lin. aï* ou *unau*.

aucun animal du genre des *felis* n'offre de dents pareilles a celle-ci. Leurs incisives sont simples et tranchantes, leurs canines sont en crochets; Leurs Molaires sont comprimes, aigues et a trois pointes.

par sa forme a la surface Cette dent approche des incisives des chevaux, Mais ses bords sont tranchants et sa base n'a point de racine distincte. de plus elle est convexe d'une coté en D et concave de L'autre en E, et sa base est creuse ainsi que les Molaires de plusieurs autres animaux tels que le rat Commun, le rat Musqué, le lapin et plusieurs autres. je pense donc que cette dent ne peut-etre qu'une dent Molaire; ce qui me conduit a la troisieme question. je n'ai point encore eu occasion d'Examiner des dents de *bradypus*. ainsi je ne me sens pas en etat de prononcer. mais nous ne connaissons que deux bradypus. Laï et L'unau. ni L'un ni l'autre n'approche de la dimension de l animal en question. Serait-ce une espece inconnue et non decrite? M. peale a dans son Museum un aï (Sloth) peut-etre Vous pourriés Examiner ses dents et par comparaison juger si il y a quelqu'analogie entre cette dent et les siennes; Mais il n'en resultera pas Moins en supposant qu'il y ait analogie (car j'ai de la peine a me figurer par l'inspection des ongles qu'il puisse etre de cette famille) il n'en resultera pas moins que c'est une Espece au Moins immense et non décrite. et comment ses ossemens se trouvent-ils a green briar, c. a. d. par les 38′ nord environ, lorsque les bradypus connus n'ont jusqu'a present été trouvés que sous la zone torride entre les 5 et 12 degres environ L'un en Amérique, L'autre a Ceyland.

j'ai L'honneur d'etre avec un attachement respectueux Monsieur.

Votre tres humble et tres obeisst. serviteur Palisot-Beauvois

EDITORS' TRANSLATION

Sir,   Richmond 25 April 1798.

Being convinced that you will learn with pleasure new details on different natural objects, and especially concerning the curious animal whose bones you gave to the philosophical society, I hasten to advise you by letter, because of my uncertainty about finding you still in Philadelphia when I go there to take my passage for France.

In a last circuit I have just made, in which I was well rewarded for the troubles and obstacles which I underwent by the spectacle, absolutely bewitching for me, of all the kinds of beauty nature offered continuously to my eyes, greedy for their contemplation, I stopped for some time at Greenbriar. Col. Stuart, our worthy colleague, gave of himself with all the kindliness and gentlemanliness one could imagine in accompanying me everywhere he thought my taste would find some satisfaction. I shall not detail all the curious things that attracted my attention and which I collected, but you will doubtless not be vexed to learn that this county is extremely rich in plants and in all kinds of natural products. Among other things, the kind of blue marble or limestone that is abundant there is covered with different products of the sea. I distinctly recognized in it sea worms, lithophytes, madrepores, etc. The petrosilex that one finds rather frequently distributed on the surface of the earth is there transformed into agate;

sometimes it forms geodes striped and covered in the center with small crystals.—In a cavern located at four miles from Col. Brown, and the entrance to which is 50 to 60 perpendicular feet, there was found the nearly complete skeleton of an elk (*cervus elephas Canadensis? Lin. genes*). Notice that for around 30 years these animals have no longer been seen in this area. The horns or antlers, attached to one side of this cavern, were covered with stalactites; the bones of the skull were decomposed and almost reduced to a state of lime. All the circumstances indicate that the animal, having probably fallen accidentally, had been there a long time; nevertheless, one of the thigh-bones, which someone chanced to find, was full of marrow. It was whitish like tallow, the odor of which it retained. I shall make no reflection on this fact for the information of the inhabitants of Lewisburg and the surrounding country. But to me it seems interesting to note.

I come now to the main subject of my letter. I betook myself into the cavern where were found the bones of that curious animal which you showed me at Monticello in 1796, when I had the honor of paying my respects to you, and about which your love for the sciences subsequently impelled you to present the society with a memoir which it hastened to order printed. One of the workers in the saltpeter which is abundantly mined in that underworld showed me and gave me a tooth that he had found a few days before *in the same place*. I caused some digging to be done in the hope of finding there the jaws which probably would have enabled me to determine to what family that animal belongs. But all I found was a small broken bone of little interest (I learned that Mr. Alexandre Courré, who lives 8 or 10 miles from Stanton has several remains of that same animal).

As there are some probabilities for believing that the tooth that I was shown belonged to the same animal, I am sending you a life-size sketch of it. According to the form of the claws or nails you thought reasonably enough that that animal belongs to the family of the carnivora, with retractable nails, consequently to the genus *felis* of Linnaeus. But what will be your surprise upon the inspection of this tooth which appears to be that of an animal of the family of the ruminants (Linnean *pecora*) whose feet, consequently, are hoofed, or ungulate.

This quite singular fact naturally presents several questions.

1o. Can this tooth belong to an animal of the genus *felis*?

2o. Is this tooth an incisor or a molar.

3o. Finally, would it not indicate that the animal is of the genus *bradypus* of Linnaeus, the *aï* or *unau*?

No animal of the genus *felis* shows teeth like this one. Their incisors are simple and cutting, their canines are curved; their molars are flattened on the sides, sharp, and with three points.

In the shape of its surface this tooth approximates horses' incisors, but its edges are sharp and its base has no distinct root at all. Moreover, it is convex on one side (D) and concave on the other (E), and its base is hollow like the molars of several other animals, such as the common rat, the muskrat, the rabbit, and several others. So I think that this tooth can be only a molar, which brings me to the third question. I have not yet had the chance to examine any *bradypus* teeth, hence I do not feel myself to be in a position to make a judgment. But we know only two bradypus, the aï and the unau. Neither one comes near the dimension of the animal in question. Could it be a species unknown and not described? Mr. Peale has in his museum an aï (sloth). Perhaps you could examine its teeth and judge by comparison whether there is some analogy between its teeth and this one; but the result will nonetheless be, supposing that there is some analogy (for I have difficulty imagining from the inspection of the nails that it can be of that family) the result will nonetheless be that it is a species at the least immense and undescribed. And how do these bones come to be in Greenbrier, that is to say at approximately 38° North, when the known bradypus until now have been found only in the torrid zone between approximately 5 and 12 degrees, one in America, the other in Ceylon.

I have the honor of being with a respectful attachment Sir.

Your very humble and obdt. servant   PALISOT-BEAUVOIS

RC (PPAmP); addressed: "The honble. Thomas Jefferson vice president of the united states and president of the philosophical society Philadelphia"; endorsed for the American Philosophical Society as having been read at a meeting of 4 May 1798 and referred to Caspar Wistar. Noted in the minutes of the society as relating to "Natural Curiosities" of Greenbrier County, Virginia, in particular "a tooth of a large non descript animal"; on 22 June 1798 Wistar reported that the paper was "worthy of publication," but it did not appear in the society's *Transactions* (APS, *Proceedings*, 22, pt. 3 [1884], 270-1, 273). Enclosure not found.

A French baron originally trained in the law, Ambroise Marie François Joseph Palisot de Beauvois (1752-1820) devoted himself to botany after inheriting his family's estates and income. In 1786 he accompanied a trading expedition to the Gulf of Guinea. After over a year of collecting and describing plants in Africa, he went to Saint-Domingue, where he continued his observations in natural history and obtained offices within the colonial government. Traveling to Philadelphia in 1791 to solicit aid in behalf of the ruling elite, he became a member of the American Philosophical Society. On his return to Saint-Domingue in June 1793 he found the island in turmoil, his home and scientific collections ruined. The new regime deported him to the United States, where he learned that the French revolutionary government had also proscribed him. Caspar Wistar took him in as a guest, and Palisot earned income by cataloging a portion of Charles Willson Peale's museum, tutoring, and working as a musi-

cian. He again collected biological specimens, and with the support of Pierre Auguste Adet traveled to the western frontiers and from New York to Georgia. He wrote papers for the APS and attended several of its meetings, including the presentation of TJ's report on the megalonyx fossils on 10 Mch. 1797. In the summer of 1798, with the proscription against him lifted, Palisot returned to France and thereafter continued his work in botany. Most of the specimens he had collected so assiduously in North America, Africa, and Haiti were either lost at sea or destroyed by political upheaval and military conflict (APS, *Proceedings*, 22, pt. 3 [1884], 201, 220, 225, 233, 247, 248, 249, 252-3, 255; E. D. Merrill, "Palisot de Beauvois as an Overlooked American Botanist," in same, 76 [1936], 899-907; APS, *Transactions*, 4 [1799], 173-7, 277-81, 362-81; Hoefer, *Nouv. biog. générale*, 39:86-8).

L'ANIMAL CURIEUX: the megalonyx. For TJ's MEMOIRE to the American Philosophical Society, see Memoir on the Megalonyx, [10 Feb. 1797].

On 20 Apr. 1798 TJ signed a resolution of the APS of that date authorizing him as the society's president to sign any loan contract or mortgage that the treasurer, John Vaughan, might arrange according to a resolution of the previous November calling for the payment of a £500 loan made by Benjamin Franklin a decade earlier. Benjamin Franklin Bache had instituted legal action to spur repayment of his grandfather's loan, which provided funds for the completion of the society's building (MS in PPAmP, in Vaughan's hand and signed by TJ, endorsed; APS, *Proceedings*, 22, pt. 3 [1884], 155-6, 262, 270).

From Edmund Pendleton

MY DEAR SIR   Richmond April 25. 1798.

I have received yr. Friendly Card of Salutation, & was much concerned at the information that the Fall of Stock was below all price in Phila.—we have made Enquiry here & find that there is no Market at any price; At the same time we have in Vain endeavoured to borrow the money to accommodate Mr. Short, and it being said that the price at Phila. for 6 pr. Cents was 16/. & so in proportion For the others, we have procured a friend who corresponds there, to get information what is the best price that can be had there, as after the sudden shock wch. occasioned the Stagnation, was past, business in that way might revive.

In this state of the case can't you venture in behalf of Mr. Short to allow the U.S.s Credit For the Amount of this demand, or get it suspended, so as to receive the Ballce. due to him? In either case we pledge the whole Funds of Mr. Robinson's estate remaining, as well as the Stock, For payment out of the first money we can recieve by Collection, or a Sale of the stock when such can be made without a ruinous loss, in wch. we as Trustees could not be justified. I am

Dr. Sir, Yr. Affe. & Obt. Servt.   EDMD PENDLETON

RC (DLC: Short Papers); endorsed by TJ as received 1 May 1798 and so recorded in SJL.

YR. FRIENDLY CARD OF SALUTATION: TJ to Pendleton, 2 Apr. 1798.

From Timothy Pickering

SIR,   Department of State April 25. 1798.

Since sending you this morning a concise statement of Mr. Short's claim for nine thousand dollars, *as it appeared from the books in my office*, I have received from the Secretary of the Treasury the following memorandum:

"Mr. Jefferson has had a conversation with Mr. Harrison, Auditor, in which it was understood that Mr. Randolph had applied Two thousand pounds for Mr. Short's use, for which Randolph would be entitled to credit."—This information the Secretary of the Treasury received from the Comptroller; and I have thought it necessary to communicate the same to you without delay.

I am, sir, your most obt. servant,   TIMOTHY PICKERING

RC (DLC: Short Papers); at foot of text: "The Honble. Thomas Jefferson Esq."; endorsed by TJ as received 25 Apr. 1798 and so recorded in SJL. FC (MHi: Pickering Papers); in a clerk's hand.

In the CONCISE STATEMENT relating to SHORT'S CLAIM FOR NINE THOUSAND DOLLARS, Pickering summarized and quoted from correspondence between his predecessor as secretary of state, Edmund Randolph, and Short from June 1794 to December 1795 and concluded: "Upon this view of the subject, I have no hesitation in expressing my opinion, That Mr. Short is still entitled to receive the nine thousand dollars, and that the United States are responsible to him for that sum: But Mr. Randolph claims a credit for the same, as applied to Mr. Short's use; and as the suit against him for the money he owes to the U. States (which involves the 9000 dollars) remains undecided, the Secretary of the Treasury wishes the actual payment may be for the present suspended" (MS in DLC: Short Papers; in Pickering's hand, signed by him, and dated 25 Apr. 1798; at head of text: "Claim of William Short Esqr. late minister of the U. States at Madrid, for nine thousand dollars credited in his account, but not received by him"; at foot of text: "For Mr. Jefferson, Attorney to Mr. Short"; endorsed by TJ as received 25 Apr. 1798).

To James Madison

Philadelphia. Apr. 26. 98.

I wrote you last on the 19th. since which your's of the 15th. is recieved. I well remember the recieving that which inclosed a letter to Muhlenberg, but do not exactly recollect how I sent it. yet I have no doubt I sent it by my servant, that being my constant practice. your note from[1] Baily I shewed to Genl. Van Cortlandt who was going to N. York. on his return he told me he would pay the note himself before the rising of Congress, since which I have said nothing to him more, as I doubt not he will do it. not knowing however the precise object of your letter to Bailey, I have sent it to the post office.

The bill for the naval armament (12. vessels) passed by a majority of about 4. to 3. in the H. of R. all restrictions on the objects for which the vessels should be used were struck out. the bill for establishing a department of Secretary of the navy was tried yesterday on it's passage to the 3d. reading & prevailed by 47. against 41. it will be read the 3d time to day. the Provisional army of 20,000 men will meet some difficulty. it would surely be rejected if our members were all here. Giles, Clopton, Cabell, & Nicholas are gone, & Clay goes tomorrow. he recieved here news of the death of his wife. Parker is completely gone over to the war-party. in this state of things they will carry what they please. one of the war-party, in a fit of unguarded passion declared some time ago they would pass a citizen bill, an alien bill, & a sedition bill. accordingly some days ago Coit laid a motion on the table of the H. of R. for modifying the citizen law. their threats point at Gallatin, & it is believed they will endeavor to reach him by this bill. yesterday mr Hillhouse laid on the table of the Senate a motion for giving power to send away suspected aliens. this is understood to be meant for Volney & Collot. but it will not stop there when it gets into a course of execution. there is now only wanting, to accomplish the whole declaration beforementioned, a sedition bill which we shall certainly soon see proposed. the object of that is the suppression of the whig presses. Bache's has been particularly named. that paper & also Cary's totter for want of subscriptions. we should really exert ourselves to procure them, for if these papers fall, republicanism will be entirely brow-beaten. Cary's paper comes out 3. times a week @ 5. D. the meeting of the people which was called at New York did nothing. it was found that the majority would be against the Address. they therefore chose to circulate it individually. the committee of ways & means have voted a land tax. an additional tax on salt will certainly be proposed in the House, and probably prevail to some degree. the stoppage of interest on the public debt will also perhaps be proposed, but not with effect. in the mean time that paper cannot be sold. Hamilton is coming on as Senator from N. York. there has been so much contrivance & combination in that as to shew there is some great object in hand. Troup the district judge of N. York, resigns towards the close of the session of their assembly. the appointment of mr Hobart, then Senator, to succeed Troup, is not made by the President till after the assembly had risen. otherwise they would have chosen the Senator in place of Hobart. Jay then names Hamilton Senator, but not till a day or two before his own election as Governor was to come on, lest the unpopularity of the nomination should be in time to affect his own election. we shall see in what all this is to end. but surely in something. the popular movement in the eastern states is checked as we expected: and war addresses are showering in from New Jersey & the great trading towns. however we still trust that a nearer view of the war & a land tax will oblige the great mass of the people to attend. at present the war-hawks talk of Septembrizing, Deportation, and the examples for quelling sedition set by the French Executive. all the firmness of the human mind is now in a state of requisition.—salutations to mrs Madison & to yourself friendship & Adieu.

P.M. The bill for the naval department is passed.

RC (DLC: Madison Papers); addressed: "James Madison junr. near Orange court-house." PrC (DLC); lacks postscript.

On 30 Apr. President Adams signed the bill that created the Department of the NAVY (U.S. Statutes at Large, 1:553-4). For an account of the passage of the bill, see Smelser, *Navy*, 150-9. The act authorizing the president to raise a PROVISIONAL ARMY was approved on 28 May, but the House of Representatives had reduced the size of the force from 20,000 to 10,000 men and had amended the president's power to raise troops from "whenever he shall judge the public safety shall require the measure" to a declaration of war, actual invasion by a foreign power, or evidence that the country was in imminent danger of an invasion. The legislation, which limited the executive authority to times when Congress was not in session, would expire after three years. Republicans failed by a 56 to 37 vote on 16 May to delete the third section of the act, which gave the president power to accept companies of volunteers and appoint commissioned officers (U.S. Statutes at Large, 1:558-61; JHR, 3:296-302; *Annals*, 8:1725-72). For the debates on the constitutionality of giving the president the right to raise troops, see Notes on Federalist Arguments in Congressional Debates, [after 3 Aug. 1798].

Perhaps the impetus for TJ's charge that Josiah PARKER had COMPLETELY GONE OVER TO THE WAR-PARTY was an announcement in the *Gazette of the United States* of 11 Apr. that "Col. P—" of Virginia had organized a meeting of House Republicans at which he noted the importance of unanimity during the crisis with France and encouraged them, as the minority party, to join with the majority "in favor of measures of general defence." For Parker's party identification and voting record, see Dauer, *Adams Federalists*, 170-1, 309.

On 17 Apr. Joshua COIT LAID A MOTION ON THE TABLE proposing that the naturalization act then in effect be referred to a committee for study. On 1 May the committee on protection of commerce and defense of the country recommended amending the law to increase the term of residence required for citizenship. In the ensuing debate Robert Goodloe Harper declared that it was time to change the law "to declare, that nothing but birth should entitle a man to citizenship in this country." Harrison Gray Otis proposed a resolution denying future naturalized citizens from "holding any office of honor, trust, or profit." The naturalization bill, signed by President Adams on 18 June, called for the registration of all aliens and included a 14-year residence requirement (*Annals*, 8:1566-70; U.S. Stat-

utes at Large, 1:566-9). For TJ's report on the attempts to cut the waiting period to 7 years, see TJ to Madison, 14 June, and JS, 2:506. For an account of the passage of the naturalization act, see Smith, *Freedom's Fetters*, 26-34.

On 19 Apr., the same day the resolution for revising the naturalization law was sent to committee, the Geneva born Albert GALLATIN spoke against the use of convoys to protect American trade. Federalists used this to challenge his patriotism. Speaker of the House Dayton charged that Gallatin had never acquainted himself with the "principles that actuated the Americans in 1776," and John Allen of Connecticut queried, "Is this the language of an American who loves his country? No, sir, it is the language of a foreign agent" (*Annals*, 8:1427, 1453, 1473-83; JHR, 3:266). For the resolution by James HILLHOUSE designed to give POWER TO SEND AWAY SUSPECTED ALIENS, see Smith, *Freedom's Fetters*, 51-3. In his arguments before the House on 20 Apr., Allen clearly had BACHE's *Aurora* in mind when he described "a vile incendiary paper published in this city, which constantly teems with the most atrocious abuse of all the measures of the Government, and its administrators." Making reference to the infamous conversation between "Y" and the American envoys, Allen identified (by insinuation, not name) the *Aurora* and the paper's supporters in the House as "the fruits of 'the diplomatic skill of France' " (*Annals*, 8:1482, 1484-5). CARY'S PAPER: *Carey's United States Recorder*, published at Philadelphia by James Carey, survived only from January to August 1798. In a draft on John Barnes on 5 May 1798 TJ ordered payment of $20 to Carey, to cover two subscriptions for TJ and one each for James Monroe and Wilson Miles Cary (MS in ViU: Edgehill-Randolph Papers, written and signed by TJ, endorsed by Barnes, canceled, with receipt on verso by Carey; MB, 2:982-3).

For the MEETING held on 20 Apr. in NEW YORK and the ADDRESS that was to be circulated through the wards of the city, see *Gazette of the United States*, 23 Apr. Adams appointed New York Senator John Sloss HOBART to succeed Robert Troup as judge of the United States District Court of New York on 11 Apr. His appointment was confirmed the next day. On the 16th TJ laid Hobart's letter of resignation before the Senate. In the missive, Hobart thanked TJ "for the politeness and attention" with which TJ, as the president of the Senate, had treated him during his short tenure as senator (RC in DNA: RG 46, Senate Records, 5th Cong., 2d sess.; addressed: "The Honble Thomas Jefferson Vice President of the United States And President of the Senate"; endorsed by clerk). Three days later Governor JAY wrote Hamilton encouraging him to accept appointment to the vacant Senate seat but Hamilton declined. William North, a Federalist leader in the New York Assembly from Duanesburg, was subsequently appointed and took his seat on 21 May. He resigned it two months later to accept a post as adjutant general of the provisional army (DAB; JEP, 1:269; JS, 2:472, 490; Syrett, Hamilton Papers, 21:433-4, 447).

The TALK OF SEPTEMBRIZING referred to the consequences of the *coup d' état* in France of 18 Fructidor (4 Sep. 1797), including the passage of a law that authorized the arrest and DEPORTATION of 2 members of the Directory, 53 deputies from the Council of 500, and other government critics. The FRENCH EXECUTIVE also obtained the power to ban newspapers. Most of the officials listed for deportation escaped arrest but news of the arrival in French Guiana of those who did not was carried in Philadelphia newspapers. In his attack on the *Aurora*, Congressman Allen declared, "In another country, this printer and his supporters would long ago have found a *fourth of September*" (Stinchcombe, *XYZ Affair*, 52-3; Scott and Rothaus, *Historical Dictionary*, 1:265-7; *Gazette of the United States*, 14 Apr. 1798; *Annals*, 8:1485).

[1] Preceding two words interlined in place of "first letter to."

From John Page

MY DEAR JEFFERSON   Rosewell Apl. 26th. 1798

I have just received the Instructions to our Envoys & their Dispatches inclosed under two blank Covers, for which I thank you—for as much as I wish for your Correspondence, I can not desire you to withdraw your attention from the greatly important Business of your Office, from the interesting subjects of various kinds which must[1] be presented to you every day at Philada. & from your favorite Studies, & possibly from an intended Vindication of your Character against the provoking & indecent Attacks lately made by Mr. Harper, & the Author of Americanus—I confess I did suppose that some one in the Senate, or in the House of Representatives would have made a Motion, respecting Harper's Attack upon you, similar to that which he has made concerning Findley's Letter—I confess too my Friend, that I think it time, you should silence such clamour against you; the public Happiness is interested in your retaining the Confidence of the People: & indeed the present critical Situation of our Country seems to require that an Explanation of the conduct & Views of the Parties in the Ud. S—s should be fairly laid open before the People; in such a manner as not to provoke & embitter the Resentment of either of them—I think you could shew that your Principles were such as appeared to you, & will appear to the People upon examination[2] to be best calculated to produce their Independence, secure their Liberty, & promote their permanent Interests & Happiness—that although you had entertained Republican Jealousies founded on the great & sudden change in the Constitution & Govt. of the Ud. S—s, on the Propositions made in the Convention, by Col. Hamilton, & on his monarchical Systems of Finance, you had like a good Citizen submitted to the Will of the Majority & had supported the Measures of Government according to the Duties of your Office. that (if you were the Author of *the* Letter to Mazzei) you used strong metaphorical Expressions suited to the Taste & disposition of your Correspondent, & though expressive of your private Sentiments, they were such as were not intended for public View, & never did in any manner proceed from a Wish[3] injurious to the Government, or even[4] to the Persons therein alluded to. You might shew indeed, what the Change was in our Constitution & Govt. of the U.S. at Which you had expressed your Surprise, & may point out by what means & on what pretexts this Change was made. You may shew I think in delicate language that an anglo-monarchico-party did effect this Change & may satisfy [Duty] itself that by this Phrase is not meant a party influenced by Britain, but by an Opinion which coinciding with that on which the british Government is supported may fitly be termed an Anglo-monarchico-aristocratic party—You may with Truth & Sincerity I have no doubt declare your respect & Friendship for those from whom you differ in political Opinion, & your unalterable determination to support the Constitution of the U.S. You may treat with candor the Sentiments of those who differ from you, & allow them the Exercise of their Judgment on Matters which they may suppose calculated to promote public Happiness. You may if you can too forgive the intemperate mistaken Zeal of those who have persecuted you. I beg your pardon for runing on in this manner & appearing to dictate to you what you should say—It proceeds from my Friendship for you, & my Wish to see the Spirit & Views of the Parties laid open to each other & to the People, & in such a manner as may possibly reduce them to proper limits & keep them within the bounds of good policy & decency.

I have enquired where ever I thought I had a chance of receiving the Information which you requested, but could receive nothing like it. On the contrary Mr. M. Anderson our Friend informed me that his Brother Col. Rd. Anderson, now of Kentucky, had told him that you had been led into a mistake by Captain Gibson—that Gibson had reported some such Speech, as that which you have published in your

Notes on Virginia, as delivered to him by Logan; but, that Logan did not appear remaining in the Woods where Cap. Gibson said he had met him & received his Talk or Speech which he gave in at the time you mentioned.[5]

Richmond May 28th 1798

I have been twice interrupted in writing, & had laid aside my Letter so long that I had determined not to send but on shewing it to a Friend to day who advised me to send it to you I have consented—

I am here endeavouring to sell my Interest in the Frying-pan Co. & happened to have this Scrawl amongst my papers. I can only add that I am yr. Friend JOHN PAGE

RC (DLC); torn; endorsed by TJ as received 2 June 1798 and so recorded in SJL.

The ATTACKS on the Republicans by Robert Goodloe HARPER took aim at TJ on 2 Mch. Harper, in a long speech in the House of Representatives on the foreign intercourse bill, declared that TJ had returned from France in 1789 as the "missionary" of its revolution, becoming "the author and secret mover" of a plan to subvert Washington's policy of neutrality and bring the United States into war with Britain to suit the purposes of a revolutionary cadre in France (Annals, 7:1192-3). For the letter of AMERICANUS, see 10 Apr.

MOTION . . . SIMILAR TO THAT WHICH HE HAS MADE CONCERNING FINDLEY'S LETTER: on 12 Apr. Porcupine's Gazette printed a letter of 21 Feb., said to be from William Findley to one of his constituents in western Pennsylvania. Referring to it on 13 Apr. Harper stated his intention to offer a motion "for the reprimand, at the bar of the House, of one of its members, for the most vile and unfounded slanders against sundry members of this House." After the motion was introduced, Findley had leave of absence for the rest of the session to attend to a pressing family matter (Annals, 8:1415, 1701).

For Harper's comments on TJ's LETTER TO MAZZEI, see Vol. 29:789.

INFORMATION WHICH YOU REQUESTED: TJ to Page, 2 Jan. 1798.

[1] Page here first began to write "engage your Attention," and deleted it.
[2] Preceding two words interlined.
[3] Preceding two words interlined in place of "Sentiments."
[4] Preceding word interlined.
[5] Judging from the appearance of Page's handwriting, he wrote this paragraph between the two interruptions in his composition of the letter.

To Thomas Mann Randolph

TH:J. TO TMR. Philadelphia Apr. 26. 98.

Your last of the 14th. was acknoleged in mine of the 19th. the bill for 12. armed vessels passed by about 4. to 3. in the H. of R. that for the establishment of a Secretary of the navy was tried yesterday on it's passage to the 3d. reading, and prevailed by 47. against 41. it will be put on it's passage to-day. the bill for a provisional army of 20,000. men is somewhat doubtful in event. the expence of this is calculated from 4. to

6. millions of Dollars a year. a land tax is voted in the committee, and must be passed. an additional tax on salt will probably be laid. the stoppage of public interest will be proposed, but will hardly prevail. motions are made for modifying the rights of citizenship, and for giving a power to send away suspected aliens. they talk of proposing a sedition bill, the object of which is to suppress the whig-presses. they have now such a majority by the going over to them of all wavering members, and the departure of others (no less than 5. of the Virginia) delegation are gone home) that they can carry any thing. our only hope is that the downfall of wheat & flour, a heavy land tax, & a near view of war will rouse the main body of the people to see at length to what objects the public measures have for some time been leading them. Hamilton is appointed by Govr. Jay to the Senate of the US. in the place of Hobart who is made a judge. nobody doubts that this portends some great and mischievous enterprize. the time of our rising is conjectured from the middle to the last of May. war addresses are coming in from New Jersey & the great trading towns. but this paroxysm will be short. the only fear is of irretrievable injury while it prevails. my warmest love to my ever dear Martha & the little ones. affectionate salutations & friendship to yourself. Adieu.

RC (DLC); endorsed by Randolph. PrC (CSmH); endorsed by TJ in ink on verso.

From John Heckewelder

SIR   Bethlehem Apr. 28th. 1798.

In compliance to Your request, I have communicated what came to my knowledge respecting the Murder of Logans family in the Year 1774. I have shewn by what Opportunity's reports were brought in the Indian Country—how they circulated—& what effect it had from time to time on the minds of the Indians—But Sir! altho I have no hesitation to bear testimony to the truth, I wish to inform You, that my situation is such, that would not admit of publishing the whole of my relation, & therefore beg You to consider the enclosed communication as Confidential. I am engaged in commencing a Settlement in the Western Country, & my business will render it necessary for me to be at times in the *very* Country, (& by the by) among the *very* People to whoom I have in my report alluded, as perpetraters of Murderous acts, especially such as were engaged in Murdering the Moravian Indians on Muskingum, & who, unprincipled as many of them may be to *this* day, might unite against me &c. Yet, whatever in Your Judgement, shall seem necessary to *prove*, that the account You gave in Your Notes on Virginia, of the Murder of Logan's family, *was* the prevailing report of that day, I cannot object to Your publishing. And as to the Account I have given of Logans Character I have no reason to object to Your publishing the whole as I have given it; if You chuse.

In my Opinion there must be yet People living in or about Pittsburg who have some knowledge of the subject in question. I should think Genl. Gibson one.

I have only to add; that Your complying with my request will put me under great Obligations to You.

I have the honour to be Sir Your most obedt humble servt.

JOHN HECKEWELDER

P.S. Next Monday I propose leaving home for Detroit & Muskingum

RC (DLC); at foot of text: "Honble. Thomas Jefferson Esqr."; endorsed by TJ as received 1 May 1798 and so recorded in SJL.

YOUR REQUEST: see TJ to Heckewelder, 11 Apr. 1798.

MURDERING THE MORAVIAN INDIANS ON MUSKINGUM: in March 1782 militiamen from Washington County, Pennsylvania, killed over ninety unarmed Delaware Indian converts at the Moravian town of Gnadenhutten, in what is now the state of Ohio. At the time Heckewelder, one of the missionaries to the settlements in the Muskingum valley, was under British custody at Detroit, but he later wrote the definitive account of the incident (John Heckewelder, *Narrative of the Mission of the United Brethren among the Delaware and Mohegan Indians, from its Commencement, in the Year 1740, to the Close of the Year 1808* [Philadelphia, 1820], 308-28; White, *Middle Ground*, 389-90; Abernethy, *Western Lands*, 267-8).

ENCLOSURE

Heckewelder's Memorandum on the Logan Affair

Communication (Confidential)

In the Spring of the Year 1774—at a time when in the interior parts of the Indian Country all seemed Peace & Tranquil, the Villages on Muskingum were suddenly allarmed by 2 Runners (Indians) who reported: "that the big Knifes (Virginians) had attacked the Mingo Settlement on Ohio, & butchered even the Women with their Children in their Arms—and that Logans family were among the Slain.   A day or 2 after this several Mingoes made their appearance, among whoom were one or two Wounded, who had in this manner effected their escape. Exasperated to a high degree—after relating the particulars of this transaction, (which for humanity sake I forbear mentioning.)—after resting some time on the treachery of the big Knifes—of their Barbarity to those who are their friends, they gave a figurative description of the perpetrators, & Named Cressap,[1] as having been at the head of this Murdering Act. They made mention of Nine being killed, & two wounded, & were prone to take revenge on any Person of a white Colour, for which reason, the Missionaries had to shut

[306]

themselves up during their stay. From this time, terror daily encreased—The exasperated friends & Relations of these murdered Women & Children, with the Nations to whoom they belonged passed & repassed thro the Villages of the quiet Delaware Towns in search of White People, making Use of the most abusive Language to these (the Delawares) since they would not join in taking revenge—Traders had either to hide themselves, or try to get out of the Country the best way they could, & even at this time, they yet found such true friends among the Indians, who, at the risk of their own Lives, conducted them, with the best part of their Property to Pittsburg, altho' (shameful to relate) these Benefactors were on their return from this Mission, *way laid*, & fired upon by Whites, while crossing Big Beaver in a Canow, & had one Man, a Shawnee, named Silverheels, (a Man of Note in his Nation) Wounded in the Body. This exasperated the Shawnees so much so that they, (or at least a great part of them) immediately took an active part in the cause; & the Mingoes, (nearest connex-ted with the former,) became unbounded in their Rage. A Mr. Jones, Son to a respectable family of this Neighborhood (Bethlehem) who was then on his pas-sage up Muskingum with two other Men was fortunately espied by a friendly Indian Woman, at the falls of Muskingum[2] who thro motives of Humanity alone, informed Jones of the Nature of the times, & that he was running right in the hands of the enraged—& put him on the way, where he might perhaps escape the Vengeance of the stroling Parties. One of Jones's Men, fatiegued by travelling in the Woods, declared he would rather Die, than remain longer in this Situation, & hitting accidentally on a Path, he determined to follow the same—few hundred Yards decided *his* fate. He was met by a party of about 15 Mingoes, (& as it happened, almost within sight of White-Eyes Town) Mur-dered, & cut to pieces, & his Limbs & flesh stuk up on the Bushes. White-Eyes on hearing the Scalp Halloo, ran immediately out with his Men to see what the matter was, & finding the mangled Body in this Condition, gathered the whole & buried it. But next day, when some of the above Party found on their return the Body interred: they instantly tore up the Ground, & endeavoured to destroy or scatter about the Parts at a greater distance. White-Eyes, with the Delawares watching their motions, gathered & interred the same a second time. The War party finding this out, ran furiously into the Del. Village, exclaiming against the conduct of these People—setting forth the cruelty of Cressap towards Women & Children, & declaring at the same time, that they would, in consequence of this cruelty, serve every White Man they should meet with in same manner.[3] The Delawares, by the care & industry of their Chieffs, succeeded amazingly in quieting the minds of their Nation, & much credit is due to some private Indi-viduals at Pittsburg for their exertions to bring about an accomodation. A Mr. Duncan of that place, at the risk of his Life, undertook to carry a Message with Captn. White-Eyes to the Enemy, but on his way between Cooshachking & Waketameki, he was fired at, & compelled to make his escape the best way he could. White Eyes's conduct on this as well as every other occasion in this affair does him honor. Times grew worse & worse—War parties went out & took Scalps & Prisoners, & the latter, in hopes it might be of service in saving their Lives, exclaimed against the barbarous Act which gave rise to these troubles, & against the Perpetraters. The Name, of Greathouse[4] was mentioned as having been an accomplice to Cressop. So detestable became the latter Name among the Indians, that I have frequently heard them apply it to the worst of things. also, in quieting and stilling their Children I have heard them say: hush! Crissop will fetch You; whereas otherwise, they name the Owl.   The Warriors having afterwards bent their course more towards the Ohio & down the same; Peace seemed with Us already on the return, & this became the case soon after the decided Battle fought on Conhawa.   Traders now returning into the Indian Country again, related the Story of the above mentioned Massacree, *after the same manner*, & *with the same words* we had heard it related hitherto. *So* the report remained, & was believed by all who resided in the Indian Country—*So* it was represented, numbers of times in the Peacable Delaware Towns by the Enemy—*So* the Christian Indians were continually told they would one Day be served—With *this* impression a petty Chieff hurried all the way from Wabash in 1779 to take his relations (who were living with the peacable Delawares near Coshachking) out of the reach of the big Knifes, in whose friendship he nevermore would place any confidence—And when this Man found, that his numerous Relations, would not break friendship with the Americans, nor be removed; he took two of his relations (Women) off by force, saying: "The whole Crop shall not be destroyed; I will save Seed out of it for a new Crop,"[5] alluding to, & repeatingly reminding these of the Murder of the family of Logan, who he said had been real friends to the Whites & yet were most cruelly Murdered by them.[6] (It turned out in end as he had predicted.) *Such* was also the Language of 80 Warriors in the Year 1781 in Apr. to the Christn. Indians on Muskingum, all cruelties heretofore committed by Whites on harmless, friendly Indians were represented to *these* People in order to induce them to move off while it was yet time; and when they could not prevail upon them to stir, they being told, they were not concious of Guilt, & therefore had nothing to fear—they returned again in August same Year, with their Number encreased to upwards of 300, *determined*, that if they would not be removed *this* time, they should be killed on the Spot. *Yet*, before they took rash measures, they spent 22 days in representing facts of the most cruel kind committed by Whites on Innocent, harmless Indians, mentioning the Names of the ringleaders of these Gangs, and declaring there was no faith to be placed in the big Knifes. (NB by this time all the Americans were called big Knifes)—They prognosticated how they would one day be rewarded for their friendship, but the latter remaining unshaken, they took off evry Soul by force, after first having made the Missionaries Prisoners, & robbed them of all they had. They were left in upper Sandusky thro the Winter, where they lived in the greatest Poverty immaginable—The Barbarous Massacree committed on upwards of 90 Christian Indians, (the greatest part Women & Children) in the Spring of the Year 1782 on Muskingum, I pass over in silence[7]—In Detroit where I arrived the same Spring, the report respecting the Murder of the Indians on Ohio, (amongst whoom was Logans family,) was the same as related above; & on my return to the United States in the fall of 1786—& from that time—whenever & wherever in my presence, this subject was the topic of Conversation: I found, the report still the same, vizt: that a Person, bearing the Name of Cressop was the author or perpetrator of this Deed.

Note. In relating the above reports, I have, for truth sake, made use of the *same* Words & expressions uttered by the Parties. Much abusive Language by Indians on the Name & Character of the Man in question, I have, for decency's sake, omitted.[8] That the Virginians had, long since, by means of their wearing Swords been universally called big Knifes, or more properly long Knifes, is, I imagine generally known. From the commencement of the American Revolution the People througought the U. States are called big Knifes by them.

JOHN HECKEWELDER

Logan was the seccond Son of *Shikéllemus*, a celebrated Chieff of the Cajuga Nation. This Chieff, on account of his attachment to the English Government was of great service to the Country. Having the confidence of all the 6 Nations, as well as that of the English, he was very useful in settling disputes &c &c. He was highly esteemed by Conrad Weisser Esqr. (an Officer for Government in the Indian Department) with whoom he acted conjunctly; & was faithful unto his Death. His residence was at Shamokin, where he took great delight in acts of hospitality to such of the White People, whose Business led them that Way*—His Name & fame was so high on record: that Count Zinzendorf, when in this Country in 1742, became desirous of seeing him, & actually visited him at his House in Shamokin.†

About the Year 1772 Logan was introduced to me by an Indian friend, as Son to the late reputable Chieff Shikellemus—& as a friend to the White People. In the course of conversation, I thought him a Man of superior talents, than Indians generally were. The subject turning on vice & immorality, he confessed his too great share of this, especially his fondness of Liquor—He exclaimed against the White People, for imposing Liquors upon the Indians—He otherwise admired their ingenuity—spoke of Gentlemen; but observed, the Indians unfortunably had but seldom these as their Neighbours &c. He spoke of his friendship to the White People—wished always to be a Neighbour to them—intended to settle somewhere on Ohio below big Beaver—was, (to the best of my recollection) then encamped at the Mouth of this River, (Beaver)—urged me to pay him a Visit &c. *Note*. I was then, living at the Moravian-Town on this River, in the Neighbourhood of Cuskuskee.   In Apr. 1773, while on my passage down the Ohio for Muskingum: I called at Logan's Settlement, where I recieved evry civility I could expect from such of the family as were at home.

Indian reports concerning Logan, after the Death of his family ran to this: that he exerted himself during the Shawnee War, (then so called) to take all the revenge he could, declaring he had lost all confidence to the White People—At the time of Negociation, he declared his reluctance in laying down the Hatchet, not having (in his Opinion) yet taken ample Sattisfaction—Yet, for the sake of the Nation, he *would* do it. His expressions from time to time, denoted a deep Melancholy. Life, (said he) had become a Torment to him—He knew no more what pleasure was—He thought it had been better, if he had never existed. &c &c. Report further stated: that he became in some measure delirious—declared he would kill himself—went to Detroit—drank very freely & did not seem to care what he did; & what became of himself. In this condition he left Detroit, & on his way between that place and Miami, was murdered.[9] In Oct. 1781, (while as Prisoner on my way to Detroit,) I was shown the spot where this shall have happened.[10]

JOHN HECKEWELDER

* The preceding account of Shikéllemus, (Logans Father) is coppied from Manuscrips of Revd. C. Pyrlæus, written between the Years 1741—& 1748.

† See G. H. Loskiel's history of the Mission of the United Brethren &c. Part II. Chap. II. page 31.

MS (DLC); endorsed by TJ. Printed, with minor variations in spelling, punctuation, and capitalization not recorded here, in *Appendix to the Notes on Virginia*, with the omission of three passages and insertion of text from another document as noted below (*Notes*, ed. Peden, 246-50).

During both Dunmore's War and the American Revolutionary War, WHITE-EYES, a leader of the Delaware Indians in Ohio, strove to maintain his group's neutrality. Despite those efforts, his death in 1778 may have been a murder by American militiamen (ANB). DECIDED BATTLE FOUGHT ON CONHAWA: on 10 Oct. 1774 at Point Pleasant, where the Kanawha River joins the Ohio, Shawnees unsuccessfully attempted to overpower Virginia militia in what proved to be the primary battle of Dunmore's War (Abernethy, *Western Lands*, 111-12). BARBAROUS MASSACREE: the Gnadenhutten massacre.

CELEBRATED CHIEFF OF THE CAJUGA NATION: Logan's mother was a Cayuga, but his father, Shikellamy, was of another Iroquois tribe, the Oneidas (ANB, 13:836). Nikolaus Ludwig von ZINZENDORF, the Saxon patron of the United Brethren who did much to recast them into the missionizing Moravian Church, was in Pennsylvania from December 1741 to January 1743 and made extended visits to Indian tribes along the frontier (ANB). During the 1740s also, Moravian scholar John Christopher PYRLÆUS studied American Indian languages in Pennsylvania (James Grant Wilson and John Fiske, eds., *Appletons' Cyclopædia of American Biography*, 6 vols. [New York, 1887-89], 5:145).

[1] Heckewelder wrote the remainder of the sentence in the margin, keyed for insertion at this point.

[2] Preceding five words written in margin and keyed for insertion at this point.

[3] Next three sentences lacking in *Appendix*.

[4] Heckewelder first wrote "A Name, something like *Long*[. . .]," before changing the name to "Longhouse" and finally altering the phrase to read as above.

[5] Remainder of sentence written in margin and keyed for insertion at this point.

[6] Text from this point to next note lacking in *Appendix*.

[7] In *Appendix* text resumes at this point with no break.

[8] Heckewelder evidently added the remainder of this "Note" after signing the document. Entire paragraph and signature that follows are lacking in *Appendix*.

[9] Heckewelder first wrote "did either murder his Companion, or at least attempt it (I forget which) when he was murdered himself," then altered the sentence to read as above.

[10] In *Appendix* TJ here inserted, with no break, the body of Heckewelder's letter to him of 24 Feb. 1800.

To Sir John Sinclair

DEAR SIR   Philadelphia. April 28. 1798.

I had the honor on the 23d. of March of addressing a letter to y[ou on] some subjects of agriculture, which was committed to the care of mr Tho[rnton] Secretary to the British legation here, who went over in the packet. Th[is is?] merely to cover the bill of lading for a box put on board the ship Act[. . .] bound to London, in which are the Drill & Mouldboard spoken of in [my?] former letter. my friend in Richmond has forwarded two barrels [of] Virginia May wheat to Norfolk (in that state) to be shipped thence [on?] two different ships to your address. it will probably therefore not [be in] my power to give you advice of the occasions by which th[ey?] are sent. I hope however all will arrive safe, and shall be glad at all times to be charged with any services here which can be rendered to your society.

I have the honor to be with great & sincere esteem [&] respect Dear Sir

Your most obedt. & most humble servt   Th: Jefferson

PrC (DLC); margin frayed; at foot of text: "Sr. John Sinclair."

From James Madison

Dear Sir   Apl. 29. 1798

My last was on the 22d. Yours recd. by the last mail was of the 19th. instant. The despatches have not yet come sufficiently to the knowledge of the bulk of the people to decide the impression which is to result from them. As far as I can infer from the language of the few who have read the Newspapers, there will be a general agreement as to the improper views of our Executive party, whatever difference of opinion there may be as to the purity of the French Councils. Indeed the reflexion of others as well as my own traces so many absurdities & improbabilities in many of the details that the injustice seems equal to the[1] temerity of publishing such a libel on the French Government. Col. Monroe lodged with me last night on his way to the District Court at Fredg. He considers the transaction as evidently a swindling experiment, and thinks the result will bring as much derision on the Envoys, as mischief the Country. I am sorry to learn that the naval bill is likely to be carried, & particularly that any of our friends should by their leaving Congs. be accessary to it. The public sentiment here is unquestionably opposed to every measure that may increase the danger of war. Petitions expressive of it will be signed by all to whom they are presented, with such exceptions only as may be guessed at. It appears however that the crisis is over for their effect on Congs. if[2] there were a disposition there to listen to them.

I take the liberty of subjoining a list of a few articles not to be got out of Philada. & so important to my present object, that I break thro' every restraint from adding to the trouble of which you have more than enough. I hope the commission may be facilitated by your previous acquaintance with the places at which they are to be had, and that you will be able to make use of the time of others chiefly for the purpose. If J. Bringhurst should be in the way, he will readily relieve you from all attention to the details. I wish them to be forwarded "to Fredg. to the care of Robert Dunbar Esqr. at Falmouth." The inclosed draught will be a fund for the purchase. Adieu affly.   Js. M. Jr.

	Inches
100 Panes Window Glass	$15\frac{1}{2}$ by $12\frac{1}{2}$ *precisely*.
80 do.	$12\frac{5}{8}$ by $12\frac{1}{2}$ do.
10 do.	$17\frac{1}{2}$ by $9\frac{1}{2}$ do.

3. Brass locks of good size & quality—3. do of smaller size—with screws &c.

Brass spiral Hinges for 8 doors with do.

RC (DLC: Madison Papers); endorsed by TJ as received 8 May 1798 and so recorded in SJL. Enclosed draft not found.

[1] Madison here canceled "folly of."

[2] Here Madison canceled "they [w]ould otherwise" but neglected to delete a second "if."

From Thomas Mann Randolph

ThM.R. to Th: Jefferson,   Belmont Ap. 29th. :98

yours of 12th. inst. reached us the 25th. that of 19th. last night. Nothing of Arnold yet—the trees had a long passage from Richmond; we lost not a moment but could not get them in the ground till the 24th.—they were in such excellent condition and the Earth in so good order that I have no doubt this will be the most successfull planting you ever made—the Harpsichord did not receive the smallest injury from its double voyage, land carriage or unpacking. Davenport has done nothing at Mont'o. since your departure—he is not at work there now—he has got 3000 Chesnut shingles for you & has cut a number of Stocks at Pounceys but has not yet begun to saw them—in my next I hope to be able to inform you of some sure engagement for the plank you want. George has not yet prized his Tobacco tho' I urge him to it every time I meet him—I wish he may not have suffered it to spoil during the winter, that was hinted to me today and I intended to have examined it this forenoon but had not time I was so long engaged in the Library: he is not careless in general tho' he procrastinates too much. I expect the Beef and Bacon every day, Fleming whose boats had just gone down when I rec'd. Clarkes letter engaged to bring it up on their return. Upon your letter of the 12th. I bought 2 large young horses immediately one for 120$ Cash the other $126:66 cts. pay'le. the 1st. of July—I put them into the Waggon and gave George the Mules—he was under great apprehension his Corn w'd. be lost before you came home from the weakness of his ploughs—he *must* make a crop of it this year for every body seems to be neglecting it for Tob'o. I have bought 40 Barrells for him @ 15/. & had it hauled to him by James: he was quite out.

I fear no more can be had for that. With pain I mention Darlington: anticipating your kindness I took him early in the Winter to ride being absolutely on foot—he had not been long at Belmont before he came in the way of my Dun horse (tho' I kept him allways chained; he unluckily got loose) & rec'd. a bite from him on the middle of the neck which was very near killing him and has greatly injured his appearance—he is quite well now & in far better plight & health than I ever saw him—I keep him still and as the depression in his neck will not spoil him for me, beg you to take Meriwethurs horse in exchange for him: I can have *him* at a short warning. Darlington will allways be dull & a stumbler, he needs keen spurs & a heavy Bridle but with those is the finest riding horse I know & except the bite an elegant Animal. I am sorrier for the accident as I fear you cannot get a better just now notwithstanding his failings. I thank you heartily for your trouble respecting the books.—I wish Richardson w'd. send a brick to Duke.

I cannot by the most diligent search find Escarbot tho I see it in the Catalogue [a 12 mo.] which makes me hope it is not out and I may yet find it.

Champlain I send as directed & shall look again before next post for Escarbot.

 With the most sincere & warm affection Th: M. Randolph

RC (ViU: Edgehill-Randolph Papers); brackets in original; addressed: "Thomas Jefferson Vice-president Philad'a."; franked; endorsed by TJ as received 8 May 1798 and so recorded in SJL.

Power of Attorney
from Tadeusz Kosciuszko

Know all men by these presents that I Thaddeus Kosciusko late of Poland, but now at Philadelphia in the United States of America do hereby constitute & appoint Thomas Jefferson of Monticello in Virginia my attorney in fact and proxy in all cases within the United States giving him full power & authority over all the property real or personal, in possession right, title or action which I now have, or hereafter may have within the United States, and of and touching the same to enter into and conclude any transactions which he may think expedient for my interest with any person or[1] persons, body politic or corporate, or any state or the United States,[2] and the said property to preserve in the same form or to change into any other for my use; as also on my behalf to demand sue for, recover, recieve, dispose of, transfer & convey the same in all

[313]

cases whatsoever, & to give, make & take in every case full and valid transfers, conveyances,[3] discharges & acquittances, as to any thing touching the premisses.

And further to enable the said Thomas Jefferson to transact the said matters as well by others as by himself, he is hereby fully authorized to appoint & substitute under himself other attornies or proxies by way of deputation, from time to time, as he shall think proper, giving to him or them on my behalf the same or any lesser powers over the premisses, as is herein before given to himself, and such deputed powers again to revoke, or to renew, as he may think best for my interest.

And moreover to provide against the contingency of death or disability of the said Thomas to transact the said business, I do further authorize the said Thomas, by any sufficient instrument under his hand & seal, for me, & on my behalf, to nominate & appoint another attorney in chief to succeed, on the contingency of his death or other disability, to all the powers herein given to the said Thomas; the same however remaining in suspense, and of no activity during his own life or ability to act.

And I do hereby ratify and confirm all the acts and proceedings of the said Thomas & of those acting under him, or in pursuance of his appointment, as fully & absolutely as if done by myself. And inasmuch as the sd Thomas undertakes to act in the premisses without fee or reward, & purely and sincerely from motives of friendship & esteem which he bears to me the said Thaddeus Kosciusko, & it would therefore be unjust that he should be chargeable for any accidents or losses which may happen herein, not through his wilful default or gross negligence, now therefore, that it may not be in the power of my representatives or others, on the event of my death, or any other event, to molest or damnify the sd Thomas or his representatives for such cause, Know ye, that from all responsibility for such accidents & losses not happening through his wilful default or gross negligence as aforesaid I do for myself my heirs executors & administrators hereby fully exonerate & acquit him the said Thomas, his heirs, executors & administrators for ever. And I do expressly reserve to myself the legal right to revoke these presents whensoever to me it shall seem expedient. Witness my[4] hand & seal at Philadelphia this 30th day of April one thousand seven hundred & ninety eight.   T KOSCIUSZKO

Witnesses
J DAWSON
JOHN BARNES

MS (PPRF); in TJ's hand, leaving blanks for day and month which were filled by an unidentified hand; signed and sealed by Kosciuszko; signed by Dawson and

Barnes; indented; notarized with seal on verso by Peter Lohra, Philadelphia, 15 June 1798, attesting Dawson's signed and sworn statement that affirms his and Barnes's witnessing of the document; endorsed in an unknown hand: "Power for Dividends &ca. Thaddeus Kosciusko to Thomas Jefferson with his Substitution to John Barnes April 30 1798" (see below). PrC (MHi); letterpressed on a sheet too small to accommodate the full text. MS (same); in TJ's hand; blanks for date filled by same unidentified hand as in MS in PPRF; signed and sealed as above; indented; signed statement by Dawson on verso notarized by Lohra, 15 June 1798, identically to MS in PPRF; endorsed by TJ: "Koscuszko to Jefferson Power of Atty." PrC (National Museum, Cracow, Poland); blanks for date not filled; unsigned. Dft (MHi); entirely in TJ's hand and endorsed by him.

On 12 June TJ made Barnes "attorney under myself & on behalf of" Kosciuszko in matters relating to the latter's shares in the Bank of Pennsylvania, to include the receipt of dividends and voting for officers of the bank (MS in PPRF, entirely in TJ's hand, signed by him and by Dawson as witness, notarized by Lohra on 15 June, with seals).

[1] In Dft TJ interlined the words from "and of and touching" to this point in place of: "of whatsoever the same may consist, whether of money, stock, shares, dividends, interest or other thing, due or to become due from any."

[2] Here in Dft TJ canceled: "or deposited or to be deposited in any public treasury, bank, association, or company within the US."

[3] Preceding three words interlined in Dft in place of "perfect."

[4] PrC in MHi ends here.

To Van Staphorst & Hubbard

GENTLEMEN   Philadelphia Apr. 30. 1798.

Your favor of June 26. reached me Sep. 22. in Virginia. having settled the interest on the account inclosed in it agreeably to a statement which will be at the foot of this letter, I prepared a bond for the amount, which I brought on to this place, and have kept by me till the present season which gives a better chance for a safe conveyance than a winter passage.

A paragraph in your letter has given me uneasiness, lest you might have supposed I could consider you as involved in the practices of which I therein spoke. nothing could be farther from my thought; and the intention of my observations was, besides giving you a general view of the speculating practices going on here, as a general caution for the government of your affairs, to designate more particularly the conduct of one individual (mr Greenleaf) whom I had formerly understood to have been trusted by you in some matters. his catastrophe, as well as that of some others, has been what all prudent men might foresee. indeed the shock which has resulted from the state of things mentioned in my letter, has been very great, & severely felt by our merchants in general, not only those who directly participated in these matters, but those also who had kept clear themselves, but were affected by the failure of others. this was considerably hastened and increased by the French &

British spoliations on our commerce. these have been most scandalous indeed: and [tho?] both nations [still continue] their outrages on us, yet those of the one are considerably more in amount than the other. a great degree of impatience under these sufferings has consequently siezed our merchants, who openly call for war, and some think our government has too readily yielded to their views. the farmers, who know that they must pay the expence, wish a continuance of peace. this occasions some difference of sentiment among us; but should war be declared against us there will be but one sentiment pervading every description of men, that of uniting cordially to repel an invader. this is the true clue to the present state of opinion with us. the expences of preparation we have already incurred are very great, and give much uneasiness to those who are anxious to see our public debt discharged.

I take the liberty of inclosing & recommending to your care a letter to a friend of mine, Baron Von Geissmar, at Hanau, which is very interesting to him. I am in hopes you can give it a safe conveyance.

I am with great esteem Gentlemen Your most obedient & most humble servt Th: Jefferson

			florins	sols
1792	May 16.	the balance per acct rendered was in my favor	656–	2
	Sep. 27.	By my draught in favor of Dobson *f* 1014–		
	Nov. 23.	By my do. in favr of the bankers of the US.	2221–14	3235–14
		balance now against me		2579–12
1795.	Oct. 13.	Int. on do. @ 6. per cent to this date is		447– 2
				3026–14
		To remittance of this date through Maury £50. 5s 5d st.		553–
		balance then remaining due		2473–14
1797.	Dec. 25.	Int. on do. @ 6. pr. cent to this date is		326– 6
		balance for which a bond is now inclosed		2800–

payable Dec. 25. 1802. with int. @ 6 per cent from Dec. 25. 1797.

PrC (DLC); torn; at foot of first page: "Messrs. Nicholas & Jacob Van Staphorst & Hubbard." Enclosures: (1) Bond to Van Staphorst & Hubbard, 25 Nov. 1797. (2) Probably TJ to Baron von Geismar, 13 Feb. 1798, recorded in SJL but not found. Enclosed in TJ to Jacob Van Staphorst, 30 May 1798.

James GREENLEAF had spent the years from 1789 to 1793 in Amsterdam marketing U.S. government securities. He then became the associate of Robert Morris and John Nicholson in their notorious speculation in Federal District real estate, but was forced to default when he failed to induce Dutch investors to purchase Washington city lots (Shaw Livermore, *Early American Land Companies: Their Influence on Corporate Development* [New York, 1939], 164–

5). MY LETTER: TJ to Van Staphorst & Hubbard, 27 Mch. 1797.

TJ's FRIEND, the Baron von Geismar, had written a letter of 15 Oct. 1796 that has not been found, but according to SJL it was received on 11 July 1797 from Hanau. Evidently he and TJ had not corresponded since 1789, although they had become acquainted ten years earlier when the baron, a German officer who surrendered with Burgoyne at Saratoga, had been quartered near Monticello awaiting parole (Marie Kimball, *Jefferson, War and Peace: 1776 to 1784* [New York, 1947], 40-5; TJ to Richard Henry Lee, 21 Apr. 1779; Geismar to TJ, 13 Apr. 1789). Also noted in SJL, but missing, are letters from Geismar to TJ of 11 July, 7 Aug. 1798, and 20 Feb. 1799, received, respectively, from Hanau on 22 Jan., 30 Mch., and 30 Aug. 1799, and one from TJ to Geismar dated 23 Feb. 1799.

A bond of £500 sterling from TJ to Farell & Jones, representing the first installment of TJ's portion of the debt owed to that firm by John Wayles's estate, had been assigned to John DOBSON, a London merchant (MB, 2:839; Vol. 15:674-6).

To William Short

DEAR SIR   Philadelphia May. 1. 98.

My last letters to you have been of Mar. 12, & June 30. 97. since which I have recieved yours of Dec. 27. 97. & Jan. 23. 98. I write to you from this place, because I can myself chuse the channel of conveyance. but it is subject to the material inconvenience of writing where I have not a single paper to turn to, & therefore I can only write from memory, & mine is not an exact one.   I have at length got a written acknolegement from the Secretary of state that the US. are liable to you for the 9000. Dollars. but as E.R. claims a credit against them for that sum, & their suit against him will be decided this summer, they desire the paiment to be suspended till that decision. in the mean time E.R. has sent me the assumpsit of old mr Pendleton & Peter Lyons to pay about 6000. Dollars of the money. I expect daily to recieve this sum. before I agreed to accept, I went to the Secretary of state and Auditor, & took from them their agreement that the recieving that sum from E.R. should not be construed into an admission that he was your debtor, but that it should be recieved only on account of the US. & placed by you to their credit. still the article of interest on the 9000. D. is unsettled. the public you know never pay interest. but if they recover interest from E.R. they ought not to pocket it,[1] and I shall endeavor to obtain it for you, on the ground of their recieving it as your fiduciary. these 6000. D. shall be instantly laid out in Pensylvania bank stock. this is now about 23. per cent above par. yet the dividends are such as to yield a clear 7. per cent on the money laid out in it. this is the safest paper in the world. it depends on a single state only, and a state which has never failed in it's engagements. it has no connection with the government, & therefore will not be affected by war. whereas the bank of the US. is chained to the government, & will be run hard by it for money in any event of war. the moment war became probable, I endeavored to sell out your paper in the public funds, in order to buy into the Pensylvania bank. but I could not be quick enough. the six per cents fell in the first instant from 16/8 to 15/. your certificates being at my house, & not here, obstructed the sale. I will not sell them to a loss, but should the appearances of war grow less, and this paper rise again to it's true level, I will convert it into Pensylvania bank stock.—your accounts with the treasury must lie till you come yourself, or send me your vouchers. if any trusty person should come over, you had better send them to my address to be lodged with mr John Barnes Merchant, South 3d. street Philadelphia, to be retained by him till my orders, if I should not be here when they come. your James river canals have not yet begun to bring in any revenue. on the contrary I found it to your interest to subscribe to the company, in common with many other members, a sum of about six, or nine hundred dollars (I write from memory & cannot be exact) at an interest of 6. per cent. whenever the work is entirely compleated, the profits will richly repay the suspension of interest. I have hitherto entered on no reformation of the leases of your Indian camp lands, tho' they needed it greatly; because I was in constant expectation of your coming yourself. but the present dangers of the seas are so great, that I scarcely expect you will commit yourself to them: & indeed the misunderstanding between this country & France is so serious, and a war, if it takes place, agitates us so much to our center, that I do not know, as it would probably be very short, whether you may not think it better not to displace yourself. I shall therefore proceed to get all your affairs into the best shape I can, as if I did not expect you at all. the Indian camp shall be laid out into tenements; all your interest accruing, as well as the mortgage money, as it shall come in, shall be invested in Pensylvania bank stock, which will always be as cash whenever advantageous offers of land shall arise. it is not easy to lease lands well in Virginia: and it is now become less so from the extraordinary price of tobacco ($13\frac{1}{2}$ Dollars per hundred) which is drawing our people back again to that culture. one would not chuse to lease to a mere tobacco maker: because he ruins the land with tobacco & Indian corn. I doubt therefore whether I shall venture to invest your money in lands further than great bargains may render adviseable. I will immediately write to Colo. Harvey on the subject of your green sea lands, & have them taken care of. I have forwarded both your letters to your brother in Kentuckey, & have no doubt he will attend to your lands there. Colo. Campbell is still living. I have no doubt that Colo. H. Skipwith has been exact in turning over what he had in his hands to Donald & Brown. how far their transfer of stock to you (of which I informed you some years ago) was of the exact balance, I know not. Brown is in flourishing circumstances. so is Colo. Skipwith. he has lately sustained a loss in his family. mrs Skipwith, after having for some time been hypocondriacally insane, died some few months ago. he has a daughter married to a son of T. Randolph of Dungeoness. while on this kind of subject, I may mention to you the marriage of my younger daughter with the son of mr Eppes of Eppington. they live with me.   the affairs of this country, as they respect France, have got into a deplorable state. distant as we are from Europe, nature seemed to have put it peculiarly in our power to keep ourselves unmixed in their broils. yet we have not turned that circumstance to best account. without descending to particulars, one may safely pronounce that when two nations who had so cordial an affection for each other as France & the US. are nevertheless brought into a war against each other, their public affairs must have been miserably mismanaged. no doubt there have been faults on both sides. 'delirant reges, plectuntur Achivi.' the present state of the public mind here is an extremely painful one, some eager for war, others anxious for peace. however, if war takes place, there can then be no division. many French are about to leave this country. among these Volney will probably go. Genl. Kosciusko will also, I believe, leave us soon for Europe. I recommend to you to make a point of seeing those two gentlemen, who are well acquainted with what has been passing here.—I communicated the proposals of M. Pougens for printing English authors, to the principal bookseller here. but he says that printing, both here and in Ireland, comes cheaper than he proposed, & therefore that it will not answer to take from him. I am very glad myself to have a good correspondent in that line proposed to me. when the ocean becomes safe, I shall trouble him with some commissions for myself. I am struck however with the advance in the price of books since I left France. be so good as to mention the above to him as an answer to his letter, till something more agreeable shall occur to furnish matter for a particular letter to him. I hope that this summer will give peace on the ocean, & open a safe communication between the two shores of the Atlantic. as you say you were never furnished with a copy of the President's message to Senate when he appointed mr Pinckney to go to Madrid, I now inclose you a copy, duly authenticated.

Present my respectful salutations to Madame de la Rochefoucault. the difficulty of communicating my ideas justly in a foreign language often prevented my indulging myself in conversation with persons whose acquaintance I wished to cultivate; & with none more than Madame de la

Rochefoucault. but it did not prevent my being entirely sensible of her merit, & entertaining for her the highest esteem. she has now survived to a threefold portion of it, as being alone left of a family, which of all others was the most dear to me. accept yourself assurances of my constant & sincere affections. Adieu.   TH: JEFFERSON

P.S. since writing the preceding, mr Pendleton informs me that the fall of stock has prevented their selling the funds destined to make the paiment for E.R. they will wait for a rise. I do not think that will happen soon, & therefore expect now to recieve only from the US. after the trial of their suit against E.R.

Dupl (DLC: Short Papers); at foot of first page: "Mr. Short"; at head of text: " Duplicata"; endorsed by Short. PrC of Dupl (same). PrC of RC (same). Enclosure: a copy, not found, of George Washington's message to the U.S. Senate, 21 Nov. 1794, nominating Thomas Pinckney as envoy extraordinary to Spain (see Short to TJ, 30 Sep. 1795).

For the ACKNOLEGEMENT FROM THE SECRETARY OF STATE, see Pickering to TJ, 25 Apr. 1798. TJ's letter to John Harvie of 6 May and Harvie's reply of 15 May discuss Short's GREEN SEA LANDS. DONALD & BROWN: some of Short's business dealings

had involved Alexander Donald of the English firm of Donald & Burton and James Brown, who acted for the company in Richmond (Short to TJ, 7 Oct. 1793, 30 Sep. 1795; TJ to Alexander Donald, 30 May 1795).

DELIRANT REGES, PLECTUNTUR ACHIVI: "the Greeks suffer for their kings' follies," from the *Epistulae* of Horace, book 1, second letter, line 14. MR PENDLETON INFORMS ME: Edmund Pendleton to TJ, 25 Apr. 1798.

[1] Preceding six words lacking in PrC of RC.

To Van Staphorst & Hubbard

GENTLEMEN   Philadelphia May 1. 1798.
   I wrote you yesterday, acknoleging the reciept of your favor of June 25 and answering it's contents.
   General Kosciusko, who has been some time with us, has invested his effects in the bank of Pensylvania, and is about to return to Europe. he has left with me a power of attorney for the superintendance of his interests here, which I shall have specially transacted by mr John Barnes merchant of this place. I have proposed to General Kosciusko, as he may not be fixed in any one place in Europe, to make you the center for his remittances from this place. mr Barnes will therefore regularly remit to you every six months the Generals dividends which will be drawn halfyearly, and you will be so good as to pay them when recieved to the order of the General.

[320]

In this letter I enclose you for General Kosciusko the two following bills of exchange, to wit,   florins sols

Pratt & Kintzing on Kunckle,

Ruys & co. Amsterdam for	6315 – 16.	Apr. 14. 98
E: Dutilh on I. F. & J. Dutilh Amsterdam	3157 – 18.	Apr. 19. 98
	9473 – 14	

both at sixty days sight, which be pleased to negociate, and to hold the proceeds subject to the order of General Kosciusko. those which I enclose you are the triplicates. he will himself carry to Europe the 1st. & 2d. of each, and forward them to you on his arrival. letters of advice will accompany [each], as they do the present.

The character of this patriotic officer is too well known to you to need anything in his favor from me. you will find that his integrity is proportioned to his other good qualities for which he has been known to the world.

I am with great esteem Gentlemen Your most obedient & most humble servt   Th: Jefferson

PrC (DLC); faint; at foot of text: "Messrs. Nicholas & Jacob Van Staphorst & Hubbard"; endorsed by TJ in ink on verso. Enclosures not found, but see below.

As TJ indicated, each of the BILLS OF EXCHANGE for Kosciuszko was issued in multiples. TJ retained the fourth bill of each set (both in MHi; on printed forms with blanks filled, each bill matching the specifications in the letter above, the amounts being the same but called guilders rather than florins; signed and dated at Philadelphia by the issuing firms; each bill endorsed on verso by Kosciuszko).

From St. George Tucker

Dear Sir,   Fredericksburg May 2d. 1798.

Mr. Lewis of this town this morning mentioned to me, that it might be an acceptable information to you to know of any person who recollected the publication of Logan's Speech at the time when it first appeared in the Virginia papers.

A few years ago, not more than three or four, being engaged in some enquiries relative to the Adoption of our State Constitution I had recourse to the papers of those times. In the research I met with the Account of Logan's Speech, & the Speech itself at full length, verbatim, *I think*, as given in your notes on Virginia, in a Virginia paper printed just after Lord Dunmore's return from the western Country, by Purdie & Dixon, or by Mrs. Rind, but I am rather inclined to believe in the former. I Strongly incline to believe I have the paper still in my possession—but it is possible that it might have been among some that I borrowed of Mr. John Byrd deceased. If it would be of any service to you to find the paper, I will on my return (which will not be till the beginning of next month) endeavour to find it.—But should I fail to do so, if this Letter can be of service to you, you may freely make such use of it as you think proper.—In addition to what I have said on this subject, I will add, that my recollection of the publication, before the publication of your notes, appears to be perfectly familiar. Our mutual friend John Page of Rosewell I am inclined to think will be able to add more satisfactory Information on this subject.

Having thus intruded upon you, I beg leave to mention another subject, at the request of a most respectable litterary Character in Boston, Doctor Belknap with whom I have for some years occasionally corresponded.— In your notes—about page 200 (I think) of the paris Edition you mention—"that the Histories & records of our Country contain Evidences of repeated *purchases* from the Indian natives."—Doctor Belknap requests (after desiring his respectful Compliments to you) to be informed of the particular sources & Authorities from which you derive this Information. Any Communication from you on the subject will I am sure be thankfully recieved by him. I am respectfully, Dear Sir, your obed Servt. &c   S G TUCKER

RC (DLC); endorsed by TJ as received 8 May 1798 and so recorded in SJL.

To James Madison

Philadelphia. May. 3. 98.

I wrote you last on the 26th. since which yours of the 22d. of April is recieved acknowleging mine of the 12th. so that all appear to have been recieved to that date. the spirit kindled up in the towns is wonderful. these and N. Jersey are pouring in their addresses offering life & fortune. even these addresses are not the worst things. for indiscreet declarations and expressions of passion may be pardoned to a multitude acting from the impulse of the moment. but we cannot expect a foreign nation to shew that apathy to the answers of the President, which are more Thrasonic than the addresses. whatever chance for peace might have been left us after the publication of the dispatches is compleatly lost by these answers. nor is it France alone but his own fellow-citizens against whom his threats are uttered. in Fenno of yesterday you will see one wherein he says to the Address from Newark 'the delusions & misrepresentations, which have misled so many citizens, must be discoun-

tenanced by authority as well as by the citizens at large,' evidently alluding to those letters from the representatives to their constituents which
they have been in the habit of seeking after & publishing. while those
sent by the Tory part of the house to their constituents are ten times
more numerous, & replete with the most atrocious falsehoods & calumnies. what new law they will propose on this subject has not yet leaked
out. the citizen bill sleeps. the alien bill proposed by the Senate has not
yet been brought in. that proposed by the H. of R. has been so moderated that it will not answer the passionate purposes of the war-gentle-
men. whether therefore the Senate will push their bolder plan, I know
not. the provisional army does not go down so smoothly in the R. as it
did in the Senate. they are whitling away some of it's choice ingredients.
particularly that of transferring their own constitutional discretion over
the raising of armies to the President. a commee of the R. have struck
out his discretion, and hang the raising of the men on the contingencies
of invasion, insurrection, or declaration of war. were all our members
here the bill would not pass. but it will probably as the house now is. it's
expence is differently estimated from 5. to 8. millions of dollars a year.
their purposes before voted require 2. millions above all the other taxes,
which therefore are voted to be raised on lands, houses, & slaves. the
provisional army will be additional to this. the threatening appearances
from the Alien bills have so alarmed the French who are among us that
they are going off. a ship chartered by themselves for this purpose will
sail within about a fortnight for France with as many as she can carry.
among these I believe will be Volney, who has in truth been the principal object aimed at by the law. notwithstanding the unfavorableness of
the late impressions, it is believed the New York elections, which are
over, will give us two or three republicans more than we now have. but
it is supposed Jay is re-elected. it is said Hamilton declines coming to
the Senate. he very soon stopped his Marcellus. it was rather the sequel
that was feared than what actually appeared. he comes out on a different
plan in his Titus Manlius, if that be really his. the appointments to the
Missisipi territory were so abominable that the Senate could not swal-
low them. they referred them to a commee to enquire into characters,
and the P. withdrew the nomination, & has now named Winthrop Serjeant Governor, Steele of Augusta in Virginia, Secretary, Tilton
&   two of the judges, the other not yet named. as there is nothing
material now to be proposed, we generally expect to rise in about three
weeks. however I do not yet venture to order my horses.   my respectful salutations to mrs Madison. to yourself affectionate friendship
& Adieu.

Perhaps the P's expression, before quoted, may look to the Sedition bill which has been spoken of, and which may be meant to put the Printing presses under the Imprimatur of the Executive. Bache is thought a main object of it.—Cabot of Massachusets is appointed Secretary of the navy.—it is said Hamilton declines coming to the Senate.

RC (DLC: Madison Papers); addressed: "James Madison junr. near Orange courthouse"; franked. PrC (DLC); lacks final sentence of postscript.

Many of the New Jersey ADDRESSES OFFERING LIFE & FORTUNE were sent to Congress as well as to President Adams. Senator Richard Stockton presented the first from Princeton and Kingston on 23 Apr. and others on 30 Apr., 1, 10, 15, 16, and 21 May, the last being signed by 700 inhabitants of Elizabeth pledging "to aid their country against the machinations of its enemies, and in support of the national councils" (JS, 2:476, 482, 483, 487, 489, 491). The address from the 5 May meeting at New Brunswick, delivered on 10 May, was specifically addressed to the president of the Senate (MS in DNA: RG 46, Senate Records, 5th Cong., 2d sess.). For a review of the addresses, see Thomas M. Ray, " 'Not One Cent for Tribute': The Public Addresses and American Popular Reaction to the XYZ Affair, 1798-1799," *Journal of the Early Republic*, 3 (1983), 389-412. On 2 May the *Gazette of the United States* printed three of the president's ANSWERS to addresses, one dated 27 Apr. in response to an address from Georgetown and the other two dated 1 May in response to addresses from Bridgeton and Newark, New Jersey. In his response to the ADDRESS FROM NEWARK Adams noted that the MISREPRESENTATIONS, WHICH HAVE MISLED SO MANY CITIZENS, were "very serious evils."

On 25 Apr. William Cobbett published two circular letters sent by Virginia REPRESENTATIVES TO THEIR CONSTITUENTS, the first by Matthew Clay dated 15 Feb. and the second by Anthony New dated 20 Mch. Cobbett described the letters as "false and inflammatory epistles" designed "to keep alive an attachment to France, and a disaffection to the Federal government." He compared them to the earlier circular letter attributed to William Findley printed in *Porcupine's Gazette* on 12 Apr. (see John

Page to TJ, 26 Apr. 1798). On 30 Apr. Cobbett printed a fourth Republican circular letter, dated 6 Apr. 1798, from Virginia Representative Samuel J. Cabell. Cobbett noted that this letter deserved special attention because it was written after the publication of the dispatches from the United States envoys and indicated the grounds on which the "French faction" hoped "to justify themselves in the eyes of their constituents."

ALIEN BILL PROPOSED BY THE SENATE: the act originating in the upper house concerning aliens, known as the Alien Friends Act, allowed the president, in times of peace or war, to order all aliens "as he shall judge dangerous to the peace and safety of the United States" to leave the country. If evidence satisfactory to the executive were presented indicating that the targeted alien was not a threat, the president could issue a license allowing the person to stay. Without a special license, the suspected alien had to depart by the appointed day or face imprisonment for up to three years. An unlawful return to the United States after deportation called for imprisonment as long as the president thought the public safety required it. The legislation also required the captains of incoming vessels to provide a list of all aliens on board (U.S. Statutes at Large, 1:570-2). For a description of the original more arbitrary and rigorous bill presented by the Senate committee on 4 May—the complete text of which was published in the Philadelphia *Aurora* four days later—and for a detailed examination of the passage of the legislation that was approved on 25 June 1798, see Smith, *Freedom's Fetters*, 50-5, 58-93. For the bill PROPOSED by the House of Representatives that became the Alien Enemies Act, see same, 35-49. As approved on 6 July, this bill provided guidelines for the removal of enemy aliens upon an invasion or declaration of war (U.S. Statutes at Large, 1:577-8).

For the APPOINTMENTS to Mississippi Territory, see TJ to Madison, 19 Apr. (second letter). Peter Bryan Bruin was the second of the two JUDGES nominated by Adams on 2 May.

George CABOT of Massachusetts declined Adams's appointment of 1 May. The Sen-

ate, on 21 May, approved the president's second nomination to the post, Benjamin Stoddert of Maryland (JEP, 1:272, 275-6).

Notes on Presidential Appointments

May. 3. the Presidt. some time ago appd. Steele of Virga a Commr. to the Indians, & now Secretary of the Missisipi territory. Steele was a Counsellor of Virga, and was voted out by the assembly because he turned tory. he then offered for Congress & was rejected by the people. then offered for the Senate of Virga & was rejected. the Presidt. has also appd. Joseph Hopkinson Commr. to make a treaty with the Oneida Indns. he is a youth of about 22. or 23. and has no other merit than extreme toryism, & the having made a poor song to the tune of the President's march.

MS (DLC: TJ Papers, 102:17525); entirely in TJ's hand; on same sheet as Notes on Conversation with Tench Coxe, [25 Apr. 1798], being the final memorandum of notes on that page.

Near the end of March, before the occasion arose to nominate John STEELE as secretary of Mississippi Territory, Adams had appointed him to a three-person commission to negotiate an acquisition of land from the Cherokee Nation. On 3 May the president nominated twenty-seven-year-old JOSEPH HOPKINSON, a Philadelphia attorney and the son of Francis Hopkinson, to supervise a treaty for the sale of land from the ONEIDA tribe to the state of New York (ASP, Indian Affairs, 1:636, 639-40; ANB).

Opinions on Hopkinson's SONG, "Hail Columbia," which was introduced in Philadelphia on 25 Apr., split along party lines. As a favor to an actor friend Hopkinson had penned lyrics to go with THE PRESIDENT's MARCH, a melody already popular with Federalists. William Cobbett's Porcupine's Gazette praised the new song even before its premiere, and soon printed the lyrics. The Aurora, on the other hand, declared that the work "contained, amidst the most ridiculous bombast, the vilest adulation to the Anglo-Monarchical Party." The song was an instant hit at its inaugural performance before a boisterous crowd in the New Theatre on Chestnut Street (Porcupine's Gazette, 24, 28 Apr. 1798; Aurora, 27 Apr. 1798; Burton Alva Konkle, Joseph Hopkinson, 1770-1842: Jurist, Scholar, Inspirer of the Arts [Philadelphia, 1931], 73-84).

To Thomas Mann Randolph

TH:J. TO TMR.   Philadelphia. May 3. 98.

I wrote you last on the 26th. since which yours of the 22d. was recieved, to wit on the Tuesday. you will have found before this that the Fredericksburg post also is to deliver a mail at Milton. I am very thankful to you for your attention to my affairs, for in truth this state of long abandonment of them on my part gives me great uneasiness. I am in

[325]

hopes that Page & George will give you but little trouble. as to the Carpenters, I must the next winter put them on a different establishment. with respect to the price of tobacco, tho' I am satisfied it must still rise from permanent causes, yet there is no foreseeing what check may be given to it's price here by the event of a war. I am therefore thinking to write to George Jefferson on the subject of selling mine, contrary to what I had determined on if the madness of our government was not hastening as it is to ruin our private fortunes as well as the public interests. whatever chance was left us, of escaping war, after the publication of the dispatches, the President's answers to the addresses pouring in on him from the great towns & N. Jersey, are pushing the irritation to a point to which nobody can expect it will be borne. the provisional army of 20,000. men will probably be carried, by the thinness of the H. of R. it's expence is now estimated from 5. to 8. millions. besides these, two millions over & above all our other taxes, are wanted for the naval & other expenditures, and are voted to be raised by a tax on land houses & slaves. when the provisional army bill passes, the sum must be augmented to provide for that also. resolutions for an alien bill have been originated in both houses. that of the Senate was broad. that of the lower house more restricted. these have so alarmed the French here that they are going off to France. a ship load of them sails in about a fortnight. among these I believe Volney will go, who was in fact the chief object of the law. it suffices for a man to be a philosopher, and to believe that human affairs are susceptible of improvement, & to look forward, rather than back to the Gothic ages, for perfection, to mark him as an anarchist, disorganiser, atheist & enemy of the government.—Winthrop Sargeant is made Governor of the Missisipi territory, & Steele of Augusta Secretary. Cabot of Massachusets is Secretary of the Navy here. in Steele's appointment, first as Commissioner to the Indians, & now Secretary of the Missisipi territory, you will see the adherence of the government to their uniform plan of rewarding with their favors all those whom the people by their votes reject as not to be trusted with their interests. the President's answers to the addresses are full of extraordinary things. among these is a declaration in one of them 'that the delusions & misrepresentations which have misled so many citizens must be discountenanced by authority as well as by our citizens in general.' whether this looks to the letters of the representatives to their constituents, or to the putting the printing presses under the Imprimatur of the government, or both, is doubted.—notwithstanding the momentary phrenzy prevailing in some places, the New York elections, which took place last week, are supposed to have given us two or three whigs more than we have had.   To return to the subject of my tobacco I am offering mine here for the present old-tobacco price ($13\frac{1}{2}$ D.) to deliver it immediately & wait for the money till it will be old tobacco, that is, till Octob. 1. I suppose this would be equal to 12.50 or 12.75 at Richmond. but as yet nobody has encouraged the offer. if I cannot sell thus, I will sell in Richmond. if I can sell on these terms I will leave an opening for yours, so as to make it optional for you to accept or not. we have nothing material now but the Provisional army bill, & land tax, so that every body counts on getting away in three weeks. perhaps however it may be the last of the month. when the day is fixed I shall write to you to send off my horses. therefore be so good as to be on the look-out for my letters, & to make Jupiter keep himself & horses in readiness to come off at 24. hours warning. I shall want all 3. of my horses on account of the workman whom I carry with me. I am in hopes from Davenport's account that I shall find the house nearly covered, and that we shall not be long without a shelter to unite under. 'oh! welcome hour whenever!' I never was so sick to the heart as of the scene here. never felt the endearments of my family so necessary for my existence. deliver my warmest love to my ever dear Martha & the little ones, and accept yourself assurances of my most affectionate esteem. Adieu.

RC (DLC); endorsed by Randolph as received 5 June 1798. PrC (MHi); endorsed by TJ in ink on verso.

William DAVENPORT'S ACCOUNT in a letter to TJ of 22 Apr. 1798, recorded in SJL as received 1 May from Charlottesville, has not been found. Letters from TJ to Davenport, recorded in SJL under 3 and 9 May 1798, are also missing.

WELCOME HOUR WHENEVER: John Milton, *Paradise Lost*, 10:771.

From James Lewis, Jr.

SIR   Fredericksburgh 4th. May 98

At this momentous crisis, when one party style themselves the enemies to abuse, and the friends of Reform; and the other party are contending for the continuance of their degraded institutions and unrelenting usurpations, the powers of man are every where in action. The struggle is, who shall prevail? the passions of men are no less active, than their understandings. No example can more effectually exhibit this activity, than a furious invective of Luther Martin, publicly applauded by Francis Corbin, a man of some conspicuity in our state, against you. At such a period, the friends of reform should let be known, that they act from the enlightened convictions of truth & justice and from the respectable motives, that such principles necessarily inspire; our motives should be pure and our integrity unimpeached. That publication has attempted to attach to you, the degraded motive of endeavouring in your notes to raise your Literary fame, at the expence of Another's reputation and to effect it, have not stopped at misrepresentation & calumny. I will not, enlightened friend of man and your Country, decide as to the mode of repelling, this charge, designed for this period—By a Letter of yours to our friend M Page your mode of resisting it, is known to me. Let me do my duty, by notifying to you, the existence of a document, wch. in my estimate, will be greatly servicable.

St. George Tucker is here attendg. in his official character, as Judge of this District: Conversing with him, he authorises me, to communicate to you, that he thinks he possesses, a paper Contemporary with the facts alluded to, wch details them, as your Virginia Notes do: if he should have it not, his recollection of having read such detail, in such paper, within a short time, is thoroughly vivid—If the possession of such paper or his Certificate can be beneficial to you, at your notification thereof, he will transmit them or either of them to you. It is unnecessary for me to add, that my services are at your disposal.

In the above conduct my motives cannot be scanned. I am determined to devote my life to the cause of equality, Justice & mankind & thus my duty is, that the votaries of such principles, should always be enabled to shield their characters & exhibit their genuine features.

I am, Sir,—your mo: ob: JAMES LEWIS JUNR.

RC (DLC); endorsed by TJ as received 8 May 1798 and so recorded in SJL.

This James Lewis, mentioned by Monroe in the letter that follows as a young attorney of Fredericksburg, was not the same as James Lewis of Charlottesville. The latter served as the guardian of William Wood, from whom TJ hired slaves in 1796-97, and seems likely to have been the James Lewis with whom TJ exchanged three letters listed in SJL but not found: one from Lewis to TJ of 15 Mch. 1794, recorded incongruously as received on 14 Mch.; a letter from TJ to Lewis of 14 July 1795; and one from Lewis to TJ dated 15 July 1795 and received on 21 July of that year (MB, 2:947, 968; Lewis to TJ, 5 Dec. 1806).

A PAPER CONTEMPORARY WITH THE FACTS: see St. George Tucker to TJ, 2 May 1798.

From James Monroe

DEAR SIR   Fredb'g May 4. 1798.

I have yours of 19. ulto. I rejoice that my affr. with M. is settled, since being a youth of good heart pushed on by others, I had no wish to injure him, and was satisfied he had none to injure me. In no view cod. I be benefited by a collision with him, & my only concern is respecting

Giles, who I hope is satisfied with the paper furnished by Mr. Dawson. I will come up in abt. three weeks at furthest. I wod. immediately had I my papers here, but being forced back for them, & the chancery term on the point of commencing, I think it best to attend its earlier days & then proceed to Phila.: being however resolved to do it sooner if invited so to do by yrself or mr Dawson. I shall make no difficulty with Mr. Pickering as to the mode of settlement, by wh. I mean that I will *pay* now & claim the right of reimbursement when vouchers are produced; however unjust the claim for such a mode shall be.

The course of the admn. does not surprise me. It is a consistint one. I think however the admn. will overwhelm itself by its folly & madness. We are preparing for a war wh. does not exist, expending millions wh. will have no other effect than to bring it on, wh. cannot produce, in any possible event when brot. on, any good & will produce much harm. Present accts. announce the commencmt. of a negotiation. What will be the effect of the late publicatn. upon that negotiation when it reaches France. Our ministers to have completed the business shod. not have entered into the negotiation but withdrawn when their letter was written. To remain after that document was committed to their employers, a document wh. was sure to terminate the negotiation (for the publication was to be counted on) was to commit to hasard the otherwise successful project of the admn.; for every thing wh. afterwards turned up was likely to diminish the force of what they had already gained. To expose the iniquity of the project, & the injury of the policy the call shod. be continued for papers, upon every rumour of the arrival of new dispatches.

A young man here of the name of Lewis, who studied the law with Mr. Minor, (not of the family with wh. you are acquainted by that name, yet of good connections) shewed me a letter he had written you respecting the attack of L. Martin in the statemt. given in yr. notes of the conduct of Cressap toward the Indian Logan & his family. His motive in interfering is no other than that wh. his letter bespeaks, a great interest in whatever concerns yr. welfare, to promote wh. he is particularly stimulated by youthful ardor, and zeal in the cause of republn. govt.—I thot. proper to let him forward the letter rather than prevent it, lest it might hurt his feelings. You will easily gratify his mind. Mr. Tyler the judge, likewise informs me to be communicated to you, that he possesses the paper containing the same document, or such knowledge of the fact as will enable him to establish it. You had better write him on the subject.

upon reflection as the cts. are sitting & my absence might be hurtful,

I have hinted to Mr. Dawson a possibility I may authorise him to adjust my acct. with T.P. without my attendance. I mention this to shew that my trip is a thing rather in contemplation than decided on.

RC (DLC); endorsed by TJ as received 8 May 1798 and so recorded in SJL.

м.: William White Morris.

LATE PUBLICATN.: the administration's release on 3 Apr. of papers relating to the XYZ imbroglio, including the LETTER to Pickering on 22 Oct. 1797 in which Pinckney, Marshall, and Gerry first reported the conditions for negotiation laid down by the

cryptic intermediaries (ASP, *Foreign Relations*, 2:157-60).

On this day TJ wrote to Spotsylvania County commmonwealth's attorney John MINOR, Jr., at Fredericksburg, who had written a letter of 3 Apr. that TJ received on 10 Apr. Both letters are recorded in SJL but neither has been found (for Minor, see Madison, *Papers*, 14:228n).

т.p.: Timothy Pickering.

To Edmund Pendleton

DEAR SIR   Philadelphia May 4. 98.

Your favor of April 25. has been duly recieved. were the case of mr Short's demand one wherein he had left me to decide, I should not hesitate to accept the assurance in your letter in discharge of the US. but mr Short has peremptorily protested against acquitting the US. there was a hesitation on the part of the Secretary of state, whether mr Randolph's receipt of the money was not by some letter of mr Short's made tantamount to a paiment to the latter. but a rigorous examination of his letters has proved there was no foundation for this hesitation, and I have from the Secretary of state a written acknolegement that the US. are liable to mr Short. when therefore I recieved from mr Randolph your note, I called on the Secretary of state and Auditor and informed them I would do no act which should absolve the US. from that ultimate responsibility on which mr Short insisted: and they agreed that I might recieve the money & only give credit for it when recieved, and they in like manner would credit mr R. when it should be recieved. mr Short therefore having peremptorily protested against a change of his debtor, and against releasing the US. I do not feel myself at liberty to do it. but you will have time yet, before the suit against mr Randolph comes to trial, to dispose of your funds and make the paiment. if this should be done in Richmond, mr George Jefferson is my agent there; if here, mr John Barnes merchant South 3d. street acts for me. so far as you depend on the sale of stock, I am persuaded they will not rise again, but continue to sink through the ensuing war, if we are to be engaged in it, as the measures every day render more & more probable, because the paiment of interest must immediately stop, & the capital depreciate as all our paper did in the former war. the publication of the dispatches of our envoys was thought to have been so much a measure of irritation as to have left little hope of our escaping war. the P's answers to the addresses from the trading towns & from N. Jersey, seem to be lessening that hope. the Provisional army is still undecided on in the lower house. they are proceeding to raise 2. millions on lands houses & slaves, which must however be greatly augmented if the army be raised. the army & the tax will give the appointment of 2500. officers to the Executive. accept assurances of the high esteem of Dear Sir

Your affectionate friend & servt   TH: JEFFERSON

RC (MHi: Washburn Collection); addressed: "The honble Edmund Pendleton Caroline near the Bowling green"; franked and postmarked; endorsed by Pendleton. PrC (DLC: Short Papers); endorsed by TJ in ink on verso.

A WRITTEN ACKNOLEGEMENT: see note to Timothy Pickering to TJ, 25 Apr. 1798.

From Tadeusz Kosciuszko

SIR   [before 5 May 1798]

Give me leave to present you a Fur for experiment Sake to try whither the hops in this Country will have the same effect as it is in mine. you must spread with it the whole surface of the fur, and once or twice in the summer in Sun shine day bit out accumulated dust and pact up in the same maner again as i related before—when ever you will have a time in the daytime for a quarter of hour I beg you would grante me to finish what i have begone   wyth Respect and Esteem your Humble and Obedient

Servant   T. KOSCIUSZKO

RC (MHi); undated, but written before Kosciuszko's departure from Philadelphia; endorsed by TJ.

It is uncertain if the FUR mentioned in this letter is the one, reputedly a gift from Kosciuszko, that appears on the collar of TJ's coat in the well-known portraits by Rembrandt Peale (1805) and Thomas Sully (1821). According to the grandson of Margaret Ellis White and General Anthony Walton White, whom Kosciuszko visited at their home in New Brunswick, New Jersey, Kosciuszko gave TJ and Margaret White "some very rich and valuable furs"

that Emperor Paul I had bestowed upon him in Russia (Anthony Walton White Evans, *Memoir of Thaddeus Kosciuszko, Poland's Hero and Patriot* [New York, 1883], [3-4], 24; Haiman, *Kosciuszko*, 51-4, 58-60, 79; Bush, *Life Portraits*, 54, 76). See also TJ to Kosciuszko, 30 May 1798 and 21 Feb. 1799.

If Kosciuszko's desire for TJ's aid TO FINISH WHAT I HAVE BEGONE refers to the arrangement of the exile's affairs prior to his departure from the United States, this letter likely dates from the latter part of April or the first few days of May 1798. A brief note from Kosciuszko to New York merchant

Henry Gahn, who was a friend of Julian Niemcewicz and whose business interests took him as far south as Baltimore, may date from the same period. Kosciuszko, who in addition to sketching enjoyed shaping small wooden items on a lathe, wrote to Gahn: "Be so good to order your Servants for delivering my two boxes wyth turning instruments to Mr: Niemcewicz. wyth my best thanks, for you" (RC in MHi, signed, addressed: "to Mr: Gahn Esqre.," endorsed by TJ: "Thaddeus Kosciuszko"; Haiman, *Kosciuszko*, 57, 110; Niemcewicz, *Under their Vine*, 17, 24, 73, 125, 129, 299).

Preliminary Will
of Tadeusz Kosciuszko

[before 5 May 1798]

I beg Mr. Jefferson that in case I should die without will or testament he should bye out of my money So many Negroes and free them. that the restante Sums should be Sufficient to give them aducation and provide for thier maintenance. that is to say. each should know before; the duty of a Cytysen in the free Government. that he must defend his Country. against foroign as well internal Enemies who would wish to change the Constitution for the worst. to inslave them by degree afterwards. to have good and human heart Sensible for the Sufferings of others. each must be maried and have 100. Ackres of Land. wyth instruments. Cattle for tillage and know how to manage and Gouvern it as well to know behave to neybourghs. always wyth Kindnes. and ready to help them to them selves frugal. to ther Children give good aducation i mean as to the heart, and the duty to ther Country, in gratitude to me to make thems'elves hapy as possible.   T KOSCIUSZKO

MS (MHi); entirely in Kosciuszko's hand; undated, being supplied on the basis of the document that follows and Kosciuszko's departure from Philadelphia on 5 May 1798.

Will of Tadeusz Kosciuszko

5th day of May 1798

I Thaddeus Kosciuszko being just in my departure from America do hereby declare and direct that should I make no other testamentory disposition of my property in the United States I hereby authorise my friend Thomas Jefferson to employ the whole thereof in purchasing Negroes from among his own or any others and giving them Liberty in my name, in giving them en education in trades or othervise and in having them instructed for their new condition in the duties of morality which may make them good neigh bours good fathers or moders, husbands or vives and in their duties as citisens teeching them to be defenders of their Liberty and Country and of the good order of Society and in whatsoever may Make them happy and useful, and I make the said Thomas Jefferson my executor of this   T. KOSCIUSZKO

MS (Albemarle County Circuit Court, Charlottesville, on deposit ViU); entirely in Kosciuszko's hand; subjoined in hand of John Carr and signed by him is a statement of 12 May 1819 that the will was produced in the Albemarle County Court, determined to be in the hand of Kosciuszko, ordered to be recorded, "and thereupon Thomas Jefferson the executor therein named, refused to take upon himself the burthen of the execution of the said Will"; endorsed in a clerk's hand: "Kosciusko's will 12th May 1819 proved & ordered to be recorded." Tr (Albemarle County Circuit Court Clerk's Office: Will Book No. 1, p. 42).

After Kosciuszko's death in 1817 an aging TJ hoped to persuade John Hartwell Cocke to assume the executorship of this will. When Cocke declined, TJ sought the advice of William Wirt and had the will entered in the Orphan's Court of the District of Columbia, which in 1821 appointed Benjamin L. Lear of Washington as administrator of the estate. Maryland law applied to the District in such matters, and Lear anticipated that it would be difficult, either there or in Virginia, to carry out the educational provisions of the will. He therefore planned the endowment of a school to be named for Kosciuszko and organized in New Jersey under the auspices of the African Education Society, which sought to educate freed slaves for colonization in Africa. However, in the end Kosciuszko's American assets

were not put to that purpose. Litigation among disputing claimants eventually came before the U.S. Supreme Court for the determination, among other questions, of which of four wills should govern the disposition of his estate. Kosciuszko evidently expected the terms of the will printed above to control the allocation of his financial holdings in the United States, no matter what other disposition might be made of his European assets. In a letter to TJ in 1817 about the management of his shares of stock, Kosciuszko alluded to the unchanged purpose to which the funds should be applied after his death: "du quel après ma mort vous savez la destination invariable." Nevertheless, in a decision handed down in 1852 the Supreme Court held that the language of a will Kosciuszko made in 1816 revoked all earlier testaments, including his American will of 1798, and his assets in the United States were distributed among his heirs (Haiman, *Kosciuszko*, 125-8; Benjamin C. Howard, *Reports of Cases Argued and Adjudged in the Supreme Court of the United States, December Term, 1852*, 2d ed. [New York, 1885], 399-433; James S. Pula, "The American Will of Thaddeus Kosciuszko," *Polish American Studies*, 34 [1977], 16-25; Marion Manola Thompson, *The Education of Negroes in New Jersey* [New York, 1941], 90-7; Kosciuszko to TJ, 15 Sep. 1817; Cocke to TJ, 3 May 1819; TJ to Wirt, 27 June 1819; Lear to TJ, 19 Sep. 1821).

From James Madison

DEAR SIR   May 5. 98

I have to thank you for your favor of the 26th Ult: My last was of the 29th. The success of the War party in turning the Despatches to their inflammatory views is a mortifying item agst. the enlightened character of our Citizens. The analysis of the Despatches by Sidney, cannot fail to be an effectual antidote, if any appeal to sober reflexion can prevail agst occurrences which are constantly addressing their imaginations & feelings. The talents of this writer make it lucky that the task has not been taken up by other hands. I am glad to find in general that every thing that good sense & accurate information can supply is abundantly exhibited by the Newspapers to the view of the public. It is to be regretted that these papers are so limited in their circulation, as well as that the mixture of indiscretions in some of them should contribute to that effect. It is to [be] hoped however that any arbitrary attacks on the freedom of the press will find virtue eno' remaining in the public mind to make them recoil on the wicked authors. No other check to desperate projects seems now to be left. The Sanguinary faction ought not however to adopt the spirit of Roburespierre without recollecting the shortness of his triumphs & the perpetuity of his infamy. The contrivance of Jay for reproducing Hamilton into office & notice suggests, no doubt, a variety of conjectures. If the contrivance is to be ascribed chiefly to Jay, it probably originated in the alarm into which the consequences of the Treaty have thrown its author, & the new demand for the services of its champion. Events have so clearly demonstrated the great objects of that Treaty to have been, to draw us into a quarrel with the Enemies of G.B. and to sacrifice our navigation to hers, that it will require greater efforts than ever to skreen the instrument & author much longer from the odium due to them. The late acts of the B. Parlt. would before this, have unmasked the character of the Treaty even to the people of N. Engd. if adventitious circumstances had not furnished its partizans with fresh dust for their eyes. A tax on land, with a loss of market for its produce, will put their credulity & blindness, to a test that may be more dreadful to the Deluders. We have had a dry spell latterly which succeeding the effects of the frost, will affect every species of crop that depends on the favor of this Season. I write to Mr. Dawson by this post for a small balance, between 30 & 40 dollars which I beg you to receive. Should the funds in your hands admit, you will further oblige me by havg my brother William's name subscribed to Cary's paper & paying the necessary advance; the paper to be sent to Orange-Court-House.

RC (DLC: Madison Papers); with word omitted by Madison supplied in brackets by Editors; endorsed by TJ as received 15 May 1798 and so recorded in SJL.

On 14 Apr. 1798 the first ANALYSIS OF THE DESPATCHES signed BY SIDNEY appeared in the Philadelphia *Aurora* under the headline "Examination of the dispatches from our Commissioners in France." Sidney questioned whether the publication of the communications was not "a last link in the systematic chain of measures pursued by the Tories to alienate this country from France, draw its connection with Britain closer" and "pave the way for a subversion or total perversion of our constitution?" A Federalist party measure, it sacrificed "peace and prosperity" for the benefit of the party. In the articles, seven in all, Sidney declared that the "swindling agents" with whom the envoys were negotiating were not agents of the Directory and perhaps not even of Talleyrand. By listening to these unofficial agents, however, the envoys gave recognition to the "insinuations and assertions" they made that were "injurious to the character of the French nation" (Philadelphia *Aurora*, 16, 20, 23 Apr., 18, 21 May, 1 June 1798).

To John Wayles Eppes

DEAR SIR   Philadelphia May 6. 98.

I wrote you last on the 11th. of April, & the day after recieved yours of Apr. 4. I inclosed you at the same time the communications just then recieved from our envoys. others are lately recieved, but, as far as made known to us, they contain only a long memorial given in by them, justifying all our complaints, and repelling those of France. it takes up the subject from the time of Genet's coming, & comes down to the last orders. offering however no new arguments. they were still in Paris as the mercantile information says the 10th. of March. the ferment excited here by the publication of the dispatches, caught all the great trading towns, and is still kept up there & here, by anonymous letters of French conspirators who are to burn the city, by newspaper declarations from Victor Hughes &c. and such other artifices. war-addresses pour in from the towns under these impressions and from the country of N. Jersey, a state which has always had peculiar politics. but the country in general seems not moved. they have abated of their admiration for the French, more or less in proportion as they[1] confine their suspicions to the swindlers, or extend them to the minister, or even the directory. the event of the elections of New York, favorable generally to the whigs, shews the small effect these communications had on the people, who were called to their elections fresh from reading them. the near prospect of war, the stamp act coming into operation, the land tax now laying will produce serious & general reflection. however actual war may destroy the fruits of it. we now learn the effects of the President's speech of November on the French legislature, which they had just got by the way of England, and concieved from it great anger. whatever chance we might have had for their not declaring war, lessens daily by the messages & answers to addresses which bid fair to carry irritation to a point beyond the possibility of bearing. indeed some of the war-members begin to avow that they are ready for declaring war themselves, & such is their majority that we begin to fear they intend it. should this not be attempted, we have only two bills of consequence to pass. the one for a provisional army of 20,000. men (the expence 6. to 8. millions of dollars a year) and the land tax, which is for 2. Millions, but must still be augmented by whatever sum the provisional army may render necessary. it is generally believed these will be got through in 2. or 3. weeks, so that the time of adjournment is pretty generally spoken of as for the last of this month. I do not yet venture to write for my horses. whenever I do, I will at the same moment write to you, in hopes of meeting yourself & Maria at Monticello. I never was more home-sick, or heart-sick. the life of this place is peculiarly hateful to me, and nothing but a sense of duty & respect to the public could keep me here a moment. I shall be disappointed, by the delay here, in my hope of going by the way of Eppington. before I can get home by the straitest road, we shall have begun our harvest. express to mr & mrs Eppes my regrets on this subject, reserving my visit for another occasion. my most friendly salutations attend them & the family. all my love to my dear Maria, and sincere affections to yourself. Adieu.

RC (ViU); at foot of first page: "J. W. Eppes." PrC (MHi); endorsed by TJ in ink on verso.

Eppes's letter to TJ of APR. 4, which according to SJL was received on 11 not 12 Apr., has not been found.

On 4 May President Adams sent Congress new communications from France consisting primarily of a LONG MEMORIAL from the American envoys to Talleyrand dated 17 Jan. Written primarily by Marshall, the document attempted to reconcile the Jay Treaty with the French-American treaties of 1778 and, using the neutrality policy developed by TJ in response to Great Britain in 1793, reiterated the basis for America's COMPLAINTS against France. The Senate promptly ordered the publication of 500 copies of the communication (*Message of the President of the United States, to Both Houses of Congress. May 4th, 1798* [Philadelphia, 1798]; Marshall, *Papers*, 3:330-81; JS, 2:485; Stinchcombe, *XYZ Affair*, 107-8).

ANONYMOUS LETTERS OF FRENCH CONSPIRATORS: on 30 Apr. the *Philadelphia Gazette* reported that three letters had been directed to the president "threatening to set fire to the city" on 9 May, the day Adams had designated as a national fast day. Philadelphians were urged to display the "utmost vigilance" to protect their lives and property and warned that "One unguarded hour may lay your city in ashes." Two of the letters are printed in Richard N. Rosenfeld, *American Aurora: A Democratic-Republican Returns* (New York, 1997), 77, 96. According to the missives, a "very numerous party of Frenchmen" was planning to set the conflagration and massacre all except those friendly to their interests (same; Charles Ellis Dickson, "Jeremiads in the New American Republic: The Case of National Fasts in the John Adams Administration," *New England Quarterly*, 60 [1987], 187-207).

On 28 Apr. *Claypoole's American Daily Advertiser* cited a letter from St. Martin's to a merchant in New York reporting that the French commissioner, VICTOR HUGHES (Hugues), had ordered all French privateers "to capture indiscriminately, American vessels, without examining or paying the smallest respect to rolls of equipage, or protections of any kind." During debate on the provisional army bill, South Carolina congressman Robert Goodloe Harper repeated reports that Hugues had command of 5,000 black troops ready to invade the southern states (*Annals*, 8:1529, 1531, 1539-40; Bowman, *Neutrality*, 346).

[1] TJ here canceled "imagine."

To John Harvie

DEAR SIR   Philadelphia May 6. 98.

Mr. Short has an interest in some Green sea lands, which I think he derived from you. he has written to me to attend to them, but has given me no information respecting them. I must therefore take the liberty of asking you to inform me, where they lie, how much there is of them, what is the state of the title, whether he is a sole or joint holder with others & whom, whether they are laid off, taxes due or paid, and whatever other information you can give me relative to the subject will be thankfully recieved. I shall still be here two or three weeks (for Congress expect to rise within that time) so that if you can favor me with an immediate answer I may recieve it here. I am with great esteem & respect Dear Sir

Your friend & servt   TH: JEFFERSON

PrC (DLC: Short Papers); at foot of text: "Colo. John Harvie"; endorsed by TJ in ink on verso.

TJ wrote a letter to Harvie on 14 Jan. 1798 that is recorded in SJL but has not been found.

To George Jefferson

DEAR SIR   Philadelphia May 6. 98.

I have to acknolege the reciept of your favors of Mar. 15. 26. & Apr. 11. and to thank you for your attention to the several commissions, & particularly the May wheat. every thing I have sent at different times appears to have got to your hands, except a Windsor couch & mattras, which went under the care of mr Lewis in a ship by which he went passenger to Richmond. the day after tomorrow a vessel sails hence for Richmond, and will take for me from 20. to 25. packages, great & small, containing chiefly groceries & stores for family use, which I hope will be in time to get up by the boats before they cease to run, and to be at home as early as I shall. as they contain articles very tempting to the depredations of watermen be so good as to attend to the condition of the packages, having them put into good order if otherwise, and to be particular in taking the reciepts. I will send you by post the bill of lading as soon as it is made out.—the price of old tobacco here (of good quality) is 14 Dollars. I have had a thought (as mine is new) of offering to deliver it immediately to a purchaser, at the old tobo. price, waiting for the money till it becomes old tobacco, that is to say till Octob. 1. however I would rather sell it in that way in Richmond, if I could get an equivalent price, allowing for the expences of bringing here. there is a little upwards of

16 M̶ from Bedford, & will be 5. or 6. M̶. from Monticello. I will thank you to inform yourself what price I can get at Richmond on a credit till Oct. 1. and to let me know as soon as possible, that if I do not sell there, I may be able to sell here before my departure. the Bedford tobo. weighs an average upwards of 1600. ℔ per hogshead. I am with great esteem Dr. Sir

Your friend & servt   TH: JEFFERSON

P.S. mr Brown has often bought my tobacco, and knowing it's quality is generally eager for it.

writing this I am told [10?] D. cash have been given in Richmond for tobacco, and that probably 13 D. credit 1. Oct. might be got. if you can get that, be so good as to sell at once without waiting to [consult me,] only giving me [. . .] notice to prevent a sale here. a credit might also be given for 6 months from the date of the contract

PrC (MHi); blurred and faint, including last three sentences written in margin; at foot of text: "Mr. G. Jefferson"; endorsed by TJ in ink on verso.

From Peter Carr

P: CARR To TH: JEFFERSON.   Carrsbrook. May. 7th. 98
By some irregularity in the post, your letter of 12th. April was not received till the first of this month. The papers inclosed form a very interesting part of the history of the present, as connected with the late administration. Under the garb of conciliation and friendship to France, there appear to me in the instructions themselves opinions advanced, and maxims sanctioned, which can only tend to widen the breach between the two countries. The declaration, "that the war in which France is engaged is not a defensive one," seems to me to be one of these. The coalesced powers at the beginning of the war, declared the same thing; and the Executive of the U. States appears all along, as far as it dared, to have acted upon their principles and policy. But, upon what plausible pretext can it be insisted that the present is not a defensive war, on the part of France? Because in the course of it, she has slaughtered her enemies, carried the war into their own countries, and obliged them to sue for peace? or is it because she has made acquisitions of territory? upon none of these grounds, in my opinion can it be with reason insisted. I suppose one of the motives of this declaration of our government has been, to keep clear of the guarantee: for if it were admitted to be a defensive war, the casus fœderis has occurred—and in that case, there seems to be no question but we might have been called on to execute the article of our treaty with France, which relates to that.

From whatever causes it may have arisen, the dilemma to which we are reduced is an embarrassing one. It is easier however, to say what we should not do, than to point out what should be done. I should without hesitation, oppose the giving money in any shape whatever—convinced that every compliance with a demand of that sort, invites to a repetition more burdensome and more dishonorable. I do not see either, upon what ground a disavowal of any parts of Mr. A's speech can be made;—if however any eligible mode of doing that could be hit upon, and the French are disposed to be satisfied with it, it would seem the lesser evil.

The proceedings of our commissioners, appear to me in a very questionable point of view. After a residence of three months in Paris, we find them still higgling with a parcel of swindlers, who had in the outset of the business told them explicitly they were clothed with no authority from the government. We find one of them listening to, and even encouraging a proposal for money, from one of these informal gentry. The publication of these dispatches too, marks in a branch of our government hostility to France, and indisposition to peace. With respect to the ultimate effect which these communications will have upon the public mind, it is difficult to say any thing with certainty. The first impressions have certainly been unfavorable to France, and the Republican party in this country. But, I am inclined to believe, that with the mass of the people this has arisen more from a misapprehension of the real state of the case, than any thing else: for I have found in the circles where I have been, that whenever the subject has been fairly represented, these impressions have generally been weakened, and in some cases entirely effaced. What do you think will be the probable issue of the present state of our affairs with France? Will congress authorise the arming of Merchantmen? If they should will it not lead to War? any information [which] your leisure will permit you to give [me on] these subjects, will be thankfully receive[d. Accept] dear Sir, assurances of my perfect esteem.

RC (DLC); torn at seal, with words in brackets supplied by Editors; addressed: "Thomas Jefferson, Vice-President of U. States. Philadelphia"; franked; endorsed by TJ as received 22 May 1798 and so recorded in SJL.

To James Lewis, Jr.

DEAR SIR   Philadelphia May 9. 98.

I am much obliged by your friendly letter of the 4th. inst. as soon as I saw the first of mr Martin's letters, I turned to the newspapers of the day & found Logan's speech as translated by a common Indian inter-

preter. the version I had used had been made by Genl. Gibson. finding
from mr Martin's article that his object was not merely truth, but to
gratify party passions, I never read another of his letters. I determined
to do my duty by searching into the truth & publishing it to the world,
whatever it should be. this I shall do at a proper season. I am much
indebted to many persons who without any acquaintance with me have
voluntarily sent me information on the subject. party passions are indeed high. no body has more reason to know it than myself. I recieve
daily bitter proofs of it from people who never saw me, nor knew any
thing of me but thro' Porcupine & Fenno. at this moment all the passions are boiling over, and one who keeps himself cool and clear of the
contagion, is so far [behind?] the point of ordinary conversation that he
finds himself insulated in every society. however the fever will not last.
war, landtax, & stamp act, are [pallia]tives which must calm it's ardor.
they will bring on reflection, and that with information is all which our
countrymen need to bring themselves and their affairs to rights. they are
essentially republican. they retain unadulterated the principles of 75.
and those who are conscious of no change in themselves, have nothing
to fear in the long-run. it is our duty still to endeavor to avoid war: but
if it shall actually take place, no matter by whom brought on, we must
defend ourselves. if our house be on fire, with[out] enquiring whether
it was fired from within or without, we must try to extinguish it. in that
I have no doubt we shall act as one man. But if we can ward off actual
war till the crisis of England is over, I [shall hope] we [may escape] it
altogether. I am with much esteem Dear Sir

Your most obedt. humble servt   TH: JEFFERSON

PrC (DLC); faint; at foot of text: "Mr. James Lewis junr."

Notes on Insects

1798. May. 9.
The insect which lays it's egg in the plumb, apricot, nectarine peach,
&c. is a Curculio. William Bartram. probably the Curculio Cerasi. [note
the Curculio segetum is the weavil.)

---

that which destroys the Peach tree is an Ichneumon. Wm. Bartram. it
lays it's egg in the peach tree a little within the surface of the earth soon
after harvest. it hatches. the worm eats downwards, and becomes
winged & escapes in May following. Moses Bartram. boxing round the
root, with 4. shingles or boards staked down & filled with dung, prevents the insect. idem.

MS (DLC); entirely in TJ's hand; bracket and parenthesis as in original; endorsed: "Natural history."

On another occasion also TJ discussed the pest of the PLUMB, APRICOT, NECTARINE PEACH, &c. with WILLIAM BARTRAM; see TJ to Thomas Mann Randolph, Jr., 1 May

1791. MOSES BARTRAM, an apothecary and former mariner, displayed some of his brother's proclivity for observing natural subjects such as insects (Edmund Berkeley and Dorothy Smith Berkeley, eds., *The Correspondence of John Bartram, 1734-1777* [Gainesville, Fla., 1992], 697, 700, 703, 784).

To Thomas Mann Randolph

Th:J. to TMR. Philadelphia May 9. 98.

My last to you was of the 3d. instant. yours of the 29th. April is now recieved. Champlain came perfectly safe: and I am in hopes you will have found Escarbot as I know it is in the library, and I think in one of the 3. presses fronting the door: I mean those near the commode, but the North East range of them. you will see in Bache an Alien bill worthy of the 8th. or 9th. century. it will pass the Senate probably by a majority of 3. to 1. but not the H. of R. they are preparing a reasonable one. the bill for the Provisional army, will be very hard run. if our members were here it would be easily rejected. the tax on lands houses & negroes goes on. there will be no questions on that but of modification. there is a rumour from Baltimore of peace between France & England on terms entirely dictated by the former. but nobody knows how it came, nor pays the least attention to it. the famous dispatches checked the addresses for peace as we expected, but did not produce any for war from the *country in general*, except New Jersey, a state entirely agitated from this city. the body of the people are still firm for peace. so they remain even in this city. the young men who addressed the President mounted the black (understood to be English) cockade. numbers of the people the next day appeared with the tricolor (or French) cockade. the same thing happened yesterday evening, being the fast day. a fray ensued & the light horse was called in. I write in the morning and therefore do not yet know the details. but it seems designed to drive the people into violence. this is becoming fast a scene of tumult & confusion. my tenderest love to my ever dear Martha & the little ones. cordial affections & Adieu to yourself.

RC (DLC); written partly or entirely on 10 May (see note below), recorded in SJL under 9 May but after entry for Madison under 10 May; endorsed by Randolph as received 5 June 1798.

For the Senate's ALIEN BILL printed in the

Philadelphia *Aurora* on 8 May, see TJ to Madison, 3 May.

On 7 May up to 1,200 YOUNG MEN of Philadelphia marched before thousands of spectators from City Tavern to the president's house and presented Adams, dressed for the occasion in full military attire, with

To St. George Tucker

DEAR SIR   Philadelphia May 9. 98.

I am much obliged by your friendly letter of the 2d. inst. and your attention to mr Martin's libels on the subject of Logan, the first only of which I have ever read: for when I found by his stile that truth was not his object, but to gratify party passions, I determined to read no more, but to make proper enquiries into the fact he questioned, & in due time publish it. I turned to the papers of the day (in my own possession) & found Logan's speech, as interpreted by the common Indian interpreter. I used Genl. Gibson's version. but in the paper I have there is no statement of facts. if there be one in the paper you have seen, you would infinitely oblige me by procuring the paper itself, or a copy of the statement.

At an early part of my life, from 1762. to 1775. I passed much time in going through the public records in Virginia, then in the Secretary's office, and especially those of a very early date of our settlement. in these are abundant instances of purchases made by our first assemblies of the indians living around them. the opinion I formed at the time was that if the records were complete & thoroughly searched, it would be found that nearly the whole of the lower country was covered by these contracts. sometimes, at the conclusion of a war, land would be ceded by them as an indemnification, but I think there were few instances of this. in general the colony lived in peace with the Indians, their habitations touched one another, & the latter receded gradually & peaceably. I do not know in what state the public records are since the British invasion, but if preserved, the facts I state may be abundantly verified from them.—we are here struggling hard to avert war; till that point we are a divided people, because some wish to bring it on. if it actually takes place, we shall defend ourselves as one man. when our house is on fire, it matters little whether fired from without or within, or both. the first object is to extinguish it. if we can keep it off till the crisis of England is over perhaps we may escape it altogether. I am with great esteem Dear Sir

Your friend & servt   TH: JEFFERSON

RC (ViW photostat); addressed: "The honble St. George Tucker Williamsburg"; franked and postmarked; endorsed by Tucker. PrC (DLC).

To George Jefferson

DEAR SIR   Philadelphia May 10. 98.

According to [advices] in my letter of the 6th. inst. I now inclose to you the bill of lading for 28. packages & 1. doz. chairs by the sloop Sally capt. Potter, which sails tomorrow morning. be so good as to forward them, when recieved, by the Milton boats. No. 28. will perhaps require new wrapping, being hinges done up in paper, as they were not thought of till all the other packages were aboard. I am with great esteem Dear Sir

Your friend & sert.   TH: JEFFERSON

PrC (MHi); faint; at foot of text: "Mr. George Jefferson"; endorsed by TJ in ink on verso. Enclosure not found.

To James Madison

                                                      May 10. 98.

I wrote you last on the 3d. inst. since which yours of Apr. 29. is recieved. a day or two after I arrived here J. Bringhurst called on me. since that moment I have never seen him nor heard of him. he cannot therefore be here. but I have put your letter & draught into the hands of mr Barnes, & desired him to get Bohemian glass from Donath. I will myself look to the locks & hinges. but both articles would have been better with further explanation. 'brass locks.' do you mean mortise-locks, or locks cased in brass and to be screwed on the outside of the door. the former are generally preferred, but require a thick door. 'brass spiral hinges.' I do not know what these are, by that name; but perhaps the shop-keepers can tell me. if you mean the dove-tail rising hinge, which raises the door as it opens, I can assure you from my own experience as well as that of others that they do not answer. the weight of the door raised by the dovetail joint wears it out very soon, and often (if there happens any little obstruction) bursts off the axis. the hinges now universally used are 5 inch butt hinges screwed on the edge of the door with stout screws. they shew only the joint which is of polished iron. mortise brass hinges are still somewhat in use. they shew only their joint. as I shall probably be here till you can send an answer to this, if you do it by return of post, I will defer getting the locks & hinges, in hopes of further explanation.

No bill has past since my last. the alien bill now before the Senate you will see in Bache. I shall make no comment on it. the first clause was debated through the whole of Tuesday. to judge from that we cannot expect above 5 or 6. votes against it. we suppose the lower house will throw it out & proceed on that which they have prepared. the bill for the provisional army is under debate. it will probably pass or be rejected by a very minute majority. if our members were here it would be rejected with ease. the tax on lands, slaves & houses is proceeding. the questions on that will only be of modification. the event of the N. York elections is not yet absolutely known, but it is still believed we have gained 2. more republicans to Congress. Burr was here a day or two ago. he says they have got a decided majority of whigs in their state H. of R. he thinks that Connecticut has chosen one whig, a mr Granger, and calculates much on the effect of his election. an election here of town-officers for Southwark, where it was said the people had entirely gone over to the tory side, shewed them unmoved. the whig ticket was carried by 10. to 1. the informations are so different as to the effect of the late dispatches on the people here that one does not know what to conclude: but I am of opinion they are little moved. some of the young men who addressed the President on Monday, mounted the Black (or English) cockade. the next day numbers of the people appeared with the tricoloured (or French) cockade: yesterday, being the fast day, the black cockade again appeared. on which the tricolor also shewed itself. a fray ensued, the light horse were called in, & the city was so filled with confusion from about 6. to 10. oclock last night that it was dangerous going out. I write in the morning & therefore know nothing of the particulars as yet. but as I do not send my letter to the post office till night, I shall probably be able by that time to add some details; it is also possible some question may be taken which may indicate the fate of the provisional army. there is a report, which comes from Baltimore, of peace between France & England on terms entirely dictated by the former. but we do not hear how it comes, nor pay the least attention to it.

P.M. by the proceedings in Senate to-day, I conclude the alien bill will pass 17 to 6. the Provisional army has been under debate in the

lower house. a motion was made to strike out the first section, professedly for the purpose of trying the fate of the bill. the motion was lost
by 44. to 47. had all the members in town been present, and the question in the house instead of the committee, the vote would have been 45.
against the bill & 46. for it.—no further particulars about the riot
appear.—Barnes has recieved for you from Moylan 158.33 D which he
will place to your credit in account. the ironmongers to whom I have
been since writing in the morning know nothing of *spiral hinges*.

RC (DLC: Madison Papers, Rives Collection); addressed: "James Madison junr.
near Orange court house"; franked. PrC
(DLC).

TJ developed notes relating to procedural matters that arose during the 10 and
29 May debates in the Senate on the ALIEN
BILL (MS in DLC; TJ Papers, 82:14221).
He recorded the following notes on "equivalent questions" from the 29 May debate:
"Where questions are perfectly equivalent,
so that the negative of the one amounts to the
affirmative of the other & leaves no other alternative, the decision of the one concludes
necessarily the other. thus the negative of
striking out amounts to the affirmative of
agreeing, and therefore to put a question on
agreeing after that on striking out would be

to put the same question in effect twice over.
not so in questions on amendments between
the two houses. a motion to recede being
negatived does not amount to a positive vote
to *insist*, because there is another alternative, viz. to *adhere*" (same). For the history
of this fragment from TJ's rough notes that
he used in compiling his *Manual of Parliamentary Practice*, see PW, 342. TJ does not
appear to have included the notes taken on
10 and 29 May in his *Manual*, but those
taken on 30 and 31 May, again on debates
on the alien friends bill, included on the
same fragment, are found in PW, 399-400.

On 9 May the Philadelphia *Aurora* reported that Republicans had carried the
election in the SOUTHWARK district of Philadelphia by the "proportion of about *Nine* to
one."

To Timothy Pickering

May 11. 98. Philadelphia

Th: Jefferson presents his compliments to the Secretary of state [&]
sends him Champlain's travels which he recieved by the last post. the
person whom he desired to search his library, could not, on his first
[look], find Escarbot: but promised to examine again, before the next
post. Th:J. knows that it is in the library, and therefore hopes it will be
found. he is happy in this occasion of rendering them useful to the public, which was the very motive inducing him while in Europe to make
great sacrifices of time & money to collect whatsoever related to the
antient history of America. no sacrifice whatever will ever enable such
another collection to be made; which consideration induces him to wish
that the Secretary of state will be so good as to recommend that after
being used for all the public purposes, they may be carefully returned to
this place, from whence he can send them on to their proper deposit.

PrC (DLC); faint.

PERSON WHOM HE DESIRED TO SEARCH HIS LIBRARY: Thomas Mann Randolph. On 24 Jan. 1799 Pickering sent his compliments and returned the books by Marc Les-carbot and Samuel de Champlain that TJ had "obligingly lent for the information of the Commissioners on the St. Croix boundary" (PrC in MHi: Pickering Papers; FC, Lb in DNA: RG 59, DL).

From Martha Jefferson Randolph

DEAREST FATHER   Bellmont May 12 1798

Nothing makes me feel your absence so sensibly as the beauty of the season; when every object in nature invites one into the fields, the close monotonous streets of a city which offers no charms of society with in doors to compensate for the dreariness of the scene with out, must be absolutely intolerable: particularly to you who have such interesting employment at home. Monticello shines with a transcendent luxury of vegetation above the rest of the neighbourhood as yet, we have been entirely supplied with vegetables from there having no sort of a garden here nor any prospect of one this year. I am glad to have it in my power to give you a more favorable account of things than Mr Randolph did in his last which was written immediately after a frost that blasted every appearance of vegetation, but John informs me alltho the peaches cherries (except the kentish) and figs which had been uncovered were gone past recovery for *this* year, yet of strawberries, raspberries, currants &c &c &c there will be more than common—I dined at Monticello a fortnight ago and saw Maria's harpsichord which arrived safe except the lock and 1 or 2 pieces of the moulding which got torn off some way. it is a charming one I think tho certainly inferior to mine. you have probably not heard of the death of poor Aunt Fleming. that of Mrs. Archer (Polly Bolling that was) is still more recent it took place at her Father's house a few weeks since. we have been all well but Jefferson who had declined rapidly for some time from a disorder which had baffled every attention and change of diet, the only remedy we ventured to try; but Mr Sneed opening school and Jeffy being hurried out of bed every morning at sunrise and obliged after a breakfast of bread and milk to walk 2 miles to school: his spirits returned his complexion cleared up and I am in hopes that his disorder has left him entirely. he is much mended in appearance strength & spirits, which had been low to an alarming degree—Anne Just begins to read and little Ellen points at grand Papa's picture over the chimney when ever she is asked where he is. adieu my dearest Father blest as I am in my family you are still wanting to compleat my happiness. Monticello will be interesting indeed when with the prospect of it the loved idea of yourself and Dear Maria will be so intimately blended as they will in a few weeks I hope. once more adieu and believe me with every sentiment of affection yours

M RANDOLPH

RC (MHi); endorsed by TJ as received 29 Apr. but recorded in SJL under 29 May 1798.

GRAND PAPA'S PICTURE: probably the 1786 portrait in oil by Mather Brown (Bush, *Life Portraits*, 3-4; Bear, *Family Letters*, 161).

From John Taylor

JOHN TAYLOR TO THOMAS JEFFERSON   [before 13 May 1798]
Having removed to some distance from Mr: Martin's, his consideration of your letter of the 6th. of April, and the drawing it covered, has been somewhat delayed.

He says, as indeed you will discover, that his amended machine, of which a drawing was lately sent you, has anticipated several of your objections, by having dispensed with the screw, and some of the wheels—that he had in the course of his experiments and reflections, fully discussed the points of an inclined plane, and of causing the axis of the great spur wheel, to be a feeding cylinder—and that the velocity and execution of his machine will he thinks, considerably exceed the English invention, in proportion to the force applied.

He therefore earnestly requests you to obtain a patent for him, pursuant to his drawing, by which means the invention will be refered to the ground of merit. If it wants it, he can derive no benefit from it; otherwise, he thinks it not amiss, that his mechanical efforts in favor of agriculture; many impliments of which he has considerably improved, should for once retribute him in some small degree.

To this I will add, that all those who have seen the machine work, are in raptures with it. That above 500 are already applied for. That he has now 40 workmen employed—and that by inventing new modes for making each peice of his invention, he has enabled his people to finish the work, in the time usually employed in laying it off, without using compass rule or square.

Mr: Martin regrets that he had adapted the workmanship of the drill to the purposes of husbandry, for which he supposed it to be intended, instead of having directed it to be finished in the stile of a model. He thinks he can extend his drill to any number of rows, and says that if you will exactly describe such a drill as you wish for, he will endeavour to supply it. The reason of this enquiry is, that your letter contains two ideas upon the subject, and he is at a loss to know, to which you would give the preference.

We have had the instructions and negociations of our French mission for some time. They do not allay our suspicions of our domestic politicks. a calm or apathy seems to be the prevailing impression. Both parties are stun'd by the very expectation of what may happen. I see nothing to change the opinions which have long obtruded themselves upon my mind—namely—that the southern states must lose their capital and commerce—and that America is destined to war—standing armies—and oppressive taxation, by which the power of the few here, as in other countries, will be matured into an irresistible scourge of human happiness.

Will you be so good as to let me hear from you on the subject of Martin's patent as soon as it is convenient?

Farewell.

RC (DLC: TJ Papers, 105:18035-6); undated; with calculations in TJ's hand on address sheet on verso; addressed: "The Vice president of the United States Philadelphia"; endorsed by TJ as received 13 May 1798 and so recorded in SJL.

From James Madison

DEAR SIR   May 13. 1798

I have recd. your favor of the 3d. instant. My last acknowledged your preceding one. The successful use of the Despatches in kindling a flame among the people, and of the flame in extending taxes armies & prerogative, are solemn lessons which I hope will have their proper effect when the infatuation of the moment is over. The management of foreign relations appears to be the most susceptible of abuse, of all the trusts committed to a Government, because they can be concealed or disclosed, or disclosed in such parts & at such times as will best suit particular views; and because the body of the people are less capable of judging & are more under the influence of prejudices, on that branch of their affairs, than of any other. Perhaps it is a universal truth that the loss of liberty at home is to be charged to provisions agst. danger real or pretended from abroad. The credit given to Mr. A. for a spirit of conciliation towards France is wonderful, when we advert to the history of his irritations from the first name in the Envoyship, down to his last answer to the addressers. If he finds it thus easy to play on the prepossessions of the people for their own Govt. agst. a foreign, we ought not to be disappointed if the same game should have equal success in the hands of the Directory.   We have had little or no rain for a month, and the evil has been increased by much windy & cold weather. The Thermr. yesterday morning was at 38°. and the frost such as to kill the leaves of tender trees in low situations. I hope now you will soon be released from the thorny seat in which you are placed, and that I shall not be disappointed of the pleasure of seeing you on your way. You must so arrange your time as to be able to ride a mile while with me to see a Threshing machine I have lately built on Martins plan. It is worked & attended by five or six hands at most, and I think promises more for general use than all the other modifications. I shall not describe it, because your own inspection will so soon give you a more perfect idea of it.

Yrs. always & affey. Js. MADISON JR

I recd. no paper by last mail but Fenno's. I hope the bridle is not yet put on the press.

RC (DLC: Madison Papers); endorsed by TJ as received 22 May 1798 and so recorded in SJL. MY LAST: Madison to TJ, 5 May 1798.

From George Jefferson

DEAR SIR, Richmond May 14th. 1798

Your favor of the 6th. came duly to hand. I have in conformity to your direction disposed of your Tobacco at $:13. payable the 1st. of Octr. & the 12th. of Novr., to a Mr. Hooper. I offered it to every person who I thought was acquainted with it's superior quality, except to Mr. Brown—to whom Mr. Randolph (who is now in Town) offered it with his own. Mr. B. having refused positively to give the price, Mr. R. had a thought (for his own) of accepting an offer he made him of 11$: certain & the rise—but upon reflection he concluded to let it go with yours, as from your letter he feared you apprehended a fall—which had much weight with me, as he informed me that you had been very sanguine in your expectations respecting it.

I am sorry to inform you Mr: R. tells me that so far from there being 5 or 6000 at Monticello, there will not be saved more than 1 Hhd: which I included in the sale with the rest—this he says is owing to it's having been neglected: the snow having driven in upon it, so as to rot at least two thirds.

The Mattrass you mention Mr. Lewis call'd with, about ten days after he came to Town—which was the first intimation I had of his arrival—indeed I did not even then know who he was, as he went away without making himself known—but as I supposed it was him, I made enquiry & called on him. he appeared to be very indifferent about engaging in business. he said nothing about the Couch, & it was not until after the receipt of your letter that I found it had been left at Mr. Brydie's by the Captain, who did not know to whom it belonged. it shall be forwarded by the first opportunity.

I enclose you one of the bills of lading for the May wheat; I have had it for some time & have kept it in expectation of soon getting the other—wishing to send them together. but as you talk of soon leaving Philada. & must be anxious to write concerning it before you come away, I send the one—but hope still it will be in my power to send the other in time—perhaps in a post or two. Mr. R. desired me to inform you that he left Mrs. R. & the children well the 6th. he is gone to Varina, & had not time to write to you:

I am most sincerely Dear Sir Your Very Hbl: servt.

GEO: JEFFERSON

The price I gave for the wheat is so enormous, & especially appears so now— that altho' it is of but little consequence I am almost ashamed to tell you—the Man however said as the quantity was so small, as the wheat was of a very superior quality, & as he had 16 miles to bring it, he could not take for 6 Bushels less than 10/.	£3— —
The Cooper was as extravagant in his charge for the barrels—but was at considerable trouble ea: 7/6	—15—
Of the freight to Norfolk we are not advised	———

RC (MHi); addressed: "Thomas Jefferson, esquire Philadelphia"; franked and postmarked; endorsed by TJ as received 20 May 1798 and so recorded in SJL. Enclosure not found.

From James Monroe

DEAR SIR   Fredbg May 14 1798.

Since my last I have been here attending this court, being detained by a cause of Colo. Mercer wh. was argued yesterday. I leave town to day on my way home. Your letters if you have written me any since I came here are at Charlottesville, so that they cannot be answered till after my arrival there. After perusing Pickering's objections to my advances abroad &ca, comprised in my acct., I can best determine whether it will be necessary for me to proceed to Phila. or not. In consideration of the acct. alone I wod. much rather not go there, since I wod. rather lose much than leave it open, & even pay the same sum three times over, subject to rectification hereafter, than accept any thing as a condesention from the admn.—or any of its members. But if there is any other object the case is altered relative to wh., & the nature of the object if any such there be I shall doubtless be advised by yr letters in Alb: when I arrive there.   There is a meeting in town to day of the merchants to address the President as other places have done Eastward of this approving his measures. There is a party in opposition of young respectability, so that the issue is uncertain. I avoid the whole of this business, having nothing to do with it; I mention this circumstance lest being here, tho' on my duty of a nature too indispensable, having two causes to argue this day before I leave town, the contrary shod. be insinuated.

RC (DLC); endorsed by TJ as received 20 May 1798 and so recorded in SJL.

MY LAST: Monroe to TJ, 4 May 1798.

In announcing the MEETING to be held at the Market House on the evening of 14 May to consider "the present interesting and critical situation of the United States, with respect to their Foreign Relations," the mayor of Fredericksburg, Fontaine Maury, said that he had been "induced" to issue the call. The group responsible for the gathering had prepared an address to Adams deeming his actions toward France "wise and prudent" and declaring a readiness to commit "our lives and fortunes" in the event of war. The PARTY IN OPPOSITION, however, including Monroe's client John Francis Mercer, also attended the meeting. They proposed in place of the address a set of six resolutions that criticized the administration for willfully bringing the nation "to the verge of destruction" by its policies toward France, declared the militia to be "the only safe and constitutional defence of these states," and pledged "firmly to support our national rights and independence whenever assailed by foreign invasion or domestic usurpation." When put to a vote, the resolutions won the approval of two-thirds of those in attendance and were published over Maury's signature as chairman of the meeting. The gathering was marked by "the most perfect order and decorum." Outmaneuvered in their own public meeting, the Federalists spent the next several days collecting signatures to their address (*Virginia Herald*, 12, 16 May 1798).

From John Harvie

DR SIR   Belvedere May 15th. 1798

In payment to Mr Short for his Mush Island Lands, was a Survey of Green Sea Lands made for me by One Bell, my Right to which Survey I transferr'd to Mr Short without any Warranty of Title—a Grant issued in the name of Mr Short (so well as I Recollect) & was deliver'd to Benjamin Harrison, who then Acted as his Agent—I do not Remember the Quantity of Land but I think about 2000 Acres—neither do I know what Attention Mr Harrison has pd. to it, the Value of the Land I Consider as of little Worth—what is called the Green Sea being Immense ponds of Water which probably will not be Drain'd in a Century—Mr Henry Obtain'd Grants for a Considerable Quantity of Green Sea Lands & made a Nominal Sale of them to judge Willson for I beleive a very small Consideration.

When I see Mr Harrison I will request him to give you Information what he has done with Mr Shorts patent.

I am Dr Sir with the truest Respect & Regard yr Most Obt Servt.

JNO. HARVIE

RC (DLC: Short Papers); addressed: "Thomas Jefferson Esqr. president of the Senate Philadelphia"; postmarked and franked; endorsed by TJ as received 29 Apr. but recorded in SJL under 29 May 1798.

In the 1780s William SHORT sold lands he had inherited in North Carolina, where MUSH ISLAND was located, to Harvie in exchange for Virginia land certificates, a large tract of land in Kentucky, and acreage in the GREEN SEA, a vast, reedy marsh within the Dismal Swamp in Norfolk County, Virginia. The expectation of Short and other investors, never fully realized, was that a Dismal Swamp canal, which both Virginia and North Carolina authorized in 1790,

would unlock the area's potential as an agricultural and timber-producing region. In 1795 Patrick HENRY, who had immersed himself in Green Sea speculation only to find the lands impossible to resell at a profit, sold his Dismal Swamp holdings to James Wilson (Charles Royster, *The Fabulous History of the Dismal Swamp Company: A Story of George Washington's Times* [New York, 1999], 82, 292, 317, 334-5, 340-3, 362, 379, 388; Shackelford, *Jefferson's Adoptive Son*, 15; William S. Powell, *The North Carolina Gazetteer* [Chapel Hill, 1968], 343; TJ to Short, 13 Apr. 1800).

A letter from Harvie to TJ of 24 June 1798, which according to SJL TJ received while passing through Baltimore on 28 June, has not been found.

From James Lewis, Jr.

DR SIR   Fredsbg 15th. May 98

Your Letter of the 9th. Inst. is at this late hour before me. In reply, I say, as a young man & a Citizen of a Country, where the hopes of every person ought to be, for the advancement of knowledge, justice & liberty I felt myself sincerely gratified by your Letter—But my heart exults when I know that you are enabled, at the proper time, to repel the attacks wch. my solicitude meant to remove.

Permit me Sir to introduce to you a young man, Mr James Walker a relation of mine, a fellow thinker & labourer in the cause of equality, who will remain in Phila. a few days.

I am DSir with that respect that proper motives inspire Yrs

JAS LEWIS JR

RC (MoSHi: Jefferson Papers); endorsed by TJ as received 21 May 1798 and so recorded in SJL.

To James Madison

My last to you was of the 10th. since that I have recieved yours of the
5th. I immediately sent a note to Carey to forward his paper to your
brother as you desired. the first vote of any importance on the alien bill
was taken yesterday. it was on agreeing to the 1st. section, which was
carried by 12. to 7. if all the Senators in town had been present it would
have been 17.[1] to 7. the Provisional army gets along. the Rep. have
reduced the 20. to 10. M̶. they have struck out the clauses for calling out
& exercising 20,000. militia at a time. the 1st. Volunteer clause has
been carried by a great majority. but endeavors will be made to render
it less destructive & less injurious to the militia. I shall inclose you a
copy of the land-tax bill. in the first moments of the tumults here, mentioned in my last, the cockade assumed by one party was mistaken to be
the tricolor. it was the old blue and red adopted in some places in an
early part of the revolution war. however it is laid aside. but the black is
still frequent. I am a little apprehensive Burr will have miscalculated on
Granger's election in Connecticut. however it is not yet known here. it
was expected Hillhouse would have been elected their Lt. Govr. but
Treadwell is chosen. we know nothing more certain yet of the New
York elections. Hamilton declined his appointment as Senator, & Jay
has named North, a quondam Aid of Steuben. all sorts of artifices have
been descended to, to agitate the popular mind. the President recieved
3 anonymous letters (written probably by some of the war-men) announcing plots to burn the city on the fast-day. he thought them worth
being made known. and great preparations were proposed, by way of
caution and some were yielded to by the Governor. many weak people
packed their most valuable moveables to be ready for transportation.
however the day past without justifying the alarms. other idle stories
have been since circulated, and the popular mind has not been proof
against them. the addresses & answers go on. some parts of[2] Maryland
& of this state are following the example of N. Jersey. the addresses are
probably written here; those which come purely from the country are
merely against the French. those written here are pointed with acri-
mony to party. you will observe one answer in which, a most unjustifiable mention has been made of Monroe, without the least occasion leading to it from the address. it is now openly avowed by some of the
Eastern men that Congress ought not to separate. and their reasons are
drawn from circumstances which will exist through the year. I was in
hopes that all efforts to render the sessions of Congress permanent were

abandoned: but a clear profit of 3. or 4. Dollars a day is sufficient to reconcile some to their absence from home. a French[3] privateer has lately taken 3. American vessels from N. York & Philada, bound to England. we do not know their loading, but it has alarmed the merchants much. wheat & flour are scarcely bought at all. tobacco, old, of the best quality, has long been 14. D. my respects to mrs Madison & to the family. affectionate Adieux to yourself.

P.M. the Provisional army bill has this day passed to it's 3d. reading. the volunteer corps remains a part of it.

RC (DLC: Madison Papers, Rives Collection); addressed: "James Madison junr. near Orange courthouse"; franked. PrC (DLC); lacks postscript. Enclosure not found, but see note below.

TJ's NOTE TO James CAREY is not recorded in SJL and has not been found. Also missing is a missive from TJ to Carey of 13 July 1798, with the entry in SJL indicating that it was for Archibald Stuart's subscription to *Carey's United States Recorder*.

LAND-TAX BILL: on 6 Apr. the House of Representatives instructed the ways and means committee to report on the need for further revenues. Committee chairman Robert Goodloe Harper submitted the report on 1 and 2 May recommending that two million dollars in additional revenues be raised by a direct tax "to be laid, by uniform assessment, on lands, houses and slaves," the tax to be apportioned among the several states according to the number of inhabitants at the last census (*Report of the Committee of Ways and Means, Instructed on the Sixth Ultimo, to Enquire Whether Any and What Additional Revenues, will be Wanted for the Public Service* [Philadelphia, 1798]; JHR, 3:280, 282). On 7 May the committee was ordered to bring in bills to implement the resolutions. Eight days later, Harper presented a bill for a direct tax. It was probably a copy of this bill, printed for the use of the House, that TJ enclosed to Madison. After debating the bill for some weeks, the House, by a 45 to 39 vote on 30 May, struck out the controversial thirteenth section of the bill that classified houses and valued them on a different scale from lands and, according to one calculation, placed three-fourths of the proposed tax on them. President Adams signed the act that provided the structure for the valuation of lands and houses and the enumeration of slaves on 9 July and the act for laying and collecting the direct tax five days later. The amount to be raised by the tax remained at two million dollars, the figure given in the original report (JHR, 3:289, 295; *Annals*, 8:1837-55, 1893-6, 1898-9, 1917-25, 2049-61; U.S. Statutes at Large, 1:580-91, 597-604).

[1] TJ first wrote "16" before altering the number to read as above.
[2] Preceding three words interlined.
[3] Word interlined.

To Martha Jefferson Randolph

MY DEAR MARTHA   Philadelphia May 17. 98.

Having nothing of business to write on to mr Randolph this week I with pleasure take up my pen to express all my love to you, and my wishes once more to find myself in the only scene where, for me, the sweeter affections of life have any exercise. but when I shall be with you seems still uncertain. we have been so long looking forward from 3.

weeks to 3. weeks, & always with disappointment, that I know not now what to expect. I shall immediately write to Maria & recommend to mr Eppes and her to go up to Monticello as soon as my stores, which went from here a week ago, shall be sent on from Richmond; because our groceries &c. were pretty well exhausted when I left home. these may well arrive at Richmond by about the 20th. instant, so that if my recommendation is adopted they may be soon with you, and contribute some variety to your scene. for you to feel all the happiness of your quiet situation, you should know the rancorous passions which tear every breast here, even of the sex which should be a stranger to them. politics & party hatreds destroy the happiness of every being here. they seem, like salamanders, to consider fire as their element. I am in hopes you make free use of the garden & any other resources at Monticello. the children I am afraid will have forgotten me. however my memory may perhaps be hung on the game of the goose which I am to carry them. kiss them for me, and present me affectionately to mr Randolph. to yourself my tenderest love & Adieu.   TH: JEFFERSON

P.S. since writing the above, Richardson has called on me. he has recieved a letter from mr Duke expressing doubts whether he shall be able to go & do mr Randolph's work. he has therefore determined to leave this place in the first vessel, and you may expect him in 3. or 4. weeks to be with you ready for work, & much improved, from what he has seen & done here.

RC (NNPM); at foot of text: "Mrs. Randolph." PrC (ViU: Edgehill-Randolph Papers); lacks postscript; endorsed by TJ in ink on verso.

To Mary Jefferson Eppes

MY DEAR MARIA   Philadelphia May 18. 98.
It is very long since I have heard from Eppington. the last letter I [recieved?] was from mr Eppes dated Apr. 4. so long without hearing from you, I cannot be without uneasiness for your health. I have been constantly in the hope that we were within 3. or 4. weeks of rising, but so often disappointed I begin to lose my faith as to any period of adjournment; and some begin now openly to avow that it would not be proper for Congress to separate. under this uncertainty I would wish you not to put off your return to Monticello, if mr Eppes & yourself would find it agreeable to be there and indeed I think his experience of ill health in the lower country should urge him to quit it before the hot weather comes

on. I sent from here on the 10th. instant the necessary groceries & stores for the use of the family. these will probably be arrived at Richmond by the time you recieve this, and I have desired mr Jefferson to forward them up by water immediately, and to give mr Eppes notice; in order that you may time your journey so as to find them there. all other necessaries, either in the house or farms, have administered to you as if I were there. I have given notice to them at home that you will come and I shall have the pleasure of finding you there as soon as I can get from here, and in the mean time brood over the pain of being uselessly kept from the society and scene for which alone I would wish to prolong life one moment. for here it is worse than nothing. you will find your harpsichord arrived at Monticello, and without injury as mr Randolph informed me. I shall go of necessity by the shortest route to Monticello, & of course must deny myself the pleasure of taking Eppington in my way this time. present my friendly salutations to mr & mrs Eppes; as also to our mr Eppes & the family. to yourself my tenderest love & Adieu.

TH: JEFFERSON

PrC (ViU: Edgehill-Randolph Papers); at foot of text: "Mrs. M. Eppes"; endorsed by TJ in ink on verso.

The letter from John Wayles EPPES to TJ

of 4 Apr. 1798, recorded in SJL as received seven days later, has not been found. MR RANDOLPH INFORMED ME: see Thomas Mann Randolph to TJ, 29 Apr. 1798.

To Aaron Burr

DEAR SIR   Philadelphia May 20. 98.
When I had the pleasure of seeing you here, I spoke to you on the case of a friend of mine, Dr. James Currie of Richmond [in Virginia] and asked the favor of you to proceed, in the way then spoken of, [to] recover against Robert Morris, Dr Currie's demand, the paper establishing which you had recieved. I have just recieved a letter from him wishing this matter to be pressed. I take the liberty therefore of repeating my request, and that you will be so good as to send to mr John Barnes, merchant South 3d. street, who is my agent here, a note of your own fee and of any costs which it may be necessary to advance and he will answer them now & from time to time on my account, whether I am here or not.   I have not heard from mr Burwell: but I know it to be his wish to have the same proceedings as shall be pursued for Dr. Currie. mr Barnes is his agent in his money matters at this place, so that his costs you will be so good as to note separately to him. his name is Lewis Burwell. he is also of Richmond.

This being merely a letter of business I shall only add assurances of the esteem & respect with which I am Dr. Sir Your most obedt. & most humble servt   TH: JEFFERSON

PrC (DLC); faint; at foot of text: "Colo. Burr"; endorsed by TJ in ink on verso.

TJ hoped that Burr might be able to obtain judgments against property that ROBERT MORRIS owned in New York State

(Kline, *Burr*, 1:358-9n). JUST RECIEVED A LETTER FROM HIM: probably a letter from Currie, dated 13 May and received by TJ on the 20th, which is recorded in SJL but has not been found.

To George Jefferson

DEAR SIR   Philadelphia May 20. 98.

I recieved yesterday your favor of the 14th. and am well pleased with the sale of my tobacco: for tho' if no check were to happen I think it would continue to rise, yet considering the critical affairs of this country, & still more of England, I think a check very possible, & that it must take place this summer, if at all. the price obtained secures my making two paiments of 1200. D. each in autumn, about which I was anxious. I inclose you the manifest for the Bedford tobacco, 16446 ℔. I have directed that from Monticello, whatever it is, to be forwarded immediately. I must ask you for information of the highest price which has been given for wheat and flour at Richmond or Manchester from Dec. 1. to Apr. 30. as I sold in Albemarle with a reference to that, & shall have to settle immediately on my return. I think I wrote to you before to attend to the price for me, and stated the times, & perhaps more exactly than I do now, as I write from memory at present, & may have forgotten.—a workman (Richardson) to whom I owed 11. D. 72 c wishing to recieve it in Richmond I have given him an order on you. I am afraid I am near the bottom of my funds in your hands for tho' one of the bonds for which they were destined will not be called for, yet the wheat & other small expences of which I have no account must have been of some amount. I will thank you for a statement. I inclosed you on the 10th. a bill of lading for between 20. & 30. packages by the sloop Sally, desiring them to be forwarded by the first Milton boats. I will thank you, as soon as they are forwarded to drop a line of information to mr J. W. Eppes, at his father's in Chesterfield, because as soon as he knows they are forwarded up the river, I have proposed to him & my daughter to proceed to Monticello. There is a weekly rider from the post office to mr Eppes's neighborhood in Chesterfield. I am with great esteem Dr. Sir

Your friend & servt   TH: JEFFERSON

P.S. I have opened my letter to ask whether it will be practicable and will not be prudent to have some guarantee of mr Hooper. I know nothing of him, having never before heard of him: but the credit is so long & the times so perilous, that it would be desireable. it is the usage here to require two guarantors with every transaction of any length. one I should think proper, but I leave it to yourself altogether.

PrC (MHi); postscript written in left margin; at foot of text: "Mr. George Jefferson"; endorsed by TJ in ink on verso. Enclosure not found, but see note below.

SECURES MY MAKING TWO PAIMENTS: see TJ to James Lyle and TJ to John Wickham, 15 June 1798. TJ took the following notes on the MANIFEST FOR THE BEDFORD TOBACCO from Poplar Forest before enclosing it:

"weights of tobo. from P.F. of which the manifests were sent to G. Jefferson, May 20. 98.

P.F	32.	137.	1568.	
T.I.	44.	137.	1641.	} 26th. Feb. 98
	52.	137.	1603	
	53.	137.	1573	
	54.	137.	1626	
	63.	137.	1641.	} 25th. Feb.
	95.	137.	1725.	
	96.	137.	1787.	
	109.	137.	1613	
	110.	137.	1669.	} 24th. Mar.
			16,446	

Spring Warehouse.
signed
Martin & Douglas.
sold by G. Jefferson to mr Hooper @ 13. D. paiable 1st. Oct. & 12th. Nov.
16446 ℔ @ 13. D = 2137.98
suppose 1400. Monticello   182.
2319.98"

(MS in MHi; on small scrap of paper; entirely in TJ's hand, with last two lines, including total, written in pencil).

On 18 May 1798 TJ had John Barnes pay Richard RICHARDSON $60. The next day TJ gave Richardson an order on George Jefferson for the balance of $11.72 (MB, 2:983). TJ also wrote drafts on Barnes on 9, 18 Apr., and 1 May, each one for $10 in favor of Richardson (MSS in MHi, written and signed by TJ, endorsed by Barnes and canceled).

From James Madison

DEAR SIR   May 20. 1798

Your favor of the 3d. was acknowledged in my last. I am now to thank you for that of the 10th. You must ascribe my inaccuracy as to the locks & hinges partly to myself, & partly to my workman. Four of the doors will be thick eno' for mortise locks which I accordingly prefer, and of the quality which you think best. Three of the doors will be about $1\frac{1}{4}$ inch thick only. If this thickness be insufficient for mortise locks, I must get the favor of you to order brass locks of moderate size to be screwed on the outside. There will be also 2 outside folding doors about the thickness of $1\frac{3}{4}$ inch for which I wish you to order such locks & Bolts as your better judgment may chuse. "Spiral hinges" were a misnomer for the dovetail rising hinge. Your objection to that sort is so deci-

sive that I can not hesitate to change it for the 5 inch Butt hinge, shewing an iron joint. The 7 doors & two folding doors will require 22
hinges, or 33 if more than two be thought necessary for all the doors, or
30 if more than two for the thick, & two only for the $1\frac{1}{4}$ doors. Being
disappointed in getting pullies for windows in Fredg. I must extend my
tax on your kindness, to the procuring that supply also. Three dozen
will be wanted, of about $1\frac{3}{8}$ inch diameter. The brass pullies I suppose are the proper sort, but relying more on your knowledge than my
own or my workman's, I must beg you to substitute a better if there be
one.

The Alien bill proposed in the Senate is a monster that must for ever
disgrace its parents. I should not have supposed it possible that such an
one could have been engendered in either House, & still persuade myself, that it can not possibly be fathered by both. It is truly to be deplored
that a standing army should be let in upon us by the absence of a few
sound votes. It may however all be for the best. These addresses to the
feelings of the people from their enemies, may have more effect in opening their eyes, than all the arguments addressed to their understandings
by their friends. The President also seems to be co-operating for the
same purpose. Every answer he gives to his addressers, unmasks more
& more his principles & views. His language to the young men of Pha.
is the most abominable & degrading that could fall from the lips of the
first magistrate of an independent people, & particularly from a Revolutionary patriot. It throws some light on his meaning when he remarked
to me, "that there was not a single principle the same in the American
& French Revolutions," & on my alluding to the contrary sentiment of
his predecessor expressed to Adet on the presentment of the Colours,
added, "that it was false let who would express it." The abolition of
Royalty was it seems not one of his Revolutionary principles. Whether
he always made this profession is best known to those, who knew him
in the year 1776.—The turn of the elections in N.Y. is a proof that the
late occurrences have increased the noise only & not the number of the
Tory-party. Besides the intrinsic value of the acquisition, it will encourage the hopes & exertions in other States. You will see by the Newspapers the turn which a Town Meeting took in Fredericksbg. I forgot to
acknowledge the pamphlet containing the last Despach from the Envoys recd. with your letter of the 10th. It is evidently more in the foren-
sic than Diplomatic stile and more likely in some of its reasonings to
satisfy an American Jury, than the French Government. The defence of
the provision-article is the most shallow that has appeared on that subject. In some instances the reasoning is good, but so tedious & tautolo-
gous as to insult the understanding as well as patience of the Directory,

if really intended for them, and not for the partial ear of the american public. The want of rain begins to be severely felt, and every appearance indicates a continuance of it. Since the 10th. of April there has fallen but one inch of water, except a *very* partial shower of less than $\frac{1}{2}$ an inch.

Adieu Affecly.   Js. MADISON JR

RC (DLC: Madison Papers); endorsed by TJ as received 29 Apr. but entered in SJL under 29 May 1798.

In his 7 May response to the YOUNG MEN of Philadelphia, Adams noted that as a REVOLUTIONARY PATRIOT he was called to act "not from a desire of innovation, not from discontent with the Government under which we were born and bred, but to preserve the honour of our Country, and vindicate the immemorial Liberties of our Ancestors" (*Gazette of the United States*, 7 May 1798). Adams's remark indicating THAT THERE WAS NOT A SINGLE PRINCIPLE THE SAME IN THE AMERICAN & FRENCH REVOLUTIONS was perhaps made when Madison dined with Adams on 26 Feb. 1796 (Madison, *Papers*, 17:135). For Washington's response to Pierre Auguste ADET on the PRESENTMENT of the French flag, see Madison to TJ, 10 Jan. 1796. For the PAMPHLET containing the last dispatches FROM THE ENVOYS, see TJ to John Wayles Eppes, 6 May 1798.

To James Monroe

Philadelphia May 21. 98.

Yours of Apr. 8. 14. & May 4. & 14 have been recieved in due time. I have not written to you since the 19th. Ult. because I knew you would be out on a circuit, and would recieve the letters only when they would be as old almanachs. the bill for the Provisional army has got through the lower house, the regulars reduced to 10,000. and the volunteers unlimited. it was carried by a majority of 11. the land-tax is now on the carpet to raise 2. millions of dollars, yet I think they must at least double it as the expences of the provisional army were not provided for in it, and will require of itself 4. millions a year. I presume therefore the tax on lands, houses & negroes will be a dollar a head on the population of each state. there are alien bills, sedition bills &c. also before both houses. the severity of their aspect determines a great number of French to go off. a ship load sails on Monday next; among them Volney. if no new business is brought on I think they may get through the tax-bill in 3. weeks.   You will have seen among numerous addresses & answers one from Lancaster in this state, and it's answer, the latter travelling out of the topics of the address altogether to mention you in a most injurious manner. your feelings have no doubt been much irritated by it, as in truth it had all the characters necessary to produce irritation. what notice you should take of it is difficult to say. but there is one step in which two or three with whom I have spoken concur with me, that feeble as the hand is from which this shaft is thrown, yet with a great mass of our citizens, strangers to the leading traits of the character from which it came, it will have considerable effect; & that in order to replace yourself on the high ground you are entitled to, it is absolutely necessary you should re-appear on the public theatre, & take an independant stand from which you can be seen & known to your fellow-citizens. the H. of Repr. appears the only place which can answer this end, as the proceedings of the other house are too obscure. Cabell has said he would give way to you whenever you should chuse to come in. and I really think it would be expedient for yourself as well as the public that you should not wait till another election but come to the next session. no interval should be admitted between this last attack of enmity and your re-appearance with the approving voice of your constituents & your taking a commanding attitude. I have not before been anxious for your return to public life, lest it should interfere with a proper pursuit of your private interests. but the next session will not at all interfere with your courts because it must end Mar. 4. and I verily believe the next election will give us such a majority in the H. of R. as to enable the republican party to shorten the alternate unlimited session, as it is evident that to shorten the sessions is to lessen the evils & burthens of the government on our country. the present session has already cost 200,000 D. besides the wounds it has inflicted on the prosperity of the union. I have no doubt Cabell can be induced to retire immediately, & that a writ may be issued at once. the very idea of this will strike the public mind & raise it's confidence in you. if this be done I should think it best you should take no notice at all of the answer to Lancaster. because were you to shew a personal hostility against the answerer, it would deaden the effect of every thing you should say or do in your public place hereafter. all would be ascribed to an enmity to mr A. and you know with what facility such insinuations enter the minds of men. I have not seen Dawson since this answer has appeared, & therefore have not yet learnt his sentiments on it. my respectful salutations to mrs Monroe, & to yourself affectionately Adieu.

RC (DLC: Monroe Papers); addressed: "Colo. James Monroe Charlottesville"; by TJ below seal: "always examine the seal before you open my letters"; endorsed by Monroe. PrC (DLC).

AMONG THEM VOLNEY: the *Benjamin Franklin*, with Volney among its passengers, did not leave until 7 June. Owned by Francis Breuil, an American citizen, the vessel carried a safe-conduct request from the secretary of state and traveled to Bordeaux under a flag of truce. Volney, the subject of acerbic comments by the Federalist press, had feared that passage of an alien act might result in his arrest and the seizure of his papers. Moreau St. Méry confirmed after Volney's departure that Volney and Victor Collot, who did not return to France until 1800, were high on a list of people whom Adams wished to see deported (Gilbert Chinard, *Volney et l'Amérique d'après des documents inédits et sa correspondance avec Jefferson*, The Johns Hopkins Studies in Romance Literatures and Languages, 1 [Baltimore, 1923], 99-100; Frances Sergeant Childs, *French Refugee Life in the United States, 1790-1800: An American Chapter of the French Revolution* [Baltimore, 1940], 189-90; Kenneth Roberts and Anna M. Roberts, eds. and trans., *Moreau de St. Méry's American Journey* [*1793-1798*] [Garden City, N.Y., 1947], 253; George W. Kyte, "A Spy on the Western Waters: The Military Intelligence Mission of General Collot in 1796," MVHR, 34 [1947], 441; *Porcupine's Gazette*, 31 May, 7 June 1798).

In his 14 May response to an address of support from LANCASTER County, Pennsylvania, Adams alluded to the French government's dismay over his message to Congress of 16 May 1797. Referring to the attention the French gave Monroe on 30 Dec. 1796, when the recalled minister and the Directory exchanged praiseful addresses of farewell, the president noted the umbrage he felt at "the honour done, the publicity and solemnity given to the audience of leave to a disgraced minister, recalled in displeasure, for misconduct." Adams considered the occasion to have been "a studied insult to the government of my country," a provocation greater than anything he had expressed in his message. Timothy Pickering, a month before Adams sent that message to Congress, had labeled Monroe's address on leaving Paris "unpardonable" (*Porcupine's Gazette*, 16 May 1798; Ammon, *Monroe*, 155-6, 167-8, 171, 606n).

MR A.: John Adams.

From George Jefferson

DEAR SIR,   Richmond May 23d. 1798.

Capt. Potter arrived to day with the things mentioned in the bill of lading which you enclosed in your letter of the 10th.—

They shall be forwarded by the first boat going to Milton.   I wish the beer which you desired Mr. Hay should have bottled for you could accompany them, but fear it will not—as it appears as if I shall not be able to prevail on Mr. H. to have it done; he has frequently promised to attend to it as soon as he possibly could, but constantly delayed it. I shall continue to press him.

I am Dear Sir Your Very Obt. servt.   GEO. JEFFERSON

RC (MHi); at foot of text: "Thomas Jefferson esqr."; endorsed by TJ as received 29 Apr. but recorded in SJL under 29 May 1798.

From Aaron Burr

24 May 98

Have the goodness to inform me how long you will remain in Phila. if till the close of the Session, I hope to come & pass an hour with you. No freedom of communication, by letter, can be indulged consistently with any degree of discretion

Be assured of my very great attachment & esteem   A. BURR

RC (DLC); endorsed by TJ: "Burr Aaron. recieved in his lre of May 24. 98. forwarded to Dr Currie," which along with TJ's reply to Burr of 26 May implies that a letter from Burr that is recorded in SJL as having been received from New York on 25 May was not the above note but a longer letter enclosing it, now missing, that TJ sent on to James Currie.

To James Madison

May. 24. 98.

My last was of the 17th. since which yours of the 13th. is recieved. the Alien bill of the Senate still hangs before them. some of it's features have been moderated, which has so much disgusted it's warmest friends that some of them have declared they will vote against it, so that I think it possible they may reject it. they appear to be waiting for one from the house of repr. worse I think than theirs, which got on to it's third reading; but in that stage was recommitted by a majority of 2. yesterday. I suppose it will be softened a little on the recommitment. the Senate yesterday passed their bill for capturing any French cruisers, who shall have taken our vessels, or who shall be found hovering on our coast for that purpose. Sitgreaves's resolutions proposed to the H. of R. of nearly the same tenor, were yesterday debated but no question taken. if these bills pass, and place us in a state of war, it may truly be ascribed to the desertion of our members. of 14. who are absent, 10 are from the republican side of the house. had every one been in his place not a single one of the dangerous measures carried or to be carried would have prevailed. even the provisional army would have been rejected, for it was carried but by a majority of 11. the absentees are Freeman, Skinner, Livingston, S. Smith, Nicholas, Giles, Cabell, Clay, Finlay, &¹ Swanwick sick.   the news from Amsterdam from our Consul Bourne, which you will see in the papers, has every appearance of truth. the war-men however are very unwilling to have it believed. the flame kindled by the late communications, has from the nature of them, and the unparalleled industry of the war party, spread more even in the country than I had expected. addresses continue to be poured in on us. I mentioned in my last the P's attack on Monroe. his friends here think that nothing can save him from the impression of that, but his coming into the H. of R. taking his stand on an independant theatre, from which his countrymen will see what are his principles. it has been said Cabell will give place to him. on that hypothesis I have counselled him strongly to come to the next session. such a recruit is immensely wanted here. it is believed we have gained 2. members in the N. York election. salutations to the family & friendly Adieux to yourself.

Mr. Adams, in a conversation in the Statehouse yard with Blair Mc.lanachan, declared that such was his want of confidence in the faith of France, that were they to agree to a treaty ever so favourable, he should think it his duty to reject it.

P.M. Sitgreave's resolns were moved to be postponed to a very distant day in June. the question was this day lost 51. to 40. had all been here it would have been carried.—Tracey (one of the war-commee of the Senate) told Anderson yesterday that he had drawn a bill for declaring our treaty with France void, & commencing hostilities but the commee thought the bill now past by the Senate would answer the same end & give less alarm.—Stockton told Tazewell yesterday he should be for a Declaration of war before Congress should separate. it is now declared by several Senators that they would not accept any treaty which France could offer.

RC (DLC: Madison Papers, Rives Collection); postscripts in margin; addressed: "James Madison junr. near Orange courthouse"; franked. PrC (DLC).

On 18 May Benjamin Goodhue introduced legislation that authorized the capture of armed vessels WHO SHALL HAVE TAKEN OUR VESSELS, OR WHO SHALL BE FOUND HOVERING ON OUR COAST FOR THAT PURPOSE. The bill's preamble made it clear that the legislation was aimed at the French, who were capturing American ships near the coast in violation of the law of nations and treaties between the United States and France. A motion on 23 May by North Carolina Senator Alexander Martin to have the preamble expunged was defeated by a 7 to 16 vote. An attempt to postpone the bill until word was received of the "total failure" of negotiations with France was defeated by the same margin. The Senate then passed the legislation, 16 yeas to 7 nays. The same bill, "An act more effectually to protect the commerce and coasts of the United States," passed the House on 26 May by a 50 to 40 vote (JS, 2:490-3; JHR, 3:313-16; U.S. Statutes at Large, 1:561). Samuel SITGREAVES'S RESOLUTIONS, allowing armed vessels, private as well as public, to capture French armed cruisers preying on American shipping, were introduced on 22 May. The Philadelphia Aurora referred to them as the "war resolutions." On 24 May, a mo-

tion to postpone consideration of the resolutions until 12 June was defeated by a 43 to 37 vote, not 51 to 40 as TJ indicated. The House then sent them to the committee that was considering the bill passed by the Senate (Annals, 8:1783, 1812; Philadelphia Aurora, 25 May 1798). For TJ's revision of the consequences of the DESERTION of Republican MEMBERS on the votes in the House of Representatives, see TJ to Madison, 31 May.

Newspapers in Philadelphia reprinted a letter FROM AMSTERDAM from United States CONSUL Sylvanus BOURNE to Boston merchant Benjamin Russell of 20 Mch. indicating that the envoys had recently had several conferences with the French minister of foreign affairs with unknown results. A summary of a second letter from Bourne gave news from Elbridge Gerry that the envoys had had three conferences with Talleyrand "and that the negociation appeared to be in good train." The Gazette of the United States observed that Bourne's letter did not give the date or indicate whether the conferences were official or informal. Fenno wondered whether the meetings referred to were those already described in the published dispatches (Gazette of the United States, 21 May 1798; Philadelphia Aurora, 22 May 1798).

CONVERSATION IN THE STATEHOUSE YARD: the Philadelphia Aurora of 24 May reported that in conversing with "a republi-

Thomas Jefferson by Robert Field

Luther Martin

"Cinque-Tetes, or The Paris Monster"

Tadeusz Kosciuszko by Benjamin West

West's "The Fright of Astyanax"

Thomas Jefferson
A Philosopher a Patriote and a Friend
Dessiné par son ami Tadée Kosciuszko.
Et Gravé par Mr Sokolnicki.

Jefferson by Tadeusz Kosciuszko

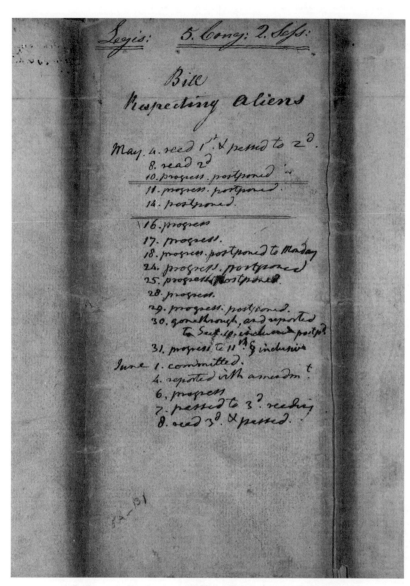

Legis: 5. Cong: 2. Sess:

Bill
Respecting Aliens

May. 4. recd 1st. & passed to 2d.
    8. read 2d
    10. progress. postponed
    11. progress. postponed.
    14. postponed.

    16. progress
    17. progress.
    18. progress. postponed to Monday
    24. progress. postponed
    25. progress postponed.
    28. progress.
    29. progress. postponed.
    30. gone through, and reported
            to Sect. 10. inclusive and postpd
    31. progress to 11th. § inclusive
June 1. committed.
    4. reported with amendmt.
    6. progress
    7. passed to 3d. reading
    8. read 3d. & passed.

Jefferson's Docketing of Senate Bill Concerning Aliens

"The Times; A Political Portrait"

can member of congress," President Adams noted "that he could not answer it to his conscience, his country, or his God, to enter in *any* treaty with the present government of France."

[1] TJ here canceled: "some others whom I do not recollect" and interlined the remainder of the sentence.

To Thomas Mann Randolph

Th:J. to TMR.   Philadelphia May 24. [1798]

My last was to my dear Martha, of the 17th. the last recieved from you was of the 29th. of Apr. acknoleged in mine of May 9. the severe alien bill of the Senate still hangs before them, & one rather worse in the H. of R. which had got on to it's 3d. reading, was in that stage recommitted yesterday by a majority of 2. it will perhaps be a little softened. the Senate yesterday passed a bill for capturing French armed vessels making prize on us, or hovering on our coasts. if this passes the H. of R. we consider it as war. all this is owing to the absence of our members. of 14. absent from the H. of R. 10. are from the republican side. even the Provisional army would have been rejected if all had been here, for it was carried but by a majority of 11. we consider the news from Consul Bourne which you will see in the papers, to be true. the war-party however are desirous of discountenancing it. the flame kindled by the late communications has extended more into the country than had been expected. the war-men have been indefatigable in the use they have made of them with the people, who are not in the habit of analysing things of that kind. still we have gained 2. members as is believed in the late elections of New York. addresses continue to be poured in on us, all offering lives & fortunes. one counter-address only has come from Maryland, and 3. from Virginia. a prospect of the measures contemplated, induced me to have my tobacco sold in Richmond for 13. Dol. as a war with France, or even the invasion of England may check the price for this summer. I sent from 20. to 30. packages of groceries &c. from hence about the 12th. I think they may be arriving at Milton by the time you get this. I shall be obliged to you to have them safely deposited at home. I have pressed mr Eppes & Maria to go to Monticello immediately. as soon as the land-tax passes we shall see whether Congress means to adjourn at all, as after that they will have no specified object. as soon as it is evident they mean to make their session permanent, I shall go home for the season. not having a vote but in cases of division, & the majority in the Senate being about 3. to 1. my presence here is useless to the public. my love to my ever-dear Martha & the children, & to yourself affectionately Adieu.

RC (DLC); partly dated; endorsed by Randolph as received 2 June 1798. PrC (MHi); year added by TJ in ink; endorsed by TJ in ink on verso.

To Aaron Burr

DEAR SIR   Philadelphia May 26. 98.

I recieved yesterday your favor of the 24th. the notes [delivered by] mr Burwell to mr Ludlow belonged three of them to Dr. Currie, & the [rest to] himself. to wit

Doll.

Dr. Currie's. { John Nicholson's note to Rob. Morris dated Nov. 18. 94 for 3500. payable in 3.

years

do.   to do.   Nov. 18. 94.   3500. do.

do.   to do.   Nov. 18. 94.   4000. do.

11,000

Mr. Burwell's. { John Nicholson's note to Rob. Morris dated Nov. 20. 94. for 4000. payable in 3.

years

do.   to do.   Nov. 30. 94.   4000. do.

do.   to do.   Jan. 15. 95.   2500. do.

do.   to do.   Mar. 21. 95.   4000. do.

14,500

this last one of mr Burwell's was not delivered to mr Ludlow, but will be forwarded to him by mr Barnes by this day's post. you will therefore be pleased to proceed in the name of Dr. James Currie for the three first notes, amounting to 11,000 Dollars; you mention that discretionary powers must be given to some person in N. York in order that you may be able to associate these gentlemen in a general compromise with some others for whom you will obtain judgment in July. Dr. Currie has given me full powers to act for him, and I hereby give you full and discretionary powers to do for him whatever you may think for his interest. I inclose you one of his letters to me sufficiently evidencing his committing the matter to me. mr Barnes is authorised by mr Burwell to take the same steps for him which I do for Dr. Currie. he will therefore write to you this day. Dr. Currie has another claim by judgment recovered here against Griffin & Morris which may be the subject of a future letter to you perhaps, after I shall have seen mr Ingersol his attorney (now absent from town.)

If Congress mean to adjourn at all (which I doubt) I shall stay here till they adjourn. if they do not after passing the land tax, I shall consider it as evidence they mean to make their sessions permanent, and shall then go home for the season. I am with great & sincere esteem Dr. Sir
Your friend & servt   TH: JEFFERSON

P.S. since writing the above I have seen mr Barnes, & find he wrote yesterday to yourself & mr Ludlow.

RC (CtHi: Aaron Burr Papers); torn, with four missing words supplied in brackets from PrC; at foot of text: "Colo. Burr." PrC (DLC); lacks postscript; endorsed by TJ in ink on verso. Enclosure not found; James Currie wrote TJ letters, now missing, of 11 Apr. received on 17 Apr. and 13

May received seven days later (see Currie to TJ, 11 Mch. 1798).

A letter from Lewis BURWELL to TJ, written on 29 May and received from Richmond on 6 June 1798, is recorded in SJL but has not been found.

From Mary Jefferson Eppes

DEAR PAPA   Eppington May 27th 98
In hopes every day of recieving the long wish'd for & long expected summons to meet you at Monticello, I have delayed answering your last letter which you in laughing at reproved me so justly for my negligence & inattention in writing. from your last to Mr Eppes he does not expect that you will come in till near the 20th of next month, till which time unless your return should be sooner we shall stay down, as he is obliged to be here at that time. I have been to Petersburg, lately with the girls, Bolling, & Tabby Walker, one of her cousins, to take the smallpox which they have had most favourably; & from there we went to Shirley with my mother who is an old acquaintance & was recieved with much pleasure. we there met with Mr John Walker & his lady, the latter seem'd pleas'd to see me & press'd me to visit her at her house, but I was not sorry that her husband did not think proper to invite me, for it would have been disagreeable to be forced to invent excuses where there was one so evident & so insurmountable. I suppose you have not heard of Polly Archers death, render'd more afflicting to Aunt Bolling from her just suspicions that she hasten'd it by her intemperance in eating. she died of a bilious fever, a fortnight after her child was born, which is now alive & well, &, seems allready to afford much consolation to my aunt. she intends to go up this summer. I heard very lately from Mr Randolph that my Sister & her children were well, Mr Eppes met him in Richmond, but amongst the many enquiries he made, he forgot to ask

if my harpsichord had arrived safe at Monticello, Mr Jefferson had before sent me word it was gone up. Adieu dear Papa Aunt Carr is here & waits as impatiently as myself for the welcome letter that will inform us you are on your way home

Adieu once more & believe me your truly affectionate daughter

M. EPPES

RC (ViU: Edgehill-Randolph Papers); endorsed by TJ as received 5 June 1798 and so recorded in SJL.

TJ's LETTER that his daughter delayed

answering was most likely his of 1 Apr. For TJ's last to John Wayles EPPES, see 6 May 1798.

MY MOTHER: her mother-in-law, Elizabeth Wayles Eppes.

From James Madison

DEAR SIR   May 27. 98

I have duly recd. yours of the 17th. accompanied by the Direct tax bill which I have not yet been able to run thro'. Every thing I perceive is carried as the war party chuse. They will of course be the more responsible for consequences. The disposition to continue the Session is a proof that the operation of the irritating proceedings here on those of France is expected to furnish fresh fuel for the popular flame & to favor the success of the Executive projects in the Legislature. It is to be deplored that we have no authentic & impartial channel thro' which the true state of things in Europe, particularly in France can reach the public mind of this Country. The present temper of the Envoys cannot fail to discolour all that passes thro' them; and if this were not the case, the obvious policy of the Ex is a compleat bar to the disclosure of all other than inflammatory communications.

The inclosed accurate & authentic view of that "stupendous fabric of human wisdom" which Mr. A idolizes so much deserves I think the public attention at the present moment. At the request of Calander I promised several years ago to send it to him, but never could lay my hand on it, till a few days ago when it fell in my way without being sought for. If you have an oppy & think it worth while you can let the public have a sight of it; & for the reason just mentioned I could wish if there be no objection that it might pass thro' his hands. As the paper is of some value, it may be well to preserve it in case it should not be republished, or in case a part only should be so.

There have been pretty extensive, but not universal rains since my last. This neighbourhood has been but barely touched by them. I have not heard from yours. Adieu affecly.   J M. JR

[368]

RC (DLC: Madison Papers); addressed: "Thomas Jefferson," with *"private"* written above; endorsed by TJ as received 5 June 1798 and so recorded in SJL. Enclosure not found, but see note below.

John Adams's VIEW of the English constitution as "the most stupendous fabric of human invention" is expressed in his *Defence of the Constitutions of Government of the United States of America*. He observed that "Americans ought to be applauded instead of censured, for imitating it as far as they have done." TJ described Madison's

enclosure as the "petition for the reform of the British parliament" (Adams, *Works*, 4:358; TJ to Madison, 7 June 1798). The editors of the Madison papers have tentatively identified the PAPER as a "Petition praying for a Reform in Parliament, presented to the House of Commons by Charles Grey, Esq. on Monday, 6th May, 1793; and signed only by the Members of the Society of the Friends of the People, associated for the Purpose of obtaining a Parliamentary Reform" in *Annual Register . . . for the Year 1793* (Madison, *Papers*, 17:138).

From Julian Ursin Niemcewicz

MONSIEUR   Fœderal City le 27 Mai 1798.

Au milieu de l'Inquietude et de l'Anxiété que vous eprouvez Monsieur sur le sort de vôtre Ami, exposé à plus d'un Naufrage, peut être ne serez vous pas fâché de savoir ce qu'est devenu Celui qui depuis tant d'années a été son Compagnon d'Infortunes et de Voyage: je m'empresse à vous satisfaire ladessus. Selon les Intentions du G.K. j'ai pris (comme pour le suivre) le chemin du Sud, j'étois à Baltimore et me voila depuis quinze jours à Federal City dans la maison de Mr. Law. Partout j'ai été accablé de questions, je ne sais comment je m'en suis tiré, tout ce que je sais c'est que le métier de Menteur (pour qui n'y est pas accoutumé) est aussi difficile qu'il est humiliant. Soyez cependant sur que le Secret est réligieusement gardé, personne ne se doute de la verité: les uns le croyent vraiment sur les chemins des Eaux, d'autres imaginent que nous sommes brouillés et separés; enfin on a ecrit ici de Philadelphie que Vous l'aves enlevé et caché à Monti Celli. Vous voila donc accusé de rapt et de Viol, tachez de vous en laver comme vous pourrez. Le Gl: Washington et son Epouse ont été dans la Citée pour voir leurs petites filles Mrs. Peeters et Mrs Law, je lui ai été presenté, il m'a reçu très honetement, s'est informé de la Santé du Gl: K. avec Interet, mais en général il a été très reservé, et beaucoup moins curieux et inquisitive que je ne le croyois. Malgré la bonté et l'hospitalité de mes hôtes, je ne puis sans indiscretion rester trop longtems chez Eux, mais ou aller et Comment je n'en sais rien, je ne voudrois pas passer par Philad: ni demeurer (comme je l'avois projetté tout auprès) tant que le Congrès y siegera, et je crains qu'il n'y siege longtems, mon sejour la, occasioneroit des Caquets et des Soupçons sans fin; je suis en verité dans une Situation bien à pleindre, mon Coeur est blessé jusqu'au Vif, mon esprit est agité et inquiet, je ne puis ni rester encore moins m'etablir ici, ni m'en retourner chez moi, pour me livrer entre les mains de mes Geoliers, (les Despotes sont si soupçoneux) Parti de l'Europe sans avoir arrangé mes affaires, uniquement pour accompagner et soigner un ami malade, mes parents mes Amis ne pourroient jamais s'imaginer que je me trouverois dans la Situation ou je suis.

Je voudrois perdre jusqu'au souvenir le traitement que j'ai eprouvé, mais helas! il n'est pas aussi facile d'oublier que de se taire. Pardonnez Monsieur ces plaintes involontaires, vous Etes le seul devant qui Elles m'ont echapé, vous êtes le seul devant qui j'ose parler de ma Situation, et de mes projets. En attendant que je réçoive des nouvelles et des Secours de chez moi, j'ai pris le parti, tant pour me distraire, que pour ne pas perdre mon tems inutilement, j'ai pris le parti dis-je, de voir un peu l'Amérique, je voudrois aller jusqu'au Boston: pourriez vous avoir la bonté de me preter pour cet Effet 150, ou 200 Doll: je promets de vous les rendre en Automne, je serois même très heureux de pouvoir vous rapporter ma dête moi-même. Excusez Monsieur la hardiesse de ma demarche, des raisons que vous ne desaprouveriez pas m'ont em-peché de demender ce service à d'autres, il m'en Couteroit de m'ouvrir la dessus à qui que ce soit, mais Vous qui inspirez de l'Attachement et du respect à tous Ceux qui ont le bonheur de vous connoître, ne vous étonnez pas si vous leur inspirez aussi de la Confiance. Agréez les Senti-ments respectueux de Celui qui a l'honneur d'être

Monsieur Vôtre très humble et très obeissant Serviteur

JULIEN NIEMCEWICZ

Si vous avez la bonté de me repondre adressez vôtre lettre to the Care of Thomas Law Federal City. N'oubliez pas surtout de me donner des nouvelles du G.K aussitot que vous en sauréz quelque chose, il doit être près du but de son voyage. Il est très probable qu'au bureau de Poste de Philadelphie, il y aura quelques paquets de lettres adressées au Gl: Kos: ayez la bonté de les ouvrir, car il y aura certainem[ent] sous son Envel-lope des lettres pour moi, et dans ce Cas je vous supplie de vouloir bien me les envoyer.

EDITORS' TRANSLATION

SIR   Federal City, 27 May, 1798
   In the midst of the disquiet and anxiety that you feel Sir over the fate of your friend, exposed to more than one shipwreck, perhaps you will not be annoyed to learn what has happened to the one who for so many years has been his companion in misfortunes and travels. I am hastening to satisfy you on that

account. According to the intentions of G.K. I set out (as though following him) on the road south, I was in Baltimore and now I have been for two weeks in the Federal City in the house of Mr. Law. Everywhere I have been overwhelmed with questions, I don't know how I made out, all that I know is that the role of liar (to which I am not accustomed) is as difficult as it is humiliating. Rest assured, however, that the secret has been religiously kept: no one suspects the truth: some believe him truly on the paths of the waters, others have imagined that we have quarreled and are separated; finally, someone wrote here from Philadelphia that you carried him off and hid him at Monticello. So there you are, accused of kidnaping and ravishing, try to wash yourself clean however you can. Gl: Washington and his wife have been in the city to see their granddaughters, Mrs. Peter and Mrs. Law, I was presented to him, he received me in a very gentlemanly way, inquired about the health of Gl: K. with interest, but in general was very formal and much less curious and inquisitive than I had believed. Despite all the kindness and hospitality of my hosts, I cannot, without indiscretion, remain too long with them, but where to go and how I have no idea, I would not like to go by Philad: nor remain (as I had planned) nearby as long as Congress is in session, and I fear that it may stay there for a long time, my stay there would give rise to wagging tongues and endless suspicions; I am truly in a very pitiable condition, my heart is wounded to the quick, my mind is agitated and restless, I can neither remain even less settle here, nor return home, to give myself over to my jailers, (despots are so suspicious) having left Europe without settling my affairs, solely to accompany and care for a sick friend, my family, my friends could never imagine that I would be in my present situation.
I should like to erase even the memory of the treatment I have undergone, but alas! it is not so easy to forget as it is to be silent. Pardon Sir these involuntary complaints, you are the only one before whom they have escaped me, you are the only one before whom I dare to speak of my situation and my plans. While waiting to receive news and help from home, I have made the decision, as much to distract myself as not to lose my time uselessly, I have made the decision, I say, to see a bit of America, I should like to go as far as Boston: would you have the kindness to lend me 150 or 200 dollars for that project: I promise to pay them back to you in autumn, I should even be very happy to return this debt to you in person. Excuse Sir the boldness of my procedure, reasons of which you would not disapprove have prevented me from asking this service of others, it would cost me to speak freely about it to others, but you who inspire affection and respect in all those who have the good fortune to know you, do not be surprised if you also inspire confidence in them. Accept the respectful sentiments of the one who has the honor of being
Sir Your very humble and very obedient Servant   JULIEN NIEMCEWICZ

If you have the kindness to answer me address your letter to the care of Thomas Law Federal City. Above all, remember to give me information about G.K. as soon as you know something, he must be near the end of his travel. It is very likely that at the Post Office of Philadelphia there are some packets of letters addressed to Gl: Kos: have the kindness to open them, for in his envelope there are certainly some letters for me, and in that case I beg you to kindly send them to me.

RC (DLC); endorsed by TJ as received 31 May 1798 and so recorded in SJL.

TJ first became acquainted with Julian Ursin Niemcewicz (1758-1841) in Paris in 1787. A member of the Polish-Lithuanian nobility, as a young man Niemcewicz came under the patronage of Prince Adam Kazimierz Czartoryski, who made Niemcewicz part of his household, sponsored his travel to other European capitals, and encouraged his early writing. In the Four Years' Diet that first met in Warsaw in 1788 Niemcewicz joined with the reformist "Patriot" element and became one of the most vocal advocates of expanded political rights, speaking ardently and penning a variety of works, including a popular stage comedy, to promote the cause of constitutional reform. He fled Poland upon the Russian occupation in 1792, returning from Italy two years later to join Kosciuszko's insurgency movement. Like Kosciuszko, who named him adjutant and secretary of state, Niemcewicz was wounded at Maciejowice in 1794 and made a Russian prisoner. Held in solitary confinement under harsh conditions for two years, he was released upon Kosciuszko's entreaties and in 1797 accompanied the general to the United States. Elected to membership in the American Philosophical Society on 20 Apr. 1798, he returned from the society's meeting on the evening of 4 May to learn, "as a bolt from the blue," of Kosciuszko's secret plans to leave Philadelphia before daybreak. They would meet again only once, briefly, before Kosciuszko's death. Niemcewicz settled in Elizabeth, New Jersey, and in 1800 married Susan Livingston Kean, the widow of John Kean, cashier of the Bank of the United States and an acquaintance of Kosciuszko from the American Revolution. Niemce-

wicz, who upon his marriage renounced any claim to his wife's property, visited Poland, 1802-04, to settle his father's estate. Never entirely comfortable in the United States, he parted amicably with his wife and her son in 1807, after the formation of the Grand Duchy of Warsaw, and returned to Europe for good. He again entered politics, but is remembered chiefly as a prolific author of poetry, novels, plays, and history (Niemcewicz, *Under their Vine*, xix-xxxii, lii, 65; Palmer, *Democratic Revolution*, 1:423-6, 2:90-2; APS, *Proceedings*, 22, pt. 3 [1884], 270; Vol. 12:387, 460).

Writing in French early in his correspondence with TJ, Niemcewicz most often signed his name "Julien Niemcewicz," as in the letter above. He subsequently adopted the spelling "Julian" and made increased use of his middle name, which he wrote as "Ursin" but is frequently given as "Ursyn" (see his letter of 4 Sep. 1810).

G.K.: General Kosciuszko. LE SECRET EST RÉLIGIEUSEMENT GARDÉ: on leaving Philadelphia, Kosciuszko instructed Niemcewicz to wait three days and then begin traveling southward, giving out that he was following Kosciuszko SUR LES CHEMINS DES EAUX, to the springs of western Virginia. DE ME PRETER POUR CET EFFET 150, OU 200 DOLL: Kosciuszko had dismissed his servant, Stanislas Dombrowski, with $100 and left his former adjutant $200. When the manservant complained of being cut off so abruptly, Niemcewicz, offended at what he interpreted to be his own exclusion from the general's confidence, gave his $200 to Dombrowski. The terms of his release from imprisonment having precluded a return to Russian-occupied Polish territory, Niemcewicz was without ready means of support in the U.S. (Niemcewicz, *Under their Vine*, xxvii, 65-6).

From George Jefferson

DEAR SIR   Richmond May 28th. 1798.

I was by last post favor'd with yours of the 20th. inclosing manifests for 10 Hhds: Tobacco weighing 16447 ld. which I have delivered to Mr. Hooper.

I am extremely sorry that I could not with the smallest degree of propriety even hint it was my wish (because it is yours) that he should give security; much less could I demand it. although it is customary in Philadelphia to have some guarantee, it is so far from being so here, that to intimate such a thing would be considered by a merchant of credit as an insult; and if it would have been so considered when I was making the bargain, to attempt now to change it by demanding a guarantee, would be entirely out of the question. but for this circumstance, I surely would have ask'd for security in the first instance; as in these times it is undoubtedly a prudent measure even from the most wealthy.

For your satisfaction however I will inform you that Mr. Hooper is a man in high credit here. I do not believe there is a merchant in the place who would not gladly have trusted him for a much larger sum on the same terms. we ourselves have had considerable dealings with him, and have found him perfectly punctual heretofore. and this is said of him universally by those with whom he has had dealings. He is a man who, from his great industry & frugality has within a few years raised himself from obscurity & indigence, to his present credit & some little wealth— the general opinion being that he cannot be worth less than 4 or 5000£—such men, who have once known the want of money, seldom lose what they have gained. It may be observed however that he is rather too adventurous for his capital—having been hitherto successful in his business he appears not to apprehend the possibility of a change in his good fortune. he is for instance shipping Tobo. rather largely in these precarious times. the same objection however would hold good against any one who would give an extra price for a credit—for altho' their capitals may be larger, the generality of them go on in proportion to it's extent. Your acquaintance Mr. B. for instance I understand shipped last year about 1500 Hhds: Tobacco; this year it is supposed he will ship more. so that for myself I would prefer Hooper's notes to his— for nothing but a *very* heavy loss on shipments could in my opinion endanger property in H's hands—and such losses would expose it to the same hazard in B's—indeed in my opinion to greater; as in addition to H's other recommendations, I have the most perfect confidence in his integrity—greater than I have in B's—and much may be expected from a young man who sets out with a determination to do that which is right & to work through all difficulties—even should he prove unfortunate. should you continue to have any doubts respecting Mr. H—I hope they will be removed when you see Mr. Randolph—as after I had informed him of every thing I knew both for & against H. he made enquiry of several respecting him, & particularly of Mr. Brown with whom he has had very extensive dealings—they all concurred in speaking very favorably of him—and it was then, in addition to other considerations, that he concluded to let his Tobacco go with yours. If you are acquainted with Messrs. Walker & Kennedy of Philada. they can give you a satisfactory account of H., they being his correspondents there.

I have made enquiry respecting the price of wheat & flour as you requested, & find that flour sold in January last at 7$: for fine, & $7\frac{1}{2}$ $: for superfine—a small quantity of the latter I myself sold at that price. wheat about the same time sold as high as 7/6 for red, & 7/9 for white—this information I obtained from Gallego & Chevallie who are the principal purchasers here—as well as from others, & which I believe to be correct. should I hear of any higher price I will write to meet you at Monticello. I enclose your account having included every thing except the freight of the goods which came the other day. for which Capt. Potter has not yet applied.

I am Dear Sir Your Very Obt. servt.   GEO. JEFFERSON

RC (MHi); at foot of text: "Thos. Jefferson esqr:"; endorsed by TJ at head of second page: "Gibson & Jefferson. series of accts. from 1797. Dec. 30. to 1798. May 28."; endorsed by TJ as received 2 June 1798 and so recorded in SJL.

Statement of Account with George Jefferson

Thomas Jefferson Esquire in Acct: Currt: with George Jefferson & Co.

Dr.			Cr.
1797		1798	
Dec. 30 To Cash pd. his Order to F: Walker	31. 3. 6	Jany. 4 By Cash recd. for Jno. Barnes dft on Boyce	60. –. –
1798		Feby. 9 By do. for ditto on Hopkins	150. –. –
Jany. 1 To do. pd. to I: Miller's order	22. 1. 8	Mar: 26 By do. for 1 Ble. Nail rod short deld.	1. –. –
" 27 To do. pd. his dft: to P: Derieux	15. –. –	May 28 By Balance due G J & Co.	3. 1. –
Feby. 5 To do. pd. do. to James Brown	65. 5.10		
" 7 To do. pd. do. to John Forbes	6.18. –		
" 9 To do. pd. do. to Coll. Harvie	14. 5. 8		
Mar: 2 To do. pd. freight of an Anvil vice beak-iron & Case from Philada:	1. 2.10		
Drayage of do. from Rockets	–. 2. –		
" 9 To do. pd. Canal toll of do. & draye:	–. 4. 1		
" 26 To do. pd. his Note to Lucy Wood	33. –. –		
" " To do. pd. fret: of 3 tons nail rod. 1 hhd: 1 Barrel & box from Philada:	3.16. 6		
Drayage from Rockets	–.14. 9		
Canal toll of do. & draye:	1.10. 7		
April 11 To do. pd. fret. of 1 hhd. & 119 Bles. nail-rod to Milton 3/ pr hundd.	11.10. 4		
freight of Harpsichord &c fm: Phila: do.	1.17. 6		
do. to Milton	–.18. –		
Canal toll & drayage	–. 4. 9		
" " To do. pd. for 6 Bushs. Wheat 10/. £ 3. 15.			
2 barrels	3.15. –		
freight to Norfolk	£214. 1. –		£214. 1. –
May 28 To Balance due G J & Co.	3. 1. –		

MS (MHi); on verso of final page of letter above; in Patrick Gibson's hand; endorsed by TJ: "Jefferson George December 30. 97. May 28. 98."

From Lord Somerville

Board of Agriculture
32 Sackville Street

SIR,   28 May 1798.

At the last Meeting of the Board of Agriculture, a very interesting letter from you, to Sir John Sinclair, was read, and I am requested to inform you, that the Board, are much obliged to you, for having communicated so many useful observations.—The letter was referred to a Committee, who may probably wish for some explanations, but I am desirous of immediately transmitting the thanks of the Board, and expressing how much we esteem the honour of your correspondence.—

I have the honour to be, Sir, Your very Obedient servant.

SOMERVILLE
President.—

RC (MHi); in clerk's hand, signed by Somerville; at foot of text: "Thomas Jefferson Esqe: &c &c &c"; endorsed by TJ as received 27 Sep. 1798 and so recorded in SJL. FC (Board of Agriculture Lb in University of Reading: Rural History Centre); in same hand; at head of text: "Jefferson Thos. Esqe. America."

Born at Fitzhead Court in Somersetshire, England, John Southey, Lord Somerville (1765-1819), received an M.A. from Cambridge University in 1785. Upon the death of his uncle in 1796, he became the fifteenth Lord Somerville and was at once elected to serve as a representative of Scotland in the House of Lords. One of the founding members of the British Board of Agriculture, he served as the society's second president from 1798 to 1800, succeeding Sir John Sinclair. Somerville was backed by William Pitt, who sought to reprimand Sinclair for his criticism of the government's taxation policies in Parliament. A prominent agriculturalist, Somerville was a leading owner and breeder of merino sheep in England and the inventor of an improved plow (DNB; Rosalind Mitchison, *Agricultural Sir John: The Life of Sir John Sinclair of Ulbster, 1754-1835* [London, 1962], 173-4). Somerville's publications included *Facts and observations relative to sheep, wool, ploughs and oxen: in which the importance of improving the short-woolled breeds, by a mixture of the Merino blood is deduced from actual practice* (London, 1803) and annotation in Robert Bakewell's *Observations on the Influence of Soil and Climate upon Wool* (London, 1808). For the last, see Sowerby, No. 797.

LETTER FROM YOU: TJ to Sir John Sinclair, 23 Mch. 1798.

To Tadeusz Kosciuszko

Philadelphia. May 30. 98.

Mr. Volney's departure for France gives me an opportunity of writing to you. I was happy in observing many days after your departure that our winds were for you. I hope therefore you quickly passed the cruising grounds on our coast [and] are safely arrived at the term of your journey. *your departure*[1] is not yet known or even suspected. *Niem-*

cewicz was much affected. *he is now* at the federal city. *he desired me* [to have] some things taken care of for you. these were some kitchen furniture, backgammon [table] and chess men, and a [pelisse] of fine fur. the latter I have had [taken to my own apartment and] had packed in hops and sewed up, the former are put into a warehouse of mr Barnes all subject to your future orders. some letters came for you soon after [your departure:] the person who delivered them said there were inclosed in them some for your friend whom you left here, and desired I would open them. I did so in his presence, found only one letter for your friend, took it out & sealed the letters again in the [presence] of the same person, without reading a word or looking who they were from. I [now] forward them to you, as I do this to my friend Jacob [Van Staphorst at Paris]. our alien bill struggles hard for a passage. [it has been considerably mollified. it] is not yet through the Senate. [we are proceeding further & further] *in war measures. I consider that event as almost inevitable.* I am extremely anxious to hear from [you, to] know what sort of a passage you had, how you find yourself, and the state & prospect of things in Europe. I hope I shall not be long without hearing from you. the first dividend which will be drawn for you & remitted will be in January, and as the winter passages are dangerous it will not be forwarded till April[:] after that [regu]larly from six months to six months. this will be done by mr Barnes. I shall leave this place in three weeks. the times do not permit an indulgence in political disquisitions. but they forbid not the effusion of friendship. [accept] my warmest towards you, which no time will alter. your principles & dispositions were made to be honored, revered & loved. true to a single object the freedom & happiness of man, they have not veered about with the changelings and apostates of our acquaintance. may health, & happiness ever attend [you. accept] sincere assurances of my affectionate esteem & respect. Adieu.

PrC (DLC); faint, with words in brackets supplied from TJR, 3:395-6; at foot of text: "General Kosciusko"; words in italics written in code (see TJ to Kosciuszko, 18 June 1798); those words appear *en clair* in the TJR transcription and also on an undated slip in TJ's hand that contains nothing except the words and phrases that are enciphered in the letter above (MS in DLC: TJ Papers, 104:17913); the code, which unlike many others used by TJ simply replaced each letter of the alphabet with a symbol rather than representing words and syllables by groups of digits, was retained by TJ on an undated strip of paper with no other markings (MS in MHi). Enclosures not found. Enclosed in the following letter.

Barnes made a list of the KITCHEN FURNITURE, including pans, kettles, pewter plates, and other miscellaneous effects Kosciuszko had left behind, labeling it an "Inventory sundry Kitchen (or, Camp.) furtiture G.K." (in MHi; in Barnes's hand, with TJ's notation on first page: "kitchen furniture"; signed and dated by Barnes at Philadelphia, May 1798).

[1] These and subsequent italicized words are written in code and supplied here as noted above.

To Jacob Van Staphorst

DEAR SIR   Philadelphia. May 30. 98.

My friend General Kosciusko placed his funds here in the bank of Pennsylvania, under my direction, with a desire to remit the dividends arising from them regularly to Europe. as he had no particular correspondent in any [of] the great seaports of Europe, I recommended that your house [in Amsterdam] should be made the deposit, and accordingly forwarded some bills [on Amster]dam and a letter, to your house there. [. . .]¹ in any one place of Europe we took the [liberty to make your house] also the center for our correspondence. he left [this place the 5th. inst. in a] vessel bound for Oporto, from whence he meant to proceed to Paris by land, and if he is not there when you recieve this, he shortly will be. I therefore take the liberty of putting under cover to you a letter to him from myself, and [some] which came here for him after his departure. as I presume you will [. . .] of his arrival in Paris, I must beg leave to give you the trouble [of having?] these letters delivered to him. perhaps you [could be] useful to [him] [. . .] advising him how to draw on Amsterdam for the proceeds of the bills I forwarded to your house for collection. I think this my safest opportunity of forwarding a letter from myself to your house, covering papers of consequence which have lain by me some time for want of a safe conveyance.   the situation of this country with respect to the war of Europe gives me the most solicitous concern. I hope that measures for [keeping our] peace may still be found in the prudence & the interests of all parties. permit me here to renew my assurances of a personal interest and esteem for yourself, and also for those connected with you in Amsterdam. I shall never be unmindful of your civilities or services, and remain with sentiments of constant esteem & regard Dear Sir

Your friend & servt   TH: JEFFERSON

PrC (DLC); faint; at foot of text: "Mr. Jacob Van Staphorst. Paris."; endorsed by TJ in ink on verso. Recorded in SJL as carried "by Volney." Enclosures: (1) TJ to Van Staphorst & Hubbard, 30 Apr. 1798, and enclosures. (2) TJ to Tadeusz Kosciuszko, 30 May 1798, and enclosures.

¹ Several words illegible.

To James Madison

                                                Philadelphia May 31. 98.

I wrote you last on the 24th. since which yours of the 20th. is recieved. I must begin by correcting two errors in my last. it was false arithmetic to say that two measures therein mentioned to be carried by majorities of 11. would have failed if the 14. absentees (wherein a majority of 6. was ours) had been present. 6 coming over from the other side would have turned the scale, and this was the idea floating in my mind, which produced the mistake. the 2d. error was in the version of mr A's expression which I stated to you. his real expression was 'that he would not unbrace a single nerve for any treaty France could offer; such was their entire want of faith, morality' &c.

The bill from the Senate for capturing French armed vessels found hovering on our coast, was past in two days by the lower house without a single alteration, and the Ganges, a 20. gun sloop fell down the river instantly to go on a cruise. she has since been ordered to New York to convoy a vessel from that to this port. the Alien bill will be ready to-day probably for it's 3d. reading in the Senate. it has been considerably mollified; particularly by a proviso saving the rights of treaties. still it is a most detestable thing. I was glad in yesterday's discussion to hear it admitted on all hands that laws of the US. subsequent to a treaty, controul it's operation, and that the legislature is the only power which can controul a treaty. both points are sound beyond doubt. this bill will unquestionably pass the H. of R. the majority there being decisive, consolidated, and bold enough to do any thing. I have no doubt, from the hints dropped they will pass a bill to declare the French treaty void. I question if they will think a declaration of war prudent, as it might alarm, and all it's effects are answered by the act authorising captures. a bill is brought in for suspending all communication with the dominions of France, which will no doubt pass. it is suspected they mean to borrow money of individuals in London, on the credit of our land tax, & perhaps the guarantee of G. Britain. the land tax was yesterday debated and a majority of 6. struck out the 13th. section for the classification of houses and taxing them by a different scale from the lands. instead of this is to be proposed a valuation of the houses & lands together. Macon yesterday laid a motion on the table for adjourning on the 14th. some think they do not mean to adjourn; others that they wait first the return of the envoys, for whom it is now avowed the brig Sophia was sent. it is expected she would bring them off about the middle of this month. they may therefore be expected here about the 2d. week of July. whatever be their decision as to adjournment I think it probable my next letter will convey orders for my horses and that I shall leave this place from the 20th. to the 25th. of June. for I have no expectation they will actually adjourn sooner. Volney & a ship load of others sail on Sunday next. another ship load will go off in about 3. weeks. it is natural to expect they go under irritations calculated to fan the flame. not so

Volney. he is most thoroughly impressed with the importance of preventing war, whether considered with reference to the interests of the
two countries, of the cause of republicanism, or of man on the broad
scale. but an eagerness to render this prevention impossible leaves me
without any hope. some of those who have insisted that it was, long
since, war on the part of France are candid enough to admit that it is
now begun on our part also.—I inclose for your perusal a poem on the
alien bill written by mr Marshall. I do this as well for your amusement
as to get you to take care of this copy for me till I return; for it will be
lost by lending if I retain it here, as the publication was suppressed after
the sale of a few copies of which I was fortunate enough to get
one.   your locks, hinges &c. shall be immediately attended to. my
respectful salutations & friendship to mrs Madison, to the family, & to
yourself. Adieu.

P.S. the President, it is said, has refused an Exequatur to the new
Consul-general of France, Dupont.

P.P.S. this fact is true. I have it this moment from Dupont, and he
goes off with Volney to France in two or three days.

RC (DLC: Madison Papers); addressed:
"James Madison junr. near Orange court
house"; franked. Enclosure: *The Aliens: A
Patriotic Poem, By H. Marshall, A Senator of
the United States. Occasioned by the Alien
Bill, Now before the Senate, May 15th, 1798*
(Philadelphia, 1798); see note to Samuel
Brown to TJ, 4 Sep. 1798.

PROVISO SAVING THE RIGHTS OF TREA-
TIES: in the debate on the alien friends bill
on 30 May TJ cast the deciding vote in favor
of adding the clause "And provided, That
nothing in this act contained shall be construed to contravene any provision of any
treaty subsisting between the United States
and any foreign nation." This provision was
not part of the final bill (JS, 2:498; U.S. Statutes at Large, 1:570-2). On 30 May Massachusetts Congressman Samuel Sewall
brought in the bill for SUSPENDING "commercial intercourse between the United
States and France, and the dependencies
thereof." The House passed the bill on 1
June and the Senate six days later, but with
amendments. Agreed to by both Houses, it
was sent to President Adams on 13 June
(JHR, 3:319-21; JS, 2:502, 505, 508; U.S.
Statutes at Large, 1:565-6).

Upon Adams's refusal to accept his cre-
dentials and grant him an EXEQUATUR, the
recently appointed CONSUL-GENERAL OF
FRANCE, Victor Marie du Pont, made arrangements to return home on the *Benjamin
Franklin*. In a report to Talleyrand, which
the French minister presented to the Directory on 27 July, du Pont used his conversations with TJ and others, shortly before his
departure, to recommend policies to prevent war between the two republics. He
emphasized that the damage to relations between the two countries was being aggra-
vated by the French depradations upon
American trade, especially in the West Indies, where agents such as Victor Hugues at
Saint-Domingue "encouraged the indiscriminate seizure" of American vessels and
then had the crews thrown into prison and
used for prisoner exchanges with the English (Bowman, *Neutrality*, 345-8; Samuel
Eliot Morison, "Du Pont, Talleyrand and
the French Spoliations," Massachusetts
Historical Society, *Proceedings*, 49 [1915-
16], 63-79; E. Wilson Lyon, "The Directory and the United States," AHR, 43
[1938], 528-9).

To Martha Jefferson Randolph

My dear Martha   Philadelphia May 31. 98.

My letter by the last post was to mr Randolph, dated May 24. yours of the 12th. inst. did not get to hand till the 29th. so it must have laid by a post somewhere. the receipt of it, by kindling up all my recollections increases my impatience to leave this place & every thing which can be disgusting, for Monticello and my dear family, comprising every thing which is pleasurable to me in this world. it has been proposed in Congress to adjourn on the 14th. of June. I have little expectation of it myself: but whatever be their determination, I am determined myself; and my letter of next week will probably bring orders for my horses. Jupiter should therefore be in readiness to depart on a night's warning, with three horses, as a workman accompanies me from here. it will be necessary also to send for my letter to the post office the evening of it's arrival, or rather to order him to attend the arrival of the post at Milton, & carry the letters to Belmont to recieve his orders if any. some think Congress will wait here till their envoys return from France, for whom a vessel was sent the 1st. of April, so that they may be here the 2d week of July. others think they will not adjourn at all, as they have past a bill for capturing French armed vessels found near our coast, which is pretty generally considered as a commencement of war without a declaration. so that we consider war as no longer doubtful. Volney & a ship load of others of his nation will sail from hence on Sunday. another ship load will go in about 3. weeks. a bill is now brought in to suspend all communication with France & her dominions: and we expect another to declare our treaty with her void. mr Randolph will percieve that this certainty of war must decide the objects of our husbandry to be such as will keep to the end of it.—I am sorry to hear of Jefferson's indisposition, but glad you do not physic him. this leaves nature free and unembarrassed in her own tendencies to repair what is wrong. I hope to hear or to find that he is recovered. kiss them all for me. remember me affectionately to mr Randolph and be assured yourself of my constant & tenderest love. Adieu.   TH: JEFFERSON

P.S. it would be well that Davenport should be immediately informed that I am coming home. since writing this I have recieved a letter from mr Eppes, informing me that all are well there. he & Maria will set out for Monticello June 20th.

RC (NNPM); with postscript written in left margin; at foot of text: "Mrs. Randolph."

A LETTER FROM John Wayles EPPES to TJ of 20 May, recorded in SJL as received from Eppington on 31 May 1798, has not been found.

From George Jefferson

DEAR SIR,   Richmond June 1st. 1798.

Concluding you will be anxious to know when the things go up which came by Capt. Potter, I have to inform you that there is a boatman now down who has engaged to take them, & who sets off up tomorrow.

They should have been forwarded sooner, but that most of the Milton boats had stopped running, in consequence of the water having been very low. there is now a little swell in the river which has brought them down.

I will write to Mr. Eppes as you direct by next post—unless I meet with an earlier opportunity.

I am very respectfully Dear Sir Your Mt. Hbl: servt.

GEO. JEFFERSON

RC (MHi); at foot of text: "Thomas Jefferson esqr."; endorsed by TJ as received 7 June 1798 and so recorded in SJL.

From James Monroe

DEAR SIR   June 1. 1798. Richmond.

I have yours of 21. ulto. and very sincerely thank you for the interest you take in what concerns my welfare, of which indeed I have heretofore had so many proofs as long since to have ceased to make acknowledgments. The cause of irritation to wh. you allude is indeed a serious one, considering the station from whence it emanated: considering the person, only an object of contempt. I had seen the paper only the day before I got yr. letter, having lately arrived here. For the present however I cannot enter on the subject, or the other to wh. I refer. I will do it by the post wh. departs the day after to morrow. I beg of you to deliver the enclosed to Mr. Dawson & believe me yr. very affectionate

friend & servant   JAS. MONROE

RC (DLC); endorsed by TJ as received 5 June 1798 and so recorded in SJL. Enclosure not found, but see below.

CAUSE OF IRRITATION: Adams's 14 May reply to the address from Lancaster, Pennsylvania (see TJ to Monroe, 21 May 1798). The OTHER subject was the prospect of Monroe entering Congress.

Monroe sent John DAWSON vouchers and other records to settle his accounts from his service as minister to France (see Monroe to [Dawson], 1 June 1798, printed in Monroe, *Writings*, 3:123-5, where TJ is mistakenly identified as the recipient [see note to TJ to Monroe, 27 Dec. 1797], and Dawson to Monroe, 29 July 1798; both letters are in DLC: Monroe Papers).

To Julian Ursin Niemcewicz

DEAR SIR   Philadelphia June 1. 98.

Your favor of the 27th. came to hand last night, and my occupations of the day have been so incessant as to leave me but a short moment to answer in time for the post. as far as I have heard there is not the [smallest suspicion] here but that our friend is gone to Virginia. it is fortunate for me; for of all men living I am the most awkward at parrying interrogatories which are not to be answered directly. mr Gahn took some letters to G.K. from the post office & brought them to me. I opened them in his presence, found one for you, delivered it to him according to your desire, & I hope you have recieved it from him. I resealed the letters and they will go off by mr Volney the day after tomorrow. I think it probable I shall leave this place within a fortnight or three weeks. I shall therefore hope to see you either here on your way to Boston, or at the Federal city on my way to Virginia and that in the course of the summer you will be able to pass some time with me at Monticello, where I will endeavor to have a *gite* of some sort for you. the news from Europe by the packet is that the [French] on the channel are in motion & England under an awful impression of their danger. Ireland too on the brink of a convulsion. about the last of this month we may expect to hear of great events, but to which party favorable is not for us to predetermine. I inclose you the sum of two hundred dollars according to desire. I had them procured in Baltimore & Alexandria bills which I expected would suit you best. I would caution you however to change there any surplus of them which may remain on your hands as they do not pass readily on this side Baltimore. I am with great esteem Dear Sir

Your friend & servt   TH: JEFFERSON

PrC (MHi); faint; at foot of text: "Julien Niemcewicz"; endorsed by TJ in ink on verso. Addressed, according to SJL, to Niemcewicz at the Federal City.

OUR FRIEND: Tadeusz Kosciuszko, also called here G.K. for "General Kosciuszko." GITE: home, resting place. According to TJ's financial memoranda he requested John Barnes to draw the TWO HUNDRED DOLLARS "on Kosciuszko's account, . . . so need not enter into my accounts"; but when Niemcewicz repaid the money in February 1799 TJ recorded it as a credit for money loaned to Niemcewicz "by Barnes on my acct." (MB, 2:984, 998).

From James Madison

DEAR SIR   June 3. 1798.

Friday's mail brought me your favor of May 24. The letter from S. Bourne had previously reached us thro' a Fredg. paper. It is corroborated I find by several accounts from different sources. These rays in the prospect will if I can judge from the sensations in this quarter, have an effect on the people very different from that which appears in the public counsels. Whilst it was expected that the unrelenting temper of France would bring on war, the mask of peace was worne by the war party. Now that a contrary appearance on the side of France is intimated, the mask is dropped, and the lye openly given to their own professions by pressing measures which must force France into War.[1] I own I am not made very sanguine by the reported amendment in the posture of our negociators, first because the account may not be very correct, and next because there are real difficulties to be overcome, as well as those which the pride of one or other of the parties may create:[2] not to mention the probable arrival of what has passed here before the scene is closed there. But the palpable urgency of the Ex. & its partizans to press war in proportion to the apparent chance of avoiding it, ought to open every eye to the hypocrisy & perfidy[3] which has hitherto deceived so many good people. Should no such consequence take place it will be a proof of infatuation which does not admit of human remedy. It is said, and there are circumstances which make me believe it, that the hotheaded proceedings of Mr. A are not well relished in the cool climate of Mount Vernon. This I think may fairly be inferred from the contrast of characters and conduct, but if it has been expressed it must have been within a very confidential circle. Since my last there has been a sequel of fine & extensive rains. We have had a tolerable, tho' not an equal or sufficient share of them. Your neighbourhood I fancy has fared better.

Very affy. Yrs.   Js. M. Jr.

If Barnes has not sent off the glass pullies &c. please to order as much of the proper chord as will be wanted for the latter.

RC (DLC: Madison Papers); addressed: "Thomas Jefferson Vice President of the United States Philadelphia"; endorsed by postmaster: "O.Ct.H.Va. 4th June 1798"; endorsed by TJ as received 12 June 1798 and so recorded in SJL.

The LETTER FROM Sylvanus BOURNE was published in the Fredericksburg *Virginia Herald* on 26 May 1798.

COOL CLIMATE OF MOUNT VERNON: see Madison, *Papers*, 17:142n.

[1] Written over partially erased word.
[2] Remainder of sentence interlined by Madison.
[3] Preceding word and ampersand canceled, but probably at a much later date when other emendations (not recorded) were also made.

From Janet Livingston Montgomery

SIR   Rhinbeck House June the 3d 99 [i.e., 1798]

Having not readily the address of Mr. Monroe May I trespass so fare on my former acquaintance with you as to commend my letter to your care—the satisfaction I, once enjoyed in that acquaintance makes the idea of brightening the chain most pleasant yet I ought not to flatter myself with being equally recolected—since but a few Years back you pass'd through my Domain and with in ken of my house without remembering it however at Rhinbeck, who would have been most happy to have received you—and gratified to have enjoyed that society— Which she participated for a Moment—at N York with her friends and which she has never forgotten

should fortune ever induce you to turn your stepes this road again I shall hope you will not pass me by and praying you to pardon this interruption I remain

Sir with sentiments of esteem   J MONTGOMERY

RC (ViW); endorsed by TJ as received 25 June 1798 and so recorded in SJL. Enclosure not found.

The widow of General Richard Montgomery of Revolutionary War fame and the sister of Chancellor Robert R. Livingston and Edward Livingston, Janet Livingston Montgomery owned tracts of land in the Hudson Valley and elsewhere. She had first made the acquaintance of James MONROE in 1784. Her only previous correspondence with TJ was a letter of 9 Dec. 1785 that enclosed one to the Marquis de Lafayette (Katherine M. Babbitt, *Janet Montgomery: Hudson River Squire* [Monroe, N.Y., 1975], 15, 17, 19).

From Thomas Mann Randolph

TH:M.R. TO TH: JEFFERSON;   Belmont June 3. :98

A few days since I returned from a journey of 3 weeks into the lower country during which from perpetual hurry and weariness I failed to write to you. Your favor of Ap. 26. I rec'd. May 5th. the Evening before I sat out; that of May 24th. yesterday; the intermediate letters passed me on the road, in the mail for Richmond, whither Martha had sent them not expecting me so soon, my absence being much shortened by the failure of the Foederal Court to hold its usual session.—I have found Lescarbot & forward it.—Your affairs at Shadwell go on well; the whole crop of Tobacco (46000) is planted & stands—George is not so forward—he cannot command his force: there were in my absence some instances of disobedience so gross that I am obliged to interfere & have them punished myself. Several of the people had actually planted considerable crops of Tobacco before I knew they designed it—I have refused permission to cultivate it, & insist on their planting something which you have allways suffered when at home, in its place. Martha and the children are well.

The republicans here are in dismay at the law impowering the President to take Volunteer Corps into his service: he may fill the Country with his armed servants; for nothing will be easier than to create these corps every where himself. The people are as supine as ever.

Yours most affectionately   TH: M. RANDOLPH

RC (ViU: Edgehill-Randolph Papers); endorsed by TJ as received 12 June 1798 and so recorded in SJL.

INTERMEDIATE LETTERS: TJ to Randolph, 3 and 9 May 1798.

Certificate for George Logan

I Thomas Jefferson do hereby certify that George Logan the bearer hereof, who is about to visit Europe on matters of business, is a citizen of the commonwealth of Pennsylvania and United States of America, of one of the most antient & respectable families of the said commonwealth, of independant fortune, good morals, irreproacheable conduct, and true civism; and as such he is recommended to the attention of all those who from principles of humanity, or a desire to attach to their country the respect of others, would interest themselves in seeing the protection & hospitality of their laws extended to a worthy & unoffending stranger placed under their safeguard. Given under my hand and seal at Philadelphia this 4th. day of June 1798.   TH: JEFFERSON

MS (PHi: Dickinson-Logan Papers); in TJ's hand; with subjoined French translation in unknown hand; with TJ's seal affixed; endorsed: "Certificate of Thos: Jefferson." Not recorded in SJL.

GEORGE LOGAN departed Philadelphia on his peace mission to France on board the *Iris*, a neutral vessel bound for Hamburg, on 12 June, carrying this and a similar certificate of citizenship from his friend Pennsylvania Chief Justice Thomas McKean. He also brought two letters of introduction from the French consul in Philadelphia, Philippe de Létombe, one for Talleyrand and the other for Philippe Antoine Merlin de Douai, member of the Directory. The Federalist press, discovering Logan's de-

parture less than a week later, depicted his mission as traitorous and warned "that seditious Envoys from all the Republics that France has subjugated first went to Paris and *concerted measures* with the despots." The newspaper accounts noted that Logan had informed McKean of his plans and had visited Létombe at daybreak on the day of his clandestine departure. In a letter to Secretary of State Pickering on 6 Aug. William Vans Murray, American minister at the Hague, characterized Logan's passports from TJ and McKean as being written "in very general terms, as a man of science and a friend of humanity—a *philosophical* sort of thing—its *real* object must therefore be suspected" (Murray to Pickering, 29 July and 6 Aug. 1798, in MHi: Pickering Papers;

TJ to Logan, 4 May 1793; *Porcupine's Ga-* *zette,* 18 June 1798; *Gazette of the United* *States,* 18, 23 June 1798; Tolles, *Logan,* 155-6). See also TJ to Aaron Burr, 12 Nov. 1798, and Monroe to TJ, 26 Jan. 1799.

From Sir John Sinclair

DEAR SIR/.   Whitehall. London. 4th. June—1798

I had the pleasure of receiving your very interesting communication, which I had the honour of laying before the Board of Agriculture, the members of which, heard, so valuable a paper read, with much satisfaction.—If, in addition to the Mass of information collected at home, we had some foreign correspondents like you, we should soon find little difficulty, in bringing agricultural knowledge, to a very considerable degree of perfection.

We hope soon to have the satisfaction of receiving, the Wheat, and the Drill machine, you propose transmitting to the Board.—It will always give me particular pleasure, to hear from you, from time to time, as opportunities offer.—

With much truth and regard, believe me,—Dear Sir/. your faithful, and obedient Servant   JOHN SINCLAIR

RC (DLC); endorsed by TJ as received 1 Nov. 1798 and so recorded in SJL.

YOUR VERY INTERESTING COMMUNICA-TION: TJ to Sinclair, 23 Mch. 1798.

To John Taylor

TH: JEFFERSON TO J. TAYLOR.   Philadelphia June 4. 98.

I now inclose you mr Martin's patent. a patent had actually been made out on the first description, and how to get this suppressed and another made for a second invention without a second fee was the difficulty. I practised a little art in a case where honesty was really on our side & nothing against us but the rigorous letter of the law, and having obtained the 1st. specification, and got the 2d. put in it's place, a second patent has been formed which I now inclose with the first specification.—I promised you long ago a description of a mould board. I now send it. it is a press copy & therefore dim. it will be less so by putting a sheet of white paper behind the one you are reading. I would recommend to you first to have a model made of about 3. I. to the foot, or $\frac{1}{4}$ the real dimensions, and to have two blocks, the 1st. of which, after taking out the pyramidal piece, & sawing in crosswise above & below, should be preserved in that form, to instruct workmen in making the large & real one. the 2d. block may be carried through all the operations, so as to present the form of the mould board complete. if I had an opportunity of sending you a model I would do it. it has been greatly approved here, as it has been before by some very good judges at my house, where I have used it for 5. years with entire approbation.

Mr. New shewed me your letter on the subject of the patent, which gave me an opportunity of observing what you said as to the effect with you[1] of public proceedings, and that it was not unusual now to estimate the separate mass of Virginia and N. Carolina, with a view to their separate existence. it is true that we are compleatly under the saddle of Massachusets & Connecticut, and that they ride us very hard, cruelly[2] insulting our feelings as well as exhausting our strength and substance. their natural friends, the three other Eastern states, join them from a sort of family pride, and they have the art to divide certain other parts of the Union, so as to make use of them to govern the whole. this is not new. it is the old practice of despots to use a part of the people to keep the rest in order. and those who have once got an ascendancy, and possessed themselves of all the resources of the nation, their revenues and offices, have immense means for retaining their advantages. but our present situation is not a natural one. the body of our countrymen is substantially republican through every part of the union. it was the irresistable influence & popularity of Genl. Washington played off by the cunning of Hamilton[3] which turned the government over to antirepublican hands, or turned the republican members chosen by the people into anti-republicans. he delivered it over to his successor in this state, and very untoward events since, improved with great artifice, have produced on the public mind the impression we see. but still, I repeat it, this is not the natural state. time alone would bring round an order of things more correspondent to the sentiments of our constituents. but are there not events impending which will do it within a few months? the invasion of England, the public and authentic avowal of sentiments hostile to the leading principles of our constitution, the prospect of a war in which we shall stand alone, landtax, stamp-tax, increase of public debt &c. be this as it may, in every free & deliberating society, there must from the nature of man be opposite parties, & violent dissensions & discords; and one of these for the most part must prevail over the other for a longer or shorter time. perhaps this party division is necessary to induce each to watch & debate to the people the proceedings of the other. but if on a temporary superiority of the one party, the other is to resort to a scission of the union, no federal government can ever exist. if to rid ourselves of the present rule of Massachusets & Connecticut, we break the union, will the evil stop there? suppose the N. England states alone cut off, will our natures be changed? are we not men still to the South of that, & with all the passions of men? immediately we shall see a Pennsylvania & a Virginia party arise in the residuary confederacy, and the public mind will be distracted with the same party spirit. what a game too will the one party have in their hands by eternally threatening the other that unless they do so & so, they will join their Northern neighbors. if we reduce our Union to Virginia & N. Carolina, immediately the conflict will be established between the representatives of these two states, and they will end by breaking into their simple units. seeing therefore that an association of men who will not quarrel with one another is a thing which never yet existed, from the greatest confederacy of nations down to a town meeting or a vestry, seeing that we must have somebody to quarrel with, I had rather keep our New-England associates for that purpose, than to see our bickerings[4] transferred to others. they are circumscribed within such narrow limits, & their population so full, that their numbers will ever be the minority, and they are marked, like the Jews, with such a peculiarity of character, as to constitute from that circumstance the natural division of our parties. a little patience and we shall see the reign of witches pass over, their spells dissolve, and the people recovering their true sight, restore their government to it's true principles. it is true that in the mean time we are suffering deeply in spirit, and incurring the horrors of a war, & long oppressions of enormous public debt. but who can say what would be the evils of a scission and when & where they would end? better keep together as we are, hawl off from Europe as soon as we can & from all attachments to any portions of it, and if we feel their power just sufficiently to hoop us together, it will be the happiest situation in which we can exist. if the game runs sometimes against us at home, we must have patience, till luck turns, & then we shall have an opportunity of winning[5] back the *principles* we have lost. for this is a game where principles are the stake. better luck therefore to us all, and health happiness & friendly salutations to yourself. Adieu.

P.S. it is hardly necessary to caution you to let nothing of mine get before the public. a single sentence got hold of by the Porcupines will suffice to abuse & persecute me in their papers for months.

RC (MHi: Washburn Collection); addressed: "John Taylor Caroline near Portroyal"; endorsed by Taylor. Recorded in SJL under 1 June 1798. Enclosures not found, but see note below.

The DESCRIPTION OF A MOULD BOARD enclosed by TJ may have been a press copy of

"Description of a Mouldboard of the least resistance, & of the easiest & most certain construction," read before the American Philosophical Society on 4 May 1798 (APS, *Proceedings*, 22, pt. 3 [1884], 271). For the document, originally paragraphs of a letter, see TJ to Sir John Sinclair, 23 Mch. 1798. THAT IT WAS NOT UNUSUAL NOW: in the

1829 edition of TJ's papers, Thomas Jefferson Randolph, using the very faint press copy as his source text, substituted "unwise" for "unusual" and assigned the letter a date of 1 June (as recorded in SJL). When George Tucker quoted this passage from Randolph's edition in his own two-volume work on TJ's life to differentiate TJ's views on the union from Taylor's, Taylor's descendants challenged him. Tucker acknowledged that the word was clearly "unusual" not "unwise" in TJ's "original letter" (the recipient's copy in the hands of Taylor's family) and noted that the transcription error made Taylor appear to express as his own sentiments those which he merely attributed to others. Meanwhile the press copy of the letter apparently was lost or destroyed before TJ's papers were sold to the government in 1848, and subsequent editions of TJ's papers continued to rely on Randolph's erroneous transcription (TJR, 3:393; L & B, 10:44; Ford, 7:263-6; Tucker, *Life*, 2:36; *Southern Literary Messenger*, 4

[1838], 344). In 1900 the Massachusetts Historical Society printed a transcription of the recipient's copy under the correct date of 4 June in its *Collections*, 7th ser., 1 (1900), 61-4. For the perpetuation of the inaccurate transcription by historians, see WMQ, 3d ser., 7 (1950), 631.

BODY OF OUR COUNTRYMEN: in the transcription based on the press copy the sentence begins "The republicans, through every part of the Union, say, that it was."

PECULIARITY OF CHARACTER: transcription based on press copy reads "perversity of character" (TJR, 3:393-4; Ford, 7:263, 265).

[1] Preceding two words interlined.
[2] Word interlined.
[3] Preceding seven words interlined.
[4] Preceding two words interlined by TJ in place of "it."
[5] Word interlined in place of "recovering."

To Mary Jefferson Eppes

MY DEAR MARIA.   Philadelphia [June 6. 98.]

I wrote you last on the 18th. of May since which [I have recieved mr Eppes's] letter of May 20. and yours of May 27. I have deter[mined to set out from] this place on the 20th. inst. and shall, in my letters of tomorrow, [order my horses] to meet me at Fredericksburg on the 24th.[1] and may therefore be at home on the 26th. or 27th.[2] where I shall hope to have the happiness of meeting you. I can supply the information you want as to your harpsichord. your sister writes me it is arrived in perfect safety except the lock & a bit of a moulding broke off. she played on it and pronounces it a very fine one, though without some of the advantages of hers, as the Celestine for instance. if I did not mistake it's tone, it will be found sweeter for a moderate room, but not as good as hers for a large one.

I forward for mr Eppes some further dispatches from our envoys. to this it is said in addition that mr Pinckney is gone into the South of France for the health of his daughter, Mr. Marshall to Amsterdam, perhaps to come home for orders, and mr Gerry remains at Paris. they have no idea of war between the two countries, and much less that we have authorized the commencement of it.

I will convince you at Monticello whether I jested or was in earnest about your writing. and as, while it will relieve me, it may habituate you to an useful exercise, I shall perhaps be less scrupulous than you might wish. my friendly salutations to mrs Eppes, the two gentlemen & family. to yourself the most tender & constant affection & Adieu

TH: JEFFERSON

RC (ViU); torn, with words in brackets supplied from PrC; addressed: "Mrs. Maria Eppes Eppington"; franked. PrC (MHi: Coolidge Collection); with alteration of several dates by TJ in ink; endorsed by TJ in ink on verso.

For John Wayles EPPES'S LETTER of 20 May, see TJ to Martha Jefferson Randolph, 31 May 1798. YOUR SISTER WRITES: Martha Jefferson Randolph to TJ, 12 May 1798.

On 5 June 1798, President Adams presented to Congress FURTHER DISPATCHES FROM OUR ENVOYS. The same day the Senate ordered 500 copies to be printed (JS, 2:501). The message included a letter from Pinckney, Marshall, and Gerry to Pickering of 9 Mch. 1798 and a narrative, indicating that when they threatened to demand their passports Talleyrand responded by granting them interviews on 2 and 6 Mch. in which he informed them that the Direc-

tory wanted a solid friendship between France and the United States. He sought a loan from the United States, noting that it could be seen as a credit to be used by the French government for payment of claims "for property taken from American citizens," and seemed surprised that the envoys had not received further instructions for negotiation. Gerry observed that the United States, as well as the envoys, were "earnestly solicitous to restore friendship between the two republics" (Message of the President of the United States to Both Houses of Congress. June 5th, 1798 [Philadelphia, 1798], 3-15; see Evans, No. 34821).

[1] TJ first wrote "23d" before altering it to read as above. In PrC TJ altered date in ink to read "24d."
[2] TJ first wrote "25th. or 26th." before altering the dates to read as above. In PrC TJ altered dates in ink to read as above.

From James Fennell

SIR   Philadelphia June 6th. 1798

To you as a philosopher, and a man of science I take the liberty of submitting the treatise which accompanies this letter; and, urged by a consideration that the subject is of consequence to the United States, I further presume to request that you will be good enough to favour me with such observations as may occur to you on the perusal of it, tending to designate error or facilitate improvement.

I am Sir With the greatest respect Your obedient humble Servant

JAMES FENNELL
129. Chesnut St near 4th. St.

RC (DLC); at foot of text: "Thomas Jefferson Esqr."; endorsed by TJ as received 6 June 1798 and so recorded in SJL. Enclosure: James Fennell, Description of the Principles and Plan of Proposed Establishments of

Salt Works; for the Purpose of Supplying the United States with Home Made Salt [Philadelphia, 1798]. See Sowerby, No. 1203.

The English-born actor James Fennell

(1766-1816) first took to the stage in Great Britain, then in 1793 went to Philadelphia to perform under contract at the Chestnut Street Theatre. He remained in the United States for the rest of his career. A performance by Fennell, incorporating the oration of Logan as printed in TJ's *Notes on the State of Virginia*, prompted Luther Martin to write his vitriolic public letters to TJ (see TJ to John Gibson, 31 May 1797, and Martin to TJ, 24 June 1797). Although successful on the stage, Fennell often neglected acting to pursue other ventures, and over a course of years he lost a considerable amount of his own and other investors' money in ambitious but failed projects to extract salt from seawater (DAB).

To John Page

MY DEAR OLD FRIEND   Philadelphia June 6. 98.

Your favor of Apr. 26. & May 28. is duly recieved, and I sincerely thank you for your kind interest in the injurious slanders against me in[1] the public papers. with respect to Logan's speech I am preparing materials, not to answer mr Martin, but to state to those who have read the Notes on Virginia, the exact fact respecting Logan, whatever it shall turn out to be. for as yet I have not collected full evidence. I inclose you a letter I wrote to a friend on that subject, of which I had a few copies printed to send to friends who would communicate it's contents to whomsoever they should think good occasionally, but would take care not to let it get into a newspaper. for indeed it must be something more serious than common lies which should draw me into the newspapers. while I should be collecting evidence to refute one lie, the Porcupines would publish twenty new ones. this indeed would be attempting to cleanse the Augean stables. and what is so delicious to a pack of hounds as their game fairly committed in the midst of them to bay and bite at pleasure? on this subject I took pretty early[2] one great and serious deliberation, and concluded that unmerited slanders are soonest forgotten when neglected. leaving all their lies uncontradicted, the world will know some of them, of themselves, to be what they are, and these will be evidence against the rest, supported by what they have seen of my conduct through life, which has been much under their eye. those who will not consider this as better evidence than Porcupine or Fenno have prejudices or enmities which defy all evidence, & would not therefore be converted by any thing I could say. in confirmation of my own judgment on this subject, many friends have strongly recommended silence, and indeed experience seems to confirm the expediency of the determination.—I inclose you some further dispatches from our envoys. you will percieve that they do not dream of a war between the two countries. to the information contained in these, I believe I may add with certainty, that Pinckney is gone to the South of France for the health of his daughter, Marshall to Amsterdam perhaps to come here for orders, & Gerry remains at Paris. it is even whispered that Gerry is in opposition to his collegues. this may produce accomodation with the directory. at any rate it gives a chance that we shall have the facts and opinions on both sides. my best respects to mrs Page and constant friendship to yourself. Adieu affectionately   TH: JEFFERSON

P.S. be on your guard that no one catches a word of this for the newspapers. this consideration obliges me to be very circumspect what & to whom I write. indeed it obliges me to write very little.

RC (NjMoHP: Lloyd W. Smith Collection); at foot of text: "John Page." Enclosures: (1) TJ to John Henry, 31 Dec. 1797 (printed copy). (2) *Message of the President of the United States to Both Houses of Congress, June 5th, 1798* (see TJ to Mary Jefferson Eppes, 6 June 1798).

[1] Preceding three words interlined to replace "of."
[2] Preceding two words interlined.

To James Madison

Philadelphia June 7. 98.

I wrote you last on the 31st. since which yours of the 27th. of May is received. The alien bill, when we had nearly got through it, on the 2d. reading, (on a report from the commee of the whole) was referred to a special committee, by a vote of it's friends (12) against 11. who thought it could be rejected on the question for the 3d. reading. it is reported again, very much softened, and if the proviso can be added to it, saving treaties, it will be less objectionable than I thought it possible to have obtained. still it would place [1] aliens not protected by treaties under absolute government. they have brought into the lower house a sedition bill, which among other enormities, undertakes to make printing certain matters criminal, tho' one of the amendments to the constitution has so expressly taken religion, printing presses &c. out of their coercion. indeed this bill and the Alien bill both are so palpably in the teeth of the constitution as to shew they mean to pay no respect to it. the citizen bill passed by the lower house sleeps in a committee of the Senate. in the meantime Callendar, a principal object of it, has eluded it by getting himself made a citizen. Volney is gone. so is Dupont the rejected Consul. the bill suspending intercourse with the French dominions will pass the Senate to-day with a small amendment. the real object of this bill is to evade the counter-irritations of the English, who under the late orders for taking all vessels from French ports, are now taking as many of our vessels as the French. by forbidding our vessels to go to or from French ports we remove the pabulum for these violations of our rights by the English, undertaking to do the work for them ourselves in another way. the tax on lands, houses & slaves is still before the H. of R. they have determined to have the houses & lands valued separately, though to pay the same tax ad valorem. but they avow that when they shall have got at the number & value of houses, they shall be free hereafter to tax houses separately, as by indirect tax. this is to avoid the quotaing of which they cannot bear the idea. rogueries under a quota-ing law can only shift the burthen from one part to another of the same state; but relieve them from the bridle of the quota, and all rogueries go to the relief of the state. so odious is the quota to the N.E. members that many think they will not pass the bill at all. the question of adjournment was lost by two votes. had our members been here it would have been carried and much mischief prevented. I think now they will make their session permanent. I have therefore in my letters of to-day ordered my horses to be at Fredsbg on the 24th. [2] and shall probably be with you the 25th. or 26th. [3] I send you further communications from our envoys. to these I believe I may add on good grounds that Pinckney is gone with his family into the South of France for the health of his daughter, Marshal to Amsterdam (but whether coming here for instructions or not is a secret not entrusted to us) and Gerry remains at Paris. it is rumored, and I believe with probability, that there is a schism between Gerry & his colleagues. perhaps the Directory may make a treaty with Gerry, if they can get through it before the brig Sophia takes him off. she sailed the 1st. of April. it is evident from these communications that our envoys have not the least idea of war between the two countries; much less that their dispatches are the cause of it. I mentioned to you in my last that I expected they would bring in a bill to declare the treaty with France void. Dwight Foster yesterday brought in resolutions for that purpose, and for authorising general reprisals on the French armed vessels: and such is their preponderance by the number & talents of our absentees withdrawn from us that they will carry it. never was any event so important to this country since it's revolution, as the issue of the invasion of England. with that we shall stand or fall.—Colo. Innes's situation is desperate. every day now is expected to be his last. the petition for the reform of the British parliament, inclosed in your last shall be disposed of as you desire: and the first vessel for Fredericksburg will carry your locks, hinges, pullies & glass. my respectful salutations to mrs Madison & the family, and sincere friendship and Adieux to yourself.

RC (DLC: Madison Papers, Rives Collection); addressed: "James Madison junr. near Orange courthouse"; franked. PrC (DLC); at foot of first page in ink: "Madison James." Enclosure: *Message of the President of the United States to Both Houses of Congress, June 5th, 1798* (see TJ to Mary Jefferson Eppes, 6 June 1798).

On 4 June Samuel Sewall brought in a SEDITION BILL, entitled "a bill for the prevention and restraint of dangerous and seditious persons," which pertained primarily to aliens. The second section, however, called for fines and imprisonment of "any persons, whether aliens or citizens" who combined or conspired to oppose "any measures" of the United States government, or who by writing, printing, or speaking threatened the character, person, or property of those "in public trust." Aliens convicted under the law would be deported. On 6 June the Philadelphia *Aurora* printed the bill immediately following a quotation of the First Amendment. A lengthy debate took place in the House on 16 June but it was then superseded by other legislative matters (JHR, 3:322, 342-3, 370-1; *Annals*, 8:1954-71). For the bill that originated in the Senate, see John Brown to TJ, 29 June 1798.

Among the COUNTER-IRRITATIONS OF THE ENGLISH was the condemnation by a British court in the West Indies of a majority of the 22 American ships brought in by British privateers. On 7 June John Dawson introduced a resolution, which was defeated the next day by a 47 to 38 vote, calling on the president to lay before the House information on the conduct of the British government "towards the neutral rights" of American commerce since the ratification of Jay's Treaty. Thomas Blount of North Carolina then introduced a resolution for the abrogation of treaties with Great Britain because the express stipulations of the treaties had been violated (*Annals*, 8:1874, 1877, 1892).

BILL TO DECLARE THE TREATY WITH FRANCE VOID: on 8 June the House postponed action on the three resolutions dealing with relations with France introduced by Dwight Foster of Massachusetts. The Senate, however, passed on 25 June, by a 14 to 5 vote, a bill brought in by Benjamin Goodhue that called for abrogating the treaties with France. It included a long preamble detailing French actions against the United States. The House passed the bill, 47 yeas to 37 nays, on 6 July, but with a much shorter introduction. The act was signed by President Adams the next day (JS, 2:514, 516; *Annals*, 8:1870-1, 2035-7, 2116-28; U.S. Statutes at Large, 1:578). For the politics behind the postponement of Foster's resolutions, see Smelser, *Navy*, 167-8.

¹ TJ first wrote "places" before deleting the "s" and interlining "would."

² TJ first wrote "23d" before altering it to read as above. In PrC TJ altered date in ink to read as above.

³ TJ first wrote "24th. or 25th." before altering the dates to read as above. In PrC TJ altered dates in ink to read as above.

To Thomas Mann Randolph

Th:J. to TMR.   Philadelphia June 7. 98.

I wrote to my dear Martha on the 31st. of May. hers of the 12th. May is the last I have recieved from Belmont. I have now determined to leave this on the 20th. inst.¹ I shall be obliged to you therefore to order Jupiter to set out in time to be² at Fredericksburg on Sunday the 24th. instant. he must bring my chair, and three horses, because I have a workman to carry with me. this admits him to set out on Saturday morning the 23d. and consequently allows another post to arrive at Milton with any change of orders should any thing arise the ensuing week to occasion a change, though I have not the least idea any thing will. yet be so good as to call for your letters arriving at Milton Friday the 22d. in time to give Jupiter his final orders that evening.   I send you some further dispatches from our envoys. to the intelligence these contain, I may add I believe on good grounds (tho not quite certain) that Pinckney is gone to the South of France for the health of his family, Marshall to Amsterdam (but whether on his way here for orders or not is not entrusted to us) and Gerry remains at Paris. it is suspected, & indeed believed that a schism has taken place between Gerry & his colleagues. possibly therefore Gerry may make a treaty with the Directory if the brig Sophia does not arrive too soon to let it be compleated. it is evident that a relinquishment of claims for spoliations (which the instructions to our envoys authorised) might have been proposed as an equivalent for the loan the French asked as a token of friendship. yet this relinquishment appears never to have been offered by the envoys. it is clear however they did not dream of war between the two countries, much less that it would be commenced by us & bottomed on what they had written. however it is pretty substantially begun by the several bills past; & to put it beyond the possibility of avoidance you will see in the papers resolutions brought in to declare the treaty void, & to authorize general reprisals. the President refused to recieve a new Consul general (Dupont) from France, who in consequence departed with Volney & others for France last Monday. Colo. Innes's situation is desperate. we look to every day to be his last. my tenderest affections to my dearest Martha, and to the little ones, and every cordial wish for yourself. Adieu.   P.S. mr Eppes & Maria set out the 20th. inst. from Eppington for Monticello. mrs Trist & mr Trist leave this in a few days for Albemarle.

RC (DLC); endorsed by Randolph as received 16 June 1798. Enclosure: *Message of the President of the United States to Both Houses of Congress, June 5th, 1798* (see TJ to Mary Jefferson Eppes, 6 June 1798).

[1] TJ here canceled "so as to be at Fredericksburg on Saturday evening the [23d]."
[2] Remainder of sentence interlined in place of "there that day."

To Archibald Stuart

DEAR SIR   Philadelphia June 8. 98.

I inclose you some further communications from our envoys at Paris. to the information contained in these I can add that by the latest accounts mr Pinckney was gone into the South of France for the health of his family, mr Marshall to Amsterdam, and mr Gerry remained at Paris. it appears that neither themselves nor the French government dreamt of war between the two countries. it seems also fairly presumeable that the douceur of 50,000 Guineas mentioned in the former dispatches, was merely from X. and Y. as not a word is ever said by Taleyrand to our envoys, nor by them to him on the subject. it is now thought possible that Gerry may be pursuing the treaty, for he was always viewed with more favor by the French government than his collegues whom they considered as personally hostile to them. it seems they offer to pay in time for unjustifiable spoliations, and insist on a present loan. our envoys reject the loan. should Gerry offer to relinquish the spoliations, which the instructions authorize to be done, as an equivalent to the loan (and it would be much more than an equivalent) there seems nothing to prevent a conclusion, unless indeed the brig Sophia should arrive too soon & bring him away. she sailed from hence the 1st. of April with positive orders to the envoys to come away. in the mean time, besides accumulating irritations we are proceeding to actual hostilities. you will have seen in the papers the bills already past, and the measures now proposed. every thing will be carried which is proposed. nobody denies but that France has given just cause of war. but so has Gr. Britain & she is now capturing our vessels as much as France. but the question was one merely of prudence, whether seeing that both powers in order to injure one another, bear down every thing in their way, without regard to the rights of others, spoliating equally Danes Swedes & Americans, it would not be more prudent in us to bear with it as the Danes & Swedes do, curtailing our commerce, and waiting for the moment of peace, when it is probable both nations would for their own interest & honour retribute for their wrongs. however the public mind has been artfully inflamed by publications well calculated to decieve them & them only and especially in the towns, and irritations have been multiplied so as to shut the door to accomodation, and war is now inevitable. I imagine that France will do little with us till she has made her peace with England, which, whether her invasion succeeds or fails, must be made this summer and autumn. the game on both sides is too heavy to be continued. when she shall turn her arms on us, I imagine it will be chiefly against our commerce and fisheries. if any thing is attempted by land it will probably be to the westward. our great expence will be in equipping a navy to be lost as fast as equipped, or to be maintained at an expence which will sink us with itself, as the like course is sinking Great Britain. of the two millions of Dollars now to be raised by a tax on lands houses & slaves, Virginia is to furnish between 3. & 400,000. but this is not more than half of the actual expence if the provisional army be raised, nor one tenth of what must be the annual expences. I see no way in which we can injure France so as to advance to negociation (as we must do in the end) on better ground than at present. and I believe it will thus appear to our citizens generally as soon as the present fervor cools down. and there will be many sedatives to effect this. for the present however nothing can be done. silence & patience are necessary for a while; and I must pray you, as to what I now write, to take care it does not get out of your own hand, nor a breath of it in a newspaper.

I wrote to mr Clarke sometime ago mentioning that I had been here for six months advancing for all the nail rods for my nailery, without the possibility of recieving any thing from it till my return. that this will render it necessary to recieve immediately on my return whatever sums my customers may have on hand for me. I yesterday recieved a letter from him informing me he had left Staunton, & with your approbation had turned over my matters to a mr John Mc.Dowell. as I am not acquainted with him, nor as yet in correspondence with him, will you be so good as to mention to him that I shall have great need of whatever sum he may have in hand for me, as soon as I return, and should be very glad if he could lodge it with Colo. Bell by our July court, at which I shall be, or if no conveyance occurs he can send me a line by post to Charlottesville, informing me what sum I may count on. his future orders for nails I shall be able to attend to in person. I leave this for Monticello on the 20th. inst. the adjournment of Congress is not yet fixed. I am with great & constant esteem Dr Sir

Your friend & servt.   TH: JEFFERSON

RC (ViHi); addressed: "Archibald Stuart Staunton." PrC (DLC). Enclosure: *Message of the President of the United States to Both Houses of Congress. June 5th, 1798* (see TJ to Mary Jefferson Eppes, 6 June 1798).

Neither the letter from TJ to Samuel CLARKE of 24 May nor the LETTER FROM Clarke to TJ of 1 June, recorded in SJL as received 7 June 1798, has been found.

From Julian Ursin Niemcewicz

MONSIEUR   le 9 Juin 1798. Mount Vernon
Votre lettre Monsieur ne m'a été remise qu'hier, vous aurez donc la bonté de m'excuser si ma reponse vous parvient tard. Daignez agreer mes remerciments pour la somme de 200 Doll: que vous aves bien voulu m'avancer, cette lettre servira de réçu, car je ne sais comment le faire en due forme: j'espere sous peu de tems m'acquitter de ma dête j'ai rèçu des lettres de mes parents du Pologne qui m'annonçent, que quelques secours pécuniers, m'alloient être envoyés sans delais, je con-

serverai à jamais le souvenir de cette preuve d'amitié et de bonté de vôtre part; sans Vous je ne sais ce que j'aurois fait, vous m'aves mis à même de voir un pays qui merite si fort d'être connu. J'étois invité par Le Gl: Washington de venir le voir chez lui, je m'y suis rendu avec la famille de Mr Law, nous partons après demain. Je quitterai aussitôt Le fœderal City pour aller [à] Frideriks Town, Lankaster, Bethlem, je retourne de la à Philadelphie, je n'y m'arreteraî qu'un jour, et j'espere avoir encore le plaisir de vous y trouver, si non je ferai mon possible pour venir en Automne Vous presenter mes devoirs à Monti Celli. Les Evenements en Europe paroissent être près de leur denouement, il semble que la Scene va être transferée en Egypte, ce projet me fait grand plaisir si on parvient à le conquerir et à chasser Les Turcs de l'Europe, je vois la plus grande probabilité, qu'en donnant de ce Côté des Compensations à la maison d'Autriche et à la Russie, on pourra leur faire lacher leur proïe de la Pologne, et ma pauvre patrie renaîtroit encore. Vous aurez sans doute lu dans Les papiers publics, que Le Sabre que le Whig Club en Angleterre avoit voté pour Le Gl: K. est arrivé dans Le navire Adriana Cpt: Lee. comme Le G.K. sera bien aise de conserver ce temoignage de l'Estime public, il vous Sera j'en suis sûr, très reconnoissant, Si vous avies La bonté, de le faire retirer des mains du Cpt: Lee, et de lui donner une place parmi les autres Effets, que vous eutes la bonté de faire garder pour lui. J'espere qu'il est dejà arrivé à bon port, il me tarde de voir cet Espoir confirmé. Veuillez être persuadé Monsieur que ma reconnoissence ne peut être egalée que par Le respect que je porte à Vos Vertus. J'ai l'honneur d'être

Monsieur Votre très humble et tres Obeissant Serviteur

JULIEN NIEMCEWICZ

EDITORS' TRANSLATION

SIR   9 June 1798. Mount Vernon
    Your letter Sir was delivered to me only yesterday, so you will kindly forgive me if my answer gets to you late. I beg you to accept my thanks for the sum of 200 dollars that you graciously advanced to me, this letter will serve as a receipt, for I do not know how to make it out in proper form: I hope to settle my debt in a short time I have received letters from my family in Poland advising me, that some pecuniary assistance, was going to be sent to me without delay, I shall forever preserve the memory of that proof of friendship and kindness on your part; without you I do not know what I should have done, you have enabled me to see a country that so strongly deserves to be known. I was invited by Gl: Washington to come and see him at home, I traveled there with the family of Mr. Law, we are leaving the day after tomorrow. I shall immediately leave the Federal City to go to Frederick, Lancaster, Bethlehem, I return from there to Philadelphia, I shall stop there only one day, and I hope to have the pleasure again of finding you there, if not I shall do my very best to come to see you in

autumn and pay you my respects at Monticello. The events in Europe seem to be near their term, it seems that the scene will be transferred to Egypt, this project gives me great pleasure if there is success in conquering and chasing the Turks from Europe, I see the greatest probability, that by giving on that side some compensations to the house of Austria and to Russia, we can make them abandon Poland as their prey, and my poor homeland would be reborn again. You have no doubt read in the papers that the saber the Whig Club of England voted for Gl: K. has arrived in the ship Adriana Cpt: Lee. As G.K. will be very content to keep this evidence of public esteem, he will be very grateful to you, I am certain, if you should have the kindness, to retrieve it from the hands of Cpt: Lee, and to place it among the other effects, that you had the kindness to place in safekeeping for him. I hope that he has already arrived in a safe harbor, I am impatient to hear that hope confirmed. Kindly be assured Sir that my gratitude can be equaled only by the respect in which I hold your virtues. I have the honor to be

Sir Your very humble and very Obedient Servant   JULIEN NIEMCEWICZ

RC (DLC); endorsed by TJ as received 14 June 1798 and so recorded in SJL.

VOTRE LETTRE: TJ to Niemcewicz, 1 June 1798. Niemcewicz visited WASHINGTON at Mount Vernon from 2 to 14 June in the company of Thomas and Elizabeth Parke Custis LAW (Washington, *Diaries*, 6:299-301; Niemcewicz, *Under their Vine*, 95-108).

Niemcewicz could have learned from the Philadelphia *Aurora* of 5 June, which cited a Paris newspaper, that a French expedition "at once of a military and scientific nature," with scholars to accompany an army of 20,000, was in preparation for EGYPTE. What that early report did not comprehend was that the expeditionary force was larger than first supposed, it was under Bona-

parte's command, and it was a surrogate for the invasion of England, which the mercurial general had successfully argued was not feasible. The armada of transports and warships had actually departed Toulon for the eastern Mediterranean beginning 20 May, and by about a month later had landed the troops in Egypt (T. C. W. Blanning, *The French Revolutionary Wars, 1787-1802* [London, 1996], 189-90; Stewart, *French Revolution*, 717-20).

American newspapers noted the arrival of the fine presentation SABRE, an homage to Kosciuszko from the WHIG CLUB of England. Niemcewicz was familiar with the ADRIANA and its master, Frederick LEE, for he and Kosciuszko had come to the U.S. aboard the American vessel in 1797 (Haiman, *Kosciuszko*, 33, 36-9, 42-3, 80).

From James Monroe

DEAR SIR   Richmond [before 10] June 1798.

I wrote you by the last post & enclosed a small packet for Mr. Dawson wh. I hope was recd., as it respects my affr. with the department of State. Fortunately I found vouchers for all but one item; this however was a heavy one being £150. Strg. I hope the acct. will be closed & the fund assigned to Mr. D. prove adequate. I prefer to pay the money & close the acct. receiving reimbursement hereafter when the voucher is produc'd rather than retain the money & let the acct. lie open.

As to my coming into the H. of R. it is difficult for me to decide how far it is an elegible measure at present. To my family it wod. be an injurious measure, for from former experience I know it wod. amount to an abandonment of my profession. The expectation that I shall enter agn into publick life injures me every where at present: but this wod. be worse if I had actually embarked. Formerly I encountered the two-fold duties of Lawyer & publick agent—but then I was younger, & the pressure of publick affrs. less urgent. So much as it respects my private interest. In a publick view I candidly own to you that I can conceive no possible benefit resulting from it, & possibly some injury may accrue. In this light the subject is to be contemplated first as it respects the publick & secondly myself. So far as I can judge of the present state of affrs. I rather think my appearance on that theatre wod. do harm than good. There is a decided preponderance in the H. of R. agnst our principles, & this is supported by the full weight of the Executive & two thirds of the Senate. The republican force in the H. of R. on wh. the publick mind rested whilst it furnished a hope of success, seems to be broken & in consequence the great bulk of the people in the Estern quarter, or rather Eastward of the Potowk., to have fall'n in with the measures of the admn. Thus it appears as if those councils wod. prevail till the course of publick events shall produce a change. These may be of a foreign or domestic nature—The foreign the issue of the contest between France & Engld.—domestic, a more thorough disclosure of the views of the preponderating party than has yet been given, with an increased pressure of distress, wh. the policy of that party must produce. I do not think that any change is to be expected before one or other of these causes begins to operate. I think also that the change must begin to the Eastward by the direct operation of these causes; and that it wod. even be impeded by a new pressure from the South especially this State. It is doubtful with me whether if the republican party had rose in a body, when its opponant violated the rules of decorum (and appealed as it were to arms, attempting to intimidate the republican party) and told that opponant, "if civil war is yr. object proclaim it: we will consider what it becomes us to do in such a situation—If regular debate is yr. object confine yr.selves to the rules of the House & the manners & language of gentn, but here we will not sit to bear such insolence & outrage." It is probable that an absolute secession wod. have produced [. . .] than has occurred. It is plain that the whole session has exhibited a departure from the ordinary rules of proceeding observed by legislative bodies that in truth it has exhibited a scene of violence on the one side & moderation on the other, and that the violent party has triumphed, its success being much owing to its violence. A course of proceeding so unusual with us & so irregular any where, will probably have a vibration in an opposit direction after awhile; but the time will not arrive till one or other of the above mentioned incidents shall occur. Indeed now all their measures are carried or will be soon, so that there cod. not be a ground whereon to make an effort for the publick interest, nor will there be untill some change takes place in the state of affrs. To oppose their measures in the interval will not only be ineffectual, but subject the opponant to imputations wh. tho' unjust tend to lessen him in the publick opinion. Those who are on the theatre must do their duty, but I really think none who are opposed to present measures, especially myself, shod. press himself forward there. And with respect to myself I cannot perceive how my taking a seat in that branch wod. advance my interest or do away calumny. If my agency produc'd no effect it wod. hurt my credit not advance it. The Eastern people wod. not have clung so long to their representatives, if the *latter* had not been opposed by the Southern. The more therefore that party is left to itself, the sooner will its ruin follow. If I have been injured, the greater the injury, and the more intemperate the aggressors the better—I was attacked by the late President & censured—I replied to the denunciation; criminating the adverse party—to wh. they [have not] replied. Mr. A. has volunteered it agnst me and taken in that respect the ground of his predecessor. But this in truth is no new ground for him, for altho' his speech to congress at the extry. session was not so harsh & illiberal as his late reply to the people of Lancaster; yet it was in principle the same. His conduct towards me was equally hostile: he took all his measures before my arrival, tho' it was known [I] had sailed & wod. soon arrive, and altho' (if peace was his object or reconcil'ment of any kind) it was to be presumed, from the manner of my farewell from the French govt., that I cod. give useful council to promote that end. His language too was as harsh towards me as he cod. well make it, by indirect allusion, if such it cod. be called. Now indeed he has been more explicit, owing I presume to the dominant fortunes of his party, having a decided preponderance in the H. of Reps. as well as in the Senate, and according to appearance if not in truth the publick opinion on his side. It is possible this attack may be made as the fore,runner to other measures agnst me, such as an impeachmt. & trial by the Senate. Be the object what it may it becomes me to act with mature council in the course I take. A conflict with him & his party at the present time must be on terms disadvantageous to me: yet I am not afraid of it. I may have erred, and can myself name acts wh. as now advised from prudential motives I wod. have avoided but I was true to my country. I do not think a pursuit of me can benefit them with an impartial or even an honest publick; certainly it cannot with posterity. It may even injure them and the *more* according to the violence of it. There are two ways of acting, one by taking no notice of this outrage: the other by calling on the author for an explanation of his motive. For the first it may be urged that as he has only echoed the calumny of his predecessor in a manner as loose and vague as his predecessor urged it, that it does not become me to notice it, or any other attack not accompanied with a specific charge. For the 2d. it may be urged that by not calling on him, I rather decline a revival of the controversy & leave the adversary in some sort in possession of the ground. The question shod. be examined not by the impression of the moment but mathematically, if I may so say, and the course taken wh. will bear the test hereafter when our heads are deposited below the surface. I am ready to take any course wh. you advise & suggest those hints for consideration. As things stand am I a defendant or otherwise, and if so what the charge? Does not A's situation and age preclude the idea of making the affr. personal, and if it does can I approach him otherwise than to vindicate myself agnst a charge? If their object is to push the affr. will they not be gratified that I agn. furnish them with a pretext? Will they not in that case push forward whether I do or not, & whether will it be better to meet than wait the attack? You will readily see that these questions turn on the effect which any measure may have on the publick mind, without much regard to the merits of the controversy. I enclose a piece taken from Davis's paper, wh. may merit attention, especially if written by a member, or by order of the faction.

I do not know what they have to alledge agnst. me. That they had spies who caught up every incautious expression whilst I was there, and have been reinforced since by what cod. be gather'd, I make no doubt. Standing however on upright ground, and knowing that my conduct was useful to my country, I am ready if deemed adviseable to repair immediately to Phila., and push Mr. A to an expln.—Perhaps the discussion might be of real & essential publick utility, as the incident might be taken advantage of, to tell some truths as well as develope some principles of importance at the present time. But of this you will be a better judge than myself.

With respect to my coming forward in the place referred to, or in the other branch, if a vacancy existed, is it not correct that in such an appeal as I have made my abstraction from *either* at the moment, is in itself proper? And wod. it not be better for me to be brot. forward by the State at home, in the first instance, if I come into publick life at all for the present? Having long served the State with fidelity, I think I have a just claim to attention from it under existing circumstances. But this is only for consideration. Consulting my own wish, it is to remain in tranquility at home: it is to seek peace which can be found there only. Yet it is possible if I remain at home it may be injurious to my good name calumniated as I am, and even hurtful to a publick case. And I am not one to withdraw myself in such a case or withhold my services when duty calls for them in either line. Let me come forward where I may I consider it as an abandonment of my profession, for really the two objects cannot be pursued at the same time.

With respect to my private affrs. they are sound in the main: I am only embarrassed by some debts attendant on my mission to France, and these I hope to be able to discharge by the sale of some of my western property, to accomplish which I have an agent now in that country. If I succeed in the sale I shall be at ease, provided it be an advantageous one, or even such, as cannot be called a sacrifice. In any event a regard for private interest shall not restrain me from giving up my profession & taking the other course, if you think it adviseable, in regard to the considerations in question.   I have thus thrown loosely before you what has occurred to me on this topic. I hope you will be able to understand what I have said, tho' indeed I doubt it, as I have been repeatedly called off in the course of the morning. I shall have this in a day or two and return to albemarle whither be pleased to address yr. reply. Be[1] me yr. affectionate friend and servt

PS. My candid opinion is that the tone given or rather the evidence exhibited of publick opinion by addresses &ca is fallacious. The publick opinion in this State is decidedly otherwise if fairly taken.

RC (DLC); day of month omitted by Monroe; torn; endorsement by TJ partially torn away; recorded in SJL as a letter of unspecified date in June received on 10 June 1798.

READY TO TAKE ANY COURSE WH. YOU ADVISE: Monroe drafted a memorandum that identified Adams's attack on him as a continuation of Washington's criticisms and evaluated different courses of action he might take in response ("A note founded on the denuciation, by Mr Adams, in his reply to an address from the people of Lancaster," undated, probably May or June 1798 but endorsed as "1800," in DLC: Monroe Papers). The PIECE TAKEN FROM DAVIS'S PAPER was a call by "A Friend to Justice," 26 May 1798, for the House of Representatives to investigate the "misconduct" by Monroe that Adams had alluded to in his reply to the Lancaster address, and to impeach Monroe if the charges merited (Monroe, *Writings*, 3:133-4n).

[1] That is, "Believe."

From James Madison

DEAR SIR   June 10. 1798

I have duly recd. your favor of 31 Ult: & am glad to find mine are recd. as regularly as yours. The law for capturing French privateers may certainly be deemed a formal commencement of hostilities, and renders all hope of peace vain, unless a progress in amicable arrangements at Paris not to be expected, should have secured it agst. the designs of our Govermt. If the Bill suspending commerce with the French Dominions passes as it doubtless will, the French Goverment will be confirmed in the suspicion begotten by the British Treaty, of our coalition in the project of starving their people; and the effect of the measure will be to feed the English at the expence of the farmers of this Country. Already flour is down, I hear at 4 dollars a barrel. How far the views of the Govt. will be answd. by annihilating the ability to pay a land tax at the very moment of imposing it, will be best explained by the experimt. Looking beyond the present moment it may be questioned whether the interest of G.B. will be as much advanced by the sacrifice of our trade with her enemies as may be intended. The use of her manufactures here depends on our means of payment, & these on the sale of our produce to the markets of her enemies. There is too much passion it seems in our Councils to calculate consequences of any sort. The only hope is that its violence by defeating itself may save the Country. The answers of Mr. Adams to his addressers form the most grotesque scene in the tragicomedy acting by the Governt. They present not only the grossest contradictions to the maxims measures & language of his predecessor, and the real principles & interests of his Constituents, but to himself. He is verifying compleatly the last feature in the character drawn of him by Dr. F. however his title may stand to the two first. "Always an honest man, often¹ a wise one, but sometimes wholly out of his senses." I thank you for the offspring of the Senatorial Muse, which shall be taken care of. It is truly an Unique. It is not even prose run mad.—Monroe is much at a loss what course to take in consequence of the wicked assault on him by Mr. A. and I am as much so as to the advice that ought to be given him. It deserves consideration perhaps that if the least occasion be furnished for reviving Governmental attention to him, the spirit of party revenge may be wreaked [thro'] the forms of the Constitution. A majority in the H. of R. & $\frac{2}{3}$ of the Senate seem to be ripe for every thing. A temperate & dignified animadversion on the proceeding, published with his name, as an appeal to the candor & justice of his fellow Citizens, agst. the wanton & unmanly treatment, might perhaps be of use. But it wd. be difficult to execute it in a manner to do justice to himself, & inflict it on his adversary, without clashing with the temper of the moment. Hoping for the pleasure of congratulating you soon, on your release from your painful situation, I close with the most affectionate assurances that I am yours   Js M Jr.

RC (DLC: Madison Papers); torn; addressed: "Thomas Jefferson Vice President of the U. States Philadelphia"; endorsed by postmaster: "O.Ct.H.Va. 11th. June

1798"; franked; endorsed by TJ as received 19 June 1798 and so recorded in SJL.

For the characterization of Adams as DRAWN by Benjamin Franklin in his letter to Robert R. Livingston, 22 July 1783, see Albert Henry Smyth, ed., *The Writings of Ben-*

jamin Franklin, 10 vols. (New York, 1905-7), 9:62. SENATORIAL MUSE: Humphrey Marshall.

[1] Word interlined by Madison in place of "sometimes."

From Thomas Mann Randolph

TH: M. RANDOLPH TO TH: JEFFERSON, Belmont June 10th. 98

Your letter of the 31. May to Martha arrived yesterday with the pleasant news that your horses w'd. be wanted in the course of another week. Your directions shall be implicitly followed and the horses ready to depart next Saturday Morning. We rejoice here that such wild and ruinous measures as are now taking are to be no longer sanctioned by your presence. While it was possible to avert the calamity we wished you to remain; for alltho' you had no voice yet it gave satisfaction to know that you were at hand to aid with your advice the cool and disinterested party; now that is completely oppressed no one expects you to stay; to behold the detestable triumph of principles which your heart has allways abhorred and your head opposed: no one can wish you longer to forego happiness yourself and keep joy from your connexions.

I inclose a note for Mr. Trist which you will oblige me by presenting sealed, if the application it will occasion to you should be entirely indifferent.

We are all well—they are so likewise at Dunlora Carrsbrook &c.

Yours most affectionately   TH: M. RANDOLPH

I remind you of Medicines—the few simples we want here can be had cheaper & better in Philad'a. than in Richmond I suppose—You have not, nor have I incurred a single fee since you left us, one Syphilitic case from Shadwell sent up twice to Charle'lle. to Wardlaw's excepted

RC (ViU: Edgehill-Randolph Papers); endorsed by TJ as received 19 June 1798 and so recorded in SJL. Enclosure not found, but see note below.

Randolph's NOTE FOR Hore Browse TRIST probably concerned Trist's purchase of "horseman's apparatus" for Randolph for which TJ provided reimbursement with an order on Barnes for $79 on 23 June, to be charged to Randolph's account (MB, 2:985). TJ paid Dr. David Jackson $.75 for MEDICINES on 27 June 1798 (same, 986).

To John Beckley

DEAR SIR   Philadelphia June 12. 98.

In consequence of my undertaking to mr Trigg, I wrote to my manager near Lynchburg to know if he could pay him 240. Dollars the 1st. of July. he has informed me he could not; but that, according to my directions in that case, he had engaged a merchant of Lynchburg to do it, in exchange for my draught for that sum in Richmond. I have accordingly made provision for the payment in Richmond. on collating my bills here with my resources, (as I shall leave this place the beginning of next week) I find I can have some of them deferred beyond the 1st. of July, if it will be a convenience to you to accept my order for the sum payable at some further day suitable to you, rather than to provide the money for the 1st. of July as proposed in one of your letters to me. it would have given me greater pleasure to have let it lie, sine die, but that my bills, on being collected, call for all the means I have. I am with great esteem Dr. Sir

Your most obedt. servt   TH: JEFFERSON

PrC (MHi); at foot of text: "Mr. Beckley"; endorsed by TJ in ink on verso. Not recorded in SJL.

I WROTE TO MY MANAGER NEAR LYNCH-BURG: according to SJL, TJ wrote Bowling Clark, his overseer at Poplar Forest, on 19 Apr. 1798. TJ received Clark's reply of 8 May on the 26th, but neither letter has been found. On 26 June TJ gave John Trigg an order on Clark for $100, part of TJ's payment as security for Beckley. To complete the payment to Trigg, TJ sent Clark an order for $140, which he entered in his account book on 31 July (MB, 2:988). According to SJL TJ wrote Trigg on 26 June and Clark on 1 Aug., but neither letter has been located. ONE OF YOUR LETTERS TO ME: see TJ to Beckley, 17 Apr. 1798 (first letter). A letter from Beckley to TJ of 14 June 1798, recorded in SJL as received the same day, has not been found.

To James Fennell

                                                   Philadelphia June 12. 98

Th: Jefferson returns his thanks to mr Fennel for the Dissertation on his method of making salt. the theory is certainly promising. what may be the actual result depends on so many circumstances as to require experiment to found an estimate. having no experience on the subject himself, he is entirely unable to give an opinion: but doubts not that mr Fennel has sufficiently verified his process by experiment to justify his conclusions. he sincerely wishes him success, and apprehends the circumstances of the times are likely to befriend his undertaking.

PrC (DLC); endorsed by TJ in ink on verso: "Fennel James. June 12. 98." Not recorded in SJL.

To James Madison

June 14. 98.

I wrote you last on the 7th. since which yours of the 3d. is recieved. your next (which I shall still be here to recieve on the 19th) will probably acknolege mine of May 31. and will perhaps be your last as you would see by mine of the 7th. that I should leave this on the 20th. which I still purpose. the new citizen or naturalization bill is past the Senate also. it requires 14. years residence to make a citizen. it had friends in both parties. the whigs apprehended that the success of the invasion of England would drive all their aristocracy here. their opponents believing still in the final failure of the revolution of France, & the safety of England, apprehended a deluge of the democrats of both countries. we were within one vote however in the Senate of striking out *14* years & inserting *7*. Langdon who would have been for it had previously declined voting on the bill at all, because he had just taken his seat. his vote would have divided the Senate 12. & 12. the bill suspending intercourse with the French dominions is signed by the President. the bill for assessing lands houses & slaves came up to the Senate yesterday. the classification of houses had been struck out of it. the second bill, for laying the tax on these subjects, is still before the R. the Senate have brought in a bill authorizing the President to accept of any number of armed vessels, not exceeding 12, & carrying not less than 22. nine pounders, which any individuals may build and cede on terms he shall approve, by way of loan. but neither the terms as to interest or paiment of the principal, nor the maximum of size are limited, but a proposition to limit was rejected. some treated the apprehension that large ships might be obtained as chimerical, while others wished they might be all of the line, and at least 3, 4, or a half a dozen 74s. this bill is in fact to open *a loan* in the form of ships. Harper has brought in resolutions for authorising the President to borrow money for the excess of this year's expences above the taxes. no other limitation of sum. I do not believe we can borrow any considerable sum but in London. some think the bank of the US. may lend as far as a couple of millions. the opinion of their connection with the government has already sunk their shares from 23. to 20. while those of Pennsylvania have risen from 23. to 25. above par. the British captures of our vessels have multiplied greatly. our stopping intercourse with France will keep that portion of our vessels out of their way. they will still take those bound to Dutch & Spanish ports.   the committees of the two houses appointed jointly to propose a time of adjournmt. have not yet reported; so that it is still uncertain whether & when they will adjourn. my horses are to meet me at Fredericksburg on Sunday the 24th.

whether I can reach you the next day is uncertain. probably not. Innes is still living. he has been carried into the country.—the window cord shall be added to the other articles. no vessel for Fredericksburg has yet occurred. this of course will be my last to you from hence. friendly salutations to mrs Madison the family & yourself and affectionately Adieu.

P.S. flour at Baltimore 4.50 D here 5 D. the farmers of this state have almost universally their last year's crop of wheat & flour still in their own hands.

P.M. the joint committees for adjournmt have reported that they think it not improbable that Congress may adjourn from the middle of July to the 1st. of October, but they do not think it prudent to fix a day at present.

RC (DLC: Madison Papers, Rives Collection); addressed: "James Madison junr. near Orange court house"; franked. PrC (DLC); endorsed by TJ in ink on verso.

On 6 June Benjamin Goodhue brought in a BILL AUTHORIZING THE PRESIDENT TO ACCEPT OF ANY NUMBER OF ARMED VESSELS, either as a gift or a loan. Sent back to committee, the bill was amended on 12 June to limit the number of vessels to 12, with the force of at least "twenty guns, nine pounders." The next day a motion to limit interest on vessels loaned to the government to six percent and a PROPOSITION TO LIMIT the number of guns were defeated. On 14 June the Senate passed the bill, 16 to 7, and sent it to the House (printed bill with TJ's notations in DNA: RG 46, Senate Records, 5th Cong., 2d sess.; JS, 2:502, 505, 507-8). The House passed a bill of its own as a supplement to the "act to provide an additional armament for the further protection of the trade of the United States," that, like the Senate bill, authorized the president to obtain 12 vessels in addition to the 12 agreed to in April 1798 but limited interest to six per-

cent and set gun sizes for the 24 vessels—6 not to exceed 18 guns each, another 6 at 32 or more guns each, and 12 at 20 to 24 guns each. On 28 June the Senate agreed to the bill with minor changes (printed bill with TJ's notations in DNA: RG 46, Senate Records, 5th Cong., 2d sess.; JHR, 3:339, 343, 349-51, 356; JS, 2:519-21; U.S. Statutes at Large, 1:552, 575-6). For the Navy's acquisition of vessels under this legislation, see Smelser, Navy, 170.

On 12 June Robert Goodloe Harper offered two RESOLUTIONS, one AUTHORISING THE PRESIDENT TO BORROW MONEY to cover government expenses for 1798. The act, as finally approved on 16 July, allowed the president to borrow a sum not to exceed five million dollars from the Bank of the United States and elsewhere on such terms as he judged most advantageous. The second resolution called for monies for the new regiment of artillerists and engineers raised under the act of 27 Apr. 1798. On 28 June, the president signed legislation appropriating $88,000 for the regiment (Annals, 8:1899; U.S. Statutes at Large, 1:552-3, 575, 607-8).

To Julian Ursin Niemcewicz

DEAR SIR   Philadelphia June 14. 98

Your favor of the 9th. is but this moment put into my hands, so that I have barely time to get an answer in for the first post. I percieve by your letter that I shall probably fail of the pleasure of meeting you. I shall leave this on Wednesday the 20th. and pass through Georgetown on the 22d. at the Stage hour. before that time I apprehend you will have left it. I have this day recieved the sword for Genl. Kosciuszko, and put it in the care of a trusty person. Capt. Lee who delivered it to me, tells me he has a letter for you from England, which he will bring me tomorrow morning. I will leave it in the care of my landlord, mr Francis, to be kept till you call or send for it. I am sorry you were so long getting my letter, as it must have [occasioned] you some uneasy [sensations]. it was sent by the first post after the reciept of yours. I shall [count] on the pleasure of seeing you at Monticello. the hour of the post obliges me to conclude with assurances of the great esteem & attachment of Dr Sir

Your most obedt. servt. TH: JEFFERSON

PrC (DLC); faint; at foot of text: "Mr. Niemcewicz"; endorsed by TJ in ink on verso.

To Thomas Mann Randolph

TH:J. TO TMR. Philadelphia June 14. 98.

I wrote you last on the 7th. inst. since which yours of the 3d. is recieved. I shall certainly leave this on the 20th. and be at Fredericksburg on the 23d.[1] consequently one day before my horses, which in my last I desired might set out Saturday the 23d. & be there Sunday the 24th. in the mean time I thank you for putting an end to the cultivation of tobacco as the peculium of the negroes. I have ever found it necessary to confine them to such articles as are not raised for the farm. there is no other way of drawing a line between what is theirs & mine.

The new naturalization bill is passed. it requires 14. years to make a citizen. the bill for suspending intercourse with the French is signed by the President. this will lessen the English captures, for they have for some time been more considerable than the French. they take all trading with French, Spanish or Dutch colonies. our bill will prevent the odium which would have attended their captures of those bound to the French: and the friends of it would have extended it to Spanish & Dutch if they could have found any pretext, merely to screen the English from censure. a bill is brought in to allow the President to recieve any number of armed vessels (not over 12. in number) and carrying not less metal than 22. ninepounders, which may be built in the US. and to agree to such paiments of the interest & principal of their cost as he thinks proper. mr Harper has also brought in resolutions to authorize the President to borrow whatever money may be necessary for the expences of this year

[410]

over & above the taxes. the bill for assessing lands, houses, & slaves is passed the H. of R. that for levying 2. millions on them, is still before that house. it is not yet decided when they will adjourn. Innes is still living. he is sent into the country. my warmest affections to my dear Martha, and the little ones. cordial Adieu to yourself.

P.S. mr Lott will furnish money for Jupiter's road expences. 4. or 5. dollars will be enough. perhaps he can find it himself & recieve it from me.

Flour at Baltimore 4.50. D here 5. D

RC (DLC); endorsed by Randolph as received 23 June 1798. PrC (CSmH); lacks final sentence of postscript; endorsed by TJ in ink on verso.

[1] Date altered by TJ from "24th."

To Benjamin Harrison, Jr.

DEAR SIR   Philadelphia June 15. 98.

Having occasion to enquire into the situation of mr Short's Green sea lands, I wrote to Colo. Harvie on the subject, who refers me to you. I wish to be informed of the quantity, county, and whether the taxes have been paid. I will thank you for information on these points addressed to me at Monticello, and also for the patent if in your hands, having been desired by mr Short to look into the matter and save the lands for him. this request will I hope apologize to you for the trouble I take the liberty of giving you. I am with esteem Dear Sir

Your most obedt. & most humble servt   TH: JEFFERSON

PrC (DLC: Short Papers); at foot of text: "Benjamin Harrison esq."; endorsed by TJ in ink on verso.

On 14 June TJ sent an order to Comp-troller John Steele authorizing John Barnes to receive any interest and principal to be paid 1 July on U.S. certificates held by William SHORT (RC in ViU; endorsed by Steele, 2 July 1798).

To George Jefferson

DEAR SIR   Philadelphia June 15. 1798.

My last to you was of the 20th. of May, since which I have recieved yours of May 23. and 28. and June 1. I am entirely satisfied with the sale to mr Hooper; the chance run, being one of those necessary to meet in the ordinary course of business. as this sale was made to meet two paiments of 1000. Doll. each to mr Wickam and mr James Lyle which were in fact stipulated for earlier days, I am desirous, tho' I do not put the cash into their hands, yet to put the order for it before the day, as it may be satisfactory to them to know with certainty the term of the delay. I have accordingly inclosed them orders payable on the 1st. of Oct. and 12th. of Nov. which I hope it [will] not be disagreeable to mr Hooper to accept. I inclose you a [letter] for him, which, when read, be so good as to seal and deliver, as [the] orders go by this post & probably will be presented to him immediately. I leave this on the 20th. and shall be at home on [the] 27th. Congress expects to adjourn about three weeks after that. I am with great esteem Dear Sir

Your friend & servt   TH: JEFFERSON

PrC (MHi); faint; at foot of text: "Mr. George Jefferson"; endorsed by TJ in ink on verso. Enclosure: TJ to Thomas Hooper, 15 July 1798 (recorded in SJL but not found).

To James Lyle

DEAR SIR   Philadelphia June 15. 1798.

Having been three times called to this place the last year, and now kept here on a session of 6. months, the expences attending this have so far exceeded what were to have been expected in the ordinary course of things, that they put it out of my power to make the first payment promised in my letter of the last year, in time. I had calculated on one trip only to this place, and a short session as has been usual. I have lately sold my tobacco to mr Hooper in Richmond and now give you an order on him for one thousand dollars payable the 12th. of November, being the term of credit allowed him on the sale. as you will be on the spot & I shall probably be here at that time I thought it best to put the matter into your hands at once. the prospect is that tobacco will continue to rise, and keep high till the supply can once more equal the demand, which it does not now by probably 40,000 hhds a year, and never will again till the new countries get into the business. the efforts I am making to avail myself of that interval, by aiming entirely at tobacco, will I hope enable me to fetch up the paiment to you which is in arrear, so as to compleat my matter within the period proposed. with wishes for your health & life I am with constant & sincere esteem Dear Sir

Your friend & servt   TH: JEFFERSON

PrC (MHi); at foot of text: "James Lyle esq"; endorsed by TJ in ink on verso. Enclosure: order by TJ to Thomas Hooper of Richmond, 15 June 1798, for payment to Lyle as specified above; recorded in TJ's financial memoranda as "to credit of my bonds to Henderson & McCaul" (PrC in MHi, endorsed by TJ on verso; MB, 2:985).

MY LETTER OF THE LAST YEAR: TJ to Lyle, 12 Feb. 1797.

To John Wickham

DEAR SIR   Philadelphia June 15. 1798.

In a former letter I informed you of the circumstances which would postpone my annual paiment somewhat later than the day fixed for it, and I recieved your answer that you had communicated my letter to mr Waller. I have lately sold my tobacco to mr Hooper of Richmond and now inclose you an order on him for one thousand dollars payable Octob. 1st. the term of credit allowed him. as you will be on the spot and I shall be here probably at the time, I have thought it best to put the matter at once into your hands: for though I have not heard from mr Waller, I presume that what is done with you will meet his approbation. I am with great esteem Dr. Sir

Your most obedt. servt.   TH: JEFFERSON

PrC (MHi); at foot of text: "Mr. Wickam"; endorsed by TJ in ink on verso. Enclosure not found, but see note below.

FORMER LETTER: TJ to Wickham, 25 Mch. 1798. YOUR ANSWER: Wickham to

TJ, 2 Apr. 1798. The ORDER enclosed by TJ was to discharge the first of four bonds given by him on 20 Jan. 1797, this one due on 1 July 1798, in payment of the Wayles estate debt owed to Wakelin Welch (TJ to Wickham, 20 Jan. 1797; MB, 1:985).

To Aaron Burr

DEAR SIR   Philadelphia June 16. 98.

In my letter of May 26. I mentioned to you that Dr. Currie had another demand by judgment against John Tayloe Griffin as principal, and Robert Morris garnishee, which should be the subject of a future letter to you. I now inclose you a transcript of the record of the supreme court of this state. It seems by this (I have not examined the record with minute attention) that the court have considered Robert Morris as holding property of Griffin's to the amount of £4305. Pensva currency = 11480. Doll. not due, as stated on interrogatory, till Dec. 3. 1800. but that interest at 5. per cent must have been payable annually, as he confesses judgment for £959.8.8. interest on that sum to Dec. 3. 95. which was paid to mr Ingersoll, and a scire facias for the interest of the year 1796. being £215.5. has been since issued. on this last, nothing has been done, as no effects here can be got at. this interest therefore for the year 1796. and now also for the year 1797. is due and immediately recoverable. as to the principal, I know not how the laws may be with you: but in Virginia, where we have courts of chancery on the principles of that of England, tho' in a court of law the principal could not be demanded before due, yet the Chancery, in consideration of the hazard in which it is placed by the change of circumstances of Rob. Morris, would either oblige him to give security, or sequester any property of his which the plaintiff would point out. if it be so with you, then we may hope that the principal may be secured so as to be recieved in 1800. and the interest for 96. & 97. immediately recovered. I will pray you however to have done for Dr. Currie both as to principal and interest whatever your laws will authorize for the best. I inclose you a letter from him referring you to me, and I hereby give you as full powers to act herein as he has given to me. I leave this place in the morning of the 20th. and would thank you to be informed what prospect you think there is for these several matters. if I am gone, the letter will follow & find me at home. I am with great esteem Dr. Sir

Your friend & servt.   TH: JEFFERSON

RC (CtHi); at foot of text: "Colo. Burr." PrC (DLC); endorsed by TJ in ink on verso. Enclosures not found; second enclosure possibly James Currie to TJ, 3 June 1798, now missing, recorded in SJL as received 9 June.

From James Monroe

DEAR SIR   Albemarle June 16. 1798.

The last communication of our Envoys was the last from you. By it nothing is more obvious than that France intends not to make war on us, so that our admn. has the merit exclusively of precipitating us into that state; if it exists, or takes place hereafter, of wh. there can be little doubt, if there is any of its existence, at the present time. France has been roused agnst us by the admn., who have never lost a moment to keep her resentment at the height, by multiplying[1] the causes of irritation daily, for otherwise the contempt she naturally has for the admn. & respect she naturally has for the nation, wod. wear it away & leave us in peace. But since the late acts of Congress the appeal is to another tribunal. The triumph of the admn. in the representative branch, cuts asunder the only remaining link between the two nations, & gives to the American people *war* wh. with the admn. they now invite. we are of course thrown upon Engld. as a subaltern dependant power. If she prevails we follow her, for sometime at least, as a feeble contemptible satellite: unless indeed the discovery of other views in the admn., than the mass of those who support its measures believe it has, shod. separate that mass from the admn. & give a new spring to republican councils: admitting that the American people are the people they were 20. years ago. And if France prevails we are then to experience that fate wh. she will prescribe. and what that will be it is very difficult to say. I believe it will be admitted there is not a noble sentiment in her councils to wh.

[414]

we can appeal. Still if we wod. skulk off with the same ignominy we have borne, thro' the whole of the war, tis posible we might escape a terrible scourging. For that state, I think the former admn. wod. be disposed so to do, declaring at the same time, it meant nothing by the late acts beyond the limits of the strictest neutrality. But our present Viceroy wod. I think even in that state be for fighting, to make the last effort in favor of his book that the state of the world wod. admit of, in the hope also of displaying himself to the same advantage in the field as a soldier, as he thinks he has done as a man of science in the republick of letters. It is really an astonishing spectacle to behold such a nation as this is, containing so many enlightened men, such a virtuous & intelligent yeomanry, such an active and grasping body of merchants, dandled about agnst the obvious interest & principles of every class, as it were by an old woman! But such is the state of things that the infatuation or disorder of the nation must be managed with skill & gently, or it will grow worse & become incurable. And I am very much inclined to think that the patient must find out his own disorder, if not by himself, yet that he must think so: that the phisician must not appear, or if at all by no means as a prominent character.

With respect to myself I am inclined to think I shod. take no step in consequence of the late attack of Adams, but remain as I am quiet. A further attack on me of the violent kind if not supported by proof cannot otherwise than injure them. Shod. however the subject come before the H. of R. I am of opinion my friends shod. unite in a call for the charge agnst me &ca and promote otherwise so far as depends on them in *any form most elegible* to the other party an enquiry. The late outrage if they do not go further, must appear intemperate & dishonorable. And if they go further I think it will appear worse, for it will make the subject better understood by the people. For me to come forward will place me in some degree in the attitude of an assailant, I mean by calling on Adams in any form, and circumstanc'd as the countries are make me appear as fighting the cause of France agnst my own country. It will be proper I think, that such a coloring to the adverse party however unjustly in fact shod. be avoided. This is idea wh. I suggest for consideration only. we are taught to expect you home soon wh. personally I sincerely wish. You have doubtless weighed it in a publick view, and so far as it is likely to secure you personally the friendly salutations wh. a host of saints never fail to greet you with, do what you will. Believe me sincerely yr. friend & servant

RC (DLC: Monroe Papers); endorsed by TJ as received 26 June 1798 and so recorded in SJL.

Evidently TJ had sent Monroe, without any cover letter recorded in SJL, the 5 June message from Adams to Congress that TJ enclosed to John Page on 6 June. It contained the LAST COMMUNICATION of the envoys in France.

OUR PRESENT VICEROY: John Adams, whose BOOK was *A Defence of the Constitu-* *tions of Government of the United States of America.*

[1] Monroe first wrote "adding" before revising to read as above.

To Tadeusz Kosciuszko

Philadelphia. June 18. 98.

I wrote to you my dear & respectable friend on the 30th. of May by Volney, putting it under cover, as I do this, to our friend Jacob Van Staphorst, at Paris. Capt. Lee of the ship Adriana has brought for you as a present from the whig club of England an elegant Sabre, mounted in gold, and inscribed 'the whig club of England to General Kosciuzko' said to have cost two hundred guineas. Capt. Lee understanding according to the general opinion that you were gone to the medicinal springs in Virginia deposited it with me for you. were I sure it would find you at Paris I should have sent it by this opportunity: but it is a thing which ought not to be put to hazard. I will therefore wait your orders. it would be easiest for us to send it to Amsterdam to N. & Jac. V. Staphorst & Hubbard, but this you will decide on. in the mean time I send you a letter which accompanied it. not a doubt is entertained here but that you are gone to the springs. our affairs continue to go on from bad to worse. if we can remain at peace this year, our citizens will see through the delusions of the present moment, and republicanism will be saved in this country. if we are invaded, an union comes on of necessity with a power under whose auspices every thing fatal to republicanism is to be apprehended. meaning to leave this place the day after tomorrow, I had packed away our cypher with my papers which puts it out of my power to avail myself of that. I am extremely anxious to hear of you & from you, never having heard a tittle since you left us. my sincere prayers for your health & life attend you, and the most affectionate Adieux.

PrC (DLC); unaddressed, but recorded in SJL as a letter to Kosciuszko.

To James Madison

Philadelphia June 21. 98.

Yours of the 10th. inst. is recieved. I expected mine of the 14th. would have been my last from hence, as I had proposed to have set out on the 20th. but in the morning of the 19th. we heard of the arrival of Marshall at New York, and I concluded to stay & see whether that circumstance would produce any new projects. no doubt he there recieved more than hints from Hamilton as to the tone required to be assumed. yet I apprehend he is not hot enough for his friends. Livingston came with him from New York. M. told him they had no idea in France of a war with us. that Taleyrand sent passports to him & Pinckney, but none for Gerry. upon this Gerry staid without explaining to them the reason. he wrote however to the President by Marshall, who knew nothing of the contents of the letter. so that there must have been a previous understanding between Taleyrand & Gerry. M. was received here with the utmost eclat. the Secretary of state & many carriages, with all the city cavalry went to Frankfort to meet him, and on his arrival here in the evening the bells rung till late in the night, & immense crowds were collected to see & make part of the shew, which was circuitously paraded through the streets before he was set down at the city tavern. all this was to secure him to their views, that he might say nothing which would expose the game they have been playing. since his arrival I can hear of nothing directly from him, while they are disseminating through the town things, as from him, diametrically opposite to what he said to Livingston. Dr. Logan about a fortnight ago sailed for Hamburgh. tho for a twelvemonth past he had been intending to Europe as soon as he could get money enough to carry him there, yet when he had accomplished this, and fixed a time for going, he very unwisely made a mystery of it, so that his disappearance without notice excited conversation. this was seised by the war-hawks, and given out as a secret mission from the Jacobins here to sollicit an army from France, instruct them as to their landing &c. this extravagance produced a real panic among the citizens, & happening just when Bache published Taleyrand's letter, Harper on the 18th. gravely announced to the H.R. that there existed a traiterous correspondence between the Jacobins here and the French Directory, that he had got hold of some threads & clues of it, and would soon be able to develope the whole. this increased the alarm; their libellists immediately set to work directly & indirectly to implicate whom they pleased. Porcupine gave me a principal share in it as I am told, for I never read his papers. this state of things added to my reasons for not departing at the time I intended. these follies seem to have died away in some degree already. perhaps I may renew my purpose by the 25th. their system is professedly to keep up an alarm. Tracy at the meeting of the joint committee for adjournment declared it necessary for Congress to stay together to keep up the inflammation of the publick mind; and Otis expressed a similar sentiment since. however they will adjourn. the opposers of adjournment in Senate yesterday agreed to adjourn on the 10th. of July: but I think the 1st. of July will be carried. that is one of the objects which detains myself as well as one or two more of the Senate who had got leave of absence. I imagine it will be decided tomorrow or next day. to separate Congress now will be withdrawing the fire from under a boiling pot.

Your commissions here are all in readiness, but no vessel for Fredericksburg has yet occurred. my respectful salutations to mrs Madison & the family, and cordial friendship to yourself.

P.M. a message to both houses this day from the Pr. with the following communications.

Mar. 23. Pickering's letter to the envoys, directing them if they are not actually engaged in negociation with authorised persons, or not conducted bonâ fide & not merely for procrastination, to break-up & come home. and at any rate to consent to no loan.

Apr. 3. Talleyrand to Gerry. he supposes the other two gentlemen, percieving that their known principles are an obstacle to negociation, will leave the republic, and proposing to renew the negociations with Gerry immediately.

Apr. 4. Gerry to Taleyrand. disclaims a power to conclude any thing separately. can only confer informally & as an unaccredited individual, reserving to lay every thing before the government of the US. for approbation.

Apr. 14. Gerry to the President. he communicates the preceding and hopes the President will send other persons instead of his collegues & himself if it shall appear that any thing can be done. the President's message says that as the instructions were not to consent to any loan, he considers the negociation as at an end; and that he will never send another minister to France until he shall be assured that he will be recieved & treated with the respect due to a great, powerful, free & independant nation.

A bill is brought into the Senate this day to declare the treaties with France void, prefaced by a list of grievances in the style of a manifesto. it passed to the 2d. reading by 14. to 5.

a bill for punishing forgeries of bank paper passed to the 3d reading by 14. to 6. three of the 14 (Laurence, Bingham & Read) bank directors.

RC (DLC: Madison Papers); addressed: "James Madison junr. near Orange court house"; franked. PrC (DLC); added by TJ in ink at foot of first page: "Madison James."

The CONVERSATION over George Logan's departure led TJ to visit Deborah Logan at Stenton on 22 or 23 June, using a circuitous route to elude "his spies." TJ advised Logan to express her "thorough consciousness" of her husband's innocence and honor by showing herself in Philadelphia "as one not afraid nor ashamed to meet the public eye." She made the trip shortly thereafter (Logan, *Memoir*, 75-6). On 21 July *Porcupine's Gazette* reported that TJ "went to his friend Doctor Logan's farm, and spent three days there, soon after the Doctor's departure for France. *Quere:* What did he do there? Was it to arrange the Doctor's *valuable manuscripts?*"

On 16 June BACHE PUBLISHED a letter from Talleyrand to the American envoys dated 18 Mch., before it had been officially released by the Adams administration. This convinced William Cobbett and the Federalists that Bache had received it from France or from a French agent in America "for the express purpose of *drawing off the people from the Government*, of exciting discontents, of strengthening opposition, and to procure a *fatal delay of preparation for war.*" According to Deborah Logan one of the reasons TJ had prolonged his stay in Philadelphia was to learn how Robert Goodloe HARPER would "make out with his conspiracy" announcement (*Porcupine's Gazette*, 16 June 1798; Logan, *Memoir*, 75). On 19 June *Porcupine's Gazette* announced that TJ was seen going into Bache's house "on the very day that the dispatches appeared." For the controversy surrounding Bache's publication of the Talleyrand letter and the efforts to associate TJ with treasonous correspondence, see note to Fulwar Skipwith to TJ, 17 Mch. 1798. For Harper's charges in the House, see *Annals*, 8:1972, and Smith, *Freedom's Fetters*, 102-6.

Upon receiving the message and COMMUNICATIONS from the president, the Senate voted to have 500 copies printed (JS, 2:513-14). See Evans, No. 34825. The letter from GERRY TO THE PRESIDENT was dated 16 not 14 Apr. 1798 (*Message of the President of the United States, to Both Houses of Congress June 21st, 1798* [Philadelphia, 1798], 2).

On a printed copy of the bill TO DECLARE THE TREATIES WITH FRANCE VOID, TJ recorded changes as the Senate considered the preamble or MANIFESTO, which consisted of 92 lines of text (DNA: RG 46, Senate Records, 5th Cong., 2d sess.). See also TJ to Madison, 7 June.

FORGERIES OF BANK PAPER: the bill "to punish frauds committed on the Bank of the United States" passed the Senate on 22 June and the House four days later. Senators John Laurance, William Bingham, and Jacob Read were DIRECTORS of the Bank of the United States as was Representative Harrison Gray Otis (JS, 2:515, 518; U.S. Statutes at Large, 1:573-4; *Longworth's American Almanack, New-York Register, and City Directory, for the Twenty-third Year of American Independence* [New York, 1798], 65). A letter from Bingham to TJ of 13 Feb. 1797, recorded in SJL as delivered "by Hope, Baring & Beecker" on 30 Apr. of that year, has not been found.

From John Page

MY DEAR JEFFERSON   Rosewell June 21st. 1798

Your Letter of the 6th. Instt. inclosing your Letter to a Friend respecting the malicious Attack on a Passage in your Notes on Virginia, & the President's last Communication to Congress of the Proceedings of our Envoys happily came safe to Hand—Of the former I think it fully sufficient for your Purpose—it will satisfy every one who is not by the infernal Spirit of Party hardened against Conviction—it may I think be shewn to such Persons as are worthy of your Regard, & hereafter be added, with any other Remarks you may think proper, to a future Edition of your Notes on Virginia. Observe, when I say the infernal Spirit of Party, I do not mean to reflect upon *Party*, but to distinguish between the celestial Spirit which influences pure patriotic Party & that Spirit which in all Countries & in all Ages has been found inflating agitating & infatuating Factions against the Liberty & true Interests of the People. No I think a Party is necessary in a free State to preserve its Freedom—The truely virtuous should firmly unite & form a Party capable at all Times of frustrating the wicked Designs of the Enemies of the Doctrine of Equallity & the Rights of Man. I have ever attributed the rapid Propagation of anglo-monarchico-aristocractical Principles amongst us to the Abolition of the Republican & Democratic Societies. Had they boldly done their Duty, Government would have been taught theirs; & the People would have learned their Rights, & understood their Interests better than to have reelected Men who had voted for the Funding System, the Bank &c & who justified the Secretary of the Treasury in his bold Violations of Acts of Appropriation; & Men too, who, whilst they sacrificed their Country's best Interest without the least Necessity that they might (as they told us) avoid War with Britain, have manifested an astonishing Degree of Impatience to plunge their Country into a War with France; a War which must in its Consequences be far more injurious to the commercial Interest of the United States than a War with Britain, & which must be most pernicious to their political & republican Interests. If vanquished, they (the Ud. States) may be most deservedly chastised for their Folly, & perhaps divided between their Enemies & their Allies: if compleatly successful, & victorious, they may ruin the only Republic which could oppose & check the Enemies of Free Governments; & thus pave the way to the compleat Establishment of Despotism not only in America but throughout the World! But to return—I attribute Mr. Martins Attack upon your Notes as proceeding altogether from party-spirit, & not from a spirit of Delicacy; as I have been informed he has not been so sensible of Reflections, cast on what most nearly concerned him: which, if Sensibility & not party-Spirit, influenced him should have arroused a Resentment against others which he has not thought proper to shew.

As to the Communications of the P—t I will only remark that I wish to know how he can reconcile them to his Declaration before the call on him for [Instrucn.] that there was an End to all Negociation—that nothing more could be done &c, & that I think the People must be blind if they do not see, that if half the Pains had been taken to sooth the justly irritated Mind of the French Republic, as was assiduously used to appease the insolent Rage of Britain, they might be at this day in a flourishing & happy commercial Connection with France & her Allies, & Dependencies & in a dignified State of Neutrality & Amity with Britain; instead of being on the Point of a War with France, of losing perhaps forever a Chance of that commercial Connection, & of becoming dependent on Britain for our commercial & even political Existence!

But—I will turn away from the Scene which my Imagination begins to set before me. I admire your philosophical Contempt of the malicious tales which party-Spirit has indefatigably propagated respecting you—but I much doubt whether that philosophical Disposition ought to be so much indulged, when the public-Good requires that the Calumnies of a dangerous Faction should be exposed in their true Colours to the public View—However, I am willing to yield to the better Judgemt. of yourself & the Friends you have alluded to—but I must insist on this—if they advise you not to defend yourself, that *they* shall defend you, and shall come forward and tell the Faction the bold Truths which they have advised you not to tell—

Adieu! my Friend—believe me yours—   JOHN PAGE

RC (DLC); endorsed by TJ as received 12 July 1798 and so recorded in SJL.

To Thomas Mann Randolph

TH:J. TO TMR.   Philadelphia June 21. 98.

Your's of the 10th. is recieved. I had expected mine of the 14th. would have been my last from here, as I had taken measures for my departure on the 20th. but on the 19th. in the morning we heard of mr Marshal's arrival at New-York, and I thought it better to remain and see whether that circumstance might engender any thing new, and in which I could be of any service. I have reason to believe he is much cooler than his friends wish. he certainly said, before he came here, that in France they had not the least idea of war with us. as yet I know not what are his informations to the government, nor in what shape they will use them to keep up the artificial inflammation they have excited. if nothing interesting to the public should be likely to arise, I may set out on Monday the 25th. in which case I should be with you on the 30th. but this is a little uncertain. mr Trist had been accidentally detained here longer than his day fixed for departure. I put your letter into his hands yesterday morning & he immediately set about procuring the articles. they will go round in the first vessel, in which I believe my workman will go also, rather than with me by the way of the stage. I am in hopes mr Eppes & Maria arrive with you this day and that I shall find them at Monticello. my tender love to my dear Martha & the little ones, and affectionate Adieu to yourself.   TH: JEFFERSON

Afternoon.

A message to both houses this day from the President with the following communications.

Mar. 23. Pickering's letter to the envoys, directing them if they are not actually engaged in negociation with authorised persons, or not conducted bonâ fide, & not merely for procrastination, to break up & come home, and at no rate to consent to any loan.

Apr. 3. Talleyrand to Gerry. he supposes the other two gentlemen, percieving that their known principles are an obstacle to negociation, will leave the republic, & proposes to renew the negociations with Gerry immedly.

Apr. 4. Gerry to Taleyrand. disclaims a power to conclude any thing separately. can only confer informally, & as an unaccredited individual, reserving to lay every thing before the government of the US. for approbation.

Apr. 14. Gerry to the Presidt. communicates the preceding & hopes the Presidt. will send other persons instead of his collegues & himself, if it shall appear that any thing can be done.

The President's message says that as the instructions were not to consent to any loan, he considers the negociation as at an end, & that he will never send another minister to France until he shall be assured that he will be recieved & treated with respect.

A bill is brought into the Senate this day to declare the treaty with France void, prefaced by a list of grievances in the style of a Manifesto. it passed to the 2d. reading by 14. to 5.

RC (DLC); endorsed by Randolph as received 30 June 1798. PrC (MHi); endorsed by TJ in ink on verso.

A letter from John Wayles EPPES to TJ of 6 June 1798, recorded in SJL as received by TJ on 19 June, has not been found.

To Peter Carr

DEAR SIR   Philadelphia June [2]2. [1798]

It is my expectation to leave this on the 25th. and to be at our July court. but something may very possibly arise which may keep me a few days longer. I must ask the favor of you therefore to press Kinsolving at court to pay up his balance, as I have considerable paiments to make immediately on my arrival at home. he may lodge the money with Colo. Bell. this being the last moment of the post I must refer you for news to mr Randolph to whom I have stated some interesting dispatches from mr Gerry. I am Dear Sir

Your affectionate friend & servt   TH: JEFFERSON

PrC (DLC); faint; at foot of text: "P. Carr"; endorsed by TJ in ink on verso as "June 22. 98."

TJ received £8 from James KINSOLVING during the summer—four transmitted by Thomas Carr on 12 Aug. and four by Wil-

liam Page on 4 Sep. 1798 (MB, 2:989, 990). For the Kinsolving debt, see TJ to James Lyle, 10 July 1795. REFER YOU FOR NEWS: see the preceding document.

A letter from TJ to Carr of 31 May 1798, recorded in SJL, has not been found.

From John Wickham

DEAR SIR,   Richmond 22d. June 1798.

By your Letter of the 15th. I find I did not make myself understood in my reply to your Letter requesting an Extension of the Time of payment of your Debt to Mr. Welch—though Counsel for Welch in all his Suits in the superior Courts I have nothing to do with the Collection of his Debts, that Business is done exclusively by Mr. Waller, to whom You will be pleased to address yourself on the Subject—I return You the order on Mr. Hooper which no doubt Mr. Waller will readily receive from You—

With much respect & Esteem I am Your obedt. Sevt

JNO WICKHAM

RC (MHi); at foot of text: "The Honble. Thos. Jefferson"; endorsed by TJ as received 12 July 1798 and so recorded in SJL. Enclosure not found.

To John Marshall

June 23. 98.

Th: Jefferson presents his compliments to General Marshall. he had the honor of calling at his lodgings twice this morning, but was so unlucky[1] as to find that he was out on both occasions. he wished to have expressed in person his regret that a preengagement for to-day which could not be dispensed with would prevent him the satisfaction of dining in company with Genl. Marshall, and therefore begs leave to place here the expressions of that respect which in common with his fellow citizens he bears him.

RC (Association for the Preservation of Virginia Antiquities, on deposit ViHi); addressed: "General Marshall at Oellers' hotel." Not recorded in SJL.

Marshall did not overlook the slip of the pen by which TJ initially declared himself

LUCKY to have missed seeing the returned envoy. According to Marshall's great-granddaughter, later in his life he "frequently laughed over it, saying, 'Mr. Jefferson came very near writing me the truth' " when he omitted the negative prefix, which "policy alone demanded" (Sallie E. Marshall Hardy, "John Marshall," *The Green Bag*, 8 [1896], 482-3; Marshall, *Papers*, 3:471n).

A letter from Marshall to TJ of 12 Apr.

1797, recorded in SJL as received on 21 Apr. of that year, has not been found.

[1] First syllable and hyphen interlined.

From Martha Jefferson Randolph

Bellmont Saturday Morning [23 June 1798]

It is easier to concieve than express the sensations with which the sight of the preparations for your return inspires us. I look forward to Theusday with raptures and palpitations not to be described; That day which will once more reunite me to those most dear to me in the world. adieu Dearest and adored Father the heart swellings with which I address you when absent and look forward to your return convince me of the folly or want of feeling of those who dare to Think that any *new* ties can weaken the first & best of nature—the first sensations of my life were affection and respect for you and none others in the course of it have weakened or[1] surpassed them.—The children all send there love to grand Papa and count the days with infinite anxiety. yours with the tenderest Love and reverence   M RANDOLPH

RC (MHi); partially dated, with 23 June being most likely; addressed: "Thomas Jefferson Vice President," with notation "by Jupiter"; endorsed by TJ as received 1 July 1798 and recorded in SJL as received at Fredericksburg.

[1] MS: "of."

From John Marshall

[24 June 1798]

J Marshall begs leave to accompany his respectful compliments, to Mr. Jefferson with assurances of the regret he feels at being absent when Mr. Jefferson did him the honor to call on him.

J Marshall is extremely sensible to the obliging expressions contain in Mr. Jeffersons polite billet of yesterday.

He sets out tomorrow for Winchester & woud with pleasure charge himself with any commands from Mr. Jefferson to that part of Virginia.

RC (DLC: TJ Papers, 102:17542); undated, but assigned on the basis of the internal reference to TJ to Marshall, 23 June 1798; endorsed by TJ: "Marshal John. probably in 97."

To Philip Nolan

SIR   Philadelphia June 24. 1798

It is some time since I have understood that there are large herds of horses, in a wild state, in the country West of the Missisipi, and have been desirous of obtaining details of their history in that state. mr Brown, Senator from Kentuckey, informs me it would be in your power to give interesting information on this subject, and encourages me to ask it. the circumstances of the old world have, beyond the records of history, been such as admitted not that animal to exist in a state of nature. the condition of America is rapidly advancing to the same. the present then is probably the only moment in the age of the world, and the herds abovementioned the only subjects, of which we can avail ourselves to obtain what has never yet been recorded and never can be again in all probability. I will add that your information is the sole reliance, as far as I can at present see, for obtaining this desideratum. you will render to Natural [his]tory a very acceptable service therefore, if you will enable our Philosophical-society to add so interesting a chapter to the history of [. . .] animal. I need not specify to you the particular facts asked [for?] as your knowledge of the animal in his domesticated, as well as [his] wild state, will naturally have led your attention to those particulars in the manners, habits, & laws of his existence, which are peculiar to his wild state. I wish you not to be anxious about the form of your information. the exactness of the substance alone is material: and if, after giving in a first [. . .] all the facts you at present possess, you could be so good, on subsequent occasions as to furnish such others in addition as you may acquire from time to time, your communications will always be thankfully recieved. if addressed to me at Monticello & put into any post office of Kentucky or Tenissee, they will reach me speedily & safely, and will be considered as obligations on Sir

Your most obedt. humble servt   TH: JEFFERSON

PrC (DLC); torn; at foot of text: "Mr. Nolan."

Little is known of the origins of Philip Nolan (ca. 1771-1801), a native of Northern Ireland. By the late 1780s he served as James Wilkinson's bookkeeper and business agent in New Orleans, where he disguised Spanish payments to Wilkinson as the proceeds of tobacco speculation. In 1791 Nolan began the first of a series of prolonged trading forays from Natchez, entering Texas with goods and returning with mustang horses. When TJ wrote the above letter Nolan was on an expedition in which he collected more than a thousand horses. Although Nolan obtained passports for his early trips, Spanish authorities grew suspicious of his facility at playing different officials off against one another and his evident connection to the American surveyor Andrew Ellicott. With a party of armed men but lacking safe-conduct papers, Nolan again went to Texas in the autumn of 1800 and began to round up horses. In March of the following year he was killed by soldiers

[425]

dispatched from Nacogdoches. The expectation of TJ and others that Nolan might provide detailed information about various aspects of the natural history of the western regions was never realized (ANB, 16:479-81; William Dunbar to TJ, 22 Aug. 1801).

At a small dinner party hosted on 1 Mch. 1798 by geologist William Maclure, TJ exhibited his interest in the wild HORSES that roamed the western plains. A year earlier Wilkinson had informed TJ of Nolan's travels, and in all likelihood Volney had encountered Nolan in Kentucky in 1796. On 12 Feb. 1799 Daniel Clark of New Orleans answered the above letter on behalf of Nolan, who seems never to have written TJ himself. Over a year later Wilkinson expected the horsetrader, one of whose associates also knew about American Indian sign languages of interest to TJ, to pay the vice president a visit. However, Nolan apparently changed his plans and never made the call, disappointing TJ in his hope of purchasing a mustang for use as a saddle horse (Niemcewicz, *Under their Vine*, 46-7; Dan L. Flores, ed., *Jefferson & Southwestern Exploration: The Freeman & Custis Accounts of the Red River Expedition of 1806* [Norman, Okla., 1984], 32-3, 131-2n; Dan L. Flores, ed., *Journal of an Indian Trader: Anthony Glass and the Texas Trading Frontier, 1790-1810* [College Station, Tex., 1985], 13, 103-4n; Volney to TJ, 24 Aug. 1796; TJ to Dunbar, 16 Jan. 1800; Wilkinson to TJ, 22 May, 1 Sep. 1800).

To John Read

SIR   Philadelphia June 25. 1798

I have read & considered the paragraph extracted from a letter written by me while in Europe to Mr Jones, of the house of Farrell & Jones of Bristol: and though I have not here the whole letter to turn to, I recognize the paragraph, & what it's meaning was. it is shortly expressed; but so as to have been well understood by Mr Jones & myself, who knew the facts & the laws alluded to—to others to whom these are less known, some explanation may be necessary.

Mr Wayles died in 1773. indebted to Farrell & Jones about 8 or 9000 £ sterling the third of this debt devolved on me. I sold lands in 1774. more than sufficient to discharge my portion of it, & took bonds for the price. Mr Evans, named in the paragraph, was the then agent of F. & J. I pressed him to accept an assignment of the bonds and to discharge me, observing that the obligors were as sure as myself, & that it would relieve me, without injuring his employers. he refused. on the first appearance of troubles (in 1775. I think) he went off to England. I cannot here state the time when the debtors paid me their money: but it was after great depreciation incurred, & before the law of Virginia was passed establishing a scale of depreciation. on these facts, well known to Mr Jones & myself, the true meaning of the paragraph will be intelligible to others also. had Evans accepted assignments of the bonds, so that the debts would have been turned over to F. & J. as he immediately went off and no other agent was appointed by them, till Mr Hanson was, after the peace, the debts would have remained unpaid till the peace for want of a receiver, and then would have been recoverable by Jones in sterling Money under the treaty: or if the debtors had paid into the treasury in depreciated money, their debts would still have been recovered under the treaty in sterling money. in either case, I should have been saved from a second sale of property which I was obliged to make after the peace, to pay the debt a second time; Mr Jones would have received, and the debtors would have paid their debt fully, & thus justice would have been done all round. as it was, I lost the amount of the debt, because it was paid to me nominally before the Virginia depreciation law was passed. & when that was enacted it did not authorize a retrospect on debts nominally paid up, tho in depreciated paper.

I will take this occasion of adding some further particulars on the subject of this debt. it was amicably settled with Mr Hanson immediately on my return to America, in Jan. or Feb. 1790. about a twelve-month after the commencement of the present government. the whole debt was by that time got up again, I think to about £9000 ster. (without war interest) according to their statement. the war-interest he agreed readily to relinquish. and, within the time stipulated with Mr Hanson I put into his hands bonds, under my ultimate guarantee, for property again sold, to the whole amount of my portion of the debt, except £80 or £100. which I wished him to receive from the treasury of Virginia. he agreed not to call on us for the money, unless the obligors failed after full prosecutions at law by him. these prosecutions have taken time; but the debts were so solid that not a shilling of them will be lost.

It may be asked why should the Agent of Mr Jones have accepted any thing short of ready money paiment? I answer, on principles of morality, as well as of expedience. Mr Wayles had for a very great number of years been a most friendly, meritorious, and valuable customer to F. & J. as a shipper of tobacco. they had made a great deal of money out of him. there is a moral duty of indulgence towards such a customer. Moreover, the year after he died, we shipped them 400 hhds of tobo. most of which they credited after the peace, only at antient prices. we believed that such probable proof of the real proceeds of this tobacco could have been obtained as would have convinced impartial judges that the debt was fully discharged. we waived however all dispute of the account, and accepted the accommodations yielded us on the other side.

The other case on which you ask information was this. a consignment was made to mr Wayles and Richard Randolph for sale & collection. these two gentlemen had no connection in any business with one another, nor were previously consulted about being made joint consignees on this occasion, it was an association of the Consignor's own choice, flowing from his seperate confidence in each they sold the property, but, before collection, mr Wayles died, and the whole authority and profit of the consignment survived to Randolph, who collected the debts, as has been said, and, before accounting for them, died, under great embarrasments if not bankrupt. it was never pretended, by any body, that one joint consignee, under these circumstances, is responsible for the proceedings of the other, any more than one executor or attorney is for the waste of another. but mr Hanson laid hold of a loose expression in a letter of mr Wayles's to F. & J. by which he contended that mr Wayles had assumed upon himself to answer for Randolph, tho never desired by F. & J. and tho' the letter was after the consignment made. it is unnecessary here to go into the many circumstances of evidence that this letter was no assumpsit. mr Hanson however sued on it. mr Wayles's exors denied that their testator was bound for Randolph. and so 11. of the jury, & the court agreed, at the first hearing. but one juror dissenting, the cause laid over, and was tried again at the next Federal court, when a second jury, with the approbation of the court, found a verdict in favor of Wayles's exors, to wit, that their testator was not answerable.

I am not able at this time & place to give a certain answer as to the remaining part of your letter. it shall be the subject of my enquiry when I return to Virginia, & if I can obtain information of precision to be relied on, I will communicate it.

I am with esteem Sir your most obedt. servt.   TH: JEFFERSON

Tr (PRO: T 79/30); part of the claim of John Tyndale Warre; in an unidentified hand; at foot of first page: "Mr Read"; endorsed in a clerk's hand.

Delaware native John Read (1769-1854), the son of George Read, practiced law in Philadelphia beginning in 1792. From 1797 to 1809 he was general agent for the settlement of British debt claims under Article 6 of the Jay Treaty. Afterward he held office at the city and state level and was a bank director and president (DAB). The PARAGRAPH EXTRACTED FROM A LETTER that TJ wrote to William JONES, then the surviving partner of Farell & Jones, was probably the third paragraph of a letter of 5 Jan. 1787; see Vol. 11:15-16. Thomas EVANS had acted as the English firm's agent in Virginia until his death, ca. 1778 (Vol. 15:673). In 1790 TJ and the other executors of John Wayles's estate, Frances Eppes and Henry Skipwith, AMICABLY SETTLED

their father-in-law's debt to the firm, the result of Wayles's marketing of tobacco to Farell & Jones in exchange for goods and credit, by agreeing on terms with Evans's successor, Richard Hanson. Each executor undertook to pay one-third of the principle and the accrued interest, which would not be charged for the period of the American Revolution, and each would pay in installments guaranteed by bond (see Vol. 15:674-6).

The OTHER CASE involved the CONSIGNMENT of 280 Africans brought to Virginia aboard The Prince of Wales in 1772. The consignors were not Farell & Jones but another Bristol firm, John Powell & Co., which had experience in the African and West Indian trade and owned the ship. But Farell & Jones arranged the transaction, pairing two of their Virginia customers, Wayles and Richard Randolph, as agents for the sale of the Africans into slavery. Powell required security, and Farell & Jones undertook that obligation, as they informed Wayles and Randolph, *"on your behalf's."* After Wayles's death in 1773, however, almost no remittance from the sales, which totaled more than £7,000 sterling, arrived from Virginia. Although there was no bond securing the obligation, Farell & Jones paid more than £6,000 sterling to Powell's firm. "We can truly say we never experienced a more disagreeable transaction in our Lives," Farell & Jones complained (Walter Minchinton, Celia King, and Peter Waite, eds., *Virginia Slave-Trade Statistics 1698-1775* [Richmond, 1984], 184-5; David Richardson, ed., *Bristol, Africa and the Eighteenth-Century Slave Trade to America*, Vol. 4: *The Final Years, 1770-1807* [Bristol, 1996], 37; Kenneth Morgan, *Bristol and the Atlantic Trade in the Eighteenth Century* [Cambridge, 1993], 144; Vol. 15:651-5, 664, 666, 676-7).

As the agent and attorney of Farell & Jones, Hanson sought compensation from Randolph, from his estate after his death, and from Wayles's estate, and after Farell's and Jones's deaths Hanson pursued the claim on behalf of John Tyndale Warre, Jones's executor. Throughout, TJ argued that responsibility for the collection of the sale payments, and for remittance of the money to England, had on Wayles's death devolved entirely upon Randolph. Wayles's estate could only be held accountable if he had collected payments and failed to remit the money, which was not the case. Hanson founded the firm's claim on the statement by Wayles that TJ dismissed as a LOOSE EXPRESSION: Wayles had offered Farell & Jones "every Assurance," as he wrote them on 14 May 1772, "that whatever engagement you may be kind enough to enter into on our behalf shall be complied with without inconvenience or prejudice to yourselves" (Vol. 15:653). In a detailed letter of 6 May 1791 TJ assured Skipwith that neither under common law nor in equity could that comment, which in any event was made after the consignment had already been arranged, place Wayles's estate under an obligation to make good on Randolph's sale of the slaves. John Marshall, who with Andrew Ronald acted as legal counsel for Wayles's executors, initially thought the Farell & Jones claim might have some validity, but by 1796 he agreed with TJ. Yet

while staunchly holding to his position TJ recognized that "all things are possible," including a legal victory for Hanson. Therefore in 1796 he quietly mortgaged most of his slaves to prevent their seizure if Hanson succeeded in winning a court judgment (TJ to James Lyle, 12 May 1796; Marshall, *Papers*, 2:89-90, 304; Vol. 29:197n).

Disputing the estate's responsibility for the *Prince of Wales* consignment, TJ and his brothers-in-law specifically excluded the transaction from the 1790 agreement with Hanson that resolved payment of Wayles's individual trading debts to Farell & Jones. Recognizing along with many others in Virginia that Randolph's disposition of property before his death in 1786 had sheltered his estate's assets from seizure by creditors (see Bill in Chancery of Wayles's Executors against the Heirs of Richard Randolph, [on or before 2 Mch. 1795]), Hanson aggressively sought to make Wayles's estate liable. Even before American courts opened to British creditors he yearned to bring suit. Declaring that he would "not be trifled with," he brushed aside TJ's "absurd arguments" and stated that "as the proofs are so numerous and Clear . . . it is one of the first suits I shall bring" (Hanson to the firm, 20 Dec. 1784, 25 Oct. 1785, 20 Dec. 1788, 8 May 1789, extracts in Warre claim papers, PRO: T 79/30). Obtaining Jerman Baker's services as attorney, in 1790 Hanson filed lawsuits against Wayles's and Randolph's estates in U.S. Circuit Court. Wayles's executors seemed as eager as Hanson was to go to trial: he thought they were anxious to resolve the matter before all hope of recovery from Randolph's assets drained away, in case a judgment should go against both estates. Yet as the suit progressed Hanson found that presenting his case required depositions and original documents not easily obtained from overseas. The press to resolve the matter worked in the defendants' favor, and Hanson repeatedly found himself asking for continuations. Finally, the FIRST HEARING of the suit against TJ and his fellow executors came during the May 1797 term, occupying a full day of the court's calendar. By this time Hanson's counsel included U.S. Attorney General Charles Lee, who could not attend. The court refusing Hanson's request for a jury consisting entirely of merchants, he instead saw his case given to a panel of "Brutes," who after five days of deliberation could not resolve a split of eleven to one against his cause. "A Jury of a very low Class of people," Hanson declared it, "many of which attends every Court to get a Dollar a day for serving and determined not to give a Verdict for a British debt." The suit was retried in December 1797, when the SECOND JURY found that Wayles's estate owed nothing to Farell & Jones for the slave cargo of *The Prince of Wales*. In the separate lawsuit against Randolph's executors, a jury awarded Hanson and his employers a judgment for more than $52,000, but only because, Hanson was convinced, the Randolph estate was insolvent and no money would actually change hands (Hanson to the firm, 1, 17 Mch., 3 June, 26 July 1790, 31 Dec. 1794, 10 July, 30 Nov. 1795, 2 June, 15 Dec. 1797, extracts in same; Rule Book No. 1 and Order Books Nos. 1-3 in Vi: USCC).

As early as July 1795 Hanson viewed the bilateral commission provided for by the Jay Treaty, which first met in Philadelphia in May 1797, as his recourse for any debt claims rejected by the American courts. "My great dependance is on the Commissioners," he noted after the first trial of the suit against Wayles's executors ended in the deadlocked jury. By early in June 1798 he gave Read vouchers for the many claims that were still outstanding in the American accounts of Farell & Jones. It was evidently an inquiry from Read that prompted TJ to write the letter above. However, the debts commission, rent by disagreement between its American and British members, dissolved before it could rule on most of the applications before it (see TJ to Madison, 16 Jan. 1799). In 1802 the U.S. agreed to pay British creditors an indemnification of £600,000 sterling, to be allocated by a panel in Britain. The claims allowed by that new commission totaled a vastly larger sum, more than £1.4 million sterling. Warre's claims were for at least £89,800 sterling, of which the commission allowed £35,000, entitling him to a £16,255 share of the indemnification (Hanson to Warre, 21 July 1795, 2 June 1797, 25 June 1798, 8 Aug. 1799, in Warre claim, PRO: T 79/30; John Bassett Moore, ed., *International Adjudications: Ancient and Modern, History and Documents*, 6 vols. [New York, 1929-33] 3:9, 22, 339, 340, 422, 430; Perkins, *First Rapprochement*, 117-19, 140-1).

Documents relating to the trial are in Vi: USCC. In those records another suit by Farell & Jones against Wayles's executors, involving a bond of John Randolph, is similarly titled and appeared in some of the same terms of the court (for that case, see TJ to Francis Eppes, 28 Aug. 1794). In the voluminous papers of Warre's claims in behalf of Farell & Jones in PRO: T 79/30, including Hanson's correspondence, the *Prince of Wales* debt is sometimes labeled the "African" account, evidently so called because the firm's transactions did not usually involve slaves.

YOUR LETTER: Read's letter to TJ, which according to SJL was written and received on this day, has not been found.

From John Taylor

JOHN TAYLOR TO THE VICE PRESIDENT   Caroline June 25. 1798.

The observations contained in yours of the 4th. instant, upon my letter to Colo. New, induce me to say something respecting our political situation, explanatory of one idea in that letter, of which you evidently disapprove. Convinced of the caution imposed on you by the malevolence of party, I have forborne the liberty I am now about to take; but considering your interrogations as permissive, I will candidly state some of the considerations, which may perhaps have led me into error.

The party spirit amongst us is geographical or personal. If geographical, its superiority in either hemisphere, will beget the insolence of tyranny and the misery of slavery. A fluctuation of this superiority, will enlist revenge as an auxiliary passion, and annihilate the chance for human happiness.

If our party spirit is personal, it must arise from interest. This interest proceeds also from some cause. If the evil is in human nature, it may yet admit of alleviation. But if it springs from political encouragement, it is the work of art, and by art may be counteracted.

That parties, sufficiently malignant to destroy the public good, are not naturally the issue of every popular government, seems to be evinced by the examples of the State governments, and particularly by the eminent example of Connecticut, which has for about two centuries enjoyed a compleat unanimity under a government, the most democratic of any representative form which ever existed. And that parties may be artificially produced by the scheme of ballancing power against power, is equally evinced by the example of England. Is it not possible, that our great error has been an imitation of the latter precedent, by counterpoising power against power, instead of securing to liberty an ascendant over power, whether simple or complex.

What are checks and ballances, but party and faction? If a good form of government too often fails, in making bad men good; a bad form of government will too often succeed in making good men bad. Activity can only be bestowed upon these checks and ballances by the exhibition of a prize. The prize can only consist of public property. This activity is then an Evidence, that a constitution has staked its existence, upon the existence of faction and party, and that it ensures their existence, by purchasing it with public rights and wealth.

If in case of a scission of the union, party spirit would still be natural, how can it be said that our present situation, the characteristic of which is party spirit, is unnatural? Admiting the former position, nature, and not [the] administration, is accountable for the evil. Admiting the idea of geographical parties, as unavoidable in any stated association, it allows that such an association is geographically unnatural, as would be an union between France and England. Under either admission, a reference to corruption and cupidity as the cause of party, is defeated, whence it would result, that all complaints of mal-administration, are groundless.

Indeed I am unable to discuss any natural political state; not only as a political state is the antithesis to a state of nature, but as all countries and nations seem liable to revolutions in government, and even in character, from artificial causes.

Can even a good administration defeat a constitutional encouragement of wicked propensities; or does a change of men, operate any lasting change of government?

Admiting (as is conceded by a portion of your observations) that individuals have robbed liberty of its ascendancy, so as to be able to convert the resources of the nation to the purpose of buying and supporting a party, can any remedy exist, except that of depriving individuals of this ascendency, and restoring it, not to other individuals, but to liberty? What endowed them with it? The form of government. What will deprive them of it? A reformation in that form.—A transference of this ascendency to other individuals, will change the tyrant, but not remove the Evil. Did the British people ever gain by a change of ministry? Saturated, are preferable to hungry flies. A southern aristocracy, oppressing the northern States, would be as detestable, as a northern, domineering over the Southern States.

And what is the proper time for opposing this ascendancy? Shall it be suffered to run through its natural course? How many years will bring it to decrepitude? Let England and all personal ascendancies reply. Let the ancient and modern systems of villenage, illustrate. Let them prove that such usurpations upon the rights of man, are more assailable, the more they are matured.

If the mass of our citizens are now republican, will submission to ante-republican measures, encrease that mass? Where are the converts made during the late eventful periods by this policy? Has it not already lost the advantage of the locality of political opinion in some degree? A fact, which violently opposes the idea, that party spirit is simply the child of nature, and evidently refers its origin to artifice and management.

To preserve therefore the purity of the sound members, which now comprise a majority, and by their help to administer medicine to the unsound, seems to be the only mode of restoring the body to health, before the primæ vitæ are irreparably contaminated.

For it is my poor impression, both that parties, sufficiently malignant to End in political exacerbation, are not natural to a republican government, really dependant on natural will, and also that there is nothing supernatural in the party paroxysm which now exists. If it arises from political causes, the cure must lie in the abolition of those causes; but if it is indeed owing to witchcraft, the spell must be broken by incantations on the part of the republic. Every common rifle-man knows, that when his gun is deprived of its propine by a spell, his remedy is to call in the aid of some conjurer, more powerful than him who laid it on.

Does not your position "that the party game is for principles," countenance this current of ideas? Is it natural for all republicks to be divided upon fundamental principles? May not art and corruption produce such a division? Is man's natural propensity for liberty, a sufficient curb upon this art and corruption? Monarchy will answer these questions. And let it prove if it can, that an union in political principle is natural to man under a monarchy, but unnatural, under a republick. of this I must doubt, until I see a republick so organized by annual & rotary offices— by breaking the intail of tax laws—and by equal representation, as to retain for the people, a real influence over the government. Constitutional paper vetos, are nothing, compared with a solid check, so woven into the form of government, as to be incapable of a separation from it.

You will evidently see, that the perfection, and not the scission of the union, was the object of the letter you[1] refer to; to which End, an appretiation of the strength of its soundest parts, will probably tend. A probability, of which the reigning power is so well convinced, that it omits no means tending to its depreciation.

If persons, as well as principles are threatened, does not even self-preservation call for some measures. As to these I have opinions, but unless you should patronize efforts of the kind, I am convinced that they will prove abortive, and would of [course] aggravate the Evil. For I must candidly declare, that I believe the chance is against a hope, that an individual will in a century, again unite the principles, powers, and confidence, adequate to such an undertaking.

These measures ought to lead to an amendment of the constitution, if party and persecution are its offspring. A variety of alterations might apply to the evil.

1. An extension of the right of suffrage, and an abbreviation of the term of service.
2. Rotation in office. If kings find it necessary to change vicegerents to preserve power, let the people proffit from the prudence of princes. Is not merit in office more likely to seduce the people, than to deceive kings? The sole subject upon which talents operate, whether they be exerted to usurp upon despotism, or upon liberty, is the people.
3. A new mode of abrogating law. Why ought not the mode of repeal, to be naturalised with the mode of legislating? The concurrence in favor of existence, ought to be the same, with that necessary for creation. The existence of a bad law, cannot require a less check than its passage, unless experience is more liable to error, than speculation; unless mankind are more injured by the creation of bad laws, than by their continuance.

[433]

If each enacting power could discontinue a law, it would beget a new check upon party and faction, by rendering advantages obtained under the influence of circumstances, by fraud, or by surprise, more insecure.

4. Annual tax laws. Standing armies are one cause of oppressive taxation. We prohibit one cause, but tolerate the evil. Armies shall only be temporary, lest they perpetuate oppressive taxes, yet the taxes may be perpetuated under any other pretext.

Taxes are the subsistence of party. As the miasma of marshes contaminate the human body, those of taxes corrupt and putrify the body politic. Taxation transfers wealth from a mass to a selection. It destroys the political Equality, which alone can save liberty; and yet no constitution, whilst devising checks upon power, has devised checks sufficiently strong upon the means which create it. Government, endowed with a right to transfer, bestow, and monopolise wealth in perpetuity is in fact, unlimited. It soon becomes a feudal lord over a nation in villenage. Proffit, to be derived from a combination between the soil and the cultivator, constituted the essence of villenage. Power has altered the mode of extorting this proffit, from a regard to the interest of the master, and not to the interest of the slave. Ignorant and barbarous power adheres to the ancient system of villenage, whilst the more artful, but not less despotic rulers of man, have discovered that he may be turned to greater account, by allowing him a nominal liberty, as an excitement to labor. Thus a nation becomes the vassal of a combination, cold, pitiless and insatiable. Thus a temporary mitigation from individual benevolence, with which the feudal system was adorned; and a chance of its subversion from its solitary weakness, by which it was restrained, are ravished from hopeless man. Avarice and ambition, entrenched behind perpetual taxation, in a disciplined corps, have become the Lords paramount of the creation.

The limits of a letter forbid an enumeration of other remedies for the evil of party. The right of the State governments to expound the constitution, might possibly be made the basis of a movement towards its amendment. If this is insufficient, the people in state conventions, are incontrovertibly the contracting parties, and possessing the impinging rights, may proceed by orderly steps to attain the object.

I doubt whether I ought to apologise for this letter, long as it is, because Every one has a right to explain himself—because your letter seemed to invite me to it—and because your charity will indulge me in the relief, afforded by prefering a portion of my political grief, towards the great hope for redress. But since government is geting into the habit of peeping into private letters, and is manufacturing a law, which may even make it criminal to pray to God for better times, I shall be careful not to repeat so dangerous a liberty.—I hope it may not be criminal to add a suplication for an individual—not—for I will be cautious—as a republican, but as a man.

May happiness & prosperity be your lot.

RC (DLC); frayed margins; endorsed by TJ as received 19 July 1798 and so recorded in SJL.

[1] Taylor here canceled several illegible words.

To George Jefferson

DEAR SIR   Philadelphia June. 26. 98.

This will be handed you by mr James Dinsmore, a housejoiner whom I have engaged to live with me. he goes by water to Richmond and on his arrival there, being a stranger, I have desired him to ask your aid to get him a passage by a waggon or boat to our neighborhood. he has in his charge some articles of mine, of value, which I wish him to keep with him to my house. I wish him not to delay in Richmond. I do not know that he will want any pecuniary aid, as he will recieve here what he may think he will have occasion for. but should he need any small matter & ask for it, be so good as to let him have it on my account. I am Dr. Sir

Your's affectionately   TH: JEFFERSON

P.S. I set out for Monticello tomorrow morning.

PrC (MHi); torn; in ink at foot of text: "Mr. G. Jeffe[rson]"; endorsed by TJ in ink on verso.

Statement of Account from John Francis

1798 Thos. Jefferson Esqr. Vice President of the United
    States to John Francis   Dr.
    To Use of his rooms & Board for himself & Servant
    from the 12th. of Decr. 1797 to the 19th. of June 1798.

27 weeks at 26 Dollars per week	D 702.
Wine "&" Poter @ *2.80. D per week or .40 c per day*[1]	75.50
Candles @ *.27 cents per week*	7.25
Fire-wood 20 Weeks @ *3.60 D*	72
To pd. for Magazines	1
	857.75
Cr. by Cash	620.
due	237.75
To rooms 4 Weeks at 13 Dollars	52.
	289.75
To week 26. D. wine &c. 3.25	*29.25*
	319

MS (MHi); date supplied from TJ's financial memoranda (see below); in an unknown hand, with additions by TJ shown in italics (see note 1); endorsed by TJ: "Francis John."

Before his departure from Philadelphia on 27 June TJ made an order on John Barnes for $319 to pay Francis "in full." Since his last settlement of accounts with the hotelkeeper on 3 July 1797, TJ had written drafts on Barnes to pay Francis $120 on 14 Jan., $200 on 17 Feb., $100 on 6 Apr., and $200 on 9 May (all in MHi, written and signed by TJ, endorsed by Barnes and canceled; MB, 2:965, 977, 979, 981, 983, 986). In another draft on Barnes written on 9 Jan. 1799 TJ ordered payment of $150 to Francis (MS in ViU: Edgehill-Randolph Papers, written and signed by TJ, endorsed by Barnes and signed by Francis on verso).

[1] Here and below, text and figures in italics are in TJ's hand.

From John Brown

DEAR SIR.   Phila. 29th. June 1798

    The Letter herewith inclosed was this day handed to me by Mr Baldwin to be forwarded to you. He recd. it from Mr Lee through a Chanel which forbids him to suspect that it has passed through the hands of the *Inquisition.* To avoid the probable effects of illiberal curiosity so prevalent at the present day, I shall put this packet under Cover addressed to our mutual friend Colo. Bell of Charlottesville with request to give it a safe conveyance to you—

Mr Sedgewick (ex Member) was by 12 Votes placed in the Chair as President pro tem—From the symptoms he exhibits I fear his Head, of which you know he has been long complaining, will derive no advantage from this elevation.—Lloyds famous Treason Bill is still with the Committee to whom it was refered. It excites much attention in this City, & having been extensively circulated in connection with Traceys Speech, will make in all probability considerable impression upon the public Mind.

No arrivals from Europe since you left us.—

I have the Honor to be with esteem Sir Yo Mo Obt. & Hble Sert.

J. BROWN

RC (DLC); at foot of text: "Tho Jefferson Esqr."; endorsed by TJ as received 26 July 1798 and so recorded in SJL. Enclosures: Joel Barlow to TJ, 12 Mch. 1798 (two letters), and enclosure.

On 27 June, the day TJ left Philadelphia, the Senate elected Theodore Sedgwick president pro tempore. James Lloyd had introduced his TREASON BILL the day before, and on 27 June it was referred to a committee consisting of Lloyd, Uriah Tracy, and other Federalists. As introduced, the bill defined the giving of "aid and comfort" to the government or people of France or its dependencies as treason, punishable by death, and provided a definition and punishment for sedition. The committee dropped the sections relating to treason, but retained the provisions on seditious libel. The Senate

passed the bill on 4 July, the House approved it, and on 14 July it went into effect as the Sedition Act (JS, 2:518-20; Smith, *Freedom's Fetters*, 107-11; Syrett, *Hamilton*, 21:522-3n; U.S. Statutes at Large, 1:596-7; MB, 2:986).

TRACEYS SPEECH: in the Senate on 23 June, in debate on the bill to void the treaties with France, Tracy called the French "a race of reprobates" marked by "their notorious baseness, their perfidy, their audacity and their want of all sense of religious or moral obligation." He called for "a war of EXTINGUISHMENT" and, as reported by the *Aurora* on 26 June, declared his wish "to put arms in the hand of every man, *every woman* and of *every child* in America, against every man, *every woman* and *every child* in France."

Certificate for
John and Gabriella Brockenbrough

The bearers hereof Doctr. Brockenborough and mrs Gabriella Brockenborough his lady, proposing to visit Europe for the benefit of mrs Brockenborough's health, I Thomas Jefferson hereby certify to all whom it may concern, that they are citizens of the commonwealth of Virginia in the United States of America, of distinction for their wealth, connections & respectability of character, & worthy the hospitality & protection of the laws, government & citizens of the countries they may have occasion to visit; and as such they are recommended, with an assurance that the laws, government & citizens of the United states are in the habit of reciprocating to strangers the good offices which it is pleasing to them should be rendered to their fellow citizens travelling in foreign countries. Given under my hand and seal at Alexandria in Virginia this 29th. day of June 1798   TH: JEFFERSON

MS (NHi); entirely in TJ's hand; with TJ's seal affixed. Not recorded in SJL.

John Brockenbrough, Jr., son of Dr. John Brockenbrough of Tappahannock, Virginia, received his medical degree from Edinburgh in 1795. He settled and developed a medical practice in Richmond, where he served as president of the Bank of Virginia for almost 40 years. Active in Virginia Republican party politics as a member of the Richmond or Essex junto, he became a close friend of John Randolph of Roanoke and supported Monroe in his 1808 campaign for the presidency. Gabriella Brockenbrough was the daughter of John Harvie, Jr., and the second wife of Thomas Mann Randolph, Sr., whom she married in 1790, reportedly being less than half his age. They had a daughter, who died in infancy, and one son, Thomas Mann Randolph, a half-brother of TJ's son-in-law of the same name, before Randolph's death in 1793. Randolph of Roanoke described her as "a mind of a very high order: well improved and manners that a queen might envy" (Wyndham B. Blanton, *Medicine in Virginia in the Eighteenth Century* [Richmond, 1931], 86-7, 337; same, *Medicine in Virginia in the Nineteenth Century* [Richmond, 1933], 367; Thomas Mann Randolph, Jr. to TJ, 30 Nov. 1793; WMQ, 1st ser., 11 [1903], 125; Ammon, *Monroe*, 273; Gaines, *Randolph*, 32, 38; Hugh A. Garland, *The Life of John Randolph of Roanoke*, 2 vols. [New York, 1857], 2:22; Jonathan Daniels, *The Randolphs of Virginia* [New York, 1972], xii, 130-1, 133, 143, 195, 256; Virginius Dabney, *Richmond: The Story of a City* [New York, 1976), 66, 84.

From Stevens Thomson Mason

DEAR SIR   Phila. June 29th 1798

Your prediction was speedily verified, the same day you left us, Fenno's paper contained an address to you. pressing you not to go. and honoring You with some of their common-place abuse. we have no late intelligence from Europe. a number of Refugees, (Royalists & Negroes) from Port au Prince. have on the evacuation of that place by the British been sent here with a letter of introduction to R Liston. who has been interceding with the Executive for their admission the subject has been referred by the Presdt to Congress and yesterday a Bill was introduced in the Senate to restrain their landing (except such as the Presdt may permit) this Bill is prefaced by a long preamble abusing the *French* and justifying the act as a measure of retaliation or revenge or something agt them. tho' it is notoriously a British favor attempted to be conferred on us. I am Dear Sir

With great respect & esteem Your Obt Sert

               STES: THON: MASON

RC (DLC); endorsed by TJ as received 18 July 1798 and so recorded in SJL.

The ADDRESS to TJ, which took the form of a letter from "Pliny" dated 26 June, mockingly beseeched him not to leave Philadelphia "at this critical period," and particularly when Bache was about to stand trial for libel. The letter emphasized TJ's connections to the *Aurora*, along with his and Bache's support of Monroe, George Logan, and France. "Pliny" also presumed—probably incorrectly, as indicated in the note to TJ's letter to John Wise of 12 Feb. 1798—that TJ was the author of letters to correspondents in Baltimore and Delaware that had appeared in the *Aurora* in March and April (*Gazette of the United States*, 27 June 1798).

Adams notified Congress of the situation regarding the REFUGEES from Saint-Domingue on 27 June. The committee to which the matter was referred reported the BILL the following day, and by unanimous consent the Senate waived a second reading. On the 29th Mason attempted to amend the bill's PREAMBLE, which stated that although the United States had extended hospitality to French citizens seeking asylum, it was prudent to "guard against the arrival and admission of such evil disposed persons as, by their machinations, may endanger the internal safety and tranquillity of the country," but his effort lost on a tie vote. The bill, which would have empowered the president to "prevent or regulate the landing of French passengers," passed the Senate on 30 June, but the House declined to consider the matter during the current session (JS, 2:520-3, 525).

A letter from Mason to TJ, written and received on 2 Feb. 1798, is recorded in SJL but has not been found.

Memorandum of Expenses in Philadelphia

[June 1798]

Expences. Philada.

Dawson gives for 2. furnished rooms on the second floor in 8th. street 7. Doll. a week, without board.[1] Innes & his son give 14. D. a week for board & 2. excellent rooms furnishd. at mrs Lawson's 4th. street. 2 very good rooms therefore genteely furnished, without board may be said 10.

Bossèe (5th. street) will furnish a soupe, 2 dishes of meat [entrées] (of which one may be Bouillie if desired) & 2 dishes of vegetables [   ] for one person 2. D. a day, per week 14.

2 ℔ butter .50 7 ℔ bread .50 coffee .18 sugar .18   1.36

2. servants. board   5.

    wages for 1. of them, being extra. <u>2.50</u>   <u>7.50</u>

                                                           32.86

I pay Francis for rooms, & board for self & servt.   30.

MS (DLC); entirely in TJ's hand; undated; brackets in original; endorsed by TJ: "Expences. Phila. estimate June. 1798."

[1] TJ here canceled "this is reckoning the room."

BOUILLIE: stewed beef.

From Henry Tazewell

DEAR SIR   Philadelphia 5. July 1798.

The inclosed, will shew you the state in which the Senate yesterday passed Mr Loyd's Sedition Bill—The passage of this Bill thro the Senate excited some clamour in the City, and this has begotten a belief that the measure will not obtain the sanction of the H of R—The question however for its second reading obtained to day 36 to 47—I am not quite sure that the Bill will finally assume the shape of a Law—My present beleif is, that it will pass, and that it will be executed with unrelenting fury—Its passage thro the Senate is an unauspicious event to have happened on the 4th. of July—

A very few days after you left us, General Washington was nominated as Lieutenant Genl. and Commander in chief of the armies raised, and to be raised in the UStates—There was no objection made to this nomination in the Senate, except as to the manner of it—By some of us, it was supposed that the Constitution had made the President Commander in cheif of the Armies, and that that power could not be transferred to another—I moved a concurrence under that Idea, but my proposition was determined not to be in order, and could not find a place on the Journal—After some verbal protests agt. the form of the nomination, it was acceded to, una voce, and Genl Washington is again the chief Commander of the Armies of the UStates—I do not beleive it is known whether he will, or will not, accept this appointment,—No answer could be obtained to that inquiry—and Reed being among the number of the inquirers, led me to suspect that the fact had not been ascertained—Report says he will accept, and that Hamilton & Lee are to be the next in Command—Already it is discoverable that Mr Adams's fame will merge in that of Genl Washington's—

The day after you left us some Vessels arrived in the Delaware with a number of whites and Blacks from Port Au Prince who had taken refuge with the british forces in that place and who were compelled to leave St. Domingo on the evacuation of Port Au Prince—The English refused them permission to go either to their ports in Europe or the W Indies—They preferred the UStates to Nova Scotia, and were assisted in coming hither—Their arrival occasioned a new source of alarm, which was at first turned to the prejudice of France—a Bill was introduced into the Senate to authorize the President to prohibit their landing—and was pressed for three readings in the same day—I objected to the Bill, not with a wish to permit these Emigrants to land, but because I deemed the power to prohibit their landing to belong to the States, and not to the UStates—and that the States were competent to protect themselves in such like instances—In the course of this discussion the whole truth came out, and the british, not the French, were found to be the authors of the injury which all apprehended—Still the Bill made its way successfully thro the Senate—The merchants petitioned the H of R agt it, and Mr Liston was seen to be busy in aid of their petition—It was at last rejected by the votes of the very Men who had been most active in bringing forward the measure—I do not think it unlikely that a part of this Band of Emigrants may have gone to the Southern States—If so, they cannot be too fearful of their landing—It is but one of the means used by the british to bring upon us the dangers with which they have threatened us from France—and the Southern States have much to dread from the well trained Negroes that may be thus distributed among them

We were induced to expect a formal declaration of War on the 4th. of July—The War party held a Caucus on Sunday last upon that subject— but I learn that such a difference of opinion existed among them, as to occasion the abandonment of the project—This is the report—I myself beleive, that the project is not intirely laid aside—All the Senators North of the Potomack have been privately summoned, and now we have not one of them absent but Ross, who is daily expected—The Southern Representatives are every day going home,—The formerly absent Eastern Representatives are every day coming in—and I beleive so soon as a Majority can be secured, War will be openly declared— This would not be done, if Treason could be got at without a declaration of War—for every effect of a declaration of War is now under the controul of the Executive; except that which affects our own Citizens— declared Enimies, are necessary to give being to that species of Treason which consists in adhering to those who are considered as Enimies— This circumstance, added to that of destroying the hopes of an amicable accommodation with France, will I think produce a declaration of War before we adjourn—

We have heard nothing from Europe since you left us—but from what has leaked out here, it may be inferred, that Gerry & the other Envoys parted in extreme ill temper, and that it is highly probable the former will conclude a Treaty—

In discussing the Bill for the valuation of Houses and Lands—the exemption of wild Lands, was warmly contended for, in the Senate—A majority however rejected the proposition—This vote excited the resentment of the holders of wild lands—and by way of retaliation they urged an indiscriminate tax on Negroes from the breast to the grave—

The object was to produce a compromise between the Negroes, and wild Land, holders—Our friend Brown, and the Maryland Solomon, voted for this latter proposition, which occasioned an equal division of the Senate, and as the temporary President had not two votes the proposition was lost, and the Bill has passed nearly as you left it—The contest will be renewed in the Bill for apportioning the Tax—As wild Lands are included, it will be attempted to throw a greater burthen on Slaves—In proportion as the tax on Slaves is increased, that on Land will be diminished—for Land is only to pay the remnant of the Tax after deducting the product of Houses and Negroes—Instead of a capitation Tax on Negroes of 50 Cents—a dollar will be proposed—and at present I see no way of avoiding it, but by consenting to leave wild Lands to be exempt at the discretion of the State Legislatures—The relative effect of such an exemption is intirely confined to a State, and therefore I think it may fairly be left to the State, to make it, or not—I very much doubted the propriety of exempting infirm and disabled Negroes from the Tax,—for it occurred to me that a Tax upon unproductive Negroes, must have the effect of emancipating them—since it would be better for the owner to pay the expence of feeding and cloathing an unproductive Negroe, when liberated, than when a Slave, since thereby he would avoid the Tax—If to avoid the Tax unproductive Negroes were emancipated, the representation of the Negroe States would necessarily be increased—Might not this Idea be used to advantage in the States holding Negroes? It is very unimportant to the Negroe holder, if his Slave is unproductive whether he is or is not emancipated,—He ought in either case to maintain him—but in a political view it is important to the State, for by emancipating such Negroes their influence in the general Govt. will be increased—This Idea might be extended to those Negroes who are above 50 years of age whether infirm or not—for if able to labour their owners could indent them to serve a reasonable time, and still the State would have a benifit, as having so many freed Men—Upon the Eve of a Census is not this worth attention?

The Massachusets Legislature have rejected Sedgewick's proposition for altering their election districts—so that probably Varnum is secure—The present Scheme of the federalists and of the british, is however, to make an impression upon the next elections, and no Stone will be left unturned in any state to effect their object—My fear is, that North Carolina will most sensibly feel their effects—Madison in our State must come forward—He should not be permitted to remain at home under any circumstances—I shall write to him on this subject by the next mail—

Our regular military establishment will be increased about 12 Regiments, and that will end the expensive and needless projects in the military line of this Session, which I think will terminate in about a fort night—No event can be more desired by

Your ob Svt HENRY TAZEWELL

RC (DLC); endorsed by TJ as received 19 July 1798 and so recorded in SJL. Enclosure not found, but see note below.

On 7 July the *Philadelphia Gazette* printed the SEDITION BILL, as passed by the Senate and sent to the House, under its official title "A Bill In addition to the Act entituled 'An act for the Punishment of certain crimes against the United States.'" Tazewell evidently enclosed a copy of the bill as printed by the Senate.

President Adams nominated Washington to serve as LIEUTENANT GENL. AND COMMANDER IN CHIEF OF THE ARMIES on 2 July, with the Senate unanimously approving the appointment the next day. As Tazewell noted the JOURNAL gave no indication that a debate took place (JEP, 1:284). Secretary of War James McHenry delivered the commission to Washington at Mount Vernon on 11 July. For Washington's acceptance of the appointment, see Washington, *Papers: Ret. Ser.*, 2:368.

For the bill authorizing the PRESIDENT TO PROHIBIT the LANDING of French passengers from the West Indies, see Stevens Thomson Mason to TJ, 29 June 1798. In the Senate debate on 29 June, Tazewell introduced an amendment that preserved the right to regulate immigration to the respective STATES. MERCHANTS PETITIONED: on 29 June the House received a memorial from Philadelphia ship owners noting that vessels had already arrived or were en route with passengers and valuable cargos from

Saint-Domingue and praying for relief (JS, 2:522; JHR, 3:357).

Theodore Sedgwick wrote Rufus King that Speaker of the House Dayton presumed that a DECLARATION OF WAR would be brought forward in the House on 4 July. But in a CAUCUS at William Bingham's home on SUNDAY, 1 July, in which Federalists from both houses of Congress were present, the party leadership's call for war was reportedly rejected by five votes. Bingham was the only senator among those present who voted against it. Sedgwick, who believed "wise policy required a declaration of war," wrote King that some believed it would make them the party of war and "discredit them among their constituents" (King, *Life*, 2:352-3; Robert C. Alberts, *The Golden Voyage: The Life and Times of William Bingham, 1752-1804* [Boston, 1969], 340-1; Dauer, *Adams Federalists*, 168-71).

On 2 July the Senate considered striking from the tax bill the provision that called for the enumeration only of those slaves who were over 12 and under 50 years of age. John BROWN of Kentucky and James Lloyd, the MARYLAND SOLOMON, were among those who voted for the deletion of that provision. Sedgwick, president pro tempore of the Senate, had already cast a vote with those in favor of striking the clause and as he HAD NOT TWO VOTES he could not cast another to break the 11 to 11 tie. Thus the provision remained in the bill (JS, 2:525-6).

From Stevens Thomson Mason

DEAR SIR Philadelphia July 6th 1798

Since my last we have heard nothing from France, except that the Toulon fleet (including the Venetian Ships) had joined that of Brest. the capture of the British Jamaica fleet of 28 Sail is given *as a report* by Fenno last evening

Lloyds Bill was reported by the committee in substance as at first introduced exceptg what related to treason which was entirely stricken out. and the 4th. of July passed the Senate. there seemed to be a particular solicitude to pass it on that day. the House of Reps had risen without doing any business. the drums Trumpets and other Martial music which surrounded us, drown'd the voices of those who spoke on the Question. the military parade so attracted the attention of the majority that much the greater part of them stood with their bodies out of the windows and could not be kept to order. to get rid of such a scene of uproar and confusion an attempt was made at adjournment & then of a postponement of that question. these were both over-ruled and the final decision taken. our friend M. in character with himself made a speech of $\frac{3}{4}$ of an hour to prove the Bill unconstitutional, which after he had repeatedly asserted and almost sworn to, he voted for the passage of the Bill to evince his determination *to support Government.* and was afterwards silly enough to declare publickly to declare that he gave his vote under a perfect conviction that the Bill was unconstitutional but that it was a lesser evil to violate the constitution than to suffer the printers to abuse the Govt. he has brought the N Carolina Delegation upon his back. who are determined to exert themselves agt him at their ensuing election for Governor. at which office it seems he is aiming.

The Tory leaders had certainly fixed on the 4th Inst. for making a formal declaration of war agt France but a previous meeting of their party on Sunday some of the most timid of them were not quite ready to yeild their assent, they required a few days more of high keeping to fit them for the race. they were therefore immediately put in a high course of preparation. Harper brought forward his resolutions for raising the provisional army to 50,000 adding ten ships of war not less than 32 Guns &c. yesterday a resolution passed the H of Reps for raising immediately 12 new Regts of Infantry & 6 troops of Cavalry. and at the close of the Session a Resolution was laid on the table for the appointment of a Commee to enquire into and report the present situation of A & F as they relate to each other. then will follow I imagine the declaration of war, so long panted for. they seem every day more afraid that Mr Gerry may conclude a Treaty. they not only declare that however favorable it might be that it cannot be ratified. and a resolution moved by Livingston for an address to the Presdt. requesting that Mr Gerry might be authorized and directed to accept of a treaty if to be obtained within the limits of the first instructions. was most indecently scoff'd at. it was called infamous scandalous wicked &c and even treason. the sedition Bill yesterday brought up personal abuse and with more violence than ever. it evident that the political delerium which has for some time raged has not yet got to its highest pitch.

Genl Washington you will see is appointed Lt General and *commander in chief* of the army. this stile was objected to. but we were told that the nomination had not been drawn up inadvertently that the Presdt had been applied to for an explanation and replied that he had chosen that mode for its peculiar propriety. for tho' by the Constn he is declared to be Commander in Chief of the army. it is no more than what all chief Executive Magistrates (Kings &c) in Europe are understood to be and yet they all appoint Commanders in chief of their forces. we know not whether Genl Washington will accept the apt tho' it is believed he will

I am Dear Sir With great respect & regard Your Obt Sert

STES. THON. MASON

RC (DLC); endorsed by TJ as received 30 July 1798 and so recorded in SJL.

The rumored consolidation of the French FLEET at BREST, where Bonaparte was supposed to have gone to prepare for a massive assault on England, and a report of the capture by French privateers of a convoy from JAMAICA appeared in the "Marine List" of the *Gazette of the United States* on 5 July. The information came by way of Charleston, from verbal accounts of people on a ship from Bordeaux.

OUR FRIEND M.: Alexander Martin, who voted with Mason, Tazewell, and five others in a failed attempt to soften the provisions of the sedition bill but ultimately sided with the majority in passing the measure (JS, 2:527-8).

Robert Goodloe HARPER introduced his RESOLUTIONS to augment the provisional army on 3 July. The House took up the subject two days later and passed, on a tie vote

broken by Speaker Dayton, the motion to increase the number of INFANTRY regiments to twelve. At the CLOSE of that day's business John Allen of Connecticut, pressing for recognition of a state of war, introduced a resolution for the appointment of a committee "to consider upon the expediency of declaring, by Legislative act, the state and relation subsisting between the United States and the French Republic." Taken up the next day, 6 July, the matter was subsumed by discussion of the Senate bill to void the treaty with France. Earlier in the week, on Monday the 2d, Edward LIVINGSTON introduced his resolution to allow Elbridge Gerry to negotiate a new concord with France. Federalists vilified the measure during debate the following day and defeated it, 51 to 30. The sedition bill became the subject of extended discussion in the House on 5 July (*Annals*, 8:2083-114, 2116-28).

From George Jefferson

DEAR SIR,   Richmond July 9th. 1798.

I am much surprised at not having yet heard any thing of the order which you mentioned having sent me on Mr. Hopkins. I however suppose it cannot have miscarried, & therefore conclude that you must have *directed* it to be forwarded, & it has been delayed.

Have the goodness if you please to send me an order by next post on the Inspectors at Shockoe for a Hhd: Tobo. of yours—I did not suppose as they knew I had the direction of it that an order would have been necessary, or it should have been inspected in my own name—but they inform me that the law is very strict.

I am mt. sincerely Dear Sir Your Very Obt. servt.

GEO. JEFFERSON

RC (MHi); at foot of text: "Thos. Jefferson, esqr."; endorsed by TJ as received 12 July 1798 and so recorded in SJL.

From Samuel Clarke

DEAR SIR   Staunton July 10th. 1798

I herewith enclose a Statement of our acct. by which you will find the balance in your favr. to be £90.18.8.$\frac{1}{2}$ I am truly sorry I have it not in my power to remit you the whole, or any part thereof at this time. at least one half of it is yet to collect & although it is in good hands, the Scarcity of money renders it extremely dificult to be come at, you may however rest assured, that I will use every industry, to raise & forward it as soon as possible, In mean time I will write my brother who has the Management of my Store in Amherst to raise what money he can for you by the first of Augt. he has but Just return'd from Market consequently will require a little time, to collect

I am with Esteem & Respect Your Obdt. Hble. Servt.

SAML. CLARKE

RC (MHi); at foot of text: "Thomas Jefferson Esqr."; endorsed by TJ as received 12 July 1798 and so recorded in SJL. Enclosure not found, but see below.

When TJ determined in 1796 to sell nails through merchants at Milton, Charlottesville, and Staunton, Samuel Clarke undertook the sales at Staunton. TJ prepared his own STATEMENT of the account between them, recording casks of a variety of sizes of nails sold to Clarke between 29 Feb. 1796 and 13 Sep. of the following year, offset by cash, by Clarke's assumption of payments to others, by his paying for transportation of some of the nails, and by his five percent commission on sales. On 19 Mch. 1798 TJ

credited Clarke for more than £124 for the value of nails delivered to John McDowell, who took over the sales in Staunton. TJ's final entry in his statement of account notes the balance in his favor acknowledged above by Clarke. It was nine years before Clarke could REMIT the last of the funds due to TJ (statement of account in MHi, entirely in TJ's hand, final entry and total added in pencil; MB, 2:939, 942, 944, 947, 949, 950, 953, 958, 969, 970, 988, 1211; TJ to Archibald Stuart, 3 Jan. 1796).

None of TJ's previous correspondence with this Samuel Clarke, which according to SJL consisted of 34 letters exchanged between 11 Mch. 1796 and 1 June 1798, has been found.

From Henry Tazewell

Dear Sir   Philadelphia 12. July 1798.

Since I last wrote you, the H of R have passed our Sedition Bill, with the inclosed amendments—The amendments were this day agreed to in the Senate; So that when the President has approved the act it will be composed of those parts of our Bill which were retained, and the inclosed amendments unaltered by us—That he will approve it, is not doubtful—The principle being established, it is but of little moment to compare the modifications made in the two Houses—but as you have our Bill as it was sent to the House of R, you will readily discover the changes which the amendments have made—I sent the original Bill to you by the last Friday's mail—

Two or three days ago Captain Decatur of the Ship Delaware captured and brought into this port, a French privateer with 70 men, and 12—6 pounders—Not a Gun was fired—and all here, are not free from suspicions that this privateer has been fitted out under british influence, and permitted to be captured, as a means of hastening a rupture between the UStates and France. I have heard that the Captain is an Englishman and that the mate is an American, and that the Vessel was built and fitted in Baltimore, but I will not vouch for these facts—

Since you left us, both the naval and military forces have been augmented, So that now we have in the public service, or rather we may have, upwards of 60 Vessels, Large and small—and the military regular establishment may consist of 22000 men in addition to the former establishment—To defray the necessary expenses, appropriations have been made of the surplus of the Revenues of the last year supposed to be worth 1,500.000. doll: of the stamp Tax the amount of which is uncertain—calculated at 2,000.000—of 2,000.000 to be raised by a direct Tax on Lands Houses and Negroes—and of 5000.000 dollars to be borrowed by the President without limitation of interest—Still a very large deficiency is counted upon, but which would be too alarming to announce to the public—It is left to be provided for at the next Session—The direct Tax Bills have passed nearly as you left them—but in their discussion very strong feelings were excited among the friends of those measures which had rendered them necessary—They augur the destruction of that unanimity which has hitherto prevailed in that party—

Both Houses of Congress have at length agreed to a Resolution for the adjournment of Congress, on Monday the 16 (instant)—It was with some difficulty that this Resolution passed—and the opposition came from a quarter which excited a fear that either a Decln of War, or a british allyance was wished before we adjourned—for knowing that the business before us could not reasonably keep us together longer than the 16th. the anxiety to keep us together could only be attributed to something which was expected but which could not then be divulged— A majority of the H of R could not be procured to favour an open Decln of War—The experiment was made in a Caucus—To wait for some intelligence which might favour the object, or weary out certain members opposed to it was I beleive the true ground of opposing the adjournment—But the Resolution for adjournment was carried, and if the members stay together until Monday—I beleive we shall hear no more of the Decln of War—which indeed is but of little moment under present circumstances—when the adjournment had been agreed upon—we were told that the Senate would be detained after the 16th. for some time—I inquired of the cause—& was informed—That the Secretary at War had gone to Mount Vernon with Genl Washington's Commission—That he had carried a List of all those who were desireous of taking a Command, in the army to Mount Vernon, to consult Genl Washington on the fitness of the nominations—That until his return the nominations could not be made, and that the President did not choose to make appointments dependent on the Senate at a future day—This was assigned as the reason for keeping the Senate together—I do not know these facts with certainty—I give them to you as I myself have received them—I understand it is yet uncertain whether Genl. Washington will accept his appointment—and as Hamilton has been here for several days past, I am inclined to beleive that he is anxious to get the efficeint command of the Army, and that it is not quite certain that he will succeed—Some believe that this business of appointing the officers—is but a pretext for keeping the Senate together—and that the real object is a british Treaty—They go so far as to say that it has been formed, and that it is a defensive, not an offensive allyance—I can plainly discover that some cause of disquiet exists between the Members of the majority in the Senate—My own conjectures are, that a part of them are extremely anxious for a british Treaty, probably pushed on by Mr Liston—That another part are very averse to it at any rate, and that if it must be resorted to, that they are determined to wait until contingencies shall make it acceptable to the People—This circumstance makes me beleive that we shall not hear of a british Treaty at present, whatever may happen, after the present European storm has blown over I shall be able by the next weeks mail to give you better information on these points—

Some incidents appear to have taken place in Europe lately, that are not yet fully explained and which furnish much food for conjecture here—The French Minister Barnadotte at Vienna, was insulted in his own House by a Mob—which occasioned him to retire to Rastadt—The Emperor alarmed at this, apologized to the Directory, and disclaimed any knowledge of the affair until after it had happened—He went so far as to displace his cheif minister who was supposed to be privy to the transaction—The Directory have taken no notice of it, and at present no appearance exists of its causing a rupture between the two Countries— By some the insult offered to the French Minister has been attributed to the intriegues of the british Minister at Vienna. By others, to a design in the Emperor to recommence hostilities with France—and by others to a design in France to begin a Revolution in Austria—Whether any of these Motives have existed, it seems for the present at least that no effects will follow that can commence a New War—

The Dey of Algiers because the French Consul at Algiers had formed a political association in that place which was displeasing to the Dey, caused his head to be cut off—But whether this fact has been truly stated, or what has been the result, we have no evidence upon which to form a correct opinion—We have also seen in the European Prints that some corrispondence has taken place between Spain and England, and it is said a seperate peace between those two Nations is talked of—From those things a beleif is inculcated here, that a new coalition is forming agt. France—and this delusion appears to be used to induce us to become a party to it—A delusion which has already done us much mischeif, and will eventually plunge us into incalculable calamities—

There are European papers here as late as the 22d. May—We have had from them but few details relative to the affairs of France and England,—and between France and the UStates—On the first of May M Gerry is said to have been in Paris, and to have been engaged in Negotiation—The Brig Sophia arrived at Havre about the middle of May— and if she has not been detained, she may hourly be expected in America—but we learn that all the French privateers had been called in for 6 Months—and that an Embargo had probably taken place—That Ireland was in an actual state of revolt, and that the invasion of England was hourly expected to be attempted—It is reported that the French have actually taken possession of Jersey—We cannot be long without some very interesting intelligence from England or France—The Toulon and Venetian Ships had joined the Brest fleet—

If I remain here during the next week I will again write to you—If not, this is the last time you will hear from me during my stay at this

Session—Should you see Colo Monroe, make my respects to him, and assure him of my esteem—

yours very sincerely
HENRY TAZEWELL

We are to adjourn to the first Monday in December.

RC (DLC); addressed: "Thomas Jefferson Esq Monticello Virginia"; endorsed by TJ as received 30 July and so recorded in SJL. Enclosure: see note below.

INCLOSED AMENDMENTS: for a copy of the changes to the Senate's sedition bill as passed by the House on 10 July and agreed to by the Senate two days later, see *National State Papers: Adams*, 9:256-7.

The adjournment of BOTH HOUSES OF CONGRESS took place on 16 July but Adams kept the SENATE TOGETHER on executive business. On 17 July the Senate approved the commissioners nominated by the president the previous day to oversee the valuation of lands and houses and the enumeration of slaves. On 19 July the Senate concluded its work with the approval of Adams's military appointments, except for that of his son-in-law, William S. Smith. Hamilton, as inspector general of the Army with the rank of major general, was the first on the list of appointments (JEP, 1:286-93). For the continuing controversy over whether Hamilton should be second in command to Washington and gain effective control of the army instead of Henry Knox or Charles C. Pinckney, see Kohn, *Eagle and Sword*, 230-8.

The FRENCH MINISTER, General Jean Baptiste Bernadotte, arrived in Vienna in February 1798. When he raised a large French tricolor at his residence on 13 Apr., demonstrators forcibly removed and destroyed the flag and began to ransack the embassy. For a description of the event and the subsequent diplomatic crisis and maneuvers, including Austrian Foreign Minister Baron von Thugut's short-lived resignation, see Karl A. Roider, Jr., *Baron Thugut and Austria's Response to the French Revolution* (Princeton, 1987), 274-80. On 10 July, the *Philadelphia Gazette* carried a report from Vienna describing the event, including Bernadotte's departure for Rastadt and reports of Thugut's resignation. It also noted talk of a new coalition between Austria, Prussia, Russia, and Great Britain. The same newspaper published the false report that André Jeanbon Saint André, the FRENCH CONSUL AT ALGIERS, had been decapitated by the dey. On 29 Oct. 1797 the consul had been transferred to Smyrna, where he was imprisoned on 17 Nov. 1798 (*Philadelphia Gazette*, 9 July 1798; Scott and Rothaus, *Historical Dictionary*, 2:859-60).

To Mary Jefferson Eppes

MY DEAR MARIA.   Monticello July 13. 98.

I arrived here on the 3d. inst. expecting to have found you here and we have been ever since imagining that every sound we heard was that of the carriage which was once more to bring us together. it was not till yesterday I learnt by the reciept of mr Eppes's letter of June 30th. that you had been sick, and were only on the recovery at that date. a preceding letter of his, referred to in that of the 30th. must have miscarried. we are now infinitely more anxious, not so much for your arrival here as your firm establishment in health, and that you may not be thrown back by your journey. much therefore, my dear, as I wish to see you, I beg you not to attempt the journey till you are quite strong enough, & then only by short day's journies. a relapse will only keep us the longer asunder and is much more formidable than a first attack. your sister & family are with me. I would have gone to you instantly on the reciept of mr Eppes's letter, had that not assured me you were well enough to take the bark. it would also have stopped my workmen here, who cannot proceed an hour without me, and I am anxious to provide a cover which may enable me to have my family & friends about me. nurse yourself therefore with all possible care for your own sake, for mine, and that of all those who love you, and do not attempt to move sooner or quicker than your health admits. [1] present me affectionately to Mr. Eppes father & son, to mrs Eppes & all the family, and be assured that my impatience to see you can only be moderated by the stronger desire that your health may be safely & firmly re-established. Adieu affectionately   TH:J.

RC (NRom); addressed: "Mrs. Maria Eppes at Eppington Chesterfield"; franked. PrC (CSmH); endorsed by TJ in ink on verso. Enclosed in TJ to George Jefferson, 14 July 1798.

John Wayles EPPES'S LETTER of 30 June, recorded in SJL as received 12 July 1798, has not been found.

[1] Word interlined in place of "requires."

To Mary Jefferson Eppes

Monticello July 14. 1798

I arrived here, my dear Maria, on the 3d. inst. and was in the daily hope of recieving you, when mr Eppes's letter of June 30. by the post of day before yesterday, gave us the first notice of your being sick. some preceding letter we infer had explained the nature of your indisposition, but it has never come to hand. we are therefore still uninformed of it. your sister & myself wrote yesterday to you by post, but I have concluded to-day to send express that we may learn your situation of a certainty, and in a shorter time. I hope the bearer will find you so advanced in recovery as to be able ere long to set out for this place. yet anxiously as we wish to see you, I must insist on your not undertaking the journey till you are quite strong enough, and then only by very short stages. to attempt it too soon will endanger a relapse which will keep us longer apart, and is always more tedious than the original attack. I have been confined some days by very sore eyes. this is the first day they seem to have mended. I should otherwise probably have set out to see you immediately on reciept of mr Eppes's letter. my workmen too are unable to proceed one day without me, and I am anxious to have a cover for my family & friends. I shall continue in great uneasiness till the return of the bearer by whom I shall hope to know the truth of your situation, and in every event to learn that you maintain good spirits and do every thing necessary to restore yourself to health and to those who love you with the tenderest sensibility. Adieu my dear, and ever dear Maria; let me know that you are well, or bravely determined to be so speedily; (for these things depend much on our own will) and to shorten our longing expectations of seeing you. again Adieu.

Your's affectionately   TH: JEFFERSON

RC (Shattuch School, Faribault, Minnesota, 1950). PrC (CSmH); endorsed by TJ in ink on verso.

On 14 July TJ gave his slave Phill, the BEARER of this letter, two dollars for expenses to Eppington (MB, 2:988).

To George Jefferson

[DEAR] SIR   Monticello July 14. 1798.

Your favor of the 9th. is at hand. mr Randolph informs me he has sent you an order for the hogshead of tobo. but lest the inspection in my name should render his order insufficient I inclose you one from myself, to be used or not as you shall find necessary.

[I also] observe that 'you have not yet heard any thing of the order which I mentioned having sent you [by] mr Hopkins.' This must relate to what passed between us as to the partial paiment proposed by mr Pendleton. [you] must have mistaken me. I did not [speak?] of having sent you any order on Hopkins. I have authorised mr Pendleton to make paiment to you. and you asked me, as from him, whether partial paiments might be received, to which I answered in the affirmative. but no other order has passed from me, except a letter to mr Pendleton authorising paiment to you. you will be so good as to notify me from time to time as you recieve paiments. I trouble you with the inclosed letter [to my daughter, not] knowing whether the weekly rider from the post [road?] to Eppington still continues [on or has?] been detained there by [sickness?]. I [am] Dr. Sir

Your [. . .] servt   TH: JEFFERSON

PrC (MHi); faint; at foot of text: "Mr. George Jefferson"; endorsed by TJ in ink on verso. Enclosure: TJ to Mary Jefferson Eppes, 13 July 1798. Other enclosure not found.

From Tadeusz Kosciuszko

[15 July-5 Aug. 1798]

the obligation i ow to you it will be ever lasting in my heart, and shall always take the uportunity to show it venever the acasion will present or require it—I am happy to find that your Character is in So high esteem here every body from the first to the last give a testy monie in expresing the greatust respect and regard for you—as to the efects left by Niem: be so good to seel it for any monay be cause it will be spild by time, if he left the boxe with Plates turn in money also—I wisch that my first dividend should be remited rather in January because i will vanted the money. I cannot yet give you acount of the afaires concerning America and Europe, but will indevour to stat the interest of both republiqus to be in friendship and peace I beg you would be so kind to mention me in the next Letter, to what Banker in Amsterdam my Dividend will be remited that in case i should want the monay i might draw upon him. you may rely upon my partiality towards america that i will do every thing in my power to prevent a war so injurious to both republiqus. and in that respect you will be my Star that will gide my indevours as you are True American Patriot, and so desinteresd man who chuse only the hapines of your own Contry. be assured also of my friendship, respect and Esteem for you—the time will prouve the inward sentyments towards you, and the time Show thier reality as well the sincerity of my affection and my heart Mr Shorte will deliver this and will say Some things my time is So taken at present that prevent me to say more and to give you an Acount of my voyage but hoever i am here in good health and sperit ready to serve my Contry, again. do what is in your pouwer that i may recive my money in due time and regularly. yours for ever.—

RC (MHi); entirely in Kosciuszko's hand; undated, the date being assigned on the basis of internal evidence discussed below; addressed: "to Mr: Jefferson Vice President of the United States of America"; endorsed by TJ as received 25 Dec. 1798 and recorded in SJL as an undated letter from Kosciuszko received on that day.

NIEM: Julian Niemcewicz. Kosciuszko's references to his possessions transferred to TJ's care by Niemcewicz and to the stock dividend expected in JANUARY imply that he wrote this letter after receiving TJ's communication of 30 May. His inquiry about WHAT BANKER IN AMSTERDAM might handle his funds appears to signify that he had

not yet seen TJ's letter of 18 June. MR SHORTE WILL DELIVER THIS: after postponing his plans to travel to the United States in the spring, William Short went to Vichy during June and remained there at least until mid-July. At some point he determined to travel to America with Elbridge Gerry, who received his passports from the French government on 15 July. Short went to Havre to embark, but by 5 Aug. changed his mind again and decided not to go. Presumably Kosciuszko wrote the above letter during the second half of July or very early in August, when he might have expected Short to make the journey. This letter was probably among papers that Gerry carried to Boston and asked Samuel Otis to convey to TJ, who returned to Philadelphia on Christmas Day (see Short's letter to TJ of 6 Aug. and Gerry's of 12 Nov. 1798; Shackelford, *Jefferson's Adoptive Son*, 129-30; Short to Fulwar Skipwith, 13 July, 5 Aug. 1798, in DLC: Short Papers; DAB, 7:226; MB, 2:995).

From Tadeusz Kosciuszko

DEAR SIR   [15 July-5 Aug. 1798]

I forgot to beg you in inquiring from the Treasurer of the U:S: of my interest that was paid in Amsterdam by Mr Pickney wether this money is returned to America for me if not i would wish to know the name of the Banker, as well to have the Certificate from mr Pickney to whom he gave because, this that hi gave mi in Philhadelphia i lost it. do me the favour also to turn in money thos things that are delivered by Mr: Niemcewicz

wyth real afection Esteem and respect your for ever Friend.

T KOSCIUSZKO

RC (MHi); date assigned on the basis that this document appears to be an addendum to the preceding letter, TJ recorded the receipt of two letters from Kosciuszko under the same date in SJL, and by its contents this letter most likely precedes Kosciuszko to TJ, [24-29 Aug. 1798]; endorsed by TJ as received 25 Dec. 1798 and recorded in SJL as an undated letter from Kosciuszko received on that day.

PAID IN AMSTERDAM BY MR PICKNEY: from London in 1793 Thomas Pinckney had arranged for a bill of exchange of more than 7,000 florins banco to be drawn on Grand & Cie. in Paris and deposited by the Willink, Van Staphorst & Hubbard firm in either Leipzig or Dresden as payment of interest due Kosciuszko from the United States through 1792. During Kosciuszko's residence in America both Pinckney and Wolcott had written to the Dutch firm to request that the funds be returned to the U.S. for Kosciuszko (Pinckney to Willink, Van Staphorst, & Hubbard, 7 Dec.1797, Tr in MHi; Kosciuszko to TJ, [on or before 23 Mch. 1798]). Kosciuszko wrote the letter above before he learned that the bankers had returned the money long before; see his letter printed below under an inferred date of 24 Aug. 1798 or after.

From James Monroe

DEAR SIR   July 16. 1798.

I shall see Mr. Strother and others and shall be able without compromitting you in a direct manner to forward Mercers views as well as if you were to write. and I shall be able also to satisfy Mercer of yr. good wishes and endeavors as fully as if you did write. I shall be back in a week. I send yr. books by the bearer. yrs affecy.   J. MONROE

RC (DLC); endorsed by TJ as received on the same date as written, and so recorded in SJL.

From William Strickland

Dear Sir/   York July 16th: 1798—

Your letter of the 23d. of March last I had the pleasure of receiving some time since; but deferred answering it till I could give some account of my success in cultivating the seeds you were so obliging as to send me last year.—

I am sorry to find that my letter of the 4th: of June 97. has fallen into the hands of the plunderer, a fate that has attended several letters I sent by the same conveyance as well as others written at different times; I do not know that the loss is of any moment, as it contained little beyond acknowledgement of the receipt of the seeds which accompanied your letter of March 12th: 97; except an answer to the request you made that I would give you some farther information respecting the ice-caves, as you had enquired concerning them without success; They were mentioned to me in company at Winchester in Virginia by a Gentleman who said he had been at them but a short time before; I am not certain of my informant, but think it was Mr: Alex: White who resides near that place, or they were mentiond in his company; You no doubt are acquainted with him, & I am pretty confident that you will obtain from him the information you are in want of. I have lately read a new publication; Travels in Hungary by a person of the name of Townson, wherein accounts are given of Caves in the Carpathian Mountains which contain Ice in the summer time, & they are attempted to be accounted for, by the supposition that the Ice is formed in the winter in such quantities, & in situation, so far out of the reach of the sun, or the influence of the external air, that tho' they continue in a thawing state during the summer, they are not entirely consumed till the near approach of winter, or perhaps new Ice is formed by the succeeding winter, before that of the last disappears; the Caves of Hungary are described to be of great capacity & extent, those of the Cacapon only to be small fissures or appertures in the Mountain lined with Ice; If you can prove the reality of these curious caves, I have no doubt but that you will farther investigate the nature of them.—As far as I have yet heard accounts of them they appear among the most remarkable of the Phenom[ena] of your country.—

The seeds you sent me under the name of Varina Vetch & which in your last letter you inform me that Mr: Randolph apprehends to be an ononis hitherto undiscribed, proves to be a more valuable plant than any nondiscript would probably have turned out; in it you have what you have been so earnestly wishing for, the true winter vetch; it is the Vicia sativa in its wild state the parent of a numerous proginy of cultivated varieties, the mere effects of the industry of man, improving upon & diverting the course of nature to their own advantage; the Parent having become so completely naturalized to your climate as to grow spontaneously, there is no reason to suppose that the cultivated descendent will not thrive equally under your ardent Sun; but should it prove otherwise there is so little difference between the winter vetch, we cultivate, & the original vetch, the spontaneous product of our fields, that in my opinion he that has the last may be satisfied, as it will answer every purpose of the other.—You may at first possibly doubt my account, but if you will examine this plant the Vicia sativa, you will find it so strongly & peculiarly marked that it cannot be mistaken; the specific character is that, *the stipula, at the foot of every leaf is marked on the under side with a brown or black indented spot of about this size* (●) *having the appearance of being burnt*; this mark cannot be mistaken & it runs through every variety of this vetch.   It is remarkable what little alteration takes place in the habit of a plant from being transplanted into a new climate & then returned to its own; this vetch undoubtedly of European origin and probably carried by accident into Virginia many ages since, unless it be the cultivated variety, which having sometime experienced the farmer's care in that country & afterwards having been neglected has, if I may be allowed the expression, *degenerated into what it was originally formed*, seems to have suffered no alteration in its nature by the great change; it flowerd in the middle of May with the wild vetch in neighbouring field, & in the last week in June both ripend their seed together; & the unwillingness of plants to change their habits is exemplified in the wild Pea, & Buffalo clover you sent me. These are undoubtedly Americans tho they belong to families of plants extremely numerous in the old world, & they shew strong dislike to our chilly & humid atmosphere; they have grown indeed, but made such little progress, as yet to have indicated no inclination for flowering; it cannot therefore yet be ascertained what they are.—From this accidental proof of the Vicia sativa thriving so well with you I am in hopes, that some others of the papilionacious tribe which I have sent you may prosper equally well as under emigration; some other varieties I may possibly have it in my power to send to you.

I am glad to find that you approve of the little treatise on manures which I sent you; it is held here to be an ingenious performance, & to unfold the effects & mode of operation of manures on vegitation more fully & more scientifically than any former publication; nothing else on any subject connected with rural improvement has been since published worthy of your inspection otherwise I should have had pleasure in presenting it to you.

I am much obliged to you for the seed of the Wabash melon, any thing new or interesting as objects of cultivation or ornament will always be acceptable; the seed I have not yet received, but it will be taken care of by the President of the Board for me; your model of the mould board cannot but be acceptable; when I saw it at Montecello it struck me as formed upon the truest and most mechanical principle of any I had seen; whenever I start again as a farmer, & it may not be long first, I shall undoubtedly follow your plan of a plough; I have an exact drawing of it which I took when with you, as well as a small model, which I prize much, as having been the work of your own hands presented to me.

I called upon Faden about two months since concerning your map; his map of S: America is not yet finished; yours therefore is still in his Hands.—

Attached as I am to a country life & rural improvements & sensible as I am, that these do not sufficiently attract the attention of your country men, for the real & substantial good of the State, I am sorry to find, that from a situation in which your example would have done much, & your knowledge & taste done more in correcting those habits, the Station which you now fill, will so frequently call you away, & be likely to interrupt that system of agricultural improvement which you had adopted on your farms, & those embellishments of your domain which you had planned, & for which your situation in a country surpassed by none in natural luxuriance of soil, in grandure & variety of feature, held out such great temptations & promised such ample reward—But your country has destined you to occupy a more important station in a period the most important & eventful, to that decree therefore you must submit, ballancing the good that may be performed in an office so honourable & conspicuous, against the loss of personal comforts & the sacrifice of favourite pursuits. I wish, who am situated so much nearer than yourself to the interesting scenes that are acting on the eventful theatre of Europe (tho perhaps not equally well acquainted with the secret springs that give life to the Drama) that I could form a reasonable conjecture on the time, when we might again recline on the lap of Peace, & again forging our Swords into plowshares might sow our crops without the apprehension of an enemy reaping the harvest or the dread of a taxation that may damp the ardor of improvement, or make the Husbandman tremble for the consequences of his exertion; but the storm no longer confined to our side of the Atlantic seems at length louring on yours, & you may unfortunately soon feel, what we feel now; the day of Peace seems still far removed.   You cannot but know that an insurrection of a portentous aspect is now raging in Ireland & foreign assistance alone appears wanting for it to proceed to any length the promoters of it may chuse; & foreign assistance it is not impossible to procure.—

Our neighbours bending all their powers to injure us after shutting us out of many of the Ports of Europe, are now attempting to exclude us from many of those of Asia & Africa, & a most important step towards this they have accomplished in the recent capture of Malta. This mass of fortifications which once withstood the Turks in a seige of many months when in the Zenith of their glory, & from before which they were compelled to retire with defeat & disgrace, has submitted in the best state of defence & preparation to France without an effort; They have thus obtained possession of the Key of the Lavant, & probably will endeavour to turn the lock against our entrance. In the midst of a prospect in many instances gloomy & unpropitious we have still our Navy to rely on, which like an individual gaining additional strength & bodily powers from a temporary illness, has acquired additional energy & additional inducements to discipline & exert[ion] from a temporary derangment & misconduct; to it we can still look with confidence to bear us thro our difficulties, & the world may still be protected by it against the inordinate pretentions & the inordinate ambition of our Neighbours.—

The mysterious expedition of Buonoparte still keeps us in suspence, he has not been heard of since quitted Malta about the 14th: of last month; by his preparations & equipment his plans are of no ordinary import; but as to what they may be the conjectures of the publick are as wide asunder as East & West; the most prevailing opinion however is, that having read of an Alexander, a Zinghis or a Tamerlane, he is willing to try whether at the end of the eighteenth century they may not be rivalled or surpassed in feats beyond previous calculation.—

I shall always be happy to hear of your welfare & be of any service to you in my power; these the hospitality & civilities I received from you during my short stay at Montecello would require, independent of the esteem & respect attached to a character distinguished for liberality & science. I beg my best Respects to Mr: Randolph, who I hope will pardon me for a botanical difference of opinion with him; & also to Miss Jefferson & I am with sincere regard

Dear Sir Yours very sincerely & faithfully   WM: STRICKLAND

RC (DLC); frayed margin and portions of several words obscured by tape; endorsed by TJ as received 2 Nov. 1798 and so recorded in SJL.

For the ICE-CAVES near Winchester, Virginia, see Strickland to TJ, 28 May 1796. NEW PUBLICATION: Robert Townson, *Travels in Hungary, With a Short Account of Vienna in the Year 1793* (London, 1797). In his letter to Strickland of 23 Mch. 1798 TJ

reacted favorably to Richard Kirwan's LITTLE TREATISE ON MANURES.

The French Directory sought to disrupt British trade with ASIA & AFRICA by ordering Bonaparte to seize Egypt. This, they hoped, would make it financially impossible for Britain to continue the war. The French force of more than 30,000 men that sailed from Toulon in May occupied MALTA on 10-11 June en route to Egypt (Scott and Rothaus, *Historical Dictionary*, 1:80-1).

From John Wickham

DEAR SIR,   Richmond 16th. June [i.e. July] 1798.

In reply to your Letter of the 15th. Ulto. inclosing a Bill on Mr. Hooper to be applied to the payment of your Debt to Mr. Welch I wrote to You on the 22d. Informing You that I had no concern with the collection of Mr. Welch's Debts, being only engaged as his Counsel, & that the Business of collection belonged wholly to Mr. Waller; In my Letter I returned You the order on Mr. Hooper. My Letter, I believe, did not find you at Philadelphia, but I presume it will follow You to Monticello. Since it was written Mr. Waller has been in Richmond and engaged me to take wholly on myself the Collection of the Debt due from yourself and the other Representatives of Mr. Wayles to Mr. Welch, the Bonds are also in my possession. You will therefore be pleased to consider me in future as the person to whom the Payments are to be made.—

With much Esteem & Respect I am Your obedt. Servant

JNO WICKHAM

RC (MHi); with "July," in TJ's hand, appearing above "June" in the dateline; at foot of text: "The Hon T. Jefferson Esq"; endorsed by TJ as received 19 July and recorded in SJL as a letter of "*June* 16. for July 16."

From Benjamin Harrison, Jr.

DEAR SIR   Richmond 18th July 1798

I received your favor of 15th Ulto from Philada in due course of Post & having lately heard of your return to Monticello I reply—that enclosed herein you will find, a Patent dated 10th Decr 1784 to Wm Short Assignee of John Harvie for 1000 Acres of Land in Norfolk County, which I suppose to be in the Green Sea, & the Land that you enquire about—

I also enclose to you a Note under date of 18th June 1782—Wm Long to Wm Short for £4 Specie—which I have never been able to do any thing with, not knowing Long or where he lived—you will do me the favor to acknowledge the Rect of these papers they being the last of Mr Shorts that I had in my Hands & believe me Sir

your very Respectful Srt   BENJ HARRISON JR

RC (DLC: Short Papers); endorsed as received 27 July 1798 and so recorded in SJL. Enclosures: (1) Virginia land patent, 10 Dec. 1784, to William Short as assignee of John Harvie, for 1,000 acres in Norfolk County with surveyed bounds, the property adjoining tracts owned by Patrick Henry "& Company" (DLC: Short Papers; in a clerk's hand, signed by Lieutenant Governor Beverly Randolph; endorsement by

[459]

clerk, signed by Harvie: "William Short is Intitled to the within mentioned Tract of Land"). (2) Note by W. Long, 10 June 1782, promising to pay Short or order the sum indicated above, no terms of payment being specified (DLC: Short Papers; among endorsements one in TJ's hand: "sent by B.H. to Th:J.").

From Archibald Hamilton Rowan

SIR   Wilmington Delawar [before 19] July 1798

If I have not too much sense, I hope I have not enough of vanity to attribute the very kind & flattering message delivered to me by Dr: Reynolds in your name, to any but the true cause; the exagerated encomia of a most eloquent pleader.

I came here as I thought to a country of Liberty and equality, phrases that may, & have been much distorted but can not be dishonoured, I do not find it such & my sense of duty bids me withdraw rather than remonstrate. But whither to go I know not. By no means satisfied with French Political morality & certain that my going to that country would irritate the Brittish Government, which as my wife informs me is about to make over to her and to our children my late property I will not remove thither. My present intention is to remove to New Orleans as soon as I can wind up a business which I had hopes would have rendered me independent of Brittish clemency for support, even thro the medium of Mrs H. R. And that it might not be said hereafter if ever I should return to my own country that I had been abject enough to receive favours & base enough to forget them

With the most sincere good wishes for your personal happiness and without the most minute doubt of the ultimate success of the friends of universal freedom, I beg leave to subscribe myself your attached friend & obedient servant   ARCHD: HAMILTON ROWAN

RC (ViW); day of month lacking in dateline; at foot of text: "Thomas Jefferson Esqr."; endorsed by TJ as received 19 July 1798 and so recorded in SJL.

After escaping from imprisonment in Dublin, where he was confined for distributing seditious literature and feared that he might eventually be executed, Archibald Hamilton Rowan (1751-1834) had gone first to France, then to the United States in 1795. He had been secretary of the Dublin branch of the Society of United Irishmen, and in America he reunited for a time with other fugitive or exiled leaders of that movement, including Theobald Wolfe Tone, James Napper Tandy, and Dr. James REYNOLDS. Seeing the effects of the Terror in France and of factionalism there and in America, Rowan abated his earlier radicalism and tried unsuccessfully to become a calico printer in Delaware. The inheritor of landed estates in Ireland, he had pledged security for good conduct as part of his sentence in Dublin, but the Earl of Clare protected his property from sequestration. Rowan left the United States for Europe in 1800 and six years later, after the reversal of his sentence, returned to Ireland (DNB; David A. Wilson, *United Irishmen, United*

States: Immigrant Radicals in the Early Republic [Ithaca, New York, 1998], 18-22, 37-8, 154-5; William H. Drummond, ed., *The Autobiography of Archibald Hamilton Rowan* [Dublin, 1840; repr. Shannon, Ireland, 1972], 380).

From George Jefferson

DEAR SIR,   Richmond July 23d: 1798.

At the request of Mr. Darmsdatt I send you the enclosed account.

I this morning forwarded your nail-rod (3 Ton) and a Tea-chest—having informed the boatmen that I would not engage to give them 3/. ℔ hundred as I had done in several instances, because you generally had it carried up for less—and that they must therefore settle it with you.

I advanced one of them (P. Gibson, alias Mingo Jackson) four dollars. I am mt. sincerely Dear Sir Your Very Obt. servt.

GEO. JEFFERSON

Be pleased to send an order on the Shockoe Inspectors for your Hhd: of Tobo.—Mr. R's order will not do   G.J.

RC (MHi); at foot of text: "Thomas Jefferson esqr."; endorsed by TJ as received 27 July 1798 and so recorded in SJL. Enclosure not found.

On 12 Dec. TJ had Thomas Mann Randolph pay Joseph DARMSDATT, the merchant in Richmond who supplied Monticello with salt fish, £41, probably in payment of the ENCLOSED ACCOUNT (MB, 2:916, 994; TJ to Darmsdatt, 27 May 1810). Letters from TJ to Darmsdatt (Darmstadt) of 17 July 1796, 3 May, 18 July, and 25 Aug. 1797, recorded in SJL, have not been found. Letters from Darmsdatt to TJ of 20 July 1796 and 26 July 1797, recorded in SJL as received 22 and 28 July respectively, are also missing. On 28 Aug. TJ gave Thomas GIBSON, alias Moses JACKSON, an order on Fleming & McClenahan for £4–7 for storing and transporting nailrod to Monticello (MB, 2:989).

From Jacob Van Staphorst

DEAR SIR: Paris the 25th. July 1798.

Your much esteemed favor of the 30th. may with your inclosed to my house of Amsterdam, together with a packet of letters you have addressed to me for Genl. Kosciuszko have duly come to hand the 20th. Instt. As the General himself had arrived here Some days before and was introduced to me for information, how he could best dispose here of the Bills he brought with him on Amsterdam, and of which you have remitted the Triplicates to the House under his endorsement, I happily had the opportunity of fulfilling your intention before knowing it, of giving him the necessary assistance, and addressed him for that purpose to my good friends Mess. Hottinguer & Co., one of the best houses here, for the negotiation of those Bills and to furnish him in the meantime with the money, he should Stay in need of; and you may depend upon Sir, that as well the house in Amsterdam, as myself here Shall, agreable to your desire render the General every further Services in our power, as your honorable Recommandation and his own personal worthy Caracter merit.

Knowing your Sentiments and Zeal for the welfare and happiness of your Country I do easily conceive Sir, that the Situation of it with respect to the War of Europe must give you the most Sollicitous concern. I hope however with you, that measures for keeping your Peace may still be found in the prudence and the Interests of all parties, and this hope has increased with me by the letter of the minister of foreign affairs of this Republick to Mr. Gerry, published here this day in the papers, which Shews at least the good disposition of this Government.

I am with Sentiments of the greatest Esteem & regard Dear Sir! Your devoted friend & Servt.   JACOB VAN STAPHORST

RC (DLC); at foot of text: "Thos. Jefferson Esqe. Philadelphia"; endorsed by TJ as received 25 Dec. 1798 and so recorded in SJL.

Talleyrand and GERRY had continued to correspond through the spring and into the summer. In his most recent communication on 22 July, PUBLISHED in Paris three days later, Talleyrand excused as politically expedient Adams's replies to the various addresses from American communities, reiterated the Directory's desire to settle differences between the two countries, and stated that negotiations could resume at Paris. He also indicated that the depreda-

tions against American shipping had recently been called to his attention (see TJ to John W. Eppes, 6 May, and to Madison, 31 May 1798), and he noted that the French GOVERNMENT was taking steps to correct that problem. On 31 July an *arrêté* by the Directory disavowed letters of marque previously issued in the French colonies, confined the power to issue new ones to the Directory's own agents, took steps to curtail any private interest that French officials may have had in the arming of privateers, and directed that the interests and property of neutrals and allies be respected (ASP, *Foreign Relations*, 2:200, 208-23; Duvergier, *Lois*, 10:321).

From Pierre Auguste Adet

Paris Le 9° Thermidor An 6eme.
MONSIEUR   27 juillet 1798. (v.s.)
Si Les intrigues du Cabinet de st james ont Reussi en amérique, Si Elles ont contribué à faire prendre un gouvernement américain des mesures à la fois hostiles contre La france, et destructives de la liberté aux Etats unis, elles n'ont point été ici couronnées de Succès. Le directoire a vu bien evidemment que L'angleterre Seule avoit interet à diviser deux peuples faits pour être unis, et il a Senti que c'eut eté Seconder Ses vües

que de Répondre par une déclaration de guerre aux provocations qu'elle avoit engagé Les Etats unis de nous faire. L'opinion que Le directoire a adoptée a été celle des amis de La liberté, Et de ceux qui connoissoient Les vrais interets des Etats unis et de La france. mais pour faire triompher cette opinion il Leur a fallu Lutter contre Les amis Secrets de L'angleterre. qui pour Seconder Les efforts des artisans de discorde que cette puissance Salarie chès vous, cherchoient a exciter Le Ressentiment du directoire dans Le même temps que Les derniers ne negligoient rien pour Soulever en amérique toutes Les passions particulieres, et tous Les interets particuliers contre La République. Si Se Couvrant du masque trompeur du patriotisme, ils ont pu avoir pendant quelque temps un peu d'influence, Leur Regne a été de Courte durée. Les Sentiments qui attachent La nation française Et Le directoire au peuple américain ont triomphé de toutes Leurs Suggestions perfides, et il ne Leur Restera pour prix de leurs manœuvres ténébreuses que La honte de L'insuccès. Les notes que m. gerry a Reçues du Ministre des Relations extérieures Vous en Seront de Surs garants, ainsi que Les mesures Repressives qui vont être adoptées contre Les violences et Les vexations de nos corsaires. Soyés en convaincu, Monsieur, et que tous Les amis de La Liberté Le Soient comme vous. Le Directoire veut rester en paix avec Les Etats unis. il veut maintenir notre ancienne alliance Et il ne veut pas donner à L'univers Le Scandaleux Spectacle de deux peuples freres S'entredéchirant à La Satisfaction de leur Ennemi commun. certes Si toute autre puissance que Les Etats unis Se fussent joués des Ses traités avec La france comme La faction angloise L'a fait en amérique, on croira aisément qu'un gouvernement qui tient dans Ses mains Les destinées de L'europe, ne L'eut pas Souffert. mais aussi juste que puissant, il n'a pas voulu faire peser Sur Le peuple que cette faction trompe, Sur Les amis de La liberté qu'elle persécute, Les fleaux qui devroient la frapper Seule; il a pensé en même temps que La magnanimité bien connüe détruiroit Les prestiges de L'erreur, triompheroit de La Calomniè, briseroit Les armes qu'on a dirigées contre Lui, Et donneroit aux amis de La Liberté des moyens de resister aux méchants qui conspirent Leur Ruine, Et qui cherchent à desunir Les Etats unis de La france, que pour pouvoir etablir chès vous Leur Tyrannie Sous Les dehors trompeurs d'une amitié protectrice.

j'ai appris avec un chagrin bien vif, Les persécutions que vous éprouviés parceque vous aimés La Liberté, parceque vous connoissés Les interets de votre pays, et que vous y êtes attaché. il est donc vrai que L'homme de bien est partout La proie du méchant! La probité, Les Lumieres La philosophie, voila donc Le But vers Lequel tous les vices dirigent Leurs attaques. La ou il existe un gracchus qui porte en même temps le cœur de Lycurgue, il doit donc exister une foule d'opimius. Si La Liberté fuit de chès vous, Si Ses amis fuient aussi avec elle, ou La trouvera-t-on? . . . . mais non j'espere qu'elle triomphera chès vous comme En france, Et que des Liens plus Etroits, Réuniront Et ceux qui En ont donné Les premieres Leçons au monde, et ceux qui Les premiers aussi ont Sçu en profiter.

je tacherai de vous faire passer Copie de La derniere note que Le ministre a ecrite à m. gerry. elle vous confirmera Les intentions du directoire. je vous Le Repete il veut la paix, et fera tout cequi Sera compatible avec La dignité et L'interet de la nation pour L'obtenir. il est Loin d'être aussi exigeant qu'on a voulu Le faire croire. il sait ménager L'amour propre de ses amis. et il [a] abandonné. surtout peut point en conséquence d'exiger des Réparations pour Les expressions outrageantes dont on peut s'être servi envers lui. Gémissant de L'erreur dans La quelle vos Commissaires ont été entrainés par des intrigants qui Se Sont joués de leur Bonne foi, il ne veut pas faire Soupçonner même qu'ils connoissoient Ses intentions, et toute demande d'emprunt, ou d'argent, Sera Bannie des négociations. des explications franches et amicales, voila cequi doit Rapprocher des peuples amis. Les vaincus seuls payent des contributions; ainsi

EDITORS' TRANSLATION

Paris 9th Thermidor Year 6th.
Sir
27 July 1798. (o.s.)

If the intrigues of the Cabinet of St. James have succeeded in America, if they have contributed to causing the American government to take measures hostile towards France and destructive of liberty in the United States, they have not been crowned with success here. The Directory quite obviously saw that only England had any interest in dividing two peoples made to be united, and it felt that it would be aiding those views to reply by a declaration of war to the provocations which she had engaged the United States into making towards us. The opinion which the Directory adopted was that of the friends of liberty, and of those who knew the real interests of the United States and France. But to bring about the triumph of that opinion they were required to struggle against the secret friends of England, who to back up the efforts of the partisans of discord which that power hires in your homeland, sought to inflame the resentment of the Directory at the same time as those latter neglected nothing to arouse in America all the private passions, and all the private interests against the Republic. If, covering themselves with the false mask of patriotism, they were able for a while to have some influence, their reign was of short duration. The sentiments that bind the French nation and the Directory to the American people have triumphed over all their perfidious suggestions, and as the prize of their shadowy maneuvers they will have merely the shame of failure. The notes that Mr. Gerry received from the minister of foreign affairs will be for you a sure guarantee, as well as the repressive measures that are going to be adopted against the acts of violence and vexations of our corsairs. Be convinced thereof, Sir, and may all the friends of liberty be so likewise with you. The Directory wishes to remain in peace with the United States. It wishes to maintain our former alliance and does not wish to present to the universe the scandalous spectacle of two fraternal peoples tearing each other apart for the satisfaction of their common enemy. Clearly if any other power save the United States had mocked its treaties with France as the English faction did in America, it is easy to conceive that a government that holds in its hands the destiny of Europe would not have suffered it. But as just as it is powerful, it did not wish to bring down on the people which that faction dupes, on the friends of liberty that she persecutes, the scourges which should strike it alone; it thought at the same time that magnanimity, well understood, would destroy the vestiges of error, would triumph over calumny, would shatter the arms directed against itself, and would give to the friends of liberty the means of resisting the wicked who conspire for their ruin, and who seek to disunite the United States and France, solely to be able to establish in your country their tyranny under the specious cover of a protective friendship.

I learned with sharp sorrow of the persecutions that you were undergoing because you love liberty, because you are aware of the interests of your country, and because you are attached to them. It is true then that the good man is everywhere the prey of the wicked man! Probity, enlightenment, philosophy, those are the target towards which all the vices direct their attacks. Where there exists a Gracchus who bears simultaneously the heart of Lycurgus, there must also exist a crowd of Opimius. If liberty flees your country, if her friends also flee with her, where can one find her? . . . . But no, I hope that she will triumph in your country as she does in France, and that firmer bonds will unite those who have given the first lessons about her to the world, together with those who first knew how to profit from them.

I shall try to pass on to you a copy of the most recent note the minister wrote to Mr. Gerry. It will confirm for you the intentions of the Directory. I repeat to you that it wants peace, and will do everything compatible with the dignity and interest of the nation to obtain it. It is far less demanding than people have tried to make it out to be. It wants to be considerate of its friends' self-respect. Consequently, it has given up on all accounts its demand for reparations for the humiliating expressions which may have been used against it. Moaning for the error into which your commissioners have been dragged by conspirators who made sport of their good faith, it does not wish to breathe the suspicion that they knew its intentions, and any request for a loan, or for money, will be banished from the negotiations. Frank and friendly explanations, that is what will bring back together friendly nations. Only the vanquished pay reparations; hence

RC (DLC); incomplete; ellipsis in original; word in brackets supplied by Editors. Recorded in SJL as a letter from Adet received 29 Nov. 1798.

For the NOTES exchanged by GERRY and Talleyrand, see the preceding letter.

Gaius Sempronius GRACCHUS, a Roman tribune of the second century B.C., instituted agrarian and other reforms. Lycurgus (LYCURGUE) had rooted out corruption in Athens two centuries earlier. Gracchus died when Lucius OPIMIUS, a consul armed with an emergency decree from the Senate, crushed an uprising fostered by Gracchus in 121 B.C. (Simon Hornblower and Antony Spawforth, eds., *The Oxford Classical Dictionary*, 3d ed. [Oxford, 1996], 897-8, 1069, 1384, 1388).

To John Barnes

DEAR SIR   Monticello July 27. 98.

I was taken on my journey with sore eyes, and have continued so ill with them, & still am, as to be unable to do business almost entirely. nevertheless my anxiety on account of payments I have to make in Philadelphia obliges me to address you. on sending my accounts to my nailcustomers on my return home, I find them as much unprepared for prompt paiment as if they had never expected my return. they make me good promises for the ensuing month. but if they perform them, it will not be in time for my Philadelphia purposes. I had therefore hoped to have heard from you whether my note for a sum at 60 days from Aug. 1. could be discounted at the bank. perhaps the derangement of our post, which now takes 15. days to bring a letter has prevented my hearing from you. I therefore inclose you such a note for 1250. D. payable 60. days from Aug. 4. for discount at the bank, where as they know they will have the money in their own hands, I imagine they will discount [. . .]. in that case be so good as to pay Joseph Roberts 370. Doll. [. . .] Charles Wharton 69 $\frac{45}{100}$ Millreas at the proper [exchange], & [remit] 200. Dollars to Chas. Johnston & co. keeping the residue first to [make] up whatever balance you may have against [. . .]. satisf[. . .] [this?] [. . .] subject to my order if you have [. . .]ed the [two sums?] of 250. & 240. D. I left you the notes for, they [. . .] [have rec]overed your advances. I shall be very anxious to hear from you, and to know that these deficits of mine are made up: and as soon as I hear from you, & not before, I will write to the persons. I am with great esteem Dear [Sir]

Your friend & servt   TH: JEFFERSON

PrC (CSmH); faint; at foot of text: "Mr. John Barnes"; endorsed by TJ in ink on verso. Enclosure: Promissory note, 4 Aug. 1798, to pay $1,250 to Barnes's order at the Bank of the United States in 60 days "for value received" (MS in MHi; entirely in TJ's hand; signed; canceled).

According to TJ's financial memoranda, the payment to JOSEPH ROBERTS was for nailrod furnished on 1 Apr. and that to CHARLES WHARTON was for John Bulkeley & Son of Lisbon. After making those payments and the one to Johnston, Barnes was to apply the remainder of the note to "any balance due to himself." As indicated by TJ's letter to Barnes at 31 Aug. below, the merchant returned the promissory note because it was not on stamped paper as the law required (MB, 2:812, 829, 988, 989-90).

According to SJL TJ's only correspondence with Charles Wharton was a letter from TJ to Wharton of 29 Sep. 1798 that has not been found.

Earlier in 1798 TJ wrote the following drafts on Barnes: one of 5 Jan. 1798 to pay Dr. David Jackson $125.75 for an obligation from TJ to Dr. William Wardlaw; drafts of 9 Jan. and 26 Feb. 1798, $18.50 and $21.50, respectively, to pay Thomas Dobson for books; another dated 9 Jan. 1798 for $18.00 to John Innes, a purveyor of copying presses who was to pay blacksmith and printing press maker Henry Ouram "for alteration of copying press"; one of 19 Jan. 1798 for payment of $25 to Thomas Leiper "in Charity"; a draft of 25

Jan. 1798 to pay E. Vredenburgh $50.70 for the purchase of "3. pieces furniture cotton"; one dated 21 Feb. 1798 to pay Joseph B. Barry $39 "for mahogany work"; one of 27 Feb. 1798 ordering Barnes to pay Edward Shoemaker $200 for Fleming & McClenahan, and another on 17 Apr. 1798 for payment of $7.50 to Shoemaker for a bridle; one of 3 May 1798 to pay Philadelphia saddler and harness maker William Phillips $23 "for a saddle &c."; and one dated 5 May 1798 for $9 to china merchant Andrew Stevenson "for 9 china dishes" (all in MHi, entirely in TJ's hand and signed by him, endorsed by Barnes and canceled; for details of the transactions, see MB, 2:973, 976, 977, 978, 979, 981, 982).

A letter from Barnes to TJ, written at Philadelphia on 7 Mch. 1798 and received the following day, and another of 18 July received on 12 Aug., are recorded in SJL but have not been found.

From George Jefferson

DEAR SIR,   Richmond July 30th. 1798

Your favor of the 14th. inclosing an order on the Inspectors for a Hhd: of Tobacco I did not receive until friday last, it having been sent from Milton to Philadelphia.

I return you the letter to Mrs. E. which was also inclosed, being informed she is gone to Monticello.

I am Dear Sir Your Very Obt. servt.   GEO. JEFFERSON

RC (MHi); at foot of text: "Thomas Jefferson esqr."; endorsed by TJ as received 2 Aug. 1798 and so recorded in SJL. Enclosure: TJ to Mary Jefferson Eppes, 13 July 1798.

Declaration of Hanbury's Executor against Wayles's Executors

[July 1798]

United States Middle Circuit District of Virginia to wit } John Lloyd a subject of the King of Great Britain exor of Osgood Hanbury who was surviving partner of John Hanbury & Compy complains of Thomas Jefferson Francis Eppes & Henry Skipwith executors of John Wayles deceased in custody &c. for that whereas the said John Wayles deceased on the 31st. day of October 1770 at Richmond in the county of Henrico and district aforesaid was indebted to the said Capel and Osgood Hanbury in the sum of £226.14.3. sterling of the value of $1007. for the like sum of money by the said Capel and Osgood Hanbury before that time at the special instance and request of the said John Wayles deceased and to the use of the said John Wayles deceased paid laid out and expended and being so indebted he the said John Wayles deced. in consideration of the same afterwards

that is to say the same day and year aforesaid at Richmond aforesaid
undertook and faithfully promised the said Capel and Osgood Hanbury
that he the said John Wayles deceased would well and truly content and
pay them the said Capel and John Hanbury & Co the said sum of
£226.14.3 stg whenever after he should be thereto required. And
whereas the said John Wayles deceased afterwards that is to say the
same day and year aforesaid at Richmond aforesaid was indebted to
the said John Hanbury & Co in the further sum of £226.14.3 stg. of the
value aforesaid for divers goods wares and merchandizes of them the
said John Hanbury & Co before that time sold and delivered to the said
John Wayles deceased at his special instance and request and being so
indebted he the said John Wayles deceased in consideration of the same
afterwards that is to say the same day and year aforesaid at Richmond
aforesaid undertook and faithfully promised to the said John Hanbury
& Co that he the said John Wayles deceased would well and truly content and pay them the said Capel and Osgood Hanbury the said last
mentioned sum of money whenever after he should be thereto required.
And whereas the said John Hanbury afterwards that is to say the same
day and year aforesaid at the special instance and request of the said
John Wayles deceased sold and delivered to him divers other goods
wares and merchandizes of them the said John Hanbury & Co he the
said John Wayles deceased in consideration of the same afterwards that
is to say the same day and year aforesaid at Richmond aforesaid undertook and faithfully promised the said John Hanbury & Co that he the
said John Wayles deceased would well and truly content and pay them
the said John Hanbury & Co so much money as such goods wares and
merchandizes so sold to the sd. John Wayles deceased by them the said
John Hanbury & Co as above last mentioned would be reasonably
worth at the time of the sale and delivery of the same whenever after he
the said John Wayles deceased should be thereto required. And the said
Plfs avers in fact that the said goods wares and merchandizes sold to the
sd. John Wayles deceased as last above mentioned were at the time of
the sale and delivery of the same reasonably worth the further sum of
£226.14.3 stg. of the value aforesaid of which the said John Wayles
deceased the same day and year aforesaid at Richmond aforesaid had
notice. Nevertheless the said John Wayles deceased not regarding his
several promises and undertakings aforesaid made in form aforesaid but
contriving and fraudulently intending craftily and subtilly to deceive
and defraud the said John Hanbury & Co in this particular did not in his
life time pay or have the said defendants or has either of them since his
death paid the said several sums of money or either of them or any part
of either of them to the said John Hanbury & Co or to either of them or

to the plaintiff but the said John Wayles during his life and after his death the said defendants altogether refused to pay the same to the said John Hanbury & Co during the respective lives of the said John Hanbury & Co and after their death to the plaintiff and still do the said defendants refuse to pay the same to the plfs. to the damage of the plfs $ and therefore he brings suit &c. WICKHAM P Q

John Doe ⎫
Richard Roe ⎭ pledges of prosecution

MS (Vi: USCC); date assigned on basis of endorsement and Rule Book No. 1, p. 328-9, in same; in an unknown hand, signed by John Wickham; monetary figures inserted in blanks by Wickham, who also changed multiple references from "Capel and Osgood Hanbury" to "John Hanbury & Co."; endorsed by Wickham as a declaration in Hanbury's executor v. Wayles's executors; also endorsed by a clerk:
"1798
June.   Contd. for decln.
July.   Decln: & Com: Ord:
August. Com: Ord: Confd. & W. Inqy.
May 1799—Continued";
an additional endorsement, in a clerk's hand and signed by Reuben George, states the jury's finding of damages.

The mercantile firm begun by JOHN HANBURY of London in the 1720s became one of the most successful companies to deal in the exchange of British goods for American tobacco. Beginning in 1747 Hanbury was also involved in the Ohio Company as a shareholder, lobbyist, and supplier of ships and goods. His cousin, Capel Hanbury, became his partner, and John's son Osgood continued the firm with Capel after John's death in 1758. Following Capel's death in 1769, Osgood Hanbury ended the family's direct involvement in the Chesapeake trade and joined members of the Lloyd family, to which he was linked by marriage, in banking. He died in 1784, and John Lloyd was an executor of his estate (Jacob M. Price, *Capital and Credit in British Overseas Trade: The View from the Chesapeake, 1700-1776* [Cambridge, Mass., 1980], 21, 73-4; A. Audrey Locke, *The Hanbury Family*, 2 vols. [London, 1916], 249-54, 289; Kenneth P. Bailey, *The Ohio Company of Virginia and the Westward Movement, 1748-1792: A Chapter in the History of the Colonial Fron-

tier* [Glendale, Calif., 1939], 25-7, 35, 69-70, 157, 298-303, 304-9).

By 1759 John Wayles traded with the Hanburys, who furnished him with goods, made payments in his behalf, and received shipments of his tobacco between 1762 and 1767. As early as 1763 the firm began to charge him interest on sums advanced, and by the time of his death in 1773 there was a balance in the company's favor of approximately £260 sterling (account with Capel & Osgood Hanbury, 1759-85, in Vi: USCC). In the November 1792 term of the U.S. Circuit Court in Richmond, Lloyd acted through Virginia attorney Burwell Starke to bring suit against Wayles's estate. Starke filed a declaration similar in form to the one above, asking £600 in damages from Eppes, TJ, and Skipwith as Wayles's executors, who were represented by John Marshall (MS in same, undated, endorsement indicating a filing date of 1792, in Starke's hand leaving blanks for dates and other facts, signed and endorsed by Starke, endorsed by clerks noting actions in the suit, 1792-95; Rule Book No. 1, p. 80-1, 92-3, in same). Notice of the suit was officially served on Eppes and Skipwith, but evidently not on TJ. In 1793, after Starke gave Eppes notice of depositions to be taken in Britain, Eppes "replied that the commissioners might meet when & where they pleased, that he had neither agent nor correspondent in London, & that he should give himself no trouble about the business, as he conceived it unnecessary." A former clerk of the Hanbury firm was deposed in England to assert the authenticity of the firm's account with John Wayles (Starke statement, 25 Oct. 1793, on a commission of 8 July 1793; deposition of Thomas Ceal, 22 May 1794; and capias writs of 7 Apr. 1792 and 12 Jan. 1793, all in same). However, when a jury was impaneled in November 1795 Lloyd's attorney did not appear to present the plaintiff's case and the action was nonsuited (Order Book No. 1, p. 131, 226-7; Order Book No. 2, p. 21, in same).

The declaration printed above pertains to a rekindling of the suit in the Circuit Court. Officially Lloyd's renewed case, in which Bushrod Washington represented Wayles's executors, first appeared in the May 1796 term of the court (Rule Book No. 1, p. 248-9, in same). Earlier in the year notice had been served on Eppes and Skipwith, but not TJ. Two other writs were issued later in the year in an effort to notify TJ, but both failed of their mark: the deputy marshal who was to serve the notice recorded "Not time" on a writ issued in July and, on one of December, that TJ was "Not found" (capias writs, 22 Mch., 7 July, and 30 Dec. 1796, in same).

According to the clerk's endorsements on it, the declaration printed above was probably entered in court during July 1798. John Wickham was a newcomer to

the case, at least in a leading role. After a series of continuations the case was finally heard in court and went against TJ, Eppes, and Skipwith. A jury decided on 28 May 1800 that Wayles's estate owed the plaintiff $1,812 plus costs. The judgment was to be administered against any of Wayles's property still held by his executors, or if his assets were unavailable the executors would themselves have to pay the costs of the suit. Apparently the defendants almost immediately filed a motion for a new trial, in light of which Lloyd's counsel on 12 June 1800 agreed to release $400 of the verdict (Order Book No. 3, p. 379, 409, in same). Although the surviving records do not elaborate further upon the motion or its outcome, in other instances Eppes, TJ, and Skipwith resisted the payment of interest accrued during the Revolutionary War on debts to British creditors, which was perhaps a factor in this case (Order Book No. 3, p. 409, in same; Vol. 15:674-6; MB, 1:616n; Wickham to TJ, 8 Dec. 1796).

To St. George Tucker

Thursday Aug. 2. 98.

Th: Jefferson presents his respectful compliments to mr Tucker and through him to mrs Tucker, mr & mrs Carter and will be made very happy by seeing them at Monticello tomorrow.

RC (ViW); addressed: "The honourable Judge Tucker Vieu-mont"; endorsed by Tucker. Not recorded in SJL.

MRS TUCKER, Lelia Skipwith Carter Tucker, was a daughter of Sir Peyton Skipwith and the widow of George Carter of Corotoman. View Mount was a Fauquier

County property of the Carter family, and the Carters mentioned above may have been her late husband's father and stepmother, Charles Carter of Shirley and Ann Butler Carter, or one of Lelia Tucker's brothers-in-law and his wife (VMHB, 9 [1901], 63n; 22 [1914], 380-1n; 31 [1923], 53-5; WMQ, 1st ser., 2 [1894], 202n).

To John Wickham

DEAR SIR   Monticello Aug. 2. 1798.

Your favor of June 22. not having found me at Philadelphia came after me to this place, since which I have recieved that also of July 16. in which I learn with pleasure that it will be yourself I am hereafter to consider as the person to whom my payments for mr Welsh are to be

made. I now therefore return you the same order on mr Hooper for 1000. D. which I had before inclosed to & recieved back from you. with the indulgence desired in my letter of Mar. 25. I hope I shall be able to comply with my instalments. the sale on a credit till Octob. this year instead of July, made the difference of 13. instead of 10. Dollars the hundred. from my knowlege of mr Welsh I am certain he will not hesitate to give a few months delay to save me this sacrifice, when that delay is to be compensated to him by interest. I am with great esteem Dear Sir
Your most obedt. servt   TH: JEFFERSON

PrC (MHi); at foot of text: "John Wickham esq."; endorsed by TJ in ink on verso. Enclosure not found.

Notes on Federalist Arguments in Congressional Debates

[after 3 Aug. 1798]

Principles.

Dayton naval armamt.
    Apr. 19. 98.
Otis contra.
Sedgwick. & Stockton.
    on same bill.

the legislature may raise armies, but cannot prescribe the purposes for which they shall be used. the army being raised the constn transfers the use of them to The President, which is paramount to any law limiting the use.

Stockton. on Tazew's
    amdmt to Reed's
    judiciary bill. about
    Apr. 20. 98.

the legislature may erect offices. but they cannot restrain the appmt of the officers to any qualification of persons; for this would be to restrain a power given by the constn to the Presidt. without restraint.

deb. on Intercourse
    bill.   98.

the constn authorises the P. to appoint foreign ministers. the legislature cannot refuse giving money for them without breech of a moral oblign.

if a law raises an army for a long term of years, tho' the constn forbids an approprian for them for more than 2. years, yet they cannot refuse to renew it every 2. years without breech of a moral obligation.

deb. on British treaty.

the constn gives the P. & S[1] a power to make treaties. if in these they give subsidies, or money for other purposes, the Legislature cannot refuse the money without a breech of moral oblign.

the constn[2] leaves the raising armies to the discretion of Congress. therefore Congress may leave it to the

[471]

discretion of the President. [so argued by[3] Ross Reid, Sedgwick, Stockdon &c. in the Senate on the Provisional army and by Otis Dana, Sewall, Harper, Rutledge, Craik &c. in the debate on the same bill Apr. 24[4] and by mr Pinckney in the debate on the bill for the Provisional army May. 10. 98.]

the constn leaves the levying taxes to the discretion of Congress. therefore Congress may leave it to the discretion of the President. [Harper in the same debate]

the Constn leaves the power of legislation to Congress. therefore Congress may leave it to the President. [necessary consequence from the premises.]

if the President informs Congress that *in his opn* there is imminent danger of invasion, Congress are bound to act in conformity to it, without examining the grounds of the opinion. said by Otis. see Gallatin's speech on the Provisional army May 10. 98.

juries

see Bayard's speech against juries & the superior advantages of a trial by the court. Aurora. Aug. 2.

MS (DLC: TJ Papers, 104:17916); entirely in TJ's hand, including brackets within body of text; likely composed in multiple sittings, perhaps beginning as early as the latter part of April 1798, the final paragraph being written after the *Aurora* of 3 Aug. came to TJ's attention (see below).

On 19 Apr. 1798, in debate in the House of Representatives on the bill for "additional armament for the further protection of the trade," Speaker DAYTON said that when circumstances required augmentation of the armed forces it was "the duty of Congress to establish and provide for it, but that here their powers ceased." It exceeded the "proper province" of Congress, according to Dayton, "to declare who shall be authorized and empowered to employ and direct such force, and more especially the manner in which it shall be employed." However, later that day Harrison Gray OTIS declared that although the president might employ armed vessels in convoys, "yet it does not follow that the Legislature shall not point out the particular manner in which they shall be employed, and under what restric-

tions convoys shall or shall not be granted. The President is Commander-in-Chief of the Army, and of the Militia when called out, but Congress might, nevertheless, direct the use of them." Comments by SEDGWICK and STOCKTON when the Senate discussed that bill four days later, like the remarks of other senators referred to by TJ in the document above, were not recorded (*Annals*, 7:545-6; 8:1454, 1460). The Senate considered two JUDICIARY bills in April. A committee chaired by Jacob Read had reported one of the measures in response to a December 1797 motion calling for revision of the judicial system. On 25 Apr. the Senate postponed further debate on that bill to the next session of Congress. Another bill, supplemental to the existing judiciary act and introduced by John Laurance, had been similarly postponed on the 20th (*Annals*, 7:478, 480, 518, 526, 527, 543, 545, 548). For the INTERCOURSE BILL, see TJ to Madison, 24 Jan. 1798. In April 1796, responding to attempts in the House to block the appropriations necessary for the Jay TREATY, Fisher Ames took the lead in propounding the theme that "a Treaty imposes an obligation on the American nation" (*Annals*, 5:1253; Perkins, *First Rapprochement*, 38-42).

In debates over the PROVISIONAL ARMY bill on 24 Apr. and 10 May, Otis and the other congressmen named by TJ above resisted Gallatin's contention that the measure was unconstitutional and bestowed too much authority on the president. Gallatin asserted that "if Congress were once to admit the principle that they have a right to vest in the President powers placed in their hands by the Constitution, that instrument would become a piece of blank paper," and he inquired: "if they could delegate the power of raising an army to the President, why not do the same with respect to the power of raising taxes?" In response, Robert Goodloe HARPER "had no hesitation in saying, that he believed this might be done," suggesting that the president could be authorized to collect a tax at his discretion. On 8 May, declaring that any member of Congress "must in some measure depend upon the President for his information," Otis thought that it would be irresponsible to oppose the raising of an army "if it was the opinion of the President that the country was in imminent danger of being invaded" (*Annals*, 8:1526-31, 1534-5, 1641-2, 1657, 1659-64).

James A. BAYARD's remarks in the House of Representatives on 9 July appeared in the AURORA on 3 Aug. 1798, the newspaper having obtained them the day before. Debating a proposal to give juries the power to determine law as well as fact in cases of libel, Bayard declared it "utterly impossible . . . that unlettered men can be competent to decide justly as to questions of law." According to the Delaware congressman, "a power of this kind is much more safely lodged in the hands of learned and upright Judges, than it could possibly be in those of an unlettered and perhaps prejudiced jury" (*Annals*, 8:2136).

¹ Ampersand and "S" interlined.
² TJ here canceled "gives."
³ TJ here canceled "all the m."
⁴ Remainder of bracketed passage interlined.

From William Short

MY DEAR SIR   Jagouville near Havre, Aug. 6. 1798

You recieve a letter from me dated at this place because I had proceeded thus far with an intention to return to America in company with Mr Gerry—My intention of returning as well as the object of it has been for some time announced to you. When I left Spain near three years ago it was with the intention of going to arrange my affairs in America—different & successive circumstances have successively postponed my departure as you have been successively informed—I concieved it at present invariably fixed, & the advantage of so agreeable a companion as Mr Gerry probably aided me to resist the sollicitation of a person whose desire has a right to be a law for me—As she is goodness & prudence itself she yielded to the arguments which I made use of in favor of the propriety & necessity in some measure of this voyage, but on the express condition of my returning here early the next spring—I consented to this & under this engagement left Paris—The pain which this separation cost us, added to the reflexions which have since presented themselves, resulting not only from our own personal situation—but the likelihood of the voyage proving not adequate to its object from the

shortness of its duration—& also the considerations as to the state of
the public mind in the U.S.—& more particularly if war should take
place—all these things together & many others which have gradually
arisen in my mind day after day since our arrival here have induced me
to yield to the wishes of my friend, & abandon a plan which was concieved for our mutual advantage, but which insures our present unhappiness, with only a probability of ameliorating & securing our future
situation—My ideas as to the uncertainty of property in the old world
had made me determine to secure & fix mine in the new, in the most
advantageous manner—& with that view to make a voyage there before
forming those connexions, which render absence still more painful—It
is this consideration which has prevented the last hand being put to
them heretofore—Particular considerations of different kinds determined us as to the propriety of keeping this subject to ourselves & it is
for that reason my dear Sir that I have never before mentioned it to
you—& not from any want of an absolute confidence in your friendship—had you been on the spot it would have certainly been mentioned
to you long ago—Notwithstanding our general reserve on the subject,
it having been never communicated by us but to a few friends, I observe
it has not only got abroad, but also passed the Atlantic—one of her
relations sent her his congratulations a long time ago from America; &
one of your letters gave me reason to believe you expected it as you
speak of the probability of my not residing in America—As to our future residence it is as uncertain as all future circumstances are at present—I beg you to be assured however that I have in no way consented
to renounce my country & the future partner of my life has consented
that our residence shall be fixed there whenever I shall insist on it—As
I feel how great a sacrifice this will be to her on account of the sea & her
peculiar situation I shall not insist on it lightly or immediately—but if
we were well settled there & my friend found herself happy & contented
so far removed from her friends & country, my happiness would be
complete—Should this take place, our residence for a part of the year
shall be certainly my dear Sir, in your neighborhood—& I must add
that this would be not only my choice but that of my friend, who in all
our projects exacts this as a condition in the case of our going to settle
in America—She feels herself sensibly affected by your kind remembrance, & the friendly expressions you use as to her—Intending to proceed on the subject of business in this letter I will conclude what relates
to the subject above, by only observing that particular circumstances,
wch. may still last some time having determined us not to render what
relates to us publick, wch. circumstances I shall hereafter explain to
you, I will beg you to consider this as for you alone, until I shall say the

contrary—In communicating to you our intentions I follow the desire of my friend, who requested me to do it on my seeing you.

I had the satisfaction my dear Sir of recieving from the hands of their respective bearers, the original & duplicate of your friendly favor of the 1st. of May last—I have postponed answering it because I expected to arrive myself before any letter would—I have it now before me—Since my letters which you there mention having recieved, I have written to you Feb. 27. a very long tedious & prolix letter—& April 15.—the former sent by a Mr. Higginson of Boston, the latter by Mr. Marshall—both mentioned my determination of going out this spring—I shall be sorry if they change your determination mentioned in yours of getting all my affairs into the best shape as if you did not expect me at all—Your plan of renting out Indian camp—& investing my disponible cash in the Pennsylvania bank—is that which I shd. chuse if I were on the spot—also that of not purchasing land (at the present low price of funds, & the difficulty of leasing) except as great bargains may render advisable—I doubt whether it be possible to find such bargains, under present circumstances—for although lands will probably fall with funds I suppose it will not be in so rapid a proportion—& as funds bring in an immediate, & clear revenue, they have an immense advantage over property which bring in little or none & that not with exactitude & certainty—I concieve it probable that this difference between a dead & an active property is seldom as much attended to as it deserves to be—It is true also that the less solidity of funds is a matter of serious consideration—Upon the whole at this distance I do not see any change I have to propose to your plan abovementioned—namely of purchasing in the Penn. bank—& of purchasing lands only in the case of advantage such as shall render it advisable—As to lands the first thing after security of title, that strikes me, is the certainty of their clear revenue—as to other advantages of situation, future prospects such as the probability of a growing value &c. &c. they can only be judged of on the spot; it is impossible from hence—Coeteris paribus, I like what is in your neighborhood as being more under your control, but I fear the difficulty & uncertainty of good & sure tenants so far south—The experiment you will have made as to Indian camp will perhaps be some guide—if it be favorable I should like adding to my property in that quarter, such as other parts of the Blenheim tract, or of Coles' or the Nicholas's, or towards Fredericksburg such as the Walkers—In general if the case would admit of it I should like to have a statement of the proposed purchase, that I might decide on it at the time—& particularly if a conditional bargain could be made, subject to my adoption—In that case it would be well to have sent to me a duplicate of your letter for greater security & expedition——The pres-

ent moment I apprehend to be a critical one as to property of all kinds—
at present even in the U.S. which I had for a long time considered as a
rock of safety—I know not what I should prefer even if I were on the
spot—& much less at this distance—if we are menaced there with high
parties—with dreadful war, & perhaps even with internal convulsions,
worse than all, what can be safe & solid?——I shall have other funds
which I wish to be disposed of & vested either in lands, or something
else in America—they will be in the form of the public domestic funds—
must they be left in that form to weather through the storm, or transferred in their present low state into something else—It will be impossible to decide here, & it would give me great pleasure to have a constant
& uninterrupted correspondence with America on this subject—it will
be the only means of coming at some reasonable conjecture—this kind
of correspondence my dear Sir, is out of your way; it would be neither
right or reasonable to expect it from you—& the time you are obliged to
devote to public affairs, cannot leave you any for this—besides it is necessary to be constantly on the spot, & in the habit of daily correspondence—I ask the favor of you therefore to select a good agent for the
purpose of details at Philadelphia & to direct him to correspond with
me—if you are satisfied with Mr Barnes, he would be the proper person—I beg you to let a precise article of his instructions to be to send me
every three months a regular account of the cash he recieved for interest
& its application (I think it is recd. every three months) or if the acct.
was sent every six months it would suffice—These persons have a right
of course to a commission on the money which passes through their
hands—& this profit insures their regularity—The capital of the funds
I understood from your former letters is on the books in my name; of
course these agents are only intrusted with the interest periodically—
My power of attorney[1] to you sent from Spain I take it for granted has
proved sufficient for all purposes & particularly for the transferring or
selling the capital of the funds wch. stand on the books in my name—
but if any thing further should prove necessary I hope you will let me
know it—trusting you will be so good as to consent to continue to represent me as to the great points of purchase sale &c.—& particularly as I
now beg you to give the irksome details of the statement of accts. &c. to
some agent who may be paid for the purpose—By this means I shall be
able to have always & successively under my view a statement of my
avoir[2] & its progress—this is so clearly & concisely expressed by a
regular acct. such as merchants keep, that it is the easiest & shortest way
to information—I feel myself inadequate to such regularity & know that
only mercantile people can subject themselves to such details, & not
even all of them among our countrymen.——As to the purchase of land

there is a tract the situation of which pleases me & wch. I shd. like to own, if a great bargain could be had in it & if I could learn the security of the title &c. wch. can be only learned in America—the owner is here & would I believe be disposed to sell, but as he purchased it at double its worth, he wd. probably not yet consent to lose so much of his purchase as to give an acceptable bargain—but as he will probably be more & more disgusted with it, seeing he recieves no kind of income from it I should be very glad if you could without inconvenience get information as to the title, the value—the extent &c. of this tract & inform me of it—I mean the Dover tract[3]—G. Morris as agent of Robt. sold it to the present owner for four hundred thousd. livres, or thereabouts—& at the same time Robt. obliged himself to be the tenant for nine years at 20,000^{tt}. p. ann—so that the purchaser thought he had placed his money at an int. of 5. p. ct.—whilst it may only turn out a trick to borrow 400,000^{tt}. at an int. of 5. p. ct. for nine years, & then to repay the capital by a tract of land not worth the half of the sum—as yet he holds the land as tenant, but does not pay the money as I understand—perhaps his farmer does not pay him—for he has let it out to one Baker—I lately saw an extract of a letter from him in wch. he says the farmer keeps it in fine order—I enquired into the title & value of this land, of Marshall—he said the title to Morris he was convinced was good, but further he did not know—he thought the extent about 3000. acres—& conjectured it to be worth from 12. to 14000 £. Virga. currency—If I could know the value of the land, & the income clear, to be got from it, I might judge what sum in our funds bringing in or quarterly interest I might offer for it, & I imagine the owner would prefer recieving the same sum (that is to say the real income of the land) in a regular interest payable quarterly & wch. he could have remitted to him & count on it—but this would not be whilst there should be any danger of French property being sequestered, & wch. we learn a member of Congress has proposed—I hope no such proposition has been made, as the meer proposition wd. do infinite harm to the honor, & particularly to the pecuniary credit of our country—I am convinced no country ever gains any thing by sequestering enemy's property—but on the contrary that it is the worst financial & political operation possible.

I enquired of Mr. Marshall of the amount of the canal shares[4]—he was not sure but thought each was £50—a book I have with me of a late voyage in America, states the original plan to be 700. shares making 240,000. doll—of course each share is more than £50.—I know not wch. is right—I shall be much obliged to you to let me know what was the original amount, & at what price the shares were purchased for me, whether above or below—& whether they have fallen since wch. I suppose of course must be the case, as all kinds of funds have fallen since then—your letter of May 95. stated the number of shares you had then purchased & mentioned the intention of purchasing more—of which I shd. be glad to be informed—I am glad that you subscribed to the loan of the canal you mention—& it will give me great pleasure to learn the progress of the canal, both on public & private acct.—I shd. be very glad also to know if lands have fallen in your neighborhood[5]—Mr. Gerry thinks they will every where have been sensibly affected by the fall in the funds & thinks that a person having funds might transfer them into land as advantageously in their present low state as when they were at par—I cannot help however thinking that he is mistaken—As I have mentioned Mr. G. I cannot help adding how much he seems to be really attached to you[6]—& how true & good a friend he appears to me to be to his country—For a few months past I have seen him, & we have communicated together most intimately & unreservedly—I am probably indebted in a great degree for the marks of unbounded confidence he has given me, to the knowlege he had of your kindness & friendship for me—I shall be happy if he should proceed to Philadelphia—from him you will know my dear Sir, my real sentiments on many political subjects—& wch. I have forborne putting to paper, since I have seen the danger of such things & known the difficulty not to say the impossiblity of giving a true & correct idea of them in such multiform times, within the compass of letters—I have seen so many things pass as it were under my eyes my dear Sir, since you left me on this wide ocean, that I may be said to have lived an age—I concieve it a misfortune to gain experience & particularly in morals & politics so fast—there are certain illusions that should be retained as long as possible, for our own sakes, & those circumstances are as cruel as the efficious friend which Horace mentions, which awake us up from them—How many times have I sighed my Dr. Sir after a few hours conversation with you—how have I often felt myself pressed with the need as it were of unbosoming myself to you—I should have disclosed to you many things, now out of date, & wch. have been retained as far as possible to myself alone—I have found so few of my countrymen in the true line of moderation—all judging of things not as they suited America—but as proper & suitable to one or other of the foreign countries, which seem to have swallowed up every thing American—It is humiliating to suppose that we should be like the United Provinces, which have been formerly[7] always governed by some foreign power, & where the people have been always divided into one or other foreign faction, scarcely taking into account the Dutch name— How happy would it have been for us if we could have supported the line traced out by you my dear Sir, in your official correspondence at

Philadelphia—I can assure you it has always been admired, by all parties where I have been as a *chef d'oeuvre* of able discussion & sound & honest policy—& preserving the true middle line—Mr. G. seems to feel sensibly all the efforts that will have been made to separate you & the Prest. from each other—he is equally a friend to both & regrets for his own sake & that of his country, that two of the most upright disinterested & enlightened patriots that any country can boast, men that would do honor to any age—men that have been so useful by their joint exertions—men that have the same decided object, the good of their country, as their only aim, should risk being put asunder, & as it were pitted one against the other; & all this by men, who perhaps have different views from both—but so go the affairs of man—he is & has ever been, all history shews it, an active enterprising intriguing animal, who can never be kept together & made to act in concert for the general good, from meer motives of virtue, reason, & disinterestedness—the few honorable exceptions to this rule, are meer exceptions, & never to be counted on as applicable to a number even if that number be a few families within the walls of a little hamlet—this is what we have seen from the beginning of the world to the present time, so far as we can rely on history—whether man will change in future, is for futurity to shew—I pretend not to decide—I for a long time indulged myself with the pleasing idea of human perfectibility—& I know not how my prejudices in favor of my own country got so far the better of me; but I really believed that a state of perfection in morals & government existed there—For some years past I have scarcely seen a countryman who has not contributed to wipe off the illusion—for whilst each exalts his own party he assures me that for vile & base intrigue—avidity & corruption, the opposite party far surpass any thing I can form an idea of from what I have seen in the old countries of Europe.—& as I have seen my country men of all parties, I should if I believed them all, suppose there was no virture or patriotism left in a country, where for a long time I supposed there was nothing else—but I recieve all this with great caution, knowing that where party spirit takes possession of the mind it sees nothing but through that medium—What I think every American had a right to count on, is that no party spirit should make any of us desirous of seeing our country entangled in European politics—but this I fear is not the case, as I see real danger of our being embroiled, where I am sure it might have been avoided—& which I fear will sow the seeds that will hereafter produce some voracious plant, that may perhaps devour us all—If true liberty, & by this I mean not the meer word but the substance contained in the security of persons & of things, be lost in America, I shall give up all hopes of its ever existing permanently in this world—I know not why I have gone so far into politics—It is a subject I wish always to reserve for free oral communications, because you may then prevent any misconception as to your ideas & which there is always a great difficulty in conveying with precision & accuracy at a distance——I repeat my wish that you may see Mr G. who seems to be of no party but that of his country, & who will be able to give you a great deal of intelligence, such as you will like to recieve as it will be true & to be relied on.

I have a thousand thanks to give you my dear Sir, for the friendly exertions you have been so good as to make as to the 9. m. dollars, & the progress you have made[8]—I had no right to expect such delay after being put to such inconvenience & loss for the want of the money at Madrid—but I am not accustomed to be spoiled by our Government—if you can recover the principal I must be satisfied without interest though I paid it on the money I took up—but if I get the principal & it be well vested I shall be no great loser, as I had desired it to be vested in 9[4] in the funds wch. have since much fallen—I like much what you say of the Penn. bank—but I think it right to add that in accidental conversation with Mr G.—he said he remembered there was something mysterious & what he did not like in this bank, but he could not recollect at this distance what it was—he considers the Massachusetts bank[9] as founded on the best & safest principles & from its manner of being conducted, to be preferred for solidity & safety to any other—I think he said there were two State banks in Massachusetts—I do not know to which he alluded—— As to my accounts I wish them to be finally settled, & particularly to get the vouchers out of my hands—but I fear sending them without an authorization from Govet.—even by the safest hand— because if perchance they should be lost, I might be embarassed—I have long ago & at different times written to the Dept of State, to be autho- rized to take this measure, but have never had any answer—I hope how- ever that they will decide something general on such subjects & allow the vouchers to be deposited somewhere in Europe & examined—I have with me all mine from the time of your leaving me—& they now form a large packet—I shall keep up also the constant hope of revisiting my native shores—It is a painful idea to have the appearance of being estranged from my country, which I have felt most sensibly since I have been not in employment—So long as one is employed abroad, he has not the appearance of not belonging to his country—& it is therefore I own sometimes a matter of pain not to be employed—though I know from experience how many disagreeable circumstances accompany public life abroad—I may say without vanity also, that I have seen more than once where I could have rendered real service, & at least have avoided real ill—but I have no expectation of ever being again employed—my long absence wd. be perhaps objected—but I feel that it ought not to be an objection if real public service is required—but if places are to be given as a governmental machine & in order to obtain governmental partisans at home it may be different, as long absence disqualifies one for such purposes—as he will of course be less known & have less partisan influence—& this mode of being employed is what I certainly do not desire—When I sent my resignation from Madrid, I did not expect ever to be employed again abroad—I did not know then or suspect the changes wch. have since taken place—nor had I experienced the painful sensation of being in such a manner abroad as to appear in some degree a stranger to one's country—

I am much obliged to you my dr. Sir for having written to Colo. Harvie as to my green sea lands[10] & shall be happy to hear the result—I mentioned to you how ignorant I was as to the papers or conveyance from him—this of course it is useless to let go further—either my brother or Mr Skipwith I hope will have had them recorded, or done what was necessary—I write to my brother again as to the western lands[11]—— I mentioned to Mr. Pougens the contents of your letter—he was astonished to learn the low prices of books with you— before your letter he had made out the two memda. inclosed, as to the re-impression here—& the forming libraries for America—the first seems at an end—the second object is still worthy of attention—I was to have carried these papers with me—I think I cannot do better than to inclose them to you—you will see that you are mistaken in supposing that books have advanced in price since you left France—Mr. Pougens has annexed as you will find the rate of prices—I inclose you also four letters wch. were committed to my care three for you, & one for a Pole—I thank you sincerely for the copy of the message wch. interested me; it is the first time I have seen it—& I do not find as warm in my favor as E.R gave me reason to suppose—but I imagine it expressed as favorable sentiments as were felt for me & I do not desire more on any occasion——I give in charge to Mr G. a little box of wood addressed to you.[12] it contains two watches—one of gold & the other of enamel with two chains one of gold & the other in cornaline & gold—I intended carrying them out for my two sisters—as I do not go I know no better way than asking the favor of Mr G. to have them delivered to you at Philadelphia by a safe hand wch. he promises me to do as well as this letter—I hope you will find without inconvenience some means of having them safely conveyed to Kentuckey to my brother, to whom I send a letter here inclosed, informing him that the watches are for my sisters Eliza & Jenny, both of whom are married & settled in Kentuckey—I know neither of their husbands—but learn that they are happy, wch. has given me an inexpressible degree of satisfaction——I must here close this long letter, begging you to excuse all the trouble I take the liberty of giving you—& hoping my dear Sir, you will command me in every thing—In the present unsettled state of affairs it will be best I imagine to send my letters to the care of Messrs. V. Staphorst & Hubbard—but if the war shd. take place it would be best I imagine to send them to some sure house at Hamburgh—I shd. in the case of war, go into Germany & employ the time in travelling there—I know no house particularly at Hamburgh, but from Philadelphia it wd. be easy to find one wch. wd. recieve my letters, & give me notice of their having such by dropping a line either to Messrs. V. Staphorst & Hubbard; or Messrs. J A Gautier & C. of Paris, who wd. always know where to find me—Adieu my dr. Sir I am happy to learn that your second daughter is married to your satisfaction & forms a part of your family—no body can know better than I do how to appreciate the worth & merit of your amiable daughters—or the happiness of forming a part of your family— May you ever my dear Sir, as I do not doubt, find all those who become connected with you worthy of you & their friendship esteem & affection—It will be ever the ardent wish of your friend & servant

W: Short

RC (DLC: Short Papers); at foot of first page: "Mr. Jefferson &c &c &c"; with marginal notations by TJ recorded in notes below; endorsed by TJ as "recd. Dec." and recorded in SJL as received 25 Dec. 1798. FC (same); an abbreviated summary entirely in Short's hand, in his epistolary record of 26 Dec. 1797 to 9 Oct. 1798. Enclosures were probably: (1) Projet de réimpression d'écrivains classiques Anglais by Charles Pougens, an undated proposal to reprint the best works of prose and verse in English for the American market more economically than books could be supplied from London (MS in DLC: TJ Papers, 125:21522-3; in French in a clerk's hand). (2) Idée sur la formation et la complétion des bibliothéques publiques de l'Amérique Septentrionale, another undated proposal by Pougens, describing categories of books that could be furnished to supply the needs of public libraries in America (MS in same, 125:21524-5; in French in a different clerk's hand; endorsed by TJ: "⟨books⟩ Pougens"). (3) Fulwar Skipwith to TJ, not found, but recorded in SJL as a letter of 6 Aug. 1798 received from Paris on 25 Dec. 1798. (4) Jacob Van Staphorst to TJ, 25 July 1798. (5) Tadeusz Kosciuszko to TJ, [15 July-5 Aug. 1798], two letters evidently counted as one by Short. (6) An unidentified letter from Kosciuszko to Julian Ursin Niemcewicz (see TJ to Niemcewicz, 16 Jan. 1799). (7) William Short to Peyton Short, 7 Aug. 1798 (MS in DLC: Short Papers; consisting of a summary in the same epistolary record as the FC above, with notation: "inclose it with above to Mr J.").

PERSON WHOSE DESIRE HAS A RIGHT TO BE A LAW FOR ME: Alexandrine Charlotte Sophie de Rohan-Chabot, the Duchesse de La Rochefoucauld. MR. HIGGINSON OF BOSTON may have been Stephen Higginson, Jr. He was a merchant like his father, who in the summer of 1798 was in the U.S. serving as agent of the Navy Department (Thomas Wentworth Higginson, *Descendants of the Reverend Francis Higginson* [Cambridge, Mass., 1910], 21-2; Tilden G. Edelstein, *Strange Enthusiasm: A Life of Thomas Wentworth Higginson* [New Haven, 1968],

7-8; Thomas Wentworth Higginson, *Life and Times of Stephen Higginson* [Boston, 1907], 197, 208-13).

COETERIS PARIBUS: "all things being equal."

Apprehensions of FRENCH PROPERTY BEING SEQUESTERED may have arisen from the remarks of Nathaniel Smith, a MEMBER OF CONGRESS from Connecticut, on the floor of the House on 21 June. Taking a position too extreme even for most Federalists, he hoped that amendments to the alien enemies bill would not impose "any restraint" on what the government might do with the property of noncitizens. Smith declared his wish "to reserve the right to Government of seizing the property of aliens, if they shall think proper to do so" (*Annals*, 8:2000; Smith, *Freedom's Fetters*, 59-60).

For TJ's LETTER OF MAY 95, see TJ to Short, 25 May 1795. A POLE: Julian Niemcewicz. Regarding the COPY OF THE MESSAGE, see the enclosure listed at TJ to Short, 1 May 1798. E.R: Edmund Randolph. For

the delivery of the WATCHES, see Elbridge Gerry to TJ, 12 Nov.

[1] Here in margin TJ placed an asterisk and wrote: "power of Atty."
[2] That is, property or worth.
[3] Here in margin TJ placed an asterisk and wrote: "Dover."
[4] Here in margin TJ placed an asterisk and wrote: "Canal shares."
[5] In margin, by TJ: "price of lands."
[6] In margin, by TJ: "mr Gerry."
[7] Preceding three words interlined in place of "[are]."
[8] TJ placed an asterisk in the margin here and wrote: "9 M̶."
[9] TJ wrote here in margin: "Mass. bank."
[10] Here in margin TJ placed an asterisk and wrote: "Green sea."
[11] Here in margin TJ placed an asterisk and wrote: "Western lands."
[12] Here in margin TJ placed an asterisk and wrote: "watches."

To Martha Jefferson Randolph

TH:J. TO HIS DEAR MARTHA.   Wednesday. Aug. 15. 98.

Ellen appeared to be feverish the evening you went away: but visiting her a little before I went to bed, I found her quite clear of fever, & was convinced the quickness of pulse which had alarmed me had proceeded from her having been in uncommon spirits and been constantly running about the house through the day & especially in the afternoon. since that she has had no symptom of fever, and is otherwise better than when you left her. the girls indeed suppose she had a little fever last night, but I am sure she had not, as she was well at 8. aclock in the evening & very well in the morning, and they say she slept soundly through the night. they judged only from her breathing. every body else is well: and only wishing to see you. I am persecuted with questions 'when I think you will come'? my respects to mr & mrs Carter & affectionate salutations to our more particular friends. if you set out home after dinner be sure to get off between four & five. Adieu my dear.

RC (NNPM); endorsed by Randolph. Not recorded in SJL.

To Samuel Smith

Dear Sir   Monticello Aug. 22. 98.

Your favor of Aug. 4.[1] came to hand by our last post, together with
the 'extract of a letter from a gentleman of Philadelphia dated July 10.'
cut from a newspaper, stating some facts which respect me. I shall notice these facts. the writer says that 'the day after the last dispatches were
communicated to Congress Bache, Leib &c. and a Dr. Reynolds were
closeted with me.' if the reciept of visits in my public room, the door
continuing free to every one who should call at the same time, may be
called *closeting*, then it is true that I was *closeted* with every person who
visited me; in no other sense is it true as to any person. I sometimes
recieved[2] visits from mr Bache & Dr. Leib. I recieved them always
with pleasure, because they are men of abilities, and of principles the
most friendly to liberty & our present form of government. mr Bache
has another claim on my respect, as being the grandson of Dr. Franklin,
the greatest man &[3] ornament of the age and country in which he lived.
whether I was visited by mr Bache or Dr. Leib the day after the communication referred to, I do not remember. I know that all my motions at
Philadelphia, here, and every where, are watched & recorded. some of
these spies therefore may remember, better than I do, the dates of these
visits. if they say these two gentlemen visited me the day after the communications, as their trade proves their truth,[4] I shall not contradict
them, tho' I affirm that I do not recollect it. however as to Dr. Reynolds
I can be more particular, because I never saw him but once, which was
on an introductory visit he was so kind as to pay me. this I well remember was before the communication alluded to, & that during the short
conversation I had with him, not one word was said on the subject of
any of the communications. not that I should not have spoken freely on
their subject to Dr. Reynolds, as I should also have done to the letter
writer or any other person who should have introduced the subject. I
know[5] my own principles to be pure, and therefore am not ashamed
of them. on the contrary I wish them known, & therefore willingly express them to every one.[6] they are the same I have acted on from the year
75. to this day, and are the same, I am sure, with those of the great body
of the American people. I only wish the real principles of those who
censure mine were also known. but, warring against those of the people,
the delusion of the people is necessary to the dominant party. I see the
extent to which that delusion has been already carried, and I see there
is no length to which it may not be pushed by a party in possession of
the revenues & the legal authorities of the US. for a short time indeed,
but yet long enough to admit much particular mischief. there is no event

therefore, however atrocious, which may not be expected. I have contemplated every event which the Maratists of the day[7] can perpetrate, and am prepared to meet every one in such a way[8] as shall not be derogatory either to the public liberty, or my own personal honour.   the letter writer says I am 'for peace; but it is only with France.' he has told half the truth. he would have told the whole, if he had added England. I am for peace with both countries. I know that both of them have given, & are daily giving, sufficient cause of war: that in defiance of the laws of nations, they are every day trampling on the rights of all the neutral powers, whenever they can thereby do the least injury either to the other. but, as I view a peace between France & England the ensuing winter to be certain, I have thought it would have been better for us to have continued to bear from France through the present summer, what we have been bearing both from her & England these four years and still continue to bear from England, and to have required indemnification in the hour of peace, when I verily believe it would have been yielded by both. this seems to be the plan of the other neutral nations; and[9] whether this, or the commencing war on one of[10] them, as we have done, would have been wisest, time & events must decide. but I am quite at a loss on what ground the letter writer can question the opinion that France had no intention of making war on us, & was willing to treat with mr Gerry, when we have this from Taleyrand's letters & from the written and verbal information of our envoys.[11] it is true then that, as with England we might of right have chosen either peace or war, & have chosen peace; and prudently in my opinion; so with France we might also of right have chosen either peace or war, & we have chosen war.[12] whether the choice may be a popular one in the other States I know not. here it certainly is not;[13] & I have no doubt the whole American people will rally ere long to the same sentiment, & rejudge those who at present think they have all judgment in their own hands.

These observations will shew you how far the imputations in the paragraph sent me approach the truth. yet they are not intended for a newspaper. at a very early period of my life, I determined never to put a sentence into any newspaper. I have religiously adhered to the resolution through my life, and have great reason to be contented with it. were I to undertake to answer the calumnies of the newspapers, it would be more than all my own time, & that of 20. aids could effect. for while I should be answering one, twenty new ones would be invented. I have thought it better to trust to the justice of my countrymen, that they would judge me by what they *see* of my conduct on the stage where they have placed me, & what they knew of me *before* the epoch since which a particular party has supposed it might answer some view of theirs to vilify me in the public eye. some, I know, will not reflect how apocryphal is the testimony of enemies so palpably betraying the views with which they give it. but this is an injury to which duty requires every one to submit whom the public think proper to call into it's councils.   I thank you, my dear Sir, for the interest you have taken for me on this occasion. though I have made up my mind not to suffer calumny to disturb my tranquillity, yet I retain all my sensibilities for the approbation of the good & just. that is indeed the chief consolation for the hatred of so many who, without the least personal knowledge, & on the sacred evidence of Porcupine & Fenno alone, cover me with their implacable hatred. the only return I will ever make them will be to do them all the good I can, in spite of their teeth. [14]

I have the pleasure to inform you that all your friends in this quarter are well, and to assure you of the sentiments of sincere esteem & respect with which I am Dear Sir

Your friend and servt.

TH: JEFFERSON

RC (PPAmP); at foot of first page: "Honble Samuel Smith"; endorsed. PrC (DLC). Dft (same).

Smith's FAVOR OF AUG. 4, recorded in SJL as received on the 16th, has not been found. A letter from TJ to Smith of 19 Mch. 1796, recorded in SJL, is also missing.

The EXTRACT OF A LETTER FROM A GENTLEMAN OF PHILADELPHIA to a friend in Frederick, Maryland, dated 10 July was published first in a local Maryland newspaper, in John Fenno's *Gazette of the United States* on the 28th, and in the *Federal Gazette & Baltimore Daily Advertiser* on 1 Aug. Smith probably sent the letter, which included two paragraphs critical of the vice president, from the *Federal Gazette*. Maryland Senator John E. Howard admitted to writing the missive, which described TJ as "unquestionably, the very soul of the party," as evidenced by his connections with Bache, George Logan, and others who were doing everything in their power to serve the French cause. Noting that the vice president had left Philadelphia before the closing of Congress, Howard concluded: "Fortunately he does not possess strong nerves.— 'The spirit is willing, but the flesh is weak.' " He went on to charge that while most "democrats" were silent after the publication of the dispatches from the envoys to France, it was because they were "waiting for the watchword from their leaders." The word came after TJ was CLOSETED with Bache, Michael Leib, Dr. James Reynolds, and others on 21 June, the day on which Adams presented to Congress the letters that John Marshall brought from France (see TJ to Madison, 21 June). After the secret meeting, Senator Howard asserted, TJ and the others began circulating rumors that the Directory had NO INTENTION OF MAKING WAR on the United States, that the French were willing to treat with Gerry, and that an accommodation with France was expected from the negotiations. The extracted letter enclosed by Smith, a wealthy Baltimore merchant who was in a hotly contested reelection campaign, also included a paragraph on a conversation he reportedly had at a dinner with the president in which the Maryland congressman indicated that he wished the "envoys had given the French the money they demanded—that it would have been cheaper than war." The president reportedly replied "that he would not *give* the value of the duty *on a pound of tea!* for the *principal* was every thing" and, Adams continued, "*he had hoped, and believed, that no virtuous American would have entertained such sentiments!!!*" (*Federal Gazette & Baltimore Daily Advertiser*, 1-4 Aug. 1798; Frank A. Cassell, *Merchant Congressman in the Young Republic: Samuel Smith of Maryland, 1752-1839* [Madison, 1971], 83-9).

¹ In Dft TJ first wrote "dated Apr. 4. (for Aug. 4. I presume)" before altering it to read as above.

² In Dft TJ began this sentence "I was in the habit of recieving" before altering it to read as above.

³ Preceding word and ampersand lacking in Dft.

⁴ Preceding six words interlined in Dft in place of "they are doubtless very honourable [avid?] witnesses &."

⁵ Interlined in Dft in place of "consider."

⁶ Preceding seven words and ampersand interlined in Dft in place of "to all the world."

⁷ In Dft TJ first canceled "their vindictive spirit" and then "the spirit of party hostility [rage?]" before interlining the preceding five words.

⁸ In Dft TJ here interlined and canceled "I hope."

⁹ Sentence to this point interlined in Dft.

¹⁰ Preceding two words interlined in RC and Dft.

¹¹ In Dft TJ here canceled "and the verbal information of mr Marshall who declared to several gentlemen ⟨that at Phila⟩ after his return that France had no idea of a war with us. every evidence therefore is true and we are safe in affirming that it was war of our own choice."

¹² Word overwritten by TJ in place of partially erased "peace." Dft: "war."

¹³ In Dft TJ first wrote "but here it certainly will not be" before altering the passage to read as above.

¹⁴ In Dft TJ here canceled "the deep rooted disgust produced in this state by the Alien & Sedition acts is beyond any thing ever seen since the days of the Stamp act."

From William Short

DEAR SIR   Paris Aug. 24. 1798

I have already had the pleasure of acknowleging by Mr Gerry the original & duplicate of your friendly favor of May 1. last—the two preceding which you had been so kind as to write me in the year 97—you had then had the acknowlegement of in mine of Dec. 27. 97. & Jan. 23. 98.—Mine which I have since had the pleasure of addressing you were dated Feb. 27. April 15. & Aug. 6.—Between the two last I did not write because I was constantly under the idea that I should arrive in America as soon as any letter I could write. My last will have informed you before you will recieve the present how I came to postpone my voyage at the eve of embarking. I could have wished much to have made that voyage before adopting a measure which will necessarily render it more difficult hereafter, & regret sincerely at present not having accomplished it in 96 & 97. as I had intended—& which I should certainly have done notwithstanding every obstacle, if I could have foreseen events.—The idea of having been so long absent from my country without interruption, so as to have in some degree the appearance of being a stranger to it is disagreeable beyond any thing I had concieved—It makes me sometimes regret having not continued in my place at the Hague—A residence there, though much less convenient & agreeable than here, would have been compatible with the situation & affairs of my friend; & I should on the whole I think, prefer the inconvenience of transferring our residence there, to the disagreeable idea of appearing a stranger to my country—& for this reason alone, for I have no disposition otherwise to enter again into public life—The time I was employed in it, was in a manner so precarious, so painful in many respects & so unjust at last, after having done every thing in my power, & after having recieved the most flattering compliments on my zeal, talents &c. &c— that it was well adapted to drive off any desire I might have had to have continued—The more I reflect on the conduct of the person then at the head of the Government the more I consider it weak, vacillating, & ignorant as to foreign affairs—the more I consider it a misfortune for his reputation, & what is still more important, a misfortune for his country that he had not retired four years sooner—It is possible however & even probable that I may be mistaken, for I do not know that I have found any body who blames him precisely on the same points or on the same principles that I do—Be it as it may I feel a full conviction that if he had been possessed of a proper knowlege of European affairs, or would have listened to those who were, & had preserved a dignified uniformity in his conduct as to those affairs, he might have avoided the debasing diffi- culties into which his country was drawn & which hurried him from bad to worse, until he had shewn to all the belligerent powers equally one after another that they might treat his country with injustice & con- tempt.——But I am getting into the chapter of politics, & which I have for a long time past endeavored to avoid on all occasions—To return to myself & my private affairs; I mentioned to you in my last what I had before then, for the reasons there mentioned, abstained from communi- cating, my intention of associating myself to a partner for life—particu- lar considerations which have induced us to postpone the accomplish- ment of this purpose hitherto have equally induced us to avoid making it known generally, & I therefore request you to consider this as be- tween ourselves for the present—The moment that these considerations shall cease I will not fail to communicate it—In the mean time my friend begs me to recall her to your recollection & to assure you how much she is flattered by the kind & friendly expressions of your letter.—We have just read the travels of her relation in America & dwelt on that part wch. relates to Monticello, & where she considered herself as it were in my paternal habitation—these travels have not yet been published here— they are now printing—the five first volumes only are struck off—they will be eight in all—I fear they will be too voluminous & too minutious for the greater number of readers—there is a great degree of candor & moderation throughout which must command confidence as to the veracity of the author—& this is a great point, more particularly in an author of travels.—

The object of my voyage as I informed you was principally to arrange my affairs & place them in some stable & secure form—& particularly to endeavor to convert them into an advantageous & profitable landed estate—one which would offer at all times a safe & solid retreat from the storms of this world—my friend who is mildness & prudence combined had consented to this voyage, on my earnest representations, under the solemn engagement which I took to return in the spring—In proportion as my departure was retarded, & as the cloud thickened in America it became less probable that I should be able to realize my plan in the time first proposed, wch. added to the other considerations mentioned, induced me to change it—This however was not without mixture, for my desire to see my native country from which nothing can ever estrange me, remains in all its force—I hope & trust too that the time will come when it will be more agreeable to be seen, when the present rage of party-spirit will have subsided, & when all honest & true Americans will be just towards each other, notwithstanding any shades of opinion which may distinguish them on foreign subjects.——I hope one great cause will be removed by the steps which this Government has lately taken, which shew that they do not wish for war with the U.S.—I do not enter into what has preceded for some time past—there has been on both sides ill will & ill management—I see several ways in which the U.S. might have avoided a great deal of insult & injury—in which they might have gained ground in the world instead of losing it—I was almost induced at different times to draw up a *memoire* on the subject & send it to the Prest.—but an aversion to the appearance of officiousness on one hand, & an apprehension that my situation might prevent confidence in the *moyens*[1] I should have proposed, induced me always to decline it, notwithstanding the conviction I felt on the subject—I have accordingly remained, as I still do, quite a stranger to politics, with however my most ardent wishes for the happiness tranquillity & prosperity of my country, which now depend on them so far as relates to their *demélés*[2] with this Government—Mr. Gerry received in time to carry out with him, the *arrèté* as to their cruisers in our hemisphere— On my return here after his departure I found that Dr Logan had arrived & as it appeared merely on his own ground, in order to endeavor to ward off the impending blow—I have seen him but once—he seems a true friend to his country & to be pushing with great zeal to prevail on this government to take some measure which may calm the public mind in America—I learn that he is well recieved & that the singularity of his mission has obtained attention—& that the embargo which had been put on our vessels is removed—I write this letter to go by him, as he has promised to take charge of it, & will set out in a day or two—We at present stand on the footing of other neutral powers, & there is reason to believe that they have determined here to change the system adopted some time ago as to them—It is easy to demonstrate that that system so far from injuring the British commerce, is on the contrary compara- tively beneficial; & injurious only to the neutral powers & to France herself—this evil then will find its remedy by the joint operations of the parties injured, & by the operation of reason & reflexion. It depends at present on our government to get things if not absolutely right, at least to avoid great evil—much will depend on the manner of renewing the negotiation, & the person or persons employed—If it should be offered to you my dear Sir & you should decline it, you would have great re- proaches to make to yourself & so would your friends & your country— I have good reason to believe that this was done last year—It is probably known to few—& I hope will not be known, for you would be blamed by all the friends to peace & good will between the two countries, on both sides of the Atlantic—In such cases one has hardly a right to con- sult one's own personal situation, risk or feelings—The prospect is much less gloomy at present, & on the whole I have little hope, that the same offer will be again made, for a variety of reasons; otherwise I should press you on the subject even to importunity—I never turn my views back to the year 94, when it was reported that you were coming here, without deploring with bitterness that that event had not taken place—Never no never my dear Sir, would greater good have been in the power of an individual, or more evil avoided—I do not know whether it was really question of your coming here, or whether it was meer report at that time—If it had taken place how differently would our affairs have been arranged with Spain—we might most unquestion- ably have been now carrying on a lawful commerce with her West-India Islands—with the Floridas—with the Philippines—& perhaps even with all her other possessions—& I do believe that we should have avoided all the losses, or almost all, that our commerce has been since recieving from the spoliations of the French cruisers—It would require time to develope all this, & it would be now useless, I therefore avoid it.——If this mission should be offered to Mr. Gerry alone I have good reason to believe he would accept it—There are few persons I under- stood from him with whom he would consent again to act jointly, & that I was one of those few—He concieved that if I had been one of the three last year, a great deal of evil would have been avoided,—& when I con- sider the necessity of one of a commission at least, understanding the usages & particularly the language of the country where they are sent, & of those with whom they are to treat I may without vanity suppose I should have been of use—The inconvenience as to language in such cases must have been well understood by the President, & of course I imagine he must have had some particular reason for appointing one of those he did, or for not appointing one who stood in the circumstances of experience & knowlege of this country in which I did—otherwise it is reasonable to suppose he would have turned his views towards me in the present scarcity of that kind of experience—It is possible however he had forgotten that I existed or did not know where I might be found—It is certain I did not expect any such appointment & did not know that any would be made until I heard the commission of the three named—Mr. Gerry wished me much to continue my voyage, because he thought my presence there would be of use, in the case of an intention to renew the negotiation—He told me it was his opinion & that he should press on the Prest. that I was the person who ought to be employed—I know not what effect my having not continued the voyage may have had on him—nor did I chuse to dwell on the matter—but sure I am that it ought to be far from being an objection—I am sure I should do as well, & probably much better than if I had made the voyage—As to my part I had rather in such a case be joined in a commission with others than be employed alone—& I think it certain that if a proper commission properly formed were to be sent, the business would be soon advantageously settled for the U.S. & to the satisfaction of all parties.—I have no idea however that the Prest. will be induced to think of me, as I have no kind of communication with him for ten years back, & as I suppose of course, I pass with him for a Jacobin &c &c. as it is probable I did or do with others for an Aristocrat, Royalist & God knows what—This is the fate of all moderate people in time of parties, & who pretend to judge of the merits of each question, & without regard to any party—They are sure to find themselves passed & repassed at different times & in all the different tacks that are taken—It is a curious thing for me to reflect on the squeamishness of the late Prest. in '92. (who was afraid of the company that a foreign minister shd. keep & of the simple chit chat conversation he should hold, lest it should displease the foreign agent of a foreign power) & compare that state of his mind with his last will & dying speech made in 96.—& yet such is the way of the world, that this man will go down to posterity as a great General, a disinterested patriot, a firm & enlightened statesman—As to the two former I am not a competent judge—but the last four years of his administration, render it impossible for an impartial & examining mind to subscribe to his reputation as a statesman of that high order, notwithstanding he possesses certainly many of those requisites which enable one man to take & keep an higher station than others, & to inspire such a degree of respect as in many cases may supply the place of abilities, & be used as a substitute for them—& this is often one of the most essential secrets of those who pass for great men & great statesmen———But enough of useless digression.—

The chapter of my private affairs which you are so good as to take under your care, is more agreeable & at the same time more useful for me to dwell on. I shall have other funds hereafter to add to those already under your friendly direction—my intention is, & particularly if the danger of war should subside to vest in America whatever I shall have disponible—I consider vestments there as the best & securest—my only doubt is in what to make those vestments—there appear to me to be a mixture of advantages & disadvantages, in both real & personal effects—The funds are undoubtedly the best as to revenue, when one is so far removed as I am & probably shall necessarily be for some time—but funds do not appear to me so solid, as lands where the title is clear & undisputed—the management however of these must be attended with great inconvenience at such a distance—for I observe even in this country where lands are leased out, & more especially when they lye in those parts where the tenants are poor & rent in part produce, the distance of the proprietor makes a difference, in the revenue he really recieves, beyond all imagination—I shd. imagine it would be still worse with lands in our country[3]—but the certainty of the gradual rise in the price of lands if purchased with judgement, would compensate in the long run the present modicity of revenue.—I should be much obliged to you my dear Sir, to take information so far as you can do it without too much trouble or inconvenience, & communicate to me your ideas on the most advantageous mode of vesting cash in lands of the U.S: & which of the States—I should be glad to have the information as well with respect to small sums, say ten or fifteen thousand dollars, as any larger sums—It is possible I might be joined by others, if some good & sure prospect offered for making one or more vestments—In such a case I suppose some new country would offer the best resource; such as the back parts of N. York, Pennsylvania—or the Western waters—the two former particularly, because those countries are limited & of course the population must increase in a greater degree being in some measure confined to them, than on the Western waters, where there are no limits, & where of course the population must be dispersed for ages to come—I should long ago have written to my brother on the subject & joined him in some purchase there, if I had not feared that his imagination was apt to decieve him & draw him into false speculations—I learn however from others & I learn with great pleasure that he has succeeded in his pur-

chases—though it was a bold & adventurous thing in a young & unex-
perienced man to sell his whole patrimony & place it on a new ground,
& there where the titles were so unsettled that I have understood from
a person who was in Kentuckey in 94-95, his whole estate as well as
that of many others depended on a vote of the assembly—It turned favorably for him at that time; but it may turn against him at another,—It
may be allowed to play that high game with a part of one's estate, but I
do not think that the most complete success can justify its being done
with the whole—I hope & trust experience will bring on sober reflexion
& prudence, wch. crown the works of activity & enterprize.——I will
thank you also to let me hear from you (always understood so far as can
be done without too much trouble) as to the vestment of any given sum
in Virginia or the upper part of Maryland—that is to say among the
mountains in your neighborhood, such as Nicholas's, Coles, or Carters
tract, or the North or South gardens, or between you & Fredericksburg,
or between there & the Potowmac, or in fine on the other side of the
Potowmac—I have little expectation that any thing lower down the
country would answer, that is to say towards Richmond or further
north, on account of the advanced price in proportion to the revenue—
& of the necessity of having slaves to cultivate them unless perhaps the
Dover tract of wch. I wrote to you in my last.—Is Curles for sale or any
of those large estates in a body? What the price & number of Acres?
what the probability of good tenants, & what the probable revenue? [4]—
The points I wish to be informed of would be the price of the purchase
compared with the revenue to be expected—& the manner of procuring
that revenue—that is to say the possibility of finding tenants, & the
manner of leasing whether by *metairie*, [5] or in cash, & if the former what
proportion of the produce goes to the proprietor—&c. &c.—The experiment you are so good as to undertake as to Indian camp will be a good
guide—if it should answer I should like to extend the purchase further
in the same tract, & particularly on the same side of the mountain &
contiguous—the more such purchases are compact & contiguous the
better, on account of your tenants being more removed from the
grounds cultivated by slaves—their neighborhood must be inevitably
an inconvenience to the cultivators not slaves—Suppose for instance
one was possessed of all Carters tract on the same side of the mountain,
the tenants would form a body a part as it were, & would be in contact
with the slaves only on the borders of Coles & your estate—this would
be much less in proportion than where a small tract & of course a few
tenants are in the center & surrounded on all sides by slaves.—I wait
with impatience to hear something from you on these subjects—the
constant expectation of going myself has made me in some degree

hitherto suspend attention to such enquiries—As far as I can judge or rather conjecture from hence I should suppose the best chance for an advantageous purchase, would be somewhere within a line drawn from Fredericksburg to the Blue ridge, from thence to the Potowmac, down the Potowmac to the new City & from thence to Fredericksburg—the prices would be lower there than on the other side of the Potowmac & tenants more likely to be found than further south or east.—Monroe spoke to me of a purchase he made somewhere on that quarter at a price inconcievably low—I think it was of old Blaise Carter—& I suppose in general it is in the *debris* of these old & large landed fortunes where purchases may be best made—I think Genl. Nelson had formerly a large estate somewhere there, which would be probably to be bought— These I mention as meer conjectures—for after all, it is only information taken on the spot that can be relied on.—When I shall have had the pleasure of recieving sufficient lights from you I will form some settled plan which may in future perhaps be extended.

I am ashamed of all the trouble I give you who have certainly little or none to spare from your public & private occupations—I mentioned in my last what I repeat here my request that you would appoint some confidential person at Philadelphia, who might relieve you from all the trouble of details in the business to be done there, in the purchase of funds receiving of interest &c. It would be proper to require of him a regular acct. kept in the mercantile way, which is the shortest mode of having under one's eyes a constant *tableau* of the business—He will of course expect & has a right to a commission which I belive is a fixed so much p. cent on the money wch. passes through his hands.——You mention in your last that you know not how far D & B.'s transfer to me was of the exact balance—I know not either, from the nature of their or Browne's correspondence with me—which consisted in two or three scattering letters on the subject, as well as I recollect & meerly mentioning the sum recieved from Colo. Skipwith—I have these letters among my papers, & will send you a copy of them if necessary—they are at present packed up & on the road from Havre here—I am fully disposed to believe that both Colo. Skipwith & they have been exact—but it would be satisfactory for all parties I shd. suppose & particularly for them to state some account where proceedings have been complicated—With respect to Colo. Skipwith I have ceased correspondence for a great many years back—I did not wish to importune him uselessly—& as he promised from time to time an account wch. he never sent, & as from his own letters it appeared he pretended to keep at interest cash of mine, after declaring he could not pay interest beyond a certain time, & after insisting on my pointing out how he shd. dispose of that cash, & after recieving my letters directing him to vest that cash in funds at all risks &c. &c.—I know not what are his intentions—In his gestion there are two distinct periods—the first where he had *carte blanche*—of course I took it for better for worse—the second where at his own request, & to avoid his responsability as he termed it, I took on myself to precise what was to be done—viz to purchase without the loss of a moment, funds with every shilling I had disponible—This was during the rapid rise—from his letters it would seem, that it was precisely after recieving my directions in answer to his declaring he could no longer pay interest on my cash & that I must give him precise directions how to dispose of it, that he avoided this, & kept the money at interest— If this be the case, it was neither just or justifiable—It has been a long time since I have read his letters, but this is the idea I have retained— If necessary I will send you extracts of them—At any rate I should suppose for his own satisfaction he would chuse to state some account of his gestion for me—in however general terms it may be.—It might be well perhaps to employ Mr. B. Harrison to settle the business as well with Colo. Skipwith as with Browne—that is to say to draw out an account of the business until the time you were so good as to recieve the translation from Browne—Mr. Harrison is acquainted with the whole, or at least better than any body else—He has a small balance also himself to account for, wch. he acknowleged in a letter to me a great many years ago—It was not comprehended in the funds he turned over to Colo. Skipwith, because as he mentioned me he had omitted entering it on his books, wch. arose from my giving him the trifle a few days before I left Richmond—we did not recollect the sum exactly—he agreed it might be considered as an £150—It was at least that—& the interest from that time will constitute the balance he owes me—If you think it necessary I will write to him on the subject, as well as what relates to Colo. Skipwith & Browne—You mentioned in your first letter as to Browne, that you were not certain whether an item in his acct. was due me or not— you purposed then writing to him on the subject, wch. I will thank you to do if it was not then done.

I repeat here what was mentioned in my last, my satisfaction with the plan you propose for getting my affairs into some fixed shape—I like the idea of the bank stock of Pennsylvania, you mention—I thought it right at the same time to mention that Mr. Gerry, as well as he could recollect, thought there was something objectionable in the origin, wch. prevented his taking a part therein—he concieved one of the Massachusetts banks, on the surest & most solid establishment possible—I shall be extremely happy to hear what is the information you recieve from Harvie as to the Green sea land—& in general any steps that may have been taken or projected in my affairs; on which I am really ashamed to take up so much of your time—Be so good as to address my letters either to Mess. V. Staphorst & Hubbard—or to J. A. Gautier & Cie. of this place—or in the case of war (which God forbid & wch. it now depends on the U.S. to avoid) to some house at Hamburgh—I shd. go to Germany in the case of war—the house of Hamburgh shd. keep the letter until they know where I may be from one of the two houses above-mentioned——I fear your patience will be now exhausted & I therefore finish my letter in assuring you my dear Sir of the unalterable friendship & constant gratitude of your affectionate   W Short

Aug. 27.

P.S. Dr. Logan has just now called on me for the first time & informs me he goes off to-morrow morning for America—I met with him only once before—he seems to be a true friend to the peace & happiness of his country—& to her independance of all foreign influence of every kind & every nation whatever—This is the principle wch. every true American shd. profess—& in the end I am sure every Government of every kind will respect & esteem us the more,—This has been ever my opinion—& I am more & more every day confirmed in it——I live out of the world of politics & have done so for years past; indeed ever since my quitting Madrid—but still I see & hear enough to have the fullest conviction that this Govet. wishes sincerely & truly at present to be on good & honorable terms with America—I hope our Governt. will have no hesitation to forget all that has passed—& to make one more effort to reconciliation, wch. cannot now fail, & wch. will be as honorable for the U.S. as it will be advantageous—putting us on a truly dignified ground as a Nation, & at the same securing all the benefits of peace & tranquillity—I cannot allow myself to believe that such an opportunity will be lost or not made the most of by the Prest.——Mr. Gerry & myself promised to write to each other—I take the liberty of inclosing you my first letter wch. I ask the favor of you to forward to him—

RC (DLC: Short Papers); at foot of first page: "Mr. Jefferson. Vice Prest. of the U.S."; endorsed by TJ as received 2 Jan. 1799 and so recorded in SJL. FC (same); a summary in Short's epistolary record of 26 Dec. 1797-9 Oct. 1798. Enclosure: Short to Elbridge Gerry, 27 Aug. 1798, expressing a wish that Gerry might return to France to negotiate for the United States, Short offering his own services and authorizing Gerry to make any arrangement for him in that regard, praising George Logan, and sending the good wishes of the Duchesse de La Rochefoucauld, who hopes to become acquainted with Gerry (FC in same, a summary in the same epistolary record).

The two letters that TJ wrote to Short in the year 97 were dated 12 Mch. and 30 June. my friend: the Duchesse de La

Rochefoucauld. PERSON THEN AT THE HEAD OF THE GOVERNMENT: George Washington. As Short indicated, when publication was completed in Paris in 1799 the account of the American TRAVELS of the duchesse's RELATION, François Alexandre Frédéric, Duc de La Rochefoucauld-Liancourt, occupied eight volumes under the title, *Voyage dans les États-Unis d'Amérique.*

For the ARRÊTÉ of 31 July curtailing the operation of CRUISERS from French colonies, see note to Jacob Van Staphorst to TJ, 25 July 1798. On 16 Aug. 1798 the Executive Directory lifted an EMBARGO which on 9 July it had placed on American ships in French ports (De Conde, *Quasi-War*, 147, 153; ASP, *Foreign Relations*, 2:229).

HIS LAST WILL & DYING SPEECH MADE IN 96: Washington's Farewell Address. D & B: Donald & Burton (see TJ to Short, 1 May 1798).

[1] Means.
[2] Quarrels (*démêlés*).
[3] Here in margin Short wrote: "lands in difft. states."
[4] Short inserted the three questions in the margin.
[5] A small farm (*métairie*) occupied on the sharecropping principle of *métayage*.

From Tadeusz Kosciuszko

MY DEAR FRIEND   [24-29 Aug. 1798]

The Amicable disposition of the Gouvernement of france are realy favorable to the interest of the United States, by the recent prouves they give, you ought not to doubt that they choose tobe in pease and in perfect harmonie with America. before it was misrepresented by some the facts relative to your Contry, but now they are perfectly acquiented wyth yours and their interest and Mr: Logan [as a?] vitnes of the Sentyment they have towards the Nation Of the United States. At present itis a duty of every true American as you, to publishe and propagate their friendship, and to Compele your Gouvernement by the Opinion of the Nation to the pacifique Masures with Republique of France, othervise you cannot but to loose every thing even your Liberty by a conexion so intimet wyth England which increasing son influence can easily subdue and exercise son despotiquc pouver as before. write me soon as possible of the effects which the news by Logans' arival will produce in America, as well as by the Election of the members for Congress, you may rely upon my indevours here but you most work in America wyth your friends and Republicans and state their reall interest, I will not hasard my Opinion concerning the affaires of different Nations in Europe. Mr: Logan, can give Some Scachess as tomy pecuniary affaires. I beg you would pay a friendly attention that i may receive punctualy my money here at Paris. inclosed I send a letters recived from Amsterdam by which it apear that the money was returned tothe Treasury long ago. but they had not inclination to pay me. now I beg you would receive from Mr Wolcott and to send me immidiatly by Amsterdam to Paris. if you will find a dificulty to receive the money please to publishe thos

Letters that the public should know their Characters. if the sword which was ofered tome by Patriots in England arived in America beso good to Send me to Paris

Your for ever Sincier Friend   T. KOSCIUSZKO

The Compliments to all my friends Mall and femell

RC (MHi); dated on the basis of the enclosure and internal evidence cited below; endorsed by TJ as "written from Paris" and received on 2 Jan. 1799, and recorded in SJL under that date. Enclosure: Jean Conrad Hottinguer to Kosciuszko, 7 Fructidor Year 6 (i.e., 24 Aug. 1798), transmitting letters, not found but evidently from Van Staphorst & Hubbard, indicating that they had written to Thomas Pinckney and Oliver Wolcott on 14 May to explain that the payment due to Kosciuszko was no longer on deposit in Europe (RC in same, in French).

Kosciuszko's implication that George LOGAN would convey information about him means that he probably wrote this letter sometime after receiving Hottinguer's letter of 24 Aug. but before Logan's departure from Paris on the 29th (Tolles, *Logan*, 169). His query about the English SWORD suggests that he had not yet received TJ's letter of 18 June.

From Sir Peyton Skipwith

DEAR SIR.   Prestwould. August 25th. 1798

Sometime ago you were so obliging as to say, you would mention to Mr Short my claim against him. I wish to have his answer, & should he have advised the payment of the debt, the bearer Major Nelson is furnished with the amount of the claim & will do me the favour to receive it for me.

I am with every sentiment of regard & esteem your obt. Sert.

                                                  PEYTON SKIPWITH

RC (DLC: Short Papers); endorsed by TJ as received 29 Aug., although recorded in SJL as received on the same day as written.

YOU WERE SO OBLIGING: TJ to Skipwith, 24 Dec. 1795. For Skipwith's CLAIM against William Short, see Skipwith to TJ, 9 Dec. 1795.

On 30 Aug. TJ wrote a note to John NELSON of Mecklenburg County inviting him to dinner, and to meet Thomas Mann Randolph, at three o'clock (RC owned by Mrs. E. C. Davis illustrated in *Atlanta Constitution*, 10 June 1951; not recorded in SJL).

From Nathaniel Cutting

SIR,   Paris, 27th. August, 1798.

Under the 19th. Feby. ulto. I took the liberty of communicating to you some of the reflections excited in my mind by the critical and alarming state of the political relation between the United States of America and France. The vessel which conveyed the original of that Letter was conducted into England; but I hope that a duplicate, which went by a Mr. Lee, whose arrival in America I have heard of, has had the honor to salute you.—

It is probable that long before this can reach you, Mr. Gerry will have communicated to you in detail many political occurrences which for five or six months last past have contributed to agitate the minds of the friends of the United States in this Country.—I will not presume to intrude upon your valuable moments by attempting a recapitulation of any of those interesting circumstances; but merely sieze the present occasion by Doctor Logan to felicitate you on the recent dawn of an amicable disposition in the present Government of France.

I have so much charity for *the supreme magistrates* of this Republique as to think that, till very lately, they have been ignorant of, or misinformed respecting, those vexations and iniquities exercised in the West Indies under colour of *their* authority.

I flatter myself that Doctor Logan, and Mr. Joseph Woodward of Boston, carry with them respectively to America some unequivocal proofs that a majority of the members of the French Directory are emerging from that cloud of error in which some of their artful and interested Subalterns have long strove to envelope them; and I please myself with the hope that things have not yet been carried to such extremity on your side the Atlantic as to preclude the probability of an amicable adjustment of all existing differences between the two Republiques.—

We owe much of the present favorable prospect to the accurate & candid information & judicious counsel of Victor Dupont, late French Consul at Charleston.—

General Kosciuszko likewise has, I am persuaded, improved every opportunity of pleading our cause at the Fountain-head of Power in this Country & with good effect.—Mr. Adet, late Minister Plenipotentiary at Philadelphia, has also been remarkably assiduous [in][1] his endeavours to promote a right understanding.—And our estimable friend and fellow-citizen, Joel Barlow, has been indefatigable in exerting his eminent talents & the influence that his literary reputation has justly acquired him, to co-operate in the desireable work of Peace and Reconciliation.

Doctor Logan's independent principles and liberal patriotism do honor to himself, and, I hope, will be productive of great benefit to our[2] Country.—He has spoken to the first authorities here, in the tone and manner of a plain, modest, but free and firm Republican;—and has represented the Union and Resources of the United States in as fair a point of view as the most spirited of our rational Citizens could desire.—He has judiciously inculcated the opinion that their whole energy would be exerted against any power on Earth which might attempt to invade the United States;—but he has at same time deprecated the miseries inseparable from a state of War, and has uttered conciliatory sentiments, with such unaffected sincerity as appears to have made very favorable impressions at the Luxembourg.—

The cordial reception he has met with here, as a private individual, furnishes an indubitable proof of the readiness with which this Government would now receive & give eclaircissements, and agree to mutual concessions, provided the mode and organs of communication were calculated to inspire confidence.—

No doubt the Government of the French Republique, like most other Governments in the world, is influenced more by what is thought to be its Interest, or what is called "good policy,"—than by any principles of Justice or Generosity.—Doubtless it would be very injurious to France at any time,—more particularly at the present moment, for the United States to be *forced* to Unite their Power & Resources with those of Great Britain.—I hope also that the Government of the United States is properly imprest with the idea that we ought at present to keep aloof from too intimate a connexion with either of those great belligerent Powers:—Sound *Policy* dictates that we should stand upon good terms with them both,—though our true *interest*, would certainly be to prefer a free Commercial intercourse with France, as presenting less Rivality and more extensive and important advantages.

The present is perhaps the most favorable moment we can ever expect to adjust our differences, and to define our Political Relation with France.—I hope sincerely that the present indications of the favorable disposition of the French Directory[3] towards the United States, will be properly appreciated & seconded with dignified cordiality by our Government. The way appears to me to be sufficiently paved for both Parties to march on with manly promptitude towards a rational accommodation, without being obliged to make, or to insist on receiving, any humiliating concessions.—I cannot boast an acquaintance with the science of Diplomacy; but to my plain understanding it appears that if an honest, candid, well-informed man on each part, could meet together and agree to pass an act of oblivion with respect to a thousand unimportant circumstances that have only served to irritate the passions on both sides, they might proceed with facility to adjust the great & essential points in dispute. I think the French Directory are now in a disposition to meet such a proposition in all good faith.—If the Government of the United States should evince a similar disposition by once more sending a Negociator to this Country,—I take the liberty of recommending that *Joel Barlow* be joined in the Commission.—His talents will not be disputed; and those who know him most intimately are thoroughly convinced that his patriotism is pure, his principles independent, and that he would with proper firmness support the true honor & interest of his Country. His long residence in different parts of *Europe* has enabled him to acquire a competent knowledge of the relative interests of the United States with most parts of *it*:—more particularly with France; and his acquaintance with many influential characters in, or connected with, the French Government, might essentially facilitate the Negociation.—

I pray you to accept my most respectful salutations.

NAT. CUTTING.

Dupl (DLC); at head of text: "Duplicate"; at foot of first and third pages: "M. Jefferson"; endorsed by TJ as received 22 Nov. 1798 and so recorded in SJL. RC (same); endorsed by TJ as received 2 Jan. 1799 and so recorded in SJL.

Concerning the fate of many of the letters that William LEE had carried from France to the United States, see note to Fulwar Skipwith to TJ, 17 Mch. 1798. George LOGAN and JOSEPH WOODWARD OF BOSTON, who had strong Federalist connections, returned from Paris with similar documents and information about the French government's position toward the United States. Woodward's earlier arrival took some of the drama away from Logan's return from France with what Republicans interpreted as hopeful news (Tolles, *Logan*, 175, 179-80, 191).

[1] MS torn; word supplied from RC.
[2] RC: "his."
[3] RC: "Government."

From Pierre Samuel Du Pont de Nemours

MONSIEUR,   Paris 10 Fructidor de l'an 6. [27 Aug. 1798]

Le Docteur *Logan* vous dira qu'il a trouvé en France de bons et zélés amis de l'Amérique; et vous ne serez pas Surpris que j'aie été du nombre, ainsi que mon fils. Vous m'avez vu pendant votre Ambassade lutter en faveur de votre Patrie et pour les principes de liberalité, d'amitié Sincere entre les deux Nations, contre tous les préjugés fiscaux et mercantiles qu'avait alors notre gouvernement.

Vous avez vu ma joie quand nos efforts n'ont pas été vains.

Ce Sentiment d'un profond interêt pour votre pays ne peut pas être diminué chez moi. Je Suis chargé par l'Institut national d'y faire un voyage qui a pour objet une communication et des recherches utiles aux Sciences; et c'est mon intention de prolonger ce voyage autant que ma vie.

Je veux mourir dans un Pays où la liberté ne Soit pas Seulement dans les loix, toujours plus ou moins bien, plus ou moins mal exécutées; mais principalement dans les constantes habitudes de la nation.

Je compte me fixer dans la haute Virginie, en ses comtés de l'ouest.

Je me flatte d'y retrouver votre durable amitié et le secours de vos lumieres.

Je vous envoie ceux de mes discours dont le conseil des anciens a ordonné l'impression, et ma *philosophie* qui, je l'espere, ne déplaira point à la vôtre.

Salut et respectueux attachement.   DuPont (de nemours)

EDITORS' TRANSLATION

Sir,   Paris 10 Fructidor of Year 6.

Doctor *Logan* will tell you that he found in France good and zealous friends of America; and you will not be surprised that I was among that number, as well as my son. You saw me during your embassy struggle in favor of your homeland and for the principles of liberality, of sincere friendship between the two nations, against all the fiscal and mercantile prejudices held at that time by our government.

You saw my joy when our efforts were not in vain.

This feeling of a strong interest for your country could not wane in me. I have been charged by the National Institute to make a voyage there with the object of a communication and research useful for the sciences; and it is my intention to prolong this voyage for as long as my life.

I want to die in a country where liberty is not only in the laws, always more or less well, more or less poorly executed; but is principally in the constant habits of the nation.

I expect to settle in upper Virginia, in its western counties.

I am convinced that I shall find there once again your lasting friendship and the help of your learning.

I am sending you those of my speeches that the Council of Elders ordered to be printed, and my *Philosophie*, which I hope will not displease yours.

Greetings and respectful affection.   DuPont (de nemours)

RC (DLC); Gregorian date supplied; at head of text below dateline: "DuPont (de Nemours) a Thomas Jefferson President du Senat des Etats unis"; endorsed by TJ as received 20 Jan. 1799 and so recorded in SJL; in pencil below dateline, probably in TJ's hand: "27 August 1798." Enclosures: (1) "Extrait du discours de Mr. Dupont de Nemours sur les droits a imposer à l'entrée des Tabacs étrangers," extracting Du Pont's comments before the Council of Elders, 23 Nov. 1796, arguing against an intended two hundred percent customs duty on tobacco that would catch by surprise a number of American and other vessels already at sea; Du Pont declaring that since the United States depends on selling only rice, cod, and tobacco in exchange for French wine, silk, and other products, this Carthaginian ruse ("ruse Carthaginoise") will have bad consequences at a time when the United States is choosing a successor to Washington and its politics is increasingly defined as a contest between parties favoring Britain and France (MS in same; in French in an unidentified hand; titled as an extract from a speech published in its entirety in *L'Historien* [a serial published by Du Pont], 9:315-28). (2) Pierre Samuel Du Pont de Nemours, *Philosophie de L'Univers*, 2d ed. (Paris, 1796), which the author inscribed in French to TJ as president of the U.S. Senate (see Sowerby, No. 1264).

ENTRE LES DEUX NATIONS: in 1786 the French government had appointed Du Pont to a committee examining trade relations between France and the United States. While TJ was minister to France he and Du Pont corresponded on commercial matters, including French importation of American products, and also on political philosophy (Vol. 9:338n; Vol. 12:211-12, 325-9, 595-6; Vol. 13:53-4n, 61; Vol. 15:446n). Regarding L'INSTITUT NATIONAL of Arts and Sciences established in 1795, see Alexandre Lerebours to TJ, 17 May 1796.

Fifty-eight years of age when he penned the above letter, Du Pont embarked on his VOYAGE in September 1799 with his sons, Victor and Éleuthère Irénée du Pont de Nemours, and their families, intending to remain in the United States. Buffeted by shifts in political power in France through the Revolution, Pierre Samuel and Irénée had been briefly jailed, and their Paris publishing establishment ransacked, as recently as September 1797. Originally expecting to establish an agricultural colony in America, the family determined instead to concentrate on manufacturing, especially gunpowder, and other endeavors. In 1802 Pierre Samuel went back to France to attend to business matters, returning to the United States in 1815, two years before his death (*Dictionnaire*, 12:472-5; Gilbert Chinard, *The Correspondence of Jefferson and Du Pont de Nemours* [Baltimore, 1931], xxiii-xxv, 215; ANB, 7:115-17).

The elder Du Pont capitalized the article in his surname even though his sons favored the form "du Pont." The father also often wrote the name as one word, as in the signature above. Pierre Samuel had appended "de Nemours" to his name to distinguish himself from other Du Ponts in France, and members of his family did not always use the expanded form. Victor, for example, generally omitted "de Nemours" from his own signature but included it in the name of a company he formed in the nineteenth century (John K. Winkler, *The Du Pont Dynasty* [New York, 1935], 34, 42; DAB, 5:533; Victor du Pont to TJ, 7 May 1803, and enclosure).

From Van Staphorst & Hubbard

SIR! Amsterdam 28 August 1798

We have before us your very esteemed favors of 30 April and 1 May.

You have greatly obliged us by your explanation of the paragraph in a former letter, concerning Land Speculators. We are entirely of your opinion on that Subject. With Mr. Greenleaf We never had any the least dealings.

We close your account Current with us, by the Bond You have forwarded for ƒ2800.– payable the 25 December 1802 to our order.

Owing to the failure of our late Correspondents Messs: Harrison & Sterett of Philadelphia, We beg of you to pay as they fall due the Interest and Reimbursments of the aforegoing and of your two preceeding Bonds in our favor, for $1000 each, unto Messs: Danl. Ludlow & Co. of New York; whose receipts for same, We do hereby promise and engage ourselves to hold of equal validity, as if they had been Signed by ourselves.

Your Letter to the Baron von Geissmar was forwarded and inclosed you have his reply to it.

General Kosciuszko negotiated in Paris, by the assistance of our Jacob van Staphorst the Bills of which you inclosed us the Thirds.

ƒ6315.16.– on Kunckel Ruys & Co.
3157.18.– " I. F. & I. Dutilh } which were duly honored.

Whenever We shall receive any remittance for the Dividends on his effects in the Bank of Pennsylvania, you may depend upon our holding their amount at his immediate disposal, as well as of our readiness to render him the useful or agreeable Services in our Power; of which We a few days ago had the opportunity to furnish him a proof.

We are with greatest esteem Sir! Your mo. ob: hb: Servants

N & J. VAN STAPHORST & HUBBARD

Dupl (DLC); in a clerk's hand, signed by the firm; at head of text: "Dupl."; at foot of first page: "Ths. Jefferson Esqr. Philadelphia"; endorsed by TJ as a letter of 22 Aug. 1798 received 22 Jan. 1799 and so recorded in SJL. RC (same); in a clerk's hand, signed by the firm. Tripl (same); in a clerk's hand, signed by the firm; at head of text: "Orig: Via New York ⅌ Nordiske Uänskape. SkiogStrom. Dupl: New York ⅌ Union. Phipps" and "Tripl." Enclosure: Baron von Geismar to TJ, 11 July 1798 (see note to TJ to Van Staphorst & Hubbard, 30 Apr. 1798).

Sometime probably between mid-July 1798 and mid-January 1799 John Barnes made a rough note of the proceeds of DIVI-

DENDS on Tadeusz Kosciuszko's BANK OF PENNSYLVANIA stock. Barnes calculated that the half-yearly dividend on 30 shares would be $480, which after the deduction of his own commission of one-half of one percent would be $477.60. With the addition of a similar dividend expected on 14 Jan. 1799 the total would come to $955.20. Barnes added an "advance" of $184.80 to bring the total to $1,140, the amount that according to his calculation would purchase 3,000 guilders (MS in MHi; in Barnes's hand on a scrap, endorsed: "Memdm. G K—"; with unrelated calculation of figures, probably by TJ, on verso).

OPPORTUNITY TO FURNISH HIM A PROOF: see Tadeusz Kosciuszko to TJ, [24-29 Aug. 1798].

To Thomas Mann Randolph

TH:J. TO TMR.   [29 Aug. 1798]

I find that the Ogee plain I sent you, was for the architraves of my doors as well as your windows. as we are now about these, I must borrow it of you again. what is become of the Carr's brook expedition, and what the present intentions on that subject? we are always ready. loves & kisses to Martha & the little ones. Adieu.

RC (DLC); date supplied from endorsement; addressed: "Mr. Randolph Belmont"; endorsed by Randolph: "Aug. 29. 98." Not recorded in SJL.

I MUST BORROW IT: at the same time the renovations were taking place at Monticello, Randolph began building a house, designed by TJ, at Edgehill, the estate across the Rivanna River just two miles from Monticello. It became the Randolph family's permanent residence in 1800 (Gaines, *Ran-* *dolph*, 44; Kimball, *Jefferson, Architect*, 61, plate 170).

To John Barnes

DEAR SIR   Monticello Aug. 31. 98.

A most astonishing derangement of our post has rendered it almost useless as the channel of communication. your letter of July 18. was 25 days on it's passage to me, that of Aug. 9. was 16 days; so that instead of 8. days as formerly letters are now never received under 16. days from Philadelphia & from that up to 22. and this is not all; for I recieve those letters now by a return post, so that a week more is lost before I can answer. when I recieved your favor of July 18. tho' it intimated that my note to the bank must be on stamped paper, yet as I had sent it on in mine of July 27. I expected you would have got it stamped as the law admits. the return of it (besides the delay of paiment to yourself and the persons named in my letter of July 27.) finds me unable to obtain proper stamped paper in time for this post. the distributor of stamps for this county lives 20. or 30. miles up among the mountains, and the sending to him would cost ten times the amount of the stamp. I have however borrowed two stamps of 10. cents each from a neighbor, which of course will only bear notes of 500. D. each. These (the only ones I could procure) I send you to avoid the inconveniences of further delay, tho' on account of the delays already incurred (unavoidably by me) I am sensible you will recieve them but three weeks before the whole quarter's salary can be drawn without a note. I wish you therefore to use them only so far as is necessary to replace your own and Joseph Roberts's advances for my [expences?] are greater than I had hoped by the failure of mr Beckley's paiment of 250. D. but for this, the balance would have been only 82.85 D instead of 332.85 as by the inclosed account, which, agreeing exactly with your's rendered me, I forward for your security. to this balance against me be pleased to add 200. Dollars which I was to answer you for mr Lott. I will avoid making any draught on you payable earlier than Octob. 5. I will by the next post inclose to mr Wharton & C. Johnston & co. draughts on you payable at that date. the mortification I have experienced at leaving my engagements to yourself & those gentlemen unfulfilled so long, will be a caution to me hereafter not to pay other people's debts for them, till I am sure I have funds enough to answer my own also.—I am sincerely concerned at the revisitation of your city by the yellow fever. I wish you were in some of the higher streets of the city. your danger must be considerable, but I hope your prudence will be the greater. I have no news yet of our friend the General. I wrote you last on the 3d. inst. I have no doubt your answer is on the road, but from the derangement of the post the time of it's reciept is uncertain.—our crops of tobacco are most flattering. near half is secured, & the remainder beyond the reach of every injury. the quality too promises to be extraordinary. I hope to have between 50. & 60. thousand made this year. the next I shall go on tobacco fully and entirely, laying aside all attention to wheat. I am with great esteem Dear Sir

Your friend & servt   TH: JEFFERSON

PrC (DLC); faint; at foot of first page: "Mr. Barnes"; endorsed by TJ in ink on verso. Enclosure not found.

For Barnes's unlocated LETTER OF JULY 18, see note to TJ to Barnes, 27 July. According to SJL TJ received THAT OF AUG. 9, which is also missing, on 25 Aug. TJ's letter of 27 July discusses the payments to JOSEPH ROBERTS, Charles Wharton, and Charles Johnston & Co. For TJ's furnishing of ready money to ease John BECKLEY's situation, see his three letters to Beckley at 16-17 Apr. above. TJ used the interest payments on William Short's securities to open a line of credit with Barnes for Charlottesville merchant Peter LOTT, who performed a similar function locally for TJ (TJ to Barnes, 11 Dec. 1796, 25 Sep. 1797; TJ to Thomas Mann Randolph, 29 Mch. 1798).

In response to the outbreak of YELLOW FEVER along Water Street, early in the second week of August the Philadelphia Health Office ordered ships away from the wharves and recommended, on the advice of the College of Physicians, that inhabitants leave the area. As the epidemic progressed, many of the stricken who remained behind were left without sufficient care. One-third of those who stayed in the city through the epidemic died, a mortality rate greater than that of the yellow fever epidemic of 1793 (*Philadelphia Gazette*, 8 Aug. 1798; Anita DeClue and Billy G. Smith, eds., "Wrestling the 'Pale Faced Messenger': The Diary of Edward Garrigues During the 1798 Philadelphia Yellow Fever Epidemic," *Pennsylvania History*, 65, supp. [1998], 243-5).

OUR FRIEND THE GENERAL: Tadeusz Kosciuszko. TJ's letter to Barnes of THE 3D. INST. is recorded in SJL but has not been found.

From Julian Ursin Niemcewicz

MONSIEUR   3 Sbr. 1798. Elizabeth Town

Me voila enfin de retour de ma tournée vers l'Est, j'ai été jusqu'à Boston & Porthsmuth, de la à travers les montagnes à Albany, d'ou j'ai descendu la riviere jusqu'à New York. Partout j'etois brulé par le Soleil et quelque fois ecorché par Les Yankis. Je me suis arreté quelques Jours chez le Chancellier Levingston et Le General Armstrong, Mr. Dawson m'y avoit dépassé, et j'ai trouvé ces Messieurs instruits du depart et de la destination du G.K. Le Secret etant entre de bonnes mains, je n'en fus nullement inquiet; mais quelle fut ma Surprise lorsqu'arrivé à Elizabeth

[506]

Town j'ai trouvé cet Endroit rempli de Contes les plus absurdes. On me dit que Le Major Touzard ayant passé par içi il y a dix jours, et s'etant arreté chez Mr. Dayton le Speaker, a assuré tout le monde avoir vu une lettre ecrite de Virginie, qui annonçoit que Le G.K. avoit quitté ce pays tout seul et dans le plus grand Secret possible; qu'on croyoit qu'il etoit allé en France ou à ce qu'il etoit dit dans La lettre en Irland pour y commander Les Insurgents. Tout cela passe, mais quelle fut mon Indignation et mon Etonnement lorsque j'appris que Le Major Touzard a eu la hardiesse de dire que les blessures et l'Etat cruel d'Invalide et d'estropié ou se trouvoit le Général n'etoit qu'une farce, une fainte, et qu'on l'a vu marcher à New Castel. J'ai nié la Calomnie comme absurde et injurieuse au Caractere du Gl: assurant tous ces Messieurs, que le jour du depart du Gl: pour les Eaux, je l'ai vu comme toujours porté à la Voîture dans les bras de son domestique. Voyez Monsieur jusqu'ou la Calomnie et la méchanceté des hommes peuvent aller. Il n'en est pas moins vrai que ces Contes absurdes du Major ont donné lieu içi, à des propos et Comerages, qui me blessent et me mortifient cruelment. Je crains qu'il n'en soit pire encore dans les grandes villes, aussi suis-je decidé à m'en tenir bien eloigné. Je n'ai rien [reçu] de ma famille, ce qui ajoute encore à ma triste position. Je vous supp[lie] de Vouloir bien m'excuser, si je ne puis Satisfaire à la dette que j'ai contractée envers Vous, j'espere pouvoir m'en acquitter sous peu, [et] être alors en Etat de faire mon pelerinage à Monti Celli. Pour a present je suis decidé de passer mon temps entre Elizabeth Town et Brunswick[,] les situations en sont charmantes, la Vie à bon marché, et comme disent Les Italiens Il primo bisbiglio di Chiacere una volta pass[ata] je pourrai y vivre oublié et tranquille, jusqu'à ce que mon devoir [ne] me rappelle chez moi, ou l'Espoir perdu pour toujours, ne me fixe [ici.]

Si le Dr: [Bache] et Mr. Maclure Sont chez vous je vous prie de me rappeller à leur Souvenir; je ne sais ce qu'est devenu Le Dr. Scandella. Si vous avez appris Monsieur quelques nouvelles du Voyageur, et si vous voulez bien m'ecrire un mot je vous prie de tout adresser chez Mrs. Bache, epouse du Docteur. J'ai reçu dernièrement de ses nouvelles, elle est en bonne Santé à la Campagne de son pere. Philadelphie est entierement deserte l'herbe croit dans les Rüës, on n'y compte que 10 m. habitants, et il en meurt encore Cent par jour, et la moitié de ce nombre à New York. S'il faut absolument des Victimes à la Colere Celeste, pourquoi ne s'exerce t-elle pas plustôt en Russie, en Autriche, en Prusse?

Veuillez Monsieur agreer les assurances de mon Attachement et de mon respect et croyez moi pour toujours Vôtre très humble et très Obeissant Serviteur   J: U. NIEMCEWICZ

SIR   3 September 1798. Elizabeth Town

Here I am at last returned from my travels to the east, I went as far as Boston and Portsmouth, from there across the mountains to Albany, whence I went down the river to New York. Everywhere I was burned by the sun and sometimes skinned by the Yankees. I stopped for a few days with Chancellor Livingston and General Armstrong, Mr. Dawson having preceded me there, and I found those gentlemen aware of the departure and the destination of G.K. the secret being in good hands, I was in no way upset; but what was my surprise when having arrived in Elizabeth Town I found that place full of the most absurd stories. They told me that Major Touzard having passed through here ten days ago, and having stayed with Mr. Dayton the speaker, assured everyone that he had seen a letter written from Virginia, which announced that G.K. had left this country alone and with the greatest possible secrecy; that it was believed that he had gone to France or, as it said in the letter, to Ireland to command the insurgents there. All of that can be passed over, but what was my indignation and my astonishment when I learned that Major Touzard had the audacity to say that the wounds and the cruel invalid and crippled condition of the General were mere comedy, a ruse, and that he had been seen walking at New Castle. I denied the calumny as being absurd and injurious to the character of the Gl: assuring all those gentlemen that on the day of departure of the Gl: for the waters, I saw him as usual carried to the coach in his servant's arms. Behold, Sir, how far the calumny and the wickedness of men can go. It is nonetheless true that these absurd stories of the major have given rise here, to talk and gossip, which wound and mortify me cruelly. I fear that it may be even worse in the big cities, so I am determined to keep myself well away from them. I received nothing from my family, which adds even more to my pitiable situation. I kindly beseech you to forgive me, if I cannot satisfy the debt that I contracted with you, I hope to be able to acquit myself of it soon, and at that time to be in a position to make my pilgrimage to Monticello. For now I am determined to spend my time between Elizabeth Town and Brunswick, their locations are charming, life is inexpensive, and as the Italians say the first whisper of gossip once passed I can live there forgotten and at peace, until my duty calls me back home, or hope being lost forever, I settle here for good.

If Dr: Bache and Mr. Maclure are with you I beg you to pay them my respects; I do not know what has happened to Dr. Scandella. If you have heard Sir some news of the traveler, and if you would kindly write me a note please address everything care of Mrs. Bache, the wife of the doctor. I have recently had news of her, she is in good health at her father's country place. Philadelphia is totally deserted, grass grows in the streets, it numbers only 10 m. inhabitants, and still one hundred die every day, and half of that number in New York. If the wrath of heaven ineluctably requires victims, why does it not take them in Russia, in Austria, in Prussia?

Please Sir accept the assurances of my affection and respect and consider me forever Your very humble and very Obedient Servant   J: U. NIEMCEWICZ

RC (DLC); torn; endorsed by TJ as re-   G.K.: General Kosciuszko. LE MAJOR
ceived on 27 Sep. and so recorded in SJL.   TOUZARD: Anne Louis de Tousard, who

had served as an officer under Lafayette in the American Revolution and commanded troops in Saint-Domingue, had accepted a commission as an artillery major in the United States Army in 1795 and oversaw construction at various fortifications (DAB).

Niemcewicz had become acquainted with William BACHE, who was a medical doctor and a brother of Benjamin Franklin Bache; William MACLURE; and Giambattista (or J. B.) SCANDELLA, who had studied medicine in London while serving as the secretary of the embassy of the Republic of Venice. Scandella, who lodged with Maclure while in Philadelphia, had been elected to the American Philosophical Society at the same time as Niemcewicz, in a meeting presided over by TJ in April 1798.

He considered TJ to be one of a small number of Virginians who had been open to him after his arrival in the United States in 1797. After passage of the alien acts Scandella determined to return to Europe, but in September 1798 he died of yellow fever in New York before he could embark. MRS. BACHE was Catharine Wistar Bache, a sister of Dr. Caspar Wistar (Niemcewicz, *Under their Vine*, 38, 60-1, 304n, 308n; Latrobe, *Virginia Journals*, 2:329n, 331; Leonard W. Labaree and others, eds., *The Papers of Benjamin Franklin*, 36 vols. to date [1959-], 1:lxiii; Richard Wistar Davids, *The Wistar Family: A Genealogy of the Descendants of Caspar Wistar, Emigrant in 1717* [Philadelphia, 1896], 7; APS, *Proceedings*, 22, pt. 3 [1884], 261-2, 270).

From Samuel Brown

DEAR SIR. Lexington Sept. 4th 1798—

The letter you did me the honor of writing me, in March last, I intended to have answered long since; & to enable me to do so, the more to your satisfaction, I took the earliest opportunities of informing General Clarke & several other gentlemen, who had been the companions of his youthful campaigns, of the illiberal attack made on you, by the Attorney General of Maryland. I have defered replying to your friendly letter hetherto, from an expectation of collecting from different sources, a variety of statements & facts relative to the murder of Logans family. But as most of the Gentlemen to whom I wrote on the subject, reside in remote parts of the country, at a distance from post Roads, I am induced to attribute their silence to the want of safe modes of conveying their letters to Lexington. I am, however, happy, in having it in my power to transmit to you, an interesting letter, from your freind General Clarke, which, indeed, appears to me, to render further investigation quite unnecessary. The only point for which you contend (viz) that Logan is really the Author of the Speech ascribed to him, in your Notes on Virginia is now established beyond the possibility of contradiction. The incidents in General Clarkes narrative follow each other in a manner so simple & so natural as to afford, to every liberal & candid enquirer, the highest internal evidence of thier reality. To those who have the happiness of being acquainted with that truely great man, his statement will bring the fullest conviction. His memory is singularly accurate, his veracity unquestionable. To such respectable authority I can suppose no one capable of objecting, except Mr Luther Martin. I have shewn General Clarkes letter to Major Morrison, the Supervisor of the Ohio District, who resided near Pittsburg, when the transactions respecting Logan occurred. He assures me that he knows most of them as stated in the letter to be true for they are within his own recollection. Colo. Paterson who likewise lived in that Country about that time mentioned to me a circumstance which appears worthy of notice. There were, then, in that, as in almost every other frontier, two parties—By the one Capt. Cresap was considered as a wanton Violator of Treaties as a man of a cruel & inhuman disposition; By the other he was esteem[ed] as an intrepid warrior & as a just avenger of savage barbarities. You probably became first acquainted with his character at Williamsburg the seat of Government; General Clarke joined him in the War Path. This circumstance will, perhaps, in some measure, account for the very different sentiments, which two Gentlemen so perfectly capable of appreciating Cresaps character, may have entertained respecting it—

Should you judge it adviseable, at the present time, I could easily obtain from General Clarke the substance of his narrative & have it published here as—an answer to spontaneous enquiries of my own. It can be done without your appearing at all in the business. This however I shall not attempt to do without your permission; yet I wish that Genl Clarkes statement could be made public in some shape or other, as it would doubly mortify Mr Martin to have his assertions refuted without receiving a reply from you whom he has so assiduously laboured to draw forth into the field of controversy. I can assure that your friends in this quarter are highly gratified at the silent contempt with which you have treated that redoutable Hero of Federalism—And it is with heartfelt pleasure that I further assure you, that nothing which old Tories, Aristocrats & governmental Sycophants can say against you, will in any degree, diminish the confidence, which the good Citizens of this state repose in your abilities & patriotism. Never was a State more unanimous in execrating the measures supported by your Enemies who, I trust, will soon prove themselves to be, what I have long thot. them, the enemies of Liberty & thier Country. The Resolutions which I take the freedom of enclosing will shew you what we think of Federal measures. Attempts will, no doubt, be made, may indeed, have already been made, to lessen the weight of our proceedings by representing our meetings as disorderly & factious. But it is most certain that greater order & decorum never were observed at any public Meetings than at those which have been held in Kentucky. I fondly hope that our Legislature will soon be called & that the constituted authorities will give such solemnity to the voice of the people, as will arrest the attention of our infatuated Rulers. Republicans ought not to despair. The Irish are fighting for us. The French can never be conquered & Woe be to those who foolishly mistake the convulsive struggles of expiring Despotism, in England, for a Renovation of healthful Spirits & national Vigor.

I am happy to learn that Co[lo.] Monroe will be returned for your District. His virtues have been often tried & his Book which has been much read in this Country, has made him a great favorite with Kentucky Republicans.

I believe no change will take place in the Representation of this State. I wish our *Bard* could be detained in this "fertile Land planting or corn or hay." He came to Lexington a few Evenings ago & the young men assembled in considerable numbers for the purpose of singing to him his own Poem, the Aliens, by way of Serenade. Whilst they were tuning their instruments & distributing thier parts, he unfortunately stole out of town—for Modesty always accompanies poetic Genius—It is still however intended to pay him that compliment to which his singular performance entitles him—

With sincerest wishes for your welfare & with sentiments of the most perfect esteem I have Sir The honor To be Yo. Mo Obt

SAM BROWN

RC (DLC); damaged; at foot of text: "The Honble. Thos Jefferson"; endorsed by TJ as received 1 Oct. 1798 and so recorded in SJL. Enclosed resolutions not identified, but see below. Other enclosure printed below.

TJ's LETTER of MARCH LAST is at 25 Mch. 1798 above. Another from TJ to Brown of 5 Dec. 1798 is recorded in SJL but has not been found. The next installment in their correspondence, from TJ to Brown on 10 May 1800, suggests that Brown's brother John, who as a U.S. senator traveled back and forth between Philadelphia and Kentucky, conveyed information between TJ and Samuel Brown relating to the SPEECH of the Mingo Indian Logan. When in Philadelphia TJ and John Brown both roomed at Francis's hotel (see note to Account with John Francis, 3 July 1797). It was perhaps through Senator Brown that a document containing statements of James Smith and Andrew Rodgers came to TJ's hands. The affidavit, which was solicited by James Brown, a brother of John and Samuel Brown, contains a copy of the portion of

TJ's *Notes on Virginia* relating to Logan's speech, followed by a note requesting Smith and Rodgers "to Subjoin what they have heard and know respecting the above Statement and Speech." Smith's appended statement, dated 25 May 1798, declares that he was a captive of the Six Nations from 1755 to 1760—"untill thier tongue became natural to me"—and that in 1774 he "commanded a large party of riphelmen on the alegany above fort pitt." With regard to the murder of Logan's kin, he stated: "all I can say at this time is that from the unanimus reports of Indiens and whites at that time which I never heard contredicted I have reason to belive that said Logans family was masecreed altho said Logan had been a friend to the whites. but wether it was Crisaps party or Greathouses or Lins I do not know; but this I know by conversing with the Indiens; that as Chrisap had been an old warier the Indiens blamed him with Commiting this murder, and further I know not." Rodgers, writing his statement on the same paper, attested that he had been with the Virginia volunteers at the conclusion of Dunmore's War. Stating that "I did not hear logan make the above speech but from the unanimus accounts of those in camp I have reason to think that said speech was delivered to Dunmore," he recalled that he heard "the very things contained in the above speech, related by some of our people in camp at that time" (MS in DLC: TJ Papers, 104:17776-7; Smith and Rodgers each writing and signing his own statement; endorsed in an unknown hand as "recd. Sepr. 7th [1]798," with notation in same hand that Smith "is a representative in the Kentucky Legislature for Bourbon County"). TJ included Rodgers's statement, but not Smith's, in his *Appendix* in 1800 (*Notes*, ed. Peden, 246). In 1799 Smith published what came to be a well-known memoir of his captivity and long involvement in the frontier wars, *An Account of the Remarkable Occurrences in the Life and Travels of Col. James Smith* (ANB, 20:211-12).

On 24 July 1798 a gathering in Clark County, Kentucky, passed ten RESOLUTIONS that among other things condemned the Alien Friends Act as "unconstitutional, impolitic, unjust and disgraceful to the American character" and the Sedition Act—which as far as the Kentuckians knew was still pending as a bill—as "the most abominable, that was ever attempted to be imposed upon a nation of free men." PUBLIC MEETINGS that followed in Lexington and elsewhere adopted resolutions of a similar tenor (*Kentucky Gazette*, 1 Aug. 1798; Ethelbert Dudley Warfield, *The Kentucky Resolutions of 1798: An Historical Study* [New York, 1887], 41-3). See also Editorial Note to the Kentucky Resolutions of 1798.

OUR BARD: U.S. Senator Humphrey Marshall of Kentucky, who had earlier been the target of public demonstrations protesting his support of the Jay Treaty, composed *The Aliens: A Patriotic Poem* (Philadelphia, 1798) as the Senate considered the alien friends bill in May (Evans, No. 34048; DAB, 12:310). The work included the lines "From distant clime, and fertile land, / In Philadelphia sings the bard"; and: "Then through the States, they take their way; / Some here, some there, as fancy leads, / Sit down; and plant, or corn, or hay, / To raise their flocks of various breeds."

ENCLOSURE

George Rogers Clark to Samuel Brown

SIR   June 17th. 1798.

Your Letter was handed to me by Mr. Thruston, the Matter therein contained was new to me; I find myself hurt that Mr. Jefferson should have been Attacked with so much Virulence on a Subject which I know he was not Author of, but except a few Mistakes of Names of Person & Places, the Story is substantially true; I was of the first and last of the active Officers who bore the Weight of that War, and on perusing some old Papers of that Date I find some Memoirs, but indepedent of them I have a perfect Recollection of every Transaction relative to Logans Story—The Conduct of Cresap I am perfectly acquainted with, he was not the Author of that Murder, but a Family of the Name of Greathouse—But some Transactions that happened under the Conduct of Captn. Cresap a few Days previous to the Murder of Logan's Family gave him sufficient Ground to suppose that it was Cresap who had done him the Injury; But to enable you fully to understand the Subject of your Enquiry, I shall relate the Incidents that gave Rise to Logan's Suspicion; and will enable Mr. Jefferson to do Justice to himself and the Cresap Family, by being made fully acquainted with Facts.

Kentucky was explored in 1773; A Resolution was formed to make Settlements in the Spring following—& the Mouth of the little Kenhawa was appointed the Place of general Rendevouz—in Order to descend the River from thence in a Body; Early in the Spring the Indians had done some Mischief, Reports from their Towns were alarming which caused many to decline Meeting and only eighty or ninety Men assembled at the Place of Rendevous, where we lay some Days; A small Party of Hunters which lay about ten Miles below us were fired on by the Indians whom the Hunters beat off and returned to our Camp; This and many other Circumstances led us to believe that the Indians were determined to make War; the wh[ole] of our Party was exasperated, and resolved n[ot] to be disappointed in their Project of forming a Settlement in Kentucky, as we had every necessary Store that could be thought of—

An Indian Town called Horse-head Bottom on the Siotho and nearest its mouth lay most in our Way, we resolved to cross the Country & surprize it; Who was to command was the Question; there were but few among us who had experience in Indian Warfare, and they were such as we did not chuse to be commanded by—We knew of Capt. Cresap being on the River about 15 Miles above with some Hands settling a new Plantation and intending to follow us to Kentucky as soon as he had fixed his People, we also knew that he had had Experience in a former War. It was proposed & unanimously agreed on to Send for him to command the Party; A Messenger was dispatched and in half an Hour returned with Cresap; he had heard of our Resolution by some of his Hunters who had fallen in with those from our Camp, and had Set out to come to us; We now thought our little Army (as we called it) compleat, and the Destruction of the Indian Town inevitable; A Council was call'd and to our Astonishment our intended General was the Person who dissuaded us from the Enterprize, alledging that appearances were suspicious, but that there was no Certainty of a War, that if we made the Attempt proposed he had no Doubt of Success, but that a War at any Rate would be the Result, that we should be blamed for it and perhaps justly; but that if we were determined to execute the Plan, he would lay aside all Considerations, send for his People and share our Fortunes; he was then asked what Measure he would recommend to us, his Answer was that we should return to Wheeling a convenient Post to obtain Intelligence of what was going forward, that a few Weeks would determine the Matter, and as it was early in the Spring, if we should find that the Indians were not hostilely disposed we should have full Time to prosecute our entended Settlements in Kentucky; This Measure was adopted and in two Hours the whole Party was under Way; As we ascended the River we met Killbuck and Indian Chief (Delaware) with a small Party; We had a long Conference but obtained very little Satisfaction from him—It was observed that Cresap did not attend this Conference but Kept on the opposite Side of the River, he said that he was afraid to trust himself with the Indians; that Killbuck had frequently attempted to waylay & kill his Father, & that he was doubtful that he should tempted to put Killbuck to Death—On our arrival at Wheeling, the whole Country being pretty well settled thereabouts, the Inhabitants appeared to be much alarmed, and fled to our Camp from every Direction—we offered to cover their Neighbourhood with Scouts, until we could obtain further Information, if they would return to their Plantations; but Nothing we could say would prevail; By this Time we got to be a formidable Party, as all the Hunters & Men without Families &c., in that Quarter joined us—Our Arrival at Wheeling was soon known at Pittsburgh, the whole of that Country at that time being under the Jurisdiction of Virginia Doctor Connelly had been appointed by Dunmore Capt. Commandant of the District then called West Augusta; He Connelly hearing of us

sent a Message addressed to the Party, informing us that a War was to be apprehended, and requesting that we would Keep our Position for a few Days, that
Messengers had been sent to the Indian Towns whose Return he daily expected, and the Doubt respecting a War with the Indians would then be cleared
up—The Answer we returned was that we had no Inclination to decamp for
some time, and during our Stay we should be careful that the Enemy should not
harrass the Neighbourhood—But before this Answer could reach Pittsburgh,
he had sent a second Express addressed to Capt. Cresap as the most influential
Man amongst us informing him that the Messengers had returned from the
Indian Towns and that a War was inevitable and begg'd him to use his Influence with the Party to get them to cover the Country until the Inhabitants could
fortify themselves—The Time of the Reception of this Letter was the Epoch of
open Hostilities with the Indians—the War Post was planted a Council called
and the Letter read and the Ceremonies used by the Indians on so important an
Occasion acted, and War Was formally declared—The same Evening two
Scalps [1] were brought into Camp—The following Day some Canoes of Indians
were discovered [2] descending the River, taking Advantage of an Island to cover
themselves from our View. They were chased by our Men 15 Miles down the
River they were forced ashore and a Battle ensued a few were wounded on both
Sides and we got one Scalp only; On Examining their Canoes we found a con-
siderable quantity of ammunition and other warlike Stores—On our Return to
Camp a Resolution was formed to march next Day and attack Logan's Camp,
on the Ohio about 30 Miles above Wheeling—We actually march about five
Miles, and halted to take some Refreshment, here the Impropriety of executing
the proposed Enterprize was argued the Conversation was brought forward by
Cresap himself; it was generally agreed that those Indians had no hostile Intentions, as it was a hunting Camp composed of Men Women and Children with
all their Stuff with them—This we knew as I myself and others then present had
been at their Camp about four weeks before that Time on our way down from
Pittsburgh; In short every Person present particularly Cresap (upon Reflection)
was opposed to the projected Measure—We returned & on the same Evening
decamped and took the Road to Red Stone—It was two Days after this [3] that
Logan's Family was killed, and from the Manner in which it was done it was
viewed as a horrid Murder by the whole Country—From Logan's hearing that
Cresap was at the Head of this Party at Wheeling it was no wonder that he
considered Cresap as the Author of his Family's Destruction—

Since the Receipt of your Letter I have procured the Notes on Virginia, they
are now before me; the Action was more barbarous than therein related by Mr.
Jefferson; those Indians used to visit & receive Visits from the neighbouring
Whites on the opposite Shore, they were on a Visit at Greathouses at the Time
they were massacre'd by those People and their associates. The War now raged
with all its Savage Fury until the following fall, when a Treaty of Peace was
held at Dunmore's Camp within five Miles of Chilicothe the Indian Capital on
the Siotho—Logan did not appear—I was acquainted with him & wished to be
informd of the Reason of his absence by one of the Interpreters—The Answer
he gave to my Enquiry was "that he was like a Mad Dog, that his Bristles had
been up were not yet quite fallen—but that the good Talks now going forward
might allay them"—Logan's Speech to Dunmore now came forward as related
by Mr. Jefferson, and was generally believed & indeed not doubted to have been
genuine and dictated by Logan—The Army knew it was wrong so far as it

respected Cresap and afforded an Opportunity of rallying that Gentleman on the Subject—I discovered that Cresap was displeased and told him that he must be a very great Man, that the Indians shouldered him with every Thing that had happened—he smiled & said that he had a great Mind to tomahawk Greathouse about the Matter—What is here related is Fact, I was intimate with Cresap, and better acquainted with Logan at that Time than with any other Indian in the Western Country, and had a knowledge of the Conduct of both Parties. Logan is the author of Speech as related by Mr. Jefferson, and Cresap's Conduct was such as I have herein related—

I have gone through a Relation of Every Circumstance that had any Connection wi[th] the Information you desire & hope it will be satisfactory to yourself & Mr. Jefferson.—

I am your mo. obt. Servt.   G: R: CLARK

RC (DLC); torn; in a clerk's hand, signed by Clark; at foot of text: "Doctr Saml Brown"; endorsed in an unknown hand: "Genl Clarkes Letter to Sam Brown—on the subject of Logans Speech."

TJ's omission of this narrative from the *Appendix* to the *Notes on the State of Virginia* in 1800 became controversial half a century later when Brantz Mayer, president of the Maryland Historical Society, surmised that TJ had unscrupulously ignored Clark's letter because it exonerated Michael Cresap of culpability for the killing of Logan's family and did not tie him to other incidents of violence against Indians. TJ's marginal numbering on Clark's letter (see below) indicates that he did consider it in context with other statements concerning the Logan-Cresap controversy. He informed Samuel Brown of his reasons for excluding Clark's account from the *Appendix*, but apparently did so orally through Brown's brother, Sen-

ator John Brown, and they were not recorded (TJ to Samuel Brown, 10 May 1800). Evidence that TJ included in the *Appendix* absolved Cresap of blame for the deaths of Logan's kin at Yellow Creek, although TJ still held him accountable for inciting the chain of events of which that incident was a part. For refutations of Mayer's charges, see *Notes*, ed. Peden, 299-300; Brant, *Madison*, 1:281-91; Malone, *Jefferson*, 3:353-5.

[1] Here in margin TJ wrote: "1." These digits in the margin (two others are noted below) correspond to the numbering system by which TJ, in the *Appendix* to the *Notes on Virginia*, distinguished among different attacks on Native Americans along the Ohio River in the spring of 1774 (*Notes*, ed. Peden, 231).

[2] Here in margin TJ wrote: "2."

[3] Here in margin TJ wrote: "3."

From Palisot de Beauvois

MONSIEUR,   Bordeaux 18 fructidor an 6—(4 Sept. 1798)

Je pense que d'après les honnetetés et amitiés que Vous m'avez toujours temoignées Vous apprendrés avec quelqu'interet mon heureuse et sauve arrivée en cette Ville après 37 jours de traversée. je serais bien flatté que Vos occupations et les Circonstances me permissent de recevoir de Vos nouvelles et de Correspondre avec le digne president de la societé philosophique et le successeur du Celebre franklin.

Mon peu de sejour dans ma patrie que j'avais quitté il y a douze ans ne me permet pas de Vous informer des progrès journalliers qu'y font les sciences, mais je ne manquerai pas de Vous en informer apres mon arrivée et quelque sejour a Paris.

je n'ecris point a M. Dérieux ne pouvant agir pour lui qu'a Paris. j'apprens avec plaisir a mon arrivée que notre gouvernement est dans le desir de Conserver l'union et la paix entre deux Nations faites pour s'aimer et s'estimer. je souhaite bien ardemment que Cet Espoir n'eprouve aucun obstacle.

j'ai L'honneur d'etre Avec les sentimens les plus distingués, Monsieur, Votre tres humble et tres obeisst serviteur   DE BEAUVOIS

Cit.en. B.ois. associé de L'institut National, correspondant du Museum d'hist.re. Nat.le. rue S.t. Claude Au Marais a Paris.

EDITORS' TRANSLATION

SIR,   Bordeaux 18 Fructidor Year 6—(4 September 1798)
I believe that in light of the courtesies and acts of friendship that you have always shown me you will learn with some interest of my happy and safe arrival in this city after a crossing of 37 days. I should be very gratified if your occupations and circumstances should permit me to receive news of you and to correspond with the worthy president of the philosophical society and the successor of the famous Franklin.

The short time that I have spent in my fatherland which I had left twelve years ago does not allow me to inform you of the daily progress made there by the sciences, but I shall not fail to inform you of them after my arrival and some time spent in Paris.

I am not writing to M. Derieux, since I can act for him only in Paris. I have learned with pleasure upon my arrival that our government desires to preserve the union and peace between two nations made to love and esteem each other. I most ardently wish that this hope will encounter no obstacle.

I have the honor to be, with the highest sentiments, Sir, your very humble and very obedient servant   DE BEAUVOIS

Citizen Beauvois, associate of the National Institute, correspondent of the Museum of Natural History, St. Claude Street in the Marais, Paris.

RC (DLC); endorsed by TJ as received 2 Jan. 1799 and so recorded in SJL.

To Janet Livingston Montgomery

DEAR MADAM   Monticello Sep. 4. 98.
The letter of June 3. with which you were pleased to honor me, came to hand in the moment I was stepping into the carriage at Philadelphia on my return home. that which it inclosed for Colo. Monroe was delivered immediately on my arrival, and I should sooner have had the pleasure of informing you of it, but that I have been confined from reading

or writing ever since by an inflammation in my eyes which began on the road & is but now wearing off.

I passed through the state of New York in the year 1791. together with mr Madison; but it was not known to either of us that we passed near your residence, or most assuredly we should have taken the liberty of paying our respects to you at your seat. there exist too many motives of respect and esteem for yourself and the different members of your family not to have rendered such an opportunity of testifying them highly gratifying. time is every day adding to the improbabilities of my undertaking long journies. but should any circumstance ever place it again as much in power, I shall assuredly take the liberty of expressing to you in person the sentiments of respect & esteem with which I have the honour to be Dear Madam

Your most obedt. & most humble servt   TH: JEFFERSON

RC (John Ross Delafield, New York, 1945); at foot of text: "Mrs. Montgomery"; endorsed. PrC (MHi); endorsed by TJ in ink on verso.

To Sir Peyton Skipwith

DEAR SIR   Monticello Sep. 4. 98.

Your favor of Aug. 25. has been handed me by Majr. Nelson. after the reciept of your former letter on the subject of your demand against mr Short I wrote to him informing him of it: and I am almost certain that in some letter to me since he has answered the article. but though I have spent near half a day in searching his letters (which are voluminous & written in a microscopic hand which renders it difficult to go over them) yet I cannot find the letter. however his letters of last winter & spring, down to Apr. 15. assure me he will be here this summer, and the war between this country & France renders it more certain, as the Americans will of course be obliged to quit France; & indeed the papers already announce that they have been ordered to do so. as soon as he arrives I will call his attention to the subject & deliver him your account & letter, & have no doubt you will immediately hear from him. I should add that tho I do not recollect precisely what he wrote me on the subject, yet I am sure it was not of a nature which enabled me to do any thing on it, or you would immediately have heard from me. I have the honour to be with great esteem & respect Dr. Sir

Your most obedt & most humble servt   TH: JEFFERSON

PrC (DLC: Short Papers); at foot of text: "Sr. Peyton Skipwith"; endorsed by TJ in ink on verso.

Certificate for Alexander Spotswood

Virginia, to wit

I hereby certify that on an invasion of this state by the British troops under the command of Genl. Leslie, the continental officers retired from service within this state were requested by me as Governor of Virginia to take commands of the militia called into the field on that occasion; that Genl. Alexander Spotswood, in compliance with that request, repaired to the militia and remained with them during the continuance of the invasion: that it appears by the newspapers of the times, which I believe to be correct as to this matter, that Leslie's troops entered the Chesapeake Oct. 20. 1780. & landed immediately, & that they got under weigh on their departure the 24th. of Novemb. following; that it is probable the militia were discharged soon after their departure was known at Richmond, and certainly before Arnold's invasion which took place on the 30th. of Decemb., at which time it is well remembered there was no militia ready in the field to oppose the invaders. Given under my hand this 12th. day of September 1798.

Th: Jefferson

MS (DNA: RG 233, House Records, 5th Cong., 2d sess.); entirely in TJ's hand; at foot of text in unknown hand:

"Genl. Spotswood servd to
the battle of german town
2 years & 5– 2–5
under Jefferson 2
under Harrison 3–
  5–5."

Enclosed in TJ to Spotswood, 12 Sep. 1798 (recorded in SJL but not found).

This certificate was one of the supporting documents presented to the House on 28 Feb. 1799 with Spotswood's petition (now missing) for a grant of 6,000 acres of land from the United States for his service as colonel in the Continental Army. It was referred to the committee of claims in December, and on 16 Apr. 1800 was forwarded to the committee of the whole to be considered with similar claims. The same day the House authorized the president to grant patents to those officers of the Continental Army from Virginia who had received warrants from the state legislature for lands that were subsequently ceded to the federal government. On 13 May 1800, Adams signed an act setting aside up to 60,000 acres to honor the Virginia land grants, although it was estimated that the officers held claims for up to 100,000 acres (*National State Papers: Adams*, 9:320; JHR, 3:501, 545, 666; *Annals*, 10:668-9, 672; U.S. Statutes at Large, 2:80).

For the invasion of the British forces commanded by General Alexander LESLIE, see James Innes to TJ, [21? Oct. 1780]. Letters from Spotswood to TJ of 9 July and 30 Aug. 1798, recorded in SJL as received 12 July and 6 Sep., respectively, have not been found. A letter from TJ to Spotswood of 2 Aug. 1798, recorded in SJL, is also missing.

From John Brown

DEAR SIR   Frankfort 15th: Septr 1798

Since my return to this State many opportunities of collecting the sense of the people have offered, & I can now with confidence assure you that they are almost unanimous in their opposition to a War with France, also in thier disapprobation of several Acts of the Genl Government as being unconstitutional. At almost every Court House crouded meetings have been held for the purpose of taking into consideration the State of the Nation & Resolutions have adopted with scarce a desenting voice, deprecating War, & denouncing the Alien & Sedition laws in the strongest terms, but at the same time expressing a determination to repel invasion & to obey all constitutional laws—Here & there an Individual is to be found who from the love of singularity, or the hope of Governmental favor undertakes to approbate the Measures adopted at the last Session. But altho their Numbers are, few yet they have been extremely active. They at first attempted to introduce the Cockade. Fifteen only could be mounted & they droped off in a few days. The next step was to prepare an Address of approbation to be presented to the Presadent. This was couched in terms the most general and in order to obtain Signatures it was sent by special Messengers into every County in the State, but I am assured that not more than 250 or 300 could be collected in the whole Country, & not twenty of these by men of respectability & fortune. I doubt not but the people of Kentucky will be represented as hostile to the Union, & to the Goverment & tending to insurrection & revolt. I assure you there exists no foundation for such calumnies. They are warmly attached to the Union & to the Constitution of the U. States, but they are equally determined to defend thier Rights & to resist every attempt to violate the fundamental principles of their freedom. Have you seen George Nicholas's Political Creed? I beleive his object in publishing it was to draw into question the constitutionality of the Sedition law. Should the Executive direct a prosecution against him he is prepared for his defence, provided the attack is made upon his own ground—

Fowler & Davis will I expect be reelected without much opposition. Many of my friends have urged me to offer at the ensuing election for a Senator, but I have not yet come to a final determination. My Interest & my present inclinations lead me to decline all thoughts of serving beyond the expiration of my present term.—

Some circumstances have lately been related to me which in my opinion go far in support of your conjecture that the species of Animal whose Bones were found in Green briar, still exists in the Western Country. I was this day informed by a Man of much respectability that a Young Man who was taken from this State by the Indians & remained prisoner with them for several years, lately returned & now lives at the Red Banks on Hendersons Grant near the mouth of Green River. He says that he lived for sometime with a Tribe of Indians, ignorant of fire Arms who inhabit a Country, far up the Misouri river in which an Animal is found of a brown colour, much larger than a Bear, of astonishing strength, activity, & fierceness. He brought with him & now has in his possession a Nail taken from the Claw of one killed by the party of Indians to which he belonged but not before it had torn several of them into pieces. This Nail or horny part of the Claw is said to measure six inches in length. Before my return to Phila. I will endeavour to obtain from him a full account of this extraordinary Animal & will if possible procure the Nail.

On my return to this Country I was informed at Mr Langfords who lives near Rockcastle on the Wilderness road that shortly before, an unknown Animal had been discovered at that place. That it had approached the house in the Night & roared or made a Noise resembling the braying of an Ass but louder & so terrible that 'tho' there were a number of men in the house they were all struck with dismay & did no venture to open the door. That the next day a man was walking at some little distance from the house & saw the Animal cross the road about forty yards in front of him, but without appearing to have observed him it laid itself down at the root of a tree. He shot at it with his Rifle—it only turned its head round & appeared to bite the place where he supposes the Ball struck it. He loaded & fired at it a second time, but it did not move. He shot at it a third time when it sprang from its situation thirty five feet at the first Jump & ran off leaping in the most astonishing manner. He described, as being very large, hump-backed, in colour resembling the Panther, & its head larger than a half Bushel. Mr Langford & eight or ten men & a number of Dogs returned with him to the place where they found Blood. The Dogs soon started it again & pursued it into a Cave in a rock. It was now almost dark & they sent for fire, but before it arrived the Animal rushed out of the Cave & 'tho shot at by some of the Party, it soon dispersed all the Dogs, & escaped, & has not since been heard of. nor can I learn that it or any of the discription had ever been seen or heard of before in that part of the Country. I have given you this information as I recd it from two men who live at Langfords & say they were witnesses to what they related. I shall endeavour to see the man who shot at the Animal in the first instance, & obtain a more particular discription of it from him. I shall also offer a reward for the Skeleton, thinking it probable that it died of its wounds, & may be found in that Nieghbourhood.

I have been informed that Mr Nolan is on his return to this Country with a large Number of Horses; & have in consequence detained your letter to him. Should he not arrive before my return to Phila. shall forward it to the care of General Wilkinson

I have the honor to be with great respect Sir Yr very Hble Servt.

J: BROWN

RC (DLC); at foot of text: "Thomas Jefferson Esqr"; endorsed by TJ as received 15 Oct. 1798 and so recorded in SJL.

For the CROUDED MEETINGS in Kentucky, see also the letter from Brown's brother Samuel at 4 Sep. On 1 Aug. the *Kentucky Gazette* printed the POLITICAL CREED of George Nicholas, an elder brother of Wilson Cary Nicholas who had relocated to Kentucky from Virginia some years earlier. In it, Nicholas declared his belief that in

voting for the Sedition Act the majority of Congress had violated the First Amendment of the Constitution, adding that if the president had signed the act and any judges acted to enforce it "they have also violated that part of the Constitution" (Ethelbert Dudley Warfield, *The Kentucky Resolutions of 1798: An Historical Study* [New York, 1887], 44-5; *Kentucky Gazette*, 1 Aug. 1798; ANB).

ANIMAL WHOSE BONES WERE FOUND IN GREEN BRIAR: the megalonyx.

From James Thomson Callender

SIR   Rasberryplain 22d. Septr. 1798

I request Your indulgence for a few lines. I Shall be as concise as possible.

A few days after I had the honour of Seeing You last, a very particular reason made it proper for me to quit the City next day. I consulted on this emergency, M Leiper, and General Mason. The former offered to take charge of my children, the latter to give me, or find me lodgings, if I came to Virginia. Accordingly, I walked down to this place. The General, in a few days, came after me, and has in every way behaved with the utmost kindness. He proposes that I Should Stay here till winter, and go back with him to town, to try my fortune. There is, however, no more Security in returning than there would have been in Staying. It was M Leiper's parting injunction not to come back, because there is no more Safety in Philadelphia than in Constantinople. Besides I am entirely sick even of the Republicans, for some of them have used me so dishonestly, in a word I have been so severely cheated, and So often, that I have the Strongest inclination, as well as the best reason, for wishing to Shift the Scene.

Since I came here, the Aristocracy in this Neighbourhood, which is one of the vilest in America, has never ceased to abuse General Mason and myself. They have found means to make me very uneasy at being the Cause of so much noise. Horace brags of being pointed at. My Ambition does not run in that way. I engaged in American Controversies not from choice, but necessity; for I dislike to make enemies, and in this Country, the Stile of writing is commonly So gross, that I do not think the majority of such a public worth addressing. I hope another couple of years will put it in my power to go home again, but I must, if possible, provide for myself in the mean time. It is needless, even were it Safe, to write any more. The party are doing their own business as fast as can be.

If I were in any part of the Country, where I could be permitted to live in peace, which here I cannot, I think that I could win my bread, I mean my own individually, either by keeping a School, or assisting to keep a Store, or in some other way, (as I have not the happiness of being able to go through Country work,) till matters clear up on the other Side of the Atlantick. You will easily see that I am aiming at some assistance in this matter from You, and if You Can think of any one way in which I can be worth my room, I Care very little what it is, providing that I am in a Republican part of the Country, for I find by wretched experience, in other instances, as well as at present, [1] that I can go to no place where my name is unknown. This has hindered me from going to Winchester as I designed, and from writing to Richmond and some other places, till I hear (if I am worthy of an answer) from You.

I am Sir Your most obedient servant   JAS. T. CALLENDER

P.S. The Scenes of printing, and swearing, and flat perjury that we have had here, if acted in Elysium, would make any man sick of it. The General,[2] took my cause with more keenness than I wished, [but perhaps because Your name also was brought in]. He is on his own ground, but as Ossian says "I am alone in the land of Strangers."

I request the inclosed to be put into the fire, as soon as read. Since writing the above, I have reason to hope we Shall make no more Replies, though *they* have had one out, some days ago.

RC (DLC); brackets in original; addressed: "Thomas Jefferson Esquire, Vice President of the United States, Charlottesville Marlborough County Virginia"; endorsed by TJ as received 4 Oct. and so recorded in SJL. Enclosure not found.

QUIT THE CITY: Callender left Philadelphia shortly before President Adams signed the Sedition Act on 14 July. Heeding Thomas LEIPER'S PARTING INJUNCTION, Callender never returned (Durey, *Callender*, 109; *Gazette of the United States*, 13 July 1798). Callender's host, Stevens Thomson Mason, lived in Loudoun County, Virginia, a Federalist stronghold. Newspapers in Philadelphia carried reports of the ABUSE suffered by Callender and his benefactor, the most publicized being Callender's detention on 2 Aug. for vagrancy "at a whiskey distillery" near Leesburg. Writing John Fenno about the incident, "A Virginian" described Callender as a dirty little man "with shaved head and greasy jacket" who was an "apostle of sedition." He also reported that, upon examination by the municipal authorities, Callender revealed that he was staying in Virginia at the invitation of his friend Mason. The Virginia senator was upbraided for giving asylum to the "notorious Scotch fugitive, the calumniator of Washington, Adams, law, order, government, God," and the "panegyrist of Jefferson." When the Leesburg magistrates required

Callender to produce his papers, Mason reportedly appeared with his guest's certificate of naturalization and vouched for his character (*Gazette of the United States*, 9 Aug. 1798; *Porcupine's Gazette*, 22 Aug. 1798). See also Callender's letter to James Carey dated 18 Aug. 1798, printed in *Carey's United States' Recorder* on 28 Aug. and in Bache's *Aurora* two days later.

HORACE BRAGS OF BEING POINTED AT: Horace, *Odes*, 4:3, l. 22-3, where the poet thanks the muse for the gift that allows him to be pointed out as "the minstrel of the Roman lyre" by those passing by.

TOOK MY CAUSE: William Cobbett printed Mason's response to an article in the *Columbian Mirror and Alexandria Gazette*, signed by "A," relating to Callender's de-

tention at Leesburg (*Porcupine's Gazette*, 22 Aug. 1798). I AM ALONE IN THE LAND OF STRANGERS: in the seventh book of Ossian's poem "Timora" Sul-malla pleads as she awaits the return of Cathmor from battle, "But if thou shouldst fall, I am in the land of strangers," and at the close of Ossian's "The Battle of Lora," Lorma exclaims, "I am in the land of strangers; where is my friend, but Aldo?" (*The Poems of Ossian, the Son of Fingal*, trans. James Macpherson [Philadelphia, 1790], 250, 333).

[1] Preceding eight words interlined.
[2] Callender here canceled "who" and at the end of the sentence deleted "is going to write another piece this week."

From Benjamin H. Latrobe

DEAR SIR,   Richmond Septr. 22d 1798

A round-about application has just now been made to me respecting a navigation in your neighbourhood, between Milton and Charlotte's ville, for which, I am told, a very considerable subscription is already raised. It comes from a very honest work man here, who presses me to go up, & see it. But as the thing seems to stand not quite upon so good as footing as the negociations of Messrs. W X Y & Z and the Lady &c, I take the liberty to mention it to you, & if my talents as an Engineer can be of the smallest service to you,—for I take it for granted that you are at the head of any work of public utility within your sphere of agency—I beg you will draw upon them to any amount.—I consider our improvements in navigation in their infancy, to require a little *nursing* by the hand of public spirit,—& to speak plainly,—when I offer my assistance to you, it is infinitely more with a view to be useful than to exhaust your funds by my emoluments. Little can be done this Year, if any thing be intended, but I shall be happy to wait upon you to *advise* or to plan for the next season, if you think proper.—

Since I had the pleasure to see you at Fredericsburg, I have been upon a strange errand at Norfolk,—to survey & report upon the fortifications at that place.—I spent about three Weeks in performing this service,—& having plann'd a new Fort for Point Nelson, & alterations for Fort Norfolk, & besides, designed Barracks for both places, an officer carried my papers to the Secretary at War. All that I had proposed was ordered to be carried into immediate execution, &—strange to tell,—the business was taken out of the hands of the Military Commander of the Garrison, & put into those of the Collector of the port. All this was consistent with the operations of a Government for the sake of a Revenue.—Of myself not the slightest notice has been taken,—*because a man of my politics is not to be trusted in so important a case as the defence of the Country against the French*. My *politics* I presume have been found out since my appointment to survey & report, for surely there was as much danger in permitting me to design,—as to construct a Work.—

The late accounts of the Paris negociation have made some impression here.—Marshall stands for Henrico district,—but his election is doubtful. Bushrod Washington, who offers for Westmoreland district stands little chance. His zeal against *the subverters of all Government*, has decided the wavering John Heath against him,—than whom, no one in the District has more influence, so that we shall most likely see Dr Jones again in Congress. Upon the whole, I think the aspect of things in this part of the country favors the republican side. But you have no doubt better intelligence from your more informed correspondents than I can give you.—John Mayo,—had distributed 500 Copies of the Cannibals progress in Henrico district to pave the way for himself. Captn. Billy Austin has sent a packet of Addison's pedantry to Bedford,—Carrington scatters X W Y Z over the state, & another packet consisting of the speeches of Goodloe Harper & Ames is dispersed by a subscription of citizen subjects. But little I believe is effected by all this expence.—

I have taken the liberty to have several of your mould boards made for my friends. I do not apologize to you to so doing, as I know that your object is to be extensively useful. I have been astonished at their performance.

As I am somewhat uncertain whether or no you will ever receive these lines I forbear enclosing in them the drawings of the Philadelphia Nail cutting Machine which I have long made for you, but which I have never had an opportunity to send.—

I have now only to beg that you will excuse the liberty I have taken to write to you upon the subject of your Navigation upon the very informal application to me, & to assure you of the truth of the sentiments of esteem & respect with which I am

Your faithful Servant　　　　　　　　　　B. HENRY LATROBE

RC (DLC); endorsed by TJ as received 1 Oct. 1798 and so recorded in SJL.

NEGOCIATIONS OF MESSRS. W X Y & Z AND THE LADY &C: a statement by Charles C.

Pinckney enclosed in the American envoys' dispatch no. 4 of 24 Dec. 1797 reported that a few days before "a lady, who is well acquainted with M. Talleyrand," had coaxed Pinckney that "all matters would be adjusted" if the U.S. would grant France a loan. Although often presumed to have been Madame de Villette, Marshall's and Gerry's landlady, the mysterious woman may actually have been the wife of Charles Mathurin de la Forest, who had held consular positions in the United States (ASP, *Foreign Relations*, 2:166-7; Stinchcombe, *XYZ Affair*, 35, 47n, 65, 66-8, 75-6n).

John MARSHALL won a seat in the Sixth Congress, BUSHROD WASHINGTON did not (*Biog. Dir. Cong.*, 64, 1426). For Marshall's campaign, see Marshall, *Papers*, 3:494-502.

During the summer of 1798 William Cobbett published a pamphlet he called THE CANNIBALS PROGRESS, presented as an abridged and translated German account, originally issued in London, of French depredations in Swabia. Cobbett considered the work an example of "how I am working against the French. I have published 25 thousand of this work, and about as many more have issued, by my permission, from the German and other presses in the States. It has been, and long will be, a mighty engine. The little boys and the poor people buy it, and it is read in every family." In 1801 Cobbett asserted that "upwards of a *hundred thousand copies* were printed and sold in the United States of America, besides a large edition in the German language" (G. D. H. Cole, ed., *Letters from William Cobbett to Edward Thornton Written in the Years 1797 to 1800* [London, 1937], 4; William Cobbett, *Porcupine's Works; Containing Various Writings and Selections, Exhibiting a Faithful Picture of the United States of America*, 12 vols. [London, 1801], 8:320n; *The Cannibals' Progress; or The Dreadful Horrors of French Invasion, as Displayed by the Republican Officers and Soldiers, in their Perfidy, Rapacity, Ferociousness and Brutality, Exercised towards the Innocent Inhabitants of Germany. Translated from the German, by Anthony Aufrer, Esq.* [Philadelphia, 1798]; see Evans, Nos. 33325-38).

ADDISON'S PEDANTRY: probably *An Infallible Cure, for Political Blindness, if Administered to Patients Possessing Sound Minds, Honest Hearts, and Independent Circumstances*, an "oration" by Pennsylvania judge Alexander Addison published in Richmond in July, and printed also in Philadelphia under another title (see Evans, Nos. 33269, 33270, 33873). Other addresses and writings by Addison also appeared in print during 1798. During the summer Timothy Pickering had sent 1,800 copies of the dispatches relating to the XYZ affair to Edward C. CARRINGTON, the federal supervisor of the revenue for Virginia, for distribution in the state (Marshall, *Papers*, 3:475; JEP, 1:82).

Sometime before the end of April TJ had furnished Latrobe with what the architect described as "the 3 Wise mens of the East's Instructions"—apparently the instructions to Marshall, Pinckney, and Gerry as envoys to France (Latrobe, *Virginia Journals*, 2:384).

To John Barnes

DEAR SIR   Monticello Sep. 25. 98

I wrote you last on the 31st. of Aug. acknoleging your's of Aug. 9. that of the 11th. of Aug. did not get to me till the 4th. inst. having been 24. days on it's passage owing to the derangement of our post which still continues & almost annihilates all benefit from it. it does not, I believe affect the passage of letters from hence to Philadelphia. by the time you recieve this you will be able to draw from the treasury my quarter's salary. I also now inclose you a letter in the usual form to the Comptroller for mr Short's quarter. these sums will replace your advances for me, and enable you to pay Joseph Roberts a further sum of 369.50 D for his last nail rod forwarded to me, which will be due the 1st. of October, which be so good as to do.

The letter promised in yours of Aug. 11. is not yet come to hand. it is of no consequence on account of the trifle which was to be the subject of it, but it's delay gives me fears for your health. in fact I hope you have had the prudence to leave the city. the mortality of the fever this year, and it's seising on every part of the city renders it quite unsafe to be in any part of it. what will be the effects of these visitations on that place? it will naturally deter [. . .]. but will it not also drive off some of the present inhabitants [. . .] of what descriptions?—I hope I shall hear from you [so that I may?] be relieved from my fears for you personally. I am with [. . .] esteem Dear Sir

Your friend & servt.   TH: JEFFERSON

PrC (CSmH); faint; at foot of text: "Mr. John Barnes"; endorsed by TJ in ink on verso. Enclosure: Order by TJ to John Steele, 21 Sep. 1798, requesting, under his power of attorney from William Short, that all dividends due 1 Oct. on Short's certificates be paid to Barnes (RC in PP: Carson Collection; at foot of text: "John Steele esq. Comptroller of the US."; endorsed by Steele; also at foot, order by Barnes, signed at Trenton, 2 Oct., for payment to his credit; endorsed as paid on 23 Oct. 1798).

For Barnes's letter OF AUG. 9, see TJ's of the 31st. According to SJL, TJ received THAT OF THE 11TH. on 4 Sep. 1798, but it has not been found. Another missing letter from Barnes to TJ, written on 8 Sep. 1798 and received on 27 Sep., is also recorded in SJL.

TJ wrote a promissory note, dated "Sep.   1798," to pay $500 to Barnes's order at the Bank of the United States in sixty days (MS facsimile in Sotheby's, Catalogue No. 6761, 13 Dec. 1995, Lot 187; entirely in TJ's hand; signed; canceled; on paper bearing embossed stamp for ten-cent tax).

To Samuel Clarke

DEAR SIR   Monticello Sep. 25. 98.

I duly recieved your favor of July 10. with the account inclosed, authorising me to debit mr John Mc.Dowell for nails delivered over to him £124.2.7 leaving a balance in your hands of £90.18.8 $\frac{1}{2}$. having recieved nothing of the earnings of my nailery during my absence from Decemb. last, & little since my return, and constantly to make advances for nailrod I am under a necessity of solliciting your remittance of the balance at the first possible moment. I shall be much pressed by a paiment to be made at our next court (Oct. 1.) when the reciept of your balance would be peculiarly acceptable. however, then, or as soon after as you can make it convenient will oblige Dr. Sir

Your most obedt. servt   TH: JEFFERSON

PrC (MHi); at foot of text: "Mr. Samuel Clarke"; endorsed by TJ in ink on verso.

To John McDowell

Sir   Monticello Sep. 25. 98.

I recieved by mr Stuart your note, as also the sum of £34. 13. s 9 d which is duly entered to your credit. mr Clarke had before informed me that, on his quitting business you had undertaken to dispose of my nails, recieving from him to the amount of £124– 2. s 7 d which I have accordingly debited you. I sent you also some time ago 3. casks of nails as stated below. there has been, since the reciept of your note, such a demand from the tobacco planters for nails to build their tobacco houses, & the season pressing hard on them, that I have been unable to get ready a barrel of twelves as desired in your note: but we shall be able to go about them soon. I take for granted mr Clarke informed you that the retail of my nails was to be for ready money only, as nothing but quick returns of my advances could support the business at so low prices as I charge. having been without any receipts from my nailery during my absence from December last, and constantly advancing largely for it, I am particularly pressed at present, and shall therefore be obliged to you for any balance in your hands on the sales you have made. I am Sir

Your most obedt. servt   Th: Jefferson

Mr. John Mc.Dowell to Th:J.			Dr.		
			£ s d		£ s d
1798. Mar. 19. To nails from mr Clarke			124. 2.7	Cr. July 12. by Cash	
	℔	s d.		by mr Stuart	34.13.9
July	To a cask do. 440. Viii. @ 13		23.16.8	by 7½ pr.Ct. commn. do.	2.16.
	do.	460. Vi. @ 13½	25.17.6		
	do.	200. XVI.br @ 11½	9.11.8		
			£183.8.5		

PrC (DLC); endorsed by TJ in ink on verso.

John McDowell, son of Staunton property owner and merchant William and Alice McDowell, corresponded with TJ concerning the sale of nails at his store in Staunton until November 1800 and finally settled his account in 1807 (Lyman Chalkley, *Chronicles of the Scotch-Irish Settlement in Virginia Extracted from the Original Court Records of Augusta County, 1745-1800*, 3 vols. [Rosslyn, Va., 1912-13], 3:227, 549, 575; Staunton *Spirit of the Press*, 18 May 1811; MB, 2:1211; TJ to McDowell, 13 Nov. 1800; TJ to John Coalter, 8 May 1807).

McDowell's NOTE that TJ received by Archibald Stuart was not recorded in SJL and has not been found. For the three CASKS OF NAILS sent by TJ to McDowell in July 1798, see TJ's nailery account book, 1796-1800, in CLU-C.

To Archibald Hamilton Rowan

Sir   Monticello Sep. 26. 98.

To avoid the suspicions & curiosity of the post office which would have been excited by seeing your name and mine on the back of a letter, I have delayed acknoleging the receipt of your favor of July last, till an occasion to write to an inhabitant of Wilmington gives me an opportunity of putting my letter under cover to him. the system of alarm & jealousy which has been so powerfully plaid off in England, has been mimicked here, not entirely without success. the most long sighted politician could not, seven years ago, have imagined, that the people of this wide extended country could have been inveloped in such delusion and made so much afraid of themselves and their own power as to surrender it spontaneously to those who are maneuvring them into a form of government the principal branches of which may be beyond their controul. the commerce of England however has spread it's roots over the whole face of our country. this is the real source of all the obliquities of the public mind: and I should have had doubts of the ultimate [term] they might attain. but happily the game, to be worth the playing of those engaged in it, must flush them with money. the authorised expences of this year are beyond those of any year in the late war for independance & they are of a nature to beget great & constant expence. the purse of the people is the real seat[1] of sensibility. it is to be [drawn upon] largely, and they will then listen to truths which could not excite them through any other organ. in this state however the delusion has not prevailed. they are sufficiently on their guard to have justified the assurance that should you chuse it for your asylum, the laws of the land, administered by upright judges would protect you from every exercise of power unauthorised by the constitution of the United [sta]tes. the Habeas corpus secures every man here, alien or citizen, against every thing which is not law, whatever shape it may assume. should this or any other circumstance draw your footsteps this way, I shall be happy to be among those who may have an opportunity of testifying by every attention in our power the sentiments of esteem & respect which the circumstances of your history have inspired, and which are peculiarly felt by Sir

Your most obedt. & most humble servt   Th: Jefferson

PrC (DLC); faint; at foot of first page: "A. H. Rowan esq."

According to SJL, the inhabitant of wilmington, Delaware, to whom TJ wrote enclosing the above letter was probably John Bringhurst, whose family had ties to both Philadelphia and Wilmington. On 27 Sep. TJ wrote Bringhurst a letter that has not been found (Henry Clay Reed, ed., *Delaware: A History of the First State*, 3 vols. [New York, 1947], 3:119).

[1] TJ first wrote "place."

[528]

From John McDowell

Sɪʀ   Staunton Sept. 27. 1798

I received your favour this morning by post wishing me to send what money there is my hands arising from the sales of your Nails there is at present between Eighteen & Twenty pounds which you can have at any time Mr Clarke inform.d me that they was onely to be sold for Cash I have done so and that is the verry reason there is not more sold the scarsity of Cash with us at present and another reason the Assortment of Nails not kept up the kind that I receved last excepting the brads is that which there is most of tens & Eights Verry few sold of them which was got from Mr Clarke however as quick as there is any sold I shall let You know by post and you can send for the money or at least every two Months you shall know the Amount of sales as that the time Mr Clarke informed me he settle with you the twelve penny Nails 6d & flouring brads is only kind that sells well I should be glad you would send the 12d as soon as possible—from your humbe Set

JOHN McDOWELL

paid waggoner	£1:13:0
Ditto man & horse to Millers	0: 7:6
	£2: 0:6

RC (MHi); endorsed by TJ as received 1 Oct. 1798 and so recorded in SJL.

The Kentucky Resolutions of 1798

I. JEFFERSON'S DRAFT, [BEFORE 4 OCT. 1798]

II. JEFFERSON'S FAIR COPY, [BEFORE 4 OCT. 1798]

III. RESOLUTIONS ADOPTED BY THE KENTUCKY GENERAL ASSEMBLY, 10 NOV. 1798

EDITORIAL NOTE

For all the significance of the Kentucky Resolutions, Jefferson's papers reveal little about their composition. This is due in part to his caution about what he revealed in his letters at the time he wrote the resolutions. Too, for the remainder of his life he showed little interest in avowing or explaining his original authorship of the document. He did not seem displeased with the changes made to the resolutions after they left his hands and was content to have the attribution of authorship lie elsewhere. He in fact called them "the Kentuckey resolves" before he even knew of their adoption by both houses of the Kentucky legislature (TJ to Madison, 17 Nov. 1798). To compound the weakness of the documentary record, when he did recount, years later, the creation of the resolutions, his recollection was faulty and he recast the story to give John Breckinridge a role in the earliest manifestation of the resolutions that the Kentucky politician did not play. Moreover, after Jefferson's death some of his admirers, uncomfortable with theoretical and practical consequences of nullification, rather than establishing and developing the story of his authorship sought to distance themselves and him from his draft resolutions of 1798.

For many years Jefferson's authorship was known only to a limited number of confidants. In 1814 John Taylor named Jefferson as the author of the resolutions, but without belaboring the issue (Taylor, *An Inquiry into the Principles and Policy of the Government of the United States* [Fredericksburg, Va., 1814], 174, 649). Jefferson later acknowledged that through the years he saw "repeated imputations" in newspapers, but, "as has been my practice on all occasions of imputation, I have observed entire silence" (TJ to Joseph Cabell Breckinridge, 11 Dec. 1821). Only late in his life would he feel a need to acknowledge his composition of the resolutions to anyone outside the circle of those who already knew. In 1821 a piece that he allowed to appear in the *Richmond Enquirer* led to assertions by that newspaper's zealous editor, Thomas Ritchie, that Jefferson was the author of the Kentucky Resolutions (*Richmond Enquirer*, 3 Aug., 4 Sep. 1821; Malone, *Jefferson*, 6:357-9). In the wake of Ritchie's announcement Joseph Cabell Breckinridge, the son of John Breckinridge, who had introduced the resolutions in the Kentucky House of Representatives in 1798 and died eight years afterward, wrote Jefferson seeking clarification. The son was puzzled that his father would seemingly accept credit for something so important if he had not in fact crafted the resolutions. Some years before, when the younger Breckinridge asked for information about his father's political career, Jefferson had said nothing about them (J. C. Breckinridge to TJ, 14 May 1815, 19 Nov. 1821, and TJ to Breckinridge, 12 June 1815). On 11 Dec. 1821, declaring that the direct question from Breckinridge had put him "under a dilemma which I cannot solve but by an exposition of the naked truth," Jefferson said that "I would have wished this rather to have remained as hitherto, without inquiry, but your inquiries have a right to be answered." Admitting that he had penned the resolutions, he noted that despite the rumors in newspapers "the question indeed has never before been put to me, nor should I answer it to any other than yourself, seeing no good end to be proposed by it and the desire of tranquility inducing with me a wish to be withdrawn from public notice."

Still, Jefferson's role in the creation of the Kentucky Resolutions continued to be poorly understood. After his death, as nullification and states' rights became central issues in the early 1830s, his grandson Thomas Jefferson Randolph was prompted to seek evidence of Jefferson's authorship of the resolutions. Randolph examined "the MSS. in my possession," noted the differences between the eighth and ninth resolutions as Jefferson wrote them and as they were adopted by the Kentucky assembly under the elder Breckinridge's stewardardship, and noticed his grandfather's use of the term "nullification." Randolph also furnished a copy of Jefferson's "original draught"—probably Document II—which newspapers published in 1832. Then in the 1850s H. A. Washington's edition of Jefferson's papers and Henry S. Randall's *Life of*

Thomas Jefferson printed Jefferson's version of the resolutions and helped fix
the document's place in the Jefferson canon (*United States Telegraph*, 12 Mch.,
4 Apr. 1832; *Niles' Weekly Register*, 43 [1832], suppl. 22-4; Malone, *Jefferson*,
3:406n).

Jefferson put no date on his draft resolutions, and the only thing certain about
when he composed them is that some version was in the hands of Wilson Cary
Nicholas, and available to be given to John Breckinridge, by the time Nicholas
wrote Jefferson on 4 Oct. 1798. Jefferson and Madison could have discussed
the strategy that underlay the resolutions on 2-3 July when Jefferson stopped at
Montpelier on his way home from Philadelphia (Madison, *Papers*, 17:186;
Malone, *Jefferson*, 3:400; MB, 2:987). But the earliest extant draft of the resolutions (Document I) contains references to the approval on 14 July 1798 of the
Sedition Act, which Jefferson referred to in the resolutions by its official title,
"An Act in addition to the act, entitled 'An Act for the punishment of certain
crimes against the United States.'" Jefferson therefore wrote the resolutions
sometime after receiving at Monticello news of the passage of the Sedition Act,
despite the fact that he left blank the 27 June date of approval of the act concerning frauds on the Bank of the U.S. and gave the date of the Alien Friends Act,
which became law on 25 June, as "the   day of July 1798." He referred to
the dates of the three acts in exactly the same way in his fair copy (Document II),
which means that little time passed between his composition of Document I and
his making the clean copy, or that he simply did not take the trouble to find and
fill in the missing information.

The evidence is far from conclusive, but some characteristics of Document I
suggest that Jefferson may have begun it as a fair copy of a now-missing earlier
draft. He first wrote the original core of resolutions in Document I (those numbered 1-2, 4-5, and 7-9, along with the canceled resolution reported in note 2 to
Document I) in a neat hand without extensive redrafting as he wrote. In that
initial casting of the document he eschewed abbreviations except for "&" and
"US," and in the opening phrase of the fourth resolution, the first time the word
appears, he printed the word "Alien" rather than writing it in cursive. These
signs may mean that he worked from a composition draft and originally intended Document I to be the final version. If so, Document I became a draft
nonetheless, Jefferson adding what became the third resolution on a separate
sheet, crowding the sixth resolution in a smaller hand in space below the seventh, making wholesale changes to the eighth, and numbering the resolutions
(see textual notes to Document I). Document II then became the fair copy, a neat
rewriting of the emended Document I.

After Wilson Cary Nicholas informed Jefferson on 4 Oct. 1798 that John
Breckinridge could furnish a means of introducing the resolutions in the Kentucky legislature, Jefferson replied that "I had imagined it better those resolutions should have originated with N. Carolina. but perhaps the late changes in
their representation may indicate some doubt whether they would have passed"
(TJ to Nicholas, 5 Oct. 1798). It seems unlikely, however, that Jefferson had
North Carolina in mind when he penned the resolutions. In the resolves he
almost exclusively characterized the state that would pass them as "this commonwealth," a term that had no particular reference to North Carolina. Moreover, in his third resolution Jefferson, discussing encroachments on religious
freedom, noted that "this state, by a law passed on the general demand of it's
citizens, had already protected" religious exercise and opinion "from all human

restraint or interference." No North Carolina statute of the time, and for that matter none passed by Kentucky, matched that description. The reference actually seems to point to the Statute for Establishing Religious Freedom drafted by Jefferson and passed into law in Virginia in 1785. If that is the case, then Virginia was the "commonwealth" Jefferson had in mind as he drafted the resolutions.

This notion is reinforced by the fact that he sent the document to Nicholas. A member of the Virginia House of Delegates from Albemarle, Nicholas in other instances conveyed key instruments to that house, notably Jefferson's petition on the election of jurors and Madison's draft resolves that late in the year became the Virginia Resolutions. The decision to send Jefferson's resolutions to another state may in the end have been determined by legislative calendars. In 1798 the House of Delegates did not meet until December, but earlier, in August, Virginia's Republicans thought that they might be able to have the legislature convened early, as soon as the first days of September, before some Federalist members could arrive. At Charlottesville on 1 Sep. "a vast number of the inhabitants of Albemarle" met to consider the constitutionality of the Alien and Sedition Acts, overwhelmingly adopting resolutions that "went to reprobate those diabolical acts" and calling for a remonstrance to be sent to the legislature. The attempt at an early convening date failed, however, and the assembly did not gather until its usual time late in the year. If Jefferson composed his resolutions with the expectation that the assembly would convene early, not long after the beginning of September, he very likely wrote them in August. Then as the hope of an early meeting of the legislature faded, he and Nicholas probably looked at other states and left the way open in Virginia for Madison's resolutions, written a little later than Jefferson's (Malone, *Jefferson*, 3:401; *Virginia Herald*, 18 Sep. 1798; note to Petition to the General Assembly of Virginia, [2 or 3 Nov. 1798]; TJ to Nicholas, 29 Nov. 1798).

Nicholas's letter to Jefferson on 4 Oct. 1798 does not illuminate the extent to which they might have anticipated sending the resolutions to Kentucky. Nicholas emphasized the fortuitous availability of John Breckinridge to take the resolutions under his wing, and Jefferson's reply on 5 Oct. confirms that he had not conceived the resolutions with Kentucky in mind. Unfortunately, when he wrote to Breckinridge's son decades later Jefferson said the opposite, confessing a weak recollection of some other points but declaring that he, Nicholas, and the elder Breckinridge had conferred before he wrote the resolutions, the intent from the start being to introduce them in the legislature of Kentucky. For a long time Jefferson's 1821 letter to Joseph Cabell Breckinridge confused historians' understanding of the circumstances surrounding the writing of the resolutions. Compounding the problem, for much of the nineteenth century it was mistakenly thought that Jefferson had written that letter not to Breckinridge's son but to a son of Wilson Cary Nicholas's brother George (see Adrienne Koch and Harry Ammon, "The Virginia and Kentucky Resolutions: An Episode in Jefferson's and Madison's Defense of Civil Liberties," wmq, 3d ser., 5 [1948], 149-50; Paul Leicester Ford printed the 1821 letter as a footnote to the Kentucky Resolutions: Ford, 7:290-1n).

By the time Wilson Cary Nicholas wrote to him on 4 Oct. 1798 Jefferson would have had some notion of the favorable ground that Kentucky presented at that moment, for on the first of the month he received Samuel Brown's 4 Sep. letter from Lexington. While it is not clear which local resolves Brown sent to Jefferson with that letter, they along with Brown's characterization of activity in the state would have given the impression that Kentucky was afire over the Alien and Sedition Acts. Resolutions adopted in Clark and other counties appeared in print in Lexington in time for Brown to have enclosed them to Jefferson, and in his letter Brown wished that the legislature would meet and "give such solemnity to the voice of the people, as will arrest the attention of our infatuated Rulers" (*Kentucky Gazette*, 1, 8, 29 Aug. 1798; Brown to TJ, 4 Sep. 1798). On 13 Aug. in Lexington, George Nicholas addressed an outdoor meeting attended by several thousand people, and John Breckinridge, who corresponded with Monroe that summer although not with Jefferson, was involved in the creation of some of the local resolutions. In the spring of 1798 Breckinridge had been elected to the Kentucky House of Representatives from Fayette County, where he lived outside Lexington, but his papers contain a draft of the resolutions adopted by an adjoining county, Woodford, on 6 Aug., and a draft set of resolves for Clark different from those adopted in that nearby county on 24 July (DLC: Breckinridge Family Papers). Coughing blood, very likely suffering from tuberculosis, Breckinridge left home on 22 Aug. for a recuperative trip to Sweet Springs, Virginia. Little is known of his itinerary on that journey other than what Wilson Cary Nicholas mentioned to Jefferson on 4 Oct. (Lowell H. Harrison, *John Breckinridge: Jeffersonian Republican* [Louisville, 1969], 72, 74-5, 89n, 110; James Morton Smith, "The Grass Roots Origins of the Kentucky Resolutions," wmq, 3d ser., 27 [1970], 221-45; *Kentucky Gazette*, 1, 8 Aug. 1798; anb).

Nicholas probably had in his possession, and "put into the hands of" Breckinridge, some version of Jefferson's fair copy of the resolutions. An undated copy in Breckinridge's handwriting and retained within his papers follows Jefferson's text with almost no substantive variation (see notes to Document ii). If Breckinridge saw the fair copy itself, the document was subsequently returned to Jefferson's papers. Jefferson sent a press copy to Madison in November 1798 (see below), but given its condition, even when new, it seems unlikely that Breckinridge and Nicholas used the press copy as their source for the text. Whether Breckinridge made his copy of the resolutions at Nicholas's house or took a version of Jefferson's fair copy with him back to Kentucky, by 10 Oct. Nicholas in a letter to Breckinridge referred to "the paper that you have," saying also that Jefferson regretted not seeing the Kentucky traveler but understood the reasons for their not meeting. Nicholas noted too that Jefferson "suggests nothing further upon the subject" (Harrison, *Breckinridge*, 76, 89n).

It was after Breckinridge copied them, therefore, that Jefferson's resolutions became the Kentucky Resolutions—that is to say, as illustrated by Document iii, his long, substantive eighth resolution and short, procedural ninth one became a short and procedural eighth resolve followed by a substantive final resolution that rearranged Jefferson's eighth and omitted, most notably, the reference to nullification. That recasting of the key section occurred before Breckinridge introduced the resolutions in the Kentucky House of Representatives on 8 Nov., to judge from a broadside version printed in Kentucky (Evans, No. 48494; see notes to Document iii). One change that did occur during the consideration of the resolutions by the legislature was the addition of the word "tamely" in the phrase "tamely to submit" in the ninth resolution (see Document iii, note 4).

Breckinridge returned to Kentucky before the seventh General Assembly convened in Frankfort early in November. In his address to the assembly on 7 Nov., Governor James Garrard noted that the state, "being deeply interested in the conduct of the national government, must have a right to applaud or to censure that government, when applause or censure becomes its due." Paying particular notice to the Alien Friends Act, the Sedition Act, and Kentucky's reputation as a place "if not in a state of insurrection, yet utterly disaffected to the federal government," Garrard urged the legislature to declare the state's support for the U.S. Constitution while "entering your protest against all unconstitutional laws and impolitic proceedings" (*Kentucky Gazette*, 14 Nov. 1798). The same day, Breckinridge gave notice in the state House of Representatives that he would bring in resolutions addressing that theme of the governor's message. Introduced on the 8th and immediately considered by a committee of the whole, the resolutions passed the House on 10 Nov., received the unanimous concurrence of the state senate three days later, and were approved by Garrard on the 16th (see descriptive note to Document III). It was in that form, as the legislature passed them, that the Kentucky Resolutions would be known until Thomas Jefferson Randolph delved into his grandfather's papers in the 1830s.

Nothing in Jefferson's correspondence indicates that he consulted Madison about the resolutions before they went to Kentucky with Breckinridge. On 5 Oct., in fact, he asked Nicholas to discuss them with Madison, which implies that such a consultation had not yet occurred. The first unmistakable reference to the document in his correspondence with Madison came on 17 Nov. 1798, when he enclosed "a copy of the draught of the Kentuckey resolves." That enclosure seems likely to have been the press copy of Document II (and see Madison, *Papers*, 17:175-81; the presumption that Jefferson had written the 17 Nov. letter in 1799 rather than 1798 caused some confusion even for Madison in later years as he attempted to sort out what Jefferson had sent him about the resolutions: Gaillard Hunt, *The Writings of James Madison*, 9 vols. [New York, 1900-10], 9:394-6n). The press copy is in the Rives Collection of Madison's papers at the Library of Congress. In that collection also is another copy of the resolutions, a later, handwritten composite incorporating both Jefferson's text and that adopted by the Kentucky legislature, using different scripts and other means to delineate the two texts. Some historians, noting the provenance of this composite document within a section of Madison's papers, have concluded that Jefferson enclosed it along with the press copy in his letter of 17 Nov. in order to show Madison the changes made to the resolutions before their passage (Koch and Ammon, "Virginia and Kentucky Resolutions," 159; Malone, *Jefferson*, 3:406). That, however, seems nearly impossible. Whoever made the composite document used a printed version of the Kentucky Resolutions that dated no earlier than 10 Nov. 1798, and notes written at the beginning of the document, evidently contemporary with its creation, demonstrate a knowledge of the Virginia Resolutions (passed in December 1798). The composite document is the result of a comparison of a printed copy with not just any version of Jefferson's text, but with the press copy of Document II, the composite distinguishing even those places in the press copy where individual lines were lost at the edges of the sheets due to imperfect pressing. Nothing about the handwriting of the composite, nor any endorsement or notation on it, indicates that Jefferson sent or Madison received the document. It seems most plausible to associate the composite not with Jefferson and Madison in 1798 but with William Cabell Rives (1793-1868). An ardent protegé of first Jefferson and then Madison, Rives studied law under Jefferson and in the 1820s, before embarking on a career in politics and diplomacy, became a political associate of Thomas

Ritchie, the editor of the *Enquirer*. A devotee of Madison's political thought, Rives was an early editor of Madison's letters and undertook a multivolume biography that was only partially completed at the time of Rives's death (ANB; Drew R. McCoy, *The Last of the Fathers: James Madison and the Republican Legacy* [Cambridge, 1989], 327-67). Involvement by Rives in the creation of the composite document would explain how its author had access to the press copy Jefferson sent in November 1798 as well as the fact that the press copy and the later composite ended up in proximity to one another in Rives's collection of Madison documents.

Although the porous documentary record is largely to blame, a thorough understanding of Jefferson's resolutions has also been impeded by the fact that even some of his strongest advocates, for reasons having to do with the sectional conflict resulting eventually in secession and civil war, have been loathe to embrace his authorship of the document—especially that portion of his eighth resolution that dealt with nullification. Jefferson was gone by the time sectional friction and political events focused attention on the use he had made of the concept and term "nullification," and it fell to Madison to explain. Striving in 1830 and after to forestall southern nullifiers who depicted Jefferson as their progenitor, Madison, who in any event surely knew the resolutions adopted by the Kentucky General Assembly better than he knew Jefferson's draft, initially denied that his friend had used the word (McCoy, *Last of the Fathers*, 139-151; Merrill D. Peterson, *The Jefferson Image in the American Mind* [New York, 1960], 51-9; William W. Freehling, *Prelude to Civil War: The Nullification Controversy in South Carolina, 1816-1836* [New York, 1966], 207-10; Hunt, *Writings*, 9:383-403). Later, Dumas Malone attributed Jefferson's draft resolutions to "impatience" and an "excess of zeal in defense of freedom." Expressing relief that "wise counsel" moderated the resolutions, Malone deemed it "a pity" that Madison had not written the original Kentucky Resolutions as well as those adopted in Virginia (Malone, *Jefferson*, 3:408). The regret of a towering Jefferson scholar that his subject had actually penned the Kentucky Resolutions stands in contrast to the detailed analysis scholars have given to Jefferson's authorship of other major documents. Malone considered Jefferson's resolutions uncharacteristically "prolix and repetitious" (same, 405), overlooking their similarity to the mannered and repetitious statements of the Declaration of Independence and their function as a quasi-legal document, a structured set of indictments and explications meant to justify extraordinary action. So meticulous was Jefferson in challenging the legality of the federal statutes in question, in the margins of his draft he changed "law," which might imply a legitimacy of natural law and right, to "act," which did not carry the same inherent authority (see notes 2, 4, and 8, Document I). He marshaled a variety of arguments, too, in his brief against the Alien and Sedition Acts. Some, such as the fifth resolution's creative indictment of the Alien Friends Act because it contradicted the constitutional protection of the slave trade until 1808, surely had no chance of standing on their own. But as with the Declaration's long list of charges against the crown, the combined array of arguments in the resolutions, the repeated intonation that the laws were "void & of no force," had cumulative impact. And by his actions Jefferson showed that he did not mind if portions of what he had written fell by the wayside. He accepted without protest the Kentuckians' modifications, including the omission of the tactic of "nullification," and in the bargain never explained what he meant by asserting a state's power to annul federal law.

I. Jefferson's Draft

[before 4 Oct. 1798]

1. Resolved that the several states composing the US. of America are not united on the principle of unlimited submission to their general government; but that, by a compact under the style & title of a Constitution for the US. and of Amendments thereto, they constituted a general government for special purposes, delegated to that government certain definite powers, reserving, each state to itself, the residuary mass of right to their own self-government; and that whensoever the General government assumes undelegated powers, it's acts are unauthoritative, void, & of no force.

   that to this compact each state acceded as a state, and is an integral party, it's co-states forming, as to itself, the other party. [1]

   that the government created by this compact was not made the exclusive or final judge of the extent of the powers delegated to itself; since that would have made it's discretion, & not the constitution the measure of it's powers: but that, as in all other cases of compact among powers having no common judge, each party has an equal right to judge for itself, as well of infractions, as of the mode & measure of redress. [2]

2. Resolved that, the Constitution of the US. having delegated to Congress a power to punish treason, counterfieting the securities & current coin of the US. piracies & felonies committed on the high seas, and offences against the law of nations, & no other crimes whatsoever, and it being true as a general principle, and one of the Amendments to the constitution having also declared, that 'the powers not delegated to the US. by the constitution, nor prohibited by it to the states, are reserved to the states respectively, or to the people,' therefore, the act of Congress passed on the 14th day of July 1798. and intituled 'an Act in addition to the act intituled an Act for the punishment of certain crimes against the US.' as also the act passed by them on the ___ day of June 1798. intituled 'an Act to punish frauds committed on the bank of the US.' [and all other their acts which assume to create, define, or punish crimes, other than those so enumerated in the Constitution][3] are altogether void and of no force, and that the power to create, define, & punish such other crimes is reserved, and of right appurtains solely and exclusively to the respective states, each within it's own territory. [4]

3. Resolved that it is true as a general principle and is also expressly declared by one of the amendments to the constitution that 'the powers not delegated to the US. by the constitution, nor prohibited by it to the states, are reserved to the states respectively or to the people': and that no power over the freedom of religion, freedom of speech, or freedom of

the press being delegated to the US. by the constitution, nor prohibited by it to the states, all lawful powers respecting the same did of right remain, & were reserved, to the states or the people: that thus was manifested their determination to retain to themselves the right of judging how far the licentiousness of speech and of the press may be abridged without lessening their useful freedom, and how far those abuses which cannot be separated from their use should be tolerated rather than the use be destroyed; and thus also they guarded against all abridgement by the US. of the freedom of religious opinions and exercises, & retained to themselves the right of protecting the same, as this state, by a law passed on the general demand of it's citizens, had already protected them, from all human restraint or interference: And that in addition to this general principle & express declaration, another & more special provision has been made by one of the amendments to the constitution which expressly declares that 'Congress shall make no law respecting an establishment of religion, or prohibiting the free exercise thereof, or abridging the freedom of speech or of the press,' thereby guarding in the same sentence & under the same words the freedom of religion, of speech & of the press. insomuch that whatever violates either throws down the sanctuary which covers the others, and that[5] libels, falsehood and defamation equally with heresy & false religion are witheld from the cognisance of federal tribunals; that therefore the act of the Congress of the US. passed on the 14th. day of July 1798. intituled 'an act in addition to the act intituled an act for the punishment of certain crimes against the US.' which does abridge the freedom of the press is not law but is altogether void and of no force.[6]

4. Resolved that ALIEN-friends are under the jurisdiction and protection[7] of the laws of the state wherein they are; that no power over them has been delegated to the US. nor prohibited to the individual states distinct from their power over citizens: and it being true as a general principle, and one of the Amendments to the constitution having also declared, that 'the powers not delegated to the US. by the constitution, nor prohibited by it to the States, are reserved to the states respectively, or to the people,' the act of the Congress of the US. passed on the ___ day of July 1798. intituled 'an Act concerning Aliens' which assumes powers over Alien-friends not delegated by the constitution is not law, but is altogether void & of no force.[8]

5. Resolved that in addition to the general principle, as well as the express declaration, that powers not delegated are reserved, another and more special provision, inserted in the constitution from abundant caution, has declared that 'the migration or importation of such persons as any of the states now existing shall think proper to admit, shall not be prohib-

ited by the Congress prior to the year 1808,' that this commonwealth does admit the migration of Alien-friends, described as the subject of the said act concerning aliens; that a provision against prohibiting their migration, is a provision against all acts equivalent thereto, or it would be nugatory; that to remove them when migrated is equivalent to a prohibition of their migration, and is therefore contrary to the said provision of the constitution, and void.[9]

6. Resolved that the imprisonment of a person under the protection of the laws of this commonwealth on his failure to obey the simple *order* of the President to depart out of the US. as is undertaken by the said act intituled 'an act concerning Aliens' is contrary to the constitution, one Amendment to which has provided that 'no person shall be deprived of liberty without due process of law.' and that another having provided that 'in all criminal[10] prosecutions the accused shall enjoy the right to a public trial, by an impartial jury, to be informed of the nature & cause of the accusation to be confronted with the witnesses against him, to have compulsory process for obtaining witnesses in his favor, & to have the assistance of counsel for his defence' the same act undertaking to authorize the President to remove a person out of the US. who is under the protection of the law, on his own suspicion, without accusation, without jury, without public trial, without confrontation of the witnesses against him, without hearing witnesses in his favor, without defence, without counsel, is contrary to these provisions also of the constitution, is therefore not law, but utterly void & of no force.

that transferring the power of judging any person who is under the protection of the law, from the courts to the President of the US. as is undertaken by the same act concerning Aliens, is against the article of the constitution which provides that 'the judicial power of the US. shall be vested in courts the judges of which shall hold their offices during good behavior,' & that the sd act is void for that reason also. and it is further to be noted that this transfer of judiciary power is to that magistrate of the general government who already possesses all the Executive, and a negative on all the Legislative powers.[11]

7. Resolved that the construction applied by the general government, (as is evidenced by sundry of their proceedings) to those parts of the constitution of the US. which delegate to Congress a power 'to lay & collect taxes, duties, imposts, & excises, to pay the debts & provide for the common defence & general welfare of the US.' and 'to make all laws which shall be necessary & proper for carrying into execution the powers vested by the constitution in the government of the US. or in any department or officer thereof,' goes to the destruction of all the limits prescribed to their power by the constitution; that words meant by that

instrument to be subsidiary only to the execution of limited powers, ought not to be so construed as themselves to give unlimited powers, nor a part to be so taken as to destroy the whole residue of that instrument: that the proceedings of the general government under colour of these articles, will be a fit & necessary subject of revisal & correction at a time of greater tranquility[12] while those specified in the preceding resolutions, call for immediate redress.

8. Resolved that a committee of conference & correspondence be appointed, who shall have in charge to communicate the preceding resolutions to the legislatures of the several states, to assure them that this commonwealth continues in the same esteem for their friendship & union which it has manifested from that moment at which a common danger first suggested a common union: that it considers union, for specified national purposes, and particularly for those specified in their late federal compact, to be friendly to the peace, happiness and prosperity of all the states: that faithful to that compact, according to the plain intent & meaning in which it was understood & acceded to by the several parties, it is sincerely anxious for it's preservation: that it does also believe that to take from the states all the powers of self-government, & transfer them to a general & consolidated government, without regard to the special delegations & reservations solemnly agreed to in that compact, is not for the peace, happiness or prosperity of these states: and that therefore this commonwealth is determined, as it doubts not it's co-states are, to submit to undelegated & consequently unlimited powers in no man, or body of men on earth: that in cases of an abuse[13] of the delegated powers, the members of the[14] general government being chosen by the people, a change by the people would be the constitutional remedy; but where powers are assumed which have not been delegated a nullification of the act is the rightful remedy: that every state has a natural right, in cases not within the compact [casus non foederis][15] to nullify of their own authority all assumptions of power by others within their limits: that without this right, they would be under the dominion, absolute and unlimited, of whosoever might exercise this right of judgment for them: that nevertheless this commonwealth, from motives of regard & respect for it's co-states has wished to communicate with them on the subject; that with them alone it is proper to communicate, they alone being parties to the compact, & solely authorised to judge in the last resort of the powers exercised under it; Congress being not a party, but merely the creature of the compact, & subject, as to it's assumptions of power, to the final judgment of those by whom & for whose use itself[16] and it's powers were all created and modified: that if those acts before specified should stand,[17] these conclusions would flow from

them; that the General government may place any act they think proper on the list of crimes, and punish it themselves, whether enumerated, or not enumerated by the constitution as cognisable by them; that they may transfer it's cognisance to the President, or any other person, who may himself be the accuser, counsel, judge & jury, whose *suspicions* may be the evidence, his *order* the sentence, his officer the executioner, & his breast the sole record of the transaction: that a very numerous & valuable description of the inhabitants of these states being, by this precedent reduced as Outlaws [18] to the absolute dominion of one man, and the barrier of the constitution thus swept away for us all, no rampart now remains against the passions and the power [19] of a majority in Congress, to protect from a like exportation or other more grievous punishment, the Minority of the same body, the legislatures, judges, governors, & counsellors [20] of the states, nor their other peaceable inhabitants, who may venture to reclaim the constitutional rights and liberties of the states and people, or who for other causes, good or bad, may be obnoxious to the views, or marked by the suspicions of the President, or be thought dangerous to his or their elections or other interests public or personal: that the friendless alien has indeed been selected as the safest subject of a first experiment; but the citizen will soon follow, or rather has already followed; for already has a Sedition act marked him as it's prey: that these & successive acts of the same character, unless arrested at the threshold necessarily drive these states into revolution and blood, and will furnish new calumnies against republican government, and new pretexts for those who wish it to be believed that man cannot be governed but by a rod of iron: that it would be a dangerous delusion were a confidence in the men of our choice to silence our fears for the safety of our rights: that confidence is every where the parent of despotism; free government is founded in jealousy and not in confidence; it is jealousy & not confidence which prescribes limited constitutions to bind down those whom we are obliged to trust with power: that our constitution has accordingly [21] fixed the limits to which, and no further, our confidence may go: and let the honest advocate of confidence read the Alien & Sedition acts, and say if the constitution has not been wise in fixing limits to the government it created, and whether we should be wise in destroying those limits? let him say what the government is, if it be not a tyranny, which the men of our choice have conferred on the President, and the President of our choice has assented to and accepted over the friendly strangers to whom the mild spirit of our country & it's laws had pledged hospitality & protection: that the men of our choice have more respected the bare *suspicions* of the President, than the solid rights of innocence, the claims of justification, [22] the sacred force of truth, and the forms & substance of law & justice: in questions of power then, let no more be heard of confidence in man, but bind him down from mischief by the chains of the constitution:[23] that this commonwealth does therefore call on it's co-states for an expression of their sentiments on the acts concerning aliens and for the punishment of certain crimes, herein before specified, plainly declaring whether these acts are, or are not, authorised by the federal compact? and it doubts not that their sense will be so enounced as to prove their attachment unaltered to limited government whether general or particular; & that the rights & liberties of their co-states will be exposed to no dangers by remaining embarked in a common bottom with their own:[24] that they will concur with this comm. in[25] considering the said acts as so palpably against the constn as to amount to an undisguised declarn that that compact is not meant to be the measure of the powers of the genl. govm't, but that it will proceed in the exercise over these states of all powers whatsoever, that they will view this as seizing the rights of the states & consolidating them in the hands of the genl govm't with a power assumed[26] to bind the states (not merely in the cases made federal, but) in all cases whatsoever, by laws made not with their consent, but by others against their consent; that this would be to surrender[27] the form of govmt we have chosen, & to live under one deriving it's powers from it's own will & not from our authority, and that the costates, recurring to their natural right in cases not made federal, will concur in declaring these acts void & of no force & will each take measures of it's own for providing that neither these acts nor any others of the genl. government not plainly & intentionally authorised[28] by the constn shall be exercised within their respective territories.

9. That the said committee be authorised to communicate, by writing or personal conferences, at any times or places whatever, with any person or persons who may be appointed by any one or more of the co-states to correspond or confer with them; & that they lay their proceedings before the next session of assembly:[29] that the members of the said committee, while acting within the state, have the same allowance as the members of the General assembly, and while acting without the commonwealth, the same as members of Congress: and that the Treasurer be authorised, on warrants from the Governor, to advance them monies on account for the said services.

Dft (DLC: TJ Papers, 93:16003, 16003-a, 16004); undated, but antecedent to Document II; entirely in TJ's hand, the first, second, and fourth through seventh resolutions written on both sides of one narrow sheet, the eighth resolution (as originally composed) and the ninth on a similar sheet; those two sheets were a single leaf when TJ composed the sixth resolution; three additional smaller pieces (two of which have been attached to the primary sheets) hold what became the third resolution and substantial alterations to the eighth (see notes 6, 16, and 24 below); one word in TJ's hand printing shown in small capitals; TJ's square brackets in text identified in notes 3, 15, and 24 below; TJ placed all the digits numbering the resolutions either in the margins or within paragraph indentations, which implies that he originally wrote the resolutions before deciding to number them; the number of one resolution may have been changed (see note 4 below); in TJ's original sequence the sixth resolution followed the seventh and he subsequently transposed them, numbering them after making that decision (notes 9 and 11).

[1] In the margin, keyed for insertion between this and the next clause, TJ wrote and canceled: "That the constitutional form of action for this commonwealth as a party with respect to any other party is by it's organised powers & not by it's citizens in a body."

[2] Following this paragraph TJ wrote and subsequently struck through: "2. Resolved that, one of the Amendments to the Constitution having declared that 'Congress shall make no law respecting an establishment of religion, or prohibiting the free exercise thereof, or *abridging the freedom of speech, or of the press,*' the Act of the Congress of the US. passed on the 14th. day of July 1798. intituled 'An act in addition to the act intituled an Act for the punishment of certain crimes against the US.' which does abridge the freedom of speech & of the press, is not law, but is altogether void and of no force." Vertically in the margin alongside this resolution he wrote "Sedition law," changing the second word to "Act."

[3] TJ's brackets.

[4] The number of this resolution was likely a "3" originally, reworked to "2." Vertically in the margin alongside this resolution TJ wrote "Sedition law, & Counterfeits of the bank," again changing "law" to "Act."

[5] Word interlined. Here TJ first wrote "placing" and then substituted "witholding," which he also canceled.

[6] TJ wrote this resolution on a separate piece that has been affixed at one end to the sheet with the preceding resolutions.

[7] Preceding two words interlined.

[8] TJ wrote "Alien⟨-*law*⟩ act" vertically in the margin alongside this resolution.

[9] TJ wrote "Alien act" vertically in the margin alongside this resolution. He inserted an arrow and the numeral "6." between this resolution and the seventh, which follows next on the page, to indicate the placement of the sixth resolution.

[10] Here TJ canceled "[cases]."

[11] Although TJ finally made this the sixth resolution it follows the one he labeled number 7. He numbered the sixth and seventh resolutions after determining their final sequence.

[12] TJ originally wrote the preceding six words following "under colour of these articles" earlier in the sentence, then transposed the phrase to this location.

[13] TJ originally wrote "that in abuses." Preceding this phrase he canceled "that it ought not."

[14] Three words interlined.

[15] TJ's brackets.

[16] The long passage that begins after this word and runs through "bind him down from mischief by the chains of the constitution" (see note 23 below) is an insertion that TJ wrote on both sides of a separate sheet. He originally wrote here "& it's powers were all created & modified: that this commonwealth does therefore call," probably continuing to the conclusion of the eighth resolution as he first composed it. In his original text he interlined "that if the acts should stand &c" following the word "modified" to key the location of the long insertion.

[17] TJ first wrote "those acts should stand" before altering the clause to read as above.

[18] Two words interlined.

[19] TJ first wrote "the will and the passions" before altering the phrase to read as above.

[20] Word and ampersand interlined.

[21] TJ here canceled "set."

[22] Above this word TJ interlined but canceled "exculpation."

[23] The long insertion ends here, TJ placing a line of flourishes and then the words "that this" to confirm the resumption of his original text.

[24] Remainder of resolution written on a small sheet that has been attached to the main page and begins with a canceled rep-

etition of the phrase, "in a common bottom with their own." This insertion is in substitution for the following paragraph, which TJ originally wrote as part of the eighth resolution but then canceled:

"But that however confident at other times this commonwealth would have been in the deliberate judgment of the co-states, and that but one opinion would be entertained on the unjustifiable character of the acts herein specified, yet it cannot be insensible that circumstances do exist, & that passions are at this time afloat which may give a biass to the judgment to be pronounced on this subject, that times of passion are peculiarly those when precedents of wrong are yielded to with the least caution, when encroachments of power are most usually made & principles are least watched. that whether the coincidence of the occasion & the encroachment in the present case, has been from accident or design, the right of the commonwealth to the government of itself in cases not parted with, is too vitally important to be yielded from temporary or secondary considerations: that a fixed determination therefore to retain it requires us in candor & without reserve to declare, & to warn our co-states that considering the said acts to be so palpably against the constitution as to amount to an undisguised declaration that that compact is not meant to be the measure of the powers of the general government, but that it is to proceed in the exercise over these states of any & all powers whatever, considering this as seizing the rights of the states & consolidating them in hands of the general government, with power to bind the states (not merely in the cases made federal [casus federis] but) in all cases whatsoever, by laws not made with their consent, but by other states against their consent; considering all other consequences as nothing in comparison with that of yielding the form of government we have chosen, & of living under one deriving it's powers from it's own will and not from our authority, this commonwealth, as an integral party, does in that case protest against such opinions & exercises of undelegated & unauthorised power, and does declare that, recurring to it's natural right of judging & acting for itself, it will be constrained to take care of itself, & to provide by measures of it's own, that no power not plainly & intentionally delegated by the constitution to the general government, shall be exercised within the territory of this commonwealth." Immediately following this passage, which TJ ended with a colon, is the ninth resolution. The brackets around "casus federis" are TJ's, the word "vitally" in the phrase "too vitally important" is an interlineation, and he considered using "measuring" instead of "deriving" in the phrase, "under one deriving it's powers."

[25] Preceding four words and abbreviation interlined.

[26] Word interlined.

[27] Word interlined in place of "yield."

[28] Word interlined in place of "delegated."

[29] TJ drew an incomplete box around the remainder of the resolution.

II. Jefferson's Fair Copy

[before 4 Oct. 1798]

1. Resolved that the several states composing the US. of America are not united on the principle of unlimited submission to their general government; but that by a compact under the style and title of a Constitution for the US. and of amendments thereto, they constituted a general government for special purposes, delegated to that government certain definite powers, reserving, each state to itself, the residuary mass of right to their own self-government; & that whensoever the General government assumes undelegated powers, it's acts are unauthoritative, void, &

of no[1] force: that to this compact each state acceded as a state, and is an integral party, it's co-states forming, as to itself, the other party: that the government created by this compact was not made the exclusive or final judge of the extent of the powers delegated to itself; since that would have made it's discretion, & not the constitution, the measure of it's powers; but that, as in all other cases of compact among powers having no common judge, each party has an equal right to judge for itself, as well of infractions, as of the mode & measure of redress.

2. Resolved that the constitution of the US. having delegated to Congress a power to punish treason, counterfieting the securities & current coin of the US. piracies & felonies committed on the high seas, & offences against the law of Nations, & no other crimes whatsoever, and it being true as a general principle, and one of the Amendments to the constitution having also declared, that 'the powers not delegated to the US. by the constitution, nor prohibited by it to the states,[2] are reserved to the states respectively, or to the people' therefore the act of Congress passed on the 14th. day of July 1798 and intituled 'an Act in addition to the act intituled an Act for the punishment of certain crimes against the US.' as also the act passed by them on the   day of June 1798. intituled 'an Act to punish frauds committed on the bank of the US.' [and all other their acts which assume to create, define or punish crimes, other than those so enumerated in the Constitution] are altogether void & of no force, & that the power to create, define & punish such other crimes is reserved, & of right appurtains solely & exclusively to the respective states, each within it's own territory.

3. Resolved that it is true as a general principle, and is also expressly declared by one of the Amendments to the Constitution that 'the powers not delegated to the US. by the constitution, nor prohibited by it to the states, are reserved to the states respectively or to the people'; and that no power over the freedom of religion, freedom of speech, or freedom of the press being delegated to the US. by the constitution, nor prohibited by it to the states, all lawful powers respecting the same did of right remain, & were reserved, to the states or the people: that thus was manifested their determination to retain to themselves the right of judging how far the licentiousness of speech & of the press may be abridged without lessening their useful freedom, and how far those abuses which cannot be separated from their use should be tolerated rather than the use be destroyed; and thus also they guarded against all abridgment by the US. of the freedom of religious opinions and exercises, & retained to themselves the right of protecting the same, as this state, by a law passed on the general demand of it's citizens, had already protected them from all human restraint or interference: And that in addition to this general

principle and express declaration, another & more special provision has
been made by one of the amendments to the constitution which expressly declares that 'Congress shall make no law respecting an establishment of religion, or prohibiting the free exercise thereof or abridging the freedom of speech or of the press,' thereby guarding in the same
sentence, & under the same words, the freedom of religion of speech &
of the press: insomuch that whatever violates either throws down the
sanctuary which covers the others, and that libels, falsehood & defamation, equally with heresy & false religion, are witheld from the cognisance of federal tribunals: that therefore the act of Congress of the US.
passed on the 14th. day of July 1798. intituled 'an Act in addition to the
act intituled an act for the punishment of certain crimes against the US,'
which does abridge the freedom of the press, is not law, but is altogether
void & of no force.

4. Resolved that ALIEN friends are under the jurisdiction and protection of the laws of the state wherein they are; that no power over them
has been delegated to the US. nor prohibited to the individual states
distinct from their power over citizens: and it being true as a general
principle, & one of the amendments to the constitution having also declared that 'the powers not delegated to the US. by the constitution, nor
prohibited by it to the States, are reserved to the states respectively, or
to the people,' the act of the Congress of the US. passed on the   day
of July 1798 intituled 'an Act concerning Aliens,' which assumes powers over Alien-friends not delegated by the constitution, is not law, but
is altogether void & of no force.

5. Resolved that in addition to the general principle, as well as the
express declaration, that powers not delegated are reserved, another and
more special provision, inserted in the constitution from abundant caution, has declared that 'the migration or importation of such persons as
any of the states now existing shall think proper to admit, shall not be
prohibited by the Congress prior to the year 1808'; that this commonwealth does admit the migration of Alien-friends, described as the subject of the said act concerning aliens; that a provision against prohibiting their migration, is a provision against all acts equivalent thereto, or
it would be nugatory; that to remove them when migrated is equivalent
to a prohibition of their migration, and is therefore contrary to the said
provision of the constitution, and void.

6. Resolved that the imprisonment of a person under the protection
of the laws of this commonwealth on his failure to obey the simple *order*
of the President to depart out of the US. as is undertaken by the said act
intituled 'an Act concerning Aliens,' is contrary to the constitution, one
Amendment to which has provided that 'no person shall be deprived of

liberty without due process of law.' and that another having provided that 'in all criminal prosecutions the accused shall enjoy the right to a public trial, by an impartial jury, to be informed of the nature and cause of the accusation, to be confronted with the witnesses against him, to have compulsory process for obtaining witnesses in his favor, & to have the assistance of counsel for his defence,' the same act, undertaking to authorize the President to remove a person out of the US. who is under the protection of the law, on his own suspicion, without accusation, without jury, without public trial, without confrontation of the witnesses against him, without hearing witnesses in his favor, without defence, without counsel, is contrary to these provisions also of the constitution, is therefore not law, but utterly void & of no force. that transferring the power of judging any person, who is under the protection of the laws, from the courts to the President of the US. as is undertaken by the same act concerning Aliens, is against the article of the constitution which provides that 'the judicial power of the US. shall be vested in courts the judges of which shall hold their offices during good behavior' and that the said act is void for that reason also. and it is further to be noted that this transfer of judiciary power is to that magistrate of the general government who already possesses all the Executive, and a negative on all the Legislative powers.

7. Resolved that the construction applied by the General government (as is evidenced[3] by sundry of their proceedings) to those parts of the constitution of the US. which delegate to Congress a power 'to lay & collect taxes, duties, imposts & excises, to pay the debts & provide for the common defence & general welfare of the US.' and 'to make all laws which shall be necessary & proper for carrying into execution the powers vested by the constitution in the government of the US. or in any department or officer thereof' goes to the destruction of all the limits prescribed to their power by the constitution; that words meant by that instrument to be subsidiary only to the execution of limited powers, ought not to be so construed as themselves to give unlimited powers, nor a part to be so taken as to destroy the whole residue of that instrument: that the proceedings of the General government under colour of these articles, will be a fit & necessary subject of revisal and correction, at a time of greater tranquility, while those specified in the preceding resolutions, call for immediate redress.

8. Resolved that a committee of conference & correspondence be appointed, who shall have in charge to communicate the preceding resolutions to the legislatures of the several states, to assure them that this commonwealth continues in the same esteem for their friendship and union which it has manifested from that moment at which a common

[546]

danger first suggested a common union: that it considers union, for specified national purposes, & particularly for those specified in their late federal compact, to be friendly to the peace, happiness & prosperity of all the states; that faithful to that compact, according to the plain intent & meaning in which it was understood & acceded to by the several parties, it is sincerely anxious for it's preservation: that it does also believe that to take from the states all the powers of self government, & transfer them to a general & consolidated government, without regard to the special delegations & reservations solemnly agreed to in that compact, is not for the peace, happiness or prosperity of these states: & that therefore this commonwealth is determined, as it doubts not it's co-states are, to submit to undelegated, & consequently unlimited powers in no man, or body of men, on earth:[4] that in cases of an abuse of the delegated powers the members of the general government, being chosen by the people, a change by the people would be the constitutional remedy; but, where powers are assumed which have not been delegated, a nullification of the act is the rightful remedy: that every state has a natural right, in cases not within the compact [casus non foederis][5] to nullify of their own authority all assumptions of power by others within their limits: that without this right, they would be under the dominion, absolute and unlimited, of whosoever might exercise this right of judgment for them: that nevertheless this commonwealth, from motives of regard & respect for it's co-states, has wished to communicate with them on the subject; that with them alone it is proper to communicate, they alone being parties to the compact, & solely authorized to judge in the last resort of the powers exercised under it, Congress being not a party, but merely the creature of the compact, & subject, as to it's assumptions of power, to the final judgment of those by whom, & for whose use, itself, & it's powers, were all created & modified:[6] that if the acts before specified should stand, these conclusions would flow from them; that the General government may place any act they think proper on the list of crimes, & punish it themselves, whether enumerated or not enumerated by the constitution as cognisable by them; that they may transfer it's cognisance to the President, or any other person, who may himself be the accuser, counsel, judge & jury, whose *suspicions* may be the evidence, his *order* the sentence, his officer the executioner, & his breast the sole record of the transaction: that a very numerous & valuable description of the inhabitants of these states being, by this precedent, reduced, as Outlaws, to the absolute dominion of one man, & the barrier of the constitution thus swept away for us all, no rampart now remains against the passions & the power of a majority in Congress, to protect from a like exportation, or other more grievous punishment, the minority of the same body, the legislatures, judges, governors & counsellors of the states, nor their other peaceable inhabitants, who may venture to reclaim the constitutional rights & liberties of the states & people, or who for other causes, good or bad, may be obnoxious to the views, or marked by the suspicions of the President, or be thought dangerous to his or their elections, or other interests public or personal: that the friendless alien has indeed been selected as the safest subject of a first experiment; but the citizen will soon follow, or rather has already followed; for already has a Sedition act marked him as it's prey: that these & successive acts of the same character, unless arrested at the threshold, necessarily drive these states into revolution & blood, & will furnish new calumnies against republican government, & new pretexts for those who wish it to be believed that man cannot be governed but by a rod of iron: that it would be a dangerous delusion, were a confidence in the men of our choice to silence our fears for the safety of our rights; that confidence is every where the parent of despotism; free government is founded in jealousy, and not in confidence; it is jealousy & not confidence which prescribes limited constitutions, to bind down those whom we are obliged to trust with power: that our constitution has accordingly fixed the limits to which, & no further, our confidence may go: and let the honest advocate of confidence read the Alien and Sedition acts, and say if the constitution has not been wise in fixing limits to the government it created, & whether we should be wise in destroying those limits? let him say What the government is, if it be not a tyranny, which the men of our choice have conferred on our President, and the President of our choice has assented to, & accepted over the friendly strangers, to whom the mild spirit of our country, & it's laws had pledged hospitality & protection: that the men of our choice have more respected the bare *suspicions* of the President, than the solid rights of innocence, the claims of justification, the sacred force of truth, & the forms and substance of law & justice: in questions of power then, let no more be heard of confidence in man, but bind him down from mischief by the chains of the constitution: that this commonwealth does therefore call on it's co-states for an expression of their sentiments on the acts concerning aliens, and for the punishment of certain crimes, herein before specified, plainly declaring whether these acts are, or are not authorised by the federal compact? and it doubts not that their sense will be so enounced⁷ as to prove their attachment unaltered to limited government, whether general or particular; and that the rights and liberties of their co-states will be exposed to no dangers by remaining embarked in a common bottom with their own: that they will concur with this commonwealth in considering the said acts as so palpably against

[548]

the constitution as to amount to an undisguised declaration that that compact is not meant to be the measure of the powers of the General government, but that it will proceed in the exercise, over these states, of all powers whatsoever; that they will view this as seizing the rights of the states, and consolidating them in the hands of the General government with a power assumed to bind the states (not merely in the cases made federal [casus foederis][8] but) in all cases whatsoever, by laws made, not with their consent, but by others against their consent; that this would be to surrender the form of government we have chosen, & to live under one deriving it's powers from it's own will & not from our authority, and that the co-states, recurring to their natural right in cases not made federal, will concur in declaring these acts void and of no force, & will each take measures of it's own for providing that neither these acts, nor any others of the general government, not plainly & intentionally authorised by the constitution, shall be exercised within their respective territories.

9. Resolved that the said committee be authorised to communicate, by writing or personal conferences, at any times or places whatever, with any person or persons who may be appointed by any one or more of the co-states to correspond or confer with them; & that they lay their proceedings before the next session of assembly.

MS (DLC: TJ Papers, 104:17906-11); undated, but written before 4 Oct. (see Wilson Cary Nicholas to TJ of that date); a fair copy entirely in TJ's hand; one word in TJ's block printing shown in small capitals; square brackets in body of text are TJ's. PrC (DLC: Madison Papers, Rives Collection); faint, smudged, and with some text at edges of pages missed in pressing; with later notations not by TJ; enclosed in TJ to Madison, 17 Nov. 1798. MS (DLC: Breckinridge Family Papers, 18:3011-16); entirely in Breckinridge's hand; merges ninth resolution, unnumbered, into conclusion of eighth; the most substantive other variations are recorded in notes below; some minor variations, not recorded, also appear in the version adopted by the Kentucky legislature (Document III); endorsed by Breckinridge in ink: "resolutions"; endorsement page also contains a faint pencil list, not by Breckinridge, of people and their places of residence in Tennessee, which predates Breckinridge's endorsement and appears to be unrelated to the resolutions.

[1] Breckinridge in his copy here canceled "effect."
[2] Before the comma TJ canceled "respectively," probably a copying error.
[3] Breckinridge MS: "evinced."
[4] In Breckinridge MS the passage that follows, from "that in cases of" through "all created & modified," is enclosed in square brackets.
[5] TJ's brackets; enclosed phrase lacking in Breckinridge MS.
[6] In Breckinridge MS the bracketed passage ends here.
[7] Breckinridge MS: "anounced."
[8] TJ's brackets; enclosed phrase lacking in Breckinridge MS.

III. Resolutions Adopted by the Kentucky General Assembly

In the House of Representatives,
November 10th, 1798.

I. Resolved, that the several states composing the United States of America, are not united on the principle of unlimited submission to their General Government; but that by compact under the style and title of a Constitution for the United States and of amendments thereto, they constituted a General Government for special purposes, delegated to that Government certain definite powers, reserving each state to itself, the residuary mass of right to their own self Government; and that whensoever the General Government assumes undelegated powers, its acts are unauthoritative, void, and of no force: That to this compact each state acceded as a state, and is an integral party, its co-states forming as to itself, the other party: That the Government created by this compact was not made the exclusive or final *judge* of the extent of the powers delegated to itself; since that would have made its discretion, and not the constitution, the measure of its powers; but that as in all other cases of compact among parties having no common Judge, each party has an equal right to judge for itself, as well of infractions as of the mode and measure of redress.

II. Resolved, that the Constitution of the United States having delegated to Congress a power to punish treason, counterfeiting the securities and current coin of the United States, piracies and felonies committed on the High Seas, and offences against the laws of nations, and no other crimes whatever, and it being true as a general principle, and one of the amendments to the Constitution having also declared, "that the powers not delegated to the United States by the Constitution, nor prohibited by it to the states, are reserved to the states respectively, or to the people," therefore also the same act of Congress passed on the 14th day of July, 1798, and entitled "An act in addition to the act entitled an act for the punishment of certain crimes against the United States;" as also the act passed by them on the 27th day of June, 1798, entitled "An act to punish frauds committed on the Bank of the United States" (and all other their acts which assume to create, define, or punish crimes other than those enumerated in the constitution) are altogether void and of no force, and that the power to create, define, and punish such other crimes is reserved, and of right appertains solely and exclusively to the respective states, each within its own Territory.

III. Resolved, that it is true as a general principle, and is also expressly declared by one of the amendments to the Constitution that "the

[550]

powers not delegated to the United States by the Constitution, nor prohibited by it to the states, are reserved to the states respectively or to the people;" and that no power over the freedom of religion, freedom of speech, or freedom of the press being delegated to the United States by the Constitution, nor prohibited by it to the states, all lawful powers respecting the same did of right remain, and were reserved to the states, or to the people: That thus was manifested their determination to retain to themselves the right of judging how far the licentiousness of speech and of the press may be abridged without lessening their useful freedom, and how far those abuses which cannot be separated from their use, should be tolerated rather than the use be destroyed; and thus also they guarded against all abridgement by the United States of the freedom of religious opinions[1] and exercises, and retained to themselves the right of protecting the same, as this state by a Law passed on the general demand of its Citizens, had already protected them from all human restraint or interference: And that in addition to this general principle and express declaration, another and more special provision has been made by one of the amendments to the Constitution which expressly declares, that "Congress shall make no law respecting an Establishment of religion, or prohibiting the free exercise thereof, or abridging the freedom of speech, or of the press," thereby guarding in the same sentence, and under the same words, the freedom of religion, of speech, and of the press, insomuch, that whatever violates either, throws down the sanctuary which covers the others, and that libels, falsehoods, and defamation, equally with heresy and false religion, are withheld from the cognizance of federal tribunals. That therefore the act of the Congress of the United States passed on the 14th day of July 1798, entitled "An act in addition to the act for the punishment of certain crimes against the United States," which does abridge the freedom of the press, is not law, but is altogether void and of no effect.[2]

IV. Resolved, that alien friends are under the jurisdiction and protection of the laws of the state wherein they are; that no power over them has been delegated to the United States, nor prohibited to the individual states distinct from their power over citizens; and it being true as a general principle, and one of the amendments to the Constitution having also declared, that "the powers not delegated to the United States by the Constitution nor prohibited by it to the states are reserved to the states respectively or to the people," the act of the Congress of the United States passed on the 22d day of June, 1798, entitled "An act concerning aliens," which assumes power over alien friends not delegated by the Constitution, is not law, but is altogether void and of no force.

V. Resolved, that in addition to the general principle as well as the express declaration, that powers not delegated are reserved, another and more special provision inserted in the Constitution from abundant caution has declared, "that the *migration* or importation of such persons as any of the states now existing shall think proper to admit, shall not be prohibited by the Congress prior to the year 1808." That this Commonwealth does admit the migration of alien friends described as the subject of the said act concerning aliens; that a provision against prohibiting their migration, is a provision against all acts equivalent thereto, or it would be nugatory; that to remove them when migrated is equivalent to a prohibition of their migration, and is therefore contrary to the said provision of the Constitution, and void.

VI. Resolved, that the imprisonment of a person under the protection of the Laws of this Commonwealth on his failure to obey the simple *order* of the President to depart out of the United States, as is undertaken by the said act entitled "An act concerning Aliens," is contrary to the Constitution, one amendment to which has provided, that "no person shall be deprived of liberty without due process of law," and that another having provided "that in all criminal prosecutions, the accused shall enjoy the right to a public trial by an impartial jury, to be informed of the nature and cause of the accusation, to be confronted with the witnesses against him, to have compulsory process for obtaining witnesses in his favour, and to have the assistance of counsel for his defence," the same act undertaking to authorize the President to remove a person out of the United States who is under the protection of the Law, on his own suspicion, without accusation, without jury, without public trial, without confrontation of the witnesses against him, without having witnesses in his favour, without defence, without counsel, is contrary to these provisions also of the Constitution, is therefore not law but utterly void and of no force.

That transferring the power of judging any person who is under the protection of the laws, from the Courts to the President of the United States, as is undertaken by the same act concerning Aliens, is against the article of the Constitution which provides, that "the judicial power of the United States shall be vested in Courts, the Judges of which shall hold their offices during good behaviour," and that the said act is void for that reason also; and it is further to be noted, that this transfer of Judiciary power is to that magistrate of the General Government who already possesses all the Executive, and a qualified negative in all the Legislative powers.

VII. Resolved, that the construction applied by the General Government (as is evinced[3] by sundry of their proceedings) to those parts of the

Constitution of the United States which delegate to Congress a power to lay and collect taxes, duties, imposts, and excises; to pay the debts, and provide for the common defence, and general welfare of the United States, and to make all laws which shall be necessary and proper for carrying into execution the powers vested by the Constitution in the Government of the United States, or any department thereof, goes to the destruction of all the limits prescribed to their power by the Constitution—That words meant by that instrument to be subsiduary only to the execution of the limited powers, ought not to be so construed as themselves to give unlimited powers, nor a part so to be taken, as to destroy the whole residue of the instrument: That the proceedings of the General Government under colour of these articles, will be a fit and necessary subject for revisal and correction at a time of greater tranquility, while those specified in the preceding resolutions call for immediate redress.

VIII. Resolved, that the preceding Resolutions be transmitted to the Senators and Representatives in Congress from this Commonwealth, who are hereby enjoined to present the same to their respective Houses, and to use their best endeavours to procure at the next session of Congress, a repeal of the aforesaid unconstitutional and obnoxious acts.

IX. Resolved lastly, that the Governor of this Commonwealth be, and is hereby authorised and requested to communicate the preceding Resolutions to the Legislatures of the several States, to assure them that this Commonwealth considers Union for specified National purposes, and particularly for those specified in their late Federal Compact, to be friendly to the peace, happiness, and prosperity of all the states: that faithful to that compact, according to the plain intent and meaning in which it was understood and acceded to by the several parties, it is sincerely anxious for its preservation: that it does also believe, that to take from the states all the powers of self government, and transfer them to a general and consolidated Government, without regard to the special delegations and reservations solemnly agreed to in that compact, is not for the peace, happiness, or prosperity of these states: And that therefore, this Commonwealth is determined, as it doubts not its Co-states are, tamely[4] to submit to undelegated & consequently unlimited powers in no man or body of men on earth: that if the acts before specified should stand, these conclusions would flow from them; that the General Government may place any act they think proper on the list of crimes & punish it themselves, whether enumerated or not enumerated by the Constitution as cognizable by them: that they may transfer its cognizance to the President or any other person, who may himself be the accuser, counsel, judge, and jury, whose *suspicions* may be the evidence, his order the sentence, his officer the executioner, and his breast the sole record of the transaction: that a very numerous and valuable description of the inhabitants of these states, being by this precedent reduced as outlaws to the absolute dominion of one man and the barrier of the Constitution thus swept away from us all, no rampart now remains against the passions and the power of a majority of Congress, to protect from a like exportation or other more[5] grievous punishment the minority of the same body, the Legislatures, Judges, Governors, & Counsellors of the states, nor their other peaceable inhabitants who may venture to reclaim the constitutional rights & liberties of the states & people, or who for other causes, good or bad, may be obnoxious to the views or marked by the suspicions of the President, or be thought dangerous to his or their elections or other interests public or personal: that the friendless alien has indeed been selected as the safest subject of a first experiment: but the citizen will soon follow, or rather has already followed; for, already has a Sedition Act marked him as its prey: that these and successive acts of the same character, unless arrested at the threshold, may tend to[6] drive these states into revolution and blood, and will furnish new calumnies against Republican Governments, and new pretexts for those who wish it to be believed, that man cannot be governed but by a rod of iron: that it would be a dangerous delusion were a confidence in the men of our choice to silence our fears for the safety of our rights: that confidence is every where the parent of despotism: free government is founded in jealousy and not in confidence; it is jealousy and not confidence which prescribes limited Constitutions to bind down those whom we are obliged to trust with power: that our Constitution has accordingly fixed the limits to which and no further our confidence may go; and let the honest advocate of confidence read the Alien and Sedition Acts, and say if the Constitution has not been wise in fixing limits to the Government it created, and whether we should be wise in destroying those limits? Let him say what the Government is if it be not a tyranny, which the men of our choice have conferred on the President, and the President of our choice has assented to and accepted over the friendly strangers, to whom the mild spirit of our Country and its laws had pledged hospitality and protection: that the men of our choice have more respected the bare suspicions of the President than the solid rights of innocence, the claims of justification, the sacred force of truth, and the forms & substance of law and justice. In questions of power then let no more be heard of confidence in man, but bind him down from mischief by the chains of the Constitution. That this Commonwealth does therefore call on its Co-states for an expression of their sentiments on the acts concerning Aliens, and for the punishment of certain crimes herein before specified, plainly declaring whether these acts are or are not authorised by the Federal Compact? And it doubts not that their sense will be so announced as to prove their attachment unaltered to limited Government, whether general or particular, and that the rights and liberties of their Co-states will be exposed to no dangers by remaining embarked on a common bottom with their own: That they will concur with this Commonwealth in considering the said acts as so palpably against the Constitution as to amount to an undisguised declaration, that the Compact is not meant to be the measure of the powers of the General Government, but that it will proceed in the exercise over these states of all powers whatsoever: That they will view this as seizing the rights of the states and consolidating them in the hands of the General Government with a power assumed to bind the states (not merely in cases made federal) but in all cases whatsoever, by laws made, not with their consent, but by others against their consent: That this would be to surrender the form of Government we have chosen, and to live under one deriving its powers from its own will, and not from our authority; and that the Co-states recurring to their natural right in cases not made federal, will concur in declaring these acts void and of no force, and will each unite with this Commonwealth in requesting their repeal at the next session of Congress.

Text from a broadside printed by Hunter and Beaumont, Frankfort, Kentucky (Evans, Nos. 33952, 33953, apparently both printed from the same lines of type, the columns differently arranged for the two printings); across top of page: "Legislature of Kentucky" (Evans, No. 33952), "Kentucky Legislature" (Evans, No. 33953); between dateline and text: "The House according to the standing Order of the Day, resolved itself into a Committee of the Whole on the state of the Commonwealth, Mr. CALDWELL in the Chair, And after sometime spent therein the Speaker resumed the Chair, and Mr. Caldwell reported, that the Committee had according to order had under consideration the Governor's Address, and had come to the following Resolutions thereupon, which he delivered in at the Clerk's table, where they were twice read and agreed to by the House"; at foot of text: names of Edward Bullock, speaker of the Kentucky House of Representatives, and John Campbell, speaker pro tem of the Senate; attestation by clerks that the resolutions were passed by the House on 10 Nov. and the Senate unanimously concurred on 13 Nov.; approval by Governor James Garrard, 16 Nov., certified by Harry Toulmin, secretary of state; near the end of the final resolution the phrase "deriving its powers from its own will" appears in the originals as "deriving it powers. . . ." Broadside (Evans, No. 48494); also by Hunter and Beaumont; at head of text: "Wednesday, Nov. 7, 1798. Mr. BRECK-ENRIDGE gave notice that he would on To-morrow move the House to go into a Committee of the whole on the state of the Commonwealth, on that part of the Governor's address which relates to certain unconstitutional laws passed at the last session of Congress, and that he would then move certain resolutions on that subject. Thursday, Nov. 8. The House according to the order of the day resolved itself into a Committee of the whole on the state of the Commonwealth, and Mr. Breckenridge according to his notice yesterday moved the following **RESOLUTIONS**, which were seconded by Mr. Johnson"; substantive differences between this version and that passed by the assembly are noted below.

¹ Evans, No. 48494: "principles."
² Evans, No. 48494: "force."

³ Evans, No. 48494: "evident."
⁴ Word lacking in Evans, No. 48494, and in the resolutions as printed in *Kentucky Gazette*, 14 Nov. 1798.
⁵ Word lacking in Evans, No. 48494.
⁶ In place of the preceding three words Evans, No. 48494, has "necessarily."

From Wilson Cary Nicholas

DEAR SIR   Warren Octr. 4th. 1798

I have taken the liberty to put into the hands of Mr. John Breckinridge a copy of the resolutions that you sent me, he says he is confident that the legislature of Kentucky (of which he is a member)¹ will adopt them. he was very anxious to pay his respects to you but we both thought it was best that he shou'd not see you, as we believed if he did the resolutions wou'd be attributed to you. I ventured to inform him that they came from you, I did this both because, I knew him to be worthy of confidence, and suppos'd he cou'd not mistake the source from whence they came. I thought it best to be frank with him, and to prevent his mentioning his conjectures even, he has given me the most Solemn assurances upon the subject. I flatter myself you will not disapprove of my conduct I shall not be perfectly reconciled to it myself, until I receive your approbation, be assur'd Sir, my chief inducement was to shield you from the invective, that I feared you might be exposed to if I had pursued a different course. I thought the opportunity a happy one, to have the subject taken up in the way that you seemed to think most advis'able. B, says we may expect their proceedings by the commencement of our session.

I am Dear Sir with the greatest respect your hum. Servt.

WILSON CARY NICHOLAS

If any thing new shou'd have occured to you I can communicate it to Breckinridge, he does not leave Buckingham until the 10th. instant.

RC (DLC); endorsed by TJ as received 5 Oct. 1798 and so recorded in SJL.

RESOLUTIONS THAT YOU SENT ME: see the Kentucky Resolutions of 1798, the group of documents preceding this letter. SJL does not indicate when TJ conveyed the resolutions to Nicholas.

¹ Words in parentheses interlined.

To Wilson Cary Nicholas

Dr. Sir   Monticello Oct. 5. 98.

I entirely approve of the confidence you have reposed in mr Brackenridge, as he possesses mine entirely. I had imagined it better those resolutions should have originated with N. Carolina. but perhaps the late changes in their representation may indicate some doubt whether they would have passed. in that case it is better they should come from Kentuckey. I understand you intend soon to go as far as mr Madison's. you know of course I have no secrets for him. I wish him therefore to be consulted as to these resolutions. the post boy waiting at the door obliges me to finish here with assurances of the esteem of Dr. Sir

    Your friend & servt   Th: Jefferson

FC (DLC); above dateline in TJ's hand: "Copy of a letter to Wilson C. Nicholas. time not permitting a press copy, this was immediately written from recollection and is nearly verbal"; at foot of text: "Wilson Cary Nicholas," immediately below which TJ wrote: "see his letter of Oct. 4. 98. to which this is an answer."

LATE CHANGES IN THEIR REPRESENTATION: in the North Carolina election of 1798 only four of the incumbents in the House of Representatives were reelected, one of those being William B. Grove, the sole state congressman who usually voted with the Federalists in the Fifth Congress. Republicans who lost their seats included Thomas Blount, Joseph McDowell, Dempsey Burges, James Gillespie, and Matthew Locke. The election of William R. Davie as governor and the passage of an address in support of the Adams Administration by the assembly also indicated the increasing influence of the Federalists in the state. When Davie laid the Kentucky Resolutions before the House of Commons on 21

Dec., the representatives immediately sent them to the Senate where they were tabled and never considered. However, although a local newspaper predicted that seven members of the newly elected North Carolina delegation would vote with the Federalists, in fact only four frequently did so during the Sixth Congress. The North Carolina House of Commons voted overwhelmingly against the Alien and Sedition Acts, calling them a "violation of the principles of the Constitution." The resolution directed the state's senators and congressmen to seek repeal of the acts without delay. The North Carolina senate, however, defeated the resolution by a 31 to 9 vote (*Journal of the House of Commons. State of North-Carolina* [Wilmington, N.C., 1798], 25, 68, 70, 76-8; see Evans, No. 34244; Dauer, *Adams Federalists*, 307-8, 313, 324; Delbert H. Gilpatrick, *Jeffersonian Democracy in North Carolina, 1789-1816* [New York, 1931], 100-2). For the Federalist surge in North Carolina following the XYZ affair, see Rose, *Prologue to Democracy*, 169-70, 172-9, 212.

From William Short

Jefferson. Oct. 9.—letters written & recd.—prudential motives prevent friend & myself giving publicity to our intentions—have seen a pamphlet from wch. it appears that party spirit has entered into the banks at Phi. as to discounts—inclose the copy legalised of Paskies papers—if good beg him to send them to my brother—inclose extracts of Colo. S. letters—& go into long details on that subject—shall employ my brother[1] to settle with him & will write to him on the subject Colo. Skip's conduct neither generous nor friendly—shd. be glad if he wd. settle the matter of himself—but from his past conduct towards me cannot hope it—besides Harvies bond, has never accted. for the int. warrty. of Jan 1. 88—&c &c.—the £150 of B. Harrison—if not paid by Harrison beg him to receive it with the interest—if paid to Colo. S. to enter into the general settlement—inclose the extracts of Brown's letters—the bonds there mentioned never accted. for by him nor Colo. S.—sorry to be so long without hearing from him—our correspondence being private can give umbrage to nobody—hope that the usual intercourse will be restored—this Go. desires it & hope our's will keep us out of the broils of Europe—&c.—

FC (DLC: Short Papers); entirely in Short's hand, the final entry in a group of epistolary summaries beginning 26 Dec. 1797; at foot of text: "(End)"; recorded in SJL as received from Paris 27 Jan. 1799. Enclosures not found, but see below.

FRIEND: the Duchesse de La Rochefoucauld.

PASKIES PAPERS: on 16 Oct. 1799 TJ wrote to Short's BROTHER, Peyton Short, enclosing the documentation sent by William Short concerning his title to a tract of military land purchased from Captain Paskie. This may have been Frederick Paschke, a captain in Count Pulaski's legion, 1777-80, and a member of the quartermaster department of the Southern Army, 1780-83 (JCC, 26:36; Paschke memorial to Congress, 30 Oct. 1784, DNA: RG 360, PCC; Leszek Szyma'nski, *Kazimierz Pulaski in America: A Monograph, 1777-1779* [San Bernardino, Calif., 1988], 192-3). COLO. S.: Henry Skipwith. In October 1799 TJ solicited a statement of James BROWN's accounts with Short (TJ to Brown, 16 Oct., Brown to TJ, 27 Oct. 1799).

[1] Word canceled in MS.

To James Thomson Callender

DEAR SIR   Monticello Oct. 11. 98.

Your favor of Sep. 22. came to hand only by our last post. I had before been informed through the channel of the newspapers of the insult committed on you. outrages against the laws may take place in every country, because in every country there are people of every character. but I hope it will appear in the issue that such a breach of the laws & hospitality of the state cannot be committed with impunity and that a proper proceeding has been instituted for that purpose. I wish I could at once have gratified your desire of getting into some temporary employment. in this part of the country there is little resource in either of the two lines you mention, of the compting house or instruction. the inhabitants of this quarter are entirely agricultural, employed mostly in raising tobacco, and not enough at their ease to go beyond the first rudiments of education for their children. in the two little villages near me, Charlottesville & Milton, do not contain more than half a dozen families each. there are a store or two, a taylor, shoemaker &c. I should suppose Alexandria, Richmond or Norfolk the most likely to offer you a resource in business. but with these Genl. Mason is much better acquainted than I am, as I have not been a day in either of them these twenty years to make any stronger acquaintance at all. should any thing be procurable within my reach, I shall certainly apprise you of it with pleasure. in the meantime as you may have wants till you can settle yourself, I have desired Genl. Mason to draw on my correspondent at Richmond for 50. Dollars, which may be some aid for the moment. uninformed of the cause which occasioned you [to leave] Philadelphia I can only express my regret that any thing should have happened to withdraw you from the place where above all others you have it in your power to render services to the public liberty, and to add my hopes that the causes are not permanent, as the meeting you there in the ensuing winter would give real satisfaction to Dr. Sir

Your most obedt. servt   TH: JEFFERSON

PrC (DLC); faint; at foot of first page: "Mr. Callender." Enclosed in TJ to Stevens Thomson Mason, 11 Oct. 1798.

MY CORRESPONDENT AT RICHMOND: George Jefferson (see letter below). This transaction was not recorded in TJ's financial accounts.

To Stevens Thomson Mason

DEAR SIR   Monticello Oct. 11. 98.

I recieved lately a letter from mr Callender to which the inclosed is an answer. after perusing it, be so good as to stick a wafer in it and (after it is dry) deliver it. you will percieve that I propose to you the trouble of drawing for 50. D. for mr Callender on my correspondent in Richmond, George Jefferson, merchant. this is to keep his name out of sight. make your draught if you please in some such form as this 'Pay to —— or order [or 'Send me in bank bills by post][1] 50. Dollars on account of Thomas Jefferson according to advice received from him &c.' I shall immediately direct him to pay such a draught from you, without mentioning to him the purpose.

I have to thank you for your favor of July 6. from Philadelphia. I did not immediately acknolege it, because I knew you would be come away. the X.Y.Z. fever has considerably abated through the country, as I am informed, and the Alien & Sedition laws are working hard. I fancy that some of the state legislatures will take strong ground on this occasion. for my own part I consider these laws as merely an experiment on the American mind to see how far it will bear an avowed violation of the constitution. if this goes down, we shall immediately see attempted another act of Congress declaring that the President shall continue in Office during life, reserving to another occasion the transfer of the succession to his heirs, and the establishment of the Senate for life. at least this may be the aim of the Oliverians, while Monk & the Cavaliers (who are perhaps the strongest) may be playing their game for the restoration of his most gracious majesty George the third. that these things are in contemplation I have no doubt, nor can I be confident of their failure, after the dupery of which our countrymen have shewn themselves susceptible.

You promised to endeavor to send me some tenants. I am waiting for them, having broken up two excellent farms with 12. fields in them of 40. acres each, some of which I have sowed with small grain. tenants of any size may be accomodated with the number of fields suited to their force. only send good people and write me what they are. Adieu.

Your's affectionately   TH: JEFFERSON

PrC (DLC); at foot of text: "Mr. Mason." Enclosure: TJ to James Thomson Callender, 11 Oct. 1798.

LETTER FROM MR CALLENDER: Callender to TJ, 22 Sep. 1798.
TJ here seems to depict John Adams and his supporters as OLIVERIANS in the aftermath of the English Civil War—Adams to assume Oliver Cromwell's role as lord protector. Alexander Hamilton and his allies would be MONK & THE CAVALIERS: initially a Royalist, then a commander under Cromwell, George Monck (Monk), Duke of Albemarle, was instrumental in the restoration of the monarchy in 1660 (DNB).

[1] TJ's brackets.

From George Jefferson

DEAR SIR,   Richmond 15th. Octr. 1798.
Mr. Hooper has at length after disappointing me several times, taken up his note for your Tobacco which became due the 1st. instant—after deducting your draft in favor of Mr. Wickham for $:1000—which he informs me was paid at maturity.

I hope he will be more punctual in the next payment, as his failure in this instance I am certain was owing to the fever in Philada. & N. York—which prevented his friends from disposing of bills which he had drawn on his Tobacco, and on which he depended to fulfil his contracts here; the same cause I know has occasioned several of the most respectable Merchants in this place to fail in complying with their engagements.

I have heard nothing further from Mr. Pendleton & Mr. Lyons respecting Mr. Shorts money; when I do you shall be of course advised.

I am Dear Sir Your Very Obt. Hbl: servt.   GEO. JEFFERSON

16th.

Since writing the preceding I have seen Mr. Wickham who informs me that Mr. Hooper has taken up your dft: as he informed me he had done   G.J.

RC (MHi); at foot of first page: "Thos. Jefferson esqr."; postscript on verso; endorsed by TJ as received 19 Oct. 1798 and so recorded in SJL.

To George Jefferson

DEAR SIR   Monticello Oct. 18. 98.

I have occasion to pay to Genl. Stephen Thompson Mason a sum not exceeding 50. dollars, which lying across the country cannot be done from hence for want of mercantile connections. presuming you have recieved mr Hooper's first paiment which furnished a surplus after mr Wyckham's order would be satisfied, I have taken the liberty of desiring Genl. Mason to draw on you in his own name for the sum before mentioned, stating it to be on my account, which I pray you therefore to honour, should it be done, for I am not sure it will be called for at all. I am Dear Sir

Your affectionate friend & servt   TH: JEFFERSON

PrC (MHi); at foot of text: "Mr. George Jefferson"; endorsed by TJ in ink on verso.

To Benjamin H. Latrobe

DEAR SIR   Monticello Oct. 18. 98.

I have to acknolege the reciept of your favor of Sep. 22. the canal which is the subject of it is a very small affair, the whole fall about 30. feet, of which two thirds are past by my mill canal 1200 yds long, and one third by Henderson's canal 200 yds long. all between us is dead water. doubling the breadth of our canals would make them wide enough for batteaux, and this we know from the actual work in making our canals would not cost £1000. then is to be added the expence of locks in a country where building stone (rough) is every where at hand, and lime within 3. or 4. miles. as the whole of this work would pass through my lands, except a few hundred yards, it connects itself in different ways with some petty interests of mine, not enough to be felt by myself, yet quite enough to enable those, so disposed, to ascribe any thing I should do to interested views, and perhaps to injure the undertaking were I to meddle. I sincerely wish it done on the broad principle of general good, which must also effect particular good. but I have avoided taking any active part in it, wishing that others should do it whose situations clear them of particular imputations. I have made your letter the occasion of spurring them up, but I am very doubtful whether it will be with effect. if any thing should be done, as I know the benefit they would derive from your aid, I shall not fail to acquaint them with [your] kind offers. I am glad the works at Norfolk were put into so good hands for projection. that the execution should have been given to others may be consistent with the new code of morality the principles of which are daily developed to us in the practices of the exclusive friends of order & religion. mr Taleyrand seems determined to disappoint their wishes.—success to all yours, health and friendly salutations.

TH: JEFFERSON

PrC (DLC); faint; at foot of text: "Mr. La Trobe"; endorsed by TJ in ink on verso.

Not until 1806 would the Rivanna Navigation Company be incorporated to make the river suitable for boats between Milton and Charlottesville, a project that required construction of LOCKS in TJ's mill canal to allow passage around his milldam (Latrobe, *Virginia Journals*, 2:431n; Betts, *Farm Book*, 343-4).

To Samuel Clarke

DEAR SIR   Monticello Oct. 22. 98.

Having occasion to make a considerable paiment immediately I send the bearer Jupiter, a trusty servant, to recieve whatever money may be lying for me in Staunton. any sum which you can furnish will be acceptable, and will be safely brought by him. be so good as to let it be in cash, & not in paper which nobody here recieves. I am with esteem Dear Sir

Your most obedt. servt   TH: JEFFERSON

PrC (MHi); at foot of text: "Mr. Samuel Clarke"; endorsed by TJ in ink on verso.

Clarke's brother William replied on his behalf on the 23d: "I have just Recd. your Yesterday's favour to my brother, He is gone to Greenbriar & I expect him back in a few days his business was with a view of making some Collections Upon his Return I am in hopes he will be enabled to furnish you with some Cash With my Respects to your family I am Dr sir Yr. Most Obedt. Servt." (MS in same; at foot of text: "Col. Thos. Jefferson"; endorsed by TJ as received 24 Oct. 1798 and so recorded in SJL).

To John McDowell

DEAR SIR   Monticello Oct. 22. 98.

Your favor of Sep. 27. was duly recieved, and having [now] to make a paiment, I send the bearer, Jupiter, a trusty servant express, to recieve and bring any sum you may have in readiness for me. be so good as to let it be in hard cash, as no [. . .] is recieved here. I will hereafter ask of you only quarterly settlements & paiments if you please, fixing them in the months of March, June, Septemb. & December, because these falling in with our docket & district courts give a chance of conveying the money without my sending express for it. the manager of my nailery has been sick upwards of a month, & is but just getting about. this has occasioned less work to be done, and not well enough done to trust it to a distant market, where the cause not being known to be temporary might give a permanent discredit to our work. as soon as he can attend to business you shall be furnished with the kinds of nails you desire. I am Sir

Your most obedt. servt   TH: JEFFERSON

PrC (DLC); faint; at foot of text: "Mr. John Mc.Dowell"; endorsed by TJ in ink on verso.

MANAGER OF MY NAILERY: on 25 Nov. TJ paid Sam, a black doctor, $10 for his care of the slave known as smith George or Little George (MB, 2:992).

From John McDowell

SIR   Staunton Oct: 23. 1798

I have Sent you all the Cash that is in my hands at present by Jupiter which is Ninety two Dollars & $\frac{2}{3}$ you mentiond you will be Satisfyed to receve payments quarterly any time that will answer you I shall be Satisfyed as I only retail your Nails for Cash And I can remit the money at any time however When It best Suits you you will please to send me one Cask of 12 d and one 20 d—as I have None of either of them And they are much wanted I expect I Shall be able to dispose a Large quantity If the Assortment is kept up—from your hmbe

Svt   JOHN MCDOWELL

92$\frac{2}{3}$ Dollars   £27:16—

RC (MHi); endorsed by TJ as received 24 Oct. 1798 and so recorded in SJL.

From Benjamin Smith Barton

DEAR SIR,— Germantown, October 26th, 98.

I have lately published a new edition of my *New Views*. I shall endeavour, by the first private conveyance, to forward to you a copy of it. It is very greatly enlarged. I am extremely anxious to pursue this subject much farther. I shall, therefore, be much obliged to you for the sight of your *Vocabularies*, when you shall come—to town. All mine are at your service. Will it not be possible to procure some words in the dialects of the Pamunkies, Màttaponies, and Nottoways, mentioned in your *Notes*? I find, by comparing the language of the Powhatans, that it is very nearly allied to the Delaware language.

I have, for some time, been employed upon an extensive work on the subject of *Instinct*.

I have the honour to be, with great respect, Dear Sir,

Your very humble & obliged friend, &c.

BENJAMIN SMITH BARTON.

Please to make my best respects to your two sons-in-law, Mr. Randolph & Mr. Eppes.—

RC (DLC); endorsed by TJ as received on 16 Nov. 1798 and recorded in SJL as received from Philadelphia on that day.

The NEW EDITION of Barton's *New Views of the Origin of the Tribes and Nations of America* (Philadelphia, 1798) expanded the first edition, which the author had dedicated to TJ the previous year (see Book

Dedication from Benjamin Smith Barton, 21 June 1797; Evans, No. 33378). For TJ's own assembling of VOCABULARIES of Native American languages, see his letter to William Linn on 5 Feb. 1798. In *Notes on the State of Virginia* TJ referred to the drastically reduced numbers of PAMUNKIES and other Virginia Indians (*Notes*, ed. Peden, 96-7).

From James Thomson Callender

SIR Rasberryplain 26 October, 1798.

I am Sensible that this freedom needs an [appology]. I wrote You a letter In last month and if nothing can be done, or ought to be done, in one quarter, *it is time* that I Should be making application, in another, if I can say that I can have another; for I have not only motives of one kind, but others quite different, for not wishing to revisit that sink of destruction Philadelphia; for whose inhabitants I at present Sympathize as much as, and not more than, I would do for those of Grand Cairo, in the same Situation. If any body can believe in *judgements*, I think that the two Newspapers printed in that porch of perdition were sufficient for bringing on a yellow fever, if all their other enormities were extinguished. I hope that this pestilence, so justly deserved by all the male adults, will prove a happy check to a much worse one, the black Cock-ade fever, I mean the fever that, under the pretence of defending us from a *foreign* war, aims at promoting a *civil* one.

In Europe it is understood, and I mean, if I ever get into the press again, to tell the people of this Country, for the sake of giving them information, In Europe it is understood, that if a political party does not support their assistant writer, they at least do not crush him, whereas I have been crushed by the very Gentry whom I was defending. I have actually vindicated the political character of a man, after I knew that he was in his private Capacity, doing his utmost to injure me, and of course a dying woman and 4 innocent children, and I did so, because though I knew him to be in private a Rascal, yet I knew him to be an useful public character, and in that light an injured man. This Shews that I was superior to personal Revenge.

I am sure that You will be shocked to hear the treatment I have met with even from Men, whom I really consider As good men. For in-stance, M Giles, in Congress, made a Splendid reference to the esteem in which Muir and Palmer were held in America; vid: debate on Demo-cratic Societies. I was their intimate friend, and quite as deep in the unlucky business as they were. This same Mr. Giles I had taken some Small pains in praising, and the defect of performance might have been palliated by the kindness of my intention. A man has no merit in telling truth, but he may claim the priviledge of not being the object of persecu-tion, from the hero of his encomium. This I was; for Mr. Giles, (the printed debates attest it) joined as a leader in the conspiracy with Doc-tor Phocion for getting me out of Congress. The man offered afterwards to speak to me on the Street! He was aided in this affair, by an old and intimate friend of yours, a real and worthy man, whom I respect and love at this moment, and who, 14 days before, had told me, with the tear half in his eye, that my minutes of Congress were of essential service to the Country, and who yet, without pretending provocation did this. The latter was not a member, but I Suppress his name, as he has since obliged me. Now I would be glad to hear how M Giles Made his enco-mium on Mr. Palmer Square with his attack on me, an attack so scouted, that he and his Six per Cent Ally durst not risk a division on it. If Such was my treatment from men who were good men, what was I to have from those who were constitutionally, and Systematically Rascals. I am Sure that, at least I hope that, if Giles had known the distress he was to bring upon my family, he would have bit his tongue rather than have Said what he did on that day.

Bache is buried, and I wish that I Could *bury* the consequences of his behaviour to me. I know that he had many useful and many pleasing qualities; but I was never the better for the one, or the other. He would not extract from my publications, a matter most essential. He would not let me advertise my last in his name, [none of the booksellers durst do so, excepting honest James Carey][1] although he was to be defended in it. But he knew very well how to get books, without the least concern as to paying for them. In July last, just after I came away, Mr. Fenno printed an attack on me, which, callous as I am, hurt me sensibly. I instantly sent up an answer which this worthy Republican refused to print, but which I must take some notice of, with an explanation, that Bache would not print it, as a reason why I did not answer it sooner. This was my thanks for the multitudinous columns I have wrote for him, and the blame which I have incurred as author of pieces in his paper I had nothing to do with, such as Dr. Jones's profound observations on Mr. Adams wanting his teeth, and being bald; while this Representative was himself attacking, or at least snubbing me, on account of my Stile, as if a man in rags were to upbraid another for wearing an unfashionable Coat. This Sir (I ask pardon for the length of the detail) is a part of my obligations to the democracts; and though I have not the egotistical effrontery of Dr. Priestley, I Shall contrive to give a general and genuine character of democrats, which will hit *my* friends the harder, because it is known, though not always confessed, that I write truth, and am not a commonplace railer! Last Summer, when Giles, whom I admire, and would Scorn to speak to, was vilely abused by Brookes, I wrote a defence, which Bache (Oh Such Republicans!) would not print, because Brookes was "a fighting man," and so I had to print it in my last volume, a stranger in the Country, without 6 people in it, who care a farthing if I were gibbetted, while the mighty Republican, with half of Philadelphia at his back, durst not defend one of the most meritorious members that ever sat in a legislative assembly, a man whose eloquence has often made every fibre in my composition thrill with pleasure, as I yet hope to make *him* thrill with Shame. If [. . .] really had almost any tolerable writers, except James Carey, [. . .] think less of their treatment of me. I am, with much respect, Sir, Your most obliged & grateful Servant   J. T. CALLENDER

RC (DLC); damaged; addressed: "Thomas Jefferson Esquire Vice-President of the United States, Charlottesville, Albemarle County, Virginia"; franked; endorsed by TJ as received 2 Nov. and so recorded in SJL.

I WROTE YOU A LETTER: see Callender to

TJ, 22 Sep. TWO NEWSPAPERS: John Fenno's *Gazette of the United States* and William Cobbett's *Porcupine's Gazette*. The DYING WOMAN was Callender's wife, who died in the spring of 1798 (Durey, *Callender*, 105-6).

Defending the democratic societies in the House on 26 Nov. 1794, William B. GILES referred to Scottish radicals Thomas MUIR and Thomas F. PALMER, who were tried, found guilty of seditious practices, and in March 1794 transported to Australia. Giles contended that these "martyrs of Scotch despotism" who were "toasted from one end of the Continent to the other" for asserting their "right of thinking, of speaking, of writing, and of printing" were treated more fairly than democratic societies, for they at least had the semblance of a trial (DNB; *Annals*, 4:918). I WAS THEIR INTIMATE FRIEND: see Durey, *Callender*, 41-3. When William L. Smith, author of the 1796 anti-Jeffersonian articles under the signature of PHOCIAN, advocated hiring stenographer David Robertson as the official House reporter in January 1796, Giles served with Smith on the committee considering the proposal and joined in criticism of the current standards of reporting congressional debates in the House. While Robertson was not hired, Callender subsequently lost the position he had held since December 1793 as congressional reporter for the *Philadelphia Gazette* (Durey, *Callender*, 56, 60-1; George C. Rogers, Jr., *Evolution of a Federalist: William Loughton Smith of Charleston (1758-1812)* [Columbia, S.C., 1962], 292; *Annals*, 5:131, 275, 280, 286). For a description of Callender's reporting on debates in the House and for his relationship with Giles, see Durey, *Callender*, 56-63. SIX PER CENT ALLY: another reference to William L. Smith, who played a prominent role in Callender's work *Sedgwick & Co. or a Key to the Six Per Cent Cabinet*, which examined the funding of the national debt and numerous other subjects.

BACHE IS BURIED: Benjamin Franklin Bache died of yellow fever on 10 Sep. and publication of the *Aurora* ceased until the first of November (Tagg, *Bache*, 396-8). On 13 July FENNO printed a very short piece in the *Gazette of the United States* entitled "Envoy Callender" in which he noted that the Republican publicist had left the city going in a westward direction on unknown business. He reported that Callender had since been sighted on the Lancaster road in a drunken state. It is not clear if Callender SENT UP AN ANSWER to this short piece or if he referred to the report of his arrest in Leesburg, Virginia, in August (see Callender to TJ, 22 Sep. 1798).

The PROFOUND OBSERVATIONS of Virginia Congressman Walter Jones appeared in the *Aurora* on 27 Apr. as an extract of a letter from a gentleman in Philadelphia to his friend in Virginia and referred to "the querulous and cankered murmurs of blind, bald, crippled, toothless Adams" (Mason, *Papers*, 1:lxvi; Dauer, *Adams Federalists*, 314). The confrontation between Giles and New York Representative David Brooks, A FIGHTING MAN, took place on 29 Mch. 1798. In his LAST VOLUME, Sedgwick & Co., Callender depicted Brooks as "an aristocratical orator of the most clownish and repulsive species" who in the confrontation with Giles unsuccessfully sought a duel. Callender praised Giles for his "nervous brevity," "persuasive modesty," and "accuracy of information" (*Annals*, 8:1345, 1352-3, 1356; Callender, *Sedgwick & Co.*, 28-9, 31).

[1] Brackets here inserted by Callender.

To James Madison

Oct. 26. 98.

The day after you left us, I sat down and wrote the petition I mentioned to you. it is not yet correct enough, & I inclose you a copy to which I pray your corrections, and to return it by the next post, that it may be set in motion. on turning to the judiciary law of the US. I find they established the designation of jurors *by lot or otherwise as now*[1] *practiced in the several states*; should this prevent, in the first moment the execution of so much of the proposed law, as respects the federal courts, the people will be in possession of the right of electing jurors as to the state courts, and either Congress will agree to conform their courts to the same rule, or they will be loaded with an odium in the eyes of the people generally which will force the matter through. I will send you a copy of the other paper by Richardson. do not send for him till Monday sennight, because that gives us another post-day to warn you of any unexpected delays in winding up his work here for the season, which, tho' I do not foresee, may yet happen. Adieu affectionately.

RC (DLC: Madison Papers, Rives Collection); addressed: "James Madison junr. near Orange court house"; franked; postmarked. PrC (DLC); in ink at foot of text: "Madison James." Enclosure: Petition to the General Assembly of Virginia, [2 or 3 Nov. 1798].

DAY AFTER YOU LEFT US: Madison visited Monticello around 15 Oct. (Madison, *Papers*, 17:xxvii). Section 29 of the JUDICIARY LAW of 1789 called for choosing federal jurors BY LOT unless another mode of selection had already been adopted by the state (U.S. Statutes at Large, 1:88). COPY OF THE OTHER PAPER: probably the Kentucky Resolutions (see TJ to Madison, 17 Nov. 1798).

[1] TJ underlined this word twice.

To Sir Herbert Croft

SIR   Monticello Oct. 30. 1798.

The copy of your printed letter on the English and German languages, which you have been so kind as to send me, has come to hand; and I pray you to accept my thanks for this mark of your attention. I have perused it with singular pleasure, and, having long been sensible of the importance of a knolege of the Northern languages to the true understanding of English, I see it, in this letter, proved and specifically exemplified by your collations of the English and German. I shall look with impatience for the publication of your 'English and American dictionary.' Johnson, besides the want of precision in his definitions, and of accurate distinction in passing from one shade of meaning to another of the same word, is most objectionable in his derivations. from a want probably of intimacy with our own language while in the Anglo-Saxon form and type, and of it's kindred languages of the North, he has a constant leaning towards Greek and Latin for English etymon. even Skinner has a little of this, who, when he has given the true Northern parentage of a word, often tells you from what Greek or Latin source it might be derived by those who have that kind of partiality. he is however, on the whole, our best etymologist, unless we ascend a step higher to the Anglo-Saxon vocabulary; and he has set the good example of collating the English word with it's kindred word in the several Northern dialects, which often assist in ascertaining it's true meaning.

Your idea is an excellent one, pa. 30. 37. in producing authorities for the meanings of words, 'to select the prominent passages in our best writers, to make your dictionary a general index to English literature and thus intersperse with verdure and flowers the barren deserts of Philology.' and I believe with you that 'wisdom, morality, religion, thus thrown down, as if without intention, before the reader, in quotations, may often produce more effect than the very passages in the books themselves'—'that the cowardly suicide, in search of a strong word for his dying letter, might light on a passage which would excite him to blush at his want of fortitude, & to forego his purpose'—'and that a dictionary with examples at the words may, in regard to every branch of knolege, produce more real effect than the whole collection of books which it quotes.' I have sometimes myself used Johnson as a Repertory, to find favorite passages which I wished to recollect, but too rarely with success.

I was led to set a due value on the study of the Northern languages, & especially of our Anglo-Saxon while I was a student of the law, by being obliged to recur to that source for explanation of a multitude of Law-terms. a preface to Fortescue on Monarchies, written by Fortescue Aland, and afterwards premised to his volume of Reports, developes the advantages to be derived, to the English student generally, and particularly the student of law, from an acquaintance with the Anglo-Saxon; and mentions the books to which the learner may have recourse for acquiring the language. I accordingly devoted some time to it's study. but my busy life has not permitted me to indulge in a pursuit to which I felt great attraction. while engaged in it however some ideas occurred for facilitating the study by simplifying it's grammar, by reducing the infinite diversities of it's unfixed orthography to single and settled forms, indicating at the same time the pronunciation of the word by it's correspondence with the characters & powers of the English alphabet. some of these ideas I noted at the time on the blank leaves of my Elstob's Anglo-Saxon grammar: but there I have left them, and must leave them, unpursued, altho' I still think them sound & useful. among the works which I proposed for the use of the A.S. student, you will find such literal & verbal translations of the A.S. writers recommended, as you have given us of the German in your printed letter. thinking that I cannot submit those ideas to a better judge than yourself, and that if you find them of any value you may put them to some use, either as hints in your dictionary, or in some other way, I will copy them as a sequel to this letter, & commit them without reserve to your better knolege of the subject. adding my sincere wishes for the speedy publication of your valuable dictionary, I tender you the assurance of my high respect and consideration.

Th: Jefferson

FC (ViU); entirely in TJ's hand; at head of text: "Copied by hand: the press-copy being illegible"; at foot of first page: "Herbert Croft esq. Ll.B. London."

YOUR PRINTED LETTER: Herbert Croft, *A Letter, from Germany, to the Princess Royal of England; On the English and German Languages* (Hamburg, 1797; see Sowerby, No. 4840). TJ's interest in Old English or ANGLO-SAXON, piqued during his early study of law, continued throughout his life. His understanding of the early development of English had limitations, particularly in terms of scholarship about, or written in, German. Moreover, his consideration of Old English was prompted at least in part by what scholars have deemed the "Saxon myth," certainly not limited to TJ, which located the origins of English democratic, legal, and constitutional traditions in the pre-Norman era. Nevertheless, TJ studied Old English, and later advocated its study at the University of Virginia, not as an aesthetic scholastic exercise but for its practical benefit to the study of law, history, and literature. Familiarity with Saxon English melded well, also, with his views of modern English as a dynamic, evolving language. When he sold his library to Congress in 1815 his collection of books in and about Old English was "by far the largest in the nation at that time" (Stanley R. Hauer, "Thomas Jefferson and the Anglo-Saxon Language," *PMLA*, 98 [1983], 879-98).

SKINNER: Stephen Skinner, *Etymologicon Linguæ Anglicanæ* (London, 1671; see Sowerby, No. 4873). FORTESCUE ON MONARCHIES: Sir John Fortescue, *The Difference between an Absolute and Limited Monarchy; As it More Particularly regards the English Constitution*, written in the fifteenth century and published in 1719 with a preface by Fortescue's descendant, Sir John FORTESCUE ALAND, who also included the preface in his *Reports of Select Cases in all the Courts of Westminster-Hall* (London, 1748). See Sowerby, Nos. 2079, 2704.

TJ's notations in ELSTOB'S ANGLO-SAXON

GRAMMAR—Elizabeth Elstob, *The Rudiments of Grammar for the English-Saxon Tongue, First Given in English: with an Apology for the Study of Northern Antiquities*, published in London in 1715—have not been located; see Sowerby, No. 4861. Well after his death, when the University of Virginia printed his work on Old English as *An Essay towards Facilitating Instruction in the Anglo-Saxon and Modern Dialects of the English Language* (New York, 1851), the published work included his letter to Croft. This pairing of the above letter and TJ's *Essay* helped establish a long-held supposition that the *Essay* was in fact the SEQUEL TJ appended to his letter to Croft (Hauer, "Jefferson and Anglo-Saxon," 885, 896n; L & B, 18:360). However, TJ likely composed most of the *Essay*, which is a fairly substantial work in several sections, over a course of years, probably 1818 to 1825, in conjunction with his inclusion of Anglo-Saxon in the curriculum of the University of Virginia. Although the *Essay* in its final form did not exist until well after 1798, a careful student of the subject has suggested that one portion, which TJ called "Observations on Anglo-Saxon grammar," may be of an earlier composition date than the other sections and could be similar to what TJ sent to Croft (Hauer, "Jefferson and Anglo-Saxon," 884-91).

The letter above is the only correspondence with Sir Herbert Croft (1751-1816) that TJ noted in his epistolary record. A baronet of limited means, Croft trained as a lawyer but took orders in the Church of England and held a nominal position as a vicar. A prolific writer in different genres, he intended to compile a dictionary of the English language but never completed the project. Ironically, a novel that he published anonymously in 1780, *Love and Madness*, contained—some years before the appearance of TJ's *Notes on the State of Virginia*—a version of Logan's lamentation of 1774. Knowledge of that fact could have reinforced TJ's contention that Logan's oration was widely circulated prior to his own publication of it, but he did not know of *Love and Madness* as he collected evidence in response to Luther Martin's newspaper attacks. When acquaintances later sent him copies of the novel he was probably unaware that Croft was its author. *Love and Madness*, the fictionalized account of a notorious case of obsessive love, is best known for Croft's treatment in its pages of the controversial poet, Thomas Chatterton (DNB; Maximilian E. Novak, "The Sensibility of Sir Herbert Croft in *Love and Madness* and the 'Life of Edward Young,' " *The Age of Johnson*, 8 [1997], 189-207; Sowerby, No. 4338; TJ to John Henry, 31 Dec. 1797).

From James Madison

DEAR SIR   Ocr. 31. 1798.

I return the draught recd. by the last post, with one or two very small alterations. The interlineated "or an alloted portion thereof," means to suggest that the whole no. might be so great as to beget objections to the expence which are always formidable in such cases. I have doubted whether the terms "ordinary" & "extraordinary" sufficiently marked the boundary between the power of the Judge & of Jurys over points of law, and whether they do not yield too much of the strict right of the latter in case they chuse to exert it. But you are so much better able to decide on this subject than myself, that I have not ventured to note any precise amendment. I shall not send for Richardson sooner than you propose; but shall then hope for the use of him for some time for plaistering as well as adjusting the Stone to the fire places. The state of the business under Mason increases my dependence on the auxiliary. Mr. R. will please to bring with him such utensils as he will need.

Yrs. affecy.   Js. MADISON JR.

The Thermr. at Sunrise Ocr.   30 — 22°
                              31.   26.

RC (DLC: Madison Papers); addressed: "Mr. Jefferson"; endorsed by TJ as received 2 Nov. 1798 and so recorded in SJL. Enclosure: Petition to the General Assembly of Virginia, [2 or 3 Nov. 1798].

DRAUGHT RECD. BY THE LAST POST: see TJ to Madison, 26 Oct. 1798.

A letter from Madison to TJ of 27 Oct., recorded in SJL as received 28 Oct. 1798, has not been found.

Petition to the General Assembly of Virginia

[2 or 3 Nov. 1798]

the Petition of sundry persons inhabitants of the county of Albemarle, and citizens of the said commonwealth, respectfully sheweth

That though civil government, duly framed & administered be one of the greatest blessings and most powerful instruments for procuring safety[1] & happiness to men collected in large societies, yet such is the proneness of those to whom it's powers are necessarily deputed to pervert them to the attainment of personal wealth & dominion, & to the utter oppression of their fellow-men,[2] that it has become questionable whether the condition of our aboriginal neighbors, who live without laws or magistracies, be not preferable to that of the great mass of the nations of the earth who feel their laws & magistrates but in the weight of their burthens: that the citizens of these United states, impressed with this mortifying[3] truth when they deposed the abusive government under which they had lived, founded their new forms, as well particular as general, in this fact & principle, that the people themselves are the safest deposit of power, & that none therefore should be trusted to others which they can competently exercise themselves: that their own experience having proved that the people are competent to the appointment or election of their agents, that of their chief executive magistrates was reserved to be made at short periods[4] by themselves, or by others chosen by themselves; as was also the choice of their legislatures, whether composed of one or more branches: that in the Judiciary department sensible[5] that they were inadequate to difficult questions of law, these were generally confided to permanent judges but reserving to juries the decision both of law and fact where in their opinion bias in the permanent judge might be apprehended, & where honest ignorance would be safer than perverted science: and reserving to themselves also the whole department of facts, which constitutes indeed the great mass of judiciary litigations. that the wisdom of these reservations will be apparent on a recurrence to the history of the country from which we chiefly emigrated, where the faint glimmerings of lib[erty] & safety now remaining to the nation are kept in [feeble] life by[6] the [reserved] powers of the people only: that [in] the establishment of the trial by jury however a great [in]consistence has been overlooked in this & some other of the states, or rather has been copied from their original without due attention; for while[7] the competence of the people to the appointment even of the highest Executive, & of the legislative agents is admitted & established, & their [compe]tence to be themselves the triers of Judiciary facts,[8] [the] appointment of the special individuals[9] from among themselves who shall be such triers of fact, has not been left in their hands, but has been placed by law in officers, dependant on the Executive or Judiciary bodies: that triers of fact are therefore habitually taken in this state from among accidental bystanders, & too often composed of [foreign]ers attending on matters of business, & of[10] idle persons, collected for purposes of dissipation; and, in cases interesting to the powers of the public functionaries, may be speci[ally] selected from descriptions of persons to be found in every co[untry] whose ignorance or dependance renders them pliable to the will and designs of power: that in others of these states[11] this germ of rottenness in the institution of juries has been carefully excluded, & their laws have provided,[12] with laudable foresight, for the appointment of jurors by select men, chosen by the people themselves; and to a like restitution of[13] principle, & salutary precaution against the abuse of power by the public functionaries, who never did yet, in any country fail to betray & oppress those for the care of whose affairs they were appointed, by force if they possessed it, or by fraud & delusion if they did not, your petitioners pray the timely attention of their legislature, while that legislature (and with a heartfelt satisfaction the petitioners pronounce it) are still honest enough to wish the preservation of the rights of the people, and wise enough to circumscribe in time[14] the spread of that gangrene which,[15] sooner than many are aware, may reach the vitals of our political existence.

And lest it should be supposed that the popular appointment of jurors may scarcely be practicable in a state so extensive & circumstanced as ours, your petitioners will undertake to suggest one mode, not presuming to propose[16] it for the adoption of the legislature, but firmly relying that their wisdom will devise a better: they observe then that by a law already passed for the establishment of schools, provision has been made for laying off every county into districts or precincts; that this division which offers so many valuable resources for the purposes of information, of justice, of order, & police, may be recurred to for the object now[17] in contemplation, and may be completed for this purpose, where it has not been done for the other; that the inhabitants of every precinct may meet at a given time & place in their precinct, and in the presence of the constable or other head officer of the precinct, elect from among themselves some one to be a juror; that, from among those so chosen in every county, someone may be designated by lot, who shall attend the ensuing session of the federal court within the state, to act as grand & petty jurors, one of these from every Senatorial district being designated by lot for a grand juror, and the residue or an allotted portion thereof[18] attending to serve as petty jurors, to be designated in like manner by lot in every particular case: that of the others so chosen in every county composing a district for the itinerant courts of this commonwealth, so many may be taken by lot as shall suffice for grand & petty juries for the district court next ensuing their election: and the residue so chosen in each county may attend their own county courts for the same purposes till another election,[19] or, if too numerous, the supernumeraries may be discharged by lot: and that such compensation may be allowed for these services as, without rendering the office an object worth canvassing, may yet protect the juror from actual loss: That an institution on this outline, or such better as the wisdom of the General assembly will devise, so modified as to[20] guard it against the intrigue of parties, the influence of power, or irregularities of conduct, and further matured from time to time as experience shall develope it's imperfections, may long preserve the trial by jury, in it's pure and original spirit, as the true tribunal of the people, for a mitigation in the execution of hard laws when the power of preventing their passage is lost, and may afford some protection to persecuted man, whether alien or citizen,[21] which the aspect of the times warns us we may want.

And your petitioners, waiving the expression of many important considerations which will offer themselves readily to the reflection of the General assembly, pray them to take the premises into deep & serious[22] consideration, and to do therein for their country[23] what their wisdom shall deem best, & they, as in duty bound, shall ever pray &c.

PrC (DLC: TJ Papers, 106:18101-4); entirely in TJ's hand; undated, but see below; faint, with words in brackets supplied from Dft; at head of text: "To the General Assembly of the Commonwealth of Virginia"; several emendations made by TJ in ink reflect changes suggested by Madison in his letter of 31 Oct., which TJ received on 2 Nov. (see notes 4, 5, and 18 below). Dft (same, 232:42018-9); undated, but see note below. MS (Vi); in two unknown hands; incorporates changes made by TJ in ink to PrC; variations in capitalization, abbreviations, punctuation, and spelling; with 23 signatures affixed; endorsed by clerk: "Albemarle Petn. December 24. 1798 whole on Friday next"; in another hand: "Nicholas."

This petition calling for the election of jurors is a successor to one TJ drafted in 1797 for the Virginia House of Delegates, in response to the grand jury presentment against Virginia Representative Samuel J. Cabell for criticizing federal policies in a letter to his constituents. The 1797 document defended the right of representatives to communicate freely with their constituents and noted defects in the method of selecting jurors that were leading to a perversion of the judicial system. TJ in early drafts sought to restrict grand jurors to "native citizens of the United States," but his recommendation was omitted from the petition as presented to the House of Delegates (Petition to Virginia House of Delegates at 3 Aug. 1797). The composition of juries remained a matter of concern to TJ, and he probably discussed the issue with Madison when he visited Monticello about 15 Oct. The day after Madison's departure, TJ drafted this petition and on 26 Oct. forwarded what was probably a fair copy of it to Montpelier for Madison's suggestions, which subsequently TJ incorporated on his press copy (Madison, *Papers*, 17:xxvii; TJ to Madison, 26 Oct. and 3 Nov., and Madison to TJ, 31 Oct. 1798). Then, as he had done in 1797 to obscure his authorship, TJ had others prepare a copy of the emended document for circulation and presentation to the Virginia Assembly. Twenty-three inhabitants of Albemarle County signed the petition including Thomas Bell, Thomas Mann Randolph, Peter Lott, and Thomas Carr, Jr. (MS in Vi, described above; TJ to Madison, 3 Nov. 1798). Perhaps to garner support in the House of Delegates TJ also enclosed a copy to his friend, Caroline County delegate John Taylor. Wilson Cary Nicholas, an Albemarle County delegate, was entrusted with carrying the petition to Richmond, where it was presented to the House on 24 December. Discussion of it, however, was continually postponed and the assembly adjourned without having taken action (JHD, Dec. 1798-Jan. 1799, 37, 51, 56, 72, 104; TJ to Taylor, 26 Nov. 1798). For the Republican response to the petition in the Virginia House of Delegates, see John Taylor's letter to TJ of 15 Feb. 1799.

Massachusetts, Vermont, and Connecticut were among the states with laws to exclude the GERM OF ROTTENNESS in the formation of juries. The Massachusetts statutes provided for the election of grand jurors from among freeholders of a town and the appointment of petit jurors "of good moral character and qualified as the constitution directs" from lists provided by the selectmen of each town. The constitution of Vermont called for the passage of legislation to insure "against every Corruption or Partiality" in the choice or appointment of juries. A state statute called for jurors to be able and substantial freeholders. In Connecticut jurors were selected at a town meeting in January from "judicious Freeholders" with a freehold estate rated at 50 shillings or more (*The Perpetual Laws of the Commonwealth of Massachusetts, from the Commencement of the Constitution, in October, 1780, to the Last Wednesday in May, 1789* [Boston, 1789], 114-19; *Acts and Laws of the State of Vermont, in America* [Dresden, Vt., 1779], 9, 65-7; *Acts and Laws of the State of Connecticut, in America* [New London, 1784], 108-10; TJ to Taylor, 26 Nov. 1798).

For the law PASSED FOR THE ESTABLISHMENT OF SCHOOLS in 1796, see Vol. 29:178n, 288n.

[1] In Dft TJ first wrote "is the most effectual instrument for the security" before altering the passage to read as above.

[2] "Men" interlined in Dft in place of "citizens."

[3] Word interlined in Dft in place of "melancholy."

[4] Preceding three words interlined in ink by TJ.

[5] From this point in Dft to ampersand TJ first wrote "of their own incompetence to the decision of questions of law, they confided [them?] in ordinary to permanent judges, reserving to themselves only ⟨in⟩ extraordinary cases where they should have reason to suspect a bias in their judges, and

reserving to themselves also" before revising it to read: "that they were inadequate to questions of law, these were in ordinary cases, confided to permanent judges, reserving to juries only extraordinary cases where a bias in the permanent judge might be suspected." At Madison's suggestion TJ altered the passage in ink in PrC to read as printed in text above.

[6] In Dft TJ first wrote "liberty now remaining are kept alive only ⟨. . .⟩ by the force of in" before altering the passage to read as above.

[7] From this point the MS in Vi is completed in a different hand.

[8] In Dft TJ first wrote "to decide themselves judiciary questions of fact" before altering the passage to read as above.

[9] Preceding three words interlined in Dft in place of "[them?]."

[10] In Dft TJ here canceled "lounging."

[11] In Dft TJ here canceled "and particulary in those to the Eastward of the union."

[12] In Dft TJ first wrote "this source of rottenness has not been [neglected?] that" before altering the passage to read as above.

[13] Preceding two words interlined in Dft in place of "attention to."

[14] Preceding three words interlined in Dft in place of "foresee."

[15] In Dft TJ first concluded this sentence "sooner than would have been believed may reach the vitals of our constitution" before altering it to read as above.

[16] Interlined in Dft in place of "prescribe."

[17] Passage from this point to semicolon interlined in Dft in place of "proposed," with interlineation extending into right margin.

[18] Preceding five words interlined by TJ in ink.

[19] Passage from this point to colon interlined in Dft.

[20] Here in Dft TJ canceled "shield."

[21] In Dft TJ first concluded this sentence "which the awfulness of the times warns us to ⟨foresee⟩ expect" before altering it to read as above.

[22] Preceding three words interlined in Dft.

[23] Preceding three words interlined in Dft.

To James Madison

Nov. 3. 98.

Your's of Oct. 31. has been duly recieved and the corrections suggested are thankfully adopted. the petition will be offered for signature at our court the day after tomorrow.   Richardson has been in a great measure prevented doing any thing this week by the weather, which has been too cold for laying mortar. he has still 2. or 3. days work of that kind to do, which is indispensable, and about as long a job in kilning some bricks which we must secure in an unburnt state through the winter. we must therefore beg you to put off sending for him till Saturday next.

Yesterday's papers bring us an account of Lyon of Vermont being indicted before Judge Patterson under the Sedition act. possibly your papers may not mention the issue. he was found guilty, fined 1000. D. and adjudged to 4. months imprisonment. he was immediately committed. the words called seditious were only general censures of the proceedings of Congress & of the President. affectionate respects to mrs Madison your father & family. Adieu.

P.S. your nails are ready

RC (DLC: Madison Papers, Rives Collection); unaddressed, but entered in SJL as a letter to Madison under this date.

TJ's PETITION advocating the election of jurors in Virginia is printed immediately above. On 19 Oct. the *Philadelphia Gazette* carried a brief notice on the sentencing of Matthew LYON OF VERMONT, the first prosecution under the Sedition Act, and four days later published a fuller account of charges against him and details of the trial. The Fredericksburg *Virginia Herald* carried the news on 23 and 26 Oct. For an analysis of the case and its political reverberations, see Smith, *Freedom's Fetters*, 225-46. Running for reelection to the House of Representatives, Lyon conducted the remainder of his campaign from the jail in Vergennes, Vermont, and received almost 4,500 votes, a majority of nearly 600 over the rest of the field (same, 241).

To Aaron Burr

Dear Sir   Monticello Nov. 12. 1798

Dr. Currie, on whose behalf I troubled you last summer, being anxious to learn something of the prospect he may have of recovery from Robert Morris, I take the liberty of asking a line directed to me at this place where I shall still be long enough to recieve it. I should not have troubled you but that you expected early in the summer to be able to judge what could be done. I am aware at the same time that the fever at New York may have disturbed all legal proceedings.

I did not mean to say a word on politics, but it seems that I have seen in the New York papers a calumny which I suppose will run through the union, that I had written by Doctr. Logan letters to Merlin and Taleyrand. on retiring from the Secretary of state's office, I determined to drop all correspondence with France, knowing the base calumnies which would be built on the most innocent correspondence. I have not therefore written a single letter to that country, within that period, except to Mr. Short on his own affairs merely which are under my direction, and once or twice to Colo. Monroe. by Logan I did not write even a letter to Mr. Short, nor to any other person whatever. I thought this notice of the matter due to my friends, though I do not go into the newspapers with a formal declaration of it. I am with sincere esteem Dear Sir

Your friend & sevt   TH: JEFFERSON

PrC (DLC); at foot of text: "Colo. Burr."

I TROUBLED YOU: TJ to Burr, 20 May 1798.

On 17 Sep. American Minister to London Rufus King reported to Alexander Hamilton the rumor that George Logan had gone to France with letters from Jefferson. The story reached NEW YORK in October. On 15 Oct. Noah Webster's New York *Commercial Advertiser* began publication of a series of articles on Logan's visit that was based on reports from Paris newspapers. On the 16th the *Advertiser* reported that Logan was not on official business, and that the Directory, afraid of a misunderstanding, wished him to complete his affairs quickly. On 5 Nov. the *Advertiser* printed a highly critical column describing Logan as the "agent of a faction." In a memoir printed in 1899, edited by Logan's great-granddaughter, Logan's wife stated that her husband carried only two letters, both from Citizen Létombe and addressed to Talleyrand and Philippe Antoine MERLIN de Douai. Merlin was a French legal authority and politician who had become minister of justice in 1795 and also served as minister of police for a few months in 1796. He was elected to the Directory in 1797 (Certificate for George Logan, 4 June 1798; Syrett, *Hamilton*, 22:183-5; Tolles, *Logan*, 153-73; Logan, *Memoir*, 57; Scott and Rothaus, *Historical Dictionary*, 2:652-3; Jean Tulard, ed., *Dictionnaire Napoléon* [Paris, 1987], 1167-8).

From Elbridge Gerry

DEAR SIR   Cambridge 12th Novr 1798

Mr Otis, secretary of the Senate, was kind eno' to take four letters, of which two were for yourself, & a small box with one or more Watches; & to promise a delivery of them, into your hands. the box, & some of the letters, were committed to my care by Mr Short; who accompanyed me to Havre, with an intention to embark in the Sophia, for the U States. he had provided every article for the Voyage, & sent his baggage to that place; but Madam Ro—f—lt,'s irrisistible letters, pursued him there, & changed his resolution. I presume he is now, in holy unison with her. he also delivered to me two books, & some papers of Mr Skipwith's, for yourself: & Monsr Latude delivered to me his memoirs, relative to his thirty five years confinement in the Bastile, with his best respects, for you. I send you the whole of these by Mr Binney: a young gentleman, who is studying law at Philadelphia. I understood, that Mr Skipwith's papers were for recovering about £8, or 900 sterling due to him from the UStates: that he advanced the money for them: & that the detention of it, is a hard case. of this, I presume you will be able to judge; & of the proper measures & time, for obtaining justice for him—Doctor Gemm, who is no longer in the practice of physic, but still a very respectable character in Paris, presents his best respects to you. I shall be much obliged to you, for the yeas & nays of my appointment, as Envoy; & for such political information, as may be interesting to myself, in regard to the embassy. during my absence I find that I have been abused alternately by both parties: but for what, I am yet to learn. send the letter by a private hand. I remain dear Sir

Your friend & very hume Sert   E GERRY

RC (DLC); at foot of text: "Honble Mr Jefferson Vice President of the U States"; endorsed by TJ as received 28 Dec. 1798 and so recorded in SJL. FC (Lb in DLC: Gerry Papers); in Gerry's hand.

For the LETTERS that Samuel A. Otis evidently handed to TJ on the vice president's arrival in Philadelphia on 25 Dec., see William Short's letter of 6 Aug. 1798. On 13 Apr. 1800 TJ informed Short that the WATCHES had been safely conveyed to Short's sisters in Kentucky. He sent the timepieces in the care of John Fowler, although the SJL entry for a 6 Feb. 1799 letter to Peyton Short, which has not been found, notes that it was carried "by mr Clay with a watch" (TJ to Peyton Short, 16 Oct. 1799; Peyton Short to TJ, 5 Dec. 1799).

MADAM RO–F–LT: the Duchesse de La Rochefoucald. The TWO BOOKS, which TJ acknowledged in that letter of 13 Apr. 1800, were the edition of Virgil (see Short's letters of 27 Feb. and 15 Apr. 1798) and a work on pisé construction, a building method in which earth or clay was packed between forms to create walls. That book was very likely École d'Architecture Rurale (Paris, 1791) by François Cointeraux; see Sowerby, No. 1177.

MONSR LATUDE DELIVERED TO ME HIS MEMOIRS: Henri Masers de Latude, previously known as Jean Danry, was first imprisoned in 1749 for pretending to reveal a plot to poison the Marquise de Pompadour, mistress of Louis XV. A perpetually difficult prisoner, he escaped from French jails several times and was eventually deemed insane by prison authorities. Attaining celebrity after the fall of the Bastille in 1789, he told the tale of his 1756 escape from that prison as Mémoire de M. Delatude, ingénieur. The book handed to Gerry may have been Le despotisme dévoilé ou Mémoires de Henri Masers de Latude, détenu pendant trente-cinq ans dans diverses prisons d'État, first published in Paris in 1790. There were other purported memoirs that Latude disavowed as apocryphal. As TJ mentioned in his famous "Head and Heart" letter to Maria Cosway on 12 Oct. 1786, Latude dined with him on occasion in Paris and regaled the American minister with stories of his imprisonment and escapes (Claude Quétel, Escape from the Bastille: The Life and Legend of Latude, trans. Christopher Sharp [Cambridge, 1990], 3-6, 11, 43-5, 62-4, 73-7, 95-6, 153-7; see also Sowerby, No. 219; and, for Latude's enigmatic persona, André Nos, Jean-Henri Masers de Latude (1725-1805), ou Le fou de la liberté: Enquête historique et psychologique [Pézenas, France, 1994], 317-59).

Eighteen-year-old Horace BINNEY had graduated from Harvard College in 1797, entering Jared Ingersoll's office in the fall of that year to read law (ANB).

From George Jefferson

DEAR SIR   Richmond 12th. Novr. 1798.

Mr. Hooper has made payment in full for your Tobacco, deducting $:1000—for your other draft, in favor of Mr. James Lyle; which he informs me he has taken up.

I subjoin an account of the sale, & am Dear Sir Your Very Obt. Hbl: servt.   GEO. JEFFERSON

Sales of Tobacco on Account of Mr. Thomas Jefferson—

1798
May 15—To Thomas Hooper—pble. 1st. Octr. & 12th. Novr.—

```
    PF
   TI – 32 —137 —1568 ⎫
Spring 44 —137 —1641 ⎪
       52 —137 —1603 ⎪
       53 —137 —1573 ⎪
       54 —137 —1627 ⎪
       63 —137 —1641 ⎬ 18129 ℔s      @ 78/ £707.–.8
       95 —137 —1725 ⎪   Duty on 10 Hhds.⎫  2.5.–
       96 —137 —1787 ⎪      @ 4/6      ⎭____£709.5.8
      109 —137 —1613 ⎪
      110 —137 —1669 ⎪
Schockoe 97 —116 —1012 ⎪
  Part of TMR N: 3.  670 ⎭   Charges—
```

```
Freight from Milton on 1 Hhd. 1128 In. 2/6    £1.8.2.
Canal toll 2/6 & draye. 1/3 on 11 Hhds.       " 2.1.3
Propn. of expences on TMR #3                  " 1.–.–    4. 9. 5
     Our Commission 2½ pr Ct.                          17.16.10   22. 6.3
                              Neat proceeds            £686.19.5
```

Errors Excepted
Richmond 30th. Septr. 1798—
GEO: JEFFERSON & CO.

RC (MHi); with account and company signature in Patrick Gibson's hand on verso; addressed: "Thomas Jefferson esquire Monticello"; franked and postmarked; endorsed by TJ as received 16 Nov. 1798 and so recorded in SJL.

To James Madison

TH:J. TO J.M.   Monticello Nov. 17. [1798]

Mr. Richardson has been detained by several jobs indispensable to the progress of the carpenters, & to the securing what is done against the winter. when will Whitton be done with you? or could you by any means dispense with his services till I set out for Philadelphia? my floors can only be laid while I am at home, and I cannot get a workman here. perhaps you have some other with you or near you who could go on with your work till his return to you. I only mention these things that if you have any other person who could enable you to spare him a few weeks, I could employ him to much accomodation till my departure in laying my floors. but in this consult your own convenience only.—I inclose you a copy of the draught of the Kentuckey resolves. I think we should distinctly affirm all the important principles they contain, so as to hold to that ground in future, and leave the matter in such a train as that we may not be committed absolutely to push the matter to extremities, & yet may be free to push as far as events will render prudent. I think to set out so as to arrive at Philadelphia the Saturday before Christmas. my friendly respects to mrs Madison, to your father & family. health, happiness & Adieu to yourself.

40. ℔. of IVy. nails @ $14\frac{1}{2}$ d per ℔ were sent this morning, being all we had. they will yield (according to the count of a single pound) 314 x 40 = 12,560.

RC (DLC: Madison Papers, Rives Collection); partially dated, with "1799" added at dateline in unknown hand, leading to a later misunderstanding by Madison as noted in his letter to Nicholas P. Trist, 23 Sep. 1830 (see Madison, *Papers*, 17:181); correct year supplied from SJL; addressed: "James Madison junr. Orange." PrC (DLC); in ink at foot of text: "Madison James." Enclosure: PrC of Document II of the group of documents on the Kentucky Resolutions of 1798, printed at 4 Oct. 1798.

Richard RICHARDSON carried this letter (Madison to TJ, 11 Dec. 1798).

A letter from Madison to TJ of 19 Nov., recorded in SJL as received 20 Nov. 1798, has not been found.

From James Thomson Callender

SIR   Rasberryplain 19 Novr. 1798.

I never write a letter, when I can avoid it. I much less desire to trouble my Superiors. But I received, some days ago, your favour of October 11th. The nature of its contents supersedes the necessity of Saying that it was welcome. I have only to add that some parts of it seem to need an explanation on my part of what brought me here. When You are quite at leisure, what follows will explain that circumstance. I did understand, in a way which admitted of no doubt, that I was very nearly in the same Situation as that in which I found myself at Edinburg, on January 2d, 1793. *Out of Sight, out of mind*, says the proverb. My immediate disappearance was likely to make the proposal, for it was but a proposal, to be dropt; and, if it Should be concluded on, I would be beyond its reach. I went very late to Genl. M. who was in bed, told him the particulars, and by his permission, set out early next morning, on foot, for this place. He was to overtake me at Lancaster, with the stage coach. I had hardly got there, when people who knew me, *met* and I was well assured that I Should not be sure of Safety. This was the natural consequence of the ballot box criticisms, as to October 1796; so bidding adieu to Messrs. Barton, and Hamilton, (printer. Vid. Ann: Register) I set out for Yorktown, having just got a letter from the General that he Could not come up, and that I must not halt at Yorktown, so I walked Straight forward. When he came here, he presented me with an account of my *Journey*, which has, I Suppose, been printed in ten newspapers by this time. I instantly wrote an answer, for very luckily every word of the Story was false, and M Leiper writes me, that with his own hand he delivered this answer to Bache. The publisher of the *Second* edition of the forged letters in the name of General Washington, (and which the General, forgetting the respect due to his character, condescended to deny) the publisher of the Second part of the Age of reason, after the *first part* had produced so much scandal, the publisher of the libel agt. M Adams for being bald and toothless, and of the ballad praying that the Queen of England's head might be tossed in a basket, and, what is hardly better, the heads of *all* the sovereigns in Europe, this publisher, who by his indiscretion, has done such infinite mischief to the Cause of liberty, refused to print my defence.

I cannot conceive that things are to go on, as they have done of late, for any considerable time. The 800,000 dollars of July 1797 are not yet borrowed. The 5 millions that are to be borrowed at any interest must, like Jupiter, descend in a [sho]wer, for they are not to be found upon earth. The 2 millions of a direct tax will not chink for 18 months. I guess another loan and tax will be adopted this winter, but the impost must, I think, be contracting, while expences are enormously augmenting, and loans cannot be raised, nor taxes realised in any effective time. In the mean while, direct taxation will force the people to think, and the prosecutions will provoke them to clamour. The System seems to be to waste money, and break the constitution as fast as can be. All this has had effect in England, where the throne rested on the Shoulders of an enormous hierarchy and Aristocracy. But even there it is like sleeping sound after swallowing 100 drops of Laudanum. It is an expedient that involves the approach of death[.] Accordingly, England is now expending for 1798 6 or 7 million[s] Sterling more than either loans or taxes can produce. I have a complete Statement of the particulars ready for the press from Accompts laid before parliament. Indeed their own Newspapers own 3 millions of *deficit* annually, but I have proved that it is not one farthing less than 6. For 99, it will be 8 millions, in spite of gifts, assessed taxes, and the very auspicious Sale of the land tax. Of this last Measure I do not know the particulars, but the very endurance of such an idea announces the consciousness of impending ruin. I do not recite this under the impertinence of pretending to inform, but merely to *remind*.

Now if England has come to this plight, She can lend nothing to America, and where we are to find money even to carry on the peace, it seems hard to say. As for War, I do not see even a Shadow of finance. My inference is that the System cannot last any time, and must land its apostles in the mire. Already, the X.Y.Z. Mania is greatly cooled. It was amusing to see how Mr. Pickering tried to conjure up this phantom in his answer to the Edward County. I felt it like "a tale of the days of old, and of the heroes that are no more." The Virginian Assembly, if they act like men, may knock this usurpation on the head by a protest to Congress. Many foolish things will be said and done in next Session at Philadelphia, and by next March, the public mind will be much riper than it is at present for the admission of truth. If I knew how to Spend the intermediate time, I would then go down to *Richmond*, and there publish a small volume. I think no Judge in this State will, by that time, dare to raise a process of Sedition. The people will be apter to take a good impression than in Philadelphia, and I would in the end of the book advertise all my former books. This could hardly fail to produce a demand for new editions, for the books have only been limited in their circulation by the ruined State of printing, the dread of the banks at Phila: and their being all published only in *one* State, nor ever taken properly by the hand of any bookseller, for *fair play* would have made them bring me a handsome income. After all I have Sold above three thousand volumes in less than 2 years, of which time one half almost has been taken up with yellow fevers. A Richmond publication would make many know the former books that never heard of them, and though they are poor enough, yet they at least are better than the Common rubbish of Newspapers. If the assembly had any good measures, I would like to go before March, indeed before they rise. But at any Rate, in Spring, I would like to print Something there, for the various reasons of—Safety—an impression—and the prospect of reprinting what is at present out *of print*. I am Sorry for having wandered into details so uninteresting to any body, but myself, but I Can not think I Should be Safe in Philadelphia, so soon as I Shall be in Richmond. Either however at the latter place, or Norfolk, or any where that I know, can I not be safe to live at peace, I mean in *a town*, till the tide turns. Among other things, I would print *Barlow's letter*, of which I would now Send a Copy but that I am Satisfied You have Seen it. If You have not seen Lyon's *Scourge*, I would Send a printed copy of that, if You chuse, as it has some articles irresistibly ludicrous, but that also I presume You have got by post. Nothing like the Colonel's Indictment was ever heard of. Barlow agrees so exactly with all I had said on the Paris embassy, that I should have a three fold pleasure in reprinting him. I would go round the Country myself with the book, for when there is a proper object in view I can promise on taking any reasonable degree of pains.

Since I Came here, I have got much information that I had not before, have made large Notes on various points entirely untouched, and would very gladly Stay here, with the advantage of a good library, till I have completed and extended an Address to the Citizens of Virginia on the present State of public affairs. The "whale caught in a net,"—The "*dust and ashes*" answer to Bath County &c. afford overwhelming materials for ridicule. I Can Speak more frankly from the internal consciousness of never having wrote an unfair thing to serve any party, if I could have been indeed capable of service.—I cannot break to the General this wish of Staying past the sitting down of Congress, though it would take at least 2 months to arrange my present materials. I would then be ready to give our rulers such a Tornado, as no Govt ever got before, for there is in American history a Species of ignorance, absurdity, and imbecillity unknown to the annals of any other nation. Before the rising of Congress I Could be completely ready. My board at 15 dols. per quarter is not the object, but I could not take away with me, a whole load of books, &c. that I have marked for reference—The General is indeed all Goodness—Without parade or effort, his benevolence, like a natural fountain flows from the Sweetness and rectitude of his primitive composition. I would like very well to be in the Situation of a lawyer's clerk, such as the General had before he gave up business. But if I could weather out 3 months, or so, till the weather clears up, as it will do, I would like printing much better. It would at least pay for itself. I have got much better since I came here of a terrible complaint that I had got in Philadelphia; and for one word, the General would bid me Stay, but *that one word I cannot get myself to pronounce.* You will see that the Aurora has got into most excellent hands—In the first Number, Liston's man looks like a bull frog in the fist of Hercules.—I have got more sound sleep since I came here than I had enjoyed for some years before. I am now master of my own time, and rid of the burden of too much Society, so that I can write at leisure, and not scrawl myself into headaches.

Sir, my anxiety to communicate some ideas has branched out into a length of which I had no design. If the letter is read at all, of which I have humilating doubts, my last and hopeless request is your pardon for its prolixity.

I am Sir Your most obliged serv.   JAMES THOMSON CALLENDER

RC (DLC); damaged; endorsed by TJ as received 29 Nov. 1798 and so recorded in SJL.

EDINBURG: Callender fled Scotland and came to the United States in 1793 to escape sedition charges (note to Callender to TJ, 28 Sep. 1797). GENL. M.: Stevens Thomson Mason.

Callender had publicized several cases of attempted BALLOT BOX fraud by Federalists in Lancaster County, Pennsylvania, during the presidential election of 1796 ([Callender], *The American Annual Register, or, Historical Memoirs of the United States, for the Year 1796*, [Philadelphia, 1797], 165-6). The charges first appeared in the Philadelphia *Aurora*, on 25 Nov. and 2 Dec. 1796. His acquaintances in Lancaster were probably William BARTON, brother of Benjamin Smith Barton, and William HAMILTON, who learned the printing business in the office of the *Aurora* before leaving Philadelphia by early 1795 and becoming first a partner and then, in 1796, the sole publisher of the *Lancaster Journal* (Philadelphia *Aurora*, 21 Apr. 1795; Brigham, *American Newspapers*, 2:869-70; Alexander Harris, *A Biographical History of Lancaster County: Being a History of Early Settlers and Eminent Men of the County* [Lancaster, 1872], 26, 38-9, 267-8).

For Washington's reaction to the new edition of FORGED LETTERS published in late 1795, see Madison to TJ, 5 Aug. 1797. In advertisements for the publication entitled *Letters from General Washington to Several of his Friends, in June and July, 1776*, Bache noted that the authenticity of the letters had been questioned "but never publicly denied" and that they bore "some intrinsic marks of authenticity" (*Aurora*, 10 Nov. 1795, 5 Jan. 1797).

To finance Great Britain's wartime expenditures and reduce the high national debt, William Pitt backed the aid and contribution bill that tripled the rate of ASSESSED TAXES and, as finally passed, included a proposal encouraging wealthier individuals voluntarily to contribute above

their payments from the assessment. On 2 Apr. 1798 Pitt also introduced the plan for the SALE OF THE LAND TAX, which commuted the tax into government stock and in the process turned the annual tax into a permanent levy (*Annual Register . . . for the Year 1798* [London, 1800], 206-7; John Ehrman, *The Younger Pitt: The Consuming Struggle* [London, 1996], 98-109).

On 29 Sep. 1798, Timothy PICKERING informed the freeholders of Prince EDWARD COUNTY, Virginia, that instead of forwarding their 21 Aug. address to Adams he was returning it because it was insulting to the president. The address called upon the president to retract the "rash resolution" he had made concerning the renewal of negotiations with France and to use his constitutional powers for the repeal of the Alien and Sedition Acts. Pickering's response countered that preparations for war were necessary to keep the United States from suffering the plight of Holland, Switzerland, and Venice, and defended the Alien and Sedition Acts. Defending the constitutionality of the Alien Friends Act, Pickering declared that the "constitution was established for the protection and security of American citizens, and not of *intriguing foreigners*" (Philadelphia *Aurora*, 6 Nov. 1798). Pickering's response was immediately published as a broadside (see Evans, No. 34378).

See the first letter from Joel Barlow to TJ, 12 Mch. 1798, for BARLOW'S LETTER to Abraham Baldwin of 4 Mch. 1798, a copy of which was enclosed in his letter to TJ. LYON'S SCOURGE: when the Rutland, Vermont, newspaper refused to publish a letter from Matthew Lyon to his constituents during his 1798 reelection campaign, the congressman established his own publication, edited by his son James, bearing the heading *The Scourge of Aristocracy, and Repository of Important Political Truths*, four numbers of which appeared between 1 Oct. and 15 Dec. 1798. The issues included Lyon's letter to his constituents, his correspondence with Stevens Thomson Mason, and news of protests against the Alien and

Sedition Acts (Smith, *Freedom's Fetters*, 227-9).

When the Philadelphia *Aurora* resumed publication on 1 Nov., William Duane published a reprimand of William Cobbett—LISTON'S MAN—for casting "base aspersions on the morals and reputation" of Bache after his death and refuted the charge from *Porcupine's Gazette* that Bache had trained a young apprentice at the *Aurora* to steal.

To John Barnes

DEAR SIR   Monticello Nov. 23. 98.

The [derangement] of our post still continuing, this is the first moment I have an opportunity of acknowleging the receipt of your favor of the 1st inst. announcing your return to Philadelphia. I hope it to have been safe from that time, tho' we have had such warm weather here as made me apprehend a revival of the fever with you. I thank you sincerely for the very kind offer of accomodations at your house. but I could not consent to displace you so inconveniently, from the apartments you occupy yourself. beside which, having hitherto lodged with mr Francis, and both himself and mrs Francis being very obliging, it would be painful to leave them. I am there also nearer to the Statehouse & Philosophical hall.—as I have not yet got my house closed against the damage of winter, and it is therefore very material for me to stay and press on the work till I shall have got it into a state of safety, I shall not set out for Philadelphia in time for the meeting of Congress. as no business is brought in during the first two or three weeks, it is probable I may not be there till the 3d week of [the] [. . .]. I will ask the favor of you therefore to inform mr Fran[cis] that I expect to occupy my former apartments with him [. . .] [and] that I shall be obliged to him to have them ready [. . .] the 2[0]th. of the month (December) and to engage a [servant?] for me at the same time. I should prefer my former one John Theodore, if to be had.—I shall write to mr Roberts by the next post for a supply of nail rod to be forwarded before the ice [shuts up?] your river. I am with affectionate esteem Dear Sir

Your friend & servt   TH: JEFFERSON

PrC (CSmH); faint; at foot of text: "Mr. Barnes"; endorsed by TJ in ink on verso.

NEARER TO THE STATEHOUSE & PHILOSOPHICAL HALL: John Francis's hotel was at numbers 11 and 13 South Fourth Street, between Market and Chestnut (Cornelius William Stafford, *The Philadelphia Directory for 1798* [Philadelphia, 1798], 57; TJ to Richard Richardson, 16 Dec. 1797).

TJ was unsuccessful in again obtaining the services of JOHN THEODORE, who for wages of $10 a month had been his servant during his earlier stays in the capital in 1797-98. On 29 Dec. he hired Jacob Lawrence, paying him $12 a month until TJ left Philadelphia on 1 Mch. 1799 (MB, 2:962, 975, 977, 979-84, 986, 995, 997-9).

According to SJL Barnes wrote TJ two letters from Trenton that have not been located, one on 29 Sep. and the other on 1 Oct., both of which TJ received on 13 Oct. Also recorded in SJL but missing are a 1 Nov. 1798 letter from Barnes, received from Philadelphia on the 16th, and one that TJ wrote to Barnes on the 30th.

From Stevens Thomson Mason

DEAR SIR   Rasberry Plain Novr 23d 1798

Having been some time absent from home your favor of the 11th Ulto did not reach me 'till last week. I have this day drawn according to your direction on your Correspondent in Richmond.

By the last post I received from an acquaintance the inclosed letter with a request to forward it to you. why it was not sent directly to you I can not divine.

I have frequently mentioned your wish to rent out your Land, and many people have expressed a desire, and some an intention of going to see you on the subject. yet none have procured letters from me. a circumstance I can only account for in one way. the great pecuniary distresses of the Farmers from the entire failure of their crops last Harvest. and consequent inability to make sale of their superfluous Stock and effects or to raise the money necessary for their removal.

I am informed of many Tenants who have been from that circumstance obliged to submit to the most intollerable increase of their Rents. and some of them very notable and industrious Farmers. I think it would not be safe to depend on a supply of Tenants from this quarter the present season, but should any offer I will still send them to you.

Lyon's trial has produced a very strong sensation here, and many who have valued themselves on being *friends of order* and *Supporters of Government* admit that this is going too far, if to a few such instances of political persecution there should be added just and reasonable overtures of peace on the part of France. I think the whole bubble of imposition and deception will be blown up at once, and tho' the connection between foreign aggression and domestic tyranny is forced and unnatural. I hope that as the Tories would marry them, they will not be divorced until the peace and liberties of this Country are fully re-established.

I am Dear Sir with the highest esteem and regard Your Obt Sert

STES. THON. MASON

RC (DLC); at foot of text: "Mr Jefferson"; endorsed by TJ as received 29 Nov. 1798 and so recorded in SJL. Enclosure not identified, but see below.

The INCLOSED LETTER may have been one, now missing, that TJ entered in his epistolary record as "Anonymous," adding in brackets "Ogden of Connecticut." TJ's record in SJL implies that the letter, which he received on 29 Nov. 1798, had no date. Episcopal clergyman John C. Ogden did not live in Connecticut in 1798 but maintained connections there from an earlier period of residence. On 20 Sep. 1798 he wrote to George Washington to denounce "the doings of Calvinists in The United States," sending TJ a copy of the letter that is recorded in SJL as received on 13 Oct. but has not been found (Washington, *Papers, Ret. Ser.*, 3:27-9). On the 26th of that month TJ noted the receipt of an undated letter from "Anonymous. Connecticut." The reference to Connecticut, the similar SJL entry under 29 Nov. that names Odgen, and the scarcity of anonymous letters recorded in SJL in this period point to Odgen as the probable author of the letter received on 26 Oct. Then on 21 Nov. TJ received a letter of the 18th

from John Strode of Culpeper County "by Ogden." That notation strongly implies, given TJ's practices in SJL, that Ogden brought him Strode's letter. The clergyman was in Philadelphia by sometime in December 1798 with a petition asking for the pardon of Matthew Lyon. Mason was a supporter of Lyon, but it is not known if Ogden was the "acquaintance" whose letter Mason forwarded to TJ. According to SJL TJ received six letters on 29 Nov. in addition to Mason's and Ogden's, but none of the others seems likely to have been the one enclosed in the letter printed above (ANB, 16:634-5; TJ to Madison, 3 Jan. 1799; Ogden to TJ, 7 Feb. 1799).

From John Wayles Eppes

Nov: 24th. 1798.

I have just time by my Father who is setting out for Richmond to acknowledge the reciept of your letter and to return Marias thanks and my own for the arrangement you have made with my Sister—The bustle of a wedding and a large company have prevented our writing for some weeks—For the future I may venture to promise we shall not neglect our friends.

Maria has been very well since leaving Monticello until within a few days. A cold caught I believe from being too thinly clad has occasioned a slight pain in her shoulder & wrist—I have recommended to her an outer waistcoat of flannel which she will put on in a few days.

My Father and myself will be at Monticello on the 12 or 13th of December which I hope will be early enough to see you before you set out. At that time I shall be ready to meet any arrangement which you have made on my part as to the road—

Be kind enough to present us affectionately to Patsy & Mr. Randolph and to accept for the happiness of all at Monticello our sincere wishes—

I am in haste yours affectionately   J: W: EPPES

RC (ViU: Coolidge Deposit); endorsed by TJ as received 29 Nov. 1798 and so recorded in SJL.

YOUR LETTER: a missive from TJ to Eppes of 17 Nov. 1798, recorded in SJL,

has not been found. On 5 Nov. Eppes's sister, Martha Bolling Eppes, married Jerman Baker, probably the son of the Richmond attorney of the same name (VMHB, 15 [1908], 359; 33 [1925], 26).

From George Jefferson & Company

Dear Sir   Richmond 26th. Novr. 1798.

We received on the 21st. instant of Messrs. Pendleton & Lyons the sum of Five hundred Pounds—in part of the judgment obtained against them as Admors: of the Estate of John Robinson by Mr. Edmd. Randolph—and assigned by him to you.

We are Very respectfully Dear Sir Your Mt. Obt. servts.

GEO. JEFFERSON & CO.

RC (MHi); at foot of text: "Thomas Jefferson esqr. Monticello"; endorsed by TJ as received 29 Nov. and so recorded in SJL.

To John Taylor

Dear Sir   November 26. 98.

We formerly had a debtor & creditor account of letters on farming; but the high price of tobo. which is likely to continue for some short time, has tempted me to go entirely into that culture and in the mean time my farming schemes are in abeyance, and my farming fields at nurse against the time of my resuming them. but I owe you a political letter. yet the infidelities of the post office and the circumstances of the times are against my writing fully & freely, whilst my own dispositions are as much against writing mysteries, innuendos & half confidences. I know not which mortifies me most, that I should fear to write what I think, or my country bear such a state of things. yet Lyon's judges, and a jury of all nations, are objects of rational fear. we agree in all the essential ideas of your letter. we agree particularly in the necessity of some reform, and of some better security, for civil liberty. but perhaps we do not see the existing circumstances in the same point of view. there are many considerations dehors of the state which will occur to you without enumeration. I should not apprehend them if all was sound within. but there is a most respectable part of our state who have been enveloped in the X.Y.Z. delusion, and who destroy our unanimity for the present moment. this disease of the imagination will pass over, because the patients are essentially republican. indeed the Doctor is now on his way to cure it, in the guise of a taxgatherer. but give time for the medicine to work, & for the repetition of stronger doses which must be administered. the principle of the present majority is *excessive expence*; money enough to fill all their maws, or it will not be worth the risk of their supporting. they cannot borrow a dollar in Europe, nor above 2. or 3.

millions in America. this is not the fourth of the expences of this year, unprovided for. paper money would be perillous even to the paper-men. nothing then but excessive taxation can get us along. and this will carry reason & reflection to every man's door, and particularly in the hour of election. I wish it were possible to obtain a single amendment to our constitution; I would be willing to depend on that alone for the reduction of the administration of our government to the genuine principles of it's constitution; I mean an additional article taking from the federal government the power of borrowing. I now deny their power of making paper money or any thing else a legal tender. I know that to pay all proper expences within the year would, in case of war, be hard on us. but not so hard as ten wars instead of one. for wars would be reduced in that proportion. besides that the state governments would be free to lend *their credit* in borrowing quotas. [1]—for the present I should be for resolving the alien & sedition laws to be against the constitution & merely void, and for addressing the other states to obtain similar declarations: and I would not do any thing at this moment [2] which should commit us further, but reserve ourselves to shape our future measures or no measures, by the events which may happen. it is a singular phaenomenon, that while our state governments are the *very best in the world* without exception or comparison, our general government has, in the rapid course of 9. or 10. years, become more arbitrary, and has swallowed more of the public liberty than even that of England. I inclose you a column cut out of a London paper to shew you that the English tho charmed with our making their enemies our enemies, yet they blush and weep over our sedition law.—but I inclose you something more important. it is a petition for a reformation in the manner of appointing our juries, and a remedy against the *jury of all nations*, which is handing about here for signature and will be presented to your house. I know it will require but little ingenuity to make objections to the details of it's execution. but do not be discouraged by small difficulties make it as perfect as you can at a first assay, and depend on amending it's defects as they develope themselves in practice. I hope it will meet with your approbation & patronage. it is the only thing which can yield us a little present protection against the dominion of a faction, while circumstances are maturing for bringing & keeping the government in real unison with the spirit of their constituents. I am aware that the act of Congress has directed that juries shall be appointed by lot or otherwise as the laws *now* [at the date of the act] [3] in force in the several states provide. the New England states have always had them elected by their selectmen, who are elected by the people. several or most of the other states have a large number appointed [I do not know how] to attend, out of whom 12. for each cause are taken by lot. this provision of Congress will render it necessary for our Senators or Delegates to apply for an amendatory law, accomodated to that prayed for in the petition. in the mean time I would pass the law as if the amendatory one existed, in reliance that, our select jurors attending, the federal judge will under a sense of right, direct the juries to be taken from among them. if he does not, or if Congress [refuses?] the amendatory law, it will serve as eye water for their constituents. health, happiness, *safety*, & esteem to yourself and my ever honored & antient friend mr Pendleton. Adieu.

PrC (DLC); faint; at foot of first page: "Mr. Taylor." Enclosure: Petition to the General Assembly of Virginia, [2 or 3 Nov. 1798]. Other enclosure not identified, but see note below.

INFIDELITIES OF THE POST OFFICE: TJ had George Jefferson see that this letter was delivered safely to Taylor (George Jefferson to TJ, 3 Dec. 1798).

IDEAS OF YOUR LETTER: see Taylor to TJ, 25 June 1798. The COLUMN CUT OUT OF A LONDON PAPER enclosed by TJ has not been found, but on 3 Nov. 1798 the Philadelphia *Aurora* noted that the London *Morning Chronicle* had praised the strong position

taken by the United States in its dispute with France but chided Congress for wishing "to shackle the liberty of the press." Such a position was to be expected in Russia or France, but it was scandalous and "fatal to liberty" for a representative government "to infringe a grand principle in order to reach a few base incendiaries."

ACT OF CONGRESS: see TJ to Madison, 26 Oct. 1798.

[1] Sentence interlined.
[2] Preceding three words interlined in place of "[for the present?]."
[3] This and following set of brackets supplied by TJ.

To Wilson Cary Nicholas

TH:J TO COLO. W. C. NICHOLAS   Nov. 29. 98

The more I have reflected on the phrase in the paper you shewed me, the more strongly I think it should be altered. suppose you were to instead of the invitation to cooperate in the annulment of the acts, to make it an invitation: 'to concur with this commonwealth in declaring, as it does hereby declare, that the said acts are, and were ab initio—null, void and of no force, or effect' I should like it better. health happiness & Adieu.

PrC (DLC).

PAPER YOU SHEWED ME: TJ had examined the Virginia Resolutions that Madison had left with Nicholas for presentation to the Virginia General Assembly. Where Madison noted that the "acts aforesaid are unconstitutional" Nicholas added the phrase "and not law, but utterly null, void and of no force or effect," thus incorporating

TJ's suggestion for change. With this addition the resolutions were introduced by John Taylor on 10 Dec. and published in the Philadelphia *Aurora* on 22 Dec. During the debate from 13 to 21 Dec., however, the House of Delegates cut TJ's alteration and passed the resolutions with Madison's more moderate language (Madison, *Papers*, 17:185-91).

To Julian Ursin Niemcewicz

DEAR SIR   Monticello Nov. 30. 98.

By a derangement of our post we have been very long getting our
Northern letters this summer, but some uncommon delay happened to
yours, as by the time I recieved it, I had reason to hope daily to see you
here. in this expectation I did not answer it as soon as it came to hand;
but as the advance of the season now forbids further hope on that subject
I do myself the pleasure of acknoleging the receipt. I had also hoped to
have seen mr Mc.lure here, but he too has failed in making our tour. I
have no letter yet from our friend Genl. Kosciusko, but find from the
newspapers he is safely arriv[ed] in a country where a due value is set,
even by those in pow[er,] on his pure and republican zeal. however cold
to that merit some in this country have been, I can assure you that the
mass of our countrymen have the highest veneration & attachment to
his character. this state would have [felt a] peculiar sensibility if he had
thought proper to make it his residence. should the war between France
& Austria revive, I shall concieve great hope that your country will
again rise into the map of the earth and there seems reason to believe
that war is reviving. on this & other subjects I shall have the pleasure of
hearing your opinions in Philadelphia, for which place I set out in about
a fortnight. permit me only in the mean time to intreat that you feel no
anxiety on the [sub]ject of the reimbursement mentioned in your letter,
[and] [. . .] assurances of the sincere esteem with which I am [. . .] your
most obedt. humble servt   TH: JEFFERSON

PrC (DLC); mutilated, including a portion of the signature; at foot of text: "Mr.
Niemcewicz."

UNCOMMON DELAY: TJ received Niemcewicz's last letter, that of 3 Sep., twenty-four
days after it was written.

From Lord Somerville

                                              Board of Agriculture
                                              32 Sackville Street
SIR/   1. Decr. 98.

The Wheat which you had the goodness to send to the Board of Agriculture, arrived safe, and in very fine order and being immediately distributed to various Members of the Board much satisfaction, was expressed at its appearance, and we were promised accurate Reports of its,
cultivation and success.—When they come to hand I will have the pleasure of communicating the result. We have been much concerned in
England at the accounts recieved from America relative to the yellow

[591]

fever, but cordially hope soon to have better advices.—Give me leave to assure you that that any farther communications from you relative to Agriculture will give us a great satisfaction.

I have the honour to be, Sir/ Your obedient servant,

SOMERVILLE
President

RC (MHi); in clerk's hand, signed by Somerville; at foot of text: "His Excellency Thomas Jefferson &c &c &c"; endorsed by TJ as received 30 Mch. 1799 and so recorded in SJL. FC (Board of Agriculture Lb in University of Reading: Rural History Centre); in same hand; at head of text: "Jefferson T. Esqe."

From George Jefferson

DEAR SIR   Richmond 3d. Decr. 1798

[I] have merely to advise you that I h[ave] to night [delive]red your letter to Colo. Taylor; presuming from the purport of your note that it may be satisfactory to you to know he has received it.

I am Dear Sir Your Very Obt. Hbl: servt.   GEO. JEFFERSON

RC (MHi); stained; at foot of text: "Thos. Jefferson esqr. Monticello." Recorded in SJL as received 6 Dec. 1798.

LETTER TO COLO. TAYLOR: TJ to John Taylor, 26 Nov. 1798. TJ's NOTE to George Jefferson was not recorded in SJL and has not been found.

To George Jefferson

DEAR SIR   Monticello Dec. 4. 1798.

I have to acknolege the reciept of your letters of Oct. 15. Nov. 12. & 26. and I do not know whether I have before formally acknoleged those of July 23. & 30th.

I yesterday drew on you in favor of Joseph Brand or order for twenty six dollars thirty three cents at sight. I have this day [ordered?] mr Randolph to call on you for three hundred dollars, and as that letter goes by a servant, apt to drink, I mention to him that I think it safest to reserve the formal order to go in this letter by post and it is accordingly [en]closed. I shall in a few days draw on you in favor of Isaac Millar or order for a sum probably not exceeding forty pounds.   I set out for Philadelphia in about ten days, from which place you will hear from me the first week in January.   my tobo. from this place & Bedford will be sent to your care as usual, and early I hope.

I am with great esteem Dear Sir Your friend & servt

TH: JEFFERSON

PrC (MHi); blurred; endorsed by TJ in ink on verso. Enclosure: TJ's order on George Jefferson & Co. at Richmond, 4 Dec. 1798, to pay Thomas Mann Randolph $300 (PrC in MHi; pressed on same sheet as letter above).

TJ settled his account with JOSEPH BRAND for the purchase of lime. On 10 Dec. TJ wrote ISAAC MILLAR an order on George Jefferson & Co. for $100.30 (MB, 2:992, 994).

To Thomas Mann Randolph

DEAR SIR   Monticello Dec. 4. 1798.

Having pressing occasion here for three hundred dollars, which I have not been able to get for an order on Richmond, I must pray you to call on mr Jefferson for that sum on my account, and to bring it to me. as Jamey, the bearer of this, sometimes drinks and might lose his papers, it will be safer for me to send the formal order to mr Jefferson by post, which I now prepare with a letter to him. this letter in the mean time will satisfy him as you may leave Richmond before the next post arrives with the order.

I inclose a letter for Darmsdat, open for your perusal, because it is for a supply you were so good as to order in my absence. when read, be pleased to deliver it. extreme disappointments in recieving money for the nails made all last winter & summer, have left me this year under painful embarrasments even for small sums, for the paiment of which I had relied as usual on my nail-money.   Patsy writes to you & of course informs you all are well here. Duke finished your chimnies and there being no more work ready for him, quitted this morning to do a day or two's work here, & then some days work at mr Meriwethers. Mc.Gee will probably finish my roof about Christmas. I am Dear Sir

Your's affectionately   TH: JEFFERSON

P.S. I had engaged to be at Philadelphia on the 22d. and consequently should have set out from here the 15th. but if mr Eppes does not come till the 14th. I shall be somewhat later.

RC (DLC). Enclosure: see note below.

TJ's LETTER to Joseph Darmsdatt is not recorded in SJL and has not been found, but see George Jefferson to TJ, 23 July 1798, for TJ's payment of the account with the Richmond merchant.

Course of Reading for William G. Munford

[5 Dec. 1798]

Mathematics, Natl Philosophy Natural history till VIII. aclock in the morning	Law from VIII. to XII. the first [2 hours] or 3 1/2 [. . .] the [longer works] in the 1st. column and the [residue] reading [. . .] in the 2d column.	
	large works	tracts.
Pike's arithmetic	Coke's four institutes	Perkins
Mussenbroeck, or Martin's	Coke's repr	Doctor & Student
Phil. Brit. or Nicholson.	Vaughan	Lambard's L'eirenarchia
Astronomy. Ferguson.	Salkeld	Dalrymple's feudal tenures
Anatomy. Cheselden.	Ld. Raymond	Hale's history of the
Nat. history. Buffon.	Strange	common law
Chemistry. Lavoisier or	Burrow.	Gilbert's Law of Devises
Fourcroy	such other later reporters	Uses.
Geograph. Guthrie	as may be pointed out by	tenures
Morse.	gentlemen better	Rents
Agriculture	acquainted with them.	Distresses
Kirwan on soils	———	Ejectments
& Manures.	Kaim's Principles of Equity	Executions
Hale's vegetable statics.	Vernon's reports	Evidence
Home's Gentleman farmer.	Peere Williams	Buller's Nisi prius.
	Tracey Atkyns.	Sayer's Law of costs.
	Vezey.	Cuningham's Law of bills.
	Abridgment of cases in	Hinde's Practice in
	equity	Chancery
	Wythe's reports.	Schomberg's hist. of [Civ. l.]
	Washington's reports.	Molloy de Jure [Mar.]
		Vattel.

[Fine Arts] from [XII.] to II.	Moral Philosophy [from?] [. . .] & [night?]
Lowthe's grammar	Condorcet's Progress of the humn.
Blair's lectures	mind
Mason on Poetic [& prosaic]	Locke's essays.
[num]bers	Ld Kaim's natural religion
Sheridan on elocution	Hume's essays.
Kaim's elements of [crit]icism	[Helveti]us's works
Cicero's orations.	Middleton's works.
Bolingbroke all his works as the	Epictetus
[. . .]	Cicero's Philosophics.
Poe[try ad] libi[tum]	Seneca.
	&c. ad libitum

	History
Politicks	Millot's antient history
Lockes [government]	[Anach]arsis
Sydney.	Li[vy]
Montesquieu	Pol[ybius]
Beccaria	[Sallust]
The Federalist	[Caesar]
Chipman	[Tacitus]
Burgh's disquisitions	Suetonius. here fill up the chasm to
Callender's P[olitical Prog.]	Gibbons, from Eu[. . .] [to] [. . .]
Turgot's distribn [of riches].	Gibbons.
Sm[ith's wealth nat.]	
Ha[tsel's Prec. in H. Comm.]	[Ma]llet's Northern antiquities
	Millot's [Modern] history
	[Voltaire]
	[Robertson] [. . .] V
	[Watson on? Ph]ilips.
	[Millot's hist of] France
	[Vertot's hist of] [Spain]
	[Hist]ory of England [. . .]
	Tacitus Germania [Agricola]
	Hume [to the] end of H[enry VI]
	[E.] IV by Habington.
	[E. V.] ⎱ Sr Thomas More
	[R. III.] ⎰
	[H. VII. Ld Bacon]
	[H. VIII. Ld. Herbert Cherbury]
	[. . .]
	[the 1st. column?]
	[. . .]
	5th. column continued.
	E. VI. ⎱ by Godwin Bp. of Hereford.
	Mary ⎰
	Eliz. by Cambden
	the Stuarts [by] Mc.Caulay & Ludlow
	Wm. ⎱ by Burnet & Belsham
	Anne ⎰
	G. I. II. & III. by Belsham
	Baxter's general hist. of [Engld]
	Buchanan's hist. of Scotld
	Robertson's [Mary]
	Wynne's hist. of Ireland
	Robertson's America.
	Douglass['s] America.
	Stith's history of Virginia
	Keith's history of Virginia

PrC (MHi); entirely in TJ's hand; undated; faint, with text in brackets supplied from FC; arranged as five columns across the page, TJ carrying the "History" entries

5 DECEMBER 1798

over from the end of the last column to the lower portion of the first column below the books on agriculture (those entries have been restored to the "History" column in the table above but TJ's notations directing the reader from the one column to the other have been retained). FC (same); entirely in TJ's hand; endorsed by him: "Munford Wm. Green course of reading"; first column labeled: "—VIII. Mathematics & Nat. Phylos."; second and third columns labeled: "Law. VIII—XII"; fourth column headed "to II," with divisions for "Fine arts," "Politicks," and "Moral Philos."; fifth column labeled "History. at night." Probably enclosed in TJ to Munford, 5 Dec. 1798 (recorded in SJL but not found; see below).

The recipient of this list was apparently William Green Munford (c. 1781?-1804), the fourth and youngest son of William Greene Munford (d. 1786) of Charles City County, who served as county sheriff, as a militia officer, and in other prominent positions in the county. The published version of the senior Munford's will gives the father's middle name as "Greene" and the son's as "Green," but it is not certain if the distinction in spelling was intentional. TJ used both spellings of the son's name almost interchangeably (wmq, 1st ser., 11 [1903], 260-1; William J. Van Schreeven et al., eds., Revolutionary Virginia: The Road to Independence, 7 vols. [Charlottesville, 1973-83], 2:201, 218, 269-70, 289; 3:218; 4:95; 6:316; and above in this series, Vol. 3:542-3; Vol. 4:304, 621, 626; Vol. 5:207, 418-19). In the spring of 1799, Carlo Bellini, a member of the faculty at the College of William and Mary, referred to the recipient of this list as "Monford" and called him "an ornament to human nature." As TJ became acquainted with young Munford he regretted that he could not supervise the young man's intellectual pursuits in person. Aaron Burr, who in October 1800 thought that Munford appeared to be "about 18 or 19 Years of age," found him "to possess handsome talents & to be modest, amiable & well informed" (Kline, Burr, 1:451; Bellini to TJ, 1 Apr., TJ to Bellini, 24 Apr. 1799).

According to SJL Munford first wrote to TJ on 20 Nov. 1798, but TJ did not receive that letter, which has not been found, until 14 Dec. There must have been earlier contact, however, for prior to the 14th TJ sent

Munford "a letter on the general subject of a course of reading," which has not been located but was most likely a communication listed in TJ's epistolary record under 5 Dec. 1798. That letter may have included the list printed above. TJ continued to advise Munford on his studies, personally scouring Philadelphia's bookshops for books to send to the young man, and in June 1799 he wrote an epistle to Munford that has been considered the epitome of TJ's thought and expression on education, scientific progress, and the role of intelligent young men in the republic (Thomas Jefferson on Science and Freedom: The Letter to the Student William Greene Munford, June 18, 1799, foreword by Julian P. Boyd [Worcester, 1964], 22; TJ to Munford, 27 Feb., 18 June 1799).

Ironically, though, while Munford's sincerity in soliciting his famous mentor's advice cannot be gauged, the young man applied his talents and channeled his ambition in directions that TJ surely did not anticipate. Not everyone at the College of William and Mary shared Bellini's exalted view of Munford, and late in 1800 one of the skeptics, Bishop James Madison, reported that the young scholar had returned from an overseas journey marked by "the most abominable swindling." TJ, now cautious, noted that Munford had appeared in Washington with " a plan as incomprehensible as it was unworthy" (Bishop James Madison to TJ, 24 Dec. 1800; TJ to Madison, 9 May 1801). Munford was now "William G. Montfort." Before arriving in the capital he had gone to New York with references from Horatio Gates and Colonel Samuel Griffin and presented himself to Burr as "abandoned by his family & friends"—he had, Burr attested, "fallen under my protection." It may be that "Montfort," who had been in France and now used a francophone version of his family name, was the source of Alexander Hamilton's declaration as "a fact" to Gouverneur Morris in January 1801 that Burr was "in frequent & close conference with a Frenchman who is suspected of being an Agent of the French Government." But sometime that month the young Virginian abruptly departed, as Burr reported to Albert Gallatin, "apparently in some agitation without assigning to me any cause and without disclosing to me his intentions or Views or even whither he was going, except that he proposed to pass through Washington." In the capital the young man stayed in the same hotel as TJ, lobbied members of the House of Representatives to vote for Burr to break the Electoral College tie for the presidency, and claimed to be "Epaminondas," whose letters, encouraging Federalists to support Burr, appeared in the *New York Gazette*. He also declared that he had seen a letter in TJ's hand that denigrated Burr. Although TJ had received the bishop's warning about Munford, when he wrote to Burr about the purported letter on 1 Feb. 1801 he betrayed no suspicion that the informant's veracity might be questioned. That circumspection seems more likely to have been the product of political wariness than of naïveté, for only after Burr wrote to Gallatin and TJ on 12 Feb. would TJ know that the New Yorker did not claim Munford as his protégé (Kline, *Burr*, 1:451, 494-5, 500-2; Syrett, *Hamilton*, 25:314-16; James Cheetham, *A View of the Political Conduct of Aaron Burr, Esq. Vice-President of the United States* [New York, 1802], 66-9).

Munford went to Dublin in 1802 and, still known as W. G. Montfort, subsequently made his way to Bordeaux, France, where he died of smallpox in December 1804. Among the dead man's effects the U.S. consul at Bordeaux, William Lee, found three unidentified letters that he sent to TJ without comment—very likely TJ's letters to Munford of 27 Feb., 18 June, and 16 Aug. 1799. Lee, who surmised from Munford's papers that he had, while in Ireland, probably worked for the French government, also reported that before he died Munford expressed great remorse for his conduct (Kline, *Burr*, 1:451-2n, 494n; William Lee to TJ, 18 Dec. 1804).

On at least one other occasion TJ framed out a course of study in columns, assigning books by topic to particular times of the student's day. The first column of that list contains 14 works on politics for the period before 8:00 A.M. The third column includes 14 works on law arranged in three groups, to occupy the time from 8:00 to 11:00 A.M., and the second column lists four works on mathematics, "to be taken up after the course of law is gone through, & to occupy those hours." In the fourth column TJ listed a dozen authors on moral philosophy allocated to the hour between 11:00 A.M. and noon. Twenty titles on history, to be read "P.M.," occupy the fifth column. The next column is blank. Finally, in the seventh column 14 authors, including Ariosto, Seneca, Euripides, and Tasso, appear under the heading "Entertt." (i.e., "Entertainment"), which TJ also assigned to the "P.M." period of the day (MS in MHi; entirely in TJ's hand; undated). Sometime probably before the death of George III in 1820 TJ also drew up a list of works on English history similar to that in the "course of reading" printed above. Following a general entry for "Saxon & Danish" history, TJ listed the abbreviated names of the monarchs of England from Edward I through George III. He indicated the year in which each reign (except the last) ended. Using braces to show which authors chronicled which eras, TJ in several cases also noted the reigns in which the authors themselves lived (MS in same; entirely in TJ's hand; undated).

From Henry Tazewell

DEAR SIR   Kings mill 7th. Decr. 1798.

My intention was to have been in Philadelphia on the first day of the present Session of Congress, if my health would have allowed me—But an autumnal fever with which I was attacked last August immediately after my return home, has not permited me to enjoy one day of health since that time—As the Winter comes on I hope I shall get the better of it—but it cannot be, that I shall be able to undertake the Journey until after 'Xmas, unless some occasion more valuable than my life requires my presence in the Senate—Towards the close of the last Session an order was passed in the Senate to enable that body to send for absent Members under grievous penalties—If this should be attempted to be executed as to me—I beg the favour of you to state my situation, and to assure the Senate that so soon as I am fit for the Journey, I will hasten to the place of my duty—Any political occurence worth knowing would be acceptable to me in my Confinement, and therefore if your leizure will permit, and any such events turn up, you will oblige me by communicating them—

You know our Ass: met last Monday—I hear that the Speaker & Clerk are reelected, the former by a Majority of 14 & I know nothing of the state of the latter vote—whether this is to be considered as a tryal of the strength of the political parties I have not heard—but my belief is, that it affords no just criterion. The election of a Senator will give a better evidence, and there is every reason to believe that the british party are using their utmost exertions to displace me—I have not heard when the election will be made, nor what the probable result maybe—If however I am discontinued, you will probably not see me this Winter in Philadelphia, as it will be a long and hazardous Journey for a short Session—

I am with great respect & esteem Your mo. obt.

HENRY TAZEWELL

RC (DLC); endorsed by TJ as received 15 Jan. 1799 and so recorded in SJL.

On 25 June 1798 the Senate amended the rule which required that a senator obtain leave before an absence and gave the sergeant at arms the power TO SEND FOR ABSENT MEMBERS at any time during the session if a quorum was not present. The order was to be carried out at the absent senator's expense unless he gave a sufficient excuse for non-attendance (JS, 2:517-18; PW, 133, 366).

The Virginia House of Delegates met on 3 Dec. and as its first order of business proceeded to elect a SPEAKER & CLERK. According to the House records, the Republicans did not nominate anyone to stand against John Stewart, who had served as clerk since 1795. John Taylor, however, nominated Wilson Cary Nicholas as qualified to discharge the duties of speaker against Federalist nominee John Wise, who had served as speaker since 1794. Wise was REELECTED. By joint ballot of the House and Senate, Tazewell was reelected as a United States SENATOR on 12 Dec. but not without EXERTIONS TO DISPLACE him. On the previous day his opponents had attempted to delay the ballot until 1 Jan. in order to investigate the charge that Tazewell had been overheard to declare in Philadelphia in the summer of 1797 "that if the French nation should land an army in these states, he would join the said army against the government of the United States." The resolution to postpone the vote was defeated, 53 yeas to 98 nays (JHD, Dec. 1798-Jan. 1799, [3], 18-20; Leonard, *General Assembly*, xv-xvi, 211).

To Mary Jefferson Eppes

MY DEAR MARIA   Monticello Dec. 8. 98.

I wrote to mr Eppes three weeks ago. immediately after the date of that letter Lucy increased her family. she is doing well except as to her breasts. the one so much out of order when you went away, still continues in the same state, and the other threatens to rise also, which would entirely prevent her giving suck. she could not be moved in their present condition. I expect to set out for Philadelphia within ten days, within which time I hope to see the two mr Eppes's here. mr Randolph is not yet returned from Richmond, tho' now expected in a day or two. his family is here & all well. Ellen continues[1] as much so as a weak digestion will permit. our house I hope will all be covered in the course of three or four weeks more so as to be out of the way of suffering, but Buck's leaving us, without laying any more floors, has prevented our getting the use of any other room. we shall hear from you I hope by mr Eppes and learn that you are well, and all the good family at Eppington. present me to them affectionately and tell[2] [mrs] Eppes [. . .] a friendly & family visit [. . .][3] let me hear from you [once again by the?] [. . .][4] be assured my dear of my [. . .] tender love, and [. . .] anxiety for your [health] & happiness. Adieu affectionately   TH: JEFFERSON

P.S. I presume that before [you recieve this] the gentlemen will be [on their] way here.

RC (ViU); bottom portion of page torn away, supplied from PrC. PrC (CSmH); blurred and faint; endorsed by TJ in ink on verso.

For TJ's letter to John Wayles EPPES, see Eppes to TJ of 24 Nov. 1798. TJ transferred the ownership of LUCY to his daughter Mary at the time of her marriage (Marriage

Settlement for Mary Jefferson, 12 Oct. 1797).

[1] TJ here canceled "tolerably."
[2] Remainder of RC torn away.
[3] Approximately seven words illegible in PrC.
[4] Four or more words illegible in PrC.

Statement of Account with William Davenport

1797.	William Davenport in acct with Th:J.	Dr. £ s d	Cr.
Aug. 12.	To cash to William Burton 10. D.	3– 0– 0	
	To a broad axe 13/ narrow do. 10/6		
	To jumping a broad axe 4/6 do. narrow do. 3/6 }	1–11– 6	

	Dr.	Cr.
31. To a poll axe. 10/6		
Sep. 16. To a tiller 2/ Sep. 20. laying an axe 4/	0–16– 6	
4. To order on P. Lott for 30. D.	9– 0– 0	
21. To nails. 84. ℔ VId. @ 12½ d £4–7–6		
60. ℔ XVId. nails 10. ℔. XVI. brads @ 10½ d 3–1–3	7– 8– 9	
23. To half a beef bought of McGehee (11. D. for 5. qrs.) 86¼ ℔	1– 6– 6	
30. To pd Rogers for 122 ℔ beef @ 3½ d (2 forequarters)	1–15– 7	
√ By 8. galls. whiskey @ 5/		2–0–0
Oct. 5. To pd Chas. McGehee 2 qrs. beef 126½ ℔ @ 3 d.	1–11– 7	
To 8. chissels £1–2 2. hammers 9	1–11– 0	
√ 16. by 8. gallons whiskey		2–0–0
20. to pd Frances Taliaferro on your order	12– 0– 0	
27. to 425¾ ℔ beef from Kindred (part of 820. ℔)[1]	4–18– 8	
to a pair of pothooks	2– 6	
Nov. 19. to your order in favor of P. Lott	6–10– 3	
Dec. 2. to your order in favor of F. Walker 100. d	30– 0– 0	
to my further assumpsit to mr Lott	5– 9– 9	
4. to Thomas Carr[2]	20– 0– 0	
1798.		
May. 3. to your order on me in favr. P. Lott 110. D	33– 0– 0	
July 9. to cash	3–12– 0	
to a saw tiller 4/6 hatchet 7/6 from George	0–12– 0	
24. to jumping a broadaxe	0– 3– 0	
Sep. 8. to allowed Colo. Bell in acct[3]	4– 0– 0	
Sep. 14. to 72. ℔ beef @ 3½ d	1– 1– 0	
√ by flooring plank		
15. to Thos. C. Fletcher's order on you	8– 1– 3	
29. to nails to Clifton Rodes on your order	3–19– 6½	
Oct. 16. to your order in favr. James Starke	1–16– 0	
Nov. 22. to nails to Clifton Rodes 26 ℔ X. @ 11½ d	1– 4–11	
to ord. for mr Lott	3– 0– 0	
to cash from mr Millar	3– 0– 0	
Dec. 10. to do. do.	5–15– 6	

MS (MHi); entirely in TJ's hand.

As TJ's correspondence with his daughters and with Thomas Mann Randolph from February through May 1798 indicates, during that period TJ wanted William Davenport of Albemarle County to see to the preparation and installation of sheathing and shingles to roof the main house at Monticello, and then to do the same for the floor planking. Davenport was to cut the roofing materials from timber on TJ's Pouncey's tract property. Although by November 1798 TJ had given the roofing work to James McGee, Davenport still furnished planks for the floors. An entry for the 12 Aug. 1797 transaction in the account above is Davenport's earliest appearance in TJ's financial memoranda. TJ and Davenport continued to have a variety of transactions at least until late 1800, TJ noting in his financial memoranda under 15 Nov. of that year that "On settlement with Wm. Davenport for sawing, I am this day in his debt £65–2–10½" (MB, 2:992, 1001, 1027, 1029; Martha Jefferson Randolph to TJ, 8 Feb. 1799; Craven Peyton to TJ, 6 Nov. 1801). None of the correspondence between TJ and Davenport has been found. Letters from TJ of 14, 22 Feb., 3, and 9 May 1798 are recorded in SJL, as well as letters Davenport wrote to TJ on 5 Mch. (received 13 Mch.) and 22 Apr. 1798 (received from Charlottesville on 1 May). Also

missing but recorded in SJL is a letter from TJ to Davenport of 7 July 1799 concerning an order from TJ to George Jefferson for $200 payable to Davenport (see also TJ to George Jefferson, 12 July 1799; MB, 2:1003).

The first purchase of BEEF recorded above was from William McGehee of Albemarle County; the purchase on 5 Oct. 1797 was from Charles McGehee (MB, 2:970, 971). For the transaction involving Francis WALKER, see TJ's letter to Walker of 21 Dec. 1797.

THOMAS CARR, a merchant in Charlottesville, was a distributor for TJ's nails (MB, 2:939). Letters from TJ to him dated 4 Jan. 1796 and 19 July 1798, recorded in SJL, are now missing.

[1] Entry written over partially erased text. Below this entry TJ wrote and canceled: "30. to assumed to F. Walker for half a beef 228 ℔ @ 4d 3–16– 0."
[2] Line inserted.
[3] Line inserted.

From John Taylor

J. TAYLOR TO THE VICE PRESIDENT.   [before 11 Dec. 1798]
It would be happy indeed for us, if agriculture and farming still continued to be interesting subjects—but alas! can we, when our house is on fire, be solicitous to save the kittens? How long is it to burn, or will it ever be extinguished? I would be almost content to save a single apartment.

If a sufficient spirit had appeared in our legislature, it was my project, by law, to declare the unconstitutional laws of congress void, and as that would have placed the State & general government at issue, to have submited the point to the people in convention, as the only reform. This measure seemed to be opposed properly to all those, which have invested one man with despotic powers; for as it was the custom of the Roman aristocracy, whenever it felt itself in danger, to appoint a dictator, to see that the commonwealth sustained no injury, so the same office seemed to be peculiarly [1] proper for a convention in a popular republic. Besides it was a measure calculated to attach to the real republicans, the physical power of the state. It was however only a provisional project, and as you seem to disaprove of pushing on at present to this ultimate

[601]

effort, I will forbear the attempt. Indeed there is yet but little prospect of its success.

An unsuccessful attempt was made to displace our speaker & clerk, and yet I believe it will produce good effects now and better in future. As however the disapointment might cause a damp on one side, and strengthen the other from the sympathy of exultation, it seemed right to me to strike out immediately some proposition, which would rally principles into a mass, and furnish matter of private discussion without looking back. Accordingly on the next day I asked leave to bring in a bill "to secure the freedom of debate & proceedings in the assembly" upon the principle and precedent of the British Law of Ph: & Mary, and up[on] that occasion hazarded some observations on the sedition law in general, & its tendency to consolidation in particular, by converting the state legislatures into simple organs of a superior power. The adversary was taken by surprise, acted distractedly, and some impression appeared to be made. The movement is very likely to succeed, because it applies force ad homines, and if it should succeed, it will be a bond and security for farther successes.

The idea of reforming our jury establishment, had struck me some time past, but was deserted on account of the difficulties which presented themselves, and the opinion that congress would disregard it. But I will try to forge something on the subject, altho' it should exhibit the rudeness of a first essay. Would it not suffice to confine it to pleas of the —— crown?

Some resolutions have appeared here from Kentucky, not passed, but on the Eve of passing that Legislature—as soon as they appear authenticated, the great effort will be directed to their approbation in the words of a *response*.

I would not wish my inclination to be gratified by the slightest risque on your part—it is obvious that the common cause would thence also be exposed to injury—but whatever can be safely said, will be highly gratifying.

Health and happiness!

RC (DLC); undated, but endorsed by TJ as received from Richmond 11 Dec. and recorded in SJL under that date; TJ later added "probably 99." to the endorsement.

For the election of the SPEAKER & CLERK, see Henry Tazewell to TJ, 7 Dec. 1798. To preserve the FREEDOM OF DEBATE in the general assembly and thus "secure the liberty of the people," Taylor introduced a bill calling for a fine and imprisonment for anyone who caused the arrest and prosecution of a member of the state Senate or House of Delegates for "any words spoken or written" or proposition made in his representative capacity. In case of arrest or imprisonment on charges related to their legislative duties, members would be able to obtain a writ of habeas corpus for their immediate release. The bill passed on 28 Dec. 1798 (Shepherd, *Statutes*, 2:150-1; JHD, Dec. 1798-Jan. 1799, [3]).

[1] Taylor here canceled "necessary."

From James Madison

DEAR SIR   Decr. 11. 1798

According to your favor by Mr. Richardson, I expect the pleasure of seeing you in the course of the present week. Be so good as to bring a memorandum from your nailery of the amount of my debt to it. I had hoped that you were possessed of the aid of Mr. Chuning & his young men, but the Bearer Mr. W. Whitten tells me the contrary. Mr. C. left this saturday was two weeks, & promised to ride up to Monticello the day following. It has been impossible to spare L. Whitten. He has been under the spur to keep the way prepared for the Plasterers, and to finish off a number of indispensable jobbs always overlooked till the execution is called for.—The Fredg paper of the 7th. inst: contains the official confirmation from Nelson of the destruction of the French fleet as first brought from Cadiz. Adieu Affecly.   Js. MADISON JR

Please to forward the inclosed safely.

[*Note by TJ:*]
[. . .] he inclosed me a draught on Moylan with orders to apply £48–11–3. balance for nails.
———
see Memm. book. 1799. Jan. 9. J. Barnes credits me 161.875 = £48–11–3 for mr Madison.

RC (ViU); with TJ's note on verso made in two undated sittings, divided by horizontal rule; initial line of note missing due to frayed margin at top of page; endorsed by TJ as received 13 Dec. 1798 and so recorded in SJL. Enclosure not found.

YOUR FAVOR: TJ to Madison, 17 Nov. 1798. PLEASURE OF SEEING YOU: TJ set out for Philadelphia on 18 Dec. and stayed at Montpelier during the first night of his trip (MB, 2:995; Madison, *Papers*, 17:xxvii).

Admiral Horatio Nelson's DESTRUCTION OF THE FRENCH FLEET occurred in the Battle of the Nile on 1 Aug. Nelson captured or destroyed 11 of the 13 French ships anchored at Aboukir Bay, thus isolating and cutting off supplies for Bonaparte's forces in Egypt (Scott and Rothaus, *Historical Dictionary*, 1:80-1; T. C. W. Blanning, *The French Revolutionary Wars, 1787-1802* [London, 1996], 189-200). For Madison's DRAUGHT ON MOYLAN, see Madison to TJ, 29 Dec. 1798.

To George Jefferson

DEAR SIR   Monticello Dec. 17. 1798.

I recieved by mr Randolph the 300. D. according to order. the money you recieved from mr Pendleton being to be trans[ferred] to Philadelphia for [. . .], I have found means of ordering here a considerable proportion of it by the draughts which are stated below which you will be pleased to honor when presented. I start for Philadelphia tomorrow where I sh[ould?] be glad to recieve a state of our account. I am Dear [Sir]

    Your affectionate friend & servt   Th: Jefferson

		£	s	d
Dec. [10] order in favor of	Isaac Millar for	35.	1.	10
13 do.	Richard Richardson	46.	1.	0
[16] do.	Wm Davenport	75.	0.	0
[17] do.	H[astings] Marks	44.	7.	2
[17] do.	Julius [Clarkson]	15.	0.	0
		£215.10.	0	

PrC (MHi); faint and torn, with bracketed dates and names in postscript supplied from TJ's financial records (MB, 2:994); endorsed by TJ in ink on verso.

TJ paid RICHARDSON for his work at Monticello and for the hire of three slaves. He still owed him £24.3. A statement of

TJ's account with William DAVENPORT is printed at 10 Dec. 1798. TJ's payment to MARKS included the balance of Thomas Mann Randolph's debt for the purchase of Critta. TJ probably paid CLARKSON, a merchant at Milton, for his share in the clearing of the Rivanna River from Milton to Charlottesville (MB, 2:994).

To Thomas Mann Randolph

Th:J. to TMR.   Thursday. Dec. 20. 98.

Mr. Dinsmore asked me to lend him Gibb's Rules for drawing, and I forgot to lay it out for him. it is a large thin folio, lying uppermost of a parcel of books laid horizontally on the shelf close to my turning chair. be so good as to give it to him. it is bound in rough calf, and one lid off.   should mr Madison send for my diamond it is in the upper part of the tool chest, in the cell adjacent to the lock of the box.—I here met with the President's speech which was certainly went to you by the last post. it is war and no war. one discovers the wish without the cause for waging it. I endeavored to arrange my matters so as to prevent your being troubled with them as I am conscious you have been. yet should any thing unexpected embarras them I must just give you the Consular commission 'to see that the republic recieves no damage.' I reached this the 2d. day, & go off this morning. my love to my dear Martha, & the little ones, & sincere affection to yourself. Adieu.

RC (DLC); endorsed by Randolph as received 21 Dec. 1798. Not recorded in SJL.

For James Gibbs's RULES FOR DRAWING (London, 1738), see Sowerby, No. 4184.

PRESIDENT'S SPEECH: Adams delivered his annual message to Congress on 8 Dec. In

it he praised the "manly sense of national honor, dignity, and independence" which had arisen in the country to defy French aggressions. He noted, on the one hand, the failure of negotiations with France, but on the other described France as appearing solicitous to avoid a rupture with the United

States. Adams affirmed, however, that until France changed policies with regard to neutral shipping and her diplomatic stance "to prescribe the qualifications" of United States ministers, the country would continue to build its defenses. He reiterated his position that "to send another minister, without more determinate assurances that he would be received, would be an act of humiliation, to which the United States ought not to submit." The president concluded that vigorous war preparations would alone give the United States "an equal treaty" with France and ensure its observance. He then advocated that Congress take further measures to strengthen the naval establishment (JS, 2:558-61).

TJ REACHED Fredericksburg on 19 Dec., the second day of his trip to Philadelphia.

To Martha Jefferson Randolph

MY DEAR MARTHA   Philadelphia Dec. 27. 98.

I reached Fredericksburg the day after I left you, and this place on Christmas-day, having (thanks to my pelisse) felt no more sensation of cold on the road than if I had been in a warm bed. nevertheless I got a small cold which brought on an inflammation in the eyes, head ach &c so that I kept within doors yesterday & only took my seat in Senate to-day. I have as yet had little opportunity of hearing news; I only observe in general that the republican gentlemen whom I have seen consider the state of the public mind to be fast advancing in their favor. whether their opponents will push for war or not is not yet developed. no business is as yet brought into the Senate, & very little into the other house: so that I was here in good time. I shall be at a loss how to direct to you hereafter, uncertain as I am whether you will leave home & where you will be. on this subject you must inform me. present me affectionately to mr Randolph, and kiss all the little ones for me, not forgetting *Elleanoroon*. be assured yourself of my constant and tender love. Adieu my ever dear Martha.

RC (NNPM). PrC (ViU); with dateline overwritten in ink by TJ; note by TJ in ink in top-left margin: "written with common ink," indicating that he had used two different inks in the letter, the last four sentences and closing being much clearer in the PrC; in ink at foot of text: "Mrs. Martha Randolph"; endorsed by TJ in ink on verso.

From James Madison

DEAR SIR   Decr. 29. 1798

I inclose a draught on Genl. Moylan out of which you will be pleased to pay yourself the price of the Nails £48–11.3. Va. Cy. to let Barnes have as much as will discharge the balance I owe him, & to let what may remain lie till I write you again.

The P.'s speech corresponds pretty much with the idea of it which was preconceived. It is the old song with no other variation of the tune than the spirit of the moment was thought to exact. It is evident also that he rises in his pitch as the Ecchoes of the S. & H. of R. embolden him, & particularly that he seizes with avidity that of the latter flattering his vigilance & firmness agst. illusory attempts on him, without noticing, as he was equally invited, the allusion to his pacific professions. The Senate as usual perform their part with alacrity in counteracting peace by dextrous provocations to the pride & irritability of the French Govt. It is pretty clear that their answer was cooked in the same shop, with the Speech. The finesse of the former calculated to impose on the public mind here, & the virulence of the latter still more calculated to draw from France the war, which can not be safely declared [1] on this side, taste strongly of the genius of that subtle & malignant [2] partizan of England who has contributed so much to the public misfortunes. It is not difficult to see how A. could be made a puppet thro' the instrumentality of creatures around him, nor how the Senate could be managed by similar artifice. I have not seen the Result of the discussions at Richmond on the Alien & Sedition laws. It is to be feared their zeal may forget some considerations which ought to temper their proceedings. Have you ever considered thoroughly the distinction between the power of the *State*, & that of *the Legislature*, on questions relating to the federal pact. On the supposition that the former is clearly the ultimate Judge of infractions, it does not follow that the latter is the legitimate organ; especially as a Convention was the organ by which the Compact was made. This was a reason of great weight for using general expressions that would leave to other States a choice of all the modes possible of concurring in the substance, and would shield the Genl. Assembly agst. the charge of Usurpation in the very act of protesting agst the usurpations of Congress.   I have not forgot my promise of McGeehee's prices, but cd. not conveniently Copy them for the present mail.

  Always affy yrs.   Js. Madison Jr

RC (DLC: Madison Papers); with calculations of price of nails in TJ's hand below endorsement (see below); endorsed by TJ as received 5 Jan. 1799 and so recorded in SJL. Enclosure not found.

TJ recorded the PRICE OF THE NAILS on 9 Jan. 1799, converting the amount in Virginia currency to $161.875 (MB, 2:996).

P.'S SPEECH: see TJ to Thomas Mann Randolph, 20 Dec. 1798. On 14 Dec. the House of Representatives delivered their response to the annual message. They upheld Adams's desire for VIGILANCE & FIRMNESS with France noting that negotiations should not take place as long as France persisted in the enforcement of decrees hostile to the rights of the United States and that whether or not negotiations were resumed "vigorous preparations for war" were indispensable. The House message concluded with an ALLUSION to the president's PACIFIC PROFESSIONS, encouraging the chief executive "to make known to the world that justice on the part of France will annihilate every obstacle to the restoration of a friendly intercourse" and that the United States would "respect the sacred rights of embassy." In his response Adams reiterated that "no illusory professions" would seduce him to abandon "the rights which belong to the United States as a free and independent nation" (JHR, 3:407-10). The Senate's response to the president's message, delivered on 12 Dec., gave no support for PEACE initiatives and instead expanded upon the reasons why further negotiations with France were harmful, noting that French initiatives were "designed to separate the people from their government, and to bring about by intrigue that which open force could not effect." In his response Adams commented upon the "officious interference of individuals, without public character or authority"—clearly with Logan's mission to France in mind—and queried whether the Senate ought not to take measures to prevent individuals from interfering in public affairs, because they, through "secret correspondence" and other means, "intended to impose upon the people, and separate them from their government" (JS, 2:562-3).

PARTIZAN OF ENGLAND: Alexander Hamilton.

For Madison's fears concerning the DISCUSSIONS AT RICHMOND on the Virginia Resolutions, see TJ to Wilson Cary Nicholas, 29 Nov. 1798.

[1] MS: "delared."
[2] Preceding ampersand and word canceled, but probably by a later hand.

To Mary Jefferson Eppes

MY DEAR MARIA   Philadelphia Jan. 1. 99.

I left Monticello the 18th. of Dec. and arrived here to breakfast on the 25th. having experienced no accident or inconvenience except a slight cold, which brought back the inflammation of my eyes and still continues it, though so far mended as to give hopes of it's going off soon. I took my place in Senate before a single bill was brought in or other act of business done, except the Address which is exactly what I ought to have nothing to do with. and indeed I might have staid at home a week longer without missing any business, for of the last 11. days the Senate have met only on 5. and then little or nothing to do. however when I am to write on politics I shall address my letter to mr Eppes. to you I had rather indulge the effusions of a heart which tenderly loves you, which builds it's happiness on your's, and feels in every other object but little interest. without an object here which is not alien to me, & barren of every delight, I turn to your situation with pleasure, in the midest of a good family which loves you, & merits all your love. go on, my dear, in cultivating the invaluable possession of their affections. the circle of our nearest connections is the only one in which a faithful and lasting affection can be found, one which will adhere to us under all changes & chances. it is therefore the only soil on which it is worth while to bestow much culture. of this truth you will become more convinced every day you advance into life. I imagine you are by this time about removing to Mont-blanco. the novelty of setting up house-keeping will, with all it's difficulties, make you very happy for a while. it's delights however pass away in time, and I am in hopes that by the spring of the year they will be no obstacle to your joining us at Monticello. I hope I shall on my return find such preparations made as will enable me rapidly to get one room after another prepared for the accomodation of our friends, and particularly of any who may be willing to accompany or visit you there. present me affectionately to mrs and Mr. Eppes, father & son, and all the family. remember how pleasing your letters will be to me, and be assured of my constant & tender love. Adieu my ever dear Maria.

Yours affectionately   TH: JEFFERSON

RC (ViU); addressed: "Mrs. Maria Eppes at Eppington in Chesterfield by the Petersburg mail"; franked.

TJ took his PLACE IN SENATE on 27 Dec. One ACT OF BUSINESS that occupied the Senate during his absence was the development of procedures for William Blount's impeachment trial, which opened on 17 Dec. according to schedule. Court sessions were held on 18 and 24 Dec. but then did not resume until 3 Jan. 1799 (JS, 2:563, 565-8, 3:483-8). See Notes on William Blount's Impeachment Trial, printed at 5 Jan. 1799. TJ's role as vice president in delivering the Senate's ADDRESS in response to President Adams's first message at the opening of Congress on 16 May 1797 is examined at Jefferson and the Senate to John Adams, [23 May 1797].

From George Jefferson & Company

DEAR SIR,   Richmond 1st. Janr. 1799.

We now forward your account—which has been delayed for some days, as we wish'd to make it up to the end of the year; and as we were desirous too, that the drafts mentioned in yours of the 17th. ultimo should be included. those in favor of Mr. Marks & Mr. Clarkson have not yet appeared.   We received yesterday of Mr. Pendleton, as you will observe from the account, the further sum of One thousand dollars.

We are most respectfully, & very sincerely Dear Sir, Your Obt. humble: servts.   GEO. JEFFERSON & CO.

RC (MHi); at foot of text: "Thomas Jefferson esqr. Philadelphia"; endorsed by TJ as received 8 Jan. 1799 and so recorded in SJL. Enclosure not found.

Notes on Comments by John Adams

[1-14 Jan. 1799]

In a conversation with Dr. Ewen, who told the Presidt one of his sons was an Aristocrat the other a Democrat, the P. asked if it was not the youngest who was the Democrat. yes, said Ewen. well said the Presidt. a boy of 15. who is not a democrat is good for nothing. & he is no better who is a democrat at 20. Ewen told Hurt, and Hurt told me.

MS (DLC: TJ Papers, 105:17951); entirely in TJ's hand, including date added in margin: "1799. Jan."; written on same sheet as, and previous to, Notes on Comments by Timothy Pickering and John Adams, 14 Jan. 1799.

DR. EWEN: John Ewing. The Reverend John HURT, a former chaplain of Virginia and U.S. troops, was an acquaintance and political supporter of TJ (Madison, *Papers*, 13:233; 17:387, 388n; Heitman, *Dictionary*, 1:559; Hurt to TJ, 31 Aug. 1801).

To George Jefferson

DEAR SIR   Philadelphia Jan. 2. 99.

I wrote you from Monticello with a statement of my draughts on you. I have this day drawn on you in favor of James Strange agent for the Donalds for £98–5 paiable at 10. days sight. the £500. which you recieved from mr Pendleton were for mr Short. as it was wanting here, & I had money here which it suited me better to transfer to Richmond, I have been able so far to make the exchange within myself. perhaps I may in the same way exchange about £50. more and sell a draught here for the balance. be so good as to send me a statement of my account to govern me in the draught as we shall immediately begin the investment of mr Short's money according to it's destination.—there was shipped hence for me on the 11th. Dec. by Joseph Roberts 120. bundles nail rod by the sloop Rising Sun capt. Adders addressed to you. she went off so quick as to give no bill of lading, and we hope (but do not know) that she got out before the river closed. be so good as to forward on the nailrod immediately on it's arrival, as I left them in want. be pleased also to note that there are only 2. sizes of rod, 10 d & 20 d. I note them because one half of the last which came to me was 30. d absolutely useless, & mr Roberts assures me he sent me none of that kind; so that it must have been exchanged in the vessel. the first opening in the river we shall send on some hoop iron & a cask of molasses in order that the latter may get to Monticello before the warm weather commences in the spring. I am Dear Sir

Your friend & servt   TH: JEFFERSON

PrC (MHi); at foot of text: "Mr. George Jefferson"; endorsed by TJ in ink on verso.

A letter from TJ to JAMES STRANGE of 2 Jan. and Strange's response of 17 Jan., which according to SJL TJ received from Manchester on 24 Jan. 1799, have not been found. Letters from TJ to Strange of 14 Mch., 3 Apr., 7 and 22 May 1796 and responses from Strange to TJ of 30 Mch., 24 Apr., and 17 May, which according to SJL

were received on 1, 30 Apr., and 21 May 1796, respectively, are also missing.

TJ's payment to the DONALDS settled an account with the local firms of James and Robert Donald & Co. and Donald, Scott & Co. for debts TJ owed or had assumed for family members. It also included payment for a telescope that Alexander Donald had obtained for TJ from London (MB, 2:945, 957, 996; TJ to Strange, 7 Oct. 1791).

To James Madison

Philadelphia Jan. 3. 99.

I have suffered the post hour to come so nearly over on me that I must huddle over what I have more than appears in the public papers. I arrived here on Christmas day, not a single bill or other article of business having yet been brought into Senate. the P's speech, so unlike himself in point of moderation, is supposed to have been written by the military conclave, & particularly Hamilton. when the Senate gratuitously hint Logan to him, you see him in his reply come out in his genuine colours. the debates on that subject & Logan's declaration you will see in the papers. the republican spirit is supposed to be gaining ground in this state & Massachusets. the taxgatherer has already excited discontent. Gerry's correspondence with Taleyrand, promised by the Presidt. at the opening of the session is still kept back. it is known to shew France in a very conciliatory attitude, and to contradict some executive assertions. therefore it is supposed they will get their war measures well taken before they will produce this damper. Vans Murray writes them that the French government is sincere in their overtures for reconciliation & have agreed, if these fail, to admit the mediation offered by the Dutch govmt. in the mean time the raising the army is to go on, & it is said they propose to build twelve 74s. insurance is now higher in all the commercial towns against British than French capture. the impresment of seamen from one of our armed vessels by a British man of war has occasioned mr Pickering to bristle up it is said. but this cannot proceed to any effect. the capture by the French of the Retaliation (an armed vessel we had taken from them) will probably be played off to the best advantage. Lyon is re-elected. his majority is great. reports vary from 600. to 900. Logan was elected into the Pensylva. legislature against F. A. Mulenburg by 1256. to 769. Livermore has been reelected in N. Hampshire by a majority of 1. in the lower & 2. in the upper house. Genl. Knox has become bankrupt for 400,000 D. & has resigned his military commission. he took in Genl. Lincoln for 150,000 D. which breaks him. Colo. Jackson also sunk with him.—it seems generally admitted that several cases of the yellow fever still exist in the city, and the apprehension is that it will re-appear early in the spring.—you promised me a copy of Mc.Gee's bill of prices. be so good as to send it on to me here. tell mrs Madison her friend Made. d'Yrujo is as well as one can be so near to a formidable crisis. present my friendly respects to her and accept yourself my sincere & affectionate salutations. Adieu.

I omitted to mention that a petition has been presented to the President signed by several thousand persons in Vermont, praying a remit-ment of Lyon's fine. he asked the bearer of the petition if Lyon himself had petitioned, and being answered in the negative, said, 'penitence must precede pardon.'

RC (DLC: Madison Papers); addressed: "James Madison junr. near Orange court house"; franked, stamped, and postmarked. PrC (DLC).

MILITARY CONCLAVE: on 10 Nov. Washington arrived in Philadelphia and during his month's stay he attended meetings with his major generals, Hamilton and Charles C. Pinckney, Secretary of War James McHenry, and other cabinet officers. When Adams delivered his annual message to Congress on 8 Dec. the former president, Hamilton, and Pinckney were sitting alongside the speaker of the House. In response to a letter from Adams in October, Oliver Wolcott had submitted ideas and a draft (evidently from Hamilton) for the message. Adams used the draft, but in altering the wording on conditions for negotiations with France, protested Hamiltonian Federalists, the president opened the door to "French diplomatic intrigues" (Freeman, *Washington*, 7:549-50, 552-6; Syrett, *Hamilton*, 25:209-10; Gibbs, *Memoirs*, 2:168-75, 180, 185-7; JS, 2:559-60; *Annals*, 9:2420).

On 3 Jan. 1799 the Philadelphia *Aurora* printed LOGAN'S DECLARATION, an address to the citizens of the United States in which George Logan defended his mission to France, noting that he undertook it as a private citizen in an effort to restore harmony between the two republics. Logan reiterated that he *"did not go* to France" at the request or direction of any other person or political party and that the two certificates of citizenship which he carried with him (see Certificate for George Logan, 4 June 1798) were addressed to no one in particular and were not used to procure interviews with French public officials.

TAXGATHERER HAS ALREADY EXCITED DISCONTENT: on 29 Dec. 1798 the *Gazette of the United States* carried news that assessors in Northampton County, Pennsylvania, had been threatened. Two days later, the Philadelphia *Aurora* noted that farmers were questioning the extravagance of the administration in supporting a house tax, a land tax, and an additional salt tax at a time when the threat of war with the French Republic had "ceased."

In July 1798 Rutger Jan Schimmelpenninck, the Dutch minister to France, approached Talleyrand and Elbridge Gerry with an offer by the Batavian Republic to serve as mediator in the dispute between the United States and France. On 23 Aug. William Vans MURRAY advised Pickering that a local newspaper carried as " 'authentic' intelligence" Talleyrand's acceptance of the Dutch proposal "provided the measures already taken to conciliate the U.S. did not succeed." Murray thought the French government was probably behind the publication to "give an *appearance* of a conciliatory disposition in the eyes of America & Europe" (Murray to Pickering, 23 Aug. 1798, in MHi: Pickering Papers; ASP, *Foreign Relations*, 2:224; Bowman, *Neutrality*, 343-4; Peter P. Hill, *William Vans Murray, Federalist Diplomat: The Shaping of Peace with France, 1797-1801* [Syracuse, N.Y., 1971], 120-1).

On 16 Nov. 1798 Captain John Loring of the Royal Navy impressed 55 SEAMEN from the *Baltimore*, one of the U.S. Navy's ARMED VESSELS near Havana. When the American commander, Isaac Phillips, protested that he did not have enough seamen left to sail the vessel properly, all but five men were returned. On 31 Dec. Pickering wrote Robert Liston a letter of protest against the "outrage." On the same day Harrison Gray Otis brought a resolution before the House of Representatives requesting the president to provide information on the incident so that Congress could take action to show the country's determination "to protect their flag against any country whatever" (King, *Life*, 2:505-8; *Annals*, 9:2546; DeConde, *Quasi-War*, 202-3; Michael A. Palmer, *Stoddert's War: Naval Operations During the Quasi-War with France, 1798-1801* [Columbia, S.C., 1987], 61-6).

The RETALIATION, commanded by William Bainbridge and formerly a French vessel captured by the *Delaware* off the coast of New Jersey in July 1798, was taken by the French frigate *L'Insurgent* in November 1798 (DeConde, *Quasi-War*, 127-8; NDQW, Nov. 1798-Mch. 1799, 40-3. For the release of the vessel, see TJ to Monroe, 11 Feb. 1798.

Samuel LIVERMORE was narrowly reelected to the New Hampshire legislature. Having no viable candidate, the Republicans in the lower house gave him their votes (Lynn Warren Turner, *The Ninth State: New Hampshire's Formative Years* [Chapel Hill, 1983], 162-3).

Unable to continue borrowing to pay off notes as they became due, Henry KNOX faced a financial crisis and was summoned to Boston by his creditors in October 1798. Since his friends and fellow Revolutionary War generals Benjamin LINCOLN, customs collector at Boston, and Henry JACKSON had endorsed many of his notes, they were also financially embarrassed, but not to the extent indicated by TJ and others. In Boston

it was rumored that Lincoln was responsible for about half of the $100,000 owed by Knox. In reality Lincoln paid about $25,000. A final settlement was not reached until 1806 (David Mattern, *Benjamin Lincoln and the American Revolution* [Columbia, S.C., 1995], 210-12). Knox resigned his military commission when Hamilton and Pinckney were ranked above him in the leadership of the new army (Kohn, *Eagle and Sword*, 243; Henry Tazewell to TJ, 12 July 1798).

The PETITION from VERMONT, printed in the Philadelphia *Aurora* on 14 Jan. 1799, was delivered by John C. Ogden (see note to Stevens Thomson Mason to TJ, 23 Nov. 1798).

To James Monroe

[MY DEAR] SIR   Philadelphia Jan. 3. 99.

Dr. Bache having determined to remove to our neighborhood, informs me he has written to you to purchase lands for him. a day or two before I left home mrs Key sent me a message that the lands on which she lives & her son Walter's were for sale. I therefore inclose you a letter to her, informg her that I have communicated it to the gentleman here whom I had under contemplation when I spoke to her & that he has authorised you to act for him. the object of this is to prevent her supposing that your application will be in competition with mine.

you know that Carter's land adjoining Moore's creek is for sale.—as it is not probable any body will sell & deliver instant possession, so as to enable Dr. Bache at once to seat himself on his own farm, I imagine the first object will be the procuring a house for him. the one in Charlottesville which chiles is building is the only one which has occurred to me: & as Dr. Bache proposes moving next month, it may be well to leave the ultimate purchase of a farm to be fixed on by himself. if you could get Carter, Catlett & Key to fix each their lowest terms, they might offer in competition against one another. I wish you could also provide for Baynham. Genl. Knox is broke for 400,000 D. and has resigned his military commission. he has broke also Genl. Lincoln & his friend Colo. Jackson. what has passed on the subject of Logan you see in the Newspapers. the county of Philadelphia have chosen him their representative in assembly by 1256. against 769. in favor of Muhlenburg. Lyon is rechosen in Vermont by a vast majority. it seems agreed that the republican sentiment is gaining ground fast in this state & in Massachusets. my respects to mrs Monroe. Adieu.

RC (DLC: Monroe Papers); torn, with portion of salutation supplied from PrC; at foot of text: "Colo. Munroe." PrC (DLC); endorsed by TJ in ink on verso. Enclosure: TJ to Ann Key, 3 Jan. 1799, which is recorded in SJL but has not been found.

When William BACHE began to relocate his household to Albemarle County in the spring of 1799 it was still uncertain where he would reside. From James Key he purchased a farm about five miles from Monticello that he named "Franklin." Bache left Virginia in 1802 (MB, 2:1037-8n; Woods, *Albemarle*, 62; TJ to Mary Jefferson Eppes, 13 Apr. 1799).

A native of Caroline County, Virginia, Dr. William BAYNHAM served a medical apprenticeship with Thomas Walker in Albemarle County before going to London, where from 1769 to 1785 he studied anatomy and surgery, worked as a dissector and preparator, and practiced surgery. He then moved to Essex County, Virginia, and gained considerable renown in the U.S. as a surgeon and an expert in anatomy (Wyndham B. Blanton, *Medicine in Virginia in the Eighteenth Century* [Richmond, 1931], 13-17; Washington, *Diaries*, 4:244-5, 6:335).

A letter from TJ to Ann Key of 18 July 1797, recorded in SJL, has not been found.

To Thomas Mann Randolph

Th:J. to TMR.   Philadelphia Jan. 3. 1799.

I wrote to Martha the last week. I believe I omitted to concur with mr Eppes in asking the favor of you as a mutual friend to have the hire of his negroes the last year estimated by any body you think a judge. the men, women, & children are known to Page, being all by this time with him except one or two of the children. perhaps mr Eppes may have left a list of them with you for this purpose. I would be glad to learn the amount as soon as possible.—I do not recollect whether I asked you to attend to the forwarding to George Jefferson the chimney piece which Dinsmore was to pack safely & direct to me here. I am much afraid of it's being thrown on my hands if not forwarded soon.—I have lately recieved a letter from Europe enquiring whether there are any fine tracts of land for sale on James river, below the falls, or even above. as the object of the person is extensive I have thought it a favorable occasion for yourself and mr Eppes [to] dispose of your lands if you desire it, and probably Dover could also be sold. it would be necessary in that case that you should send me a description of the lands, very full, and also plats of them, and the prices they are held at. the negociation could not be taken up till the fall, and the paiment would be ready money. it is desired to know also whether tenants for lands could be found in that quarter, and what they would rent for. I would be glad of your answer as soon as possible as I must write from hence early in next month. you have heard of the British impressment of seamen from on board one of our armed vessels, & observe that mr Otis is *sorry to confess* to the house that it is true. we are told that Pickering has bristled up a little on it. insurance is much higher through all the commercial towns against British than

French capture. mr Gerry's correspondence with Taleyrand, promised at the opening of the session, is not yet communicated. it is said to shew a very conciliatory disposition on the part of France. in the mean time they are proceeding with the army & navy. twelve 74s. are said to be meditated.—Genl. Knox is become bankrupt for 400,000 Dollars. he has broke his friend Genl. Lincoln for 150,000. D. and a colo. Jackson.—I shall immediately order Bache's paper for you as desired, from the 1st. inst. Cary's is likely not to be revived. Porcupine is going down hill. from 80. quires a day he is sunk to 50. my tender love to my dear Martha & the little ones. let me know how to address to you if you should go down the country. Adieu affectionately.

RC (DLC); word in brackets supplied from PrC; endorsed by Randolph as received 28 Jan. 1799. PrC (MHi); endorsed by TJ in ink on verso.

I WROTE TO MARTHA: TJ to Martha Jefferson Randolph, 27 Dec. 1798. A letter from TJ to William PAGE of 23 Jan. 1799, recorded in SJL, has not been found. LETTER FROM EUROPE: see William Short to TJ, 6 Aug. 1798.

Notes on William Blount's Impeachment Trial

Impeachmt odious. rival of trial of jury
I. None but Officer impeachble.
    Constitution says who are
    Amendmt. denies what is not given.

  for offence in office.

II. Senator not an officer
    meaning of *officer* sought in Constns of state—constn of U.S.—
    laws of Congress.
    impeachmt of him not necessary
      because expulsion equivelt.
    Legislators are the *govmt*
      not *officer* of the govmt

III. Blount is not a Senator
    not by his own act
    but by act of Senate
  1st. sentence of expulsion final
    otherwise 2d trial might have contradictory issue
    the same court cannot pass twice on same offence

Jan. 5. 99.

H.[1] considers the indepdce of Senate on people to be for tht reason the best feature in the constn

Martens. Bradford

MS (DLC: TJ Papers, 105:17952); entirely in TJ's hand; endorsed by TJ: "Impeachment."

TJ's outline above summarizes the arguments pursued by the defense in William Blount's trial, which commenced on 17 Dec. 1798, more than 17 months after he was impeached by the House and expelled from the Senate (see Resolution on William Blount, printed at 4 July 1797). During TJ's absence in December, John Laurance, president pro tempore of the Senate, was in charge of the proceedings. After the resignation of Samuel Sitgreaves, leader of the Blount investigation, the House elected Pennsylvania Federalist John W. Kittera to serve as a manager, and James A. Bayard and Robert Goodloe Harper assumed leadership of the prosecution. When Blount failed to appear before the Senate in person to face the charges, the trial managers questioned whether to proceed, but after debate in the House on 21 Dec. they accepted the Senate's decision authorizing defense attorneys Jared Ingersoll and Alexander J. Dallas to appear on Blount's behalf. On 24 Dec. Ingersoll presented Blount's plea, and it was read by the secretary of the Senate. Challenging the Senate's jurisdiction, he argued that impeachment proceedings were to be held only for high crimes and misdemeanors and only against the president, vice president, and civil officers of the United States. Even if members of Congress could be impeached, Blount was "not now a Senator" so the proceedings could not apply to him. Relying on Henry Tazewell's earlier argument (see TJ to Tazewell, 27 Jan. 1798), Blount pleaded that an amendment to the Constitution guaranteed a jury trial for criminal prosecutions, thus overriding a Senate trial. The subject of jurisdiction framed the rest of the impeachment proceedings (JHR, 3:406-7, 415; JS, 3:483-8; Annals, 9:2470-87; Melton, First Impeachment, 196-208).

When the court reconvened on 3 Jan. 1799, TJ took the prescribed oath and presided at the trial. On that day Bayard pre-

sented arguments for the managers upholding the jurisdiction of the court. The next day, TJ notified the defense counsel to proceed and Dallas presented arguments for three and one-half hours in support of Blount's plea (JS, 3:488-90; Annals, 8: 2248-78; Melton, First Impeachment, 214). On 5 Jan. Ingersoll completed the case for the defense. While both Dallas and Ingersoll addressed the points in TJ's notes, Ingersoll's arguments on constitutional matters carried additional weight because he had served as a member of the Philadelphia Convention. He began his argument by noting that while English legal sources contained much praise for a TRIAL by JURY in criminal cases, he found "none on proceedings by impeachment." Trial by jury had "preserved the liberties of the British nation during the shocks of conquest from abroad, the convulsions of civil wars within, and the more dangerous period of modern luxury," and while he acknowledged that trial by jury, "like every human institution, is liable to abuse," he thought it was "less so, infinitely less so, than trial by impeachment." Recognizing this, the framers of the Constitution designed an impeachment power that was to be "strictly construed." The Constitution provided for the "purity of the Legislature" by giving to each house the power of EXPULSION of its members. Blount had been expelled, and Ingersoll asked whether he could be "removed at one trial, and disqualified at another, for the same offence?" But rather than concluding that a second TRIAL MIGHT HAVE CONTRADICTORY ISSUE, Ingersoll closed his defense with the query: "Would not error in the first sentence naturally be productive of error in the second instance? Is there not reason to apprehend the strong bias of a former decision would be apt to prevent the influence of any new lights brought forward upon a second trial?" (Annals, 8:2279-94; Melton, First Impeachment, 219).

BEST FEATURE IN THE CONSTN: concluding the case for the House managers, on 5 Jan. Harper praised the Senate as "the sheet-anchor of our vessel of state." The more "permanent and independent" structure of the Senate rendered it "far less influenced by popular opinion or popular feeling" than the executive office (*Annals*, 8:2315).

MARTENS: Georg Friedrich von Martens, *Précis du droit des gens moderne de l'Europe*, translated by William Cobbett and published by Thomas BRADFORD in 1795 under the title *Summary of the Law of Nations, Founded on the Treaties and Customs of the Modern Nations of Europe*. Harper probably referred to this work during his remarks when he cited TJ's reference, while secretary of state, to the " 'worm-eaten volumes' of the law of nations" (*Annals*, 8:2295). At the end of the arguments, TJ inquired whether the trial managers had any additional observations. None being offered, the

court adjourned until Monday, 7 Jan. (JS, 3:490). For an analyses of arguments presented during the trial, see Melton, *First Impeachment*, 207-30; Raymond Walters, Jr., *Alexander James Dallas: Lawyer—Politician—Financier, 1759-1817* (Philadelphia, 1943), 109-10; Morton Borden, *The Federalism of James A. Bayard* (New York, 1955), 47-61; and Peter C. Hoffer and N. E. H. Hull, *Impeachment in America, 1635-1805* (New Haven, 1984), 155-63. For the conclusion of the case, see Senate Resolution on William Blount, [11 Jan. 1799].

[1] TJ here interlined "illhouse," probably at a later date. James Hillhouse served as senator from Connecticut in the Fifth Congress.

To Aaron Burr

DEAR SIR   Philadelphia Jan. 7. 99.

I wrote you some time before I left home on the subject of my friend Currie's affair but lest that letter should not have [come to hand] I trouble you with this merely to enquire in what state his suit against Morris [is]. and I should not have done it but that you had supposed that, if terminated favorably at all, it would be before this time. a line of information will be acceptable.

A want of confidence in our posts prevents my saying any thing on political subjects, further than that it is proposed (and no doubt will be agreed) to commence a great naval power by building 12 ships of [74. guns,] 12 frigates and from 25 to 30 smaller vessels, say a fleet of 50. ships. the first cost 10. millions of Doll. the annual expenses between 5. & 6 millions. thus our navy alone will cost us annually $1\frac{1}{2}$ Dollars a head besides the first cost. add the army, civil list, & interest of the debt, and estimate the amount. I am Dear Sir

Your friend & servt   TH: JEFFERSON

PrC(DLC); faint.

I WROTE YOU: TJ to Burr, 12 Nov. 1798. In response to an 8 Dec. address by Adams calling for an increase in NAVAL POWER, a House committee on 14 Dec. began to consider a bill, eventually reported on 17 Jan. and debated on 29 Jan. It authorized the president to induct revenue cutters into the Navy, "that the Navy be augmented with six ships, to carry not less than seventy-four guns, to be built within the United States, and six sloops of war, of not more than eighteen guns, to be built or purchased within the United States; and that a sum not exceeding one million of dollars, be appropriated therefore," and extra monies for docks, timber, and cannon. The Senate passed it on 19 Feb. 1799, and on the 25th Adams signed it into law (JHR, 3:410, 439, 455; JS, 2:590; U.S. Statutes at Large, 1:621).

From George Jefferson

DEAR SIR, Richmond 8th. Janr. 1799.

I was informed by Mr. Joseph Roberts in a letter of the 14th. ultimo that he had shipped on board the rising sun Capt. Adderson 120 bundles of nail-rod on your account.—I was informed some days ago upon enquiring after her, that there was a report she was lost, her hands having all deserted her—this report the norfolk paper by last post confirmed, as you will find from the inclosed. I have to day seen one of the owners, who says he understands the Capt. is within 15 or 20 miles of this place & has been for several days; he is much surprised at his not having yet arrived.

I suppose the Capt. will proceed on immediately after coming up, to claim the property—of which however I will advice you as soon as I hear from him.

I am Dr. Sir Your Mt. humble: servt. GEO. JEFFERSON

RC (MHi); with newspaper clippings pasted on verso; at foot of text: "Thomas Jefferson esqr."; endorsed by TJ as received 15 Jan. 1799 and so recorded in SJL. Enclosures: (1) Notice, undated, by Benjamin Luther, captain of the sloop Lark, advising that he had taken up a wreck at sea with no persons or papers on board, but with "Sloop Rising Sun of Richmond" painted on her stern and a message written in chalk, "Blown of the coast of Philadelphia, December 13, 1798, bound to Richmond," and he had towed the vessel to the Pasquotank River in the customs district of Camden, North Carolina. (2) Charles Grice, of Elizabeth City, North Carolina, to Charles Willett and James O'Connor, editors of the Norfolk Herald, dated 31 Dec. 1798, reporting that Captain Luther had deposited the cargo of the Rising Sun with the customs collector at Camden (both in Norfolk Herald, 3 Jan. 1799; Brigham, American Newspapers, 2:1126-7).

From James Sullivan

SIR Boston January 8th 1799

One Mr Dearborn of this Town whom I conceive to be a natural Machanic, carries this letter to Philadelphia and hopes to have the honor to deliver it to you. His object is to gain by Patents an exclusive priviledge in several inventions among which are a perpendicular wind-Mill on new & useful principles, a Steelyard calculated to prevent fraud—a Trigonometrical Instrument useful in measuration & drawing

Machine. I encourage him that he will certainly receive your countenance if he merits it—

You will allow me the honor to assure you that I am with sentiments of high respect your Most humble servt   JA SULLIVAN

RC (ViWC); at foot of text: "Honble. Mr Jefferson"; endorsed by TJ as received 24 Jan. 1799 and so recorded in SJL.

In 1799 Benjamin DEARBORN received two patents, one for his improvement in the steelyard, a portable balance for weighing, and the other for a double centered watermill or windmill (*List of Patents*, 18-19; Madison, *Papers: Sec. of State Ser.*, 4:123).

A letter from Sullivan to TJ of 12 Jan. 1798, recorded in SJL as received from Boston twelve days later, has not been found.

To George Jefferson

DEAR SIR   Philadelphia Jan. 10. 1799.

Your favor of the 1st. inst. is at hand with the account inclosed stating a balance in my favor of 581.8.8. you had probably not then recieved my draught in favor of Strange for £98.5 which of course is to lessen the balance abovementioned. having a convenient offer for transferring this money here I yesterday drew on you in favor of John Richard junr. for twelve hundred dollars at 7. days sight, which be pleased to honor.

On a view of your account I must remind you of a desire I think I once before expressed, never to pay in Richmond the freight[1] up the river. my memory decieves me if one of the persons named in your account did not apply & recieve paiment from me. besides that for my nailrod I pay less than the usual freight by agreement with most of the watermen. I believe I before informed you that the box with the chimney piece would be brought down to you to be forwarded here. I should be glad it could come on as soon as it is known to you that this river is open. I am with esteem Dr. Sir

Your friend & servt   TH: JEFFERSON

PrC (MHi); at foot of page: "Mr. George Jefferson"; endorsed by TJ in ink on verso.

[1] TJ here canceled "of what is sent."

Senate Resolution on William Blount

[11 Jan. 1799]

that the matter alledged in the plea of the def. is sufficient in law to shew that this court ought not to hold jurisdiction of the said impeachment, and that the said impeachmt[1] be dismissed

MS (DNA: RG 46, Senate Records, 5th Cong., 3d sess.); in TJ's hand in pencil; at head of text in Samuel A. Otis's hand: "This Court is of opinion"; endorsed by Otis: "Motion that Wm Blount be dismissed his bonds Jany 11th 1799"; in clerk's hand: "High Court of Impt. 5 Cong: 3d Sess." Printed in JS, 3:491.

On 7 Jan., debating a resolution to overrule Blount's plea, the Senate began deliberations on whether to go ahead with the impeachment trial. Three days later the court defeated the motion by an 11 to 14 vote. On 11 Jan. the court voted, by the same margin, that the COURT OUGHT NOT TO HOLD JURISDICTION and that the impeachment should be dismissed (JS, 3:490-1; Annals, 8:2318-19). It then "Resolved that the Senate will be ready to recieve the Managers of the H. of R. and the counsel of the def. on Monday next at 12. aclock to render judgment in the impeachment of the H. of R. against W.B." (MS in DNA: RG 46, Senate Records, 5th Cong., 3d sess.; in TJ's hand, with emendations by TJ and an unidentified hand rendering the closing passage to read "in the impeachmt. against William Blount"; endorsed by clerk). For the motion as finally adopted, see JS, 3:491. On 14 Jan. TJ addressed the trial managers and Blount's defense counsel with the following words: "The Court, after having given the most mature and serious consideration to the question, and to the full and able arguments urged on both sides, has come to the decision which I am now about to deliver." He then read the opinion agreed to on 11 Jan., copies of the judgment were delivered to the House managers and defense counsel, and the court adjourned (Annals, 8:2319; JS, 3:491).

[1] Preceding two words interlined in place of "same."

From James Madison

DEAR SIR   Jany. 12. 99.

According to a promise in my last, I inclose a copy of the rates at which McGeehee works. I inclose also a few observations on a subject which we have frequently talked of, which are submitted to your entire disposal, in whole or in part, under the sole reserve of the name of the author. In Gordon's History Vol. IV p. 399-400, is a transaction that may perhaps be properly referred to in the debate on the alien-bill. Among other names is that of Sedgwick, to a protest agst. a Bill subjecting to banishment, without trial by jury. It does not appear clearly whether the exiles were under the character of aliens or Citizens. If under the former the case is in point. In the hurry of my last, I suspect that I overrated the payments expected from Moylan & Lewis. Should they be short of the objects to which they are appropriated, I will make up the deficiency on notice. We have lately had a few days of intense cold, & now the weather is in the opposite extreme. The Thermr. on sunday morning last was at 6°. & on monday within the Bulb. Our post had not arrived at the usual hour on wednesday & I have not since heard from the office. We are consequently without any late intelligence of your proceedings. I have been disappointed in seeing no step taken in relation to Lyon. He is clearly within his privilege & it ought to be claimed for him. In the case of Wilkes, the judges were unanimously of opinion that a libel did not take away his privilege, altho it is there less definite than with us. The House of Commons voted differently, but it was the vote of a faction, & therefore of less weight than the other authority

Adieu

RC (DLC: Madison Papers); endorsed by TJ as received 20 Jan. 1799 and so recorded in SJL. Enclosed rates not found. For other enclosure, see note below.

FEW OBSERVATIONS: an essay entitled "Foreign Influence" and appearing under the signature "Enemy to Foreign Influence" that was published in the Philadelphia Aurora on 23 Jan. 1799. Identified as Madison's by the editors of the Madison Papers, the essay warned against the growing "undue and pernicious ascendency" of Great Britain in the United States (Madison, Papers, 17:211-20).

GORDON'S HISTORY: William Gordon, The History of the Rise, Progress, and Establishment, of the Independence of the United States of America: Including an account of the late war; and of the Thirteen Colonies, from their origin to that period, 4 vols. (London, 1788). See Sowerby, No. 487. Theodore SEDGWICK was among those who in 1783 protested against a bill in the Massachusetts House designed to prevent Tory refugees from returning to the state by subjecting them to BANISHMENT "by the sole judgment of two justices of the peace." The protesters argued that the bill took away "that essential right of freemen, a trial by jury" (Gordon, History, 4:399-401; Richard E. Welch, Jr., Theodore Sedgwick, Federalist: A Political Portrait [Middletown, Conn., 1965], 29-30).

John WILKES was arrested for seditious libel in 1763 when in the North Briton he criticized King George III's speech at the opening of Parliament. Accepting the argument of Wilkes's defense that his PRIVILEGE as a member of Parliament protected him from all charges except those of treason, felony, or a breach of the peace, the court ordered his release. A majority of both houses of Parliament, however, resolved that the privilege of Parliament did not extend to the "case of writing and publishing seditious libels." The House of Commons expelled Wilkes in January 1764 (George Rudi, Wilkes and Liberty: A Social Study of 1763 to 1774 [London, 1962], 18-27, 35; The Annual Register . . . for the Year 1763, 6th ed. [London, 1790], 135-41; The Annual Register . . . for the Year 1764, 4th ed. [London, 1792], 18-25).

To Jean Antoine Gautier

DEAR SIR   Philadelphia Jan. 14. 1799.

Mr Tenche Coxe, a gentleman of eminence in these [states] [. . .] in commerce & of great respectability in that line, having some business to transact in Paris, & desiring me to recommend some[one] to him on whom he may rely for negotiating it, I have taken the liberty of advising his application to you on the personal acquaintance I had the honour of having with you while at Paris, and the confidence in you which that inspired. I am in hopes the case falls within your course of business, & that he will have the benefit of your aid & influence which will be partic-

ula[rly] gratifying to me. Accept I pray you my friendly & respectful
salutations.   TH: JEFFERSON

PrC (MHi); faint; at foot of text: "Au Citoyen Gautier Banquier à Paris"; endorsed by TJ in ink on verso.

Notes on Comments by Timothy Pickering and John Adams

Jan. 14. Logan tells me that in his conversation with Pickering on his arrival, the latter abused Gerry very much, said he was a traitor to his country & had deserted the post to which he was appointed; that the French temporised at first with Pinckney but found him too much of a man for their purpose. Logan observing that notwithstandg. the pacific declarns of France, it might still be well to keep up the military ardor of our citizens & to have the militia in good order, 'the militia' said P. 'the militia never did any good to this country except in the single affair of Bunker's hill; that we must have a standing army of 50,000 men, which being stationed in different parts of the continent might serve as rallying points for the militia, & so render them of some service.—in his conversation with mr Adams, Logan mentioned the willingness of the French to treat with Gerry, 'and do you know why,' said mr A. 'why, Sir? said G.[1] 'because said mr A. they know him to have been an Antifederalist, against the constn.'

MS (DLC: TJ Papers, 105:17951); written entirely in TJ's hand on same sheet as Notes on Comments by John Adams, [1-14 Jan. 1799].

[1] Thus in MS, although TJ evidently meant Logan.

From George Jefferson

DEAR SIR,   Richmd. 15th. Janr. '99.
  The preceding is a copy of a notice which Mr. Call, (who has taken charge of Mr. Washington's business) gave me a few days ago; the original of which I forwarded by this mornings post to Mr. Randolph, with a request that he will have it executed and returned to me.   Mr. C. called to advise with me upon the subject, & concurred in opinion with me that this would be a better plan, than sending it to you, which he had a thought of doing.

I have not yet seen the Capt. of the rising sun; I went to Rocketts to day in search of him, & find he has been up, but is gone again into the Country, being in ill-health. I believe I informed you in my last that one of his owners was of opinion he would go to Carolina & take possession of the Cargo—he is still, after seeing the Capt., of the same opinion.

Mr. Pendleton yesterday paid us four hundred pounds more—if you should meet with any difficulty in disposing of dfts: on this place, I can remit you Mr. S's money in B. notes—or if you dislike that mode on acct. of the risk, I think I can at any time procure bills on Philada.

I am Dear Sir Your Very humble servt. GEO. JEFFERSON

RC (MHi); with copy of court notice in George Jefferson's hand at head of page above greeting; at foot of text: "Thos. Jefferson esqr."; endorsed by TJ as received 22 Jan. 1799 and so recorded in SJL.

COPY OF A NOTICE: the document from the Virginia High Court of Chancery concerned the suit brought by TJ as plaintiff against the heirs of Bennett Henderson in September 1795 to cease work on a dam they were erecting on the Rivanna River (Inquest on Shadwell Mill, 18 Sep. 1795). The court's notice provided the names of the Henderson heirs "upon whom an attachment for their contempt in not answering the bill of the plaintiff hath been returned executed & still failing to answer the same, the Court this 27th. day of Septr. 1798, upon the motion of the plaintiff by his councel, doth take his bill for confessed, & will proceed at a future day to decree the matter thereof; unless the said defendant, on or before the 10th. day of the term next after they shall have been served with a copy of this order, shew cause to the contrary." The copy of the order was certified by Peter Tinsley, clerk of the court. For the decree issued by the court on 1 Oct., see Daniel Call to TJ, 13 Oct. 1799.

MR. S'S MONEY: William Short's salary reimbursement.

To James Madison

Philadelphia. Jan. 16. 1799.

The forgery lately attempted to be plaid off by mr H. on the house of representatives, of a pretended memorial presented by Logan to the French government, has been so palpably exposed as to have thrown ridicule on the whole of the clamours they endeavored to raise as to that transaction. still however their majority will pass the bill. the real views in the importance they have given to Logan's enterprize are mistaken by nobody. mr Gerry's communications relative to his transactions after the departure of his collegues, tho' he has now been returned 5. months, & they have been promised to the house 6. or 7. weeks, are still kept back. in the mean time the paper of this morning promises them from the Paris papers. it is said they leave not a possibility to doubt the sincerity & the anxiety of the French government to avoid the spectacle of a war with us. notwithstanding this is well understood, the army, & a great addition to our navy are steadily intended. a loan of 5. millions is opened at 8. per cent interest! in a rough way we may state future expences thus annually, Navy $5\frac{1}{2}$ millions (exclusive of it's outfit) army (14,000 men) $6\frac{1}{2}$ millions, interest of national debt (I believe) about 4. millions, interest of the new loan 400,000. which with the expences of government will make an aggregate of about 18,000,000. all our taxes this year have brought in about $10\frac{1}{2}$ millions, to which the direct tax will add 2. millions, leaving a deficit of between 5 & 6. millions. still no addition to the taxes will be ventured on at this session. it is pretty evident from the proceedings to get at the measure & number of windows in our houses that a tax on air & light is meditated, but I suppose not till the next session. the bankrupt bill was yesterday rejected by a majority of three. the determinations of the British commissioners under the treaty (who are 3. against 2. of ours) are so extravagant, that about 3. days ago ours protested & seceded. it was said yesterday they had come together again. the demands which will be allowed on the principles of the British majority will amount to from 15. to 20. millions of Dollars. it is not believed that our government will submit to it, & consequently that this must again become a subject of negociation. it is very evident the British are using that part of the treaty merely as a political engine.—notwithstanding the pretensions of the papers of the danger & destruction of Buonaparte, nothing of that is believed. it seems probable that he will establish himself in Egypt, and that that is, at present at least, his ultimate object. Ireland also is considered as more organised in her insurrection and stronger than she has been hitherto.—as yet no tobacco has come to this market. at New York the new tobo. is at 13. D. Georgia has sent on a greater quantity than had been imagined, and so improved in quality as to take place of that of Maryland & the Carolinas. it is at 11. D. while they are about 10. immense sums of money now go to Virginia. every stage is loaded. this is partly to pay for last year's purchases, & partly for the new.—in a society of members between whom & yourself is great mutual esteem & respect, a most anxious desire is expressed that you would publish your debates of the Convention. that these measures of the army, navy & direct tax will bring about a revulsion of public sentiment is thought certain. & that the constitution will then recieve a different explanation. could those debates be ready to appear critically, their effect would be decisive. I beg of you to turn this subject in your mind. the arguments against it will be personal; those in favor of it moral; and something is required from you as a set-off against the sin of your retirement.—your favor of Dec. 29. came to hand Jan. 5. seal sound. I pray you always to examine the seals of mine to you, & the strength of the impression. the suspicions against the government on this subject are strong. I wrote you Jan. 5. accept for yourself & mrs Madison my affectionate salutations & Adieu.

RC (DLC: Madison Papers); addressed: "James madison junr. near Orange courthouse"; franked, stamped, and postmarked. PrC (DLC); endorsed by TJ in ink at foot of first page.

MR H.: Robert Goodloe Harper. On 10 Jan. 1799 during debate on the bill that became known as the Logan Act, Harper introduced a paper transmitted through unofficial channels that he identified as being "presented to the French Government by an American citizen who was lately in France." Harper's language implied that the paper WAS A MEMORIAL PRESENTED BY LOGAN to Talleyrand. In debate the next day Gallatin reported that Logan had assured him that although he had neither written nor presented the paper read by Harper he recognized it as one given to him by Richard Codman, a Boston merchant in Paris, with the request that he present it to the French government as his own. Logan refused, and he returned the document to Codman a few days later. On 14 Jan. Logan disavowed the memorial in writing and identified Congressman Harrison Gray Otis as one of Codman's correspondents and the probable source of the document (Annals, 9:2619-26, 2643-4, 2703-4; Philadelphia Aurora, 14, 15 Jan. 1799). For support of the assertion that Logan was the author of the memorial, see Samuel Eliot Morison, The Life and Letters of Harrison Gray Otis, 2 vols. (Boston, 1913), 1:170-1. The Logan Act, which made it a criminal offense for a private citizen of the United States to carry on diplomatic negotiations with a foreign power, passed the House by a 58 to 36 vote on 17 Jan. and the Senate by an 18 to 2 vote eight days later (JHR, 3:439-40; JS, 2:573; U.S. Statutes at Large, 1:613).

PAPER OF THIS MORNING: in one sentence on 16 Jan. the Philadelphia Aurora promised that the correspondence relating to negotiations with France would be published shortly. The next day a longer piece in the same newspaper indicated that a Philadelphia gentleman had received a copy of

Gerry's correspondence as it appeared in Paris and that it was "of the most consolatory nature" to the United States. William Duane argued that the public had a right to read the communications to enable them to judge whether the expensive measures being passed to augment the standing army and establish a navy were necessary.

For the legislation authorizing the LOAN OF 5. MILLIONS, see TJ to Madison, 14 June 1798. On 12 Jan. 1799 Wolcott issued a notice that subscriptions for the loan would be opened at the Bank of the United States in Philadelphia on 28 Feb., with the stock to be issued bearing an interest of 8 percent per annum (Philadelphia Gazette, 14 Jan. 1799).

FUTURE EXPENCES: see TJ to John Wayles Eppes, 21 Jan. 1799.

The direct tax act passed by Congress on 9 July 1798 provided procedures for assessing the value of land, houses, and slaves and specified that the list for houses provide information on the MEASURE & NUMBER OF WINDOWS. The discontent that the provision aroused made it difficult to obtain lists in several parts of the country because many feared the information was intended to implement a window tax. On 18 Jan. Wolcott wrote to the House committee that "popular objections" were proving to be "very embarrassing to the assessors, particularly in Pennsylvania." An act amending the 1798 statute to eliminate the requirement for information on windows was signed by the president on 28 Feb. (U.S. Statutes at Large, 1:586, 626; National State Papers: Adams, 11:206-12).

BANKRUPT BILL: defeated on its third reading by a 44-47 vote, the bill, which had also been considered during previous sessions, would have established a uniform system of bankruptcy throughout the United States (Annals, 9:2441-2, 2465-9, 2656, 2676-7).

Thomas Macdonald and Henry Pye Rich were the BRITISH COMMISSIONERS on the bilateral panel established under the Jay TREATY to arbitrate the debt claims of British merchants against American citizens. Thomas Fitzsimons, who had been an ardent supporter of Alexander Hamilton's financial policies in the House of Representatives, and Samuel Sitgreaves were the commissioners for the United States, Adams having appointed Sitgreaves in December 1798 in the place of James Innes, who had died early in August. According to the treaty a fifth commissioner was to be selected by the other four, and in May 1797, after the panel deadlocked between Englishman John Guillemard and American Fisher Ames, Guillemard had been chosen by lot. By the time Sitgreaves joined the board it was deeply divided over questions that were nominally procedural but affected the disposition of important claims. Guillemard consistently sided with the British commissioners, and Fitzsimons and Sitgreaves, advised by Timothy Pickering and Attorney General Charles Lee, began to boycott commission meetings. One of those protests, accompanied by a statement of grievance from the U.S. commissioners, took place in January 1799. The board split for good, the majority of the claims unsettled, in July of that year (John Bassett Moore, ed., *International Adjudications: Ancient and Modern, History and Documents*, 6 vols. [New York, 1929-33] 3:18, 95-7; Perkins, *First Rapprochement*, 117-19; JEP, 1:296-7; ANB, 8:67-8).

In early January Philadelphia newspapers carried conflicting news from Vienna, Constantinople, and London of the DE-STRUCTION of Bonaparte's army in Egypt. On 8 and 14 Jan. the *Philadelphia Gazette* printed accounts from Vienna that Bonaparte had been taken prisoner and his army reduced to a few thousand men. The reports turned out to be unfounded (Philadelphia *Aurora*, 2, 4 Jan.; *Gazette of the United States*, 2, 4 Jan.; *Philadelphia Gazette*, 8, 9, 14, 18 Jan.; Scott and Rothaus, *Historical Dictionary*, 1:348-9).

To Julian Ursin Niemcewicz

DEAR SIR   Philadelphia Jan. 16. 99.

Your favor which I recieved at Monticello was so long on the road that I expected you would be with us yourself very soon after. finding however the season advance beyond the time for expecting you, without these expectations being realised, I wrote to you and directed my letter to be put into mr Mc.lure's hands, and I hope you got it safely. on my arrival here I recieved a letter from Genl Kosciusko which had been brought by mr Gerry. it covered one for you. fearing to trust that by the post I detained it a few days till I got an opportunity, by a gentleman who was known to me, & who being to pass through Elizabeth town, promised to see that you should recieve it with certainty. still I am anxious till I learn from yourself that it has got to hand, as well as mine from Monticello. the General's letters to me are short, merely relating to some of his affairs here, & mentioning in general his good health. I learn through other channels that he is able to walk.—I had hoped we should have seen you here ere this, and still flatter myself you will not let the session pass over without visiting Philadelphia, and to be assured that your partialities for the Northern part of our country will not prevent your coming to see what we are in the South. there will be an inducement the more soon, as Dr. Bache & mrs Bache move in April or May to fix themselves in my neighborhood. be so good as to let me hear from you as soon as convenient as to the letters abovementioned, & to accept my friendly esteem and salutations. Th: Jefferson

PrC (DLC); at foot of text: "Mr. Niemce-wicz"; endorsed by TJ in ink on verso.

favor which i recieved at monti-cello: Niemcewicz to TJ, 3 Sep. 1798. i wrote to you: TJ to Niemcewicz, 30 Nov. 1798. The letter from genl kos-ciusko was probably the first communica-tion from Tadeusz Kosciuszko under [15 July-5 Aug. 1798] above, received by TJ on Christmas Day. mine from monti-cello: TJ's letter of 30 Nov.

To Thomas Mann Randolph

Th:J. to TMR.   Philadelphia Jan. 17. 99.

I wrote to my dear Martha Dec. 27. and to yourself Jan. 3. I am afraid my nailery will stop from the want of rod. 3 tons were sent from hence Dec. 11. the vessel was blown off the capes and deserted by the crew. she has been taken up at sea and carried into Albemarle Sound. we are in hopes however of getting off another supply from here immediately as the river bids fair to open. the shutting of the river has prevented any tobo. coming here as yet; so nothing is known about price. at New-York the new tobo. is 13. Doll. Georgia has sent a much larger quantity there than had been expected, & of such a quality as to place it next to the Virginia. it is at 11. D. while the tobo. of the Carolinas & Maryland are but 10. D. I suspect that the price will be at it's maximum this year. whether that will be more than 13. D. I do not know; but I think it will. when this city comes into the market, it must greatly increase the de-mand. we know too that immense sums of cash are gone & going on to Virginia, such as were never before heard of. every stage is loaded. some pretend here it is merely to pay for last year's tobo. but we know that that was in a considerable degree paid for; & I have no doubt that a great part of this money is to purchase the new crop. if I were offered 13. D. in Richmond, perhaps I should take it, for the sake of securing certain objects, but my judgment would condemn it. wheat here is 1.75   Dr. Bache sets out for our neighborhood next month early. having concluded absolutely to settle there. he is now breaking up his house and beginning to pack. Dr. Logan tells me Dupont de Nemours is coming over, and decided to settle in our neighborhood. I always considered him as the ablest man in France. I ordered Bache's papers for you from Jan. 1. the moment I can get answers from the Postmasters of Charlottesville & Milton to letters I wrote them a fortnight ago, we shall have the error of our mail corrected. it will turn out I believe to have taken place here by making up the mail a day too late, which occasioned a loss of a week at Fredericksburg.   the bankrupt bill was yesterday rejected in the H. of R. by a majority of 3. Logan's law will certainly pass. no body mistakes the object of it. the forgery they attempted to palm on the house, of a memorial falsely pretended to have been drawn & presented by Logan, is so completely detected, as to have thrown infamy on the whole proceeding. but a majority will still go through with it. the army & navy are steadily pursued. the former, with our old troops will make up about 14,000. men, and consequently cost annually[1] 7. millions of dollars. the navy will cost annually $5\frac{1}{2}$ millions, but as it will not be on foot for some time,[2] no addition to the direct tax will be made at this session, nor perhaps at the next. it is very evident from circumstances that a window tax is intended. a loan for 5. millions is opened at 8. per cent. the extravagance of the interest will occasion it to fill. this it is supposed will build the navy. our taxes bring in this year $10\frac{1}{2}$ millions clear, and the direct tax will add[3] 2. millions. according to the principles settled by a (British) majority of the commissioners under the treaty, that demand will be from 15. to 20. millions of D. but there is some reason to suppose our government will not yeild to it. in that case they must recur to new negotiations. notwithstanding the forgeries of London, Vienna & Constantinople, it is believed that Buonaparte will establish himself in Egypt, & that that is, for the present at least his ultimate object. also that the insurrection in Ireland is in force & better organised than before. my warmest love to my dear Martha & the little ones: to yourself affectionate salutations & Adieu.

RC (DLC). PrC (MHi); endorsed by TJ in ink on verso.

According to SJL TJ wrote Alexander Garrett and John Watson, POSTMASTERS OF CHARLOTTESVILLE & MILTON, on 3 Jan. 1799, but neither letter has been found. A letter from TJ to Garrett of 15 Feb. 1798 and letters from Garrett to TJ of 28 Jan. and 26 Feb. 1798, recorded in SJL as received on 9 Feb. and 8 Mch., and eleven other letters exchanged by TJ and Watson between 27 Aug. 1794 and 28 Mch. 1800, are also missing. For the results of TJ's inquiry, see his memorandum on postal service, 13 Mch. 1799.

[1] MS: "annuall."
[2] Preceding three words interlined; lacking in PrC.
[3] Here TJ canceled "about."

From Julian Ursin Niemcewicz

SIR   Elizabeth Town 19 Jan 1799.

It is only in the beginning of this week that I had the pleasure to receive your favor of 30 Nov: /: it having remained the whole time at the Post office in Brunswick:/ two days afterwards a gentleman on his way to Philadelphia left me a letter from General Kosciuszko, when I was to aknowledge You the receipt of both I received your kind letter of 16 present. Accept Sir my warmest thanks for the friendly expressions you honour me with. The Note of G:K: contained only a Compliment of four Linen[1] without mentioning a Single word of his health, his mysterious & wunderful recovery, or any private or political affairs. Althought the Love of tranquillity & retirement, the Political Intolerance & above all the fear of indelicat Questions render me extremely averse from visiting large Cities, the desire of seeing You Sir & some other few friends have deccided me to come to Philadelphia before the Congress breaks off. I beg you to remember me most affectionately to Dr. & Mrs. Beache I had the pleasure to see yesterday the old gentelman & his Lady on their way to New York, happy as I was to see them I was most deeply affected by finding Miss Bache in such a bad Condition of health, I hope the fine Season will restore here. Receive Sir the assurances of my best Respects.

Your most Obedient Servant J. NIEMCEWICZ

RC (DLC); endorsed by TJ as received 21 Jan. 1799 and so recorded in SJL.

DR. & MRS. BEACHE: William and Catharine Wistar Bache. The OLD GENTELMAN & HIS LADY were William's parents, Richard

Bache and Sarah Franklin Bache, MISS BACHE being one of their three daughters (Niemcewicz, *Under their Vine*, 61).

[1] That is, "lines."

From Thomas Mann Randolph

DEAR SIR, Belmont Jan. 19 :99

We remained at Monticello after you left us till Christmas day on which we paid a visit to George Divers with as many as we could carry; Virginia, Nancy & Ellen—we passed the Christmas with Divers, P. Carr, & Mrs. Trist; assisted at a ball in Charlottesville on the first day of the year and returned on the 4th. to Monticello where we found our children (whom I had not neglected to visit) in the most florid health. On the 5th. I made an arrangement with Allen & by help of a Douceur got into the house here again next day—to remain till your return. We are all well, comfortable and contented—we shall await your return where we are, having prudently resolved not to encounter the fatigues, exposures, and dangers of a long journey in Winter with a carriage full of children. Your affairs at Monticello go on as usual—I shall visit it frequently and interpose with authority if at any time that should be necessary. I have no news of your neighbourhood to give you: we shall all be pleased to receive the foreign news from you when you have leisure; for news-papers come to us so irregularly they are of no use.   Excuse my haste and slovenliness. Martha undertook to write every post since your departure but miscarried in every attempt; she resolved last night to rise very early this morning and do it but coming in to Breakfast I find she is just up and as the letters must be sent immediately I do it for her that you may have some news of us at last.

Most affectionately yours   TH: M. RANDOLPH

RC (ViU: Edgehill-Randolph Papers); addressed: "Thomas Jefferson Vice-President U.S. Philada."; franked; endorsed by TJ as received 29 Jan. 1799 and so recorded in SJL.

From John Wayles Eppes

Eppington Jan: 20th. 99.

On my return here from Bermuda-Hundred I found your last letter & as an opportunity to Petersburg offers I inclose two plats one of the Lands lying immediately at the Hundred and the other of My part of Martins Swamp. My Father has always estimated the 2 pieces at £6000—So anxious am I however to purchase higher up the Country that I would willingly make a sacrifice—You are as well acquainted with the property as I am & have full power from me to make sale of it on the best terms you can—If you can get £5000 for the Lands I shall be well contented—This will bring it to an average nearly of £5 pr. acre—

My Father has received two days ago £40 from Mr. Page for you which he has put into my hands—I hold it subject to your order & will either remit it to you or lodge it for you at any place in Richmond you may direct—

Maria is mending daily She sends her love—

Accept for your health and happiness our joint wishes—

Yours affectionately   J: W: EPPES

RC (ViU: Edgehill-Randolph Papers); endorsed by TJ as received 6 Feb. 1799 and so recorded in SJL. Enclosures not found.   YOUR LAST LETTER: a letter from TJ to Eppes, recorded in SJL at 3 Jan. 1799, has not been found.

From George Jefferson

DEAR SIR,   Richmond 20th. Janr. 1799

Your favors of the 10th. & 12th. both came to hand by last nights post—your draughts therein mentioned, in favor of Mr. Strange for £95.8., and Mr. Richard for $:1200—, are accepted.

With respect to my having paid freight on your things up the river

[629]

contrary to your direction; I have to observe—that I perfectly recollect your having given me such direction—and, as perfectly, that I have never since paid any freight, excepting in one or two instances in which I have advanced a few dollars to a fellow of the name of Jackson—who sometimes calls himself Gibson; which I did in consequence of his telling me after he had got the things into his boat, that he could not do without a little money to get provisons— In such cases I remember that I was particular in expressing in the receipt which I uniformly forwarded,[1] that so much had been advanced.   I do not recollect to a certainty at what time you gave this instruction; I thought you had written to me upon the subject—but upon referring to your letters I cannot find any thing concerning it—& am therefore inclined to think that you must have mentioned it to me when we met in Baltimore on your return from Philada.—indeed I think I have some recollection of the conversation—I find that I returned home the 4th of July—& if you will examine my account, you will perceive there is no charge for freight since that time; except the little advances I have mentioned—& which I knew could not have any influence in your fixing on the price of carriage.

I inclose you receipts for the freight charged in my last account— to enable you to ascertain whether you have paid the same yourself.   The chimney-piece has not yet come down—when it does it shall be forwarded. Your Very Obt. servt.   GEO. JEFFERSON

RC (MHi); at foot of text: "Thos. Jefferson esqr."; endorsed by TJ as received 27 Jan. 1799 and so recorded in SJL. Enclosures not found.

TJ's letter of 12 Jan. is not recorded in SJL and has not been found.

[1] Preceding four words interlined.

To John Wayles Eppes

MY DEAR SIR   Philadelphia Jan. 21. 99

I wrote to my dear Maria on the 1st. inst. and covered it in one to yourself on the 3d. I have not yet recieved any letters either from you or Monticello since I left home, now five weeks.—you will have seen the debates on Logan's law, as it is called. the forged paper they endeavored to palm on the H. of R. as if written & presented by Logan to the French directory, being made appear to have been written by a mr Codman of Paris a friend and correspondent of Otis, who pressed Logan to present it, but was refused, begins now to be thought a contrivance from this side the water to ensnare Logan. yet they had the audacity to send the paper here and to bring it forward as genuine. they were however completely discomfited & disgraced by the detection. still they brazened the law through by their majority, & it will probably pass the Senate as fast as forms will admit. on the Reports from the Secretary of the navy, purging the statements of revenue & expence from articles not permanent, the regular revenue appears to be (in round numbers) Impost $7\frac{1}{2}$ Millions of dollars, Excise, auctions, licences & carriages $\frac{1}{2}$ million, residuary taxes about $\frac{1}{8}$ of a million, making $8\frac{1}{8}$ million. the stamp act will probably bring in enough to pay the expence of collecting the direct tax, so that we may state these two at two millions clear making in the whole $10\frac{1}{8}$ millions. the expences are as follows, annually

the civil list	$\frac{3}{4}$ million
foreign intercourse	$\frac{1}{2}$ million
interest on the public debt	4. millions
the existing navy	$2\frac{1}{2}$ millions
the existing army (5000. men)	$1\frac{1}{2}$ millions
	$9\frac{1}{4}$

so that there is a surplus of near a million. but the additional army to be raised (about 9000 men) will add $2\frac{1}{2}$ millions, & the additional navy proposed by the Secretary 3. millions, so that when they are complete there will be wanting for annual expences $4\frac{1}{2}$ millions of dollars to be raised by new taxes to which add half a million nearly for the interest of the new loan. the existing taxes are $2\frac{1}{2}$ dollars ahead on a population of four millions; with the future they will be $3\frac{3}{4}$ D. a head.—we are now reading Gerry's communications of what passed between him & Taleyrand after the departure of his collegues. they shew the most anxious desire & earnest endeavors of that government to prevent a breach with us, and Gerry gives it explicitly as his opinion that a just treaty could have been obtained from them at any time before his departure. Logan's enthusiastic enterprize was fortunate, as it prevented the effect which our actual hostilities on their vessels would have produced. whether they will be able to stand the regular cruizes now established by us about their islands, & fixed there, is questionable. Gerry's communications are now in the press & I will send you a copy when done. they have opened a loan for money to raise the army & build the navy of 5. millions at 8. per cent. so it is that folly begets folly. every newspaper kills Buonaparte in a different form. but the news of London Vienna & Constantinople is merely fabricated to keep up the spirits of their own people. the last rational accounts from Buonaparte, shewed him in a very firm position. I do not believe he was destined to proceed further than Egypt. the London accounts of Irish affairs are thought equally fabulous. that rebellion is probably strong & organised. the French have certainly sustained considerable losses in endeavoring to assist them; but still in the long nights of the winter, they will be probably able to throw in considerable reinforcements. I expect to hear from you soon in answer to my letter of the 3d. relative to your lands at the Hundred. my tenderest love to Maria, and affectionate salutations to yourself. the same to the family at Eppington. TH: JEFFERSON

RC (Gilder Lehrman Collection, on deposit NNPM); addressed: "John W. Eppes near Petersburg"; franked. PrC (ViU); endorsed by TJ in ink on verso.

ONE TO YOURSELF ON THE 3D.: see Eppes to TJ, 20 Jan. 1799.

While TJ may have gleaned the information he provided on naval expenditures from detailed REPORTS FROM THE SECRETARY OF THE NAVY published by the House committee considering the president's call for augmentation of the navy, most of the information TJ provided here and in subsequent letters came from the secretary of the treasury's report on receipts and expenditures for 1798 and appropriations for 1799, enclosed in Wolcott's letter to the House of Representatives of 22 Dec. 1798 and printed as a 110-page document. TJ acknowledged this in his letter to Monroe of 23 Jan., the first of several missives in which he provided a more exact statement of revenues and expenses. It is not clear how he derived the estimates here for the CIVIL LIST, which according to the treasury report was $504,206.83, and FOREIGN INTERCOURSE, which included sums for the diplomatic department and the fulfillment of treaty engagements amounting to $53,000 and $187,500, respectively (*Report [in part] of the Committee to Whom was Referred so much of the President's Speech as Relates to the "Naval Establishment, the Augmentation of the Navy, and the Adoption of Systematic Measures for Procuring Timber, and other Supplies"* [Philadelphia, 1799], 8; see Evans, No. 36563; *Letter From the Secretary of the Treasury, Inclosing a Report and Estimates of the Sums necessary to be appropriated for the service of the year 1799: Also a Statement of the Receipts and Expenditures at the Treasury of the United States, For one year preceding the 1st of October, 1798* [Philadelphia, 1798], 4, 52-4, 92-8, 100-107; see Evans, No. 34872).

From Mary Jefferson Eppes

Eppington January 21st 99

I was writing to you My Dear Papa and apologizing for my silence which for some time past had been occasion'd by a slight indisposition when I recieved your last letter, how much does your kindness affect me my dear Papa, a kindness which I so little merit—ah surely, if the most grateful sense of it, if the tenderest love could in any degree entitle me to it, I should not be undeserving of it. suffer me dear Papa to tell you, how much above all others you are dear to me. that I feel more if possible every day how necessary your presence is to my happiness, & while blest with that & your affection I can never be otherwise, but the time is not far-distant I hope that will again reunite us all, with what pleasure do I look forward to it!, to see you once more settled at home & to be after so long an absence allways¹ within a mile or two of you &, my dear sister; ah if you are indeed with us whose happiness can be compared with ours! Mr Eppes is now at the Hundred he has turn'd off his overseer & finds his presence there indispensable & I shall join him as soon as it is in my power which will be in a week, or two at the farthest & we shall remain there till he gets another, we shall then remove to Mont Blanco, & there I hope it will not be long before we shall see you, let me remind you of your promise my dear Papa if not too inconvenient for you to perform, & tell you what delight I feel at the hope of seeing you there   Adieu my dear Papa. excuse this hasty scrawl for it is very late[2] believe me your affectionate daughter

ME

PS Mr Eppes desired me to tell you that his father expects to recieve the next Cumberland court 30 pound more for you & wishes to know in to whose he must commit it   the family here all join in love to you

RC (MHi); endorsed by TJ as received 6 Feb. 1799 and so recorded in SJL.

[1] Preceding six words interlined.
[2] Eppes here canceled several illegible words.

To George Jefferson

DEAR SIR   Philadelphia Jan. 22. 99.
    I recieved your favor of the 8th. instant announcing the misfortune of the vessel having my nail rod on board. my situation rendering it impossible to take the proper steps, I must beg the favor of you to act for me in the business, and to get the nailrod brought to Richmond & forwarded up. in the mean time, as I know my nailery will be out of rod, I will send on some from hence the moment the river opens.
    As I have both wheat & tobacco for sale, I will be obliged to you whenever you write to me to quote the prices at Richmond. I hope my tobo is mostly with you by this time. the new tobo is at 13. D. at N. York. the river being shut here none is yet come to this market. the ports of Spain being open for this article and depending entirely on us for supplies, I think it will get sensibly higher as the season advances. I am with great esteem Dr. Sir
    Yours affectionately   TH: JEFFERSON

PrC (MHi); at foot of text: "Mr. George Jefferson"; endorsed by TJ in ink on verso.

To James Monroe

DEAR SIR   Jan. 23. 99.
    The newspapers furnish you with the articles of common news as well as the Congressional. you observe the addition proposed to be

made to our navy, and the loan of 5. millions opened at 8. percent to equip it. the papers say that our agents abroad are purchasing vessels for this purpose. the following is as accurate a statement of our income & expence, *annual*, as I can form, after divesting the treasury reports of such articles as are accidental, & not properly *annual*.

	D. C			
1798. Impost	7,405,420.86	Int. & reimbursmt. of		
Excise, auctions,		domestic debt	2,987,145.48	
licences, carriages	585,879.67	Int. on domestic loans	238,637.50	
Postage	57,000.	Dutch debt	586,829.58	3,812,612.56
Patents	1,050.	Civil list		524,206.83
Coinage	10,242.	loan offices		13,000.
dividends of bank		Mint		13,300.
stock	79,920	lighthouses		44,281.08
fines	8	annuities and grants		1,603.33
	8,139,520.53	military pensions		93,400.
1799. Direct tax. } clear of		miscellaneous expences		19,000
Stamp tax } expence	2,000,000	Contingent expences of		
	10,139,520.	govmt.		20,000
		amt of civil govmt.		
		properly.	728,791.24	
		Indians		110,000
		Foreign intercourse	93,000	
		Treaties Gr. Br. Spain &		
		Meditern.	187,500	280,000
		annual expence of existing		
		navy	2,434,261.10	
		do. of existing army (5038.		
		offic. & priv.)	1,461,175.	
		do. of officers of additl.		
		army (actually commd)	217,375.	4,112,811.10
				9,044,714.90
		do. of privates of do.		
		(about 9000.)	2,523,455	
		do. of additional navy		
		(exclus. outfit)	2,949,278.96	5,472,733.96
		8 pr. Ct. int. on 5. Millions.		
		new loan		400,000
				14,917,448.86

by this you will percieve that our income for 1799. being 10. Millions, and expences 9. Million we have a surplus of 1. Million, which with the 5. millions to be borrowed it is expected will build the navy & raise the army. when they are complete we shall have to raise by new taxes about 5. millions more, making in the whole 15. millions, which if our population be 5. Millions will be 3. dollars a head. but these additional taxes will not be wanting till the session after next.—the majority in Congress being as in the last session, matters will go on now as then. I shall send you Gerry's correspondence and Pickering's report on it, by which you will percieve the unwillingness of France to break with us, and our determination not to believe it & therefore to go to war with them. for in this light must be viewed our surrounding their islands with our armed vessels instead of their cruising on our own coasts as the law directs.

According to information there is real reason to believe that the X.Y.Z. delusion is wearing off, and the public mind beginning to take the same direction it was getting into before that maneuvre. Gerry's dispatches will lend strongly to open the eyes of the people. besides this several other impressive circumstances will all be bearing on the public mind. the alien & sedition laws as before, the direct tax, the additional army & navy, an usurious loan to set those follies on foot, a prospect of heavy additional taxes as soon as they are completed, still heavier taxes if the government forces on the war, recruiting officers lounging at every court house and decoying the labourer from his plough. a clause in a bill now under debate for opening commerce with Toussaint & his black subjects now in open rebellion against France, will be a circumstance of high aggravation to that country, and in addition to our cruising round their islands will put their patience to a great proof. one fortunate circumstance is that, annihilated as they are on the ocean, they cannot get at us for some time, and this will give room for the popular sentiment to correct the imprudence. nothing is believed of the stories about Buonaparte. those about Ireland have a more serious aspect. I delivered the letter from you of which I was the bearer. no use was made of the paper, because that poor creature had already fallen too low even for contempt. it seems that the representative of our district is attached to his seat. mr Beckley tells me you have the collection of a sum of money for him which is destined for me. what is the prospect of getting it, & how much? I do not know whether I have before informed you that[1] mr Madison paid to mr Barnes 240. or 250. D. in your name to be placed to your credit with mr Short. I consequently squared that account, & debited you to myself for the balance. this with another article or two of account between us, stands therefore against the books for which I am indebted to you, & of which I know not the cost. a very important measure is under contemplation here, which if adopted will require a considerable sum of money *on loan*.[2] the thing being beyond the abilities of those present, they will possibly be obliged to assess their friends also. I may perhaps be forced to score you for 50. or 100. D. to be paid at convenience. but as yet it is only talked of. I shall rest my justification on the importance of the measure, and the Sentiments I

[635]

know you to entertain on such subjects.—we consider the elections on the whole as rather in our favor, & particularly believe those of N. Carolina will immediately come right. J. Nicholas, & Brent both offer again. my friendly respects to mrs Monroe, & to yourself affectionate salutations & Adieu.

P.S. I shall seldom write to you, on account of the strong suspicions of infidelity in the post offices. always examine the seal before you open my letters, and note whether the impression is distinct.

RC (DLC: Monroe Papers); addressed: "Colo. James Monroe near Charlottesville"; franked and postmarked; endorsed by Monroe. PrC (DLC).

The *Aurora* of 22 Jan. printed a report from an unidentified London newspaper stating that unnamed American AGENTS had purchased "several of the French, Dutch, and Spanish prizes" recently brought into British ports, the vessels to undergo conversion "to ships of force."

On Friday, 18 Jan., John Adams transmitted to Congress GERRY'S CORRESPONDENCE with Talleyrand, introduced by a long letter of 1 Oct. 1798 from Gerry to Pickering that detailed Gerry's transactions with the French government following the departure of Marshall and Pinckney. On Monday the 21st Adams sent Congress PICKERING'S REPORT assessing those papers. In the Senate the reading of the documents received on Friday was not concluded until after the receipt of the report on the 21st, and Stevens Thomson Mason immediately presented a motion to order the printing of the Gerry correspondence. That motion was postponed, and when the Senate took it up again on the 22d it was passed with the additional provision that the secretary of state's report should also be printed. On the 21st the House ordered the printing of both Gerry's correspondence and Pickering's report. An effort in the House to confine its printing only to those documents received on 18 Jan. failed to pass (Dft of Mason's motion in DNA: RG 46, Senate Records, 5th Cong., 3d sess., in TJ's hand, with emendations, endorsed by clerk; JS, 2:571-2; JHR, 3:440, 441, 443). Gerry's papers appeared under the title *Message from the President of the United States, Accompanying Sundry Papers Relative to the Affairs of the United States, with the French Republic* (Evans, Nos. 36551-2). John Fenno printed the report as *Message from the President of the United States, Accompanying a Report of the Secretary of State, Containing Observations on Some of the Documents, Communicated by the President, on the Eighteenth Instant* (Evans, No. 36546). From his examination of Gerry's letters Pickering concluded that France continued to offer "only *empty professions* of a desire to conciliate." The secretary of state closed his lengthy tract with the warning "that the Tyger crouches before he leaps upon his prey" (p. 17, 45). A subsequent printing of the pamphlet by Fenno included as an erratum page a letter from Pickering to "The Honourable the President of the Senate of the United States," 24 Jan. 1799, correcting two errors in his report and noting that "the President of the United States . . . has directed me to communicate the same to you, for the information of the Senate" (Evans, No. 36547).

SURROUNDING THEIR ISLANDS WITH OUR ARMED VESSELS: in December Secretary of the Navy Benjamin Stoddert had ordered the frigates *United States, Constellation*, and *Constitution* to the West Indies with other ships "for the protection of our Commerce, and for the Capture, or destruction of French armed Vessels." Stoddert had issued orders for the first such cruise by U.S. warships in July 1798, immediately following the approval of a statute that authorized such action (NDQW, Feb. 1797-Oct. 1798, 189-90; Nov. 1798-Mch. 1799, 70; U.S. Statutes at Large, 1:578-80).

The CLAUSE . . . FOR OPENING COMMERCE WITH TOUSSAINT was part of a bill "further to suspend" trade with France by continuing the provisions of the act of 13 June 1798 (see TJ to Madison, 31 May 1798). A section in the new bill would have allowed the president to exempt from restrictions on trade any part of the French Republic in which claimants to authority "shall clearly disavow, and shall be found to refrain from the aggressions, depredations, and hostilities" of France against American property and ships. In the House of Representatives on 22 Jan., Gallatin argued that although the provision was not couched in such terms it was meant to strike at France by endorsing and aiding the Haitian independence movement led by Toussaint-Louverture. In order to carry this line of reasoning, Gallatin argued that the independence of Saint-Domingue would be "a very problematical event." After further debate, on the 24th John Nicholas's motion to strike that portion of the bill failed, 55 to 35. The bill passed the House on 28 Jan. and became law on 9 Feb. In its final form the act did not specify conditions but simply gave the president discretion to lift restrictions on trade with any possession of the French Republic (*Annals*, 9:2747-53, 2768, 2791-2; U.S. Statutes at Large, 1:613-16).

TJ had been the BEARER of an unidentified document that had been in Madison's possession and went to John Dawson at Monroe's request. In December Monroe had been riled by a letter of "Junius" to the *Aurora* that he thought encouraged John Skey Eustace to continue a series of bitter articles in a New York newspaper denouncing Monroe's conduct as minister to France. Monroe saw Alexander Hamilton as the instigator of Eustace's attack (Madison, *Pa-*

pers, 17:182-3, 184-5, 222; Syrett, *Hamilton*, 22:216, 253-61).

THE REPRESENTATIVE OF OUR DISTRICT: Samuel J. Cabell. The payment from MADISON in June 1798 helped retire the loan that TJ made to Monroe from the stock dividends of William SHORT in October 1797 to defray the cost of publishing Monroe's *View of the Conduct of the Executive* (MB, 2:971, 977-8, 979, 986; TJ to John Barnes, 8 Oct. 1797).

The IMPORTANT MEASURE was the establishment of another newspaper in Philadelphia that TJ, Tench Coxe, and other Republicans hoped to achieve. Unable to raise sufficient funds over the spring and summer of 1799, the organizers were unsuccessful in bringing the project to fruition (Noble E. Cunningham, *Jeffersonian Republicans: The Formation of Party Organizations, 1789-1801* [Chapel Hill, 1957], 131-3; Cooke, *Coxe*, 352-3; Coxe to TJ, 14 Feb., 29 Apr., and TJ to Coxe, 21 May 1799).

John NICHOLAS was "hard run" during the election but kept his seat in Congress. Richard BRENT of Stafford and Prince William counties lost his seat but regained it for the Seventh Congress. Henry Lee's winning of what proved to be a single term in Congress signaled to TJ an unanticipated Federalist "taint" in Northern Virginia (*Biog. Dir. Cong.*, 666, 1357; TJ to Archibald Stuart, 14 May 1799).

[1] Here TJ canceled "I took on myself."
[2] Here TJ canceled "very possibly."

To Martha Jefferson Randolph

Philadelphia Jan. 23. 99.

The object of this letter, my very dear Martha, is merely to inform you I am well, and to convey to you the expressions of my love. it will not be new to tell you that your letters do not come as often as I could wish. I have not heard from Albemarle or Chesterfield since I left home, now 5. weeks. this deprives me of the gleams of pleasure wanting to relieve the dreariness of this scene, where not one single occurrence is calculated to produce pleasing sensations. tho' I hear not from you, I hope you are all well, and that the little ones, even Ellen talk of me sometimes. if your visit to Goochland has been relinquished as I expect,

I shall hope to find you on my return still at Monticello. within a post or two I shall announce to you the day for my cavalry to be sent off. in the mean time I feed myself with the pleasure which the approach of that day always gives me. I hope you will aid John in his preparations in the garden. I have heard nothing from mr Richardson about the hiring of labourers & consequently am anxious about my summer operations. Dr. Bache will set out for our neighborhood next month. I have persuaded mrs Bache to let him go first and prepare a *gite*. in the mean time they are packing their furniture. let George know that the nail rod sent from here in December has, with the vessel in which it was, been cast away at sea; and that another supply was shipped here two or three days ago, and will probably be at Richmond about the 10th. of February. present me affectionately to mr Randolph to whom I inclose Gerry's correspondence & Pickering's report. kiss all the little ones, and recieve the tender and unmingled effusions of my love to yourself. Adieu

TH: JEFFERSON

RC (NNPM); at foot of text: "Mrs. Randolph." Enclosures: (1) *Message from the President of the United States, Accompanying Sundry Papers*. (2) *Message from the President of the United States, Accompanying a Report of the Secretary of State*. For both see the preceding letter.

From John Beckley

SIR,   24. January 1799. 12 o'clock A.M.

Mr. Tazewell is no more—he this moment departed.
Will you be pleased to make this Melancholy event known to the Members of the Senate.

I have taken immediate preparatory measures for his funeral.
In great distress I am, Sir, Yrs.   JOHN BECKLEY

RC (DLC); addressed: "Thomas Jefferson, Esqre."; endorsed by TJ as received 24 Jan. 1799 and so recorded in SJL.

Upon learning of the death of Virginia Senator Henry TAZEWELL, the Senate passed three resolutions. The first, in TJ's hand, is as follows: "Resolved that a commee be appd. to take order for superintending the funeral of the sd H.T., & that this house will attend the same, and that notice of the event be given to the H. of Representatives" (MS in DNA, RG 46, Senate Records, 5th Cong., 3d sess.; with emendations by Samuel A. Otis; endorsed by clerk: "Committee on the superintendence of the funeral of Mr. Tazewell. January 24th, 1799"). For the resolution as adopted, including the appointment of Stevens Thomson Mason and Kentucky Senators John Brown and Humphrey Marshall to the committee, see JS, 2:573. The funeral was held the following afternoon. The second resolution called for members of the Senate to observe a month of mourning by "wearing a crape round the left arm" (same; *Annals*, 9:2771). For the third resolution, see enclosure to TJ to James Wood, 24 Jan. 1799.

[638]

From John Wayles Eppes

January 24th. 1799.

In my letter on the subject of Bermuda Hundred I neglected to say any thing in answer to that part of yours which relates to rent and Tenants. In this part of Virginia we are so little in the habit of leasing that it would be difficult to say what any Lands would rent for. Mine are well situated for that purpose and might be conveniently divided into four farms of 100. acres—each of which farms would have 75 acres of low grounds 25 of high Land an outlet to the river and also to the 356 acres of wood Land which might be a common of wood for the Tenants—In addition to this the Swamp which lies on James River only a mile from the Hundred would furnish an abundance of wood which might be brought by water to their doors. You will find in the plat the Low grounds divided into four fields—These fields instead of terminating at the margin of the high Land as marked in the plat extend to the wood and take in each 25 acres of high Land—In the field next appamattox on the high Land stands the small dwelling house mentioned in the plat which would answer well for a Tenant—In the next field is the Overseer's house a framed building covered with Shingles & the barn stables &c.—This would answer well for another Tenant—The other two fields might at a moderate expence be fitted for Tenants—

I know no situation in which industrious Tenants could do better—The Soil is fertile. City-point & Bermuda Hundred are the ports of entry above Norfolk and all large Vessels which pass that place stop at one or the other of the two ports—This makes a considerable market on the spot—Added to this the Town of Petersburg is near enough to go there with one tide and return with another being only 15. miles by Water.

It would however be the interest of any person who purchased with a view of leasing to send industrious and skilful Tenants from other places as in general in this part of the world only the lazy and Indolent rent Land—And indeed long leases being unusual here Tenants are not sufficiently interested to improve their property or to pursue such a course of Husbandry as would be beneficial to themselves and promote the interest of their Landlord—

I have just heard from Monticello by Lucy who has arrived at Mont-Blanco— They are well & have given up their trip down the Country— I left Maria again on the day I wrote to you and by the last of the week I shall have every thing ready for her reception at our new habitation—

We shall then have it in our power to write more regularly—With Sincere wishes for your health & happiness

I am yours affectionately   JNO: W: EPPES

RC (ViU: Edgehill-Randolph Papers); endorsed by TJ as received 6 Feb. 1799 and so recorded in SJL.

To John Page

MY DEAR FRIEND   Philadelphia Jan. 24. 99.

I inclose you a copy of Gerry's correspondence after his companions left him, and of mr Pickering's commentary on it. you will see reason to suspect (especially after what the papers say of a British alliance) that the Executive has taken some step on the presumption that France would declare war, to support which it is necessary to have it believed she will still make war. yesterday they voted in the H. of R. by a majority of 20. to retain a clause in a bill opening commerce with Toussaint, now in rebellion against France. this circumstance with the stationing our armed vessels round the French islands will probably be more than the Directory will bear. in the mean time you observe that the raising the additional army, and building a great additional navy are steadily proposed; and as these will require a great immediate supply of money, a loan of 5. millions is opened at the usurious interest of 8. per cent, for fear that an immediate addition of that to our taxes should blow up the whole object. the following is a statement (in round numbers) of our *annual* income & expenditure divested of those articles of the Treasury report which are accidental.

Income.		Expences.		
1798. Impost	$7\frac{1}{2}$ Millions	Civil list.		$\frac{3}{4}$ million
Excise, carriages &c	$\frac{5}{8}$ of a million	foreign intercourse		$\frac{1}{2}$
	$8\frac{1}{8}$	int. on public debt		4.
1799. Stamp & direct tax,		existing navy	$2\frac{1}{2}$	
clear	2	existing army (5000)	$1\frac{1}{2}$	4
	$10\frac{1}{8}$			$9\frac{1}{4}$
		addnl. army (9000)	$2\frac{1}{2}$	
		addnl. navy (exclus. outfit)	3.	
		int. of new loan	$\frac{4}{10}$	$5\frac{9}{10}$
				$15\frac{1}{7}$

it is said however that the deficit of 5. millions, need not be added to our annual taxes for a year or two. these subjects compared with Gerry's explicit assurance that France is sincere in wishing to avoid war with us, that she does not desire a breach of the British treaty but only to be put on an equal foot, and that a *liberal* treaty might have been had, I leave to your own reflections.—I am told that if you will exert yourself you may be elected to the next Congress. pray my dear Sir, leave nothing undone to effect it. we gain on the whole by the new elections, & if those of Virginia are uniform we shall have a majority. two years more of such measures as we have had lately will ruin us beyond recovery. never did so important a public duty rest on you before. for even a single vote may decide the majority. it is truly a case of moral duty, and I know your conscience will not be insensible to it, if you will indulge it's suggestions. I write to my friends seldom because of the suspected infidelity of the post office. present me respectfully to mrs Page, and accept assurances of great and unaltered affection from Dr. Sir

Yours sincerely   TH: JEFFERSON

RC (Mrs. Henry M. Sage, Albany, New York, 1954); addressed: "John Page of Rosewell in Gloucester now in Richmond"; franked, postmarked at Philadelphia 24 Jan. and at Richmond 3 Feb. 1799; endorsed by Page. PrC (DLC). Enclosures: (1) *Message from the President of the United States, Accompanying Sundry Papers.* (2) *Message from the President of the United States, Accompanying a Report of the Secretary of State.*

As well as dismissing rumors that Bonaparte had been defeated by a vast army of Turks and that France had beseeched Britain for peace, the *Aurora* of 21 Jan. 1799 rejected reports of an offensive and defensive ALLIANCE between the United States and Great Britain. The American people, the newspaper noted, "would not suffer such an outrageous attempt to involve the nation in a then inevitable war—and what would be still worse to connect us with all the vices and corruptions of the British Government."

To John Taylor

DEAR SIR   Philadelphia Jan. 24. 99.

Mr. Tazewell died about noon this day after an illness of about 36. hours. on this event, so melancholy for his family & friends, the loss to the public of so faithful and able a servant no reflections can be adequate.

The object of this letter (and which I beseech you to mention as from me[1] to no mortal) is the replacement of him *by the legislature.* many points in Munro's character would render him the most valuable acquisition the republican interest in this legislature could make. there is no chance of bringing him into the other house as some had wished, because the present representative of his district will not retire. I salute you affectionately   TH: JEFFERSON

RC (MHi: Washburn Collection); addressed: "John Taylor of Caroline now in Richmond"; endorsed by Taylor. PrC (DLC); endorsed by TJ in ink on verso.

The Virginia LEGISLATURE adjourned on 26 Jan. before receiving news of Tazewell's death. On 5 Dec. the Virginia Assembly elected Wilson Cary Nicholas to fill the vacancy (JHD, Dec. 1798-Jan. 1799, 103-4; same, Dec. 1799-Jan. 1800, 10). PRESENT REPRESENTATIVE: Samuel J. Cabell.

¹ Preceding three words interlined.

To James Wood

SIR   Philadelphia Jan. 24. 1799.

In obedience to an instruction from the Senate of the US. I am to perform the melancholy office of informing you that the honourable Henry Tazewell late a Senator of the US. from Virginia departed this life on this day. this is not a place in which I am permitted to indulge those reflections which the loss of so able and virtuous a publick servant naturally suggests. it rests with you, Sir, to make that use of this information which is necessary for supplying his place as speedily as may be in the Senate of the US.

I have the honor to be with great respect Sir
Your most obedt. & most humble servt   TH: JEFFERSON

RC (Vi); addressed: "The Governour of Virginia." Enclosure: Resolution of the Senate, 24 Jan. 1799, directing the president of the Senate to inform the executive of Virginia of the death of Senator Henry Tazewell (Tr in Vi, in hand of and attested by Samuel A. Otis, with subjoined note in Wood's hand and signed by him: "As the above Came by express who expects Compensation, I request the Board to meet this Morning 11 Oclock J Wood. Wednesday Morng"; see JS, 2:573; CVSP, 9:4).

From James Madison

DEAR SIR   Jany. 25. 1799

I have recd. your favor of the 3d. inst: but not till the day before yesterday. The same mail brought me two parcels of the Newspapers, one of which was due two mails & the other one mail sooner. The papers due at the time did not come. You see therefore the uncertain footing of the conveyance. I should be more willing to ascribe the delays to the season of the year, if there were not proofs that there has been no entire failure of the post, and that the complaint is applicable to letters as well as newspapers. All that I have recd. from Mr. Dawson have been several weeks on the passage. The two recd. along with yours were of the 2d. & 3d. instant. I have already intimated to you that Wednesday is the proper day for your letters to leave Philada. in order to avoid a halt by the way. I sent you some time ago the promised state of McGehee's prices. Some of them he signified were put down without being clear that they were the customary ones. But in general he considered them as rather below the standard of your neighbourhood, than above it.

I have long been anxious to know the real complexion of Gerry's report to the Executive. Several symtoms concur with your information, that it does not favor the position which our Govt. wishes to take. Among them is a letter from a person who says he had been shewn Gerry's journal. If truth shall be found to have been suppressed or mistated in order to trick the public into a war or an army, it will be one of the most daring experiments that has been made on the apathy of the people. You do not say whether the narrow escape of Livermore proceeded from a Republican rival or the mere declension of his personal consequence. On the former supposition the State of N. Hampshire must be on the point of abandoning the party it has hitherto been among the foremost in supporting. I see by the vote of the Senate of N.C. on the subject of the Alien & Sedition laws, that great progress has been made in that State towards throwing its weight into the scale of the Administration. What is understood to be the true result of the late elections for Congress? I have never seen a full return of it either for Massts. or S. Carolina or Georgia. I have no late information as to the prospect in the doubtful districts of this State. The opinion Still prevails that Marshal will be disappointed; but it is agreed that the maximum of effort will be used in his favor, and we know that in that case, the issue must be attended with some uncertainty. The proceedings at Richmond find their way to you immediately from thence, better than I can give them to you. Indeed I do not receive them myself, but slowly & through casual opportunitites.

Adieu with the sincerest affection   Js. Madison Jr

I have never yet learnt whether the death of Yard was a true or false report. What is the fact?

RC (DLC: Madison Papers); endorsed by TJ as received 2 Feb.1799 and so recorded in SJL.

The letter from John DAWSON to Madison of 2 Jan. 1799 is printed in Madison, *Papers*, 17:192-3. His letter of 3 Jan. has not been found (same, 17:222).

On 8 Jan. the Philadelphia *Aurora* printed an extract of a letter from Boston in which the author claimed to have seen GERRY'S JOURNAL and from it concluded that if Gerry alone had been entrusted with powers to negotiate with France the mission would have succeeded and that "the haughty conduct and repellent manners of Pinckney and Marshall were in a great degree the cause of our making no treaty."

For North Carolina's response to the ALIEN & SEDITION LAWS, see TJ to Wilson Cary Nicholas, 5 Oct. 1798.

The report of the DEATH OF YARD was false: TJ to Madison, 5 Feb. 1799.

To Henry Remsen

DEAR SIR   Philadelphia Jan. 25. 99.

I take the liberty of inclosing you a letter to be put into the mail of the British packet about to sail.

I ought sooner to have thanked you for a paper you inclosed to me in Virginia, giving the first information I had of the calumny respecting Logan's journey[1] to Europe. a few days before his departure he informed me he was going to Hamburg & thence to Paris, & asked & recieved from me a certificate of his being an American citizen of character, family & fortune, merely to serve him in case he should be questioned on his journey in the present convulsed state of Europe. I had been led to believe his object was private business & so certified; and neither counselled his journey, nor authorised him to say one word politically in my name or any body's name[2] nor wrote a scrip of a pen by him to or for any mortal. this you will have seen that he has candidly declared to the public. however it serves to keep up the ball of a French faction for the present session, and against the next they will invent some other.

I must beg the favor of you to send either to me or to mr Barnes a note of what I am indebted for the newspaper & price current, which he will immediately remit. my wish is to continue a subscriber.

I beg you to accept assurances of the unaltered & sincere esteem of Dr. Sir

Your friend & servt   TH: JEFFERSON

RC (J. M. Fox, Philadelphia, 1946); at foot of text: "Mr. Remsen"; endorsed. Enclosure: TJ to Lucy Ludwell Paradise, recorded in SJL under this date but not found.

Regarding the newspaper Remsen sent from New York concerning the CALUMNY RESPECTING LOGAN'S JOURNEY, see TJ to Aaron Burr, 12 Nov. 1798. TJ's CERTIFICATE for George Logan is printed at 4 June 1798.

By a draft on John BARNES on 9 Jan. 1799 TJ ordered payment of $150 to John Francis on account (MS in ViU: Edgehill-Randolph Papers, written and signed by TJ, endorsed by Barnes, signed on verso by Francis; MB, 2:996). TJ on the 22d requested Barnes to pay $10 "to the bearer for his mother," Henrietta Gardner, for wash-

ing. According to Barnes's endorsement the bearer was Jacob Lawrence, TJ's servant in Philadelphia early in 1799 (MS in ViU: Edgehill-Randolph Papers, written and signed by TJ, endorsed by Barnes; MB, 2:808, 962, 995, 997). On 5 Jan. TJ ordered payment of $10 to Philadelphia publishers John Thompson and Abraham Small to complete payment for a copy of the first hot-pressed Bible printed in the United States. Another draft on Barnes, dated 21 Jan., ordered payment of $13.50 to Sebastian Voight (probably connected to Philadelphia clockmaker Henry Voight) for a "clock plate & wheels" (MSS in MHi, written and signed by TJ, endorsed by Barnes; MB, 2:829, 979, 996, 997; see Sowerby, No. 1469).

NEWSPAPER & PRICE CURRENT: see TJ to Remsen, 25 Mch. 1798.

Letters from Remsen to TJ of 28 Apr. and 10 May 1798, received on 1 and 11 May respectively, are recorded in SJL but have not been found.

[1] Word written over partially erased "mission."
[2] Remainder of sentence interlined.

To Elbridge Gerry

MY DEAR SIR   Philadelphia Jan. 26. 1799.

Your favor of Nov. 12. was safely delivered to me by mr ——,[1] but not till Dec. 28. as I arrived here only three days before that date. it was recieved with great satisfaction. our very long intimacy as fellow-labourers in the same cause, the recent expressions of mutual confidence which had preceded your mission, the interesting course which that had taken, & particularly & personally as it regarded yourself, made me anxious to hear from you on your return. I was the more so too, as I had myself during the whole of your absence, as well as since your return, been a constant butt for every shaft of calumny which malice & false-hood could form, & the presses, public speakers, or private letters dis-seminate. one of these too was of a nature to touch yourself; as if, want-ing confidence in your efforts, I had been capable of usurping powers committed to you, & authorising negociations private & collateral to yours. the real truth is that though Dr. Logan, the pretended mission-ary,[2] about 4. or 5. days before he sailed for Hamburgh, told me he was going there, & thence to Paris, & asked & recieved from me a certificate of his citizenship, character, & circumstances of life, merely as a protection should he be molested on his journey in the present turbulent & suspicious state of Europe, yet[3] I had been led to consider his object as relative to his private affairs; and tho' from an intimacy of some standing, he knew well my wishes for peace, and my political sentiments in general, he nevertheless[4] recieved then no particular dec-laration of them, no authority to communicate them to any mortal, nor to speak to any one in my name, or in any body's name, on that, or any other subject what ever;[5] nor did I write by him a scrip of a pen to any person what ever. this he has himself honestly & publicly declared since his return; & from his well known character & every other[6] circum-stance, every candid man must percieve that his enterprize was dictated by his own enthusiasm, without consultation or communication with any one; that he acted in Paris on his own ground, & made his own way. yet to give some colour to his proceedings which might implicate the republicans in general, & myself particularly,[7] they have not been ashamed to bring forward a supposititious paper drawn by one of their

[645]

own party in the name of Logan, & falsely pretended to have been presented by him to the government of France; counting that the bare[8] mention of my[9] name therein would connect that in the eye of the public with this transaction. in confutation of these & all future calumnies, by way of anticipation, I shall make to you a profession of my political faith; in confidence that you will consider every future imputation on me of a contrary complexion as bearing on it's front the mask of falsehood & calumny.

I do then with sincere zeal wish an inviolable preservation of our present federal constitution, according to the true sense in which it was adopted[10] by the states, that in which it was advocated by it's friends, & not that which it's enemies apprehended, who therefore became it's enemies: and I am opposed to the monarchising it's features by the forms of it's administration, with a view to conciliate a first transition to a President & Senate for life, & from that to a hereditary tenure of these offices, & thus to worm out the elective principle. I am for preserving to the states the powers not yielded by them to the Union,[11] & to the legislature of the Union it's constitutional share in the division of powers: and I am not for transferring all the powers of the states to the general government, & all those of that government to the Executive branch. I am for a government rigorously frugal & simple, applying all the possible savings of the public revenue to the discharge of the national debt: and not for a multiplication of officers & salaries merely to make partizans, & for increasing, by every device, the public debt, on the principle of it's being a public blessing. I am for relying, for internal defence, on our militia solely till actual invasion, and for such a naval force only as may protect our coasts and harbours from such depredations as we have experienced: and not for a standing army in time of peace which may overawe the public sentiment; nor for a navy which by it's own expences and the eternal wars in which it will implicate us, will grind us with public burthens, & sink us under them. I am for free commerce with all nations, political connection with none, & little or no[12] diplomatic establishment: and I am not for linking ourselves, by new treaties[13] with the quarrels of Europe, entering that field of slaughter to preserve their[14] balance, or joining in the confederacy of kings to war against the principles of liberty. I am for freedom of religion, & against all maneuvres to bring about a legal ascendancy of one sect over another:[15] for freedom of the press, & against all violations of the constitution to silence by force & not by reason[16] the complaints or criticisms, just or unjust, of our citizens against the conduct of their agents. and I am for encouraging the progress of science in all it's branches; and not for raising a hue and cry against the sacred name of philosophy, for awing[17] the human mind, by stories of rawhead & bloody bones, to a distrust of it's own vision & to repose implicitly on that of others; to go backwards instead of forwards to look for improvement, to believe that government, religion, morality & every other science were in the highest perfection in ages of the darkest ignorance, and that nothing can ever be devised more perfect than what was established by[18] our forefathers. to these I will add that I was a sincere wellwisher to the success of the French revolution, and still wish it may end in the establishment of a free & well ordered republic:[19] but I have not been insensible under the atrocious depredations they have committed on our commerce. the first object of my heart is my own country. in that is embarked my family, my fortune, & my own existence. I have not one farthing of interest, nor one fibre of attachment out of it, nor a single motive of preference of any one nation to another but in proportion as they are more or less friendly to us. but though deeply feeling the injuries of France, I did not think war the surest mode of redressing them. I did believe that a mission sincerely disposed to preserve peace, would obtain for us a peaceable & honourable settlement and retribution; & I appeal to you to say whether this might not have been obtained, if either of your collegues had been of the same sentiment with[20] yourself.—these my friend are my principles; they are unquestionably the principles of the great body of our fellow citizens,[21] and I know there is not one[22] of them which is not yours also. in truth we never differed but on one ground, the funding system; and as from the moment of it's being adopted by the constituted authorities, I became religiously principled in the sacred discharge of it to the uttermost farthing, we are now united even on that single ground of difference.

I turn now to your enquiries. the inclosed paper will answer one of them. but you also ask for such political information as may be possessed by me & interesting to yourself in regard to your embassy. as a proof of my entire confidence in you I shall give it fully & candidly. when Pinckney, Marshal, and Dana were nominated to settle our differences with France, it was suspected by many, from what was understood[23] of their dispositions, that their mission would not result in a settlement of differences; but would produce circumstances tending to widen the breach, and to provoke our citizens to consent to a war with that nation, & union with England. Dana's resignation, & your appointment gave the first gleam of hope of a peaceable issue to the mission. for it was believed that you were sincerely disposed to accomodation: & it was not long after your arrival there before symptoms were observed of that difference of views which had been suspected to exist.—In the mean time however[24] the aspect of our government towards the French republic²⁵ had become so ardent that the people of America generally took the alarm. to the Southward their apprehensions were early excited. in the Eastern states also they at length began to break out. meetings were held in many of your towns, & addresses to the government agreed on in opposition to war. the example was spreading like wild fire. other meetings were called in other places, & a general concurrence of sentiment against the apparent inclinations of the government was imminent, when, most critically for the government, the dispatches of Oct. 22. prepared²⁶ by your collegue Marshall with a view to their being made public,²⁷ dropped into their laps. it was truly a God-send to them, & they made the most of it. many thousands of copies were printed & dispersed gratis at the public expence; & the zealots for war co-operated so heartily that there were instances of single individuals who printed & dispersed 10, or 12,000 copies at their own expence. the odiousness of the²⁸ corruption supposed²⁹ in those papers excited a general & high indignation among the people. unexperienced³⁰ in such maneuvres, they did not permit themselves even to suspect that the turpitude of private swindlers might mingle itself unobserved, & give it's own hue to the communications³¹ of the French government, of whose participation there was neither proof nor probability. it served however, for a time, the purpose intended. the people in many places gave a loose to the expressions of their warm indignation, & of their honest preference of war to dishonour. the fever was long & succesfully kept up, and in the mean time war measures as ardently crouded.—still however as it was known that your collegues were coming away, & yourself to stay, though disclaiming a separate power to conclude a treaty, it was hoped by the lovers of peace that³² a project of treaty would have been prepared, ad referendum,³³ on principles which would have satisfied our citizens, & overawed any bias of the government towards a different policy. but the expedition of the Sophia, and, as was supposed, the suggestions of the person charged with your dispatches, & his probable misrepresentations³⁴ of the real wishes of the American people, prevented these hopes. they had then only to look forward to your return for such information either through the Executive, or from yourself, as might present³⁵ to our view the other side of the medal. the dispatches of Oct. 22. 97. had presented one face. that information, to a certain degree, is now recieved; & the public will see from your correspondence with Taleyrand that France, as you testify, 'was sincere & anxious to obtain a reconciliation, not wishing us to break the British treaty, but only to give her equivalent stipulations, and in general was disposed to a liberal treaty.'³⁶ and they will judge whether mr Pickering's report shews³⁷ an inflexible determination to believe no declarations the

French government can make, nor any opinion which you, judging on the spot & from actual view, can give of their sincerity, and to meet their designs of peace with operations of war. the alien & sedition acts have already operated in the South as powerful sedatives of the XYZ. inflammation. in your quarter where violations of principle are either less regarded or more concealed, the direct tax is likely to have the same effect, & to excite enquiries into the object of the enormous expences & taxes we are bringing on. and your information supervening that we might have a liberal accomodation if we would, there can be little doubt of the reproduction of that general movement which had been changed for a moment by the dispatches of Oct. 22. and tho' small checks & stops, like Logan's pretended embassy, may be thrown in the way from time to time, & may a little retard it's motion, yet the tide is already turned and will sweep before it all[38] the feeble obstacles of art. the unquestionable republicanism of the American mind will break through the mist under which it has been clouded, and will oblige it's agents to reform the principles & practices of their administration.[39]

You suppose that you have been abused by both parties. as far as has come to my knowledge you are misinformed. I have never seen or heard a sentence of blame uttered against you by the republicans, unless we were so to construe their wishes that you had more boldly cooperated in a project of a treaty, and would more explicitly state whether there was in your collegues that flexibility which persons earnest after peace would have practised? whether, on the contrary, their demeanor was not cold, reserved and distant at least, if not backward? and whether, if they had yielded to those informal conferences which Taleyrand seems to have courted, the liberal accomodation you suppose might not have been effected, even with their agency? your fellow citizens think they have a right to full information in a case of such great concernment to them. it is their sweat which is to earn all the expences of the war, and their blood which is to flow in expiation of the causes of it. it may be in your power to save them from these miseries by full communications and unrestrained details,[40] postponing motives of delicacy to those of duty. it rests with you to come forward independantly, to take your stand on the high ground of your own character, to disregard calumny, and to be borne above it on the shoulders of your grateful fellow citizens, or to sink into the humble oblivion to which the Federalists (self-called)[41] have secretly condemned you, and even to be happy if they will indulge you with oblivion while they have beamed on your collegues meridian splendor.[42] pardon me, my dear Sir, if my expressions are strong. my feelings are so much more so, that it is with difficulty I reduce them even to the tone I use. if you doubt the dispositions towards you, look into the papers on both sides for the toasts which were given through all the states on the 4th. of July. you will there see whose hearts were with you, and whose were ulcerated against you. indeed as soon as it was known that you had consented to stay in Paris, there was no measure observed in the execrations of the war-party, they openly wished you might be guillotined, or sent to Cayenne, or any thing else: and these expressions were finally stifled [43] from a principle of policy only, & to prevent you from being urged to a justification of yourself. from this principle alone proceeds the silence, & cold respect they observe towards you. still they cannot prevent at times the flames bursting from under the embers, as mr Pickering's letters, report, & conversations testify as well as the indecent expressions respecting you indulged by some of them in the debate on these dispatches. these sufficiently shew that you are never more to be honoured or trusted by them, & that they wait to crush you for ever only till they can do it without danger to themselves. [44]

When I sat down to answer your letter, but two courses presented themselves. either to say nothing or every thing; for half-confidences are not in my character. I could not hesitate which was due to you. I have unbosomed myself fully; & it will certainly be highly gratifying if I recieve a like confidence from you. for even if we differ in principle more than I believe we do, you & I know too well the texture of the human mind, & the slipperiness of human reason, to consider differences of opinion otherwise than differences of form or feature. integrity of views, more than their soundness, is the basis of esteem.   I shall follow your direction in conveying this by a private hand; tho' I know not as yet when one worthy of confidence will occur: [45] & my trust in you leaves me without a fear that this letter, meant as a confidential communication [46] of my impressions, may ever go out of your own hand, or be suffered in any wise to commit my name. [47] indeed, besides the accidents which might happen to it even under your care, considering the accident of death to which yourself are liable, I think it safest to pray you, after reading it as often as you please to destroy at least the 2d. & 3d. leaves. the 1st. contains principles only, which I fear not to avow; but the 2d. & 3d contain facts stated for your information, and which though sacredly conformable to my firm belief, yet would be galling to some, & expose me to illiberal attacks. I therefore repeat my prayer to burn the 2d. & 3d. leaves. and did we ever expect to see the day when, breathing nothing but sentiments of love to our country & it's freedom & happiness, our correspondence must be as secret as if we were hatching it's destruction! Adieu, my friend, and accept my sincere & affectionate salutations. I need not add my signature. [48]

RC (NNPM); endorsed by Gerry: "Phi-lozette His Exy Mr Jefferson 26 Jany 1799 & copies of Answers 15 & 20 of Jany 1801." PrC (DLC); with enclosure letter-pressed on last leaf (see below). Dft (same); heavily emended, with the most significant emendations and variations recorded in notes below; variations in paragraphing not recorded.

Gerry did not reply to this letter until January 1801. RECENT EXPRESSIONS OF MUTUAL CONFIDENCE between TJ and Gerry preceding the latter's journey to France included nine letters they exchanged between 27 Mch. and 6 July 1797 (see Vol. 29:326-7, 355-6, 361-6, 387, 398-9, 402, 448-9, 475-6). Their last previous corre-spondence had been a letter from TJ to Gerry of 26 Feb. 1793.

See 4 June 1798 for TJ's CERTIFICATE for George Logan.

For Francis DANA'S RESIGNATION as envoy to France, or more properly his de-clining the nomination, and Adams's AP-POINTMENT of Gerry in his place, see Senate Resolution on Appointment of Charles C. Pinckney, [5 June 1797]. The DISPATCHES OF OCT. 22. PREPARED BY YOUR COLLEGUE MARSHALL were the reports from Marshall, Pinckney, and Gerry, dated 22 Oct. 1797 through 8 Jan. 1798, released to Congress in April 1798 (see TJ to John Wayles Eppes, 11 Apr., and Monroe to TJ, 4 May 1798).

PERSON CHARGED WITH YOUR DIS-PATCHES: Clement Humphreys.

'WAS SINCERE & ANXIOUS . . . DISPOSED TO A LIBERAL TREATY': what TJ depicted as a consolidated quotation is actually his para-phrasing of language in Gerry's correspon-dence with Talleyrand recently conveyed to Congress and published (see TJ to Monroe, 23 Jan. 1799). The intention of France to reconcile sincerely appears in item no. 14 of that correspondence, Talleyrand's letter to Gerry of 10 June 1798, and no. 23, Talley-rand's of 12 July. Gerry reported Talley-rand's declaration that France did not ex-pect the U.S. to break the Jay Treaty in his covering letter to Pickering of 1 Oct. 1798. The term "liberal" or "liberality" with re-gard to France's intent for a new treaty with the United States appeared in that cover letter as well as in no. 23 and no. 24, Gerry's reply to Talleyrand on 20 July (ASP,

Foreign Relations, 2:206, 207, 212, 219, 221).

The 2D. & 3D. LEAVES of the MS contain all of the text beginning with the paragraph that opens "I turn now to your enquiries" and continuing to the end of the letter.

[1] PrC: "Binney," which TJ almost en-tirely erased in RC and replaced with a se-ries of flourishes shown here as a dash. Dft: "Binney."

[2] Preceding three words interlined in Dft.

[3] Here in Dft TJ canceled "not a word."

[4] In Dft TJ interlined the preceding eight words in place of "yet he."

[5] Remainder of sentence interlined in Dft.

[6] Preceding six words and ampersand interlined in Dft in place of "every."

[7] In Dft TJ interlined the preceding passage beginning with "the republicans" in place of "me," and "the republicans in general" is a substitution for "republican party."

[8] In Dft TJ interlined the passage from "a supposititious" to this point in place of "a forgery committed by one of their own party, as if presented to the French govern-ment by Taleyrand, and the sentiments of which are so evidently different from their own that nothing but could have induced it's being made use of but that it."

[9] Foot of page in MS. TJ wrote the re-mainder of the paragraph in the margin.

[10] In Dft TJ interlined the remainder of this passage to the colon in place of "& which I know to have been highly re-publican."

[11] TJ interlined the preceding seven words in Dft in place of "left them by the constitution, and for."

[12] In Dft TJ interlined preceding three words and ampersand in place of "and the reduction of [. . .] expensive & mischief making."

[13] Three words interlined in Dft.

[14] Word underlined in Dft and in ink on PrC.

[15] Preceding nine words interlined in Dft in place of "on religious establish-ments."

[16] Preceding five words and ampersand interlined in Dft.

[17] Word interlined in Dft in place of "deterring."

[18] Two words interlined in Dft in place of "known to." In Dft TJ wrote the passage following this sentence, from "to these I will add" through "same sentiment with yourself," in the margin and keyed it for insertion in the body of the text.

[19] Word interlined in Dft in place of "government."

[20] Preceding five words interlined in Dft in place of "as earnest in it as."

[21] Preceding thirteen words interlined in Dft.

[22] Foot of page in MS. TJ wrote the remainder of the paragraph in the margin.

[23] In Dft TJ interlined preceding seven words in place of "believed by the republicans generally, from a knolege."

[24] In Dft TJ first wrote the long passage that follows—beginning "the aspect of our government" and ending "war measures as ardently crouded"—farther below in the letter, preceding "the alien & sedition acts have already operated in the South." He subsequently marked the passage for transposition to this point.

[25] Preceding four words interlined in Dft in place of "to a war with France."

[26] In Dft TJ interlined the preceding phrase in place of "story of W.X.Y.Z. cooked up."

[27] Here in Dft TJ interlined but canceled: "as is known to me, but I believe not to you," enclosing the insertion in square brackets.

[28] Here in Dft TJ canceled "attempt at bribery."

[29] Word interlined in Dft in place of "presented."

[30] Prefix of word interlined in Dft in place of "your town meetings were arrested, or took a contrary turn; which concealed from their minds, not."

[31] In Dft, passage from "might mingle itself" through this word is an interlineation in place of "was played off on their credulity for that."

[32] Preceding six words interlined in Dft.

[33] Two words interlined in Dft in place of "for the consideration of government."

[34] In Dft TJ first wrote "& misrepresenting to you that a momentary delusion" before altering the the clause to read as above.

[35] In Dft, the passage beginning with this word and running through "operations of war. the alien &" is on a piece TJ affixed to the original page. The passage superseded by the new text reads in part: "believed that these alone have retarded your determination: but [. . .] never will consent to remain under the cloud they have drawn over [. . .] while they have beamed on your collegues meridian splendour. it is the less [. . .] because in doing justice to yourself, you will perform a duty to your fellow citizens; who in all cases of such high concernment have a right to judge their agents, & to controul by the expressions of the public sentiments any bias eminently injurious to them. you observe that you have been abused by both parties. in this, as far as has come to my knolege, you are misinformed. I have never seen a sentence of blame uttered against you by the republicans, unless we were so to construe their wishes that you had been bolder. I shall state to you some facts, which having taken place while you were absent may not have become known to you." In Dft this passage, portions of which TJ incorporated later in the text, immediately precedes the large block that he transposed to a position earlier in the text (see note 24 above).

[36] After "in general" TJ canceled "to have." In Dft he first wrote: "in general to have concurred liberally in a treaty" before altering the passage to read as above.

[37] Here in Dft TJ canceled "them equally that our admn is invincible."

[38] TJ here canceled "artificial."

[39] Here in Dft TJ canceled: "and it rests with yourself, my dear," and in Dft the text that follows, from "You Suppose" through "meridian splendor" below (see note 42), is on a piece that TJ attached to the sheet.

[40] Preceding three words interlined in Dft in place of "if there be any thing yet untold, and by."

[41] Words in parentheses lacking in Dft.

[42] In Dft remainder of paragraph is partially obscured by the piece attached to the larger sheet as described in note 39 above.

[43] Word interlined in Dft in place of "hushed up."

[44] Preceding two sentences interlined in Dft in place of "but the known frame of your mind will prevent your being ever more troubled or honoured by them."

[45] In Dft TJ wrote the succeeding passage, through "commit my name," as an interlineation continued in the margin.

[46] Dft: "explanation."

[47] The text that follows, through "I there-

fore repeat my prayer to burn the 2d. & 3d. leaves. and," is lacking in Dft, which continues here: "but did we ever expect ⟨to live⟩ to see the day."

[48] Final sentence lacking in Dft.

Senate Votes on Gerry's Appointment as Envoy to France

Yeas.	Nays.	
Langdon ⎱ Livermore ⎰		N.H.
	Goodhue ⎱ Sedgwick ⎰	Mas.
Bradford ⎱ Foster ⎰		R.I.
Hillhouse	Tracy	Con.
Paine ⎱ Tichenor ⎰		Verm.
Laurence		N.Y.
Rutherford		N.J.
Bingham	Ross	Pens.
Latimer		Del.
Howard		Mar.
Tazewell ⎱ Mason ⎰		V.
Bloodworth ⎱ Martin ⎰		N.C
Hunter	Reade	S.C.
Tatnall		G
Blount ⎱ Cocke ⎰		Ten.
Brown	Marshall	Kentuck.

PrC (DLC); entirely in TJ's hand; letterpressed perpendicularly at bottom of last leaf of PrC of covering letter.

Responding to Gerry's 12 Nov. request "for the yeas & nays of my appointment," TJ made this list of the votes in the Senate on 22 June 1797 when it consented to Adams's nomination of Gerry as one of the three envoys extraordinary and ministers plenipotentiary to the French Republic (JEP, 1:245).

From Robert R. Livingston

DEAR SIR   ClerMont 26th. Jany 1799.

Surrounded as you are at present by the mists of politicks, & those too of a nature to defuse, like other fogs, are obscurity & gloom upon every object, I flatter myself, that it will not be unpleasing to you, to let your eyes rest for a moment upon a spot irradiated by a slight glimmering of philosophy. I therefore take the liberty to communicate & to ask your sentiments on the subject of an invention with which I have amused my leisure hours.

Physicks, & Mechanicks, never formed a nobler union, than in the invention of the steam engine. Which at once subjects the most powerful, & the most common agents to man. He reposes at ease, while fire air & water perform his most laborious tasks. The slow steps by which this engine has advanced to its present state of improvement, are realy astonishing, considering how naturally most of those improvements must have suggested themselves. But even now it appears to me very imperfect. The first defect is the want of simplicity in those forms of it in which the object is to raise water to no great heights, as this occurs very frequently, as in drying marshes, freeing dry docks, & ships from water &c. It wd be extreamly desirable to have an engine so constructed as to cost little, & not to require the care & attention of an artist. The second defect of the most improved engine (Docr. Watts) is the loss of power occasioned by the friction. The dry piston, & the working rod, exhaust near one third of his gross power, when to this is added the opposition the air gives to his air pumps, their friction, & the friction of the pumps when water is raised, it will be found that one half of the force is lost, even where his engine acts to most advantage, to wit in the raising of water.

It is still more defective when it is applied to obtain a circular motion. This it gets either by a winch or planet wheels, the latter he prefers. In this case supposing his power 2100. $\frac{1}{3}$ lost in friction—near 100 W. in friction of the air pumps, (exclusive of the opposition of the atmosphere,) the friction & vis enertiæ of the beam; have about 1200 ℔ to apply to the winch or planet wheels whose friction cannot be less than $\frac{1}{4}$ of that weight, but as in turning a winch by their means, there are two points on which the wheels do not act at all, but depend on the fly to carry them past, & only two other points on which the machine acts at right angles, the mean between nothing & 900. is the whole power directly applied to obtain a circular motion, or in other words a gross power of 2100 ℔. in the engine is reduced to 450 ℔ when it turns a wheel. I have attempted to remedy these defects in Docr. Watts engine, with what success you will judge when I explain my principles, & examine the rough sketches I shall enclose. First to obtain a simple engine, & that can be erected at a trivial expence. Take a box or hogd. of wood, of sufficient strength, & connect this with a tube of wood, which is to serve as a pump, & is imersed in water; the bore of the pump to be small,

& at the hight of 20 feet, to which the water is to be raised, let there be
a large chamber, fitted to hold so much water as is to be discharged at
every lift—Into this a valve must open from the lower or narrow part of
the pump—Let a nozel lead from this chamber, the mouth of which
must be covered with a valve that opens outward. from this chamber a
narrow pipe must lead in to the Cylinder & be furnished with a valve
that opens into it. This must be placed so high that no water can get in
to the cylinder—On the top of the pump place a valve that opens, so as
to admit air, in order that the water may run out when raised into the
chamber of the pump.

The Cylinder must be furnished with the usual snifter valves, thro'
which condensing water, & air, may be discharged. A steam cock &
condensing cock (the water for which may be taken, from the pump)
these several cocks may be worked by hand, by floats—by the water
raised (as in the plan enclose'd) or a small atmospheric engine on the top
of the cylinder—Suppose the hogd. or cylinder to contain thirty cubic
feet & the pump Chamber ten. When a vacuum is made in the cylinder,
the air will rush into it, to supply the vacuum. That is to say the air
which before occupied ten feet, will now occupy forty, & of course be
$\frac{3}{4}$ lighter than the external air. The water will of course rise about 24
feet in the pump. When the steam is agn let into the Cylinder the valve
of communication must close, & the cock on the top of the pump open,
which forces open the valve on the nozel of the pump, & drives the
water out, thus at every stroke ten cubic feet of water will be raised
upwards of twenty feet. If it is desired to raise it to a greater hight, it
may be done by enlarging the cylinder, & working several pumps at
once, the upper pump, reciving its water from the reservore of the
Lower one, & all communicating, by small channels or pipes, with the
cylinder. It is true that this engine wastes some steam, because the vacuum is only the difference between the contents of the cylinder & the
bore of the pump, which we have stated at $\frac{1}{4}$, but Docr Watts engine
looses $\frac{1}{3}$ in friction $\frac{1}{8}$ in his air pumps $\frac{1}{4}$ of the remaining power in the
friction of the forcing pump besides the vis enertæ of his beam chains
&c. So that in fact this simple engine requires less steam than his complex one to do the same work. As the cylinder is of wood, & may be
lined & covered with blankets, or matts, or any other non conductor, it
will be kept nearly of the temperature of the steam, the air which is
admitted being a bad conductor of heat, can carry off little of it. The
condensing water will be the only active agent for this purpose. but as
wood parts with its heat very slowly, much less will be lost in this, than
in NewCombs engine, tho perhaps more than in Watts. You will observe that as the only object here of the steam is to expel the air, the

[655]

water need not be more than boiling hot, so that no extraordinary strength is necessary in the boiler; In Watts machine the heat of the steam is equal to 4 ℔ more than the incumbent atmosphere. To loose less heat, & because it is cheaper, I have made a boiler of wood with a furnace in the centre. And I find when the steam is so hot as to raise a weight of 4 ℔ upon a square inch that it imparts so little heat to the wood, that you may lay the back of your hand agt the outside of two & half inch plank (of which the boiler is composed) without any inconvenience—That I may not engross too much of your very valuable time at one period, I shall defer till another opportunity, my discription of an engine, in which I think I have the full power of Docr Watts, without loosing any by friction of the piston working rod or air pumps (tho I use them) as I have contrived the whole machinery to work witht. friction. And also another in which the whole power, can be directly applied to obtain a circular motion without winch or planet wheels. prudence bids me to afford you an opportunity of detecting the faults of this, before I expose a second child of fancy to your critical inspection.

Now few people would believe that a noted Democrat shd address so long a letter to you without a word of politicks.

I have the honor to be Sir with the highest respect & esteem Your Most Obt hum: Servt   ROBT R LIVINGSTON

RC (PPAmP); at foot of text: "The honble Thoms Jefferson Esqr."; note by Livingston on verso of last page: "Should any thing in this appear to merret the notice of the Philosophical society (of which I have not the honor to be a member) you may communicate it—"; endorsed by TJ as received 20 Feb. 1799 and so recorded in SJL; endorsed for the American Philosophical Society as "Livingston on Steam Engines," read on 1 Mch. 1799 and referred to Robert Patterson and Charles Willson Peale.

NEWCOMBS ENGINE: the steam engine designed by Thomas Newcomen.

TJ departed Philadelphia for Monticello on 1 Mch. 1799 and did not attend that day's meeting of the Philosophical Society at which this paper, recorded in the minutes as "On an improved steam engine," was read. Patterson and Peale reported on Livingston's paper at a meeting of 19 Apr., and the society took no further action on the matter at that time (APS, Proceedings, 22, pt. 3 [1884], 280, 281; MB, 2:999).

On 24 Jan. 1799, Jonathan Williams wrote a letter addressed to "The President or Chairman protem of the Philosophical Society." Pleading that his residence outside Philadelphia made it impossible for him to attend even the regular meetings of the APS on any consistent basis, Williams requested that someone else be substituted for him on the standing committee appointed in 1797 to solicit natural history specimens and cultural artifacts from the frontier regions (see note to Hugh Williamson to TJ, 3 Mch. 1798). TJ made no endorsement on Williams's letter and did not enter it in SJL. When it was read at a meeting of the society on 1 Feb. 1799, with TJ presiding, the Reverend Dr. Nicholas Collin, one of the society's curators, was put on the committee in Williams's place (RC in PPAmP, endorsed for the society; APS, Proceedings, 22, pt. 3 [1884], 277, 279).

On 30 Jan. TJ paid John B. Guenat, the collection agent for the APS, two dollars for his dues subscription for 1799 (John Vaughan to Guenat, 20 Jan. 1799, MS in PPAmP; MB, 2:997).

Livingston's Steam Engine

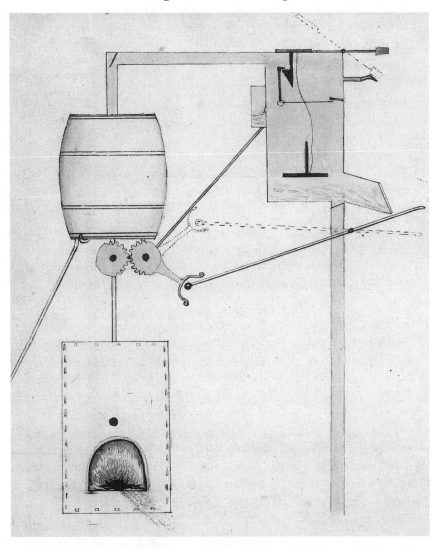

MS (PPAmP); endorsed for the APS: "Livingston's Steam Engine."

From James Monroe

Dear Sir   Albemarle Jany 26. 1799.

Yours of the 3d. reached me yesterday as did likewise that of Dr. Bache mentioned in yours. I shall do every thing in my power to fulfill the Drs. wishes & hope to procure him a settlement in our neighbourhood, such as he will approve. The plan you suggest for negotiation with the parties having land for sale is judicious & shall be followed. Tho' I fear the price of each will be high & that it will not be easy to lessen it with either. I wish also that Baynham co'd. be added to our circle, as the acquisition of him wod. be important in many respects, nor shall I fail to invite him by such services as I can render. The[1] enterprise of Logan with its consequences will not hurt any in his political sentiments, while the attempt to make it instrumental to that end will have its advantages. The ill humour shewn by the head and all the members of the opposit party, at an interference forbidden by no law, prompted by benevolent motive, & wh. was useful to the publick, is a circumstance wh. will tend to shew the views of that party. The longer there fore the debate is kept up on the resolution, and the greater the zeal of its friends the better the effect, since at best it is legislating on an abstract principle, agnst the form of a precedent shewing the folly of the law. I recd. by the post a letter of wh. I subjoin a copy, because as I recd. & opend several at the same time, I cannot say whether it came inclosed, or otherwise. If in the latter mode as it had inscribed on the seal "Directoire Executif" it may have attracted the attention of those in office & become the subject of animadvertion. If this shod. be the case you will use it as you think fit. We are all well & unite in wishes for yr. welfare.

Paris 7th. Fructidor an: 6 de la republique Francaise.
Citoyen—

Le docteur Logan que J'ai eu le plaisir de voir ici, m'offre une occasion infiniment agreable de me rapeler a votre souvenir; et J'en profit avec d'autant plus de satisfaction, que votre depart de France m'a causé de plus vifs regrets.

Le Dr. Logan vous dira qu'il a été temoin des dispositions pacifiques du gouvernement Français envers votre nation; et il en emporte des preuves non equivoques. Puisse le genie de la liberté seconder nos efforts pour dejouer les machinations britaniques contre l'independance de nos freres les Americains! Jamais elle n'a couru d'aussi grands dangers, et vous devez conceviur qu'ils doivent nous allarmer. La liberté des Etats unis nous a couté assez de sang et de trésor pour qu'elle nous soit chére.

Je vous prie de me rappeler au souvenir de Mde. M. & de lui faire agréer mon respectueux hommage. recevez mes salutations fraternelles & amicales.—Merlin

EDITORS' TRANSLATION

Paris 7th Fructidor Year 6 of the French Republic [24 Aug. 1798].
Citizen—

Doctor Logan, whom I have had the pleasure of seeing here, offers me an infinitely agreeable chance to pay you my respects; and I take advantage of it with all the more pleasure, since your departure from France caused me the sharpest of regrets.

Dr. Logan will tell you that he has been a witness to the peaceful dispositions of the French government towards your nation; and he bears away unequivocal proofs of it. May the genius of liberty assist our efforts to undo the British machinations against the independence of our brothers, the Americans! Never has it encountered such great dangers, and you must realize that they must alarm us. The freedom of the United States has cost us enough blood and treasure for it to be precious to us.

I beg you to pay my respects to Mrs. M. & to request her to accept my most respectful homage. Accept my fraternal & friendly greetings. —Merlin

RC (DLC); endorsed by TJ as received 2   [1] Monroe here canceled "whole."
Feb. 1799 and so recorded in SJL.

Notes on a Letter from Thomas Tingey to the Secretary of the Navy

Extract of a letter from Capt. Tingey, on board the Ganges at St. Thomas. 27th Jany. 1799:

I understood from Capt. Smith and the other two captain's who were on board the Hannibal [a British ship of war][1] at the time, that an almost total stagnation to the French privateering had taken place in consequence of so heavy a penalty for their behavior having been decreed, that very few were able or willing to comply with, and that not more than one in twenty of the prizes they took were French vessels. from this I could not but presage little business from[2] the Ganges.'

The war party have always insisted that the late arret by which the French government pretended to regulate & restrain their privateers was nugatory, & meant to delude, because they were still to conduct themselves by the laws of the republic, the very laws under which we have suffered so much. this authentic information shews it has been so effectual as to put down nearly the whole [. . .].—they pretend too that this disappearance of French cruisers is solely the effect of our arming. this information shews the chief cause of their disappearance is very different.

PrC (MHi); entirely in TJ's hand, including one set of brackets identified in note 1 below; faint.

The EXTRACT is from a letter Thomas Tingey wrote as a report to Benjamin Stoddert. The *Philadelphia Gazette* printed the letter in full on 16 Feb. 1799. As a young man Tingey, English-born, had served in the British naval service. He had experience as a merchant captain in the West Indies trade and was living in New Jersey in September 1798 when, during the congressional recess, John Adams named him a captain in the U.S. Navy. The *Ganges*

under Tingey's command cruised the Windward Passage during the winter of 1798-99 with particular orders "to capture or destroy the Armed Vessels fitted out under the Authority of France." Early in January 1799 he spoke to the commanders of three British warships off the coast of Saint-Domingue (NDQW, Nov. 1798-Mch. 1799, 84-5, 283-7; DAB; JEP, 1:308).

LATE ARRET: see Jacob Van Staphorst to TJ, 25 July 1798.

[1] TJ's brackets.
[2] NDQW, Nov. 1798-Mch. 1799, 284, and *Philadelphia Gazette*: "for."

From George Jefferson

DEAR SIR,   Richmond 29th. Janr. 1799

Your favor of the 22d. is duly received. I have several times seen the part owner of the sloop rising sun, whom I before mentioned to you, who informs me the Capt. has not yet recovered his health—if he does not shortly, so as to be enabled to go round to the vessel this Gentlemen has determined positively to go himself—of which I will give you information.

So far from most of your Tobo. being down, not a Hhd: has yet come—it has been owing I suppose until latterly to the river being very low—but there is now a fine tide, & has been for ten days, so that I suppose it may shortly be expected. Tobo. sells here only at 51/. Cash—$:10.—is the highest it has sold at on a credit—tho' as yet scarcely any shipments have been made—wheat would command 9/. at 90 days, & flour $7\frac{1}{2}$ & 8$:.

I am Mt. sincerely Dear Sir Your Very humble: servt.

GEO. JEFFERSON

RC (MHi); at foot of text: "Thos. Jefferson esqr."; endorsed by TJ as received 6 Feb. 1799 and so recorded in SJL.

To Edmund Pendleton

DEAR SIR   Philadelphia Jan. 29. 99.

Your patriarchal address to your county is running through all the republican papers, and has a very great effect on the people. it is short, simple and presents things in a view they readily comprehend. the character & circumstances too of the writer leave them without doubts of his motives. if like the patriarch of old you had but one blessing to give us, I should have wished it directed to a particular object. but I hope you have one for this also. you know what a wicked use has been made of the French negociation: and particularly of the XYZ dish cooked up by Marshall, where the swindlers are made to appear as the French government. art and industry combined have certainly wrought out of this business a wonderful effect on the people. yet they have been astonished more than they have understood it, and now that Gerry's correspondence comes out, clearing the French government of that turpitude & shewing them 'sincere in their dispositions for peace, not wishing us to break the British treaty, and willing to arrange a liberal one with us' the people will be disposed to suspect they have been duped. but these communications are too voluminous for them, and beyond their reach. a recapitulation is now wanting of the whole story, stating every thing according to what we may now suppose to have been the truth, short, simple & levelled to every capacity. nobody in America can do it so well as yourself, in the same character of the father of your county or any form you like better, and so concise as, omitting nothing material, may yet be printed in hand bills of which we could print & disperse 10, or 20,000 copies under letter covers through all the US. by the members of Congress when they return home. if the understanding of the people could be rallied to the truth on this subject, by exposing the dupery practised on them there are so many other things about to bear on them favorably for the resurrection of their republican spirit, that a reduction of the administration to constitutional principles cannot fail to be the effect. these are the Alien & Sedition laws, the vexations of the stamp act, the disgusting particularities of the direct tax, the additional army without an enemy & recruiting officers lounging at every court house, a navy of 50. ships, 5. millions to be raised to build it on the usurious interest of 8. per cent, the perseverance in war on our part, when the French government shew such an anxious desire to keep at peace with us, taxes of 10. millions now paid by 4. millions of people and yet a necessity in a year or two of raising 5. millions more for annual expence. these things will immediately be bearing on the public mind, and if it remain not still blinded by a supposed necessity for the purposes of maintaining our independance & defending our country, they will set things to rights. I hope you will undertake this statement. if any body else had possessed your happy talent for this kind of recapitulation,[1] I would have been the last to disturb you with the application; but it will really be rendering our country a service greater than it is in the power of any other individual to render. to save you the trouble of hunting up the several documents from which this statement is to be taken I have collected them here compleatly and inclose them to you.

Logan's bill is passed. on this subject it is hardly necessary for me to declare to you on every thing sacred, that the part they ascribed to me was entirely a calumny. Logan called on me 4. or 5. days before his departure & asked & recieved a certificate (in my private capacity) of his citizenship & circumstances of life, merely as a protection should he be molested in the present turbulent state of Europe. I have given such to an hundred others, & they have been much more frequently asked & obtained by tories than whigs. I did not write a scrip of a pen by him to any person. from long acquaintance he knew my wishes for peace & my political sentiments generally, but he recieved no particular declaration of them then, nor one word of authority to speak in my name, or any body's name on that or any other subject. it was an enterprize founded in the enthusiasm of his own character. he went on his own ground & made his own way. his object was virtuous, and the effect meritorious. accept my sincere prayers for long & happy years to you still and my affectionate salutations & Adieu.   TH: JEFFERSON

RC (MHi: Washburn Collection); addressed: "The honorable Edmund Pendleton Chief Justice of Virginia near the Bowling green"; franked and postmarked; endorsed by Pendleton with notation: "Abuses of Adams's admn—useless army & officers—had no agency in Logan's trip to France." PrC (DLC). Enclosures not found.

Pendleton's PATRIARCHAL ADDRESS "To the respectable Freeholders and other citizens of the county of Caroline" was dated "December court, 1798," and was intended to be read at a public meeting in the county. Pendleton, the chief justice of the Virginia Court of Appeals, noted that Caroline County had a long tradition of peaceful expression against distasteful federal measures. The arrival of Francis Corbin upset "this happy situation," for instead of participating "in our harmony," Corbin intended "to interrupt its progress, and raise dissen-tions and parties amongst us, those great enemies to *social*, as well as *private* happiness." Corbin opposed a memorial sent to the Virginia Assembly from Caroline County objecting to the bellicose tendencies of Congress, the Alien Friends Act, and the Sedition Act. He tried to initiate a new memorial expressing support for all of the federal government's measures, and called the meeting for which Pendleton composed his address. Pendleton laid out his reasons for opposing the strengthening of the military and the Alien and Sedition Acts, concluding that "the true character of good citizens" embodied support for the Constitution and defense of the nation coupled with diligent guardianship of citizens' rights (*Aurora*, 15 Jan. 1799).

Concerning TJ's paraphrasing of GERRY'S CORRESPONDENCE to the effect that the French were SINCERE IN THEIR DISPOSITIONS FOR PEACE, ready to tolerate the Jay TREATY, and WILLING TO ARRANGE A LIB-

ERAL ONE with the United States, see TJ to Gerry, 26 Jan. 1799.

For the STATEMENT that Pendleton wrote as a result of TJ's exhortations in the letter printed above, see Pendleton to TJ, 24 Feb. 1799.

[1] Word interlined in place of "statement."

To Nicholas Lewis

DEAR SIR   Philadelphia Jan. 30. 99

Believing that the letters of mr Gerry & Taleyrand will give you pleasure to peruse I send you a copy. you will percieve by them the anxiety of the government of France[1] for a reconciliation with us, & mr Gerry's belief of their sincerity, & that they were ready to have made a liberal treaty with us. you will also see by mr Pickering's report that we are determined to believe no declarations they can make, but to meet their peaceable professions with acts of war. an act has passed the H. of Rep. by a majority of 20. for continuing the law cutting off intercourse with France, but allowing the President by proclamation to except out of this such parts of their dominions as disavow the depredations committed on us. this is intended for St. Domingo, where Toussant has thrown off dependance on France. he has an agent here on this business. yesterday the H. of R: voted 6. ships of 74. guns & 6 of 18. making 552. guns. these would cost in England 5000. Dollars a gun. they will cost here 10,000. so the whole will cost $5\frac{1}{2}$ millions of dollars. their annual expence is stated at 1000£ Virginia money a gun, being a little short of 2. millions of dollars. and this is only a part of what is proposed; the whole contemplated being 12. 74s. 12 frigates & about 25. smaller vessels. the state of our income & expence is (in round numbers) nearly as follows.

Impost $7\frac{1}{2}$ millions of Dollars, Excise, auctions, licences, carriages $\frac{1}{2}$ a million. Postage, patents & bank stock $\frac{1}{8}$ of a million making $8\frac{1}{8}$ millions. to these the direct tax & stamp tax will add 2. millions clear of expence, making in the whole $10\frac{1}{8}$ millions. the expences are the Civil list $\frac{3}{4}$ of a million, foreign intercourse $\frac{1}{2}$ million, interest on the public debt 4. millions, the present navy $2\frac{1}{2}$ millions, the present army $1\frac{1}{2}$ million making $9\frac{1}{4}$ millions. the additional army will be $2\frac{1}{2}$ millions, the additional navy 3. millions, & interest on the new loan near $\frac{1}{2}$ a million, in all $15\frac{1}{4}$ millions so in about a year or two there will be 5 millions annually to be raised by taxes in addition to the 10. millions we now pay. suppose our population is now 5. millions, this will be 3. dollars a head. this is exclusive of the outfit of the navy, for which a loan is opened to borrow 5. millions at 8. per cent. if we can remain at peace we have this in our favor that these projects will require time to execute; that in the mean time the sentiments of the people in the middle states are visibly turning back to their former direction, the XYZ. delusion being abated, & their minds become sensible to the circumstances surrounding them, to wit, the Alien & Sedition acts, the vexations of the stamp act, the direct tax, the follies of the additional army & navy, money borrowed for these at the usurious interest of 8. per cent, and mr Gerry's communications showing that peace is ours unless we throw it away. but if the joining the revolted subjects (negroes) of France & surrounding *their* islands with our armed vessels, instead of their merely cruising on our own coasts to protect our own commerce, should provoke France to a declaration of war, these measures will become irremediable.

The English & German papers are killing and eating Buonaparte every day. he is however safe, has effected a peaceable establishment of government in Egypt, the inhabitants of which have preferred him to their Mameluke governors, and the expectation is renewed of his march to India. in that country great preparations are made for the overthrow of the English power.—the insurrection of Ireland seems to be reduced low. the peace between France & the empire seems also to be doubtful. very little is apprehended for them from any thing which the Turks & Russians can do against them. I wish I could have presented you a more comfortable view of our affairs. however that will come if the friends of reform while they remain firm, avoid every act & threat against the peace of the union. that would check the favorable sentiments of the middle states, & rally them again round the measures which are ruining us. reason, not rashness, is the only means of bringing our fellowcitizens to their true minds. present my best compliments to mrs Lewis, and accept yourself assurances of the sincere & affectionate esteem with which I am Dear Sir

Your friend & servt   TH: JEFFERSON

PrC (DLC); at foot of first page: "Colo. N. Lewis." Enclosures: (1) *Message from the President of the United States, Accompanying Sundry Papers.* (2) *Message from the President of the United States, Accompanying a Report of the Secretary of State.*

For the act concerning INTERCOURSE WITH FRANCE, see TJ to Monroe, 23 Jan.

1799. Joseph Bunel of France was the AGENT from Saint-Domingue seeking commercial relations with the United States (Madison, *Papers*, 17:224n). For the bill authorizing naval SHIPS, see TJ to Aaron Burr, 7 Jan.

[1] Two words interlined.

To James Madison

My last to you was of the 16th. since which yours of the 12th. is recieved and it's contents disposed of properly. these met such approbation as to have occasioned an extraordinary impression of that day's paper. Logan's bill is passed. the lower house, by a majority of 20. passed yesterday a bill continuing the suspension of intercourse with France, with a new clause enabling the President to admit intercourse with the rebellious negroes under Toussaint, who has an agent here, & has thrown off dependance on France. the H. of R. have also voted 6. 74s. & 6. 18s. in part of the additional navy: say 552. guns, which in England would cost 5000. D. a gun, & here 10,000. consequently more than the whole 5. millions for which a loan is now opened at 8. per cent. the maintenance is estimated at £1000. lawful a gun annually. a bill has been this day brought into the Senate for authorising the P. *in case of a declaration of war or danger of invasion by any European power*, to raise an *eventual* army of 30. regiments, infantry, cavalry & artillery, in addition to the *additional* army, the *provisional* army, & the corps of volunteers, which last he is authorised to brigade, officer, exercise, & pay during the time of exercise. and all this notwithstanding Gerry's correspondence recently read & demonstrating the aversion of France to consider us as enemies. all depends on her patient standing the measures of the present session, & the surrounding *her* islands with our cruisers & capturing her armed vessels on her own coasts. if this is borne a while, the public[1] opinion is most manifestly veering in the middle states, & was even before the publication of Gerry's correspdce. in New York, Jersey & Pensylvania every one attests this, & Genl. Sumpter, just arrived, assures me the republicans in S.C. have gained 50. per cent in numbers since their election which was in the moment of the XYZ. fever. I believe there is no doubt the republican Governor would be elected here now, & still less for next October. the gentlemen of N.C. seem to be satisfied that their new delegation will furnish but 3. perhaps only 2. antirepublicans. if so we shall be gainers on the whole. but it is on the progress of public opinion we are to depend for rectifying the proceedings of the next congress. the only question is whether this will not carry things beyond the reach of rectification. petitions & remonstrances against the alien & sedition law are coming from various parts of N.Y. Jersey & Pensva.; some of them very well drawn. I am in hopes Virginia will stand so countenanced by those states as to repress the wishes of the government to coerce her, which they might venture on if they supposed she would be left alone. firmness on our part, but a passive firmness is the true course. any thing rash or threatening might check the favorable dispositions of these middle states & rally them again round the measures which are ruining us.—Buonaparte appears to have settled Egypt peaceably & with the consent of the inhabitants, & seems to be looking towards the E. Indies where a most formidable cooperation has been prepared for demolishing the British power. I wish the affairs of Ireland were as hopeful, and the peace with the North of Europe.—nothing new here as to the price of tobo. the river not having yet admitted the bringing any to this market. Spain being entirely open to ours, & depending on it for her supplies during the cutting off of her intercourse with her own colonies by the superiority of the British at sea, is much in our favor.—I forgot to add that the bill for the *eventual* army authorises the President to borrow 2. millions more. present my best respects to mrs Madison. health & affectionate salutations to yourself. Adieu.

RC (DLC: Madison Papers, Rives Collection); addressed: "James Madison junr. near Orange court house"; franked and stamped. PrC (DLC).

On 30 Jan. Senator James Gunn introduced the bill authorizing the president under certain circumstances and for a limited period of time to RAISE AN EVENTUAL ARMY of 24 regiments of infantry and 3 of cavalry, a regiment and battalion of riflemen, and a battalion of artillerists and engineers. The president was also empowered to borrow $2 million to implement the legislation. On a printed copy TJ noted changes made to the bill by the Senate and on the docket sheet recorded the progress of the bill from its introduction to its passage by the Senate on 18 Feb. ("A Bill, Giving eventual authority to the President of the United States to augment the Army" in DNA: RG 46, Senate Records, 5th Cong., 3d sess.; JS, 2:576). On 1 Mch. the House passed the bill by a 54 to 41 vote (JHR, 3:509-10). For a delineation of the various armies as established by acts of Congress in 1798 and 1799, see Kohn, *Eagle and Sword*, 229, and TJ to Madison, 5 Feb. 1799.

PETITIONS & REMONSTRANCES AGAINST THE ALIEN & SEDITION LAW: on 30 Jan. Franklin Davenport presented and read an address and remonstrance to the Senate

from a meeting held in Essex County, New Jersey (JS, 2:575). It was enclosed in a letter from Jabez Parkhurst, clerk of the meeting, to TJ, dated 26 Jan. (RC in DNA: RG 46, Senate Records, 5th Cong., 3d sess.; addressed: "The Honble. Thomas Jefferson Esqr., Vice President of the United States & President of the Senate Philadelphia"; franked). The Essex County citizens called for the repeal of the Alien and Sedition Acts on the grounds of unconstitutionality and bad policy and argued that unless the country was in actual danger of a foreign invasion a standing army would be "dangerous to the rights and liberties of the people," load the people with taxes, and create an asylum for idle dissipation supported by "the laboring part of the Community" (MS in same; dated 17 Jan. 1799; in Parkhurst's hand, and signed by him and Amos Harrison, chairman of the meeting). The Essex remonstrance and petitions from Suffolk County, New York; Northampton, York, Dauphin, and Washington counties in Pennsylvania; and Amelia County, Virginia—all against the Alien and Sedition Acts and some also protesting the "introduction of an oppressive system of taxation" for the maintenance of a standing army and "expensive navy"— were presented and read before the House of Representatives between 25 and 31 Jan. and sent to a committee of the whole. The

Aurora printed several of these petitions as well as others from the counties of Mifflin, Chester, and Cumberland in Pennsylvania (Philadelphia *Aurora*, 10, 16, 22, 23, 30 Jan. 1799; JHR, 3:445, 452, 456-8).

¹ TJ here canceled "spirit."

To Thomas Mann Randolph

TH:J. TO TMR.   Philadelphia Jan. 30. 99.

My letters to you have been of Jan. 3. & 17. to Martha of Dec. 27. and Jan. 23. yours of the 19th. came to hand yesterday. we have now got the derangement of the post set to rights. your letters arrive on Tuesday, & the post goes out again on Thursday. he arrives in Charlottesville the Thursday following & comes away on Saturday (I believe, but perhaps Friday) and gives an answer in three weeks, allowing a day at each place to answer. I send you by this post mr Gerry's correspondence after the departure of his collegues. the bill against Loganism is past. the H. of R. by a majority of 20. passed yesterday a bill continuing the suspension of intercourse with France, but with a new clause whereby the President may open it with her revolted negroes under Toussaint, who have thrown off their dependance on France. the following is a correct statement of our income & expenditure

				D	
1798. Impost	7,405,420.86	Int. of domestic debt	2,987,145.48		
Excise, auctions,		on domestic loans	238,637.50		
licences, carriages	585,879.67	Dutch debt	586,829.58	3,812,612.56	
Postage	57,000	Civil list		524,206.83	
Patents	1,050	loan offices		13,000.	
Coinage	10,242.	Mint		13,300.	
dividends of		light houses		44,281.08	
bank stock	79,920.	annuities & grants		1,603.33	
fines	8.	military pensions		93,400.	
	8,139,520.53	miscellaneous expences		19,000	
1799. Direct tax ⎱ clear of		contingent expences of government		20,000	
Stamp tax ⎰ expence	2,000,000.	Indians		110,000.	
	10,139,520.53	Foreign intercourse		93,000.	
		Treaties with Gr. Br.			
		Spain & Meditern.		187,500.	
		annual expence of			
		existing navy	2,434,261.10		
		do. of existing army			
		(5038. officers &			
		priv.)	1,461,175.		

```
do. of officers of addnl.
   army appointed          217,375.     4,112,811.10
                                         9,044,714.90
do. of privates of do.
   (abt 9000. off. &
   priv)                   2,523,455.
do. of additional navy
   (proposed)              2,949,278.96  5,472,733.96
                                        14,517,448.86
8. per cent interest on
   new loan                                 400,000
                                        14,917,448.86
```

the new loan of 5. millions will much about equip the 6. 74s. & 6. 18s. voted yesterday in part of the additional fleet. within about one or two years we must raise 5. millions a year more by taxes in addition to the 10. millions we now pay. but I hope before these follies are carried into execution they will be corrected by a revolution in the public opinion. that is sensibly & certainly commenced in Pennsylva, Jersey, New York, and S. Carolina. and joined to Virginia N. Carolina, & Georgia will suffice to change these measures. it is most essential to give time to this progress of opinion, and not to check it by any rashness or threats which might occasion the middle states again to rally round the measures which are ruining us. firmness of opinion, but a passive firmness is what is to save us without a convulsion, the issue of which nobody can foresee. if in the mean time France is forced to declare war against us, it will increase our difficulties. I apprehend their peace with Germany is doubtful. Buonaparte has accomplished the settlement of Egypt, and it now seems as if he were looking towards India, where an immense concert has taken place for the destruction of the English power.—no tobacco yet at this market, nor any new symptoms what may be expected. the Georgia tobo. arrived at N. York I learn is of their 1st. growth, consequently their best. little more of that remains to come. when the 2d. & 3d. growths come in their quality will make them as nothing in the market. South Carolina makes about 12,000. hhds, the double of their ordinary crop. to balance these circumstances, all the markets of Spain are open to us & depend on us chiefly for their supplies, their intercourse with their own tobo. colonies being entirely at an end by the naval superiority of England. on the whole I still expect a rise of price. but I am meditating to offer my tobo. at Richd on a credit till Septemb. for the highest price which shall be given there in the mean time. I am very anxious indeed to hear it is all arrived there. wheat at N. York is about 1.60 little is doing here. my supply of nail rod got out of the river

2. or 3. days ago. I am in hopes by your saying nothing of George that he continues well. I wish you to be where you can be in greatest comfort yourselves. it would have been an additional gratification to me if the accomodations at Monticello could have been instrumental to it. I recieved a letter from mr Eppes a few days ago. Maria has been ill, & in danger of a 2d accident, but had got well & they were to remove the next day to Mont blanco. my tenderest love to my ever dear Martha, & warm affections to yourself & the little ones. Adieu.

RC (DLC). PrC (MHi); endorsed by TJ in ink on verso.

A LETTER FROM John Wayles EPPES to TJ of 18 Jan. 1799, recorded in SJL as received from Bermuda Hundred nine days later, has not been found.

To George Jefferson

DEAR SIR   Philadelphia Jan. 31. 99.

Your favors of Jan. 15. & 20. are duly recieved. it was better, as you supposed, to send the [process] against the Henderson's to Albemarle. with respect to the article of freight mentioned in your account, you have taken a great deal more trouble about it than I could have wished. I only meant to keep the thing in your mind in future, and I dare say, from an attention to dates, that it preceded my request to you.—I remark what you say of the reciept of a further [sum] of £400. from mr Pendleton. I shall be able to exchange perhaps the whole of it myself, as I shall recieve a considerable sum here in a few days which would suit me better in Richmond.—I inclose you a bill of lading for a supply of nailrod lately sent on, as my works must be stopt for want of it by this time. also a hogshead of molasses.—no tobacco is yet come to this market, so no price talked of. at New York the new tobo. is now 12. D. the crops from the different states are large, yet the magazines in Europe are in so empty & hungry a state that I do not think the supply will be equal to the demand. all the markets of Spain continue open for this article & depend on us chiefly, their communication with their own tobacco colonies being cut off by the British superiority at sea. I still think therefore that the price will rise 2. or 3. dollars this year as it has done every year for 4. years past. being anxious however to accomplish & secure certain objects, with my crop, (about 30,000. from Bedford & 20,000. Albemarle) I would sell it for *the highest price which shall be given on James river from the time of delivery till paiment* which might be the 1st. of October. I expect the tobo. at Richmond every day. if you can so dispose

[669]

of it, do so.[1] if you could make it [. . .]spective *to the whole crop of 98. tho sold before*, so much the better, as [it would secure] the highest price already given. I am Dear Sir your affectionate friend

TH: JEFFERSON

PrC (MHi); faint, with frayed right margin; at foot of text: "Mr. Jefferson"; endorsed by TJ in ink on verso. Enclosure not found.

[1] TJ here canceled several illegible words.

Appendix

Notations by Jefferson on Senate Documents

E D I T O R I A L   N O T E

As vice president of the United States, Jefferson's primary responsibility was to preside over the Senate (see Vol. 29:633). Although Jefferson did not take an active legislative role in the Senate's proceedings, he sometimes did make notes on documents that came before that body. These markings, which reflect less his own thought or opinion than his recording of the deliberations of the senators, give some indication of Jefferson's involvement in day-to-day proceedings of the Senate.

For a Senate document entirely in Jefferson's hand, see the resolution printed above at 11 Jan. 1798. An example of his emendations to the Rough Journal of the Senate is printed above at 20 Feb. The following list enumerates other motions, bills, committee reports, and acts that came before the Fifth Congress between 1 Jan. 1798 and 31 Jan. 1799 and received some written comment by the vice president. The Editors have grouped Jefferson's markings on the documents into three categories: "emendation" indicates that Jefferson recorded changes to a bill or motion, from a word or two to several sentences, often incorporating amendments passed; "notation" means that brief information on action taken by the Senate appears in Jefferson's hand, most often as "agreed" in the margin of the text of the document, or, for example, on Jacob Read's amendment of 15 June the vice president's directions to "add to the end of the bill"; and "endorsement" indicates that Jefferson provided one or more entries in the docketing or clerical record of the history of the document. Jefferson's is often only one of several hands in which the notations or endorsements appear, indicating that in addition to presiding he may have filled a clerical role on occasions when Samuel A. Otis, secretary of the Senate, and his assistants were away. During the second session of the Fifth Congress, several Senate bills bear only the title of the legislation in a clerk's hand, the endorsements being all by Jefferson. This was the case with the Alien Friends Bill (see illustration). During the third session, Jefferson sometimes provided the title as well as all other information on the panel.

The endorsement panel provides inclusive dates for a document; in the absence of such endorsements we have derived the dates from the printed *Journal of the Senate* and they are supplied in brackets. If the document marked by Jefferson was a motion or bill printed for the Senate's consideration, that fact is also noted in the description below. Motions are rendered as they appear on the endorsement panel unless clarification requires substituting the language of the motion itself.

All the documents listed below are from Senate Records, DNA: RG 46, 5th Congress. The second session ran from 13 Nov. 1797 to 16 July 1798 and the third session began on 3 Dec. 1798.

Bill Suspending, for a limited time, the second section of an act, intituled "An Act regulating foreign coins," 3-15 Jan. 1798; printed; emendations by TJ.

Motion by Mr. Paine for a committee relative to territory lying to the Southward & Westward of State of Georgia, 17 Jan. 1798; emendations by TJ. Printed copy; emendation by TJ. Printed in JS, 2:427, at 18 Jan. 1798.

Committee report on Bill for the relief of the refugees from the British provinces of Canada and Nova Scotia, 31 Jan. 1798; printed; notations and emendations by TJ.

Committee report on Bill regulating certain proceedings in cases of impeachment, [1 Feb. 1798]; printed; notations by TJ.

Committee report on form of proceedings to be adopted by the Senate in cases of impeachment, 1 Feb.1798; printed; notations and emendations by TJ.

Bill For the relief of the legal representatives of Thomas Clark, deceased, 3 Feb.-15 Mch. 1798; printed; endorsement by TJ.

Bill To erect a Light-House on Eaton's Neck, in the state of New-York, and place Beacons and Buoys in the sound, between the city of New-York, in said state, and Newport, in the state of Rhode-Island, and in the Harbours of those places, 13 Feb. 1798; printed; endorsement by TJ.

Mr Sedgwicks motion on Mr Reads motion of 14th Feby respecting the impeachment of A Senator of the US, 21 Feb. 1798; partially in TJ's hand. Printed in JS, 2:444.

Bill For an amicable settlement of limits with Georgia, and authorizing the establishment of a government in the Mississippi territory, [ca. 23-28 Feb. 1798]; printed; notations and emendations by TJ.

Committee report on rules of proceeding in the case of impeachment against William Blount, 27 Feb. 1798; emendations by TJ. Printed copy; notations and emendations by TJ.

Mr Reads motion for summons against Wm Blount, 1 Mch. 1798; emendation by TJ. Printed in JS, 2:448.

Bill For the erection of a Light-House, and placing Buoys at the several places therein mentioned, 2-5 Mch. 1798; printed; emendations and endorsement by TJ.

Bill Providing the means of Intercourse between the United States and foreign nations, 6-12 Mch. 1798; printed; endorsement by TJ.

Bill to authorize a Grant of Lands to Stephen Monot & others Inhabitants of Galliopolis Therein named, 7-14 Mch. 1798; endorsement by TJ.

Bill To amend the Act intituled "An Act laying Duties on stamped Vellum, Parchment and Paper," 8-14 Mch. 1798; printed; endorsement by TJ.

Bill For the relief of Silvanus Crowell, 12-14 Mch. 1798; printed; endorsement by TJ.

Bill Declaring the consent of Congress to an act of the commonwealth of Massachusetts, 12-20 Mch. 1798; printed; endorsement by TJ.

Bill for the relief of the legal representative of Samuel Lapsley, deceased, 19-23 Mch. 1798; endorsement by TJ.

APPENDIX

Notification by Mr Laurance to ask leave to bring in a bill on Judicial Courts, 20-21 Mch. 1798; endorsement by TJ.

Bill to enable the President of the United States to purchase or lease one or more Founderies, 20-22 Mch. 1798; emendation and endorsement by TJ.

Mr Andersons motion to request the Prest. U States to communicate Instructions, 20 Mch.-3 Apr. 1798; endorsement by TJ. Printed in JS, 2:458.

Bill Making an appropriation for completing the buildings requisite for the accommodation of the Government of the United States at the City of Washington, 20 Mch.-10 Apr. 1798; printed; endorsement by TJ.

Bill To continue in force the act, intituled "An Act prohibiting, for a limited time, the exportation of Arms and Ammunition, and for encouraging the importation thereof," 21-26 Mch. 1798; printed; emendations and endorsement by TJ.

Bill To continue in force, the fifth section of an act, intituled "An Act in addition to the act, intituled "An Act to establish the Post Office and Post Roads within the United States," 22-26 Mch. 1798; printed; endorsement by TJ.

Bill To continue in force, for a limited time, a part of an act, entitled, "An act making further provision for securing and collecting the duties on foreign and domestic distilled spirits, stills, wines, and teas," 22-30 Mch. 1798; printed; endorsement by TJ.

Bill To alter the time of making entry of stills, 22 Mch.-8 June 1798; printed; endorsement by TJ.

Committee report on petition of Joseph Nourse, [23 Mch. 1798]; notations and emendation by TJ. Printed in JS, 2:461-2.

Bill To revive and continue in force, the act respecting the compensation of clerks, 23 Mch.-2 Apr. 1798; printed; endorsement by TJ.

Bill to provide an additional Armament for the further protection of the trade of the United States, 23 Mch.-9 Apr. 1798; notations, emendations, and endorsement by TJ. Printed copy, 23-26 Mch. 1798; notations, emendations, and endorsement by TJ.

Bill Making an appropriation for the payment of a balance found due to the legal representatives of William Carmichael, deceased, 23 Mch.-19 Apr. 1798; printed; endorsement by TJ.

Motion by Mr. Marshall proposing sundry resolutions relative to the defence of the United States, 25-27 Mch. 1798; notation and endorsement by TJ. Printed in JS, 2:463.

Committee report on Bill To revive and continue in force, the act respecting the compensation of clerks, [29 Mch. 1798]; notations by TJ.

Mr. Bingham's motion for the establishment of a seperate executive department, 2-3 Apr. 1798; endorsement by TJ. Printed in JS, 2:466.

Mr. Goodhues motion to publish instructions, 5 Apr. 1798; notations by TJ. Printed in JS, 2:468.

Bill Authorizing an Expenditure, and making an Appropriation for the reimbursement of Monies advanced by the Consuls of the United States, in certain cases, 5-10 Apr. 1798; printed; endorsement by TJ.

Bill Declaring the consent of Congress to two Acts of the state of North Carolina, therein mentioned, 9-16 Apr. 1798; printed; endorsement by TJ.

Bill To authorize certain officers and other persons to administer oaths, 9-24 Apr. 1798; printed; notation and endorsement by TJ.

Committee report on Bill Making an appropriation for completing the buildings requisite for the accommodation of the Government of the United States at the City of Washington, [11 Apr. 1798]; emendation by TJ. Printed copy; notations and emendations by TJ.

Bill To establish an Executive department, to be denominated the department of the Navy, 11-16 Apr. 1798; printed; notations, emendations, and endorsement by TJ.

Bill For the relief of sick and disabled seamen, 12 Apr.-14 July 1798; endorsement by TJ.

Bill; authorizing the President of the United States, to raise a provisional Army, 13-23 Apr. 1798; endorsement by TJ.

Bill Supplementary to the act providing for the further defence of the ports and harbours of the United States, 13-27 Apr. 1798; printed; endorsement by TJ.

Motion by Mr. Brown for a Committee as to amendments necessary to Act providing for the sale of Lands North West of Ohio, 17 Apr. 1798; endorsement by TJ. Printed in JS, 2: 474.

Motion by Mr. Ross that the Secy of the Treasury report the progress of the Surveyor General in laying off & surveying certain Land, 17 Apr. 1798; endorsement by TJ. Printed in JS, 2:474.

Bill To provide an additional regiment of Artillerists and Engineers, 17-23 Apr. 1798; printed; endorsement by TJ.

Bill For erecting Light-houses, and placing buoys and stakes at the places therein mentioned, 18-20 Apr. 1798; printed; endorsement by TJ.

Bill To enable the President of the United States to procure cannons, arms and ammunition, 18-30 Apr. 1798; printed; endorsement by TJ.

Committee report on Bill To authorize certain officers and other persons to administer oaths, 20 Apr. 1798; notation by TJ.

Mr Marshalls motion respecting district Courts, 20 Apr. 1798; emendation and endorsement by TJ. Printed in JS, 2:476.

Bill For the Relief of Obadiah Brown, 24-30 Apr. 1798; printed; endorsement by TJ.

Motion by Mr. Hillhouse respecting Aliens, 25-26 Apr. 1798; endorsement by TJ. Printed in JS, 2:479.

Bill To authorize the President of the United States to cause to be purchased or built, a number of small vessels, to be equipped as Gallies, or

APPENDIX

otherwise, [ca. 25-27 Apr. 1798]; printed; notations and emendations by TJ.

Bill to amend an Act intitled an Act providing for the sale of the lands of the United States in the Territory Northwest of the River Ohio & above the mouth of the Kentucky river, 25 Apr.-5 July 1798; notation and endorsement by TJ.

Motion by Mr. Marshall for changing the districts of the United States into four Circuits, 26 Apr.-2 May 1798; endorsement by TJ. Printed in JS, 2:480.

Mr Marshalls motion respecting admission on floor of the House, 27 Apr. 1798; notation by TJ. Printed in JS, 2:481.

Bill Making appropriations for the military establishment, for the year one thousand seven hundred and ninety-eight, 27 Apr.-30 May 1798; printed; endorsement by TJ.

Bill Directing the payment of a detachment of militia, for services performed in the year one thousand seven hundred and ninety-four, under Major James Ore, 30 Apr.-3 May 1798; printed; emendation and endorsement by TJ.

Bill concerning revenue cutters, 2-4 May 1798; printed; endorsement by TJ.

A Bill, to amend, the Act intituled an Act to amend & repeal in part the Act intituled an Act to ascertain and fix the military establishment of the United States, 2-15 May 1798; endorsement by TJ.

Bill concerning aliens, 4 May-8 June 1798; endorsement by TJ. Printed copy, 4 May- [1 June] 1798; notations and emendations by TJ. Amendments on separate sheet, with TJ's emendations keyed to Sect. 2 of printed copy of bill.

Motion by Mr. Livermore for requiring attendance of absent Senators, 15 May 1798; endorsement by TJ. Printed in JS, 2:489.

Bill, more effectually to protect the Commerce and Coasts of the United States, 18-22 May 1798; endorsement by TJ.

Agreement to House of Representatives' amendments to bill sent from the Senate, intituled "An act authorizing the President of the United States to raise a provisional army," 21-22 May 1798; printed; notations and endorsement by TJ.

Bill Supplementary to, and to amend the act, intituled "An act to establish an uniform rule of naturalization, and to repeal the act heretofore passed on that subject," 22 May-12 June 1798; printed; emendations and endorsement by TJ.

Mr Anderson's motion to postpone Bill to protect Commerce, 23 May 1798; notation by TJ. Printed in JS, 2:493.

Bill Providing for the more effectual collection of certain internal revenues of the United States, 25 May-7 June 1798; printed; emendations and endorsement by TJ.

APPENDIX

Mr. Marshalls Motion to amend bill respecting Aliens, 28 May 1798; notation and emendation by TJ. Printed in JS, 2:496.

Bill Providing for the relief of persons imprisoned for debts due to the United States, 28 May-4 June 1798; printed; endorsement by TJ.

Bill Supplementary to an act, intituled "An act for the relief of persons imprisoned for debt," 28 May-4 June 1798; printed; notations, emendations, and endorsement by TJ.

Mr Laurance's motion on amendment to Alien Bill, 29 May 1798; notation and emendation by TJ. Printed in JS, 2:497.

Bill To suspend the commercial intercourse between the United States and France, and the dependencies thereof, 1-7 June 1798; printed; emendations and endorsement by TJ.

Bill For establishing and organizing a battalion of Infantry, to be called Marine Corps, 1 June-3 July 1798; printed; endorsement by TJ.

Committee report on Bill concerning aliens, 4 June 1798; printed; notations and emendation by TJ.

Bill Respecting loan-office and final settlement certificates, indents of interest, and the unfunded or registered debt credited in the books of the Treasury, 4-5 June 1798; printed; endorsement by TJ.

Committee report on Explanatory Article to the British Treaty, 5 June 1798; endorsement by TJ.

Committee report on Bill Providing for the more effectual collection of certain internal revenues of the United States, 6 June 1798; notations by TJ.

Bill Authorizing the President of the United States, to accept of any armed vessel offered for the use of the United States, 6-14 June 1798; printed; endorsement by TJ.

Mr. Mason's motion for Committee to consider of Adjournt, 7-8 June 1798; notation, emendation, and endorsement by TJ. Printed in JS, 2:503.

Bill to punish frauds committed on the Banks of the United States, 7-22 June 1798; endorsement by TJ. Printed copy, 7 June 1798; emendation by TJ.

Bill To regulate and fix the compensations of the officers employed in collecting the internal revenues of United States, and to ensure more effectually the settlement of their accounts, 8 June-7 July 1798; printed; endorsement by TJ.

Committee report on Bill Supplementary to, and to amend the act, intituled "An act to establish an uniform rule of naturalization, and to repeal the act heretofore passed on that subject," 12 June 1798; printed; notations and emendation by TJ.

Motion for a Committee on compensation of officers, 12 June 1798; endorsement by TJ. Printed in JS, 2:507.

Committee report on Bill, authorizing the President of the United States,

APPENDIX

to accept of any armed vessel offered for the use of the United States, [13 June 1798]; printed; notations and emendations by TJ.

Committee report on Bill For providing compensation for the marshals, clerks, attornies, jurors and witnesses in the courts of the United States, and to repeal certain parts of the acts therein mentioned, [13 June 1798]; printed; notation by TJ.

Vote tally sheets on Masons's motion on Bill Authorizing the President of the United States, to accept of any armed vessel offered for the use of the United States, 13 June 1798; notations by TJ.

Bill For providing compensation for the marshals, clerks, attornies, jurors and witnesses in the courts of the United States, and to repeal certain parts of the acts therein mentioned, 13-20 June 1798; printed; emendations and endorsement by TJ.

Bill To amend the act, intituled "An act providing a naval armament," and the act, intituled "An act to authorize the President of the United States to cause to be purchased or built, a number of small vessels, to be equipped as gallies, or otherwise," 14-15 June 1798; printed; endorsement by TJ.

Amendments of the Senate, to the bill, entitled, "An act providing for the more effectual collection of certain internal revenues of the United States," [14-18 June 1798]; printed; notations and emendations by TJ.

Bill in addition to the act more effectually to protect the commerce and coasts of the Unites States, 14-18 June 1798; endorsement by TJ. Printed copy; notations and emendations by TJ.

Mr Reads amendt to Bill Addition to the Act protection of Sea Coast, 15 June 1798; notation by TJ.

Bill Providing arms for the militia throughout the United States, 15 June-3 July 1798; printed; endorsement by TJ.

Bill For the relief of John Vaughan, 15 June-13 July 1798; printed; endorsement by TJ.

Committee report on Bill To authorize the defence of merchant vessels of the United States against French depredations, [18 June 1798]; printed; notations by TJ.

Mr Reads amendt to Bill Addition to "Act for protection of Commerce," 18 June 1798; notation by TJ.

Bill Supplementary to, and to amend the act, entitled, "An act authorizing the President of the United States to raise a provisional army," 18-20 June 1798; printed; notations and endorsement by TJ.

Bill To authorize the defence of the merchant vessels of the United States against French depredations, 18-20 June 1798; printed; emendations and endorsement by TJ.

Bill To extend the privilege of franking Letters and Packets to the Secretary of the Navy, 18-20 June 1798; printed; endorsement by TJ.

Committee report on Bill For the relief of sick and disabled seamen, 19 June 1798; notation by TJ.

APPENDIX

Committee report on Bill To provide for the valuation of lands and dwelling-houses, and the enumeration of slaves, within the United States, 21 June 1798; printed; notations and emendation by TJ.

Bill to declare the Treaties betwixt the United States & the Republic of France, void & of no Effect, 21-25 June 1798; emendation and endorsement by TJ. Printed copy; notations and emendations by TJ.

House Amendments to Bill concerning Aliens, 22 June 1798; notations by TJ.

Bill To provide for the valuation of lands and dwelling-houses, and the enumeration of slaves, within the United States, 22 June-2 July 1798; printed; emendations and endorsement by TJ.

Committee report on the Bill Making an appropriation for the expenses incident to the new regiment of artillerists and engineers, during the year one thousand seven hundred and ninety-eight, [25 June 1798]; notation by TJ.

Bill Making an appropriation for the expenses incident to the new regiment of artillerists and engineers, during the year one thousand seven hundred and ninety-eight, 25-26 June 1798; printed; endorsement by TJ.

Bill Providing for the enumeration of the inhabitants of the United States, 25-26 June 1798; printed; endorsement by TJ.

Bill Supplementary to the act, entitled, "An act to provide an additional armament for the further protection of the trade of the United States," 25-27 June 1798; printed; endorsement by TJ.

Bill to define more particularly the Crime of Treason and to define & punish the crime of Sedition, 26 June 1798; endorsement by TJ.

Bill Providing for the enumeration of the Inhabitants of the United States, 27 Dec. 1798-17 Jan. 1799; printed; emendations and endorsement by TJ.

Bill authorizing the acceptance from the State of Connecticut, of a cession of the jurisdiction of the territory west of Pennsylvania commonly called the western reserve of Connecticut, 31 Dec. 1798-2 Jan. 1799; endorsement by TJ. Printed copy, 31 Dec. 1798-25 Feb. 1799; notation, emendations, and endorsement by TJ.

Bill Respecting balances reported against certain states, by the commissioners appointed to settle the accounts between the United States and the several states, 3 Jan.-11 Feb. 1799; printed; endorsement by TJ.

Committee report on Bill Providing for the enumeration of the Inhabitants of the United States, 14 Jan.1799; endorsement by TJ.

Motion by Mr. Ross for a committee to repeal amendments to Bill for sale of Lands above the mouth of Kentucky river, 15 Jan. 1799; endorsement by TJ.

Mr Ross's motion for Committee to consider whether any division, or other alteration ought to be made in the Government of the Territory of the U.S. northwest of the River Ohio, 15 Jan. 1799; endorsement by TJ.

APPENDIX

Mr Masons motion Respecting Laws of North West Territory, 15-18 Jan. 1799; endorsement by TJ.

Mr Read's motion to print Constitution & Amendts. thereto, 16 Jan. 1799; entirely in TJ's hand; endorsement by TJ. Printed in JS, 2:570.

Bill For the punishment of certain Crimes therein specified, 18-25 Jan. 1799; printed; endorsement by TJ. (Logan Act)

Mr Masons Motion to print 18 Jan. message and communications of the President, 21 Jan. 1799; entirely in TJ's hand; emendation and endorsement by TJ.

Bill For the better organizing of the Troops of the United States, 21 Jan.-11 Feb. 1799; printed; notations, emendations, and endorsement by TJ.

Bill Supplementary to the Act entitled "an Act to establish the Judicial Courts of the United States," 23 Jan. 1799; endorsement by TJ.

Bill To authorize the reimbursement of monies expended in rendering aid to sick and destitute American seamen, in foreign countries, 23 Jan.-15 Feb. 1799; printed; endorsement by TJ.

Bill For the relief of Thomas Lewis, 24 Jan. 1799; endorsement by TJ.

Committee report on the Bill Respecting balances reported against certain states, by the commissioners appointed to settle the accounts between the United States and the several states, 25 Jan. 1799; printed; notation by TJ.

Bill To regulate the Medical Establishment, [25] Jan.-25 Feb. 1799; printed; notations, emendations, and endorsement by TJ.

Bill Further to suspend the Commercial Intercourse, between the United States and France, and the dependencies thereof, 29 Jan.-6 Feb. 1799; printed; notations, emendations, and endorsement by TJ.

Bill giving eventual authority to the President of the United States to augment the Army, 30 Jan.1799; emendation and endorsement by TJ. Printed copy, 30 Jan.-18 Feb. 1799; emendations and endorsement by TJ.

Bill For the relief of Gazzam, Taylor and Jones, of the City of Philadelphia, 30 Jan.-16 Feb. 1799; printed; emendations, and endorsement by TJ.

Bill Respecting quarantines, and health laws, 30 Jan.-20 Feb. 1799; printed; emendation and endorsement by TJ.

Bill To amend an act entitled an act giving effect to the Laws of the United States within the District of Tennessee, 31 Jan. 1799; endorsement by TJ.

Committee report on Bill Further to suspend the Commercial Intercourse between the United States and France, and the dependencies thereof, [31 Jan. 1799]; printed; notations and emendations by TJ.

Mr. Foster's motion on Petition of John Brown and others, 31 Jan. 1799; emendation and endorsement by TJ.

APPENDIX

Mr Tracy's motion to amend Bill to regulate Indian intercourse, 31 Jan. 1799; endorsement by TJ.

Bill For the relief of Jonathan Haskill, 31 Jan.-16 Feb. 1799; printed; endorsement by TJ.

INDEX

abolition: Short on prospects of, 149-53; advantages of gradual emancipation, 151-2; emancipation societies, 153

Abraham (TJ's slave), 269

Abridgment of Cases in Equity. See *General Abridgement of Cases in Equity*

Adams, Abigail: TJ declines invitations of, 132; TJ records comments apparently made by, 248

ADAMS, JOHN

Opinions

on celebration of Washington's birthday, 112n, 156, 221; on bank notes, 113; on France, 113, 359-60, 621; on importance of strong Senate, 113, 126-7; seen as disciple of Burke, 174n; on moving government to Washington, 228, 275-6; on British government, 368-9; on democrats, 608-9; on Gerry, 621

Politics

public's opinions of, xl; influence of Sewall on, 173

President

addresses and petitions to, vii, 268, 279-80, 322, 324, 341-2, 344, 351, 582-4; XYZ affair, vii, xl; 19 Mch. message to Congress, viii, 189-93, 227, 231, 239; on convening Congress during epidemics, 10, 11n; accused of trampling on Constitution, 22; united with Senate, 22; May 1797 address to Congress, 35n, 250, 263, 267, 269, 274-5, 339; and relations with France, 35n, 65, 66, 67, 118-19, 120, 166n, 174n, 184-6, 219, 254, 274-5, 348, 414-15, 462n, 486n, 489, 491, 496, 621; Nov. 1797 address to Congress, 46, 49n, 119, 185, 250, 335; on attack by French privateer, 88-90; and foreign diplomats, 89; sends correspondence, papers to Congress, 94, 112n, 165-6, 245-6, 673, 679; and appointments, 112n, 280-1, 323-5, 326, 331, 625n, 660n; distrusts France, 113; Madison's views on, 116-17, 384; appoints son minister to Prussia, 120, 182; 5 Mch. message to Congress, 165-6n, 170, 264n; delays sending XYZ dispatches, 166n; expects war with France, 166n, 241;

640, 647-8, 652n, 653n, 663; cabinet politics, 173, 182; criticized, 174n, 184, 420-1, 522n; and House of Representatives, 176, 395n; and arming of merchant vessels, 194, 217, 239; and patronage, 225; signs legislation, 229n, 300n, 301n, 354n, 380n, 395n, 408-9, 410, 518n, 522n, 617n, 624n; characterized, 239, 405-6; lack of communication with Washington, 248; 3 Apr. message to Congress, 263-4, 266-70, 283, 289, 290, 335, 338; sends dispatch to U.S. envoys, 271; replies to addresses on XYZ affair, 279-80, 322-4, 326, 331, 335, 353, 359-60, 362n, 363, 382n, 402-5, 462n; and publication of XYZ dispatches, 289; judicial appointments, 300, 301-2n; 4 May message to Congress, 335-6, 359-60; proclaims national Fast Day, 336, 341-2, 344, 353; receives threats of plot to burn Philadelphia, 353; and departures of French from U.S., 362n; on treaty with France, 364-5, 379; influence in Congress, 368; refuses papers for French consul general, 380, 393, 396; 5 June message to Congress, 391n, 392-8, 419-20; orders envoys to leave France, 397; authorized to raise army and borrow money, 408-11, 447, 665-6; and Gerry negotiation, communication, 417-18, 422, 444, 610, 614, 622; 21 June message to Congress, 418-19, 421-2, 484-6; and Saint-Domingue, 438-9, 665, 667; appoints Washington commander, 440, 443n, 445, 448; powers of, 441; and Sedition Act, 447; role in command of military, 471-3; and Short, 491; Ky. Federalists seek to praise, 519; TJ fears lifetime tenure for, 560, 646; described, 566-7, 581; and prosecutions under Sedition Act, 576; 8 Dec. annual message to Congress, 604-8, 610-11, 616-17n; and G. Logan's mission to France, 607n, 658; and M. Lyon's petition, 610-11; sets conditions for negotiations with France, 611n; *Message from the President of the United States, Accompanying Sundry Papers*, 631, 636n, 638n, 640-1, 648, 651n, 663-4, 667; and

Bernadotte, Jean Baptiste, 449-50
Bethlehem, Pa.: Indians residing at, 86; as
　Moravian center, 265n, 288
Bible: TJ purchases hot-pressed, 644n
Bingham, William: transmits model of
　threshing machine, 252; as bank direc-
　tor, 418-19; letter from cited, 419n; op-
　poses declaration of war, 443n; and
　Gerry's confirmation, 653; moves to es-
　tablish navy department, 673
Binney, Horace, 578, 645, 651n
Bishop Burnet's History of His Own Time
　(Gilbert Burnet), 595
blacks: colonization of American, British
　in Africa, 149, 154n, 333n; disadvan-
　tages of deportation of, 150; skin color
　and prejudice, 150-1; and plans for inva-
　sion of U.S., 336n; as refugees from
　Saint-Domingue, 441; in Haitian inde-
　pendence movement, 635, 637n
Blackstone, William: *Commentaries on the
　Laws of England*, 58-61
Blair, David, 102n
Blair, Hugh, 594
blasphemy: crime of, under British law,
　60
Bleecker (Beecker), Mr.: visits Monti-
　cello, 419n
Blenheim, Germany: astronomical obser-
　vations at, 160
Blenheim (Carter estate), 148, 475
Bloodworth, Timothy, 653
Blount, Thomas, 395n, 557
Blount, William: impeachment, trial of,
　vii, 10-11, 35, 53, 56, 84-5, 87, 90, 117,
　121, 127n, 176, 608n, 614-15, 618-19,
　672; conspiracy of, relations with Spain,
　55n, 95, 247; expulsion, impeachment,
　261-2; TJ's notes on trial of, 614-15;
　and Gerry's confirmation, 653. *See also*
　United States: Senate
Blue Ridge Mountains, 276
boatmen: characterized by TJ, 337; and
　freight charges, 461, 579, 618, 629-30
boats: carry shipments for TJ, 104, 167,
　183, 192, 220, 265, 282, 312, 343, 357,
　362, 365, 382; freight charges for, 375
Bolingbroke, Henry St. John, Viscount,
　594
Bolling, John (TJ's brother-in-law):
　drunkenness, 15-16; death of daughter,
　346
Bolling, Mary Jefferson (Mrs. John Bol-
　ling, TJ's sister): relationship with hus-
　band, 15-16; health of, 188; plans trip to
　Monticello, 367

Bonaparte, Napoleon: and plans for inva-
　sion of England, 63, 400n, 445n; in
　Paris, 65, 67; Egyptian campaign, 399,
　400, 458, 603n, 623-5, 627, 631, 664,
　666, 668; rumors of defeat of, 625n,
　627, 631, 635, 641n, 664
Bordeaux, France: U.S. vessels detained
　at, 146; Fenwick at, 147; U.S. consulate
　at, 175, 597n; and transatlantic travel,
　272, 288, 515-16
Bossee, Mr. (Philadelphia boarding-
　house), 439
Boston: Republican newspaper in, 25-6;
　reliability of foreign news from, 53, 56;
　and arming of private vessels, 88; views
　on arming merchant vessels, 90; Chari-
　table Fire Society in, 125n
Botetourt Co., Va.: mammoth bones found
　in, 178
Bouquet, Henry, 141
Bourne, Sylvanus, 363-5, 383-4
Bournonville, Charles François, 53, 54n
Boyce, Joseph: and TJ's business affairs,
　12, 29, 375
Bracken, Henry: *The Traveller's Pocket
　Farrier*, 69
Bradford, Thomas, 615-16
Bradford, William (R.I.), 653
Brand, Joseph, 592-3
Breckinridge, John: and Ky. Resolutions
　of 1798, 530-4, 549n, 555-6, 557;
　writes local resolutions, 533
Breckinridge, John Cabell: collects in-
　formation on Ky. Resolutions, 530,
　532
Bremen: observatory near, 160, 162n
Brent, Richard: as possible counter to
　"Scipio," 121; stands for election, 636,
　637n
Brest, France: and rumored invasion of
　Britain, 443, 445n, 449
Breuil, Francis, 362n
bricks: made at Monticello, 576
Bridgeton, N.J.: and XYZ affair, 324n
Bringhurst, John: and building supplies
　for Madison, 311, 343; letter to cited,
　528
Bristol, England: and slave trade, 426,
　428n
Brockenbrough, Gabriella: certificate of
　citizenship for, 437-8; travels to Europe,
　437-8; identified, 438n
Brockenbrough, John, Jr.: certificate of
　citizenship for, 437-8; travels to Europe,
　437-8; identified, 438n
Brockenbrough, John, Sr., 438n

Brooks, David, 566-7
Brown, Andrew. See *Philadelphia Gazette*
Brown, Charles Brockden, 82n
Brown, James: letter to, 28-9; handles
TJ's business affairs in Richmond, 28-9;
letter from cited, 29n; and Short's business affairs, 319, 320n, 494-5, 558; and
Donald & Burton, 320n; and TJ's to-
bacco, 338, 349; G. Jefferson's opinion
of, 373
Brown, James (1766-1835), 511n
Brown, John (Ky.): letters from, 436-7,
519-21; TJ records information from,
172-3; forwards letters, 174n, 175n,
436-7; and Nolan, 425, 521; and Direct
Tax, 442-3; carries information, 511n,
515n; stays at Francis's hotel, 511n; in
legislature, 519; on megalonyx, 519-20;
on situation in Ky., 519; on committee
for Tazewell's funeral, 638n; and
Gerry's confirmation, 653; actions in
Senate, 674
Brown, John (R.I.), 679
Brown, Mary, 167
Brown, Mather, 347n
Brown, Obadiah, 674
Brown, Samuel: letter to, 216; letter from,
509-12; and TJ's account of Logan's
speech, 216, 509-15; sends news from
Ky., 510, 512n, 532-3; letter to cited,
511n
Brown, Col. Samuel (Va.), 293, 296
Brown, Thomas (Brownsville, Pa.), 77,
78n
Brownsville (Redstone), Pa.: settlements
near, 74, 77-8; and Dunmore's War,
106, 140, 514
Bruce, Normand, 12-13
Bruin, Peter Bryan, 281n, 324-5n
Brydie, Alexander, 350
Buchanan, George: *Rerum Scoticarum
Historia*, 595
Buchanan, James (Richmond), 104, 132
Buck, John H., 599
buckwheat, 200
Buffon, Georges Louis Leclerc, Comte de:
and *Notes on Virginia*, 8, 34; *Histoire
Naturelle*, 594
Bulkeley, John, & Son (Lisbon), 466
Buller, Sir Francis: *Introduction to the Law
relative to trials at Nisi Prius*, 594
Bullock, Edward, 555n
Bunel, Joseph, 663-5
Bunker Hill, battle of, 621
Burges, Dempsey, 557
Burgh, James: *Political Disquisitions*, 595

Burke, Edmund, 174n
Burnet, Gilbert: *History of His Own Time*,
595
Burr, Aaron: letters to, 356-7, 366-7, 413-
14, 576-7, 616-17; letters from, 249,
362-3; TJ sees in Philadelphia, 131,
356-7; recommends H. Aupaumut, 249;
and relations with France, 251n; reports
on elections, 344, 353; and Currie's
claim, 356-7, 363n, 366, 413-14, 576,
616; judgments against R. Morris's
property, 357n, 366, 413-14, 576, 616;
wishes to talk with TJ in person, 362;
letters from cited, 363n; patron to
Munford, 596-7n; and election of 1800,
597n
Burrall, Charles, 9, 56
Burrow, Sir James: *Reports of Cases Adjudged in the Court of King's Bench*, 594
Burwell, Lewis: and R. Morris's debt,
171-2, 356, 366; letter from cited, 367n
Butler, Messrs. (Pittsburgh), 102, 135
Byrd, Francis Otway, 524
Byrd, John, 322

Cabell, Samuel J.: and TJ's grand jury petition, 260; absent from Congress, 279,
281, 299, 305, 311, 341, 344, 363-4,
394; sends letter to constituents, 324n;
and congressional seat for Monroe, 363;
as representative, 635, 641-2
Cabot, George, 155, 324-6
Cacapon River: ice caves on, 455
Caesar, Julius: as conqueror, 123; *Commentaries*, 595
Caffery, John, 158, 159n
Cairo: Housa compared to, 154n; Callender refers to, 564
Caldwell, John W., 555n
Caldwell, William, 76-7
calendars: changes in, 161
Call, Daniel: and suit against B. Henderson's heirs, 621-2
Callender, James Thomson: letter to, 558-
9; letters from, 188-9, 521-3, 564-7,
580-5; edits *Aurora*, 45, 100n; *Sketches
of the History of America*, 115, 188-9;
Sedgwick & Co., 188-9, 565-7; seeks, receives financial assistance from TJ, 188-
9, 277n, 522, 558-9, 561, 586; Madison
sends publication to, 368, 394; gains
U.S. citizenship, 393; children of, remain in Philadelphia, 521, 565; flees to
Va., 521-3; criticizes Republicans, 565-
7; reports on debates in House, 565-7;

INDEX

Callender, James Thomson (*cont.*)
and XYZ affair, 580-4; plans for publications, 582-3; *Political Progress of Britain*, 595
Callender, Mrs. James Thomson, 565-6
Cambridge University, 287n
Camden (Cambden), William: *History of Elizabeth*, 595
Camden, N.C.: shipwrecked vessel carried to, 617, 622
Campbell, Mrs. (Hylton's daughter), 69-70
Campbell, Arthur: letter from, 71; and foreign influence in postal service, 71
Campbell, John, 288, 318, 555n
Campoformio, Treaty of, 11-12, 47, 51
canals: in Maryland, 70n; in Batavian Republic, 149; Latrobe works on, 225, 523-4; tolls for, 375, 579; proposed, in Albemarle Co., 523-4, 561-2. *See also* James River Company
Canasatego (Onondaga Indian), 18
Cannibals' Progress (William Cobbett): influence of, xliii, 524, 525n
cannon, 229n, 280n, 674
Capitol, U.S. *See* Federal District
Carey, James: publishes *Daily Advertiser*, 159; payments to, 301n; letter to cited, 354n; praised by Callender, 566. See also *Carey's United States Recorder* (Philadelphia)
Carey, John: letters from cited, 237n; letter to cited, 237n; Lloyd's *System of Short-Hand*, 237n; *Official Letters to the Honorable American Congress*, 237n
Carey, Mathew: letter to, 237; provides TJ with brother's address, 237
Carey's United States Recorder (Philadelphia): and XYZ dispatches, 251; subscriptions to, 300, 301n, 334, 353, 354n; prints Callender letter, 523n; ceases publication, 614. *See also* Carey, James
Carlyle (Carlisle), John, 19
Carmichael, William, 673
Caroline County, Va.: E. Pendleton's address to freeholders of, 662n; opposes Alien Friends Act, 662n
Carpathian Mountains: ice caves in, 455
Carr, Hester (Hettie) Smith Stevenson (Mrs. Peter Carr): accompanies husband, 80; TJ sends respects to, 268; and TJ's plans to visit, 504
Carr, John (b.1753), 333n
Carr, Martha Jefferson (Mrs. Dabney Carr, TJ's sister), 188, 368

Carr, Peter (TJ's nephew): letters to, 266-8, 422-3; letter from, 338-9; rears son from wife's first marriage, 63; illness of, 79-80; TJ sends news of XYZ affair to, 266-8; letters to cited, 268n, 423n; views U.S. as hostile to France, 338-9; health of family, 406; and Kinsolving's debt to TJ, 422-3; and TJ's plans to visit, 504; celebrates Christmas, 628
Carr, Samuel (TJ's nephew), 406
Carr, Thomas: and TJ's accounts, 423n; signs TJ's petition, 574n
carriages: TJ's chariot, 116, 235
carriage tax: revenues from, 631, 634, 640, 663, 667
Carrington, Edward C., 524, 525n
Carrsbrook (Carr estate), 80, 406, 504
Carstairs, Thomas: letter to, 255; TJ recommends bricklayer to, 255; estimates for construction of U.S. Capitol, 255n
Carter, Ann Butler, 470
Carter, Blaise, 494
Carter, Charles (of Shirley), 470
Carter, Edward (d. 1792): estate of, 493, 613. *See also* Blenheim (Carter estate)
Carter, Edward (Ned): and land for W. Bache, 613, 658
Carter, George (of Corotoman), 470n
Carter, Maria Farley (Mrs. William Champe Carter), 483
Carter, William Champe, 483
cartoons: political, xxxix-xl, xliii, 364 (illus.)
Cary, Robert, & Co., 218
Cary, Wilson Miles, 301n
Cases Argued and Adjudged in the High Court of Chancery (Thomas Vernon), 594
Cases Argued and Determined in the High Court of Chancery (Francis Vesey), 594
Catherine II (the Great), Empress of Russia, 238
Catholic Church: M. Cosway's devotion to, 23
Catlett, Kemp: and land for W. Bache, 613, 658
cattle, 208n
Cayuga Indians, 309, 310n
census: and enumeration of slaves, 442; bill providing for, 678
Chambers, James, 285-7
Champlain, Samuel de: *Voyages de la Nouvelle France*, 284, 313, 341, 345-6
Chapman, Nathaniel, 19
Charleston, S.C.: attack by French privateer at, 88

[688]

Cobbett, William (*cont.*)
  with McKean, Irujo, 194n; mocked
  in Latrobe play, 226n; warns against
  peace petition, 229n; criticizes letters
  by Republican congressmen, 324n;
  urges wearing of black cockades,
  342n; and Callender, 523n; pro-Brit-
  ish writing, 583-5; translation by,
  616n. See also *Porcupine's Gazette*
  (Philadelphia)
cockades: worn in Philadelphia, 341-2,
  344, 353; as political symbol, 565
Cocke, John Hartwell, 333n
Cocke, William, 653
Codman, Richard, 624n, 630
coffee: effects of drinking, 79
coinage: legislation on foreign, 8, 10, 671;
  expected revenue from, 634, 671
coins: theft of TJ's, 79
Cointeraux, François: *École d'Architecture
  Rurale*, 578n
Coit, Joshua: and Naturalization Act, 299,
  301n
Coke, Sir Edward: works, 594
Coles, John, 475, 493
Collin, Nicholas, 656n
Collot, Georges Henri Victor: as Federal-
  ist target, xliii, 300, 362n
Columbian Mirror and Alexandria Gazette,
  523n
Colvard (Calvert), Benjamin, Jr., 271
Commentaries (Julius Caesar), 595
Commentaries on the Laws of England
  (William Blackstone), 58-61
Commercial Advertiser (New York), 246n,
  577n
common law: and seditious libel, 187n
comptroller. *See* Steele, John (comptroller
  of treasury)
Condorcet, Marie Jean Antoine Nicolas de
  Caritat, Marquis de: and Smith's *Wealth
  of Nations*, 194n; *Esquisse d'un tableau*,
  594
Condy, Jonathan W., 85n
Conhawa. *See* Kanawha River
Connasatego. *See* Canasatego (Onondaga
  Indian)
Connecticut: and Madison's resolutions on
  Report on Commerce, 93; mules from,
  114; protests against stamp tax in, 156-
  7; TJ characterizes politics of, 156-7;
  Republican newspapers in, 227, 228-9n,
  241; congressmen from, advocate salt
  tax, 279; elections in, 344, 353; and dis-
  agreements among states, 388-9; J.
  Taylor praises government of, 431; se-

lection of jurors in, 575n; cedes land to
  U.S., 678
Connecticut Society of Arts and Sciences,
  87n
Connolly, John: and Dunmore's War, 75,
  78n, 513-14
Constantine, 125
Constantinople: Philadelphia compared to,
  521; inaccurate news from, 625n, 627,
  631
Constellation (U.S. frigate), 636n
Constitution (U.S. frigate), 263-4, 636n
Constitutional Convention: motivations
  of delegates to, 13-14, 155n, 190-1;
  Madison's notes on, 14, 623; various
  notes on, 14n; discussions of enumerated
  powers in, 173; national bank as crucial
  issue in, 173; Hamilton's influence in,
  303
Constitution of the United States: Va. proposes amendments to, 40-1, 54; amendments to, introduced in Senate, 53-4,
  55n, 679; Sixth Amendment, 53-4, 58,
  61; and trial by jury, 53, 90, 614-15; and
  impeachment, 61, 91, 163, 405, 614-
  15; division of powers in, 98-100, 256-
  62, 301n, 323, 471-3; and the Senate,
  126; and power to erect corporations,
  173; and power to grant copyrights, patents, 173; and power to declare war,
  190, 191-2, 239-40, 279-80; and rise of
  political parties, 212-13; and republicanism, 303, 646, 651n; and Federalist
  policies, 334n; and Alien and Sedition
  Acts, 393, 519, 521n, 534, 536-55,
  557n, 584n, 589, 666n; freedom of
  speech, press, religion, 395n, 536-7,
  542n, 544-5, 551, 646, 651n; role of
  states in preserving, 434; and position of
  commander in chief, 440; clause on slave
  trade, 535, 537-8, 545, 552; as compact
  of states, 536, 539-41, 543-5, 547-9,
  550-1, 553-5, 646, 651n; TJ forecasts
  threats to, 559-60; and XYZ affair, 581;
  TJ proposes amendment to prohibit
  borrowing, 589; and Va. Resolutions,
  590; and laws of Congress, 601-2; inter-
  pretation of, 623
constitutions, 431-3
consuls, 674
Continental army, 518
Cooke, Rev. James, 252
Coolidge, Ellen Randolph. *See* Randolph,
  Ellen Wayles, II (TJ's granddaughter)
Cooschachking. *See* Coshocton, Ohio
copying press, 466n

INDEX

Darmsdatt, Joseph: supplies fish for Monticello, 461, 593; letters from cited, 461n; letters to cited, 461n
Davenport, Franklin, 666n
Davenport, William: and renovation of Monticello, 114, 128, 166-7, 232, 269, 283, 312, 327; letters to cited, 115n, 129n, 327n; letters from cited, 167n, 327n; and TJ's return to Monticello, 381; and TJ's financial transactions, 604
Davie, William R., 557n
Davis, Augustine: and annual election of state printer, 57-8; TJ refers to as Tory, 63; prints piece against Monroe, 403-4. See also *Virginia Gazette and General Advertiser* (Richmond)
Davis, Thomas T., 88n, 519
Davy, William, 83
Davy (b. 1755, TJ's slave): TJ's instructions to, 56, 114
Davy (TJ's slave): and work at Monticello, 269
Dawson, John: and Monroe, 22, 120, 222-3, 246, 247n, 281-2, 329-30, 382, 400, 637n; and Madison, 96, 334, 642-3; as possible counter to "Scipio," 121; aids Kosciuszko, 196n, 314-15, 506, 508; and U.S. relations with Britain, 395n; living arrangement in Philadelphia, 439
Dayton, Jonathan: sides with Federalists, 111, 112n; and Lyon-Griswold affair, 116; challenges Gallatin's patriotism, 301n; and declaration of war against France, 443n; votes, debates in House, 445n, 471, 472n; and rumors about Kosciuszko, 507, 508; and president's annual address, 611n
Dearborn, Benjamin, 617-18
debt: imprisonment for, 10
debts, foreign, 122-3
debts, public: plans to stop interest payments on, 279, 284, 300, 305; increased by defense measures, 388-9. See also United States: Public Finance
Decatur, Stephen, Sr., 447
Decisions of Cases in Virginia, By The High Court of Chancery (George Wythe), 594
Declaration of Independence: similarities to Ky. Resolutions, 535
Decline and Fall of the Roman Empire (Edward Gibbon), 595
Defence of the Constitutions of Government of the United States of America (John Adams), 368-9, 415-16
Dejanira, 158

De Jure Maritimo et Navali: or, A Treatise of Affairs Maritime and of Commerce (Charles Molloy), 594
Delamotte, F. C. A.: letter from, 45-9; says France will not declare war, 44-52, 245-6; letter from, translated, 50-2; as vice consul at Le Havre, 119; forwards letters, 146-7
Delaware: and Madison's resolutions on Report on Commerce, 93n
Delaware (Lenni Lenape) Indians: language, 86-7, 564; and Dunmore's War, 102, 513; J. Gibson's connections to, 288n; Christian converts killed, 305, 306n, 308; in Ohio, 305-10. See also Loskiel, George Henry
Delaware (ship), 447, 611n
Delaware River: freezes over, 9, 87, 116, 122, 127, 128, 609, 618, 626, 633, 666; beginning to open, 5-6
democratic societies, 420, 565-7
Denmark: relations with France, 47-8, 51-2, 245, 247, 248; trade with U.S., 147; and seizure of neutral vessels, 241, 397; TJ recommends Mallet's *Northern Antiquities*, 595; history of Danes in Britain, 597n
Dennis, John: and Blount impeachment, 84-5, 615n, 619n
Derieux, Justin Pierre Plumard: TJ gives financial assistance to, 29-30, 375; letter to cited, 30n; aided by Palisot de Beauvois, 516
Desear, Samuel, 104
Detroit: Heckewelder at, 291, 306, 309; and Logan, 308-9
dictionaries, 568-70
Didot, Pierre and Firmin: develop printing process, 154n, 277n. See also Virgil
Difference between an Absolute and Limited Monarchy; As it More Particularly regards the English Constitution (Sir John Fortescue), 569, 570n
Dinsmore, James: hired as housejoiner at Monticello, 249, 269, 327, 381, 395, 421; introduced by TJ, 435; borrows book from TJ, 604; sends chimney piece to TJ, 613
Dinwiddie, Gov. Robert, 19-20, 32
dipping needle. See magnetism
Direct Tax (1798): Congress considers, vii, 8, 9n, 10, 21-2, 281, 300, 327, 331, 341, 344, 360, 365, 367, 408, 411; opposition to, 158, 300, 581, 611n, 649, 664; as substitute for other revenues, 158; needed to pay for defense measures,

381, 396, 421, 467; TJ reports marriage of, 319; sister's affection for, 347; Strickland sends regards to, 458; Short's regard for, 482; plans to reside at Mont Blanco, 639-40

Eppes family: TJ's affection for, 16, 116, 214-15; TJ sends regards to, 236, 336, 391, 451, 599, 632; health of, 381

Eppington, Va.: postal service to, 452

Erie, Lake, 213

Esquisse d'un tableau historique des progrès de l'esprit humain (Marquis de Condorcet), 594

Essay on Colonization, Particularly Applied to the Western Coast of Africa (Carl Bernhard Wadström), 149

Essay on Crimes and Punishments (Cesare Bonesana Beccaria), 595

Essays on Poetical and Prosaic Numbers, and Elocution (John Mason), 594

Essays on the Principles of Morality and Natural Religion (Lord Kames), 594

Essay towards a General History of Feudal Property in Great Britain (Sir John Dalrymple), 594

Essay towards Facilitating Instruction in the Anglo-Saxon and Modern Dialects of the English Language (Thomas Jefferson), 570n

Essex Co., N.J.: petitions against Alien and Sedition Acts, 666n

Ethis de Corny, Anne Mangeot (Mme Ethis de Corny), 23

Ettwein, John, 87

Etymologicon Linguæ Anglicanæ (Stephen Skinner), 568-9, 570n

Euler, Leonard, 160, 162n

Euripides, 597n

Europe: U.S. relations with, 117; partition of, 156; scarcity of capital in, 183; and prospects of war, 227; American travelers in, 386, 437-8; plants of, compared to American, 456; British excluded from ports of, 458; support for newspapers in, 565; supply of tobacco in, 669

Eustace, John Skey, 637n

Evans, Cadwalader, 229n

Evans, Thomas: and Blount impeachment, 84-5, 615n, 619n; and TJ's comments on J. Wise, 99-100n; avoids voting on war measure, 189-90, 193-4

Evans, Thomas (agent of Farell & Jones), 426, 428n

Ewing (Ewen), John: astronomical observations, 160, 162n; conversation with Adams, 608

Facts and observations relative to sheep, wool, ploughs and oxen (Lord Somerville), 376n

Faden, William, 212, 457

Fairfax, George, 19

Farell & Jones: and Wayles estate, 317n, 426-30; market tobacco, 427, 428n

farmers: as legislators, 128; favor peace, 283, 316; plight of, 405

farm implements: Caroline drill by T. Martin, 198-9, 310, 387; TJ sends to Britain, 198-9, 310, 387; animals for, 199. *See also* plow, moldboard; plows; threshing machines

Fast Day (9 May 1798): proclaimed by Adams, 336n; in Philadelphia, 341-2, 344, 353

Fauchet, Jean Antoine Joseph: *Coup d'oeil sur l'état actuel*, 7, 8n, 43; *Sketch*, 11, 62

Federal District: U.S. Capitol, 225n, 255n; federal aid for buildings in, 228, 229n, 244-6, 673-4; Adams's views on, 275-6; investment in land in, 316n; Orphan's Court executes Kosciuszko's will, 333n; Washington visits, 369, 371; TJ expects to visit, 383

Federal Gazette & Baltimore Daily Advertiser (Baltimore), 486n

Federalist (Alexander Hamilton, John Jay, and James Madison): recommended by TJ, 595

Federalists: prevail in Congress, government, vii, 363-4, 365, 368, 379, 397, 484-5; called tories, British party, viii, 40, 63-4, 98-100, 212-13, 216, 251n, 269, 290, 323, 325, 334n, 344, 359, 420, 444, 510, 521, 586, 598, 662; and impeachment of Blount, 10; threaten disunion, 83-4, 155; divisions within, 112n, 156, 173, 175, 182, 388, 441, 443n, 448, 560; condemn Barlow's letter to Baldwin, 174n; and president's message of 19 Mch. 1798, 189-90, 193-4; referred to as war party, 189-90, 193-4, 263, 267, 270, 279, 299, 300, 301n, 333-4, 363-4, 365, 384, 441; and Kosciuszko, 196n; seek to undermine TJ, 216; mocked by Latrobe, 226n; as party of Hamilton, 245; and XYZ affair, 245-6, 250-1, 275, 333, 353, 359, 363-4, 648, 649, 652n; Monroe sees ruin of, 254; and defense measures, 268, 279; legislative program of, 299-302, 305, 323; and patriotic songs, 325n; and foreign policy, 334-5n; call for war against France, 335; and newspaper attacks on

INDEX

INDEX

FRANCE (*cont.*)

War with Britain

prospects of peace, 8, 56-7, 341, 344; preparations for conquest of Britain, 25, 62-3, 66, 67, 101, 124, 146n, 156, 168, 190, 206, 213, 357, 365, 383, 388, 394, 397, 449; treatment of neutral nations, commerce, 47, 49n, 51, 118-9, 125, 165-6, 168, 170, 221, 245, 281, 282n, 397, 490; impact on transatlantic travel, 147; conflict approaching a climax, 165, 217, 340, 343, 383; France expected to prevail, 184; attempts to disrupt British trade, 248, 457-8; as offensive or defensive, 338; and W. Indies trade, 380n; invasion of Britain abandoned, 400n; fleet assembles at Brest, 443, 445n, 449; rumors of military movements, 443, 445n; formation of new coalition, 449-50; assistance to Ireland, 460, 597n, 631-2; destruction of French fleet at Aboukir Bay, 603; rumors of French submission, 641n; and India, 664, 666, 668. *See also* Egypt

Francis, John: cares for letter, 410; account with, 436, 644n; TJ's regard for, 585

Francis, Mrs. John, 585

Francis II, Holy Roman Emperor: signs Treaty of Campoformio, 11, 47, 51; and relations with France, 449

Francis's hotel: residents at, 14n, 511n; TJ criticizes Wise at, 63, 98; TJ stays at, 436, 439, 585; TJ receives visitors at, 484; location, 585n

Franklin, Benjamin: and APS, 297n, 515-16; characterizes Adams, 405-6; praised by TJ, 484

Frederick Co., Va.: H. B. Trist's impressions of, 177

Fredericksburg, Va.: postal service at, 9, 27, 56, 88, 117, 282, 325, 627; reliable postal rider for, 90, 92; district court in, 254-5, 311; meeting of merchants in, 351; and XYZ affair, 359; and TJ's trips to, from Philadelphia, 390, 604, 605n; newspapers at, 603

Freeman, Nathaniel, Jr., 363-4

Freire, Cipriano Ribeiro: grants passport, 195n; letter from cited, 195n; letter to cited, 195n

French language: G. Taylor as translator of, 129; TJ's reticence in using, 319-20; and XYZ envoys, 490-1

French Revolution: Terror caricatured, xl, 364 (illus.); response of Adams and Washington to, 117; Palisot de Beauvois proscribed, 297n; TJ condemned as missionary of, 304n; Adams assesses, 359-60; prospects for failure of, 408; as check on European despotism, 420; TJ's support for, 647

Freneau, Philip, 226n

Friends, Society of: and votes on war measures, 194; and peace petition, 228, 229n; petition for reform of Parliament, 369n

"Friend to Justice": attacks Monroe, 404n

"Fright of Astyanax" (Benjamin West): owned by TJ, xli-xlii, 364 (illus.)

fruit, 193

fruit trees: at Monticello, 193; bloom late in Philadelphia, 248; hurt by frost, 290; pests of, 340-1

furniture: bookcases, 69; Windsor sofa, 282, 337, 350; chairs, 343, 362

furs: given by Kosciuszko, 331

Gahn, Henry, 331-2n, 383

Gale, Levin, 20

Gallatin, Albert: depicted in political cartoon, xliii, 364 (illus.); mocked by Cobbett, xliii; lays memorial before House, 229n; as target of Federalists, 299-300, 301n; opposes use of convoys, 301n; speech on provisional army bill, 472, 473n; and Munford, 596-7n; on Haitian independence, 637n

Gallego & Chevallie, 374

Ganges (ship), 379, 659-60

Gardner, Henrietta, 644n

Garnett, John, 110

Garrard, James, 533-4, 555n

Garrett, Alexander: and TJ's financial transactions, 115n; and postal service at Charlottesville, 626-7; letters from cited, 627n; letters to cited, 627n

Gates, Horatio: letter to, 123-4; letters from, 110-11, 146; invites TJ to visit, 110; and Kosciuszko, 110, 123, 146, 196n; praises Monroe, 110; and U.S. relations with France and Britain, 110, 123; health of, 124; and Munford, 596n

Gates, Mary Vallance (Mrs. Horatio Gates), 110, 124

Gatewood. *See* Greathouse, Daniel

Gautier, Jean Antoine: letter to, 620-1; and Short, 482, 496; and Coxe, 620-1

[698]

INDEX

Gazette of the United States (Philadelphia): prints essays by Federalists, 11, 245-6; seen as Adams's mouthpiece, 185; Callender's opinion of, 188, 564-6; and XYZ affair, 251, 301n; prints president's addresses and replies to addresses, 279-80, 322-4n; reports on meeting of House Republicans, 301n; TJ sends to Madison, 349; and U.S. negotiations with France, 364n; criticizes TJ, 438-9; reports world news, 443, 445n; TJ's views on, 486

Gazzam, Mr., 679

Geddy (Gaddy), Mr., 132

Geismar, Baron von: letters to cited, 316-17; letters from cited, 317n, 504

Gemm, Richard, 578

General Abridgement of Cases in Equity, 594

General History of Ireland, from the Earliest Accounts to the Death of King William III (John Huddleston Wynne), 595

Genera Plantarum (Carolus Linnaeus): ordered by T. M. Randolph, 69, 283

Genet, Edmond Charles, 335

Genghis Khan. *See* Jenghiz Khan

Gentleman Farmer (Lord Kames), 594

geography: and political parties, 431-2

George (1730-1799, TJ's slave): as manager at Monticello, 55-6, 312, 326; and tobacco crops, 56, 192, 282, 312; and altercation at Monticello, 68; T. M. Randolph's comments on, 79, 145, 312; and preparations for spring work at Monticello, 114, 128; sows clover at Monticello, 170; horses for, 177; directed to accommodate Arnold, 271; and discipline of workforce at Monticello, 385-6; health of, 669

George (1759-1799, TJ's slave): manages nailery, viii-ix, 145, 290, 563, 638; TJ sends blacksmith's equipment to, 56; and nails for Madison, 95; illness, 563

George II, King of Great Britain, 6, 18-19

George III, King of Great Britain, 560, 620n

George, Reuben, 469n

Georgetown, Md.: TJ travels through, 9, 410; TJ seeks to buy mules at, 283; and XYZ affair, 324n

Georgia: tobacco from, 623, 626, 668; and congressional elections of 1798, 643; public sentiment in, 668; motion in Senate for committee on lands adjoining, 672

Germania (Cornelius Tacitus), 595

German language, 568-71

Germany: and relations with France, 124, 666, 668; astronomy, 160-2; and prospect of war between U.S., France, 482, 496; French depredations in Swabia, 525n

Gerry, Elbridge: letter to, 645-53; letter from, 577-8; Republican spirit of, ix, 645-53; in cartoon, xl, 364 (illus.); conduct as envoy criticized, 174n, 339; characterized as weak, 185-6; and Directory, 185, 393, 394, 396, 397, 621; remains in Paris, 219, 390, 393, 394, 396, 397; on conferences with Talleyrand, 364n; relations with Pinckney, Marshall, 393, 647; correspondence with Adams, 417-18, 422; corresponds with Talleyrand, 417-18, 422, 462, 463-5, 610, 614, 622, 624n, 631, 665; continues negotiations, 441, 449, 485-6, 648; Federalists oppose independent negotiation by, 444, 445n, 650; returns to U.S., 453-4n, 473, 487, 489, 499; and Short, 478, 481, 490-1, 496, 577; as political moderate, 479, 480; on Bank of Pennsylvania, 480, 495; prospect of solo envoyship, 490; and Duchesse de La Rochefoucauld, 496n, 577; delivers items, respects from Americans in France, 577-8; Senate confirmation, 578, 653; and Dutch proposal to mediate between U.S. and France, 611n; as Antifederalist, 621; Pickering, Adams comment on, 621; and Kosciuszko, 625; reports to Pickering, 631, 635, 640-1, 643, 648; relationship with TJ, 635, 645-50; correspondence with Talleyrand published, 636n, 638, 640-1, 648, 651n, 661-4, 667; keeps journal, 643; encouraged to assume prominent role, 649-50. *See also* XYZ affair

Gibbon, Edward: *Decline and Fall of the Roman Empire*, 595

Gibbs, James: *Rules for Drawing the Several Parts of Architecture*, 604

Gibson, George, 288n

Gibson, John: letter to, 100-1; letters from, 26, 72; and Logan affair, 26, 72, 100-1, 288, 306; ties to Logan's family, 102, 135, 288n; translates Logan's speech, 102, 136-7, 142, 288n, 303-4, 340, 342

Gibson, Patrick: prepares account for TJ's tobacco, 579n. *See also* Jefferson, George, & Co.

INDEX

GREAT BRITAIN (*cont.*)
allusion to English Civil War, 560; trial by jury, 615n; and Wilkes's prosecution, 620

Public Opinion
Kosciuszko acclaimed, xl-xli, 196n

Society
TJ studies law, history of, 568-70, 594-5, 597n. *See also* Whig Club of England

U.S. Relations with
interference with U.S. shipping, 25, 168, 170, 271, 288, 315-16, 393-5, 405, 408, 410, 485, 610, 613-14; and prospects of political change in Britain, 25; Delamotte's letter comments upon, 44-52; British gather intelligence in U.S., 71; earlier responses by Congress, 84; and American politics, 110, 303, 325n, 420, 442, 528; and British policies toward neutral shipping, 125; American commercial, political dependency, 158, 420; courts condemn vessels, cargoes, 169-70n, 395n; and U.S. naturalization of British subjects, 170; rumors of alliance, 227-8, 270, 448, 640, 641n; and XYZ affair, 251, 334n; and U.S. relations with France, 290, 447, 462, 464, 497, 500, 647; TJ said to be subverting, 304n; boundary issue, 346n; and Britain's war with France, 401; aided by U.S. anti-French legislation, 408, 410; undue influence of British in U.S., 414, 619-20; and bill to prevent landing of French passengers, 438-9; and refugees from Saint-Domingue, 440-1; and impressment of sailors, 610-11, 613; U.S. expenditures for treaties, 634, 667; and American popular perceptions, 641n. *See also* Jay Treaty

War with France
prospects for peace, 8, 56-7, 341, 344, 641n; prospects of French invasion, 25, 62-3, 101, 124, 146n, 156, 161, 190, 206, 213, 357, 365, 383, 388, 394, 397, 399-400, 408, 443, 445n, 449, 457-8; treatment of neutral nations, commerce, 118-19, 165-6, 397; impact on commerce, travel, 147, 181; conflict approaching a climax, 165, 217, 340, 343, 383; France expected to prevail, 184; impact of

French operations, 242; restrictions on U.S. shipping, 271; and W. Indies trade, 380n; and efforts to form new coalition in Europe, 449-50; high cost of, 581-2, 584n; destroys French fleet at Aboukir Bay, 603; and India, 664, 666, 668

Greathouse, Daniel: and murder of Logan's kin, 39, 102, 138, 140, 142, 285-8, 307, 511n, 512, 514-15
Greek language, 568
Green, Timothy, 9, 88
Greenbrier Co., Va.: fossils, 236, 293-7, 519
Greene, Nathanael, 196n
Greenleaf, James, 315-16, 503
Greenleaf, Thomas, 217, 644
Greenleaf's New York Journal, & Patriotic Register (New York): TJ's notes from, 125; TJ subscribes to, 217, 644
Green Sea. *See* Dismal Swamp
Grey, Charles, 369n
Grice, Charles, 617n
Griffin, John Tayloe: R. Morris purchases land from, 171-2; Currie's claim against, 366, 413-14
Griffin, Samuel, 596n
Griswold, Roger: confrontation with M. Lyon, viii, 87-8, 90, 111, 115-16, 117, 133, 164, 165, 241
groceries: sent by TJ from Philadelphia, 355, 356
Grove, William B., 557
Guenat, John B., 656n
Guiana, French: French deportations to, 302n
Guillemard, John, 623-5, 627
Gun, James, 666n
guns: carried by slaves, 68; theft of, 79
Guthrie, William: *New System of Modern Geography*, 594
Gwin, Andrew: letter to, 215; letter from, 219-20; and measurement of latitude, 159-60, 177-8, 215, 219-20, 236, 273

Habington, Thomas: *Historie of Edward the Fourth*, 595
Haden, Mr.: and renovation of Monticello, 271
Hague, The: Short's service at, 487
"Hail Columbia" (Joseph Hopkinson), 325
Hale, Sir Matthew: *History of the Common Law*, 594

Hales, Stephen: *Vegetable Staticks*, 594
Hamburg, Germany: La Rochefoucauld-Liancourt writes from, 65-8; and correspondence between U.S., Europe, 482, 496; G. Logan travels through, 645
Hamilton, Alexander: at Constitutional Convention, 13-14; dispute with Monroe, 22n, 89, 637n; and Britain, monarchy, 172-3, 560, 606-7; mocked in Latrobe play, 226n; Reynolds affair, 226n; pseudonyms ascribed to, 245-6, 276, 323; offered U.S. Senate seat, 300, 302n, 305, 323-4, 334, 353; influence on American politics, 303, 388, 420; and J. Marshall, 417; appointed inspector general of army, 440, 450n; and rumor of G. Logan mission to France, 577n; on suspected French agent, 596n; and president's annual address to Congress, 610-11; and Knox's resignation from army, 612n; mentioned, viii, 625n
Hamilton, William, 581, 584n
Hanbury, Capel, 467-70
Hanbury, John, 18-19, 469n
Hanbury, John, & Co., 467-70
Hanbury, Osgood, 467-70
Hannibal (ship), 659
Hanover: and Treaty of Campoformio, 11, 46; astronomical observatory, 160, 162n
Hanse Towns, 47, 51
Hanson, Richard, 426-30
Hardin, John, 78
hardware: Madison orders, 312, 343-5, 358-9, 380, 384, 394, 409, 418
Harper, Robert Goodloe: introduces foreign intercourse bill, 54n; and Blount impeachment, 84-5, 615-16n, 619n; and Lyon-Griswold affair, 88n, 164; and Stamp Act, 156-7; on U.S. relations with France, 227, 228n, 231, 417-19; on naturalization and citizenship, 301n; attacks Findley, TJ, 302-4; and provisional army, 336n; and Direct Tax, 354n; resolutions on finances, 409n, 410-11; supports defense measures, 444, 445n, 472; supports delegation of powers to president, 473n; speeches printed, distributed, 524; praises Senate as anchor of government, 615-16; and G. Logan's mission to France, 622, 624n
Harpers Ferry: arsenal for, 224-5
harpsichords: for Mary Eppes, shipped to Monticello, 192, 215, 248, 265, 282, 312, 346, 356, 368, 375, 390; comparisons of, 215, 346, 390

Harris, Mr., 76
Harris, James, first Earl of Malmesbury, 46, 50
Harris, Jordan: and TJ's business affairs, 103, 179, 220; letters from cited, 105n, 179n; letters to cited, 105n, 179n
Harrison, Benjamin (governor of Va.), 518n
Harrison, Benjamin, Jr.: letter to, 411; letter from, 459-60; and Short's affairs, 351-2, 411, 459-60, 495, 558
Harrison, Carter Bassett, 157n
Harrison, Richard: and charges against Monroe, 246; and Short's salary, 298, 317, 330
Harrison & Sterett (Van Staphorst & Hubbard's agent), 503
Harvie, John: letter to, 337; letter from, 351-2; TJ's financial transactions with, 29-30, 375; and Short's business affairs, 318, 337, 351-2, 411, 459, 481, 496, 558; letter to cited, 337n; letter from cited, 352n; marriage of daughter, 438n
Haskill, Jonathan, 680
Hatsell, John: *Precedents of Proceedings in the House of Commons*, 595
Hauteval, Lucien: as "Z," 251n, 523. *See also* XYZ affair
Havre. *See* Le Havre, France
Hay, Mr.: bottles beer for TJ, 104, 362
Heath, John, 524
Hebrew, 86
Heckewelder, John: letter to, 264-5; letters from, 291, 305-6; observes Indians, 87; and TJ's account of Logan's speech, 264-5, 285, 288, 291, 305-10; identified, 265n; memorandum on Logan affair, 306-10
Hector, xli
Helvetic Republic, 186, 187n
Hélvetius, Claude Adrien: *Œuvres complètes*, 594
Hemings, Critta (ca. 1783-1819): purchased by T. M. Randolph, 604n
Hemings, Harriet (1795-1797), 28, 43
Hemings, John: and renovation of Monticello, 269, 271
Hemings, Sally: death of Harriet, 28, 43
Hemsley, William, Jr., 227
Henderson, Bennett (d. 1793): mill canal, 561; TJ's suit against heirs of, 622n, 669
Henderson, Bennett Hillsborough, 622n, 669
Henderson, Charles, 622n, 669

Henderson, Eliza (Elizabeth), 622n, 669
Henderson, Frances, 622n, 669
Henderson, Isham, 622n, 669
Henderson, James, 622n, 669
Henderson, John, 622n, 669
Henderson, Lucy, 622n, 669
Henderson, McCaul & Co.: TJ indebted to, 411-12, 579. *See also* Lyle, James
Henderson, Nancy Crawford, 622n, 669
Henderson, Sally (Sarah), 622n, 669
Henderson, William, 622n, 669
Henry, John: and Logan affair, 216, 392-3, 419
Henry, Patrick: debates Corbin, 287n; Green Sea land speculation, 352, 459n
Herald of Liberty (Washington, Pa.), 286n
Hercules, 158, 583
heresy, 59
Herhan, Louis Etienne: develops printing process, 154n, 277n. *See also* Virgil
Herschel, Sir William, 178
Higginbotham, David: and postal service at Milton, 27; factor of Rives & Co., 28-9; letters from cited, 29n; letters to cited, 29n
Higginson, Stephen, Jr.: carries letters, 154n, 475, 482n
Higginson, Stephen, Sr., 482n
Hillhouse, James: and alien bill, xliii, 300, 301n, 674; TJ's comments on, 84, 615-16; and aid for Federal District, 245; and Conn. election, 353; and Gerry's confirmation, 653
Hinde, Robert: *Modern Practice of the High Court of Chancery*, 594
Hindman, William, 264n
Hispaniola. *See* Saint-Domingue, W.I.
Histoire de la Nouvelle-France (Marc Lescarbot): TJ lends to Pickering, 284, 313, 341, 345-6, 385
Histoire Naturelle, générale et particulière (Comte de Buffon), 594
Historiarum (Polybius), 595
Historical and Chronological View of Roman Law (Alexander Crowcher Schomberg), 594
Historie of Edward the Fourth (Thomas Habington), 595
Historie of the Pitifull Life, and Unfortunate Death of Edward the Fifth (Thomas More), 595
Historie of the Reigne of King Henry the Seventh (Francis Bacon), 595
History of America (William Robertson), 595
History of England (David Hume), 595

History of England: from the Accession of James I to That of the Brunswick Line (Catharine Macaulay), 595
History of Great Britain, from the Revolution to the Accession of the House of Hanover (William Belsham), 595
History of King Richard III (Thomas More), 595
History of Scotland During the Reigns of Queen Mary and of King James VI (William Robertson), 595
History of the British Plantations in America (Sir William Keith), 595
History of the Common Law of England (Sir Matthew Hale), 594
History of the First Discovery and Settlement of Virginia (William Stith), 595
History of the Mission of the United Brethren among the Indians in North America (George Henry Loskiel), 86, 87n, 238, 309
History of the Most Renowned and Victorious Princess Elizabeth, Late Queen of England (William Camden), 595
History of the Reign of Philip the Second, King of Spain (Robert Watson), 595
History of the Reign of Philip the Third, King of Spain (Robert Watson), 595
History of the Reign of the Emperor Charles V (William Robertson), 595
History of the Revolutions in Spain (René Aubert de Vertot), 595
History of the Rise, Progress, and Establishment, of the Independence of the United States of America (William Gordon): Madison refers to, 619-20
H.L., Capt.: in Dunmore's War, 106
Hobart, John Sloss, 300, 302n, 305
Hockhocking River, 137, 138
Hogg, Thomas, 141
holidays: Fast Day, 336n, 341-2, 344, 353; Fourth of July, 444, 650; celebration of Christmas and New Year's, 628
Holland. *See* Batavian Republic
Holt, Charles, 228n
Holy Roman Empire. *See* Austria; Francis II, Holy Roman Emperor
Home, Francis: *Principles of Agriculture and Vegetation*, 211
Home, Henry, Lord Kames. *See* Kames, Henry Home, Lord
Hooper, Thomas: buys TJ's tobacco, 349, 357-8, 372-3, 411-12, 413, 423, 459, 471, 560-1, 579; G. Jefferson's opinion of, 373-4; letter to cited, 412n
Hoops, Adam, 281

Hope, Henry Philip, 419n

Hopkins, John: and TJ's business affairs, 29-30, 55, 375, 445, 452

Hopkinson, Francis, 325n

Hopkinson, Joseph, 325

hops, 331

Horace: *Epistulae* quoted, 319, 320n; allusions to, 478; cited by Callender, 521-3

horses: to be sent for TJ's trip home, ix, 323, 327, 336, 379, 390, 394, 406, 408, 410, 638; and farm equipment, 114, 128, 158, 177; feed for, 132; TJ seeks to purchase, 231, 249, 283, 312; Darlington described, 283, 313; of trans-Mississippi west, 425-6, 521; saddles, bridles for, 467n

Hosmer, Hezekiah L.: and Blount impeachment, 84-5, 615n, 619n

Hottinguer, Jean Conrad: rebuffed by American envoys, xl; as "X," 251n, 397, 523; and Kosciuszko's funds, 462, 498n. *See also* XYZ affair

Houghton, Daniel, 154n

Housa (Hausa): discovery of, 149, 154n

houses: rental costs in Philadelphia, 10; for tenant farmers, 639. *See also* Direct Tax (1798)

Howard, John E.: criticizes TJ, 484-6; mentioned, 39, 653

Hubbard, Nicholas: as "W," 251n, 523. *See also* XYZ affair

Hugues (Hughes), Victor, 335-6, 380n

Hume, David: essays of, 594; *History of England*, 595

Humphreys, Clement: attacks Bache, 271-2; TJ characterizes, 271; and American envoys to France, 648, 651n

Humphreys, David, 147

Hungary: ice caves in, 455

Hunter, John, 172-3, 653

Hunter, William. See *Virginia Gazette* (Dixon and Hunter)

Hunter and Beaumont (printers, Frankfort, Ky.), 555n

Huron Indians, 81

Hurt, John, 608-9

Huston, William, 285, 286n

Hylton, William, 69

Hylton, Mr. (son of William Hylton), 69-70

Iliad (Homer), xli

Illinois: Indian-white violence in, 141

Imlay, James H.: and Blount impeachment, 84-5, 615n, 619n

impeachment: right of trial by jury, vii, 53-4, 58-61, 90, 126, 162-3, 614-15; British laws on, 59-61; and partisanship, 111-12, 117; Senate procedures for, 121, 672; power of Senate in, 257-62; process of, 405. *See also* Blount, William

impressment, 610-11, 613

Independence Day: Senate passes sedition bill on, 440; plans to bring forth a declaration of war in House on, 441, 443n; military parade in Philadelphia, 444; political orations, 650

Independent Chronicle (Boston): subscriptions to, 25-6, 115, 183; T. Adams edits, 115; TJ's notes from, 124-5; carries news from France, 146n; TJ recommends, 228n

India: Britain allows trade with, 94n; British-French rivalry in, 664, 666, 668

Indian Camp. *See* Short, William

Indians: languages, viii, 81-2, 86-7, 114-15, 238, 243, 265n, 310n, 564; women, children as victims of whites, 4, 39, 102, 103, 135, 288n, 306-8, 514; and competition between colonial powers, 18, 184; and Ohio Company, 19-20, 33; and Va., 19-20, 322, 342, 564; tenor of relations with whites, 30-4, 306, 308-9, 342; in *Notes on Virginia*, 33, 34n, 322; interaction with whites in Ohio Valley, 75-7, 102, 137-9, 141-2, 285-8, 305-10, 512-15; and Christian missionary activity, 81-2n, 86-7, 238, 243, 265n, 305-10; names of tribes, 81, 86; white traders among, 102, 135, 137-8, 288n, 307-8; APS seeks information on, 159n; wars of, in Callender's publication, 188; depicted as living peacefully without laws, 206, 572; trust lands in Ohio, 265n; and savagery of frontier whites, 285-6, 287, 514; and alcoholism, 309; U.S. expenditures for, negotiations with, 325, 326, 634, 667; sign languages, 426n; white captives, 511-12n, 520; bill to regulate, 680. *See also* Delaware (Lenni Lenape) Indians; Dunmore's War; Iroquois (Six Nations) Indians; Logan (Mingo Indian); Mahican (Mohican) Indians; Miami Indians; Mingo Indians; Oneida Indians; Shawnee Indians

indigo: exported from N.C., 73

Infallible Cure, for Political Blindness, if Administered to Patients Possessing Sound Minds, Honest Hearts, and Inde-

INDEX

JEFFERSON, THOMAS (*cont.*)
11, 94; books obtained for, 69, 82-3,
284, 313, 341, 466n, 644n; TJ's catalogue of, 84, 313; Short sends new
printing of Virgil to, 153-4, 277, 577,
578n; lends Faden's map of South
America, 212, 457; lends books to
Pickering, 284, 313, 341, 345-6, 385;
Pougens supplies books for, 319, 481;
quotes Horace, 319, 320n; description of, 341; purchases magazines in
Philadelphia, 436; courses of reading
for students, 594-6, 597n; books borrowed from, 604

Nailery
nailrod and iron stock for, viii, 104,
105n, 132, 145, 154-5, 167, 180,
182-3, 220, 375, 461, 466, 525-6,
585, 609, 617, 618, 626, 633, 638,
668-9; Madison orders nails from, 9,
40, 95-6, 127, 162, 576, 580, 603,
605-6; cutting machine at, 95-6, 127,
162, 524; management of work force
at, 290; sale of nails, 398, 466, 593;
accounts with S. Clarke, McDowell,
446, 526-7, 529, 563; illness reduces
output, 563; loss of nailrod at sea,
617, 622, 633, 660

Opinions
on Adams, Adams's views, vii-ix, 113,
126, 271, 322-3, 326, 604, 605-6,
610; on XYZ affair, xxxix-xl, 165,
250-1, 267-8, 269-70, 322-3, 326,
335, 344, 363, 365, 635, 648, 652n;
on Alien and Sedition Acts, xliii, 324,
363, 365, 393; on marriage, debt, 15-
16; on political parties, politics, 23,
212-13, 388-9; distrusts foreign
news, 53, 56, 623, 627; on arming of
merchant vessels, 88, 168-9, 183,
191, 408; on power of Senate to frame
oaths, 91; on political divisions, geography, 92-4; on union, 94, 389-90n;
on relations with France, 100-1, 217,
263, 266-7, 269, 283, 319, 397-8; on
Lyon-Griswold affair, 111; on impact
of paper currency, 113; on taxes, public debt, and public opinion, 156-7,
305, 623, 627, 668; relationship of
war, peace, commercial regulation,
161; on relearning science, geography, politics, 161; on need for representatives to consult their constituents, 190, 191, 194, 227, 240; on
prospect of war with France, 190,

217, 227, 231-2, 270, 283, 318, 319,
326, 340, 377, 379-80, 392-3, 396-8;
416, 647; on war, 206, 217, 281, 635;
on relations with Britain and France,
213, 485; on threat of constitutional
abuse, 213, 559-60, 623, 646; on
aging, death, 214; on removal to Federal District, 244-5; on "Hail Columbia," 325; of Volney, 326, 379-80; on
Indian-white relations, 342; on
women in politics, 355, 607; says
Congress seems to make its session
permanent, 367; on Kosciuszko, 377,
591; on power of despots, 388; on rivalry among states, 388; on financing
government expenditures, 408, 627,
631, 646; decries Federalists' "new
code of morality," 562; on selection of
jurors, 572-4; praises state governments, 589; on republicanism in Poland, 591; on importance of family, affection, 607; on army, militia, 634-5,
646; on Republican cause, 641; defends philosophy, progress of knowledge, 646; favors limited naval force,
646; on freedom of religion, 646,
651n; on freedom of speech, press,
646; on relations with other nations,
646

Personal Affairs
studies Anglo-Saxon language, viii,
568-71; owns West drawing, xli-xlii;
in Paris, 23-4, 453; encourages family to write, 26; urges Trists to settle
near Monticello, 26; buys books for
T. M. Randolph, 69, 283, 313; declines social invitations, 112n, 132;
introduces H. B. Trist, 114; seeks employment for C. L. Lewis, 179, 220;
and Kosciuszko, 194-7, 223, 272,
288-9, 291-2, 313-15, 320-1, 331-3,
351, 376-7, 453-4; collects debts for
J. Carey, 237n; reticence in using
French, 319-20; regard for La Rochefoucauld family, 320; interest in history, historical records, 342, 345,
568-70, 594-5; accounts for shipment
of goods to Monticello, 375; provides
certificates of citizenship, 386-7, 437-
8; plans to attend court, 398, 422;
Philadelphia expenditures, 436, 439,
585; extends invitations, 498n; relations with neighbors, 561-2; knows
Latude, 578n; mentor to Munford,
594-7

[707]

INDEX

McDowell, Joseph, 557

McDowell, William, 527n

McGee (McGehee), James: works on roof at Monticello, 593; Madison sends schedule of rates for, 606, 610, 619, 642-3

McGuire, William, 281n

Machecou Indians. *See* Fox (Mechecaukis, Mechecouakis) Indians

McHenry, James: and TJ's comments on J. Wise, 99-100n; prospects for continuing in office, 111, 173, 182; and Washington, 156, 443n, 448, 611n; *Letter from the Secretary at War*, 279-80; and fortifications at Norfolk, 523-4

Machir, James, 169, 194

McKean, Sarah (Sally). *See* Irujo, Sarah (Sally) McKean

McKean, Thomas: as gubernatorial candidate in 1799, 10; charge to grand jury, 125; dispute with Cobbett, 194n; provides certificate for G. Logan, 386n

Maclay, William, 228, 229n

Maclure, William: entertains TJ, 426n; knows Niemcewicz, 507-9, 625; hopes to visit Monticello, 591

Macon, Nathaniel, 379

Madison, Dolley Payne Todd: TJ sends regards to, 11, 54, 88, 112, 127, 182, 269, 300, 323, 354, 380, 394, 409, 418, 576, 580, 624, 666; TJ sends news to, 610

MADISON, JAMES: letters to, 9-12, 53-5, 87-9, 111-12, 125-7, 156-7, 181-2, 189-91, 227-9, 244-6, 250-1, 279-80, 280-1, 299-302, 322-5, 343-5, 353-4, 363-5, 378-80, 393-5, 408-9, 416-19, 567-8, 576, 579-80, 610-12, 622-5, 665-7; letters from, 40-1, 94-6, 116-18, 162-4, 175-6, 238-40, 274-6, 289-90, 311-12, 333-5, 348-9, 358-60, 368-9, 383-4, 404-6, 571, 603, 605-7, 619-20, 642-3; letters from cited, 571n, 580n

Congress

resolutions on TJ's Report on Commerce, 84, 92-4

Opinions

compares Washington and Adams, 117, 384, 405; on conduct of Senate, 163; on Jay, Jay Treaty, 163-4, 334; on juries and impeachment trials, 163; on abuse of power by executive, 239, 348; on Adams's views and policies, 239, 275-6, 348, 359, 368, 405; inter-

prets Constitution, 239; on power to declare war, 239; on Talleyrand, 274; on XYZ affair, 275, 289, 311, 359; on role of citizenry, 333-4; on Alien Friends Act, 359; on partiality of news from Europe, 368; on powers of states, 606; on congressional privilege, 619-20

Personal Affairs

financial transactions, 9, 88, 276n, 299, 334, 345, 603, 605, 619, 635, 637n; travels to Richmond, 40; visits Albemarle Co., 95-6; and Mazzei's publication, 175-6; and F. Muhlenberg, 274, 276n; orders glass, 311-12, 343, 394; orders hardware, 312, 343-5, 358-9, 380, 384, 394, 409, 418; builds threshing machine, 349. *See also* Montpelier

Politics

depicted in political cartoon, xliii, 364 (illus.); and call for Constitutional Convention, 14; on negotiations in France, 40-1, 94-5, 274-5, 359-60, 384; on Lyon-Griswold affair, 117, 164; and comments by Hamilton, 172; on celebration of Washington's birthday, 175; supports Republican call for adjournment of Congress, 240; and Spriggs's resolution on war, 275; rumors of election to House of Delegates, 280; on Republican newspapers, 334; holds Federalists responsible for desiring war, 368, 384; on prospects for war with France, 404-5; and attacks on Monroe, 405; urged to run for office, 442; and irregular postal service in Va., 642; on apathy of people, 643

Relations with Jefferson

TJ visits, viii, 531, 603; urged to publish debates from Federal Convention, ix, 623; TJ sends congressional and political news to, xliii, 10, 87-8, 111-12, 156-7, 182, 189-90, 227-8, 244-5, 280-1, 299-300, 322-4, 344-5, 353, 363-4, 378-80, 393-4, 610-11, 622-3, 665; places orders from TJ's nailery, 9, 40, 95-6, 127, 162, 576, 580, 603, 605-6; and postal service, 9, 88, 192, 642; TJ handles orders, business affairs in Philadelphia for, 9, 88, 274, 276n, 299, 311-12, 334, 343-5, 353, 358-9, 380, 384, 394,

INDEX

the *Treaties and Customs of the Modern Nations of Europe*, 615-16
Martin, Mr., 120
Martin, Alexander: and relations with France, 364n; political ambitions, 444; wavers on sedition bill, 444, 445n; and Gerry's confirmation, 653
Martin, Benjamin: *Philosophia Britannica*, 594
Martin, Ephraim, 5
Martin, James: letter to, 131; Independence Day oration by, 131; TJ confuses with B. Vaughan, 131
Martin, John, 137, 138
Martin, Luther: letters from, 3-7, 16-21, 30-4, 73-8, 105-10, 133-43; portrait, xxxix, 364 (illus.); challenges TJ's account of Logan's speech, 3-7, 8, 34, 37-8, 73-8, 101, 108-10, 133-43, 216, 264-5, 285, 291, 327, 329, 339-40, 392, 509-10, 571n; defends Cresaps, 3-6, 16-21, 30-4, 73-8, 105-10, 133-43; mocks TJ as philosopher, 4, 6, 77, 107, 109n, 110n, 135, 143n; relationship to Cresaps, 20, 107, 264; Corbin defends, 285-7; political motives condemned, 340, 342, 420, 510; and Fennell, 392n
Martin, Maria Cresap (Mrs. Luther Martin), 20, 107
Martin, Thomas C.: threshing machine and drill by, 198-9, 217-18, 252-4, 310, 347-8, 349, 387; seeks patent, 217-18, 252-4, 347-8, 387-8
Martin & Douglas, 358n
Martin's swamp (Chesterfield Co., Va.): J. W. Eppes seeks to sell, 629; described, 639
Mary I (Mary Tudor), Queen of England, 602
Maryland: dispute with Pa., 5-6, 30-1; frontier settlements, 5-6, 17-18, 31-2, 74, 108-10; elections in, 10, 242; relations with Indians, 18, 20, 31-2; canal construction, 70n; mapping of counties, 70n; rifle companies in American Revolution, 107; Kosciuszko's will and laws of, 333n; and XYZ affair, 353, 365; land investments, 493; price of tobacco from, 623, 626. *See also* Ogle, Samuel
Mason, Mr., 571
Mason, George: relationship to S. T. Mason, 13n; and Ohio Company, 19; regard for T. Cresap, 34
Mason, John (British author): *Essays on Poetical and Prosaic Numbers*, 594
Mason, Stevens Thomson: letter to, 559-

60; letters from, 12-13, 438-9, 443-5, 586-7; and TJ's account of Logan's speech, 12-13; assists Callender, 13n, 521-3, 559, 580-4, 586; identified, 13n; and Jay Treaty, 13n; and M. Lyon, 13n, 584n, 586n; sends copy of Logan's speech, 38-9; and procedures for impeachment trials, 59n; TJ's regards to, 65; in Senate, 438-9, 445n, 676, 679; sends news, 438-9, 443-5, 586-7; letter from cited, 439n; handles TJ's financial transaction with Callender, 559, 561; and TJ's search for tenants, 560, 586; and Gerry, 636n, 653; on committee for Tazewell's funeral, 638n
Mason, Thomson, 13n
Massachusetts: and Madison's resolutions on Report on Commerce, 93; protests against stamp tax in, 157n; Republican newspapers in, 227, 228n, 241; congressional elections in, 241-2, 643; opposes war, 241-2; petitions against arming merchant vessels, 279; and disagreements among states, 388-9; election districts in, 442; selection of jurors in, 575n; growth of republicanism in, 610, 612; and Tory refugees, 619-20; congressional assent to an act of, 672
Massachusetts Historical Society, 390n
Massachusetts State Bank, 480, 495
Mathers, James, 85n
Mattaponi Indians, 564
Matthews, George, 280-1
Matthiessen & Sillem (Selem) (Hamburg), 65, 67
Maury, Fontaine, 351
Maury, James, 316, 317n
Mayer, Brantz, 515n
Mayo, John, 524
Mayo's bridge, 104
Mazzei, Philip: TJ's letter of 24 Apr. 1796, 3, 11n, 100n, 256, 303; *Recherches historiques et politiques sur les États-Unis d'Amérique*, 157, 175-6
Mease, James: *Domestic Encyclopædia*, 207-8n
medals: theft of TJ's medals, 79
medicine: description of T. M. Randolph's illness, 79; TJ's views on, 381; for syphilis, 406; purchased by TJ in Philadelphia, 406; treatment for cold, 587
megalonyx: confused with mammoth, 178, 232, 236; TJ's report to APS, 178, 232, 236-7; relationship to sloths, 294-7; tooth analyzed, 294-7; hunters' accounts associated with, 519-20

[717]

Mohegan Indians: confused with Mahicans, 86

Mohican Indians. *See* Mahican (Mohican) Indians

molasses: for TJ, 167, 170, 183, 220, 609, 669

Molloy, Charles: *De Jure Maritimo*, 594

monarchy: in Europe, 124; Hamilton on U.S. and, 172-3; Federalists associated with, 325n, 420; on abolition of, 359; and political parties, 433

Monck (Monk), George, Duke of Albemarle, 560n

money: scarcity of cash, 10, 446, 529, 562-3; paper money, 113, 589

Monford, Montfort. *See* Munford, William G. (d. 1804)

Monongahela River, 77

Monot, Stephen, 672

Monroe, Elizabeth Kortright (Mrs. James Monroe): and Mme de Corny, 23; TJ sends regards to, 90, 169, 247, 282, 612, 636; Merlin sends regards to, 659

Monroe, James: letters to, 89-90, 168-70, 191-2, 246-8, 281-2, 360-2, 612-13, 633-7; letters from, 21-2, 57-8, 120-1, 133, 221-3, 254-5, 272-3, 328-30, 350-1, 382, 400-4, 414-16, 454, 658-9; publishes *View*, 7, 8n, 637n; financial affairs, 9, 276n, 404, 635; conduct as minister to France, 11-12, 22, 89, 382, 402, 637n; *View*, 11-12, 40, 96, 246, 511; correspondence with G. Logan, 11n; on land tax, 21-2; and Dawson, 22, 281, 382, 400, 637n; dispute with A. Hamilton, 22; hopes session of Congress will end, 22; and distribution of *View*, 40, 57, 87, 89, 96, 127, 221, 223n; and Delamotte, 45, 57; draws on Barnes, 57, 88, 89; recalled from France, 83, 118-19, 174n; considers practicing law in Richmond, 89-90, 120, 133, 169, 254-5, 401-2; feted at Richmond dinner, 110-11, 225, 226n; H. Gates praises, 110; accused of financial improprieties, 221-3, 246, 247n, 272, 281-2, 329-30, 350-1, 400; Latrobe harmed by association with, 225; refuses to toast G. Washington, 246, 247n; views on Adams, 254, 329; newspaper subscription, 301n; criticizes U.S. envoys, 311; visits Madison, 311; and Mercer's case, 350; Adams's attack on, 353, 402-4, 405; prospect of entering Congress, 361, 382, 401-4, 511; political attacks on, 363; and Janet Montgomery, 385, 516;

threat of impeachment, 405; as presidential candidate in 1808, 438n; TJ criticized for connections to, 439n; and Tazewell, 450, 641; sends books to TJ, 454; buys land, 494; and J. Breckinridge, 533; acts as agent for W. Bache, 612-13, 658; TJ sends statement on income, expenses to, 633-4; and Madison, 637n; and G. Logan affair, 658-9; sends TJ letter from Merlin de Douai, 658-9

Mont Blanco: as new residence for Mary and J. W. Eppes, 607-8, 633, 639, 669

Montesquieu, Charles Louis de Secondat, Baron de: works, 595

Montgomery, Janet Livingston: letter to, 516-17; letter from, 385; asks TJ to forward letter to Monroe, 385, 516; identified, 385n

Montgomery, Richard, 385n, 517

Monticello: break-in at, viii, 68-9, 78-9; renovation and expansion of, viii, 92, 114, 128, 166-7, 188, 215, 235, 249, 269-71, 312, 326-7, 451-2, 504, 585, 593, 599, 603, 608; TJ longs for, plans return to, viii-ix, 327, 336, 381, 394, 406, 410-11, 412, 421, 435; art displayed at, xli-xlii; sale of furnishings from, xli-xlii; plants, trees for, 42n, 183, 192-3, 211, 248-9, 265, 282, 312; tools for blacksmith, 55, 56, 104, 167, 180, 375; flooring for, 56, 269-71, 312, 579-80; guns at, 68-9; management of, 79, 325-6, 385-6, 628; horses and mules for farm work at, 114, 128, 158, 177, 249; items in TJ's study, 114; carriages repaired at, 116; chimney piece for, 167-8, 180, 192, 613, 618, 630; molasses for, 170, 183, 609, 669; construction of roads at, 200-1; use of moldboard plow at, 207-8n, 388; various visitors to, 213, 419n, 458, 498, 587, 591; spring at, compared to Philadelphia, 248; brickmasons, stonemasons at, 255, 283, 313, 568, 571, 576, 579, 593; furniture, furnishings for, 282, 337, 343, 350, 362, 461, 466-7n; TJ and summers at, 290; carpenters at, 326-7, 579-80, 619, 642-3; groceries and supplies for, 337, 343, 355, 356, 357, 362, 365, 382, 461; supplies abundance of vegetables, 346; TJ invites family to, 357, 365, 382, 396, 421, 669; Niemcewicz hopes to visit, 399, 400, 410, 507, 508, 591; described by La Rochefoucauld-Liancourt, 488; Madison visits, 567-8

to maintain, 336n. *See also* France: Directory; France: War with Britain

New, Anthony: sends letter to constituents, 324n; and J. Taylor's politics, 388, 430; and T. Martin's patent, 388

New and Complete System of Arithmetic, Composed for the Use of the Citizens of the United States (Nicolas Pike), 594

New and Impartial History of England (John Baxter), 595

Newark, N.J., 322-4, 326

New Brunswick, N.J., 324n

New Castle, Del., 196n

Newcomen, Thomas, 655

New England: and navigation bill, 72, 93-4; and prospects of war with Spain, 95; and XYZ affair, 275; and Jay Treaty, 334; characterized by TJ, 388-9; selection of juries in, 589-90; opposition to administration policies, 648

New Hampshire: views on arming private vessels, 88, 90; and Stamp Act, 156; elections in, 610-12; politics in, 643

New Jersey: and Madison's resolutions on Report on Commerce, 93n; electoral districts, 169; congressional elections, 242; and XYZ affair, 300, 305, 322, 324n, 326, 335, 341, 353, 665; addresses to president, 331; and administration of Kosciuszko's will, 333n; petitions against Alien and Sedition Acts from, 665-6; public sentiment in, 668

New Jersey (ship), 170n

newspapers: *Independent Chronicle*, 26n; as source of congressional news, 56; laws on public printers in Va., 57-8, 89; anti-French bias of, 174n; print Barlow's letter to Baldwin, 174n; and seditious libel, 187n; treatment of Kosciuszko by Federalist, 196n; TJ's subscription to New York, 217, 644; establishment of Republican, 227, 228-9n, 241, 635-7; coverage of Lyon-Griswold affair, 241; and government patronage, 275; Republican, as target of Sedition Act, 300, 305; power to ban in France, 302n; and letters from congressmen to constituents, 323; limited circulation of Republican, 334; and attacks on TJ, 340, 392-3, 484-6; report Callender's arrest, 558; supported by political parties in Europe, 565; carry inaccurate foreign news, 623-5, 631; irregular delivery of, in Va., 628-9, 642

New System of Modern Geography (William Guthrie), 594

New Theatre. *See* Chestnut Street Theatre (New Theatre; Philadelphia)

New Views of the Origin of the Tribes and Nations of America (Benjamin Smith Barton), 564

New York: growing support for Republicans in, 10; monarchists from, at Annapolis and Constitution Convention, 13-14; views on arming merchant vessels, 90; and Madison's resolutions on Report on Commerce, 93n; protests against stamp tax in, 157n; field peas grown in, 210; elections in, 279, 323, 326-7, 335, 344, 353, 359, 363, 365; political appointments in, 300, 301-2n, 305; Oneida lands, 325; land investments in, 492; abatement of XYZ fever in, 665; and opposition to Alien and Sedition Acts, 665-6; increasing Republican public sentiment in, 668

New York City: price of tobacco at, 10, 623, 626, 633, 669; price of wheat, flour at, 10, 668; society and politics in, 23; Longworth's directory, 82n; and arming of private vessels, 88; as port, 147; Congress meets in, 175; petition from merchants on XYZ affair, 279; suspends shipments to W. Indies, 283; and XYZ affair, 300, 301n; yellow fever in, 507-8, 509n, 560; news of G. Logan affair reaches, 576-7; as market for tobacco, 668; lighthouses for harbor of, 672

New York Gazette (New York), 597n

New York Missionary Society: collects Indian vocabularies, 81-2n, 87, 238, 243

New York Price-Current (New York): TJ subscribes to, 217, 644

Nicholas, George: Charlottesville house of, 236; "political creed," 519, 521n; as key figure in Ky., 532-3

Nicholas, John (brother of W. C. Nicholas): amendment on diplomatic establishment, 54n, 165; as possible counter to "Scipio," 121; absent from Congress, 299, 305, 311, 341, 344, 363-4, 394; stands for election, 636, 637n; in debate on Haitian independence, 637n

Nicholas, John, Jr. (clerk of Albemarle County Court): as "Americanus" criticizes TJ, 255-62

Nicholas, Wilson Cary: letters to, 557, 590; letter from, 556; elected to Va. Assembly, 290; and Ky. Resolutions, 531-4, 556, 557; and TJ's petition on jurors, 574n; and Va. Resolutions, 590;

INDEX

Nicholas, Wilson Cary (*cont.*)
and Va. Assembly, 598n; named to
succeed Tazewell, 642n
Nicholas family, 475, 493
Nicholson, John: and R. Morris's debt,
171-2, 366; financial failure, 316n
Nicholson, William: *Introduction to Natural Philosophy*, 594
Nicklin, Philip, 170n
Niemcewicz, Julian Ursin: letters to, 383,
409-10, 591, 625-6; letters from, 369-
72, 398-400, 506-9, 627-8; reports on
M. Cosway, 23; and Kosciuszko's departure, 196n, 332n, 369-72, 376-7,
383, 453, 506-9; borrows money, 371,
383, 398-9, 507, 508, 591; identified,
372n; hopes to visit TJ, 399, 400, 409-
10, 507, 508, 591, 625, 628; visits
Mount Vernon, 399; correspondence
with Kosciuszko, 481, 482n, 625, 627-8
Niemcewicz, Susan Livingston Kean,
372n
Nile, battle of the, 603n, 635
Nimmo, William, 19
Nolan, Philip: letter to, 425-6; identified,
425-6n; and trans-Mississippi west,
425-6, 521
Nordiske Uäskape (ship), 504n
Norfolk, Va.: TJ expects to pass through,
9; and transatlantic trade, 147; fortifications, 523-4, 562; employment in,
559; Callender considers working at,
582
Norfolk Co., Va.: Short's Green Sea investments in, 352n, 459. *See also* Dismal Swamp
Norfolk Herald, 617
North, William, 302n, 353
Northampton Co., Pa., 611n
North Briton, 620n
North Carolina: exports, 72-3; and Madison's resolutions on Report on Commerce, 93; and Dismal Swamp, 352n;
and disagreements among states, 388-9;
politics, elections in, 442, 557, 665,
668; divisions within congressional delegation, 444; and Ky. Resolutions, 531-
2, 557; price of tobacco from, 623, 626;
support for Alien and Sedition Acts,
643; congressional acts on Senate bills
pertaining to, 674
*Northern Antiquities: or, A Description of
the Manners, Customs, Religion and
Laws of the Ancient Danes, and Other
Northern Nations* (Paul Henri Mallet),
595

northern states: and navigation bill, 72,
92-4; and political power, parties, 173,
432; and Direct Tax, 649
North Star: position of, 160-2
Northwest Territory, 674-5, 678-9
Notes on the State of Virginia: and Logan's
speech, 3-4, 34, 101, 103n, 134, 216,
264, 291, 303-4, 306, 321-2, 328, 392,
419, 509, 511n, 514, 570-1n; and TJ's
criticism of Buffon, 8, 34; depiction of
Indians in, 33, 34n, 81; S. T. Mason's
text of Logan's speech, 38-9; L. Martin
mocks, 77, 108; information on Ky. imperfect, 216; utilized by Latrobe, 226n;
on mammoth, 236; on purchases of land
from Indians, 322; on Native American
tribes, 564. *See also Appendix to the
Notes on Virginia Relative to the Murder of Logan's Family; Logan (Mingo
Indian)*
Nottoway Indians, 564
Nourse, Joseph, 673
Nova Scotia, 440, 672
nullification: and Ky. Resolutions, 530,
535, 539, 547

oaths: TJ's notes on, vii, 91; at impeach-
ment trials, 87, 90, 91, 121n; authoriza-
tion of authorities to administer, 674
*Observations on the Influence of Soil and
Climate upon Wool* (Robert Bakewell),
376n
*Observations on the Language of the Muhhe-
kaneew Indians* (Jonathan Edwards,
Jr.), 86, 87n, 238, 243
O'Connor, James, 617n
Oellers's hotel: site of Washington birth-
day ball, 132n; Marshall stays at, 423n
Œuvres complètes (Claude Adrien
Hélvetius), 594
*Official Letters to the Honorable American
Congress* (John Carey), 237n
Ogden, John C.: letters from cited, 586-
7n; writes TJ, Washington, 586-7; sup-
ports Lyon, 586n; delivers petition,
611-12
Ogle, Samuel (governor of Md.), 6, 20, 32
Ohio: Indians, missionaries in, 86, 106,
136-8, 265n, 288, 305-10, 513-14;
grant of lands at Gallipolis, 672
Ohio Company, 18-20, 33, 469n
Ohio River: Indian-white interactions
along, 75-7, 102, 137-9, 141-2, 285-8,
305-10, 512-15; fossils, artifacts near,
159n

INDEX

Randolph, Elizabeth Nicholas (Mrs. Edmund Randolph), 36

Randolph, Ellen Wayles, II (TJ's granddaughter): and sale of Monticello furnishings, xli-xlii; TJ's affection for, 26, 57, 115, 128, 158, 171, 183, 232, 249, 270, 284, 305, 327, 341, 366, 381, 396, 411, 421, 504, 604, 614, 627, 637-8, 669; cuts teeth, 28; game of goose for, 44, 92, 355; health of, 63, 79, 92, 96, 350, 367, 386, 483, 593, 599, 628; affection for TJ, 346, 424; visits Monticello, 451, 483, 599

Randolph, John (d. 1784), 430n

Randolph, John (of Roanoke), 438n

Randolph, Martha Jefferson (Patsy, Mrs. Thomas Mann Randolph, TJ's daughter): letters to, 91-2, 248-9, 354-5, 381, 483, 605, 637-8; letters from, 43-4, 346-7, 424; as slaveholder, viii-ix; criticizes Kosciuszko portrait of TJ, xlii; and C. Church, 24-5; TJ's affection for, 26, 57, 91-2, 115, 128, 158, 171, 183, 232, 249, 270, 284, 305, 327, 341, 354-5, 366, 396, 411, 421, 504, 604, 614, 627, 669; correspondence with TJ, 27, 114, 145, 270, 365, 395, 406, 613-14, 626, 629, 630, 637-8, 667; health of, 28, 63, 79, 96, 350, 367, 386; requests items from Philadelphia, 43-4, 69; awaits TJ's return, 44, 346-7, 381, 424; expresses affection for father, 44, 424; relationship with sister, 44, 347, 451, 632; supervises garden work at Monticello, 114; TJ urges to stay at Monticello, 166-7; unpleasant situation at Belmont, 187; and harpsichord, 215, 390; at Monticello, 346, 451, 593, 599; forwards letters, 385; Short's regard for, 482; regards sent to, 587; social life, 628; postpones trip to Goochland Co., 639

Randolph, Mary Skipwith, 319

Randolph, Richard (d. 1786), 427-30

Randolph, Thomas Jefferson (TJ's grandson): and portrait of TJ, xlii; TJ's affection for, 26, 57, 115, 128, 158, 171, 183, 232, 249, 270, 284, 305, 327, 341, 366, 396, 411, 421, 504, 604, 614, 627, 637-8, 669; health of, 28, 63, 79, 92, 96, 350, 367, 386, 593, 628; game of goose for, 44, 92, 355; fails to wear shoes, 63; suffers from baffling disorder, 346, 381; 1829 edition of TJ's papers, 390n; sends love to TJ, 424; visits Monticello, 451, 599; examines TJ's papers, 530, 534

Randolph, Thomas, Jr. (of Dungeness), 319

Randolph, Thomas, Sr. (of Dungeness), 319

Randolph, Thomas Mann, Sr., 438n

Randolph, Thomas Mann (TJ's son-in-law): letters to, 25-6, 55-7, 114-15, 127-8, 128-9, 158, 170-1, 182-3, 192-4, 231-2, 269-71, 282-4, 304-5, 325-7, 341-2, 365-6, 395-6, 410-11, 421-2, 504-5, 593, 604-5, 613-14, 626-7, 667-9; letters from, 26-8, 62-3, 68-9, 78-80, 145, 177, 290-1, 312-13, 385-6, 406, 628-9; as slaveholder, viii-ix, 28, 604n; TJ makes political comments to, xliii; as TJ's neighbor, 24-5; subscribes to newspapers, 25, 115, 183, 614, 626; and H. B. Trist, 26, 114, 177, 406, 421; and postal service, 26-7, 56, 192, 282, 325, 626-7, 628-9, 667; sells wheat, 27-8; weather diary, 27, 56, 80; cares for TJ's affairs at Monticello, Shadwell, 28, 55-6, 79, 114, 128, 145, 158, 170, 177, 192-3, 238, 248-9, 282-4, 290, 312-13, 325-6, 341, 345-6, 349, 356, 365, 385-6, 406, 410-11, 452, 604, 613, 628, 669; seeks blacksmith, stonemason, 28, 56, 145, 183, 355; and TJ's financial transactions, 43-4, 115, 231, 410, 461, 592-3, 603-4; and renovation of Monticello, 56, 114, 128, 269-71, 312, 326-7; expresses hostility towards Britain, 62-3, 290; reads Fauchet's pamphlet, 62; TJ sends publications to, 62-3, 115, 170-1, 269-70, 283, 396, 667; health of, 63, 69, 79, 92, 96; reports on theft at Monticello, 68-9, 78-9; orders items from Philadelphia, 69, 283, 313, 406, 421; Madison visits, 96; TJ sends news on Congress, politics, and foreign affairs to, 127-8, 170, 193-4, 231-2, 269-70, 304-5, 326-7, 341, 365, 396, 410-11, 421-2, 613-14, 627, 667-8; letters from cited, 129n, 194n, 249n, 270n, 284n, 346n; and correspondence with TJ, 145, 354, 381, 630; and TJ's nailrod, nailery, 145, 154-5, 182-3, 626; grows barley, 210; and seeds from Strickland, 210; provides botanical description, 211-12, 214n, 455-6; TJ sends regards to, 249, 355, 381; and TJ's horses, 255, 283, 312-13; and sale of tobacco, 290, 326, 349, 365, 373-4, 579, 626, 668; reports on health of children, 367; travels in Va., 385, 599; on TJ's role in Senate, 406; family background, 438n;

Randolph, Thomas Mann (*cont.*):
visits Monticello, 451, 498n; regards
sent to, 458, 564, 587; signs TJ's petition, 574n; and sale of land, 613;
cares for TJ's legal affairs, 621, 669;
celebrates Christmas, 628; postpones
trip to Goochland Co., 628, 637-8,
639. *See also* Edgehill (Randolph
estate)

Randolph, Virginia (sister of Thomas
Mann Randolph), 628

raspberries: Antwerp, TJ praises, 193; at
Monticello, 249, 346

Raspberry Plain (Loudoun Co., Va.):
Mason estate, 13n

Rastadt, 156-7

Raymond, Robert, Lord Raymond: *Reports of Cases Argued and Adjudged*, 594

Read, George, 428n

Read (Reed, Reid), Jacob: on power to impeach senators, 126-7, 672; as bank director, 418-19; and Washington's appointment, 440; judiciary bill, 471,
472n; in Senate, 472, 677, 679; and
Gerry's confirmation, 653

Read, John: letter to, 426-30; and British
debt claims, 426-30; letter from cited,
428, 430n; identified, 428n

*Recherches historiques et politiques sur les
États-Unis d'Amérique* (Philip Mazzei),
157, 175-6

Red Hawk (Shawnee Indian), 141

Redick, David: letter from, 285-7; letter
to Fenno, 285, 287-8; son mentioned,
285; and TJ's account of Logan affair,
285-8

Redstone. *See* Brownsville (Redstone), Pa.

*Reflections on Monroe's View, of the Con-
duct of the Executive* (Uriah Tracy), 11-
12n

*Réflexions sur la formation et la distribution
de richesses* (Anne Robert Jacques Turgot), 595

religion: offenses against, under British
law, 59-60; and oaths, 91; and Sabbath,
125; Conn. described as priest-ridden,
156-7; and U.S. Constitution, 393; proposed law interfering with freedom of,
434-5

Remsen, Henry: letters to, 217, 644-5; TJ
orders newspapers from, 217, 644; forwards correspondence, news, 644

Report (in part) of the Committee: TJ collects information from, 631-2

Reports and Arguments (Sir John
Vaughan), 594

*Reports of Adjudged Cases in the Courts
of Chancery, King's Bench, Common
Pleas and Exchequer* (Sir John Strange),
594

*Reports of Cases Adjudged in the Court of
King's Bench* (William Salkeld), 594

Reports of Cases Argued and Adjudged
(Lord Raymond), 594

*Reports of Cases Argued and Determined in
the Court of Appeals of Virginia*
(Bushrod Washington), 594

*Reports of Cases Argued and Determined in
the High Court of Chancery* (William
Peere Williams), 594

*Reports of Select Cases in all the Courts of
Westminster-Hall* (Sir John Fortescue
Aland), 569, 570n

Reports of Sir Edward Coke (Sir Edward
Coke), 594

republicanism: spread of, 25; in Va. Assembly, 63, 89; and free discussion, 120;
"Americanus's" comments on, 255-62;
and political parties, 432-4; and conventions of the people, 601-2; and Constitution, 646, 651n

Republicans: absent from Congress, vii-
viii, 279, 281, 299, 305, 311, 341, 344,
363-4, 365, 394, 441; and TJ's draft of
Ky. Resolutions, ix; growing support
for, 10, 267, 610, 665-6; and Blount impeachment, 11; fear alliance with Great
Britain, 40, 227-8, 270, 448, 640, 641n;
in Va., 40, 110-11, 225, 226n, 386,
438n, 524, 574-5n, 598, 641; Madison's
recommendations to, 95; TJ distin-
guishes from Federalists, Tories, 98-
100; called whigs, 156, 175, 194, 269,
284, 326, 335, 344, 408; and celebration of Washington's birthday, 156, 175;
and president's message of 19 Mch.
1798, 189-90, 193-4, 227, 228n, 231-2;
called peace party, 193-4, 231, 263,
267, 268; as protectors of Constitution,
239; and XYZ affair, 245-6, 263-4, 267-
8, 269-70, 339, 353, 647, 652n; accused
of pro-French sentiments, 250-1, 324n,
341-2, 417-19; hold caucuses, 264n,
301n; urged to stand firm, 272; and
measures before Congress, 284, 408; in
Pa., 286n; and newspapers, public opinion, 300, 302-3, 334, 635-7; and N.Y.
elections, 323, 326-7, 359, 363, 365;
represent true sentiments of nation, 340,
388, 416, 588, 649; and 1798 elections,
344, 643; lack of power in Congress,
401-2, 444, 445n; TJ as leader of, 406,

rotation in office, 433

Rowan, Archibald Hamilton: letter to, 528; letter from, 460-1; visits Kosciuszko, xli; exile in U.S., 460-1, 528; identified, 460n

Rowan, Sarah Anne Dawson Hamilton, 460

Roxbury, Mass.: opposes arming merchant vessels, 242n

Royle (Royal) v. Robinson Administrators, 35-6, 64

Rudiments of Grammar for the English-Saxon Tongue, First Given in English (Elizabeth Elstob), 569, 570n

Rules for Drawing the Several Parts of Architecture (James Gibbs), 604

Rush, Benjamin, xli, 248

Russell, Benjamin, 364n

Russell, Henry, 141

Russell, Capt. William, 141

Russia: and military movements, 156; defeats, partitions Poland, 196n, 372n, 399, 400, 507, 508; and comparative studies of languages, 238; furs, 331n; and talks of new coalition against France, 449-50; lack of freedom of press in, 590n; and France, 664

Rutherfurd, John, 653

Rutledge, John, Jr., 173, 181-2, 472

"Sabbaticus" (pseudonym), 125

saddles, 467n

Saint André, André Jeanbon, 449-50

Saint Croix River, 284, 346n

Saint-Domingue, W.I.: blacks caricatured, xl, 364 (illus.); relations with France, xl; and problems of sudden emancipation, 151; natural history of, 297n; political upheaval, 297n; refugees from, seek asylum in U.S., 438-41; independence for, 635, 637n, 640, 663-5, 667; U.S. trade with, 640, 663, 665, 667; British, U.S. warships off coast of, 659-60; mentioned, 70n, 509n. *See also* Toussaint-Louverture

Saint German, Christopher: *Doctor and Student*, 594

St. Thomas, W.I., 659

Salkeld, William: *Reports of Cases*, 594

Sallust: works of, 595

Sally (sloop): carries shipment for TJ, 192, 265, 343, 357

Salmagundi (Washington Irving, William Irving, and James Kirke Paulding), 82-3n

salt: taxes on, 279, 281, 300, 305, 611n; extracted from seawater, 391-2, 407

Salzburg, 12n

Sam: cares for TJ's slave, George, 563n

Sandusky, Northwest Terr.: Indians, missionaries at, 86, 308

Sappington, John, 136, 138

Sargent, Winthrop: appointed governor of Miss. Terr., 281n, 323, 326

Sawyer, Enoch, 617n

Saxe-Coburg-Saalfeld, Francis Frederick, Duke of, 161n

Saxons: histories of, 597n

Sayer, Joseph: *Law of Costs*, 594

Scandella, Giambattista (J. B.), 507-9

Schimmelpenninck, Rutger Jan, 611n

Schomberg, Alexander Crowcher: *Historical and Chronological View of Roman Law*, 594

Schröter, Johann Hieronymus: studies Jupiter's moons, 160-2, 178

Scioto River: and Dunmore's War, 106, 137, 138, 513, 514

"Scipio" (Uriah Tracy): criticizes Monroe's *View*, 11-12, 57, 89, 120-1, 221, 223n, 246; essays ascribed to C. Lee, 87; essays ascribed to Pickering, 96; rebutted, 223n

Scotland, 206, 565-7

Scott, James, 19

Scourge of Aristocracy, and Repository of Important Political Truths, 583-5

seamen, U.S.: impressment of, 610-11, 613; bill for relief of sick and disabled, 674, 679

seaports: and stamp tax, 157n; fortification of harbors, 182, 228, 280n, 674; quarantine of, 679. *See also* lighthouses

Sedgwick, Theodore: and impeachment procedures, 127n, 619-20, 672; fails to attend Washington's birthday celebration, 156; and aid for Federal District, 245; president pro tem of Senate, 437; and Direct Tax, 442-3; and election districts in Mass., 442; considers declaration of war, 443n; in Senate debates, 471-2; and Gerry's confirmation, 653

Sedgwick & Co. or a Key to the Six Per Cent Cabinet (James Thomson Callender), 188-9, 565-7

sedition: common law prosecutions for, 187n; as crime in Scotland, 567n; prosecuted in Britain for, 620

Sedition Act (1798): prosecutions under, 174n, 576, 586, 619-20; as part of Fed-

INDEX

Tazewell, Henry: letter to, 58-61; letters from, 440-3, 447-50, 597-8; and procedures for impeachment trials, 58-9, 62, 126, 162-3, 261, 615n; TJ sends regards to, 65; health, death of, 96, 597-8, 638, 641-2; Madison sends regards to, 96; and Jay Treaty, 155; opposes J. Q. Adams's appointment, 182; votes, acts in Senate, 229n, 445n; and TJ's conversation with T. Coxe, 293; and relations with France, 364; and right of states to regulate immigration, 440-3; and Sedition Act, 440, 447; and taxes on slaves, 441-2; and judiciary bill, 471; reelected to Senate, 598; successor in Congress for, 641-2; and Gerry's confirmation, 653

tea: duties on foreign, 673

tea chest, 461

telescopes, 160, 178, 609n

tenancy: high cost of house rent, 113; in Va., 148, 318, 493-4, 613, 639; relationship to slavery, 152, 493; and landlord's income, 492; TJ seeks farm tenants, 560, 586

Tennessee: early exploration of, 75, 76, 106-7, 139; mammoth remains in, 158, 159n; and U.S. laws, 679

Texas, 425-6n

textiles, 158

theft: at Monticello, 68-9, 79

Theodore, John: TJ's servant in Philadelphia, 436, 439, 585

Thomas, George, 6

Thompson, John (Philadelphia), 644n

Thornton, Edward, 227, 310

Thornton, Francis, 19

Thornton, Presley, 19

Thornton, William, xlii

Thornton, Col. William, 19

"Thrasybulus": rebuts "Scipio," 223

threshing machines: T. Martin's patent for, 217-18, 252-4, 347-9, 387-8; TJ's drawing of, 253

Thruston, Buckner, 512

Thugut, Franz Maria, Baron von, 449-50

Tichenor, Isaac, 10, 653

Tilghman, William, 293

Tillinghast, Thomas, 157n

Tilton, Daniel, 280-1, 323

timber: for use of tenant farmers, 639

Timbuktu. See Tombouctou (Timbuktu)

"Times; A Political Portrait": cartoon, xliii, 364 (illus.)

Timur (Timour Beg; Tammerlane), 458

Tingey, Thomas, 659-60

Tinsley, Peter, 622n

"Titus Manlius" (Alexander Hamilton), 246n, 323

tobacco: and individual cultivation by slaves, viii, 385-6, 410; TJ's dependence on, viii, 192, 412, 506, 588, 626, 669-70; price of, 10, 54, 56, 116, 128, 157, 158, 171, 192, 282, 318, 327, 349, 354, 365, 412, 588, 623, 626, 633, 660, 666; storage and inspection of, 27, 445-6, 452, 461, 467; shipment, sale of TJ's, 56, 181n, 218, 266, 282, 326, 337-8, 349, 357-8, 365, 372-4, 411-12, 413, 423, 441, 459, 560-1, 579, 592, 633, 660, 668, 669-70; exported from N.C., 73; French duties on, 124, 502n; as crop at Monticello, Poplar Forest, 145, 192, 312, 349, 385, 506, 669; T. M. Randolph seeks advice on sale of, 290; ruins land, 318; sold to English firms, 427, 428n, 469n; planters require nails, 527; as major crop in Va., 558-9; Spain as market for U.S., 633, 666, 668, 669

Tom (TJ's slave), 43

Tombouctou (Timbuktu): and European explorations in Africa, 154n

Tomlinson, Benjamin, 135-7, 142

Tomlinson, Nathaniel, 102, 138

Tone, Theobald Wolfe, 460n

tonnage duties, 84

"To the respectable Freeholders and other citizens of the county of Caroline" (Edmund Pendleton), 661-2

Toulmin, Harry, 555n

Toulon, France: French expedition departs from, 400n, 443, 458n; ships from, join French fleet at Brest, 449

Tousard (Touzard), Anne Louis de, 507-9

Toussaint-Louverture: relations with U.S., 635-7, 640, 663, 665, 667; leads Haitian independence movement, 637n

Townsend, Capt., 146

Townson, Robert: *Travels in Hungary, With a Short Account of Vienna in the Year 1793*, 455, 458n

Tracy, Uriah: "Scipio" essays by, 11-12, 57, 87, 96; and procedures for impeachment trials, 58, 62; fails to attend Washington's birthday celebration, 156; criticizes House of Representatives, 176; debate, motions in Senate, 228, 680; favors war with France, 364, 437; opposes adjournment of Congress, 417; and Gerry's confirmation, 653

INDEX

Traité élémentaire de chimie, présenté dans un ordre nouveau et d'après les découvertes modernes (Antoine Laurent Lavoisier), 594
Traveller's Pocket Farrier (Henry Bracken), 69
Travels in Hungary, With a Short Account of Vienna in the Year 1793 (Robert Townson), 455, 458n
Travels in the Interior Districts of Africa (Mungo Park), 154n
Travels through the United States of North America, the Country of the Iroquois, and Upper Canada (Duc de La Rochefoucauld-Liancourt), 488-9
Treadwell, John, 353
treason: under British law, 60-1; in early version of sedition bill, 437, 443-4, 445n; as crime during war, 441; and congressional privilege, 620n
Treasury, U.S. Department of the: Congress publishes statements of, 238, 240n. *See also* Wolcott, Oliver, Jr.
treaties: and House appropriations, 41n; U.S. abrogation of, with France, 364, 379, 418-19, 422, 678; laws subsequent to, 379; expenditures for, 634, 667
Treatise of Tenures (Sir Geoffrey Gilbert), 594
Treatise on Government (John Locke), 595
Treatise on Rents (Sir Geoffrey Gilbert), 594
Tree of Liberty (Pittsburgh, Pa.), 286n
trees: varieties of, planted at Monticello, 193, 312; and restoration of soil, 210-11
Trenton, N.J.: as refuge from yellow fever, 526n, 585n
Trigg, John: lends money to J. Beckley, 278, 407; letter to cited, 407n
Trist, Elizabeth House, 396, 628
Trist, Hore Browse: travels to, plans to settle in Albemarle Co., 26, 114, 167, 231, 236, 396; and T. M. Randolph, 177, 406, 421
Tronchin, Jean Armand: letter to, 122-3; and foreign creditors' recovery of funds in U.S., 122-3
Troup, Robert, 300, 301n
Trumbull, John: visits Kosciuszko, xl
Tucker, Frances Bland Randolph, 151
Tucker, Lelia Skipwith Carter, 470
Tucker, St. George: letters to, 342-3, 470; letter from, 321-2; and TJ's account of Logan's speech, 321-2, 328, 342; invited to Monticello, 470
Tumblestone. *See* Tomlinson, Nathaniel

Turgot, Anne Robert Jacques: *Réflexions sur la formation et la distribution de richesses*, 595
Turkey. *See* Ottoman Empire
Turner, George: and APS, 39-40n, 159n; calls on TJ in Philadelphia, 39; letter from cited, 39n
turpentine: exported from N.C., 73
Tyler, John, 329

Union (ship), 504n
United Brethren. *See* Moravians
United Irishmen, Society of, 460n

UNITED STATES

Agriculture
impact of foreign policy on, 123-4

Army
augmentation of, vii, 614, 635; Washington's appointment, vii, 440, 443n, 445, 448; arms and ammunition for, 228, 229n, 280n, 673-4; bill for marine corps, 276; cost of, 280n, 398, 616; new regiments, 280n, 348, 409n, 442-3, 444, 445n, 610, 674; appointments, 302n, 448, 450n; opposition to augmentation of, 348, 610, 661-2, 664; views on standing army, 348, 621, 646, 666n; appropriations, expenditures for, 409n, 623, 627, 631, 634, 640, 663, 667-8, 675, 678; obligation to fund, 471; leadership of, 612n; organization of, 675, 679; military hospitals, 679. *See also* United States: Congress, Fifth (4 Mch. 1797-3 Mch. 1799); McHenry, James

Confederation Congress
threats to authority of, 13-14

Congress, First
(4 Mch. 1789-3 Mch. 1791)
meets in N.Y., 175

Congress, Fourth
(4 Mch. 1795-3 Mch. 1797)
defense of democratic societies in, 565-7

Congress, Fifth
(4 Mch. 1797-3 Mch. 1799)
and arming of merchant vessels, vii, 10, 11n, 88-9, 111, 170, 181, 183, 189-90, 217, 228-9n, 239, 279, 339, 676; little business in, vii, 26, 115, 128, 157, 161, 171; and bill giving currency to foreign coins, 8, 10, 671;

[736]

INDEX

INDEX

INDEX

Vaughan, Benjamin, 131
Vaughan, John, 297n, 656n, 677
Vaughan, Sir John: *Reports and Arguments*, 594
Vegetable Staticks (Stephen Hales), 594
Venice: and Treaty of Campoformio, 12n; fleet controlled by France, 443, 449; embassy in London, 509n; and relations with France, 584n
Venus (planet): 1769 transit of, 160, 162n
Vermont: elections in, 10, 584n, 610; protests against stamp tax in, 156-7; selection of jurors in, 575n; prosecutions under Sedition Act, 576; shows support for M. Lyon, 610-12
Vernon, Thomas: *Cases Argued and Adjudged*, 594
Vertot, René Aubert de: *History of the Revolutions in Spain*, 595
Vesey (Vezey), Francis: *Cases Argued and Determined*, 594
vetch, winter: TJ exchanges seed of, with Strickland, 170, 210, 455-6; identified as ononis by T. M. Randolph, 211-12, 214n, 455-6
Vienna: inaccurate news from, 625n, 627, 631
View of the Conduct of the Executive (James Monroe). *See* Monroe, James
View of the Soil and Climate of the United States of America (Constantin François Chasseboeuf Volney), 82n
Villette, Reine Philiberte Rouph de Varicourt, Marquisse de, 523, 524-5n
vineyards, 42
Virgil: new French edition of works of, 154n, 277n, 577, 578n

VIRGINIA

Agriculture
condition of crops in, 27, 176, 276; May wheat in, 198; tobacco in, 318, 558-9, 626; and possibility of war with France, 381; and plants from Europe, 456

British Invasions
and hostility against Britain, 62; effect on state records, 342; under commands of Leslie and Arnold, 518

Constitution
calls for revision of, 41n

Courts
courts of chancery, 179, 413-14; Federal court fails to meet in, 385; and selection of jurors, 568, 572-4, 576; pre-

sentment against S. Cabell, 574n; TJ's suit against Henderson heirs, 621-2, 669; Court of Appeals, 662n

Description
boundaries, 162n; ice caves, 455

Economy
difficulty of landed estates in, 15-16; western land claims, 18-20; and farm tenancy, 148, 560, 586, 613, 639; Green Sea land investments, 318, 337, 351-2, 411, 459, 481, 496; sale, investments in land, 318, 493, 613, 629, 639; share of Direct Tax to be raised in, 397-8; transportation, sale of slaves, 428-30n; regional variation in land prices, 493-4; canals, 523-4, 561-2; employment in, 558-9; influx of tobacco money, 623, 626. *See also* James River Company

Education and Science
lack of emphasis upon education, 558-9; act for establishment of schools, 573-5

Federal Convention
Va. issues call for, 13

General Assembly
crowded living conditions during sessions, 43; on election of state printer, 57-8, 89; called republican, 63, 89; and Va. Resolutions, 532, 534, 590, 606-7; and TJ's petition on jurors, 567-8, 571-5, 576, 589-90, 602; and Prince Edward Co. petition, 582; and election of U.S. senators, 598, 641-2; and declaring U.S. laws unconstitutional, 601-2; bill to secure freedom of debate in, 602; adjournment, 642n; memorial from Caroline Co., 662n

House of Delegates
and TJ's grand jury petition, 22, 40-1, 57, 255-62, 574n; debates selling church lands, 40-1; proposal for amendments to U.S. Constitution, 40-1, 54; members, 280, 287n, 290; election of speaker and clerk for, 598, 602

Indians
tribes, 19-20, 564; acquisition of lands from, 322, 342

Laws
Statute for Establishing Religious Freedom, 41n, 532; and Kosciuszko's will, 333n; enforcement of, 558

[740]

Wardlaw, William, 406, 466n
Wardrop, James, 19
Warre, John Tyndale, 428-30n
Washington, Augustine, 19
Washington, Bushrod: retires from law practice, 89, 621; represents Wayles estate, 470n; runs for Congress, 524, 525n; *Reports of Cases*, 594

WASHINGTON, GEORGE

American Revolutionary War
correspondence from published by J. Carey, 237n

Commander in Chief, 1798-1799
appointed, vii, 440, 443n, 445, 448; depicted in cartoon, xliii, 364 (illus.); meets with officers in Philadelphia, 611n

Confederation Congress
refuses to join plan to overthrow, 13

Personal Affairs
honorary French citizen, 196n; and Niemcewicz, 369, 371, 399-400; visits Federal District, 369, 371

Politics
and Odgen, 587n

President
criticizes Monroe's conduct, 83, 402, 404n; compared with Adams, 117, 384, 405, 415; and Jay Treaty, 184, 240n; Monroe refuses to toast, 246, 247n; relations with France, 254, 304n, 338, 359-60; nomination of T. Pinckney, 319, 320n, 481; criticized by Short, 488, 491-2; Farewell Address, 491; Callender attacks, 522n; response to new edition of forged letters, 581, 584n

Relations with Jefferson
TJ declines to attend ball, 132

Retirement
birthday celebrations, 112, 132, 156, 175, 221; lack of communication with Adams, 248, 384; and XYZ affair, 384; popularity of, 388

Washington, Henry Augustine: *Works of Jefferson*, 530-1
Washington, Lawrence, 19
Washington, Martha Dandridge Custis: portrait by Field mentioned, xxxix; entertains, 132; visits granddaughters in Federal District, 369, 371

Washington Co., Pa.: and Republican politics, 286n; residents attack Indians, 306n
watches, 16, 481, 577, 578
Waters, Capt. (master of *Pomona*), 147
Waters, Nicholas B.: Bell's *System of Surgery*, 283
Watson, David, 114
Watson, John: and postal service at Milton, Va., 56, 626-7; handles shipments for TJ, 167; letters from cited, 627n; letters to cited, 627n
Watson, Robert: *History of Philip the Second*, 595; *History of Philip the Third*, 595
Watt, James, 654-6
Wawiaton Indians. *See* Wea (Ouiatanon) Indians
Wayles, John (TJ's father-in-law): slave trade venture, 426-30; tobacco crops, 427, 428n, 469n; indebted to Hanbury firm, 467-70
Wayles estate: payment of claims against, 218, 242-3, 357-8, 411-12, 413, 423, 459, 470-1, 560-1; claim of Farell & Jones, 317n, 426-30; and *Prince of Wales* case, 427-30; Declaration of Hanbury's Executor against Wayles's Executors, 467-70
Wayne, Anthony, 82n
Wea (Ouiatanon) Indians, 81, 86
wealth: and equality, taxation, 434
Wealth of Nations (Adam Smith), 194n, 595
Webster, Noah, 577n
Weeaw Indians. *See* Wea (Ouiatanon) Indians
Weiser, Johann Conrad, 20, 31-2, 309
Welch (Welsh), Wakelin, Jr.: and Wayles estate debt, 218, 242-3, 411-12, 413, 423, 459, 470-1, 560-1
Wells, William, 82n
West, Benjamin: portrait of Kosciuszko, xl-xli, 364 (illus.); "Fright of Astyanax," xli-xlii, 364 (illus.)
West Augusta, District of (Va.), 513
West Indies: market for N.C. products, 73; suspension of U.S. shipments to, 283; British seize American vessels in, 395n; and slave trade, 428
West Indies, British: Jamaica convoy, 443, 445n
West Indies, French: restrictions on U.S. trade, 267; privateering against American ships, 335-6, 380n, 462n, 489, 490, 499, 635, 659-60; U.S. Navy pa-

wood: pine, for flooring at Monticello, 269-71

Wood, James: letter to, 642; and TJ's account of Logan's speech, 38; TJ refers to as Tory, 63; receives news of Tazewell's death, 642

Wood, Lucy, Jr.: TJ pays for hire of slaves, 29n, 103; letter from cited, 105n; letter to cited, 105n

Wood, Lucy Henry (Mrs. Valentine Wood): TJ pays for hire of slaves, 28-30, 103, 220; letter from cited, 105n; letters to cited, 105n; TJ's payment to, 179; in TJ's accounts with G. Jefferson, 375

Wood, William: hires out slaves, 28, 30n, 328n

Wooddeson, Richard: *A Systematical View of the Laws of England; As Treated of in a Course of Vinerian Lectures*, 58-61

Woodward, Joseph, 499, 501n

Works of Thomas Jefferson (Henry Augustine Washington): and Ky. Resolutions, 530-1

Wyandot Indians, 81

Wynne, John Huddleston: *General History of Ireland*, 595

Wythe, George: *Decisions of Cases*, 594

XYZ affair: news of envoys awaited, vii, 7, 25, 29, 36, 53, 56, 57, 66, 67, 88, 94-5, 100-1, 110, 111, 115, 123, 125, 128, 157, 158, 161, 165; seems to vindicate Federalist predictions, vii; "Cinque-Têtes" cartoon, xxxix-xl, 364 (illus.); depicted as fever, delusion, xxxix, 384, 559-60, 588, 635, 664, 665-7, 668; TJ's opinions on, xxxix-xl, 165, 250-1, 267-8, 269-70, 290, 322-3, 326, 335, 344, 363, 365, 635, 648, 652n; "not six pence" retort, xl; envoys arrive in Paris, 7-9, 11; envoys' relations, negotiations with Talleyrand, 11, 53, 219, 363-4, 365, 384, 391n, 397, 417-19; prospects, reception of envoys in Paris, 35-6, 40, 46, 50, 64-5, 66, 67; envoys' communications published in April, 99n, 245-6, 247, 250-1, 252, 263-4, 266-70, 283-4, 289, 302, 324n, 326, 329, 330n, 331, 333-5, 348, 648, 651n; Marshall, Gerry keep journals, 99n, 643; French assessments of, reactions to U.S. envoys, 119, 174n, 185, 219, 397; congressional, executive responses, 165-6, 245-6, 275,

311, 363-4, 365, 379, 406, 582; first dispatches received, printed, 165-6, 168, 170; instructions to envoys, 166n, 264n, 266-9, 283, 289, 338, 396, 397, 418, 421-2, 444, 525n, 673; president announces failure of mission to France, 166n, 189-90; envoys' conduct criticized, 174n, 185-6, 329, 339, 490-1, 643n; influence of envoys on U.S. policy, 174n; France wants loans, 184, 391n, 464, 465, 524-5n; rumored intrigues of Marshall, C. C. Pinckney, 185; agents approach U.S. envoys, 250-1, 339, 397, 523; Talleyrand, agents demand payment, 250-1, 263, 267-8, 269; agents identified, 251n; agents depicted as swindlers unauthorized by French government, 263, 266-7, 269, 290, 311, 334-5n, 339, 397; envoys' dispatches received, published, 263-4, 281, 289, 290, 329, 363; envoys reveal French demands, 263-4, 266-7, 268, 269; and Philadelphia, 268, 335-6, 341-2, 344-5, 353, 359; Adams sends letter, *Sophia* for envoys, 271, 379, 381, 394, 396, 397, 449, 648; C. Humphreys sent for envoys, 271, 648; envoys' disposition toward France, 274, 368, 643, 647, 649; responses to publication of dispatches, 274-5, 279, 283-4, 290, 311, 333-5, 338-9, 344, 365, 397-8; used by Federalists, 275, 333, 348, 353, 363-4, 643, 648, 652n, 661; addresses, responses to, 279-80, 300, 301n, 305, 322-4, 326, 335, 341, 353, 359-60; memorial to Talleyrand of 17 Jan. 1798, 335-6, 359-60; and accusations against Republicans, 339, 353, 417-19; impact on liberty, 348; impact on elections, 359; and Va. politics, 365, 524-5, 582-3; and news of improvement in negotiations, 384; additional dispatches from envoys, 390-3, 394, 396-7, 414, 415-16n, 419-20, 524; relations among envoys, 393, 441, 647; envoys do not anticipate war with France, 394, 396, 397; Talleyrand encourages negotiation, 462-5, 485, 562, 648-9, 651n, 663; Directory disavows, 464, 465; role of mysterious woman, 523, 524-5n; and N.C., 557n; Callender on, 580-5. *See also* Adams, John: President; France: U.S. Relations with; Gerry, Elbridge; Marshall, John; Pinckney, Charles Cotesworth; United States: Public Opinion

INDEX

A comprehensive index of Volumes 1-20 of the
First Series has been issued as Volume 21.
Each subsequent volume has its own index,
as does each volume or set of volumes
in the Second Series.